Lecture Notes in Computer Science 11405

Commenced Publication in 1973
Founding and Former Series Editors:
Gerhard Goos, Juris Hartmanis, and Jan van Leeuwen

More information about this series at http://www.springer.com/series/7410

Mitsuru Matsui (Ed.)

Topics in Cryptology – CT-RSA 2019

The Cryptographers' Track at the RSA Conference 2019
San Francisco, CA, USA, March 4–8, 2019
Proceedings

 Springer

Editor
Mitsuru Matsui
Mitsubishi Electric Corporation
Kamakura, Japan

ISSN 0302-9743 ISSN 1611-3349 (electronic)
Lecture Notes in Computer Science
ISBN 978-3-030-12611-7 ISBN 978-3-030-12612-4 (eBook)
https://doi.org/10.1007/978-3-030-12612-4

Library of Congress Control Number: 2019930584

LNCS Sublibrary: SL4 – Security and Cryptology

This Springer imprint is published by the registered company Springer Nature Switzerland AG
The registered company address is: Gewerbestrasse 11, 6330 Cham, Switzerland

Preface

The RSA conference has been a major international event for information security experts since its inception in 1991. It is an annual event that attracts several hundreds of vendors and over 40,000 participants from industry, government, and academia. Since 2001, the RSA conference has included the Cryptographer's Track (CT-RSA), which provides a forum for current research in cryptography. CT-RSA has become a major publication venue for cryptographers.

This volume represents the proceedings of the 2019 RSA Conference Cryptographer's Track, which was held in San Francisco, California, during March 4–8, 2019. A total of 75 submissions were received for review, of which 28 papers were selected for presentation and publication. As chair of the Program Committee, I would like to deeply thank all the authors who contributed the results of their innovative research.

My appreciation also goes to all the members of the Program Committee and their designated external reviewers who carefully read and reviewed these submissions. The selection process was a difficult task since each contribution had its own merits. At least three reviewers were assigned to each submission (four if the work included a Program Committee member as an author), and the selection process was carried out with great professionalism and transparency.

The submission process as well as the review process and the editing of the final proceedings were greatly simplified by the software written by Shai Halevi. I would like to thank him for his kind support throughout the entire process. In addition to the contributed talks, the program included a panel discussion moderated by Bart Preneel on "Cryptography and AI."

March 2019

Mitsuru Matsui

CT-RSA 2019

RSA Conference Cryptographer's Track 2019

Moscone Center, San Francisco, California, USA
March 4–8, 2019

Program Chair

Mitsuru Matsui — Mitsubishi Electric Corporation, Japan

Program Committee

Josh Benaloh	Microsoft Research, USA
Alex Biryukov	University of Luxembourg, Luxembourg
Alexandra Boldyreva	Georgia Institute of Technology, USA
Joppe Bos	NXP, Belgium
David Cash	University of Chicago, USA
Jung Hee Cheon	Seoul National University, South Korea
Jean-Sébastien Coron	University of Luxembourg, Luxembourg
Henri Gilbert	ANSSI, France
Helena Handschuh	Rambus Cryptography Research, USA
Tibor Jager	Paderborn University, Germany
Stanislaw Jarecki	University of California at Irvine, USA
Marc Joye	OneSpan, Belgium
Florian Kerschbaum	University of Waterloo, Canada
Xuejia Lai	Shanghai Jiao Tong University, China
Tancrède Lepoint	SRI International, USA
Michael Naehrig	Microsoft Research, USA
Miyako Ohkubo	NICT, Japan
Elisabeth Oswald	University of Bristol, UK
Léo Perrin	Inria, France
David Pointcheval	CNRS and Ecole Normale Supérieure, France
Bart Preneel	KU Leuven and iMinds, Belgium
Reihaneh Safavi-Naini	University of Calgary, Canada
Kazue Sako	NEC, Japan
Peter Scholl	Aarhus University, Denmark
Nigel Smart	KU Leuven, Belgium and University of Bristol, UK
François-Xavier Standaert	Université Catholique de Louvain, Belgium
Takeshi Sugawara	The University of Electro-Communications, Japan
Mehdi Tibouchi	NTT Corporation, Japan
Huaxiong Wang	Nanyang Technological University, Singapore

Additional Reviewers

Masayuki Abe
Mamun Akand
James Bartusek
Carsten Baum
Pascal Bemmann
Ritam Bhaumik
Jan Bobolz
Jie Chen
Hang Cheng
Wonhee Cho
Peter Chvojka
Jan Pieter Denvers
Keita Emura
Prastudy Fauzi
Kai Gellert
Benedikt Gierlichs
Johann Großschädl
Cyprien Delpech de Saint
  Guilhem
Chun Guo
Mike Hamburg
Kyoohyung Han
Minki Hhan
Viet Tung Hoang
Seungwan Hong
James Howe
Jingwei Hu
Takanori Isobe
Toshiyuki Isshiki
Jeremy Jean
Jinhyuck Jeong
Shaoquan Jiang

Zhang Juanyang
Saqib Kakvi
Sabyasachi Karati
Andrey Kim
Dongwoo Kim
Duhyeong Kim
Jaeyun Kim
Jiseung Kim
Rafael Kurek
Virginie Lallemand
Joohee Lee
Keewoo Lee
Yang Li
Benoît Libert
Fuchun Lin
Tingting Lin
Ximeng Liu
Yunwen Liu
Yiyuan Luo
Fermi Ma
Mark Marson
Marco Martinoli
Alexander May
Rui Meng
Rebekah Mercer
Yusuke Naito
Sanami Nakagawa
Khoa Nguyen
David Niehues
Ventzi Nikov
Ryo Nishimaki
Sabine Oechsner

Kazuma Ohara
Jiaxin Pan
Louiza Papachristodoulou
Romain Poussier
Emmanuel Prouff
Matt Robshaw
Dragos Rotaru
Vladimir Rozic
Yusuke Sakai
Luan Cardoso dos Santos
Tobias Schneider
André Schrottenloher
Peter Schwabe
Jae Hong Seo
Yongha Son
Koutarou Suzuki
Hiroto Tamiya
Hikaru Tsuchida
Mike Tunstall
Aleksei Udovenko
Rei Ueno
Fre Vercauteren
Giuseppe Vitto
Hendrik Waldner
Qingju Wang
Carolyn Whitnall
Keita Xagawa
Hailun Yan
Donggeon Yhee
Kazuki Yoneyama
Liang Feng Zhang

Contents

Structure-Preserving Certificateless Encryption and Its Application

Tao Zhang, Huangting Wu, and Sherman S. M. Chow[✉]

Department of Information Engineering, The Chinese University of Hong Kong,
Shatin, New Territories, Hong Kong
sherman@ie.cuhk.edu.hk

Abstract. Certificateless encryption (CLE) combines the advantages of public-key encryption (PKE) and identity-based encryption (IBE) by removing the certificate management of PKE and the key escrow problem of IBE. In this paper, we propose structure-preserving CLE schemes. Structure preservation enables efficient non-interactive proof of certain ciphertext properties, thus supporting efficient modular constructions of advanced cryptographic protocols with a simple design.

As an illustration, we propose a structure-preserving group signature scheme with certified limited (CL) opening from structure-preserving CLE. CL opening allows a master certifier to certify openers. The opener who is the designated one for a group signature can open it (i.e., revoke its anonymity). Neither the certifier nor any non-designated openers can perform the opening. The structure-preserving property of our scheme can also hide who is the designated opener among a list of possibilities.

Keywords: Structure-preserving cryptography ·
Certificateless encryption

1 Introduction

Structure-preserving cryptography is a promising paradigm which enables modular designs of advanced cryptographic protocols, due to its compatibility with efficient non-interactive zero-knowledge proof over the same structure, such as Groth-Sahai proof [21]. Abe *et al.* [3] constructed structure-preserving signature (SPS) schemes which sign on a vector of group elements. They also used SPS to design concurrently-secure group signatures among other applications. Camenisch *et al.* [10] proposed the first CCA-secure structure-preserving encryption (SPE) scheme. Specifically, their integrity check before the final step in the decryption algorithm does not hash the ciphertext, which is often required in other CCA-secure scheme and its presence may hinder its compatibility with

S. S. M. Chow—Supported by General Research Funds (CUHK 14210217) of the Research Grants Council, Hong Kong.

Groth-Sahai proof. SPE found applications in joint computation of cipher-text [10].

Many studies have been carried out on basic primitives which are structure-preserving; yet, despite the numerous applications of identity-based encryption (IBE), (fully) structure-preserving IBE (SP-IBE) has never been studied. SP-IBE requires the public parameters, the plaintext, the ciphertext, and the user identity, consists of only group elements. The user identity is of a particular interest. For existing pairing-based IBE schemes, the user identity ID is not a group element, but consists of integers or bits. Usually, these schemes hash ID to a group element or to an exponent, which kills the original structure of the identity. A notable exception is proposed by Libert and Joye [25], where everything except the user identity consists of only group element. Such a scheme found applications in group signature with message-dependent opening.

It is well known that any IBE construction implies an implicit signature scheme. One may wonder if any of the existing SPS schemes feature a signature which can be used as a decryption key for a certain SP-IBE scheme. In other words, any valid signature can recover the ephemeral session key in the SP-IBE scheme, by pairing up the signature (as a user decryption key) with the cipher-text. However, to the best of the authors' knowledge, existing SPS signatures cannot be used for this purpose. The reason is that the verification equation requires the computation of a pairing term where both of its input comes from the signature. From another perspective, if one is going to generate a ciphertext such that it is decryptable by such a decryption key, the pairing will involve an unknown term since the decryption key is unknown to the encryptor. In this paper, towards enriching the class of structure-preserving cryptographic schemes, we move our focus to structure-preserving certificateless encryption (SP-CLE).

Certificateless encryption (CLE), introduced by Al-Riyami and Paterson [5], strikes a balance between IBE and public-key encryption (PKE). In traditional PKE, an encryptor needs to verify a certificate which ensures that a given public key belongs to the recipient. This requires a public-key infrastructure to support the storage and distribution of the certificates. The sender also needs to verify the certificate before encrypting. To overcome this weakness of PKE, IBE provides another solution in which every identity string can be mapped to a public key via a publicly computable function. The corresponding private decryption key can only be generated by the key generation center (KGC). Such kind of key-escrow is inherent and introduces serious security concerns. CLE removes key-escrow by requiring both the partial decryption key from the KGC and a user secret in decryption. Yet, unlike PKE, CLE does not need any infrastructure to authenticate users' public keys. In contrast, implicit certification is ensured by the KGC since decryption would be impossible without the partial decryption key.

In the CLE formulation of Al-Riyami and Paterson [5], a user can compute and release its user public key before it obtains its partial decryption key from the KGC. Such formulation implies the existence of both PKE and IBE [18]. Indeed, CLE can be constructed generically from IBE and PKE. Baek, Safavi-Naini, and Susilo [6] formulated an alternative CLE notion in which a user must obtain its partial decryption key from the KGC before it can compute its user public key. Such formulation no longer implies IBE. Consequently, Baek *et al.* constructed CLE from Schnorr signatures and ElGamal PKE. This gives us hope in designing SP-CLE without first designing SP-IBE.

Another distinctive feature of CLE is its security under strong decryption [5]. A strong decryption oracle can provide correct decryption even when the public key of a user is replaced by the adversary, without requiring the adversary to surrender the decryption key corresponding to the replaced public key. This level of security has important applications in complete non-malleability [7,14]. Many CLE schemes, under either formulation [5,6], rely on the random oracle to simulate the strong decryption oracle. Dent *et al.* [19] proposed the first CLE scheme featuring strong decryption in the standard model. Yet, Groth-Sahai proof cannot prove about its ciphertext well-formedness due to the presence of a hash.

Our Contribution. We propose the first SP-CLE schemes over groups with bilinear map $e : \mathbb{G} \times \mathbb{H} \to \mathbb{G}_T$. We first present a construction encrypting plaintexts in $\mathbb{G}_T$ which is secure against chosen-plaintext attacks (CPA). Then, we extend it to support message space of $\mathbb{G}$ (or $\mathbb{H}$). Finally, we show how to extend it for security against replayable chosen-ciphertext attacks (RCCA). Our proofs do not rely on random oracles; yet, they are proven in the generic group model.

To illustrate the application of SP-CLE, we then build a (partially) structure-preserving group signature scheme with certified limited (CL) opening from our SP-CLE. We defer the relevant introduction and motivation to Sect. 5.

2 Preliminaries

2.1 Bilinear Group

For bilinear group context $\mathcal{G} = (\mathbb{G}, \mathbb{H}, \mathbb{G}_T, e, p, g, h)$, $\mathbb{G}, \mathbb{H}$, and $\mathbb{G}_T$ are groups of prime order p, where g and h are random generators for $\mathbb{G}$ and $\mathbb{H}$ respectively. A bilinear map $e : \mathbb{G} \times \mathbb{H} \to \mathbb{G}_T$ is a non-trivial and efficiently computable pairing function such that, for all $u \in \mathbb{G}$, $v \in \mathbb{H}$, $a, b \in \mathbb{Z}$, $e(u^a, v^b) = e(u, v)^{ab}$. In Type-I groups, $\mathbb{G} = \mathbb{H}$. For Type II, there exists an efficient mapping from $\mathbb{G}$ to $\mathbb{H}$ but not the other way around. For Type III, there exists no efficient mapping between $\mathbb{G}$ and $\mathbb{H}$. This paper uses Type-III groups which is the most efficient.

2.2 Groth-Sahai Proof System

Groth and Sahai [21] proposed several instantiations for efficient NIZK proof of knowledge, for statements about group elements satisfying a pairing product equation. Their proof system (called Groth-Sahai proof hereinafter) consists of four algorithms $\mathcal{GS} = (\texttt{Setup}, \texttt{Prove}, \texttt{Verify}, \texttt{Extract})$. $\texttt{Setup}(1^\lambda)$ generates the common reference string $\texttt{crs}$ and the extraction key $\texttt{ek}$. $\texttt{Prove}()$ takes in a witness and a statement to generate a proof of the statement w.r.t. the witness. We use the notation PoK to refer to a proof. $\texttt{Verify}()$ outputs 1 on a valid proof.

$\mathcal{GS}$ uses a commitment scheme (`Commit`() with commitment key ck) as a building block, committing the witness to prepare for an NIZK proof of knowledge. The remaining algorithm `Extract`() extracts the hidden element from a proof with the extraction key ek. The commitment key ck is publicly accessible, and the extraction key ek is only accessible to a knowledge extractor.

2.3 Structure-Preserving Signature

A signature scheme is a tuple of four algorithms (`Setup`, `KeyGen`, `Sign`, `Verify`). It is structure preserving [3] if the verification key, the messages, and the signatures consist of only group elements, and the verification algorithm only evaluates pairing product equations of the form $\prod_i \prod_j e(G_i, H_j)^{a_{ij}} = 1_{\mathbb{G}_T}$, where $G_i \in \mathbb{G}$ and $H_j \in \mathbb{H}$ are group elements forming the verification key, the message(s), and the public parameters, $a_{ij} \in \mathbb{Z}_p$ are constants, and the element $1_{\mathbb{G}_T}$ is the identity element in $\mathbb{G}_T$. An SPS is existentially unforgeable under chosen-message attack (EUF-CMA) if no probabilistic polynomial-time (PPT) adversary can output a valid forgery (M, σ), given the public parameters param, the verification key vk, and a signing oracle for adversarially chosen messages but M is never queried. If the signing oracle can only be queried once, the scheme is called one-time secure.

3   Definitions of Certificateless Encryption

We follow Baek *et al.*'s formulation [6, 31], where the user public key can only be generated after the user has interacted with the KGC. We add one algorithm `SetUserSec`() which is executed by a user and include a partial user public key ppk as part of the input of `Issue`, an algorithm executed by the KGC for the user. These changes have been discussed in the seminal work [5]. A benefit is that the CLE scheme can reach trust level 3 named by Girault [20] as a traditional PKI. The CLE definition in this paper consists of seven algorithms (`Setup`, `MKeyGen`, `SetUserSec`, `Issue`, `UKeyGen`, `Enc`, `Dec`):

- `Setup`(1^λ) $\to$ param. This algorithm takes in a security parameter 1^λ and outputs the parameter param. We assume param is an implicit input to all other algorithms.
- `MKeyGen`() $\to$ (mpk, msk). The KGC runs this algorithm. It generates the master public-private key pair. The KGC publishes the master public key mpk and keeps the master secret key msk in private.
- `SetUserSec`(mpk, ID) $\to$ (ppk, uk). A user takes as input the master public key mpk and its own identity ID, and outputs a partial user public key ppk and a user secret value uk.
- `Issue`(msk, mpk, ID, ppk) $\to$ psk. The KGC takes in the master public-private key pair, a user identity ID, and a user partial public key ppk to generate the user partial secret key psk for ID.
- `UKeyGen`(mpk, ppk, psk, uk) $\to$ (upk, usk). With respect to the master public key mpk and a partial public key ppk, the user uses its partial secret key psk

and user secret value uk to generate the user public-private key pair (upk, usk). The user publishes the user public key upk and keeps the full private key usk in private.

- Enc(mpk, upk, ID, M) → C. This algorithm takes in the master public key mpk, the user public key upk, and an identity ID, to encrypt a plaintext M.
- Dec(mpk, upk, usk, C) → M. This deterministic algorithm takes in the master public key, the user public-private key pair, and a ciphertext to recover the plaintext M, or the error symbol ⊥ when C is invalid.

A CLE scheme is said to be correct if for any integer λ, param ← Setup(1^λ), (mpk, msk) ← MKeyGen(param), any string ID, (ppk, uk) ← SetUserSec(mpk, ID), psk ← Issue(msk, mpk, ID, ppk), (upk, usk) ← UKeyGen(mpk, ppk, psk, uk), any message M, and C ← Enc(mpk, upk, ID, M), we have M ← Dec(mpk, upk, usk, C).

A CLE scheme is said to be structure-preserving if the encryption and decryption algorithms only operate on group elements. In other words, all elements in mpk, upk, and usk, the identity ID, the message M to encrypt, and the ciphertext C to be produced, are all group elements. We call a CLE scheme to be partially structure-preserving if some elements in ID, M, or C are not group elements, e.g., ID in Libert and Joye [25] and M and C in our basic scheme.

We consider two kinds of adversaries. Type-I adversary $\mathcal{A}_I$ models the malicious users who can replace the public key of a victim user to other "unauthenticated" public keys since there is no certificate. Type-II adversary $\mathcal{A}_{II}$ models an honest-but-curious KGC who can obtain partial decryption keys for the users, but cannot replace the user public key for any user. Obviously, these two types of adversaries cannot collude. We first describe the oracles available to $\mathcal{A}_I/\mathcal{A}_{II}$:

- **Replace Public Key.** The adversary submits ID and a user public key upk′ to this oracle, which replaces the previous user public key of ID to upk′.
- **Extract Partial Secret Key.** The adversary submits an identity ID to this oracle. This oracle returns the partial secret key psk generated for ID.
- **Extract Full Private Key.** The adversary supplies an identity ID to this oracle. This oracle returns the full private key usk generated for ID.
- **Strong Decrypt.** The adversary supplies an identity ID and a ciphertext C. This oracle creates a full private key usk for ID if it is not previously generated, decrypts C with usk even if upk of ID used in C has been replaced, and sends the plaintext to the adversary.
- **Weak SV Decrypt.** The adversary supplies an identity ID, a user secret uk′, and a ciphertext C to this oracle. This oracle creates usk′ for ID with the real psk and uk′, and decrypts C. The oracle returns the plaintext result.

Definition 1 (IND-CPA security against Type-I adversary). *A CLE scheme is indistinguishable under chosen-plaintext attacks (IND-CPA secure) against Type-I adversary if* $Adv_{\mathcal{A}_I}^{IND\text{-}CPA}$ *is negligible.*

Setup. The challenger $\mathcal{C}$ executes Setup() and publishes param.

Master Key Generation. $\mathcal{C}$ runs MKeyGen(), sends mpk to $\mathcal{A}_I$, and keeps msk private.

Query Phase. The adversary $\mathcal{A}_I$ first makes registration queries for a polynomial number of identities $\{ID_i\}_{i=1}^q$. $\mathcal{C}$ runs $psk_i \leftarrow$ Issue(msk, mpk, ID_i, ppk_i) and $(upk_i, usk_i) \leftarrow$ UKeyGen(mpk, psk_i), and publishes upk_i for $i \in [1, q]$. Then, $\mathcal{A}_I$ can make **Replace Public Key**, **Extract Partial Secret Key**, and **Extract Full Private Key** queries on any registered identity, but $\mathcal{A}_I$ cannot request for the partial or full private key of an identity ID after replacing its upk.

Challenge. $\mathcal{A}_I$ submits an identity ID^* and two messages M_0, M_1 to $\mathcal{C}$. $\mathcal{C}$ aborts this game if any of the following events happen.

- $\mathcal{A}_I$ made **Extract Full Private Key** query on ID^*.
- $\mathcal{A}_I$ made both **Replace Public Key** query and **Extract Partial Secret Key** query on ID^*.

$\mathcal{C}$ then randomly picks $b \xleftarrow{\$} \{0, 1\}$ and gives $C^* = $ Enc(mpk, upk^*, ID^*, M_b) to $\mathcal{A}_I$.

Guess. $\mathcal{A}_I$ receives C^* and outputs a bit b'. If $b' = b$, $\mathcal{A}_I$ wins the game. The advantage of $\mathcal{A}_I$ in this game is $Adv_{\mathcal{A}_I}^{\text{IND-CPA}} = \Pr[b' = b] - \frac{1}{2}$.

Definition 2 (IND-CPA security against Type-II adversary). *A CLE scheme is IND-CPA secure against Type-II adversary if $Adv_{\mathcal{A}_{II}}^{\text{IND-CPA}}$ defined below is negligible.*

Setup. The challenger $\mathcal{C}$ executes Setup() and publishes param.

Master Key Generation. The challenger $\mathcal{C}$ runs the algorithm (mpk, msk) $\leftarrow$ MKeyGen(param), publishes mpk, and sends msk to $\mathcal{A}_{II}$.

Query Phase. $\mathcal{A}_{II}$ and $\mathcal{C}$ interact in the same way as in the experiment in Definition 1 except for the following differences. First, $\mathcal{C}$ sends psk to $\mathcal{A}_{II}$. Second, $\mathcal{A}_{II}$ can create new psk_i for ID_i by itself. Third, $\mathcal{A}_{II}$ can only make **Extract Full Private Key** queries in this game.

Challenge and **Guess.** These two phases are the same as in the experiment in Definition 1. The advantage of $\mathcal{A}_{II}$ in this game is $Adv_{\mathcal{A}_{II}}^{\text{IND-CPA}} = \Pr[b' = b] - \frac{1}{2}$.

The indistinguishability under chosen-ciphertext attacks (IND-CCA security) games for SP-CLE against *Strong Type-I* and *Strong Type-II* adversaries are similar to the experiments in Definitions 1 and 2 respectively, except that in Query Phase, the adversaries can make **Strong Decrypt** and **Weak SV Decrypt** queries on ciphertexts of its choice except C^*. The advantage of $\mathcal{A}_I$ and $\mathcal{A}_{II}$ in IND-CCA game are defined as $Adv_{\mathcal{A}_I}^{\text{IND-CCA}}$ and $Adv_{\mathcal{A}_{II}}^{\text{IND-CCA}}$ respectively. For replayable CCA (RCCA) security [11], decryption oracle returns `replay` if the decryption result is M_0 or M_1 after the challenge phase.

4 A Specific Construction of SP-CLE

4.1 Intuition

Instead of using an SPE generically to perform encryption, we rely on the pairings computed in the SPS verification for encryption or decryption. In our scheme, a receiver generates and sends his partial public key ppk to the KGC. The KGC creates a structure-preserving signature on the receiver identity together with the partial public key. The receiver then publishes *a part* of the signature together with his partial public key while keeping the remaining signature parts.

A general verification algorithm of an SPS consists of a series of pairing product equations of the form $\prod_{i=1}^{m} \prod_{j=1}^{n} e(G_i, H_j)^{a_{ij}} = 1_{\mathbb{G}_T}$, where $G_i \in \mathbb{G}$ for $i \in [1, m]$, $H_j \in \mathbb{H}$ for $j \in [1, n]$, and $a_{ij} \in \{-1, 0, 1\}$. The group elements G_i and H_i are from the verification key of SPS, the signature being verified, or the message. The exponents a_{ij} indicate whether they should be on the left or the right side of the equation (1 or -1), or should not appear at all (0).

We divide the set $\{(G_i, H_j)\}_{(i,j)}$ into two indices sets: $\mathbf{K}$ which contains the pairings used in encryption by the sender to construct a session key (or for hiding the plaintext); and $\overline{\mathbf{K}}$ which contains the rest of the pairing that are used in decryption to recover the session key. To encrypt a plaintext M, the pairings $e(G_i, H_i)$ for $(i, j) \in \mathbf{K}$ and some randomness $r_{ij} \xleftarrow{\$} \mathbb{Z}_p$ together form a session key as $\prod_{(i,j) \in \mathbf{K}} e(G_i, H_j)^{a_{ij} \cdot r_{ij}}$. The ciphertext also contains elements exponentiated with the randomness r_{ij} ($\{x, y, z\}$ in our concrete scheme below). The remaining pairings in set $\overline{\mathbf{K}}$ can be used in the decryption algorithm to pair up the ciphertext elements and the decryption key to recover the session key.

Whether a pairing should be put in the session key, included in the other ciphertext elements, or used in decryption privately as part of the decryption key, depends on whether the input of a pairing function is public or not.

We start with the basics. To make our exposition concrete, we consider the SPS scheme due to Abe *et al.* [4]. We chose to build our SP-CLE based on this SPS for its optimality. The verification key of the SPS scheme is the master public key which should be public. This contains $(g, h, U, \tilde{V}_1, \tilde{V}_2, W_1, W_2)$. The message vector signed by SPS contains a user identity and a (partial) user public key D_α. Both elements are public. The signature $(\tilde{R}, \tilde{S}, T)$ contributes to the only parts which can be private. Now, we classify the pairings in the SPS verification. A similar classification has also been done in the literature [32] for a different purpose (delegating computations of pairings).

(1) *Both* elements in a pairing are *public*: This type of pairing includes public key-public key pairs and message-public key pairs. The involved elements are available to the encryptor, so we use *all* of them in the *session key*. In our scheme, these include $e(W_1, h)$, $e(\mathsf{ID}, \tilde{V}_1)$, $e(D_\alpha, \tilde{V}_2)$, and $e(g, h)$, where D_α is a user-chosen public key. Our scheme also includes an additional term $e(D_\alpha, h)$ to ensure that only the user but not the KGC (who can recreate the SPS signature) can decrypt. Looking ahead, our scheme publishes $\tilde{R}$ from the signature, so $e(W_2, \tilde{R})$ and $e(U, \tilde{R})$ eventually belong to this type (see "both private" below).

(2) *One* of the elements in a pairing is *public*: This type of pairing includes public key-signature pairs and message-signature pairs. In our scheme, that is $e(g, \tilde{S})$. The public element can be used to embed randomness r in the ciphertext in the form of G_i^r or H_j^r. In our scheme, such elements include g (and $\tilde{R}$ below).

(3) *Both* elements in a pairing are *private*: The private elements (from the SPS signature) are part of the user private key. This type of pairing includes only signature-signature pairs. In our scheme, $e(T, \tilde{R})$ "originally" belongs to this type. As both of the elements are private, the encryptor has no way to know what is the SPS signature (i.e., user private key) obtained by the intended decryptor. We thus publish $\tilde{R}$ as part of the user public key (which is not allowed in the IBE setting). We remark that such treatment is not possible for IBE since the user public key in IBE should be purely derived from the identity instead of any random choice made by the KGC during user private key generation.

Such a choice (over T) is due to multiple reasons. Firstly, $\tilde{R}$ is created as a random term which by itself does not relate to the private signing key in any way. It is intuitively safer to publish it instead of T which is a term created from the private signing key on top of some public information like identity. Moreover, $\tilde{R}$ is the term which "glues up" two equations in the SPS verification. If the adversary chose to manipulate this term, it needs to deal with two equations. From the efficiency perspective, publishing $\tilde{R}$ minimizes the number of public-private pairings, which reduces the ciphertext size.

With $\tilde{R}$ published in our scheme, this makes $e(T, \tilde{R})$ becomes the type of "one being public". As discussed, the ciphertext in our scheme thus includes the term $\tilde{R}$ to embed the ciphertext randomness. Also, $e(W_2, \tilde{R})$ and $e(U, \tilde{R})$ in the pairing-product equations become the type of "both being public", and hence these pairing terms appear in the session key.

4.2　CPA-Secure SP-CLE Scheme

We construct our CPA-secure SP-CLE scheme called $\mathcal{CLE}_0$ based on an existing structure-preserving signature scheme of Abe *et al.* [4].

$\mathsf{Setup}(1^\lambda) \to \mathsf{param}$. Choose a bilinear group context $\mathcal{G} = (\mathbb{G}, \mathbb{H}, \mathbb{G}_T, e, p, g, h)$, and output $\mathsf{param} = \mathcal{G}$.

$\mathsf{MKeyGen}(\mathsf{param}) \to (\mathsf{mpk}, \mathsf{msk})$. The KGC randomly picks $u, v_1, v_2, w_1, w_2 \xleftarrow{\$} \mathbb{Z}_p^*$ where $u \neq -w_2$, and computes $U = g^u$, $\tilde{V}_1 = h^{v_1}$, $\tilde{V}_2 = h^{v_2}$, $W_1 = g^{w_1}$, and $W_2 = g^{w_2}$. The master key pair is

$$\mathsf{mpk} = (U, \tilde{V}_1, \tilde{V}_2, W_1, W_2), \qquad \mathsf{msk} = (u, v_1, v_2, w_1, w_2).$$

This key pair is just the one for the SPS scheme by Abe *et al.* [4] with the message space of $\mathbb{G}^2 \times \mathbb{H}$. Specifically, U is for the $\mathbb{H}$ part of the message space, and $(\tilde{V}_1, \tilde{V}_2)$ is for $\mathbb{G}^2$. Note that $e(g, h)$ and $e(W_1, h)$ can be pre-computed, especially when W_1 is never used as is except in $e(W_1, h)$.

$\texttt{SetUserSec}(\mathsf{mpk}) \to (\mathsf{ppk}, \mathsf{uk})$. A user randomly picks $\alpha \xleftarrow{\$} \mathbb{Z}_p$, computes $D_\alpha = g^\alpha$ and $\tilde{D}_\alpha = h^\alpha$, and sets $\mathsf{ppk} = D_\alpha$ and $\mathsf{uk} = \tilde{D}_\alpha$.

$\texttt{Issue}(\mathsf{msk}, \mathsf{mpk}, \mathsf{ID}, \mathsf{ppk}) \to \mathsf{psk}$. For $\mathsf{ID} \in \mathbb{G}$ and $\mathsf{ppk} = D_\alpha \in \mathbb{G}$, the KGC randomly chooses $r \xleftarrow{\$} \mathbb{Z}_p^*$ and computes

$$\tilde{R} = h^r, \qquad \tilde{S} = h^{w_1 - r \cdot w_2} \cdot \tilde{R}^{-u}, \qquad T = (g \cdot \mathsf{ID}^{-v_1} \cdot D_\alpha^{-v_2})^{\frac{1}{r}},$$

Output $\mathsf{psk} = (\tilde{R}, \tilde{S}, T)$ as the partial secret key.

We remark that $(\tilde{R}, \tilde{S}, T)$ forms a signature on $(\mathsf{ID}, D_\alpha, \tilde{R}) \in \mathbb{G}^2 \times \mathbb{H}$ for the SPS scheme by Abe *et al.* [4] which can be verified with the equations below:

$$e(W_2, \tilde{R})e(g, \tilde{S})e(U, \tilde{R}) = e(W_1, h), \qquad e(T, \tilde{R})e(\mathsf{ID}, \tilde{V}_1)e(D_\alpha, \tilde{V}_2) = e(g, h).$$

Note that the first equation can be simplified to $e(W_2 \cdot U, \tilde{R})e(g, \tilde{S}) = e(W_1, h)$.

Different from the underlying signature scheme, we expect the signature to sign on an element $\tilde{R}$ of itself. This remains secure in the generic group model.

$\texttt{UKeyGen}(\mathsf{mpk}, \mathsf{ppk}, \mathsf{psk}, \mathsf{uk}) \to (\mathsf{upk}, \mathsf{usk})$. A user parses psk as $(\tilde{R}, \tilde{S}, T)$ and set the key pair as

$$\mathsf{upk} = (D_\alpha, \tilde{R}), \qquad \mathsf{usk} = (\tilde{D}_\alpha, \tilde{S}, T) \qquad (\text{recall: } \mathsf{ppk} = D_\alpha \text{ and } \mathsf{uk} = \tilde{D}_\alpha).$$

As $\tilde{R}$ is a part of upk, it can be replaced by an adversary. Our scheme thus also requires the KGC to "implicitly certify" $\tilde{R}$ during partial secret key generation.

$\texttt{Enc}(\mathsf{mpk}, \mathsf{upk}, \mathsf{ID}, M) \to C$. To encrypt $M \in \mathbb{G}_T$, the sender randomly picks $x, y, z \xleftarrow{\$} \mathbb{Z}_p$, and computes

$$K = \{e(W_2, \tilde{R})e(U, \tilde{R})/e(W_1, h)\}^x \{e(\mathsf{ID}, \tilde{V}_1)e(D_\alpha, \tilde{V}_2)/e(g, h)\}^y/e(D_\alpha, h)^z,$$
$$C_0 = M \cdot K, \quad C_g = g^x, \quad C_R = \tilde{R}^y, \quad C_z = g^z.$$

Output the ciphertext $C = (C_0, C_g, C_R, C_z)$.

(Note that $K = \{e(W_2 U, \tilde{R})/e(W_1, h)\}^x \{e(\mathsf{ID}, \tilde{V}_1)/e(g, h)\}^y e(D_\alpha, \tilde{V}_2^y/h^z).$)

$\texttt{Dec}(\mathsf{mpk}, \mathsf{upk}, \mathsf{usk}, C) \to M/\perp$. Parse C as (C_0, C_g, C_R, C_z). Output

$$M = C_0 \cdot e(C_g, \tilde{S})e(T, C_R)e(C_z, \tilde{D}_\alpha).$$

Analysis. **Correctness.** Recall that $D_\alpha = g^\alpha$, $\tilde{D}_\alpha = h^\alpha$, $C_0 = M \cdot K$, and

$$K = e(W_2, \tilde{R})^x e(U, \tilde{R})^x e(W_1, h)^{-x} \cdot e(\mathsf{ID}, \tilde{V}_1)^y e(D_\alpha, \tilde{V}_2)^y e(g, h)^{-y} \cdot e(D_\alpha, h)^{-z}.$$

Hence, the decryption algorithm proceeds as below.

$$C_0 \cdot e(C_g, \tilde{S})e(T, C_R)e(C_z, \tilde{D}_\alpha)$$
$$= M \cdot K \cdot e(C_g, \tilde{S})e(T, C_R)e(C_z, \tilde{D}_\alpha)$$
$$= M \cdot e(W_2, \tilde{R})^x e(U, \tilde{R})^x e(W_1, h)^{-x} e(\mathsf{ID}, \tilde{V}_1)^y e(D_\alpha, \tilde{V}_2)^y e(g, h)^{-y} e(D_\alpha, h)^{-z}$$
$$\quad e(C_g, \tilde{S})e(T, C_R)e(C_z, \tilde{D}_\alpha)$$
$$= M \cdot e(W_2, \tilde{R})^x e(U, \tilde{R})^x e(W_1, h)^{-x} e(C_g, \tilde{S})$$
$$\quad e(\mathsf{ID}, \tilde{V}_1)^y e(D_\alpha, \tilde{V}_2)^y e(g, h)^{-y} e(T, C_R) \cdot e(D_\alpha, h)^{-z} e(C_z, \tilde{D}_\alpha)$$
$$= M \cdot e(W_2, \tilde{R})^x e(U, \tilde{R})^x e(W_1, h)^{-x} e(g, \tilde{S})^x$$
$$\quad e(\mathsf{ID}, \tilde{V}_1)^y e(D_\alpha, \tilde{V}_2)^y e(g, h)^{-y} e(T, \tilde{R})^y \cdot e(g^\alpha, h)^{-z} e(g^z, h^\alpha)$$
$$= M \cdot (e(W_2, \tilde{R})e(g, \tilde{S})e(U, \tilde{R})e(W_1, h)^{-1})^x$$
$$\quad (e(T, \tilde{R})e(\mathsf{ID}, \tilde{V}_1)e(D_\alpha, \tilde{V}_2)e(g, h)^{-1})^y = M.$$

The second last equality holds because $(\tilde{R}, \tilde{S}, T)$ is a signature which satisfies the verification equations mentioned when we describe Issue().

Efficiency. We first start with some basic observations of our scheme. The user private key consists of 3 elements in base groups. The ciphertext consists of 3 group elements in base groups and 1 group element in the target group. The decryption algorithm needs 3 pairings and 4 multiplications in the target group.

Comparison with the Generic Approach. It is mandatory to compare the performance of our proposed scheme with the folklore approach of building a CLE scheme "with certificate" [12]. Specifically, one can build a CLE scheme from any SPS and SPE schemes in the following way. A user publishes an SPE public key with an SPS signature on it as his public key. An encryptor encrypts to the user using the SPE public key only if the SPS signature is verified successfully.

Instantiating this idea with the SPS due to Abe *et al.* [4] used in our concrete construction, we can see that the user public key will then consists of at least 3 elements from the SPS (and at least 1 element from the SPE public key as the CLE partial user public key). In contrast, for our concrete construction, the user public key consists of only 2 elements in base groups, which is much shorter.

The explicit certificate verification step in the folklore approach using the same SPS scheme as ours will require 3 multiplications in the target group and 5 pairings. While the complexity of the actual encryption steps depends on which SPE scheme is used to instantiate this idea, the number of pairings involved is already larger than what our proposed scheme requires. Our encryption algorithm takes 5 exponentiations and 2 multiplications in base groups, 2 exponentiations and 4 multiplications in the target group, and 3 pairing computations.

Theorem 1. $\mathcal{CLE}_0$ *is CPA-secure against Type-I and Type-II adversaries in the generic group model (without any isomorphism between the two base groups).*

To prove that $\mathcal{CLE}_0$ is CPA-secure against Type-I and Type-II adversaries, we replace the challenge ciphertext component C_0^* with a random element in $\mathbb{G}_T$

and show that the adversaries cannot distinguish this simulation with the real scheme in the generic group model. The detailed proof is in the full version.

4.3   A Variant CLE Scheme for $M \in \mathbb{G}$

This part proposes an SP-CLE scheme $\mathcal{CLE}_1$ encrypting $M \in \mathbb{G}$ building on top of $\mathcal{CLE}_0$. Based on the technique of encrypting group elements in the partially structure-preserving IBE scheme [25], we present a generic way to transform a scheme encrypting plaintexts in $\mathbb{G}_T$ to a scheme encrypting plaintexts in $\mathbb{G}$ or $\mathbb{H}$.

Setup(1^λ) $\rightarrow$ param. The KGC runs $\mathsf{param}_0 \leftarrow \mathcal{CLE}_0.\mathsf{Setup}(1^\lambda)$, picks $G_i \xleftarrow{\$} \mathbb{G}$ for $i \in [1, l]$ where l is suitably large[1], and outputs param = $(\mathsf{param}_0, \{G_i\}_{i=1}^l)$.

MKeyGen() $\rightarrow$ (mpk, msk). The KGC runs $(\mathsf{mpk}_0, \mathsf{msk}_0) \leftarrow \mathcal{CLE}_0.\mathsf{MKeyGen}$ (param_0) and outputs the master key pair mpk = $(\mathsf{mpk}_0, \{G_i\}_{i=1}^l)$, msk = msk_0.

SetUserSec(mpk) $\rightarrow$ (ppk, uk). A user runs $(\mathsf{ppk}, \mathsf{uk}) \leftarrow \mathcal{CLE}_0.\mathsf{SetUserSec}$ (mpk_0), and sets ppk, uk as its partial public key and the user secret value respectively.

Issue(msk, mpk, ID, ppk) $\rightarrow$ psk. For a user ID $\in \mathbb{H}$, the KGC runs $\mathsf{psk}_0 \leftarrow \mathcal{CLE}_0.\mathsf{Issue}(\mathsf{msk}_0, \mathsf{mpk}_0, \mathsf{ID}, \mathsf{ppk})$ and outputs the partial secret key psk = psk_0.

UKeyGen(mpk, ppk, psk, uk) $\rightarrow$ (upk, usk). The user computes its own user public-private key pair as $(\mathsf{upk}, \mathsf{usk}) \leftarrow \mathcal{CLE}_0.\mathsf{UKeyGen}(\mathsf{mpk}_0, \mathsf{psk}_0, \mathsf{ppk}, \mathsf{uk})$.

Enc(mpk, upk, ID, M) $\rightarrow$ C. To encrypt $M \in \mathbb{G}$, randomly choose $\tau_k \in \{0, 1\}$ for $k = 1, 2, \cdots, l$, and compute

$$C_0 = M \cdot \prod_{j=1}^l G_j^{\tau_j}, C_{k,M} \leftarrow \mathcal{CLE}_0.\mathsf{Enc}(\mathsf{mpk}_0, \mathsf{upk}, \mathsf{ID}, e(G_k, h)^{\tau_k}) \; \forall k \in \{1, 2, \cdots, l\}.$$

Output $C = (C_0, \{C_{k,M}\}_{k=1}^l)$ as the ciphertext (where $\{C_{k,M}\}$ are still in $\mathbb{G}_T$).

Dec(mpk, upk, usk, C) $\rightarrow$ $M/\perp$. Parse C as $(C_0, \{C_{k,M}\}_{k=1}^l)$. For $k = 1, 2, \cdots, l$, compute $M_k = \mathcal{CLE}_0.\mathsf{Dec}(\mathsf{mpk}_0, \mathsf{upk}, \mathsf{usk}, C_{k,M})$ and find τ_k such that $M_k = e(G_k, h)^{\tau_k}$. Output $M = \frac{C_0}{\prod_{k=1}^l G_k^{\tau_k}}$ as the plaintext.

The scheme $\mathcal{CLE}_1$ also supports plaintexts from $\mathbb{H}$. If we choose $\tilde{H}_k \in \mathbb{H}$ for integer $k \in [1, l]$ as part of the master public key, and encrypt the plaintext as $M \cdot \prod_{k=1}^l \tilde{H}_k^{\tau_k}$, we can then encrypt plaintext in $\mathbb{H}$.

Correctness. The correctness of $\mathcal{CLE}_1$ follows from the correctness of $\mathcal{CLE}_0$, which ensures that M_k can be calculated correctly. Thus, there is at most one series $\{\tau_k\}_{k=1}^l$ such that $M_k = e(G_k, h)^{\tau_k}$ for all $k \in [1, l]$, and this series can cancel the term $\prod_{k=1}^l G_k^{\tau_k}$ in C_0 to obtain the plaintext M. More details can be seen from the correctness analysis in our CCA-secure extension presented below, which also encrypts messages in the base group ($\mathbb{H}$).

---

[1] In the partially structure-preserving IBE scheme [25], this represents the bit-length of the identity. In our scheme, ID is a group element, so l belongs to poly(λ).

Theorem 2. *The SP-CLE scheme $\mathcal{CLE}_1$ is IND-CPA secure if $\mathcal{CLE}_0$ is IND-CPA secure.*

The proof is deferred to the full version.

4.4 RCCA-Secure Extension

Now we propose an RCCA-secure SP-CLE scheme $\mathcal{CLE}_2$ with message space $\mathbb{H}$, which uses a one-time SPS scheme $\mathcal{OTS}$ and a simulation-sound NIZK proof system $\mathcal{GS}$ as building blocks, following the idea of transforming CPA-secure IBE to CCA-secure PKE [9]. We use the SPS scheme proposed by Abe *et al.* [2] as $\mathcal{OTS}$ (which is also used in an CCA-secure SPE scheme by Libert *et al.* [27]).

Our RCCA-secure SP-CLE is derived from $\mathcal{CLE}_1$. Intuitively, the encryptor generates an $\mathcal{OTS}$ key pair (ovk, osk), binds ovk with the session key, provides extra elements computed from osk (which can be simulated without osk with the "trapdoor" in param), and proves everything is faithfully constructed using osk. We add a Groth-Sahai proof of the validity of the ciphertext embedding the plaintext as a witness. When simulating **Strong Decrypt** oracle, the challenger can extract the plaintext even for an identity with replaced user public key.

Setup(1^λ) $\to$ param. Run the two algorithms $\mathsf{param}_1 \leftarrow \mathcal{CLE}_1.\mathsf{Setup}(1^\lambda)$ and $\mathsf{param}_{OTS} \leftarrow \mathcal{OTS}.\mathsf{Setup}(1^\lambda, 1)$, and set up $\mathcal{GS}$ to generate a common reference string crs. Randomly choose $u_i \xleftarrow{\$} \mathbb{Z}_p$ for $i \in [1, 4]$ to compute $U_i = g^{u_i}$, $\tilde{H}_i = h^{u_i}$, and output the public parameter $\mathsf{param} = (\mathsf{param}_1, \mathsf{param}_{OTS}, \mathsf{crs}, \{U_i, \tilde{H}_i\}_{i=1}^4)$.

MKeyGen(param) $\to$ (mpk, msk). The KGC runs the algorithm $(\mathsf{mpk}_1, \mathsf{msk}_1) \leftarrow \mathcal{CLE}_1.\mathsf{MKeyGen}(\mathsf{param}_1)$, and outputs the master public-private key pair as $\mathsf{mpk} = (\mathsf{mpk}_1, \{U_i, \tilde{H}_i\}_{i=1}^4)$, $\mathsf{msk} = \mathsf{msk}_1$. The one-time public key ovk for $\mathcal{OTS}$ of our choice [2] consists of 4 group elements in $\mathbb{H}$. The elements $\{U_i, \tilde{H}_i\}_{i=1}^4$ are for binding ovk with a ciphertext. Generally, i can be in the range $[1, k]$ where k is the number of elements contained in ovk of the one-time SPS scheme.

SetUserSec(mpk) $\to$ (ppk, uk). A user runs $(\mathsf{ppk}, \mathsf{uk}) \leftarrow \mathcal{CLE}_1.\mathsf{SetUserSec}$ (mpk_1), and sets $(\mathsf{ppk}, \mathsf{uk})$ as its partial public key and the user secret value respectively.

Issue(msk, mpk, ID, ppk) $\to$ psk. For a user with identity $\mathsf{ID} \in \mathbb{H}$, the KGC outputs the partial secret key $\mathsf{psk} \leftarrow \mathcal{CLE}_1.\mathsf{Issue}(\mathsf{msk}_1, \mathsf{mpk}_1, \mathsf{ID}, \mathsf{ppk})$.

UKeyGen(mpk, psk, ppk, uk) $\to$ (upk, usk). The user computes its own user public-private key pair as $(\mathsf{upk}, \mathsf{usk}) \leftarrow \mathcal{CLE}_1.\mathsf{UKeyGen}(\mathsf{mpk}, \mathsf{psk}, \mathsf{ppk}, \mathsf{uk})$.

Enc(mpk, upk, ID, M) $\to$ C. To encrypt $M \in \mathbb{G}$, the sender randomly picks $\tau_k \xleftarrow{\$} \{0, 1\}$ and $x_k, y_k, z_k \xleftarrow{\$} \mathbb{Z}_p$ for $k \in [1, l]$. The set $\{x_k, y_k, z_k, \tau_k\}$ will be used as the internal randomness for $\mathcal{CLE}_1.\mathsf{Enc}()$. The sender also runs (ovk, osk) $\leftarrow \mathcal{OTS}.\mathsf{KeyGen}(\mathsf{param}_{OTS})$ of Abe *et al.*'s one-time SPS scheme [2] which the exponent $\{a_i\}$ for $i \in [1, 4]$ such that $\mathsf{ovk} = (h^{a_1}, h^{a_2}, h^{a_3}, h^{a_4})$ are available. For the ease of presentation, we use $(\tilde{A}_1, \tilde{A}_2, \tilde{A}_3, \tilde{A}_4)$ to represent ovk.

Finally, the sender computes

$$(C_0, \{C_{k,M}\}_{k=1}^l) \leftarrow \mathcal{CLE}_1.\text{Enc}(\text{mpk}_1, \text{upk}, \text{ID}, M; \{x_k, y_k, z_k, \tau_k\}),$$
$$(C'_{k,0}, C_{k,g}, C_{k,R}, C_{k,z}) \leftarrow C_{k,M},$$

$$C_{k,0} = C'_{k,0} \cdot \prod_{i=1}^4 e(U_i, \tilde{A}_i)^{-x_k} \text{ for } k \in [1, l],$$

$$C_{a,i} = \tilde{H}_i^{a_i} \text{ for } i \in [1, 4],$$

$$\pi = PoK\{(M, \{x_k, y_k, z_k, \tau_k\}_{k=1}^l, \{a_i\}_{i=1}^4):$$
$$(C_0, \{(C'_{k,0}, C_{k,g}, C_{k,R}, C_{k,z})\}_{k=1}^l)$$
$$\leftarrow \mathcal{CLE}_1.\text{Enc}(\text{mpk}_1, \text{upk}, \text{ID}, M; \{x_k, y_k, z_k, \tau_k\}_{k=1}^l)$$
$$\wedge_{k=1}^l C_0 = M \cdot \prod_{j=1}^l G_j^{\tau_j} \wedge_{i=1}^4 C_{a,i} = \tilde{H}_i^{a_i}$$
$$\wedge_{k=1}^l C_{k,0} = C'_{k,0} \cdot \prod_{i=1}^4 e(U_i, \tilde{A}_i)^{-x_k}\},$$

$$\sigma \leftarrow \mathcal{OTS}.\text{Sign}(\text{osk}, C_0).$$

Output $(C_0, \{\tilde{A}_i, C_{a,i}\}_{i=1}^4, \{C_{k,0}, C_{k,g}, C_{k,R}, C_{k,z}\}_{k=1}^l, \pi, \sigma)$ as the ciphertext.

$\text{Dec}(\text{mpk}, \text{upk}, \text{usk}, C) \rightarrow M/\bot$. The decryptor first performs the following checks.

1. Parse the ciphertext C as specified in the output of the algorithm $\text{Enc}()$.
2. Verify the equations $e(g, C_{a,i}) = e(U_i, \tilde{A}_i)$ for $i \in [1, 4]$.
3. Verify the signature σ using $\mathcal{OTS}.\text{Verify}((\tilde{A}_1, \tilde{A}_2, \tilde{A}_3, \tilde{A}_4), C_0, \sigma)$.
4. Verify the proof π using the $\mathcal{GS}.\text{Verify}()$ algorithm.

If any one of the four equations does not hold, or either σ or π does not pass the verification, output $\bot$. Otherwise, for $k \in [1, l]$, compute

$$M_k = C_{k,0} \cdot e(C_{k,g}, \tilde{S} \cdot \prod_{i=1}^4 C_{a,i})e(T, C_{k,R})e(C_{k,z}, \tilde{D}_\alpha).$$

Find τ_k such that $M_k = e(G_k, h)^{\tau_k}$. Finally, output $M = \frac{C_0}{\prod_{i=1}^l G_i^{\tau_k}}$.

Correctness. For $k \in [1, l]$,

$$C_{k,0} \cdot e(C_{k,g}, \tilde{S} \cdot \prod_{i=1}^4 C_{a,i})e(T, C_{k,R})e(C_{k,z}, \tilde{D}_\alpha)$$

$$= M_k \cdot e(W_2, \tilde{R})^{x_k} e(U, \tilde{R})^{x_k} \cdot \prod_{i=1}^4 e(U_i, \tilde{A}_i)^{-x_k} \cdot e(W_1, h)^{-x_k}$$

$$\cdot e(\text{ID}, \tilde{V}_1)^{y_k} e(D_\alpha, \tilde{V}_2)^{y_k} e(g, h)^{-y_k} e(D_\alpha, h)^{-z_k}$$

$$\cdot e(C_{k,g}, \tilde{S} \cdot \prod_{i=1}^4 C_{a,i})e(T, C_{k,R})e(C_{k,z}, \tilde{D}_\alpha)$$

$$= M_k \cdot e(W_2, \tilde{R})^{x_k} e(U, \tilde{R})^{x_k} \cdot \prod_{i=1}^{4} e(U_i, \tilde{A}_i)^{-x_k} \cdot e(W_1, h)^{-x_k} \cdot e(C_{k,g}, \tilde{S} \cdot \prod_{i=1}^{4} C_{a,i})$$

$$\cdot e(\mathsf{ID}, \tilde{V}_1)^{y_k} e(D_\alpha, \tilde{V}_2)^{y_k} e(g, h)^{-y_k} \cdot e(T, C_{k,R}) \cdot e(D_\alpha, h)^{-z_k} \cdot e(C_{k,z}, \tilde{D}_\alpha)$$

$$= M_k \cdot (e(W_2, \tilde{R}) e(U, \tilde{R}) \cdot \prod_{i=1}^{4} e(U_i, \tilde{A}_i)^{-1} \cdot e(W_1, h)^{-1} \cdot e(g, \tilde{S} \cdot \prod_{i=1}^{4} C_{a,i}))^{x_k}$$

$$\cdot (e(\mathsf{ID}, \tilde{V}_1) e(D_\alpha, \tilde{V}_2) e(g, h)^{-1} \cdot e(T, \tilde{R}))^{y_k} \cdot e(g^\alpha, h)^{-z_k} \cdot e(g^z, h^\alpha) = M_k.$$

With correct M_k, τ_k such that $M_k = e(G_k, h)^{\tau_k}$ can be correctly recovered. With all M_k for $k \in [1, l]$, $M = \frac{C_0}{\prod_{i=1}^{l} G_i'^{\tau_k}}$ can be correctly recovered as in Sect. 4.3.

Theorem 3. *The SP-CLE scheme* $\mathcal{CLE}_2$ *is RCCA-secure against* Strong Type-I *and* Strong Type-II *adversaries if* $\mathcal{CLE}_1$ *is CPA-secure against Type-I and Type-II adversaries.*

The proof is deferred to the full version.

Remark. A fully structure-preserving CLE scheme would be an overkill for our application as it does not need to hide the ciphertext and prove about its validity. Also, our application will apply yet another signature on top of the CLE ciphertext (with other parts) such that any rerandomization of the CLE ciphertext will invalidate the signature, so $\mathcal{CLE}_2$ only aimed for RCCA-security.

Nevertheless, Appendix A outlines how to use the trick of Libert and Joye [25] for converting $\mathbb{G}_T$ values into base group elements in the ciphertext of our $\mathcal{CLE}_1$.

5 Group Signatures with Certified Limited Opening

We use our SP-CLE (in Sect. 4) as a building block to construct an example application, a group signature scheme with certified limited (CL) opening, a generalization of message-dependent opening [30]. Due to the page limit, we present the formal definitions in the full version.

Group signature is a privacy-oriented signature scheme where the verifier can be convinced that a given signature is signed by a group member, but not exactly whom. Since perfect anonymity may be abused, group signatures come with an opening mechanism such that the group manager, or in general, an opening authority (OA), can use a secret key to reveal the true signer of a signature.

When there is purported abuse, we want to identify the signer of the suspicious signatures. In traditional group signatures, it means *all* signatures must be opened, which is undesirable for honest users. The notion of traceable signatures (TS) [1,23] extends that of the group signatures to mitigate this problem. In TS, when a group member is classified as a misbehaving one. A user-specific tracing trapdoor can be generated (by the group manager or the OA). Every one with this user-specific trapdoor can check if a signature is actually signed by the misbehaving user, or trace [13] the signatures generated by the misbehaving user. TS can be regarded as a group signature scheme with signer-dependent opening. Subsequently, Sakai *et al.* [30] proposed the notion of group signature with message-dependent opening (GS-MDO). In GS-MDO, apart from the OA, there is another entity called the admitter. The admitter can generate a message-dependent opening key. The real signer of a group signature signing on a given message can be revealed only when both the master opening key (of the OA) and the message-dependent opening key (provided by the admitter) are used.

Difficulty in Construction. GS-MDO schemes are often constructed by IBE since GS-MDO implies its existence (or precisely, identity-based key encapsulation) [30]. Existing schemes not relying on the pairing-based Groth-Sahai proof are either not that efficient [26] or is proven secure in the random oracle model [28]; however, typical pairing-based IBE schemes encrypt messages in the target group, which are not compatible with Groth-Sahai proof that a correct message (the signer identity in the case of GS-MDO) has been encrypted.

Consequently, the original work of Sakai *et al.* [30] proposed to use k-resilient IBE to construct GS-MDO which remains secure only when adversary obtains no more than a predefined bound of k message-dependent opening keys. Later, Ohara *et al.* [28] proposed a GS-MDO scheme with unbounded MDO in the random oracle model. A subsequent work of Libert and Joye [25] describes an unbounded GS-MDO scheme in the standard model by proposing an IBE scheme which encrypts messages in the base group. This IBE scheme is partially structure preserving in the sense that the identity is still a bit-string instead of a group element. In an IBE-based GS-MDO scheme, the identity used in IBE is the same as the message to be signed. So this scheme [25] is not structure-preserving and cannot sign on group elements. Potential higher applications of GS-MDO thus cannot hide yet prove about the message with another Groth-Sahai proof.

Certified Limited Opening. We consider an alternative way of limiting the opening power which we call certified limited (CL) opening. CL opening features an entity called a *master certifier*, who certifies *openers* case by case depending on the context. For example, consider the application of group signatures for signing on votes in electronic voting. The government can be the master certifier, and the openers can be those overseeing different districts/counties/provinces/states. When issuing a group signature, the group member can designate an *opener* during the signing process. The opener who is the designated one for a group signature can open it (i.e., revoke the anonymity of the signature). Neither the certifier nor any non-designated openers can perform opening.

CL opening is a variant of MDO which removes the reliance of a single opening authority and minimizes the disturbance of honest users. Moreover, it decouples the criteria of opening from the message being signed. In many applications, the need for opening may not be originated from the message itself. We can assign the openers depending on the applications. Consider the e-voting scenario again, where the voting software in one of the voting booths could be compromised. We can set the opener to be the authorities overseeing different booths. If some anomaly happen with a particular booth, say, the candidate is set to be an adversarially-chosen set under the hood, independent of what is the vote cast by the voters; only the signatures in the concerned booth will be opened, and only the affected voters will be asked to cast a correct vote again.

CL opening also simplifies the opening process. The existing MDO functionality [25, 30] requires the master opening key and the message-dependent key as inputs. That means the two parties holding the corresponding keys must cooperate in an honest manner. In our formulation, the master certifier and the opening authority interact once such that latter will get the opening key of limited power, instead of performing joint decryption in every opening. Dealing with a single key also allows an easier zero-knowledge proof for the opening correctness.

5.1   Our Group Signature Scheme with Certified Limited Opening

We build our group signature scheme with CL opening using SP-CLE. In a nutshell, the signing algorithm uses SP-CLE to encrypt the identity of the signer with respect to a SP-CLE user. In this way, we can realize new privacy-enhancing features easily thanks to the preserved structures. In particular, since the identity and the user public key in our SP-CLE scheme are both group elements, one can include an additional proof about them to preserve the opener privacy. For example, it can hide who is the designated opener among a list of possibilities.

Due to our formulation of the underlying SP-CLE scheme, our resulting group signature scheme with CL opening can be considered as weaker than group signatures with MDO since the message in the latter does not require prior "certification" from any party. However, in case the message domain is small, one can obtain MDO from CL opening by assigning an opener for each possible message. Also, as argued above, we decouple the message to be signed from the context of the opening. More importantly, from the technical perspective, since SP-IBE does not exist, it is unclear how to "upgrade" the existing GS-MDO schemes such that we can sign on a group element, while retaining the MDO functionality. On the other hand, our group signature scheme with CL opening is partially structure-preserving, in the sense that it can sign on group element as a message (and the public-key and the identity of the opener are also group elements, due to our SP-CLE). It can then sign on an encryption of vote (for privacy) when the resulting ciphertext consists of only group elements, and further allow a zero-knowledge proof of the message being encrypted and signed. For example, the zero-knowledge proof can be proving that the vote is a valid choice among the possible candidates. With the group structure preserved, the encrypted votes can also be homomorphically-processed (when the underlying encryption is homomorphic) such that only the aggregate results will be revealed.

Finally, as a generic construction, future constructions of SP-CLE in the original formulation can be directly plugged into our proposed design.

5.2   Construction

Design Overview. We follow the two-level signature construction [8] and use two SPS instances and one SP-CLE instance. The group manager generates an SPS signature cert_{ID} on an identity ID and a verification key vk_{ID} for an SPS scheme as part of the user private key for ID. The user with identity ID generates another SPS signature σ' on a message M, then proves the relation of $(\text{ID}, \text{vk}_{\text{ID}}, \text{cert}_{\text{ID}})$ and that of (M, σ') without revealing $\text{ID}, \text{vk}_{\text{ID}}, \text{certID}$, nor σ'.

To implement the certified limited opening feature using SP-CLE, the KGC (as the master certifier) interacts with an SP-CLE user (as an opener). After they interact in the SP-CLE key-issuing process, the opener obtains a public-private key pair. Suppose the identity of the opener is E, the user public key pk_E will be published, and the user private key osk_E will be kept secret. The signer uses pk_E to encrypt ID, then generates a proof showing that this ciphertext is well-formed. All the proofs and this ciphertext are output as the group signature. The party holding osk_E can decrypt the ciphertext to obtain ID.

Syntax. Our definition extends the one by Sakai *et al.* [30]. We replace the input of the TrapGen algorithm from a message M with an identifier E and an opener public key, and only require the output of TrapGen but not the "master" opening key in the Open algorithm. We also split the key generation into Setup, MKeyGen, and Issue. A detailed definition can be found in the full version.

Our Construction. We use an our CLE scheme for $M \in \mathbb{G}$ $\mathcal{CLE}$, two SPS schemes $\mathcal{SPS}_G$ and $\mathcal{SPS}$, and a GS-proof system $\mathcal{GS}$ as the building blocks to construct a structure-preserving group signature with certified limited opening. As Groth-Sahai proof is rerandomizable, we use a structure-preserving one-time signature $\mathcal{OTS}$ to enforce CCA-anonymity.

This scheme also achieves the "hidden identity" features as in hidden identity-based signatures [17,24] since its opening mechanism can directly recover the signer identity without relying on the existence of any membership database.

Setup(1^λ) $\rightarrow$ param. Choose a Type III bilinear group $\mathcal{G} = (\mathbb{G}, \mathbb{H}, \mathbb{G}_T, e, p, g, h)$ which is suitable for $\mathcal{CLE}$, $\mathcal{SPS}_G$, and $\mathcal{SPS}$. Generate the common reference string crs for $\mathcal{GS}$. Output param $= (\mathcal{G}, \text{crs})$.

MKeyGen() $\rightarrow$ (mpk, msk). Generate the key-pair for the underlying structure-preserving primitives as follows.

1. $(\text{vk}_G, \text{sk}_G) \leftarrow \mathcal{SPS}_G.\text{KeyGen}()$.
2. $(\text{mpk}_{\mathcal{CLE}}, \text{msk}_{\mathcal{CLE}}) \leftarrow \mathcal{CLE}.\text{MKeyGen}()$.

Output the master public-private key pair mpk $= (\text{vk}_G, \text{mpk}_{\mathcal{CLE}})$, msk $= \text{sk}_G$ to the KGC, and output the master opening key ok $= \text{msk}_{\mathcal{CLE}}$ to the master certifier.

Issue(msk, ID) $\rightarrow$ usk_{ID}. A user with identity ID and the KGC interactively compute a certificate as part of the user secret key for the user.

1. The user runs $(\mathsf{vk_{ID}}, \mathsf{sk_{ID}}) \leftarrow \mathcal{SPS}.\mathtt{KeyGen}()$, sends $(\mathsf{ID}, \mathsf{vk_{ID}})$ to the KGC.
2. The KGC runs $\mathsf{cert_{ID}} \leftarrow \mathcal{SPS}_G.\mathtt{Sign}(\mathsf{sk}_G, (\mathsf{ID}, \mathsf{vk_{ID}}))$, sends $\mathsf{cert_{ID}}$ to the user.

The user sets $\mathsf{usk_{ID}} = (\mathsf{sk_{ID}}, \mathsf{vk_{ID}}, \mathsf{cert_{ID}})$ as user private key.

$\mathtt{TrapGen}(\mathsf{mpk}, \mathsf{ok}, E) \rightarrow (\mathsf{pk}_E, \mathsf{osk}_E)$. The master certifier and an opener runs this protocol such that the opener will get an opening key for an identity $E \in \mathbb{H}$.

1. The opener first runs $(\mathsf{ppk}_E, \mathsf{uk}_E) \leftarrow \mathtt{SetUserSec}(\mathsf{mpk}_{\mathcal{CLE}}, E)$.
2. The master certifier runs $\mathsf{psk}_E \leftarrow \mathcal{CLE}.\mathtt{Issue}(\mathsf{msk}_{\mathcal{CLE}}, \mathsf{mpk}_{\mathcal{CLE}}, E, \mathsf{ppk}_E)$ and $(\mathsf{upk}_{E,\mathcal{CLE}}, \mathsf{usk}_{E,\mathcal{CLE}}) \leftarrow \mathcal{CLE}.\mathtt{UKeyGen}(\mathsf{mpk}_{\mathcal{CLE}}, \mathsf{ppk}_E, \mathsf{psk}_E, \mathsf{usk}_E)$, where ok is parsed as $\mathsf{msk}_{\mathcal{CLE}}$.
3. The master certifier outputs $\mathsf{usk}_{E,\mathcal{CLE}}$ as the certified limited opening key osk_E, and publishes $\mathsf{upk}_{E,\mathcal{CLE}}$ as pk_E for identity E.

$\mathtt{Sign}(\mathsf{mpk}, \mathsf{usk_{ID}}, \mathsf{pk}_E, E, M) \rightarrow \sigma$. The input E is the identity of the opener, and pk_E is the public key of the opener generated by the algorithm $\mathtt{TrapGen}$. To sign on a message $M \in \mathbb{H}$ by $\mathsf{usk_{ID}}$, a user performs the following steps.

1. $(\mathsf{ovk}, \mathsf{osk}) \leftarrow \mathcal{OTS}.\mathtt{KeyGen}()$,
2. $\sigma' \leftarrow \mathcal{SPS}.\mathtt{Sign}(\mathsf{sk_{ID}}, (M, E, \mathsf{ovk}))$.
3. $C \leftarrow \mathcal{CLE}.\mathtt{Enc}(\mathsf{mpk}_{\mathcal{CLE}}, \mathsf{pk}_E, E, \mathsf{ID})$.
4. Run $\mathcal{GS}.\mathtt{Prove}()$ to generate the proof

$$\pi = PoK\{(\mathsf{vk_{ID}}, \mathsf{cert_{ID}}, \mathsf{ID}, \sigma') : 1 \leftarrow \mathcal{SPS}.\mathtt{Verify}(\mathsf{vk_{ID}}, (M, E, \mathsf{ovk}), \sigma')$$
$$\wedge\, 1 \leftarrow \mathcal{SPS}_G.\mathtt{Verify}(\mathsf{vk}_G, (\mathsf{ID}, \mathsf{vk_{ID}}), \mathsf{cert_{ID}})$$
$$\wedge\, C \leftarrow \mathcal{CLE}.\mathtt{Enc}(\mathsf{mpk}_{\mathcal{CLE}}, \mathsf{pk}_E, E, \mathsf{ID})\}.$$

5. $\sigma'' \leftarrow \mathcal{OTS}.\mathtt{Sign}(\mathsf{osk}, (C, \pi))$.

Output $\sigma = (\pi, C, E, \mathsf{ovk}, \sigma'')$ as the group signature.

$\mathtt{Verify}(\mathsf{mpk}, M, \sigma) \rightarrow 1/0$. The verifier parses σ as $(\pi, C, E, \mathsf{ovk}, \sigma'')$. If the algorithm $\mathcal{OTS}.\mathtt{Verify}(\mathsf{ovk}, (C, \pi), \sigma'')$ outputs 1 and $\mathcal{GS}.\mathtt{Verify}()$ outputs 1 for π (i.e., π is a valid proof), the verifier outputs 1 and accepts the group signature σ; Otherwise, the verifier outputs 0.

$\mathtt{Open}(\mathsf{mpk}, \mathsf{pk}_E, \mathsf{osk}_E, \sigma) \rightarrow \mathsf{ID}/\bot$. An opener parses mpk as $(\mathsf{vk}_G, \mathsf{mpk}_{\mathcal{CLE}})$ and σ as $(\pi, C, E, \mathsf{ovk}, \sigma'')$. It returns $\bot$ if $0 \leftarrow \mathtt{Verify}(\mathsf{mpk}, M, \sigma)$. Otherwise, it computes $\mathsf{ID} \leftarrow \mathcal{CLE}.\mathtt{Dec}(\mathsf{mpk}_{\mathcal{CLE}}, \mathsf{pk}_E, \mathsf{psk}_E, C)$ and outputs ID.

Theorem 4. *The proposed group signature scheme with certified limited opening provides traceability, anonymity, and is existentially unforgeable against adaptive chosen-message attack (EUF-CMA secure) if $\mathcal{GS}$ is an non-interactive zero-knowledge proof, $\mathcal{CLE}$ is CPA/CCA secure, $\mathcal{SPS}_G$ and $\mathcal{SPS}$ are both EUF-CMA secure, and $\mathcal{OTS}$ is one-time secure (only for CCA-anonymity).*

The proof is deferred to the full version.

Remarks. Two specific steps of Sign(), namely, $\sigma' \leftarrow \mathcal{SPS}.\text{Sign}(\text{sk}_{\text{ID}}, (M, E, \text{ovk}))$ and $C \leftarrow \mathcal{CLE}.\text{Enc}(\text{mpk}_{\mathcal{CLE}}, \text{pk}_E, E, \text{ID})$ merit more discussion. With the use of $\mathcal{SPS}$, our group signature scheme can sign on group element $M \in \mathbb{H}$. With our SP-CLE, pk_E and E are both group elements. It is thus easy to use Groth-Sahai proof to, say prove that the opener is among one of a known list of n openers.

6   Conclusion

We propose a series of structure-preserving certificateless encryption schemes by extending an existing structure-preserving signature scheme. We illustrate their applications in group signature with certified limited opening. We leave it as a future work to use our structure-preserving certificateless encryption scheme for other accountable privacy features, e.g., escrowed linkability [16] in which two anonymous signatures from the same signer can only be linked by the one who owns the private key (in our structure-preserving certificateless encryption).

Our scheme supports typical application of CLE except "encrypt to the future" [15,22,29]. We leave it as an open problem to devise an SP-CLE under the original formulation [5]. Another future work is to propose a generic way to construct SP-CLE from any SPS scheme, without any step verifying an SPS in the encryption algorithm. A challenge is to generically "upgrade" the complexity assumption required for the SPS to its decisional variant required by SP-CLE.

A   Towards Removing $\mathbb{G}_T$ Elements from the Ciphertext

Recall that in our basic scheme (Sect. 4.2)

$$K = \{e(W_2, \tilde{R})e(U, \tilde{R})/e(W_1, h)\}^x \{e(\text{ID}, \tilde{V}_1)e(D_\alpha, \tilde{V}_2)/e(g, h)\}^y/e(D_\alpha, h)^z.$$

We include the following terms in the ciphertext such that $\prod_{i=1}^{4}\{e(C_i, \tilde{C}_i)\} = K$.

$$C_1 = ((W_2 \cdot U)^x)^{r_1}, \quad \tilde{C}_1 = \tilde{R}^{1/r_1}, \quad C_2 = (\text{ID}^y)^{r_2}, \qquad\qquad \tilde{C}_2 = \tilde{V}_1^{1/r_2},$$
$$C_3 = (D_\alpha{}^y)^{r_3}, \qquad \tilde{C}_3 = \tilde{V}_2^{1/r_3}, \quad C_4 = (W_1{}^x/g^y/D_\alpha{}^z)^{r_4}, \quad \tilde{C}_4 = h^{1/r_4}.$$

K can be recovered by $e(C_g, \tilde{S})e(T, C_R)e(C_z, \tilde{D}_\alpha)$ as in the decryption algorithm.

The idea of encryption/decryption is still about encoding/recovering the bits $\{\tau_j\}$ in $C_0 = M \cdot \prod_{j=1}^{l} G_j^{\tau_j}$ (Sect. 4.3). Roughly, the trick [25] has two steps. First, we replicate K into l versions by different randomness. Second, we replicate the master public key and the private key into two versions based on different generators. To encode $\tau_j = 0$, both encryption and decryption should use the first version of the corresponding key. Similarly, $\tau_j = 1$ takes the second version.

References

1. Abe, M., Chow, S.S.M., Haralambiev, K., Ohkubo, M.: Double-trapdoor anonymous tags for traceable signatures. Int. J. Inf. Secur. **12**(1), 19–31 (2013)
2. Abe, M., David, B., Kohlweiss, M., Nishimaki, R., Ohkubo, M.: Tagged one-time signatures: tight security and optimal tag size. In: Kurosawa, K., Hanaoka, G. (eds.) PKC 2013. LNCS, vol. 7778, pp. 312–331. Springer, Heidelberg (2013). https://doi.org/10.1007/978-3-642-36362-7_20
3. Abe, M., Fuchsbauer, G., Groth, J., Haralambiev, K., Ohkubo, M.: Structure-preserving signatures and commitments to group elements. In: Rabin, T. (ed.) CRYPTO 2010. LNCS, vol. 6223, pp. 209–236. Springer, Heidelberg (2010). https://doi.org/10.1007/978-3-642-14623-7_12
4. Abe, M., Groth, J., Haralambiev, K., Ohkubo, M.: Optimal structure-preserving signatures in asymmetric bilinear groups. In: Rogaway, P. (ed.) CRYPTO 2011. LNCS, vol. 6841, pp. 649–666. Springer, Heidelberg (2011). https://doi.org/10.1007/978-3-642-22792-9_37
5. Al-Riyami, S.S., Paterson, K.G.: Certificateless public key cryptography. In: Laih, C.-S. (ed.) ASIACRYPT 2003. LNCS, vol. 2894, pp. 452–473. Springer, Heidelberg (2003). https://doi.org/10.1007/978-3-540-40061-5_29
6. Baek, J., Safavi-Naini, R., Susilo, W.: Certificateless public key encryption without pairing. In: Zhou, J., Lopez, J., Deng, R.H., Bao, F. (eds.) ISC 2005. LNCS, vol. 3650, pp. 134–148. Springer, Heidelberg (2005). https://doi.org/10.1007/11556992_10
7. Barbosa, M., Farshim, P.: Relations among notions of complete non-malleability: indistinguishability characterisation and efficient construction without random oracles. In: Steinfeld, R., Hawkes, P. (eds.) ACISP 2010. LNCS, vol. 6168, pp. 145–163. Springer, Heidelberg (2010). https://doi.org/10.1007/978-3-642-14081-5_10
8. Bellare, M., Micciancio, D., Warinschi, B.: Foundations of group signatures: formal definitions, simplified requirements, and a construction based on general assumptions. In: Biham, E. (ed.) EUROCRYPT 2003. LNCS, vol. 2656, pp. 614–629. Springer, Heidelberg (2003). https://doi.org/10.1007/3-540-39200-9_38
9. Boneh, D., Canetti, R., Halevi, S., Katz, J.: Chosen-ciphertext security from identity-based encryption. SIAM J. Comput. **36**(5), 1301–1328 (2007)
10. Camenisch, J., Haralambiev, K., Kohlweiss, M., Lapon, J., Naessens, V.: Structure preserving CCA secure encryption and applications. In: Lee, D.H., Wang, X. (eds.) ASIACRYPT 2011. LNCS, vol. 7073, pp. 89–106. Springer, Heidelberg (2011). https://doi.org/10.1007/978-3-642-25385-0_5
11. Canetti, R., Krawczyk, H., Nielsen, J.B.: Relaxing chosen-ciphertext security. In: Boneh, D. (ed.) CRYPTO 2003. LNCS, vol. 2729, pp. 565–582. Springer, Heidelberg (2003). https://doi.org/10.1007/978-3-540-45146-4_33
12. Chow, S.S.M.: Certificateless encryption. In: Identity-Based Cryptography. Cryptology and Information Security Series, vol. 2, pp. 135–155. IOS Press (2008)
13. Chow, S.S.M.: Real traceable signatures. In: Jacobson, M.J., Rijmen, V., Safavi-Naini, R. (eds.) SAC 2009. LNCS, vol. 5867, pp. 92–107. Springer, Heidelberg (2009). https://doi.org/10.1007/978-3-642-05445-7_6
14. Chow, S.S.M., Franklin, M.K., Zhang, H.: Practical dual-receiver encryption - soundness, complete non-malleability, and applications. In: The Cryptographer's Track at the RSA Conference (CT-RSA), pp. 85–105 (2014)

15. Chow, S.S.M., Roth, V., Rieffel, E.G.: General certificateless encryption and timed-release encryption. In: Ostrovsky, R., De Prisco, R., Visconti, I. (eds.) SCN 2008. LNCS, vol. 5229, pp. 126–143. Springer, Heidelberg (2008). https://doi.org/10.1007/978-3-540-85855-3_9

16. Chow, S.S.M., Susilo, W., Yuen, T.H.: Escrowed linkability of ring signatures and its applications. In: Nguyen, P.Q. (ed.) VIETCRYPT 2006. LNCS, vol. 4341, pp. 175–192. Springer, Heidelberg (2006). https://doi.org/10.1007/11958239_12

17. Chow, S.S.M., Zhang, H., Zhang, T.: Real hidden identity-based signatures. In: Financial Cryptography and Data Security (FC), pp. 21–38 (2017)

18. Dent, A.W.: A brief introduction to certificateless encryption schemes and their infrastructures. In: Martinelli, F., Preneel, B. (eds.) EuroPKI 2009. LNCS, vol. 6391, pp. 1–16. Springer, Heidelberg (2010). https://doi.org/10.1007/978-3-642-16441-5_1

19. Dent, A.W., Libert, B., Paterson, K.G.: Certificateless encryption schemes strongly secure in the standard model. In: Cramer, R. (ed.) PKC 2008. LNCS, vol. 4939, pp. 344–359. Springer, Heidelberg (2008). https://doi.org/10.1007/978-3-540-78440-1_20

20. Girault, M.: Self-certified public keys. In: Davies, D.W. (ed.) EUROCRYPT 1991. LNCS, vol. 547, pp. 490–497. Springer, Heidelberg (1991). https://doi.org/10.1007/3-540-46416-6_42

21. Groth, J., Sahai, A.: Efficient non-interactive proof systems for bilinear groups. SIAM J. Comput. **41**(5), 1193–1232 (2012)

22. Kasamatsu, K., Matsuda, T., Emura, K., Attrapadung, N., Hanaoka, G., Imai, H.: Time-specific encryption from forward-secure encryption. In: Visconti, I., De Prisco, R. (eds.) SCN 2012. LNCS, vol. 7485, pp. 184–204. Springer, Heidelberg (2012). https://doi.org/10.1007/978-3-642-32928-9_11

23. Kiayias, A., Tsiounis, Y., Yung, M.: Traceable signatures. In: Cachin, C., Camenisch, J.L. (eds.) EUROCRYPT 2004. LNCS, vol. 3027, pp. 571–589. Springer, Heidelberg (2004). https://doi.org/10.1007/978-3-540-24676-3_34

24. Kiayias, A., Zhou, H.: Hidden identity-based signatures. IET Inf. Secur. **3**(3), 119–127 (2009)

25. Libert, B., Joye, M.: Group signatures with message-dependent opening in the standard model. In: Benaloh, J. (ed.) CT-RSA 2014. LNCS, vol. 8366, pp. 286–306. Springer, Cham (2014). https://doi.org/10.1007/978-3-319-04852-9_15

26. Libert, B., Mouhartem, F., Nguyen, K.: A lattice-based group signature scheme with message-dependent opening. In: Manulis, M., Sadeghi, A.-R., Schneider, S. (eds.) ACNS 2016. LNCS, vol. 9696, pp. 137–155. Springer, Cham (2016). https://doi.org/10.1007/978-3-319-39555-5_8

27. Libert, B., Peters, T., Qian, C.: Structure-preserving chosen-ciphertext security with shorter verifiable ciphertexts. In: Fehr, S. (ed.) PKC 2017. LNCS, vol. 10174, pp. 247–276. Springer, Heidelberg (2017). https://doi.org/10.1007/978-3-662-54365-8_11

28. Ohara, K., Sakai, Y., Emura, K., Hanaoka, G.: A group signature scheme with unbounded message-dependent opening. In: ACM SIGSAC Symposium on Information, Computer and Communications Security (AsiaCCS), pp. 517–522. ACM (2013)

29. Paterson, K.G., Quaglia, E.A.: Time-specific encryption. In: Garay, J.A., De Prisco, R. (eds.) SCN 2010. LNCS, vol. 6280, pp. 1–16. Springer, Heidelberg (2010). https://doi.org/10.1007/978-3-642-15317-4_1

30. Sakai, Y., Emura, K., Hanaoka, G., Kawai, Y., Matsuda, T., Omote, K.: Group signatures with message-dependent opening. In: Abdalla, M., Lange, T. (eds.) Pairing 2012. LNCS, vol. 7708, pp. 270–294. Springer, Heidelberg (2013). https://doi.org/10.1007/978-3-642-36334-4_18
31. Sun, Y., Zhang, F., Baek, J.: Strongly secure certificateless public key encryption without pairing. In: Bao, F., Ling, S., Okamoto, T., Wang, H., Xing, C. (eds.) CANS 2007. LNCS, vol. 4856, pp. 194–208. Springer, Heidelberg (2007). https://doi.org/10.1007/978-3-540-76969-9_13
32. Tsang, P.P., Chow, S.S.M., Smith, S.W.: Batch pairing delegation. In: Miyaji, A., Kikuchi, H., Rannenberg, K. (eds.) IWSEC 2007. LNCS, vol. 4752, pp. 74–90. Springer, Heidelberg (2007). https://doi.org/10.1007/978-3-540-75651-4_6

Public Key Encryption Resilient to Post-challenge Leakage and Tampering Attacks

Suvradip Chakraborty[✉] and C. Pandu Rangan

Department of Computer Science and Engineering, Indian Institute of Technology Madras, Chennai, India
{suvradip,rangan}@cse.iitm.ac.in

Abstract. In this paper, we introduce a new framework for constructing public-key encryption (PKE) schemes resilient to joint *post-challenge/after-the-fact* leakage and tampering attacks in the bounded leakage and tampering (BLT) model, introduced by Damgård et al. (Asiacrypt 2013). All the prior formulations of PKE schemes considered leakage and tampering attacks only *before* the challenge ciphertext is made available to the adversary. However, this restriction seems necessary, since achieving security against post-challenge leakage and tampering attacks in its full generality is impossible, as shown in previous works. In this paper, we study the post-challenge/after-the-fact security for PKE schemes against bounded leakage and tampering under a restricted yet meaningful and reasonable notion of security, namely, the *split-state leakage and tampering model*. We show that it is possible to construct secure PKE schemes in this model, tolerating arbitrary (but bounded) leakage and tampering queries; thus overcoming the previous impossibility results.

To this end, we formulate a new notion of security, which we call *entropic post-challenge* IND-CCA-BLT secure PKE. We first define a weaker notion called *entropic restricted post-challenge* IND-CCA-BLT secure PKE, which can be instantiated using the (standard) DDH assumption. We then show a generic compiler from our entropic restricted notion to the entropic notion of security using a simulation-extractable non-interactive zero-knowledge argument system. This requires an untamperable common reference string, as in previous works. Finally, we demonstrate the usefulness of our entropic notion of security by giving a simple and generic construction of post-challenge IND-CCA-BLT secure PKE scheme in the split-state leakage and tampering model. This also settles the *open problem* posed by Faonio and Venturi (Asiacrypt 2016).

Keywords: After-the-fact · Post-challenge · Entropic PKE · Split-state · Memory tampering · Related-key attacks · Bounded leakage and tampering

© Springer Nature Switzerland AG 2019
M. Matsui (Ed.): CT-RSA 2019, LNCS 11405, pp. 23–43, 2019.
https://doi.org/10.1007/978-3-030-12612-4_2

1   Introduction and Related Works

Traditionally, cryptographic schemes have been analyzed assuming that an adversary only have *black-box access* to the underlying functionality, and in no way is allowed to manipulate the internal state of the functionality. Leakage and tamper-resilient cryptography studies on designing secure protocols and primitives against an adversary who goes way beyond black-box access to protocol algorithms and gets information by directly accessing/tampering the memory or the internal computations of the system. These physical attacks can be broadly categorized into *passive* and *active* attacks. In case of passive attacks, the adversary tries to recover information via some *side-channel attacks* that include timing measurements, power analysis, electromagnetic measurements, microwave attacks, memory attacks and many more [15,17,18]. In case of active attacks, the adversary can modify the secret data/key of a targeted cryptographic scheme by applying various physical attacks, and later violate the security of the primitive by observing the effect of such changes at the output. These classes of attacks are called *memory tampering attacks* or *related key attacks* (RKA). These attacks can be launched both in software or hardware, like, injecting faults in the device, altering the internal power supply or clock of the device, or shooting the chip with a laser etc.

The formal study of security of cryptosystems, in particular block ciphers, against related key attacks was initiated by Bellare and Kohno [3]. In their setting, the adversary can continuously tamper with the secret key of the cryptosystem by choosing tampering functions from a restricted class of functions. One might hope to provably resist a cryptosystem against arbitrary efficiently computable tampering functions. Unfortunately, this type of *unrestricted tampering* is shown to be impossible by Gennaro et al. [13], without making further assumptions, like self-destruct mechanism, where the device simply blows up and erases all its intermediate values (including the secret key) after an tampering attempt is detected by the device. One useful line of research is to investigate the security of cryptosystems against *restricted* classes of tampering attacks. In most of these schemes, it is assumed that the secret key belongs to some finite field, and the allowed modifications consists of linear or affine functions, or all polynomial of bounded degree applied to the secret key.

Another interesting line of research was initiated in Asiacrypt 2013 by Damgård et al. [8], which is called the model of *bounded tampering*. In this model, the adversary is allowed to make a *bounded* number of tampering queries, however, there is no further restriction on the functions, unlike the previous works. Note that this model of bounded unrestricted tampering is orthogonal to the model of continuous but restricted tampering model of [3]. In [8], the authors showed a construction of signature scheme (in the random oracle model) and public-key encryption scheme (in the standard model) in the bounded leakage and tampering (BLT) model, where, apart from bounded unrestricted tampering, the adversary is also allowed to obtain bounded leakage from the secret key of the cryptosystem. Faonio and Venturi [12] later improved the state-of-the-art for the construction of signature schemes (in the standard model) and

PKE scheme (without involving pairings and zero-knowledge proofs) in the BLT model.

In all the above constructions of PKE schemes [8,12], the adversary is allowed to make *only* pre-challenge tampering queries. In other words, the adversary can specify a bounded number (say τ) of tampering queries T_i ($i \in [\tau]$) before the challenge phase, and gets access to the tampered decryption oracle $\mathsf{Dec}(\widetilde{sk}_i, \cdot)$, where $\widetilde{sk}_i = T_i(sk)$. However, after receiving the challenge ciphertext, the adversary is not allowed to make even a single tampering query. This severely restricts the meaning and applicability of the existing security notions and that of the resulting constructions of the cryptographic primitives satisfying these notions. In particular, this means that even if the adversary tampers with the secret key/memory only once, the secrecy of all the previously encrypted messages before that tampering attempt cannot be guaranteed. However, note that, this is not a limitation of the existing security notions or the constructions. Indeed, as shown in [16,20], tolerating *post-challenge* (also called *after-the-fact*) tampering in it full generality is *impossible*. In particular, the adversary could simply overwrite the secret key depending on the bit b that is encrypted in the challenge ciphertext c^*, and thus gain some advantage in guessing the value of b by asking additional decryption queries. We refer the reader to [8, Sect. 4.4] for the detailed attack. The above impossibility result holds even if the adversary is allowed to make even a single post-challenge tampering query followed by a single decryption query (with respect to the original secret key). Similar impossibility result is known to hold for the setting of leakage as well, in the sense that even if the adversary obtains a single bit of leakage in the post-challenge phase, this is enough to completely break the security of the PKE scheme. This is because the adversary can simply encode the decryption function with the challenge ciphertext and the two challenge messages in the leakage function and obtain exactly the bit b that the challenger tries to hide.

Halevi and Lin [16] addressed this issue of after-the-fact leakage, and defined an appropriate security model, namely the *split-state* leakage model (more on this below), and showed how to construct semantically-secure PKE scheme under this restricted security model. This was later extended to handle CCA security under the same split-state leakage model in [5,23]. However, note that, for the case of tampering, there are no suitable security notions or definitions to handle post-challenge tampering. This definitional problem was acknowledged in the prior works [8,12]. However, no solution to this issue was offered. Indeed it is mentioned in [12] that "it remains open how to obtain CCA security for PKE against "*after-the-fact*" tampering and leakage, where both tampering and leakage can still occur after the challenge ciphertext is generated".

1.1 Our Contributions and Techniques

In this work, we study post-challenge/after-the-fact leakage and tampering attacks in the context of public-key encryption. As discussed above, achieving resilience to post challenge tampering attack in its most general form is impossible. To this end, we formulate an appropriate security model that avoids the impossibility result shown in [8], and at the same time enables secure and efficient construction of PKE schemes in our new model. Our approach to the solution is *modular* in nature and is also surprisingly *simple*. In particular, we show how to effectively (and in a non-trivial way) combine together the appropriate works from the domain of leakage and tamper-resilience to arrive at our current solution. We discuss more on this below.

Split-State Leakage and Tampering Model: We draw the motivation of our work from that of Halevi and Lin [16]. To take care of after-the-fact leakage, the authors in [16] considered the *split-state leakage* model, where the secret key of the cryptosystem is split into multiple disjoint parts, and the adversary can observe (arbitrary) bounded leakage from each of these parts, but in an independent fashion. In order to take care of leakage and tampering jointly, we consider the *split-state leakage and tampering* model. Similar to the split-state leakage model, this model also considers the case where the secret key is also split into multiple disjoint parts (in our case only two, and hence optimal) and the adversary can obtain independent leakages from each of these parts. In addition, the adversary is also allowed to tamper each of the secret key components/parts independently. Note that, the split-state tampering model is already a very useful and widely used model and it captures bit tampering and block-wise tampering attacks, where the adversary can tamper each bit or each block of the secret key independently. The split-state tampering model is also well studied in the context of non-malleable codes [1, 10, 11], where similar type of impossibility results hold. We then proceed to construct our PKE scheme in this model. Lastly, one may note that, in the post-challenge setting in the context of a PKE scheme, the adversary may specify a tampering function to be an identity function and get the challenge ciphertext decrypted under the original secret keys (even in split-state model), and trivially win the security game. To avoid this, we enforce the condition that, when the adversary queries the (tampered) decryption oracle with the challenge ciphertext, the tampered keys need to be different from the original secret key. In other words, the post-challenge tampering functions must not be identity functions with respect to the challenge ciphertext[1].

Entropic Restricted Post-challenge IND-CCA-BLT PKE: We first formulate a new notion of *entropic restricted post-challenge* IND-CCA-BLT-*secure* PKE scheme. Our notion can be seen as an *entropic version* of the notion of restricted (pre-challenge) IND-CCA-BLT secure PKE of Damgård et al. [8], augmented with post challenge leakage and tampering queries. The definition of restricted IND-CCA-BLT-security [8] says that the adversary is given access to a *restricted* (faulty) decryption oracle, i.e., it is allowed to query only valid ciphertexts to the tampered decryption oracles (as opposed to any arbitrary ciphertexts as in the full fledged IND-CCA-BLT security game). Note that, in the definition

---

[1] However, note that, the tampering functions may be identity functions with respect to ciphertexts $c \neq c^*$, where c^* is the challenge ciphertext. This also emulates access to the (original) decryption oracle to the adversary.

of [8], the adversary is allowed to make only pre-challenge leakage and tampering queries. Our notion of entropic restricted post-challenge IND-CCA-BLT security captures the following intuition: Suppose we sample a message M from a high min-entropy distribution. Given a ciphertext encrypting M, and even given (bounded) leakage from the secret key and access to a restricted (tampered) decryption oracle (even if both leakage and tampering happens after observing the challenge ciphertext), the message M still retains enough min-entropy in it. We then show that the cryptosystem of Boneh et al. [4] (referred to as BHHO cryptosystem) satisfies our entropic restricted notion. The main idea of our construction is the leakage to tamper reduction for the BHHO cryptosystem as shown in [8]. Note that, using leakage to simulate tampering is non-trivial, since for each tampered secret key the adversary can make polynomially many (tampered) decryption oracle queries. Hence the amount of key-dependent information that the adversary receives cannot be simulated by a small amount of (bounded) leakage. However, as shown in [8], in case of BHHO cryptosystem for each (pre-challenge) tampering query it is possible to simulate polynomially many decryption queries under it by just leaking a single group element, thus reducing tampering to leakage. We use similar ideas and show that the BHHO cryptosystem with appropriate parameters satisfy our entropic restricted notion of security, even if leakage and tampering is allowed in the post-challenge phase. We note that, the work of Faonio and Venturi [12] gives a comparatively efficient construction of IND-CCA-BLT secure PKE scheme compared to the work of Damgård et al. [8]. Both these constructions rely on projective almost-universal hash-proof system (HPS) as a common building block, and we observe that on a high level, our entropic post-challenge BLT security relies on the *statistical soundness* property of the HPS. However, we choose to start with the construction of Damgård et al. [8] due to its simplicity.

Entropic Post-challenge IND-CCA-BLT PKE: Next, we show how to upgrade the *entropic restricted* post-challenge IND-CCA-BLT security to *entropic* post-challenge IND-CCA-BLT security. In the entropic notion, the adversary can query arbitrary ciphertexts to the (tampered) decryption oracles, as opposed to the entropic restricted notion, where the adversary can only query well-formed (valid) ciphertexts to the oracle. The adversary also has access to the normal (non-tampered) decryption oracle $\mathsf{Dec}(sk, \cdot)$ both in the pre- and post-challenge phase as in the IND-CCA security game. The transformation follows the classical paradigm of converting a CPA-secure PKE to a CCA-secure one by appending to the ciphertext a zero knowledge argument proving the knowledge of the plaintext. Similar transformation was shown in [8] for converting a restricted IND-CCA-BLT secure PKE scheme to a full fledged IND-CCA-BLT secure PKE scheme in the context of pre-challenge leakage and tampering. We observe that the same transformation goes through in the context of post-challenge leakage and tampering as well, and also when the PKE scheme is entropic.

Upgrading to Full Fledged (Non-entropic) Security: We then show how to compile such an *entropic* post-challenge IND-CCA-BLT secure PKE scheme to a *full-fledged* post-challenge IND-CCA-BLT secure PKE scheme. For this, we resort to our split-state leakage and tampering restriction[2]. On a high level, our construction bears similarity with the construction of [16], although the PKE scheme of [16] was only proven to be CPA secure against leakage attacks. We appropriately modify their construction to prove our scheme to be CCA-secure and resilient to joint leakage and tampering attacks. To make the construction more modular, we first show how to construct post-challenge IND-CCA-BLT secure key encapsulation mechanism (KEM) and later show how to compile it to a full-fledged PKE scheme.

On a high level, to generate an encapsulated symmetric key, we generate a key pair (vk, sk) of a strong one-time signature (OTS) scheme. We then use two instances of the entropic scheme to encrypt two random strings x_1 and x_2 independently, with the verification key vk as the label/tag to generate two ciphertexts c_1 and c_2 respectively. The ciphertext $c = (c_1, c_2)$ is then signed using the OTS scheme to generate a signature, say, σ. Finally, we apply a seedless 2-source extractor to both x_1 and x_2 to generate the encapsulated key. We then output the final ciphertext $c = (vk, c_1, c_2, \sigma)$. On a high level, the security of the entropic scheme guarantees that both the strings x_1 and x_2 still retain enough average min-entropy even after chosen-ciphertext leakage and tampering attacks (even in the post-challenge phase). In addition, the split-state model ensures that the strings are independent. At this point, we can use an average-case seedless 2-source extractor to extract a random encapsulation key from both the strings. The trick of generating a key pair of an OTS and setting the verification key vk as a tag/label while encrypting, ensures that, a tag cannot be re-used by an adversary in a decryption or tampering query, hence preventing "mix-and-match" attacks (In fact, to re-use that tag, the adversary essentially has to forge a signature under vk).

Compiling to a Post-challenge IND-CCA-BLT PKE: Finally, we show how to construct a IND-CCA-BLT secure PKE from a IND-CCA-BLT secure KEM as above. One natural idea to achieve this is to use standard hybrid encryption technique, where a symmetric-key encryption (SKE) scheme is used to encrypt the message using the derived encapsulation key. However, we point out, that unlike in standard PKE or even in leakage-resilient PKE settings, this transformation needs a little careful analysis in the context of tampering. This is because the adversary can also ask decryption queries with respect to the tampered keys, and the security of the challenge ciphertext should hold even given these tampered decryption oracle responses. This is not directly guaranteed by standard hybrid encryption paradigm. However, we leverage on the security guarantee of our KEM scheme and show that it is indeed possible to argue the above security. In particular, our KEM scheme guarantees that the average min-entropy of the challenge KEM key K^* is negligibly close to an uniform distribution over the KEM key space, even given many tampered keys $K = (\widetilde{K}_1, \cdots, \widetilde{K}_t)$. So, in the hybrid, we can replace the key K^* with a uniform random key. This implies that, with very high probability, K^* is independent

---

[2] For our construction the secret key is split into only *two* parts/splits, which is the optimal.

of the tampered key distribution, and hence any function of the tampered keys (in particular decryption function). We can then rely on the (standard) CCA security of the SKE to argue indistinguishability of the challenge messages.

Finally, combining all the above ideas together, we obtain the full construction of a post-challenge IND-CCA-BLT secure PKE scheme, thus solving the open problem posed by Faonio and Venturi [12] (Asiacrypt 2016).

Lastly, we note that, it is instructive to compare our approach of constructing post-challenge leakage and tamper-resilient PKE construction with that of Liu and Lysyanskaya [19]. We observe that the framework of [19] instantiated with a non-malleable extractor, would already produce a scheme with security against post-challenge tampering. However, their model is not comparable with ours in the following sense. In particular, the framework of [19] considers securing any (deterministic) cryptographic functionality against leakage and tampering attacks, where the leakage and tampering functions apply only on the memory of the device implementing the functionality, and not on its computation. This is because the construction of [19] relies on a (computationally secure) leakage-resilient non-malleable code, which allow only leakage and tampering on the memory of the device. However, in our model, we allow the adversary to leak from the memory and also allow to tamper with the internal computations (modeled by giving the adversary access to tampered decryption oracles). In this sense, our model is more general, as it also considers tampering with the computation. However, a significant feature of the framework of [19] is that, it considers the model of continual leakage and tampering (in split-state), whereas our model considers bounded leakage and tampering (as in [8]) in split-state.

1.2 Organization

The rest of the paper is organized as follows. In Sect. 2, we provide the necessary preliminaries required for our constructions. In Sect. 3, we give our definition of entropic post-challenge IND-CCA-BLT secure PKE schemes and its restricted notion. In Sect. 3.2, we show our construction of entropic restricted post-challenge IND-CCA-BLT secure PKE and show the transformation from the entropic restricted notion to the entropic notion in Sect. 3.3. In Sect. 4, we present the security definition of post-challenge IND-CCA-BLT secure KEM scheme and show a generic compiler from entropic post-challenge IND-CCA-BLT secure PKE scheme to a post-challenge IND-CCA-BLT secure PKE scheme in the standard model. Section 5 shows the generic transformation from such a KEM scheme to a full fledged IND-CCA-BLT secure PKE scheme secure against post-challenge leakage and tampering attacks. Finally Sect. 6 concludes the paper.

2 Preliminaries

2.1 Notations

For $n \in \mathbb{N}$, we write $[n] = \{1, 2, \cdots, n\}$. If x is a string, we denote $|x|$ as the length of x. For a set $\mathcal{X}$, we write $x \xleftarrow{\$} \mathcal{X}$ to denote that element x is chosen uniformly at random from $\mathcal{X}$. For a distribution or random variable X, we denote $x \leftarrow X$ the action of sampling an element x according to X. When A is an algorithm, we write $y \leftarrow A(x)$ to denote a run of A on input x and output y; if A is randomized, then y is a random variable and $A(x; r)$ denotes a run of A on input x and randomness r. An algorithm A is probabilistic polynomial-time (PPT) if A is randomized and for any input $x, r \in \{0, 1\}^*$; the computation of $A(x; r)$ terminates in at most $poly(|x|)$ steps. For a set S, we let U_S denote the uniform distribution over S. For an integer $\alpha \in \mathbb{N}$, let U_α denote the uniform distribution over $\{0, 1\}^\alpha$, the bit strings of length α. Throughout this paper, we denote the security parameter by κ. Vectors are written in boldface. Given a vector $\mathbf{x} = \{x_1, \cdots, x_n\}$, and some integer a, we write $a^{\mathbf{x}}$ to denote the vector $(a^{x_1}, \cdots, a^{x_n})$. Let D_1 and D_2 be two distributions on a finite set $\mathcal{S}$. We denote by $|D_1 - D_2|$ the statistical distance between them. For random variables X, Y, we denote min-entropy (conditional min-entropy) of X as $H_\infty(X)$ $(\tilde{H}_\infty(X|Y))$ respectively. We assume that the reader is familiar with the results related to (conditional) min- entropy, and we refer to the full version of our paper [6] for these definitions. We denote a distribution supported on $\{0, 1\}^n$ with min-entropy k to be an (n, k)-source.

2.2 Two Source Extractors

In this section, we give an overview of two-source extractors [7, 21, 22] and their generalization, which will be required for our work.

Definition 1 (Seedless 2-source Extractor). *A function* Ext2 $: \{0, 1\}^n \times \{0, 1\}^n \rightarrow \{0, 1\}^m$ *is a seedless 2-source extractor at min-entropy k and error ϵ if it satisfies the following property: If X and Y are independent (n, k)-sources, it holds that $|$ (Ext2$(X, Y) - U_m)$ $| < \epsilon$. where U_m refer to a uniform m-bit string.*

Definition 2 (Average-case Seedless 2-source Extractor). *A function* Ext2 $: \{0, 1\}^n \times \{0, 1\}^n \rightarrow \{0, 1\}^m$ *is an average-case seedless 2-source extractor at min-entropy k and error ϵ if it satisfies the following property: If for all random variables $X, Y \in \{0, 1\}^n$ and Z, such that, conditioned on Z, X and Y are independent (n, k)-sources, it holds that $|$ ((Ext2$(X, Y), Z) - (U_m, Z))$ $| < \epsilon$.*

Lemma 1 [16]. *For any $\delta > 0$, if* Ext2 $: \{0, 1\}^n \times \{0, 1\}^n \rightarrow \{0, 1\}^m$ *is a (worst-case) $(k - \log \frac{1}{\delta}, \epsilon)$-2-source extractor, then* Ext2 *is an average-case $(k, \epsilon + 2\delta)$-2-source extractor.*

2.3 True Simulation Extractable Non-interactive Zero Knowledge Argument System

In our construction, we require the notion of (same-string) *true-simulation extractable non-interactive zero knowledge argument system* (tSE-NIZK) first introduced in [9] and also its extension to support labels/tags. This notion is similar to the notion of simulation-sound extractable NIZKs [14] with the difference that the adversary has oracle access to *simulated* proofs only for *true* statements, in contrast to any arbitrary statement as in simulation-sound extractable NIZK argument system. In particular, we require the standard properties of *completeness, soundness* and *composable zero-knowledge*. Additionally, we also require the existence of another PPT *extractor* Ext which extracts a valid witness from any proof produced by a malicious prover $\mathcal{P}^*$, even if $\mathcal{P}^*$ has previously seen some *simulated proofs* for *true* statements. We refer the reader to the full version of our paper [6] for the formal definition of tSE-NIZK. For our purpose, it is sufficient to rely on the (weaker) notion of *one-time* strong true simulation extractability, where the adversary can query the simulation oracle $\mathcal{SIM}_{tk}(.)$ *only once*. Dodis et al. [9] showed how to generically construct tSE-NIZK argument systems supporting labels starting from any (labeled) CCA-secure PKE scheme and a (standard) NIZK argument system.

3 Entropic Post-challenge IND-CCA-BLT Secure PKE

In this section, we introduce the definition of *entropic post-challenge* IND-CCA-secure PKE resilient to both pre- and post-challenge bounded leakage and tampering (BLT) attacks. In Sect. 3.1, we define a relaxation of our entropic notion, which we call *entropic restricted post-challenge* IND-CCA BLT secure PKE. We show that a variant of the cryptosystem of Boneh et al. [4] with appropriate parameters, satisfies our entropic restricted notion of security (see Sect. 3.2). Finally, in Sect. 3.3, we show a generic transformation from our entropic restricted notion to the full-fledged entropic post-challenge IND-CCA-BLT secure PKE scheme. Before defining these notions, we explain the working of the leakage oracle and the tampering oracle.

The Leakage Oracle. In order to model *key leakage* attacks, we assume that the adversary may access a leakage oracle $O_{sk}^{\lambda}(.)$, subject to some restrictions. The adversary can query this oracle with arbitrary efficiently computable (polytime) leakage functions f and receive $f(sk)$ in response, where sk denotes the secret key. The restriction is that the output length of f must be less than $|sk|$. Specifically, following the works of [2,9], we require the output length of the leakage function f to be at most λ bits, which means the entropy loss of sk is at most λ bits upon observing $f(sk)$. Formally, we define the bounded leakage function family $\mathcal{F}_{bbd}(\kappa)$. The family $\mathcal{F}_{bbd}(\kappa)$ is defined as the class of all polynomial-time computable functions: $f : \{0,1\}^{|sk|} \rightarrow \{0,1\}^{\lambda}$, where $\lambda < |sk|$. We then require that the leakage function submitted by the adversary should satisfy that $f \in \mathcal{F}_{bbd}(\kappa)$.

The Tampering Oracle. To model related key attacks, the adversary is given access to a tampering oracle. Let $\mathcal{T}_{SK}$ denote the class of functions from SK to SK, where SK is the secret key space. The adversary may query the tampering oracle with arbitrary functions of its choice from $\mathcal{T}_{SK}$ and the number of such queries is *bounded* (say $t \in \mathbb{N}$). In the ith tampering query ($i \in [t]$), the adversary chooses a function $T_i \in \mathcal{T}_{SK}$ and gets access to the (tampered) decryption oracle $\mathsf{Dec}(\widetilde{sk}_i, \cdot)$, where $\widetilde{sk}_i = T_i(sk)$. The adversary may ask polynomially many decryption queries with respect to the tampered secret key $\widetilde{sk}_i$. In other words, the adversary gets access to information through decryption oracle executed on keys related to the original secret key, where the relations are induced by the tampering functions. If the encryption scheme supports labels, i.e., it is a labeled encryption scheme, the adversary gets access to the (tampered) decryption oracle $\mathsf{Dec}(\widetilde{sk}_i, \cdot, \cdot)$, where the third coordinate is a placeholder for labels. Also, the adversary gets access to the (tampered) decryption oracle both in the pre- and post-challenge phases. Another (obvious) restriction that is imposed on the tampering functions is that: In the post-challenge phase, when the adversary gets access to the (tampered) decryption oracles with respect to the challenge ciphertext c^*, it should be the case that $T_i(sk) \neq sk$, i.e., the post-challenge tampering functions T_i should not be identity functions with respect to the challenge ciphertext[3].

Definition 3 (Entropic Post-challenge IND-CCA-BLT Secure PKE).
Our definition of entropic post-challenge IND-CCA-BLT secure PKE can be seen as an *entropic version* of the notion of IND-CCA-BLT secure PKE introduced in [8], augmented with post challenge leakage and tampering queries. Informally, our definition captures the intuition that if we start with a message M with high min-entropy, the message M still *looks random* to an adversary who gets to see the ciphertext, some leakage information (even if this leakage happens after observing the ciphertext), and access to the tampering oracle (both in pre- and post-challenge phase) as defined above.

Formally, we define two games- "real" game and a "simulated" game. For simplicity, we assume the message is chosen from U_k, i.e, the uniform distribution over k bit strings. In general, it can be chosen from any arbitrary distribution as long as the message has min-entropy k. Let $(\lambda_{\mathsf{pre}}, \lambda_{\mathsf{post}})$ and $(t_{\mathsf{pre}}, t_{\mathsf{post}})$ denote the leakage bounds and the number of tampering queries allowed in the pre- and post-challenge phases respectively.

The "real" game. Given the parameters $(k, (\lambda_{\mathsf{pre}}, \lambda_{\mathsf{post}}), (t_{\mathsf{pre}}, t_{\mathsf{post}}))$ and a labeled encryption scheme E-BLT = (E-BLT.SetUp, E-BLT.Gen, E-BLT.Enc, E-BLT.Dec), the real game is defined as follows:

0. **Sampling:** *The challenger chooses a random message* $m \xleftarrow{\$} U_k$.
1. **SetUp:** *The challenger runs params* $\leftarrow$ E-BLT.SetUp(1^κ) *and sends params to the adversary* $\mathcal{A}$. *The public parameters params are taken as (implicit) input by all other algorithms.*
2. **Key Generation:** *The challenger chooses* $(sk, pk) \leftarrow$ E-BLT.Gen$(params)$ *and sends pk to* $\mathcal{A}$. *Set* $L^{\mathsf{pre}} = L^{\mathsf{post}} = 0$.

---

[3] When $T_i(sk) = sk$, and the adversary gets access to the tampering oracle with respect to c^*, it is emulating the scenario when it gets decryption oracle access with respect to sk on c^*, which is anyway disallowed in the IND-CCA-2 security game.

3. **Pre-challenge Leakage:** *In this phase, the adversary* $\mathcal{A}$ *makes a pre-challenge leakage query, specifying a function* $f_{\text{pre}}(.)$. *If* $L^{\text{pre}} + |f_{\text{pre}}(sk)| \leq \lambda_{\text{pre}}$, *then the challenger replies with* $f_{\text{pre}}(sk)$, *and sets* $L^{\text{pre}} = L^{\text{pre}} + |f_{\text{pre}}(sk)|$. *Otherwise, it ignores this query.*

4. **Pre-challenge Tampering queries:** *The adversary* $\mathcal{A}$ *may adaptively ask at most* t_{pre} *number of pre-challenge tampering queries. In the* i^{th} *tampering query* $(i \in [t_{\text{pre}}])$, *the adversary chooses* $T_i \in \mathcal{T}_{SK}$, *and gets access to the decryption oracle* E-BLT.$\text{Dec}(\widetilde{sk}_\theta, \cdot, \cdot)$[4] *(where* $1 \leq \theta \leq i$). *In other words, the decryption oracle may be queried with any of the tampered keys obtained till this point. We assume that, the total number of decryption oracle queries be* $q(k)$, *for some polynomial* $q(k)$. *Note that, when* $T_\theta(sk) = sk$, $\mathcal{A}$ *gets access to the (normal) decryption oracle.*

5. **Challenge:** *In this phase, the adversary submits a label (as a bit-string)* L^*. *The challenger encrypts the message* m *chosen at the beginning of the game as* $c^* \leftarrow$ E-BLT.$\text{Enc}(pk, m, L^*)$ *and sends* c^* *to* $\mathcal{A}$.

6. **Post-challenge Leakage:** *In this phase, the adversary* $\mathcal{A}$ *makes a post-challenge leakage query, specifying a function* $f_{\text{post}}(.)$. *If* $L^{\text{post}} + |f_{\text{post}}(sk)| \leq \lambda_{\text{post}}$, *then the challenger replies with* $f_{\text{post}}(sk)$, *and sets* $L^{\text{post}} = L^{\text{post}} + |f_{\text{post}}(sk)|$. *Otherwise, it ignores this query.*

7. **Post-challenge Tampering queries:** *The adversary* $\mathcal{A}$ *may adaptively ask* t_{post} *number of post-challenge tampering queries. In the* j^{th} *tampering query* $(j \in [t_{\text{post}}])$, *the adversary chooses* $T_j \in \mathcal{T}_{sk}$, *and gets access to the decryption oracle* E-BLT.$\text{Dec}(\widetilde{sk}_\rho, \cdot, \cdot)$ $(1 \leq \rho \leq j)$. *We assume that, the total number of decryption oracle queries be* $q'(k)$, *for some polynomial* $q'(k)$. *However, here we impose the restriction that:* $\mathcal{A}$ *is not allowed to query the pair* (c^*, L^*) *to the (tampered) decryption oracle(s)* E-BLT.$\text{Dec}(\widetilde{sk}_\rho, \cdot, \cdot)$.

Note that all these queries can be made *arbitrarily* and *adaptively* in nature. We denote the message m chosen at the onset of this game as M^{rl} to emphasize that it is used in the real game. Let the sets Q_{pre} and Q_{post} contain the tuples of the form $\left\{ (\widetilde{m}_{i_1}, (c_{i_1}, L_{i_1})), \cdots, (\widetilde{m}_{i_{q(\kappa)}}, (c_{i_{q(\kappa)}}, L_{i_{q(\kappa)}})) \right\}_{i=1}^{t_{\text{pre}}}$ and $\left\{ (\widetilde{m}_{j_1}, (c_{j_1}, L_{j_1})), \cdots, (\widetilde{m}_{j_{q(\kappa)}}, (c_{i_{q'(\kappa)}}, L_{i_{q'(\kappa)}})) \right\}_{j=1}^{t_{\text{post}}}$ respectively, for some polynomials $q(\kappa)$ and $q'(\kappa)$. Let $\mathcal{L}_{\text{pre}}$ and $\mathcal{L}_{\text{post}}$ be the random variables corresponding to the pre- and post-challenge leakages. We define the view of the adversary $\mathcal{A}$ in the real game as $\text{View}^{\text{rl}}_{\text{E-BLT}, \mathcal{A}}(\kappa) = (\text{rand}, \mathcal{L}_{\text{pre}}, Q_{\text{pre}}, c^*, \mathcal{L}_{\text{post}}, Q_{\text{post}})$, where rand denotes the random coins used by the adversary in the game. Finally, we denote by $(M^{\text{rl}}, \text{View}^{\text{rl}}_{\text{E-BLT}, \mathcal{A}})$ the joint distribution of the message M^{rl} and $\mathcal{A}$'s view in a real game with M^{rl}.

The "simulated" game: In the simulated game, we replace the challenger from above by a simulator Simu that interacts with $\mathcal{A}$ in any way that it sees fit.

---

[4] Recall when we write $\text{Dec}(\widetilde{sk}_\theta, \cdot, \cdot)$, the second coordinate is the placeholder for ciphertexts input by the adversary; whereas the third coordinate is the placeholder for labels.

Simu gets a uniformly chosen message M^{sm} as input and it has to simulate the interaction with $\mathcal{A}$ conditioned on M^{sm}. We denote the view of the adversary in the simulated game by $\mathsf{View}^{sm}_{Simu,\mathcal{A}}(\kappa) = (\mathsf{rand}^{sm}, \mathcal{L}^{sm}_{pre}, Q^{sm}_{pre}, c^{sm}, \mathcal{L}^{sm}_{post}, Q^{sm}_{post})$. Now, we define what it means for the encryption scheme ER-BLT to be entropic restricted post-challenge (bounded) leakage and tamper-resilient.

Definition 4 (Entropic restricted post-challenge IND-CCA-BLT security). *Let* $(k, (\lambda_{pre}, \lambda_{post}), (t_{pre}, t_{post}))$ *be parameters as stated above, let* $\mathcal{T}_{SK}$ *be the family of allowable tampering functions. A public key encryption scheme is said to be entropic restricted post-challenge IND-CCA-BLT secure with respect to all these parameters if there exists a simulator* Simu, *such that, for every PPT adversary* $\mathcal{A}$ *the following two conditions hold:*

1. $(M^{rl}, \mathsf{View}^{rl}_{E\text{-}BLT,\mathcal{A}}(\kappa)) \approx_c (M^{sm}, \mathsf{View}^{sm}_{Simu,\mathcal{A}}(\kappa))$, *i.e, the above two ensembles (indexed by the security parameter) are computationally indistinguishable.*
2. *The average min-entropy of the message* M^{sm} *given* $\mathsf{View}^{sm}_{Simu,\mathcal{A}}(\kappa)$ *is*

$$\widetilde{\mathsf{H}}_\infty(M^{sm} \mid \mathsf{View}^{sm}_{Simu,\mathcal{A}}(\kappa)) \geq k - \lambda_{post} - \mathcal{F}(t_{post}).$$

where $\mathcal{F}(t_{post})$ *denotes the entropy loss due to post-challenge tampering queries, and the tampering functions come from the class* $\mathcal{T}_{SK}$.[5]

Intuitively, even after the adversary sees the encryption of the message, pre- and post-challenge leakages and the output of the (tampered) decryption oracle both in the pre- and post-challenge phase, the message M^{sm} still retains its initial entropy, except for the entropy loss due to post-challenge leakage and tampering.

3.1   Entropic Restricted Post-challenge IND-CCA-BLT Secure PKE

We now define the notion of *entropic restricted* post-challenge IND-CCA-BLT secure PKE (denoted by ER-BLT), which is a relaxation of the notion of the entropic post-challenge IND-CCA-BLT secure PKE. The difference between the two notions is with respect to the working of (tampered) decryption oracle, as defined in the real game in Definition 3. In particular, in our entropic restricted notion of security, the adversary *cannot* make pre- and post-challenge decryption queries with respect to the original secret key (unlike the entropic notion in Sect. 3) and working of the (tampered) decryption oracle is *modified* as follows:

Modified Decryption Oracle: In the restricted post-challenge IND-CCA-BLT security game, the adversary is not given full access to the tampering oracle. Instead, the adversary is allowed to see the output of the (tampered) decryption oracle for only those ciphertexts c, for which he already knows the plaintext m and the randomness r used to encrypt it (using the original

---

[5] In our construction, we will show that $\mathcal{F}(t_{post}) = t_{post} \log p$, i.e., for each post-challenge tampering query we have to leak *only* one element of the base group $\mathbb{G}$ of prime order p. This single element is sufficient to simulate polynomially many (modified) decryption queries with respect to each tampering query.

public key). This restricts the power of the adversary to submit only *"well-formed"* ciphertexts to the tampering oracle. In particular, in the ith tampering query the adversary chooses a function $T_i \in \mathcal{T}_{SK}$ and gets access to a (modified) decryption oracle ER-BLT.Dec$^*(\widetilde{sk}_i, \cdot, \cdot)$, where $\widetilde{sk}_i = T_i(sk)$. This oracle answers polynomially many queries of the following form: Upon input a pair $(m, r) \in \mathcal{M} \times \mathcal{R}$, (where $\mathcal{M}$ and $\mathcal{R}$ are the message space and randomness space of the PKE respectively), compute $c \leftarrow$ ER-BLT.Enc$(pk, m; r)$ and output a plaintext $\widetilde{m} =$ ER-BLT.Dec$(\widetilde{sk}_i, c)$ under the current tampered key.

The real and simulated game for the above entropic restricted post-challenge IND-CCA-BLT game, apart from the above restrictions, is identical to the real and simulated games of the entropic post-challenge IND-CCA-BLT secure PKE as defined in Definition 3. In particular, using the same notations from Definition 3, we denote the view of the adversary in the entropic restricted game as $\mathsf{View}^{rl}_{\mathsf{ER\text{-}BLT}, \mathcal{A}}(\kappa) = (\mathsf{rand}, \mathcal{L}_{\mathsf{pre}}, Q_{\mathsf{pre}}, c^*, \mathcal{L}_{\mathsf{post}}, Q_{\mathsf{post}})$, where Q_{pre} and Q_{post} contain answers to the (tampered) decryption oracle queries as described above with respect to the tampered secret keys.

3.2 Construction of Entropic Restricted Post-challenge IND-CCA-BLT Secure PKE

In this section, we show how to construct a CCA-2 secure entropic restricted post-challenge PKE secure against bounded leakage and tampering (BLT) attacks. We show that a variant of the encryption scheme proposed by Boneh et al. (referred to as BHHO cryptosystem from herein) [4] is entropic restricted post-challenge IND-CCA-BLT secure. It was shown in [8] that the (modified) BHHO cryptosystem is a restricted (pre-challenge) IND-CCA-BLT secure PKE. However, we observe that the same variant of the BHHO cryptosystem with the parameters appropriately modified satisfies our new notion of entropic security, even when the adversary is given post-challenge leakage and access to (restricted) tampering oracle (even in the post-challenge phase).

- ER-BLT.SetUp(1^κ): Choose a group $\mathbb{G}$ of prime order p with generator g. Set $params := (\mathbb{G}, g, p)$. All the algorithms take $params$ as implicit input.
- ER-BLT.Gen$(params)$: Sample random vectors $\mathbf{x}, \boldsymbol{\alpha} \in \mathbb{Z}_p^\ell$; compute $g^{\boldsymbol{\alpha}} = (g_1, \cdots, g_\ell)$, and $h = \prod_{i=1}^\ell g_i^{x_i}$. Set $sk := \mathbf{x} = (x_1, \cdots, x_\ell)$ and $pk := (h, g^{\boldsymbol{\alpha}})$
- ER-BLT.Enc(pk, m): Sample $r \leftarrow \mathbb{Z}_p$, and return $c := (g_1^r, \cdots, g_\ell^r, h^r \cdot m)$
- ER-BLT.Dec(sk, c): Parse c as $(c_1, \cdots, c_\ell, d)$ as sk as $(x_1, \cdots, x_\ell).$, and outputs $m \leftarrow d / \prod_{i=1}^\ell (g_i^r)^{x_i}$

It is easy to verify the correctness of the above cryptosystem.

Theorem 1. *Let $\kappa \in \mathbb{N}$ be the security parameter, and assume that the* DDH *assumption holds in group $\mathbb{G}$. The* BHHO *cryptosystem is entropic restricted post-challenge* IND-CCA-$\big(k, (\lambda_{\mathsf{pre}}, \lambda_{\mathsf{post}}), (t_{\mathsf{pre}}, t_{\mathsf{post}})\big)$-BLT *secure, where*

$$\lambda_{\mathsf{pre}} + \lambda_{\mathsf{post}} \leq (\ell - 2 - t_{\mathsf{pre}} - t_{\mathsf{post}}) \log p - \omega(\log \kappa) \quad and \quad (t_{\mathsf{pre}} + t_{\mathsf{post}}) \leq \ell - 3.$$

Proof. Before proceeding with the proof of the above theorem, we prove a lemma (Lemma 2) that essentially shows that the BHHO cryptosystem is entropic leakage-resilient with respect to pre- and post-challenge leakage, i.e., it satisfies the notion of entropic restricted post-challenge IND-CCA-$(k, (\lambda'_{pre}, \lambda'_{post}), (0,0))$-BLT security (the adversary has no access to the tampering oracle), for appropriate choice of parameters. We then prove the above theorem by using Lemma 2 and showing a leakage to tamper reduction to take care of pre- and post-challenge tampering queries.

Lemma 2. *The* BHHO *cryptosystem described above is entropic restricted post-challenge* IND-CCA-$(k, (\lambda'_{pre}, \lambda'_{post}), (0,0))$-BLT *secure, where*

$$\lambda'_{pre} + \lambda'_{post} \leq (\ell - 2) \log p - \omega(\log \kappa)$$

Proof. To prove Lemma 2 we need to describe a simulator, whose answers to the adversary are indistinguishable from the real game, and at the same time leave enough min-entropy in the message m. The main idea of the proof follows from the observation that the BHHO cryptosystem can be viewed as a *hash proof system* (HPS) (see [6] for the definition of HPS), with DDH-like tuples as valid ciphertexts, and non-DDH tuples as invalid ciphertexts. In the real game, the challenger samples a valid ciphertext (along with a witness) and proceeds as in the original construction, whereas in the simulated game a random invalid ciphertext is sampled. The indistinguishability of the real and simulated games is implied by the subset membership problem. The left-over hash lemma then guarantees uniformity of the challenge message. For details of the proof, please refer to the full version of our paper [6].

We now proceed to prove our main theorem. Let us assume that there exists an adversary $\mathcal{A}$ that breaks the entropic restricted post-challenge IND-CCA $(k, (\lambda_{pre}, \lambda_{post}), (t_{pre}, t_{post}))$-BLT security with non-negligible advantage. We construct an adversary $\mathcal{A}'$ against the entropic restricted post-challenge IND-CCA $(k, (\lambda'_{pre}, \lambda'_{post}), (0,0))$-BLT security, with the same advantage. The main idea behind this proof is *leakage to tamper reduction*. For each tampering query made by the adversary, the reduction simply leaks a single group element from $\mathbb{Z}_p$, and simulates polynomially many decryption queries under that tampered key using the leaked element. Hence, the reduction has to leak $(t_{pre} + t_{post}) \log p$ bits in all. We appropriately set the parameters of BHHO to ensure that the message still has enough min-entropy, even given the responses of the tampering oracle. We refer the reader to the full version [6] for the detailed proof.

3.3 The General Transformation

In this section, we show a general transformation from an entropic-restricted post-challenge IND-CCA-BLT secure PKE to an entropic post-challenge IND-CCA-BLT secure PKE scheme (see Fig. 1). Let ER-BLT = (ER-BLT.SetUp, ER-BLT.Gen, ER-BLT.Enc, ER-BLT.Dec) be an entropic restricted post-challenge IND-CCA-$(k, (\lambda_{pre}, \lambda_{post}), (t_{pre}, t_{post}))$-BLT secure PKE scheme, and let

$\Pi = (\text{Gen}, \text{P}, \text{V})$ be a one-time strong tSE-NIZK argument system supporting labels for the following relation:

$$\mathbb{R}_{\text{ER-BLT}} = \{(m, r), (pk, c) \mid c = \text{ER-BLT.Enc}(pk, m; r)\}$$

Let E-BLT $= (\text{E-BLT.SetUp}', \text{E-BLT.Gen}', \text{E-BLT.Enc}', \text{E-BLT.Dec}')$ be an entropic post-challenge IND-CCA-BLT secure PKE.

Theorem 2. *Let* ER-BLT *be an entropic-restricted post-challenge IND-CCA-* $\left(k, (\lambda_{\text{pre}}, \lambda_{\text{post}}), (t_{\text{pre}}, t_{\text{post}})\right)$*-BLT secure PKE scheme,* Π *be a one-time strong tSE NIZK argument system supporting label for the relation* $\mathbb{R}_{\text{ER-BLT}}$, *then the above encryption scheme* E-BLT *is an entropic post-challenge IND-CCA-* $\left(k, (\lambda_{\text{pre}}, \lambda_{\text{post}}), (t_{\text{pre}}, t_{\text{post}})\right)$*-BLT secure PKE scheme.*

Define the encryption scheme E-BLT as follows:

1. E-BLT.SetUp$'(1^{\kappa})$: Obtain *params* $\leftarrow$ ER-BLT.SetUp(1^{κ}), and sample $(\text{crs}, \text{tk}, \text{ek}) \leftarrow \text{Gen}(1^{\kappa})$. Set *params'* $:= (params, \text{crs})$

2. E-BLT.Gen$'(params')$: Obtain $(pk, sk) \leftarrow$ ER-BLT.Gen$(params)$; set $pk' = pk$, and $sk' = sk$.

3. E-BLT.Enc$'(pk, m, \text{L})$: On input the public key pk, a message $m \in \mathcal{M}$ and a label L , sample $r \xleftarrow{\$} \mathcal{R}$, and compute $c \leftarrow$ ER-BLT.Enc$(pk, m; r)$, $\pi \leftarrow$ P$(\text{crs}, \text{L}, (m, r), (pk, c))$. Output $c' = (c, \pi)$

4. E-BLT.Dec$'(sk, c', \text{L})$: Parse c' as $c' = (c, \pi)$. Check if V$(\text{crs}, \text{L}, (pk, c), \pi) = 1$. If not output $\perp$, else output $m =$ ER-BLT.Dec(sk, c)

Fig. 1. Entropic post-challenge IND-CCA-BLT PKE scheme E-BLT

Proof Sketch. We now give an intuitive proof sketch of the above theorem. Informally, the zero-knowledge argument enforces the adversary to submit to the (tampered) decryption oracle only *valid* ciphertexts, for which he knows the corresponding plaintext (and the randomness used to encrypt it). The plaintext-randomness pair (m, r) (which acts as a witness) can then be extracted using the extraction trapdoor of the tSE-NIZK argument system, thus allowing to reduce entropic IND-CCA BLT security to entropic restricted IND-CCA BLT security. Since the extraction trapdoor is never used in the real encryption scheme, the adversary neither gets any leakage from it, nor gets to tamper with it. This essentially makes the (tampered) decryption oracle useless and the adversary learns *no* additional information from the decryption oracle access. The proof also relies on the fact that the CRS is untamperable, a notion that is used in all the previous works [8,12]. This can be achieved by (say) hard-coding the CRS in the encryption algorithm. The detailed proof of this theorem can be found in the full version [6] of our paper.

4   Post-challenge IND-CCA-BLT Secure KEM in Split-State Model

In this section, we present our construction of post-challenge IND-CCA-BLT secure Key Encapsulation Mechanism (KEM) in the (bounded) split-state leakage and tampering model. Note that, achieving security against post-challenge leakage and tampering in its most general form is impossible as already shown in [8, 16, 20], even if a single bit of leakage is allowed or the adversary is allowed to ask even a single tampering query after receiving the challenge ciphertext. To this end, we resort to the 2-split-state leakage and tampering model. In this model, the secret key of the KEM scheme is split into two disjoint parts, and the adversary can ask arbitrary (pre- and post-challenge) leakage and tampering queries on each of these two parts *independently*. However, the adversary is allowed to adaptively ask leakage/tampering functions depending on the answers of the previous queries. The tampering queries allow the adversary to have access to the tampered decryption oracle. The adversary also gets access to the (standard) decryption oracle by specifying the tampering functions to be identity functions. Finally, the adversary has to guess whether the challenger KEM key is a randomly sampled key or a real key. Due to space constraints, we refer the reader to the full version [6] for the formal definition and the security model for IND-CCA-BLT secure KEM.

4.1   Construction of Post-challenge IND-CCA-BLT Secure KEM

We now show the construction of our post-challenge/after-the-fact IND-CCA-BLT secure KEM scheme $\mathcal{KEM}$ = $(\mathcal{KEM}.\mathsf{Setup}, \mathcal{KEM}.\mathsf{Gen}, \mathcal{KEM}.\mathsf{Encap}, \mathcal{KEM}.\mathsf{Decap})$ (see Fig. 2).

The main ingredients required for our construction are as follows:

- An *entropic* post-challenge IND-CCA-BLT-secure PKE scheme E-BLT = (E-BLT.Setup, E-BLT.Gen, E-BLT.Enc, E-BLT.Dec), that encrypts ν bit messages, and supports labels. Also, assume that E-BLT is entropic with respect to parameters $(\lambda_{\mathsf{pre}}, \lambda_{\mathsf{post}}, t_{\mathsf{pre}}, t_{\mathsf{post}})$ (refer to Definition 3).
- A (ϑ, ε) average-case (seedless) 2-source extractor $\mathsf{Ext2} : \{0,1\}^\nu \times \{0,1\}^\nu \to \{0,1\}^u$, with $\varepsilon = 2^{-u-\omega(\log \kappa)}$ (see Sect. 2.2 for its definition).
- A strong one-time signature (OTS) scheme $\mathcal{SS} = (\mathcal{SS}.\mathsf{Gen}, \mathcal{SS}.\mathsf{Sig}, \mathcal{SS}.\mathsf{Ver})$, with message space $\mathsf{poly}(\kappa)$ (see [6] for the definition of OTS).

Design Rationale: On a high level, to generate an encapsulated symmetric key, first we generate a key pair (vk, sk) of a one-time signature (OTS) scheme. We then use an *entropic* post-challenge IND-CCA-BLT secure PKE scheme (E-BLT) to encrypt two random strings x_1 and x_2 independently with the verification key vk as the label/tag, and generate a signature on both the ciphertexts c_1 and c_2. The security of E-BLT guarantees that both the strings x_1 and x_2 still have enough average min-entropy after chosen-ciphertext leakage and tampering attacks (even in the post-challenge phase). In addition, the split-state model ensures that the two strings are independent. Hence, we can use an average-case seedless 2-source extractor to extract a random encapsulation key from both the strings. The trick of generating a key pair of an OTS and setting the verification key vk as a tag/label while encrypting, ensures that, a tag cannot be re-used by an adversary in a decryption or tampering query (In fact, to re-use that tag, the adversary essentially has to forge a signature under vk). The formal proof of our construction will follow this intuition, expect for one condition related to adaptivity of the adversary. The adversary may chose leakage and tampering functions from the two parts of the secret key after it saw the encapsulated key which was itself derived from the two parts, hence causing a circularity in the argument. This leap is handled in our proof using complexity leveraging. In particular, if the size of the extracted encapsulation key has u bits, then the adaptivity can only increase the advantage of the adversary by a factor at most 2^u. We set our parameters appropriately to handle this gap.

Theorem 3. *Let* E-BLT *be an entropic post-challenge* IND-CCA-BLT-*secure PKE scheme with parameters* $(\lambda_{\text{pre}}, \lambda_{\text{post}}, t_{\text{pre}}, t_{\text{post}})$ *and encrypting* ν *bit messages and supporting labels. Also, let* Ext2 *be a* (ϑ, ε) *average-case (seedless) 2-source extractor with parameters mentioned above, and let* SS *be a strong one-time signature scheme supporting polynomial sized message space. Then the KEM scheme* $\mathcal{KEM}$ *is* IND-CCA *secure with respect to pre- and post-challenge leakage* λ'_{pre} *and* λ'_{post} *respectively, and pre- and post-challenge tampering* t'_{pre} *and* t'_{post} *respectively, in the bounded split-state leakage and tampering model, as long as the parameters satisfy the following constraints:*

$$\lambda'_{\text{pre}} \leq \lambda_{\text{pre}}, \quad \lambda'_{\text{post}} \leq \min(\lambda_{\text{post}} - u, \ \nu - t'_{\text{post}} \log p - \vartheta - 1), \quad t'_{\text{pre}} \leq t_{\text{pre}} \ \text{and} \ t'_{\text{post}} \leq t_{\text{post}}.$$

We refer the reader to the full version [6] for the detailed proof of the above theorem.

5   Post-challenge IND-CCA-BLT Secure PKE in Split-State Model

In this section, we present our construction of post-challenge IND-CCA-BLT secure PKE scheme in split-state model, starting from a post-challenge IND-CCA-BLT secure KEM scheme (as shown in Sect. 4.1) and a (one-time) symmetric-key encryption scheme. The security model of post-challenge IND-CCA-BLT secure PKE scheme in split state model is similar to the model of post-challenge IND-CCA-BLT secure KEM scheme in split state as described in Sect. 4, with the only difference that the encapsulation and the decapsulation algorithms are replaced by the encryption and decryption algorithms respectively. The secret key of the PKE is also split into two parts, as in the KEM scheme, and the adversary can query ask arbitrary pre- and post-challenge leakage and tampering queries, provided they act independently on the secret key

Define the key encapsulation scheme $\mathcal{KEM}$ as follows:

1. $\mathcal{KEM}.\mathsf{Setup}(1^\kappa)$: On input 1^κ, run E-BLT.SetUp to get $params$. Set par $:=$ $params$.

2. $\mathcal{KEM}.\mathsf{Gen}(\mathsf{par})$: The key generation consists of two subroutines–
   $\mathcal{KEM}.\mathsf{Gen}_1$ and $\mathcal{KEM}.\mathsf{Gen}_2$, where $\mathcal{KEM}.\mathsf{Gen}_j$ on input par, samples $(pk_j, sk_j) \leftarrow$ E-BLT.Gen(par), for $j = 1, 2$. It outputs the public key as $pk = (pk_1, pk_2)$, and the secret key is $sk = (sk_1, sk_2)$.

3. $\mathcal{KEM}.\mathsf{Encap}(pk)$: On input the public key pk, do the following:
   - Run $(vk, ssk) \leftarrow \mathcal{SS}.\mathsf{Gen}(1^\kappa)$, where vk and ssk are the verification and signing keys of the strong OTS scheme respectively.
   - Choose $x_1, x_2 \xleftarrow{\$} \{0,1\}^\nu$ and compute $c_1 \leftarrow$ E-BLT.Enc(pk_1, x_1, vk) and $c_2 \leftarrow$ E-BLT.Enc(pk_2, x_2, vk), where vk is the label.
   - Compute $\sigma \leftarrow \mathcal{SS}.\mathsf{Sign}(ssk, (c_1, c_2))$ and $k = \mathsf{Ext2}(x_1, x_2)$.
   Output the ciphertext-key pair $(c = (vk, c_1, c_2, \sigma), k)$

4. $\mathcal{KEM}.\mathsf{Decap}(sk, c)$: On input the secret key sk and the ciphertext c do:
   - Parse c as $c = (vk, c_1, c_2, \sigma)$ and $sk = (sk_1, sk_2)$.
   - Run $\mathcal{SS}.\mathsf{Ver}(vk, (c_1, c_2), \sigma)$. If the verification fails, the ciphertext is $invalid$ and return $\perp$.
   - Run $x_j \leftarrow$ E-BLT.Dec$_j(sk_j, c_j)$ for $j = \{1, 2\}$.
   - Run $\mathcal{KEM}.\mathsf{Comb}(x_1, x_2)$: Compute $k = \mathsf{Ext2}(x_1, x_2)$.

Fig. 2. Post-challenge IND-CCA-BLT-secure KEM scheme $\mathcal{KEM}$.

parts and are bounded in length or number as before. Besides, he can ask arbitrary pre- and post-challenge decryption queries, with the obvious restriction that in the post-challenge phase the decryption queries are never asked on the challenge ciphertext. The challenge phase is replaced by the standard indistinguishability style definition for PKE scheme. The PKE scheme $\mathcal{BLT}$ consists of the following algorithms $\mathcal{BLT} = (\mathcal{BLT}.\mathsf{Setup}, \mathcal{BLT}.\mathsf{Gen}, \mathcal{BLT}.\mathsf{Enc}, \mathcal{BLT}.\mathsf{Dec})$. We refer the reader to [6] for the detailed model.

5.1   Construction of Post-challenge IND-CCA-BLT Secure PKE

We now show the construction of our post-challenge/after-the-fact IND-CCA-BLT secure PKE scheme $\mathcal{BLT} = (\mathcal{BLT}.\mathsf{Setup}, \mathcal{BLT}.\mathsf{Gen}, \mathcal{BLT}.\mathsf{Enc}, \mathcal{BLT}.\mathsf{Dec})$. The main ingredients of our construction are:

1. A 2-split-state IND-CCA-$(k, (\lambda'_{\mathsf{pre}}, \lambda'_{\mathsf{post}}), (t'_{\mathsf{pre}}, t'_{\mathsf{post}}))$-BLT secure KEM $\mathcal{KEM} = (\mathcal{KEM}.\mathsf{Setup}, \mathcal{KEM}.\mathsf{Gen}, \mathcal{KEM}.\mathsf{Encap}, \mathcal{KEM}.\mathsf{Decap})$ (please refer to [6] for the definition) with output space $\{0,1\}^* \times \{0,1\}^u$.

2. (One-time) symmetric encryption scheme $\varphi = (\mathcal{SKE}.\mathsf{KG}, \mathcal{SKE}.\mathsf{Enc}, \mathcal{SKE}.\mathsf{Dec})$ encrypting ω bit messages, with key space $\{0,1\}^u$. (please refer to [6] for its definition).

Construction: The construction of our 2-split-state PKE scheme $\mathcal{BLT}$ proceeds as follows:

1. $\mathcal{BLT}.\mathsf{Setup}(1^\kappa)$: Run $\mathsf{par} \leftarrow \mathcal{KEM}.\mathsf{Setup}(1^\kappa)$. Set $\mathsf{params} := \mathsf{par}$.
2. $\mathcal{BLT}.\mathsf{Gen}(\mathsf{params})$: Run $(pk, sk) \leftarrow \mathcal{KEM}.\mathsf{Gen}(\mathsf{par})$. Recall that public key $pk = (pk_1, pk_2)$ and $sk = (sk_1, sk_2)$. Set $pk' = pk$ and $sk' = sk$.
3. $\mathcal{BLT}.\mathsf{Enc}(pk', m)$: On input a message $m \in \{0,1\}^\omega$, run $(c_0, k) \leftarrow \mathcal{KEM}.\mathsf{Encap}(pk')$. Then it computes $c_1 \leftarrow \mathcal{SKE}.\mathsf{Enc}(k, m)$, and output the ciphertext $c = (c_0, c_1)$.
4. $\mathcal{BLT}.\mathsf{Dec}(sk', c)$: Parse $c = (c_0, c_1)$. Run $k \leftarrow \mathcal{KEM}.\mathsf{Decap}(sk', c_0)$, and outputs the message $m = \mathcal{SKE}.\mathsf{Dec}(k, c_1)$.

Theorem 4. *The encryption scheme* $\mathcal{BLT}$ *is post-challenge* IND-CCA- $\left(k, (\lambda''_{\mathsf{pre}}, \lambda''_{\mathsf{post}}), (t''_{\mathsf{pre}}, t''_{\mathsf{post}})\right)$-BLT *secure as long as the parameters satisfies:*

$$\lambda''_{\mathsf{pre}} \le \lambda'_{\mathsf{pre}}, \quad \lambda''_{\mathsf{post}} \le \lambda'_{\mathsf{post}} \quad \text{and} \quad t''_{\mathsf{pre}} \le t'_{\mathsf{pre}}, \quad t''_{\mathsf{post}} \le t'_{\mathsf{post}}$$

We refer the reader to the full version [6] for the detailed proof.

6 Conclusion

In this work, we study after-the-fact leakage and tampering in the context of public-key encryption schemes. To this end, we define an entropic post-challenge IND-CCA-BLT security and show how to construct full-fledged post-challenge IND-CCA-BLT secure PKE schemes under the split-state restriction. It is interesting to find other meaningful and realizable after-the-fact definitions of security for leakage and tampering. Besides, it will be interesting to define an appropriate framework for after-the-fact continuous leakage and tampering attacks, and port our construction in this setting.

Acknowledgments. We acknowledge the reviewers for their helpful comments. The authors are grateful to the project "Information Security Education and Awareness Program" of Ministry of Information Technology, Government of India for providing partial support.

References

1. Aggarwal, D., Dodis, Y., Kazana, T., Obremski, M.: Non-malleable reductions and applications. In: Proceedings of the Forty-Seventh Annual ACM on Symposium on Theory of Computing, pp. 459–468. ACM (2015)
2. Akavia, A., Goldwasser, S., Vaikuntanathan, V.: Simultaneous hardcore bits and cryptography against memory attacks. In: Reingold, O. (ed.) TCC 2009. LNCS, vol. 5444, pp. 474–495. Springer, Heidelberg (2009). https://doi.org/10.1007/978-3-642-00457-5_28
3. Bellare, M., Kohno, T.: A theoretical treatment of related-key attacks: RKA-PRPs, RKA-PRFs, and applications. In: Biham, E. (ed.) EUROCRYPT 2003. LNCS, vol. 2656, pp. 491–506. Springer, Heidelberg (2003). https://doi.org/10.1007/3-540-39200-9_31

4. Boneh, D., Halevi, S., Hamburg, M., Ostrovsky, R.: Circular-secure encryption from decision Diffie-Hellman. In: Wagner, D. (ed.) CRYPTO 2008. LNCS, vol. 5157, pp. 108–125. Springer, Heidelberg (2008). https://doi.org/10.1007/978-3-540-85174-5_7

5. Chakraborty, S., Paul, G., Rangan, C.P.: Efficient compilers for after-the-fact leakage: from CPA to CCA-2 secure PKE to AKE. In: Pieprzyk, J., Suriadi, S. (eds.) ACISP 2017. LNCS, vol. 10342, pp. 343–362. Springer, Cham (2017). https://doi.org/10.1007/978-3-319-60055-0_18

6. Chakraborty, S., Rangan, C.P.: Public key encryption resilient to post-challenge leakage and tampering attacks. Cryptology ePrint Archive, Report 2018/883 (2018). https://eprint.iacr.org/2018/883

7. Chor, B., Goldreich, O.: Unbiased bits from sources of weak randomness and probabilistic communication complexity. SIAM J. Comput. **17**(2), 230–261 (1988)

8. Damgård, I., Faust, S., Mukherjee, P., Venturi, D.: Bounded tamper resilience: how to go beyond the algebraic barrier. In: Sako, K., Sarkar, P. (eds.) ASIACRYPT 2013. LNCS, vol. 8270, pp. 140–160. Springer, Heidelberg (2013). https://doi.org/10.1007/978-3-642-42045-0_8

9. Dodis, Y., Haralambiev, K., López-Alt, A., Wichs, D.: Efficient public-key cryptography in the presence of key leakage. In: Abe, M. (ed.) ASIACRYPT 2010. LNCS, vol. 6477, pp. 613–631. Springer, Heidelberg (2010). https://doi.org/10.1007/978-3-642-17373-8_35

10. Dziembowski, S., Kazana, T., Obremski, M.: Non-malleable codes from two-source extractors. In: Canetti, R., Garay, J.A. (eds.) CRYPTO 2013. LNCS, vol. 8043, pp. 239–257. Springer, Heidelberg (2013). https://doi.org/10.1007/978-3-642-40084-1_14

11. Dziembowski, S., Pietrzak, K., Wichs, D.: Non-malleable codes. In: ICS, pp. 434–452 (2010)

12. Faonio, A., Venturi, D.: Efficient public-key cryptography with bounded leakage and tamper resilience. In: Cheon, J.H., Takagi, T. (eds.) ASIACRYPT 2016. LNCS, vol. 10031, pp. 877–907. Springer, Heidelberg (2016). https://doi.org/10.1007/978-3-662-53887-6_32

13. Gennaro, R., Lysyanskaya, A., Malkin, T., Micali, S., Rabin, T.: Algorithmic tamper-proof (ATP) security: theoretical foundations for security against hardware tampering. In: Naor, M. (ed.) TCC 2004. LNCS, vol. 2951, pp. 258–277. Springer, Heidelberg (2004). https://doi.org/10.1007/978-3-540-24638-1_15

14. Groth, J.: Simulation-sound NIZK proofs for a practical language and constant size group signatures. In: Lai, X., Chen, K. (eds.) ASIACRYPT 2006. LNCS, vol. 4284, pp. 444–459. Springer, Heidelberg (2006). https://doi.org/10.1007/11935230_29

15. Halderman, J.A., et al.: Lest we remember: cold-boot attacks on encryption keys. Commun. ACM **52**(5), 91–98 (2009)

16. Halevi, S., Lin, H.: After-the-fact leakage in public-key encryption. In: Ishai, Y. (ed.) TCC 2011. LNCS, vol. 6597, pp. 107–124. Springer, Heidelberg (2011). https://doi.org/10.1007/978-3-642-19571-6_8

17. Kocher, P., Jaffe, J., Jun, B.: Differential power analysis. In: Wiener, M. (ed.) CRYPTO 1999. LNCS, vol. 1666, pp. 388–397. Springer, Heidelberg (1999). https://doi.org/10.1007/3-540-48405-1_25

18. Kocher, P.C.: Timing attacks on implementations of Diffie-Hellman, RSA, DSS, and other systems. In: Koblitz, N. (ed.) CRYPTO 1996. LNCS, vol. 1109, pp. 104–113. Springer, Heidelberg (1996). https://doi.org/10.1007/3-540-68697-5_9

19. Liu, F.-H., Lysyanskaya, A.: Tamper and leakage resilience in the split-state model. In: Safavi-Naini, R., Canetti, R. (eds.) CRYPTO 2012. LNCS, vol. 7417, pp. 517–532. Springer, Heidelberg (2012). https://doi.org/10.1007/978-3-642-32009-5_30

20. Naor, M., Segev, G.: Public-key cryptosystems resilient to key leakage. SIAM J. Comput. **41**(4), 772–814 (2012)

21. Santha, M., Vazirani, U.V.: Generating quasi-random sequences from semi-random sources. J. Comput. Syst. Sci. **33**(1), 75–87 (1986)

22. Vazirani, U.V.: Strong communication complexity or generating quasi-random sequences from two communicating semi-random sources. Combinatorica **7**(4), 375–392 (1987)

23. Zhang, Z., Chow, S.S., Cao, Z.: Post-challenge leakage in public-key encryption. Theor. Comput. Sci. **572**, 25–49 (2015)

Downgradable Identity-Based Encryption and Applications

Olivier Blazy$^{(\boxtimes)}$, Paul Germouty, and Duong Hieu Phan

Université de Limoges, XLim, Limoges, France
olivier.blazy@unilim.fr

Abstract. In Identity-based cryptography, in order to generalize one receiver encryption to multi-receiver encryption, wildcards were introduced: WIBE enables wildcard in receivers' pattern and Wicked-IBE allows one to generate a key for identities with wildcard. However, the use of wildcard makes the construction of WIBE, Wicked-IBE more complicated and significantly less efficient than the underlying IBE. The main reason is that the conventional identity's binary alphabet is extended to a ternary alphabet $\{0, 1, *\}$ and the wildcard $*$ is always treated in a convoluted way in encryption or in key generation. In this paper, we show that when dealing with multi-receiver setting, wildcard is not necessary. We introduce a new downgradable property for IBE scheme and show that any IBE with this property, called DIBE, can be efficiently transformed into WIBE or Wicked-IBE.

While WIBE and Wicked-IBE have been used to construct Broadcast encryption, we go a step further by employing DIBE to construct Attribute-based Encryption of which the access policy is expressed as a boolean formula in the disjunctive normal form.

Keywords: Identity-based Encryption · Attribute-based Encryption

1 Introduction

Identity-based encryption (IBE) is a concept introduced by Shamir in [Sha84] allowing encrypting for a specific recipient using solely his identity (for example an email address or phone number) instead of public key. Decryption is done by using a user secret key for the said identity, obtained via a trusted authority. This concept avoids the use of Public Key Infrastructure in order to get a user's public key securely. This was the main argument to build such scheme, however a lot of works expose the fact that Identity-based Encryption schemes can be used to build other primitives like Adaptive Oblivious Transfer [GH07,BCG16].

The first instantiations of an IBE scheme arose in 2001 [Coc01,BF01,SOK00]. It was only in 2005 in [Wat05], that the first construction, with adaptive security in the standard model, was proposed. Adaptive security meaning that an

---

An extended version of this paper is available on eprint [BGP18].

© Springer Nature Switzerland AG 2019
M. Matsui (Ed.): CT-RSA 2019, LNCS 11405, pp. 44–61, 2019.
https://doi.org/10.1007/978-3-030-12612-4_3

adversary may select the challenge identity id* after seeing the public key and arbitrarily many user secret keys for identities of his choice. The concept of IBE generalizes naturally to hierarchical IBE (HIBE). In an L-level HIBE, hierarchical identities are vectors of identities of maximal length L and user secret keys for a hierarchical identity can be delegated. An IBE is simply a L-level HIBE with $L = 1$.

From One Receiver to Multi-receiver Setting: Introduction of Wildcard. As in the case of public-key encryption, passing from one receiver setting to multi-receiver setting is an important step. For this aim, wildcard IBE (WIBE) was introduced in [ACD+06] where the wildcard symbol (*) is added in identities to encrypt for a broad range of users at once. Along the same line, another generalization called WKD-IBE [AKN07] allows joker (*) symbol in users' secret keys to decrypt several targeted identities with a single key. Many others primitives, namely identity-based broadcast encryption [AKN07], identity-based traitor tracing [ADML+07], identity-based trace and revoke [PT11] schemes can be then constructed from WIBE and WKD-IBE.

Is Wildcard Really Necessary for the Multi-receiver Setting? While the introduction of wildcard is very interesting, it makes the construction of WIBE, Wicked-IBE more complicated and thus less efficient than the underlying IBE. Basically the alphabet is extended from a conventional binary alphabet to a ternary alphabet $\{0, 1, *\}$ and the wildcard $*$ is treated in a special and different way than $\{0, 1\}$. Beside the efficiency, there is often a significant loss in reducing the security of the WIBE, Wicked-IBE to the underlying IBE.

We are thus interested in the following question: can we avoid wildcard in considering IBE in multi-receiver setting? This paper gives the positive answer. We propose a new property for IBE, called downgradable IBE (DIBE). While keeping the binary alphabet unchanged, we show that downgradable IBE is not less powerful than the other wildcard based IBE: efficient transformations from downgradable IBE to wildcard based IBE schemes will be given.

Interestingly, avoiding wildcard helps us to get very efficient constructions. We simply need to show that the downgradable property can be obtained from existing constructions. A recent paper [KLLO18] found instantiations for Wicked-IBE and wildcarded IBE with good improve of the previous schemes, showing the interest of the research for this subject. Our instantiation of DIBE, once transformed into WIBE or Wkd-IBE is even more efficient allowing a constant size ciphertext, a master public key linear in the size of the identity (instead of n^2) and is fully secure under the standard assumption DLin. Indirectly our instantiation also improve the identity-based broadcast encryption, identity-based traitor tracing, identity-based trace and revoke schemes which rely on the WIBE and Wicked-IBE.

Toward Efficient Transformations from DIBE to ABE. Attribute-Based Encryption (ABE), introduced by Sahai and Waters [SW05], is a generalization of both identity-based encryption and broadcast encryption. It gives a flexible way to define the target group of people who can receive the message: the target set can be defined in a more structural way via access policies on the user's attributes. While broadcast encryption can be obtained from WIBE, as far as we know, there is still no generic construction of ABE from any variant of IBE. We will show a transformation from DIBE to ABE where the access policies is in DNF.

In the papers [AKN07, FP12], they show how some variant of IBE, WKD-IBE for the first one and HIBE for the second one, can be used to create broadcast encryption. ABE encompass the notion of Broadcast Encryption, thus our work achieves the willing of constructing the complex primitive like ABE from the much more simple IBE.

1.1 This Work

Downgradable IBE. In this work we introduce the notion of *Downgradable Identity-based Encryption* (DIBE). A downgradable IBE is an identity-based encryption where a user possessing a key for an identity $\mathsf{usk}[id]$ can downgrade his key to any identity $\tilde{id}$ with the restriction that he can only transform 1 into 0 in his identity string. More formally, the set $\tilde{\mathsf{ID}} = \{\tilde{id} | \forall i, \tilde{id}_i = 1 \Rightarrow id_i = 1\}$.

From Downgradable IBE to HIBE, WIBE, WKD-IBE. We later show that our new primitive encompasses other previous primitives, and that it can be tightly transformed into all of them. We then propose a generic framework, and an instantiation inspired by [BKP14], and show that thanks to our transform, we can obtain efficient WIBE, and WKD-IBE. This can be seen as a new method to design Wildcard-based IBE: one just need to prove the downgradable property of the IBE and then apply our direct transformation.

Moving to Attribute-Based Encryption. We also show how to generically transform a Downgradable IBE into an Attribute-based Encryption by using the properties of the DIBE and associating each attribute to a bit in the identity bit string. Our instantiation of DIBE lead to a secure ABE scheme with boolean formula in DNF (Fig. 6).

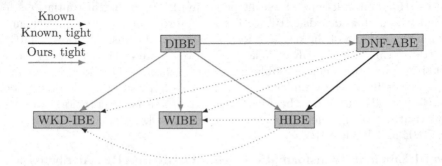

Fig. 1. Relations between primitives

1.2 Comparison to Existing Work

We propose a construction of DIBE inspired by the Hash-Proof based HIBE from [BKP14]. Interestingly, our construction combined with the WKD-DIBE, Wild-DIBE transformations are way more efficient than the existing WIBE and WKD-IBE. We compare them in Fig. 2, where we set the number of pattern and the size of the identity to the same value n, q_k correspond to the number adversary's key derivation queries. ℓ is the number of bits of identity that a user is allow to delegate a key to (e.g. his height in the hierarchical tree). A more detailed comparison can be found in Sect. 7. The improvements both in term of security and efficiency make those schemes now more suitable for practical applications.

Name	$|\mathsf{pk}|$	$|\mathsf{usk}|$	$|C|$	assump.	Loss
WKD [AKN07]	$(n+1)n+3$	$n+2$	2	BDDH	$O(q_k^n)$
our WKD-DIBE	$4n+2$	$3n+5$	5	DLin (any $k-$MDDH)	$O(q_k)$
WIBE [BDNS07]	$(n+1)n+3$	$n+1$	$(n+1)n+2$	BDDH	$O(n^2 q_k^n)$
our Wild-DIBE	$4n+2$	$3n+5$	5	DLin (any $k-$MDDH)	$O(q_k)$

Fig. 2. Efficiency comparison between our transformations and previous schemes

1.3 Open Problems

We managed to create an efficient Ciphertext Policy Attribute-based Encryption for boolean formula in DNF. This improve our knowledge of the relation Between IBE and ABE. But finally how close IBE and ABE are? Is it possible to extend efficiently our idea to fit other/any kind of access structure.

2 Definitions

2.1 Notation

- If $x \in \mathcal{BS}^n$, then $|x|$ denotes the length n of the vector. Further, $x \xleftarrow{\$} \mathcal{BS}$ denotes the process of sampling an element x from set $\mathcal{BS}$ uniformly at random.
- If $\mathbf{A} \in \mathbb{Z}_p^{(k+1)\times n}$ is a matrix, then $\overline{\mathbf{A}} \in \mathbb{Z}_p^{k\times n}$ denotes the upper matrix of $\mathbf{A}$ and then $\underline{\mathbf{A}} \in \mathbb{Z}_p^{1\times k}$ denotes the last row of $\mathbf{A}$.
- We are going to define a relation $\preceq$ between two strings s, t of the same length ℓ, such that $s \preceq t$ if and only if $\forall i \in [\![1, \ell]\!], s[i] \leq t[i]$. As an extension, given a set S of strings of length ℓ and a similarly long string t, we are going to say that $t \preceq S$, if there exists $s \in S$ such that $t \preceq s$. One has to pay attention that $\preceq$ is not total, for example, 10 and 01 can not be compared. Similarly, we define a relation $\preceq_*$ between two strings s, t of the same length ℓ, such that $s \preceq_* t$ if and only if $\forall i \in [\![1, \ell]\!], s[i] \preceq t[i] \vee s[i] = *$.

– **Games.** We use games for our security reductions. A game G is defined by
procedures Initialize and Finalize, plus some optional procedures $P_1, \ldots, P_n$.
All procedures are given using pseudo-code, where initially all variables are
undefined. An adversary $\mathcal{A}$ is executed in game G if it first calls Initialize,
obtaining its output. Next, it may make arbitrary queries to P_i (according to
their specification), again obtaining their output. Finally, it makes one single
call to Finalize(·) and stops. We define $G^{\mathcal{A}}$ as the output of $\mathcal{A}$'s call to Finalize.

2.2 Pairing Groups and Matrix Diffie-Hellman Assumption

Let GGen be a probabilistic polynomial time (PPT) algorithm that on input
$1^{\mathfrak{K}}$ returns a description $(\mathbb{G}_1, \mathbb{G}_2, \mathbb{G}_T, q, g_1, g_2, e)$ of asymmetric pairing groups
where $\mathbb{G}_1$, $\mathbb{G}_2$, $\mathbb{G}_T$ are cyclic groups of order q for a λ-bit prime q, g_1 and g_2
are generators of $\mathbb{G}_1$ and $\mathbb{G}_2$, respectively, and $e : \mathbb{G}_1 \times \mathbb{G}_2$ is an efficiently
computable (non-degenerated) bilinear map. Define $g_T := e(g_1, g_2)$, which is a
generator in $\mathbb{G}_T$.

We use implicit representation of group elements as introduced in [EHK+13].
For $s \in \{1, 2, T\}$ and $a \in \mathbb{Z}_p$ define $[a]_s = g_s^a \in \mathbb{G}_s$ as the *implicit representation*
of a in $\mathbb{G}_s$. More generally, for a matrix $\mathbf{A} = (a_{ij}) \in \mathbb{Z}_p^{n \times m}$ we define $[\mathbf{A}]_s$ as
the implicit representation of $\mathbf{A}$ in $\mathbb{G}_s$. Obviously, given $[a]_s \in \mathbb{G}_s$ and a scalar
$x \in \mathbb{Z}_p$, one can efficiently compute $[ax]_s \in \mathbb{G}_s$. Further, given $[a]_1, [a]_2$ one can
efficiently compute $[ab]_T$ using the pairing e. For $\boldsymbol{a}, \boldsymbol{b} \in \mathbb{Z}_p^k$ define $e([\boldsymbol{a}]_1, [\boldsymbol{b}]_2) :=$
$[\boldsymbol{a}^\top \boldsymbol{b}]_T \in \mathbb{G}_T$.

We recall the definition of the matrix Diffie-Hellman (MDDH) assumption
[EHK+13].

Definition 1 (Matrix Distribution). *Let $k \in \mathbb{N}$. We call $\mathcal{D}_k$ a matrix distribution if it outputs matrices in $\mathbb{Z}_p^{(k+1) \times k}$ of full rank k in polynomial time.*

We assume the first k rows of $\mathbf{A} \xleftarrow{\$} \mathcal{D}_k$ form an invertible matrix. The $\mathcal{D}_k$-Matrix
Diffie-Hellman problem is to distinguish the two distributions $([\mathbf{A}], [\mathbf{A}\boldsymbol{w}])$ and
$([\mathbf{A}], [\boldsymbol{u}])$ where $\mathbf{A} \xleftarrow{\$} \mathcal{D}_k$, $\boldsymbol{w} \xleftarrow{\$} \mathbb{Z}_p^k$ and $\boldsymbol{u} \xleftarrow{\$} \mathbb{Z}_p^{k+1}$.

Definition 2 ($\mathcal{D}_k$-Matrix Diffie-Hellman Assumption $\mathcal{D}_k$-MDDH). *Let
$\mathcal{D}_k$ be a matrix distribution and $s \in \{1, 2, T\}$. We say that the $\mathcal{D}_k$-Matrix Diffie-
Hellman ($\mathcal{D}_k$-MDDH) Assumption holds relative to GGen in group $\mathbb{G}_s$ if for all
PPT adversaries $\mathcal{D}$,*

$$\mathbf{Adv}_{\mathcal{D}_k, \mathsf{GGen}}(\mathcal{D})$$
$$:= |\Pr[\mathcal{D}(\mathcal{G}, [\mathbf{A}]_s, [\mathbf{A}\boldsymbol{w}]_s) = 1] - \Pr[\mathcal{D}(\mathcal{G}, [\mathbf{A}]_s, [\boldsymbol{u}]_s) = 1]| = \mathsf{negl}(\lambda),$$

*where the probability is taken over $\mathcal{G} \xleftarrow{\$} \mathsf{GGen}(1^\lambda)$, $\mathbf{A} \xleftarrow{\$} \mathcal{D}_k$, $\boldsymbol{w} \xleftarrow{\$} \mathbb{Z}_p^k$, $\boldsymbol{u} \xleftarrow{\$} \mathbb{Z}_p^{k+1}$.
This assumption is Random Self Reducible.*

2.3   Identity-Based Key Encapsulation

We now recall syntax and security of IBE in terms of an ID-based key encapsulation mechanism IBKEM. Every IBKEM can be transformed into an ID-based encryption scheme IBE using a (one-time secure) symmetric cipher.

Definition 3 (Identity-based Key Encapsulation Scheme). *An identity-based key encapsulation (IBKEM) scheme* IBKEM *consists of four PPT algorithms* IBKEM = (Gen, USKGen, Enc, Dec) *with the following properties.*

- *The probabilistic key generation algorithm* Gen($\Re$) *returns the (master) public/secret key* (mpk, msk). *We assume that* mpk *implicitly defines a message space* $\mathcal{M}$, *an identity space* ID, *a key space* $\mathcal{K}$, *and ciphertext space* CS.
- *The probabilistic user secret key generation algorithm* USKGen(msk, id) *returns the user secret-key* usk[id] *for identity* id $\in$ ID.
- *The probabilistic encapsulation algorithm* Enc(mpk, id) *returns the symmetric key* sk $\in \mathcal{K}$ *together with a ciphertext* C $\in$ CS *with respect to identity* id.
- *The deterministic decapsulation algorithm* Dec(usk[id], id, C) *returns the decapsulated key* sk $\in \mathcal{K}$ *or the reject symbol* $\perp$.

For perfect correctness we require that for all $\Re \in \mathbb{N}$, *all pairs* (mpk, msk) *honestly generated by* Gen($\Re$), *all identities* id $\in$ ID, *all* usk[id] *generated by* USKGen(msk, id) *and all* (sk, C) *output by* Enc(mpk, id):

$$\Pr[\mathsf{Dec}(\mathsf{usk}[\mathsf{id}], \mathsf{id}, \mathsf{C}) = \mathsf{sk}] = 1.$$

The security requirements for an IBKEM we consider here are indistinguishability and anonymity against chosen plaintext and identity attacks (IND-ID-CPA and ANON-ID-CPA). Instead of defining both security notions separately, we define pseudorandom ciphertexts against chosen plaintext and identity attacks (PR-ID-CPA) which means that challenge key and ciphertext are both pseudorandom. Note that PR-ID-CPA trivially implies IND-ID-CPA and ANON-ID-CPA. We define PR-ID-CPA-security of IBKEM formally via the games given in Fig. 3.

Procedure Initialize:	**Procedure** Enc(id*): //one query
(mpk, msk) $\xleftarrow{\$}$ Gen($\Re$)	(sk*, C*) $\xleftarrow{\$}$ Enc(mpk, id*)
Return mpk	$\boxed{\mathsf{sk}^* \xleftarrow{\$} \mathcal{K}; \mathsf{C}^* \xleftarrow{\$} \mathsf{CS}}$
	Return (sk*, C*)
Procedure USKGen(id):	
$\mathcal{Q}_{\mathsf{ID}} = \mathcal{Q}_{\mathsf{ID}} \cup \{\mathsf{id}\}$	
Return usk[id] $\xleftarrow{\$}$ USKGen(msk, id)	**Procedure** Finalize(β):
	Return (id* $\notin \mathcal{Q}_{\mathsf{ID}}$) $\wedge\ \beta$

Fig. 3. Security games PR-ID-CPA$_{real}$ and $\boxed{\text{PR-ID-CPA}_{rand}}$ for defining PR-ID-CPA-security.

Definition 4 (PR-ID-CPA Security). *An identity-based key encapsulation scheme* IBKEM *is* PR-ID-CPA-*secure if for all PPT* $\mathcal{A}$, $\mathsf{Adv}_{\mathsf{IBKEM}}^{\mathsf{pr\text{-}id\text{-}cpa}}(\mathcal{A}) := |\Pr[\mathsf{PR\text{-}ID\text{-}CPA}_{\mathsf{real}}^{\mathcal{A}} \Rightarrow 1] - \Pr[\mathsf{PR\text{-}ID\text{-}CPA}_{\mathsf{rand}}^{\mathcal{A}} \Rightarrow 1]|$ *is negligible.*

3 Downgradable Identity-Based Encryption

In this section we introduce the notion of Downgradable Identity-Based Encryption. There is a lot of different variant of IBE in the nowadays, add another one seems to be not useful but we stress that our is not here to be used as a simple scheme but as a key pillar to create ABE from IBE. Also in Sect. 4 we explain the relations between different variant of IBE and how DIBE can be transformed into them. For simplicity we are going to express in term of Key Encapsulation, as it can then be trivially transformed into an encryption.

Definition 5 (Downgradable Identity-Based Key Encapsulation Scheme). *A Downgradable identity-based key encapsulation (DIBKEM) scheme* DIBKEM *consists of five PPT algorithms* DIBKEM = (Gen, USKGen, Enc, Dec, USKDown) *with the following properties.*

- *The probabilistic key generation algorithm* Gen($\mathfrak{K}$) *returns the (master) public/secret key* (mpk, msk). *We assume that* mpk *implicitly defines a message space* $\mathcal{M}$, *an identity space* ID, *a key space* $\mathcal{K}$, *and ciphertext space* CS.
- *The probabilistic user secret key generation algorithm* USKGen(msk, id) *returns the user secret-key* usk[id] *for identity* id $\in$ ID.
- *The probabilistic encapsulation algorithm* Enc(mpk, id) *returns the symmetric key* sk $\in \mathcal{K}$ *together with a ciphertext* C $\in$ CS *with respect to identity* id.
- *The deterministic decapsulation algorithm* Dec(usk[id], id, C) *returns the decapsulated key* sk $\in \mathcal{K}$ *or the reject symbol* $\perp$.
- *The probabilistic user secret key downgrade algorithm* USKDown(usk[id], ĩd) *returns the user secret-key* usk[ĩd] *as long as* ĩd $\preceq$ id.

For perfect correctness we require that for all $\mathfrak{K} \in \mathbb{N}$, *all pairs* (mpk, msk) *honestly generated by* Gen($\mathfrak{K}$), *all identities* id $\in$ ID, *all* usk[id] *generated by* USKGen(msk, id) *and all* (sk, C) *output by* Enc(mpk, id)*:*

$$\Pr[\mathsf{Dec}(\mathsf{usk}[\mathsf{id}], \mathsf{id}, \mathsf{C}) = \mathsf{sk}] = 1.$$

We also require the distribution of usk[ĩd] *from* USKDown(usk[id], ĩd) *to be identical to the one from* USKGen(msk, ĩd).

The security requirements we consider here are indistinguishability and anonymity against chosen plaintext and identity attacks (IND-ID-CPA and ANON-ID-CPA). Instead of defining both security notions separately, we define pseudorandom ciphertexts against chosen plaintext and identity attacks (PR-ID-CPA) which means that challenge key and ciphertext are both pseudorandom. We define PR-ID-CPA-security of DIBKEM formally via the games given in Fig. 4.

Procedure Initialize:	Procedure Enc(id*): //one
$(\mathsf{mpk}, \mathsf{msk}) \overset{\$}{\leftarrow} \mathsf{Gen}(\mathfrak{K})$	query
Return mpk	$(\mathsf{sk}^*, \mathsf{C}^*) \overset{\$}{\leftarrow} \mathsf{Enc}(\mathsf{mpk}, \mathsf{id}^*)$
	$\boxed{\mathsf{sk}^* \overset{\$}{\leftarrow} \mathcal{K}; \mathsf{C}^* \overset{\$}{\leftarrow} \mathsf{CS}}$
Procedure USKGen(id):	Return $(\mathsf{sk}^*, \mathsf{C}^*)$
$\mathcal{Q}_{\mathsf{ID}} = \mathcal{Q}_{\mathsf{ID}} \cup \{\mathsf{id}\}$	
Return usk[id] $\overset{\$}{\leftarrow}$ USKGen(msk, id)	Procedure Finalize(β):
	Return $(\neg(\mathsf{id}^* \preceq \mathcal{Q}_{\mathsf{ID}})) \wedge \beta$

Fig. 4. Security games PR-ID-CPA$_{\mathsf{real}}$ and $\boxed{\text{PR-ID-CPA}_{\mathsf{rand}}}$ for defining PR-ID-CPA-security for DIBKEM.

Definition 6 (PR-ID-CPA Security). *A downgradable identity-based key encapsulation scheme* DIBKEM *is* PR-ID-CPA-*secure if for all PPT* $\mathcal{A}$, $\mathsf{Adv}^{\mathsf{pr\text{-}id\text{-}cpa}}_{\mathsf{DIBKEM}}(\mathcal{A}) := |\Pr[\text{PR-ID-CPA}^{\mathcal{A}}_{\mathsf{real}} \Rightarrow 1] - \Pr[\text{PR-ID-CPA}^{\mathcal{A}}_{\mathsf{rand}} \Rightarrow 1]|$ *is negligible.*

We stress the importance of the condition: $(\neg(\mathsf{id}^* \preceq \mathcal{Q}_{\mathsf{ID}}))$. This is here to guarantee that the adversary did not query an identity that can be downgraded to the challenge one, as this would allow for a trivial attack.

4 Transformation to Classical Primitives

Here, we are going to show how a Downgradable IBE relates to other primitives from the same family. Note that there is notions generalizing WIBE and WKD-IBE called WW-IBE described in [ACP12] and SWIBE described in [KLLO18] but their instantiation lead to not practical schemes. We can note that HIBE and WIBE have been linked in [AFL12]. In our work we are motivated in achieving a fully secure HIBE which would be inefficient using their construction.

4.1 From DIBE to WIBE

Wildcard Identity-Based Encryption is a concept introduced in [ACD+06]. The idea is to be able to encrypt message for serveral identities by fixing some identity bits and letting others free (symbolized by the $*$). Thus only people with identity matching the one used to encrypt can decrypt. We say that id matches id' if $\forall i$ $\mathsf{id}_i = \mathsf{id}'_i$ or $\mathsf{id}'_i = *$. Detailed definitions are included in the full version.

We are now given a DIBKEM(Gen, USKGen, Enc, Dec, USKDown), let us show how to build the corresponding Wild-IBKEM.

As with all the following constructions, the heart of the transformation will be to use a DIBKEM for identity of size 2ℓ to handle identities of size ℓ.

Let's consider an identity wid of size ℓ, we define $\mathsf{id} = \phi(\mathsf{wid})$ as follows:

$$\mathsf{id}[2i, 2i+1] = \begin{cases} 01 & \text{if } \mathsf{wid}[i] = 0 \\ 10 & \text{if } \mathsf{wid}[i] = 1 \\ 00 & \text{otherwise.} \end{cases}$$

Now we can define:

- WIBE.Gen($\mathfrak{K}$): Gen($\mathfrak{K}$), except that instead of defining ID as strings of size 2ℓ, we suppose the public key define WID of enriched identities of size ℓ.
- WIBE.USKGen(sk, id) = USKGen(sk, ϕ(id)).
- WIBE.Enc(mpk, id) = Enc(mpk, ϕ(id)).
- WIBE.Dec(usk[id], $\hat{\text{id}}$, C) checks if $\hat{\text{id}} \preceq$ id, then computes usk[$\phi(\hat{\text{id}})$] = USKDown(usk[ϕ(id)]). Returns Dec(usk[$\phi(\hat{\text{id}})$], $\hat{\text{id}}$, C) or rejects with $\bot$.

4.2   From DIBE to HIBE

Hierarchical Identity-Based Encryption is a concept introduced in [GS02]. The idea of this primitive is to introduce a hierarchy in the user secret key. A user can create a secret key from his one for any identity with prefix his own identity. Detailed definitions are included in the full version.

This time, we are going to map the identity space to a bigger set, with joker identity that can be downgraded to both 0 or 1.

Let's consider an identity hid of size ℓ, we define id = ϕ(hid) as follows:

$$\text{id}[2i, 2i+1] = \begin{cases} 01 & \text{if hid}[i] = 0 \\ 10 & \text{if hid}[i] = 1 \\ 11 & \text{otherwise(hid}[i] = \bot). \end{cases}$$

Now we can define:

- HIB.Gen($\mathfrak{K}$): Gen($\mathfrak{K}$), except instead of defining ID as strings of size 2ℓ, we suppose the public key define HID of enriched identities of size ℓ.
- HIB.USKGen(sk, id) = USKGen(sk, ϕ(id)). It should be noted that in case of an DIBKEM, some identities are never to be queried to the downgradable IBKEM: those with 00 is $2i, 2i+1$, or those with 11 at $2i, 2i+1$ and then a 0 (this would correspond to *punctured* identities).
- HIB.USKDel(usk[id], id $\in \mathcal{BS}^p$, id$_{p+1}$) = USKDown(usk[ϕ(id)], ϕ(id||id$_{p+1}$)). By construction we have ϕ(id||id$_{p+1}$) $\preceq \phi$(id).
- HIB.Enc(mpk, id) = Enc(mpk, ϕ(id)).
- HIB.Dec(usk[id], id, C) returns Dec(usk[ϕ(id)], ϕ(id), C) or the reject symbol $\bot$.

4.3   From DIBE to Wicked IBE

The paper [AKN07] presents a variant of Identity-based Encryption called Wicked IBE (WKD-IBE). A wicked IBE or wildcard key derivation IBE is a generalization of the concept of limited delegation concept by Boneh-Boyen-Goh [BBG05].

This scheme allows secret key associated with a pattern $P = (P_1, \ldots, P_l) \in \{\{0,1\}^* \cup \{*\}\}^l$ to be delegated for a pattern $P' = (P'_1, \ldots, P'_{l'})$ that matches P. We say that P' match P if $\forall i \leq l'$ $P'_i = P_i$ or $P_i = *$ and $\forall l'+1 \leq i \leq l$ $P_i = *$.

Here again, we are going to map the identity space to a bigger set.

Let's consider an identity id of size ℓ, we define $\text{id} = \phi(\text{wkdid})$ as follows:

$$\text{id}[2i, 2i+1] = \begin{cases} 01 & \text{if wkdid}[i] = 0 \\ 10 & \text{if wkdid}[i] = 1 \\ 11 & \text{if wkdid}[i] = * \end{cases}$$

Now we can define:

- WKDIB.Gen($\mathfrak{K}$): Gen($\mathfrak{K}$), except instead of defining ID as strings of size 2ℓ, we suppose the public key define WKDID of enriched identities of size ℓ.
- WKDIB.USKGen(msk, id) = USKGen(msk, ϕ(id)). It should be noted that in case of an WKD-DIBE, some identities are never to be queried to the downgradable IBE: those with 00.
- WKDIB.USKDel(usk[id], id, id′) = USKDown(usk[ϕ(id)], ϕ(id), ϕ(id′)).
- WKDIB.Enc(mpk, id) = Enc(mpk, ϕ(id)).
- WKDIB.Dec(usk[id], id, C) returns Dec(usk[ϕ(id)], ϕ(id), C) or the reject symbol $\perp$.

Remark 7. It can be noted, that all those transformations end up using 4 bits instead to encode a ternary alphabet. So there is a bit wasted in every given transformation. This could easily be avoided by using a more convoluted encoding, however this is already enough to show the link between the construction; also, this allows to build a scheme both wicked and wildcarded.

4.4 From Wicked IBE to DIBE

We can easily transform a Wicked IBE scheme into DIBE by using only identity made of 0 and $*$. In fact the element 1 of the DIBE play the role of the $*$ of the Wicked IBE. Morally a DIBE can be seen as a Wicked IBE where the patterns are made of only 2 distinct elements instead of 3.

5 ABE

In this section, we consider Attribute Based Encryption (ABE) and present a transformation from DIBE to ABE. We recall the definition and the security requirement:

Definition 8 (Attribute-based Encryption). *An Attribute-based encryption (ABE) scheme* ABE *consists of four PPT algorithms* ABKEM = (Gen, USKGen, Enc, Dec) *with the following properties.*

- *The probabilistic key generation algorithm* Gen($\mathfrak{K}$) *returns the (master) public/secret key* (pk, sk). *We assume that* pk *implicitly defines a message space* $\mathcal{M}$, *an Attribute space* AS, *and ciphertext space* CS.
- *The probabilistic user secret key generation algorithm* USKGen(sk, $\mathbb{A}$) *that takes as input the master secret key* sk *and a set of attributes* $\mathbb{A} \subset$ AS *and returns the user secret-key* usk[$\mathbb{A}$].

- *The probabilistic encryption algorithm* $\mathsf{Enc}(\mathsf{pk}, \mathbb{F}, M)$ *returns a ciphertext* $\mathsf{C} \in \mathsf{CS}$ *with respect to the access structure* $\mathbb{F}$.
- *The deterministic decryption algorithm* $\mathsf{Dec}(\mathsf{usk}[\mathbb{A}], \mathbb{F}, \mathbb{A}, \mathsf{C})$ *returns the decrypted message* $M \in \mathcal{M}$ *or the reject symbol* $\bot$.

For perfect correctness we require that for all $\mathfrak{K} \in \mathbb{N}$, *all pairs* $(\mathsf{pk}, \mathsf{sk})$ *generated by* $\mathsf{Gen}(\mathfrak{K})$, *all access structure* $\mathbb{F}$, *all set of attribute* $\mathbb{A} \subset \mathsf{AS}$ *satisfying* $\mathbb{F}$, *all* $\mathsf{usk}[\mathbb{A}]$ *generated by* $\mathsf{USKGen}(\mathsf{sk}, \mathbb{A})$ *and all* C *output by* $\mathsf{Enc}(\mathsf{pk}, \mathbb{F}, M)$:

$$\Pr[\mathsf{Dec}(\mathsf{usk}[\mathbb{A}], \mathbb{F}, \mathbb{A}, \mathsf{C}) = M] = 1.$$

Like before, we encompass the classical security hypotheses for an ABE, with a PR-A-CPA one as described in Fig. 5.

Procedure Initialize:
$(\mathsf{pk}, \mathsf{sk}) \xleftarrow{\$} \mathsf{Gen}(\mathfrak{K})$
Return pk

Procedure USKGen($\mathbb{A}$):
$\mathcal{Q}_A \leftarrow \mathcal{Q}_A \cup \{\mathbb{A}\}$
Return $\mathsf{usk}[\mathbb{A}] \xleftarrow{\$} \mathsf{USKGen}(\mathsf{sk}, \mathbb{A})$

Procedure Enc($\mathbb{F}^*$): //one query
$(\mathsf{sk}^*, \mathsf{C}^*) \xleftarrow{\$} \mathsf{Enc}(\mathsf{pk}, \mathbb{F}^*, M^*)$
$\boxed{\mathsf{C}^* \xleftarrow{\$} \mathsf{CS}}$
Return (C^*)

Procedure Finalize(β):
Return $(\forall \mathbb{A} \in \mathcal{Q}_A, \mathbb{A}$ doesn't verify $\mathbb{F}) \wedge \beta$

Fig. 5. Security games PR-A-CPA$_{\mathsf{real}}$ and $\boxed{\text{PR-A-CPA}_{\mathsf{rand}}}$ for defining PR-A-CPA-security.

Definition 9 (PR-A-CPA Security). *An identity-based key encapsulation scheme* ABKEM *is* PR-A-CPA-*secure if for all PPT* $\mathcal{A}$, $\mathsf{Adv}_{\mathsf{ABKEM}}^{\mathsf{PR\text{-}A\text{-}CPA}}(\mathcal{A}) :=$ $|\Pr[\text{PR-A-CPA}_{\mathsf{real}}^{\mathcal{A}} \Rightarrow 1] - \Pr[\text{PR-A-CPA}_{\mathsf{rand}}^{\mathcal{A}} \Rightarrow 1]|$ *is negligible.*

In a usual notion of (ciphertext-policy) ABE, a key is associated with a set $\mathbb{A}$ of attributes in the attribute universe $\mathcal{U}$, while a ciphertext is associated with an access policy $\mathbb{F}$ (or called access structure) over attributes. The decryption can be done if $\mathbb{A}$ satisfies $\mathbb{F}$. We can see that IBE is a special case of ABE where both $\mathbb{A}$ and $\mathbb{F}$ are singletons, that is, each is an identity in the universe $\mathcal{U}$.

In this paper, we confine ABE in the two following aspects. First, we restrict the universe $\mathcal{U}$ to be of polynomial size in security parameter; this is often called small-universe ABE (as opposed to large-universe ABE where $\mathcal{U}$ can be of super polynomial size.). Second, we allow only DNF formulae in expressing policies (as opposed to any boolean formulae, or equivalently, any access structures).

Our idea for obtaining a (small-universe) ABE scheme for DNF formulae from any DIBE scheme is as follows. For simplicity and wlog, we set the universe as

$\mathcal{U} = \{1, \ldots, n\}$. We will use DIBE with identity length n. For any set $S \subseteq \mathcal{U}$, we define $\text{id}_S \in \{0,1\}^n$ where its i-th position is defined by

$$\text{id}_S[i] := \begin{cases} 1 & \text{if } i \in S \\ 0 & \text{if } i \notin S \end{cases}.$$

To issue an ABE key for a set $\mathbb{A} \subseteq \mathcal{U}$, we use a DIBE key for $\text{id}_{\mathbb{A}}$. On the other hand, to encrypt a message M in ABE with a DNF policy $\mathbb{F} = \bigvee_{j=1}^{k}(\bigwedge_{a \in S_j} a)$, where each attribute a is in $\mathcal{U}$, we encrypt the same message M in DIBE each with id_{S_j} for all $j \in [1, k]$; this will result in k ciphertexts of the DIBE scheme. Note that k is the number of OR, the disjunction, in the DNF formula.

Decryption can be done as follows. Suppose $\mathbb{A}$ satisfies $\mathbb{F}$. Hence, we have that there exists S_j (defined in the formula $\mathbb{F}$) such that $S_j \subseteq \mathbb{A}$. We then derive a DIBE key for id_{S_j} from our ABE key for $\mathbb{A}$ (which is then a DIBE key for $\text{id}_{\mathbb{A}}$); this can be done since $S_j \subseteq \mathbb{A}$ implies that any positions of 1 in id_{S_j} will also contain 1 in $\text{id}_{\mathbb{A}}$ (and thus the derivation is possible). We finally decrypt the ciphertext associated with id_{S_j} to obtain the message M. We summarize this transformation in Fig. 6.

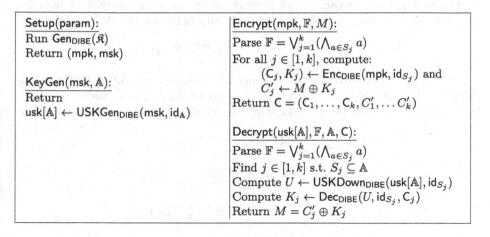

Fig. 6. ABE from DIBE

We have the following security theorem for the above ABE scheme. The proof is very simple and is done by a straightforward hybrid argument over k ciphertexts of DIBE. Note that the advantage definition for ABE is defined similarly to other primitives and is captured in The full version.

Theorem 10. *The above* ABE *from* DIBE *is* pr-a-cpa *secure under the* pr-id-cpa *security of the* DIBE *scheme used. In particular for all adversaries* $\mathcal{A}$*, we have that* $\text{Adv}_{\text{ABE}}^{\text{PR-A-CPA}}(\mathcal{A}) \leq k \cdot \text{Adv}_{\text{DIBE}}^{\text{pr-id-cpa}}(\mathcal{A})$ *where* k *is the number of OR in the DNF formula (associated to the challenge ciphertext).*

Proof. We prove our transformation via a sequence of games beginning with the real game for the pr-a-cpa security of the ABE and ending up with a game where the ciphertext of the ABE is uniformly chosen at random e.g. a game where adversary's advantage is reduce to 0.

Let $\mathcal{A}$ be an adversary against the pr-a-cpa security of our transformation. Let C be the simulator of the pr-a-cpa experience.

Game G_0: This is the real security game.

Game $G_{1.1}$: In this game the simulator generates correctly every ciphertexts but the first one. The first ciphertext is replaced by a random element of the ciphertext space. $G_{1.1}$ is indistinguishable from Game 0 if the pr-id-cpa security holds for the DIBE used.

$$\mathsf{Adv}^{G_0, G_{1.1}}(\mathcal{A}) \leq \mathsf{Adv}^{\mathsf{pr\text{-}id\text{-}cpa}}_{\mathsf{DIBE}}(\mathcal{A})$$

Game $G_{1.i}$: This game is the same than the game $G_{1.i-1}$ but the i-th ciphertext is replaced by a random element of the ciphertext space. $G_{1.i}$ is indistinguishable from $G_{1.i-1}$ if the pr-id-cpa security holds for the DIBE used.

$$\mathsf{Adv}^{G_{1.i-1}, G_{1.i}}(\mathcal{A}) \leq \mathsf{Adv}^{\mathsf{pr\text{-}id\text{-}cpa}}_{\mathsf{DIBE}}(\mathcal{A})$$

Game $G_{1.k}$: in this game all ciphertexts are random elements, $G_{1.k}$ is indistinguishable from $G_{1.k-1}$ if the pr-id-cpa security holds for the DIBE used.

$$\mathsf{Adv}^{G_{1.k-1}, G_{1.k}}(\mathcal{A}) \leq \mathsf{Adv}^{\mathsf{pr\text{-}id\text{-}cpa}}_{\mathsf{DIBE}}(\mathcal{A})$$

At this point our current game $G_{1.k}$ has for challenge encryption only random elements. This means that an adversary has no advantage in winning this game. We finally end up with the advantage of $\mathcal{A}$ in winning the original security game:

$$\mathsf{Adv}^{\mathsf{PR\text{-}A\text{-}CPA}}_{\mathsf{ABE}}(\mathcal{A}) \leq \mathsf{Adv}^{G_0, G_{1.k}}(\mathcal{A})$$
$$\leq \sum_{i=1}^{k} \mathsf{Adv}^{G_{1.i-1}, G_{1.i}}(\mathcal{A})$$
$$\leq k \times \mathsf{Adv}^{\mathsf{pr\text{-}id\text{-}cpa}}_{\mathsf{DIBE}}(\mathcal{A})$$

$\square$

6 Instantiation

Theorem 11. *Under the $\mathcal{D}_k$-MDDH assumption, the scheme presented in Fig. 7 is PR-ID-CPA secure. For all adversaries $\mathcal{A}$ there exists an adversary $\mathcal{B}$ with $\mathbf{T}(\mathcal{A}) \approx \mathbf{T}(\mathcal{B})$ and $\mathbf{Adv}_{\mathsf{DIBKEM}, \mathcal{D}_k}(\mathcal{B})^{\mathsf{PR\text{-}ID\text{-}CPA}}(\mathcal{A}) \leq (\mathbf{Adv}_{\mathcal{D}_k, \mathsf{GGen}}(\mathcal{B}) + 2q_k(\mathbf{Adv}_{\mathcal{D}_k, \mathsf{GGen}}(\mathcal{B}) + 1/q)^1$.*

The proof is detailed in the full version.

---

[1] We recall that q_k is the maximal number of query to the Eval oracle.

Gen(param):	USKDown(usk[id], ĩd):
$\mathbf{A} \xleftarrow{\$} \mathcal{D}_k, \mathbf{B} = \bar{\mathbf{A}}$	If $\neg(\tilde{\mathsf{id}} \preceq \mathsf{id})$, then return $\perp$
For $i = 0, \ldots, \ell$:	Set $\mathcal{I} = \{i \mid \tilde{\mathsf{id}}[i] = 0 \wedge \mathsf{id}[i] = 1\}$
$\quad z_i \xleftarrow{\$} \mathbb{Z}_p^{k+1 \times n}; \mathbf{Z}_i = z_i^\top \cdot \mathbf{A} \in \mathbb{Z}_p^{n \times k}$	// Downgrading the key:
$z' \xleftarrow{\$} \mathbb{Z}_p^{k+1}; \mathbf{Z}' = z'^\top \cdot \mathbf{A} \in \mathbb{Z}_p^{1 \times k}$	$\hat{v} = v + \sum_{i \in \mathcal{I}} \tilde{\mathsf{id}}_i e_i \in \mathbb{Z}_p^k + 1$
	$\hat{V} = V + \sum_{i \in \mathcal{I}} \tilde{\mathsf{id}}_i E_i \in \mathbb{Z}_p^{k \times \mu}$
$\mathsf{mpk} := (\mathcal{G}, [\mathbf{A}]_1, ([\mathbf{Z}_i]_1)_{0 \le i \le \ell}, [\mathbf{Z}']_1)$	// Rerandomization of $(\hat{v}, \hat{V})$:
$\mathsf{msk} := ((z_i)_{0 \le i \le \ell}, z')$	$s' \xleftarrow{\$} \mathbb{Z}_p^\mu; S' \xleftarrow{\$} \mathbb{Z}_p^{\mu \times \mu}$
Return $(\mathsf{mpk}, \mathsf{msk})$	$t' = t + \mathbf{T}s' \in \mathbb{Z}_p^n;$
	$T' = \hat{T} \cdot S' \in \mathbb{Z}_p^{n \times \mu}$
USKGen(msk, id $\in$ ID):	$\hat{v}' = \hat{v} + \hat{V} \cdot s' \in \mathbb{Z}_p^k;$
$t \xleftarrow{\$} \mathbb{Z}_p^n;$	$V' = \hat{V} \cdot S' \in \mathbb{Z}_p^{(k+1) \times \mu}$
$v = \sum_{i=0}^{l(\mathsf{id})} \mathsf{id}_i z_i t + z' \in \mathbb{Z}_p^{k+1}$	// Rerandomization of e_i:
$\mathbf{S} \xleftarrow{\$} \mathbb{Z}_p^{n' \times \mu}; \mathbf{T} = \mathbf{B} \cdot \mathbf{S} \in \mathbb{Z}_p^{n \times \mu}$	For $i, \tilde{\mathsf{id}}[i] = 1$:
$\mathbf{V} = \sum_{i=0}^{l(\mathsf{id})} \mathsf{id}_i \mathbf{Z}_i \mathbf{T} \in \mathbb{Z}_p^{(k+1) \times \mu}$	$e_i' = e_i + \mathbf{E}_i s' \in \mathbb{Z}_p^{k+1};$
For $i, \mathsf{id}[i] = 1$:	$E_i' = E_i \cdot S' \in \mathbb{Z}_p^{(k+1) \times \mu}$
$\quad e_i = \mathbf{Z}_i t \in \mathbb{Z}_p^{k+1}; E_i = \mathbf{Z}_i \mathbf{T} \in \mathbb{Z}_p^{k+1 \times \mu}$	$\mathsf{usk}[\tilde{\mathsf{id}}] := ([t']_2, [\hat{v}']_2)$
$\mathsf{usk}[\mathsf{id}] := ([t]_2, [v]_2) \in \mathbb{G}_2^n \times \mathbb{G}_2^{k+1}$	$\mathsf{udk}[\tilde{\mathsf{id}}] := ([T']_2, [V']_2, [e_i']_2, [E_i']_2)$
$\mathsf{udk}[\mathsf{id}] := ([T]_2, [V]_2, ([e_i]_2, [E_i]_2)_{i, \mathsf{id}[i]=1})$	Return $(\mathsf{usk}[\tilde{\mathsf{id}}], \mathsf{udk}[\tilde{\mathsf{id}}])$
$\qquad \in \mathbb{G}_2^{n \times \mu} \times \mathbb{G}_2^{(k+1) \times \mu} \times (\mathbb{G}_2^{k+1} \times \mathbb{G}_2^{(k+1) \times \mu})^{\mathsf{Ham(id)}}$	
Return $(\mathsf{usk}[\mathsf{id}], \mathsf{udk}[\mathsf{id}])$	Dec(usk[id], id, C):
	Parse $\mathsf{usk}[\mathsf{id}] = ([t]_2, [v]_2)$
Enc(mpk, id):	Parse $\mathsf{C} = ([c_0]_1, [c_1]_1)$
$r \xleftarrow{\$} \mathbb{Z}_p^k$	$\mathsf{sk} = e([c_0]_1, [v]_2) \cdot e([c_1]_1, [t]_2)^{-1}$
$c_0 = \mathbf{A} r \in \mathbb{Z}_p^{k+1}$	Return $\mathsf{sk} \in \mathbb{G}_T$
$c_1 = (\sum_{i=0}^{l(\mathsf{id})} \mathsf{id}_i \mathbf{Z}_i) \cdot r \in \mathbb{Z}_p^n$	
$K = z_0' \cdot r \in \mathbb{Z}_p.$	
Return $\mathsf{sk} = [K]_T$ and $\mathsf{C} = ([c_0]_1, [c_1]_1)$	

Fig. 7. A downgradable IBE based on MDDH. For readability, the user secret key is split here between usk for the decapsulation, and udk used for the downgrade operation.

Remark 12. This instantiation respect the formal definition of DIBKEM of Sect. 3. However for efficiency purpose one can remark that for realizing WIBE or ABE the user's secret keys does not need to be rerandomize during the delegation phase since it will not be used by another user. It introduce the concept of self-delegatable-only scheme. Thus we can avoid the heavy elements T, S, E of the user secret keys, the self-delegetable-only scheme is describe in Fig. 7 when removing the gray parts.

7 Efficiency Comparison

In this section we compare the schemes obtained by using our instantiation of DIBE (see Sect. 6) and our transformations described in the Sect. 4. We end up with the most efficient scheme for full security in the standard model and under classical hypothesis for WIBE, WKD-IBE and of similar efficiency for HIBE.

In the example of WIBE and WKD-IBE given below the parameters will grow exponentially in the number of query from the adversary, where our will be only linear. This is a parameter to take into account because the size of the keys for the same security will depend on this security loss (Fig. 8).

To compare efficiency in a simple way, we choose to consider the case where the number of pattern is maximal e.g. the size of pattern is equal to 1, thus the number of pattern is n which is the length of the identity. The value q_k correspond to the number of derivation key oracle request made by the adversary[2].

Name	$|pk|$	$|usk|$	$|C|$	assump.	Sec	Loss
WKD [AKN07]	$n+4$	$n+2$	2	BDDH	Sel. standard	$O(nq_k)$
WKD [AKN07]	$(n+1)n+3$	$n+2$	2	BDDH	Full standard	$O(q_k^n)$
WKD-DIBE	$4n+2$	$3n+5$	5	DLin (any $k-$MDDH)	Full standard	$O(q_k)$
SWIBE [KLLO18]	$n+4$	$2n+3$	4	ROM	Full	$O((n+1)(q_k+1)^n)$
WIBE [BDNS07]	$(n+1)n+3$	$n+1$	$(n+1)n+2$	BDDH	Full standard	$O(n^2q_k^n)$
Wild-DIBE	$4n+2$	$3n+5$	5	DLin (any $k-$MDDH)	Full standard	$O(q_k)$

Fig. 8. Efficiency comparison between our transformations and previous schemes

Efficiency Comparison for HIBE. The Fig. 9 compares the HIBE built via our DIBE. Our instantiation of DIBE inherit its efficiency from the HIBE from [BKP14], except we need to artificially double the size of the identities. Here ℓ is the number of free bits in an identity (the ones to delegate). Note that for the case of root of the hierarchy e.g. the user with an empty bit string as identity, $\ell = n$.

It should be noted, that while we rely on the same underlying principle, our security reduction does not need handle $\bot$ symbol as [BKP14], which allows to circumvent the worrisome parts of their proofs.

Efficiency Comparison for ABE. Our instantiation leads to a very efficient ABE scheme. This scheme would be one of the most practical. However we achieve ABE where the access structure has to be a boolean formula in the DNF which is less general than allowing any kind of access structure (which is done in others practical schemes).

Figure 10 presents a non exhaustive comparison of our ABE schemes with efficient ones. They are all full secure under the classical assumption DLin. U is the size of the universe of attributes. m is the number of attributes in a policy. t is the size of an attribute set, and T is the maximum size of t (if bounded). R is

---

[2] In the original version of [AKN07] they include an element in the ciphertext to turn their scheme into an encryption scheme. Since our scheme is a Key Encapsulation Mechanism we remove this element when comparing both schemes.

Name	|pk|	|usk|	|C|	assump.	Loss
HIBE [BBG05]	$n+4$	$2+\ell$	5	DLin	sel. $O(n \cdot q_k)$
HIBE [BKP14]	$2n+1$	$11\ell+5$	5	DLin (any $k - $ MDDH)	$O(n)$
H-DIBE	$4n+2$	$11n+5$	5	DLin (any $k - $ MDDH)	$O(q_k)$

Fig. 9. Efficiency comparison between our transformations and HIBE schemes

Name	|pk|	|sk|	|C|	pairing	exp G	exp $\mathbb{G}_t$	Reduction Loss
[OT10]	$4U+2$	$3U+3$	$7m+5$	$7m+5$	0	m	$O(q_k)$
[LW12]	$24U+12$	$6U+6$	$6m+6$	$6m+9$	0	m	$O(q_k)$
[CGW15]	$6UR+12$	$3UR+3$	$3m+3$	6	$6m$	0	$O(q_k)$
[Att16] scheme 10	$6UR+12$	$3UR+6$	$3m+6$	9	$6m$	0	$O(q_k)$
[Att16] scheme 13	$96(M+TR)^2 + log(UR)$	$3UR+6$	$3m+6$	9	$6m$	0	$O(q_k)$
Our DNF-ABE	$4U+2$	$3U+3$	$3k+2$	13	0	0	$O(q_k)$

Fig. 10. Efficiency comparison of practical CP-ABE schemes

the maximum number of attributes multi used in one policy (if bounded). q_k is again the number of all the key queries made by the adversary during security game. For our scheme, k is the number of OR, the disjunction, in the associated DNF formula.

Acknowledgements. This work was supported in part by the French ANR: IDFIX (ANR-16-CE39-0004) Project.

References

[ACD+06] Abdalla, M., Catalano, D., Dent, A.W., Malone-Lee, J., Neven, G., Smart, N.P.: Identity-based encryption gone wild. In: Bugliesi, M., Preneel, B., Sassone, V., Wegener, I. (eds.) ICALP 2006. LNCS, vol. 4052, pp. 300–311. Springer, Heidelberg (2006). https://doi.org/10.1007/11787006_26

[ACP12] Abdalla, M., De Caro, A., Phan, D.H.: Generalized key delegation for wildcarded identity-based and inner-product encryption. IEEE Trans. Inf. Forensics Secur. **7**(6), 1695–1706 (2012)

[ADML+07] Abdalla, M., Dent, A.W., Malone-Lee, J., Neven, G., Phan, D.H., Smart, N.P.: Identity-based traitor tracing. In: Okamoto, T., Wang, X. (eds.) PKC 2007. LNCS, vol. 4450, pp. 361–376. Springer, Heidelberg (2007). https://doi.org/10.1007/978-3-540-71677-8_24

[AFL12] Abdalla, M., Fiore, D., Lyubashevsky, V.: From selective to full security: semi-generic transformations in the standard model. In: Fischlin, M., Buchmann, J., Manulis, M. (eds.) PKC 2012. LNCS, vol. 7293, pp. 316–333. Springer, Heidelberg (2012). https://doi.org/10.1007/978-3-642-30057-8_19

[AKN07] Abdalla, M., Kiltz, E., Neven, G.: Generalized key delegation for hier-archical identity-based encryption. In: Biskup, J., López, J. (eds.) ESORICS 2007. LNCS, vol. 4734, pp. 139–154. Springer, Heidelberg (2007). https://doi.org/10.1007/978-3-540-74835-9_10

[Att16] Attrapadung, N.: Dual system encryption framework in prime-order groups via computational pair encodings. In: Cheon, J.H., Takagi, T. (eds.) ASIACRYPT 2016. LNCS, vol. 10032, pp. 591–623. Springer, Hei-delberg (2016). https://doi.org/10.1007/978-3-662-53890-6_20

[BBG05] Boneh, D., Boyen, X., Goh, E.-J.: Hierarchical identity based encryption with constant size ciphertext. In: Cramer, R. (ed.) EUROCRYPT 2005. LNCS, vol. 3494, pp. 440–456. Springer, Heidelberg (2005). https://doi.org/10.1007/11426639_26

[BCG16] Blazy, O., Chevalier, C., Germouty, P.: Adaptive oblivious transfer and generalization. In: Cheon, J.H., Takagi, T. (eds.) ASIACRYPT 2016. LNCS, vol. 10032, pp. 217–247. Springer, Heidelberg (2016). https://doi.org/10.1007/978-3-662-53890-6_8

[BDNS07] Birkett, J., Dent, A.W., Neven, G., Schuldt, J.C.N.: Efficient chosen-ciphertext secure identity-based encryption with wildcards. In: Pieprzyk, J., Ghodosi, H., Dawson, E. (eds.) ACISP 2007. LNCS, vol. 4586, pp. 274–292. Springer, Heidelberg (2007). https://doi.org/10.1007/978-3-540-73458-1_21

[BF01] Boneh, D., Franklin, M.: Identity-based encryption from the Weil pair-ing. In: Kilian, J. (ed.) CRYPTO 2001. LNCS, vol. 2139, pp. 213–229. Springer, Heidelberg (2001). https://doi.org/10.1007/3-540-44647-8_13

[BGP18] Blazy, O., Germouty, P., Phan, D.H.: Downgradable identity-based encryption and applications. Cryptology ePrint Archive, Report 2018/1176 (2018). https://eprint.iacr.org/2018/1176

[BKP14] Blazy, O., Kiltz, E., Pan, J.: (Hierarchical) identity-based encryption from affine message authentication. In: Garay, J.A., Gennaro, R. (eds.) CRYPTO 2014. LNCS, vol. 8616, pp. 408–425. Springer, Heidelberg (2014). https://doi.org/10.1007/978-3-662-44371-2_23

[CGW15] Chen, J., Gay, R., Wee, H.: Improved dual system ABE in prime-order groups via predicate encodings. In: Oswald, E., Fischlin, M. (eds.) EURO-CRYPT 2015. LNCS, vol. 9057, pp. 595–624. Springer, Heidelberg (2015). https://doi.org/10.1007/978-3-662-46803-6_20

[Coc01] Cocks, C.: An identity based encryption scheme based on quadratic residues. In: Honary, B. (ed.) Cryptography and Coding 2001. LNCS, vol. 2260, pp. 360–363. Springer, Heidelberg (2001). https://doi.org/10.1007/3-540-45325-3_32

[EHK+13] Escala, A., Herold, G., Kiltz, E., Ràfols, C., Villar, J.: An algebraic framework for Diffie-Hellman assumptions. In: Canetti, R., Garay, J.A. (eds.) CRYPTO 2013. LNCS, vol. 8043, pp. 129–147. Springer, Heidel-berg (2013). https://doi.org/10.1007/978-3-642-40084-1_8

[FP12] Fazio, N., Perera, I.M.: Outsider-anonymous broadcast encryption with sublinear ciphertexts. In: Fischlin, M., Buchmann, J., Manulis, M. (eds.) PKC 2012. LNCS, vol. 7293, pp. 225–242. Springer, Heidelberg (2012). https://doi.org/10.1007/978-3-642-30057-8_14

[GH07] Green, M., Hohenberger, S.: Blind identity-based encryption and sim-ulatable oblivious transfer. In: Kurosawa, K. (ed.) ASIACRYPT 2007. LNCS, vol. 4833, pp. 265–282. Springer, Heidelberg (2007). https://doi.org/10.1007/978-3-540-76900-2_16

[GS02] Gentry, C., Silverberg, A.: Hierarchical ID-based cryptography. In: Zheng, Y. (ed.) ASIACRYPT 2002. LNCS, vol. 2501, pp. 548–566. Springer, Heidelberg (2002). https://doi.org/10.1007/3-540-36178-2_34

[KLLO18] Kim, J., Lee, S., Lee, J., Oh, H.: Scalable wildcarded identity-based encryption. In: Lopez, J., Zhou, J., Soriano, M. (eds.) ESORICS 2018. LNCS, vol. 11099, pp. 269–287. Springer, Cham (2018). https://doi.org/10.1007/978-3-319-98989-1_14

[LW12] Lewko, A., Waters, B.: New proof methods for attribute-based encryption: achieving full security through selective techniques. In: Safavi-Naini, R., Canetti, R. (eds.) CRYPTO 2012. LNCS, vol. 7417, pp. 180–198. Springer, Heidelberg (2012). https://doi.org/10.1007/978-3-642-32009-5_12

[OT10] Okamoto, T., Takashima, K.: Fully secure functional encryption with general relations from the decisional linear assumption. In: Rabin, T. (ed.) CRYPTO 2010. LNCS, vol. 6223, pp. 191–208. Springer, Heidelberg (2010). https://doi.org/10.1007/978-3-642-14623-7_11

[PT11] Phan, D.H., Trinh, V.C.: Identity-based trace and revoke schemes. In: Boyen, X., Chen, X. (eds.) ProvSec 2011. LNCS, vol. 6980, pp. 204–221. Springer, Heidelberg (2011). https://doi.org/10.1007/978-3-642-24316-5_15

[Sha84] Shamir, A.: Identity-based cryptosystems and signature schemes. In: Blakley, G.R., Chaum, D. (eds.) CRYPTO 1984. LNCS, vol. 196, pp. 47–53. Springer, Heidelberg (1985). https://doi.org/10.1007/3-540-39568-7_5

[SOK00] Sakai, R., Ohgishi, K., Kasahara, M.: Cryptosystems based on pairing. In: SCIS 2000, Okinawa, Japan, January 2000

[SW05] Sahai, A., Waters, B.: Fuzzy identity-based encryption. In: Cramer, R. (ed.) EUROCRYPT 2005. LNCS, vol. 3494, pp. 457–473. Springer, Heidelberg (2005). https://doi.org/10.1007/11426639_27

[Wat05] Waters, B.: Efficient identity-based encryption without random oracles. In: Cramer, R. (ed.) EUROCRYPT 2005. LNCS, vol. 3494, pp. 114–127. Springer, Heidelberg (2005). https://doi.org/10.1007/11426639_7

Large Universe Subset Predicate Encryption Based on Static Assumption (Without Random Oracle)

Sanjit Chatterjee and Sayantan Mukherjee[✉]

Department of Computer Science and Automation,
Indian Institute of Science, Bangalore, India
{sanjit,sayantanm}@iisc.ac.in

Abstract. In a recent work, Katz et al. (CANS'17) generalized the notion of Broadcast Encryption to define Subset Predicate Encryption (SPE) that emulates *subset containment* predicate in the encrypted domain. They proposed two selective secure constructions of SPE in the small universe settings. Their first construction is based on q-type assumption while the second one is based on DBDH. Both achieve constant size secret key while the ciphertext size depends on the size of the privileged set. They also showed some black-box transformation of SPE to well-known primitives like WIBE and ABE to establish the richness of the SPE structure.

This work investigates the question of large universe realization of SPE scheme based on static assumption without random oracle. We propose two constructions both of which achieve constant size secret key. First construction SPE_1, instantiated in composite order bilinear groups, achieves constant size ciphertext and is proven secure in a restricted version of selective security model under the subgroup decision assumption (SDP). Our main construction SPE_2 is adaptive secure in the prime order bilinear group under the symmetric external Diffie-Hellman assumption (SXDH). Thus SPE_2 is the first large universe instantiation of SPE to achieve adaptive security without random oracle. Both our constructions have efficient decryption function suggesting their practical applicability. Thus the primitives like WIBE and ABE resulting through black-box transformation of our constructions become more practical.

1 Introduction

The notion of Identity-Based Encryption (IBE) [7] was generalized by Katz et al. [21] to Predicate Encryption (PE). PE emulates a predicate function $R : \mathcal{X} \times \mathcal{Y} \to \{0,1\}$ in the encrypted domain in the following sense. A key SK associated with key-index x can decrypt a ciphertext CT associated with data-index y if $R(\mathsf{x},\mathsf{y}) = 1$. In such a generalized view, IBE evaluates an equality predicate. Attribute-Based Encryption (ABE) [18] is another example of predicate encryption that emulates boolean function in the encrypted domain.

© Springer Nature Switzerland AG 2019
M. Matsui (Ed.): CT-RSA 2019, LNCS 11405, pp. 62–82, 2019.
https://doi.org/10.1007/978-3-030-12612-4_4

One can view Broadcast Encryption (BE) [8] as a simpler form of ABE where the predicate evaluated is disjunction in the form of membership checking.

Katz et al. [20] recently introduced another primitive called Subset Predicate Encryption (SPE) that allows checking for *subset containment* in the encrypted domain. More formally, in an SPE, a key SK associated with a key-index set Ω can decrypt a ciphertext CT associated with data-index set Θ if $\Omega \subseteq \Theta$. There is an obvious connection between BE and SPE in the sense that both encrypt for a privileged set Θ. However, unlike BE, the KeyGen in SPE takes input a set of identities Ω allowing a subset based testing during decryption. It is trivial to achieve subset containment check through multiple membership checks.

Thus, one may be tempted to use an efficient BE instantiation [8] to construct a small-universe SPE. In such an instantiation, KeyGen of SPE would simply be a concatenation of output of KeyGen of BE for each $x \in \Omega$ i.e. $\mathsf{SK}_\Omega = (\mathsf{SK}_{x_1}, \ldots, \mathsf{SK}_{x_k})$ where $\Omega = (x_1, \ldots, x_k)$. However, such a realization of SPE suffers from an obvious security issue. Given a ciphertext CT_Θ, an unprivileged user having secret key SK_Ω (for $\Omega \not\subseteq \Theta$), can easily derive a valid key by stripping the SK_Ω as long as $\Omega \cap \Theta \neq \phi$.

In their work, Katz et al. [20] discussed and then ruled out a few generic techniques to construct small-universe SPE from Inner-Product Encryption (IPE), Wildcard Identity-Based Encryption (WIBE) and Fuzzy Identity-Based Encryption (FIBE) due to the reason of inefficiency. They proposed two dedicated SPE constructions in the small universe settings. Both the constructions achieve constant-size secret key while the ciphertext size depends on the cardinality of the privileged set it is intended to. Informally speaking, their first construction utilized the *inversion exponent* technique [9] and the second one utilized the *commutative blinding* technique [6]. However, both the constructions were proven only *selectively secure*. The security of the first construction is based on a non-static assumption (q-BDHI) whereas the security of second construction is based on a static assumption (DBDH). The second construction of [20] can be easily modified to achieve selective security in large universe setting in the random oracle model.

Given the above results of [20], the main open question in the context of SPE is the following. Can we realize an adaptively secure SPE in the large universe setting without random oracle where security is based on some static assumption? In this paper we answer this question in the affirmative. In addition, we also ask whether one can achieve an SPE with constant-size ciphertext. On this front this paper reports some partial success through a trade-off in the security model.

We start with a rather obvious observation. Recall the connection between SPE in small universe and public key broadcast encryption mentioned above. In a similar vein, Identity-Based Broadcast Encryption (IBBE) can be seen as a special case of large-universe SPE. In particular, the KeyGen of IBBE always takes a singleton set as input. However, trivially extending the KeyGen of IBBE to that of SPE may be problematic. The security model of IBBE has a natural restriction that the intersection of challenge identity set and the set of identities compromised in the key extraction phase must be *null*. On the other hand, the corresponding natural restriction in the context of SPE would be that none of the set of identities queried in the key extraction phase should be a subset of the challenge identity set.

A constant-size ciphertext IBBE was proposed in [14] based on q-type assumption in the random oracle model. Recently, Gong et al. [17] proposed integration of [14] and Déjà Q [26] towards selective secure IBBE with constant-size ciphertext under static subgroup decision assumptions. However, unlike the IBBE KeyGen that encodes a single identity, the KeyGen in SPE encodes a set Ω into a secret key of constant-size. We notice that the KeyGen of [17] can be tweaked appropriately to generate a constant-size secret key corresponding to a set. This way we arrive at our first construction SPE_1, a constant-size ciphertext SPE in the large universe setting without random oracle.

The security reduction, closely follows that of [17]. However, the reduction faces additional hurdles in order to properly simulate KeyGen of SPE. In the usual IBBE scenario, for a challenge ciphertext CT_{Θ^*}, adversary is not allowed to make secret key queries on $x \in \Theta^*$. In case of SPE, however, it is possible to have some $x \in \Omega \cap \Theta^*$. In other words, the simulator in our SPE security argument should be able to answer for key extraction queries which were naturally ruled out in IBBE security model considered in [17].

Our Déjà Q based security argument is able to achieve the following – (i) the effect of the terms encoding $x \in (\Theta^* \cap \Omega)$ gets nullified naturally and (ii) takes into consideration of the effect of availability of admissible Aggregate function [15] to adversary. This, however, comes with a restriction on the KeyGen queries (also due to the Déjà Q approach). Informally speaking, we need the sets that are queried for key extraction: $(\Omega_1, \Omega_2, \ldots, \Omega_q)$ to be *cover-free sets* i.e. for any $i \in [q]$, $\Omega_i \setminus (\bigcup_{j \in [q] \setminus \{i\}} \Omega_j) \neq \phi$.

While pairing-based adaptive secure IBBE achieving constant size secret key as well as ciphertext remains still as an open problem; our above result indicates the limitations of the available techniques to argue even selective security for constant size ciphertext SPE.

Our main construction (SPE_2) achieves adaptive security in the prime order groups under SXDH with constant-size secret key. This construction resembles IBBE structure of [22] which extended JR-IBE [19] to achieve an efficient tag-based IBBE construction. We tweak the KeyGen algorithm of their $IBBE_1$ [22] to realize adaptive secure SPE in the large universe settings. Again, the non-triviality lies in the security argument. Precisely, in the security model of [22], for a challenge set $\Theta^* = (y_1, \ldots, y_\ell)$, the set of identities queried for key extraction should be strictly non-overlapping. However, in the security argument of (SPE_2), the query (Ω) adversary makes may contain some elements that also belong to the challenge set Θ^*.

We are able to realize the first large universe adaptive secure SPE without random oracle. Our construction is quite efficient too in terms of parameter size, encryption and decryption cost. For example, the encryption does not require any pairing evaluation while the decryption evaluates only 3 pairings. The only limitation is the obvious: ciphertext size depends on the size of the privileged set it is intended to.

We briefly discuss the effect of black-box transformations of Katz et al. [20] on our $\mathsf{SPE_2}$ constructions. We achieve first adaptive secure CP-DNF (CP-ABE with DNF policy) evaluation with constant-size secret key. We present the comparison with state of the art in Tables 1 and 2.

Organization of the Paper. In Sect. 2 we recall few definitions and present the notations that will be followed in this paper. In Sect. 3 we define the subset predicate encryption (SPE) and its security model. In Sects. 4 and 5, we present two SPE constructions along with their proofs. Section 6 concludes this paper.

2 Preliminaries

Notations. Here we denote $[a, b] = \{i \in \mathbb{N} : a \leq i \leq b\}$ and for any $n \in \mathbb{N}$, $[n] = [1, n]$. The security parameter is denoted by 1^λ where $\lambda \in \mathbb{N}$. By $s \hookleftarrow S$ we denote a uniformly random choice s from S. We use $A \approx_\epsilon B$ to denote that A and B are computationally indistinguishable such that for any PPT adversary $\mathcal{A}$, $|\Pr[\mathcal{A}(A) \to 1] - \Pr[\mathcal{A}(B) \to 1]| \leq \epsilon$ where $\epsilon \leq \mathsf{neg}(\lambda)$ for $\mathsf{neg}(\lambda)$ denoting negligible function. We use $\mathsf{Adv}_{\mathcal{A}}^i(\lambda)$ to denote the advantage adversary $\mathcal{A}$ has in security game Game_i and $\mathsf{Adv}_{\mathcal{A}}^{\mathsf{HP}}(\lambda)$ is used to denote the advantage of $\mathcal{A}$ to solve the hard problem HP.

2.1 Bilinear Groups

This paper presents two subset predicate encryption schemes. The first construction is instantiated in the composite order symmetric bilinear groups whereas the second one is instantiated in the prime order asymmetric bilinear groups.

Composite Order Bilinear Pairings. A composite order symmetric bilinear group generator $\mathcal{G}_{\mathsf{sbg}}$, apart from security parameter 1^λ takes an additional parameter n and returns an $(n+3)$-tuple $(p_1, \cdots, p_n, \mathsf{G}, \mathsf{G_T}, e)$ where both $\mathsf{G}, \mathsf{G_T}$ are cyclic groups of order $N = \prod_{i \in [n]} p_i$ where all p_i are large primes and $e : \mathsf{G} \times \mathsf{G} \to \mathsf{G_T}$ is an admissible, non-degenerate Type-1 bilinear pairing. Here, G_{p_i} denotes a subgroup of G of order p_i. This notation is naturally extended to $\mathsf{G}_{p_i \cdots p_j}$ denoting a subgroup of G of order $p_i \times \cdots \times p_j$. By convention $g_{i \cdots j}$ is an element of subgroup $\mathsf{G}_{p_i \cdots p_j}$. It is evident that $e(g_i, g_j) = 1$ if $i \neq j$.

Prime Order Bilinear Pairings. The prime order asymmetric bilinear group generator $\mathcal{G}_{\mathsf{abg}}$, takes security parameter 1^λ and returns a 5 tuple $(p, \mathsf{G_1}, \mathsf{G_2}, \mathsf{G_T}, e)$ where all of $\mathsf{G_1}, \mathsf{G_2}, \mathsf{G_T}$ are cyclic groups of order large prime p and $e : \mathsf{G_1} \times \mathsf{G_2} \to \mathsf{G_T}$ is an admissible, non-degenerate Type-3 bilinear pairing [16].

2.2   Hardness Assumptions

Composite Order Setting. Let $(p_1, p_2, p_3, G, G_T, e) \leftarrow \mathcal{G}_{\text{sbg}}(1^\lambda, 3)$ be the output of symmetric bilinear group generator where both G, G_T are cyclic groups of order $N = p_1 p_2 p_3$ where p_1, p_2, p_3 are large primes. We define two variants of subgroup decision problems [26] as follows:

DS1. $\{D, T_0\} \approx_{\epsilon_{DS1}} \{D, T_1\}$ for $T_0 \hookleftarrow G_{p_1}$ and $T_1 \hookleftarrow G_{p_1 p_2}$ given $D = (g_1, g_3, g_{12})$ where $g_1 \hookleftarrow G_{p_1}^\times$, $g_3 \hookleftarrow G_{p_3}^\times$ and $g_{12} \hookleftarrow G_{p_1 p_2}$. In other words, the advantage of any adversary $\mathcal{A}$ to solve the DS1 is

$$\text{Adv}_{\mathcal{A}}^{\text{DS1}}(\lambda) = |\Pr[\mathcal{A}(D, T_0) \to 1] - \Pr[\mathcal{A}(D, T_1) \to 1]| \leq \epsilon_{DS1}.$$

DS1 is hard if advantage of $\mathcal{A}$ is negligible i.e. $\epsilon_{DS1} \leq \text{neg}(\lambda)$.

DS2. $\{D, T_0\} \approx_{\epsilon_{DS2}} \{D, T_1\}$ for $T_0 \hookleftarrow G_{p_1 p_3}$ and $T_1 \hookleftarrow \mathbb{G}$ given $D = (g_1, g_3, g_{12}, g_{23})$ where $g_1 \hookleftarrow G_{p_1}^\times$, $g_3 \hookleftarrow G_{p_3}^\times$, $g_{12} \hookleftarrow G_{p_1 p_2}$ and $g_{23} \hookleftarrow G_{p_2 p_3}$. In other words, the advantage of any adversary $\mathcal{A}$ to solve the DS2 is

$$\text{Adv}_{\mathcal{A}}^{\text{DS2}}(\lambda) = |\Pr[\mathcal{A}(D, T_0) \to 1] - \Pr[\mathcal{A}(D, T_1) \to 1]| \leq \epsilon_{DS2}.$$

DS2 is hard if advantage of $\mathcal{A}$ is negligible i.e. $\epsilon_{DS2} \leq \text{neg}(\lambda)$.

Prime Order Setting. Let $(p, G_1, G_2, G_T, e) \leftarrow \mathcal{G}_{\text{abg}}(1^\lambda)$ be the output of asymmetric bilinear group generator where G_1, G_2, G_T are cyclic groups of order a large prime p.

Symmetric External Diffie-Hellman Assumption (SXDH). The SXDH assumption in group (G_1, G_2) is: DDH in G_1 and DDH in G_2 is hard. We rewrite DDH in G_1 in the form of 1-Lin assumption below and call it DDH_{G_1}. The DDH_{G_2} denotes the DDH problem in G_2.

- DDH_{G_1}: $\{D, T_0\} \approx_{\epsilon_{\text{DDH}_{G_1}}} \{D, T_1\}$ for $T_0 = g_1^s$ and $T_1 = g_1^{s+\hat{s}}$ given $D = (g_1, g_2, g_1^b, g_1^{bs})$ where $g_1 \hookleftarrow G_1$, $g_2 \hookleftarrow G_2$, $b \hookleftarrow \mathbb{Z}_p^\times$, $s, \hat{s} \hookleftarrow \mathbb{Z}_p$. In other words, the advantage of any adversary $\mathcal{A}$ to solve the DDH_{G_1} is

$$\text{Adv}_{\mathcal{A}}^{\text{DDH}_{G_1}}(\lambda) = |\Pr[\mathcal{A}(D, T_0) \to 1] - \Pr[\mathcal{A}(D, T_1) \to 1]| \leq \epsilon_{\text{DDH}_{G_1}}.$$

  DDH_{G_1} is hard if advantage of $\mathcal{A}$ is negligible i.e. $\epsilon_{\text{DDH}_{G_1}} \leq \text{neg}(\lambda)$.

- DDH_{G_2}: $\{D, T_0\} \approx_{\epsilon_{\text{DDH}_{G_2}}} \{D, T_1\}$ for $T_0 = g_2^{cr}$ and $T_1 = g_2^{cr+\hat{r}}$ given $D = (g_1, g_2, g_2^c, g_2^r)$ where $g_1 \hookleftarrow G_1$, $g_2 \hookleftarrow G_2$, $c, r, \hat{r} \hookleftarrow \mathbb{Z}_p$. In other words, the advantage of any adversary $\mathcal{A}$ to solve the DDH_{G_2} is

$$\text{Adv}_{\mathcal{A}}^{\text{DDH}_{G_2}}(\lambda) = |\Pr[\mathcal{A}(D, T_0) \to 1] - \Pr[\mathcal{A}(D, T_1) \to 1]| \leq \epsilon_{\text{DDH}_{G_2}}.$$

  DDH_{G_2} is hard if advantage of $\mathcal{A}$ is negligible i.e. $\epsilon_{\text{DDH}_{G_2}} \leq \text{neg}(\lambda)$.

3   Subset Predicate Encryption

We rephrase Subset Predicate Encryption (SPE) in terms of a predicate encryption [21] and formally model its security requirement.

3.1   Subset Predicate Encryption (SPE)

Let $\mathcal{ID}$ be the identity space. For a key-index set $\Omega \in \mathcal{X} \subset \mathcal{ID}$ and a data-index set $\Theta \in \mathcal{Y} \subset \mathcal{ID}$, the predicate function for SPE is

$$R_s(\Omega, \Theta) = \begin{cases} 1 & \text{if } \Omega \subseteq \Theta \\ 0 & \text{otherwise} \end{cases}.$$

The following description of SPE scheme is presented here as a Key-Encapsulation Mechanism (KEM) where $\mathcal{C}$, $\mathcal{SK}$ and $\mathcal{K}$ denote ciphertext space, secret key space and encapsulation key space respectively.

- Setup: It takes $m \in \mathbb{N}$ along with security parameter 1^λ. It outputs master secret key msk and public key mpk.
- KeyGen: It takes mpk, msk and key-index set $\Omega \in \mathcal{X}$ of size $k \leq m$ secret key SK $\in \mathcal{SK}$ corresponding to key-index set Ω.
- Encrypt: It takes mpk, data-index set $\Theta \in \mathcal{Y}$ of size $\ell \leq m$ encapsulation key $\kappa \in \mathcal{K}$ and ciphertext CT $\in \mathcal{C}$.
- Test: It takes (SK, Ω) and (CT, Θ) as input. Outputs κ or $\perp$.

Correctness. For all $(\mathsf{mpk}, \mathsf{msk}) \leftarrow \mathsf{Setup}(1^\lambda)$, all key-index set $\Omega \in \mathcal{X}$, all SK $\leftarrow \mathsf{KeyGen}(\mathsf{msk}, \Omega)$, all data-index set $\Theta \in \mathcal{Y}$, all $(\kappa, \mathsf{CT}) \leftarrow \mathsf{Encrypt}(\mathsf{mpk}, \Theta)$,

$$\mathsf{Decrypt}(\mathsf{mpk}, (\mathsf{SK}, \Omega), (\mathsf{CT}, \Theta)) = \begin{cases} \kappa & \text{if } R_s(\Omega, \Theta) = 1 \\ \perp & \text{otherwise} \end{cases}.$$

Remark 1. The Setup algorithms takes an additional parameter m along with the security parameter λ. This is because, both our constructions are large universe constructions. The cardinality of the sets processed in ciphertext generation and key generation in both of our constructions will be upper bounded by m like any other available standard model large universe constructions [4,22].

3.2   Security Notions

Adaptive CPA-Security **of SPE.** The security game for adaptive CPA-Security for SPE (SPE) is defined as following:

- **Setup:** The challenger $\mathcal{C}$ gives mpk to adversary $\mathcal{A}$ and keeps msk as secret.
- **Query Phase-I:** $\mathcal{C}$ gets a key-index set Ω and returns SK $\leftarrow \mathsf{KeyGen}(\mathsf{msk}, \Omega)$.
- **Challenge:** $\mathcal{A}$ provides challenge data-index set Θ^* (such that $R_s(\Omega, \Theta^*) = 0$ for all previous key queries). $\mathcal{C}$ then generates $(\kappa_0, \mathsf{CT}) \leftarrow \mathsf{Encrypt}(\mathsf{mpk}, \Theta^*)$ and chooses $\kappa_1 \hookleftarrow \mathcal{K}$. Finally, $\mathcal{C}$ returns (CT, κ_b) to $\mathcal{A}$ for $b \hookleftarrow \{0, 1\}$.
- **Query Phase-II:** Given a key-index Ω such that $R_s(\Omega, \Theta^*) = 0$, $\mathcal{C}$ returns SK $\leftarrow \mathsf{KeyGen}(\mathsf{msk}, \Omega)$.
- **Guess:** $\mathcal{A}$ outputs its guess $b' \in \{0, 1\}$ and wins if $b = b'$.

For any adversary $\mathcal{A}$,

$$\mathsf{Adv}^{\mathsf{SPE}}_{\mathcal{A},\mathsf{IND\text{-}CPA}}(\lambda) = |\Pr[\mathfrak{b} = \mathfrak{b}'] - 1/2|.$$

We say, SPE is Ind-CPA secure (IND-CPA) if for any efficient adversary $\mathcal{A}$, $\mathsf{Adv}^{\mathsf{SPE}}_{\mathcal{A},\mathsf{IND\text{-}CPA}}(\lambda) \leq \mathsf{neg}(\lambda)$. If there is a **Init** phase before the **Setup** where the adversary $\mathcal{A}$ commits to the challenge data-index set Θ^*, we call such security model as sInd-CPA security (sIND-CPA) model.

4 SPE_1: Realizing Constant Size Ciphertext

We present first SPE construction having constant-size secret key and constant-size ciphertext in the composite order pairing setting.

4.1   Construction

SPE_1 is defined by following four algorithms.

- $\mathsf{Setup}(1^\lambda, m)$: The symmetric bilinear group generator outputs $(p_1, p_2, p_3, \mathsf{G}, \mathsf{G}_T, e) \leftarrow \mathcal{G}_{\mathsf{sbg}}(1^\lambda, 3)$ where both G, G_T are cyclic groups of order $N = p_1 p_2 p_3$. Then pick $\alpha, \beta \hookleftarrow N$, generators $g_1, u \hookleftarrow \mathsf{G}_{p_1}$ and $g_3 \hookleftarrow \mathsf{G}_{p_3}$. Choose $\mathsf{R}_{3,i} \hookleftarrow \mathsf{G}_{p_3}$ for all $i \in [m]$. Define the $\mathsf{msk} = (\alpha, \beta, u, g_3)$ and the public parameter is

$$\mathsf{mpk} = \left(g_1, g_1^\beta, \left(G_i = g_1^{\alpha^i}, U_i = u^{\alpha^i} \cdot \mathsf{R}_{3,i}\right)_{i \in [m]}, e(g_1, u)^\beta, \mathsf{H}\right)$$

  where $\mathsf{H} : \mathsf{G}_T \to \{0,1\}^{\mathsf{poly}(\lambda)}$ is a randomly chosen universal hash function.
- $\mathsf{KeyGen}(\mathsf{msk}, \Omega)$: Given a set Ω, such that $|\Omega| = \mathfrak{k} \leq m$; define the polynomial $P_\Omega(z) = \prod\limits_{x \in \Omega} (z + x) = d_0 + d_1 z + d_2 z^2 + \ldots + d_{\mathfrak{k}} z^{\mathfrak{k}}$, pick $X_3 \hookleftarrow \mathsf{G}_{p_3}$ and define secret key as

$$\mathsf{SK}_\Omega = u^{\frac{\beta}{P_\Omega(\alpha)}} \cdot X_3 = u^{\frac{\beta}{\prod\limits_{x \in \Omega}(\alpha + x)}} \cdot X_3.$$

- $\mathsf{Encrypt}(\mathsf{mpk}, \Theta)$: Given a set Θ, such that $|\Theta| = \ell \leq m$; the polynomial $P_\Theta(z) = \prod\limits_{y \in \Theta} (z + y) = c_0 + c_1 z + c_2 z^2 + \ldots + c_\ell z^\ell$. Choose $s \hookleftarrow \mathbb{Z}_p$ and compute κ and $\mathsf{CT}_\Theta = (\mathsf{C}_0, \mathsf{C}_1)$ such that

$$\kappa = \mathsf{H}(e(g_1, u)^{s\beta}), \mathsf{C}_0 = g_1^{s\beta}, \mathsf{C}_1 = g_1^{sP_\Theta(\alpha)} = \left(g_1^{c_0} \prod_{i \in [\ell]} G_i^{c_i}\right)^s.$$

- $\mathsf{Decrypt}((\mathsf{SK}_\Omega, \Omega), (\mathsf{CT}_\Theta, \Theta))$: As $\Omega \subseteq \Theta$, compute $P_{\Theta \setminus \Omega}(\alpha) = \prod\limits_{w \in \Theta \setminus \Omega} (\alpha + w) = a_0 + a_1\alpha + a_2\alpha^2 + \ldots + a_t\alpha^t$ where $t = |\Theta \setminus \Omega|$. Then compute $\kappa = \mathsf{H}((B/A)^{1/a_0})$ where

$$A = e(\mathsf{C}_0, \prod_{i \in [t]} U_i^{a_i}), B = e(\mathsf{C}_1, \mathsf{SK}_\Omega).$$

Correctness. Notice that,

$$A = e(\mathsf{C}_0, \prod_{i \in [t]} U_i^{a_i}) = e(g_1^{s\beta}, u^{P_{\Theta \setminus \Omega}(\alpha) - a_0}) = e(g_1, u)^{s\beta(P_{\Theta \setminus \Omega}(\alpha) - a_0)},$$

$$B = e(\mathsf{C}_1, \mathsf{SK}_\Omega) = e(g_1^{sP_\Theta(\alpha)}, u^{\frac{\beta}{P_\Omega(\alpha)}} \cdot X_3) = e(g_1, u)^{s\beta P_{\Theta \setminus \Omega}(\alpha)}.$$

Then $B/A = e(g_1, u)^{s\beta a_0}$, $\mathsf{H}((B/A)^{1/a_0}) = \mathsf{H}(e(g_1, u)^{s\beta}) = \kappa$.

4.2 Security

As we already have mentioned, one can view SPE as a generalization of IBBE [14]. Recently Gong et al. [17] used Déjà Q to prove their identity-based broadcast encryption selective secure in the standard model. The crux of their proof lies in the independence of the semi-functional component of the secret keys (SK_Ω) and semi-functional components of the related public parameters $(U_i)_{i \in [m]}$. To argue that, they showed corresponding matrix representation to be non-singular (see game G_5 in the proof of [17, Theorem 1]). The proof made an implicit natural assumption that none of the secret key queries get repeated. Otherwise, the matrix will have more than one identical rows that encode the same key-index. The matrix in such case is singular and the proof fails.

SPE, being a generalization of IBBE, allows key queries on sets where same key-index can appear in different key queries. Precisely, the adversary in case of SPE, can make key extraction queries on Ω_i and Ω_j for $\Omega_i \cap \Omega_j \neq 0$. This introduces a problem here due to dependency among the secret keys of SPE_1. As a result, the matrix might become singular in one of the intermediate games of our hybrid argument to prove security of SPE_1. Here, we take a simple example to show this problem in light of one admissible Aggregate [15].

In [15], an efficient algorithm called Aggregate was introduced. Given finite sets $S = (x_i)_{i \in I}$ and $H = \left(h^{\frac{1}{z + x_i}}\right)_{x_i \in S}$, Aggregate outputs h^X where I is finite set of indices on S, z is the indeterminant, h is an element from cyclic group W and $x_i \in [\mathrm{ord}(h)]$ such that $X = \frac{1}{\prod_{x_i \in S} (z + x_i)}$. Note that this holds for any cyclic group (W) unless there exists distinct $x_i, x_j \in S$ but $x_i - x_j = 0 \mod \mathrm{ord}(W)$.

Now, notice that the secret keys of SPE_1 allow collusion similar to [15,17]. But such collusions did not create any problem in [15,17] as their KeyGen takes singleton key-index. On the other hand, as SPE_1.KeyGen takes set as input, collusion due to Aggregate creates the following problem. Suppose the adversary of SPE_1 makes following three queries: $\Omega_1 = \{1, 2\}$, $\Omega_2 = \{1, 3\}$ and $\Omega_3 = \{2, 3\}$. Given SK_{Ω_1} and SK_{Ω_2}, the adversary can easily compute SK_Ω using Aggregate function where $\Omega = \{1, 2, 3\}$. Moreover, given SK_{Ω_2} and SK_{Ω_3}, the adversary can also compute same key SK_Ω using Aggregate function. Such a query sequence causes the proof to fail as semi-functional components can no longer be proved to be independent. See the full version [11] of this work for further details. In particular, during the proof of Lemma 3 (in [11]) which is at the core of the proof of indistinguishability of Game_5 and Game_6, the matrix $\mathbf{P}'$ (and subsequently $\mathbf{A}$ in Lemma 2 in [11]) precisely would be singular. Notice that, given $(\mathsf{SK}_{\Omega_i})_{i \in I}$, one can use $\mathsf{Aggregate}$ in a cascading manner to get secret keys corresponding to other sets as well. We formally define the *claw due to* $\mathsf{Aggregate}$ as following: there exists $\Omega_i, \Omega_j, \Omega_k \subset \mathcal{ID}$ where at least two of these sets are distinct and the adversary acquired secret key on all three of them such that $\mathsf{Aggregate}(\mathsf{SK}_{\Omega_i}, \mathsf{SK}_{\Omega_j}) = \mathsf{Aggregate}(\mathsf{SK}_{\Omega_j}, \mathsf{SK}_{\Omega_k})$. In case the query sequence has such a claw, the matrix $\mathbf{P}'$ becomes singular and the proof fails. The easiest work-around would be to ensure that no two queries have any element common i.e. $\Omega_i \cap \Omega_j = \phi$ for all distinct $i, j \in [q]$.

We put a much weaker restriction on the adversary where we allow making key queries only on *cover-free* sets. Formally, after making a challenge query Θ^*, adversary $\mathcal{A}$ is allowed to make key extraction queries on $(\Omega_1, \Omega_2, \ldots, \Omega_q)$ adaptively with two restrictions. For all $i \in [q]$, the following must hold:

1. $\Omega_i \not\subset \Theta^*$,
2. $\Omega_i \setminus \left(\bigcup_{j \in [q] \setminus \{i\}} \Omega_j \right) \neq \phi$.

Notice that, the first is the natural restriction on the relation between challenge set Θ^* with secret key queries $\{\Omega_i\}_{i \in [q]}$. We say, SPE is selective* Ind-CPA secure (aka s*IND-CPA) if for any PPT adversary $\mathcal{A}$ that gives out the challenge Θ^* during **Init** and the queries it make following the above-mentioned restrictions, $\mathsf{Adv}_{\mathcal{A},\mathsf{s}^*\mathsf{IND}\text{-}\mathsf{CPA}}^{\mathsf{SPE}}(\lambda) \leq \mathsf{neg}(\lambda)$.

Here we mention that, we do not see any ready vulnerability in our construction due to $\mathsf{Aggregate}$ (or any other way for that matter). This is because, given secret keys corresponding to Ω_i and Ω_j, the $\mathsf{Aggregate}$ computes secret key for *bigger* set Ω (precisely $\Omega = \Omega_i \cup \Omega_j$ for distinct Ω_i, Ω_j). Now for a challenge Θ^*, the natural restriction ensures $\Omega_i, \Omega_j \not\subset \Theta^*$ and therefore $\Omega \not\subset \Theta^*$. Naturally, the resulting Ω is a valid key-index set. Thus, even if the $\mathsf{Aggregate}$ function is used to compute SK_Ω from SK_{Ω_i} and SK_{Ω_j}, it does not help the adversary in any way to break the security of the scheme. We reiterate that, we do not put any restriction on the relation between challenge Θ^* and secret-key queries Ω apart from the natural restriction mentioned above. This s*IND-CPA model in this respect behaves exactly the same as sIND-CPA model.

Theorem 1. *For any adversary $\mathcal{A}$ of SPE construction* SPE_1 *in the* s*IND-CPA *model that makes at most q many secret key queries, there exist adversary $\mathcal{B}_1$, $\mathcal{B}_2$ such that*

$$\mathsf{Adv}_{\mathcal{A},\mathsf{s}^*\mathsf{IND}\text{-}\mathsf{CPA}}^{\mathsf{SPE}_1}(\lambda) \leq 2 \cdot \mathsf{Adv}_{\mathcal{B}_1}^{\mathsf{DS1}}(\lambda) + (m + q + 2) \cdot \mathsf{Adv}_{\mathcal{B}_2}^{\mathsf{DS2}}(\lambda)$$
$$+ \frac{((m+q)(m+q+1)+1)}{p_2} + 2^{-\lambda}.$$

Proof Sketch. The proof is established via a hybrid argument. The idea is to modify each game only a small amount that allows the solver $\mathcal{B}$ to model the intermediate games properly. The hybrid argument is based on Wee's [25] porting of Déjà Q framework introduced by Chase and Meiklejohn [10]. Intuitively, in the first game Game_0, both the challenge ciphertext and secret keys are normal. We define three intermediate games ($\mathsf{Game}_1, \mathsf{Game}_2,$ and Game_3) to change the ciphertext to semi-functional in Game_4. We next define a sub-sequence of games $(\mathsf{Game}_{5,1,0}, \mathsf{Game}_{5,1,1}, \mathsf{Game}_{5,2,0}, \mathsf{Game}_{5,2,1}, \ldots, \mathsf{Game}_{5,m+q+1,0}, \mathsf{Game}_{5,m+q+1,1})$ to introduce enough randomness into the semi-functional components of secret key and few related public parameters. Note that till this point, we mostly have followed [17]. Such a sub-sequence of games effectively introduces enough entropy in the semi-functional component such that we can replace it by pure random choice in Game_6. The structure here is more involved than [17] and we find a trick (namely key-queries on *cover-free* sets only) that is necessary and sufficient to complete the security argument. Finally, in Game_7, we show that semi-functional components as a whole supply enough entropy to hide encapsulation key κ. The detailed proof is given in the full version of the paper ([11, Section 4.2.1]). $\qquad\square$

5   SPE$_2$: An Adaptive Secure Construction

Our second and main construction is instantiated in the prime order bilinear groups and achieves adaptive security under SXDH assumption.

5.1   Construction

SPE$_2$ is defined as following four algorithms.

– Setup$(1^\lambda, m)$: Let $(p, \mathsf{G}_1, \mathsf{G}_2, \mathsf{G}_T, e) \leftarrow \mathcal{G}_{\mathrm{abg}}(1^\lambda)$ where $\mathsf{G}_1, \mathsf{G}_2, \mathsf{G}_T$ are cyclic groups of order p. Choose generators $(g_1, g_2) \leftarrow \mathsf{G}_1 \times \mathsf{G}_2$ and define $g_T = e(g_1, g_2)$. Choose $\alpha_1, \alpha_2, c, d, (u_j, v_j)_{j \in [0,m]} \leftarrow \mathbb{Z}_p$ and $b \leftarrow \mathbb{Z}_p^\times$. For all $j \in [0, m]$, define $g_1^{w_j} = g_1^{u_j + bv_j}$ and $g_1^w = g_1^{c + bd}$. Then define $g_T^\alpha = e(g_1, g_2)^{\alpha_1 + b\alpha_2}$ via setting $\alpha = (\alpha_1 + b\alpha_2)$. Define the $\mathsf{msk} = (g_2, g_2^c, \alpha_1, \alpha_2, d, (u_j, v_j)_{j \in [0,m]})$ and the public parameter is defined as

$$\mathsf{mpk} = \left(g_1, g_1^b, \left(g_1^{w_j} \right)_{j \in [0,m]}, g_1^w, g_T^\alpha \right).$$

– KeyGen(msk, Ω) : Given a key-index set Ω of size $k \le m$, choose $r \leftarrow \mathbb{Z}_p$. Compute the secret key as $\mathsf{SK}_\Omega = (\mathsf{K}_1, \mathsf{K}_2, \mathsf{K}_3, \mathsf{K}_4, \mathsf{K}_5)$ where

$$\mathsf{K}_1 = g_2^r, \mathsf{K}_2 = g_2^{cr}, \mathsf{K}_3 = g_2^{\alpha_1 + r \sum\limits_{x \in \Omega} (u_0 + u_1 x + u_2 x^2 + \ldots + u_m x^m)},$$

$$\mathsf{K}_4 = g_2^{dr}, \mathsf{K}_5 = g_2^{\alpha_2 + r \sum\limits_{x \in \Omega} (v_0 + v_1 x + v_2 x^2 + \ldots + v_m x^m)}.$$

– Encrypt(mpk, Θ) : Given a data-index set Θ of size $\ell \le m$, choose $s \leftarrow \mathbb{Z}_p$. Compute κ and $\mathsf{CT}_\Theta = (\mathsf{C}_0, \mathsf{C}_1, (\mathsf{C}_{2,i}, t_i)_{i \in [\ell]})$ where $(t_i)_{i \in [\ell]} \leftarrow \mathbb{Z}_p$ and

$$\kappa = e(g_1, g_2)^{\alpha s}, \mathsf{C}_0 = g_1^s, \mathsf{C}_1 = g_1^{bs}, \mathsf{C}_{2,i} = g_1^{s(w_0 + w_1 y_i + w_2 y_i^2 + \ldots + w_m y_i^m + w t_i)}.$$

– Decrypt$((\mathsf{SK}_\Omega, \Omega), (\mathsf{CT}_\Theta, \Theta))$: Computes $\kappa = B/A$ where

$$A = e\left(\prod_{y_i \in \Omega} \mathsf{C}_{2,i}, \mathsf{K}_1 \right), B = e\left(\mathsf{C}_0, \mathsf{K}_3 \prod_{y_i \in \Omega} \mathsf{K}_2^{t_i} \right) e\left(\mathsf{C}_1, \mathsf{K}_5 \prod_{y_i \in \Omega} \mathsf{K}_4^{t_i} \right).$$

Correctness. As $\Omega \subseteq \Theta$,

$$B = e\left(C_0, K_3 \prod_{y_i \in \Omega} K_2^{t_i}\right) e\left(C_1, K_5 \prod_{y_i \in \Omega} K_4^{t_i}\right),$$

$$= e\left(C_0, g_2^{\alpha_1 + r \sum_{y_i \in \Omega}(u_0 + u_1 y_i + u_2 y_i^2 + \ldots + u_m y_i^m)} \cdot \prod_{y_i \in \Omega} g_2^{rct_i}\right)$$

$$\cdot\, e\left(C_1, g_2^{\alpha_2 + r \sum_{y_i \in \Omega}(v_0 + v_1 y_i + v_2 y_i^2 + \ldots + v_m y_i^m)} \cdot \prod_{y_i \in \Omega} g_2^{rdt_i}\right)$$

$$= e\left(C_0, g_2^{(\alpha_1 + b\alpha_2) + r \sum_{y_i \in \Omega}((u_0 + bv_0) + (u_1 + bv_1)y_i + \ldots + (u_m + bv_m)y_i^m)} \cdot \prod_{y_i \in \Omega} g_2^{r(c + bd)t_i}\right)$$

$$= e\left(C_0, g_2^{\alpha + r \sum_{y_i \in \Omega}(w_0 + w_1 y_i + w_2 y_i^2 + \ldots + w_m y_i^m)} \cdot \prod_{y_i \in \Omega} g_2^{rwt_i}\right)$$

$$= e\left(g_1^s, g_2^{\alpha + r \sum_{y_i \in \Omega}(w_0 + w_1 y_i + w_2 y_i^2 + \ldots + w_m y_i^m + wt_i)}\right)$$

$$A = e\left(\prod_{y_i \in \Omega} C_{2,i}, K_1\right)$$

$$= e\left(g_1^{s \sum_{y_i \in \Omega}(w_0 + w_1 y_i + w_2 y_i^2 + \ldots + w_m y_i^m + wt_i)}, g_2^r\right)$$

Then $B/A = e(g_1^s, g_2^\alpha) = \kappa$.

Remark 2. We observe that our SPE$_2$ construction has a *pair encoding* [3] embedded. One can utilize the generic technique of Chen et al. [12] to get corresponding predicate encryption. The public parameter and ciphertext size, however, will be significantly larger than that of SPE$_2$. Precisely, both the public parameter and ciphertext contain additional m G$_1$-elements. Although the secret key requires one less G$_2$ element, the decryption is costlier as it takes one extra pairing evaluation. In addition, one can apply such pair encoding on framework by Chen and Gong [13] to generalize our SPE$_2$ construction further in terms of security.

5.2 Security

Theorem 2. *For any adversary $\mathcal{A}$ of SPE construction* SPE$_2$ *in the* IND-CPA *model that makes at most q many secret key queries, there exist adversary $\mathcal{B}_1$, $\mathcal{B}_2$ such that*

$$\mathsf{Adv}^{\mathsf{SPE}_2}_{\mathcal{A},\mathsf{IND\text{-}CPA}}(\lambda) \leq \mathsf{Adv}^{\mathsf{DDH}_{\mathsf{G}_1}}_{\mathcal{B}_1}(\lambda) + q \cdot \mathsf{Adv}^{\mathsf{DDH}_{\mathsf{G}_2}}_{\mathcal{B}_2}(\lambda) + 2/p.$$

Proof Sketch. We propose a hybrid argument based proof that uses dual system proof technique [24] at its core. This hybrid argument follows the proof strategy of [22]. In this sequence of game based argument, in the first game (Game$_0$)

both the challenge ciphertext and secret keys are normal. In Game_1, we first make the challenge ciphertext semi-functional. Then all the keys are changed to semi-functional via a series of games namely $(\mathsf{Game}_{2,1}, \ldots, \mathsf{Game}_{2,q})$. In any $\mathsf{Game}_{2,k}$, for any $k \in [q]$, all the previous (i.e. $1 \le j \le k$) secret keys are semi-functional whereas all the following (i.e. $k < j \le q$) secret keys are normal. We continue this till $\mathsf{Game}_{2,q}$ where all the keys are semi-functional. In the final game (Game_3), the encapsulation key κ is replaced by a uniform random choice from $\mathcal{K}$. We show that the semi-functional components of challenge ciphertext and secret keys in Game_3 supply enough entropy to hide the encapsulation key κ; hence it is distributionally same as random choice from $\mathcal{K}$. Note that, we denote Game_1 by $\mathsf{Game}_{2,0}$.

We first recall the crucial tactics [22] used to prove their IBBE adaptive CPA-secure as we already have mentioned that our large-universe SPE_2 construction uses IBBE [22] as a starting point. The crux of the proof of IBBE in [22] is a linear map that reflects the relation between tags $(t_1, \ldots, t_\ell)$ that encoded $(y_1, \ldots, y_\ell)$ respectively and semi-functional component (π) in the secret key SK_x that encoded queried key-index x. This scenario occurs when a normal secret key is translated into corresponding semi-functional form. At this point, [22] showed that such linear map is non-singular following Attrapadung and Libert [5]. Such a property of the linear map effectively ensures that semi-functional component of the key has enough entropy to hide the encapsulation key κ.

However, following their proof technique verbatim does not work in our case as the semi-functional component π no longer encodes only one identity rather it has to encode multiple identities belonging to the queried set Ω. Let us consider a case where, $x \in (\Theta^* \cap \Omega)$, i.e. $\exists j \in [\ell], x = y_j$. In other words $\exists j \in [\ell]$ such that tag t_j encodes $y_j(= x)$ where $x \in \Omega$. As the semi-functional component π, that encodes queried set Ω, will also contain some information about x (i.e. y_j), it is not clear if $(t_1, \ldots, t_\ell)$ and π are still independent.

The novelty in our proof technique is that we proceed in a different manner where we argue independence of $(t_1, \ldots, t_\ell)$ and π^* as well as the independence of $\hat{\pi}$ and π^* where π^* encodes $x^* \in \Omega \setminus \Theta^*$ and $\hat{\pi}$ encodes all $x \in \Omega \setminus \{x^*\}$. Notice that such a x^* will always exist as $\Omega \not\subset \Theta^*$. This therefore ensures that the linear map reflecting the relation between $(t_1, \ldots, t_\ell)$ and π to be non-singular.

Now, we define the semi-functional ciphertext and semi-functional secret keys.

5.2.1 Semi-functional Algorithms

– $\mathsf{SFKeyGen}(\mathsf{msk}, \Omega)$: Let the normal secret key be $\mathsf{SK}'_\Omega = (\mathsf{K}'_1, \mathsf{K}'_2, \mathsf{K}'_3, \mathsf{K}'_4, \mathsf{K}'_5) \leftarrow \mathsf{KeyGen}(\mathsf{msk}, \Omega)$ where r is the randomness used in KeyGen. Choose $\hat{r}, \pi \hookleftarrow \mathbb{Z}_p$. Compute the semi-functional trapdoor as $\mathsf{SK}_\Omega = (\mathsf{K}_1, \mathsf{K}_2, \mathsf{K}_3, \mathsf{K}_4, \mathsf{K}_5)$ such that

$$\mathsf{K}_1 = \mathsf{K}'_1 = g_2^r, \mathsf{K}_2 = \mathsf{K}'_2 \cdot g_2^{\hat{r}} = g_2^{cr + \hat{r}},$$
$$\mathsf{K}_3 = \mathsf{K}'_3 \cdot g_2^{\hat{r}\pi} = g_2^{\alpha_1 + r \sum_{x \in \Omega} (u_0 + u_1 x + u_2 x^2 + \ldots + u_m x^m) + \hat{r}\pi},$$

$$K_4 = K_4' \cdot g_2^{-\hat{r}b^{-1}} = g_2^{dr - \hat{r}b^{-1}},$$

$$K_5 = K_5' \cdot g_2^{-\hat{r}\pi b^{-1}} = g_2^{\alpha_2 + r \sum_{x \in \Omega} (v_0 + v_1 x + v_2 x^2 + \ldots + v_m x^m) - \hat{r}\pi b^{-1}}.$$

- SFEncrypt(mpk, msk, Θ): Let the normal encapsulation key and normal ciphertext be $(\kappa', CT_\Theta') \leftarrow$ Encrypt(mpk, msk, Θ) where s is the randomness and $(t_i)_{i \in [\ell]}$ are the random tags used in Encrypt such that $CT_\Theta' = (C_0', C_1', (C_{2,i}', t_i)_{i \in [\ell]})$. Compute the semi-functional encapsulation key κ and semi-functional ciphertext $CT_\Theta = (C_0, C_1, (C_{2,i}, t_i)_{i \in [\ell]})$ as follows:

$$\kappa = \kappa' \cdot g_T^{\alpha_1 \hat{s}} = e(g_1, g_2)^{\alpha s + \alpha_1 \hat{s}}, C_0 = C_0' \cdot g_1^{\hat{s}} = g_1^{s + \hat{s}}, C_1 = g_1^{bs},$$

$$C_{2,i} = C_{2,i}' \cdot g_1^{\hat{s}(u_0 + u_1 y_i + u_2 y_i^2 + \ldots + u_m y_i^m + ct_i)},$$

$$= g_1^{s(w_0 + w_1 y_i + w_2 y_i^2 + \ldots + w_m y_i^m + wt_i) + \hat{s}(u_0 + u_1 y_i + u_2 y_i^2 + \ldots + u_m y_i^m + ct_i)}. \qquad \square$$

5.2.2 Sequence of Games

The idea is to change each game only by a small margin and prove indistinguishability of two consecutive games.

Lemma 1 (Game$_0$ to Game$_1$). *For any efficient adversary $\mathcal{A}$ that makes at most q key queries, there exists a PPT algorithm $\mathcal{B}$ such that* $|Adv_{\mathcal{A}}^0(\lambda) - Adv_{\mathcal{A}}^1(\lambda)| \leq Adv_{\mathcal{B}}^{DDH_{G_1}}(\lambda).$

Proof. The solver $\mathcal{B}$ is given the DDH_{G_1} problem instance $D = (g_1, g_2, g_1^b, g_1^{bs})$ and the target $T = g_1^{s + \hat{s}}$ where $\hat{s} = 0$ or chosen uniformly random from $\mathbb{Z}_p^\times$.

Setup. $\mathcal{B}$ chooses $\alpha_1, \alpha_2, (u_i, v_i)_{i \in [0,m]}, c, d \leftarrow \mathbb{Z}_p$. As both α_1 and α_2 are available to $\mathcal{B}$, it can generate $g_T^\alpha = e(g_1^{\alpha_1} \cdot (g_1^b)^{\alpha_2}, g_2)$. Hence, $\mathcal{B}$ outputs the public parameter mpk. Notice that the master secret key msk is available to $\mathcal{B}$.

Phase-I Queries. Since $\mathcal{B}$ knows the msk, it can answer with normal secret keys on any query of Ω.

Challenge. Given the challenge set $\Theta^* = (y_1, \ldots, y_\ell)$ for $\ell \leq m$, $\mathcal{B}$ chooses $(t_i)_{i \in [\ell]} \leftarrow \mathbb{Z}_p$. It then computes the challenge as κ_0 and $CT_{\Theta^*} = (C_0, C_1, (C_{2,i}, t_i)_{i \in [\ell]})$ using the problem instance as follows.

$$\kappa_0 = e(C_0, g_2)^{\alpha_1} \cdot e(C_1, g_2)^{\alpha_2}, C_0 = T, C_1 = g_1^{bs},$$

$$C_{2,i} = C_0^{u_0 + u_1 y_i + u_2 y_i^2 + \ldots + u_m y_i^m + ct_i} \cdot C_1^{v_0 + v_1 y_i + v_2 y_i^2 + \ldots + v_m y_i^m + dt_i}$$

where $i \in [\ell]$. $\mathcal{B}$ then chooses $\kappa_1 \leftarrow \mathcal{K}$ and returns $(\kappa_\mathfrak{b}, CT_{\Theta^*})$ as the challenge ciphertext for $\mathfrak{b} \leftarrow \{0, 1\}$.

Phase-II Queries. Same as Phase-I queries.

Guess. $\mathcal{A}$ output $\mathfrak{b}' \in \{0, 1\}$. $\mathcal{B}$ outputs 1 if $\mathfrak{b} = \mathfrak{b}'$ and 0 otherwise.

Notice that, if $\hat{s}$ in $\mathsf{DDH}_{\mathsf{G}_1}$ problem instance is 0, then the challenge ciphertext CT_{Θ^*} is normal. Otherwise the challenge ciphertext CT_{Θ^*} is semi-functional. If $\mathcal{A}$ can distinguish these two scenarios, the solver $\mathcal{B}$ will use it to break $\mathsf{DDH}_{\mathsf{G}_1}$ problem. Thus, $\left|\mathsf{Adv}_{\mathcal{A}}^0(\lambda) - \mathsf{Adv}_{\mathcal{A}}^1(\lambda)\right| \leq \epsilon_{\mathsf{DDH}_{\mathsf{G}_1}}$. $\qquad\square$

Lemma 2 (Game$_{2,k-1}$ to Game$_{2,k}$). *For any efficient adversary $\mathcal{A}$ that makes at most q key queries, there exists a PPT algorithm $\mathcal{B}$ such that* $|\mathsf{Adv}_{\mathcal{A}}^{2,k-1}(\lambda) - \mathsf{Adv}_{\mathcal{A}}^{2,k}(\lambda)| \leq \mathsf{Adv}_{\mathcal{B}}^{\mathsf{DDH}_{\mathsf{G}_2}}(\lambda)$.

Proof. The solver $\mathcal{B}$ is given the $\mathsf{DDH}_{\mathsf{G}_2}$ problem instance $D = (g_1, g_2, g_2^c, g_2^r)$ and the target $T = g_2^{cr+\hat{r}}$ where $\hat{r} = 0$ or chosen uniformly random from $\mathbb{Z}_p^\times$.

Setup. $\mathcal{B}$ chooses $b \xleftarrow{} \mathbb{Z}_p^\times$, $\alpha, \alpha_1, w, (p_i, q_i, w_i)_{i \in [0,m]} \xleftarrow{} \mathbb{Z}_p$. It sets $\alpha_2 = b^{-1}(\alpha - \alpha_1)$, $d = b^{-1}(w - c)$, $u_i = p_i + cq_i$, $v_i = b^{-1}(w_i - u_i)$. Note that, as c explicitly is unknown to $\mathcal{B}$, all but α_2 assignment has been done implicitly. The public parameters mpk are generated as $(g_1, g_1^b, (g_1^{w_i})_{i \in [0,m]}, g_1^w, g_T^\alpha)$ where $g_T = e(g_1, g_2)$. Here note that, not all of msk is available to $\mathcal{B}$. Still we show that, even without knowing $(d, (u_i, v_i)_{i \in [0,m]})$ explicitly, $\mathcal{B}$ can simulate the game.

Phase-I Queries. Given the jth key query on Ω_j s.t. $|\Omega_j| = \hbar_j \leq m$,

- If $j > k$: $\mathcal{B}$ has to return a normal key. We already have mentioned that $(d, (u_i, v_i)_{i \in [0,m]})$ of msk are unavailable to $\mathcal{B}$. Thus $\mathcal{B}$ simulates the normal secret keys as follows.

  $\mathcal{B}$ chooses $r_j \xleftarrow{} \mathbb{Z}_p$. Computes the secret key $\mathsf{SK}_{\Omega_j} = (\mathsf{K}_1, \mathsf{K}_2, \mathsf{K}_3, \mathsf{K}_4, \mathsf{K}_5)$ where,
  $$\mathsf{K}_1 = g_2^{r_j}, \mathsf{K}_2 = (g_2^c)^{r_j},$$
  $$\mathsf{K}_3 = g_2^{\alpha_1} \cdot \mathsf{K}_1^{\sum\limits_{x \in \Omega_j}(p_0 + p_1 x + p_2 x^2 + \ldots + p_m x^m)} \cdot \mathsf{K}_2^{\sum\limits_{x \in \Omega_j}(q_0 + q_1 x + q_2 x^2 + \ldots + q_m x^m)},$$
  $$= g_2^{\alpha_1 + r_j \sum\limits_{x \in \Omega_j}(u_0 + u_1 x + u_2 x^2 + \ldots + u_m x^m)},$$
  $$\mathsf{K}_4 = \mathsf{K}_1^{b^{-1}w} \cdot \mathsf{K}_2^{-b^{-1}} = g_2^{dr_j},$$
  $$\mathsf{K}_5 = g_2^{b^{-1}\alpha} \cdot \mathsf{K}_1^{b^{-1}\sum\limits_{x \in \Omega_j}(w_0 + w_1 x + w_2 x^2 + \ldots + w_m x^m)} \cdot \mathsf{K}_3^{-b^{-1}}$$
  $$= g_2^{b^{-1}\alpha + r_j b^{-1} \sum\limits_{x \in \Omega_j}(w_0 + w_1 x + w_2 x^2 + \ldots + w_m x^m)}$$
  $$\cdot g_2^{-b^{-1}(\alpha_1 + r_j \sum\limits_{x \in \Omega_j}(u_0 + u_1 x + u_2 x^2 + \ldots + u_m x^m))}$$
  $$= g_2^{\alpha_2 + r_j \sum\limits_{x \in \Omega_j}(v_0 + v_1 x + v_2 x^2 + \ldots + v_m x^m)}.$$
  Notice that SK_{Ω_j} is identically distributed to output of $\mathsf{KeyGen}(\mathsf{msk}, \Omega_j)$. Hence $\mathcal{B}$ has managed to simulate the normal secret key without knowing the msk completely.

- If $j < k$: $\mathcal{B}$ has to return a semi-functional secret key. It first creates normal secret keys as above and chooses $\hat{r}, \pi \xleftarrow{} \mathbb{Z}_p$ to create semi-functional secret keys following $\mathsf{SFKeyGen}$.

- If $j = k$: $\mathcal{B}$ will use $\mathsf{DDH}_{\mathsf{G}_2}$ problem instance to simulate the secret key. It sets,

$$\mathsf{K}_1 = g_2^r, \; \mathsf{K}_2 = T = g_2^{cr+\hat{r}} = \mathsf{K}_2' \cdot g_2^{\hat{r}},$$

$$\mathsf{K}_3 = g_2^{\alpha_1} \cdot \mathsf{K}_1^{\sum\limits_{x \in \Omega_j}(p_0+p_1 x+p_2 x^2+\ldots+p_m x^m)} \cdot \mathsf{K}_2^{\sum\limits_{x \in \Omega_j}(q_0+q_1 x+q_2 x^2+\ldots+q_m x^m)},$$

$$= g_2^{\alpha_1+r \sum\limits_{x \in \Omega_j}(u_0+u_1 x+u_2 x^2+\ldots+u_m x^m)+\hat{r} \sum\limits_{x \in \Omega_j}(q_0+q_1 x+q_2 x^2+\ldots+q_m x^m)},$$

$$= \mathsf{K}_3' \cdot g_2^{\hat{r} \sum\limits_{x \in \Omega_j}(q_0+q_1 x+q_2 x^2+\ldots+q_m x^m)}.$$

$$\mathsf{K}_4 = \mathsf{K}_1^{b^{-1}w} \cdot \mathsf{K}_2^{-b^{-1}} = g_2^{dr} \cdot g_2^{-b^{-1}\hat{r}} = \mathsf{K}_4' \cdot g_2^{-b^{-1}\hat{r}}.$$

$$\mathsf{K}_5 = g_2^{b^{-1}\alpha} \cdot \mathsf{K}_1^{b^{-1} \sum\limits_{x \in \Omega_j}(w_0+w_1 x+w_2 x^2+\ldots+w_m x^m)} \cdot \mathsf{K}_3^{-b^{-1}},$$

$$= g_2^{\alpha_2+r \sum\limits_{x \in \Omega_j}(v_0+v_1 x+v_2 x^2+\ldots+v_m x^m)} \cdot g_2^{-b^{-1}\hat{r} \sum\limits_{x \in \Omega_j}(q_0+q_1 x+q_2 x^2+\ldots+q_m x^m)},$$

$$= \mathsf{K}_5' \cdot g_2^{-b^{-1}\hat{r} \sum\limits_{x \in \Omega_j}(q_0+q_1 x+q_2 x^2+\ldots+q_m x^m)}.$$

Here, $\mathcal{B}$ has implicitly set $\pi = \sum\limits_{x \in \Omega_j}(q_0+q_1 x+q_2 x^2+\ldots+q_m x^m)$. Notice that if $\hat{r} = 0$ then the key is normal; otherwise it is semi-functional secret key.

Challenge. Given the challenge set Θ^*, of size $\ell \leq m$, $\mathcal{B}$ chooses $s, \hat{s} \hookleftarrow \mathbb{Z}_p$. It then defines the challenge as κ_0 and $\mathsf{CT}_{\Theta^*} = (\mathsf{C}_0, \mathsf{C}_1, (\mathsf{C}_{2,i}, t_i)_{i \in [\ell]})$ such that,

$$\kappa_0 = g_{\mathsf{T}}^{(\alpha s+\alpha_1 \hat{s})}, \; \mathsf{C}_0 = g_1^{s+\hat{s}}, \; \mathsf{C}_1 = g_1^{bs},$$

$$\mathsf{C}_{2,i} = g_1^{s(w_0+w_1 y_i+w_2 y_i^2+\ldots+w_m y_i^m+wt_i)+\hat{s}(u_0+u_1 y_i+u_2 y_i^2+\ldots+u_m y_i^m+ct_i)},$$

$$= g_1^{s(w_0+w_1 y_i+w_2 y_i^2+\ldots+w_m y_i^m+wt_i)+\hat{s}(p_0+p_1 y_i+p_2 y_i^2+\ldots+p_m y_i^m)}$$

$$\cdot g_1^{c\hat{s}(q_0+q_1 y_i+q_2 y_i^2+\ldots+q_m y_i^m+t_i)}.$$

However, g_1^c is not available to $\mathcal{B}$. We here implicitly set $t_i = -(q_0 + q_1 y_i + q_2 y_i^2 + \ldots + q_m y_i^m)$ for each $i \in [\ell]$.

Then, $\mathsf{C}_{2,i} = g_1^{s(w_0+w_1 y_i+w_2 y_i^2+\ldots+w_m y_i^m+wt_i)+\hat{s}(p_0+p_1 y_i+p_2 y_i^2+\ldots+p_m y_i^m)}$

where i^{th} element of the challenge set Θ^* is denoted by y_i. $\mathcal{B}$ then chooses $\kappa_1 \hookleftarrow \mathcal{K}$ and returns $\left(\kappa_{\mathfrak{b}}, \mathsf{C}_0, \mathsf{C}_1, (\mathsf{C}_{2,i}, t_i)_{i \in [\ell]}\right)$ as the challenge ciphertext. Notice that, the challenge ciphertext $(\kappa_0, \mathsf{CT}_{\Theta^*})$ is identically distributed to the output of $\mathsf{SFEncrypt}(\mathsf{mpk}, \mathsf{msk}, \Theta^*)$. Hence, the ciphertext is semi-functional.

Phase-II Queries. Same as Phase-I queries.

Guess. $\mathcal{A}$ output $\mathfrak{b}' \in \{0, 1\}$. $\mathcal{B}$ outputs 1 if $\mathfrak{b} = \mathfrak{b}'$ and 0 otherwise.

As noted earlier, if $\hat{r}$ in $\mathsf{DDH}_{\mathsf{G}_2}$ problem instance is 0, then the kth secret key is normal. Otherwise the kth secret key is semi-functional. The challenge ciphertext is also constructed semi-functional.

However, we need to argue that the tags $(t_i)_{i \in [\ell]}$ output as the challenge ciphertext component are uniformly random to the view of adversary $\mathcal{A}$ who has got hold of the semi-functional k^{th} secret key containing π. This is because, according to Sect. 5.2.1, the tags that are used in the semi-functional secret key and semi-functional ciphertext, should also be uniformly random and independent.

Recall that, $\pi = \sum_{x \in \Omega_k} (q_0 + q_1 x + q_2 x^2 + \ldots + q_m x^m)$ and $t_i = -(q_0 + q_1 y_i + q_2 y_i^2 + \ldots + q_m y_i^m)$ for all $y_i \in \Theta^*$. As $\Omega_k \not\subset \Theta^*$, due to natural restriction of the security game, there exists an $x^* \in \Omega_k$ but $x^* \notin \Theta^*$. Then, $\pi = \sum_{x \in \Omega_k} (q_0 + q_1 x + q_2 x^2 + \ldots + q_m x^m) = \sum_{\substack{x \in \Omega_k \\ x \neq x^*}} (q_0 + q_1 x + q_2 x^2 + \ldots + q_m x^m) + (q_0 + q_1 (x^*) + q_2 (x^*)^2 + \ldots + q_m (x^*)^m)$. Let us denote $\pi^* = (q_0 + q_1 (x^*) + q_2 (x^*)^2 + \ldots + q_m (x^*)^m)$ and $\hat{\pi} = \sum_{x_i \in \Omega_k \setminus \{x^*\}} \pi_i$ where $\pi_i = (q_0 + q_1 x_i + q_2 x_i^2 + \ldots + q_m x_i^m)$.

Next we argue that π^* is independent of all the tags $(t_i)_{i \in [\ell]}$. The relation between π^* and $(t_1, t_2, \ldots, t_\ell)$ can be expressed as the following linear system of equations $\mathbf{t} = \mathbf{Vq}$.

$$
\begin{pmatrix} \pi^* \\ t_1 \\ t_2 \\ \vdots \\ t_\ell \end{pmatrix} = \begin{pmatrix} 1 & x^* & (x^*)^2 & \cdots & (x^*)^m \\ 1 & y_1 & (y_1)^2 & \cdots & (y_1)^m \\ 1 & y_2 & (y_2)^2 & \cdots & (y_2)^m \\ \vdots & \vdots & \vdots & \ddots & \vdots \\ 1 & y_\ell & (y_\ell)^2 & \cdots & (y_\ell)^m \end{pmatrix} \cdot \begin{pmatrix} q_0 \\ q_1 \\ q_2 \\ \vdots \\ q_m \end{pmatrix} \tag{1}
$$

Notice that $\mathbf{V}$ is Vandermonde matrix of rank $(\ell + 1)$ as $x^* \notin \Theta^* = \{y_1, y_2, \ldots, y_\ell\}$. The vector $\mathbf{q}$ is completely hidden from adversary $\mathcal{A}$ and was chosen uniformly at random. Therefore, π^* is independent of $(t_1, t_2, \ldots, t_\ell)$ and uniformly random in the view of $\mathcal{A}$.

Recall that, $\pi = \hat{\pi} + \pi^*$ where $\hat{\pi}$ is linear combination of $(k - 1)$ many m-degree polynomials as $|\Omega_k| = k$. The collection $\pi_1, \ldots, \pi_{k-1}$ and π^* also result in a full rank matrix as each encodes m-degree polynomial evaluated on distinct k points. This effectively ensures that π^* is independent of $\hat{\pi}$ as well. Thus, $\pi = \hat{\pi} + \pi^*$ is now a one-time-pad evaluation in the view of $\mathcal{A}$. Hence, π is uniformly random and independent choice from $\mathbb{Z}_p$. This completes the proof as $(\pi, (t_i)_{i \in [\ell]})$ are uniformly random quantities. Thereby, the ciphertext and k^{th} secret key is properly simulated.

If $\mathcal{A}$ can distinguish normal and semi-functional secret keys, the solver $\mathcal{B}$ will use it to break $\mathsf{DDH}_{\mathsf{G}_2}$ problem. Thus, $\left| \mathsf{Adv}_{\mathcal{A}}^{2,k-1}(\lambda) - \mathsf{Adv}_{\mathcal{A}}^{2,k}(\lambda) \right| \leq \epsilon_{\mathsf{DDH}_{\mathsf{G}_2}}$. □

Lemma 3 (Game$_{2,q}$ to Game$_3$). *For any efficient adversary $\mathcal{A}$ that makes at most q key queries,* $\left| \mathsf{Adv}_{\mathcal{A}}^{2,q}(\lambda) - \mathsf{Adv}_{\mathcal{A}}^{3}(\lambda) \right| \leq 2/p$.

Proof. In Game$_{2,q}$, all the queried secret keys and the challenge ciphertext are transformed into semi-functional. To argue that the challenge encapsulation key κ is identically distributed to uniformly random G_T element, we perform a conceptual change on the parameters of Game$_{2,q}$.

Setup. Choose $b \hookleftarrow \mathbb{Z}_p^\times$, $\alpha_1, \alpha, c, w, (u_i, w_i)_{i \in [0,m]} \hookleftarrow \mathbb{Z}_p$. It sets $\alpha_2 = b^{-1}(\alpha - \alpha_1)$, $d = b^{-1}(w - c)$, $v_i = b^{-1}(w_i - u_i)$. The public parameters are generated as $(g_1, g_1^b, (g_1^{w_i})_{i \in [0,m]}, g_1^w, g_T^\alpha)$ where $g_T = e(g_1, g_2)$. Notice that g_T is independent of α_1 as α was chosen independently.

Phase-I Queries. Given key query on Ω, choose $r, \hat{r}, \pi' \hookleftarrow \mathbb{Z}_p$. Compute the secret key $\mathsf{SK}_\Omega = (\mathsf{K}_1, \mathsf{K}_2, \mathsf{K}_3, \mathsf{K}_4, \mathsf{K}_5)$ as follows.

$$\mathsf{K}_1 = g_2^r, \mathsf{K}_2 = g_2^{cr+\hat{r}}, \mathsf{K}_3 = g_2^{\pi'} \cdot g_2^{r \sum\limits_{x \in \Omega} (u_0 + u_1 x + u_2 x^2 + \ldots + u_m x^m)},$$

$$\mathsf{K}_4 = g_2^{dr - \hat{r}b^{-1}}, \mathsf{K}_5 = g_2^{b^{-1}(\alpha - \pi')} \cdot g_2^{r \sum\limits_{x \in \Omega} (v_0 + v_1 x + v_2 x^2 + \ldots + v_m x^m)}.$$

The reduction sets $\pi' = \alpha_1 + \hat{r}\pi$. Therefore, if $\hat{r} = 0$, π can take any uniformly random value from $\mathbb{Z}_p$. On the other hand, if $\hat{r} \neq 0$, due to the independent random choice of both π' and α_1, π is uniformly random and independent. Therefore no matter what value $\hat{r}$ takes, π is uniformly random and independent. As a result, the secret keys are simulated properly.

Here the point of focus is that both K_3 and K_5 are generated using randomly chosen π' that is independent of α_1 as long as $\hat{r} \neq 0$ and none of the other key components contain α_1. The secret key SK_Ω therefore, is independent of α_1 if $\hat{r} \neq 0$. This happens with probability $1 - 1/p$.

Challenge. On challenge Θ^*, choose $s, \hat{s} \hookleftarrow \mathbb{Z}_p$ and $(t_i)_{i \in [\ell]} \hookleftarrow \mathbb{Z}_p$. Compute the ciphertext $\mathsf{CT}_{\Theta^*} = (\kappa_0, \mathsf{C}_0, \mathsf{C}_1, (\mathsf{C}_{2,i}, t_i)_{i \in [\ell]})$ where,

$$\kappa_0 = e(g_1, g_2)^{\alpha s + \alpha_1 \hat{s}} = g_T^{\alpha s} \cdot g_T^{\alpha_1 \hat{s}}, \mathsf{C}_0 = g_1^{s + \hat{s}}, \mathsf{C}_1 = g_1^{bs},$$

$$\mathsf{C}_{2,i} = g_1^{s(w_0 + w_1 y_i + w_2 y_i^2 + \ldots + w_m y_i^m + wt_i) + \hat{s}(u_0 + u_1 y_i + u_2 y_i^2 + \ldots + u_m y_i^m + ct_i)}.$$

Phase-II Queries. Same as Phase-I queries.

Guess. $\mathcal{A}$ output $\mathfrak{b}' \in \{0, 1\}$. Output 1 if $\mathfrak{b} = \mathfrak{b}'$ and 0 otherwise.

All the scalars used in mpk and $(\mathsf{SK}_{\Omega_i})_{i \in [q]}$ are independent of α_1 as we already have seen. Notice that none of the ciphertext components but κ_0 contain α_1. The entropy due to α_1 thus makes κ_0 random as long as $\hat{s} \neq 0$. In fact, this allows the replacement of κ_0 by a uniform random choice $\kappa_1 \hookleftarrow \mathcal{K}$ provided $\hat{s} \neq 0$. Recall that, this exactly is the situation of Game_3. Thus, $\left|\mathsf{Adv}_{\mathcal{A}}^{2;q}(\lambda) - \mathsf{Adv}_{\mathcal{A}}^3(\lambda)\right| \leq \Pr[\hat{r} = 0] + \Pr[\hat{s} = 0] \leq 2/p$.

Notice that, $\kappa_\mathfrak{b}$ output in Game_3 completely hides $\mathfrak{b}$. Thus, for any adversary $\mathcal{A}$, the advantage $\mathsf{Adv}_{\mathcal{A}}^3(\lambda) = 0$. $\qquad\square$

5.3 Applications

Katz et al. [20] described a few black-box transformations from SPE to well known cryptographic protocols. We can perform those transformations on our adaptive-secure SPE_2 construction. Note that, all these transformations were designed for small-universe SPE. We therefore restrict our large-universe SPE_2 construction to small universe. This is done by considering the universes $\mathcal{U} = \{1, \cdots, n\}$ and $\mathcal{U}' = \{1, \cdots, \mathfrak{n}\}$ where $\mathcal{U}$ is universe for protocol to be designed and $\mathcal{U}'$ is the universe for underlying SPE_2 for some $\mathfrak{n} \in \mathbb{N}$. Note that, we formalize the black-box transformation [20] as a function called Encode.

WIBE. The generic transformation of [20] allows construction of WIBE [1] which supports presence of wildcard in the data-index. Here, any index (key-index, data-index alike) will be first processed bit-wise into a ordered set of double size (i.e. $\mathfrak{n} = 2n$). Informally, Encode expands $z \in \{0, 1, *\}^n$ to $T \in \{0, 1\}^{\mathfrak{n}}$ where $T[2i - 1]$ stores z_i and $T[2i]$ stores $\bar{z}_i$ if $z_i \in \{0, 1\}$. In case of $z_i = *$, both $T[2i-1]$ and $T[2i]$ stores 1. Then $S^{(z)}$ is defined as the set that stores all indexes that are set in T. The WIBE KeyGen and Encrypt is defined as $\mathsf{SPE_2.KeyGen}$ and $\mathsf{SPE_2.Encrypt}$ running on such set S respectively. We can achieve a WKD-IBE [2] in a similar way with the exception that now, the wildcard is present in the key-index.

CP-ABE. As [20] mentions, the most interesting black-box transformation of SPE is that it can achieve a secure CP-ABE (though restricted to DNF formula only) with constant-size key. Intuitively, an attribute set A can satisfy a DNF formula $C_1 \vee C_2 \vee \cdots C_t$ where each C_j represents a conjunction over some subset of the attributes if $\exists j \in [t]$ such that $C_j \subseteq \mathsf{A}$. This is done by associating the clauses C_j as well as A to corresponding *revocation list* i.e. $\mathcal{U} \setminus C_j$ and $\mathcal{U} \setminus \mathsf{A}$ and perform the subset predicate evaluation: $\mathcal{U} \setminus \mathsf{A} \subseteq \mathcal{U} \setminus C_j$ where $\mathcal{U}$ denotes the attribute universe of size n. Precisely, Encode takes input $Z \in \{C_1, \cdots, C_t, \mathsf{A}\}$ and outputs $S^{(Z)} = \{i \in \mathcal{U}' : T^{(Z)}[i] = 1\}$ where for all $i \in \{1, 2, \cdots, \mathfrak{n}\}$ (here $\mathfrak{n} = n$).

$$T^{(Z)}[i] = \begin{cases} 0 & \text{if } i \in Z, \\ 1 & \text{if } i \notin Z. \end{cases}$$

Table 1. Comparison of efficient standard model WIBE schemes.

WIBE schemes	|mpk|	|SK|	|CT|	Decrypt	Security	Assumption
BBG-WIBE [1]	$(n + 4)\mathsf{G}$	$(n + 2)\mathsf{G}$	$(n + 2)\mathsf{G} + \mathsf{G_T}$	2[P]	Adaptive	n-BDHI
Wa-WIBE [1]	$((\ell + 1)n + 3)\mathsf{G}$	$(n + 1)\mathsf{G}$	$((\ell + 1)n + 2)\mathsf{G} + \mathsf{G_T}$	$(n + 1)$[P]	Adaptive	DBDH
SPE-1 [20]	$(2n + 2)\mathsf{G_1} + \mathsf{G_T}$	$\mathsf{G_2} + \mathbb{Z}_p$	$(2n + 1)\mathsf{G_1} + \mathsf{G_T}$	1[P]	Selective	q-BDHI
SPE-2 [20]	$(2n + 1)\mathsf{G_1} + 2\mathsf{G_2}$	$\mathsf{G_1} + \mathsf{G_2}$	$2n\mathsf{G_1} + \mathsf{G_2} + \mathsf{G_T}$	2[P]	Selective	DBDH
SPE$_2$	$(2n + 6)\mathsf{G_1} + \mathsf{G_T}$	$5\mathsf{G_2}$	$(n + 2)\mathsf{G_1} + \mathsf{G_T} + n\mathbb{Z}_p$	3[P]	Adaptive	SXDH

Table 2. Comparison of efficient standard model DNF schemes.

DNF schemes	|mpk|	|SK|	|CT|	Decrypt	Security	Assumption
SPE-1 [20]	$(n + 2)\mathsf{G_1} + \mathsf{G_T}$	$\mathsf{G_2} + \mathbb{Z}_p$	$\gamma((n + 1)\mathsf{G_1} + \mathsf{G_T})$	1[P]	Selective	q-BDHI
SPE-2 [20]	$(n + 1)\mathsf{G_1} + 2\mathsf{G_2}$	$\mathsf{G_1} + \mathsf{G_2}$	$\gamma(2n\mathsf{G_1} + \mathsf{G_2} + \mathsf{G_T})$	2[P]	Selective	DBDH
SPE$_2$	$(n + 3)\mathsf{G_1} + \mathsf{G_T}$	$5\mathsf{G_2}$	$\gamma((n + 2)\mathsf{G_1} + \mathsf{G_T} + n\mathbb{Z}_p)$	3[P]	Adaptive	SXDH

We now compare the black-box transformation [20] applied on SPE$_2$ in terms of performance to previous WIBE and DNF schemes (both dedicated and due to black-box transformation [20]). From Table 1, we see that both adaptive secure BBG-WIBE and Wa-WIBE attain much bigger secret key size. Although, other parameter sizes are quite competitive to ours, Wa-WIBE is proved secure under parameterized assumption. In case of the second one however, the all the parameters blow up. Our construction not only attains similar parameter size as the selective secure constructions due to black-box transformation [20], is also proved adaptive secure under standard assumption. In case of DNF in Table 2, ours is the only scheme that achieve adaptive security and still enjoy constant-size key and constant number of pairing evaluations during decryption. Again, as compared to black-box transformation [20], our parameter sizes are quite competitive. We denote size of public key by $|\mathsf{mpk}|$, size of secret key by $|\mathsf{SK}|$, size of ciphertext by $|\mathsf{CT}|$, number of primitive operations required in Decrypt. Here n denotes depth of hierarchy, ℓ is bit-length of identity in Wa-IBE [23], γ is number of disjunctive clauses in a DNF formula and [P] denotes number of pairing operations.

6   Conclusion

We presented two large universe constructions of subset predicate encryption (SPE). Both the constructions achieve constant-size secret key and efficient decryption. First construction achieves constant-size ciphertext as well and is proven selectively secure in a restricted model. Our second and main construction achieves adaptive security in the asymmetric prime order bilinear group setting under the SXDH assumption. The ciphertext size in this construction is of $\mathcal{O}(|\Theta^*|)$. It is an interesting open problem to design an SPE with constant-size ciphertext without the kind of restriction we imposed in the selective security model so is any improvement of our second construction in terms of the ciphertext size.

References

1. Abdalla, M., Catalano, D., Dent, A.W., Malone-Lee, J., Neven, G., Smart, N.P.: Identity-based encryption gone wild. In: Bugliesi, M., Preneel, B., Sassone, V., Wegener, I. (eds.) ICALP 2006. LNCS, vol. 4052, pp. 300–311. Springer, Heidelberg (2006). https://doi.org/10.1007/11787006_26
2. Abdalla, M., Kiltz, E., Neven, G.: Generalized key delegation for hierarchical identity-based encryption. In: Biskup, J., López, J. (eds.) ESORICS 2007. LNCS, vol. 4734, pp. 139–154. Springer, Heidelberg (2007). https://doi.org/10.1007/978-3-540-74835-9_10
3. Attrapadung, N.: Dual system encryption via doubly selective security: framework, fully secure functional encryption for regular languages, and more. In: Nguyen, P.Q., Oswald, E. (eds.) EUROCRYPT 2014. LNCS, vol. 8441, pp. 557–577. Springer, Heidelberg (2014). https://doi.org/10.1007/978-3-642-55220-5_31
4. Attrapadung, N.: Dual system encryption framework in prime-order groups. In: IACR Cryptology ePrint Archive 2015, 390 (2015)

5. Attrapadung, N., Libert, B.: Functional encryption for inner product: achieving constant-size ciphertexts with adaptive security or support for negation. In: Nguyen, P.Q., Pointcheval, D. (eds.) PKC 2010. LNCS, vol. 6056, pp. 384–402. Springer, Heidelberg (2010). https://doi.org/10.1007/978-3-642-13013-7_23

6. Boneh, D., Boyen, X.: Efficient selective-ID secure identity-based encryption without random oracles. In: Cachin, C., Camenisch, J.L. (eds.) EUROCRYPT 2004. LNCS, vol. 3027, pp. 223–238. Springer, Heidelberg (2004). https://doi.org/10.1007/978-3-540-24676-3_14

7. Boneh, D., Franklin, M.: Identity-based encryption from the Weil pairing. In: Kilian, J. (ed.) CRYPTO 2001. LNCS, vol. 2139, pp. 213–229. Springer, Heidelberg (2001). https://doi.org/10.1007/3-540-44647-8_13

8. Boneh, D., Gentry, C., Waters, B.: Collusion resistant broadcast encryption with short ciphertexts and private keys. In: Shoup, V. (ed.) CRYPTO 2005. LNCS, vol. 3621, pp. 258–275. Springer, Heidelberg (2005). https://doi.org/10.1007/11535218_16

9. Boyen, X.: General *Ad Hoc* encryption from exponent inversion IBE. In: Naor, M. (ed.) EUROCRYPT 2007. LNCS, vol. 4515, pp. 394–411. Springer, Heidelberg (2007). https://doi.org/10.1007/978-3-540-72540-4_23

10. Chase, M., Meiklejohn, S.: Déjà Q: using dual systems to revisit q-type assumptions. In: Nguyen, P.Q., Oswald, E. (eds.) EUROCRYPT 2014. LNCS, vol. 8441, pp. 622–639. Springer, Heidelberg (2014). https://doi.org/10.1007/978-3-642-55220-5_34

11. Chatterjee, S., Mukherjee, S.: Large universe subset predicate encryption based on static assumption (without random oracle). Cryptology ePrint Archive, Report 2018/1190 (2018). https://eprint.iacr.org/2018/1190

12. Chen, J., Gay, R., Wee, H.: Improved dual system ABE in prime-order groups via predicate encodings. In: Oswald, E., Fischlin, M. (eds.) EUROCRYPT 2015. LNCS, vol. 9057, pp. 595–624. Springer, Heidelberg (2015). https://doi.org/10.1007/978-3-662-46803-6_20

13. Chen, J., Gong, J.: ABE with tag made easy. In: Takagi, T., Peyrin, T. (eds.) ASIACRYPT 2017. LNCS, vol. 10625, pp. 35–65. Springer, Cham (2017). https://doi.org/10.1007/978-3-319-70697-9_2

14. Delerablée, C.: Identity-based broadcast encryption with constant size ciphertexts and private keys. In: Kurosawa, K. (ed.) ASIACRYPT 2007. LNCS, vol. 4833, pp. 200–215. Springer, Heidelberg (2007). https://doi.org/10.1007/978-3-540-76900-2_12

15. Delerablée, C., Paillier, P., Pointcheval, D.: Fully collusion secure dynamic broadcast encryption with constant-size ciphertexts or decryption keys. In: Takagi, T., Okamoto, E., Okamoto, T., Okamoto, T. (eds.) Pairing 2007. LNCS, vol. 4575, pp. 39–59. Springer, Heidelberg (2007). https://doi.org/10.1007/978-3-540-73489-5_4

16. Galbraith, S.D., Paterson, K.G., Smart, N.P.: Pairings for cryptographers. Discrete Appl. Math. **156**(16), 3113–3121 (2008). Applications of Algebra to Cryptography

17. Gong, J., Libert, B., Ramanna, S.C.: Compact IBBE and Fuzzy IBE from simple assumptions. In: Catalano, D., De Prisco, R. (eds.) SCN 2018. LNCS, vol. 11035, pp. 563–582. Springer, Cham (2018). https://doi.org/10.1007/978-3-319-98113-0_30

18. Goyal, V., Pandey, O., Sahai, A., Waters, B.: Attribute-based encryption for fine-grained access control of encrypted data. In: ACM CCS, pp. 89–98 (2006)

19. Jutla, C.S., Roy, A.: Shorter quasi-adaptive NIZK proofs for linear subspaces. J. Cryptol. **30**(4), 1116–1156 (2017)

20. Katz, J., Maffei, M., Malavolta, G., Schröder, D.: Subset predicate encryption and its applications. In: Capkun, S., Chow, S.S.M. (eds.) CANS 2017. LNCS, vol. 11261, pp. 115–134. Springer, Cham (2018). https://doi.org/10.1007/978-3-030-02641-7_6
21. Katz, J., Sahai, A., Waters, B.: Predicate encryption supporting disjunctions, polynomial equations, and inner products. In: Smart, N. (ed.) EUROCRYPT 2008. LNCS, vol. 4965, pp. 146–162. Springer, Heidelberg (2008). https://doi.org/10.1007/978-3-540-78967-3_9
22. Ramanna, S.C., Sarkar, P.: Efficient adaptively secure IBBE from the SXDH assumption. IEEE IT **62**(10), 5709–5726 (2016)
23. Waters, B.: Efficient identity-based encryption without random Oracles. In: Cramer, R. (ed.) EUROCRYPT 2005. LNCS, vol. 3494, pp. 114–127. Springer, Heidelberg (2005). https://doi.org/10.1007/11426639_7
24. Waters, B.: Dual system encryption: realizing fully secure IBE and HIBE under simple assumptions. In: Halevi, S. (ed.) CRYPTO 2009. LNCS, vol. 5677, pp. 619–636. Springer, Heidelberg (2009). https://doi.org/10.1007/978-3-642-03356-8_36
25. Wee, H.: Dual system encryption via predicate encodings. In: Lindell, Y. (ed.) TCC 2014. LNCS, vol. 8349, pp. 616–637. Springer, Heidelberg (2014). https://doi.org/10.1007/978-3-642-54242-8_26
26. Wee, H.: Déjà Q: Encore! un petit IBE. In: Kushilevitz, E., Malkin, T. (eds.) TCC 2016. LNCS, vol. 9563, pp. 237–258. Springer, Heidelberg (2016). https://doi.org/10.1007/978-3-662-49099-0_9

An Improved RNS Variant of the BFV Homomorphic Encryption Scheme

Shai Halevi[1], Yuriy Polyakov[2(✉)], and Victor Shoup[3]

[1] IBM Research, Yorktown Heights, USA
[2] New Jersey Institute of Technology, Newark, USA
polyakov@njit.edu
[3] New York University, New York, USA

Abstract. We present an optimized variant of the Brakerski/Fan-Vercauteren (BFV) homomorphic encryption scheme and its efficient implementation in PALISADE. Our algorithmic improvements focus on optimizing decryption and homomorphic multiplication in the Residue Number System (RNS), using the Chinese Remainder Theorem (CRT) to represent and manipulate the large coefficients in the ciphertext polynomials. These improvements are based on our original general-purpose techniques for CRT basis extension and scaling that can be applied to many other lattice-based cryptographic primitives. Our variant is simpler and significantly more efficient than the RNS variant proposed by Bajard *et al.* both in terms of noise growth and the computational complexity of the underlying CRT basis extension and scaling procedures.

Keywords: Lattice-based cryptography · Homomorphic encryption · Post-quantum cryptography · Residue number systems · Software implementation

1 Introduction

Homomorphic encryption has been an area of active research since the first design of a Fully Homomorphic Encryption (FHE) scheme by Gentry [9]. FHE allows performing arbitrary secure computations over encrypted sensitive data without ever decrypting them. One of the potential applications is to outsource computations to a public cloud without compromising data privacy.

A salient property of contemporary FHE schemes is that ciphertexts are "noisy", where the noise increases with every homomorphic operation, and decryption starts failing once the noise becomes too large. This is addressed by setting the parameters large enough to accommodate some level of noise,

S. Halevi—Supported by the Defense Advanced Research Projects Agency (DARPA) and Army Research Office (ARO) under Contract No. W911NF-15-C-0236.
Y. Polyakov—Supported by the Sloan Foundation and Defense Advanced Research Projects Agency (DARPA) and Army Research Office (ARO) under Contracts No. W911NF-15-C-0226 and W911NF-15-C-0233.

© Springer Nature Switzerland AG 2019
M. Matsui (Ed.): CT-RSA 2019, LNCS 11405, pp. 83–105, 2019.
https://doi.org/10.1007/978-3-030-12612-4_5

and using Gentry's "bootstrapping" technique to reduce the noise once it gets too close to the decryption-error level. However, the large parameters make homomorphic computations quite slow, and so significant effort was devoted to constructing more efficient schemes. Two of the most promising schemes in terms of practical performance have been the BGV scheme of Brakerski, Gentry and Vaikuntanathan [6], and the Fan-Vercauteren variant of Brakerski's scale-invariant scheme [5,8], which we call here the BFV scheme. Both of these schemes rely on the hardness of the Ring Learning With Errors (RLWE) problem.

Both schemes manipulate elements in large cyclotomic rings, modulo integers with many hundreds of bits. Implementing the necessary multi-precision modular arithmetic is expensive, and one way of making it faster is to use a "Residue Number System" (RNS) to represent the big integers. Namely, the big modulus q is chosen as a smooth integer, $q = \prod_i q_i$, where the factors q_i are same-size, pairwise coprime, single-precision integers (typically of size 30–60 bits). Using the Chinese Remainder Theorem (CRT), an integer $x \in \mathbb{Z}_q$ can be represented by its CRT components $\{x_i = x \bmod q_i \in \mathbb{Z}_{q_i}\}_i$, and operations on x in $\mathbb{Z}_q$ can be implemented by applying the same operations to each CRT component x_i in its own ring $\mathbb{Z}_{q_i}$.

Unfortunately, both BGV and BFV feature some scaling operations that cannot be directly implemented on the CRT components. In both schemes there is sometimes a need to interpret $x \in \mathbb{Z}_q$ as a rational number (say in the interval $[-q/2, q/2)$) and then either lift x to a larger ring $\mathbb{Z}_Q$ for $Q > q$, or to scale it down and round to get $y = \lceil \delta x \rfloor \in \mathbb{Z}_t$ (for some $\delta \ll 1$ and accordingly $t \ll q$). These operations seem to require that x be translated from its CRT representation back to standard "positional" representation, but computing these translations back and forth will negate the gains from using RNS to begin with.

While implementations of the BGV scheme using CRT representation are known (e.g., [10,13]), implementing BFV in this manner seems harder. One difference is that BFV features more of these scaling operations than BGV. Another is that in BGV numbers are typically scaled by just single-precision factors, while in BFV these factors are often big, of order similar to the multi-precision modulus q. An implementation of the BFV scheme using CRT representation was recently reported by Bajard et al. [3], featuring significant speedup as compared to earlier implementations such as in [16]. This implementation, however, uses somewhat complex procedures, and moreover these procedures incur an increase in the ciphertext noise.

In the current work we propose simpler and more efficient procedures for the CRT-based scaling and lifting as compared to the procedures in [3]. The same techniques are also applicable to other scale-invariant homomorphic encryption schemes, such as YASHE and YASHE' [4], and many other lattice-based cryptographic primitives that require CRT-based scaling.

We implemented our procedures in the PALISADE library [19]. We evaluate the runtime performance of decryption and homomorphic multiplication in the range of multiplicative depths from 1 to 100. For example, the runtimes for depth-20 decryption and homomorphic multiplication are 3.1 and 62 ms, respectively, which can already support outsourced-computing applications with latencies up to few seconds, even without bootstrapping.

Our Contributions. We propose new procedures for CRT basis extension and scaling in RNS using floating-point arithmetic for some intermediate computations. Our procedures have a low probability of introducing small approximation errors, but in the context of homomorphic operations these errors are inconsequential. As we explain in Sect. 4.5, they increase the ciphertext noise after homomorphic multiplications by at most 2 bits for any depth of the multiplication circuit (typically significantly less than 1 bit), and those contributions were not observable in our experiments. We apply these techniques to develop:

- A BFV decryption procedure supporting CRT moduli up to 59 bits, using extended precision floating-point arithmetic natively available in x86 architectures[1].
- A BFV homomorphic multiplication procedure that has practically the same noise requirements as the textbook BFV.
- A multi-threaded CPU implementation of our BFV variant in PALISADE.

Comparison with the RNS Variant by Bajard et al. [3][2]. Al Badawi *et al.* [2] compare the complexity and performance of decryption and homomorphic multiplication in our variant and the one proposed in [3]. For the experimental comparison, they implemented both variants in PALISADE (CPU) and DSI_BFV (GPU). Their analysis shows that the practical (experimentally observed) noise growth of our variant is much lower. For instance, our variant supports the multiplicative depth of 35 at $n = 2^{15}$ and $\log_2 q = 600$ while the Bajard *et al.* variant can support only the depth of 26. They also demonstrate that the computational complexity and actual runtimes for our variant both in GPU and CPU are lower (even when the noise growth difference is ignored) in all cases, except for the decryption when the size of CRT moduli is 60 bits. The combined effect of smaller noise growth and computational complexity is a speed-up of 2x or more in homomorphic multiplication for the same depth.

2   Notations and Basic Procedures

For an integer $n \geq 2$, we identify below the ring $\mathbb{Z}_n$ with its representation in the symmetric interval $\mathbb{Z} \cap [-n/2, n/2)$. For an arbitrary real number x, we denote by $[x]_n$ the reduction of x into that interval (namely the real number $x' \in [-n/2, n/2)$ such that $x' - x$ is an integer divisible by n). We also denote by $\lfloor x \rfloor$, $\lceil x \rceil$, and $\lceil x \rfloor$ the rounding of x to an integer down, up, and to the nearest integer, respectively. We denote vectors by boldface letters, and extend the notations $\lfloor x \rfloor$, $\lceil x \rceil$, $\lceil x \rfloor$ to vectors element-wise.

---

[1] Larger CRT moduli can be supported using "double double" floating-points.
[2] A more detailed comparison is presented in the extended version of this paper [12].

Throughout this paper we fix a set of k co-prime moduli $q_1, \ldots, q_k$ (all integers larger than 1), and let their product be $q = \prod_{i=1}^{k} q_i$. For all $i \in \{1, \ldots, k\}$, we also denote

$$q_i^* = q/q_i \in \mathbb{Z} \quad \text{and} \quad \tilde{q}_i = q_i^{*-1} \pmod{q_i} \in \mathbb{Z}_{q_i}, \tag{1}$$

namely, $\tilde{q}_i \in \left[-\frac{q_i}{2}, \frac{q_i}{2}\right)$ and $q_i^* \cdot \tilde{q}_i = 1 \pmod{q_i}$.

Complexity Measures. In our setting we always assume that the moduli q_i are single-precision integers (i.e. $|q_i| < 2^{63}$), and that operations modulo q_i are inexpensive. We assign unit cost to mod-q_i multiplication and ignore additions, and analyze the complexity of our routines just by counting the number of multiplications. Our procedures also include floating-point operations, and here too we assign unit cost to floating-point multiplications and divisions (typically in "double float" format as per IEEE 754) and ignore additions.

2.1 CRT Representation

We denote the CRT representation of an integer $x \in \mathbb{Z}_q$ relative to the CRT basis $\{q_1, \ldots, q_k\}$ by $x \sim (x_1, \ldots, x_k)$ with $x_i = [x]_{q_i} \in \mathbb{Z}_{q_i}$. The formula expressing x in terms of the x_i's is $x = \sum_{i=1}^{k} x_i \cdot \tilde{q}_i \cdot q_i^* \pmod{q}$. This formula can be used in more than one way to "reconstruct" the value $x \in \mathbb{Z}_q$ from the x_i's. In this work we use in particular the following two facts:

$$x = \Big(\sum_{i=1}^{k} \underbrace{[x_i \cdot \tilde{q}_i]_{q_i} \cdot q_i^*}_{\in \mathbb{Z}_q} \Big) - v \cdot q \text{ for some } v \in \mathbb{Z}, \tag{2}$$

$$\text{and} \quad x = \Big(\sum_{i=1}^{k} \underbrace{x_i \cdot \tilde{q}_i \cdot q_i^*}_{\in \left[-\frac{q_i q}{4}, \frac{q_i q}{4}\right)} \Big) - v' \cdot q \quad \text{for some } v' \in \mathbb{Z}. \tag{3}$$

2.2 CRT Basis Extension

Let $x \in \mathbb{Z}_q$ be given in CRT representation $(x_1, \ldots, x_k)$, and suppose we want to extend the CRT basis by computing $[x]_p \in \mathbb{Z}_p$ for some other modulus $p > 1$. Using Eq. 2, we would like to compute $[x]_p = \left[\left(\sum_{i=1}^{k} [x_i \cdot \tilde{q}_i]_{q_i} \cdot q_i^* \right) - v \cdot q \right]_p$. The main challenge here is to compute v (which is an integer in $\mathbb{Z}_k$). The formula for v is:

$$v = \left\lceil \Big(\sum_{i=1}^{k} [x_i \cdot \tilde{q}_i]_{q_i} \cdot q_i^* \Big) / q \right\rfloor = \left\lceil \sum_{i=1}^{k} [x_i \cdot \tilde{q}_i]_{q_i} \cdot \frac{q_i^*}{q} \right\rfloor = \left\lceil \sum_{i=1}^{k} \frac{[x_i \cdot \tilde{q}_i]_{q_i}}{q_i} \right\rfloor.$$

To get v, we compute for every $i \in \{1, \ldots, k\}$ the element $y_i := [x_i \cdot \tilde{q}_i]_{q_i}$ (using single-precision integer arithmetic), and next the rational number $z_i := y_i / q_i$

(in floating-point). Then we sum up all the z_i's and round them to get v. Once we have the value of v, as well as all the y_i's, we can directly compute Eq. 2 modulo p to get $[x]_p = \left[\left(\sum_{i=1}^{k} y_i \cdot [q_i^*]_p \right) - v \cdot [q]_p \right]_p$.

In our setting p and the q_i's are parameters that can be pre-processed. In particular we pre-compute all the values $[q_i^*]_p$'s and $[q]_p$, so the last equation becomes just an inner-product of two $(k+1)$-vectors in $\mathbb{Z}_p$.

Complexity Analysis. The computation of v requires k single-precision integer multiplications to compute the y_i's, then k floating-point division operations to compute the z_i's, and then some additions and one rounding operation. In total it takes k integer and $k+1$ floating-point operations. When p is a single-precision integer, the last inner product takes $k+1$ integer multiplications, so the entire procedure takes $2k+1$ integer and $k+1$ floating-point operations.

For larger p we may need to do $k+1$ multi-precision multiplications, but we may be able to use CRT representation again. When $p = \prod_{j=1}^{k'} p_j$ for single-precision co-prime p_j's, we can compute v only once and then compute the last inner product for each p_i (provided that we pre-computed $[q_i^*]_{p_j}$'s and $[q]_{p_j}$ for all i and j). The overall complexity in this case will be $kk' + k + k'$ integer operations and $k+1$ floating-point operations.

Correctness. The only source of errors in this procedure is the floating-point operations when computing v: Instead of the exact values $z_i = y_i/q_i$, we compute their floating-point approximations z_i^* (with error ϵ_i), and so we obtain $v^* = \lceil \sum_i (z_i + \epsilon_i) \rceil$ which may be different from $v = \lceil \sum_i z_i \rceil$.

Since the z_i's are all in $[-\frac{1}{2}, \frac{1}{2})$, then using IEEE 754 double floats we have that the ϵ_i's are bounded in magnitude by 2^{-53}, and therefore the overall magnitude of the error term $\epsilon := \sum \epsilon_i$ is bounded, $|\epsilon| < k \cdot 2^{-53}$. If we assume $k \leq 32$, this gives us $|\epsilon| < 2^{-48}$. (Similarly, if we use single floats we get $|\epsilon| < 2^{-19}$.)

When applying the procedure above, we should generally check that the resulting v^* that we get is outside the possible-error region $\mathbb{Z} + \frac{1}{2} \pm \epsilon$. If v^* falls in the error region, we can re-run this procedure using higher precision (and hence smaller ϵ) until the result is outside the error region.

It turns out that for our use cases, we do not need to check for these error conditions, and can often get by with a rather low precision for this computation. One reason for this is that for our uses, even if we do incur a floating-point approximation error, it only results in a small contribution to ciphertext noise, which has no practical significance.

Moreover, we almost never see these approximation errors, because the value $\sum_i z_i$ that we want to approximate equals x/q modulo 1. When we use that procedure in our implementation, we sometimes have (pseudo)random values of $x \in \mathbb{Z}_q$, in which case the probability that the result falls in the error region is bounded by $2|\epsilon|$. In other cases, we even have a guarantee that $|x| \ll q$ (say $|x| < q/4$), so we know a-priori that the value will always fall outside of the error region. For more details, see Sects. 2.4 and 4.5.

Comparison to Other Approaches for Computing v. Two exact approaches for computing v are presented in [22] and [15]. The first approach introduces an auxiliary modulus and performs the CRT computations both for p and the extra modulus, thus significantly increasing the number of integer operations and also increasing the implementation complexity [22]. The second approach computes successive fixed-point approximations until the computed value of v is outside the error region (in one setting) or computes the exact value (in another setting with higher complexity) [15]. Both of these techniques incur higher computational costs than our method.

2.3   Simple Scaling in CRT Representation

Let $x \in \mathbb{Z}_q$ be given in CRT representation $(x_1, \ldots, x_k)$, and let $t \in \mathbb{Z}$ be an integer modulus $t \geq 2$. We want to "scale down" x by a t/q factor, namely to compute the integer $y = \lceil t/q \cdot x \rfloor \in \mathbb{Z}_t$. We do it using Eq. 3, as follows:

$$y := \left\lceil \frac{t}{q} \cdot x \right\rfloor = \left\lceil \left(\sum_{i=1}^{k} x_i \cdot (\tilde{q}_i \cdot \frac{t}{q_i}) \right) \right\rfloor - v' \cdot t = \left[\left\lceil \left(\sum_{i=1}^{k} x_i \cdot (\tilde{q}_i \cdot \frac{t}{q_i}) \right) \right\rfloor \right]_t. \quad (4)$$

The last equation follows since the two sides are congruent modulo t and are both in the interval $[-t/2, t/2)$, hence they must be equal.

In our context, t and the q_i's are parameters that we can pre-process (while the x_i's are computed on-line). We pre-compute the rational numbers $t\tilde{q}_i/q_i \in [-t/2, t/2)$, separated into their integer and fractional parts:

$$t\tilde{q}_i/q_i \;=\; \omega_i + \theta_i, \quad \text{with}\, \omega_i \in \mathbb{Z}_t \text{ and } \theta_i \in [-\tfrac{1}{2}, \tfrac{1}{2}).$$

With the ω_i's and θ_i pre-computed, we take as input the x_i's, compute the two sums $w := \left[\sum_i x_i \omega_i \right]_t$ and $v := \left\lceil \sum_i x_i \theta_i \right\rfloor$, (using integer arithmetic for w and floating-point arithmetic for v), then output $[w + v]_t$.

Complexity Analysis. The procedure above takes k floating-point multiplications, some additions, and one rounding to compute v, and then an inner product mod t between two $(k+1)$-vectors: the single-precision vector $(x_1, \ldots, x_k, 1)$ and the mod-t vector $(\omega_1, \ldots, \omega_k, v)$. When the modulus t is a single-precision integer, the ω_i's are also single-precision integers, and hence the inner product takes k integer multiplications. The total complexity is therefore $k + 1$ floating-point operations and k integer modular multiplications.

For a larger t we may need to do $O(k)$ multi-precision operations to compute the inner product. But in some cases we can also use CRT representation here: For $t = \prod_{j=1}^{k'} t_j$ (with the t_j's co-prime), we can represent each $\omega_i \in \mathbb{Z}_t$ in the CRT basis $\omega_{i,j} = [\omega_i]_{t_j}$. We can then compute the result y in the same CRT basis, $y_j = [y]_{t_j}$ by setting $w_j = \left[\sum_i x_i \omega_{i,j} \right]_{t_j}$ for all j, and then $y_j = [v + w_j]_{t_j}$. This will still take only $k + 1$ floating-point operations, but kk' modular multiplications.

Correctness. The only source of errors in this routine is the computation of $v := \lceil \sum_i x_i \theta_i \rceil$: Since we only keep the θ_i's with limited precision, we need to worry about the error exceeding the precision. Let $\tilde{\theta}_i$ be the floating-point values that we keep, while θ_i are the exact values ($\theta_i = t\tilde{q}_i/q - \omega_i$) and ϵ_i are the errors, $\epsilon_i = \tilde{\theta}_i - \theta_i$. Since $|\tilde{\theta}_i| \leq \frac{1}{2}$, then for IEEE 754 double floats we have $|\epsilon_i| < 2^{-53}$. The value that our procedure computes for v is therefore $\tilde{v} := \lceil \sum_i x_i(\theta_i + \epsilon_i) \rfloor$, which may be different from $v := \lceil \sum_i x_i \theta_i \rfloor$.

We can easily control the magnitude of the error term $\sum x_i \epsilon_i$ by limiting the size of the q_i's: Since $|x_i| < q_i/2$ for all i, then $|\sum_i x_i \epsilon_i| < 2^{-54} \cdot \sum_i q_i$. For example, if $k < 32$, as long as all our moduli satisfy $q_i \leq 2^{47} < 2^{54}/4k$, we are ensured that $|\sum x_i \epsilon_i| < 1/4$.

If we use the extended double floating-point precision ("long double" in C/C++) natively supported by x86 architectures, which stores 64 bits in the significand as compared to 52 bits in the IEEE 754 double float, we can increase the upper bound for the moduli up to $q_i \leq 2^{59}$.

When using the scaling procedure for decryption, we can keep $y' = \lceil t/q \cdot x \rfloor$ close to an integer by controlling the ciphertext noise. For example, we can ensure that y' (and therefore also v) is within $1/4$ of an integer, and thus if we also restrict the size of the q_i's as above, then we always get the correct result. Using the scaling procedure in other settings may require more care, see the next section for a discussion.

2.4 Complex Scaling in CRT Representation

The scaling procedure above was made simpler by the fact that we scale by a t/q factor, where the original integer is in $\mathbb{Z}_q$ and the result is computed modulo t. During homomorphic multiplication, however, we have a more complicated setting: Over there we have three parameters t, p, q, where $q = \prod_{i=1}^{k} q_i$ as before, we similarly have $p = \prod_{j=1}^{k'} p_j$, and we know that p is co-prime with q and $p \gg t$.

The input is $x \in \mathbb{Z} \cap [-qp/2t, qp/2t) \subset \mathbb{Z}_{qp}$, represented in the CRT basis $\{q_1, \ldots, q_k, p_1, \ldots, p_{k'}\}$. We need to scale it by a t/q factor and round, and we want the result modulo q in the CRT basis $\{q_1, \ldots, q_k\}$. Namely, we want to compute $y := \left[\lceil t/q \cdot x \rfloor \right]_q$. This complex scaling is accomplished in two steps:

1. First we essentially apply the CRT scaling procedure from Sect. 2.3 using $q' = qp$ and $t' = tp$, computing $y' := [\lceil tp/qp \cdot x \rfloor]_p$ (which we can think of as computing y' modulo tp and then discarding the mod-t CRT component). Note that since $x \in [-qp/2t, qp/2t)$ then $\lceil tp/qp \cdot x \rfloor \in [-p/2, p/2)$. Hence even though we computed y' modulo p, we know that $y' = \lceil t/q \cdot x \rfloor$ without modular reduction.
2. Having a representation of y' relative to CRT basis $\{p_1, \ldots, p_{k'}\}$, we extend this basis using the procedure from Sect. 2.2, adding $[y']_{q_i}$ for all the q_i's. Then we just discard the mod-p_j CRT components, thus getting a representation of $y = [y']_q$.

The second step is a straightforward application of the procedure from Sect. 2.2, but the first step needs some explanation. The input consists of the CRT components $x_i = [x]_{q_i}$ and $x'_j = [x]_{p_j}$, and we denote $Q := qp$, $Q_i^* := Q/q_i = q_i^* p$, $Q_j'^* := Q/p_j = qp_j^*$, and also $\tilde{Q}_i = [(Q_i^*)^{-1}]_{q_i}$ and $\tilde{Q}'_j = [(Q_j'^*)^{-1}]_{p_j}$. Then by Eq. 3 we have

$$\frac{t}{q} \cdot x = \frac{t}{q}\Big(\sum_{i=1}^{k} x_i \tilde{Q}_i Q_i^* + \sum_{j=1}^{k'} x'_j \tilde{Q}'_j Q_j'^* - v'Q\Big) = \sum_{i=1}^{k} x_i \cdot \frac{t\tilde{Q}_i p}{q_i} + \sum_{j=1}^{k'} x'_j \cdot t\tilde{Q}'_j p_j^* - tv'p.$$

Reducing the above expression modulo any one of the p_j's, all but one of the terms in the second sum drop out (as well as the term $tv'p$), and we get:

$$[[t/q \cdot x]]_{p_j} = \Big[\Big[\sum_{i=1}^{k} x_i \cdot \frac{t\tilde{Q}_i p}{q_i}\Big] + x'_j \cdot [t\tilde{Q}'_j p_j^*]_{p_j}\Big]_{p_j}.$$

As in Sect. 2.3, we pre-compute all the values $\frac{t\tilde{Q}_i p}{q_i}$, breaking them into their integral and fractional parts, $\frac{t\tilde{Q}_i p}{q_i} = \omega'_i + \theta'_i$ with $\omega'_i \in \mathbb{Z}_p$ and $\theta'_i \in [-\frac{1}{2}, \frac{1}{2})$. We store all the θ'_i's as double (or extended double) floats, for every i,j we store the single-precision integer $\omega'_{i,j} = [\omega'_i]_{p_j}$, and for every j we also store $\lambda_j := [t\tilde{Q}'_j p_j^*]_{p_j}$. Then given the integer x, represented as $x \sim (x_1, \ldots, x_k, x'_1, \ldots, x'_{k'})$, we compute

$$v := \Big\lceil\sum_i \theta'_i x_i\Big\rfloor, \text{ and for all } j \ w_j := \Big[\lambda_j x'_j + \sum_i \omega'_{i,j} x_i\Big]_{p_j} \text{ and } y'_j := [v + w_j]_{p_j}.$$

Then we have $y'_j = [[t/q \cdot x]]_{p_j}$, and we return $y' \sim \{y'_1, \ldots, y'_{k'}\} \in \mathbb{Z}_p$.

Correctness. When computing the value $v = \lceil\sum_i \theta'_i x_i\rfloor$, we can bound the floating-point inaccuracy before rounding below $1/4$, just as in the simple scaling procedure from Sect. 2.3. However, when we use complex scaling during homomorphic multiplication, we do not have the guarantee that the exact value before rounding is close to an integer, and so we may encounter rounding errors where instead of rounding to the nearest integer, we will round to the second nearest. Contrary to the case of decryption, here such "rounding errors" are perfectly acceptable, as the rounding error is only added to the ciphertext noise.

We remark also that in the second CRT basis extension (from $\mathbb{Z}_p$ to $\mathbb{Z}_{pq}$, before discarding the mod-p components), we regain the guarantee that the exact value before rounding is close to an integer: This is because the value that we seek before rounding is $v = x/p \pmod 1$, we have the guarantee that $|x| \le q/2$, and our parameter choices imply that $p > q$ (by a substantial margin). Since $|\frac{x}{p}| \le \frac{q}{2p} \ll \frac{1}{2}$, we are ensured to land outside of the error region of $\mathbb{Z} + \frac{1}{2} \pm \epsilon$. See Sect. 4.5 for more details of our parameter choices.

Complexity Analysis. The complexity of the first step above where we compute $y' = [[t/q \cdot x]]_p$, is similar to the simple scaling procedure from Sect. 2.3. Namely we have $k + 1$ floating-point operations when computing v, and then for each modulus p_j we have $k + 1$ single-precision modular multiplications to compute w_j. Hence the total complexity of this step is $k+1$ floating-point operations and $k'(k + 1)$ modular multiplications.

The complexity of the CRT basis extension, as described in Sect. 2.2, is $k + 1$ floating-point operations and $k'(k + 1) + k$ single-precision modular multiplications. Hence the total complexity of complex scaling is $2(k + 1)$ floating-point operations and $2k'(k + 1) + k$ modular multiplications.

3   Background: Scale-Invariant Homomorphic Encryption

For self-containment we briefly sketch Brakerski's "scale-invariant" homomorphic encryption scheme from [5]. Then we discuss the Fan-Vercauteren variant of the scheme and some optimizations due to Bajard et al. [3].

3.1   Brakerski's Scheme

The starting point for Brakerski's scheme is Regev's encryption scheme [21], with plaintext space $\mathbb{Z}_t$ for some modulus $t > 1$, where secret keys and ciphertexts are dimension-n vectors over $\mathbb{Z}_q^n$ for some other modulus $q \gg t$. (Throughout this section we assume for simplicity of notations that q is divisible by t. It is well known that this condition in superfluous, however, and replacing q/t by $\lceil q/t \rceil$ everywhere works just as well.)

The decryption invariant of this scheme is that a ciphertext $\mathbf{ct}$, encrypting a message $m \in \mathbb{Z}_t$ relative to secret key $\mathbf{sk}$, satisfies

$$[\langle \mathbf{sk}, \mathbf{ct} \rangle]_q = m \cdot q/t + e, \text{ for a small noise term } |e| \ll q/t,$$

where $\langle \cdot, \cdot \rangle$ denotes inner product. Decryption is therefore implemented by setting $m := \left[\left\lfloor \frac{t}{q} \cdot [\langle \mathbf{sk}, \mathbf{ct} \rangle]_q \right\rceil \right]_t$.[3] Homomorphic addition of two ciphertext vectors $\mathbf{ct}_1, \mathbf{ct}_2$ consists of just adding the two vectors over $\mathbb{Z}_q$, and has the effect of adding the plaintexts and also adding the two noise terms. Homomorphic multiplication is more involved, consisting of the following parts:

Key Generation. In Brakerski's scheme, the secret key $\mathbf{sk}$ must also be small, namely $\|\mathbf{sk}\| \ll q/t$. Moreover, the public key includes a "relinearization gadget", consisting of $\log q$ matrices $W_i \in \mathbb{Z}_q^{n \times n^2}$. Denoting the tensor product of $\mathbf{sk}$ with itself (over $\mathbb{Z}$) by $\mathbf{sk}^* = \mathbf{sk} \otimes \mathbf{sk} \in \mathbb{Z}^{n^2}$, the relinearization matrices satisfy

$$[\mathbf{sk} \times W_i]_q = 2^i \mathbf{sk}^* + \mathbf{e}_i^*, \text{ for a small noise term } \|\mathbf{e}_i^*\| \ll q/t.$$

---

[3] We ignore the encryption procedure in this section, since it is mostly irrelevant for the current work. For suitable choices, Regev proved that this encryption scheme is CPA-secure under the LWE assumption.

Homomorphic Multiplication. Let $\mathbf{ct}_1, \mathbf{ct}_2$ be two ciphertexts, satisfying the decryption invariant $[\langle \mathbf{sk}, \mathbf{ct}_i \rangle]_q = m_i \cdot q/t + e_i$. The multiplication consists of:

1. **Tensoring.** Taking the tensor product $\mathbf{ct}_1 \otimes \mathbf{ct}_2$ *without modular reduction*, then scaling down by t/q, hence getting $\mathbf{ct}^* := \left[\lfloor t/q \cdot \mathbf{ct}_1 \otimes \mathbf{ct}_2 \rfloor \right]_q$.
2. **Relinearization.** Decomposing $\mathbf{ct}^*$ into bits $\mathbf{ct}_i^* \in \{0,1\}^{n^2}$ (where $\mathbf{ct}^* = \sum_i 2^i \mathbf{ct}_i^*$), then setting $\mathbf{ct}^{\times} := [\sum_i W_i \times \mathbf{ct}_i^*]_q$.

To see that $\mathbf{ct}^{\times}$ is indeed an encryption of the product $m_1 m_2$ relative to $\mathbf{sk}$, denote the rational vector before rounding by $\mathbf{ct}' = t/q \cdot \mathbf{ct}_1 \otimes \mathbf{ct}_2$, and the rounding error by ϵ (so $\mathbf{ct}^* = \epsilon + \mathbf{ct}' + q \cdot \text{something}$), and we have

$$\langle \mathbf{sk}^*, \mathbf{ct}' \rangle = \left\langle \mathbf{sk} \otimes \mathbf{sk}, \tfrac{t}{q} \mathbf{ct}_1 \otimes \mathbf{ct}_2 \right\rangle = t/q \cdot (\langle \mathbf{sk}, \mathbf{ct}_1 \rangle \cdot \langle \mathbf{sk}, \mathbf{ct}_2 \rangle$$
$$= t/q \cdot (m_1 \cdot q/t + e_1 + k_1 q)(m_2 \cdot q/t + e_2 + k_2 q)$$
$$= m_1 m_2 \cdot q/t + \underbrace{e_1 m_2 + m_1 e_2 + e_1 e_2 t/q + t(k_1 e_2 + k_2 e_1)}_{e' \ll q/t} + q \cdot \text{something}.$$

Including the rounding error, and since $\mathbf{sk}$ is small (and hence so is $\mathbf{sk}^*$), we get

$$\langle \mathbf{sk}^*, \mathbf{ct}^* \rangle = \langle \mathbf{sk}^*, \epsilon + \mathbf{ct}' + \mathbf{k}^* q \rangle = m_1 m_2 \cdot q/t + \underbrace{e' + \langle \mathbf{sk}^*, \epsilon \rangle}_{e'' \ll q/t} + q \cdot \text{something}, \quad (5)$$

so $\mathbf{ct}^*$ encrypts $m_1 m_2$ relative to $\mathbf{sk}^*$. After relinearization, we have

$$\langle \mathbf{sk}, \mathbf{ct}^{\times} \rangle = \mathbf{sk} \times \sum_i W_i \times \mathbf{ct}_i^* = \sum_i \langle (2^i \mathbf{sk}^* + \mathbf{e}_i^*), \mathbf{ct}_i^* \rangle$$
$$= \langle \mathbf{sk}^*, \sum_i 2^i \mathbf{ct}_i^* \rangle + \sum_i \langle \mathbf{e}_i^*, \mathbf{ct}_i^* \rangle = m_1 m_2 \cdot q/t + e'' + \underbrace{\sum_i \langle \mathbf{e}_i^*, \mathbf{ct}_i^* \rangle}_{\tilde{e}} \quad (\text{mod } q).$$

Since the $\mathbf{ct}_i^*$'s are small then so is the noise term $\tilde{e}$, as needed.

3.2   The Fan-Vercauteren Variant

In [8], Fan and Vercauteren ported Brakerski's scheme to the ring-LWE setting, working over polynomial rings rather than over the integers. Below we let $R = \mathbb{Z}[X]/\langle f(X) \rangle$ be a fixed ring, where $f \in \mathbb{Z}[X]$ is a monic polynomial of degree n (typically an m-th cyclotomic polynomial $\Phi_m(x)$ of degree $n = \phi(m)$). We use some convenient basis to represent R over $\mathbb{Z}$ (most often just the power basis, i.e., the coefficient representation of the polynomials). Also, let $R_t = R/tR$ denote the quotient ring for an integer modulus $t \in \mathbb{Z}$ in the same basis.

The plaintext space of this variant is R_t for some $t > 1$ (i.e., a polynomial of degree at most $n - 1$ with coefficients in $\mathbb{Z}_t$), the secret key is a 2-vector $\mathbf{sk} = (1, s) \in R^2$ with $\|s\| \ll q/t$, ciphertexts are 2-vectors $\mathbf{ct} = (c_0, c_1) \in R_q^2$ for another modulus $q \gg t$, and the decryption invariant is the same as in

Brakerski's scheme, namely $\left[\left\lfloor \frac{t}{q}[\langle \mathbf{sk}, \mathbf{ct}\rangle]_q \right\rceil\right]_t = \left[\left\lfloor \frac{t}{q}[c_0 + c_1 s]_q \right\rceil\right]_t = m \cdot \frac{q}{t} + e$ for a small noise term $e \in R, \|e\| \ll q/t$.

For encryption, the public key includes a low-noise encryption of zero, $\mathbf{ct}^0 = (\mathbf{ct}_0^0, \mathbf{ct}_1^0)$, and to encrypt $m \in R_t$ they choose low-norm elements $u, e_1, e_2 \in R$ and set $Enc_{\mathbf{ct}^0}(m) := [u \cdot \mathbf{ct}^0 + (e_0, e_1) + (\Delta m, 0)]_q$, where $\Delta = \lfloor q/t \rfloor$. Homomorphic addition just adds the ciphertext vectors in R_q^2, and homomorphic multiplication is the same as in Brakerski's scheme, except (a) the special form of $\mathbf{sk}$ lets them optimize the relinearization "matrices" and use vectors instead, and (b) they use base-w decomposition (for a suitable word-size w) instead of base-2 decomposition[4]. In a little more detail:

(a) For the secret-key vector $\mathbf{sk} = (1, s)$, the tensor product $\mathbf{sk} \otimes \mathbf{sk}$ can be represented by the 3-vector $\mathbf{sk}^* = (1, s, s^2)$. Similarly, for the two ciphertexts $\mathbf{ct}^i = (c_0^i, c_1^i)$ $(i = 1, 2)$, it is sufficient to represent the tensor $\mathbf{ct}_1 \otimes \mathbf{ct}_2$ by the 3-vector $\mathbf{ct}^* = (c_0^*, c_1^*, c_2^*) = [c_0^1 c_0^2, (c_0^1 c_1^2 + c_1^1 c_0^2), c_1^1 c_1^2]_q$.

(b) For the relinearization gadget, all they need is to "encrypt" the single element s^2 using $\mathbf{sk}$. When using a base-w decomposition, they have vectors (rather than matrices) $W_i = (\beta_i, \alpha_i)$, with uniform α_i's and $\beta_i = [w^i s^2 - \alpha_i s + e_i]_q$ (for low-norm noise terms e_i).

After computing the three-vector $\mathbf{ct}^* = (c_0^*, c_1^*, c_2^*)$ as above during homomorphic multiplication, they decompose c_2^* into its base-w digits, $c_2^* = \sum_i w^i c_{2,i}^*$. Then computing $\mathbf{ct}^\times = \sum_i W_i \times \mathbf{ct}_i^*$ only requires that they set

$$\tilde{c}_0 := [\sum_{i=1}^k \beta_i c_{2,i}^*]_q, \ \tilde{c}_1 := [\sum_{i=1}^k \alpha_i c_{2,i}^*]_q, \quad \text{and then } \mathbf{ct}^\times := [(c_0^* + \tilde{c}_0, c_1^* + \tilde{c}_1)]_q.$$

3.3 CRT Representation and Optimized Relinearization

Bajard et al. described in [3] several optimizations of the Fan-Vercauteren variant, centered around the use of CRT representation of the large integers involved. (They called it a *Residue Number System*, or RNS, but in this writeup we prefer the term CRT representation.) Specifically, the modulus q is chosen as a product of same-size, pairwise coprime, single-precision moduli, $q = \prod_{i=1}^k q_i$, and each element $x \in \mathbb{Z}_q$ is represented by the vector $(x_i = [x]_{q_i})_{i=1}^k$.

One significant optimization from [3] relates to the relinearization step in homomorphic multiplication. Recall that in that step we decompose the ciphertext $\mathbf{ct}^*$ into low-norm components $\mathbf{ct}_i^*$, such that reconstructing $\mathbf{ct}^*$ from the $\mathbf{ct}_i^*$'s is a linear operation, namely $\mathbf{ct}^* = \sum_i \tau_i \mathbf{ct}_i^*$ for some known coefficients τ_i. Instead of decomposing $\mathbf{ct}^*$ into bit or digits, Bajard et al. suggested to use its CRT components $\mathbf{ct}_i^* = [\mathbf{ct}^* \tilde{q}_i]_{q_i}$ and secret key components $s_i^2 = [s^2 q_i^*]_q$

---

[4] Fan and Vercauteren described in [8] a second relinearization procedure, using a technique of Gentry et al. from [10]. We ignore this alternative procedure here.

when computing the relinearization key, and rely on the reconstruction from Eq. 3 (which is linear).

We remark that it is more efficient to use the CRT components $\mathbf{ct}_i^* = [\mathbf{ct}^*]_{q_i}$ and secret key components $s_i^2 = [s^2 \tilde{q}_i q_i^*]_q$. The latter corresponds to $[s^2]_{q_i}$ for the i-th modulus and 0's for all other moduli. This optimization removes one scalar multiplication in each $\mathbf{ct}_i^*$ term (as compared to [3]) and eliminates the need for any precomputed parameters in the relinearization procedure.

As in [3], we also apply digit decomposition to the residues, thus allowing a more granular control of noise growth at small multiplicative depths. A detailed discussion of this technique is provided in Appendix B.1 of [3].

4 Our Optimizations

4.1 The Scheme that We Implemented

The scheme that we implemented is the Fan-Vercauteren variant of Braker-ski's scheme (we refer to this variant as the "BFV scheme"), with a modified CRT-based relinearization step of Bajard et al. We begin with a concrete stand-alone description of the functions that we implemented, then describe our simpler/faster CRT-based implementation of these functions.

Parameters. Let $t, m, q \in \mathbb{Z}$ be parameters (where the single-precision t determines the plaintext space, and $m, |q|$ depend on t and the security parameter), such that $q = \prod_{i=1}^{k} q_i$ for same-size, pairwise coprime, single-precision moduli q_i.

Let $n = \phi(m)$, and let $R = \mathbb{Z}[X]/\Phi_m(X)$ be the m-th cyclotomic ring, and denote by $R_q = R/qR$ and $R_t = R/tR$ the quotient rings. In our implementation we represent elements in R, R_q, R_t in the power basis (i.e., polynomial coefficients), but note that other "small bases" are possible (such as the decoding basis from [18]), and for non-power-of-two cyclotomics they could sometimes result in better parameters. We let χ_e, χ_k be distributions over low-norm elements in R in the power basis, specifically we use discrete Gaussians for χ_e and the uniform distribution over $\{-1, 0, 1\}^n$ for χ_k.

Key Generation. For the secret key, choose a low-norm secret key $s \leftarrow \chi_k$ and set $\mathbf{sk} := (1, s) \in R^2$. For the public encryption key, choose a uniform random $a \in R_q$ and $e \leftarrow \chi_e$, set $b := [-(as + e)]_q \in R_q$, and compute $\mathbf{pk} := (b, a)$.

Recall that we denote $q_i^* = \frac{q}{q_i}$ and $\tilde{q}_i = [q_i^{*-1}]_{q_i}$. For relinearization, choose a uniform $\alpha_i \in R_q$ and $e_i \leftarrow \chi_e$, and set $\beta_i = [\tilde{q}_i q_i^* s^2 - \alpha_i s + e_i]_q$ for each $i = 1, \ldots, k$. The public key consists of $\mathbf{pk}$ and all the vectors $W_i := (\beta_i, \alpha_i)$.

Encryption. To encrypt $m \in R_t$, choose $u \leftarrow \chi_k$ and $e_0', e_1' \leftarrow \chi_e$ and output the ciphertext $\mathbf{ct} := [u \cdot \mathbf{pk} + (e_0', e_1') + (\Delta m, 0)]_q$, where $\Delta = q/t$.

Decryption. For a ciphertext $\mathbf{ct} = (c_0, c_1)$, compute $x := [\langle \mathbf{sk}, \mathbf{ct} \rangle]_q = [c_0 + c_1 s]_q$ and output $m := [\lfloor x \cdot t/q \rceil]_t$.

Homomorphic Addition. On input $\mathbf{ct}^1, \mathbf{ct}^2$, output $[\mathbf{ct}^1 + \mathbf{ct}^2]_q$.

Homomorphic Multiplication. Given $\mathbf{ct}^i = (c_0^i, c_1^i)_{i=1,2}$, do the following:

1. **Tensoring:** Compute $c_0' := c_0^1 c_0^2$, $c_1' := c_0^1 c_1^2 + c_1^1 c_0^2$, $c_2' := c_1^1 c_1^2 \in R$ without modular reduction, then set $c_i^* = [[t/q \cdot c_i']]_q$ for $i = 0, 1, 2$.
2. **Relinearization:** Decompose c_2^* into its CRT components $c_{2,i}^* = [c_2^*]_{q_i}$, set $\tilde{c}_0 := [\sum_{i=1}^k \beta_i c_{2,i}^*]_q$, $\tilde{c}_1 := [\sum_{i=1}^k \alpha_i c_{2,i}^*]_q$, output $\mathbf{ct}^\times := [(c_0^* + \tilde{c}_0, c_1^* + \tilde{c}_1)]_q$.

4.2 Pre-computed Values

When setting the parameters, we pre-compute some tables to help speed things up later. Specifically:

- We pre-compute and store all the values that are needed for the simple CRT scaling procedure in Sect. 2.3: For each $i = 1, \ldots, k$, we compute the rational number $t\tilde{q}_i/q_i$, split into integral and fractional parts. Namely, $\omega_i := \left[t \cdot \frac{\tilde{q}_i}{q_i} \right] \in \mathbb{Z}_t$ and $\theta_i := \frac{t \cdot \tilde{q}_i}{q_i} - \omega_i \in [-\frac{1}{2}, \frac{1}{2})$. We store ω_i as a single-precision integer and θ_i as a double (or long double) float.
- We also choose a second set of single-precision coprime numbers $\{p_j\}_{j=1}^{k'}$ (coprime to all the q_i's), such that $p := \prod_j p_j$ is bigger than q by a large enough margin. Specifically we will need to ensure that for $c_0^1, c_1^1, c_0^2, c_1^2 \in R$ with coefficients in $[-q/2, q/2)$, the element $c^* := c_0^1 c_1^2 + c_1^1 c_0^2 \in R$ (without modular reduction) has coefficients in the range $[-qp/2t, qp/2t)$. For our setting of parameters, where all the q_i's and p_j's are 55-bit primes and t is up to 32 bits, it is sufficient to take $k' = k + 1$. For smaller CRT primes or larger values of t, a higher value of k' may be needed.

  Below we denote for all j, $p_j^* := p/p_j$ and $\tilde{p}_j := [(p_j^*)^{-1}]_{p_j}$. We also denote $Q := qp$, and for every i, j we have $Q_i^* := Q/q_i = q_i^* p$, $Q_j'^* := Q/p_j = qp_j^*$, and also $\tilde{Q}_i = [(Q_i^*)^{-1}]_{q_i}$ and $\tilde{Q}'_j = [(Q_j'^*)^{-1}]_{p_j}$.
- We pre-compute and store all the values that are needed in the procedure from Sect. 2.2 to extend the CRT basis $\{q_1, \ldots, q_k\}$ by each of the p_j's, as well the values that are needed to extend the CRT basis $\{p_1, \ldots, p_{k'}\}$ by each of the q_i's. Namely for all i, j we store the single-precision integers $\mu_{i,j} = [q_i^*]_{p_j}$ and $\nu_{i,j} = [p_j^*]_{q_i}$, as well as $\phi_j = [q]_{p_j}$ and $\psi_i = [p]_{q_i}$.
- We also pre-compute and store all the values that are needed for the complex CRT scaling procedure in Sect. 2.4. Namely, we pre-compute all the values $\frac{t\tilde{Q}_i p}{q_i}$, breaking them into their integral and fractional parts, $\frac{t\tilde{Q}_i p}{q_i} = \omega_i' + \theta_i'$ with $\omega_i' \in \mathbb{Z}_p$ and $\theta_i' \in [-\frac{1}{2}, \frac{1}{2})$. We store all the θ_i''s as double (or long double) floats, for every i, j we store the single-precision integer $\omega_{i,j}' = [\omega_i']_{p_j}$, and for every j we also store $\lambda_j := [t\tilde{Q}'_j p_j^*]_{p_j}$.

4.3 Key-Generation and Encryption

The key-generation and encryption procedures are implemented in a straightforward manner. Small integers such as noise and key coefficients are drawn from χ_e

or χ_k and stored as single-precision integers, while uniform elements in $a \leftarrow \mathbb{Z}_q$ are chosen directly in the CRT basis by drawing uniform values $a_i \in \mathbb{Z}_{q_i}$ for all i.

Operations in R_q are implemented directly in CRT representation, often requiring the computation of the number-theoretic-transform (NTT) modulo the separate q_i's. The only operations that require computations outside of R_q are decryption and homomorphic multiplications, as described next.

4.4   Decryption

Given the ciphertext $\mathbf{ct} = (c_0, c_1)$ and secret key $\mathbf{sk} = (1, s)$, we first compute the inner product in R_q, setting $x := [c_0 + c_1 s]_q$. We obtain the result in coefficient representation relative to the CRT basis $q_1, \ldots, q_k$. Namely for each coefficient of x (call it $x_\ell \in \mathbb{Z}_q$) we have the CRT components $x_{\ell,i} = [x_\ell]_{q_i}$, $i = 1, \ldots, k, \ell = 0, \ldots, n-1$.

We then apply to each coefficient x_ℓ the simple scaling procedure from Sect. 2.3. This yields the scaled coefficients $m_\ell = [[t/q \cdot x_\ell]]_t$, representing the element $m = [[t/q \cdot x]]_t \in R_t$, as needed.

As we explained in Sect. 2.3, in the context of decryption we can ensure correctness by controlling the noise to guarantee that each $t/q \cdot x_\ell$ is within $1/4$ of an integer, and limit the size of the q_i's to 59 bits to ensure that the error is bounded below $1/4$.

Decryption Complexity. The dominant factor in decryption is NTTs modulo the individual q_i's, that are used to compute the inner product $x := [c_0 + c_1 s]_q \in R_q$. Specifically we need $2k$ of them, k in the forward direction (one for each $[c_1]_{q_i}$) and k inverse NTTs (one for each $[c_1 s]_{q_i}$). These operations require $O(kn \log n)$ single-precision modular multiplications, where $n = \phi(m)$ is the degree of the polynomials and k is the number of moduli q_i. Once this computation is done, the simple CRT scaling procedure takes $(k+1)n$ floating-point operations and kn integer multiplications modulo t.

4.5   Homomorphic Multiplication

The input to homomorphic multiplication is two ciphertexts $\mathbf{ct}^1 = (c_0^1, c_1^1), \mathbf{ct}^2 = (c_0^2, c_1^2)$, where each $c_b^a \in R_q$ is represented in the power basis with each coefficient represented in the CRT basis $\{q_i\}_{i=1}^k$. The procedure consists of three steps, where we first compute the "double-precision" elements $c_0', c_1', c_2' \in R$, then scale them down to get $c_i^* := [[t/q \cdot c_i']]_q$, and finally apply relinearization.

Multiplication with Double Precision. We begin by extending the CRT basis using the procedure from Sect. 2.2. For each coefficient x in any of the c_b^a's, we are given the CRT representation $(x_1, \ldots, x_k)$ with $x_i = [x]_{q_i}$ and compute also the CRT components $(x_1', \ldots, x_{k'}')$ with $x_j' = [x]_{p_j}$. This gives us a representation of the same integer x, in the larger ring $\mathbb{Z}_{qp}$, which in turn yields a representation of the c_b^a's in the larger ring R_{qp}.

Next we compute the three elements $c'_0 := [c_0^1 c_0^2]_{pq}$, $c'_1 := [c_0^1 c_1^2 + c_1^1 c_0^2]_{pq}$ and $c'_2 := [c_1^1 c_1^2]_{pq}$, where all the operations are in the ring R_{qp}. By our choice of parameters (with p sufficiently larger than q), we know that there is no modular reduction in these expressions, so in fact we obtain $c'_0, c'_1, c'_2 \in R$. These elements are represented in the power basis, with each coefficient $x \in \mathbb{Z}_{qp}$ represented by $(x_1, \ldots, x_k, x'_1, \ldots, x'_{k'})$ with $x_i = [x]_{q_i}$ and $x'_j = [x]_{p_j}$.

Scaling Back Down to R_q. By our choice of parameters, we know that all the coefficients of the c'_ℓ's are integers in the range $[-qp/2t, qp/2t)$, as needed for the complex CRT scaling procedure from Sect. 2.4. We therefore apply that procedure to each coefficient $x \in \mathbb{Z}_{qp}$, computing $x^* = [[t/q \cdot x]]_q$. This gives us the power-basis representation of the elements $c^*_\ell = [[t/q \cdot c'_\ell]]_q \in R_q$ for $\ell = 0, 1, 2$.

Relinearization. For relinearization, we use a modification of the technique by Bajard et al. [3] discussed in Sect. 3.3. Namely, at this point we have the elements $c^*_0, c^*_1, c^*_2 \in R_q$ in CRT representation, $c^*_{\ell,i} = [c^*_\ell]_{q_i}$ (for $\ell = 0, 1, 2$ and $i = 1, \ldots, k$). To relinearize, we use the relinearization gadget vectors (β_i, α_i) that were computed during key generation. For each q_i, we first compute $\tilde{c}_{0,i} := \left[\sum_{j=1}^{k} [\beta_j]_{q_i} \cdot c^*_{2,j} \right]_{q_i}$ and $\tilde{c}_{1,i} := \left[\sum_{j=1}^{k} [\alpha_j]_{q_i} \cdot c^*_{2,j} \right]_{q_i}$, and then $c^\times_{0,i} := [c^*_{0,i} + \tilde{c}_{0,i}]_{q_i}$ and $c^\times_{1,i} := [c^*_{1,i} + \tilde{c}_{1,i}]_{q_i}$.

This gives the relinearized ciphertext $\mathbf{ct}^\times = (c^\times_0, c^\times_1) \in R_q^2$, which is the output of the homomorphic multiplication procedure.

Correctness. Correctness of the CRT basis-extension and complex scaling procedures was discussed in Sects. 2.2 and 2.4, respectively. Though both CRT basis extension and scaling procedures may introduce some approximation errors due to the use of floating-point arithmetic, these errors only increase the ciphertext noise by a small (practically negligible) amount.

To illustrate the small contribution of approximation errors, consider the noise estimate for the original Brakerski's scheme described in Sect. 3.1. (Similar arguments apply to any other scale-invariant scheme, including BFV and YASHE.) The approximation error in the CRT basis extension before the tensor product can change the value of v at most by one, with probability $\approx 2^{-48}$. This means that the value of k_1 or k_2 may grow by one with the same probability, thus increasing the noise term $t(k_1 e_2 + k_2 e_1)$ in Eq. 5 to $t((k_1 + \epsilon_1)e_2 + (k_2 + \epsilon_2)e_1)$, where $\epsilon_i \in \{0, 1\}$ and $\Pr[\epsilon_i \neq 0] \approx 2^{-47+\log n}$. Recall that $k_i \approx \lceil \langle \mathbf{sk}, \mathbf{ct}_i \rangle / q \rfloor$, so $\|k_i\|_\infty$'s are at least $\sqrt{n}$. As n in all practical cases is typically above 1024 (and often much higher), the difference between $k_1 e_2 + k_2 e_1$ and $(k_1 + \epsilon_1)e_2 + (k_2 + \epsilon_2)e_1$ is less than 3% (and even this only occurring with probability $2^{-47+\log n}$). In our experiments we never noticed this effect.

To study the effect of the approximation error introduced by scaling, we replace the term $\mathbf{ct}^* = \epsilon + \mathbf{ct}' + q \cdot \mathbf{something}$ for Brakerski's scheme (Sect. 3.1) with $\mathbf{ct}^* = \epsilon + \epsilon_\mathbf{s} + \mathbf{ct}' + q \cdot \mathbf{something}$, where $\epsilon_\mathbf{s}$ is the scaling error. To ensure that the noise growth is not impacted, it suffices to ensure that the added noise term $|\mathbf{sk}^2 \cdot \epsilon_s|$ (corresponding to the term $\langle \mathbf{sk}^*, \epsilon_s \rangle$ in the description from Sect. 3.1) is smaller than the previous noise term of $t(k_1 e_2 + k_2 e_1)$. This is always the case if we have $\|\epsilon_\mathbf{s}\|_\infty < 1/4$ (as we do for decryption), but in some cases we can also handle larger values of ϵ_s (e.g., later in the computation where the terms e_1, e_2 are already larger, or when working with a large plaintext-space modulus t).

Finally, we note that the floating-point arithmetic in the second CRT-basis extension (inside complex scaling) does not produce any errors. This is because we use $p \gg q$ (to ensure that all the coefficients before scaling fit in the range $[-pq/2t, +pq/2t]$). The analysis from Sect. 2.2 then tells us that when computing the CRT basis extension from mod-p to mod-pq we never end up in the error region.

Multiplication Complexity. As for decryption, here too the dominant factor is the NTTs that we must compute when performing multiplication operations in R_q and R_{qp}. Specifically we need to transform the four elements $c_b^a \in R_{qp}$ after the CRT extension in order to compute the three $c_\ell' \in R_{qp}$, then transform back the c_ℓ''s before scaling them back to R_q to get the c_ℓ^*'s. For relinearization we need to transform all the elements $c_{2,i}^* \in R_q$ before multiplying them by the α_i's and β_i's, and also transform c_0^*, c_1^* before we can add them. Each transform in R_q takes k single-precision NTTs, and each transform in R_{qp} takes $k + k'$ NTTs, so the total number of single-precision NTTs is $k^2 + 9k + 7k'$. Each transform takes $O(n \log n)$ multiplications, so the NTTs take $O(k^2 n \log n)$ modular multiplications overall. In our experiments, these NTTs account for 58–77% of the homomorphic multiplication running time.

In addition to these NTTs, we spend $4(k + k')n$ modular multiplications computing the c_ℓ''s in the transformed domain and $2k^2 n$ modular multiplications computing the products $c_{2,i}^* \beta_i$ and $c_{2,i}^* \beta_i$ in the transformed domain. We also spend $4n(kk' + k + k')$ modular multiplications and $4(k + 1)n$ floating-point operations in the CRT-extension procedure in Sect. 4.5, and additional $3n(2k'(k+1)+k)$ modular multiplications and $3(k' + k + 2)n$ floating-point operations in the complex scaling in Sect. 4.5. Hence other than the NTTs, we have a total of $(7k + 3k' + 10)n$ floating-point operations and $(2k^2 + 10kk' + 11k + 14k')n$ modular multiplications.

4.6   Noise Growth

We show that our decryption and homomorphic multiplication procedures introduce almost no extra noise (up to 2 bits) as compared to the textbook BFV.

Textbook BFV. The worst-case noise bound for correct decryption using textbook BFV is written as [16]:

$$\|v\|_\infty < (\Delta - r_t(q))/2, \tag{6}$$

where $r_t(q) = t(q/t - \Delta)$.

The initial noise in $[c_0 + c_1 s]_q$ is bounded by $B_e (1 + 2\delta \|s\|_\infty)$, where B_e is the effective (low-probability) upper bound for Gaussian errors, and δ is the polynomial multiplication expansion factor $\sup \{\|ab\|_\infty / \|a\|_\infty \|b\|_\infty : a, b \in R\}$. The initial noise is the same in all three BFV variants as the first RNS procedure is introduced at the scaling step of decryption.

The noise bound for binary tree multiplication of depth L is given by [16]

$$\|v_{\text{mult}}\|_\infty < C_1^L V + L C_1^{L-1} C_2, \tag{7}$$

where $\|v_1\|_\infty, \|v_2\|_\infty < V$ and

$$C_1 = (1 + \epsilon_2) \delta^2 t \|s\|_\infty, \epsilon_2 = 4 (\delta \|s\|_\infty)^{-1}, \tag{8}$$

$$C_2 = \delta^2 \|s\|_\infty (\|s\|_\infty + t^2) + \delta \ell_{w,q} w B_e. \tag{9}$$

Here $\ell_{w,q}$ is the number of base-w digits in q.

Our RNS Variant. Our RNS variant has the following requirement for correct decryption:

$$\|v'\|_\infty < (\Delta - r_t(q))/4. \tag{10}$$

Here the denominator is 4 (rather than 2 in the textbook BFV) to guarantee that the simple scaling procedure does not approach the possible-error region $\mathbb{Z} + \frac{1}{2} \pm \epsilon$. This adds at most 1 bit of noise to the textbook BFV bound.

The low-probability (around 2^{-48} in our implementation) approximation error in CRT basis extension before computing the tensor product without modular reduction simply changes the value of ϵ_2 to $5 (\delta \|s\|_\infty)^{-1}$, which can be easily shown using the same procedure as in Appendix I of [4] for the YASHE' scheme and the same logic as described for Brakerski's scheme in Sect. 4.5. Note that the value of $\epsilon_2 \ll 1$, which implies that the change of the factor from 4 to 5 should have no practical effect, especially considering the low probability of this approximation error. We did not observe any practical noise increase due to this error in our experiments.

The effect of the scaling approximation error can be factored into the existing term $\delta^2 \|s\|_\infty^2$ in C_2, which corresponds to the error in rounding $t/q \cdot \mathbf{ct}_1 \otimes \mathbf{ct}_2$. In our case, we need to multiply this term by $(1 + 2 \|\epsilon_s\|_\infty)$, as explained in Sect. 4.5. As $\|\epsilon_s\|_\infty < 1/4$ when we use the same floating-point precision as in decryption, this term is smaller than $C_1' V$ in all practical settings, including the case of fresh ciphertexts at $t = 2$ (see Sect. 4.5 for a more detailed discussion). We add 1 more bit to the textbook BFV noise to account for the potential extra noise during first-level multiplications, especially if larger values of $\|\epsilon_s\|_\infty$ are selected to use a lower precision for floating-point arithmetic. For homomorphic multiplications at higher levels, we will always have $\|\epsilon_s\|_\infty \ll C_1' V$.

The relinearization term $\delta \ell_{w,q} w B_e$ in the textbook BFV expression gets replaced with $\delta \ell_{w,2^\nu} w k B_e$, where ν is the CRT moduli bit size, which is the same as for the Bajard et al. variant and the same as for the textbook BFV if $w \leq \nu$.

In summary, the binary tree multiplication noise constraint for our RNS variant is given by

$$\|v'_{mult}\|_\infty < C'^L_1 V + LC'^{L-1}_1 C'_2, \tag{11}$$

$$C'_1 = (1 + \epsilon'_2) \delta^2 t \|s\|_\infty, \epsilon'_2 = 5 (\delta \|s\|_\infty)^{-1}, \tag{12}$$

$$C'_2 = \delta^2 \|s\|_\infty (\{1 + 2 \|\epsilon_s\|_\infty\} \|s\|_\infty + t^2) + \delta \ell_{w,2^\nu} wkB_e. \tag{13}$$

5   Implementation Details and Performance Results

5.1   Parameter Selection

Tighter Heuristic (Average-Case) Noise Bounds. The polynomial multiplication expansion factor δ in Eqs. 8 and 9 is typically selected as $\delta = n$ for the worst-case scenario [3,16]. However, our experiments for the textbook BFV, our BFV variant, and products of discrete Gaussian and ternary generated polynomials showed that we can select $\delta = C\sqrt{n}$ for practical experiments, where C is a constant close to one (for the case of power-of-two cyclotomics). This follows from the Central Limit Theorem (or rather subgaussian analysis), since all dominant polynomial multiplication terms result from the multiplication of polynomials with zero-centered random coefficients.

The highest experimental value of C for which we observed decryption failures was 0.9. We also ran numerous experiments at n varying from 2^{10} to 2^{17} for the cases of (1) multiplying a discrete Gaussian polynomial by a ternary uniform polynomial and (2) multiplying a discrete uniform polynomial by a ternary uniform polynomial, which cover the dominant terms in the noise constraints for BFV. The highest experimental value of C (observed for the product of a discrete Gaussian polynomial by a ternary uniform polynomial at $n = 1024$) was 1.75. Therefore, we selected $C = 2$ for our experiments, i.e., we set $\delta = 2\sqrt{n}$.

Security. To choose the ring dimension n, we ran the LWE security estimator[5] (commit f59326c) [1] to find the lowest security levels for the uSVP, decoding, and dual attacks following the standard homomorphic encryption security recommendations [7]. We selected the least value of the number of security bits λ for all 3 attacks on classical computers based on the estimates for the BKZ sieve reduction cost model.

The secret-key polynomials were generated using discrete ternary uniform distribution over $\{-1, 0, 1\}^n$. In all of our experiments, we selected the minimum ciphertext modulus bitwidth that satisfied the correctness constraint for the lowest ring dimension n corresponding to the security level $\lambda \geq 128$.

Other Parameters. We set the Gaussian distribution parameter σ to $8/\sqrt{2\pi}$ [7], the error bound B_e to 6σ, and the lower bound for p to $2tnq$. For the digit decomposition of residues in the relinearization procedure, we used the base w of 30 bits for the range of multiplicative depths from 1 to 10. For larger multiplicative depths, we utilized solely the CRT decomposition.

---

[5] https://bitbucket.org/malb/lwe-estimator.

5.2   Implementation Details

Software Implementation. The BFV scheme based on the decryption and homomorphic multiplication algorithms described in this paper was implemented in PALISADE [19], a modular C++11 lattice cryptography library that supports several SHE and proxy re-encryption schemes based on cyclotomic rings [20]. The results presented in this work were obtained for a power-of-two cyclotomic ring $\mathbb{Z}[x]/\langle x^n + 1\rangle$, which supports efficient polynomial multiplication using nega-cylic convolution [17]. For efficient modular multiplication implementation in NTT, scaling, and CRT basis extension, we used the Number Theory Library (NTL) function MULMODPRECON, which is described in Lines 5–7 of Algorithm 2 in [14]. All single-precision integer computations were done in unsigned 64-bit integers. Floating-point computations were done in IEEE 754 double-precision and extended double-precision floating-point formats. Our implementation of the BFV scheme is publicly accessible (included in PALISADE starting with v1.1).

Loop Parallelization. Multi-threading in our implementation is achieved via OpenMP. The loop parallelization in the scaling and CRT basis extension operations is applied at the level of single-precision polynomial coefficients (w.r.t. n). The loop parallelization for NTT and component-wise vector multiplications (polynomial multiplication in the evaluation representation) is applied at the level of CRT moduli (w.r.t. k).

Experimental Setup. We ran the experiments in PALISADE version 1.1, which includes NTL version 10.5.0 and GMP version 6.1.2. The evaluation environment for the single-threaded experiments was a commodity desktop computer system with an Intel Core i7-3770 CPU with 4 cores rated at 3.40 GHz and 16 GB of memory, running Linux CentOS 7. The compiler was g++ (GCC) 5.3.1. The evaluation environment for the multi-threaded experiments was a server system with 2 sockets of 16-core Intel Xeon E5-2698 v3 at 2.30 GHz CPU (which is a Haswell processor) and 250 GB of RAM. The compiler was g++ (GCC) 4.8.5.

5.3   Results

Single-Threaded Mode. Table 1 presents the timing results for the range of multiplicative depths L from 1 to 100 for the single-threaded mode of operation. It also demonstrates the contributions of CRT basis extension, scaling, and NTT to the homomorphic multiplication time (excluding the relinearization).

Table 1 suggests that the relative contribution of CRT basis extension and scaling operations to the homomorphic multiplication runtime (without relinearization) first declines from 42% at $L = 1$ to 37% at $L = 10$, and then grows up to 50% at $L = 100$. The remaining execution time is dominated by NTT operations. Our complexity and profiling analysis indicated that the initial decline is caused by a decreasing contribution (w.r.t. to modular multiplications in NTTs) of the linear terms of k and k' to the computational complexity of homomorphic multiplication as k increases from 1 to 4. The subsequent increase in relative execution time is due to the $O(k^2n)$ modular multiplications needed for CRT basis extension and scaling operations, which start contributing more than the $O(kn \log n)$ modular multiplications in the NTT operations for polynomial multiplications as k further increases.

Table 1. Timing results for decryption, homomorphic multiplication, and relinearization in the single-threaded mode; $t = 2$, $\log_2 q_i \approx 55$, $\lambda \geq 128$

L	n	$\log_2 q$	k	Dec. [ms]	Mul. [ms]	Relin. [ms]	Multiplication [%]		
							CRT ext.	Scaling	NTT
1	2^{11}	55	1	0.15	3.16	0.41	34	8	52
5	2^{12}	110	2	0.49	10.1	2.58	29	9	56
10	2^{13}	220	4	1.89	38.9	18.7	27	10	56
20	2^{14}	440	8	8.3	174	78.3	27	14	54
30	2^{15}	605	11	25.8	555	332	27	15	52
50	2^{16}	1,045	19	95.8	2,368	2,066	30	20	46
100	2^{17}	2,090	38	409	12,890	16,994	30	20	46

Table 2. Timing results with multiple threads for decryption, multiplication, and relinearization, for the case of $L = 20, n = 2^{14}, k = 8$ from Table 1

# of threads	Dec. [ms]	Mul. [ms]	Relin. [ms]	Mul. + Relin. [ms]
1	9.83	178.6	95.8	274.4
2	5.90	114.1	53.8	168.0
3	4.93	79.5	49.6	129.1
4	3.92	66.3	37.4	103.7
8	3.13	43.3	29.2	72.5
9	3.17	38.0	31.4	69.5
16	3.37	34.9	32.7	67.6
17	3.46	32.0	33.2	65.2
32	3.47	29.2	33.1	62.4

Our profiling analysis showed that the contributions of floating-point operations to CRT basis extension and scaling were always under 5% and 10% (under 5% for $k > 5$), respectively. This corresponded to at most 2.5% of the total homomorphic multiplication time (typically the value was closer to 1%). This result justifies the practical use of our much simpler algorithms, as compared to [3], considering that our approach has lower computational complexity.

Table 1 also shows that the contribution of the relinearization procedure to the total homomorphic multiplication time grows from 11% ($L = 1$) to 57% ($L = 100$) due to the quadratic dependence of the number of NTTs in the relinearization procedure on the number of coprime moduli k.

The profiling of the decryption operation showed that only 8% ($L = 100$) to 18% ($L = 1$) was spent on CRT scaling while at least 60% was consumed by NTT operations and up to 10% by component-wise vector products. This supports our analysis, asserting that the decryption operation is dominated by NTT, and the effect of the scaling operation is insignificant.

Multi-threaded Mode. Table 2 illustrates the runtimes for $L = 20$ on a 32-core server system when the number of threads is varied from 1 to 32. The highest runtime improvement factors for decryption and homomorphic multiplication (with relinearization) are 3.1 and 4.4, respectively.

The decryption runtime is dominated by NTT, and the NTTs are parallelized at the level of CRT moduli (parameter k, which is 8 in this case). Table 2 shows that the maximum improvement is indeed achieved at 8 threads. Any further increase in the number of threads increases the overhead related to multi-threading without providing any improvement in speed. The theoretical maximum improvement factor of 8 is not reached most likely due to the distribution of the load between the cores of two sockets in the server. A more careful fine-tuning of OpenMP thread affinity settings would be needed to achieve a higher improvement factor, which is beyond the scope of this work.

The runtime of homomorphic multiplication (without relinearization) shows a more significant improvement with increase in the number of threads: it continues improving until 32 threads and reaches the speedup of 6.1 compared to the single-threaded execution time. This effect is due to the CRT basis extension and scaling operations, which are parallelized at the level of polynomial coefficients (parameter $n = 2^{14}$). However, as the contribution of NTT operations is high (nearly 70% for the single-threaded mode, as illustrated in Table 1), the benefits of parallelization due to CRT basis extension and scaling are limited (their relative contribution becomes smaller as the number of threads increases).

The relinearization procedure is NTT-bound and, therefore, shows approximately the same relative improvement as the decryption procedure, i.e., a factor of 2.9, which reaches its maximum value at 8 threads.

In summary, our analysis suggests that the proposed CRT basis extension and scaling operations parallelize well (w.r.t. ring dimension n) but the overall parallelization improvements of homomorphic multiplication and decryption largely depend on the parallelization of NTT operations. In our implementation, no intra-NTT parallelization was applied and thus the overall benefits of parallelization were limited.

6   Conclusion

In this work we described simpler alternatives to the CRT basis extension and scaling procedures of Bajard et al. [3], and implemented them in the PALISADE library [19]. These procedures are based on the use of floating-point arithmetic for certain intermediate computations. These procedures are not only simpler but also have lower computational complexity and noise growth than the procedures proposed in [3].

Our single- and multi-threaded experiments suggest that the main bottleneck of the implementation of our BFV variant is NTT operations. In other words, the cost of the CRT maintenance procedures, i.e., CRT basis extension and scaling, is relatively small. Therefore, further improvements in the BFV runtimes can be achieved by optimizing the NTT operations, focusing on their parallelization.

We have shown that our procedures can be applied to any scale-invariant homomorphic encryption scheme based on Brakerski's scheme, including YASHE. The CRT basis extension and scaling procedures may also be utilized in other lattice-based cryptographic constructions; for instance, scaling is a common technique used in many lattice schemes based on dual Regev's cryptosystem [11,21].

References

1. Albrecht, M., Scott, S., Player, R.: On the concrete hardness of learning with errors. J. Math. Cryptol. **9**(3), 169–203 (2015)
2. Badawi, A.A., Polyakov, Y., Aung, K.M.M., Veeravalli, B., Rohloff, K.: Implementation and performance evaluation of RNS variants of the BFV homomorphic encryption scheme. Cryptology ePrint Archive, Report 2018/589 (2018)
3. Bajard, J.-C., Eynard, J., Hasan, M.A., Zucca, V.: A full RNS variant of FV like somewhat homomorphic encryption schemes. In: Avanzi, R., Heys, H. (eds.) SAC 2016. LNCS, vol. 10532, pp. 423–442. Springer, Cham (2017). https://doi.org/10.1007/978-3-319-69453-5_23
4. Bos, J.W., Lauter, K., Loftus, J., Naehrig, M.: Improved security for a ring-based fully homomorphic encryption scheme. In: Stam, M. (ed.) IMACC 2013. LNCS, vol. 8308, pp. 45–64. Springer, Heidelberg (2013). https://doi.org/10.1007/978-3-642-45239-0_4
5. Brakerski, Z.: Fully homomorphic encryption without modulus switching from classical GapSVP. In: Safavi-Naini, R., Canetti, R. (eds.) CRYPTO 2012. LNCS, vol. 7417, pp. 868–886. Springer, Heidelberg (2012). https://doi.org/10.1007/978-3-642-32009-5_50
6. Brakerski, Z., Gentry, C., Vaikuntanathan, V.: (Leveled) fully homomorphic encryption without bootstrapping. In: ITCS 2012, pp. 309–325 (2012)
7. Chase, M., Chen, H., Ding, J., Goldwasser, S., et al.: Security of homomorphic encryption. Technical report, HomomorphicEncryption.org, Redmond WA, July 2017
8. Fan, J., Vercauteren, F.: Somewhat practical fully homomorphic encryption. Cryptology ePrint Archive, Report 2012/144 (2012)
9. Gentry, C.: Fully homomorphic encryption using ideal lattices. In: STOC 2009, pp. 169–178 (2009)
10. Gentry, C., Halevi, S., Smart, N.P.: Homomorphic evaluation of the AES circuit. In: Safavi-Naini, R., Canetti, R. (eds.) CRYPTO 2012. LNCS, vol. 7417, pp. 850–867. Springer, Heidelberg (2012). https://doi.org/10.1007/978-3-642-32009-5_49

11. Gentry, C., Peikert, C., Vaikuntanathan, V.: Trapdoors for hard lattices and new cryptographic constructions. In: STOC 2008, pp. 197–206 (2008)
12. Halevi, S., Polyakov, Y., Shoup, V.: An improved RNS variant of the BFV homomorphic encryption scheme. Cryptology ePrint Archive, Report 2018/117 (2018)
13. Halevi, S., Shoup, V.: Design and implementation of a homomorphic-encryption library (2013). https://shaih.github.io/pubs/he-library.pdf
14. Harvey, D.: Faster arithmetic for number-theoretic transforms. J. Symb. Comput. **60**, 113–119 (2014)
15. Kawamura, S., Koike, M., Sano, F., Shimbo, A.: Cox-rower architecture for fast parallel montgomery multiplication. In: Preneel, B. (ed.) EUROCRYPT 2000. LNCS, vol. 1807, pp. 523–538. Springer, Heidelberg (2000). https://doi.org/10.1007/3-540-45539-6_37
16. Lepoint, T., Naehrig, M.: A comparison of the homomorphic encryption schemes FV and YASHE. In: Pointcheval, D., Vergnaud, D. (eds.) AFRICACRYPT 2014. LNCS, vol. 8469, pp. 318–335. Springer, Cham (2014). https://doi.org/10.1007/978-3-319-06734-6_20
17. Longa, P., Naehrig, M.: Speeding up the number theoretic transform for faster ideal lattice-based cryptography. In: Foresti, S., Persiano, G. (eds.) CANS 2016. LNCS, vol. 10052, pp. 124–139. Springer, Cham (2016). https://doi.org/10.1007/978-3-319-48965-0_8
18. Lyubashevsky, V., Peikert, C., Regev, O.: A toolkit for ring-LWE cryptography. In: Johansson, T., Nguyen, P.Q. (eds.) EUROCRYPT 2013. LNCS, vol. 7881, pp. 35–54. Springer, Heidelberg (2013). https://doi.org/10.1007/978-3-642-38348-9_3
19. Polyakov, Y., Rohloff, K., Ryan, G.W.: PALISADE lattice cryptography library. https://git.njit.edu/palisade/PALISADE. Accessed Sept 2018
20. Polyakov, Y., Rohloff, K., Sahu, G., Vaikuntanathan, V.: Fast proxy re-encryption for publish/subscribe systems. ACM Trans. Priv. Secur. **20**(4), 14:1–14:31 (2017)
21. Regev, O.: On lattices, learning with errors, random linear codes, and cryptography. J. ACM **56**(6), 34 (2009)
22. Shenoy, A.P., Kumaresan, R.: Fast base extension using a redundant modulus in RNS. IEEE Trans. Comput. **38**(2), 292–297 (1989)

New Techniques for Multi-value Input Homomorphic Evaluation and Applications

Sergiu Carpov[1], Malika Izabachène[1(✉)], and Victor Mollimard[1,2]

[1] CEA LIST, Point Courrier 172, 91191 Gif-sur-Yvette Cedex, France
malika.izabachene@gmail.com
[2] Univ. Lyon, ENS de Lyon, 15 Parvis Renè Descartes, 69342 Lyon Cedex, France

Abstract. In this paper, we propose a new technique to perform several homomorphic operations in one bootstrapping call over a multi-value plaintext space. Our construction relies on the FHEW-based gate bootstrapping; we analyze its structure and propose a strategy we call *multi-value bootstrapping* which allows to bootstrap an arbitrary function in an efficient way.

The security of our scheme relies on the LWE assumption over the torus. We give three possible applications: we first describe how to efficiently evaluate an arbitrary boolean function (LUT) and combine LUTs in circuits. We also explain how to apply our procedure to optimize the circuit bootstrapping from (Asiacrypt'2017) which allows to compose circuits in a leveled mode. And we finally present a simple method which makes use of the multi-value bootstrapping to evaluate a encrypted neural network. We have implemented the proposed method and were able to evaluate an arbitrary 6-to-6 LUTs under 1.6 s. Our implementation is based on the TFHE library but can be easily integrated into other homomorphic libraries based on the same structure, such as FHEW (Eurocrypt'2015). The number of LUT outputs does not influence the execution time by a lot, e.g. evaluation of additional 128 outputs on the same 6 input bits takes only 0.05 more seconds.

Keywords: LWE-based FHE · Multi-value bootstrapping · Homomorphic LUT

1 Introduction

Fully homomorphic encryption (FHE) allows to perform arbitrary computations directly over encrypted data. The first FHE scheme has been proposed by Gentry [16]. The construction relies on a technique called *bootstrapping*, which handles noise increase in FHE ciphertexts. This construction theoretically enables to execute any computation directly over encrypted data but remains slow in practice. Several works ([6,15,18,19,22] for example) followed Gentry's initial proposal and contributed to further improve FHE efficiency.

© Springer Nature Switzerland AG 2019
M. Matsui (Ed.): CT-RSA 2019, LNCS 11405, pp. 106–126, 2019.
https://doi.org/10.1007/978-3-030-12612-4_6

Fully homomorphic encryption schemes are divided in two types of constructions. The first one is based on Gentry's initial proposal, where basically the bootstrapping procedure consists of the evaluation of the decryption circuit at gate level. In this case, the operations remain slow but their design allows to pack data efficiently using batching techniques. The second one is based on the Gentry, Sahai and Waters Somewhat homomorphic scheme [17] proposed in 2013 which supports branching programs with polynomial noise overhead and deterministic automata logic. Alperin-Sheriff and Peikert [3] improved the bootstrapping by implementing an efficient homomorphic arithmetic function, showing that boolean function and Barighton circuit can be avoided in bootstrapping. In 2015, Ducas and Micciancio [14] gave a construction of bootstrapping with NAND gate evaluation, named FHEW, and suggested extension for larger gates. They provided an implementation for their scheme taking less than a second per bootstrapping on a single core. Biasse and Riuz [4] adapted the FHEW construction for arbitrary gates. Recently, Chillotti, Gama, Georgieva and Izabachène [10,12] also improved the bootstrapping procedure and provided a construction named TFHE. Their implementation [13] runs in less than 13ms for any binary gate and 26 ms for the MUX gate. They also proposed new techniques for the TFHE toolbox which allow to pack data and compose bootstrapped gates in a leveled mode with a new procedure they called *circuit bootstrapping*. Recently, Bonnoron, Ducas, and Fillinger [5] introduced a FHEW-based type scheme which allows to perform more computation per bootstrapping call. They implemented their method for the evaluation of a 6-to-6 bit LUT in about 10 s.

Our multi-value bootstrapping is built from the same line of scheme as the FHEW bootstrapping. In order to explain our contribution, we first review its basic construction and give later a more detailed description. The FHEW-based boostrapping algorithms are implemented via an homomorphic accumulator which evaluates the linear part of decryption function followed by a non-linear part. Given an LWE ciphertext of m and GSW encryptions of the secret key, we want to homomorphically evaluate a known arbitrary function f on m where $f : \mathbb{Z}_t \to \mathbb{Z}_t$. We define $F = f \circ r$ where r is the rounding function which corresponds to the final non-linear step of the ciphertext $\mathbf{c}$ decryption function. We write $F : \mathbb{Z}_T \to \mathbb{Z}_T$. To be as clear as possible, we depict the bootstrapping algorithm in three steps: Setp (1) the input ciphertext of m is rescaled modulo T and the operations are mapped over a cyclic group $\mathcal{G}$. We explain later how $\mathcal{G}$ is constructed; Step (2) the accumulator ACC is computed using blind shift operations in $\mathcal{G}$ which uses encryptions of the secret key; Step (3) a test polynomial TV_F is then applied to ACC and an LWE ciphertext of $f(m)$ is extracted. Here TV_F encodes the possible output values of the function f, i.e. the correspondence between the message m encoded in the input ciphertext and the output ciphertext of $f(m)$. Note that the test polynomial TV_F can also be applied before the blind shift operations.

Our Contribution. In this work, we show how to construct and chose TV_F in order to optimize the evaluation of arbitrary functions in one bootstrapping call. In order to do so, we analyze the structure of FHEW-based bootstrapping algorithms and make a comparison in term of noise overhead output and modularity, i.e. the functions they allow to evaluate. To be efficient, our solution should output a small noise while being able to 'statistically' encode all the possible values of the function. As a first proof concept and for sake of comparison, we implement a 6-to-6 LUT which runs in 1.6 s for a concrete security of about 128 bits (asserted using the estimator from [1]) compared to a timing of about 10 s at a security level of about 100 bits for the implementation of [5]. Our construction makes it possible to evaluate several arbitrary functions on the same set of inputs by calling only once the main subroutine of the TFHE bootstrapping. The name multi-value is derived from many-valued logic which is a propositional calculus with more than two values. We give examples of possible applications of our procedure in this paper: we explain how to efficiently compose homomorphic LUTs and we give an idea on how to optimize the circuit bootstrapping proposed in Sect. 4 of [12] which can be used to compose circuits in a leveled mode. We finally show an application to the homomorphic evaluation of a neural network where the linear part is evaluated using a generalization of the key-switching procedure and the non-linear part is evaluated with our multi-value bootstrapping.

Our Technique and Comparisons to Other Works. In previous constructions, except [13], test polynomial TV_F is integrated at the end, after the accumulator is computed, we have $\mathsf{ACC} \cdot \mathsf{TV}_F$ [1]. In the TFHE gate bootstrapping of [13], the test polynomial TV_F is embedded in the accumulator from the very start when the accumulator is still noiseless and, at step 2 the accumulator is $\mathsf{TV}_F \cdot \mathsf{ACC}$. This allows to save a factor $\sqrt{N}$, where N is the dimension. On the other end, they are only able to encode two possible values in TFHE gate bootstrapping. A naive idea for computing multi-value input function f would be to decompose f into p Mux gate functions and then combine the results of the p gate bootstrapping calls, but this method is quite inefficient. To optimize this naive construction, we define a common factor $\mathsf{TV}_F^{(0)}$ which is shared between all the p calls. The most expensive part is made once for the p calls. Then the specification with respect to the 2-value functions is made at the end using a second test polynomial $\mathsf{TV}_F^{(1)}$. This last step consists only of a multiplication by constant polynomial, which is much cheaper than p blind rotations. We manage to decrease the output ciphertext noise by choosing a low-norm second-stage test polynomials when compared to previous methods integrating the test polynomial at the end.

Organization of the Paper. We first describe the high level structure of FHEW based bootstrapping algorithms and provide a comparison between the different scheme in the literature. Then, our preliminary section reviews the mathematical backgrounds for LWE and GSW encryption over the torus and gives the building blocks from the TFHE framework [13] used in our constructions. In Sect. 3, we present the optimized multi-value bootstrapping together with test

---

[1] In this paragraph only the evaluation order of an expression matters and is used for a better illustration.

polynomial factorization. In Sect. 4, we present applications to the homomorphic evaluation of arbitrary functions and describe our implementation results for the case of a 6-to-6 LUT function. Finally, we explain how to apply the multi-value bootstrapping and extended keyswitching to optimize the circuit bootstrapping from [12] and to evaluate a encrypted neural network system.

2   Preliminaries

Notation. The set $\{0,1\}$ is written as $\mathbb{B}$. The set of vectors of size n in E is denoted E^n, and the set of $n \times m$ matrices with entries in E is noted $\mathcal{M}_{n,m}(E)$. The real torus $\mathbb{R} \mod 1$ is denoted $\mathbb{T}$. $\mathbb{T}_N[X]$ denotes the $\mathbb{Z}$-module $\mathbb{R}[X]/(X^N+1) \mod 1$ of torus polynomials, here N is a fixed power of 2 integer. The ring $\mathbb{Z}[X]/(X^N+1)$ is denoted $\mathfrak{R}$. The set of polynomials with binary coefficients is denoted $\mathbb{B}_N[X]$.

2.1   High Level Structure of FHEW-based Bootstrapping

We first describe the high level structure of the FHEW-based bootstrapping algorithms. The procedure can be split in three steps we detail below. We explain later how schemes in this line can be instanciated using this formalism. Figure 1 gives a schematic overview of the bootstrapping steps.

1. In the first step, the coefficients $(\mathbf{a}, b)$ of input LWE ciphertext $\mathbf{c} = (\mathbf{a}, b)$ are mapped to $\mathbb{Z}_T$. A cyclic multiplicative group $\mathcal{G}$, where $\mathbb{Z}_T \simeq \mathcal{G}$, is used for an equivalent representation of $\mathbb{Z}_T$ elements. The group $\mathcal{G}$ contains all the powers of X: $X^0, \ldots, X^{T-1}$ and T is defined as the smallest integer verifying $X^T \mod \Phi(X) = 1$ where $\Phi(X)$ is the quotient polynomial defining the input Ring-LWE scheme. Most of the times $\Phi(X)$ is the T-th cyclotomic polynomial.
2. In this step, the message m encrypted as $\mathbf{c} = (\mathbf{a}, b)$ is transformed to an intermediary GSW encryption of X^m. Message $m \in \mathbb{Z}_T$ is obtained from $\mathbf{c} = (\mathbf{a}, b)$ using the linear transformation $b - \mathbf{a} \cdot \mathbf{s} \equiv m$ (i.e. the linear part of the decryption algorithm). Given encryptions of X^{s_i} one can homomorphically apply linear mapping φ to $\mathbf{c}$. We obtain the so-called accumulator ACC which contains an encryption of $X^{\varphi(\mathbf{c})} \in \mathcal{G}$.
3. At the third step, a test polynomial $\mathsf{TV}_F \in \mathcal{G}$ is multiplied to ACC. The test polynomial encodes output values of a function F for each possible input message $m \in \mathbb{Z}_T$. Here F is a function from $\mathbb{Z}_T$ to $\mathbb{Z}_T$. It finally extracts an LWE encryption of $F(m)$ from $\mathsf{TV}_F \cdot \mathsf{ACC}$ (or from $\mathsf{ACC} \cdot \mathsf{TV}_F$ if TV_F is applied after computing the accumulator) with a modified noise. As input message m is a noised version of the actual message encrypted in $\mathbf{c} = (\mathbf{a}, b)$ function F is a composition of a 'payload' function $f : \mathbb{Z}_t \to \mathbb{Z}_t$ and a rounding function $r : \mathbb{Z}_T \to \mathbb{Z}_t$.

For example, in [5], step (1) corresponds to a modulus switching from Q to $T = pq$, step (2) computes the accumulator operation in the groups

$\mathcal{G} = \{1, \ldots, X^p - 1\}$ and $\mathcal{G} = \{1, \ldots, Y^q - 1\}$ for primes p and q and recomposes the result in the circulant ring $\mathbb{Z}[Z]/(Z^{pq} - 1)$; at step (3), a test polynomial (encoding $F(x) = f(\lfloor tx/pq \rceil)$ where f is an arbitrary function) is applied to the accumulator and a LWE ciphertext of $f(m)$ is extracted, where the extraction is implemented by the trace function. In [13], $\mathcal{G}$ is the multiplicative group $\{1, X, \ldots, X^{2N-1}\}$ where N is a power of 2. Function f implements a rounding (i.e. torus most significant bit extraction); step (1) does the rounding from $\mathbb{T}$ to $\mathbb{Z}_{2N}$ and the test polynomial is applied before the computation of the accumulator ACC; step (2) computes $\mathsf{ACC} \in \mathcal{G}$ with a blind rotation; step (3) extracts $\mathsf{LWE}(f(m))$ by extracting the constant coefficient of $\mathsf{TV}_F \cdot \mathsf{ACC}$. Our multi-value bootstapping is instanciated using [13].

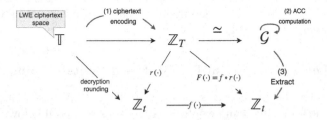

Fig. 1. Structure of the bootstrapping Algorithm. Setp (1): The ciphertext of m is rescaled modulo T and the operations are mapped over the cyclic group $\mathcal{G}$ where $\mathcal{G} = \langle X \rangle$ is the group of T-th roots of unity associated to the cyclotomic polynomial $\Phi_T(X)$ (for example). Step (2): the accumulator ACC is computed using blind shift operations in $\mathcal{G}$ which uses encryptions of the secret key in the powers of X. Step (3): a test polynomial is applied to ACC, it can also be applied before blind shift operations, and an LWE ciphertext of $f(m)$ is extracted from ACC using the encoding of an alternative representation of f over $\mathbb{Z}_T$.

2.2   Backgrounds on TFHE

In this work, we will use the torus representation from [10] of the LWE encryption scheme introduced by Regev [21] and the ring variant of Lyubashevsky et al. [20].

Distance, Norm and Concentrated Distribution. We use the ℓ_p distance for torus elements. By abuse of notation, we denote as $\|x\|_p$ the p-norm of the representative of $x \in \mathbb{T}^k$ with all its coefficients in $]-\frac{1}{2}, \frac{1}{2}]$. For a torus polynomial $P(X)$ modulo $X^N + 1$, we take the norm of its unique representative of degree $\leq N - 1$. A distribution on the torus is concentrated iff its support is included in a ball of radius $\frac{1}{4}$ of $\mathbb{T}$ except with negligible probability. In this case, we can define the usual notion of expectation and variance over $\mathbb{T}$. Let $\mathcal{N}(0, \sigma^2)$ be a normal distribution centered in 0 and of variance σ^2. We denote $\kappa(\varepsilon) = \min_k \{\Pr_{X \leftarrow \mathcal{N}(0,\sigma^2)} [|X| > k \cdot \sigma] < \varepsilon\}$. In this case, we have $\Pr_{X \leftarrow \mathcal{N}(0,\sigma^2)} [|X| > k \cdot \sigma] = \mathrm{erf}(k/\sqrt{2})$. For example, for $\varepsilon = 2^{-64}$ (this paper), we can take $\kappa(\varepsilon) > 9.16$ and for $\epsilon = 2^{-32}$, we can take $\kappa(\varepsilon) > 6.33$.

A real distribution X is said σ-subgaussian iff for all $t \in \mathbb{R}$, $\mathbb{E}(\exp(tX)) \leq \exp(\sigma^2 t^2/2)$. If X and X' are two independent σ and σ' subgaussian variables, then for all $\alpha, \gamma \in \mathbb{R}$, $\alpha X + \gamma X'$ is $\sqrt{\alpha^2\sigma^2 + \gamma^2\sigma'^2}$-subgaussian. All the errors in this document will follow subgaussian distributions. In what follows, we review TFHE for encryption of torus polynomial elements.

TRLWE Samples. To encrypt a message $\mu \in \mathbb{T}_N[X]$, one picks a Gaussian approximation of the preimage of $\varphi_s^{-1}(\mu)$ over the Ω-probability space of all possible choices of Gaussian noise. If the Gaussian noise α is small, we can define the expectation and the variance over the torus. The expectation of $\varphi_s(c)$ is equal to μ and its variance is equal to the variance of α. We refer to [10] for a more complete definition of the Ω-probability space.

Definition 2.1 (TRLWE). *Let $\mathcal{M}$ be a discrete subspace of $\mathbb{T}_N[X]$ and $\mu \in \mathcal{M}$ a message. Let $s \in \mathbb{B}_N[X]^k$ a TRLWE secret key, where each coefficient is chosen uniformly at random. A TRLWE sample is a vector $c = (\mathbf{a}, b)$ of $\mathbb{T}_N[X]^{k+1}$ which can be either :*

- *A trivial sample: $\mathbf{a} = 0$ and $b = \mu$. Note that this ciphertext is independent of the secret key.*
- *A fresh TRLWE sample of μ of standard deviation α: $\mathbf{a}$ is uniformly chosen in $\mathbb{T}_N[X]^k$ and b follows a continuous Gaussian distribution of standard deviation α centered in $\mu + \mathbf{s} \cdot \mathbf{a}$ and of variance α^2.*
- *Linear combination of fresh or trivial TRLWE samples.*

We define the phase $\varphi_s(c)$ of a sample $c = (\mathbf{a}, b) \in \mathbb{T}_N[X]^k \times \mathbb{T}_N[X]$ under key $s \in \mathbb{B}_N[X]^k$ as $\varphi_s(c) = b - \mathbf{s} \cdot \mathbf{a}$. Note that the phase function is a linear $(kN + 1)$-lipschitzian function from $\mathbb{T}_N[X]^{k+1}$ to $\mathbb{T}_N[X]$. We say that c is a valid TRLWE sample iff there exists a key $s \in \mathbb{B}_N[X]^k$ such that the distribution of the phase $\varphi_s(c)$ is concentrated over the Ω-space around the message μ, i.e. included in a ball of radius $< \frac{1}{4}$ around μ. Note that $c = \sum_{j=1}^p r_j \cdot c_j$ is a valid TRLWE sample if $c_1, \ldots, c_p$ are valid TRLWE samples (under the same key) and $r_1, \ldots, r_p \in \mathfrak{R}$. We also use the function msg() defined as the expectation of the phase over the Ω-space. If μ is in $\mathcal{M}$, one can decrypt a TRLWE sample c under secret key $\mathbf{s}$ with small noise (smaller that the packing radius) by rounding its phase to the nearest element of the discrete message space $\mathcal{M}$. We also use the function error Err($\cdot$) of a sample defined as the difference between the phase and the message of the sample. We write Var(Err(X)) the variance of the error of X and $\|\text{Err}(X)\|_\infty$ its amplitude. When X is a normal distribution we have $\|\text{Err}(X)\|_\infty \leq \kappa(\varepsilon) \cdot \text{Var}(\text{Err}(X))$ with probability $1 - \varepsilon$.

Given p valid and independent TRLWE samples $c_1, \ldots, c_p$ under key s, if $c = \sum_{i=1}^p e_i \cdot c_i$, then $\text{msg}(c) = \sum_{i=1}^p e_i \cdot \text{msg}(c_i)$ with $\|\text{Err}(c)\|_\infty \leq \sum_{i=1}^p \|e_i\|_1 \cdot \|\text{Err}(c_i)\|$ and $\text{Var}(\text{Err}(c)) = \sum_{i=1}^p \|e_i\|_2^2 \cdot \text{Var}(\text{Err}(c_i))$.

The TRLWE problem consists of distinguishing TRLWE encryptions of **0** from random samples in $\mathbb{T}_N[X]^k \times \mathbb{T}_N[X]$. When $N = 1$ and k is large, the TRLWE problem is the Scalar LWE problem over the torus and the TRLWE encryption is the LWE encryption over the torus. We denote it TLWE. When N is large and

$k = 1$, the TRLWE problem is the LWE problem over torus polynomials with binary secrets. In addition, the TLWE and the TRLWE correspond to the Scale invariant variants defined in [7,9,11] and to the Ring-LWE from [20]. We refer to Sect. 6 of [10] for more details on security estimates on the LWE problem of the torus.

TRGSW Samples. We define a gadget matrix that will be used to decompose over ring elements and to reverse back. Other choices of gadget basis are also possible.

$$\mathbf{H} = \begin{pmatrix} 1/B_g & \cdots & 0 \\ \vdots & \ddots & \vdots \\ 1/B_g^\ell & \cdots & 0 \\ \hline \vdots & \ddots & \vdots \\ 0 & \cdots & 1/B_g \\ \vdots & \ddots & \vdots \\ 0 & \cdots & 1/B_g^\ell \end{pmatrix} \in \mathcal{M}_{(k+1)\ell, k+1}(\mathbb{T}_N[X]).$$

A vector $v \in \mathbb{T}_N[X]^{k+1}$ can approximately be decomposed as $Dec_{H,\beta,\epsilon}(\boldsymbol{v}) = \boldsymbol{u}$ where $\boldsymbol{u} \in \mathfrak{R}^{(k+1)\ell}$, s.t. $\|\boldsymbol{u}\|_\infty \leq \beta$ and $\|\boldsymbol{u} \cdot H - \boldsymbol{v}\|_\infty \leq \epsilon$. We call $\beta \in \mathbb{R}_{>0}$ the quality parameter and $\epsilon \in \mathbb{R}_{>0}$ the precision of the decomposition. In this paper, we use the gadget H where the decomposition in base B_g is a power of 2. We take $\beta = B_g/2$ and $\epsilon = 1/2B_g^\ell$.

Definition 2.2 (TRGSW Sample). *Let ℓ and $k \geq 1$ be two integers and $\alpha \geq 0$ be a noise parameter. Let $\mathbf{s} \in \mathbb{B}_N[X]^k$ be a TRLWE key, we say that $\mathbf{C} \in \mathcal{M}_{(k+1)\ell, k+1}(\mathbb{T}_N[X])$ is a fresh TGSW sample of $\mu \in \mathfrak{R}/\mathbf{H}^\perp$ with standard deviation α iff $\mathbf{C} = \mathbf{Z} + \mu \cdot \mathbf{H}$ where each row of $\mathbf{Z} \in \mathcal{M}_{(k+1)\ell, k+1}(\mathbb{T}_N[X])$ is a TRLWE sample of $\mathbf{0}$ with Gaussian standard deviation α. Reciprocally, we say that an element $\mathbf{C} \in \mathcal{M}_{(k+1)\ell, k+1}(\mathbb{T}_N[X])$ is a valid TRGSW sample iff there exists a unique polynomial $\mu \in \mathfrak{R}/\mathbf{H}^\perp$ and a unique key $\mathbf{s}$ such that each row of $\mathbf{C} - \mu \cdot \mathbf{H}$ is a valid TRLWE sample of 0 under the key $\mathbf{s}$. We call the polynomial μ the message of $\mathbf{C}$.*

Since a TRGSW sample consists of $(k + 1)\ell$ TRLWE under the same secret key, the definition of the phase, message, error, norm and variance and the result on the sum of TRLWE samples can easily be extended for TRGSW samples.

External Product. We review the module multiplication of the messages of TRGSW and TRLWE samples from [8,10]. This operation is called external product operation and is defined as: $\boxdot : \mathbb{T}_N[X]^{k+1} \times \mathcal{M}_{(k+1)\ell, k+1}(\mathbb{T}_N[X]) \to \mathbb{T}_N[X]^{k+1}$. The operation $\boxdot$ has the following property:

Theorem 2.3 (Homomorphic module multiplication). *If A is a valid* TRGSW *sample of μ_A and b is a valid* TRLWE *sample of μ_b. Then, if $\|Err(A \boxdot b)\|_\infty \leq \frac{1}{4}$, $A \boxdot b$ is a valid* TRLWE *sample of $\mu_A \cdot \mu_b$.*

We have $Var(Err(A \boxdot b)) \leq (k+1)\ell N \beta^2 Var(Err(A)) + (1+kN)\|\mu_A\|_2^2 \epsilon^2 + \|\mu_A\|_2^2 Var(Err(b))$ where β and ϵ are the parameters used in the decomposition $Dec_{h,\beta,\epsilon}()$.

Assumption 2.4 (Independence heuristic). All the previous results rely on the Gaussian Heuristic: all the error coefficients of TRLWE or TRGSW samples of the linear combinations we consider are independent and concentrated. In particular, we assume that they are σ-subgaussian where σ is the square-root of their variance.

2.3   TFHE Gate Bootstrapping

We review the TFHE gate bootstrapping and the key-switching procedure from [10,12]. The TFHE gate bootstrapping changes the noise of the LWE input to bring it to a fix noise; it can also change the dimension of the ciphertexts. We specify with an under-bar the input parameters and with an upper-bar the output parameters when needed.

Definition 2.5. *Let $\underline{\mathfrak{K}} \in \mathbb{B}^n$, $\bar{\mathfrak{K}} \in \mathbb{B}_N^k$ and α be a noise parameter. We define the bootstrapping key $BK_{\underline{\mathfrak{K}} \to \bar{\mathfrak{K}}, \alpha}$ as the sequence of n TGSW samples $BK_i \in TGSW_{\bar{\mathfrak{K}}, \alpha}(\underline{\mathfrak{K}}_i)$.*

TFHE Gate Bootstrapping. The ternary Mux gate takes three boolean values c, d_0, d_1 and returns $Mux(c, d_0, d_1) = (c \wedge d_1) \oplus ((1 - c) \wedge d_0)$. We also write $Mux(c, d_0, d_1) = c?d_1 : d_0$.

The controlled Mux gate, CMux takes in input samples $\mathbf{d_0}, \mathbf{d_1}$ of messages μ_0, μ_1, a TRGSW sample $\mathbf{C}$ of a message bit m and returns a TRLWE sample of message μ_0 if $m = 0$ and μ_1 if $m = 1$. Lemma 2.6 gives the error propagation of CMux.

Lemma 2.6. *Let $\mathbf{d_0}, \mathbf{d_1}$ be* TRLWE *samples and $\mathbf{C} \in TGSW_s(m)$ where message $m \in \{0, 1\}$. Then, $msg(CMux(\mathbf{C}, \mathbf{d_1}, \mathbf{d_0})) = msg(\mathbf{C})?msg(\mathbf{d_1}) : msg(\mathbf{d_0})$ and we have: $Var(Err(CMux(\mathbf{C}, \mathbf{d_1}, \mathbf{d_0}))) \leq \max(Var(Err(\mathbf{d_0})), Var(Err(\mathbf{d_1}))) + \vartheta(\mathbf{C})$ where $\vartheta(\mathbf{C}) = (k+1)\ell N \beta^2 Var(Err(\mathbf{C})) + (1+kN)\epsilon^2$.*

The gate bootstrapping from [12] also uses the BlindRotate algorithm. Assuming $\mathbf{c} = (a_1, \ldots, a_p, b)$ is a LWE ciphertext under secret key $\mathbf{s}$, Algorithm 1 computes the blind rotation of v by the phase of $\mathbf{c}$.

Theorem 2.7. *Let $\alpha > 0 \in \mathbb{R}$ be a noise parameter, $\mathfrak{K} \in \mathbb{B}^n$ be a* TLWE *secret key and $K \in \mathbb{B}_N[X]^k$ be its* TRLWE *interpretation. Given one sample $\mathbf{c} \in TRLWE_K(v)$ with $v \in \mathbb{T}_N[X]$, $p+1$ integers $a_1, \ldots, a_p, b \in \mathbb{Z}/2N\mathbb{Z}$, and p* TRGSW *ciphertexts $\mathbf{C_1}, \ldots, \mathbf{C_p}$ where each $\mathbf{C_i} \in TRGSW_{K,\alpha}(s_i)$ for $s_i \in \mathbb{B}$ the* BlindRotate *algorithm outputs a sample $ACC \in TRLWE_K(X^{-\rho} \cdot v)$ where $\rho = b - \sum_{i=1}^p a_i s_i$ such that $Var(Err(ACC)) \leq Var(Err(\mathbf{c})) + p(k+1)\ell N \beta^2 \vartheta_C + p(1+kN)\epsilon^2$ where $\vartheta_C = \alpha^2$.*

Algorithm 1. BlindRotate

Input: A TRLWE sample c of $v \in \mathbb{T}_N[X]$ with key K.
  1: $p+1$ int. coefficients $a_1, \ldots, a_p, b \in \mathbb{Z}/2N\mathbb{Z}$
  2: p TRGSW samples $C_1, \ldots, C_p$ of $s_1, \ldots, s_p \in \mathbb{B}$ with key K
Output: A TRLWE sample of $X^{-\rho}.v$ where $\rho = b - \sum_{i=1}^{p} s_i.a_i \mod 2N$ with key K
  3: $\mathsf{ACC} \leftarrow X^{-b} \cdot c$
  4: **for** $i = 1$ **to** p
  5:      $\mathsf{ACC} \leftarrow \mathsf{CMux}(C_i, X^{a_i} \cdot \mathsf{ACC}, \mathsf{ACC})$
  6: **return** ACC

TRLWE-to-TLWE Sample Extraction. Given one TRLWE sample of message $\mu \in \mathbb{T}_N[X]$ the SampleExtract procedure allows to extract a TLWE sample of a single coefficient of polynomial μ. Indeed, a TRLWE ciphertext of message $\mu \in \mathbb{T}_N[X]$ of dimension k under a secret key $K \in \mathbb{B}_N[X]$ can alternatively be seen as N TLWE ciphertexts whose messages are the coefficients of μ. It is of dimension $n = kN$ and the secret key $\mathfrak{K}$ is in $\mathbb{B}^n$, where $K_i = \sum_{j=0}^{N-1} \mathfrak{K}_{N(i-1)+j+1} X^j$.

Functional Key-Switching. The functional key-switching procedure allows to switch between different parameter sets and between scalar and polynomial message space. It allows to homomorphically evaluate a morphism from $\mathbb{Z}$-module $\mathbb{T}^p$ to $\mathbb{T}_N[X]$. We recall in Algorithm 2 the functional keyswitching algorithm (from Sect. 2.2 of [12]) where the morphism f is public; we adapt its definition to be able to use other decomposition basis of the key than the decomposition in base 2.

Algorithm 2. TLWE-to-TRLWE public functional key-switch

Input: p TLWE samples $\mathfrak{c}^{(z)} = (\mathfrak{a}^{(z)}, \mathfrak{b}^{(z)}) \in \mathsf{TLWE}_{\mathfrak{K}}(\mu_z)$ for $z = 1, \ldots, p$, a public R-lipschitzian morphism f from $\mathbb{T}^p$ to $\mathbb{T}_N[X]$, $\mathsf{KS}_{i,j} \in \mathsf{TRLWE}_K(\frac{\mathfrak{K}_i}{\mathsf{base}^j})$, where base is an integer.
Output: A TRLWE sample $c \in \mathsf{TRLWE}_K(f(\mu_1, \ldots, \mu_p))$
  1: **for** $i \in [\![1, n]\!]$ **do**
  2:      Let $a_i = f(\mathfrak{a}_i^{(1)}, \ldots, \mathfrak{a}_i^{(p)})$
  3:      Let $\tilde{a}_i$ be the closest multiple of $1/\mathsf{base}^t$ to a_i (i.e. $\|\tilde{a}_i - a_i\|_\infty < \mathsf{base}^{-(t+1)}$)
  4:      Binary decompose each $\tilde{a}_i = \sum_{j=1}^{t} \tilde{a}_{i,j} \cdot \mathsf{base}^{-j}$ where $\tilde{a}_{i,j} \in \mathbb{Z}_N[X]$ and each of its coefficient is in $\{0, \ldots, \mathsf{base} - 1\}$.
  5: **end for**
  6: **return** $(0, f(\mathfrak{b}^{(1)}, \ldots, \mathfrak{b}^{(p)})) - \sum_{i=1}^{n} \sum_{j=1}^{t} \tilde{a}_{i,j} \times \mathsf{KS}_{i,j}$

Theorem 2.8 *(Public functional key-switch). Given p TLWE samples $\mathfrak{c}^{(z)}$ under the same key $\mathfrak{K}$ of μ_z with $z = 1, \ldots, p$, a public R-lipschitzian morphism f from $\mathbb{T}^p$ to $\mathbb{T}_N[X]$, and a family of samples $\mathsf{KS}_{i,j} \in \mathsf{TRLWE}_{K,\gamma}(\frac{\mathfrak{K}_i}{\mathsf{base}^j})$ with standard deviation γ and where base is an integer, Algorithm 2 outputs a TRLWE sample $c \in \mathsf{TRLWE}_K(f(\mu_1, \ldots, \mu_p))$ with $\mathsf{Var}(\mathsf{Err}(c)) \leq R^2 \mathsf{Var}(\mathsf{Err}(\mathfrak{c})) + ntN\vartheta_{\mathsf{KS}} + nN\mathsf{base}^{-2(t+1)}$, where $\vartheta_{\mathsf{KS}} = \gamma^2$ is the variance of the error of KS.*

For $p = 1$ and f the identity function, we retrieve the classical key-switching where the $\mathsf{KS}_{i,j}$ is a sample $\mathsf{TLWE}_{s,\gamma}(c_i \cdot \mathsf{base}^{-j})$ for $i \in [\![1, n]\!]$ and $j \in [\![1, t]\!]$. In this case, the output is a TLWE sample $\mathbf{c}$ of the same input message μ_1 and secret s, with $\mathsf{Var}(\mathsf{Err}(\mathbf{c})) \leq \mathsf{Var}(\mathsf{Err}(\mathbf{c})) + nt\gamma^2 + n\mathsf{base}^{-2(t+1)}$.

We are now ready to recall the TFHE gate bootstrapping in Algorithm 3. The TFHE gate bootstrapping algorithm takes as inputs a constant $\mu \in \mathbb{T}$, a TLWE sample of $x \cdot \frac{1}{2}$ with $x \in \mathbb{B}$, a bootstrapping key and returns a TLWE sample of $x \cdot \mu$ with a controlled error.

Algorithm 3. TFHE gate bootstrapping

Input: A constant $\mu \in \mathbb{T}$, a TLWE sample $\underline{\mathbf{c}} = (\underline{\mathbf{a}}, \underline{b}) \in \mathsf{TLWE}_{\underline{\mathfrak{K}}, \eta}(x \cdot \frac{1}{2})$ with $x \in \mathbb{B}$,
   a bootstrapping key $\mathsf{BK}_{\underline{\mathfrak{K}} \to \bar{\mathfrak{K}}, \alpha} = \left(\mathsf{BK}_i \in \mathsf{TRGSW}_{\bar{K}, \alpha}(\underline{\mathfrak{K}}_i) \right)_{i \in [\![1,n]\!]}$ where $\bar{K}$ is the
   TRLWE interpretation of $\bar{\mathfrak{K}}$.
Output: A TLWE sample $\bar{\mathbf{c}} = (\bar{a}, \bar{b}) \in \mathsf{TLWE}_{\bar{\mathfrak{K}}, \bar{\eta}}(x \cdot \mu)$
   1: Let $\hat{\mu} = \frac{1}{2}\mu \in \mathbb{T}$ (Pick one of the two possible values)
   2: Let $b = \lfloor 2N\underline{b} \rceil$ and $a_i = \lfloor 2N\underline{a}_i \rceil \in \mathbb{Z}$ for each $i \in [\![1, n]\!]$
   3: Let $\mathsf{TV}_F := (1 + X + \cdots + X^{N-1}) \cdot X^{\frac{N}{2}} \cdot \hat{\mu} \in \mathbb{T}_N[X]$
   4: $\mathsf{ACC} \leftarrow \mathsf{BlindRotate}((\mathbf{0}, v), (a_1, \ldots, a_n, b), (\mathsf{BK}_1, \ldots, \mathsf{BK}_n))$
   5: Return $(\mathbf{0}, \hat{\mu}) + \mathsf{SampleExtract}(\mathsf{ACC})$

Lines 1 to 4 compute a TRLWE sample of message $X^{\varphi} \cdot v$ where φ is the phase of $\underline{\mathbf{c}}$ (actually an approximated phase because of rescaling in line 2). The $\mathsf{SampleExtract}$ extracts its constant coefficient ($\hat{\mu}$ if $x = 1$ and $-\hat{\mu}$ if $x = 0$) encrypted in a TLWE sample. The final addition allows to either obtain a TLWE sample of 0 or a TLWE sample of $2 \cdot \hat{\mu} = \mu$. The error of the output ciphertext is obtained from the combination of the output error of Theorem 2.7 and the error of the $\mathsf{SampleExtract}$ procedure. An internal cumulated error δ is introduced in line 2 by the rescaling. We have $\delta \leq \frac{h+1}{4N}$ where h is the number of non-zero coefficients of TLWE secret key $\underline{\mathfrak{K}}$ and $4N$ comes from the rescaling by $2N$ and rounding of $(\underline{\mathbf{a}}, \underline{b})$ coefficients. This error does not influence the output.

Theorem 2.9 (TFHE gate boostrapping). *Let $\underline{\mathfrak{K}} \in \mathbb{B}^n$ and $\bar{\mathfrak{K}} \in \mathbb{B}^{kN}$ be two* TLWE *secret keys, $\bar{K} \in \mathbb{B}_N[X]^k$ be the* TRLWE *interpretation of $\bar{\mathfrak{K}}$ and $\alpha > 0 \in \mathbb{R}$ a noise parameter. Let* $\mathsf{BK}_{\underline{\mathfrak{K}} \to \bar{\mathfrak{K}}, \alpha}$ *be a bootstrapping key, i.e n samples* $\mathsf{BK}_i \in \mathsf{TRGSW}_{\bar{K}, \alpha}(\underline{\mathfrak{K}}_i)$ *for $i \in [\![1, n]\!]$. Given a constant $\mu \in \mathbb{T}$ and a sample $\underline{\mathbf{c}} \in \mathbb{T}^{n+1}$, Algorithm 3 outputs a* TLWE *sample $\bar{\mathbf{c}} \in \mathsf{TLWE}_{\bar{\mathfrak{K}}}(\bar{\mu})$ where $\bar{\mu} = 0$ if $|\varphi_{\underline{\mathfrak{K}}}(\underline{\mathbf{c}})| < \frac{1}{4} - \delta$ and $\bar{\mu} = \mu$ if $|\varphi_{\underline{\mathfrak{K}}}(\underline{\mathbf{c}})| > \frac{1}{4} + \delta$. We have $\mathsf{Var}(\mathsf{Err}(\bar{\mathbf{c}})) \leq n(k+1) \ell N \beta^2 \vartheta_{BK} + n(1 + kN)\epsilon^2$ where ϑ_{BK} is $\mathsf{Var}(\mathsf{Err}(\mathsf{BK}_{\underline{\mathfrak{K}} \to \bar{\mathfrak{K}}, \alpha})) = \alpha^2$.*

3   Multi-value Bootstrapping

In the previous section, we recall the bootstrapping procedures based on an auxiliary GSW scheme. Instead of the bootstrapping procedures where only a 're-encryption' of input ciphertext is made, we explain here how to bootstrapp an arbitrary function of the input message. For example in [10] the arbitrary function was the rounding (or modulus switching) of ciphertext decryption function. Recall, $\mathcal{G} = \langle X \rangle$ is the group of powers of X where X is a $2N$-th root of unity. This corresponds to the cyclotomic polynomial $\Phi_{2N}(X) = X^N + 1$ defining the TRLWE ciphertext polynomials. The bootstrapping procedure consists of a linear step where an approximate phase $m \in \mathbb{Z}_{2N}$ of the input ciphertext $\mathbf{c}$ is computed followed by a non-linear step described by the following relation, here $R(X) \in \mathbb{Z}_N[X]$ is a polynomial with zero-degree coefficient equal to zero:

$$\mathsf{TV}_F(X) \cdot X^m \equiv F(m) + R(X) \mod \Phi_{2N}(X) \tag{1}$$

To ease the exposition, only the plaintext counterpart is presented. The BlindRotate procedure is used to obtain ACC which encrypts the phase m in the form of a power of X. This new representation is then multiplied by a test polynomial TV_F, for a function $F : \mathbb{Z}_{2N} \to \mathbb{Z}_{2N}$. In the zero-degree coefficient of the resulting polynomial the evaluation of function F in point m is obtained. Several possibilities to evaluate relation (1) exist. Hereafter we present 3 different ways to perform this evaluation and discuss their advantages and drawbacks.

$\mathsf{TV}_F(X) \cdot X^m$ – The first one is to start the BlindRotate procedure with TV_F already encoded in ACC. The main advantage is that the output noise is independent of the test polynomial and is the lowest possible. The drawback is that only one function can be computed per bootstrapping procedure. This is how TV_F is encoded in the bootstrapping of [10].

$X^m \cdot \mathsf{TV}_F(X)$ – Another possibility is to integrate TV_F after the BlindRotate procedure is performed. In this case, one can use several test polynomials and thus, compute several functions in the same input. This is how TV_F is encoded in the bootstrapping of [4,5,14]. The main drawback is that output ciphertext noise depends on test polynomial coefficient values.

$\mathsf{TV}^{(0)}(X) \cdot X^m \cdot \mathsf{TV}_F^{(1)}(X)$ – Finally, we can split test polynomial TV_F into two factors, with a first-phase factor $TV^{(0)}$ and a second-phase factor $\mathsf{TV}_F^{(1)}(X)$ test polynomials. The first-phase factor $\mathsf{TV}^{(0)}$ does not depend on the evaluated function F. Thus, as in the previous case, using different second-phase test polynomials we are able to evaluate several functions on the same input. Another condition when performing the factorization is to obtain the second-phase factors with low-norm coefficients. This is needed in order to obtain small noise increase in output ciphertexts. We conclude that this new evaluation technique allows to leverage the best of the first two possibilities.

The test polynomial is specific to a function f we want to evaluate. As the phase m is a noised version of the message of the input $\mathbf{c}$, it should be rounded before function f is applied to. We have $F = f \circ \mathbf{round}$, where the function F is a composition of a rounding function and the "payload" function.

In the next subsection, we give a possible way to factorize test polynomials. Afterwards, we examine an updated version of Algorithm 3 which implements a bootstrapping procedure where the test polynomials are split.

3.1   Test Polynomial Factorization

Hereafter, we examine the conditions a function F should verify and we introduce a "half-circle" factorization of the test polynomial.

Theorem 3.1. *Let $F : \mathbb{Z}_{2N} \to \mathbb{Z}_{2N}$ be a function to be evaluated in a bootstrapping procedure using relation* (1). *Function F must satisfy relation $F(m+N) = -F(m)$ for $0 \le m < N$.*

Proof. Let $P(X)$ be a polynomial from $\mathbb{Z}_N[X]$. Multiplying it by X^N gives the initial polynomial with negated coefficients, i.e. $P(X) \cdot X^N \equiv -P(X) \in \mathbb{Z}_N[X]$. This is due to relation $X^N = -1$ defining cyclotomic polynomial $\Phi_{2N}(X)$, i.e. the negacyclic property of the ring $\mathbb{Z}_N[X]$. If we apply this observation to the left-hand side of Eq. (1) we have:

$$\mathsf{TV}_F(X) \cdot X^{(m+N)} \equiv -TV_F(X) \cdot X^m \quad \text{mod } \Phi_{2N}(X), \ 0 \le m < N$$

Respectively, the right-hand side must satisfy the condition $F(m+N) = -F(m)$ for $0 \le m < N$. □

In what follows we restrict Eq. (1) to values of m belonging to $\mathbb{Z}_N$. In this way, the condition $F(m+N) = -F(m)$ is automatically verified.

Half-Circle Polynomial Bootstrapping. Let TV_F be a test polynomial defined as $\mathsf{TV}_F = \sum_{i=0}^{N-1} t_i X^i$, where $t_0 = F(0)$ and $t_i = -F(N-i)$ for $1 \le i < N$. Thus, TV_F equals to $F(0) - \sum_{i=1}^{N-1} F(i) \cdot X^{N-i}$. It is straightforward to see that the relation $\mathsf{TV}_F \cdot X^m = F(m) + R(X) \mod \Phi_{2N}(X)$ is satisfied for any $0 \le m < N$.

The test polynomial TV_F must be factored into two polynomials such that the first one $\mathsf{TV}^{(0)}$ does not depend on the evaluated function F. We did not mentioned earlier but the factorization can be fractional. Let τ denote the least common multiple of the factorization such that $TV^{(0)}, TV_F^{(1)} \in \mathbb{Z}_N[X]$:

$$\tau \cdot TV^{(0)} \cdot TV_F^{(1)} \equiv TV_F \quad \text{mod } \Phi_{2N}(X)$$

We define the first-phase test polynomial as $TV^{(0)} = \sum_{i=0}^{N-1} X^i$ and $\tau = 1/2$.

Let second-phase test polynomial be $TV_F^{(1)} = \sum_{i=0}^{N-1} t_i' \cdot X^i$. Polynomials $\mathsf{TV}^{(0)}$ and $\mathsf{TV}_F^{(1)}$ being factors of TV_F we have:

$$\sum_i t_i \cdot X^i \equiv 1/2 \cdot \sum_i t_i' \cdot X^i \cdot \sum_i X^i \quad \text{mod } \Phi_{2N}(X)$$

Using the fact that $X^N = -1$, we obtain the following system of linear equations with N unknowns t_i', $0 \le i < N$:

$$\sum_{0 \le i \le k} t_i' - \sum_{k < i < N} t_i' = 2t_k, \ 0 \le k < N \tag{2}$$

Theorem 3.2. *The system of linear equation* (2) *admits an analytical solution given by:* $t'_0 = t_0 + t_{N-1}$ *and* $t'_k = t_k - t_{k-1}$ *for* $k \geq 1$.

Proof. Observe that two consecutive t_{k-1} and t_k differ only by t'_k element sign. Computing their difference, we have $2 \cdot (t_k - t_{k-1}) = \sum_{0 \leq i \leq k} t'_i - \sum_{k < i < N} t'_i - \sum_{0 \leq i \leq k-1} t'_i + \sum_{k-1 < i < N} t'_i = 2t'_k$. The case for t'_0 is equivalently proved except that for t_0 and t_{N-1} only the sign of t'_0 is the same.

Property 1. Suppose that function F has the same output value for consecutive points $N - k$ and $N - k + 1$, thus $F(N - k) = F(N - k + 1)$. Observe that $t'_k = t_k - t_{k-1} = -F(N - k) - F(N - k + 1) = 0$. We deduce that the second-phase test polynomial coefficient t'_k is zero in this case. More generally, this test polynomial has exactly s non-zero coefficients where s is the number of transitions of function F, i.e. $s = |\{F(k) \neq F(k + 1) : 0 \leq k < N\}|$.

The test polynomial factorization introduced earlier can be graphically interpreted as follows:

1. The first-phase test polynomial divides the torus in two parts. The bootstrapping with test polynomial $\tau \cdot TV^{(0)}$ returns $+\tau$ for first half-circle $[0, 1/2[$ of torus and $-\tau$ for the other part.
2. The second-phase test polynomial builds a linear combination of such half-circles, thus the half-circles from step 1 are rotated by X^i and scaled by t'_i.

Example. We give in Fig. 2 an example over $\mathbb{T}$ of the previously explained procedure. We ignore the coefficient τ in this illustration. On the top torus circle are denoted values returned by the first-phase test polynomial, i.e. test polynomial values projected on torus circle. The second-phase test polynomial has 3 terms and is equal to $t'_a X^a + t'_b X^b + t'_c X^c$. The 3 bottom torus circles denote the linear mapping performed by each monomial of the second-phase test polynomial. Summing up these terms gives a torus circle values illustrated on the rightmost part of the figure. Observe the negacyclic property of cyclotomic polynomial $X^N + 1$ on the torus circles from the fact that symmetric output values are negated.

Function Evaluation with Rounding. Let f be a function from $\mathbb{Z}_t$ to $\mathbb{Z}_q$ for $t < 2N$ and $q \leq 2N$. Let r be a rounding function which takes as input a message from $\mathbb{Z}_{2N}$ and outputs a rounded message belonging to $\mathbb{Z}_t$. Function r is defined as $r(m) = \lfloor m \cdot t/2N \rceil$. This function corresponds to the rounding performed on TLWE ciphertext phase in order to obtain the plaintext message.

Test polynomial $TV_{for} = \sum_i t_i$ for the composed function $f \circ r$ is defined as: $t_0 = f \circ r(0)$ and $t_k = -f \circ r(N - k)$ for $1 \leq k < N$. Building the system of linear equation (2) and using explicit solution given in Theorem 3.2 we can deduce the coefficients for second-phase test polynomial.

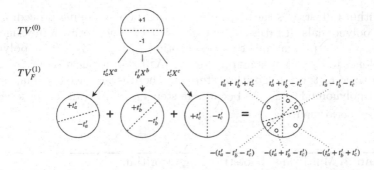

Fig. 2. Illustration of the high-level strategy for the multi-value bootstrapping

Proposition 1 (Second-phase test polynomial norm). *Let f be a function from $\mathbb{Z}_s$ to $\mathbb{Z}_q$ and let $TV_{for}^{(1)}$ be the corresponding second-phase test polynomial. The squared norm of this polynomial is given by:* $\left\| TV_{for}^{(1)} \right\|_2^2 \leq s \cdot (q-1)^2$.

Proof. (Number of non-zero coefficients) From the definition of the rounding function r we have $r(k) = l$ for any k such that $l \cdot 2N/t \leq k < (l+1) \cdot 2N/t$. Without loss of generality we suppose here that t divides $2N$. Composed function $f \circ r$, denoted by F, has the same output value for $2N/t$ consecutive input messages from $\mathbb{Z}_{2N}$, i.e. $F(k) = f \circ r(k) = f(l)$ for $l \cdot 2N/t \leq k < (l+1) \cdot 2N/t$. Using Property 1 we deduce that the $TV_{for}^{(1)}$ polynomial is sparse and has exactly s non-zero coefficients. Let $S, |S| = s$, be the set of indexes of non-zero coefficients, we have $TV_{for}^{(1)} = \sum_{i \in S} t_i' X^i$.

(Coefficient range) Each non-zero coefficient t_i', $i \in S$, is defined as the difference between consecutive output values of function $f \circ r$, or equivalently function f. Refer to Theorem 3.2 and TV_{for} definition. We have $(t_i')^2 \leq (f(k) - f(k'))^2$ for any $k, k' \in \mathbb{Z}_t$. As function f is defined over $\mathbb{Z}_q$ relation $0 \leq f(.) \leq q-1$ is verified. We deduce $(t_i')^2 \leq (q-1)^2$. Combining these results we obtain the bound expression:

$$\left\| TV_{for}^{(1)} \right\|_2^2 = \left\| \sum_{i \in S} t_i' X^i \right\|_2^2 = \sum_{i \in S} (t_i')^2 \leq s \cdot (q-1)^2$$

3.2 Optimized Multi-value Bootstrapping

In this subsection we focus on multi-value bootstrapping procedure for Torus FHE where the $2N$-th cyclotomic polynomial $X^N + 1$ defines TRLWE samples. We assume that first and second phase test polynomials, $TV^{(0)}, TV_F^{(1)} \in \mathbb{Z}_N[X]$, together with scale factor τ verifying condition (3) are given.

$$\tau \cdot TV^{(0)}(X) \cdot X^m \cdot TV_F^{(0)}(X) \equiv F(m) + R(X) \mod \Phi_{2N}(X) \qquad (3)$$

Algorithm 4 illustrates the steps of optimized bootstrapping procedure using split test polynomials. It takes as input a ciphertext encrypting a message $m/2N$, $m \in \mathbb{Z}_{2N}$, and outputs a ciphertext encrypting $F(m) \in \mathbb{Z}_{2N}$. Test polynomial $TV^{(0)}$ belongs to $\mathbb{Z}_N[X]$. It is mapped to $\mathbb{T}_N[X]$ by multiplication with $1/2N \in \mathbb{T}$ and with scale factor τ (algorithm step 2). There is not need to map second-phase test polynomial to $\mathbb{T}_N[X]$ because in step 4 a linear transformation of ACC by $TV_F^{(1)}$ is performed.

Algorithm 4. Multi-value bootstrapping algorithm

Input: A TLWE sample $\underline{c} = (\underline{a}, \underline{b}) \in \text{TLWE}_{\underline{\mathfrak{K}}, \eta}(\mu)$ where $\mu = m/2N$, $m \in \mathbb{Z}_{2N}$

Input: First, second phase test polynomials $TV^{(0)}, TV_F^{(1)} \in \mathbb{Z}_N[X]$ and scale factor τ

Input: A bootstrapping key $\text{BK}_{\underline{\mathfrak{K}} \to \bar{\mathfrak{K}}, \alpha} = \left(\text{BK}_i \in \text{TRGSW}_{\bar{K}, \alpha}(\underline{\mathfrak{K}}_i) \right)_{i \in [\![1,n]\!]}$ where $\bar{K}$ is the TRLWE interpretation of $\bar{\mathfrak{K}}$.

Output: A TLWE sample $\bar{c} \in \text{TLWE}_{\bar{\mathfrak{K}}, \bar{\eta}}(F(m)/2N)$

1: Let $b = \lfloor 2N\underline{b} \rceil$ and $a_i = \lfloor 2N\underline{a}_i \rceil \in \mathbb{Z}_{2N}$ for each $i \in [\![1,n]\!]$
2: Let $v \leftarrow TV^{(0)} \cdot 1/2N \cdot \tau \in \mathbb{T}_N[X]$
3: $\text{ACC} \leftarrow \text{BlindRotate}((\mathbf{0}, v), (a_1, \ldots, a_n, b), (\text{BK}_1, \ldots, \text{BK}_n))$
4: $\text{ACC} \leftarrow TV_F^{(1)} \cdot \text{ACC}$
5: Return $\bar{c} = \text{SampleExtract}(\text{ACC})$

Theorem 3.3. *Given a TLWE input ciphertext $\underline{c}$ of message $\mu = m/2N$, $m \in \mathbb{Z}_{2N}$, first-phase $TV^{(0)} \in \mathbb{Z}_N[X]$, second-phase $TV_F^{(1)} \in \mathbb{Z}_N[X]$ test polynomials, factorization factor τ verifying condition (3) and a valid bootstrapping key $\text{BK}_{\underline{\mathfrak{K}} \to \bar{\mathfrak{K}}, \alpha} = (\text{BK}_i)_{i \in [\![1,n]\!]}$, Algorithm 4 outputs a valid TLWE ciphertext $\bar{c}$ of message $F(m)/2N$ with error distribution variance verifying: $\text{Var}(\text{Err}(\bar{c})) \le \left\| TV_F^{(1)} \right\|_2^2 \left(n(k+1)\ell N\beta^2 \vartheta_{\text{BK}} + n(1+kN)\epsilon^2 \right)$ where ϑ_{BK} is the variance of bootstrapping key $\text{Var}(\text{Err}(\text{BK}_{\underline{\mathfrak{K}} \leftarrow \bar{\mathfrak{K}}, \alpha})) = \alpha^2$.*

Proof. (Correctness) The first 3 lines of Algorithm 4 compute a TRLWE ciphertext of message $X^{b-a\underline{\mathfrak{K}}} \cdot TV^{(0)} \cdot 1/2N \cdot \tau$. Line 4 applies a linear transformation to it and message $\tau/2N \cdot X^{b-a\underline{\mathfrak{K}}} \cdot TV^{(0)} \cdot TV_F^{(1)}$ is obtained. Input message μ is a multiple of $1/2N$ on the torus so we have $b - a\underline{\mathfrak{K}} = \mu \cdot 2N$. Recall that $\tau \cdot TV^{(0)} \cdot TV_F^{(1)} \cdot X^m \equiv F(m) + \ldots$ for any $m \in \mathbb{Z}_{2N}$ and $m = \mu \cdot 2N$. Thus, ACC at line 5 contains an encryption of a polynomial whose zero-degree coefficient is $F(m)/2N$. The SampleExtract function from the last line extracts from ACC a TLWE sample of message $F(m)/2N$.

(Error Analysis) The error analysis for this method follows from the error analysis of the TFHE gate bootstrapping. It adds one multiplication by a constant polynomial $TV_F^{(1)}$ and gives the following variation of error distribution: $\text{Var}(\text{Err}(\bar{c})) \le \left\| TV_F^{(1)} \right\|_2^2 \left(n(k+1)\ell N\beta^2 \vartheta_{\text{BK}} + n(1+kN)\epsilon^2 \right)$.

Theorem 3.4. *Under the same hypothesis as in Theorems 2.8 and 3.3, when given a correct input ciphertext $\underline{c}$ of message μ, $m = \mu \cdot 2N \in \mathbb{Z}_{2N}$, the multi-value bootstrapping of Algorithm 4 followed by the classical key-switching outputs a ciphertext $\bar{c}$ of message $F(m)/2N$ with error distribution variance:*

$$Var(Err(\bar{c})) \leq \left\| TV_F^{(1)} \right\|_2^2 \left(n(k+1)\ell N\beta^2\vartheta_{\mathsf{BK}} + n(1+kN)\epsilon^2 \right) +$$
$$n t\vartheta_{\mathsf{KS}}^2 + n2^{-2(t+1)} \quad (4)$$

where ϑ_{BK} and ϑ_{KS} are respectively the variances of bootstrapping and key-switching keys error distributions.

Multi-output Version. In many cases one needs to evaluate several functions over the same encrypted message. The naive way is to execute bootstrapping Algorithm 4 several times for each function. Remark that for equal first-phase test polynomials $TV^{(0)}$ Algorithm 4 performs the same computations up to line 3. Thus, until second-phase test polynomial integration into the accumulator. By repeating steps 4–5 for several second-phase test polynomials $TV_{F_1}^{(1)}, \ldots, TV_{F_q}^{(1)}$ the bootstrapping algorithm outputs encryptions of messages $F_1(m), \ldots, F_q(m)$. Figure 3 is a schematic view of the bootstrapping procedure which evaluates several functions over same input message.

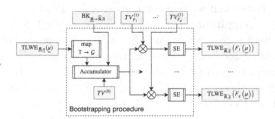

Fig. 3. Multiple output multi-value bootstrapping overview. Test polynomials $TV_{F_1}^{(1)}, \ldots, TV_{F_q}^{(1)}$ correspond to q functions evaluated over message $\underline{\mu}$ encrypted in the input ciphertext.

4   Homomorphic LUT

In this section, we show how to use the multi-value bootstrapping introduced earlier to homomorphically evaluate r-bit LUT functions over encrypted data.

4.1   Homomorphic LUT Evaluation

A boolean LUT is a function defined as $f : \mathbb{Z}_2^r \to \mathbb{Z}_2^q$. At first we focus on single-output LUTs, i.e. the case $q = 1$. Afterwards we show how to efficiently evaluate multi-output LUTs. It is straightforward to see an equivalent formulation for f over the ring of integers modulo 2^r using $F : \mathbb{Z}_{2^r} \to \mathbb{Z}_2$ and the linear mapping $\phi(m_0, \ldots, m_{r-1}) = \sum_{j=0}^{r-1} m_j \cdot 2^j$ from $\mathbb{Z}_2^r$ to $\mathbb{Z}_{2^r}$. We have $F \circ \phi(m_0, \ldots, m_{r-1}) \equiv f(m_0, \ldots, m_{r-1})$ for any $(m_0, \ldots, m_{r-1}) \in \mathbb{Z}_2^r$. The multi-value bootstrapping is used to evaluate LUT function F as follows. We encode integers over the torus as multiples of $1/2^{r+1}$. Only the first half-circle of torus is used for input and output message spaces. In this way any function can be evaluated using bootstrapping procedure - refer to restrictions from Theorem 3.1. Full message space is used for the input $j/2^{r+1}$ for $j \in \mathbb{Z}_{2^r}$ and only the first 2 elements are used for the output messages $j/2^{r+1}$ for $j \in \mathbb{Z}_2$. Test polynomial factorization described in previous section is used. Recall, the first-phase test polynomial $\mathsf{TV}^{(0)}$ is $\sum_i X^i$ and scaling factor is $\tau = 1/2$. The second-phase test polynomial is computed using Theorem 3.2 for LUT function F composed with a rounding function. From Proposition 1 this test polynomial norm verifies relation $\left\| TV_{For}^{(1)} \right\|_2^2 \le 2^r$.

4.2   LUT Circuits

A naive solution for multi-output LUT evaluation is to map $\mathbb{Z}_2^q$ to $\mathbb{Z}_{2^q}$. Doing so, we would be able evaluate functions $F : \mathbb{Z}_{2^r} \to \mathbb{Z}_{2^q}$ where $q \le r$. The drawback of this method appears when we need to compose LUTs into a circuit and evaluate it. A reverse mapping from $\mathbb{Z}_{2^q}$ to $\mathbb{Z}_2^q$ would be needed. It will be an overkill to use another function to extract bits from $\mathbb{Z}_{2^q}$ messages, because it implies to use another multi-value bootstrapping. Let $F^{(\ell)} : \mathbb{Z}_{2^r} \to \mathbb{Z}_2$ be a multi-value input function computing the ℓ-th output bit of LUT function $f : \mathbb{Z}_2^r \to \mathbb{Z}_2^q$, $\ell = 1, \ldots, q$. Each of these functions, $F^{(1)}, \ldots, F^{(q)}$, is evaluated as described previously. Note that the expensive blind rotate part from the bootstrapping is performed once. Only the multiplication by second-phase test vector and sample extract is done for each evaluated function. Figure 4 illustrates intermediary steps for interfacing LUTs. Firstly, ciphertexts encrypting messages $m_1, \ldots, m_r \in \mathbb{B}$ obtained from several bootstrapping procedures are combined together into a multi-value message m using the linear transformation ϕ. Note that this transformation is performed in the output key space of the bootstrapping procedure under the secret key $\overline{\mathfrak{K}}$. Next, a key-switching procedure is performed and a ciphertext of the same message m under the secret $\underline{\mathfrak{K}}$ is obtained. This ciphertext is fed into the next bootstrapping and the process can be repeated. It is possible to reorder the linear mapping evaluation and the key-switching, i.e. perform key-switching directly after the bootstrapping and evaluate the linear mapping afterwards. Besides the fact that r times more key-switching procedures are performed the noise increase will also be larger. Actually, the linear map evaluation noise increase is multiplicative compared to the additive key-switching noise. In the next subsection, we describe implementation in more details.

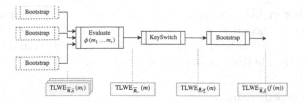

Fig. 4. LUT composition into circuits. On top are shown executed algorithms and at the bottom obtained ciphertexts.

4.3 Implementation Details and Performance

We implement the previous method for $r = 6$. The parameters of samples are:

- TLWE – $n = 803$, noise standard deviation 2^{-20} and $h = 63$ (TLWE key non-zero coefficient count),
- TRLWE – $N = 2^{14}$ and noise standard deviation 2^{-50},
- TRGSW – decomposition parameters $\ell = 2^3$ and $B_g = 2^6$.

To estimate the security, we used the `lwe-estimator` script[2] from [1] which includes the recent attacks on small LWE secrets [2]. We found that our instances achieve at least 128 bits of security which is better than to the concrete security level (about 100 bits) of the 6-to-6 LUT implementation of [5]. The keyswitch parameters are $t = 4$ and decomposition base 2^4. We have implemented the multi-value bootstrapping technique proposed above on-top of the TFHE library [13] and a test implementation is available in the `torus_generic` branch. Several modifications were performed in order to support 64-bit precision torus. Approximate sample sizes are: TLWE 6.3 kB, TRLWE 256 kB and the TRGSW 2 MB. As for the keys we have: multi-value bootstrapping key <2GB and the switching key ≈6GB. The key sizes can be reduced using a pseudo-random number generator as in [10]. Our experimental protocol consisted in: (i) a 6 bit multi-value message is encrypted, (ii) parameters (i.e. second-phase test polynomials) for several LUTs are generated randomly, (iii) the multi-value bootstrapping is executed on this encrypted message (several ciphertexts encrypting boolean messages are obtained), (iv) a weighted sum is used to build a new multi-value message ciphertext from 6 of the output boolean messages obtained previously, (v) finally a key-switching procedure is performed in order to regain the bootstrapping input parameter space. We executed the algorithms on a single core of an Intel Xeon E3-1240 processor running at 3.50 GHz. The bootstrapping and switching keys are generated in approximatively 66 s. Multi-value bootstrapping on 6 bit words with 6 boolean outputs runs in ≈1.57 s with the bit combination plus key-switching phase and in under 1.5 sec. without the key-switching. For comparison the gate bootstrapping from TFHE library takes 15 ms on the same machine. We did not observed a significant increase in the execution time

---

[2] Available at https://bitbucket.org/malb/lwe-estimator. Our estimation were performed using commit `76d05ee`.

when the number of LUT outputs augments. For example computing 128 different functions on the same input message increased the execution time only by 0.05 s, almost for free! We shall note that the combination and key-switching was performed a single time in this last experiment.

4.4 Further Applications

We present here possible applications of the multi-value bootstrapping. We do not implement them but give a brief overview on the multi-bootstrapping could be used and leave the model analysis and teh implementation for a future independent work. The first one concerns the optimization of the circuit bootstrapping from [12, Sec. 4.1] which allows to compose circuits in a leveled mode by turning a TLWE sample into a TRGSW sample. The first step of the *circuit bootstrapping* consists to ℓ TFHE gate bootstrapping calls on the same TLWE input sample. Here each bootstrapping call is associated to a different test polynomial. We can apply the multi-value bootstrapping to optimize this step: since the LWE input sample is the same, the idea is to perform Algorithm 1 only once for the ℓ bootstrapping calls, and to adapt the output using corresponding test polynomials $\mathsf{TV}_F^{(1)}$ as in Subsect. 3.2. We then obtain the ℓ desired outputs. This allows to save a factor ℓ in one of the circuit bootstrapping phases. The second one relates to homomorphic evaluation of neural networks. Our multi-value bootstrapping can also be used to homomorphically evaluate a neural network. Assume neurons $x_1, \ldots, x_p$ inputs and output y are encrypted as TLWE ciphertexts. The computational neuron network functionality is defined by two functions, a linear function $f : \mathbb{T}^p \mapsto \mathbb{T}$ and an activation function $g : \mathbb{T} \mapsto \mathbb{T}$. The result is a TLWE sample of $y = g(f(x_1, \ldots, x_p))$. Function f is usually implemented as an inner-product. We can compute the inner-product between p neuron inputs and a fixed weight vector using a functional key-switch, and afterwards extract the TLWE encryption from the TRLWE key-switch output. Note that the public functional key-switch allows to compute up to N inner-products. Thus, using a single key-switch procedure we can compute all the linear functions of a whole neural network layer! Afterwards, using our multi-value bootstrapping, we compute a TLWE sample of $g(.)$ which is not an arbitrary function. Usually a threshold function is used for g. In this particular case, the multi-value bootstrapping can be more efficiently instantiated than for an arbitrary function.

5 Conclusion

We introduced a bootstrapping procedure based on TFHE scheme with split test polynomials which can be used to evaluate multi-value functions and increase the evaluation efficiency of multi-output functions. We notice that this method (the test polynomial split trick) can be easily adapted to other FHEW-based bootstrapping algorithms. We show how to apply the multi-value bootstrapping to execute arbitrary LUT functions on encrypted data and implement the evaluation of a 6-to-6 LUT which takes under 1.6 s; the evaluation of additional outputs on the same input comes at virtually no cost.

Acknowledgements. We acknowledge the support of the french Programme d'Investissement d'Avenir under the national project RISQ.

References

1. Albrecht, M., Player, R., Scott, S.: On the concrete hardness of learning with errors. J. Math. Cryptol. **9**, 169–203 (2015). ePrint Archive 2015/046
2. Albrecht, M.R.: On dual lattice attacks against small-secret LWE and parameter choices in HElib and SEAL. In: Coron, J.-S., Nielsen, J.B. (eds.) EUROCRYPT 2017. LNCS, vol. 10211, pp. 103–129. Springer, Cham (2017). https://doi.org/10. 1007/978-3-319-56614-6_4
3. Alperin-Sheriff, J., Peikert, C.: Faster bootstrapping with polynomial error. In: Garay, J.A., Gennaro, R. (eds.) CRYPTO 2014. LNCS, vol. 8616, pp. 297–314. Springer, Heidelberg (2014). https://doi.org/10.1007/978-3-662-44371-2_17
4. Biasse, J.-F., Ruiz, L.: FHEW with efficient multibit bootstrapping. In: Lauter, K., Rodríguez-Henríquez, F. (eds.) LATINCRYPT 2015. LNCS, vol. 9230, pp. 119–135. Springer, Cham (2015). https://doi.org/10.1007/978-3-319-22174-8_7
5. Bonnoron, G., Ducas, L., Fillinger, M.: Large FHE gates from tensored homomorphic accumulator. In: Joux, A., Nitaj, A., Rachidi, T. (eds.) AFRICACRYPT 2018. LNCS, vol. 10831, pp. 217–251. Springer, Cham (2018). https://doi.org/10. 1007/978-3-319-89339-6_13
6. Brakerski, Z., Gentry, C., Vaikuntanathan, V.: (Leveled) fully homomorphic encryption without bootstrapping. In: ITCS, pp. 309–325 (2012)
7. Brakerski, Z., Langlois, A., Peikert, C., Regev, O., Stehlé, D.: Classical hardness of learning with errors. In: STOC, pp. 575–584 (2013)
8. Brakerski, Z., Perlman, R.: Lattice-based fully dynamic multi-key FHE with short ciphertexts. In: Robshaw, M., Katz, J. (eds.) CRYPTO 2016. LNCS, vol. 9814, pp. 190–213. Springer, Heidelberg (2016). https://doi.org/10.1007/978-3-662-53018-4_8
9. Cheon, J.H., Stehlé, D.: Fully homomophic encryption over the integers revisited. In: Oswald, E., Fischlin, M. (eds.) EUROCRYPT 2015. LNCS, vol. 9056, pp. 513–536. Springer, Heidelberg (2015). https://doi.org/10.1007/978-3-662-46800-5_20
10. Chillotti, I., Gama, N., Georgieva, M., Izabachène, M.: Faster fully homomorphic encryption: bootstrapping in less than 0.1 seconds. In: Cheon, J.H., Takagi, T. (eds.) ASIACRYPT 2016. LNCS, vol. 10031, pp. 3–33. Springer, Heidelberg (2016). https://doi.org/10.1007/978-3-662-53887-6_1
11. Chillotti, I., Gama, N., Georgieva, M., Izabachène, M.: A homomorphic LWE based E-voting scheme. In: Takagi, T. (ed.) PQCrypto 2016. LNCS, vol. 9606, pp. 245–265. Springer, Cham (2016). https://doi.org/10.1007/978-3-319-29360-8_16
12. Chillotti, I., Gama, N., Georgieva, M., Izabachène, M.: Faster packed homomorphic operations and efficient circuit bootstrapping for TFHE. In: Takagi, T., Peyrin, T. (eds.) ASIACRYPT 2017. LNCS, vol. 10624, pp. 377–408. Springer, Cham (2017). https://doi.org/10.1007/978-3-319-70694-8_14
13. Chillotti, I., Gama, N., Georgieva, M., Izabachène, M.: TFHE: fast fully homomorphic encryption library, August 2016. https://tfhe.github.io/tfhe/
14. Ducas, L., Micciancio, D.: FHEW: bootstrapping homomorphic encryption in less than a second. In: Oswald, E., Fischlin, M. (eds.) EUROCRYPT 2015. LNCS, vol. 9056, pp. 617–640. Springer, Heidelberg (2015). https://doi.org/10.1007/978-3-662-46800-5_24

15. Fan, J., Vercauteren, F.: Somewhat practical fully homomorphic encryption (2012). https://eprint.iacr.org/2012/144
16. Gentry, C.: Fully homomorphic encryption using ideal lattices. In: STOC, vol. 9, pp. 169–178 (2009)
17. Gentry, C., Sahai, A., Waters, B.: Homomorphic encryption from learning with errors: conceptually-simpler, asymptotically-faster, attribute-based. In: Canetti, R., Garay, J.A. (eds.) CRYPTO 2013. LNCS, vol. 8042, pp. 75–92. Springer, Heidelberg (2013). https://doi.org/10.1007/978-3-642-40041-4_5
18. Halevi, S., Shoup, I.V.: Helib - an implementation of homomorphic encryption, September 2014. https://github.com/shaih/HElib/
19. Lepoint, T.: FV-NFLlib: library implementing the Fan-Vercauteren homomorphic encryption scheme, May 2016 https://github.com/CryptoExperts/FV-NFLlib
20. Lyubashevsky, V., Peikert, C., Regev, O.: On ideal lattices and learning with errors over rings. In: Gilbert, H. (ed.) EUROCRYPT 2010. LNCS, vol. 6110, pp. 1–23. Springer, Heidelberg (2010). https://doi.org/10.1007/978-3-642-13190-5_1
21. Regev, O.: On lattices, learning with errors, random linear codes, and cryptography. In: STOC, pp. 84–93 (2005)
22. SEAL. Simple encrypted arithmetic library. https://sealcrypto.codeplex.com/

Efficient Function-Hiding Functional Encryption: From Inner-Products to Orthogonality

Manuel Barbosa[1], Dario Catalano[2], Azam Soleimanian[3,4](✉),
and Bogdan Warinschi[5]

[1] INESC TEC and FCUP, Porto, Portugal
mbb@fc.up.pt
[2] Università di Catania, Catania, Italy
catalano@dmi.unict.it
[3] Kharazmi University, Tehran, Iran
std_a.soleimani@khu.ac.ir
[4] École Normale Supérieure, Paris, France
[5] University of Bristol, Bristol, UK
csxbw@bristol.ac.uk

Abstract. We construct functional encryption (FE) schemes for the orthogonality (**OFE**) relation where each ciphertext encrypts some vector **x** and each decryption key, associated to some vector **y**, allows to determine if **x** is orthogonal to **y** or not. Motivated by compelling applications, we aim at schemes which are *function hiding*, i.e. **y** is not leaked.

Our main contribution are two such schemes, both rooted in existing constructions of FE for inner products (**IPFE**), i.e., where decryption keys reveal the inner product of **x** and **y**. The first construction builds upon the very efficient **IPFE** by Kim *et al.* (SCN 2018) but just like the original scheme its security holds in the generic group model (GGM). The second scheme builds on recent developments in the construction of efficient **IPFE** schemes in the standard model and extends the work of Wee (TCC 2017) in leveraging these results for the construction of FE for Boolean functions. Conceptually, both our constructions can be seen as further evidence that *shutting down* leakage from inner product values to only a single bit for the orthogonality relation can be done with little overhead, not only in the GGM, but also in the standard model.

We discuss potential applications of our constructions to secure databases and provide efficiency benchmarks. Our implementation shows that the first scheme is extremely fast and ready to be deployed in practical applications.

1 Introduction

Consider the following scenario inspired from the literature on privacy preserving cryptographic role-based access control. The file storage of an organization is

---

A. Soleimanian—Work done while visiting student at the Università di Catania, Italy.

M. Matsui (Ed.): CT-RSA 2019, LNCS 11405, pp. 127–148, 2019.
https://doi.org/10.1007/978-3-030-12612-4_7

structured following a role-based access control, where users have associated one or more roles and each file can be accessed by users with a certain role (or combination of roles). Storage of the files is outsourced to a cloud which needs to serve files to users that request them. In particular, the cloud needs to determine, for each request, if it complies with the access control structure. In this scenario it is important to empower the cloud to perform such checks but, crucially, the cloud should not have information regarding the roles that can access each file. Indeed, access privileges may indicate which files are critical and may be linked, semantically, with the content of the files (e.g. revealing which patient files can be accessed by psychiatrists is clearly undesirable).

A similar scenario arises in the context of outsourcing file storage in a way that enables keyword search. A solution is to reveal to the cloud, for each file deterministic encryptions of the keywords which occur in that file. Even if the actual keywords are hidden, this solution reveals co-occurrence information, i.e. which files share keywords and how many keywords are shared. In turn this may reveal sensitive information about the semantics of the encrypted keywords.

The two scenarios are conceptually quite close and, unsurprisingly, share a similar solution. The information associated to a file f can be encoded as a binary vector r_f which encodes the subset of roles that can access a file. Similarly, to each user u one can then associate a binary vector r_u, which encodes the roles associated to that user. User u has access to file f if $\langle r_u, r_f \rangle \neq 0$.[1] The challenge is to encode r_u and r_f in a way that prevents unnecessary leaks. In particular, given encodings of r_{f_1} and r_{f_2} the precise relation between the vectors (i.e. their dot-product) should not be revealed. More interestingly, while the cloud should learn that $\langle r_u, r_f \rangle \neq 0$ it should not learn the precise value of $\langle r_u, r_f \rangle$: this reveals the number of roles associated to a user that allow accessing that file.

Technically, the above functionality can be achieved using functional encryption for the orthogonality relation (OFE). Here, each ciphertext encrypts a vector $\mathbf{x}$ in $\mathbb{Z}_q^n$. Each secret key $\mathsf{sk_y}$ is also associated with a vector $\mathbf{y}$ in $\mathbb{Z}_q^n$ defines a function $f_{\mathbf{y}}(\mathbf{x})$ that returns 1 iff $\langle \mathbf{x}, \mathbf{y} \rangle = 0$, and returns 0 otherwise. We write $\mathbf{x} \perp \mathbf{y}$ for the orthogonality predicate between vectors $\mathbf{x}$ and $\mathbf{y}$.[2]

Despite the close relation between orthogonality and inner products, OFE is a different primitive from Functional Encryption for Inner-Products (IPFE): in the latter schemes a decryption key permits recovering the value of the inner-product $\langle \mathbf{x}, \mathbf{y} \rangle$. Intuitively, IPFE schemes should be easier to construct than OFE schemes, since they leak much more information about the encrypted data. A cursory look at the state of the art shows that this the case. For IPFE schemes, recent works [1–6] propose surprisingly efficient constructions of IPFE schemes with strong security guarantees and comparatively simple security proofs. More recent extensions to these constructions also covered the function-hiding case

---

[1] Here $\langle \cdot, \cdot \rangle$ denotes the inner-product.

[2] In other works this type of OFE has been referred to predicate-hiding attribute-hiding predicate-only predicate encryption, but we prefer the view that we are dealing with a particular case of functional encryption rather than a particular case of attribute-based or predicate encryption.

where decryption keys do not reveal information about the function to which they are associated. The most efficient scheme to date offering this level of security is based on a modular construction proposed by Lin [15] that converts two instances of a non-function hiding IPFE into a function hiding IPFE in an elegant way.

In contrast, most of the existing OFE schemes are instantiated in (three-factors) composite-order bilinear groups [10,12] or dual paring vector space on prime-order bilinear groups [17,18]. All of these schemes share an uncomfortably high level of conceptual complexity which explains perhaps the slow progress in this area. Indeed, till the recent work by Wee [22] there had been little progress on the design of (non function-hiding) OFE schemes. Wee shows that it is possible to port the rationale underlying the family of constructions of IPFE initiated by Abdalla et al. [1] to build more efficient OFE schemes from standard assumptions and using simpler proof techniques. The main result of this line of work is a family of simple OFE schemes in prime-order bilinear groups under the matrix-DDH (MDDH) assumption, using an insightful randomization technique to reduce inner-product leakage (in the exponents) to the orthogonality leakage allowed by OFE.

In this paper we extend this line of works, by considering the following two main questions in the context of OFE schemes that are function hiding:

Question 1. Can the relation between OFE and IPFE hinted at by Wee's construction be generalized to obtain black-box constructions of OFE from IPFE simply by "shutting down" the excessive leakage?

Question 2. Can one combine the new techniques by Lin [15] and Wee [22] in the construction of OFE, giving rise to new families of schemes and proof techniques?

1.1 Our Contributions

SIMPLE CONSTRUCTIONS: GOOD AND BAD. We start by looking at the relation between OFE and IPFE and give a negative result that excludes a simplistic approach to constructing a function hiding OFE from any IPFE. Specifically, we look at black-box constructions that deterministically encodes the key $\mathbf{y}$ for the orthogonality relation as a set of keys $\{\mathbf{y}_1, \mathbf{y}_1, \ldots, \mathbf{y}_k\}$ for the inner product computation. We show that, even starting from a secure IPFE that also guarantees function hiding (FH-IPFE, for short), it is impossible to construct in this way a function hiding OFE even if security should only hold for a single ciphertext. We then extend the results to the case where the transformation is randomized, but multiple challenge queries are allowed. We stress that other black-box transformations, e.g. some which combine multiple instances of an IPFE scheme, are not ruled out by these results.

Next, we show that this negative result is tight: we provide a construction of an OFE from a FH-IPFE via a randomized transformation which is secure but only for the single-challenge case. While not all-encompassing, these negative results suggest ways around them. On the positive side, we first show how to overcome this negative result when working in the generic group model and slightly deviating from the simplistic black-box construction above. We give a highly efficient secure OFE in the generic group model (that also achieves function hiding) via a simple modification of the FH-IPFE scheme put forth by Kim et al. [14]. After these warm up results we move on to construct a fully secure OFE from standard assumptions. Our solution builds on results by Wee [22] and Lin [15] and extends them to the setting of function hiding OFE. We start by briefly discussing these two results separately.

RECENT DEVELOPMENTS IN IPFE. In [22] Wee shows how a family of (public-key) OFE schemes can be constructed from the MDDH assumption. The schemes are inspired by recent results in constructing IPFE in which the inner-product result is recovered in the exponent. Wee's crucial observation is that it is possible to use randomization to preserve the orthogonality relation in the decrypted result, while ensuring that no additional leakage exists under the DDH assumption. The resulting schemes are elegant and have a relatively simple security proof when compared to constructions relying on alternative techniques such as composite-order bilinear groups and dual pairing vector spaces over prime-order bilinear groups. The caveat is that these schemes are semi-adaptive secure (selective after seeing the master public key).

Lin [15] gave a generic construction of (secret-key) FH-IPFE from (public-key) IPFE schemes with a particular structure (similar in spirit to those explored by Wee). The construction (roughly) uses two instances of the same scheme on top of each other (the encryption algorithm of one scheme is used to protect keys and the other scheme is used to encrypt messages) and then takes advantage of the algebraic structure of such schemes to ensure the correctness of the construction via a combination of key extraction and decryption. Again, the security proof is simple and elegant.[3]

MAIN CONSTRUCTION. We show how to combine the two techniques by Wee and Lin to give a modular construction of a new family of function-hiding OFE via the following partial results, which add up to our main technical contribution.

First, we extend Lin's generic construction from the IPFE to the OFE setting, showing that the construction also works if one starts from two instances of a OFE scheme to obtain a (weakly) function hiding OFE. We also observe that this transformation has a downside: if starting from a semi-adaptively secure OFE, one obtains a weakly secure OFE, where the adversary must be restricted to selectively commit to *both* keys and indices. Interestingly, our transform differs from Lin's original one in two main points. First, it does not induce additional levels of multi-linearity. Starting from two OFE in the bilinear group setting, the transformation produces a (weak) function hiding OFE that also relies on pairings. This is in sharp contrast with the basic IPFE setting [15] and similar

---

[3] A (small) caveat of Lin's transform is that it only achieves *weak* function hiding. This is a relaxation of the FH notion that imposes some additional constraints on the key derivation queries that the adversary is allowed to ask. This restriction is not too severe as generic (yet efficient) transforms to fully fledged (strong) function hiding are known [16].

Table 1. Comparison of our generic group model (GGM) and standard model (SM) constructions with prior constructions. Full security refers to unrestricted indistinguishability-based function-hiding. For the case of our standard-model scheme, we signal with * the (controlled) impact of complexity leveraging in our proof of security. Selective security refers to the setting where the attacker commits to the challenge message ahead of time. Sizes are given in terms of group element counts and the costs of key generation, extraction and encryption are expressed in group operation counts. For our standard model scheme we take $k = 2$.

Scheme	Ours (GGM)	Ours (SM)	[20]	[13]
Security	Full	Full*	Selective	Full
Group order	Prime	Prime	Composite	Prime
Assumption	GGM	MDDH, DDH	C3DH, DLIN	DLIN
Key size	n	$6n + 6$	$4n + 4$	$6n$
Ciphertext size	n	$6n + 6$	$4n + 4$	$6n$
Key extraction	n	$12n + 9$	$32n + 4$	$6n$
Encryption	n	$12n + 9$	$24n + 16$	$6n$
Decryption	n	$6n + 6$	$4n + 4$	$6n$

to the multi-input IPFE setting [3]. Second, to guarantee correctness, the two underlying OFE need to be instantiated with different, but matching parameters.

Thus, to concretely instantiate our transform we modify Wee's OFE construction in two ways: i. we make it compatible with our extension of Lin's construction and ii. we use complexity leveraging to get adaptive (rather than semi-adaptive) security. As a result we get a new family of (function hiding) OFE schemes based on the MDDH assumption with a simple and modular proof of security and whose practical efficiency compares favorable with existing solutions (see Table 1 for comparisons with previous work). We remark that our usage of complexity leveraging *does not* degrade security too much (at least when restricting, as we do in our applications, to small norm vectors). To see why this is the case let us describe our techniques a bit more in detail.

JUST ENOUGH COMPLEXITY LEVERAGING. In general, any selective (or semi-adaptive) secure scheme can be turned into an adaptively secure one by essentially guessing the challenges in advance. Complexity leveraging typically induces an exponential factor (in the length of the challenge) loss in the quality of the reduction, often resulting in meaningless security guarantee for practical parameters. At the same time if one applies complexity leveraging to small size challenges, the security loss might become tolerable, thus making the technique relevant also from a practical perspective. A naive application of complexity leveraging to the scheme resulting from our transformation would lead to an unacceptably high security loss. Indeed, as we are dealing with a symmetric and function-hiding scheme, the reduction would need to guess in advance *all* the challenge messages and secret key queries that the adversary is allowed to ask. Even when restricting to small norm vectors this results in a huge exponential loss that destroys security completely. Our key observation is to "anticipate" complexity leveraging to a stage where it can be made much less harmful. Concretely, we apply the complexity leveraging step to the basic (semi-adaptive secure) OFE scheme. This scheme is secure in the public-key setting and therefore only one challenge query needs to be guessed by the reduction.[4] Moreover, we show that the next steps in our construction (namely our Lin-style function-hiding transform) easily extends to the adaptive setting without introducing exponential losses. Hence the final loss essentially matches the possibilities for a single message vector, which is tolerable for small norm vectors.

APPLICATIONS AND IMPLEMENTATION. As a final result we put forward applications of OFE in the area of access-control and conjunctive keyword search. We focus on applications where our usage of complexity leveraging step does not reduce security too much, which is the case for both applications because they depend only on the ability to compute the subset relation. Indeed, when encoding the subset relation over n keywords/roles we can show that our loss in reduction tightness is only 2^{2n} and is independent of the size of the finite-field in which the orthogonality relation is computed.

We implement both our scheme in the generic group model and our main constructions and give benchmarking results for subset keyword search. The generic group model construction is very fast and it can be used in practical applications: all operations are in the range of 100 ms for vectors of size 256. Operations in our standard model construction are roughly 6 times slower.

ORGANIZATION. After we establish notation and introduce preliminary definitions in Sect. 2 we present our generic group model construction is presented in Sect. 4 and our standard model construction in Sect. 5. Finally in Sects. 6 and 7, respectively, we present our experiment results and discuss applications of our schemes.

2   Preliminaries

We write $y \leftarrow x$ for assigning a value to variable x and $x \twoheadleftarrow X$ when sampling x from the set X uniformly at random. For an integer n, we let $[n]$ denote the set $\{1, \ldots, n\}$. If $\mathcal{A}$ is a probabilistic algorithm, we also write $y \twoheadleftarrow \mathcal{A}(x_1, \ldots, x_n)$ for the action of running $\mathcal{A}$ on inputs $x_1, \ldots, x_n$ with random coins chosen uniformly at random, and assigning the result to y. We use ppt for probabilistic polynomial-time. All algorithms are ppt unless stated otherwise.

We use lowercase bold font for vectors x and uppercase bold font for matrices A. $|x|$ denotes vector length and $x \parallel y$ is used for vector concatenation. We use $\langle \mathbf{x}, \mathbf{y} \rangle$ to denote the inner-product of two vectors. We write $\mathbf{x} \perp \mathbf{y}$ for orthogonality of two vectors, which takes the value 1 if $\langle \mathbf{x}, \mathbf{y} \rangle = 0$, and 0 otherwise.

Throughout we let $\mathcal{PG} = (e, G_1, G_2, G_T, q, g_1, g_2)$ denote a pairing group, where G_1, G_2, G_T are cyclic groups of prime order q, g_1 and g_2 are generators of

---

[4] Recall that in the public key setting, adaptive single message indistinguishability implies adaptive many message indistinguishability via a standard hybrid argument.

G_1 and G_2 respectively, and $e : G_1 \times G_2 \to G_T$ is an admissible bilinear map. For $a \in \mathbb{Z}_q$ and $i = \{1, 2, T\}$ we write $[a]_i$ for encoding a using the group operation $[a]_i = g_i^a$ and extend this notation naturally for the component-wise encoding of vectors and matrices. We will assume that the following computational assumption holds in both G_1 and G_2.[5]

Definition 1 (Matrix Distribution). *Let* $l, k \in \mathbb{N}$ *with* $l > k$. *We call* $\mathcal{D}_{l,k}$ *a matrix distribution if it outputs (in polynomial time and with overwhelming probability) matrices in* $\mathbb{Z}_q^{l \times k}$ *of full rank* k. *We define* $\mathcal{D}_k = \mathcal{D}_{k+1,k}$.

Definition 2 ($\mathcal{D}_{l,k}$-Matrix Diffie-Hellman Assumption [11]). *Let* $\mathcal{D}_{l,k}$ *be a matrix distribution. We say that the* $\mathcal{D}_{l,k}$-*Matrix Diffie-Hellman Assumption* ($\mathcal{D}_{l,k}$-*MDDH) holds in* G *if, for all ppt adversaries* D, *this definition of advantage is small*

$$\mathsf{Adv}_{\mathcal{D}_{l,k},G}(D) := \Pr[D(\mathcal{G}, [A], [As]) = 1] - \Pr[D(\mathcal{G}, [A], [c]) = 1].$$

The probability space is that induced by the following sampling operations $A \leftarrow \mathcal{D}_{l,k}$, $s \leftarrow \mathbb{Z}_q^k$, *and* $c \leftarrow \mathbb{Z}_q^l$ *and the coin tosses of adversary* D.

In this paper we consider the case $l = k + 1$ referred as $\mathcal{D}_k$-MDDH assumption. Note that, to simplify notation, we omit the security parameter in the previous assumption and throughout the paper. Asymptotic definitions of security can be recovered by considering a family of bilinear groups indexed by the security parameter.

Experiment $\mathsf{IND}_{\mathcal{FE},\mathcal{A}}^b()$:

$(\mathsf{mpk}, \mathsf{msk}) \leftarrow \mathsf{Setup}()$

$b' \leftarrow \mathcal{A}^{\mathsf{LoR}_y(\cdot,\cdot), \mathsf{LoR}_x(\cdot,\cdot)}(\alpha)$

Output b'

Fig. 1. Game defining indistiguishability-based security of a functional encryption scheme. An admissible adversary will ensure that $F_{y_0^j}(\mathsf{x}_0^i) = F_{y_1^j}(\mathsf{x}_1^i)$ for all i queries to LoR_x and all j queries to LoR_y. Furthermore, we also impose that the attacker never queries the all-zeroes to either the key extraction or the encryption oracle.

Functional Encryption. We briefly overview relevant concepts from the area of functional encryption, following the formalization introduced by Boneh, Sahai, Waters [9] and O'Neill [19]. We start with the syntax of this primitive.

SYNTAX. A functional encryption scheme $\mathcal{FE}$ for a family of functions $F_y X \to \Sigma$, for $y \in Y$, is a tuple $\mathcal{FE} = (\mathsf{Setup}, \mathsf{KeyGen}, \mathsf{Enc}, \mathsf{Dec})$ of ppt algorithms, where:

- $\mathsf{Setup}()$ is the setup algorithm, which outputs a master public key mpk and a master secret key msk.

---

[5] This implies that our scheme requires an asymmetric Type-III pairing group.

- KeyGen(msk, y), is the key extraction algorithm, which on input a master secret key msk and key $y \in Y$ outputs a secret key sk_y associated with F_y.
- Enc(mpk, x) is the encryption algorithm, which on input a public key mpk and a message $msk \in X$ outputs a ciphertext ct.
- Dec(mpk, ct, sk_y) is the deterministic decryption algorithm, which on input a master publik key mpk, a ciphertext ct and a secret key sk_y outputs $z \in \Sigma$ or an abort symbol $\perp$.

We note that when $\Sigma = \{0, 1\}$ the syntax considered above matches predicate-only encryption schemes [12].

CORRECTNESS. A scheme $\mathcal{FE}$ as above is correct if, for all (mpk, msk) in the range of Setup( ), all $x, y \in X$, all sk_y in the range of KeyGen(msk, y) and all ct in the range of Enc(mpk, x), we have that Dec(ct, sk_y) $= F(x, y)$.

INDISTINGUISHABILITY-BASED SECURITY. Consider the experiment defined in Fig. 1, parametrised by a functional encryption scheme $\mathcal{FE}$, an attacker $\mathcal{A}$ and a secret bit b. The LoR_x oracle receives two messages (x_0, x_1) and returns a fresh encryption of x_b and the LoR_y oracle receives two keys (y_0, y_1) and returns a secret key sk_b corresponding to a fresh extraction of y_b.

Several variants of IND-based security can be defined based on this experiment:

- Public-key security: the input to the attacker is $\alpha = $ mpk. In the secret key setting, we have $\alpha = \epsilon$. We use SK to refer to the latter weaker setting.
- Semi-adaptive security: the attacker places all calls to LoR_x before calling LoR_y. We use SAD to refer to the weaker setting where this restriction is enforced.
- Non function-hiding (standard) security: the attacker is restricted to making $y_0 = y_1$ in all calls to LoR_y. We use FH to denote the stronger setting where this restriction is *not* enforced.
- Weak function-hiding: the attacker is restricted by the stronger requirement $F_{y_0^j}(x_0^i) = F_{y_1^j}(x_0^i) = F_{y_1^j}(x_1^i)$ for all i queries to LoR_x and all j queries to LoR_y. We use wFH to distinguish this case from the full function-hiding case.
- Single-message security: the attacker places only one call to LoR_x. We will use one to indicate when we are in the weaker setting where this restriction is enforced.

For all such variants, the advantage of an an attacker $\mathcal{A}$ against $\mathcal{FE}$ is defined by the following difference of conditional probabilities, where xx will specify the security variant according to the above conventions.

$$\mathbf{Adv}_{\mathcal{FE},\mathcal{A}}^{\mathsf{xx\text{-}IND}}( ) = \left| \Pr[\mathsf{IND}_{\mathcal{FE},\mathcal{A}}^1( ) \Rightarrow 1] - \Pr[\mathsf{IND}_{\mathcal{FE},\mathcal{A}}^0( ) \Rightarrow 1] \right|.$$

DISCUSSION. As examples of the use of our notation for security definitions, the strongest notion of security is function hiding public-key FE, denoted FH-IND, which is actually impossible to achieve; the weakest notion is single-message, semi-adaptive single-key security in the secret-key setting, denoted

Experiment Real$_{\mathcal{FE},\mathcal{A}}(\ )$:	Experiment Ideal$_{\mathcal{FE},\mathcal{A},\mathcal{S}}(\ )$:
$(\mathsf{mpk}, \mathsf{msk}) \twoheadleftarrow \mathsf{Setup}(\ )$	$(\mathsf{mpk}, \mathsf{msk}) \twoheadleftarrow \mathsf{Setup}(\ )$
$b \twoheadleftarrow \mathcal{A}^{\mathsf{KeyGen}(\mathsf{msk},\cdot),\mathsf{Enc}(\mathsf{mpk},\cdot)}(\alpha)$	$b \twoheadleftarrow \mathcal{A}^{\mathcal{S}(\mathsf{key},\varPhi(\cdot)),\mathcal{S}(\mathsf{msg},\varPhi(\cdot))}(\alpha)$
Output b	Output b

Fig. 2. Games defining simulation-based security of an FE scheme. On the i-th (resp. j-th) Enc query (resp. KeyGen query) the (stateful) simulator $\mathcal{S}$ receives as side information leakage $\varPhi$: a matrix of values such that $\varPhi[i, j] = F_{y_j}(x_i)$, for all (i, j) combinations of all key extraction and encryption queries placed by $\mathcal{A}$ (including the current one). Furthermore, we also impose that the attacker never queries the all zeroes vector to either the key extraction or the encryption oracle.

one-SAD-SK-IND. Note that in the public key setting the single-message and multi-message are equivalent via a standard hybrid argument (for all variants of security) whereas in the symmetric key setting this is not the case since the attacker cannot obtain arbitrary encryptions of chosen messages. Note also that, as mentioned above, function-hiding functional encryption cannot be satisfied in the public-key setting: once an adversary is provided with a secret key sk_y for some y and public encryption key mpk, it can learn $F_y(x)$ for arbitrary x. Finally, note that in the secret-key setting, semi-adaptive security is the same as *selective* security, where the adversary needs to commit to the LoR$_x$ queries without any side information about the global parameters. A further weakening of this notion is *fully selective* security, where all queries are provided upfront and the adversary gets a set of challenge ciphertexts and keys in batch to conduct its attack.

SIMULATION-BASED SECURITY. Consider the experiments defined in Fig. 2, which are parametrised by functional encryption scheme $\mathcal{FE}$, adversary $\mathcal{A}$ and simulator $\mathcal{S}$.

As before, the following variants of simulation-based security can be defined based on this experiment:

- Public-key security: the attacker is parametrised with $\alpha = \mathsf{mpk}$. In the secret key setting (SK), we have $\alpha = \epsilon$.
- Semi-adaptive security (SAD): the attacker places all calls to Enc before calling KeyGen.
- Non function-hiding (standard) security: leakage $\varPhi$ is extended to also provide the inputs to the KeyGen oracle (i.e., the keys are explicitly given to the simulator). Again we use FH to denote the stronger function-hiding setting.
- Single-message security (one): the attacker places only one call to LoR$_x$.

For all such variants, the advantage of an an attacker $\mathcal{A}$ against $\mathcal{FE}$ is defined by the following difference of probabilities, where xx will specify the security variant according to the above conventions.

$$\mathbf{Adv}^{\text{xx-SIM}}_{\mathcal{FE},\mathcal{A}}(\ ) = |\Pr[\mathsf{Real}_{\mathcal{FE},\mathcal{A}}(\ ) \Rightarrow 1] - \Pr[\mathsf{Ideal}_{\mathcal{FE},\mathcal{A},\mathcal{S}}(\ ) \Rightarrow 1]|.$$

For the same set of adversarial restrictions, simulation-based security implies indistinguishability-based security. To see this, observe that any IND attacker $\mathcal{A}$ can be used to construct a SIM attacker $\mathcal{B}$ as follows. $\mathcal{B}$ initially chooses a bit b uniformly at random and converts the left-right calls placed by $\mathcal{A}$ into encryption and key extractions calls x_b (resp. y_b) that depend on b. By giving the oracle answers back to $\mathcal{A}$, our SIM adversary ensures that, when running in the real world, it perfectly simulates the environment in the IND experiment for $\mathcal{A}$. The output of $\mathcal{A}$, which $\mathcal{B}$ uses as its own will therefore be correlated with b in a visible way if $\mathcal{A}$ is a successful IND attacker. Consider now the ideal world and *any* simulator Sim. It is easy to see that, given the restrictions on the left-or-right calls placed by $\mathcal{A}$, the input to the simulator will be information-theoretically independent of b, which means that the output of $\mathcal{A}$ will also be independent of b. The bias in the real-world output would therefore give $\mathcal{B}$ a visible advantage in breaking SIM security. In other words, the existence of an IND attacker with large advantage contradicts the existence of a successful simulator.

3   IPFE vs OFE

Perhaps the first question elicited by the close relationship between IPFE and OFE is whether generic transformations of one scheme into the other one are possible. We briefly explore a couple of simple transformations where one attempts to construct an OFE from an IPFE by somehow encoding an OFE key y as a vector of keys y_i for the underlying IPFE. We provide negative results which show that no deterministic transformation (even one which depends on a secret key) cannot yield a function-hiding OFE, independent of the security level offered by the starting IPFE.

These negative results heavily rely on the determinism of the transformation and suggest that one way around them would be to consider randomized transformations. Indeed, for warm-up we present a simple OFE scheme constructed, generically, from an IPFE scheme: the OFE key for some vector y is simply the IPFE key for $r \cdot y$ for some randomly selected scalar r: decryption of a ciphertext which encrypts x is either 0 when $x \perp y$ or uniformly random otherwise. Clearly, as soon as the adversary has more than one ciphertext, which each encrypts messages known to the adversary, then can recover information about r and y. In effect, we can only prove that the scheme is one-SAD-FH-IND-secure.

For space reasons we describe the negative results and the construction in the full version of this paper. Nonetheless, even the cursory discussion above indicates that one needs additional randomization also in the ciphertexts. The scheme which we present next implements this intuition.

4   A Construction in the Generic Group Model

In this section we describe a simple construction which satisfies simulation-based security in the generic group model (GGM). Our starting point is recent work by Kim et al. [14] who propose a FH-IPFE scheme that is simulation-based secure in the GGM. The construction follows the pattern of recent schemes where the inner-product is recovered by solving a discrete logarithm problem over a small domain by exhaustive search. Here we show that, by a simple adaptation where we omit one group element in both keys and ciphertexts (which are the values used to compute the basis for the discrete logarithm problem) we obtain a fully secure OFE. Indeed, the information leaked by the scheme of Kim et al. is accessible to the GGM attacker only via a zero-testing oracle which becomes useless if the basis for the discrete logarithm problem is hidden.

Our construction works as follows:

- Setup($1^\lambda, n$): On input the security parameter λ, the setup algorithm samples an asymmetric bilinear group (G_1, G_2, G_T, q, e) and chooses generators $g_1 \in G_1$ and $g_2 \in G_2$. Then, it samples an invertible square matrix $B \in \mathbb{Z}_q^{n \times n}$ uniformly at random and sets $B^\star = \det(B) \cdot (B^{-1})^\top$. The algorithm outputs the public parameters pp $= (G_1, G_2, G_T, q, e, n)$ and the master secret key msk $= (\text{pp}, g_1, g_2, B, B^\star)$.
- KeyGen(msk, y): On input the master secret key msk and a vector $y \in \mathbb{Z}_q^n$, the key generation algorithm chooses an element $\alpha \in \mathbb{Z}_q$ uniformly at random and outputs $\text{sk}_y = [\alpha \cdot y^\top \cdot B]_1$, i.e., a vector of encodings in G_1.
- Enc(msk, x): On input the master secret key msk and a vector $x \in \mathbb{Z}_q^n$, the encryption algorithm chooses an element $\beta \in \mathbb{Z}_q$ uniformly at random and outputs ct $= [\beta \cdot x^\top \cdot B^\star]_2$, i.e., a vector of encodings in G_2.
- Dec(pp, sk, ct): On input the public parameters pp, a secret key sk and a ciphertext ct, the algorithm computes $\prod_{i=1}^n e(\text{sk}[i], \text{ct}[i])$ and returns $\top$ if the result is equal to 1_{G_T} and $\bot$ otherwise.

Correctness of the scheme follows from the fact that the output value computed by decryption encodes $[\alpha\beta \cdot x^\top \cdot B \cdot B^{\star\top} \cdot y]_t$, which therefore includes $\langle x, y \rangle$ as a multiplicative factor. The following theorem establishes the security of the scheme.

Theorem 1. *The above OFE scheme is simulation-based secure OFE in the GGM.*

Sketch. The proof is an adaptation of the original argument in [14]. Specifically, we describe a simulator that, not only answers key extraction and encryption queries in a way which is identical to what happens in the real world, it also simulates the operation of the generic bilinear group operations in a way which is indistinguishable from what the attacker sees in the real world. Due to the operation of the generic group model, all queries that the adversary makes can be perfectly simulated by returning fresh random labels for all group elements resulting from key extraction, encryption, and bilinear group operations bar zero testing. Simulating zero-test queries in the source groups is natural: the simulator answers zero if and only if the queried label corresponds to a formal polynomial that is identically zero; all non-zero answers can be justified by the Schwartz-Zippel lemma. The more intricate part of the simulation lies in zero-test queries for the target group, where one must take into account that formal

Setup( ):	Enc(mpk, x):
$A \twoheadleftarrow \mathbb{Z}_q^{k+1 \times k}$	$s \twoheadleftarrow \mathbb{Z}_q^k$
For $i \in [n]$:	$U \twoheadleftarrow \mathbb{Z}_q^{k+1 \times k+1}$
$\quad W_i \twoheadleftarrow \mathbb{Z}_q^{k+1 \times k+1}$	$M_0 \leftarrow s^\top A^\top$
msk $\leftarrow (A, \{W_i\}_{i=1}^n)$	ct $\leftarrow [M_0 \| \{M_0(x_i U + W_i)\}_{i=1}^n]_1$
mpk $\leftarrow ([A^\top]_1, \{[A^\top W_i]_1\}_{i=1}^n)$	Return ct
Return (msk, mpk)	
KeyGen(msk, y):	Dec(sk, ct):
$r \twoheadleftarrow \mathbb{Z}_q^{k+1}$	Return $\langle \text{ct}, \text{sk} \rangle = 1$
sk $\leftarrow [-\sum_{i=0}^n y_i W_i r \| \{y_i r\}_{i=1}^n]_2$	
Return sk	

Fig. 3. First variant of Wee's scheme. Decryption is presented using inner-product notation, denoting in compact form the pointwise pairing of ciphertext and key components (each comprising $(n+1)(k+1)$ group elements), followed by a product to obtain a single group element.

polynomials that are *not* identically zero in the simulator's view, correspond to cancellations in the real world. Here we show that the simulator can identify *honest* evaluations of inner products between orthogonal vectors (these cases can be detected because orthogonality is revealed in the leakage provided to the simulator) and correctly answer *zero* to linear combinations of such cases. We adapt the argument in [14] to show that all other cases can be answered as non-zero. The details are deferred to the full version of this paper.   □

5   A Construction in the Standard Model

In this section we show a construction of a function hiding OFE that is provably secure in the standard model. Our construction is developed in several steps.

Intuitively, our goal is to adapt a technique originally developed by Lin [15] in the context of functional encryption for inner products to the case of OFE. Recall that Lin's technique allows to combine two instances of a functional encryption scheme for inner products to obtain a (secret key) functional encryption scheme for inner products that also provides function hiding guarantees.

Aiming at the simplest possible solution, the natural approach would be to try to combine Lin's technique with the clever OFE recently proposed by Wee in [22]. Interestingly, adapting Lin's transform to the orthogonality setting is not at all immediate. Indeed, to guarantee correctness, the two instances of the OFE need to be instantiated with different, but matching, parameters. This is in sharp contrast with the basic IPFE setting where the transformation is less demanding on the underlying encryption schemes. In particular, we need to develop two novel variants of the basic Wee's scheme, both of which we discuss next.

5.1   First Scheme

The first scheme closely follows the blueprint of Wee's original scheme. The difference is that matrices U and W_i are uniformly chosen in $\mathbb{Z}_q^{k+1 \times k+1}$, rather

Setup( ):	Enc(mpk, $\boldsymbol{X}$):
$\boldsymbol{A} \twoheadleftarrow \mathbb{Z}_q^{k+1 \times k}$	$\boldsymbol{s} \twoheadleftarrow \mathbb{Z}_q^k$
For $i \in [n]$:	$\boldsymbol{U} \twoheadleftarrow \mathbb{Z}_q^{k+1}$
$\quad \boldsymbol{W}_i \twoheadleftarrow \mathbb{Z}_q^{k+1 \times k+1}$	$\boldsymbol{M}_0 \leftarrow \boldsymbol{s}^\top \boldsymbol{A}^\top$
msk $\leftarrow (\boldsymbol{A}, \{\boldsymbol{W}_i\}_{i=1}^n)$	ct $\leftarrow [\boldsymbol{M}_0 \| \{\boldsymbol{M}_0(\boldsymbol{U}\boldsymbol{X}_i + \boldsymbol{W}_i)\}_{i=1}^n]_2$
mpk $\leftarrow ([\boldsymbol{A}^\top]_2, \{[\boldsymbol{A}^\top \boldsymbol{W}_i]_2\}_{i=1}^n)$	Return ct
Return (msk, mpk)	
KeyGen(msk, $\boldsymbol{y}$):	Dec(sk, ct):
$r \twoheadleftarrow \mathbb{Z}_q$	Return $\langle \text{ct}, \text{sk} \rangle = 1$
sk $\leftarrow [-\sum_{i=0}^n r\boldsymbol{Y}_i^\top \boldsymbol{W}_i^\top \| \{r\boldsymbol{Y}_i^\top\}_{i=1}^n]_1$	
Return sk	

Fig. 4. Second variant of Wee's scheme. Decryption notation is as in Fig. 3.

than in $\mathbb{Z}_q^{k+1 \times k}$ as in Wee's scheme. This is shown in Fig. 3. Correctness follows from the fact that the result of decryption includes $\langle \mathbf{x}, \mathbf{y} \rangle$ as a multiplicative factor in the exponent. Indeed, decryption computes in the exponents:

$$\sum_{i=1}^n \mathbf{y}_i \boldsymbol{M}_0(\mathbf{x}_i \boldsymbol{U} + \boldsymbol{W}_i)r - \boldsymbol{M}_0 \sum_{i=0}^n \mathbf{y}_i r^\top \boldsymbol{W}_i^\top = \boldsymbol{M}_0 \boldsymbol{U} r \langle \mathbf{x}, \mathbf{y} \rangle \in \mathbb{Z}_q.$$

The following theorem establishes security and follows an argument similar to Wee's construction [22]. A sketch of the proof is given in the full version of this paper.

Theorem 2. *If MDDH and DDH assumptions hold respectively in G_1 and G_2 then the modified scheme of Wee in Fig. 3 is one-SAD-SIM secure.*

5.2 Second Scheme

The second construction modifies Wee's scheme in the sense that it allows to compute $\sum_i \boldsymbol{X}_i \boldsymbol{Y}_i$ for $\boldsymbol{X} = (\boldsymbol{X}_1, \ldots, \boldsymbol{X}_n)$ and $\boldsymbol{Y} = (\boldsymbol{Y}_1, \ldots, \boldsymbol{Y}_n)$ where for all $i \in [n]$, $\boldsymbol{X}_i \in \mathbb{Z}_q^{1 \times k+1}$ and $\boldsymbol{Y}_i \in \mathbb{Z}_q^{k+1}$. Intuitively, this corresponds precisely to the computation carried out in the exponents by the decryption algorithm of the first variant of Wee's scheme we presented above. The scheme can be found in Fig. 3.

Correctness can be verified by rewriting the decryption operation as

$$\sum_{i=1}^n (r\boldsymbol{M}_0(\boldsymbol{U}\boldsymbol{X}_i + \boldsymbol{W}_i)\boldsymbol{Y}_i) - \boldsymbol{M}_0 \sum_{i=0}^n r\boldsymbol{W}_i\boldsymbol{Y}_i = r\boldsymbol{M}_0\boldsymbol{U} \sum_{i=1}^n \boldsymbol{X}_i\boldsymbol{Y}_i$$

Again, the following theorem shows that these modifications do not affect security. The proof is similar to the scheme of Wee [22] and is given in the full version of this paper.

Theorem 3. *If DDH and MDDH assumptions hold respectively in G_1 and G_2, then the modification of Wee's scheme in Fig. 4 is one-SAD-SIM secure.*

As a simple corollary of Theorems 2 and 3 we have the following

Corollary 1. *The two modifications of Wee's scheme are (many) SAD-IND secure.*

5.3   Weak Function-Hiding Functional Encryption for Orthogonality

Now, we can give the details of our new Lin-like transform for orthogonality. For simplicity, we present our results in the fully selective setting, but the proof easily generalises to the fully adaptive setting if the underlying constructions are themselves fully adaptive. Moreover, for clarity of exposition, we present the transform in an abstract, generic way. In particular we first establish a set of conditions (see Definition 3 below) for which the transformation works and then show that our two schemes from Sects. 5.1 and 5.2 trivially satisfy these conditions. We stress that the transformation produces a scheme that is *weakly* function hiding. Still, this is enough for us as we can move to a full-fledged FH solution using the efficient Lin and Vaikuntanathan [16] compiler.[6]

Definition 3. *Let $\Gamma = (\mathsf{Setup}, \mathsf{KeyGen}, \mathsf{Enc}, \mathsf{Dec})$ be a Functional Encryption scheme for orthogonality (OFE), we say that Γ is $[\cdot]_{\alpha\beta}$-OFE, for $\alpha, \beta \in \{1, 2\}$ if the following properties are satisfied.*

1. *There are ppt algorithms RowKey and RowEnc such that,*

   $$\mathsf{Enc}(\mathsf{mpk}, \cdot) = [\mathsf{RowEnc}(\mathsf{msk}, \cdot)]_\alpha \ \text{and} \ \mathsf{KeyGen}(\mathsf{msk}, \cdot) = [\mathsf{RowKey}(\mathsf{msk}, \cdot)]_\beta$$

   for all $(\mathsf{mpk}, \mathsf{msk})$ in the support of $\mathsf{Setup}()$.
2. *There are efficiently computable functions F_e and F_k such that*

   $$\mathsf{Enc}(\mathsf{mpk}, \cdot) = F_e(\mathsf{mpk}, [\cdot]_\alpha) \ \text{and} \ \mathsf{KeyGen}(\mathsf{msk}, \cdot) = F_k(\mathsf{msk}, [\cdot]_\beta).$$

3. *For both schemes, and for all ciphertexts in the support of $\mathsf{Enc}(\mathsf{mpk}, \mathbf{x})$ and keys in the support of $\mathsf{KeyGen}(\mathsf{msk}, \mathbf{y})$, there exists some scalar δ that is a function of the randomness used in algorithms Enc and KeyGen, such that decryption returns $[\langle \mathbf{x}, \mathbf{y} \rangle]_T^\delta$ computed as*

   $$\mathsf{Dec}(\mathsf{Enc}(\mathsf{mpk}, \mathbf{x}), \mathsf{KeyGen}(\mathsf{msk}, \mathbf{y})) = [\langle \mathsf{RowEnc}(\mathsf{mpk}, \mathbf{x}), \mathsf{RowKey}(\mathsf{msk}, \mathbf{y}) \rangle]_T.$$

It is easy to see that our first and second modification of Wee's scheme are respectively $[\cdot]_{12}$-OFE and $[\cdot]_{21}$-OFE schemes. We now show that, if Γ_1 and Γ_2 are two $[\cdot]_{12}$ and $[\cdot]_{21}$ OFE schemes, respectively, then the generic OFE construction in Fig. 5 is a secret-key (weakly) function hiding OFE. Correctness of the construction follows from the following derivation:

$$\Gamma_2.\mathsf{Dec}(\mathsf{sk}, \mathsf{ct}) = [\langle \mathsf{sk}_2, \mathsf{ct}_1 \rangle]_T^{\delta_2} = [\langle \mathbf{x}, \mathbf{y} \rangle]_T^{\delta_1 \delta_2}$$

---

[6] The compiler has been proposed in the IPFE setting, but trivially extends to the OFE setting.

Setup( ):	Enc(msk, **x**):
$(\text{msk}_1, \text{mpk}_1) \twoheadleftarrow \Gamma_1.\text{Setup}(n)$	$(\text{msk}_1, \text{msk}_2) \leftarrow \text{msk}$
$(\text{msk}_2, \text{mpk}_2) \twoheadleftarrow \Gamma_2.\text{Setup}(n+1)$	$\text{ct}_1 \twoheadleftarrow \Gamma_1.\text{RowEnc}(\text{msk}_1, \mathbf{x})$
Return $(\text{msk}_1, \text{msk}_2, \text{mpk}_2)$	$\text{ct} \twoheadleftarrow \Gamma_2.\text{KeyGen}(\text{msk}_2, \text{ct}_1)$
	Return ct
KeyGen(msk, **y**):	Dec(sk, ct):
$(\text{msk}_1, \text{msk}_2) \leftarrow \text{msk}$	Return $\Gamma_2.\text{Dec}(\text{sk}, \text{ct})$
$\text{sk}_1 \twoheadleftarrow \Gamma_1.\text{RowKey}(\text{msk}_1, \mathbf{y})$	
$\text{sk} \twoheadleftarrow \Gamma_2.\text{Enc}(\text{mpk}_2, \text{sk}_1)$	
Return sk	

Fig. 5. Lin-like transform for orthogonality. We slightly abuse notation by using $\Gamma_1.\text{Setup}(n)$ and $\Gamma_2.\text{Setup}(n+1)$ to denote the size of message and key vectors supported by each scheme when constructing a function-hiding OFE for vectors of size n.

Theorem 4. *If Γ_1 and Γ_2 are SAD-IND secure OFE schemes then our scheme is selectively secure OFE with (weak) function hiding.*

Proof. The proof follows from a sequence of games, where Game_0 is the real game in the definition of indistinguishability-based security, when $b = 0$, Game_1 is the same game when $b = 1$, and Game_h is a hybrid game that proceeds as Game_0, except that Enc is run on inputs $\mathbf{x}_1^j$. Thus, for the security proof it is enough to prove that Game_h is computationally indistinguishable from both Game_0 and Game_1.

Indistinguishability of Game_0 and Game_h: Let $\mathcal{A}_{0-h}$ be any adversary that is able to distinguish between these two games. We construct $\mathcal{B}$ that breaks the SAD-IND-security of Γ_1. $\mathcal{B}$ runs $\mathcal{A}_{0-h}$, interpolating between the two games while interacting with the experiment SAD-IND, as follows.

$\mathcal{B}$ gets the the public key mpk_1 of scheme Γ_1 and challenges $(\mathbf{x}_0^j, \mathbf{x}_1^j)$ and $(\mathbf{y}_0^i, \mathbf{y}_1^i)$ from $\mathcal{A}_{0-h}$. Then $\mathcal{B}$ runs $\Gamma_2.\text{Setup}$ itself to get a pair $(\text{msk}_2, \text{mpk}_2)$, calls the external $\text{LoR}_\mathbf{x}$ oracle to get encryptions under Γ_1 of all the challenges $[\text{ct}_1^j]_1 = \Gamma_1.\text{Enc}(\text{mpk}_1, \mathbf{x}_b^j)$, and computes $\text{ct}^j = \Gamma_2.\text{KeyGen}(\text{msk}_2, \text{ct}_1^j) = F_k(\text{msk}_2, [\text{ct}_1^j]_1)$, where F_k comes from Definition 3. Then, $\mathcal{B}$ sends queries $\mathbf{y}_0^i$ to key extraction in the external game, receives secret keys $[\text{sk}_1^i]_2 = \Gamma_1.\text{KeyGen}(\text{msk}_1, \mathbf{y}_0^i)$ and computes

$$\text{sk}^i = \Gamma_2.\text{Enc}(\text{mpk}_2, \text{sk}^i) = F_e(\text{mpk}_2, [\text{sk}_1^i]_2)$$

It provides all ciphertexts and keys to the attacker, waits for the adversary's choice, and uses this as it's own output. It is easy to see that any change in the behaviour of $\mathcal{A}_{0-h}$ between the two games is immediately translated into a distinguishing advantage against Γ_1. This is because all queries placed by $\mathcal{B}$ are admissible: $\mathcal{B}$ must satisfy restriction $\mathbf{x}_0^j \perp \mathbf{y}_0^i = \mathbf{x}_1^j \perp \mathbf{y}_0^i$ on all queries and this is guaranteed because $\mathcal{A}_{0-h}$ has output challenges that satisfy $\mathbf{x}_0^j \perp \mathbf{y}_0^i = \mathbf{x}_1^j \perp \mathbf{y}_0^i = \mathbf{x}_1^j \perp \mathbf{y}_1^i$.

Indistinguishability of Game_h and Game_1: Let $\mathcal{A}_{h-1}$ be any adversary that is able to distinguish between these two games. We construct $\mathcal{B}$ that breaks the

SAD-IND-security of Γ_2. $\mathcal{B}$ runs $\mathcal{A}_{h-1}$, interpolating betweeen the two games while interacting with the experiment SAD-IND, as follows.

$\mathcal{B}$ gets the the public key mpk_2 of scheme Γ_2 and challenges $(\mathbf{x}_0^j, \mathbf{x}_1^j)$ and $(\mathbf{y}_0^i, \mathbf{y}_1^i)$ from $\mathcal{A}_{h-1}$. Then $\mathcal{B}$ runs Γ_1.Setup itself to get a pair $(\mathsf{msk}_1, \mathsf{mpk}_1)$, computes

$$\mathsf{sk}_{1,c}^i = \Gamma_1.\mathsf{RowKey}(\mathsf{msk}_1, \mathbf{y}_c^i) \text{ for all } i \text{ and } c \in \{0,1\},$$

and calls $\mathsf{LoR_x}$ in the external game on $(\mathsf{sk}_{1,0}^i, \mathsf{sk}_{1,1}^i)$ to get $\mathsf{sk}^i = \Gamma_2.\mathsf{Enc}(\mathsf{mpk}_2, \mathsf{sk}_{1,b}^i)$.

$\mathcal{B}$ then computes $\mathsf{ct}_1^j = \Gamma_1.\mathsf{RowEnc}(\mathsf{mpk}_1, \mathbf{x}_1^j)$, calls key extraction in the external game to obtain $\mathsf{ct}^j = \Gamma_2.\mathsf{KeyGen}(\mathsf{msk}_2, \mathsf{ct}_1^j)$. Finally, $\mathcal{B}$ provides all ciphertexts and keys to the attacker, waits for the adversary's choice, and uses this as it's own output.

It is easy to see that any change in the behaviour of $\mathcal{A}_{h-1}$ between the two games is immediately translated into a distinguishing advantage against Γ_2. This is because all queries placed by $\mathcal{B}$ are admissible, which we now justify. $\mathcal{B}$ must satisfy restriction $\mathsf{ct}_1^j \bot \mathsf{sk}_{1,0}^i = \mathsf{ct}_1^j \bot \mathsf{sk}_{1,1}^i$ on all queries. Note that $[\langle \mathsf{ct}_1^j, \mathsf{sk}_{1,b}^i \rangle]_T = [\langle \mathbf{x}_1^j, \mathbf{y}_b^i \rangle]_T^{\delta_1}$, so restriction $\mathsf{ct}_1^j \bot \mathsf{sk}_{1,0}^i = \mathsf{ct}_1^j \bot \mathsf{sk}_{1,1}^i$ is equivalent to $\mathbf{x}_1^j \bot \mathbf{y}_0^i = \mathbf{x}_1^j \bot \mathbf{y}_1^i$. Furthermore, $\mathcal{A}_{h-1}$ outputs challenges that satisfy $\mathbf{x}_0^j \bot \mathbf{y}_0^i = \mathbf{x}_1^j \bot \mathbf{y}_0^i = \mathbf{x}_1^j \bot \mathbf{y}_1^i$. Thus, all queries placed by $\mathcal{B}$ are admissible. $\qquad\square$

5.4   Achieving Adaptive Security

An obvious way to make the scheme given in Sect. 5.3 adaptive secure, would be to employ complexity leveraging.

However, a naive application of complexity leveraging to the scheme from Sect. 5.3 would result in a security loss 2^τ where $\tau = q_e|\mathbf{x}| + q_s|\mathbf{y}|$, (here q_e and q_s are, respectively, the maximum number of encryption queries and secret key queries allowed). This is because the scheme is selective both with respect to challenge messages and with respect to challenge keys. Furthermore, since it lives in the symmetric setting we need to guess *all* the challenges in advance. Notice that, while in our setting both $|\mathbf{x}|$ and $|\mathbf{y}|$ might be small, this is not necessarily the case for τ.

We overcome this by "anticipating" the complexity leveraging step to the basic schemes. Recall that the construction from Sect. 5.3 builds upon two schemes Γ_1 and Γ_2 that are in the public key setting. These latter schemes, in turn, are assumed to guarantee SAD-IND security, which means they also guarantee one-SAD-IND security.

Our key observation is to apply complexity leveraging to these basic one-SAD-IND secure building blocks. This means that assuming that $\mathbf{x}$ (resp. $\mathbf{y}$) is sufficiently small, complexity leveraging induces only a polynomial $2^{2|\mathbf{x}|}$ (resp. $2^{2|\mathbf{y}|}$) loss, as one single challenge query has to be guessed. Next, we build our way towards a fully fledged (adaptively secure) construction via the following two observations. First, in the public key setting, one-IND implies (many) IND via a standard hybrid argument that only induces a polynomial loss in the security reduction. Second, Theorem 4 trivially extends to the adaptive setting without introducing additional losses.

All these observations combined mean that the resulting scheme achieves adaptive security with only a $\max(2^{2|x|}, 2^{2|y|})$ security loss with respect to the selective secure solution we started from. In what follows we prove this formally. We start with the following theorem (its proof appears in the full version of this paper).

Theorem 5. *Let n, be a integer bound on the max size of admissible messages. If Γ is a ϵ one-SAD-IND-secure functional encryption for orthogonality (where ϵ denotes the advantage of adversary attacking the security of the scheme), then Γ is also $2^{2n}\epsilon$ one-IND-secure.*

Claim. If Γ is a ϵ'-one-IND-secure functional encryption for orthogonality, then it is also $(q + 1)\epsilon'$-IND-secure (where q is the number of ciphertext challenges).

The proof is a straightforward hybrid argument.

Claim. If Γ_1 and Γ_2 are respectively ϵ_1 and ϵ_2-IND-secure functional encryption schemes for orthogonality, then the construction from Sect. 5.3 is $(\epsilon_1 + \epsilon_2)$-IND-secure.

The proof is the same as that given in Sect. 5.3 and is, therefore, omitted. Putting together all the claims we have the following result.

Corollary 2. *If Γ_1 and Γ_2 are ϵ-one-SAD-IND-secure OFE, then our proposed construction is $2^{2n}((q_x + 1) + (q_y + 1))\epsilon$-IND-secure FH-OFE scheme (where n is the length of the messages and q_x and q_y are respectively the number of ciphertext and secret key challenges).*

Thus, the total factor of security that we will lose is $2^{2n}((q_x + 1) + (q_y + 1))$.

6 Experimental Evaluation

We have implemented our new OFE schemes in C++ starting from Shoup's Number Theory Library[7] (NTL) on top of the GNU Multiprecision Library[8] (GMP), and in integration with and the SCIPR Lab's library for Finite Fields and Elliptic Curves[9] (libff). We used NTL to deal with matrix and vector operations carried out in the exponents, and libff as a provider for the pairing group. Conversions between the NTL representations and the libff representations make the implementation sub-optimal in terms of performance in key generation and encryption. No such conversions are needed for decryption. We used the pairing

---

[7] https://www.shoup.net/ntl/.
[8] https://gmplib.org/.
[9] https://github.com/scipr-lab/libff.

group over a curve known as BN128 from libff, aka BN254,[10] which is deployed for example in ZCash but gradually being abandoned due to the fact that it offers less than 128 bits of security.[11] All our implementations are single-threaded, and could be further optimized via parallelization. For all of these reasons, we present this implementation as a proof of concept, aiming to give an approximate idea of the performance one might get if deploying such schemes. The implementation is available upon request.

Our benchmarking results were collected in a standard MacBook Pro machine with a 2.9 GHz Intel Core i5 and 16 GB or RAM. For every chosen set of parameters, we repeated the experiment 10 times, and took the median of the timings. In all cases we observed a coefficient of variation below 10%. Table 2 provides execution times and key/ciphertext lengths for growing sizes of key/message vectors. For our standard model construction, note that we are actually using double-sized vectors, in order to guarantee full security according to the discussion in Sect. 5. We observe the linear growth in both execution times and key/ciphertext length, which is to be expected, and highlight the fact that the overhead of going for a standard-model security guarantee is roughly 6-fold. The most interesting conclusion we can draw, although not surprising due to the close match between our GGM scheme and that proposed in [14], is that our implementation is roughly twice as fast for the same security level (112-bits) than the results reported for the original inner-product encryption scheme. This shows that we bridged the gap between the two primitives with essentially no efficiency loss (this is explained by the fact that we deal with a generic attacker).

Table 2. Benchmarking results for our generic-group-model construction (GGM) and our standard-model construction (SM). On the left-hand side, timing values are given in milliseconds. On the righ-hand side, key and ciphertext lengths are given in kilobytes. Each row corresponds to an increasing vector size N. Although similar in terms of group operations, the execution times and sizes for keys and ciphertexts differ due to the different sizes of representations of G_1 and G_2 elements in an asymmetric pairing.

	GGM			SM				GGM		SM	
N	Extract	Encrypt	Decrypt	Extract	Encrypt	Decrypt	N	Keys	Cph	Keys	Cph
16	6	2	10	36	15	60	16	0,99	0,50	6,34	3,18
32	12	4	19	71	28	116	32	1,99	1,00	12,30	6,16
64	22	9	37	139	60	231	64	3,98	1,99	24,23	12,14
128	46	20	73	270	112	463	128	7,95	3,98	48,09	24,09
256	100	44	155	558	229	968	256	15,91	7,97	95,81	48,00

---

[10] https://github.com/zcash/zcash/issues/2502.
[11] https://twitter.com/pbarreto/status/779852921135476738.

7   Applications of Function-Hiding OFE

Our function-hiding OFE constructions can be applied in all the scenarios where secret-key functional encryption for hyperplane-membership [8,12] and hidden-vector encryption [10] are used. These include outsourcing of computations of CNF/DNF Boolean formulas, outsourcing subset relations and range queries on encrypted data. In particular, in the latter example no information is leaked about encrypted data and the query, besides the value of the predicate itself. Indeed, since our constructions are function-hiding, they also imply property-revealing encryption schemes [7] for such predicates. To see this, consider the construction of a property-revealing encryption scheme where an encryption of message x consists of *both* an encryption and a key token for x under our function-hiding OFE. Then, the orthogonality relation can be publicly computed over all pairs of encrypted messages as in the property revealing setting. In fact, this construction gives rise to a single-key two-input functional encryption scheme, which in turn implies a property-revealing encryption scheme [14].

Furthermore, both our GGM construction and our standard model construction are the most efficient to date under comparable assumptions. However, our standard model construction comes with a message space constraint due to the application of a complexity leveraging argument that we use to achieve full adaptivity.

We therefore focus our attention on applications of function-hiding OFE where this constraint is not a limitation. Our goal is to emphasize that the optimized complexity leveraging argument that we give in Sect. 5 is crucial to validate our standard model construction for applications where adaptive security is a requirement.

We recall that all our schemes can securely operate over message sizes of roughly $|\mathcal{M}| = q^n$, where q is the cardinality of the cyclic groups over which the schemes are implemented and n is the vector length. However, our standard model scheme from Sect. 5 achieves only selective security for both keys and messages. A naive complexity leveraging argument to obtain adaptive security would therefore lead to a security loss in the range of $|\mathcal{M}|^{k+1}$, where k is an upper bound on the number of key extraction queries that the scheme should tolerate. However, in Sect. 5 we have shown how to obtain adaptive security with only $|\mathcal{M}|$ loss. This motivates our analysis of applications of function-hiding OFE where only a small fraction of the full message space $|\mathcal{M}| \approx 2^n \ll q^n$ is used. We stress that no such restrictions apply to our GGM construction, which therefore can be used to replace with better performance all applications of OFE proposed in the literature.

PRIVACY-PRESERVING SUBSET RELATION. Let us consider a universe $\mathcal{U}$ of n elements $u_1, \ldots, u_n$ and the following two representations of sets $A, B \subseteq \mathcal{U}$ in this universe as vectors x, y of length $n + 1$ such that

$$\mathsf{mRep}(A) := \begin{cases} x_i = 1 & \text{if } u_i \in A, 1 \le i \le n \\ x_i = 0 & \text{if } u_i \notin A, 1 \le i \le n \\ x_{n+1} = -1 \end{cases}$$

$$\mathsf{kRep}(B) := \begin{cases} y_i = 1 & \text{if } u_i \in B, 1 \leq i \leq n \\ y_i = 0 & \text{if } u_i \notin B, 1 \leq i \leq n \\ y_{n+1} = |B| \end{cases}$$

Clearly, $\langle \mathsf{mRep}(A), \mathsf{kRep}(B) \rangle = 0$ if and only if $B \subseteq A$. Furthermore, the power set $\mathcal{P}(\mathcal{U})$ has size 2^n and both of these representations give injective mappings from $\mathcal{P}(\mathcal{U})$ to $\mathbb{F}_q^{n+1}$. This means that, by using these encodings to compute the subset relation over $\mathcal{P}(\mathcal{U})$, we are in effect operating over a message space of size 2^n.

The computation of the subset relation over a universe of small size can therefore be securely outsourced to an untrusted server with full adaptivity (i.e., new messages can be encrypted interleaved with query evaluations) with the guarantee that the orthogonality predicate over all message/key pairs is leaked to the untrusted server. Furthermore, no information is leaked to an external observer or a snapshot adversary that just observes encrypted messages at rest.

One direct application of this primitive is to allow topological sorting over encrypted data, as any partial order can be computed by using the subset relation. Another application of the subset relation is conjunction keyword search: fix a dictionary of keywords of size n and for each document in a database, encrypt the set of keywords that match that document; then the subset relation can be used to identify all the documents that match *all* the keywords in the set associated with an extracted key. This subsumes the simplest form of single-key symmetric searchable encryption and reduces leakage for conjunctive queries by hiding the size of the matched subset. However, the security loss of our scheme requires impractically small dictionaries. Next however, we consider two other applications of the subset relation where this is not the case.

RANGE QUERIES. A standard method to encode range queries of the sort $a < x < b$ is to partition the range of values that x can take into n disjoint intervals of equal size $0 < i_1 < i_2 < \ldots$, and then encode x as the singleton $\{i_k\}$ such that $i_{k-1} \leq x < i_k$. Let I_x be the representation of a value x. Then, the check $i_a \leq x < i_b$ can be computed as $I_x \subseteq \{i_a, \ldots, i_b\}$. This also applies to cases where x is represented in generalized form as belonging to a range of more than one intervals. Our standard-model function-hiding OFE therefore permits dealing with range queries whenever the granularity of the used intervals is acceptable for reasonably small n. In particular, for x coming from a small domain, the same technique can be used to implement the comparison operator and therefore implies a standard order revealing encryption scheme. For implications and optimized variants of these techniques we refer the interested reader to, e.g., [21].

ACCESS CONTROL. It is well known that access-control and, more generally, data-flow control restrictions can be represented as partial orders, and therefore implemented using a set representation and the subset relation. Then, the enforcement of an access control mechanism can be outsourced to an untrusted remote server, while keeping the details of the security lattice secret. For example, consider a database of encrypted resources stored in the remote server, each along with an encryption of the point in the access-control lattice that defines the minimal set of permissions A required to access it. Then, by providing the server with a decryption key for an OFE that encodes the set of permissions assigned to a user B, the server can decide whether the operation is allowed by computing $A \subseteq B$. Any security lattice with n nodes is isomorphic to a partially ordered subset of the power set $\mathcal{P}([n])$, and can be therefore outsourced with our standard model scheme if n is reasonably small.

Acknowledgements. This work was supported in part by Royal Society grant for international collaboration and by the European Union Horizon 2020 Research and Innovation Programme under grant agreement 780108 (FENTEC). The first author is financed by Project NanoSTIMA (NORTE-01-0145-FEDER-000016) through the North Portugal Regional Operational Programme (NORTE 2020), under the PORTU-GAL 2020 Partnership Agreement and the ERDF.

References

1. Abdalla, M., Bourse, F., De Caro, A., Pointcheval, D.: Simple functional encryption schemes for inner products. In: Katz, J. (ed.) PKC 2015. LNCS, vol. 9020, pp. 733–751. Springer, Heidelberg (2015). https://doi.org/10.1007/978-3-662-46447-2_33
2. Abdalla, M., Bourse, F., Caro, A.D., Pointcheval, D.: Better security for functional encryption for inner product evaluations. IACR Cryptology ePrint Archive 2016, 11 (2016)
3. Abdalla, M., Catalano, D., Fiore, D., Gay, R., Ursu, B.: Multi-input functional encryption for inner products: function-hiding realizations and constructions without pairings. In: Shacham, H., Boldyreva, A. (eds.) CRYPTO 2018. LNCS, vol. 10991, pp. 597–627. Springer, Cham (2018). https://doi.org/10.1007/978-3-319-96884-1_20
4. Abdalla, M., Gay, R., Raykova, M., Wee, H.: Multi-input inner-product functional encryption from pairings. In: Coron, J.-S., Nielsen, J.B. (eds.) EUROCRYPT 2017. LNCS, vol. 10210, pp. 601–626. Springer, Cham (2017). https://doi.org/10.1007/978-3-319-56620-7_21
5. Agrawal, S., Gorbunov, S., Vaikuntanathan, V., Wee, H.: Functional encryption: new perspectives and lower bounds. In: Canetti, R., Garay, J.A. (eds.) CRYPTO 2013. LNCS, vol. 8043, pp. 500–518. Springer, Heidelberg (2013). https://doi.org/10.1007/978-3-642-40084-1_28
6. Agrawal, S., Libert, B., Stehlé, D.: Fully secure functional encryption for inner products, from standard assumptions. In: Robshaw, M., Katz, J. (eds.) CRYPTO 2016. LNCS, vol. 9816, pp. 333–362. Springer, Heidelberg (2016). https://doi.org/10.1007/978-3-662-53015-3_12
7. Boneh, D., Lewi, K., Raykova, M., Sahai, A., Zhandry, M., Zimmerman, J.: Semantically secure order-revealing encryption: multi-input functional encryption without obfuscation. In: Oswald, E., Fischlin, M. (eds.) EUROCRYPT 2015. LNCS, vol. 9057, pp. 563–594. Springer, Heidelberg (2015). https://doi.org/10.1007/978-3-662-46803-6_19
8. Boneh, D., Raghunathan, A., Segev, G.: Function-private subspace-membership encryption and its applications. In: Sako, K., Sarkar, P. (eds.) ASIACRYPT 2013. LNCS, vol. 8269, pp. 255–275. Springer, Heidelberg (2013). https://doi.org/10.1007/978-3-642-42033-7_14

9. Boneh, D., Sahai, A., Waters, B.: Functional encryption: definitions and challenges. In: Ishai, Y. (ed.) TCC 2011. LNCS, vol. 6597, pp. 253–273. Springer, Heidelberg (2011). https://doi.org/10.1007/978-3-642-19571-6_16

10. Boneh, D., Waters, B.: Conjunctive, subset, and range queries on encrypted data. In: Vadhan, S.P. (ed.) TCC 2007. LNCS, vol. 4392, pp. 535–554. Springer, Heidelberg (2007). https://doi.org/10.1007/978-3-540-70936-7_29

11. Escala, A., Herold, G., Kiltz, E., Ràfols, C., Villar, J.L.: An algebraic framework for diffie-hellman assumptions. J. Cryptol. **30**(1), 242–288 (2017)

12. Katz, J., Sahai, A., Waters, B.: Predicate encryption supporting disjunctions, polynomial equations, and inner products. J. Cryptol. **26**(2), 191–224 (2013)

13. Kawai, Y., Takashima, K.: Predicate- and attribute-hiding inner product encryption in a public key setting. In: Cao, Z., Zhang, F. (eds.) Pairing 2013. LNCS, vol. 8365, pp. 113–130. Springer, Cham (2014). https://doi.org/10.1007/978-3-319-04873-4_7

14. Kim, S., Lewi, K., Mandal, A., Montgomery, H.W., Roy, A., Wu, D.J.: Function-hiding inner product encryption is practical. IACR Cryptology ePrint Archive 2016, 440 (2016)

15. Lin, H.: Indistinguishability obfuscation from SXDH on 5-linear maps and locality-5 PRGs. In: Katz, J., Shacham, H. (eds.) CRYPTO 2017. LNCS, vol. 10401, pp. 599–629. Springer, Cham (2017). https://doi.org/10.1007/978-3-319-63688-7_20

16. Lin, H., Vaikuntanathan, V.: Indistinguishability obfuscation from DDH-like assumptions on constant-degree graded encodings. In: Proceedings of IEEE 57th Annual Symposium on Foundations of Computer Science, FOCS 2016, pp. 11–20 (2016)

17. Okamoto, T., Takashima, K.: Adaptively attribute-hiding (hierarchical) inner product encryption. In: Pointcheval, D., Johansson, T. (eds.) EUROCRYPT 2012. LNCS, vol. 7237, pp. 591–608. Springer, Heidelberg (2012). https://doi.org/10.1007/978-3-642-29011-4_35

18. Okamoto, T., Takashima, K.: Efficient (hierarchical) inner-product encryption tightly reduced from the decisional linear assumption. IEICE Trans. **96-A**(1), 42–52 (2013)

19. O'Neill, A.: Definitional issues in functional encryption. IACR Cryptology ePrint Archive 2010, 556 (2010)

20. Shen, E., Shi, E., Waters, B.: Predicate privacy in encryption systems. In: Reingold, O. (ed.) TCC 2009. LNCS, vol. 5444, pp. 457–473. Springer, Heidelberg (2009). https://doi.org/10.1007/978-3-642-00457-5_27

21. Shi, E., Bethencourt, J., Chan, T.H.H., Song, D., Perrig, A.: Multi-dimensional range query over encrypted data. In: Proceedings of the 2007 IEEE Symposium on Security and Privacy, SP 2007, pp. 350–364. IEEE Computer Society, Washington, DC, USA (2007). https://doi.org/10.1109/SP.2007.29

22. Wee, H.: Attribute-hiding predicate encryption in bilinear groups, revisited. In: Kalai, Y., Reyzin, L. (eds.) TCC 2017. LNCS, vol. 10677, pp. 206–233. Springer, Cham (2017). https://doi.org/10.1007/978-3-319-70500-2_8

Robust Encryption, Extended

Rémi Géraud[1][(✉)], David Naccache[1][(✉)], and Răzvan Roşie[1,2][(✉)]

[1] ENS, CNRS, INRIA, PSL Research University, Paris, France
{remi.geraud,david.naccache,razvan.rosie}@ens.fr
[2] University of Luxembourg, Esch-sur-Alzette, Luxembourg

Abstract. Robustness is a notion often tacitly assumed while working with encrypted data. Roughly speaking, it states that a ciphertext cannot be decrypted under different keys. Initially formalized in a public-key context, it has been further extended to key-encapsulation mechanisms, and more recently to pseudorandom functions, message-authentication codes and authenticated encryption. In this work, we motivate the importance of establishing similar guarantees for *functional encryption* schemes, even under adversarially generated keys. Our main security notion is intended to capture the scenario where a ciphertext obtained under a master key (corresponding to Authority 1) is decrypted by functional keys issued under a different master key (Authority 2). Furthermore, we show there exist simple functional encryption schemes where robustness under adversarial key-generation is not achieved. As a secondary and independent result, we formalize robustness for digital signatures – a signature should not verify under multiple keys – and point out that certain signature schemes are not robust when the keys are adversarially generated.

We present simple, generic transforms that turn a scheme into a robust one, while maintaining the original scheme's security. For the case of public-key functional encryption, we look into ciphertext anonymity and provide a transform achieving it.

Keywords: Robustness · Functional encryption · Signatures · Anonymity

1 Introduction

Cryptographic primitives, such as encryption and signature schemes, provide security guarantees under the condition, often left implicit, that they are "used correctly". Fatal examples of cryptographic misuse abound, from weak key generation to nonce-reuse. This reliance on operational security has attracted attackers, who can for instance impose faulty or backdoored random number generators to erode cryptographic protections. At the same time, the social usage of technology leans towards a more open environment than the one in which historic primitives were designed: keys are generated by one party, shared with another, certified by third... These two observations raise new interesting questions, which

© Springer Nature Switzerland AG 2019
M. Matsui (Ed.): CT-RSA 2019, LNCS 11405, pp. 149–168, 2019.
https://doi.org/10.1007/978-3-030-12612-4_8

have only recently been addressed in the cryptographic literature. For instance, if Alice generates keys that she is using, but doesn't share, can an adversary (observing Alice or influencing her in some way) nevertheless generate a *different* set of keys, which would allow decryption (maybe only partial)? Intuitively this should not be the case, but it was not until the seminal work of Abdalla, Bellare and Neven [1], that this situation was formally analysed. They introduced the notion of robustness, which ensures that a ciphertext cannot be decrypted under multiple keys.

Is ROBUSTNESS DESIRABLE? Imagine a scenario where users within a network exchange messages by broadcasting them, and further encrypt them with the public key of the recipient to ensure confidentiality. If this is the case, we usually assume that there is only one receiver, by arguing that no other members apart from the intended recipient can decrypt the ciphertext and obtain a valid (non-$\perp$) plaintext. But if the adversary can somehow tamper with the key generation process, she may "craft" keys that behave unexpectedly for some messages, or design alternative keys that give at least some information on some of the messages.

Farshim et al. [12] refined the original definition of robustness, by covering the cases where the keys are adversarially generated, under a master notion called "complete robustness". Mohassel addressed the question in the context of key-encapsulation mechanisms [19]. More recently, Farshim et al. also defined robustness for symmetric primitives [13], motivated by the security of oblivious transfer protocols [9] or message authentication codes. Further extensions of their security notions found applications in novel password-authenticated key-exchange protocols described by Jarecki et al. [17] or (fast) message-franking schemes [16]. The above line of work, however, leaves open several questions. Indeed, to the best of our knowledge there has been no notion of robustness defined for digital signatures [15], functional signatures [7] or functional encryption [6,20]. Yet, some existing schemes seem to be vulnerable to attacks that a proper notion of robustness would prevent.

Consider digital signature schemes (DS), that are used to authenticate electronic documents. The textbook notion, capturing the *existential unforgeability* of a DS ensures that an adversary, interacting with *one* signing oracle, cannot forge a signature (for a message he did not previously query). On the other hand, a real-world scenario is placed in a multi-user context, where it is often assumed (but not necessarily proven) that a signature can *only* be verified under the issuer's key.

Example 1: Consider a practical situation where a clerk has *acquired* a digital signature for daily use, with a third party generating the pairs of keys. Even if the scheme remains unforgeable according to the classical definition, we do not have formal guarantees that two pairs of keys—(sk, pk) and (sk', pk')—generated by the third party (potentially *malicious*), cannot be used to produce a signature σ for some *chosen message* M, verifiable under both pk and pk'—something completely undesirable in practice. To be fully explicit with our example, let us suppose one pair of keys (pk, sk) is given to the clerk and the second pair (pk', sk'), is issued by the third party and is covertly used by a local/global security agency. When needed (and if needed), an operator can issue a signature (using sk') for the message: "I attest [...] is true." which can later be verified under pk, thus having baleful consequences for the clerk.

To give a flavour of a signature scheme where such an attack is feasible, consider the one obtained from a toy version of the Boneh–Boyen scheme [4]. The construction is *pairing*-based and can be summarized as follows: (1) key-generation samples two group generators $g_1 \in \mathbb{G}_1$ and $g_2 \in \mathbb{G}_2$, both of prime order p, and publishes as a public key $(g_1, g_2, g_2^x, e(g_1, g_2))$—for a uniformly sampled x over $\mathbb{Z}_p$—keeping x as a secret key. To sign the message M, one computes $\sigma \leftarrow g_1^{1/(x+M)}$. A robustness attack against this simple signature scheme exploits the randomness in choosing the secret keys, observing that for a different pair (pk', sk'), one can choose $g_1' \equiv g_1^t \pmod{p}$ and then can set $x' \equiv t(x + M) - M \pmod{p}$ such that $\sigma \equiv g_1'^{1/(x'+M)}$.

The above example provides the intuition that robustness has practical consequences. As expected, under *correct* key generation, standard unforgeability *does imply* robustness. But it fails in a malicious setting. Fortunately, we can provide a trivial construction that generically transforms any unforgeable signature scheme into a completely robust one (allowing for adversarial, yet well-formed keys). As we prove in Sect. 4.1, the natural idea of including the public key (or a collision-resistant hash of it) in the signature is indeed sufficient.

Speaking roughly about robustness as the property of a ciphertext of not being decryptable under multiple keys, then, when it comes to decryption, an FE scheme trivially does not exhibit this property. The reason resides in the broken symmetry to the way decryption works in symmetric/public-key schemes. Through its purpose, a functional ciphertext can be decrypted under multiple keys [6,20]. In this respect, an adversary holding multiple functional keys (which is not a restriction by itself) will be able to decrypt under multiple keys. Therefore, defining robustness in terms of decryption itself is fallacious. Instead, an appropriate definition should ensure the FE ciphertext can be decrypted only by the intended set of receivers.

Example 2: Consider a simple use case of a functional encryption scheme for the "inner product" function (IP FE) [2,3]. From a technical perspective, suppose the ciphertext is generated by encrypting a plaintext M as $C \leftarrow \text{FE.Enc}(\text{mpk}, M; R)$. If msk is somehow corrupted[1] to msk', then is it possible that performing decryption under sk_y' reveals a different plaintext $M' \neq M$? Intuitively, if the functional encryption scheme meets robustness, we expect that no ciphertext can be decrypted under functional keys issued by a *different* master secret keys.

As a concrete scenario, consider a Computer Science (CS) department's registry, which holds the marks obtained by each student in the Crypto course, the final grade being computed as a weighted average of the stored marks (i.e. homework counts 30%, midterm 20% and final 50%). *A priori* established confidentiality rules ask that a clerk should not have access to the marks, but still,

---

[1] There are several scenarios leading to such corruption, including memory corruption.

it must be possible to compute the final grade. Therefore, considering the set of marks as the vector x and the weights as y, one can use an IP FE scheme, to obtain the final grade, its formula mapping to $x^\top \cdot y$. In order to achieve this, for each course: (1) the course leader encrypts the marks; (2) later, the clerk obtains a new key sk_y (depending on the established course weights), and uses it to obtain the final average. A failure to guarantee robustness could result in decryption to succeed, but the final average being incorrect (and possibly under the control of an adversary). To illustrate this, consider the (bounded-norm) IP FE scheme instantiated from ElGamal and introduced in [2]: encrypting a plaintext under $\mathsf{mpk} = (g^{s_1}, \dots, g^{s_n})$—where $\mathsf{msk} = s = (s_1, \dots, s_n)$—is done as follows: $C \leftarrow_\$ (g^{-r}, g^{r \cdot s_1 + x_1}, \dots, g^{r \cdot s_n + x_n})$, for r sampled uniformly at random in $\mathbb{Z}_p$. If an attacker wishes to obtain the same C, then r remains the same, but it can use different s' and x', implicitly changing the value of msk. As expected, even if FE.KDer is correct, and the queried key is indeed issued for the vector y, the final decrypted result corresponds to $x'^\top \cdot y$ rather than to $x^\top \cdot y$.

OUR CONTRIBUTIONS. We begin by motivating and defining the notion of robust signature schemes under honest and adversarial keys, denoted as strong (SROB) and complete (CROB) robustness (Sect. 3.1). A natural question is whether existing schemes already possess a form of robustness: we show that while SROB is indeed typically guaranteed, it is not the case of CROB, thus providing a separation between the two security concepts. Fortunately, there exist a simple generic transform, in the standard model, that turn a SROB signature scheme into a CROB one (Sect. 4.1).

In Sect. 3.2, we define robustness for functional encryption in a multi-authority context. The strongest security notion we propose (FEROB) is intended to capture adversaries able to generate the keys and the randomness used during encryption and key-derivation, while remaining as simple as possible. As regards the generic transforms, we provide them in the public and private-key paradigms Sect. 4.2. The case for private-key FE schemes [8,18] relies on right-injective PRGs and collision-resistant PRFs, concepts that we review in Sect. 2. Finally, in the original spirit of the security notion we consider, we discuss anonymity for the context of functional encryption schemes.

2   Preliminaries

NOTATIONS. We denote the security parameter by $\lambda \in \mathbb{N}^*$ and we assume it is implicitly given to all algorithms in the unary representation 1^λ. An algorithm is equivalent to a Turing machine. Algorithms are assumed to be randomized unless stated otherwise; PPT stands for "probabilistic polynomial-time," in the security parameter (rather than the total length of its inputs). Given a randomized algorithm $\mathcal{A}$ we denote the action of running $\mathcal{A}$ on input(s) $(1^\lambda, x_1, \dots)$ with uniform random coins r and assigning the output(s) to $(y_1, \dots)$ by $(y_1, \dots) \leftarrow_\$ \mathcal{A}(1^\lambda, x_1, \dots; r)$. When $\mathcal{A}$ is given oracle access to some procedure $\mathcal{O}$, we write $\mathcal{A}^\mathcal{O}$. For a finite set S, we denote its cardinality by $|S|$ and the action of sampling a uniformly at random element x from X by $x \leftarrow_\$ X$.

We define $[k] := \{1, \ldots, k\}$. A real-valued function $\text{NEGL}(\lambda)$ is negligible if $\text{NEGL}(\lambda) \in \mathcal{O}(\lambda^{-\omega(1)})$. We denote the set of all negligible functions by NEGL. Throughout the paper $\perp$ stands for a special error symbol, while $||$ denotes concatenation. For completeness, we recall below definitions for the more important concepts to be used throughout the paper.

2.1 (Right-Injective) Pseudorandom Generators

Definition 1. *A pseudorandom generator* $\text{PRG} : \{0,1\}^n \to \{0,1\}^{n+\ell}$ *takes as input a random seed s of length n and outputs a pseudorandom binary string of length $n + \ell$. We require a negligible advantage for any PPT adversary $\mathcal{A}$ against the PRG security experiment defined in Fig. 1:*

$$\text{Adv}_{\mathcal{A},\text{PRG}}^{\text{PRG}}(\lambda) := 2 \cdot \Pr\left[\text{PRG}_{\text{PRG}}^{\mathcal{A}}(\lambda) = 1\right] - 1 \in \text{NEGL}(\lambda).$$

RIGHT-INJECTIVE PRGS. We will make use of length-doubling, right-injective PRGs, where the right-injectivity condition is defined as

$$R_2 = R_2' \implies s = s'$$

for $R_1 || R_2 \leftarrow \text{PRG}(s)$ and $R_1' || R_2' \leftarrow \text{PRG}(s')$. Such constructions can be achieved assuming the existence of one-way permutations, as shown by Yao [21].

2.2 (Collision-Resistant) Pseudorandom Functions

The notion of a pseudorandom function (PRF), introduced in the seminal work of Goldreich, Goldwasser, and Micali [14], is a foundational building block in theoretical cryptography. A PRF is a *keyed* functionality guaranteeing the randomness of its output under various assumptions. PRFs found applications in the construction of both symmetric and public-key primitives.

Definition 2. *A PRF is a pair of PPT algorithms* (PRF.Gen, PRF.Eval) *such that:*

- sk $\leftarrow_{\$}$ PRF.Gen(1^λ): *is the randomized procedure that samples a secret key* sk, *given as input the unary version of the security parameter.*
- $y \leftarrow$ PRF.Eval(sk, M): *is the deterministic procedure that outputs y, corresponding to the evaluation of M under* sk.

We require the advantage of any PPT adversary $\mathcal{A}$ in the PRF security experiment defined in Fig. 1 to be negligible:

$$\text{Adv}_{\mathcal{A},\text{PRF}}^{\text{PRF}}(\lambda) := 2 \cdot \Pr\left[\text{PRF}_{\text{PRF}}^{\mathcal{A}}(\lambda)\right] - 1 \in \text{NEGL}(\lambda).$$

COLLISION-RESISTANT PRFS. We make use of collision-resistant PRFs [13]. The collision-resistance property is defined over both the secret-keys and the inputs:

$$\text{PRF.Eval}(\text{sk}, M) = \text{PRF.Eval}(\text{sk}', M') \implies (\text{sk}, M) = (\text{sk}', M').$$

Such constructions can be obtained for instance from key-injective PRFs via the GGM construction - see for instance [10, Appendix C] and length-doubling right-injective PRGs.

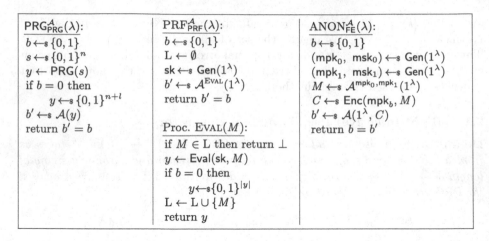

$\mathrm{PRG}^{\mathcal{A}}_{\mathsf{PRG}}(\lambda)$:	$\mathrm{PRF}^{\mathcal{A}}_{\mathsf{PRF}}(\lambda)$:	$\mathrm{ANON}^{\mathcal{A}}_{\mathsf{FE}}(\lambda)$:
$b \leftarrow_{\$} \{0,1\}$	$b \leftarrow_{\$} \{0,1\}$	$b \leftarrow_{\$} \{0,1\}$
$s \leftarrow_{\$} \{0,1\}^n$	$L \leftarrow \emptyset$	$(\mathsf{mpk}_0, \mathsf{msk}_0) \leftarrow_{\$} \mathsf{Gen}(1^\lambda)$
$y \leftarrow \mathsf{PRG}(s)$	$\mathsf{sk} \leftarrow_{\$} \mathsf{Gen}(1^\lambda)$	$(\mathsf{mpk}_1, \mathsf{msk}_1) \leftarrow_{\$} \mathsf{Gen}(1^\lambda)$
if $b = 0$ then	$b' \leftarrow_{\$} \mathcal{A}^{\mathrm{EVAL}}(1^\lambda)$	$M \leftarrow_{\$} \mathcal{A}^{\mathsf{mpk}_0, \mathsf{mpk}_1}(1^\lambda)$
$\quad y \leftarrow_{\$} \{0,1\}^{n+l}$	return $b' = b$	$C \leftarrow_{\$} \mathsf{Enc}(\mathsf{mpk}_b, M)$
$b' \leftarrow_{\$} \mathcal{A}(y)$		$b' \leftarrow_{\$} \mathcal{A}(1^\lambda, C)$
return $b' = b$	Proc. $\mathrm{EVAL}(M)$:	return $b = b'$
	if $M \in L$ then return $\bot$	
	$y \leftarrow \mathsf{Eval}(\mathsf{sk}, M)$	
	if $b = 0$ then	
	$\quad y \leftarrow_{\$} \{0,1\}^{|y|}$	
	$L \leftarrow L \cup \{M\}$	
	return y	

Fig. 1. Experiments defining pseudorandomness for PRGs (left) and PRFs (middle). Anonymity for public-key functional encryption is defined on the right.

2.3 Functional Encryption

Definition 3 (Functional Encryption Scheme - Public-Key Setting).
A functional encryption scheme FE *in the public-key setting consists of a tuple of* PPT *algorithms* (Setup, Gen, KDer, Enc, Dec) *such that:*

- pars $\leftarrow_{\$}$ *FE*.Setup(1^λ): *we assume the existence of a* Setup *algorithm producing a set of public parameters which are implicitly given to all algorithms. When omitted, the output of FE*.Setup *is* $\emptyset$.
- (msk, mpk) $\leftarrow_{\$}$ *FE*.Gen(1^λ) : *takes as input the unary representation of the security parameter* λ *and outputs a pair of master secret/public keys.*
- sk$_f$ $\leftarrow_{\$}$ *FE*.KDer(msk, f): *given the master secret key and a function* f, *the (possibly randomized) key-derivation procedure outputs a corresponding* sk$_f$.
- $C \leftarrow_{\$}$ *FE*.Enc(mpk, M): *the randomized encryption procedure encrypts the plaintext* M *with respect to* mpk.
- *FE*.Dec(sk$_f$, C): *decrypts the ciphertext* C *using the functional key* sk$_f$ *in order to learn a valid message* $f(M)$ *or a special symbol* $\bot$, *in case the decryption procedure fails.*

A functional encryption scheme is s-IND-FE-CPA-*secure if the advantage of any* PPT *adversary* $\mathcal{A}$ *against the* IND-FE-CPA-*game defined in* Fig. 2 *is negligible:*

$$\mathsf{Adv}^{\text{s-IND-FE-CPA}}_{\mathcal{A}, \textit{FE}}(\lambda) := 2 \cdot \Pr\left[\text{s-IND-FE-CPA}^{\mathcal{A}}_{\textit{FE}}(\lambda) = 1\right] - 1 \in \mathrm{NEGL}(\lambda).$$

Similarly we say that it is adaptive IND-FE-CPA-*secure if*

$$\mathsf{Adv}^{\text{IND-FE-CPA}}_{\mathcal{A}, \textit{FE}}(\lambda) := 2 \cdot \Pr\left[\text{IND-FE-CPA}^{\mathcal{A}}_{\textit{FE}}(\lambda) = 1\right] - 1 \in \mathrm{NEGL}(\lambda).$$

$\text{s-IND-FE-CPA}_{\text{FE}}^{\mathcal{A}}(\lambda)$:	$\text{IND-FE-CPA}_{\text{FE}}^{\mathcal{A}}(\lambda)$:
$b \leftarrow_\$ \{0,1\}$	$b \leftarrow_\$ \{0,1\}$
$L \leftarrow \emptyset$	$L \leftarrow \emptyset$
$(M_0, M_1; \text{state}) \leftarrow_\$ \mathcal{A}(1^\lambda)$	$\boxed{(\text{mpk}, \text{msk})}\ \text{msk} \leftarrow_\$ \text{FE.Gen}(1^\lambda)$
$\boxed{(\text{mpk}, \text{msk})}\ \text{msk} \leftarrow_\$ \text{FE.Gen}(1^\lambda)$	$(M_0, M_1) \leftarrow_\$ \mathcal{A}^{\text{KDER}_{\text{msk}}(\cdot), \text{FE.ENC}_{\text{msk}}(\cdot)}(1^\lambda)$
$C^* \leftarrow_\$ \text{FE.Enc}(\text{msk}, M_b)$	$\boxed{(M_0, M_1) \leftarrow_\$ \mathcal{A}^{\text{KDER}_{\text{msk}}(\cdot), \text{mpk}}(1^\lambda)}$
$b' \leftarrow_\$ \mathcal{A}^{C^*, \text{KDER}_{\text{msk}}(\cdot), \text{ENC}_{\text{msk}}(\cdot)}(1^\lambda, \text{state})$	$C^* \leftarrow_\$ \text{Enc}(\text{msk}, M_b)$
$\boxed{b' \leftarrow_\$ \mathcal{A}^{C^*, \text{KDER}_{\text{msk}}(\cdot), \text{mpk}}(1^\lambda, \text{state})}$	$b' \leftarrow_\$ \mathcal{A}^{\text{KDER}_{\text{msk}}(\cdot), \text{ENC}_{\text{msk}}(\cdot)}(1^\lambda)$
if $\exists \text{sk}_f \in L$ s.t. $f(\text{sk}_f, M_0) \neq f(\text{sk}_f, M_1)$	$\boxed{b' \leftarrow_\$ \mathcal{A}^{C^*, \text{KDER}_{\text{msk}}(\cdot), \text{mpk}}(1^\lambda, \text{state})}$
$\quad\quad$ return 0	if $\exists \text{sk}_f \in L$ s.t. $f(\text{sk}_f, M_0) \neq f(\text{sk}_f, M_1)$:
return $b = b'$	$\quad\quad$ return 0
	return $b = b'$
Proc. $\text{KDER}_{\text{msk}}(f)$:	Proc. $\text{KDER}_{\text{msk}}(f)$:
$L \leftarrow L \cup \{f\}$	$L \leftarrow L \cup \{f\}$
$\text{sk}_f \leftarrow_\$ \text{FE.KDer}(\text{msk}, f)$	$\text{sk}_f \leftarrow_\$ \text{FE.KDer}(\text{msk}, f)$
return sk_f	return sk_f

Fig. 2. The selective and adaptive indistinguishability experiments defined for a functional encryption scheme. The difference between the private-key and the public settings are marked in $\boxed{\text{boxed}}$ lines of codes, corresponding to the latter notion.

Functional encryption can be defined in a private-key setting: the master secret key msk is used to encrypt the plaintext M, as there is no mpk.

ANONYMITY. We define the classical notion of anonymity to the context of functional encryption and its security experiment in Fig. 1 (right). We point out that usually, in an FE scheme, a central authority answers key-derivation queries from a potential set of users $\mathcal{U}$, therefore it is unnatural to assume that a user does not know from whom it received the functional key. What we want to ensure is that an adversary $\mathcal{A} \notin \mathcal{U}$ cannot tell *which* central authority has issued a ciphertext, without interacting with the key-derivation procedures, otherwise the game becomes trivial. As an easy consequence, anonymity makes sense only in the context of public-key FE, as for a private scheme, the adversary uses encryption oracles to obtain a ciphertext. Thus, anonymity requires that a PPT bounded adversary can tell which mpk was used to encrypt a ciphertext only with negligible probability: $\text{Adv}_{\mathcal{A}, \text{FE}}^{\text{ANON}}(\lambda) := 2 \cdot \Pr\left[\text{ANON}_{\text{FE}}^{\mathcal{A}}(\lambda) = 1\right] - 1 \in \text{NEGL}(\lambda)$.

3   Robustness: Definitions, Implications and Separations

Robustness guarantees hardness in finding ciphertexts (resp. signatures) generated under adversarial, but well-formed keys, decryptable (resp. verifiable) under multiple secret (resp. public) keys. As stated in the introductory part, this property is often tacitly presumed, but almost as often left without a proof. In this work, we capture two levels of strengths of an adversary: *strong* robustness models the case where the keys are honestly generated and the adversary is agnostic of their actual values, the interaction being interfaced through decryption/signing oracles. A related, stronger notion, dubbed *complete* robustness gives an adversary the ability to generate keys (not necessarily honestly). In this work, we restrict to the cases where the keys are malicious, but well-formed[2].

We commence by presenting the security definition for digital signatures in Sect. 3.1, and then for functional encryption in Sect. 3.2.

3.1 Warm-Up: Robustness for Digital Signatures

The case for digital signatures is treated with respect to two security notions, which we denote strong and complete robustness. The winning condition remains the same in both experiments: that of obtaining a signature/message pair in such a way that it verifies under both public keys. In the SROB experiment, two signing oracles under sk_1, sk_2 are given to the adversary, while a CROB adversary generates its intrinsic keys for accomplishing essentially the same break.

$\mathrm{SROB}_{\mathsf{DS}}^{\mathcal{A}}(\lambda)$:	$\mathrm{CROB}_{\mathsf{DS}}^{\mathcal{A}}(\lambda)$:
$(\mathsf{pk}_1, \mathsf{sk}_1) \leftarrow\!\!\text{\$}\ \mathsf{Gen}(1^\lambda)$	$(\mathsf{pk}_1, \mathsf{pk}_2, \sigma, M) \leftarrow\!\!\text{\$}\ \mathcal{A}(1^\lambda)$
$(\mathsf{pk}_2, \mathsf{sk}_2) \leftarrow\!\!\text{\$}\ \mathsf{Gen}(1^\lambda)$	if $\mathsf{pk}_1 = \mathsf{pk}_2$:
$(M, \sigma) \leftarrow\!\!\text{\$}\ \mathcal{A}^{\mathsf{Sign}_{\mathsf{sk}_1}(\cdot), \mathsf{Sign}_{\mathsf{sk}_2}(\cdot)}(1^\lambda, \mathsf{pk}_1, \mathsf{pk}_2)$	$\quad$ return 0
if $\mathsf{Ver}(\mathsf{pk}_1, \sigma, M) = 1 \wedge$	if $\mathsf{Ver}(\mathsf{pk}_1, \sigma, M) = 1 \wedge$
$\qquad \mathsf{Ver}(\mathsf{pk}_2, \sigma, M) = 1$:	$\qquad \mathsf{Ver}(\mathsf{pk}_2, \sigma, M) = 1$:
$\quad$ return 1	$\quad$ return 1
return 0	return 0

Fig. 3. Games defining strong robustness SROB (left) and complete robustness CROB (right) for a digital signature scheme DS. We assume a negligible probability of sampling $\mathsf{pk}_1 = \mathsf{pk}_2$ in the SROB game.

Definition 4 (SROB and CROB Security). *Let* DS *be a digital signature scheme. We say* DS *achieves complete robustness if the advantage of any* PPT *adversary* $\mathcal{A}$ *against the CROB game depicted in Fig. 3 (right side) is negligible:* $\mathsf{Adv}_{\mathcal{A},\mathsf{DS}}^{\mathrm{CROB}}(\lambda) := \Pr\left[\mathrm{CROB}_{\mathsf{DS}}^{\mathcal{A}}(\lambda) = 1\right]$. SROB-*security is defined similarly, the* $\mathrm{SROB}_{\mathsf{DS}}^{\mathcal{A}}(\lambda)$ *game being defined in Fig. 3 (left side).*

Notice the *difference* to the classical unforgeability game where the adversary obtains signatures issued under the *same* secret key. We prove any EUF-scheme is implicitly strong-robust, and show there exist signature schemes that fail to achieve complete robustness (thus providing a separation between the two).

---

[2] We may assume that malformed keys would be easily recognisable and rejected.

Proposition 1. *Let* DS *be a* CROB-*secure digital signature scheme. Then* DS *is also* SROB-*secure, the advantage of breaking the strong robustness game being bounded as follows:* $\mathsf{Adv}^{\mathrm{SROB}}_{\mathcal{A},\mathsf{DS}}(\lambda) \leq \mathsf{Adv}^{\mathrm{CROB}}_{\mathcal{A}',\mathsf{DS}}(\lambda)$.

Proof (Proposition 1). Suppose DS is not SROB-secure. Let $\mathcal{A}$ be a PPT adversary that wins the SROB game with advantage at most ϵ_{SROB}. We construct a PPT adversary $\mathcal{A}'$ against the CROB game as follows: (1) sample two pairs of keys $(\mathsf{sk}_1, \mathsf{pk}_1), (\mathsf{sk}_2, \mathsf{pk}_2)$ using $\mathsf{Gen}(1^\lambda)$; (2) $\mathcal{A}'$ publishes $\mathsf{pk}_1, \mathsf{pk}_2$ and constructs the signing oracles $\mathsf{Sign}_{\mathsf{sk}_1}(\cdot)$ and $\mathsf{Sign}_{\mathsf{sk}_2}(\cdot)$; (3) $\mathcal{A}'$ runs $\mathcal{A}$ w.r.t. signing oracles and public-keys to obtain (M, σ); (4) $\mathcal{A}'$ constructs the tuple $(\mathsf{pk}_1,\ \mathsf{pk}_2,\ \sigma,\ M)$ and outputs it. We obtain that $\mathsf{Adv}^{\mathrm{SROB}}_{\mathcal{A}',\mathsf{DS}}(\lambda) \leq \mathsf{Adv}^{\mathrm{CROB}}_{\mathcal{A},\mathsf{DS}}(\lambda)$. $\qquad\square$

Of interest, is a minimal level of robustness achieved by any digital signature scheme, and as it turns out, SROB is accomplished.

Lemma 1. *Any* EUF-*secure digital signature scheme* DS *is* SROB-*secure. The advantage of breaking the* SROB *game is bounded by the advantage of breaking the* EUF *game:* $\mathsf{Adv}^{\mathrm{SROB}}_{\mathcal{A},\mathsf{DS}}(\lambda) \leq 2 \cdot \mathsf{Adv}^{\mathrm{EUF}}_{\mathcal{A}',\mathsf{DS}}(\lambda)$.

> Algorithm $\mathcal{A}'_{\mathcal{A}}(\lambda, \mathsf{pk}_1, \mathsf{Sign}_{\mathsf{sk}_1}(\cdot))$:
> $(\mathsf{pk}_2, \mathsf{sk}_2) \leftarrow_\$ \mathsf{Gen}(1^\lambda)$
> build $\mathsf{Sign}_{\mathsf{sk}_2}(\cdot)$
> $(M, \sigma) \leftarrow_\$ \mathcal{A}^{\mathsf{Sign}_{\mathsf{sk}_1}(\cdot), \mathsf{Sign}_{\mathsf{sk}_2}(\cdot)}(\mathsf{pk}_1, \mathsf{pk}_2)$
> if $M \in \mathsf{Sign}_{\mathsf{sk}_1}(\cdot).\mathsf{SignedMessages}()$
>   abort
> return (M, σ)

Fig. 4. The reduction $\mathcal{A}'$ in Lemma 1.

Proof (Lemma 1). Let $\mathcal{A}$ be a PPT adversary against the strong robustness game. Let $\mathcal{A}'$ stand for an adversary against the unforgeability of the digital signature. We assume without loss of generality that $\mathcal{A}$: (1) never queries a "winning" message M to the second signing oracle after it has been signed by the first oracle (since it can check it right away) and (2) it never queries a "winning" message M to the first oracle after it has been signed by the second oracle (for the same reason). We present the reduction in Fig. 4 and describe it below:

1. The EUF game proceeds by sampling $(\mathsf{sk}_1, \mathsf{pk}_1)$ and builds a signing oracle $\mathsf{Sign}_{\mathsf{sk}_1}(\cdot)$.
2. The reduction $\mathcal{A}'$ is given pk_1 and oracle access to the $\mathsf{Sign}_{\mathsf{sk}_1}(\cdot)$. $\mathcal{A}'$ samples uniformly at random $(\mathsf{sk}_2, \mathsf{pk}_2)$ via DS.Gen and constructs a second signing oracle $\mathsf{Sign}_{\mathsf{sk}_2}(\cdot)$.
3. $\mathcal{A}'$ runs $\mathcal{A}$ w.r.t. the two $(\mathsf{pk}_1, \mathsf{pk}_2)$ and the corresponding signing oracles $\mathsf{Sign}_{\mathsf{sk}_1}(\cdot), \mathsf{Sign}_{\mathsf{sk}_2}(\cdot)$. $\mathcal{A}'$ keeps track of the queried messages to each oracle.
4. $\mathcal{A}$ returns a pair (σ, M) which verifies under both public keys with probability ϵ_{SROB}, s.t. M has been queried to either $\mathsf{Sign}_{\mathsf{sk}_1}$ or $\mathsf{Sign}_{\mathsf{sk}_2}$ but not to both.
5. $\mathcal{A}'$ returns (σ, M). If $M \in \mathsf{Sign}_{\mathsf{sk}_1}(\cdot).\mathsf{SignedMessages}()$, $\mathcal{A}'$ aborts and runs $\mathcal{A}$ again. With probability $\frac{1}{2}$, M was not queried before to $\mathsf{Sign}_{\mathsf{sk}_1}(\cdot)$. The tuple (σ, M) wins the EUF game w.r.t. $(\mathsf{pk}_1, \mathsf{sk}_1)$ with probability $\geq \frac{1}{2} \cdot \epsilon_{\mathrm{SROB}}$.

Thus, the reduction (Fig. 4) shows the advantage of breaking SROB is bounded by advantage breaking EUF, which completes the proof.   □

We also show a separation between the SROB and CROB, by pointing to a signature scheme that is not CROB secure (but already SROB).

Proposition 2. *There exist DS schemes that are not CROB-secure.*

Proof (Proposition 2). We provide a simple counterexample as follows. Consider the digital signature scheme in [5]:

- Gen: selects uniformly at random $g_1 \leftarrow_s \mathbb{G}_1, g_2 \leftarrow_s \mathbb{G}_2$ and $(x, y) \leftarrow_s \mathbb{Z}_p^2$. Set sk $\leftarrow (x, y)$ and pk $\leftarrow (g_1, g_2, g_2^x, g_2^y, e(g_1, g_2))$, where $e : \mathbb{G}_1 \times \mathbb{G}_2 \rightarrow \mathbb{G}_T$ is a pairing[3].
- Sign: given a message M, sample $r \leftarrow_s \mathbb{Z}_p$ and compute $\sigma \leftarrow g_1^{1/(x+M+yr)}$. Note that with overwhelming probability, $x + M + yr \neq 0 \mod p$, where p is the order of $\mathbb{G}_1$. The signature is the pair (σ, r).
- Verify: check that $e\left(\sigma, g_2^x \cdot g_2^M \cdot (g_2^y)^r\right) \overset{?}{=} e(g_1, g_2)$.

To win the CROB game, an adversary $\mathcal{A}$ proceeds as follows:

1. $\mathcal{A}$ samples a key-pair: sk $\leftarrow_s (x, y)$; pk $\leftarrow (g_1, g_2, g_2^x, g_2^y, e(g_1, g_2))$ and a message $M \in \mathbb{Z}_p$.
2. $\mathcal{A}$ samples $r \leftarrow_s \mathbb{Z}_p$ and computes σ under sk$_1$. Since g'_1 can be written as g_1^t, $\mathcal{A}$ sets t, x', y' such that $1/(x + M + yr) = t/(x' + M + y'r)$ (equate the exponents to obtain the same σ corresponding to M). This can be done by assigning random values to x', y' and setting $t \leftarrow (x' + M + y'r)/(x + M + yr)$.
3. $\mathcal{A}$ sets sk$' \leftarrow_s (x', y')$; pk$' \leftarrow (g'_1, g'_2, g'_2^{x'}, g'_2^{y'}, e(g'_1, g'_2))$, for some uniformly sampled generator $g'_2 \leftarrow_s \mathbb{G}_2$.
4. Finally, observe that (σ, r) verifies under (sk$_1$, pk$_1$) through the correctness of the signature scheme, but also under (pk$_2$, sk$_2$), since

$$e\left(g_1^{t/(x'+M+y'r)}, g'_2^{x'} \cdot g'_2^M \cdot (g'_2^{y'})^r\right) = e(g_1^t, g'_2).$$

$\mathcal{A}$ halts and returns (pk, pk$'$, (σ, r), M). Note that $\mathcal{A}$ runs in probabilistic polynomial time.   □

3.2   Robustness for Functional Encryption

As discussed in the motivational part of Sect. 1, robustness should be considered as a security notion achieved by a functional encryption scheme. In what follows, we define it for the public/private key settings. We stress about the existence of essentially two major paths one can explore. A first stream of work would study the meaning of robustness in a single-authority context.

---

[3] See for instance [5] for the definition and usage of a cryptographic pairing.

MULTI-AUTHORITY SETTING. A second path is placed in a multi-authority context—that is, assuming there exist multiple pairs (msk, mpk). Aiming for a correct definition, one property that should be guaranteed is that a ciphertext should not be decryptable under *two* (*or more*) functional keys issued via *different* master secret keys. Stated differently, if msk_1 produces sk_{f_1} and $msk_2 \neq msk_1$ produces sk_{f_2} for two functionalities f_1, f_2, we do not want that C (say encrypted under mpk_1) to be decrypted under sk_{f_2} (it already decrypts under sk_{f_1} with high probability due to the correctness of the scheme). We follow the lines of Definition 4, and propose two new flavours of robustness, corresponding to the cases where the adversary has oracle access to the (encryption, if in a private key setting case), key-derivation and decryption oracles. The security experiments are depicted in Fig. 5. The difference between the two paradigms may seem minor (for our purpose), but in fact having a *public* master key confers a significant advantage when it comes to deriving a generic transform for achieving complete robustness, as detailed in Sect. 4. In what follows, we will explore the multi-authority path, since it naturally maps to our motivational examples.

INTERMEDIATE NOTIONS. Intermediate notions considering robustness under adversarially generated keys introduced in [12]—such as full-robustness or mixed robustness—do not generalize well to functional encryption (or attribute-based encryption). The notion we consider, namely FEROB is in fact the generalization of KROB (key-less robustness), as introduced for PKE by Farshim et al. [12].

Definition 5 (SROB and FEROB Security for FE). *Let FE be a functional encryption scheme. We say FE achieves functional robustness if the advantage of any PPT adversary $\mathcal{A}$ against the FEROB game defined in Fig. 5 (bottom) is negligible:* $\mathsf{Adv}^{\mathrm{FEROB}}_{\mathcal{A},\mathsf{Pub/PrvFE}}(\lambda) := \Pr\left[\mathrm{FEROB}^{\mathcal{A}}_{\mathsf{Pub/PrvFE}}(\lambda) = 1\right]$. *SROB-security is defined similarly, the* $\mathrm{SROB}^{\mathcal{A}}_{\mathsf{Pub/PrvFE}}(\lambda)$ *game being defined in Fig. 5 (top).*

As stated in the algorithmic description of the security experiment, an adversary against the strongest notion of FEROB attempts to find colliding ciphertexts, which decrypt under two msk-separated keys sk_{f_1}, sk_{f_2}.

Lemma 2 (Implications). *Let FE denote a functional encryption scheme. If FE is FEROB-secure, then it is also SROB-secure.*

Proof (Lemma 2). We prove the implication holds in both the public and private key settings:

PUBLIC-KEY FE. We take the contrapositive. For a scheme FE, we assume the existence of an adversary $\mathcal{A}$ winning the SROB-game with non-negligible advantage ϵ_{SROB}. A reduction $\mathcal{A}'$ that wins the FEROB game is built as follows: (1) $\mathcal{A}'$ samples uniformly at random $(msk_1, mpk_1, msk_2, mpk_2)$; (2) the corresponding oracles for key-derivation are built; (3) $\mathcal{A}$ runs with access to the aforementioned oracles, returning (C, sk_{f_1}, sk_{f_2}). If $\mathcal{A}$ outputs a winning tuple, then $\mathcal{A}'$ wins the FEROB game by releasing the messages and the randomness terms used to construct (C, sk_{f_1}, sk_{f_2}). Hence, $\mathsf{Adv}^{\mathrm{SROB}}_{\mathcal{A},\mathsf{FE}}(\lambda) \leq \mathsf{Adv}^{\mathrm{FEROB}}_{\mathcal{A}',\mathsf{FE}}(\lambda)$.

<table>
<tr><td>

$\mathrm{SROB}^{\mathcal{A}}_{\mathsf{PubFE}}(\lambda):$

$L_1 \leftarrow \emptyset$
$L_2 \leftarrow \emptyset$
$(\mathsf{mpk}_1, \mathsf{msk}_1) \leftarrow_\$ \mathsf{Gen}(1^\lambda)$
$(\mathsf{mpk}_2, \mathsf{msk}_2) \leftarrow_\$ \mathsf{Gen}(1^\lambda)$
$(C, \mathsf{sk}_{f_1}, \mathsf{sk}_{f_2}) \leftarrow_\$$

$$\leftarrow_\$ \mathcal{A} \begin{pmatrix} \\ \\ \mathrm{KDER}_{\mathsf{msk}_1}(\cdot), \\ \mathrm{KDER}_{\mathsf{msk}_2}(\cdot) \\ \end{pmatrix} (\mathsf{mpk}_1, \mathsf{mpk}_2)$$

if $\mathsf{sk}_{f_1} \in L_2 \vee \mathsf{sk}_{f_2} \in L_1:$
 return 0
if $\mathsf{Dec}(C, \mathsf{sk}_{f_1}) \neq \perp \wedge$
  $\mathsf{Dec}(C, \mathsf{sk}_{f_2}) \neq \perp:$
 return 1
return 0

</td><td>

$\mathrm{SROB}^{\mathcal{A}}_{\mathsf{PrvFE}}(\lambda):$

$L_1 \leftarrow \emptyset$
$L_2 \leftarrow \emptyset$
$\mathsf{msk}_1 \leftarrow_\$ \mathsf{Gen}(1^\lambda)$
$\mathsf{msk}_2 \leftarrow_\$ \mathsf{Gen}(1^\lambda)$
$(C, \mathsf{sk}_{f_1}, \mathsf{sk}_{f_2}) \leftarrow_\$$

$$\leftarrow_\$ \mathcal{A} \begin{pmatrix} \mathrm{ENC}_{\mathsf{msk}_1}(\cdot), \\ \mathrm{ENC}_{\mathsf{msk}_2}(\cdot), \\ \mathrm{KDER}_{\mathsf{msk}_1}(\cdot), \\ \mathrm{KDER}_{\mathsf{msk}_2}(\cdot) \\ \end{pmatrix} (1^\lambda)$$

if $\mathsf{sk}_{f_1} \in L_2 \vee \mathsf{sk}_{f_2} \in L_1:$
 return 0
if $\mathsf{Dec}(C, \mathsf{sk}_{f_1}) \neq \perp \wedge$
  $\mathsf{Dec}(C, \mathsf{sk}_{f_2}) \neq \perp:$
 return 1
return 0

</td></tr>
<tr><td>

$\mathrm{KDER}_{\mathsf{msk}_i}(f):$

$\mathsf{sk}_f \leftarrow_\$ \mathsf{KDer}(\mathsf{msk}_i, f)$
$L_i \leftarrow L_i \cup \{(\mathsf{sk}_f, f)\}$
return sk_f

$\mathrm{ENC}_{\mathsf{mpk}_i}(M):$

$C \leftarrow_\$ \mathsf{Enc}(\mathsf{mpk}_i, M)$
return C

</td><td>

$\mathrm{KDER}_{\mathsf{msk}_i}(f):$

$\mathsf{sk}_f \leftarrow_\$ \mathsf{KDer}(\mathsf{msk}_i, f)$
$L_i \leftarrow L_i \cup \{(\mathsf{sk}_f, f)\}$
return sk_f

$\mathrm{ENC}_{\mathsf{msk}_i}(M):$

$C \leftarrow_\$ \mathsf{Enc}(\mathsf{msk}_i, M)$
return C

</td></tr>
<tr><td>

$\mathrm{FEROB}^{\mathcal{A}}_{\mathsf{PubFE}}(\lambda):$

$(\mathsf{mpk}_1, \mathsf{msk}_1, R_1, M_1, f_1, R_{f_1},$
 $\mathsf{mpk}_2, \mathsf{msk}_2, R_2, M_2, f_2, R_{f_2}) \leftarrow_\$ \mathcal{A}(1^\lambda)$
$C_1 \leftarrow_\$ \mathsf{Enc}(\mathsf{mpk}_1, M_1; R_1)$
$C_2 \leftarrow_\$ \mathsf{Enc}(\mathsf{mpk}_2, M_2; R_2)$
if $C_1 = C_2 \wedge \mathsf{mpk}_1 \neq \mathsf{mpk}_2:$
 $\mathsf{sk}_{f_1} \leftarrow_\$ \mathsf{KDer}(\mathsf{msk}_1, f_1; R_{f_1})$
 $\mathsf{sk}_{f_2} \leftarrow_\$ \mathsf{KDer}(\mathsf{msk}_2, f_2; R_{f_2})$
 if $\mathsf{Dec}(C, \mathsf{sk}_{f_1}) \neq \perp \wedge$
  $\mathsf{Dec}(C, \mathsf{sk}_{f_2}) \neq \perp:$
  return 1
return 0

</td><td>

$\mathrm{FEROB}^{\mathcal{A}}_{\mathsf{PrvFE}}(\lambda):$

$(\mathsf{msk}_1, R_1, M_1, f_1, R_{f_1},$
 $\mathsf{msk}_2, R_2, M_2, f_2, R_{f_2}) \leftarrow_\$ \mathcal{A}(1^\lambda)$
$C_1 \leftarrow_\$ \mathsf{Enc}(\mathsf{msk}_1, M_1; R_1)$
$C_2 \leftarrow_\$ \mathsf{Enc}(\mathsf{msk}_2, M_2; R_2)$
if $C_1 = C_2 \wedge \mathsf{msk}_1 \neq \mathsf{msk}_2:$
 $\mathsf{sk}_{f_1} \leftarrow_\$ \mathsf{KDer}(\mathsf{msk}_1, f_1; R_{f_1})$
 $\mathsf{sk}_{f_2} \leftarrow_\$ \mathsf{KDer}(\mathsf{msk}_2, f_2; R_{f_2})$
 if $\mathsf{Dec}(C, \mathsf{sk}_{f_1}) \neq \perp \wedge$
  $\mathsf{Dec}(C, \mathsf{sk}_{f_2}) \neq \perp:$
  return 1
return 0

</td></tr>
</table>

Fig. 5. We introduce FEROB and SROB in the context of FE schemes defined both in the public and private key setting. For the SROB games, we give the oracles implementing Enc and KDer procedures, mentioning that each query to the latter oracle adds an entry of the form (f, sk_f) in the corresponding list L_i—where $i \in \{1, 2\}$ stands for the index of the used master keys.

PRIVATE-KEY FE. We take the contrapositive. For a scheme FE, we assume the existence of an adversary $\mathcal{A}$ winning the SROB-game with non-negligible advantage ϵ_{SROB}. A reduction $\mathcal{A}'$ that wins the FEROB game is built as follows:

(1) $\mathcal{A}'$ samples uniformly at random $(\mathsf{msk}_1, \mathsf{msk}_2)$; (2) $\mathcal{A}'$ constructs the encryption and key-derivation oracles under the two keys; (3) $\mathcal{A}'$ runs $\mathcal{A}$ with these oracles, records the random coins used and obtains $(C, \mathsf{sk}_{f_1}, \mathsf{sk}_{f_2})$. Finally $\mathcal{A}'$ wins the FEROB game by issuing the FEROB tuple, using the random coins used to derive the functional keys and the ciphertext and therefore we have:
$\mathsf{Adv}_{\mathcal{A},\mathsf{FE}}^{\mathsf{SROB}}(\lambda) \leq \mathsf{Adv}_{\mathcal{A}',\mathsf{FE}}^{\mathsf{FEROB}}(\lambda)$. □

Proposition 3 (Separations). *There exist functional encryption schemes in the public/private-key setting that are not FEROB-secure.*

Proof (Proposition 3). As sketched in Sect. 1, a DDH instantiation for the FE scheme of [2] is not FEROB-secure. The adversary is built upon the idea presented in the introduction and is shown in Fig. 6. Given that any public-key functional encryption scheme can be trivially converted into one in the private-key setting simply by making mpk private, we obtain an FE scheme for the inner product functionality in the private-key setting that is not FEROB-secure.

FEROB adversary $\mathcal{A}_{\mathsf{FE}}^{\mathsf{FEROB}}(\lambda)$:

1. $(g^{\boldsymbol{s}}, \boldsymbol{s}, r, \boldsymbol{x}, \boldsymbol{y}, \emptyset$
   $\qquad g^{\boldsymbol{s}'}, \boldsymbol{s}', r, \boldsymbol{x}', \boldsymbol{y}, \emptyset) \leftarrow_{\$} \mathsf{Gen}(1^\lambda)$
   $\qquad$ such that $r \cdot s_i + x_i = r \cdot s_i' + x_i'$ and $\boldsymbol{s} \neq \boldsymbol{s}'$
2. observe that $\mathsf{Enc}(g^{\boldsymbol{s}}, \boldsymbol{x}) = (g^{-r}, g^{r \cdot s_1 + x_1} \ldots, g^{r \cdot s_n + x_n}) =$
   $\qquad\qquad\qquad (g^{-r}, g^{r \cdot s_1' + x_1'} \ldots, g^{r \cdot s_n' + x_n'}) = \mathsf{Enc}(g^{\boldsymbol{s}'}, \boldsymbol{x}')$
3. $\mathsf{sk}_y \leftarrow \boldsymbol{s}^\top \cdot \boldsymbol{y}$
4. $\mathsf{sk}_y' \leftarrow \boldsymbol{s}'^\top \cdot \boldsymbol{y}$
5. $\mathsf{Dec}(C, \mathsf{sk}_y) = \boldsymbol{y}^\top \cdot \boldsymbol{x} \neq \perp$
6. $\mathsf{Dec}(C, \mathsf{sk}_y') = \boldsymbol{y}^\top \cdot \boldsymbol{x}' \neq \perp$

Fig. 6. A FEROB adversary against the DDH instantiation of the bounded-norm inner product scheme in [2].

□

4 Achieving Robustness via Generic Transforms

4.1 Robust Digital Signatures

We put forward a generic transform similar in spirit to the original work of Abdalla, Bellare, and Neven [1] in the context of digital signatures. For a digital signature scheme, we benefit from the fact that pk acts as an "immutable" value to which one can easily commit to, while signing a message. Thus, checking if a message verifies under another public key implicitly breaks the binding property of the commitment scheme. For simplicity, we use a hash instead of a commitment scheme.

$$
\begin{array}{lll}
\overline{\mathsf{Gen}}(1^\lambda): & \overline{\mathsf{Sign}}(\overline{\mathsf{sk}}, M): & \overline{\mathsf{Ver}}(\overline{\mathsf{pk}}, \overline{\sigma}, M): \\
(\mathsf{sk}, \mathsf{pk}) \leftarrow_\$ \mathsf{DS.Gen}(1^\lambda) & \mathsf{sk} \leftarrow \overline{\mathsf{sk}} & \mathsf{pk} \leftarrow \overline{\mathsf{pk}} \\
\overline{\mathsf{pk}} \leftarrow \mathsf{pk} & \sigma_1 \leftarrow_\$ \mathsf{DS.Sign}(\mathsf{sk}, M) & (\sigma_1, \sigma_2) \leftarrow \overline{\sigma} \\
\overline{\mathsf{sk}} \leftarrow \mathsf{sk} & \sigma_2 \leftarrow \mathsf{H}(\mathsf{pk}) & \text{return } \mathsf{DS.Ver}(\mathsf{pk}, \sigma_1) = 1 \wedge \\
\text{return } (\overline{\mathsf{sk}}, \overline{\mathsf{pk}}) & \overline{\sigma} \leftarrow (\sigma_1, \sigma_2) & \qquad\qquad \sigma_2 \stackrel{?}{=} \mathsf{H}(\mathsf{pk}) \\
& \text{return } \overline{\sigma} &
\end{array}
$$

$$
\begin{array}{l}
\overline{\mathsf{Setup}}(1^\lambda): \\
K \leftarrow \mathsf{H.Gen}(1^\lambda); \ \mathsf{H} \leftarrow \mathsf{H}_K; \ \text{return } \mathsf{H}
\end{array}
$$

Fig. 7. A generic transform that turns any digital signature scheme DS into one that is, in addition, CROB-secure. The (publicly available) collision-resistant hash function H can be based on claw-free permutations in the standard model, as shown in the seminal work of Damgård [11]. It is used as a commitment to the public-key.

Lemma 3. *Let* DS *be an EUF-secure digital signature scheme. Let* H *denote a collision-resistant hash function. The digital signature* $\overline{\mathsf{DS}}$ *obtained through the transform depicted in Fig. 7 is CROB-secure.*

Proof (Lemma 3). We prove both the unforgeability and the complete robustness of the newly obtained construction:

UNFORGEABILITY. Assume the existence of a PPT adversary $\mathcal{A}$ against $\overline{\mathsf{DS}}$. We build an adversary $\mathcal{A}'$ against the EUF of the underlying DS. The unforgeability experiment EUF for DS samples $(\mathsf{pk}, \mathsf{sk})$ and constructs a signing oracle under sk, which is given to $\mathcal{A}'$. $\mathcal{A}'$ is given a collision resistant hash function H and builds its own signing oracle $\overline{\mathsf{Sign}}$; when queried, $\overline{\mathsf{Sign}}$ returns the output of Sign concatenated to the value of $\mathsf{H}(\mathsf{pk})$. When $\mathcal{A}$ replies with $(\overline{\sigma}, M)$, it must be the case that $\mathsf{Ver}(\mathsf{pk}, \sigma, M)$ passes, which breaks EUF for DS. Thus we conclude that: $\mathsf{Adv}_{\mathcal{A}, \overline{\mathsf{DS}}}^{\mathsf{EUF}}(\lambda) \leq \mathsf{Adv}_{\mathcal{A}', \mathsf{DS}}^{\mathsf{EUF}}(\lambda)$.

CROB. To show robustness, we rely on the collision-resistance of H. The CROB game in Fig. 3 specifies that the adversary $\mathcal{A}$ against the CROB game finds $\mathsf{pk}_1 \neq \mathsf{pk}_2$ such that $\overline{\mathsf{Ver}}$ passes. The latter implies $\mathsf{H}(\mathsf{pk}_1) = \mathsf{H}(\mathsf{pk}_2)$, trivially breaking the collision-resistance of H, giving us: $\mathsf{Adv}_{\mathcal{A}, \overline{\mathsf{DS}}}^{\mathsf{CROB}}(\lambda) \leq \mathsf{Adv}_{\mathcal{A}', \mathsf{H}}^{\mathsf{CR}}(\lambda)$.   □

4.2 Achieving Robustness for Functional Encryption

The ABN Transform [1] Adapted to Public-Key FE. As for the case of digital signatures, one can reuse the elegant idea rooted in the *binding* property of a commitment scheme. Concretely, we start from a FE scheme, encrypt the plaintext, and post-process the resulting ciphertext through the use of a public-key encryption scheme. The transform consists in committing to the two public keys (corresponding to FE and PK) and encrypting the resulting decommitment together with the output of FE.Enc under pk. For decryption, in addition to the functional key, the secret key sk^4 is needed to recover the decommitment from

---

[4] sk is common to all users querying a sk_f.

the "middle" part of the ciphertext. A key difference to the ABN transform is rooted in the innate nature of FE: we cannot encrypt the plaintext under pk, as this would break indistinguishability. For space reasons, we defer such a construction to the full version of this work.

Simple Robustness Transforms in the Public-Key Setting. A simpler idea makes use of a collision-resistant hash function and simply appends the hash of mpk$\|C$ to the already existing ciphertext.

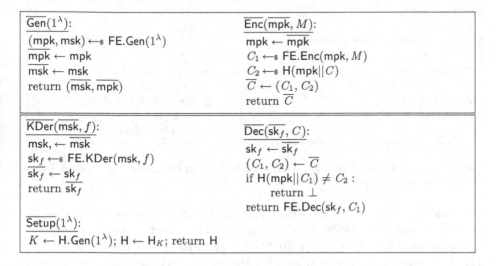

Fig. 8. Generic transform that turns an FE scheme into a FEROB scheme $\overline{\mathsf{FE}}$.

Lemma 4. *Let* FE *be an* IND-FE-CPA-*secure functional encryption scheme in the public setting and let* H *denote a collision-resistant hash function. The functional encryption scheme* $\overline{\mathsf{FE}}$ *obtained through the transform depicted in* Fig. 8 *is* FEROB-*secure, while preserving the* IND-FE-CPA-*security.*

Proof (Lemma 4). ROBUSTNESS. To show the transform achieves FEROB, we argue that if an adversary concludes with $(\overline{\mathsf{mpk}_1}, R_1, M_1, \overline{\mathsf{mpk}_2}, R_2, M_2, \ldots)$ such that $\overline{\mathsf{FE}}.\mathsf{Enc}(\overline{\mathsf{mpk}_1}, M_1; R_1) = \overline{\mathsf{FE}}.\mathsf{Enc}(\overline{\mathsf{mpk}_2}, M_2; R_2)$, then the adversary is essentially able to find two tuples such that $\mathsf{H}(\mathsf{mpk}_1\|\mathsf{FE}.\mathsf{Enc}(\mathsf{mpk}_1, M_1; R_1)) = \mathsf{H}(\mathsf{mpk}_2\|\mathsf{FE}.\mathsf{Enc}(\mathsf{mpk}_2, M_2; R_2))$ which cannot happen with non-negligible probability down to the collision-resistance of H.

INDISTINGUISHABILITY. The proof follows easily down to the indistinguishability of the underlying scheme FE: during the challenge phase, the reduction will be given the C^* corresponding to M_b (chosen by $\mathcal{A}$); after appending $\mathsf{H}(C^*\|\mathsf{mpk})$, the adversary will be given $\overline{C^*}$. Also, that the reduction can answer all the functional key-derivation queries the adversary makes. Hence the advantage in winning the IND-FE-CPA game against $\overline{\mathsf{FE}}$ is bounded by the advantage of winning the IND-FE-CPA game against FE.

FEROB Transform in the Private-Key FE Setting. In this part, we provide a similar generic transform for turning any FE scheme into one that is FEROB-secure, in the private-key framework.

$\overline{\mathsf{Gen}}(1^\lambda)$:	$\overline{\mathsf{Enc}}(\overline{\mathsf{msk}}, M)$:
$R \leftarrow_\$ \{0,1\}^\lambda$	$(\mathsf{msk}, \mathsf{sk}) \leftarrow \overline{\mathsf{msk}}$
$R_1 \| R_2 \leftarrow \mathsf{PRG}.\mathsf{Eval}(R)$	$C_1 \leftarrow_\$ \mathsf{FE}.\mathsf{Enc}(\mathsf{msk}, M)$
$\mathsf{msk} \leftarrow \mathsf{FE}.\mathsf{Enc}(1^\lambda; R_1)$	$C_2 \leftarrow_\$ \mathsf{PRF}.\mathsf{Eval}(\mathsf{sk}, C_1)$
$\mathsf{sk} \leftarrow R_2$	$\overline{C} \leftarrow (C_1, C_2)$
$\overline{\mathsf{msk}} \leftarrow (\mathsf{msk}, \mathsf{sk})$	return $\overline{C}$
return $\overline{\mathsf{msk}}$	
$\overline{\mathsf{KDer}}(\overline{\mathsf{msk}}, f)$:	$\overline{\mathsf{Dec}}(\overline{\mathsf{sk}_f}, \overline{C})$:
$(\mathsf{msk}, \mathsf{sk}) \leftarrow \overline{\mathsf{msk}}$	$(\mathsf{sk}_f, \mathsf{sk}) \leftarrow \overline{\mathsf{sk}_f}$
$\mathsf{sk}_f \leftarrow_\$ \mathsf{FE}.\mathsf{KDer}(\mathsf{msk}, f)$	$(C_1, C_2) \leftarrow \overline{C}$
$\overline{\mathsf{sk}_f} \leftarrow (\mathsf{sk}_f, \mathsf{sk})$	if $\mathsf{PRF}.\mathsf{Eval}(\mathsf{sk}, C_1) \neq C_2$:
return $\overline{\mathsf{sk}_f}$	return $\bot$
	return $\mathsf{FE}.\mathsf{Dec}(\mathsf{sk}_f, C_1)$

Fig. 9. A generic transform that turns a FE scheme in the private-key setting into a FEROB-secure scheme $\overline{\mathsf{FE}}$.

Lemma 5. *Let* FE *be an* IND-FE-CPA *functional encryption scheme in the private-key setting. Let* PRG *denote a right-injective length doubling pseudorandom generator from* $\{0,1\}^{|1^\lambda|}$ *to* $\{0,1\}^{2 \cdot |1^\lambda|}$ *and* PRF *a collision-resistant* PRF. *The functional encryption scheme* $\overline{\mathsf{FE}}$ *obtained through the transform depicted in* Fig. 9 *is* FEROB-*secure, while preserving* IND-FE-CPA-*security.*

Proof (Lemma 5). ROBUSTNESS. Assuming the FEROB adversary $\mathcal{A}$ outputs $(\overline{\mathsf{msk}_1}, R_1, M_1, f_1, R_{f_1}, \overline{\mathsf{msk}_2}, R_2, M_2, f_2, R_{f_2})$ such that $\overline{\mathsf{FE}}.\mathsf{Enc}(\overline{\mathsf{msk}_1}, M_1; R_1) = \overline{\mathsf{FE}}.\mathsf{Enc}(\overline{\mathsf{msk}_2}, M_2; R_2)$, we argue that:

- $C_2 = \mathsf{PRF}.\mathsf{Eval}(\mathsf{sk}_1, C_1) = \mathsf{PRF}.\mathsf{Eval}(\mathsf{sk}_2, C_1)$. Down to the collision-resistance (over both keys and inputs) property of the PRF, it results that $\mathsf{sk}_1 = \mathsf{sk}_2$.
- the $\overline{\mathsf{Gen}}$ function makes use of a right injective pseudorandom generator. Since the right half is exactly $\mathsf{sk}_1(= \mathsf{sk}_2)$, through the injectivity property, it must be the case that the seed R used to feed the PRG is the same.
- since the randomness R is the same for both cases, it results that the random coins used by FE.Gen are the same, implying that $\mathsf{msk}_1 = \mathsf{msk}_2$.
- finally, we obtain that $\overline{\mathsf{msk}_1} = \overline{\mathsf{msk}_2}$, which is not allowed in the robustness game.

Therefore, the advantage of breaking the FEROB game is bounded by the union bound applied on the collision-resistance of the PRF and right-injectivity of the PRG: $\mathsf{Adv}_{\mathcal{A},\overline{\mathsf{FE}}}^{\mathsf{FEROB}}(\lambda) \leq \mathsf{Adv}_{\mathcal{A}',\mathsf{PRG}}^{\mathsf{INJ}}(\lambda) + \mathsf{Adv}_{\mathcal{A}'',\mathsf{PRF}}^{\mathsf{CR}}(\lambda)$.

IND-FE-CPA-SECURITY. The reduction proceeds via one game hop:

- Game_0: is the game, where the adversary runs against the scheme depicted in Fig. 9—the output of the PRG is the expected one.

– Game$_1$: based on the pseudorandomness property of the PRG, we change the output to a truly random string, ensuring independence between msk and sk. The distance to Game$_0$ is bounded by the pseudorandomness advantage against PRG. We now show the advantage of an adversary winning the IND-FE-CPA experiment against $\overline{\text{FE}}$ in this setting is negligible.

Assume the existence of a PPT adversary $\mathcal{A}$ against the IND-FE-CPA of $\overline{\text{FE}}$. We build an adversary $\mathcal{A}'$ against the IND-FE-CPA of the underlying FE scheme. The IND-FE-CPA experiment samples a bit b', the key msk and constructs a key-derivation oracle KDer under msk, which is given to $\mathcal{A}'$. The reduction then proceeds as follows:

1. $\mathcal{A}'$ chooses uniformly at random sk to key the PRF utility.
2. $\mathcal{A}'$ builds the $\overline{\text{FE}}$.Enc oracle and the $\overline{\text{FE}}$.KDer oracle by querying the given FE.Enc, FE.KDer. The PRF is evaluated under sk.
3. $\mathcal{A}'$ runs $\mathcal{A}$, obtains a tuple (M_0, M_1) and gets back the encryption of $M_{b'}$ (say C^*) by querying FE.Enc(msk, $M_{b'}$). $\mathcal{A}'$ computes the corresponding $\overline{C^*}$, which is passed to $\mathcal{A}$.
4. finally, $\mathcal{A}$ returns a bit b, which constitutes the output of $\mathcal{A}'$.

Analysis of the Reduction. The correctness of the reduction follows trivially. Thus we conclude that in Game$_1$, the probability of winning is:

$$\Pr[\text{Game}_1^{\mathcal{A}}(\lambda) \Rightarrow 1] \leq \text{Adv}_{\mathcal{A}',\text{FE}}^{\text{IND-FE-CPA}}(\lambda).$$

For the analysis, we also include the fact that the transition between Game$_0$ and Game$_1$ is bounded as follows:

$$\Pr[\text{Game}_0^{\mathcal{A}}(\lambda) \Rightarrow 1] - \Pr[\text{Game}_1^{\mathcal{A}}(\lambda) \Rightarrow 1] \leq \text{Adv}_{\mathcal{A}'',\text{PRG}}^{\text{PRG}}(\lambda).$$

We apply the Union Bound and conclude:

$$\text{Adv}_{\mathcal{A},\overline{\text{FE}}}^{\text{IND-FE-CPA}}(\lambda) \leq \text{Adv}_{\mathcal{A}',\text{FE}}^{\text{IND-FE-CPA}}(\lambda) + \text{Adv}_{\mathcal{A}'',\text{PRG}}^{\text{PRG}}(\lambda).$$

$\square$

5   Anonymity and Robustness

Interestingly, FEROB does not imply anonymity as defined in Fig. 1 (right) for the public-key case. And based on FEROB $\Rightarrow$ SROB, it follows that SROB does not imply anonymity in a generic fashion. Therefore, we have the following separation:

Proposition 4. *There exist FEROB transforms for public-key functional encryption that do not ensure anonymity (as defined in Fig. 1).*

Proof (Proposition 4). We consider the scheme in Fig. 8 and observe that the anonymity game can be easily won as follows: an adversary, given two master public keys and the ciphertext $\overline{C} \leftarrow (C_1, C_2)$, decides the issuer by checking whether $H(C_1 \| \mathsf{mpk}_1) \stackrel{?}{=} C_2$ or $H(C_1 \| \mathsf{mpk}_2) \stackrel{?}{=} C_2$, via the publicly available H.   □

Finally, we give a generic construction of an anonymous FEROB scheme. Reaching both anonymity and robustness for FE is non-trivial: on one hand, we expect the ciphertext to be "robust" w.r.t. a sole authority (mpk), but the "link" should not be detectable when included in the ciphertext (anonymity). Therefore, we attempt to embed such a link in the functional key. Our solution ensures FEROB through the means of a collision-resistant PRF with keys K generated on the fly. An independent functional key to compute the PRF value is issued via a second FE supporting general circuits, while the PRF key K is encrypted under the additional mpk.

$\underline{\mathsf{Gen}(1^\lambda)}:$

$(\mathsf{mpk}, \mathsf{msk}) \leftarrow_\$ \mathsf{FE}.\mathsf{Gen}(1^\lambda)$
$(\mathsf{mpk}', \mathsf{msk}') \leftarrow_\$ \mathsf{FE}'.\mathsf{Gen}(1^\lambda)$
$\overline{\mathsf{mpk}} \leftarrow (\mathsf{mpk}, \mathsf{mpk}')$
$\overline{\mathsf{msk}} \leftarrow (\mathsf{msk}, \mathsf{msk}')$
return $(\overline{\mathsf{msk}}, \overline{\mathsf{mpk}})$

$\underline{\mathsf{Enc}(\overline{\mathsf{mpk}}, M)}:$

$(\mathsf{msk}, \mathsf{msk}') \leftarrow \overline{\mathsf{msk}}$
$(\mathsf{mpk}, \mathsf{mpk}') \leftarrow \overline{\mathsf{mpk}}$
$C_1 \leftarrow_\$ \mathsf{FE}.\mathsf{Enc}(\mathsf{mpk}, M)$
$K \leftarrow_\$ \mathcal{K}$
$C_2 \leftarrow \mathsf{PRF}(K, \mathsf{mpk})$
$C_3 \leftarrow_\$ \mathsf{FE}'.\mathsf{Enc}(\mathsf{mpk}', K)$
$\overline{C} \leftarrow (C_1, C_2, C_3)$
return $\overline{C}$

$\underline{\mathsf{KDer}(\overline{\mathsf{msk}}, f)}:$

$\mathsf{msk} \leftarrow \overline{\mathsf{msk}}$
$\mathsf{sk}_f \leftarrow_\$ \mathsf{FE}.\mathsf{KDer}(\mathsf{msk}, f)$
$\mathsf{sk}_g \leftarrow_\$ \mathsf{FE}'.\mathsf{KDer}(\mathsf{msk}', \mathcal{C}_{\mathsf{PRF}(\cdot, \mathsf{mpk})})$
$\overline{\mathsf{sk}}_f \leftarrow (\mathsf{sk}_f, \mathsf{sk}_g)$
return $\overline{\mathsf{sk}}_f$

$\underline{\mathsf{Dec}(\overline{\mathsf{sk}}_f, C)}:$

$(\mathsf{sk}_f, \mathsf{sk}_g) \leftarrow \overline{\mathsf{sk}}_f$
$(C_1, C_2, C_3) \leftarrow \overline{C}$
if $\mathsf{FE}.\mathsf{Dec}(\mathsf{sk}_g, C_3) \neq C_2$:
    return $\bot$
return $\mathsf{FE}.\mathsf{Dec}(\mathsf{sk}_f, C_1)$

Fig. 10. A generic transform that converts an FE scheme into a FEROB scheme $\overline{\mathsf{FE}}$, *without* ensuring anonymity. Here $\mathcal{C}_{\mathsf{PRF}}$ denotes the circuit that computes the PRF value, where mpk is hard-coded in the circuit.

Theorem 1. *Let* FE' *be an* ANON-*secure functional encryption scheme supporting (at least) one functional-key for general circuits and* PRF *denote a collision-resistant* PRF. *Given an* ANON, IND-FE-CPA-*secure scheme* FE, *the functional encryption scheme obtained from the transform in* Fig. 10 *is* FEROB-*secure while preserving the original scheme's security guarantees.*

Proof (Theorem 1). ROBUSTNESS. FEROB follows from the collision resistance of the PRF: if an adversary $\mathcal{A}$ is able to find $(K, C_1), (K', C_1)$ such that $\mathsf{PRF}(K, C_1) = \mathsf{PRF}(K', C_1)$, then $\mathcal{A}$ wins the collision resistance game against the PRF.

INDISTINGUISHABILITY. Follows from the IND-FE-CPA-security of the underlying scheme. For any adversary $\mathcal{A}$ against the IND-FE-CPA-security of the scheme $\overline{\mathsf{FE}}$ in Fig. 10, we build the reduction $\mathcal{A}'$ that wins the IND-FE-CPA game against FE. When $\mathcal{A}$ sends the challenge tuple (M_0, M_1), $\mathcal{A}'$ obtains C_1 from IND-FE-CPA challenger, samples its own Ks, $\mathsf{msk}', \mathsf{mpk}'$ and computes C_2, C_3, which are forwarded to $\mathcal{A}$. Whenever $\mathcal{A}$ makes a functional key query for f, then $\mathcal{A}'$ forwards two functional queries for f and for $C_{\mathsf{PRF}(\cdot, \mathsf{mpk})}$, a circuit that is designed to compute C_2 (the PRF value) over the encrypted K. Thus, whenever $\mathcal{A}$ returns b, $\mathcal{A}'$ returns the same bit and wins under the same advantage.

ANONYMITY. Follows from the anonymity of the underlying FE scheme. We use a hybrid argument. We start from a setting corresponding to $b = 0$ in the $\mathsf{ANON}_{\overline{\mathsf{FE}}}^{\mathcal{A}}$ game (Game_0).

- Game_1: in Game_1, we change C_3 from $\mathsf{FE}'.\mathsf{Enc}(\mathsf{mpk}_0, K)$ to $\mathsf{FE}'.\mathsf{Enc}(\mathsf{mpk}_1, K)$, based on the ANON property of FE', the hop between the two games being bounded by $\mathsf{Adv}_{\mathcal{A}, \mathsf{FE}'}^{\mathsf{ANON}}(\lambda)$.
- Game_2: we change C_1 from $\mathsf{FE}.\mathsf{Enc}(\mathsf{mpk}_0, M)$ to $\mathsf{FE}.\mathsf{Enc}(\mathsf{mpk}_1, M)$, based on the anonymity of the underlying FE scheme, the distance to the previous game being bounded by $\mathsf{Adv}_{\mathcal{A}, \mathsf{FE}}^{\mathsf{ANON}}(\lambda)$. Implicitly, in Game_2, the reduction updates the value of the PRF from $\mathsf{PRF}(K, \mathsf{FE}.\mathsf{Enc}(\mathsf{mpk}_0, C_1))$ to $\mathsf{PRF}(K, \mathsf{FE}.\mathsf{Enc}(\mathsf{mpk}_1, C_1))$.

Finally observe that Game_2 maps to the setting where $b = 1$ in the anonymity game for the $\overline{\mathsf{FE}}$ scheme. Therefore, $\mathsf{Adv}_{\mathcal{A}, \overline{\mathsf{FE}}}^{\mathsf{ANON}} \leq \mathsf{Adv}_{\mathcal{A}_1, \mathsf{FE}'}^{\mathsf{ANON}}(\lambda) + \mathsf{Adv}_{\mathcal{A}_2, \mathsf{FF}}^{\mathsf{ANON}}(\lambda)$. □

Acknowledgements. The authors thank to anonymous reviewers for valuable comments. Roşie was supported by EU Horizon 2020 research and innovation programme under grant agreements No H2020-ERC-2017-ADG-787390 CLOUDMAP and No H2020-MSCA-ITN-2014-643161 ECRYPT-NET.

References

1. Abdalla, M., Bellare, M., Neven, G.: Robust encryption. In: Micciancio, D. (ed.) TCC 2010. LNCS, vol. 5978, pp. 480–497. Springer, Heidelberg (2010). https://doi.org/10.1007/978-3-642-11799-2_28

2. Abdalla, M., Bourse, F., De Caro, A., Pointcheval, D.: Simple functional encryption schemes for inner products. In: Katz, J. (ed.) PKC 2015. LNCS, vol. 9020, pp. 733–751. Springer, Heidelberg (2015). https://doi.org/10.1007/978-3-662-46447-2_33

3. Agrawal, S., Libert, B., Stehlé, D.: Fully secure functional encryption for inner products, from standard assumptions. In: Robshaw, M., Katz, J. (eds.) CRYPTO 2016. LNCS, vol. 9816, pp. 333–362. Springer, Heidelberg (2016). https://doi.org/10.1007/978-3-662-53015-3_12

4. Boneh, D., Boyen, X.: Short signatures without random oracles. In: Cachin, C., Camenisch, J.L. (eds.) EUROCRYPT 2004. LNCS, vol. 3027, pp. 56–73. Springer, Heidelberg (2004). https://doi.org/10.1007/978-3-540-24676-3_4

5. Boneh, D., Boyen, X.: Short signatures without random oracles and the SDH assumption in bilinear groups. J. Cryptol. **21**(2), 149–177 (2008)
6. Boneh, D., Sahai, A., Waters, B.: Functional encryption: definitions and challenges. In: Ishai, Y. (ed.) TCC 2011. LNCS, vol. 6597, pp. 253–273. Springer, Heidelberg (2011). https://doi.org/10.1007/978-3-642-19571-6_16
7. Boyle, E., Goldwasser, S., Ivan, I.: Functional signatures and pseudorandom functions. In: Krawczyk, H. (ed.) PKC 2014. LNCS, vol. 8383, pp. 501–519. Springer, Heidelberg (2014). https://doi.org/10.1007/978-3-642-54631-0_29
8. Brakerski, Z., Komargodski, I., Segev, G.: Multi-input functional encryption in the private-key setting: stronger security from weaker assumptions. In: Fischlin, M., Coron, J.-S. (eds.) EUROCRYPT 2016. LNCS, vol. 9666, pp. 852–880. Springer, Heidelberg (2016). https://doi.org/10.1007/978-3-662-49896-5_30
9. Chou, T., Orlandi, C.: The simplest protocol for oblivious transfer. In: Lauter, K., Rodríguez-Henríquez, F. (eds.) LATINCRYPT 2015. LNCS, vol. 9230, pp. 40–58. Springer, Cham (2015). https://doi.org/10.1007/978-3-319-22174-8_3
10. Cohen, A., Holmgren, J., Nishimaki, R., Vaikuntanathan, V., Wichs, D.: Watermarking cryptographic capabilities. In: Wichs, D., Mansour, Y. (eds.) 48th ACM STOC, pp. 1115–1127. ACM Press, June 2016
11. Damgård, I.B.: Collision free hash functions and public key signature schemes. In: Chaum, D., Price, W.L. (eds.) EUROCRYPT 1987. LNCS, vol. 304, pp. 203–216. Springer, Heidelberg (1988). https://doi.org/10.1007/3-540-39118-5_19
12. Farshim, P., Libert, B., Paterson, K.G., Quaglia, E.A.: Robust encryption, revisited. In: Kurosawa, K., Hanaoka, G. (eds.) PKC 2013. LNCS, vol. 7778, pp. 352–368. Springer, Heidelberg (2013). https://doi.org/10.1007/978-3-642-36362-7_22
13. Farshim, P., Orlandi, C., Roşie, R.: Security of symmetric primitives under incorrect usage of keys. IACR Trans. Symm. Cryptol. **2017**(1), 449–473 (2017)
14. Goldreich, O., Goldwasser, S., Micali, S.: How to construct random functions. J. ACM **33**(4), 792–807 (1986)
15. Goldwasser, S., Micali, S., Rivest, R.L.: A "Paradoxical" solution to the signature problem. In: Blakley, G.R., Chaum, D. (eds.) CRYPTO 1984. LNCS, vol. 196, p. 467. Springer, Heidelberg (1985). https://doi.org/10.1007/3-540-39568-7_37
16. Grubbs, P., Lu, J., Ristenpart, T.: Message franking via committing authenticated encryption. In: Katz, J., Shacham, H. (eds.) CRYPTO 2017. LNCS, vol. 10403, pp. 66–97. Springer, Cham (2017). https://doi.org/10.1007/978-3-319-63697-9_3
17. Jarecki, S., Krawczyk, H., Xu, J.: OPAQUE: an asymmetric PAKE protocol secure against pre-computation attacks. In: Nielsen, J.B., Rijmen, V. (eds.) EUROCRYPT 2018. LNCS, vol. 10822, pp. 456–486. Springer, Cham (2018). https://doi.org/10.1007/978-3-319-78372-7_15
18. Komargodski, I., Segev, G.: From minicrypt to obfustopia via private-key functional encryption. In: Coron, J.-S., Nielsen, J.B. (eds.) EUROCRYPT 2017. LNCS, vol. 10210, pp. 122–151. Springer, Cham (2017). https://doi.org/10.1007/978-3-319-56620-7_5
19. Mohassel, P.: A closer look at anonymity and robustness in encryption schemes. In: Abe, M. (ed.) ASIACRYPT 2010. LNCS, vol. 6477, pp. 501–518. Springer, Heidelberg (2010). https://doi.org/10.1007/978-3-642-17373-8_29
20. O'Neill, A.: Definitional issues in functional encryption. Cryptology ePrint Archive, Report 2010/556 (2010). http://eprint.iacr.org/2010/556
21. Yao, A.C.-C.: Theory and applications of trapdoor functions (extended abstract). In: 23rd FOCS, pp. 80–91. IEEE Computer Society Press, November 1982

Tight Reductions for Diffie-Hellman Variants in the Algebraic Group Model

Taiga Mizuide[1], Atsushi Takayasu[2,3(✉)], and Tsuyoshi Takagi[2]

[1] Department of Creative Informatics, The University of Tokyo, Tokyo, Japan
[2] Department of Mathematical Informatics, The University of Tokyo, Tokyo, Japan
[3] National Institute of Advanced Industrial Science and Technology, Tokyo, Japan
`takayasu@mist.i.u-tokyo.ac.jp`

Abstract. Fuchsbauer, Kiltz, and Loss (Crypto'18) gave a simple and clean definition of an *algebraic group model (AGM)* that lies in between the standard model and the generic group model (GGM). Specifically, an algebraic adversary is able to exploit group-specific structures as the standard model while the AGM successfully provides meaningful hardness results as the GGM. As an application of the AGM, they show a tight computational equivalence between the computing Diffie-Hellman (CDH) assumption and the discrete logarithm (DL) assumption. For the purpose, they used the square Diffie-Hellman assumption as a bridge, i.e., they first proved the equivalence between the DL assumption and the square Diffie-Hellman assumption, then used the known equivalence between the square Diffie-Hellman assumption and the CDH assumption. In this paper, we provide an alternative proof that directly shows the tight equivalence between the DL assumption and the CDH assumption. The crucial benefit of the direct reduction is that we can easily extend the approach to variants of the CDH assumption, e.g., the bilinear Diffie-Hellman assumption. Indeed, we show several tight computational equivalences and discuss applicabilities of our techniques.

1 Introduction

1.1 Background

Diffie-Hellman Problem in the Generic Group Model. The discrete logarithm (DL) assumption and the computational Diffie-Hellman (CDH) assumption including its variants have been devoted to constructing numerous cryptographic protocols. Hence, estimating the computational hardness of solving the problems is a fundamental research topic in cryptography. For the purpose, the *generic group model* (GGM) [Nac94, BL96, Sho97, MW98, Mau05] over cyclic groups is a wonderful tool and has successfully provided several fantastic results in the context. Generic algorithms are not able to exploit specific structures of cyclic groups in the sense that the algorithms are given group elements only via abstract handles. Then, the algorithms are able to output only group elements which are computed by interacting with an oracle and applying group operations

© Springer Nature Switzerland AG 2019
M. Matsui (Ed.): CT-RSA 2019, LNCS 11405, pp. 169–188, 2019.
https://doi.org/10.1007/978-3-030-12612-4_9

to given elements. Therefore, generic algorithms such as a baby-step giant-step algorithm, the Pohlig-Hellman algorithm [PH78] (in composite-order groups), and Pollard's rho algorithm [Pol78] work in any cyclic groups.

Furthermore, the most substantial benefit of the GGM is that we are able to derive information theoretic lower bounds of computational problems, where analogous analyses seem infeasible in the standard model. For example, any generic algorithms require at least $O(\sqrt{p})$ group operations to solve the DL problem in cyclic groups of a prime-order p. Analogous analyses have also been made for the CDH problem and its variants in an ad-hoc manner. Thus far, the GGM has been extended and used for studying computational problems in bilinear (and multilinear) groups [BB08, Boy08, KSW13, MRV16, EHK+17].

One main criticism of the GGM is that computational problems that are generically hard may not be hard when instantiated in concrete groups. Jager and Schwenk [JS13] proved that computing a Jacobi symbol of an integer modulo a composite n generically is equivalent to factorization; however, the computation is easy when given an actual representation of $\mathbb{Z}_n$. Similarly, the number field sieves [Gor93] in specific groups are able to solve the DL problem in subexponential time in $\log p$, i.e., faster than the generic algorithms. Hence, the GGM gives us certain confidence of computational hardness while we want to obtain analogous results in the standard model or less restricted models than the GGM.

Algebraic Group Model. In Crypto'18, Fuchsbauer, Kiltz, and Loss [FKL18] introduced an *algebraic group model* (AGM). The definition of the AGM lies in between the standard model and the GGM. Like the standard model and unlike the GGM, an algebraic algorithm is given an actual representation of cyclic groups. On the other hand, like the GGM and unlike the standard model, an algebraic algorithm is able to output only group elements by applying group operations to given elements. Although the algebraic algorithm is not required to interact with an oracle for the computation, it should output a record of a group operation which Fuchsbauer et al. called a *representation*. Let $\mathcal{G} := (\mathbb{G}, G, p)$ be a group description, where $\mathbb{G}$ is an additive cyclic group of a prime-order p and G is a generator. When an algebraic algorithm is given $\left(\mathcal{G}, \vec{X} := (X_1, \ldots, X_\ell) \in \mathbb{G}^\ell\right)$ and outputs $Z \in \mathbb{G}$, it has to also output a vector $\vec{z} := (z_0, z_1, \ldots, z_\ell) \in \mathbb{Z}_p^{\ell+1}$ as a representation of Z with respect to $\vec{X}$ such that $Z = \sum_{i=0}^\ell z_i X_i$, where $X_0 := G$. Similar definitions of an algebraic algorithm are already known in [BV98, PV05]; however, Fuchsbauer et al.'s definition is simpler and clearer.

The AGM is not allowed to derive computational lower bounds as the standard model. In turn, as opposed to the standard model, Fuchsbauer et al. showed that the AGM is able to make a tight reduction from the DL to the CDH. To be precise, they used the square Diffie-Hellman (DH) problem [MW96, BDS98] as an intermediate step. They first proved a tight reduction from the DL to the square DH in the AGM. Let $(\mathcal{G}, X)$ be a DL instance such that $X := xG$. The reduction algorithm gives $(\mathcal{G}, X)$ to a square DH algorithm and receives an answer $Z = x^2 G$ along with a representation vector $\vec{z}$. Fuchsbauer et al. showed that the vector $\vec{z}$ and the relation $z_0 G + z_1 X = Z$ are sufficient to recover the DL solution x by solving an equation modulo a prime p. Then, due to the known computational equivalence between the square DH and the CDH [MW99, BDZ03], their reduction implies a tight reduction from the DL to the CDH in the AGM. Furthermore, a valuable feature of the result is that the reduction algorithm is *generic*. Due to the fact, an existence of the tight reduction implies an information theoretic lower bounds of the CDH as $O(\sqrt{p})$ in the GGM.

Fuchsbauer et al. claimed that a benefit of the AGM is that we are able to derive information theoretic lower bounds of the CDH in the GGM via *quite simple* arguments. Indeed, Fuchsbauer et al.'s reduction in the AGM is much simpler than the analysis in the GGM. Therefore, providing generic reductions from the DL to other computational problems of the CDH family in the AGM has to be an interesting open problem.

1.2 Our Contributions

In this paper, we provide generic and tight reductions from the DL to several computational problems of the CDH family in the AGM. A starting point of our technique is a *direct* reduction from the DL to the CDH *without* using the square DH as the intermediate step. Given the DL instance $(\mathcal{G}, X)$, our reduction algorithm randomly samples $r \in \mathbb{Z}_p$ and gives $(\mathcal{G}, (X_1, X_2))$ to a CDH algorithm, where $X_1 := X = xG$ and $X_2 := X + rG = (x + r)G$. Here, $(\mathcal{G}, (X_1, X_2))$ is a properly distributed CDH instance in the sense that x and $x + r$ are independently distributed to uniform in $\mathbb{Z}_p$ from the CDH algorithm's view. Then, the reduction algorithm receives a solution of the CDH $Z = x(x + r)G$ along with a representation vector $\vec{z}$. We show that the vector $\vec{z}$ and the relation $z_0 G + z_1 X_1 + z_2 X_2 = Z$ are sufficient to recover x by solving an equation modulo a prime p. The approach is very simple as Fuchsbauer et al.'s one and easily applicable to several CDH variants which are not studied in [FKL18]. We believe that the simple approach is a main benefit of our result. To explain our technique as simple as possible, we consider only *tight* reductions in the sense that the reduction algorithm uses an algorithm for CDH variants only once.

Furthermore, we extend the AGM to an *algebraic bilinear group model* (ABGM) for studying computational problems in symmetric bilinear groups equipped with a map $e : \mathbb{G} \times \mathbb{G} \to \mathbb{G}_T$. We define an algebraic bilinear algorithm so that it is given $(\mathcal{G} := (\mathbb{G}, \mathbb{G}_T, G, e, p), \vec{X} := (X_1, \ldots, X_k) \in \mathbb{G}^k, \vec{Y} := (Y_1, \ldots, Y_\ell) \in \mathbb{G}_T^\ell)$ and outputs $Z \in \mathbb{G}_T$ along with a representation vector $\vec{z}$ that indicates how Z is computed by the given elements. Then, we extend the approach used in cyclic groups and provide generic and tight reductions from the DL to several computational problems of the CDH family including the bilinear Diffie-Hellman problem.

Finally, we provide our master theorems that indicate what kind of computational assumptions can be reduced to from the DL assumption both in cyclic groups and bilinear groups of a prime-order.

We should note that the master theorem does not capture the standard k-linear assumption. Hence, we slightly modify the above approach and successfully provide a tailor-made reduction from the DL to the k-linear assumption.

1.3   Organization

In Sect. 2, we recall several computational problems which we study in this paper. Then, we show a definition of algebraic group models defined by Fuchsbauer et al. In Sects. 3 and 4, we show our technique to provide generic and tight reductions from the DL to the CDH family in cyclic groups and bilinear groups along with a master theorem, respectively. In Sect. 5, we provide a tailor-made reduction from the DL to the k-linear assumption.

2   Preliminaries

In Sect. 2.1, we review several computational problems in cyclic groups and in bilinear groups. In Sect. 2.2, we recall a basic notion of security games, the generic group model, and the algebraic group model. The contents of this section heavily refer to [Boy08, KSW13, EHK+17, FKL18].

Notations. We use $x \xleftarrow{\$} \mathbb{Z}_p$ to denote a uniformly random sampling from $\mathbb{Z}_p$ and $(x_1, \ldots, x_\ell) \xleftarrow{\$} \mathbb{Z}_p^\ell$ to denote every element is sampled by $x_i \xleftarrow{\$} \mathbb{Z}_p$ independently. For a positive integer $\ell > 0$, we use $[\ell]$ to denote a set of integers $\{1, 2, \ldots, \ell\}$. For an $(m + n)$-variate polynomial $f(x_1, \ldots, x_m, y_1, \ldots, y_n)$, we use $\deg f$ to denote a degree of a polynomial and $\deg_{x_1, \ldots, x_m} f$ to denote a degree of the polynomial only with respect to variables $x_1, \ldots, x_m$. As an example for $f(x, y, z) := x^2 yz$, we use the notations $\deg f = 4$, $\deg_x f = 2$, and $\deg_{x,y} = 3$.

2.1   Computational Problems

We first review computational problems in cyclic groups, then do them in bilinear groups.

Computational Problems in Cyclic Groups. We review computational problems in cyclic groups. Let $\mathcal{G} := (\mathbb{G}, G, p)$ be a group description, where $\mathbb{G}$ is an additive group generated by G and has a prime-order p.[1] We first define a discrete logarithm problem to which other problems will be reduced.

Definition 1 (Discrete Logarithm (DL) Problem). *Given a group description $\mathcal{G} := (\mathbb{G}, G, p)$ and a group element $X := xG \in \mathbb{G}; x \xleftarrow{\$} \mathbb{Z}_p$, compute $x \in \mathbb{Z}_p$.*

Then, we summarize the CDH problem and its variants which we study in this paper.

Definition 2 (Computational Diffie-Hellman (CDH) Problem [DH76]). *Given a group description $\mathcal{G} := (\mathbb{G}, G, p)$ and group elements $(X_1 := x_1 G, X_2 := x_2 G) \in \mathbb{G}^2; (x_1, x_2) \xleftarrow{\$} \mathbb{Z}_p^2$, compute $Z := x_1 x_2 G \in \mathbb{G}$.*

---

[1] To construct a reduction, we solve an equation modulo an order of $\mathbb{G}$. Hence, if the order is composite, we do not know how to solve it in general. Hence, as [FKL18] we study only a prime-order group in this paper.

Definition 3 (k-party Diffie-Hellman (k-PDH) Problem [Bis08]**).** *Given a group description* $\mathcal{G} := (\mathbb{G}, G, p)$ *and group elements* $(X_1 := x_1 G, \ldots, X_k := x_k G) \in \mathbb{G}^k; (x_1, \ldots, x_k) \xleftarrow{\$} \mathbb{Z}_p^k$, *compute* $Z := x_1 \cdots x_k G \in \mathbb{G}$.

The following k-exponent Diffie-Hellman assumption for $k = 2$ called the square Diffie-Hellman assumption was used in [MW96, BDS98].

Definition 4 (k-exponent Diffie-Hellman (k-EDH) Problem). *Given a group description* $\mathcal{G} := (\mathbb{G}, G, p)$ *and a group element* $X := xG \in \mathbb{G}; x \xleftarrow{\$} \mathbb{Z}_p$, *compute* $Z := x^k G \in \mathbb{G}$.

The following k-th root Diffie-Hellman problem for $k = 2$ called the square root Diffie-Hellman problem was used in [KMS04].

Definition 5 (k-th Root Diffie-Hellman (k-RDH) Problem). *Given a group description* $\mathcal{G} := (\mathbb{G}, G, p)$ *and a group element* $X := x^k G \in \mathbb{G}; x \xleftarrow{\$} \mathbb{Z}_p$, *compute* $Z := xG \in \mathbb{G}$.

Next, we recall a *decisional* k-linear problem.

Definition 6 (Decisional k-Linear Problem [BBS04]**).** *Given a group description* $\mathcal{G} := (\mathbb{G}, G, p)$ *and group elements* $(X_1 := x_1 G, \ldots, X_k := x_k G, Y_1 := x_1 y_1 G, \ldots, Y_k := x_k y_k G, Z) \in \mathbb{G}^{2k+1}; (x_1, \ldots, x_k, y_1, \ldots, y_k) \xleftarrow{\$} \mathbb{Z}_p^{2k}$, *distinguish whether* $Z := (y_1 + \cdots + y_k)G$ *or* Z *is a random element in* $\mathbb{G}$.

In this paper, we define computational variants of the k-linear problem in the following two ways.

Definition 7 (Computational k-Linear (k-Lin$^{(1)}$) Problem). *Given a group description* $\mathcal{G} := (\mathbb{G}, G, p)$ *and group elements* $(X_1 := x_1 G, \ldots, X_k := x_k G, Y_1 := x_1 y_1 G, \ldots, Y_k := x_k y_k G) \in \mathbb{G}^{2k+1}; (x_1, \ldots, x_k, y_1, \ldots, y_k) \xleftarrow{\$} \mathbb{Z}_p^{2k}$, *compute* $Z := (y_1 + \cdots + y_k)G$.

Definition 8 (Computational k-Linear (k-Lin$^{(2)}$) Problem). *Given a group description* $\mathcal{G} := (\mathbb{G}, G, p)$ *and group elements* $(X_1 := x_1 G, \ldots, X_k := x_k G, Y_1 := x_1 y_1 G, \ldots, Y_{k-1} := x_{k-1} y_{k-1} G, Y' := (y_1 + \cdots + y_k)G) \in \mathbb{G}^{2k}; (x_1, \ldots, x_k, y_1, \ldots, y_k) \xleftarrow{\$} \mathbb{Z}_p^{2k}$, *compute* $Z := x_k y_k G$.

A natural definition of a computational variant should be k-Lin$^{(1)}$; however, our master theorem will not capture the problem. Therefore, we also define k-Lin$^{(2)}$ which is included in the master theorem. The difference may be a good example to give an intuitive understanding of our master theorem. We will later provide a tailor-made reduction for k-Lin$^{(1)}$ by slightly modifying our technique.

To provide our master theorem in cyclic groups, we define a generalized version of the Diffie-Hellman problem as follows.

Definition 9 (Generalized Diffie-Hellman (GDH) Problem). *Let*
$f_1(x_1, \ldots, x_m, y_1, \ldots, y_n), \ldots, f_\ell(x_1, \ldots, x_m, y_1, \ldots, y_n)$ *and* $g(x_1, \ldots, x_m)$ *be*
known fixed non-zero polynomials. Given a group description $\mathcal{G} := (\mathbb{G}, G, p)$ *and*
group elements

$$(X_1 := f_1(x_1, \ldots, x_m, y_1, \ldots, y_n)G, \ldots, X_\ell := f_\ell(x_1, \ldots, x_m, y_1, \ldots, y_n)G) \in \mathbb{G}^\ell;$$

$$(x_1, \ldots, x_m, y_1, \ldots, y_n) \xleftarrow{s} \mathbb{Z}_p^{m+n},$$

compute

$$Z := g(x_1, \ldots, x_m)G.$$

Our master theorem will indicate that when the GDH problem can be reduced
to from the DL.

Computational Problems in Bilinear Groups. We review computational
problems in bilinear groups. For simplicity, we focus only on *symmetric* bilinear
maps $e : \mathbb{G} \times \mathbb{G} \to \mathbb{G}_T$ throughout this paper. Let $\mathcal{G} := (\mathbb{G}, \mathbb{G}_T, G, e, p)$ be a
bilinear group description, where $\mathbb{G}$ is an additive group generated by G and has
a prime-order p, and $\mathbb{G}_T$ is a multiplicative group of order p associated with a
non-degenerate bilinear map $e : \mathbb{G} \times \mathbb{G} \to \mathbb{G}_T$, i.e., $e(G, G)$ is a generator of $\mathbb{G}_T$
and $e(xG, yG) = e(G, G)^{xy}$.

We will provide a reduction from the DL in source groups $\mathbb{G}$ to CDH variants.
Hence, we define a bilinear discrete logarithm problem as follows.

Definition 10 (Bilinear Discrete Logarithm (BDL) Problem). *Given a*
bilinear group description $\mathcal{G} := (\mathbb{G}, \mathbb{G}_T, G, e, p)$ *and a group element* $X := xG \in$
$\mathbb{G}; x \xleftarrow{s} \mathbb{Z}_p$, *compute* $x \in \mathbb{Z}_p$.

Then, we summarize the CDH variants in bilinear groups.

Definition 11 (Bilinear Diffie-Hellman (BDH) Problem [BF03, Jou04]).
Given a bilinear group description $\mathcal{G} := (\mathbb{G}, \mathbb{G}_T, G, e, p)$ *and group elements*
$(X_1 := x_1 G, X_2 := x_2 G, X_3 := x_3 G) \in \mathbb{G}^3; (x_1, x_2, x_3) \xleftarrow{s} \mathbb{Z}_p^3$, *compute*
$Z := e(G, G)^{x_1 x_2 x_3} \in \mathbb{G}_T$.

The following ℓ-weak bilinear Diffie-Hellman inversion problem is a *paramet-*
ric problem defined with a fixed integer ℓ. Although we define the problem with
general ℓ, our technique will be able to provide generic reductions from the DL
problem to the parametric problem only for $\ell = 1$.

Definition 12 (ℓ-weak Bilinear Diffie-Hellman Inversion (ℓ-wBDHI)
Problem [Boy08]). *Given a bilinear group description* $\mathcal{G} := (\mathbb{G}, \mathbb{G}_T, G, e, p)$
and group elements $(X_1 := x_1 G, X_2 := x_1^2 G, \ldots, X_\ell := x_1^\ell G, X_{\ell+1} := x_2 G) \in$
$\mathbb{G}^{\ell+1}; (x_1, x_2) \xleftarrow{s} \mathbb{Z}_p^2$, *compute* $Z := e(G, G)^{x_1^{\ell+1} x_2} \in \mathbb{G}_T$.

To provide our master theorem in bilinear groups, we define a generalized
version of the bilinear Diffie-Hellman problem as follows.

Definition 13 (Generalized Bilinear Diffie-Hellman (GBDH) Problem). *Let* $f_1(x_1, \ldots, x_m, y_1, \ldots, y_n), \ldots, f_k(x_1, \ldots, x_m, y_1, \ldots, y_n), g_1(x_1, \ldots, x_m, y_1, \ldots, y_n), \ldots, g_\ell(x_1, \ldots, x_m, y_1, \ldots, y_n),$ *and* $h(x_1, \ldots, x_m)$ *be known fixed non-zero polynomials. Given a bilinear group description* $\mathcal{G} := (\mathbb{G}, \mathbb{G}_T, G, e, p)$ *and group elements*

$$
\begin{pmatrix}
X_1 := f_1(x_1, \ldots, x_m, y_1, \ldots, y_n)G, \ldots, X_k := f_k(x_1, \ldots, x_m, y_1, \ldots, y_n)G, \\
Y_1 := e(G,G)^{g_1(x_1,\ldots,x_m,y_1,\ldots,y_n)}, \ldots, Y_\ell := e(G,G)^{g_\ell(x_1,\ldots,x_m,y_1,\ldots,y_n)}
\end{pmatrix}
$$

$$
\in \mathbb{G}^k \times \mathbb{G}_T^\ell; (x_1, \ldots, x_m, y_1, \ldots, y_n) \xleftarrow{\$} \mathbb{Z}_p^{m+n},
$$

compute

$$
Z := e(G,G)^{h(x_1,\ldots,x_m)}.
$$

2.2 Algebraic Group Model

In this subsection, we review the GGM and the AGM in cyclic groups.

Algebraic Security Game. Let $\mathbf{G}_\mathcal{G}$ be an *algebraic* security game relative to a group description $\mathcal{G} := (\mathbb{G}, G, p)$; an adversary A receives $\mathcal{G}$ and an instance of the problem $\vec{X}$ from a challenger, then returns an output. For example, we use $\mathbf{CDH}_\mathcal{G}$ to denote security games of the CDH problem relative to $\mathcal{G}$; an adversary A receives $\mathcal{G}$ and (X_1, X_2) from a challenger, then returns an output Z. We use $\mathbf{G}_\mathcal{G}^A$ to denote an output of a game $\mathbf{G}_\mathcal{G}$ between a challenger and an adversary A. A is said to win if $\mathbf{G}_\mathcal{G}^A = 1$; $\mathbf{CDH}_\mathcal{G}^A = 1$ when $Z = x_1 x_2 G$. We define an advantage and a running time of an adversary A in $\mathbf{G}_\mathcal{G}$ as $\mathsf{Adv}_{\mathcal{G},A}^G := \Pr[\mathbf{G}_\mathcal{G}^A = 1]$ and $\mathsf{Time}_{\mathcal{G},A}^G$, respectively.

Generic Group Model (GGM). In the GGM, an adversary $\mathsf{A}_{\mathsf{gen}}$ is not given actual representations of group elements but the elements via abstract handles. For example, an adversary $\mathsf{A}_{\mathsf{gen}}$ in a security game $\mathbf{CDH}_\mathcal{G}$ receives a group description $\mathcal{G} := (\mathbb{G}, 00, p)$ and $(01, 02)$ from a challenger. Here, $\mathbb{G}$ only contains an information of an additive cyclic group of a prime-order p. The adversary $\mathsf{A}_{\mathsf{gen}}$ is able to perform group operations only via oracle queries, e.g., a generic adversary $\mathsf{A}_{\mathsf{gen}}$ queries $(01, 02, +)$ to an oracle and obtains 03, where $01 = X_1, 02 = X_2$, and $03 = X_1 + X_2$. Since a behavior of the generic adversary $\mathsf{A}_{\mathsf{gen}}$ is independent of actual group representations, it works in any groups.

Some computational problems that are hard in the GGM may not be hard when instantiated in concrete groups. However, the GGM is still useful since it enables us to obtain information theoretic lower bounds. We use a notion of (ε, t)-*hard* if for all generic algorithms $\mathsf{A}_{\mathsf{gen}}$ in a game $\mathbf{G}_\mathcal{G}$

$$
\mathsf{Time}_{\mathcal{G},\mathsf{A}_{\mathsf{gen}}}^G \le t \quad \Rightarrow \quad \mathsf{Adv}_{\mathcal{G},\mathsf{A}_{\mathsf{gen}}}^G \le \varepsilon
$$

holds. The following fact is known for the discrete logarithm problem.

Lemma 1 (Generic Hardness of DL [Sho97, Mau05]). *The discrete logarithm problem is* $(t^2/p, t)$-*hard in the GGM.*

Algebraic Algorithm. Now, we review a notion of an *algebraic algorithm* defined by Fuchsbauer et al. [FKL18]. An algebraic algorithm is able to output group elements only via group additions of given elements. Furthermore, the algebraic algorithm should also output a *representation* which indicates how outputted group elements are calculated with respect to given elements.

Definition 14 (Algebraic Algorithm, Definition 2.1 of [FKL18]). *An algorithm* A_{alg} *executed in an algebraic security game* $\mathbf{G}_{\mathcal{G}}$ *in a cyclic group* $\mathcal{G} := (\mathbb{G}, G, p)$ *is called* algebraic *if for all group elements* $Z \in \mathbb{G}$ *that* A_{alg} *outputs, it additionally returns the representation of* Z *with respect to given group elements. Specifically, if* $\vec{X} := (X_0, \dots, X_\ell) \in \mathbb{G}^{\ell+1}$, *where* $X_0 := G$, *is the list of group elements that* A_{alg} *has received so far, then* A_{alg} *must also return a vector* $\vec{z} := (z_i)_{0 \le i \le \ell} \in \mathbb{Z}_p^{\ell+1}$ *such that* $Z = \sum_{i=0}^{\ell} z_i X_i$. *We use* $[Z]_{\vec{z}}$ *to denote such an output.*

We remark that every generic algorithm A_{gen} can be modeled as an algebraic one. A generic algorithm A_{gen} is able to output only group elements which are derived from group additions of given elements as an algebraic algorithm. Furthermore, by keeping a record of all oracle queries, a generic algorithm A_{gen} is able to output a group element Z along with its representation $\vec{z}$. Hence, a generic algorithm A_{gen} is able to behave as an algebraic algorithm. Moreover, let A_{alg} and B_{gen} be an algebraic and a generic algorithm, respectively. Then, $B_{alg} := B_{gen}^{A_{alg}}$ is also an algebraic algorithm.

Reduction Between Algebraic Security Games. Let $\mathbf{G}_{\mathcal{G}}$ and $\mathbf{H}_{\mathcal{G}}$ be two algebraic security games. Please keep in mind that $\mathbf{G}_{\mathcal{G}}$ and $\mathbf{H}_{\mathcal{G}}$ will be the game for the CDH variants and the (B)DL, respectively. We use $\mathbf{H}_{\mathcal{G}} \Rightarrow_{alg} \mathbf{G}_{\mathcal{G}}$ to denote an existence of a *generic* and tight reduction algorithm R_{gen} such that for every algorithm A, an algorithm $B := R_{gen}^A$ satisfies

$$\mathsf{Adv}_{\mathcal{G},B}^{\mathbf{H}} = \mathsf{Adv}_{\mathcal{G},A}^{\mathbf{G}} \quad \text{and} \quad \mathsf{Time}_{\mathcal{G},B}^{\mathbf{H}} = \mathsf{Time}_{\mathcal{G},A}^{\mathbf{G}}.$$

The crucial point of the definition is that a reduction algorithm R_{gen} is generic. Hence, if $A = A_{alg}$ is algebraic, $B = B_{alg}$ is also algebraic. Furthermore, if $A = A_{gen}$ is generic, $B = B_{gen}$ is also generic. Thanks to the generic reduction algorithm R_{gen}, we are able to obtain information theoretic lower bounds of CDH variants as follows by combining with Lemma 1.

Lemma 2 (Lemma 2.2 of [FKL18]). *Let* $\mathbf{G}_{\mathcal{G}}$ *and* $\mathbf{H}_{\mathcal{G}}$ *be algebraic security games such that* $\mathbf{H}_{\mathcal{G}} \Rightarrow_{alg} \mathbf{G}_{\mathcal{G}}$ *and winning* $\mathbf{H}_{\mathcal{G}}$ *is* (ε, t)-*hard in the GGM. Then,* $\mathbf{G}_{\mathcal{G}}$ *is* (ε, t)-*hard in the GGM.*

3   Reduction from DL in Cyclic Groups

In this section, we show several generic and tight reductions from the DL to the CDH variants in cyclic groups. We first provide a direct reduction to the CDH in Sect. 3.1. Then, we provide our master theorem in Sect. 3.2.

3.1   Basic Reduction: From DL to CDH

In this section, we show a basic approach of this paper by providing a generic and tight reduction from the DL to the CDH in the AGM.

Theorem 1. $\mathbf{DL}_{\mathcal{G}} \Rightarrow_{\mathsf{alg}} \mathbf{CDH}_{\mathcal{G}}$.

Proof. We construct a generic and tight reduction algorithm $\mathsf{R}_{\mathsf{gen}}$. Specifically, the reduction algorithm $\mathsf{R}_{\mathsf{gen}}$ uses an algebraic adversary $\mathsf{A}_{\mathsf{alg}}$ on the $\mathbf{CDH}_{\mathcal{G}}$ only once and construct an algebraic adversary $\mathsf{B}_{\mathsf{alg}} := \mathsf{R}_{\mathsf{gen}}^{\mathsf{A}_{\mathsf{alg}}}$ on the $\mathbf{DL}_{\mathcal{G}}$.

The reduction algorithm $\mathsf{R}_{\mathsf{gen}}$ is given a group description $\mathcal{G} := (\mathbb{G}, G, p)$ and an instance of the $\mathbf{DL}_{\mathcal{G}}$, i.e., $X := xG \in \mathbb{G}$ for an unknown $x \in \mathbb{Z}_p$. Then, the reduction algorithm $\mathsf{R}_{\mathsf{gen}}$ creates an instance of the $\mathbf{CDH}_{\mathcal{G}}$ as follows: Pick a random $r \xleftarrow{\$} \mathbb{Z}_p$ and compute

$$X_2 := X + rG = (x + r)G \in \mathbb{G},$$

then set

$$(X_1 := X, X_2) \in \mathbb{G}^2.$$

The reduction algorithm $\mathsf{R}_{\mathsf{gen}}$ gives a group description $\mathcal{G} := (\mathbb{G}, G, p)$ and group elements $(X_1, X_2) \in \mathbb{G}^2$ to $\mathsf{A}_{\mathsf{alg}}$. Observe that (X_1, X_2) is a valid CDH instance by implicitly setting

$$(x_1, x_2) = (x, x + r)$$

since x_2 is independently distributed of x_1 to uniform in $\mathbb{Z}_p$ from $\mathsf{A}_{\mathsf{alg}}$'s view. Hence, an algebraic adversary $\mathsf{A}_{\mathsf{alg}}$ outputs a correct solution $[Z]_{\vec{z}}$ with an advantage $\mathsf{Adv}_{\mathcal{G},\mathsf{A}_{\mathsf{alg}}}^{\mathbf{CDH}}$ and a running time $\mathsf{Time}_{\mathcal{G},\mathsf{A}_{\mathsf{alg}}}^{\mathbf{CDH}}$.

Next, the reduction algorithm $\mathsf{R}_{\mathsf{gen}}$ uses $[Z]_{\vec{z}}$ outputted by an algebraic adversary $\mathsf{A}_{\mathsf{alg}}$ on the $\mathbf{CDH}_{\mathcal{G}}$ and computes a solution of the $\mathbf{DL}_{\mathcal{G}}$. Assume the output is a correct solution of the CDH, i.e., $Z = x_1 x_2 G$. It holds with probability $\mathsf{Adv}_{\mathcal{G},\mathsf{A}_{\mathsf{alg}}}^{\mathbf{CDH}}$. Then, the representation vector $\vec{z} := (z_0, z_1, z_2)$ satisfies

$$x_1 x_2 G = x(x + r)G = z_0 G + z_1 X + z_2 Y$$
$$= (z_0 + z_1 x + z_2(x + r))G.$$

Hence, the reduction algorithm $\mathsf{R}_{\mathsf{gen}}$ obtains the following univariate equation modulo a prime p:

$$x(x + r) = z_0 + z_1 x + z_2(x + r) \mod p$$
$$\Leftrightarrow x^2 + (r - z_1 - z_2)x - z_0 - z_2 r = 0 \mod p.$$

Observe that the left hand side is a degree 2 monic polynomial; hence, a non-zero polynomial. Since the reduction algorithm $\mathsf{R}_{\mathsf{gen}}$ knows a value of r, it is able to find all solutions for x in polynomial time. By checking $xG = X$, the reduction algorithm $\mathsf{R}_{\mathsf{gen}}$ successfully finds a correct solution of the $\mathbf{DL}_{\mathcal{G}}$. □

By combining with Lemmas 1, 2, and Theorem 1, we are able to obtain an information theoretic lower bound for the CDH.

Theorem 2 (Generic Hardness of CDH). *The computational Diffie-Hellman problem in Definition 2 is $(t^2/p, t)$-hard in the generic group model.*

3.2   Master Theorem in Cyclic Groups

In this subsection, we provide the following master theorem in cyclic groups to indicate the power of our technique.

Theorem 3 (Master Theorem in Cyclic Groups). $\mathbf{DL}_{\mathcal{G}} \Rightarrow_{\mathsf{alg}} \mathbf{GDH}_{\mathcal{G}}$ *holds when the following conditions hold:*

(1) $\deg_{x_1,\dots,x_m} f_i(x_1,\dots,x_m,y_1,\dots,y_n) \in \{0,1\}$ *for all* $i \in [\ell]$,
(2) $\deg g(x_1,\dots,x_m) > 1$.

Before providing a proof, we summarize the CDH variants which we studied in Sect. 3 and the conditions of Theorem 3 in Table 1. As the table shows, CDH, k-PDH, k-EDH, and k-Lin$^{(2)}$ satisfy the conditions (1) and (2) in Theorem 3. Hence, as immediate corollary of the master theorem, we are able to provide generic and tight reductions from the DL to the k-PDH, k-EDH, and k-Lin$^{(2)}$. Unfortunately, the k-Lin$^{(1)}$ does not satisfy the condition (2). Hence, we will provide a tailor-made reduction for the k-Lin$^{(1)}$ later.

Table 1. Applicability of our technique in cyclic groups

Problem	$(f_i)_{i\in[\ell]}$	g	max deg f_i	deg g	Reduction?
CDH	(x_1, x_2)	$x_1 x_2$	1	2	Yes
k-PDH	$(x_i)_{i\in[k]}$	$x_1 \cdots x_k$	1	k	Yes
k-EDH	x	x^k	1	k	Yes
k-Lin$^{(1)}$	$((x_i)_{i\in[k]}, (x_i y_i)_{i\in[k]})$	$\sum_{i=1}^{k} y_i$	1	1	No
k-Lin$^{(2)}$	$\begin{pmatrix} (x_i)_{i\in[k]}, (x_i y_i)_{i\in[k-1]}, \\ \sum_{i=1}^{k} y_i \end{pmatrix}$	$x_k y_k$	1	2	Yes

Then, we show a proof of Theorem 3. In advance, we claim that the condition (1) will be used to ensure that the reduction algorithm is able to produce all group elements of the GDH during a reduction, while both the conditions (1) and (2) will be used to ensure that the modular equation never becomes a zero polynomial.

Proof. We construct a generic and tight reduction algorithm $\mathsf{R}_{\mathsf{gen}}$. Specifically, the reduction algorithm $\mathsf{R}_{\mathsf{gen}}$ uses an algebraic adversary $\mathsf{A}_{\mathsf{alg}}$ on the $\mathbf{GDH}_{\mathcal{G}}$ only once and construct an algebraic adversary $\mathsf{B}_{\mathsf{alg}} := \mathsf{R}_{\mathsf{gen}}^{\mathsf{A}_{\mathsf{alg}}}$ on the $\mathbf{DL}_{\mathcal{G}}$.

The reduction algorithm $\mathsf{R}_{\mathsf{gen}}$ is given a group description $\mathcal{G} := (\mathbb{G}, G, p)$ and an instance of the $\mathbf{DL}_{\mathcal{G}}$, i.e., $X := xG \in \mathbb{G}$ for an unknown $x \in \mathbb{Z}_p$. Then, the reduction algorithm $\mathsf{R}_{\mathsf{gen}}$ creates an instance of the $\mathbf{GDH}_{\mathcal{G}}$ as follows: Pick random $(r_2,\dots,r_m,s_1,\dots,s_n) \xleftarrow{\$} \mathbb{Z}_p^{m+n-1}$ and compute

$$X_i := f_i(x_1,\dots,x_m,y_1,\dots,y_n)G \in \mathbb{G}$$

for all $i \in [\ell]$ by implicitly setting

$$(x_1, x_2, \ldots, x_m, y_1, \ldots, y_n) = (x, x + r_2, \ldots, x + r_m, s_1, \ldots, s_n).$$

The reduction algorithm $\mathsf{R}_{\mathsf{gen}}$ is able to compute all the group elements thanks to the condition (1). Then, the reduction algorithm $\mathsf{R}_{\mathsf{gen}}$ gives a group description $\mathcal{G} := (\mathbb{G}, G, p)$ and group elements $(X_1, \ldots, X_\ell) \in \mathbb{G}^\ell$ to $\mathsf{A}_{\mathsf{alg}}$. Observe that $(X_1, \ldots, X_\ell)$ is a valid GDH instance since $(x_2, \ldots, x_m)$ is independently distributed of x_1 to uniform in $\mathbb{Z}_p^{m-1}$ from $\mathsf{A}_{\mathsf{alg}}$'s view. Hence, an algebraic adversary $\mathsf{A}_{\mathsf{alg}}$ outputs a correct solution $[Z]_{\vec{z}}$ with an advantage $\mathsf{Adv}_{\mathcal{G},\mathsf{A}_{\mathsf{alg}}}^{\mathsf{GDH}}$ and a running time $\mathsf{Time}_{\mathcal{G},\mathsf{A}_{\mathsf{alg}}}^{\mathsf{GDH}}$.

Next, the reduction algorithm $\mathsf{R}_{\mathsf{gen}}$ uses $[Z]_{\vec{z}}$ outputted by an algebraic adversary $\mathsf{A}_{\mathsf{alg}}$ on the $\mathbf{GDH}_{\mathcal{G}}$ and computes a solution of the $\mathbf{DL}_{\mathcal{G}}$. Assume the output is a correct solution of the GDH, i.e., $Z = g(x_1, \ldots, x_m)G$. It holds with probability $\mathsf{Adv}_{\mathcal{G},\mathsf{A}_{\mathsf{alg}}}^{\mathsf{GDH}}$. Then, the representation vector $\vec{z} := (z_0, z_1, \ldots, z_\ell)$ satisfies

$$
\begin{aligned}
&g(x_1, \ldots, x_m)G \\
&= z_0 G + z_1 X_1 + \cdots + z_\ell X_\ell \\
&= (z_0 + z_1 f_1(x_1, \ldots, x_m, y_1, \ldots, y_n) + \cdots + z_\ell f_\ell(x_1, \ldots, x_m, y_1, \ldots, y_n))G.
\end{aligned}
$$

Hence, the reduction algorithm $\mathsf{R}_{\mathsf{gen}}$ obtains the following univariate equation modulo a prime p:

$$
\begin{aligned}
&g(x, x + r_2, \ldots, x + r_m) \\
&= z_0 + \sum_{i=1}^{\ell} z_i f_i(x, x + r_2, \ldots, x + r_m, s_1, \ldots, s_n) \mod p.
\end{aligned}
$$

Observe that a degree of the left and the right hand side with respect to a variable x is strictly larger than 1 and exactly 1 respectively due to the conditions (1) and (2). Hence, the modular equation never becomes a zero polynomial. Since the reduction algorithm $\mathsf{R}_{\mathsf{gen}}$ knows values of $(r_2, \ldots, r_m, s_1, \ldots, s_n)$, it is able to find all solutions for x in polynomial time. By checking $xG = X$, the reduction algorithm $\mathsf{R}_{\mathsf{gen}}$ successfully finds a correct solution of the $\mathbf{DL}_{\mathcal{G}}$.   □

By combining with Lemmas 1, 2, and Theorem 3, we are able to obtain an information theoretic lower bound for the GDH as follows.

Theorem 4 (Generic Hardness of GDH). *The generalized Diffie-Hellman problem in Definition 9 is $(t^2/p, t)$-hard in the generic group model.*

4   Reduction from BDL in Bilinear Groups

In this section, we show tight reductions from the bilinear discrete logarithm problem to the bilinear Diffie-Hellman problem in an *algebraic bilinear group model* which we define in Sect. 4.1. In Sect. 4.2, we provide a reduction to the BDH. Finally, we provide our master theorem in Sect. 4.3.

4.1   Algebraic Bilinear Group Model

In advance of the reduction, we define an algebraic bilinear algorithm. The definition is analogous to Definition 14 in the sense that the algebraic bilinear algorithm is able to output only group elements which are derived from group additions in $\mathbb{G}$, group multiplications in $\mathbb{G}_T$, and pairing e of given elements. Furthermore, the algebraic bilinear algorithm should also output a *representation* which indicates how outputted group elements are calculated. In this paper, we study computational problems in bilinear groups whose solutions Z are elements in $\mathbb{G}_T$. Hence, we define a representation so that it records how Z is computed by group multiplications of given elements in $\mathbb{G}_T$ and pairing of given elements in $\mathbb{G}$. We formally provide a definition as follows.

Definition 15 (Algebraic Bilinear Algorithm). *An algorithm* $\mathsf{A}_{\mathsf{alg}}$ *executed in an algebraic security game* $\mathbf{G}_{\mathcal{G}}$ *for* $\mathcal{G} := (\mathbb{G}, \mathbb{G}_T, G, e, p)$ *is called algebraic if for all group elements* $Z \in \mathbb{G}_T$ *that* $\mathsf{A}_{\mathsf{alg}}$ *outputs, it additionally return the representation of* Z *with respect to given group elements. Specifically, if* $\vec{X} := (X_0, \ldots, X_k) \in \mathbb{G}^{k+1}$, *where* $X_0 := G$, *and* $\vec{Y} := (Y_1, \ldots, Y_\ell) \in \mathbb{G}_T^\ell$ *are the list of group elements that* $\mathsf{A}_{\mathsf{alg}}$ *has received so far, then* $\mathsf{A}_{\mathsf{alg}}$ *must also return a vector* $\vec{z} := ((z_{ij})_{0 \le i \le j \le k}, (z_i')_{1 \le i \le \ell}) \in \mathbb{Z}_p^{\frac{(k+1)(k+2)}{2} + \ell}$ *such that* $Z = \left(\prod_{0 \le i \le j \le k} e(X_i, X_j)^{z_{ij}} \right) \cdot \left(\prod_{i=1}^{\ell} Y_i^{z_i'} \right)$. *We denote such an output as* $[Z]_{\vec{z}}$.

We note that the BDH and the ℓ-wBDI does not take elements in $\mathbb{G}_T$ as the input. Therefore, the algorithm outputs Z along with a vector $\vec{z} \in \mathbb{Z}_p^{\frac{(k+1)(k+2)}{2}}$.

4.2   From BDL to BDH

In this subsection, we extend the approach in Sect. 3 and prove the following reduction.

Theorem 5. BDL$_{\mathcal{G}}$ $\Rightarrow_{\mathsf{alg}}$ BDH$_{\mathcal{G}}$.

Proof. We construct a generic and tight reduction algorithm $\mathsf{R}_{\mathsf{gen}}$. Specifically, the reduction algorithm $\mathsf{R}_{\mathsf{gen}}$ uses an algebraic adversary $\mathsf{A}_{\mathsf{alg}}$ on the **BDH$_{\mathcal{G}}$** only once and construct an algebraic adversary $\mathsf{B}_{\mathsf{alg}} := \mathsf{R}_{\mathsf{gen}}^{\mathsf{A}_{\mathsf{alg}}}$ on the **BDL$_{\mathcal{G}}$**.

The reduction algorithm $\mathsf{R}_{\mathsf{gen}}$ is given a bilinear group description $\mathcal{G} := (\mathbb{G}, \mathbb{G}_T, G, e, p)$ and an instance of the **BDL$_{\mathcal{G}}$**, i.e., $X := xG \in \mathbb{G}$ for an unknown $x \in \mathbb{Z}_p$. Then, the reduction algorithm $\mathsf{R}_{\mathsf{gen}}$ creates an instance of the **BDH$_{\mathcal{G}}$** as follows: Pick a random $(r, s) \xleftarrow{\$} \mathbb{Z}_p^2$ and compute

$$(X_2 := X + rG = (x + r)G, \quad X_3 := X + sG = (x + s)G) \in \mathbb{G}^2,$$

then set

$$(X_1 := X, X_2, X_3) \in \mathbb{G}^3.$$

The reduction algorithm $\mathsf{R}_{\mathsf{gen}}$ gives a bilinear group description $\mathcal{G} := (\mathbb{G}, \mathbb{G}_T, G, e, p)$ and group elements $(X_1, X_2, X_3) \in \mathbb{G}^3$ to $\mathsf{A}_{\mathsf{alg}}$. Observe that

(X_1, X_2, X_3) is a valid BDH instance since (x_2, x_3) is independently distributed of x to uniform in $\mathbb{Z}_p^2$ from $\mathsf{A_{alg}}$'s view. Hence, an algebraic adversary $\mathsf{A_{alg}}$ outputs a correct solution $[Z]_{\tilde{z}}$ with an advantage $\mathsf{Adv}^{\mathbf{BDH}}_{\mathcal{G}, \mathsf{A_{alg}}}$ and a running time $\mathsf{Time}^{\mathbf{BDH}}_{\mathcal{G}, \mathsf{A_{alg}}}$.

Next, the reduction algorithm $\mathsf{R_{gen}}$ uses $[Z]_{\tilde{z}}$ outputted by an algebraic adversary $\mathsf{A_{alg}}$ on the $\mathbf{BDH}_{\mathcal{G}}$ and computes a solution of the $\mathbf{BDL}_{\mathcal{G}}$. Assume the output is a correct solution of the BDH, i.e., $Z = e(G, G)^{x_1 x_2 x_3}$. It holds with probability $\mathsf{Adv}^{\mathbf{BDH}}_{\mathcal{G}, \mathsf{A_{alg}}}$. Then, we use $X_0 := G$ for notational convenience and the representation vector $\vec{z} := (z_{ij})_{0 \le i \le j \le 3}$ satisfies

$$
\begin{aligned}
e(G, G)^{x_1 x_2 x_3} &= e(G, G)^{x(x+r)(x+s)} \\
&= \prod_{0 \le i \le j \le 3} e(X_i, X_j)^{z_{ij}} \\
&= e(G, G)^{z_{00} + z_{01} x + z_{02}(x+r) + z_{03}(x+s) + z_{11} x^2 + z_{12} x(x+r) + z_{13} x(x+s)} \\
&\quad \cdot e(G, G)^{z_{22}(x+r)^2 + z_{23}(x+r)(x+s) + z_{33}(x+s)^2}.
\end{aligned}
$$

Hence, the reduction algorithm $\mathsf{R_{gen}}$ obtains the following univariate equation modulo a prime p:

$$
\begin{aligned}
& x(x+r)(x+s) \\
&= z_{00} + z_{01} x + z_{02}(x+r) + z_{03}(x+s) + z_{11} x^2 + z_{12} x(x+r) \\
&\quad + z_{13} x(x+s) + z_{22}(x+r)^2 + z_{23}(x+r)(x+s) + z_{33}(x+s)^2 \mod p \\
&\Leftrightarrow x^3 + (r + s - z_{11} - z_{12} - z_{13} - z_{22} - z_{23} - z_{33}) x^2 \\
&\quad + (rs - z_{01} - z_{02} - z_{03} - r z_{12} - s z_{13} - 2r z_{22} - (r+s) z_{23} - 2s z_{33}) x \\
&\quad - z_{00} - r z_{02} - s z_{03} - r^2 z_{22} - rs z_{23} - s^2 z_{33} = 0 \mod p.
\end{aligned}
$$

Observe that the left hand side is a degree 3 monic polynomial; hence, a non-zero polynomial. Since the reduction algorithm $\mathsf{R_{gen}}$ knows values of r and s, it is able to find all solutions for x in polynomial time. By checking $xG = X$, the reduction algorithm $\mathsf{R_{gen}}$ successfully finds a correct solution of the $\mathbf{BDL}_{\mathcal{G}}$. □

By combining with Lemmas 1, 2, and Theorem 5, we are able to obtain an information theoretic lower bound for the BDH.

Theorem 6 (Generic Hardness of BDH). *The bilinear Diffie-Hellman problem in Definition 11 is $(t^2/p, t)$-hard in the generic group model.*

4.3 Master Theorem in Bilinear Groups

In this subsection, we provide the following master theorem in bilinear groups to indicate the power of our technique.

Theorem 7 (Master Theorem in Bilinear Groups). $\mathbf{BDL}_{\mathcal{G}} \Rightarrow_{\mathsf{alg}}$ $\mathbf{GBDH}_{\mathcal{G}}$ *holds when the following conditions hold:*

(1) $\deg_{x_1,\ldots,x_m} f_i(x_1,\ldots,x_m,y_1,\ldots,y_n) \in \{0,1\}$ *for all* $i \in [k]$,
(2) $\deg_{x_1,\ldots,x_m} g_i(x_1,\ldots,x_m,y_1,\ldots,y_n) \in \{0,1,2\}$ *for all* $i \in [\ell]$,
(3) $\deg h(x_1,\ldots,x_m) > 2$.

Before providing a proof, we summarize the BDH and the ℓ-wBDHI which we studied in Sect. 4 and the conditions of Theorem 7 in Table 2. Since these problems do not take group elements in $\mathbb{G}_T$ as the input, we omit the condition (2) in the table. As the table shows, the BDH which we provided reductions satisfies the conditions (1) and (3) in Theorem 7. However, the ℓ-wBDHI does not satisfy the condition (1) for $\ell > 1$. Hence, as immediate corollary of the master theorem, we are able to provide generic and tight reductions from the BDL to the 1-wBDHI. In this paper, we are not able to provide a tailor-made reduction for ℓ-wBDHI for $\ell > 1$.

Table 2. Applicability of our technique in bilinear groups

Problem	$(f_i)_{i \in [k]}$	h	max deg f_i	deg h	Reduction?
BDH	$(x_i)_{i \in [3]}$	$x_1 x_2 x_3$	1	3	Yes
ℓ-wBDHI	$((x_1^i)_{i \in [\ell]}, x_2)$	$x_1^{\ell+1} x_2$	ℓ	$\ell + 2$	$\ell = 1$

Then, we show a proof of Theorem 7. In advance, we claim that the conditions (1) and (2) will be used to ensure that the reduction algorithm is able to produce all group elements of the GBDH during a reduction, while all the conditions (1), (2), and (3) will be used to ensure that the modular equation never becomes a zero polynomial.

Proof. We construct a generic and tight reduction algorithm R_{gen}. Specifically, the reduction algorithm R_{gen} uses an algebraic adversary A_{alg} on the **GBDH**$_\mathcal{G}$ only once and construct an algebraic adversary $\mathsf{B}_{alg} := \mathsf{R}_{gen}^{\mathsf{A}_{alg}}$ on the **BDL**$_\mathcal{G}$.

The reduction algorithm R_{gen} is given a bilinear group description $\mathcal{G} := (\mathbb{G}, \mathbb{G}_T, G, e, p)$ and an instance of the **BDL**$_\mathcal{G}$, i.e., $X := xG \in \mathbb{G}$ for an unknown $x \in \mathbb{Z}_p$. Then, the reduction algorithm R_{gen} creates an instance of the **GBDH**$_\mathcal{G}$ as follows: Pick random $(r_2,\ldots,r_m,s_1,\ldots,s_n) \xleftarrow{\$} \mathbb{Z}_p^{m+n-1}$ and compute

$$X_i := f_i(x_1,\ldots,x_m,y_1,\ldots,y_n)G \in \mathbb{G}$$

for all $i \in [k]$ and

$$Y_j := g_j(x_1,\ldots,x_m,y_1,\ldots,y_n)G \in \mathbb{G}_T$$

for all $j \in [\ell]$ by implicitly setting

$$(x_1,x_2,\ldots,x_m,y_1,\ldots,y_n) = (x, x + r_2,\ldots,x + r_m, s_1,\ldots,s_n).$$

The reduction algorithm R_{gen} is able to compute all the group elements thanks to the conditions (1) and (2). Then, the reduction algorithm R_{gen}

gives a bilinear group description $\mathcal{G} := (\mathbb{G}, \mathbb{G}_T, G, e, p)$ and group elements $(X_1, \ldots, X_k, Y_1, \ldots, Y_\ell) \in \mathbb{G}^k \times \mathbb{G}_T^\ell$ to $\mathsf{A}_{\mathsf{alg}}$. Observe that $(X_1, \ldots, X_k, Y_1, \ldots, Y_\ell)$ is a valid GBDH instance since $(x_2, \ldots, x_m)$ is independently distributed of x_1 to uniform in $\mathbb{Z}_p^{m-1}$ from $\mathsf{A}_{\mathsf{alg}}$'s view. Hence, an algebraic adversary $\mathsf{A}_{\mathsf{alg}}$ outputs a correct solution $[Z]_{\vec{z}}$ with an advantage $\mathsf{Adv}_{\mathcal{G},\mathsf{A}_{\mathsf{alg}}}^{\mathrm{GBDH}}$ and a running time $\mathsf{Time}_{\mathcal{G},\mathsf{A}_{\mathsf{alg}}}^{\mathrm{GBDH}}$.

Next, the reduction algorithm $\mathsf{R}_{\mathsf{gen}}$ uses $[Z]_{\vec{z}}$ outputted by an algebraic adversary $\mathsf{A}_{\mathsf{alg}}$ on the **GBDH**$_\mathcal{G}$ and computes a solution of the **BDL**$_\mathcal{G}$. Assume the output is a correct solution of the GBDH, i.e., $Z = h(x_1, \ldots, x_m, y_1, \ldots, y_n)G$. It holds with probability $\mathsf{Adv}_{\mathcal{G},\mathsf{A}_{\mathsf{alg}}}^{\mathrm{GBDH}}$. Then, the representation vector $\vec{z} :=$ $(z_0, (z_{ij})_{0 \leq i \leq j \leq k}, (z_i')_{1 \leq i \leq \ell})$ satisfies

$$e(G, G)^{h(x_1, \ldots, x_m, y_1, \ldots, y_n)}$$

$$= \left(\prod_{0 \leq i \leq j \leq k} e(X_i, X_j)^{z_{ij}} \right) \cdot \left(\prod_{1 \leq i \leq \ell} Y_i^{z_i'} \right)$$

$$= e(G, G)^{\sum_{0 \leq i \leq j \leq k} z_{ij} f_i(x_1, \ldots, x_m, y_1, \ldots, y_n) \cdot f_j(x_1, \ldots, x_m, y_1, \ldots, y_n)}$$

$$\cdot e(G, G)^{\sum_{i=1}^{\ell} z_i' g_i(x_1, \ldots, x_m, y_1, \ldots, y_n)}.$$

Hence, the reduction algorithm $\mathsf{R}_{\mathsf{gen}}$ obtains the following univariate equation modulo a prime p:

$$h(x, x + r_2, \ldots, x + r_m, s_1, \ldots, s_n)$$

$$= \sum_{0 \leq i \leq j \leq k} z_{ij} f_i(x, x + r_2, \ldots, x + r_m, s_1, \ldots, s_n)$$

$$\cdot f_j(x, x + r_2, \ldots, x + r_m, s_1, \ldots, s_n)$$

$$+ \sum_{i=1}^{\ell} z_i' g_i(x, x + r_2, \ldots, x + r_m, s_1, \ldots, s_n) \mod p.$$

Observe that a degree of the left and the right hand side with respect to a variable x is strictly larger than 2 and at most 2 respectively due to the conditions (1), (2), and (3). Hence, the modular equation never becomes a zero polynomial. Since the reduction algorithm $\mathsf{R}_{\mathsf{gen}}$ knows values of $(r_2, \ldots, r_m, s_1, \ldots, s_n)$, it is able to find all solutions for x in polynomial time. By checking $xG = X$, the reduction algorithm $\mathsf{R}_{\mathsf{gen}}$ successfully finds a correct solution of the **BDL**$_\mathcal{G}$. □

By combining with Lemmas 1, 2, and Theorem 7, we are able to obtain an information theoretic lower bound for the GBDH as follows.

Theorem 8 (Generic Hardness of GBDH). *The generalized bilinear Diffie-Hellman problem in Definition 13 is $(t^2/p, t)$-hard in the generic group model.*

5   DL to k-Lin Reduction

In this section, we provide a generic and tight reduction from the DL to the k-Lin$^{(1)}$ in an ad-hoc manner.

As described in Sect. 3.2, our master theorem (Theorem 3) does not capture the k-Lin$^{(1)}$ problem. The core trick of the above reduction for the CDH consists of the following two steps:

- embedding the DL solution x into group elements of the CDH instance (X_1, X_2),
- constructing a modular equation with a *non-zero* polynomial whose solution is x.

In particular, by following the same approach, we are not able to ensure that a modular equation becomes non-zero. For example, for simplicity we explain how the attempt fails for the 1-Lin$^{(1)}$. To provide a reduction from the DL to the 1-Lin$^{(1)}$ in the same way, we try to embed the DL solution x into x_1 *and/or* y_1 of the 1-Lin$^{(1)}$ instance. We note that the DL solution x cannot be embedded into x_1 *and* y_1, simultaneously. In particular, the reduction algorithm is not able to create group elements whose discrete logarithm have a term of x of degree 2, e.g., $x^2 G$. The intractability readily follows from the fact that the square DH is computationally equivalent to the DL.

Hence, we try to continue the approach by embedding the DL solution x into x_1 *or* y_1. When we embed x into x_1 and create a 1-Lin$^{(1)}$ instance $(X_1 = X, Y_1 = cX)$ by implicitly setting $(x_1, y_1) = (x, c)$ with a random $c \in \mathbb{Z}_p$, the 1-Lin$^{(1)}$ algorithm outputs $[Z]_{\tilde{z}}$ such that $Z = z_0 G + z_1 X_1 + z_2 Y_1$. When Z is a correct solution $Z = y_1 G$,

$$y_1 G = cG = z_0 G + z_1 X_1 + z_2 Y_1$$
$$= (z_0 + z_1 x + z_2 cx) G$$

holds and the reduction algorithm obtains a modular equation

$$c = z_0 + z_1 x + z_2 cx \mod p$$
$$\Leftrightarrow (z_1 + z_2 c)x + z_0 - c = 0 \mod p.$$

Observe that the left hand side is a zero polynomial when $z_1 + z_2 c = z_0 - c = 0$. Similarly, when we embed x into y_1 and create a 1-Lin$^{(1)}$ instance $(X_1 = cG, Y_1 = cX)$ by implicitly setting $(x_1, y_1) = (c, x)$ with a random $c \in \mathbb{Z}_p$,

$$y_1 G = xG = z_0 G + z_1 X_1 + z_2 Y_1$$
$$= (z_0 + z_1 c + z_2 cx) G$$

holds and the reduction algorithm obtains a modular equation

$$x = z_0 + z_1 c + z_2 cx \mod p$$
$$\Leftrightarrow (z_2 c - 1)x + z_0 + z_1 c = 0 \mod p.$$

Observe that the left hand side is a zero polynomial when $z_2 c - 1 = z_0 + z_1 c = 0$. Hence, the reduction algorithm may fail even when the 1-Lin$^{(1)}$ algorithm outputs a correct solution $Z = y_1 G$.

The reduction of the CDH (and our master theorem) avoids the problem by using the fact that the x_1 and x_2 which are the discrete logarithms of the input (X_1, X_2) are linear in x while $x_1 x_2$ which is the discrete logarithm of the CDH solution Z is quadratic in x. In other words, the resulting modular equation has to become a monic *non-zero* polynomial.

However, by modifying the approach, we are still able to provide a generic and tight reduction from the DL to the k-$\mathrm{Lin}^{(1)}$.

Theorem 9. $\mathbf{DL}_{\mathcal{G}} \Rightarrow_{\mathsf{alg}} k\text{-}\mathbf{Lin}_{\mathcal{G}}^{(1)}$.

Here, for simplicity we prove $\mathbf{DL}_{\mathcal{G}} \Rightarrow_{\mathsf{alg}} 1\text{-}\mathbf{Lin}_{\mathcal{G}}^{(1)}$. Note that there is a reduction from the 1-$\mathbf{Lin}_{\mathcal{G}}^{(1)}$ to the k-$\mathbf{Lin}_{\mathcal{G}}^{(1)}$ in the standard model. Hence, the proof for 1-$\mathbf{Lin}_{\mathcal{G}}^{(1)}$ is sufficient to prove Theorem 9.

Proof. We construct a generic and tight reduction algorithm $\mathsf{R}_{\mathsf{gen}}$. Specifically, the reduction algorithm $\mathsf{R}_{\mathsf{gen}}$ uses an algebraic adversary $\mathsf{A}_{\mathsf{alg}}$ on the 1-$\mathbf{Lin}_{\mathcal{G}}^{(1)}$ only once and construct an algebraic adversary $\mathsf{B}_{\mathsf{alg}} := \mathsf{R}_{\mathsf{gen}}^{\mathsf{A}_{\mathsf{alg}}}$ on the $\mathbf{DL}_{\mathcal{G}}$.

The reduction algorithm $\mathsf{R}_{\mathsf{gen}}$ is given a group description $\mathcal{G} := (\mathbb{G}, G, p)$ and an instance of the $\mathbf{DL}_{\mathcal{G}}$, i.e., $X := xG \in \mathbb{G}$ for an unknown $x \in \mathbb{Z}_p$. Then, the reduction algorithm $\mathsf{R}_{\mathsf{gen}}$ creates an instance of the 1-$\mathbf{Lin}_{\mathcal{G}}^{(1)}$ as follows: Pick random $c \xleftarrow{\$} \mathbb{Z}_p$ and compute

$$Y_1 := cG \in \mathbb{G},$$

then set

$$(X_1 := X, Y_1) \in \mathbb{G}^2.$$

The reduction algorithm $\mathsf{R}_{\mathsf{gen}}$ gives a group description $\mathcal{G} := (\mathbb{G}, G, p)$ and group elements $(X_1, Y_1) \in \mathbb{G}^2$ to $\mathsf{A}_{\mathsf{alg}}$. Observe that (X_1, Y_1) is a valid 1-$\mathrm{Lin}^{(1)}$ instance by implicitly setting

$$(x_1, y_1) = (x, c/x)$$

since y_1 is independently distributed of x_1 to uniform in $\mathbb{Z}_p$ from $\mathsf{A}_{\mathsf{alg}}$'s view. Hence, an algebraic adversary $\mathsf{A}_{\mathsf{alg}}$ outputs a correct solution $[Z]_{\vec{z}}$ with an advantage $\mathsf{Adv}_{\mathcal{G}, \mathsf{A}_{\mathsf{alg}}}^{1\text{-}\mathbf{Lin}^{(1)}}$ and a running time $\mathsf{Time}_{\mathcal{G}, \mathsf{A}_{\mathsf{alg}}}^{1\text{-}\mathbf{Lin}^{(1)}}$.

Next, the reduction algorithm $\mathsf{R}_{\mathsf{gen}}$ uses $[Z]_{\vec{z}}$ outputted by an algebraic adversary $\mathsf{A}_{\mathsf{alg}}$ on the 1-$\mathbf{Lin}_{\mathcal{G}}^{(1)}$ and computes a solution of the $\mathbf{DL}_{\mathcal{G}}$. Assume the output is a correct solution of the 1-$\mathrm{Lin}^{(1)}$, i.e., $Z = y_1 G$. It holds with probability $\mathsf{Adv}_{\mathcal{G}, \mathsf{A}_{\mathsf{alg}}}^{1\text{-}\mathbf{Lin}_{\mathcal{G}}^{(1)}}$. Then, the representation vector $\vec{z} := (z_0, z_1, z_2)$ satisfies

$$y_1 G = (c/x)G = z_0 G + z_1 X_1 + z_2 Y_1$$
$$= (z_0 + z_1 x + z_2 c)\, G$$

Hence, the reduction algorithm $\mathsf{R}_{\mathsf{gen}}$ obtains the following univariate equation modulo a prime p:

$$c/x = z_0 + z_1 x + z_2 c \mod p$$
$$\Leftrightarrow z_1 x^2 + (z_0 + z_2 c)x - c = 0 \mod p.$$

Observe that the left hand side is not a monic polynomial. However, it has to be a non-zero polynomial due to the constant term c. Since the reduction algorithm $\mathsf{R}_{\mathsf{gen}}$ knows values of c, it is able to find all solutions for x in polynomial time. By checking $xG = X$, the reduction algorithm $\mathsf{R}_{\mathsf{gen}}$ successfully finds a correct solution of the $\mathbf{DL}_{\mathcal{G}}$.   □

By combining with Lemmas 1, 2, and Theorem 9, we are able to obtain an information theoretic lower bound for the k-Lin$^{(2)}$.

Theorem 10 (Generic Hardness of k-$Lin^{(2)}$). *The computational k-linear problem in Definition 8 is $(t^2/p, t)$-hard in the generic group model.*

The DL to k-Lin$^{(1)}$ reduction implies that our master theorem is not perfect in the sense that there are other ways to provide reductions from the DL to the computational problems.

6   Conclusion

In this paper, we revisited the AGM which Fuchsbauer, Kiltz, and Loss [FKL18] gave a simple and clean definition to study the computational hardness of the CDH family. The AGM allows us to study the problem based on very simple arguments. Among their several results, we focused on the generic and tight reduction from the DL to the CDH. For the purpose, they used the square DH as the intermediate step. On the other hand, we provided the direct reduction from the DL to the CDH. We extended the approach and provided several reductions from the DL to the CDH variants in cyclic groups. By extending the definition of the AGM, we also studied the computational hardness of the BDH in the same way. Our approach was able to provide these reduction based on as simple arguments as Fuchsbauer et al.'s one. What is more, we formalized master theorems to indicate that to what kinds of computational problems can be reduced from the (B)DL by following our approach.

The additional contents of this paper may be more valuable. We claimed the limit of our master theorems by showing that we were not able to provide reductions for the standard computational variant of the k-Lin and the ℓ-wBDHI for $\ell > 1$ in the same way. We slightly modified our approach and provided a generic and tight reduction from the k-Lin to the DL in an ad-hoc manner. On the other hand, we were not able to provide such reductions for the ℓ-wBDHI.

Studying the CDH variants that were not studied in this paper is an arguably interesting topic (possibly variants which are not captured by our master theorems). One interesting open problem is formalizing a new master theorem to capture the reduction from the k-Lin to the DL simultaneously. Throughout this paper, we focused only on tight reductions so that the approach becomes as simple as possible. As opposed to our work, studying the computational hardness of CDH variants by allowing reasonable reduction loss should also be an interesting approach. The most important future directions of this work are extending the technique to *composite*-order groups and/or *decisional* problems.

Acknowledgement. We would like to thank anonymous reviewers of CT-RSA 2019 for their helpful comments and suggestions. This research was supported by JST CREST Grant Number JPMJCR14D6, Japan.

References

[BDZ03] Bao, F., Deng, R.H., Zhu, H.F.: Variations of diffie-hellman problem. In: Qing, S., Gollmann, D., Zhou, J. (eds.) ICICS 2003. LNCS, vol. 2836, pp. 301–312. Springer, Heidelberg (2003). https://doi.org/10.1007/978-3-540-39927-8_28

[Bis08] Biswas, G.: Diffie-Hellman technique: extended to multiple two-party keys and one multi-party key. IET Inf. Secur. **2**(1), 12–18 (2008)

[BB08] Boneh, D., Boyen, X.: Short signatures without random oracles and the SDH assumption in bilinear groups. J. Cryptol. **21**(2), 149–177 (2008)

[BBS04] Boneh, D., Boyen, X., Shacham, H.: Short group signatures. In: Franklin, M. (ed.) CRYPTO 2004. LNCS, vol. 3152, pp. 41–55. Springer, Heidelberg (2004). https://doi.org/10.1007/978-3-540-28628-8_3

[BF03] Boneh, D., Franklin, M.K.: Identity-based encryption from the weil pairing. SIAM J. Comput. **32**(3), 586–615 (2003)

[BL96] Boneh, D., Lipton, R.J.: Algorithms for black-box fields and their application to cryptography. In: Koblitz, N. (ed.) CRYPTO 1996. LNCS, vol. 1109, pp. 283–297. Springer, Heidelberg (1996). https://doi.org/10.1007/3-540-68697-5_22

[BV98] Boneh, D., Venkatesan, R.: Breaking RSA may not be equivalent to factoring. In: Nyberg, K. (ed.) EUROCRYPT 1998. LNCS, vol. 1403, pp. 59–71. Springer, Heidelberg (1998). https://doi.org/10.1007/BFb0054117

[Boy08] Boyen, X.: The uber-assumption family. In: Galbraith, S.D., Paterson, K.G. (eds.) Pairing 2008. LNCS, vol. 5209, pp. 39–56. Springer, Heidelberg (2008). https://doi.org/10.1007/978-3-540-85538-5_3

[BDS98] Burmester, M., Desmedt, Y., Seberry, J.: Equitable key escrow with limited time span (or, how to enforce time expiration cryptographically) extended abstract. In: Ohta, K., Pei, D. (eds.) ASIACRYPT 1998. LNCS, vol. 1514, pp. 380–391. Springer, Heidelberg (1998). https://doi.org/10.1007/3-540-49649-1_30

[DH76] Diffie, W., Hellman, M.E.: New directions in cryptography. IEEE Trans. Inf. Theory **22**(6), 644–654 (1976)

[EHK+17] Escala, A., Herold, G., Kiltz, E., Ràfols, C., Villar, J.L.: An algebraic framework for Diffie-Hellman assumptions. J. Cryptol. **30**(1), 242–288 (2017)

[FKL18] Fuchsbauer, G., Kiltz, E., Loss, J.: The algebraic group model and its applications. In: Shacham, H., Boldyreva, A. (eds.) CRYPTO 2018. LNCS, vol. 10992, pp. 33–62. Springer, Cham (2018). https://doi.org/10.1007/978-3-319-96881-0_2

[GG17] Ghadafi, E., Groth, J.: Towards a classification of non-interactive computational assumptions in cyclic groups. In: Takagi, T., Peyrin, T. (eds.) ASIACRYPT 2017. LNCS, vol. 10625, pp. 66–96. Springer, Cham (2017). https://doi.org/10.1007/978-3-319-70697-9_3

[Gor93] Gordon, D.M.: Discrete logarithms in GF(P) using the number field sieve. SIAM J. Discrete Math. **6**(1), 124–138 (1993)

[JS13] Jager, T., Schwenk, J.: On the analysis of cryptographic assumptions in the generic ring model. J. Cryptol. **26**(2), 225–245 (2013)

[Jou04] Joux, A.: A one round protocol for tripartite Diffie-Hellman. J. Cryptol. 17(4), 263–276 (2004)

[KSW13] Katz, J., Sahai, A., Waters, B.: Predicate encryption supporting disjunctions, polynomial equations, and inner products. J. Cryptol. 26(2), 191–224 (2013)

[KMS04] Konoma, C., Mambo, M., Shizuya, H.: Complexity analysis of the crypto-graphic primitive problems through square-root exponent. IEICE Trans. 87–A(5), 1083–1091 (2004)

[Mau05] Maurer, U.: Abstract models of computation in cryptography. In: Smart, N.P. (ed.) Cryptography and Coding 2005. LNCS, vol. 3796, pp. 1–12. Springer, Heidelberg (2005). https://doi.org/10.1007/11586821_1

[MW96] Maurer, U.M., Wolf, S.: Diffie-Hellman oracles. In: Koblitz, N. (ed.) CRYPTO 1996. LNCS, vol. 1109, pp. 268–282. Springer, Heidelberg (1996). https://doi.org/10.1007/3-540-68697-5_21

[MW98] Maurer, U., Wolf, S.: Lower bounds on generic algorithms in groups. In: Nyberg, K. (ed.) EUROCRYPT 1998. LNCS, vol. 1403, pp. 72–84. Springer, Heidelberg (1998). https://doi.org/10.1007/BFb0054118

[MW99] Maurer, U.M., Wolf, S.: The relationship between breaking the Diffie-Hellman protocol and computing discrete logarithms. SIAM J. Comput. 28(5), 1689–1721 (1999)

[MRV16] Morillo, P., Ràfols, C., Villar, J.L.: The Kernel Matrix Diffie-Hellman assumption. In: Cheon, J.H., Takagi, T. (eds.) ASIACRYPT 2016. LNCS, vol. 10031, pp. 729–758. Springer, Heidelberg (2016). https://doi.org/10.1007/978-3-662-53887-6_27

[Nac94] Nechaev, V.I.: Complexity of a determinate algorithm for the discrete loga-rithm. Math. Notes 55(2), 165–172 (1994)

[PV05] Paillier, P., Vergnaud, D.: Discrete-log-based signatures may not be equiva-lent to discrete log. In: Roy, B. (ed.) ASIACRYPT 2005. LNCS, vol. 3788, pp. 1–20. Springer, Heidelberg (2005). https://doi.org/10.1007/11593447_1

[PH78] Pohlig, S.C., Hellman, M.E.: An improved algorithm for computing loga-rithms over GF(p) and its cryptographic significance (corresp.). IEEE Trans. Inf. Theory 24(1), 106–110 (1978)

[Pol78] Pollard, J.: Monte carlo methods for index computation mod p. Math. Com-put. 32, 918–924 (1978)

[Sho97] Shoup, V.: Lower bounds for discrete logarithms and related problems. In: Fumy, W. (ed.) EUROCRYPT 1997. LNCS, vol. 1233, pp. 256–266. Springer, Heidelberg (1997). https://doi.org/10.1007/3-540-69053-0_18

Doubly Half-Injective PRGs for Incompressible White-Box Cryptography

Estuardo Alpirez Bock[1], Alessandro Amadori[2], Joppe W. Bos[3],
Chris Brzuska[1(✉)], and Wil Michiels[2,3]

[1] Aalto University, Helsinki, Finland
{estuardo.alpirezbock,brzuska}@aalto.fi
[2] Technische Universiteit Eindhoven, Eindhoven, The Netherlands
A.Amadori@tue.nl
[3] NXP Semiconductors, Eindhoven, The Netherlands
{joppe.bos,wil.michiels}@nxp.com

Abstract. White-box cryptography was originally introduced in the setting of digital rights management with the goal of preventing a user from illegally re-distributing their software decryption program. In recent years, mobile payment has become a popular new application for white-box cryptography. Here, white-box cryptography is used to increase the robustness against external adversaries (i.e., not the user) who aim to misuse/attack the cryptographic functionalities of the payment application. A necessary requirement for secure white-box cryptography is that an adversary cannot extract the embedded secret key from the implementation. However, a white-box implementation needs to fulfill further security properties in order to provide useful protection of an application. In this paper we focus on the popular property *incompressibility* that is a mitigation technique against code-lifting attacks. We provide an incompressible white-box encryption scheme based on the standard-assumption of one-way permutations whereas previous work used either public-key type assumptions or non-standard symmetric-type assumptions.

Keywords: White-box cryptography · Incompressibility · One-way permutations

1 Introduction

White-box cryptography was introduced by Chow, Eisen, Johnson and van Oorschot in 2002 in order to protect keys in symmetric ciphers when implemented in insecure or adversarially controlled environments [9,10]. The original proposal was motivated by Digital Rights Management (DRM), and white-box cryptography has been used in this context for many years. In recent years, mobile payment applications became popular and, originally, relied on secure

M. Matsui (Ed.): CT-RSA 2019, LNCS 11405, pp. 189–209, 2019.
https://doi.org/10.1007/978-3-030-12612-4_10

hardware that communicated via Near-Field Communication (NFC) (cf. NFC-based payment products by Mastercard, Visa and Google Wallet [38]). Android 4.4 added host-card emulation (HCE) which allows to implement the NFC protocols in software-only. Hereby, white-box cryptography has become an integral building block of mobile payment applications. Mastercard promotes the use of white-box cryptography in the payment applications that Mastercard certifies. i.e., the Mastercard security guidelines for payment applications make the use of white-box cryptography *mandatory* [30].

The wide-spread deployment of white-box cryptography stands in contrast with the state-of-the-art in white-box research. Currently, there are no long-term secure white-box implementations of standard ciphers in the academic literature. Proposed white-box constructions for both DES [10,29] and AES [8,9,26,40] have been subsequently broken by [21,25,39] and [3,28,32,33], respectively. Moreover, Bos, Hubain, Michiels, and Teuwen [7] and Sanfelix, de Haas and Mune [36] introduced Differential Computational Analysis (DCA) which is a generic approach to extract emebedded keys from a large class of white-box implementations *automatically*, i.e., without human reverse-engineering effort. As explained in [31], popular frameworks for implementing white-box cryptography are particularly vulnerable to such automated attacks.

In order to promote research on good candidates for white-box cryptography, CHES 2017 organized the white-box competition CHES 2017 Capture the Flag Challenge [13] to white-box AES-128. Unfortunately, all candidates were broken eventually. Most candidates lasted only 2 days, whereas some candidates resisted attacks for several weeks. Such a level of short-term security might already be useful, as long as the secret key and the white-box design can be updated on a regular basis. In light of these results, one might wonder whether there exists a long-term secure white-box implementation of AES. Short of being able to provide a practically secure white-box implementation of AES itself, we approach feasibility from the reduction-based approach in cryptography and aim to base secure white-box implementations on well-studied, symmetric assumptions. Whereas attacks usually focus on key extraction, positive feasibility results should aim for stronger, more useful security notions.

Definitions. Systematic definitional studies of security properties for white-box cryptography have been undertaken by Delerablée, Lepoint, Paillier, and Rivain (DLPR [11]) and Saxena, Wyseur, Preneel (SWP [37]). Some of the early definitions have been revisited and refined subsequently [4–6]. Beyond the modest goal of security against key extraction, those works cover desirable asymmetry properties: A white-box *en*cryption program should not allow to decrypt (confidentiality), and a white-box *de*cryption program should not allow to encrypt (integrity).

While asymmetry is a desirable property (and, in particular, implies security against key extraction), in practice, code-lifting attacks are more prevalent: Given a software cryptographic implementation with an embedded secret key, the adversary might simply copy the complete implementation and run it on its own device without the need to recover the embedded secret key. As a means to mitigate code-lifting attacks (and subsequently re-distribution attacks) most works discuss the notion of incompressibility. Additionally, DLPR also suggest traceability.

Incompressibility. Incompressibility aims to mitigate re-distribution attacks by building large-size white-box programs, which remain functional only in their complete form. As soon as the white-box program is compressed or fragments of the program are removed, the program loses its functionality. The intuitive justification of the usefulness of incompressibility is that if a decryption algorithm is several gigabytes large, then online re-distribution of that algorithm might not be feasible, reducing thus the chances of an adversary sharing the cryptographic code for unintended purposes. This approach is particularly useful for the case where one distributes a combination of software and hardware with large memory.

Constructions. DLPR and SWP show that public-key encryption schemes, considered as white-boxed symmetric encryption schemes, satisfy confidentiality. Interestingly, DLPR also show that the RSA function is incompressible when interpreted as a white-boxed cipher. Feasibility results are important, because they illustrate that the hardness of building a white-box version of AES does not hinge on a general impossibility of white-box encryption. In particular, the hardness of building a white-box version of AES is not subject to the general impossibility result for virtual black-box obfuscation shown in the seminal paper by Barak, Goldreich, Impagliazzo, Rudich, Sahai, Vadhan and Yang [1].

In a systematic analysis of the obstacles that white-box constructions for AES face, one might investigate the cryptographic tools and assumptions that are needed. At first sight, one might expect that white-boxing AES requires public-key type assumptions from Cryptomania (See Impagliazzo's survey on average-case complexity [22]) such as trapdoor functions. Indeed, if the white-boxed version of AES shall satisfy the same confidentiality guarantees as public-key encryption, then the oracle separation by Impagliazzo and Rudich [24] applies[1].

In turn, for less demanding notions such as incompressibility, it is conceivable that white-boxing can be based on symmetric-key type MiniCrypt assumptions alone. Indeed, an important step in that direction was made in a recent work by Fouque, Karpman, Kirchner and Minaud (FKKM [14]). FKKM present a symmetric-style cipher (i.e., a cipher that looks like a genuine cipher-design and is not built on public-key type assumptions) and show that the cipher admits an incompressible implementation, based on a novel symmetric-style assumption.

---

[1] It applies conceptually in the sense that AES is a pseudorandom permutation which is a MiniCrypt primitive that is equivalent to the existence of one-way functions. Strictly speaking, the security of AES is a much stronger assumption than merely the assumption of a one-way function, but it is fair to conjecture that one cannot turn AES into a secure public-key encryption scheme without gaining insights into the question for how to build public-key encryption from one-way functions generally.

In this work, we place feasibility of incompressible white-box cryptography fully in MiniCrypt. We provide a white-box encryption scheme and a white-box decryption scheme, whose incompressibility is based on the assumption of a one-way permutation (See Sect. 4 for a more detailed comparison between our construction and the construction by FKKM).

Summary of Contribution. We contribute to the foundations of white-box cryptography by showing that incompressible white-box encryption and decryption schemes can be built based on the assumption of one-way permutations only thereby placing incompressible white-box cryptography fully in MiniCrypt.

Taking a step back, solid definitions as well as feasibility results and impossibility for white-box cryptography are needed to clarify whether it is realistic to pursue the goal of building white-box cryptography with useful long-term security properties, with reasonable efficiency, based on standard assumptions. As the CHES Capture the Flag Challenge 2017 demonstrates, providing a secure white-box implementation of AES is tremendously difficult, and thus obtaining a solid understanding of the feasibility and limits of white-box cryptography is needed rather urgently. Our results take a step towards such an understanding and we encourage further studies on the foundations of white-box cryptography.

2   Preliminaries and Notation

1^n denotes the security parameter in unary notation. Given a bit string x, we denote by $x[j : i]$ the bits j to i of the bit string x. end denotes the index of the last bit. By $a||b$ we denote the concatenation of two bit strings a and b. For a program P, we denote by $|P|$ its bit-size. We leave the choice of encoding of the program implicit in this work. U_n denotes the uniform distribution over strings of length n.

By $\leftarrow$, we denote the execution of a deterministic algorithm while $\leftarrow_\$$ denotes the execution of a randomized algorithm. We denote by $:=$ the process of initializing a set, e.g. $S := \emptyset$, while $\leftarrow_\$$ denotes the process of randomly sampling an element from a given set, e.g. $x \leftarrow_\$ \{0, 1\}^n$. When sampling x according to the probability distribution X, we denote the probability that the event $F(x) = 1$ happens by $\Pr_{x \leftarrow_\$ X}[F(x)]$. We sometimes use $\circ$ for function composition, i.e. $g \circ f(x)$ is the same as $g(f(x))$. The latter notation is helpful to make terms easier to parse when many functions are composed, as in the standard notation, each function application introduces a layer of brackets. We write oracles as superscript to the adversary $\mathcal{A}^O$.

Definition 1. *A symmetric encryption scheme ξ consists of three polynomial-time algorithms* (Kgen, Enc, Dec) *such that* Kgen *and* Enc *are probabilistic polynomial-time algorithms (PPT), and* Dec *is deterministic. The algorithms have the syntax* $k \leftarrow_\$ \text{Kgen}(1^n)$, $c \leftarrow_\$ \text{Enc}(1^n, k, m)$ *and* $m \leftarrow \text{Dec}(1^n, k, c)$. *Moreover, the encryption scheme ξ satisfies* Correctness, *i.e., for all messages* $m \in \{0, 1\}^*$,

$$\Pr[\text{Dec}(k, \text{Enc}(k, m)) = m] = 1 \tag{1}$$

where the probability is over the randomness of Enc *and* $k \leftarrow_{\$} \mathsf{Kgen}(1^n)$.

Remark. To clarify wording (as scientific communities vary in their terminology), we consider a *cipher* a deterministic algorithm that is a *building block* for an encryption scheme, but is not an encryption scheme itself. That is, AES is a cipher, not an encryption scheme, while, e.g., AES-CBC or AES-GCM are symmetric encryption schemes. All algorithms receive the security parameter 1^n as input. For ease of notation, we omit the security parameter for the rest of the article.

We now include the definition of authenticated encryption. We use an indistinguishability definition of authenticated encryption that encodes both, the ciphertext integrity and the indistinguishability under chosen plaintext attacks (IND-CPA). Bellare and Namprempre [2] show that if a symmetric encryption scheme provides ciphertext integrity and IND-CPA security, then it is also indistinguishable under chosen ciphertext attacks (IND-CCA). We refer to their article as well as to Krawczyk [27] for more background on authenticated encryption.

Definition 2 (Authenticated encryption (AE)). *A symmetric encryption scheme* se $=$ (AKgen, AEnc, ADec) *is an authenticated encryption scheme (AE-secure) if for all adversaries* $\mathcal{A}$, *the advantage*

$$\left| \Pr\left[\mathsf{EXP}_{AE}^{\mathcal{A},\mathsf{se}}(1^n) = 1 \right] - \tfrac{1}{2} \right|$$

is negligible.

$\mathsf{EXP}_{AE}^{\mathcal{A},\mathsf{se}}(1^n)$	$\mathrm{ENC}(m)$	$\mathrm{DEC}(c)$
$k \leftarrow_{\$} \mathsf{AKgen}(1^n)$	**if** $b = 0$	**if** $b = 0$
$b \leftarrow_{\$} \{0,1\}$	$\quad c \leftarrow_{\$} \mathsf{AEnc}(k,m)$	$\quad$ **if** $c \notin C$
$b^* \leftarrow_{\$} \mathcal{A}^{\mathsf{ENC,DEC}}(1^n)$	**if** $b = 1$	$\quad\quad m \leftarrow \mathsf{ADec}(k,c)$
return $(b = b^*)$	$\quad c \leftarrow_{\$} \mathsf{AEnc}(k,0^{|m|})$	$\quad\quad$ **return** m
	$C \leftarrow C \cup \{c\}$	**return** $\perp$
	return c	

2.1 Syntax of White-Box Cryptography

Definition 3 (White-Box Encryption Scheme). *A white-box encryption scheme* WBEnc *consists of four probabilistic polynomial-time algorithms* (Kgen, Enc, Dec, Comp), *where* (Kgen, Enc, Dec) *is a symmetric encryption scheme and* Comp *is a publicly known (possibly) randomized compiling algorithm that takes as input the symmetric key* k *and generates a (probabilistic) white-box encryption algorithm* $\mathsf{Enc}_{\mathsf{WB}}$.

$$\mathsf{Enc}_{\mathsf{WB}} \leftarrow_{\$} \mathsf{Comp}(k) \tag{2}$$

For all messages $m \in \{0,1\}^*$, *the randomized program* $\mathtt{Enc_{WB}}(m)$ *produces a distribution that is statistically close to the distribution of the randomized program* $\mathtt{Enc}(k,m)$. *Moreover, the following* correctness *property holds. For all messages* $m \in \{0,1\}^*$,

$$\Pr[\mathtt{Dec}(k, \mathtt{Enc_{WB}}(m)) = m] = 1, \tag{3}$$

where the probability is over the randomness of $\mathtt{Enc_{WB}}$ *and* $k \leftarrow_\$ \mathtt{Kgen}(1^n)$.

Remark. One can use $\mathtt{Enc}(k,\cdot)$ as well as $\mathtt{Enc_{WB}}(\cdot)$ to encrypt a message under key k. Both programs require randomness, and an honest user can provide the program $\mathtt{Enc_{WB}}(\cdot)$ with uniform randomness to generate a secure distribution of ciphertexts. We will not mention this feature again, as the security properties covered in this paper are concerned with the case that the owner of $\mathtt{Enc_{WD}}(\cdot)$ misbehaves. Note that we only demand statistical closeness between $\mathtt{Enc}(k,\cdot)$ and $\mathtt{Enc_{WB}}(\cdot)$ and not full functional equivalence, as notions such as traceability benefit from flexibility on the functionality requirement.

We now define a white-box decryption scheme analogously that produces a white-box of the decryption algorithm rather than the encryption algorithm. Note that in the case of white-box *encryption*, there is a ciphertext *distribution* for each message m. In turn, in the case of white-box *decryption*, for each ciphertext c, there is merely a single plaintext. Therefore, for white-box *decryption*, no requirement on statistical closeness is needed beyond correctness.

Definition 4 (White-Box Decryption Scheme). *A white-box decryption scheme* WBDec *consists of four probabilistic polynomial-time algorithms* $(\mathtt{Kgen}, \mathtt{Enc}, \mathtt{Dec}, \mathtt{Comp})$, *where* $(\mathtt{Kgen}, \mathtt{Enc}, \mathtt{Dec})$ *is a symmetric encryption scheme and* Comp *is a publicly known (possibly) randomized compiling algorithm that takes as input the symmetric key* k *and generates a white-box decryption program* $\mathtt{Dec_{WB}}$, *such that for all messages* $m \in \{0,1\}^*$,

$$\Pr[\mathtt{Dec_{WB}}(\mathtt{Enc}(k,m)) = m] = 1, \tag{4}$$

where the probability is over the randomness of $k \leftarrow_\$ \mathtt{Kgen}(1^n)$, $\mathtt{Dec_{WB}} \leftarrow_\$ \mathtt{Comp}(k)$ *and* $\mathtt{Enc}(k,\cdot)$.

3   Definitions

Incompressibility aims to make redistribution attacks harder by making the white-box program too large to distribute. The first formalization of incompressibility was given by DLPR, and the notion has been adopted and studied in several subsequent works [4,5,14]. We adopt the incompressibility notion by DLPR with minor modifications: DLPR consider deterministic ciphers, while we consider randomized encryption schemes. Therefore, our correctness requirement will ask to produce decryptable ciphertexts rather than ciphertexts that are equal to a target value, as can be defined for deterministic ciphers. Moreover, we will add an encryption oracle for sake of completeness. As the adversary has a white-box encryption algorithm, the adversary can emulate the encryption oracle up to statistical distance and thus, our modification is merely esthetic.

In the (δ, λ)-incompressibility game, conceptually, there are two collaborating adversaries. One is the adversary $\mathcal{A}$ that is given a white-box encryption program $\mathsf{Enc_{WB}}$ and outputs some smaller value Com. The second collaborating adversary is the decompression algorithm Decomp that will try to decompress Com. The winning condition says that the pair of adversaries is successful if

(i) Com is shorter than $\mathsf{Enc_{WB}}$ by λ bits *and*
(ii) the probability that the decompressed program $\mathsf{Decomp(Com)}$ produces a valid ciphertext (i.e., a ciphertext that decrypts correctly) for a random message $m \in \{0,1\}^n$ is greater than δ.

Definition 5 (Incompressibility). *A white-box encryption scheme WBEnc is INC-(δ, λ)-secure if for all PPT adversaries $\mathcal{A}$, the success probability*

$$\left| \Pr\left[\mathsf{EXP}^{\mathcal{A}, WBEnc}_{INC\text{-}(\delta,\lambda)} = 1 \right] \right|$$

is negligible, where the experiment $\mathsf{EXP}^{\mathcal{A}, WBEnc}_{INC\text{-}(\delta,\lambda)}$ *is defined as follows:*

$\mathit{EXP}^{\mathcal{A}, WBEnc}_{INC\text{-}(\delta, \lambda)}$	$\mathsf{RCA}()$	
$k \leftarrow_\$ \mathsf{Kgen}(1^n)$	$\mathsf{Enc'_{WB}} \leftarrow_\$ \mathsf{Comp}(k)$	
$\mathsf{Enc_{WB}} \leftarrow_\$ \mathsf{Comp}(k)$	return $\mathsf{Enc'_{WB}}$	
$\mathsf{Com} \leftarrow_\$ \mathcal{A}^{\mathsf{RCA},\mathsf{ENC},\mathsf{DEC}}(\mathsf{Enc_{WB}})$		
if $\Pr_{m \leftarrow_\$ \{0,1\}^*}[\mathsf{Dec}(k, \mathsf{Decomp(Com)}(m)) = m] \geq \delta$	$\mathsf{ENC}(m)$	$\mathsf{DEC}(c)$
and if $|\mathsf{Com}| \leq |\mathsf{Enc_{WB}}| - \lambda$	$c \leftarrow_\$ \mathsf{Enc}(k, m)$	$m \leftarrow \mathsf{Dec}(k, c)$
return 1	return c	return m
else return 0		

Incompressibility for White-Box Decryption. The definition of incompressibility for white-box decryption is analogous to Definition 5, except that in the former, the compression attack targets a white-box decryption algorithm $\mathsf{WBDec_{WB}}$ and thus, the winning condition is $\Pr_{m \leftarrow_\$ \{0,1\}^*}[\mathsf{Decomp(Com)}(\mathsf{Enc}(k, (m))) = m] \geq \delta$, where the randomness is over m and Enc.

Definition 6. *A white-box decryption scheme WBDec is INC-(δ, λ)-secure if for all PPT adversaries $\mathcal{A}$, the advantage*

$$\left| \Pr\left[\mathsf{EXP}^{\mathcal{A}, WBDec}_{INC\text{-}(\delta,\lambda)} = 1 \right] \right|$$

is negligible, where the experiment $\mathsf{EXP}^{\mathcal{A}, WBDec}_{INC\text{-}(\delta,\lambda)}$ *is defined as follows:*

$\underline{\mathsf{EXP}^{\mathcal{A}, WBDec}_{INC\text{-}(\delta, \lambda)}}$

$k \leftarrow_{\$} \mathsf{Kgen}(1^n)$

$\mathsf{Dec}_{\mathsf{WB}} \leftarrow_{\$} \mathsf{Comp}(k)$

$\mathsf{Com} \leftarrow_{\$} \mathcal{A}^{\mathsf{RCA},\mathsf{ENC},\mathsf{DEC}}(\mathsf{Dec}_{\mathsf{WB}})$

if $\Pr_{m \leftarrow_{\$} \mathcal{M}}[\mathsf{Decomp}(\mathsf{Com})(\mathsf{Enc}(k, m)) = m] \geq \delta$

$\wedge |\mathsf{Com}| \leq |\mathsf{Dec}_{\mathsf{WB}}| - \lambda$

return 1

else return 0

$\underline{\mathsf{RCA}()}$

$\mathsf{Dec}'_{\mathsf{WB}} \leftarrow_{\$} \mathsf{Comp}(k)$

return $\mathsf{Dec}'_{\mathsf{WB}}$

$\underline{\mathsf{ENC}(m)} \qquad \underline{\mathsf{DEC}(c)}$

$c \leftarrow_{\$} \mathsf{Enc}(k, m) \qquad m \leftarrow \mathsf{Dec}(k, c)$

return $c \qquad\qquad$ return m

4   Constructions of White-Box Cryptography

In this section, we first discuss existing white-box constructions and then present our own construction with a security reduction for (δ, λ)-incompressibility, assuming one-way permutations.

4.1   Existing Constructions

The white-box implementations of standardized cryptographic primitives that have been published in [8–10, 26, 29, 40] unfortunately turned out insecure with respect to key extraction (see e.g. [7, 36]). In turn, more recent works [5, 6, 11] follow different approaches to construct white-box implementations for alternative (non-standardized) primitives. In [11, Sect. 6], DLPR build a white-box encryption scheme based on a public-key encryption scheme which is secure under their security notions of one-wayness under chosen plaintext attacks and incompressibility. Their implementation is based on the RSA cryptosystem [35]. They first consider the RSA cryptosystem as a symmetric cipher and then use the asymmetric properties of RSA to prove the white-box properties. Likewise, SWP [37] show that public-key encryption systems can first be interpreted as a symmetric encryption algorithm, so that one can then use the asymmetric properties to argue about IND-CPA and IND-CCA security.

Bogdanov and Isobe [5] propose a family of *white-box secure block ciphers* called SPACE, and Bogdanov, Isobe and Tischhauser [6] present an improvement of these designs called SPNbox. The authors claim that these designs are secure under their models for *weak* and *strong space hardness*, a variant of the DLPR model for incompressibility. Their designs are notable in that they present the first symmetric-style construction for an incompressible white-box encryption scheme. The security of their design is based on symmetric cryptanalysis techniques. In turn, a recent construction by FKKM [14] comes with a security reduction. The reduction reduces incompressibility to a novel symmetric-style assumption. Our construction below will improve upon FKKM by moving to the (symmetric) standard-assumption of one-way permutations. Another difference between FKKM and our construction is that FKKM restricted the adversary to return bits of the key rather than arbitrary strings. Such a restriction, potentially, could enable expansion via secret-sharing, which is highly compressible when allowing for arbitrary compression algorithms. We remove this restriction.

4.2 Incompressible Constructions for White-Box Encryption

In this subsection, we provide an incompressible white-box encryption scheme and an incompressible white-box decryption scheme. We start by introducing our main tool, namely a pseudorandom function that admits a computationally (δ, λ)-incompressible implementation. Then we show that if a PRF admits a computationally (δ, λ)-incompressible implementation, then there is a $(\delta, \lambda - o(1))$-incompressible white-box encryption scheme and a $(\delta, \lambda - o(1))$-incompressible decryption scheme. Finally, we construct a computationally incompressible PRF, assuming one-way permutations. Jumping ahead, we note that our incompressible PRF construction makes use of a length-doubling, doubly half-injective pseudorandom generator, a new tool that we introduce and construct in this work, based on one-way permutations.

Computationally Incompressible Pseudorandom Functions. In the following, we consider PRFs whose message and key length are identical, unless stated explicitly otherwise.

Definition 7 (PRF-implementation). *Let f be a PRF. We call a pair of deterministic polynomial-time algorithms $(F, \mathsf{Comp}_{\mathsf{PRF}})$ an implementation of the PRF f with expansion α if the following hold:*

Key Expansion. $\forall k \in \{0,1\}^* \; |K| = \alpha \cdot |k|$, *where* $K = \mathsf{Comp}_{\mathsf{PRF}}(k)$.
Functionality-preservation. $\forall k \in \{0,1\}^* \; \forall x \in \{0,1\}^{|k|} f(k,x) = F(K,x)$, *where* $K = \mathsf{Comp}_{\mathsf{PRF}}(k)$.

Definition 8 (computational PRF-incompressibility). *An implementation $(F, \mathsf{Comp}_{\mathsf{PRF}})$ of a PRF f with expansion factor α is called computationally (δ, λ)-incompressible, if the following hold:*

Pseudorandomness. $\mathsf{Comp}_{\mathsf{PRF}}(U_n)$ *is computationally indistinguishable from* $U_{\alpha n}$.
Incompressibility. *For any PPT computable leakage function* Leak *and any PPT computable adversary $\mathcal{S}$, it holds that, if $|\mathsf{Leak}(U_{\alpha n})| \leq \alpha n - \lambda$, then the probability that the experiment $\$\text{-}PRF\text{-}INC^{\mathsf{Leak}, \mathcal{S}}$ returns 1 is less than δ.*

$\$\text{-}PRF\text{-}INC^{\mathsf{Leak}, \mathcal{S}}$	$PRF\text{-}INC^{\mathsf{Leak}, \mathcal{S}}$
	$k \leftarrow_\$ \{0,1\}^n$
$K \leftarrow_\$ U_{\alpha n}$	$K \leftarrow \mathsf{Comp}_{\mathsf{PRF}}(k)$
$\mathsf{aux} \leftarrow_\$ \mathsf{Leak}(K)$	$\mathsf{aux} \leftarrow_\$ \mathsf{Leak}(K)$
$x \leftarrow_\$ \{0,1\}^n$	$x \leftarrow_\$ \{0,1\}^n$
$y \leftarrow_\$ \mathcal{S}(\mathsf{aux}, x)$	$y \leftarrow_\$ \mathcal{S}(\mathsf{aux}, x)$
return $(y \overset{?}{=} F(K, x))$	**return** $(y \overset{?}{=} F(K, x))$

In the \$-PRF-INC$^{\mathrm{Leak},\mathcal{S}}$ game, the key K is not generated via $\mathsf{Comp_{PRF}}$, but sampled randomly from the distribution $U_{\alpha n}$. The leakage function Leak outputs several bits of information of K, which are saved in aux. The adversary $\mathcal{S}$ tries to compute the value y by using aux instead of the complete key K. The following claim states that due to the pseudorandomness of the key, the success probability of the adversary in the PRF incompressibility game \$-PRF-INC$^{\mathrm{Leak},\mathcal{S}}$ does not depend (except for a negligible amount) on whether the game uses a real key or a random key. The statement follows directly from the pseudorandomness property of $(F, \mathsf{Comp_{PRF}})$.

Claim 1. *Let f be a PRF. If $(F, \mathsf{Comp_{PRF}})$ is a (δ, λ)-incompressible implementation of the PRF f, then for any PPT computable leakage function Leak and any PPT computable adversary $\mathcal{S}$, it holds that, if $|\mathsf{Leak}(U_{\alpha n})| \leq \alpha n - \lambda$, then the probability that the experiment PRF-INC$^{\mathrm{Leak},\mathcal{S}}$ returns 1 is at most negligibly greater than δ.*

An Incompressible White-Box Encryption Scheme. We now use an incompressible PRF to construct an incompressible white-box encryption scheme. Hereby, we focus on integrity features, i.e., the hardness of producing valid ciphertexts from a compressed algorithm. We achieve this via a message authentication code (MAC) which is generated using the large key K. Additionally, our construction achieves confidentiality via an authenticated encryption scheme which makes use of a small key k'' for encrypting the plaintext and MAC. Since the key k'' is very short in comparison to K, it does not affect the incompressibility of our scheme significantly. An authenticated encryption scheme is a symmetric encryption scheme that satisfies ciphertext integrity and indistinguishability under chosen plaintext attacks. For simplicity, in the following, we assume an authenticated encryption scheme whose key generation algorithm AKgen samples uniformly random keys of the same length as the security parameter.

Construction 1 (incompressible white-box encryption scheme). *Let $(\mathsf{AKgen}, \mathsf{AEnc}, \mathsf{ADec})$ be an authenticated encryption scheme. Let f be a PRF and let $(F, \mathsf{Comp_{PRF}})$ be an implementation of f with expansion factor α. We construct $WBEnc = (\mathsf{Kgen}, \mathsf{Enc}, \mathsf{Dec}, \mathsf{Comp})$ as given in Fig. 1.*

Theorem 1 (Incompressibility). *If PRF f admits a computationally (δ, λ)-incompressible implementation F, then white-box encryption scheme WBEnc in Construction 1 is a $(\delta, \lambda - n - o(1))$-incompressible white-box encryption scheme.*

Proof. Given a pair of adversaries $(\mathcal{A}, \mathsf{Decomp})$ against (δ, λ)-incompressibility, we need to construct a pair of adversaries $(\mathsf{Leak}, \mathcal{S})$ against the $(\delta, \lambda - n - o(1))$-incompressibility of the PRF implementation F. The adversary Leak receives as input the key K, then draws a key k'', builds $\mathsf{Enc_{WB}}$ as $C[K, k'']$ and runs $\mathcal{A}$ on $\mathsf{Enc_{WB}}$. The adversary Leak then emulates the oracles that $\mathcal{A}$ expects as follows: Comp is a deterministic algorithm and thus, the recompilation algorithm would always return the same program $\mathsf{Enc_{WB}}$ to $\mathcal{A}$ and so does Leak. Likewise, $\mathsf{Enc_{WB}}(\cdot)$

$\mathsf{Kgen}(1^n)$	$\mathsf{Enc}(k, m)$	$\mathsf{Dec}(k, c)$
$k' \leftarrow_\$ \{0,1\}^n$	$k' \leftarrow k[0 : n-1]$	$k' \leftarrow k[0 : n-1]$
$k'' \leftarrow_\$ \{0,1\}^n$	$k'' \leftarrow k[n : 2n-1]$	$k'' \leftarrow k[n : 2n-1]$
$k \leftarrow k'\|k''$	$t \leftarrow f(k', m)$	$\tau \leftarrow \mathsf{ADec}(k'', c)$
return k	$\tau \leftarrow (m, t)$	$(m, t) \leftarrow \tau$
	$c \leftarrow_\$ \mathsf{AEnc}(k'', \tau)$	**if** $t = f(k', m)$ **return** m.
	return c	**else return** $\bot$

$\mathsf{Comp}(k)$	$C[K, k''](m)$
$k' \leftarrow k[0 : n-1]$	$t \leftarrow F(K, m)$
$k'' \leftarrow k[n : 2n-1]$	$\tau \leftarrow (m, t)$
$K := \mathsf{Comp}_{\mathsf{PRF}}(k')$	$c \leftarrow_\$ \mathsf{AEnc}(k'', \tau)$
$\mathsf{Enc}_{\mathsf{WB}} := C[K, k''](.)$	**return** c
return $\mathsf{Enc}_{\mathsf{WB}}$	

Fig. 1. Construction: incompressible white-box encryption scheme based on PRF f and an authenticated encryption scheme.

and $\mathsf{Enc}(k, \cdot)$ are functionally equivalent, and thus, Leak can perfectly emulate $\mathsf{Enc}(k, \cdot)$ by running $\mathsf{Enc}_{\mathsf{WB}}(\cdot)$. Finally, to emulate the decryption oracle, the adversary Leak computes a function that is functionally equivalent to $\mathsf{Dec}(k, \cdot)$ as follows: On input a ciphertext (m, t), the adversary Leak first decrypts using k'' and then re-computes the PRF on the message m, using K, and checks whether the value is equal to t. If yes, Leak returns m. Else, Leak returns $\bot$ to the adversary. Eventually, $\mathcal{A}$ produces some output Com that Leak outputs together with k'', i.e., $\mathsf{aux} := (\mathsf{Com}, k'')$.

Finally, we need to construct the adversary $\mathcal{S}$ from the algorithm Decomp. Given the leakage aux and a value x, the adversary $\mathcal{S}$ runs Decomp on aux and obtains a ciphertext c that is an encryption of a pair (x, t) under k''. $\mathcal{S}$ decrypts c using k'' and returns t.

Analysis. Note that $\mathsf{Enc}_{\mathsf{WB}}$, encoded as a Turing machine, is a constant number of bits larger than K and thus, a compressing adversary can strip off those additional bits needed for the Turing machine encoding whence the loss of a constant in λ. By the winning condition of (δ, λ)-incompressibility, $\mathcal{S}$ returns the correct PRF value if and only if $\mathsf{Decomp}(\mathsf{Com})$ returns a ciphertext that decrypts to the correct message. Thus, if $(\mathcal{A}, \mathsf{Decomp})$ satisfies the winning condition with probability greater than δ, so does $(\mathsf{Leak}, \mathcal{S})$. $\square$

In the next subsection, we present a white-box decryption scheme based on an incompressible PRF. Afterwards, in Sect. 5, we construct an incompressible PRF.

4.3   An Incompressible White-Box Decryption Scheme

For constructing a white-box decryption scheme we focus on the hardness of recovering the message from the ciphertext. Note that analogous to our encryption scheme presented in Construction 1, our decryption scheme can be augmented by adding an authenticated encryption scheme with a comparatively short key on top of it and thus upgrade it to a full authenticated decryption scheme.

Construction 2 (incompressible white-box decryption scheme). *Let f be a PRF and let $(F, \mathsf{Comp}_{\mathsf{PRF}})$ be an implementation of f with expansion factor α. We construct $\mathsf{WBDec} = (\mathsf{Kgen}, \mathsf{Enc}, \mathsf{Dec}, \mathsf{Comp})$ as given in Fig. 2.*

$\mathsf{Kgen}(1^n)$	$\mathsf{Enc}(k, m)$	$\mathsf{Dec}(k, c)$	$\mathsf{Comp}(k)$	$C[K](c)$
$k \leftarrow_\$ \{0,1\}^*$	$r \leftarrow_\$ \{0,1\}^{|k|}$	$(r, p) \leftarrow c$	$K := \mathsf{Comp}_{\mathsf{PRF}}(k)$	$(r, p) \leftarrow c$
return k	$\mathsf{pad} \leftarrow f(k, r)$	$\mathsf{pad} \leftarrow f(k, r)$	$\mathsf{Dec}_{\mathsf{WB}} := C[K](.)$	$\mathsf{pad} \leftarrow F(K, m)$
	$p \leftarrow m \oplus \mathsf{pad}$	$m \leftarrow p \oplus \mathsf{pad}$	**return** $\mathsf{Dec}_{\mathsf{WB}}$	$m \leftarrow p \oplus \mathsf{pad}$
	$c \leftarrow (r, p)$	**return** m		**return** m
	return c			

Fig. 2. Construction of an incompressible white-box decryption scheme based on a PRF f.

Theorem 2 (Incompressibility). *If a PRF f admits a computationally (δ, λ)-incompressible implementation F, then the white-box decryption scheme WBDec in Construction 2 is a $(\delta, \lambda - o(1))$-incompressible white-box decryption scheme.*

The proof is analogous to the proof of Theorem 1 and thus omitted.

5   Incompressible PRFs from OWPs

The main theorem that we will prove in this section is the following.

Theorem 3. *Assume that one-way permutations exist. Let α be a function in the security parameter n such that for all n, $\alpha(n) > n$ and such that for all n, $\alpha(n)$ is a power of 2. Then, there exists a PRF with a (δ, λ)-incompressible implementation with $\delta = 1 - \frac{\lambda_n}{\alpha} + \mathsf{negl}(n)$, where λ_n is the largest integer such that $n \cdot \lambda_n \leq \lambda$.*

We now construct the incompressible PRF that instantiates this theorem. The writing style of this section is aimed at the parts of the cryptographic community that are familiar with the reduction-based approach to cryptography, see e.g., Goldreich's textbooks on the foundations of cryptography for an excellent introduction [17,18]. Recall that we want to construct a PRF that has its standard small key as well as a much larger, pseudorandom key that cannot be compressed. Towards this goal, we consider the PRF construction by Goldreich, Goldwasser and Micali (GGM [19]). Recall that the GGM idea is to iterate a PRG within a tree structure, where the paths within the tree is determined by the bits of the PRF input x. That is, let g be a length-doubling PRG and let g_0 be its left half and g_1 be its right half. If k is the PRF key, then the GGM PRF is computed as follows:

$$\mathsf{GGM}(k,x) := g_{x[|x|]}g_{x[|x|-1]} \circ \cdots \circ g_{x[3]} \circ g_{x[2]} \circ g_{x[1]}(k)$$

We now provide an incompressible implementation of the GGM PRF.

Construction 3. *The expansion factor of this incompressible implementation of the GGM PRF is $\alpha = 2^\ell$. For $0 \leq j \leq 2^\ell - 1$, the notation $<j>$ refers to the ℓ-bit string that encodes j in binary.*

$f(k,x)$	$\mathsf{Comp}_{\mathsf{PRF}}(k)$	$F(K,x)$
$y \leftarrow \mathsf{GGM}(k,x)$	**for** j **from** 0 **to** $2^\ell - 1$	$(x[1...\ell], x[\ell+1...|x|]) \leftarrow x$
return y	$k_j := \mathsf{GGM}(k, <j>)$	$j \leftarrow x[1...\ell]$
	$K \leftarrow k_0||...||k_{2^\ell - 1}$	$y \leftarrow \mathsf{GGM}(k_j, x[\ell+1...|x|])$
	return K	**return** y.

Fig. 3. Construction of an incompressible implementation of the GGM PRF.

For Construction 3, the key expansion property is clear, and the pseudorandomness property follows from the PRF property of the GGM construction. We thus focus on showing incompressibility properties of Construction 3. To do so, intuitively, one needs to argue that if one loses one bit of the key k_j, then one loses one bit of information about *all* PRF values that are located in the corresponding branch of the GGM PRF (which corresponds to evaluations of messages that start by $<j>$. Unfortunately, such a tight connection might not hold generally. Imagine, e.g., the case, that the PRG in the GGM construction ignores one half of its input and only expands the other half of the input hugely. Likewise, it might be the case that certain bits of the input only affect the left half of the output or the right part of the input. To avoid both of those bad properties, we will consider a PRG that is both, left-half injective and right-half injective. We call such a PRG a doubly half-injective pseudorandom generator (DPRG).

Definition 9 (Doubly Half-Injective Pseudorandom Generator). *A doubly half-injective pseudorandom generator (DPRG) is a deterministic polynomial-time computable map $g : \{0,1\}^* \rightarrow \{0,1\}^*$ such that the following three properties are satisfied:*

Length-doubling. *For all $x \in \{0,1\}^*$, it holds that $|g(x)| = 2|x|$. We write $g_0(x)$ for the left half of g and $g_1(x)$ for the right half of g.*
Doubly half-injective. *The functions g_0 and g_1 are injective.*
Pseudorandomness. *$g(U_n)$ is computationally indistinguishable from U_{2n}.*

Remark. Note that, as g_0 and g_1 are length-preserving, injectivity is equivalent to bijectivity, but we choose the term injectivity because we only need injectivity in our proofs and because one could define analogous properties also for functions with more stretch. For a further discussion of modification of this definition, see the end of this section.

We build on an observation by Garg, Pandey, Srinivasan and Zhandry [15,16] who show that the standard-construction of a PRG from a one-way permutation is left-half-injective and then transform any left-half injective PRG into a doubly half-injective PRG.

Definition 10 (Left-Half-Injective Pseudorandom Generator). *A left-half-injective pseudorandom generator is a deterministic polynomially-time computable map $g : \{0,1\}^* \to \{0,1\}^*$ such that the following three properties are satisfied:*

Length-doubling. *For all $x \in \{0,1\}^*$, it holds that $|g(x)| = 2|x|$. We write $g_0(x)$ for the left half of g and $g_1(x)$ for the right half of g.*
Half-injective. *The function g_0 is injective.*
Pseudorandomness. *$g(U_n)$ is computationally indistinguishable from U_{2n}.*

For completeness, we include the proof of left-half-injectivity by Garg, Pandey, Srinivasan and Zhandry [15,16].

Claim 2 ([15,16]). *Assuming the existence of one-way permutations, there exist left-half injective, length-doubling PRGs.*

Proof. Let $f' : \{0,1\}^* \to \{0,1\}^*$ be a one-way permutation. Then the Goldreich-Levin hardcore bit [20] implies that there exists a one-way permutation $f : \{0,1\}^* \to \{0,1\}^*$ with hardcore bit $B : \{0,1\}^* \to \{0,1\}$. We define the function $G : \{0,1\}^* \to \{0,1\}^*$, as $G(x) := f^{|x|}(x)||B(x)||B(f(x))||...||B(f^{|x|-1})$. Indeed, $|G(x)| = 2|x|$. The pseudorandomness of G follows from the security of the hardcore bit, see [17], and the left-injectivity follows, as f is a permutation and therefore, for all ℓ, f^ℓ is a permutation, too.   □

We can now prove the existence of doubly half-injective pseudorandom generators, based on one-way permutations.

Lemma 1 (Doubly Half-Injective Pseudorandom Generators). *Assuming the existence of one-way permutations, there exist DPRGs.*

The proof follows directly by combining Claim 2 and the following claim.

Claim 3. *If $G = G_0||G_1$ is a left-half injective, length-doubling PRG, where G_0 denotes its left, injective half, then g is doubly half-injective PRG, where g is defined as*

$$g(x_0||x_1) := G_0(x_0)||G_1(x_0) \oplus G_0(x_1)||G_0(x_1)||G_1(x_1) \oplus G_0(x_0),$$

where $||$ denotes concatenation and where $\oplus$ binds stronger than $||$ and where w.l.o.g., we consider even length $|x|$ and denote x_0 the left half of x and x_1 the right half of x.

Proof. Assume a left-half injective length-doubling PRG $G = G_0||G_1$, where G_0 denotes its left, injective half. We need to show that g is a doubly half-injective PRG, where g is defined as

$$g(x_0||x_1) := G_0(x_0)||G_1(x_0) \oplus G_0(x_1)||G_0(x_1)||G_1(x_1) \oplus G_0(x_0),$$

where $||$ denotes concatenation and where $\oplus$ binds stronger than $||$ and where w.l.o.g., we consider even length $|x|$ and denote x_0 the left half of x and x_1 the right half of x.

Double Half-Injectivity. We show that $g_0(x_0||x_1) = G_0(x_0)||G_1(x_0) \oplus G_0(x_1)$ is injective. The injectivity of g_1 then follows analogously. Let $w_0||w_1$ be such that $g_0(w_0||w_1) = g_0(x_0||x_1)$. Firstly note that G_0 is a permutation and therefore, $x_0 = w_0$. Plugging this equality into $G_1(w_0) \oplus G_0(w_1) = G_1(x_0) \oplus G_0(x_1)$, we obtain that $G_0(w_1) = G_0(x_1)$. As G_0 is a permutation, it follows that $w_1 = x_1$.

Pseudorandomness. We now prove the pseudorandomness property. We denote by U_n^0, U_n^{00}, U_n^{01}, U_n^1, U_n^{10}, U_n^{11} independent, uniform distributions on n bits. We use that the output of the PRG $G_0(U_n^0)||G_1(U_n^0)$ is computationally indistinguishable from $U_n^{00}||U_n^{01}$ and that $G_0(U_n^1)||G_1(U_n^1)$ is computationally indistinguishable from $U_n^{10}||U_n^{11}$. We get

$$
\begin{array}{ll}
G_0(U_n^0)||G_1(U_n^0) \oplus G_0(U_n^1)|| & G_0(U_n^1)||G_1(U_n^1) \oplus G_0(U_n^0) \\
\stackrel{c}{\approx} \quad U_n^{00}||U_n^{01} \oplus G_0(U_n^1)|| & G_0(U_n^1)||G_1(U_n^1) \oplus U_n^{00} \\
\stackrel{c}{\approx} \quad U_n^{00}||U_n^{01} \oplus U_n^{10}|| & U_n^{10}||U_n^{11} \oplus U_n^{00} \\
\stackrel{s}{\approx} \quad U_n^{00}||U_n^{01}|| & U_n^{10}||U_n^{11}
\end{array}
$$

The last step follows, as U_n^{01} and U_n^{11} are independent from the other uniform distributions. We thus proved that G is a pseudorandom generator. Note that the restriction on even input length can be removed by using G_0 and G_1 with matching input and output length (G_1 needs to output strings that are one bit longer than those output by G_0.) and by truncating the output of G_1 appropriately when creating the padding for the shorter half. This concludes the proof of Claim 3. $\square$

We now prove the incompressibility properties of the GGM pseudorandom function when based on a DPRG.

Claim 4. *Let f be the GGM PRF using a DPRG $g = g_0||g_1$. We denote by m the input length of the input x to the PRF. Then for each pair of randomized, possibly inefficient algorithms (Leak, S), there exists a randomized possibly inefficient algorithm P such that the probability that the following two experiments return 1 is equal.*

$$\underline{\$\text{-}PRF\text{-}INC^{\text{Leak},S}} \qquad \underline{\$\text{-}KEY\text{-}INC^{\text{Leak},P}}$$

$$\begin{array}{ll}
k \leftarrow_\$ U_n & k \leftarrow_\$ U_n \\
\text{aux} \leftarrow_\$ \text{Leak}(k) & \text{aux} \leftarrow_\$ \text{Leak}(k) \\
x \leftarrow_\$ \{0,1\}^m & \\
y \leftarrow_\$ S(\text{aux}, x) & k' \leftarrow_\$ P(\text{aux}) \\
\textbf{return } (y \stackrel{?}{=} f(k,x)) & \textbf{return } (k' \stackrel{?}{=} k)
\end{array}$$

Moreover, for each pair of possibly inefficient algorithms (Leak, P), there exists a randomized possibly inefficient algorithm S such that the probability that the two experiments $\$\text{-}PRF\text{-}INC^{\text{Leak},S}$ and $\$\text{-}KEY\text{-}INC^{\text{Leak},P}$ return 1 is equal.

Proof. We observe that for each $x \in \{0,1\}^m$, the function $f(\cdot, x)$ is a permutation as, depending on the bits of x, it applies the functions g_0 and g_1 several times subsequently to the input k. As g_0 and g_1 are permutations, we have a fixed sequence of permutations (depending on the bits of x) that we apply to k. A fixed sequence of permutations is a permutation as well. Therefore, any unpredictability on k immediately translates into unpredictability on the function values of the PRF. We now prove this statement formally. We use the notation $f_x(\cdot)$ for $f(\cdot, x)$ to emphasize that x is fixed and now, for each pair of algorithms (Leak, S), construct and algorithm P (left column). We also describe, how for each pair of algorithms (Leak, P), one can construct an algorithm S (right column).

$$\underline{P(\text{aux})} \qquad \underline{P(\text{aux}, x)}$$

$$\begin{array}{ll}
x \leftarrow_\$ U_n & \\
y \leftarrow_\$ S(\text{aux}, x) & k' \leftarrow_\$ P(\text{aux}) \\
k' := f_x^{-1}(y) & y := f(k', x) \\
\textbf{return } k' & \textbf{return } y
\end{array}$$

As f_x is a permutation, $k' = k$ if and only if $f(k', x) = f_x(k') = f_x(k) = f(k, x)$ and the claim follows. □

In other words, the average min-entropy (see Dodis et al. [12] and Reyzin [34]) of $f(U_n, U_m)$, conditioned on $\text{Leak}(U_n)$, is equal to the average min-entropy of U_n, conditioned on $\text{Leak}(U_n)$. We recall the definition of average min-entropy.

Definition 11 (Average Min-Entropy). *Let (Y, Z) be a pair of random variables. The average min-entropy of Y conditioned on Z is denoted $\widetilde{H}_\infty(Y|Z)$ and defined as*

$$-\log \mathbb{E}_{z \leftarrow_\$ Z} \left[\max_y \Pr[Y = y | Z = z] \right] = -\log \left(\mathbb{E}_{z \leftarrow_\$ Z} \left[2^{-H_\infty(Y|Z=z)} \right] \right),$$

where $H_\infty(Y|Z = z) = -\log(\max_y \Pr[Y = y|Z = z])$ *denotes min-entropy.*

We can now rephrase Claim 4 as

$$\widetilde{H}_\infty(f(U_n, U_m)|\mathsf{Leak}(U_n)) = \widetilde{H}_\infty(U_n|\mathsf{Leak}(U_n)). \tag{5}$$

Now, we can state the following lemma which concludes the proof of Theorem 3.

Lemma 2. *Let α be a function in the security parameter n such that for all n, $\alpha(n) > n$ and such that for all n, $\alpha(n)$ is a power of 2. Construction 3 is a (δ, λ)-incompressible PRF implementation with expansion factor α of the GGM PRF with $\delta = 1 - \frac{\lambda_n}{\alpha} - \mathsf{negl}(n)$, where λ_n is the largest integer such that $n \cdot \lambda_n \leq \lambda$.*

Proof. We need to show that for each pair of efficient algorithms (Leak, S), the probability that \$-PRF-INC$^{\mathsf{Leak}, S}$ returns 1 is smaller than $\delta + \mathsf{negl}(n)$. We will show that this statement even holds for pairs of inefficient algorithms (Leak, S). That is, the property holds statistically and we need to show that

$$\widetilde{H}_\infty(F(U_{\alpha n}, U_n)|\mathsf{Leak}(U_{\alpha n})) \geq -\log(\delta + \mathsf{negl}(n)). \tag{6}$$

First, remark that as the length of the output of Leak is upper bounded by λ, we have that

$$\lambda \leq \widetilde{H}_\infty(U_{\alpha n}|\mathsf{Leak}(U_{\alpha n})).$$

We can now split $U_{\alpha n}$ into α blocks of n bits each, where we denote the ith block as $U_{\alpha n}[i]$, and we obtain

$$\widetilde{H}_\infty(U_{\alpha n}|\mathsf{Leak}(U_{\alpha n})) \leq \sum_{i=0}^{\alpha-1} \widetilde{H}_\infty(U_{\alpha n}[i]|\mathsf{Leak}(U_{\alpha n})).$$

We denote by h_i the entropy of the conditional uniform distribution $\widetilde{H}_\infty(U_{\alpha n}[i]|\mathsf{Leak}(U_{\alpha n}))$, which, by Eq. 5, is equal to the entropy of the conditional PRF distribution $\widetilde{H}_\infty(f(U_{\alpha n}[i], U_m)|\mathsf{Leak}(U_{\alpha n}))$. Putting all together, we obtain that

$$\lambda \leq \sum_{i=0}^{\alpha-1} h_i, \text{ where} \tag{7}$$

$$\forall 0 \leq i \leq \alpha - 1 : 0 \leq h_i \leq n. \tag{8}$$

Recall that we want to show Inequality 6. Using the notation h_i, we can re-phrase Inequality 6 equivalently as

$$S(h_0, ..., h_{\alpha-1}) := \frac{1}{\alpha} \sum_{i=0}^{\alpha-1} 2^{-h_i} \leq \delta + \mathsf{negl}(n). \tag{9}$$

To summarize, we need to find $h_0,...,h_{\alpha-1}$ such that Inequality 7 and Inequality 8 are satisfied and such that the term $S(h_0, ..., h_{\alpha-1})$ on the left-hand side of Inequality 9 is maximized. On the α-dimensional domain that satisfies Inequality 8, the term $S(h_0, ..., h_{\alpha-1})$ is maximized when $h_0 = ... = h_{\alpha-1} = 0$. Moreover,

S is anti-monotone. That is, if $(h'_0, ..., h'_{\alpha-1}) \leq (h_0, ..., h_{\alpha-1})$ component-wise, then $S(h'_0, ..., h'_{\alpha-1}) \geq S(h_0, ..., h_{\alpha-1})$. Moreover, given any point $(h_0, ..., h_{\alpha-1})$ in the domain $[0, n]^\alpha$, the descent of S is least steep in the direction of the largest entry h_i. As S is symmetric, we obtain that under the constraints of Inequality 7 and Inequality 8, S is maximized at $\overline{h} = (n, ..., n, \lambda_{\mathrm{rem}}, 0, ..., 0)$, which contains λ_n entries n and where λ_{rem} is such that $\lambda = \lambda_n \cdot n + \lambda_{\mathrm{rem}}$. We obtain

$$S(\overline{h}) = \frac{1}{\alpha}(\lambda_n \cdot 2^{-n} + 2^{-\lambda_{\mathrm{rem}}} + (\alpha - \lambda_n - 1)) \leq 1 - \frac{\lambda_n}{\alpha} + \mathsf{negl}(n),$$

which concludes the proof of the lemma. □

Discussion on Stretch and Assumptions. Note that one can obtain DPRGs with more stretch from a DPRG that is length-doubling simply by first applying the original DPRG and then applying an injective PRG to the left half and an injective PRG to the right half of the output of the DPRG. Also note that a DPRG with stretch 2 implies (is actually equivalent to) the existence of one-way permutations and that one-way permutations imply injective PRGs via the Goldreich-Levin hardcore bit construction [20].

Our construction would also work with a DPRG that stretches its input by more than a factor of 2. Such a function might be constructed based on one-way functions only, as g_0 and g_1 would not be bijective anymore and thus, such a DPRG does not seem to imply one-way permutations unlike a DPRG whose stretch is exactly 2. In the rest of the paper, we consider DPRGs whose stretch exactly 2. We made no attempt to construct DPRGs based on one-way functions only, as one-way permutations are a standard symmetric-type MiniCrypt assumption[2].

References

1. Barak, B., et al.: On the (im)possibility of obfuscating programs. In: Kilian, J. (ed.) CRYPTO 2001. LNCS, vol. 2139, pp. 1–18. Springer, Heidelberg (2001). https://doi.org/10.1007/3-540-44647-8_1
2. Bellare, M., Namprempre, C.: Authenticated encryption: relations among notions and analysis of the generic composition paradigm. In: Okamoto, T. (ed.) ASIACRYPT 2000. LNCS, vol. 1976, pp. 531–545. Springer, Heidelberg (2000). https://doi.org/10.1007/3-540-44448-3_41
3. Billet, O., Gilbert, H., Ech-Chatbi, C.: Cryptanalysis of a white box AES implementation. In: Handschuh, H., Hasan, M.A. (eds.) SAC 2004. LNCS, vol. 3357, pp. 227–240. Springer, Heidelberg (2004). https://doi.org/10.1007/978-3-540-30564-4_16

---

[2] That is, one-way permutations are not known to imply trapdoor functions, and, by the seminal paper of Impagliazzo and Rudich [23], it seems unlikely that anyone would show such an implication anytime soon. See also Impagliazzo [22] for an excellent survey on cryptographic assumptions.

4. Biryukov, A., Bouillaguet, C., Khovratovich, D.: Cryptographic schemes based on the ASASA structure: black-box, white-box, and public-key (extended abstract). In: Sarkar, P., Iwata, T. (eds.) ASIACRYPT 2014. Part I, of LNCS, vol. 8873, pp. 63–84. Springer, Heidelberg (2014)
5. Bogdanov, A., Isobe, T.: White-box cryptography revisited: space-hard ciphers. In: Ray, I., Li, N., Kruegel, C. (eds.) ACM CCS 2015, pp. 1058–1069. ACM Press, October 2015
6. Bogdanov, A., Isobe, T., Tischhauser, E.: Towards practical whitebox cryptography: optimizing efficiency and space hardness. In: Cheon, J.H., Takagi, T. (eds.) ASIACRYPT 2016. LNCS, vol. 10031, pp. 126–158. Springer, Heidelberg (2016). https://doi.org/10.1007/978-3-662-53887-6_5
7. Bos, J.W., Hubain, C., Michiels, W., Teuwen, P.: Differential computation analysis: hiding your white-box designs is not enough. In: Gierlichs, B., Poschmann, A.Y. (eds.) CHES 2016. LNCS, vol. 9813, pp. 215–236. Springer, Heidelberg (2016). https://doi.org/10.1007/978-3-662-53140-2_11
8. Bringer, J., Chabanne, H., Dottax, E.: White box cryptography: another attempt. Cryptology ePrint Archive, Report 2006/468 2006. http://eprint.iacr.org/2006/468
9. Chow, S., Eisen, P., Johnson, H., Van Oorschot, P.C.: White-box cryptography and an AES implementation. In: Nyberg, K., Heys, H. (eds.) SAC 2002. LNCS, vol. 2595, pp. 250–270. Springer, Heidelberg (2003). https://doi.org/10.1007/3-540-36492-7_17
10. Chow, S., Eisen, P., Johnson, H., van Oorschot, P.C.: A white-box DES implementation for DRM applications. In: Feigenbaum, J. (ed.) DRM 2002. LNCS, vol. 2696, pp. 1–15. Springer, Heidelberg (2003). https://doi.org/10.1007/978-3-540-44993-5_1
11. Delerablée, C., Lepoint, T., Paillier, P., Rivain, M.: White-box security notions for symmetric encryption schemes. In: Lange, T., Lauter, K., Lisoněk, P. (eds.) SAC 2013. LNCS, vol. 8282, pp. 247–264. Springer, Heidelberg (2014). https://doi.org/10.1007/978-3-662-43414-7_13
12. Dodis, Y., Reyzin, L., Smith, A.: Fuzzy extractors: how to generate strong keys from biometrics and other noisy data. In: Cachin, C., Camenisch, J.L. (eds.) EUROCRYPT 2004. LNCS, vol. 3027, pp. 523–540. Springer, Heidelberg (2004). https://doi.org/10.1007/978-3-540-24676-3_31
13. ECRYPT: Ches 2017 capture the flag challenge - the whibox contest 2017. https://whibox.cr.yp.to/
14. Fouque, P.-A., Karpman, P., Kirchner, P., Minaud, B.: Efficient and provable white-box primitives. In: Cheon, J.H., Takagi, T. (eds.) ASIACRYPT 2016. LNCS, vol. 10031, pp. 159–188. Springer, Heidelberg (2016). https://doi.org/10.1007/978-3-662-53887-6_6
15. Garg, S., Pandey, O., Srinivasan, A.: Revisiting the cryptographic hardness of finding a nash equilibrium. In: Robshaw, M., Katz, J. (eds.) CRYPTO 2016. LNCS, vol. 9815, pp. 579–604. Springer, Heidelberg (2016). https://doi.org/10.1007/978-3-662-53008-5_20
16. Garg, S., Pandey, O., Srinivasan, A., Zhandry, M.: Breaking the sub-exponential barrier in obfustopia. In: Coron, J.-S., Nielsen, J.B. (eds.) EUROCRYPT 2017. LNCS, vol. 10212, pp. 156–181. Springer, Cham (2017). https://doi.org/10.1007/978-3-319-56617-7_6
17. Goldreich, O.: Foundations of Cryptography: Basic Tools, vol. 1. Cambridge University Press, Cambridge (2001)

18. Goldreich, O.: Foundations of Cryptography: Basic Applications, vol. 2. Cambridge University Press, Cambridge (2004)

19. Goldreich, O., Goldwasser, S., Micali, S.: On the cryptographic applications of random functions. In: Blakley, G.R., Chaum, D. (eds.) CRYPTO 1984. LNCS, vol. 196, pp. 276–288. Springer, Heidelberg (1984). https://doi.org/10.1007/3-540-39568-7_22

20. Goldreich, O., Levin, L.A.: A hard-core predicate for all one-way functions. In: 21st ACM STOC, pp. 25–32. ACM Press, May 1989

21. Goubin, L., Masereel, J.-M., Quisquater, M.: Cryptanalysis of white box DES implementations. In: Adams, C., Miri, A., Wiener, M. (eds.) SAC 2007. LNCS, vol. 4876, pp. 278–295. Springer, Heidelberg (2007). https://doi.org/10.1007/978-3-540-77360-3_18

22. Impagliazzo, R.: A personal view of average-case complexity. In: Proceedings of the Tenth Annual Structure in Complexity Theory Conference, Minneapolis, Minnesota, USA, 19–22 June 1995, pp. 134–147. IEEE Computer Society (1995)

23. Impagliazzo, R., Rudich, S.: Limits on the provable consequences of one-way permutations. In: 21st ACM STOC, pp. 44–61. ACM Press, May 1989

24. Impagliazzo, R., Rudich, S.: Limits on the provable consequences of one-way permutations. In: Goldwasser, S. (ed.) CRYPTO 1988. LNCS, vol. 403, pp. 8–26. Springer, New York (1990). https://doi.org/10.1007/0-387-34799-2_2

25. Jacob, M., Boneh, D., Felten, E.: Attacking an obfuscated cipher by injecting faults. In: Feigenbaum, J. (ed.) DRM 2002. LNCS, vol. 2696, pp. 16–31. Springer, Heidelberg (2003). https://doi.org/10.1007/978-3-540-44993-5_2

26. Karroumi, M.: Protecting white-box AES with dual ciphers. In: Rhee, K.-H., Nyang, D.H. (eds.) ICISC 2010. LNCS, vol. 6829, pp. 278–291. Springer, Heidelberg (2011). https://doi.org/10.1007/978-3-642-24209-0_19

27. Krawczyk, H.: The order of encryption and authentication for protecting communications (or: how secure Is SSL?). In: Kilian, J. (ed.) CRYPTO 2001. LNCS, vol. 2139, pp. 310–331. Springer, Heidelberg (2001). https://doi.org/10.1007/3-540-44647-8_19

28. Lepoint, T., Rivain, M., De Mulder, Y., Roelse, P., Preneel, B.: Two attacks on a white-box AES implementation. In: Lange, T., Lauter, K., Lisoněk, P. (eds.) SAC 2013. LNCS, vol. 8282, pp. 265–285. Springer, Heidelberg (2014). https://doi.org/10.1007/978-3-662-43414-7_14

29. Link, H.E., Neumann, W.D.: Clarifying obfuscation: improving the security of white-box encoding. Cryptology ePrint Archive, Report 2004/025 2004. http://eprint.iacr.org/2004/025

30. Mastercard: Mastercard mobile payment SDK, 2017. https://developer.mastercard.com/media/32/b3/b6a8b4134e50bfe53590c128085e/mastercard-mobile-payment-sdk-security-guide-v2.0.pdf

31. Alpirez Bock, E., Brzuska, C., Michiels, W., Treff, A.: On the ineffectiveness of internal encodings - revisiting the DCA attack on white-box cryptography. Cryptology ePrint Archive, Report 2018/301 2018. https://eprint.iacr.org/2018/301.pdf

32. Mulder, Y.D., Roelse, P., Preneel, B.: Cryptanalysis of the Xiao-Lai white-box AES implementation. In: Knudsen, L.R., Wu, H. (eds.) SAC 2012. LNCS, vol. 7707, pp. 34–49. Springer, Heidelberg (2013)

33. De Mulder, Y., Wyseur, B., Preneel, B.: Cryptanalysis of a perturbated white-box AES implementation. In: Gong, G., Gupta, K.C. (eds.) INDOCRYPT 2010. LNCS, vol. 6498, pp. 292–310. Springer, Heidelberg (2010). https://doi.org/10.1007/978-3-642-17401-8_21

34. Reyzin, L.: Some notions of entropy for cryptography. In: Fehr, S. (ed.) ICITS 2011. LNCS, vol. 6673, pp. 138–142. Springer, Heidelberg (2011). https://doi.org/10.1007/978-3-642-20728-0_13

35. Rivest, R.L., Shamir, A., Adleman, L.M.: A method for obtaining digital signature and public-key cryptosystems. Commun. Assoc. Comput. Mach. **21**(2), 120–126 (1978)

36. Sanfelix, E., de Haas, J., Mune, C.: Unboxing the white-box: practical attacks against obfuscated ciphers. Presentation at BlackHat Europe 2015 (2015). https://www.blackhat.com/eu-15/briefings.html

37. Saxena, A., Wyseur, B., Preneel, B.: Towards security notions for white-box cryptography. In: Samarati, P., Yung, M., Martinelli, F., Ardagna, C.A. (eds.) ISC 2009. LNCS, vol. 5735, pp. 49–58. Springer, Heidelberg (2009). https://doi.org/10.1007/978-3-642-04474-8_4

38. Smart Card Alliance Mobile and NFC Council. Host card emulation 101. white paper (2014). http://www.smartcardalliance.org/downloads/HCE-101-WP-FINAL-081114-clean.pdf

39. Wyseur, B., Michiels, W., Gorissen, P., Preneel, B.: Cryptanalysis of white-box DES implementations with arbitrary external encodings. In: Adams, C., Miri, A., Wiener, M. (eds.) SAC 2007. LNCS, vol. 4876, pp. 264–277. Springer, Heidelberg (2007). https://doi.org/10.1007/978-3-540-77360-3_17

40. Xiao, Y., Lai, X.: A secure implementation of white-box AES. In: 2009 2nd International Conference on Computer Science and its Applications, pp. 1–6. IEEE Computer Society (2009)

Error Detection in Monotone Span Programs with Application to Communication-Efficient Multi-party Computation

Nigel P. Smart[1,2(✉)] and Tim Wood[1,2]

[1] University of Bristol, Bristol, UK
[2] KU Leuven, Leuven, Belgium
{nigel.smart,t.wood}@kuleuven.be

Abstract. Recent improvements in the state-of-the-art of MPC for non-full-threshold access structures introduced the idea of using a collision-resistant hash functions and redundancy in the secret-sharing scheme to construct a communication-efficient MPC protocol which is computationally-secure against malicious adversaries, with abort. The prior work is based on replicated secret-sharing; in this work we extend this methodology to *any* LSSS implementing a $\mathcal{Q}_2$ access structure. To do so we need to establish a folklore property of error detection for such LSSS and their associated Monotone Span Programs. In doing so we obtain communication-efficient online and offline protocols for MPC in the pre-processing model.

1 Introduction

Secure multi-party computation (MPC) allows a set of parties to compute a function on their combined secret inputs so that all parties learn the output of the function and no party can learn anything that cannot be inferred from the output and their own inputs alone. As a field it has recently received a lot of attention and has been explored in a variety of contexts: for example, private auctions [12], secure statistical analysis of personal information [10] and protection against side-channel attacks in hardware [8,33,34].

Most MPC protocols fall into one of two broad categories: garbled circuits, and linear-secret-sharing-scheme-based (LSSS-based) MPC. The garbled-circuit approach, which began with the work of Yao [36], involves some collection of parties "garbling" a circuit to conceal the internal circuit evaluations, and then later a single party or a collection of parties jointly evaluating the garbled circuit. By contrast, the LSSS-based approach involves using a so-called linear secret-sharing scheme, in which the parties: "share" a secret into several *shares* which are distributed to different parties, perform computations on the shares, and then reconstruct the secret at the end by combining the shares to determine the output. LSSS-based MPC is traditionally presented in the context of

© Springer Nature Switzerland AG 2019
M. Matsui (Ed.): CT-RSA 2019, LNCS 11405, pp. 210–229, 2019.
https://doi.org/10.1007/978-3-030-12612-4_11

information-theoretic security, although many modern practical protocols that realise LSSS-based MPC often make use of computationally-secure primitives such as somewhat-homomorphic encryption (SHE) [23] or oblivious transfer (OT) [30]. In this paper, we focus on computationally-secure LSSS-based MPC.

An access structure for a set of parties defines which subsets of parties are allowed to discover the secret if they pool their information. Such quorums of parties are often called *qualified* sets of parties. An access structure is called $\mathcal{Q}_\ell$ (for $\ell \in \mathbb{N}$) if the union of any set of ℓ unqualified sets of parties is missing at least one party. We discuss this in some detail later, but for now the reader can think of an (n, t)-threshold scheme where $t < n/\ell$ which is where a subset of parties is qualified if and only if it is of size at least $t + 1$. Computationally-secure LSSS-based MPC has recently seen significant, efficient instantiations for full-threshold access structures [7,22,23,30], which is where the protocol is secure if at least one party is honest, even if the adversary causes the corrupt parties to run arbitrary code (though this behaviour may cause the protocol to abort rather than provide output to the parties). In the threshold case similar efficient instantiations are known, such as the older VIFF protocol [20] which uses (essentially) information-theoretic primitives only.

While protocols providing full-threshold security are an important research goal, in the real world such guarantees of security do not always match the use-cases that appear. Different applications call for different access structures, and not necessarily the usual threshold examples. For example, a company may have four directors (CEO, CTO, CSO and CFO) and access may be granted in the two combinations (CEO and CFO) or (CTO and CSO and CFO). In such a situation it may be more efficient to tailor the protocol to this structure, rather than try to shoe-horn the application into a more standard (i.e. full-threshold) structure. Indeed, while it is possible that a computation can be performed in a full-threshold setting and then the outputs distributed in accordance with the access structure, such a process requires all parties to participate equally in the computation, which may not be feasible in the real world, especially if the computing parties are distributed over a wide network, and susceptible to outages if the total number of parties is large.

Most LSSS-based MPC protocols split the computation into two parts: an *offline phase*, in which parties interact using "expensive" public-key cryptography to lay the groundwork for an *online phase* in which only "cheap" information-theoretic primitives are required. The online phase is where the actual circuit evaluation takes place. For the access structures considered in this work, namely $\mathcal{Q}_2$ structures, the offline phase is almost as fast as the online phase. Thus the goal here is to minimize the cost of communication in both phases.

Realising MPC for different access structures has been well studied: shortly following the advent of Shamir's secret-sharing scheme [9,35], the first formal MPC – as opposed to 2PC – protocols [5,15,26] were constructed, with varying correctness guarantees for different threshold structures. These works were developed by Hirt and Maurer [27], and then Beaver and Wool [3] for general access structures, culminating in Maurer's relatively more recent work [32]. In this last work it is shown that passively-secure information-theoretic MPC is possible if the access structure is Q_2, and full active security (without requiring abort) is possible if the access structure is Q_3. The latter has seen various optimisations in the literature, for example [21], making use of packed secret sharing to obtain a bandwidth-efficient perfectly-secure protocol.

In recent work [31], Keller et al. show that by generalising a method of Araki et al. [1, 25] communication-efficient computationally-secure MPC with abort can be realised for Q_2 access structures, if replicated secret-sharing is used. The methodology in [1, 25, 31] uses the explicit properties of replicated secret-sharing so as to authenticate various shares. This enables active security with abort to be achieved relatively cheaply, albeit at the expense in general of the pre-deployment of a large number, depending on the access structure, of symmetric keys to enable the generation of pseudo-random secret sharings (PRSSs) in a non-interactive manner. A disadvantage of replicated sharing is the potentially larger (than average) memory footprint needed for each party per secret, and consequently there is still a relatively large communication cost involved when the parties need to send shares across the network. In this work we extend this prior work to produce a protocol for *any* LSSS that supports the Q_2 access structure.

1.1 Authentication of Shares

Many of practical MPC protocols begin with a basic passively-secure (a.k.a. *semi-honest* or *honest-but-curious*) protocol, in which corrupt parties execute the protocol honestly but try to deduce anything they can about other parties' data from their own data and the communication tapes. Such passively-secure protocols for Q_2 access structures are highly efficient, and are information-theoretically secure. The passively secure protocols are then augmented to obtain active security with abort by using some form of "share authentication"; in this security setting, corrupt parties may deviate arbitrarily from the protocol description but if they do so the honest parties will abort the protocol.

At a high level, modern actively-secure LSSS-based MPC protocols combine:

1. A linear (i.e. additively homomorphic) secret sharing scheme;
2. A passive multiplication protocol; and
3. An authentication protocol.

The communication efficiency of the computation (usually an arithmetic or Boolean circuit) depends heavily on how authentication is performed.

In the full-threshold SPDZ protocol [23] and its successors, e.g. [22, 30], authentication is achieved with additively homomorphic message authentication codes (MACs). For each secret that is shared amongst the parties, the parties also share a MAC on that secret. Since the authentication is additively homomorphic and the sharing scheme is linear, this means that the sum (and consequently scalar multiple) of authenticated shares is authenticated "for free" by performing the addition (or scalar multiplication) on the associated MACs. More work is required for multiplication of secrets, but the general methodology for doing these operations on shared secrets is now generally considered "standard" for MPC in this setting.

One important branch of this authentication methodology contributing significantly to their practical performance is the amortisation of verification costs by batch-checking MACs, a technique developed in [6,23], amongst other works. A different approach to batch verification for authentication of shares, in the case of Q_2 access structures, was introduced by Furakawa et al. [25], in the context of the three-party honest-majority setting, i.e. a $(3,1)$-threshold access structure. This work extended a passively-secure protocol of Araki et al. [1] in the same threshold setting. This approach dispenses with the MACs and instead achieves authentication of shares using a collision-resistant hash function when authenticating an open-to-all operation, and uses redundancy of the underlying secret sharing scheme in an open-to-one operation. Their protocol can be viewed as a bootstrapping of the passively-secure protocol of Beaver and Wool [3], with an optimised sharing procedure (highly tailored to the $(3,1)$-threshold access structure), to provide a communication-efficient actively-secure protocol (with abort). By using a hash function they sacrifice the information-theoretic security of Beaver-Wool for computational security, and also use computationally-secure share generation operations to improve the offline phase.

The above protocols for replicated sharing in a $(3,1)$-threshold access structure of $[1,25]$ simultaneously reduce the number of secure communication channels needed *and* the total number of bits sent per multiplication. Recent work [31] has shown that these techniques can be generalised from $(3,1)$-threshold to *any* Q_2 access structure, using replicated secret-sharing. Both [25] and [31] make use of the fact that replicated sharing provides a trivial method to authenticate a full set of shares; i.e. it somehow offers a form of error-detection.

A recent protocol due to Chida et al. [16] also considers actively-secure honest-majority MPC and makes use of MACs. In their work, the communication cost is a constant number of elements per multiplication, but the messages are broadcast, so this cost is linear in the number of parties. Our protocol also has linear overhead, but following the methodology of [31], the total number of uni-directional channels is reduced and so the asymptotic cost is lower (for threshold access structures). The benefit of the Chida protocol is that there is no offline processing, and the total cost of active computation is less than ours (they achieve roughly twice the cost of passive multiplication as opposed to our roughly threefold cost). However, if one is interested purely in online times then our protocol is more efficient than that of Chida et al.

1.2   Our Contribution

While the replicated secret-sharing of [31] offers flexibility in being able to realise *any* access structure, unfortunately it *can* require an exponentially-large number of shares to be held by each party for each shared secret. As threshold access structures illustrate, using a general MSP may enable the same access structure to be realised in a more efficient manner, which motivates our work in this area.

The two main contributions of this work are as follows:

- Showing we can get authentication of shares almost for free for any MSP realising Q_2 access structures. Assuming an offline phase which produces Beaver triples, this gives us active security with abort, at the cost of replacing information-theoretic with computational security.
- We also provide, in the full version, a generic way to reduce the amount of communication required for the passive multiplication subprotocol in the offline phase for multiplicative MSPs.

Thus we generalise the online phase of [31] to arbitrary MSPs, hence allowing the benefits of that work to be achieved without necessarily requiring the cost of replicated secret sharing. Whereas many of the previous protocols are optimised for access structures on specific numbers of parties, or use specific secret-sharing schemes, our optimisation of the passive online multiplication is generic in the sense that it only uses the Q_2 nature of the access structure for authentication: [25] and [31] are special cases of our optimisation.

Our contribution, then, is not so much our full MPC protocol as it is the mechanism for an actively-secure multiplication in the Q_2 setting. Viewing the protocol in this more modular sense allows us to separate the LSSS from the actual multiplication and thus allows us to reduce the search for finding an efficient MPC protocol for a given Q_2 access structure to finding an LSSS with a small total number of shares.

To conclude this section, we briefly remark how our work relates to the correspondence between LSSSs and linear codes. Cramer et al. [19] showed how the correspondence between linear secret-sharing schemes and linear codes reveals an efficient method by which qualified parties can *correct* any errors in a set of shares for some secret. The ability to do so requires the access structure to be Q_3, since if this holds then a strongly-multiplicative LSSS realising it allows honest parties to correct any errors introduced by the adversary. This is not a direct connection to error-correction codes since such LSSSs do not necessarily allow unique decoding of the entire share vector: it is only the component of the share vector corresponding to the *secret* that is guaranteed to be correct. In our work we show that if the access structure is Q_2 then any LSSS realising it allows honest parties to agree on whether or not the secret is correct: thus we obtain a form of error-detection. This reveals why the protocols above (viz., [25,31]) are able to perform the error-detection causing abort. This result seems to be folklore – but we could find no statement or proof in the literature to this effect, and so we prove the required properties here.

2   Preliminaries

2.1   Notation

Let $\mathbb{F}$ denote a finite field; we write $\mathbb{F} = \mathbb{F}_q$ for q some prime power if $\mathbb{F}$ is the field of q elements. We write $r \xleftarrow{\$} \mathbb{F}$ to mean that r is sampled uniformly at random from $\mathbb{F}$. Vectors are written in bold and are taken to be column vectors. We denote by $\mathbf{0}$ a vector consisting entirely of zeros of appropriate dimension, determined by the context, and similarly by $\mathbf{1}$ a vector consisting entirely of ones. For a vector $\mathbf{x}$ we write the ith component as $\mathbf{x}_i$, whereas $\mathbf{x}^i$ denotes the ith vector from a sequence of vectors. We use the notation $\mathbf{e}^i$ for the ith standard basis vector (defined by $\mathbf{e}^i_j := \delta_{ij}$ where δ_{ij} is the Kronecker delta). We denote by $[n]$ the set $\cup_{i=1}^n \{i\}$, and by $\mathcal{P}$ the complete set of parties, which we take to be $\{P_i\}_{i\in[n]}$. Given some set S, a subset of some larger set S', we write $a \notin S$ to indicate that element a is in $S' \setminus S$; in general, S' will be implicit, according to context. We define the function $supp : \mathbb{F}^m \to 2^{\mathcal{P}}$ via $\mathbf{s} \mapsto \{i \in [m] : \mathbf{s}_i \neq 0\}$. We use the notation $A \subseteq B$ to mean that A is a (not necessarily proper) subset of B, contrasted with $A \subsetneq B$ where A is a proper subset of B. We write λ and κ for the statistical and computational security parameters respectively.

Given a vector space $V \subseteq \mathbb{F}^d$, we denote by $V^{\perp}$ the orthogonal complement; that is, $V^{\perp} = \{\mathbf{w} \in \mathbb{F}^d : \langle \mathbf{v}, \mathbf{w} \rangle = 0\}$, where $\langle \mathbf{v}, \mathbf{w} \rangle = \mathbf{v}^{\top} \cdot \mathbf{w}$ is the standard inner product. From basic linear algebra, $(V^{\perp})^{\perp} = V$. For a matrix $M \in \mathbb{F}^{m \times d}$, we write $M^{\top}$ for the transpose. If M is a matrix representing a linear map $\mathbb{F}^d \to \mathbb{F}^m$, then $\text{im}(M^{\top}) = \ker(M)^{\perp}$ by the fundamental theorem of linear algebra.

2.2 Access Structures, MSPs, LSSSs and Linear Codes

Access Structures: Fix $\mathcal{P} = \{P_i\}_{i\in[n]}$ and let $\Gamma \subseteq 2^{\mathcal{P}}$ be a monotonically increasing set, i.e. Γ is closed under taking supersets: if $Q \in \Gamma$ and $Q' \supseteq Q$ then $Q' \in \Gamma$. Similarly, let $\Delta \subseteq 2^{\mathcal{P}}$ be a monotonically decreasing set, i.e. Δ is closed under taking subsets: if $U \in \Delta$ and $U' \subseteq U$ then $U' \in \Delta$. We call the pair (Γ, Δ) a *monotone access structure* if $\Gamma \cap \Delta = \varnothing$. If $\Delta = 2^{\mathcal{P}} \setminus \Gamma$, then we say the access structure is *complete*. In this paper, we will only be concerned with complete monotone access structures and so this is assumed throughout without qualification. The sets in Γ, usually denoted by Q, are called *qualified*, and the sets in Δ, usually denoted by U, are called *unqualified*. Partial ordering is induced on Γ and Δ by the standard subset relation denoted by "$\subseteq$": we write Γ^- for the set of *minimally qualified sets* where minimality is with respect to "$\subseteq$": $\Gamma^- = \{Q \in \Gamma : \text{if } Q' \in \Gamma \text{ and } Q' \subseteq Q \text{ then } Q' = Q\}$; similarly, Δ^+ denotes the set of *maximally unqualified sets* where maximality is with respect to "$\subseteq$": $\Delta^+ = \{U \in \Delta : \text{if } U' \in \Delta \text{ and } U \subseteq U' \text{ then } U' = U\}$.

An access structure is said to be $\mathcal{Q}_2$ (resp. $\mathcal{Q}_3$) if the union of no two (resp. three) sets in Δ is the whole of $\mathcal{P}$. A consequence of this is that in a $\mathcal{Q}_2$ access structure, the complement of a qualified set is unqualified, and *vice versa*.

In an (n, t)-threshold access structure, any set of $t + 1$ parties is qualified, whilst any set of t or fewer parties is unqualified. Thus Γ^- contains $\binom{n}{t+1}$ sets in total. The term *full threshold* refers to an $(n, n-1)$-threshold access structure. For an arbitrary complete monotone access structure, the set of minimally qualified sets together with the set of maximally unqualified sets uniquely determine the entire structure. The dual access structure Γ^* of an access structure Γ is defined by $\Gamma^* := \{Q \in 2^{\mathcal{P}} : 2^{\mathcal{P}} \setminus Q \notin \Gamma\}$. Cramer et al. [19] showed that an access structure Γ is $\mathcal{Q}_2$ if and only if $\Gamma^* \subseteq \Gamma$.

Linear Secret Sharing Schemes: An LSSS is a method of sharing secret data amongst parties. It consists of three multi-party algorithms: Input, Open, and ALF (affine linear function), allowing parties to provide secret inputs, reveal (or *open*) secrets, and compute an affine linear function on shared secrets. In a practical sense, this means that the parties can add secrets, multiply by scalars, and add public constants to a shared secret, all by local computations. In this work we consider, as examples, the three most well-known secret-sharing schemes: Shamir; replicated, also known as CNF-based (conjunctive-normal-form-based); and DNF-based (disjunctive-normal-form-based). We will use the term *additive sharing* to mean that a secret s takes the value $s = \sum_{i=1}^{n} s_i$ where s_i is held by P_i and the s_i's are uniformly random subject to the constraint that they sum to s.

An LSSS is called *multiplicative* if the whole set of parties $\mathcal{P}$ can compute an additive sharing of the product of two secrets by performing only local computations. If the product is to be kept as a secret and used further in the computation, it is usually necessary for the parties to engage in one or more rounds of communication to convert the additive sharing into a sharing in the LSSS being used. A secret-sharing scheme is called *strongly multiplicative* if, for any $U \in \Delta$, the parties in $\mathcal{P} \setminus U$ can compute an additive sharing of the product of two secrets by local computations. Such schemes offer robustness, since the adversary, corrupting an unqualified set of parties, cannot prevent the honest parties from reconstructing the desired secret. Cramer et al. [18] showed that any (non-multiplicative) LSSS realising a $\mathcal{Q}_2$ access structure can be converted to a multiplicative LSSS for the same access structure so that each party holds at most twice the number of shares it held originally. There is currently no known construction to convert an arbitrary $\mathcal{Q}_3$ LSSS to a strongly multiplicative LSSS with only polynomial blow-up in the number of shares each party must hold [18,19].

Monotone Span Programs: Span programs, and monotone span programs specifically, were introduced by Karchmer and Wigderson [29] as a model of computation. It has been shown that MSPs have a close relationship to secret-sharing schemes, as discussed informally below.

Definition 1. *A Monotone Span Program (MSP), denoted by $\mathcal{M}$, is a quadruple $(\mathbb{F}, M, \varepsilon, \psi)$ where $\mathbb{F}$ is a field, $M \in \mathbb{F}^{m \times d}$ is a full-rank matrix for some m and $d \le m$, $\varepsilon \in \mathbb{F}^d$ is an arbitrary non-zero vector called the* target vector, *and $\psi : [m] \twoheadrightarrow \mathcal{P}$ is a surjective "labelling" map of rows to parties. The size of $\mathcal{M}$ is defined to be m, the number of rows of the matrix M.*

Typically, $\varepsilon = \mathbf{e}^1$ or $\varepsilon = \mathbf{1}$, but it can be an arbitrary non-zero vector: changing it simply changes how the vector $\mathbf{x}$ is selected, and corresponds to performing column operations on the columns of M, which does not change the access structure the MSP realises by results of Beimel et al. [4]. Some definitions of MSP do not require that M have full rank, since if this is not the case, one can iteratively remove any columns which are linearly dependent on preceding columns without changing the access structure $\mathcal{M}$ computes. We make this assumption for the sake of simplicity later on.

We say that the row-map ψ defines which rows are "owned" by each party. Given a set $S \subseteq \mathcal{P}$, we denote by M_S the submatrix of M whose rows are indexed by the set $\{i \in [m] : \psi(i) \in S\}$, and similarly $\mathbf{s}_S$ is the subvector of $\mathbf{s}$ whose entries are indexed by the same. Later, we will somewhat abuse notation by denoting again by M_S, where now $S \subseteq [m]$, the submatrix whose rows are indexed by S. Context will determine which matrix we mean since the indexing set is either a set of parties, or a set of row indices. If $\mathbf{s} \in \mathbb{F}^m$, then we call $\mathbf{s}_Q$ a *qualified subvector* of $\mathbf{s}$ if $Q \in \Gamma$, and an *unqualified subvector* otherwise. An MSP $\mathcal{M}$ is said to compute an access structure Γ if it holds that $Q \in \Gamma$ if and only if $\exists\ \boldsymbol{\lambda}^Q \in \mathbb{F}^m$ (i.e. depending on Q) such that $M^\top \cdot \boldsymbol{\lambda}^Q = \boldsymbol{\varepsilon}$ and $\psi(supp(\boldsymbol{\lambda}^Q)) \subseteq Q$. In other words, $\boldsymbol{\varepsilon} \in \mathrm{Im}(M_Q^\top)$ if and only if Q is qualified. Note that we write $\boldsymbol{\lambda}^Q$ to show that this vector is associated to the set Q; compare with $\boldsymbol{\lambda}_Q^Q$, which is the subvector of $\boldsymbol{\lambda}^Q$ whose co-ordinates are indexed by Q, to be consistent with the notation above. This means that the parties in the set Q "own" rows of the matrix M which can be combined in a public, known linear combination encoded as the vector $\boldsymbol{\lambda}^Q$, to obtain the target vector $\boldsymbol{\varepsilon}$.

Monotone Span Programs induce LSSSs in the following way: Sample $\mathbf{x} \xleftarrow{\$} \mathbb{F}^d$ subject to $\langle \mathbf{x}, \boldsymbol{\varepsilon} \rangle = s$, the secret. Now let $\mathbf{s} = M \cdot \mathbf{x}$ and for each $i \in [m]$, give $\mathbf{s}_i$ (that is, the ith co-ordinate) to party $\psi(i)$. Thus party P_i has the vector $\mathbf{s}_{\{P_i\}}$. We call $\mathbf{x}$ the *randomness vector* since $\mathbf{x}$ is chosen uniformly at random, subject to $\langle \mathbf{x}, \boldsymbol{\varepsilon} \rangle = s$, to generate $\mathbf{s} := M \cdot \mathbf{x}$, the *share vector*. The co-ordinates of $\mathbf{s}$ are precisely the shares of the secret which are distributed to parties according to the mapping ψ. We say that a share vector $\mathbf{s}$ *encodes* a secret s if $\mathbf{s} = M \cdot \mathbf{x}$ for some $\mathbf{x}$ where $\langle \mathbf{x}, \boldsymbol{\varepsilon} \rangle = s$. An MSP is called *ideal* if ψ is injective; since it is surjective by definition, an ideal MSP is an MSP for which ψ is bijective – i.e. each party receives exactly one share.

The associated access structure for an MSP is such that $\boldsymbol{\varepsilon}$ is contained in the linear span of the rows of M owned by any qualified set of parties, and also so that $\boldsymbol{\varepsilon}$ is *not* in the linear span of the rows owned by any unqualified set of parties. It is well known that, given a monotone access structure (Γ, Δ), there exists an MSP $\mathcal{M}$ computing it [24,28,29].

In more detail: A qualified set of parties $Q \in \Gamma$ can compute the secret from the qualified subvector $\mathbf{s}_Q$ because by construction of M there is a publicly-known recombination vector $\boldsymbol{\lambda}$ associated to this set Q such that $\psi(supp(\boldsymbol{\lambda})) \subseteq Q$ and $M^\top \boldsymbol{\lambda} = \boldsymbol{\varepsilon}$. Note that while $\psi(supp(\boldsymbol{\lambda})) \subseteq Q$, this subset of Q must still be qualified – it just may be the case that not all of the parties' shares are required to reconstruct the secret (for example, if multiple parties hold the same share). Since $\psi(supp(\boldsymbol{\lambda})) \subseteq Q$, we have $\langle \boldsymbol{\lambda}, \mathbf{s} \rangle = \langle \boldsymbol{\lambda}_Q, \mathbf{s}_Q \rangle$, so given $\mathbf{s}_Q$ the parties can compute $\langle \boldsymbol{\lambda}_Q, \mathbf{s}_Q \rangle$, and since $\langle \boldsymbol{\lambda}_Q, \mathbf{s}_Q \rangle = \langle \boldsymbol{\lambda}, \mathbf{s} \rangle = \langle \boldsymbol{\lambda}, M \cdot \mathbf{x} \rangle = \langle M^\top \boldsymbol{\lambda}, \mathbf{x} \rangle = \langle \boldsymbol{\varepsilon}, \mathbf{x} \rangle = s$, they can thus determine the secret.

Conversely, for any unqualified set of parties $U \in \Delta$, again by construction of M we have that $\boldsymbol{\varepsilon} \notin im(M_U^\top)$, which is equivalent to each of the following three statements:

- $\varepsilon \notin \ker(M_U)^{\perp}$
- $\exists\, \mathbf{k} \in \ker(M_U)$ such that $\langle \varepsilon, \mathbf{k} \rangle \neq 0$
- $\exists\, \mathbf{k} \in \mathbb{F}^d$ such that $M_U \cdot \mathbf{k} = \mathbf{0}$ with $\langle \varepsilon, \mathbf{k} \rangle = 1$

From the last statement, we can see that for any secret s, for any randomness vector $\mathbf{x} \in \mathbb{F}^d$ encoding it – i.e. where $\langle \mathbf{x}, \varepsilon \rangle = s$ – for any other secret $s' \in \mathbb{F}$ we have $M_U \mathbf{x} = M_U \mathbf{x} + \mathbf{0} = M_U \mathbf{x} + M_U((s' - s) \cdot \mathbf{k}) = M_U(\mathbf{x} + (s' - s) \cdot \mathbf{k})$. Thus if $\mathbf{x}$ encodes the secret s, then the randomness vector $\mathbf{x} + (s' - s) \cdot \mathbf{k}$ encodes s' by linearity of the inner product, but the share vectors held by parties in U are the same. Thus the set of shares received by an unqualified set of parties provides no information about the secret.

In this work we show that for any MSP computing any $\mathcal{Q}_2$ access structure, there exists a matrix N such that for any vector $\mathbf{e} \neq \mathbf{0}$ for which $\psi(supp(\mathbf{e})) \notin \Gamma$, we either have $N \cdot \mathbf{e} \neq \mathbf{0}$, or $N \cdot \mathbf{e} = \mathbf{0}$ and $\langle \mathbf{e}, \varepsilon \rangle = 0$. The matrix N is essentially the parity-check matrix of the code generated by the matrix M of the MSP and turns out to be very useful for efficiently detecting cheating behaviour.

2.3 MPC

Network: We assume secure point-to-point channels. When broadcasting shares but we do not assume broadcast channels: in this context we mean an honest party sends the same element to each other party over the given secure channel.

Security Model: Our protocols are modelled and proved secure in the Universal Composability (UC) framework introduced by Canetti [13] and we assume the reader is familiar with it. We assume static corruptions by the adversary, meaning that the adversary corrupts some set of parties once at the beginning of the protocol. We will usually denote the set of parties the adversary corrupts by $A \subseteq \mathcal{P}$. We assume the adversary is active, meaning that the corrupted parties may execute arbitrary code determined by the adversary, and additionally we allow the protocol to abort prematurely – i.e. the protocols are *actively-secure with abort*. The protocol is secure against a computationally bounded adversary, who must find a collision of the hash function to cheat without causing the protocol to abort.

Pre-processing: Many modern MPC protocols split computation into two phases, the *offline* or *pre-processing phase* and the *online phase*. In the offline phase, the parties engage in several rounds of communication to produce data which can then be used in the online phase. The purpose of doing this is that the pre-processing can be done at any time prior to the execution of the online phase, can be made independent of the function to be computed, and may use expensive public-key primitives, in order to allow the online phase to use only fast information-theoretic primitives. In our protocol design, we follow this model, although we only require symmetric-key primitives throughout since the access structure is $\mathcal{Q}_2$.

Hash Authentication: The work of Furakawa et al. [25] is in the three-party honest majority case. A secret is additively split into three parts, and each party

---

Hash API

The hash API implemented via the hash function $H : \mathbb{F}^* \to \{0,1\}^\lambda$ consists of the following three algorithms:
- $H.\mathsf{Initialise}()$: the hash function is initialised.
- $H.\mathsf{Update}(\mathbf{s})$: the hash function is updated with the vector $\mathbf{s}$.
- $H.\mathsf{Output}()$: the hash function is evaluated and output provided.

Fig. 1. Hash API

is given a different set of two of them. To open a secret, each party sends to one other party the share that party is missing, symmetrically. This suffices for all parties to obtain all shares, but does not ensure that the one corrupt party sent the correct share. This is where the hash evaluation comes in: after a secret is opened, all parties update their hash function locally with all three shares (the two they held and the one they received); after possibly many secrets are opened, the parties broadcast (here meaning each party sends to the other two parties over a secure channel) the outputs of their hash evaluations and compare what they received with what they computed themselves. If any hashes differ, they abort. This process ensures that the shares held by all parties are consistent, even though each party need only send one share to one party per opening. If many shares are opened in the execution of the protocol (as is the case in SPDZ-like protocols, since every multiplication requires two secrets to be opened), this significantly reduces communication overhead, at the cost of cryptographic assumptions for the existence of a collision-resistant hash function. This was generalised to any replicated scheme $\mathcal{Q}_2$ LSSS by Keller et al. [31].

In our work, we apply similar techniques to Furukawa et al. and Keller et al. to the problem of opening values to parties, but in a significantly more general case. We achieve this by proving the folklore results that say an LSSS is error-detecting if and only if it is $\mathcal{Q}_2$. Our protocol will use the "standard" hash function API given in Fig. 1; in brief, our methods are as follows:

- If single party P_i is required to learn a secret, all the other parties send all of their shares to P_i, and then P_i performs an error-detection check on the shares received, telling all parties to abort if errors are detected.
- If all parties are required to learn a secret, the parties engage in a round of communication in which not all parties need to communicate with each other. The parties reconstruct a view of what they think other parties have received, even if they have not communicated with all other parties. After opening possibly many secrets, each party calls Output on the hash function, broadcasts their output, and checks every other party's hash value against their own; we will see that this process authenticates the secrets.

In the next two sections we outline why the methodologies for the two cases are correct. The proof of security of our protocol can be found in the full version.

3 Opening a Value to One Party

In this section, we show that for an LSSS realising a $\mathcal{Q}_2$ access structure, if the share vector $\mathbf{s}$ for some secret s is modified with an error vector $\mathbf{e}$ with unqualified support then $\mathbf{s} + \mathbf{e}$ is either no longer a valid share vector (i.e. is not in $im(M)$), or the error vector encodes 0, and so by linearity $\mathbf{s} + \mathbf{e}$ also encodes s. In our MPC protocol, this will provide an efficient method by which a party to whom a secret is opened (by all other parties sending that party all of their shares) can check whether or not the adversary has introduced an error. The procedure of opening to a single party is necessary in order for the parties to provide input and obtain output in an actively-secure manner.

Lemma 1. *For any MSP $\mathcal{M} = (\mathbb{F}, M, \varepsilon, \psi)$ computing a $\mathcal{Q}_2$ access structure Γ, for any vector $\mathbf{s} \in \mathbb{F}^m$,*

$$\psi(supp(\mathbf{s})) \notin \Gamma \implies \begin{cases} \mathbf{s} \notin im(M), \ or \\ \mathbf{s} \in im(M) \ and \ \mathbf{s} = M\mathbf{x} \ for \ some \ \mathbf{x} \in \mathbb{F}^d \ where \ \langle \mathbf{x}, \varepsilon \rangle = 0. \end{cases}$$

Proof. If $\psi(supp(\mathbf{s})) \notin \Gamma$ then $\mathcal{P} \setminus \psi(supp(\mathbf{s})) \in \Gamma$ since the access structure is $\mathcal{Q}_2$. Thus there is at least one set $Q \in \Gamma$ where $Q \subseteq \mathcal{P} \setminus \psi(supp(\mathbf{s}))$ for which $\mathbf{s}_i = 0$ for all $i \in [m]$ where $\psi(i) \in Q$ (i.e. $\mathbf{s}_Q = \mathbf{0}$), by definition of $supp$.

Recall that for a qualified set Q of parties to reconstruct the secret, they take the appropriate recombination vector $\boldsymbol{\lambda}$ (which has the property that $\psi(supp(\boldsymbol{\lambda})) \subseteq Q$) and compute $s = \langle \boldsymbol{\lambda}, \mathbf{s} \rangle$. For this particular Q and corresponding recombination vector $\boldsymbol{\lambda}$, we have $\langle \boldsymbol{\lambda}, \mathbf{s} \rangle = \langle \boldsymbol{\lambda}_Q, \mathbf{s}_Q \rangle$ since $\psi(supp(\boldsymbol{\lambda})) \subseteq Q$, and $\langle \boldsymbol{\lambda}_Q, \mathbf{s}_Q \rangle = \langle \boldsymbol{\lambda}_Q, \mathbf{0} \rangle = 0$ by the above, so the secret is 0.

If $\mathbf{s} \in im(M)$ then every set $Q \in \Gamma$ must compute the secret as 0 by the definition of MSP (though note that it is not necessarily the case that $\mathbf{s}_Q = \mathbf{0}$ for all $Q \in \Gamma$). Thus the share vector $\mathbf{s}$ is in $im(M)$ and encodes the secret $s = 0$.

Otherwise, $\mathbf{s} \notin im(M)$, and we are done.   □

We now show that if the adversary (controlling an unqualified set of parties) adds an error vector $\mathbf{e}$ to a share vector $\mathbf{s}$, the resulting vector $\mathbf{c} := \mathbf{s} + \mathbf{e}$ will either not be a valid share vector, or will encode the same secret as $\mathbf{s}$ (by linearity). Adding in an error $\mathbf{e}$ that does not change the value of the secret can be viewed as the adversary re-randomising the shares he holds for corrupt parties.

Lemma 2. *Let $\mathcal{M} = (\mathbb{F}, M, \varepsilon, \psi)$ be an MSP computing $\mathcal{Q}_2$ access structure Γ and $\mathbf{c} = \mathbf{s} + \mathbf{e}$ be the observed set of shares, given as a valid share vector $\mathbf{s}$ encoding secret s, with error $\mathbf{e}$. Then there exists a matrix N such that*

$$\psi(supp(\mathbf{e})) \notin \Gamma \implies either \ \mathbf{e} \ encodes \ the \ error \ e = 0, \ or \ N \cdot \mathbf{c} \neq \mathbf{0}$$

Proof. Let N be any matrix whose rows form a basis of $\ker(M^\top)$ and suppose $\mathbf{e} \in \mathbb{F}^m$. By the fundamental theorem of linear algebra, $\ker(M^\top) = im(M)^\perp$, so $\mathbf{s} \in im(M)$ if and only if $N \cdot \mathbf{s} = \mathbf{0}$. Since $\psi(supp(\mathbf{e})) \notin \Gamma$, then by Lemma 1 we have that either $\mathbf{e} \notin im(M)$, or $\mathbf{e} \in im(M)$ and $e = 0$.

If $\mathbf{e} \in im(M)$ then $e = 0$ and we are done, whilst if $\mathbf{e} \notin im(M)$ then $N \cdot \mathbf{e} \neq \mathbf{0}$. In the latter case, since $\mathbf{s} \in im(M)$ we have $N \cdot \mathbf{s} = \mathbf{0}$ and hence $N \cdot \mathbf{c} = N \cdot (\mathbf{s} + \mathbf{e}) = N \cdot \mathbf{s} + N \cdot \mathbf{e} = \mathbf{0} + N \cdot \mathbf{e} \neq \mathbf{0}$.   □

The matrix N is usually called the *cokernel* of M, and can be viewed as the parity-check matrix of the code defined by generator matrix M. The method to open a secret to a single party P_i is then immediate: all parties send their shares to P_i, who then concatenates the shares into a share vector s and computes $N \cdot s$. Since the adversary controls an unqualified set of parties, if $N \cdot s = 0$ then by Lemma 2 the share vector s encodes the correct secret. In this case, P_i recalls any recombination vector λ and computes the secret as $s = \langle \lambda, s \rangle$, and otherwise tells the parties to abort.

4   Opening a Value to All Parties

To motivate our procedure for opening to all parties and to show that it is correct, we first discuss the naïve method of opening shares in a semi-honest protocol, then show how to reduce the communication, and then explain how to obtain a version which is actively-secure (with abort).

To open a secret in a passively-secure protocol, all parties can broadcast all of their shares so that all parties can reconstruct the secret. This method contains redundancy if the access structure is not full-threshold since proper subsets of parties can reconstruct the secret by definition of the access structure. This implies the existence of "minimal" communication patterns for each access structure and LSSS, in which parties only communicate sufficiently for every party to have all shares corresponding to a qualified set of parties.

When bootstrapping to active security, we see that the redundancy allows verification of opened secrets: honest parties can check *all* other parties' broadcasted shares for correctness. When reducing communication with the aim of avoiding the redundancy of broadcasting, honest parties must still be able to detect when the adversary sends inconsistent or erroneous shares. In particular, parties *not* receiving shares from the adversary must also be able to detect that cheating has occurred in spite of not directly being sent erroneous shares.

To achieve this, in our protocol each party will receive enough shares from other parties to determine "optimistically" all shares held by all parties – that is, reconstruct the entire share vector – and then all parties will compare their reconstructed share vectors. To amortise the cost of comparison, the parties will actually update a local collision-resistant hash function each time they reconstruct a new share vector and will then compare the final output of the hash function at the end of the computation, when output is required. This, in essence, is the idea behind the protocols of Furakawa et al. [25] and Keller et al. [31] that are tailored to replicated secret-sharing.

To fix ideas, consider the case of Shamir's scheme: a set of $t + 1$ distinct points determines a unique polynomial of degree at most t that passes through them. This fact not only enables the secret to be computed using $t + 1$ shares, but additionally enables determining the entire polynomial (the coefficients of which are the share vector for the scheme) and consequently all other shares.

For some LSSSs it is not the case that *any* qualified set of parties have enough information to reconstruct all shares[1].

To allow the parties to perform reconstruction, each party is assigned a set of shares that it will receive, which we encode as a map $\mathsf{q} : \mathcal{P} \to 2^{[m]}$ defined as follows: for each $P_i \in \mathcal{P}$, define $\mathsf{q}(P_i)$ to be a set $S_i \subseteq [m]$ such that:

- $\ker(M_{S_i}) = \{\mathbf{0}\}$; that is, the kernel of the submatrix M restricted to the rows indexed by S_i, is trivial; and
- $\psi^{-1}(\{P_i\}) \subseteq S_i$, where ψ^{-1} denotes the preimage of the row-map ψ; that is, each party includes all of their own shares in the set S_i.

These sets are used as follows. Each P_i receives a set of shares, denoted by $\mathbf{s}^i_{\mathsf{q}(P_i)}$, for a given secret. Then in order to reconstruct all shares, P_i tries to find $\mathbf{x}^i$ such that $\mathbf{s}^i_{\mathsf{q}(P_i)} = M_{\mathsf{q}(P_i)} \cdot \mathbf{x}^i$ and then computes $\mathbf{s}^i = M \cdot \mathbf{x}^i$ as the reconstructed share vector, which is then used to update the hash function (locally). Trivially, we can take $\mathsf{q}(P_i) = [m]$ for all $P_i \in \mathcal{P}$, which corresponds to broadcasting all shares; however, better choices of q result in better communication efficiency. In the full version we give a somewhat-optimised algorithm for finding a "good" map q for a given MSP. We remark that finding the map q is not always as straightforward as it is for replicated secret-sharing in which each party must obtain precisely all the shares it does not have; for many LSSSs, this is overkill: for example, Shamir sharing only requires receiving t shares from other parties, not all $n - 1$ other shares it does not possess.

If such an $\mathbf{x}^i$ does not exist then it must be because the adversary sent one or more incorrect shares, because $\mathbf{s}^i_{\mathsf{q}(P_i)}$ should be a subvector of *some* share vector. In this case, the party or parties unable to reconstruct tell all parties to abort.

If such an $\mathbf{x}^i$ does exist for each party then the adversary could still cause different parties to reconstruct different share vectors (and thus output different secrets), but then the hashes would differ and the honest parties would abort. The first condition, $\ker(M_{S_i}) = \{\mathbf{0}\}$, ensures that if all parties follow the protocol, they all reconstruct the *same* share vector, since there are multiple possible share vectors for a given secret, otherwise an honest execution may lead to an abort.

Indeed, the only thing the adversary can do without causing abort – either immediately or later on when hashes are compared – is to change his shares so that his shares combined with the honest parties' shares form a valid share vector. Intuitively, one can think of this as the adversary re-randomising the shares owned only by corrupt parties, which is not possible in Shamir or replicated secret-sharing, but is in DNF-based sharing, and in general is possible if and only if the LSSS admits non-trivial share vectors with unqualified support.

More formally, we have the following lemma that shows that if all parties *can* reconstruct share vectors and the share vectors are consistent, then the adversary cannot have introduced an error.

---

[1] In the full version we provide a formal description of MSPs in which all qualified sets of parties can reconstruct the entire share vector and explain how such MSPs are "good" for our protocol.

Protocol Π_{Opening}

For each $P_i \in \mathcal{P}$, the parties decide on some $\boldsymbol{\lambda}^i$, which is any recombination vector such that $supp(\boldsymbol{\lambda}^i) \subseteq \mathsf{q}(P_i)$. See Section 4 for the definition of q. We denote by H^i the hash function updated locally by P_i which will be initialised as in Figure 5, at the start of the MPC protocol. If at any point a party receives the message Abort, it runs the subprotocol **Abort**.

OpenTo(i):
If $i = 0$, the secret s encoded via share vector $\mathbf{s}$, is to be opened to all, otherwise it is to be opened only to player P_i.

If $i = 0$ then each $P_j \in \mathcal{P}$ does the following:
1. Retrieve from memory the recombination vector $\boldsymbol{\lambda}^j$.
2. For each $P_\ell \in \mathcal{P}$, for each $k \in \mathsf{q}(P_\ell)$, if $\psi(k) = P_j$ then send $\mathbf{s}_k$ to P_ℓ.
3. For each $k \in \mathsf{q}(P_j)$, wait to receive $\mathbf{s}_k$ from party $\psi(k)$.
4. Concatenate local and received shares into a vector denoted by $\mathbf{s}^j_{\mathsf{q}(P_j)} \in \mathbb{F}^{|\mathsf{q}(P_j)|}$.
5. (Locally) output $s = \langle \boldsymbol{\lambda}^j_{\mathsf{q}(P_j)}, \mathbf{s}^j_{\mathsf{q}(P_j)} \rangle$.
6. Solve $M_{\mathsf{q}(P_j)} \cdot \mathbf{x}^j = \mathbf{s}^j_{\mathsf{q}(P_j)}$ for $\mathbf{x}^j$. If there are no solutions, run **Abort**.
7. Execute $H^j.\mathsf{Update}(M\mathbf{x}^j)$.

If $i \neq 0$, the secret encoded via share vector $\mathbf{s}$ is to be opened to party P_i. The parties do the following:
1. Each $P_j \in \mathcal{P} \setminus \{P_i\}$ sends $\mathbf{s}_{\{P_j\}}$ to P_i, who concatenates local and received shares into a vector $\mathbf{s}$.
2. Party P_i computes $N \cdot \mathbf{s}$; if it is equal to $\mathbf{0}$, P_i (locally) outputs $s = \langle \boldsymbol{\lambda}^i, \mathbf{s} \rangle$, and otherwise runs **Abort**.

Verify: Each $P_i \in \mathcal{P}$ does the following:
1. Compute $h^i := H^i.\mathsf{Output}()$.
2. Send h^i to all other parties $P_j \in \mathcal{P} \setminus \{P_i\}$ over pair-wise secure channels.
3. Wait for h^j from all other parties $P_j \in \mathcal{P} \setminus \{P_i\}$.
4. If $h^j \neq h^i$ for any j, run **Abort**.

Abort: If a party calls this subroutine, it sends a message Abort to all parties and aborts. If a party receives a message Abort, it aborts.

Broadcast: When P_i calls this procedure to broadcast a value s,
1. Party P_i sends the secret s to all other players over pair-wise secure channels.
2. When party P_j receives the share, it executes $H^j.\mathsf{Update}(s)$.

Fig. 2. Protocol Π_{Opening}

Lemma 3. *Let $q : \mathcal{P} \to 2^{[m]}$ be defined as above and let $\mathbf{s}^i_{\mathsf{q}(i)}$ denote the subvector of shares received by party P_i for a given secret. Suppose it is possible for each party $P_i \in \mathcal{P}$ to find a vector $\mathbf{x}^i$ such that $\mathbf{s}^i_{\mathsf{q}(P_i)} = M_{\mathsf{q}(P_i)}\mathbf{x}^i$; let $\mathbf{s}^i := M \cdot \mathbf{x}^i$*

for each $i \in [n]$. If $\mathbf{s}^i = \mathbf{s}^j$ for all honest parties P_i and P_j, then the adversary did not introduce an error on the secret.

Proof. The existence of q follows from the fact that "at worst" we can take $\mathsf{q}(P_i) = [m]$ for all $P_i \in \mathcal{P}$. There is a unique $\mathbf{x}^i$ solving $\mathbf{s}^i_{\mathsf{q}(P_i)} = M_{\mathsf{q}(P_i)} \cdot \mathbf{x}^i$ (not *a priori* necessarily the same for all parties) because $\ker(M_{\mathsf{q}(P_i)}) = \{\mathbf{0}\}$ for all $P_i \in \mathcal{P}$ by the first requirement in the definition of q.

Let A denote the set of corrupt parties. Since A is unqualified, the honest parties form a qualified set $Q = \mathcal{P} \setminus A$ since the access structure is $\mathcal{Q}_2$.

Each honest party uses their own shares in the reconstruction process by the second requirement in the definition of q, so if $\mathbf{s}^i = \mathbf{s}^j$ for all honest parties P_i and P_j, then in particular they all agree on a qualified subvector defined by honest shares – i.e. $\mathbf{s}^i_Q = \mathbf{s}^j_Q$ for all honest parties P_i and P_j. Thus some qualified subvector of the share vector is well defined, which uniquely defines the secret by definition of MSP.   □

Functionality $\mathcal{F}_{\mathsf{Prep}}$

The functionality maintains a list Value of secrets that it stores. The set A indexes the corrupt parties (unknown to the honest parties).

Triples: On input (Triple, N_T) from all parties, the functionality does the following:
1. For i from 1 to N_T:
   (a) Sample $a^i, b^i \overset{\$}{\leftarrow} \mathbb{F}$ and compute share vectors $\mathbf{a}^i$ and $\mathbf{b}^i$.
   (b) Send $(\mathbf{a}^i_A, \mathbf{b}^i_A)$ to the adversary.
   (c) Receive a subvector of shares $\tilde{\mathbf{c}}^i_A$ from the adversary.
   (d) Compute a vector $\mathbf{c}^i = M \cdot \mathbf{x}^i_c$ such that $\langle \mathbf{x}^i_c, \boldsymbol{\epsilon} \rangle = a^i \cdot b^i$ and $\mathbf{c}^i_A = \tilde{\mathbf{c}}^i_A$. If no such vector $\mathbf{c}^i$ exists, set an internal flag Abort to true and continue.
2. Wait for a message OK or Abort from the adversary.
3. If the response is OK and the internal flag Abort has not been set to true, for each honest $P_i \in \mathcal{P}$, send $(\mathbf{a}^i_{\{P_i\}}, \mathbf{b}^i_{\{P_i\}}, \mathbf{c}^i_{\{P_i\}})_{i=1}^{N_T}$ to each honest party P_i, and otherwise output the message Abort to all honest parties and abort.

Fig. 3. Functionality $\mathcal{F}_{\mathsf{Prep}}$

As mentioned in the introduction, our results in the last two sections are somewhat analogous to the result of Cramer et al. [19, Theorem 1] which roughly shows that for a strongly multiplicative LSSS implementing a $\mathcal{Q}_3$ access structure, honest parties can always agree on the correct secret (when all parties broadcast their shares). In Fig. 2 we present the methods we use to open secret shared data in different situations.

5   MPC Protocol

We are now ready to present our protocol to implement the MPC functionality offering active security with abort as given in Fig. 4. We present the online

---

Functionality $\mathcal{F}_{\mathsf{MPC}}$

Initialise: On input Init from all parties, the functionality initialises the array Value[]. Accept a message OK or Abort from the adversary; if the message is OK then continue, and otherwise send the message Abort to all parties and abort.

Input: On input (Input, id, x) from party P_i and (Input, id, $\perp$) from all other parties, where id is a fresh identifer, the functionality sets Value[id] := x.

Add: On input (Add, $\mathsf{id}_1, \mathsf{id}_2, \mathsf{id}_3$) from all parties, if id_3 is a fresh identifier and Value[id_1] and Value[id_2] have been defined, the functionality sets Value[id_3] := Value[id_1] + Value[id_2].

Multiply: On input (Multiply, $\mathsf{id}_1, \mathsf{id}_2, \mathsf{id}_3$) from all parties, if id_3 is a fresh identifier and Value[id_1] and Value[id_2] have been defined, the functionality waits for a message OK or Abort from the adversary. If the adversary sends the message Abort, send the message Abort to all parties and the adversary and abort, and otherwise set Value[id_3] := Value[id_1] · Value[id_2].

Output: On input (Output, id, i) from all parties, if Value[id] has been defined, the functionality does the following:
- If $i = 0$, send Value[id] to the adversary and wait for a signal OK or Abort in return. If it signals Abort, send the message Abort to all parties and the adversary and abort, and otherwise send Value[id] to all parties. If not aborted, wait for another signal OK or Abort. If the adversary signals Abort, send the message Abort to all parties and the adversary and abort.
- If $i \neq 0$ and P_i is corrupt, then the functionality sends Value[id] to the adversary and waits for the adversary to signal OK or Abort. If it signals Abort, send the message Abort to all parties and abort.
- If $i \neq 0$ and P_i is honest, the functionality waits for the adversary to signal OK or Abort. If it signals Abort, send the message Abort to all parties and the adversary and abort, and otherwise send Value[id] to P_i.

Fig. 4. Functionality $\mathcal{F}_{\mathsf{MPC}}$

method here, leaving the offline method for the full version. Our offline method is much more scalable than [31] since the dependence on replicated secret-sharing is removed. The offline method implements the functionality given in Fig. 3. Our online protocol, in Fig. 5, makes use of the opening protocol Π_{Opening} given in Fig. 2 earlier. The majority of our protocol uses standard MPC techniques for secret-sharing. In particular, the equation the parties compute for the multiplication is a standard application of Beaver's circuit randomisation technique [2], albeit for a general LSSS.

Correctness of our input procedure follows from the input method given in the non-interactive pseudo-random secret-sharing protocol of [17]. In particular for party P_i to provide an input s in a secret-shared form $\mathbf{s}$, the parties will first take a secret-sharing $\mathbf{r}$ of a uniformly random secret r – which is some a or b

---

Protocol Π_{MPC}

Note that this protocol calls on procedures from Π_{Opening} in Figure 2. If a party never receives an expected message from the adversary, we assume the receiving party signals **Abort** to all other parties and aborts.

Initialise: The parties do the following:
1. Each $P_i \in \mathcal{P}$ executes $H^i.\mathsf{Initialise}()$.
2. The parties call $\mathcal{F}_{\mathsf{Prep}}$ with input (Triple, N_T) get N_T triples.
3. The parties agree on a public sharing of the secret 1, denoted by $\mathbf{u}$.
4. Each party has one random secret opened to them for every input they will provide to the protocol: the parties do the following:
   (a) Retrieve from memory a sharing $\mathbf{r}$ of a uniformly random secret r, obtained first or second random secret from a Beaver triple. (The secret used may neither be used again for input nor used in a multiplication.)
   (b) Run **OpenTo**(i) on $\mathbf{r}$ so that P_i obtains r.

Input: For party P_i to input secret s,
1. Party P_i retrieves a secret r from memory, corresponding to a share vector $\mathbf{r}$ established during **Initialise** for inputs, and all parties $P_j \in \mathcal{P}$ retrieve their shares $\mathbf{r}_{\{P_j\}}$.
2. Party P_i executes **Broadcast** to open $\epsilon := s - r$.
3. Each party $P_j \in \mathcal{P}$ computes $\mathbf{s}_{\{P_j\}} := \epsilon \cdot \mathbf{u}_{\{P_j\}} + \mathbf{r}_{\{P_j\}}$.

Add: To add secrets s and s', with corresponding share vectors $\mathbf{s}$ and $\mathbf{s}'$, for each $P_i \in \mathcal{P}$ party P_i computes $\mathbf{s}_{\{P_i\}} + \mathbf{s}'_{\{P_i\}}$.

Multiply: To multiply secrets s and s', with corresponding share vectors $\mathbf{s}$ and $\mathbf{s}'$, each $P_i \in \mathcal{P}$ does the following:
1. Retrieve from memory the shares $(\mathbf{a}_{\{P_i\}}, \mathbf{b}_{\{P_i\}}, \mathbf{c}_{\{P_i\}})$ of a triple $(\mathbf{a}, \mathbf{b}, \mathbf{c})$ obtained in **Initialise**.
2. Compute $\mathbf{s}_{\{P_i\}} - \mathbf{a}_{\{P_i\}}$ and $\mathbf{s}'_{\{P_i\}} - \mathbf{b}_{\{P_i\}}$.
3. Run **OpenTo**(0) on $\mathbf{s} - \mathbf{a}$ and $\mathbf{s}' - \mathbf{b}$ to obtain (publicly) $s - a$ and $s' - b$.
4. If the parties have not aborted, compute the following as the share of the product $\mathbf{c}_{\{P_i\}} + (s - a) \cdot \mathbf{s}'_{\{P_i\}} + (s' - b) \cdot \mathbf{s}_{\{P_i\}} - (s - a) \cdot (s' - b) \cdot \mathbf{u}_{\{P_i\}}$.

OutputTo(i): If $i = 0$, the secret s, encoded via share vector $\mathbf{s}$, is to be output to all parties, so the parties do the following:
1. Run **Verify**.
2. If the parties have not aborted, run **OpenTo**(0) on $\mathbf{s}$.
3. If the parties have not aborted, run **Verify** again.
4. If the parties have not aborted, all parties (locally) output s.
If $P_i \in \mathcal{P}$, the secret s encoded via share vector $\mathbf{s}$ is to be output to party P_i, so the parties do the following:
1. Run **Verify**.
2. If the parties have not aborted, run **OpenTo**(i) on $\mathbf{s}$.
3. If P_i has not aborted it (locally) outputs s.

Fig. 5. Protocol Π_{MPC}

from a Beaver triple – and open it by calling **OpenTo**(i). Then P_i determines the encoded secret (using any recombination vector) and broadcasts $\epsilon := s - r$. The parties compute the share vector as $\mathbf{s} := \epsilon \cdot \mathbf{u} + \mathbf{r}$ where $\mathbf{u}$ is a pre-agreed sharing of 1, which may be the same vector used to compute all inputs, by which we mean that for $i \in [m]$, party $\psi(i)$ computes $\mathbf{s}_i := \epsilon \cdot \mathbf{u}_i + \mathbf{r}_i$. Since this r is uniformly random by assumption, it hides the input s in the broadcast of ϵ. This is proved formally in our simulation proof.

We have the following proposition, which we prove in the full version under the UC framework of Canetti [14]. Here we use $(\Pi_{\mathsf{MPC}} \| \Pi_{\mathsf{Opening}})$ to mean simply that the union of the procedures from both protocols are used.

Proposition 1. *The protocol $(\Pi_{\mathsf{MPC}} \| \Pi_{\mathsf{Opening}})$ securely realises $\mathcal{F}_{\mathsf{MPC}}$ for a $\mathcal{Q}_2$ access structure in the presence of a computationally-bounded active adversary, corrupting any unqualified set of parties, in the $\mathcal{F}_{\mathsf{Prep}}$-hybrid model, assuming the existence of a collision-resistant hash function and point-to-point secure channels.*

We note that since we do not use MACs, we can also instantiate our protocol over small finite fields[2], or indeed using a LSSS over a ring. The latter will hold as long as the reconstruction vectors can be defined over the said ring. By taking a ring such as $\mathbb{Z}/2^{32}\mathbb{Z}$ we thus generalise the Sharemind methodology [11] to an arbitrary $\mathcal{Q}_2$ structure. Also note that we can extend $\mathcal{F}_{\mathsf{Prep}}$ in a trivial way so as to obtain other forms of pre-processing such shares of bits etc. as in [22].

Acknowledgements. We thank for the anonymous reviewers for their helpful comments and remarks. This work has been supported in part by ERC Advanced Grant ERC-2015-AdG-IMPaCT, by the Defense Advanced Research Projects Agency (DARPA) and Space and Naval Warfare Systems Center, Pacific (SSC Pacific) under contract No. N66001-15-C-4070, and by EPSRC via grant EP/N021940/1.

References

1. Araki, T., Furukawa, J., Lindell, Y., Nof, A., Ohara, K.: High-throughput semi-honest secure three-party computation with an honest majority. In: Weippl, E.R., Katzenbeisser, S., Kruegel, C., Myers, A.C., Halevi, S. (eds.) ACM CCS 2016, pp. 805–817. ACM Press, October 2016
2. Beaver, D.: Efficient multiparty protocols using circuit randomization. In: Feigenbaum, J. (ed.) CRYPTO 1991. LNCS, vol. 576, pp. 420–432. Springer, Heidelberg (1992). https://doi.org/10.1007/3-540-46766-1_34
3. Beaver, D., Wool, A.: Quorum-based secure multi-party computation. In: Nyberg, K. (ed.) EUROCRYPT 1998. LNCS, vol. 1403, pp. 375–390. Springer, Heidelberg (1998). https://doi.org/10.1007/BFb0054140
4. Beimel, A., Gál, A., Paterson, M.: Lower bounds for monotone span programs. In: 36th FOCS, pp. 674–681. IEEE Computer Society Press, October 1995

---

[2] If using a small ring/finite field we simply need to modify the sacrificing stage in the triple production process; no changes are needed for the online phase at all.

5. Ben-Or, M., Goldwasser, S., Wigderson, A.: Completeness theorems for non-cryptographic fault-tolerant distributed computation (extended abstract). In: 20th ACM STOC, pp. 1–10. ACM Press, May 1988

6. Ben-Sasson, E., Fehr, S., Ostrovsky, R.: Near-linear unconditionally-secure multiparty computation with a dishonest minority. In: Safavi-Naini, R., Canetti, R. (eds.) CRYPTO 2012. LNCS, vol. 7417, pp. 663–680. Springer, Heidelberg (2012). https://doi.org/10.1007/978-3-642-32009-5_39

7. Bendlin, R., Damgård, I., Orlandi, C., Zakarias, S.: Semi-homomorphic encryption and multiparty computation. In: Paterson, K.G. (ed.) EUROCRYPT 2011. LNCS, vol. 6632, pp. 169–188. Springer, Heidelberg (2011). https://doi.org/10.1007/978-3-642-20465-4_11

8. Bilgin, B., Gierlichs, B., Nikova, S., Nikov, V., Rijmen, V.: Higher-order threshold implementations. In: Sarkar, P., Iwata, T. (eds.) ASIACRYPT 2014, Part II. LNCS, vol. 8874, pp. 326–343. Springer, Heidelberg (2014). https://doi.org/10.1007/978-3-662-45608-8_18

9. Blakley, G.R.: Safeguarding cryptographic keys. In: Proceedings of AFIPS 1979 National Computer Conference, vol. 48, pp. 313–317 (1979)

10. Bogdanov, D., Kamm, L., Kubo, B., Rebane, R., Sokk, V., Talviste, R.: Students and taxes: a privacy-preserving social study using secure computation. Cryptology ePrint Archive, Report 2015/1159 (2015). http://eprint.iacr.org/2015/1159

11. Bogdanov, D., Laur, S., Willemson, J.: Sharemind: a framework for fast privacy-preserving computations. In: Jajodia, S., Lopez, J. (eds.) ESORICS 2008. LNCS, vol. 5283, pp. 192–206. Springer, Heidelberg (2008). https://doi.org/10.1007/978-3-540-88313-5_13

12. Bogetoft, P., et al.: Secure multiparty computation goes live. In: Dingledine, R., Golle, P. (eds.) FC 2009. LNCS, vol. 5628, pp. 325–343. Springer, Heidelberg (2009). https://doi.org/10.1007/978-3-642-03549-4_20

13. Canetti, R.: Security and composition of multiparty cryptographic protocols. J. Cryptology 13(1), 143–202 (2000)

14. Canetti, R.: Universally composable security: a new paradigm for cryptographic protocols. Cryptology ePrint Archive, Report 2000/067 (2000). http://eprint.iacr.org/2000/067

15. Chaum, D., Crépeau, C., Damgård, I.: Multiparty unconditionally secure protocols (extended abstract). In: 20th ACM STOC, pp. 11–19. ACM Press, May 1988

16. Chida, K., et al.: Fast large-scale honest-majority MPC for malicious adversaries. In: Shacham, H., Boldyreva, A. (eds.) CRYPTO 2018, Part III. LNCS, vol. 10993, pp. 34–64. Springer, Cham (2018). https://doi.org/10.1007/978-3-319-96878-0_2

17. Cramer, R., Damgård, I., Ishai, Y.: Share conversion, pseudorandom secret-sharing and applications to secure computation. In: Kilian, J. (ed.) TCC 2005. LNCS, vol. 3378, pp. 342–362. Springer, Heidelberg (2005). https://doi.org/10.1007/978-3-540-30576-7_19

18. Cramer, R., Damgård, I., Maurer, U.: General secure multi-party computation from any linear secret-sharing scheme. In: Preneel, B. (ed.) EUROCRYPT 2000. LNCS, vol. 1807, pp. 316–334. Springer, Heidelberg (2000). https://doi.org/10.1007/3-540-45539-6_22

19. Cramer, R., et al.: On codes, matroids and secure multi-party computation from linear secret sharing schemes. In: Shoup, V. (ed.) CRYPTO 2005. LNCS, vol. 3621, pp. 327–343. Springer, Heidelberg (2005). https://doi.org/10.1007/11535218_20

20. Damgård, I., Geisler, M., Krøigaard, M., Nielsen, J.B.: Asynchronous multiparty computation: theory and implementation. In: Jarecki, S., Tsudik, G. (eds.) PKC

2009. LNCS, vol. 5443, pp. 160–179. Springer, Heidelberg (2009). https://doi.org/10.1007/978-3-642-00468-1_10

21. Damgård, I., Ishai, Y., Krøigaard, M.: Perfectly secure multiparty computation and the computational overhead of cryptography. In: Gilbert, H. (ed.) EUROCRYPT 2010. LNCS, vol. 6110, pp. 445–465. Springer, Heidelberg (2010). https://doi.org/10.1007/978-3-642-13190-5_23

22. Damgård, I., Keller, M., Larraia, E., Pastro, V., Scholl, P., Smart, N.P.: Practical covertly secure MPC for dishonest majority – or: breaking the SPDZ limits. In: Crampton, J., Jajodia, S., Mayes, K. (eds.) ESORICS 2013. LNCS, vol. 8134, pp. 1–18. Springer, Heidelberg (2013). https://doi.org/10.1007/978-3-642-40203-6_1

23. Damgård, I., Pastro, V., Smart, N., Zakarias, S.: Multiparty computation from somewhat homomorphic encryption. In: Safavi-Naini, R., Canetti, R. (eds.) CRYPTO 2012. LNCS, vol. 7417, pp. 643–662. Springer, Heidelberg (2012). https://doi.org/10.1007/978-3-642-32009-5_38

24. van Dijk, M.: Secret key sharing and secret key generation. Ph.D. thesis, Eindhoven University of Technology (1997)

25. Furukawa, J., Lindell, Y., Nof, A., Weinstein, O.: High-throughput secure three-party computation for malicious adversaries and an honest majority. In: Coron, J.-S., Nielsen, J.B. (eds.) EUROCRYPT 2017, Part II. LNCS, vol. 10211, pp. 225–255. Springer, Cham (2017). https://doi.org/10.1007/978-3-319-56614-6_8

26. Goldreich, O., Micali, S., Wigderson, A.: How to play any mental game or a completeness theorem for protocols with honest majority. In: Aho, A. (ed.) 19th ACM STOC, pp. 218–229. ACM Press, May 1987

27. Hirt, M., Maurer, U.M.: Complete characterization of adversaries tolerable in secure multi-party computation (extended abstract). In: Burns, J.E., Attiya, H. (eds.) 16th ACM PODC, pp. 25–34. ACM, August 1997

28. Ito, M., Saito, A., Nishizeki, T.: Secret sharing schemes realizing general access structure. In: Proceedings of IEEE Global Telecommunication Conference (Globecom 1987), pp. 99–102 (1987)

29. Karchmer, M., Wigderson, A.: On span programs. In: Proceedings of Structures in Complexity Theory, pp. 102–111 (1993)

30. Keller, M., Orsini, E., Scholl, P.: MASCOT: faster malicious arithmetic secure computation with oblivious transfer. In: Weippl, E.R., Katzenbeisser, S., Kruegel, C., Myers, A.C., Halevi, S. (eds.) ACM CCS 2016, pp. 830–842. ACM Press, October 2016

31. Keller, M., Rotaru, D., Smart, N.P., Wood, T.: Reducing communication channels in MPC. In: Catalano, D., De Prisco, R. (eds.) SCN 2018. LNCS, vol. 11035, pp. 181–199. Springer, Cham (2018). https://doi.org/10.1007/978-3-319-98113-0_10

32. Maurer, U.M.: Secure multi-party computation made simple. Discrete Appl. Math. 154(2), 370–381 (2006)

33. Nikova, S., Rijmen, V., Schläffer, M.: Secure hardware implementation of nonlinear functions in the presence of glitches. J. Cryptology 24(2), 292–321 (2011)

34. Reparaz, O., Bilgin, B., Nikova, S., Gierlichs, B., Verbauwhede, I.: Consolidating masking schemes. In: Gennaro, R., Robshaw, M. (eds.) CRYPTO 2015, Part I. LNCS, vol. 9215, pp. 764–783. Springer, Heidelberg (2015). https://doi.org/10.1007/978-3-662-47989-6_37

35. Shamir, A.: How to share a secret. Commun. ACM 22(11), 612–613 (1979)

36. Yao, A.C.C.: How to generate and exchange secrets (extended abstract). In: 27th FOCS, pp. 162–167. IEEE Computer Society Press, October 1986

Lossy Trapdoor Permutations
with Improved Lossiness

Benedikt Auerbach[1]($\boxtimes$), Eike Kiltz[1], Bertram Poettering[2],
and Stefan Schoenen[3]

[1] Horst-Görtz Institute for IT Security, Ruhr University Bochum, Bochum, Germany
{benedikt.auerbach,eike.kiltz}@rub.de
[2] Royal Holloway, University of London, Egham, UK
bertram.poettering@rhul.ac.uk
[3] paluno – The Ruhr Institute for Software Technology,
University of Duisburg-Essen, Essen, Germany
stefan.schoenen@paluno.uni-due.de

Abstract. Lossy trapdoor functions (Peikert and Waters, STOC 2008 and SIAM J. Computing 2011) imply, via black-box transformations, a number of interesting cryptographic primitives, including chosen-ciphertext secure public-key encryption. Kiltz, O'Neill, and Smith (CRYPTO 2010) showed that the RSA trapdoor permutation is lossy under the Phi-hiding assumption, but syntactically it is not a lossy trapdoor function since it acts on $\mathbb{Z}_N$ and not on strings. Using a domain extension technique by Freeman et al. (PKC 2010 and J. Cryptology 2013) it can be extended to a lossy trapdoor permutation, but with considerably reduced lossiness.

In this work we give new constructions of lossy trapdoor permutations from the Phi-hiding assumption, the quadratic residuosity assumption, and the decisional composite residuosity assumption, all with improved lossiness. Furthermore, we propose the first all-but-one lossy trapdoor permutation from the Phi-hiding assumption. A technical vehicle used for achieving this is a novel transform that converts trapdoor functions with index-dependent domain to trapdoor functions with fixed domain.

1 Introduction

LOSSY TRAPDOOR FUNCTIONS. Lossy trapdoor functions (LTFs) are like classic (one-way) trapdoor functions but with strengthened security properties. Instances of an LTF can be created in two computationally indistinguishable ways: An instance generated with the standard key-generation algorithm describes an injective function that can be efficiently inverted using the trapdoor; and an instance generated with the lossy key-generation algorithm describes a "lossy" function, meaning its range is considerably smaller than its domain. The

The full version of this article can be found in the IACR eprint archive as article 2018/1183 at https://eprint.iacr.org/2018/1183.

M. Matsui (Ed.): CT-RSA 2019, LNCS 11405, pp. 230–250, 2019.
https://doi.org/10.1007/978-3-030-12612-4_12

lossiness factor $L \geq 1$, defined as the ratio of the cardinalities of domain and range, measures the LTF's quality.[1] The larger the lossiness factor, the better the cryptographic properties of the LTF. In case the non-lossy instances define permutations, we will refer to the whole object as a lossy trapdoor permutation (LTP).

Lossy trapdoor functions were introduced by Peikert and Waters [21,22] who showed that they imply (via black-box constructions) fundamental cryptographic primitives such as classic trapdoor functions, collision-resistant hash functions, oblivious transfer, and chosen-ciphertext secure public-key encryption. Furthermore, LTFs have found various other applications, including deterministic public-key encryption [7], OAEP-based public-key encryption [17], "hedged" public-key encryption for protecting against bad randomness [2,4], security against selective opening attacks [5], efficient non-interactive string commitments [20], threshold encryption [26], correlated-product secure trapdoor functions [24], adaptive trapdoor functions [16], and many others.

LTFs WITH INDEX-DEPENDENT DOMAINS. In the original definition by Peikert and Waters, all instances of an LTF are defined over the same fixed domain $\{0,1\}^k$. That is, the domain is independent of the specific index output by the key-generation algorithm ('index' is used synonym with the public key describing the instance). Subsequently, LTFs were generalized to *LTFs with index-dependent domains* [11] where the domain may depend on the function's index. To illustrate index-dependent domains, consider the well-known RSA trapdoor permutation $f_{RSA} \colon \mathbb{Z}_N \to \mathbb{Z}_N; \ x \mapsto x^e \bmod N$. Its index consists of a modulus $N = pq$ (of fixed bit-length k) and an exponent e; its domain is $\mathbb{Z}_N$, hence it is index-dependent. For $e \leq 2^{k/4}$, permutation f_{RSA} was proved to be lossy [17] with lossiness factor $L = e$ under the Phi-hiding assumption [9].[2] Similarly, constructions of trapdoor functions based on quadratic residuosity or Paillier's assumption yield LTPs with index-dependent domains [10,11].

As pointed out in [11], LTFs with index-dependent domains do not seem to be sufficient for constructing correlated-product secure trapdoor functions [24] or chosen-ciphertext secure public-key encryption [21]. The difficulty is that in these applications a fixed value has to be evaluated on many independently generated instances of the trapdoor function. It is therefore crucial that the domains are the same for all these instances. Furthermore, most constructions of deterministic encryption schemes (e.g., [3,7,8,18,23]) assume message distributions that do not depend on the public key and hence cannot be constructed from

---

[1] The original definition of lossy trapdoor functions [21,22] measures lossiness on a logarithmic scale. That is, $\ell := \log_2(L)$ is the lossiness of the LTF and L is the lossiness factor (which we use in this work).

[2] In brief, the Phi-hiding assumption states that (N, e), where $N = pq$ and $e \nmid \varphi(N)$, is computationally indistinguishable from (N, e), where $N = pq$ and $e \mid \varphi(N)$. The Phi-hiding assumption is conjectured to hold for $e \leq N^{1/4-\epsilon}$ and does not hold for $e > N^{1/4}$ (due to a Coppersmith-like attack). If $e \mid \varphi(N)$, then $f_{RSA}(x) = x^e \bmod N$ is roughly an e-to-1 function.

LTFs with index-dependent domains. Fortunately, however, LTFs with index-dependent domains turn out to be sufficient for many other applications.

In [11, Sect. 3.2], a general domain-extension technique was (implicitly) proposed that transforms an LTF $f \colon \mathbb{Z}_N \to \mathbb{Z}_N$ with index-dependent domain $\mathbb{Z}_N$ (with $2^{k-1} \leq N < 2^k$) into an LTF $f_{\mathrm{de}} \colon \{0,1\}^k \to \{0,1\}^k$ with index-independent domain $\{0,1\}^k$ by defining

$$f_{\mathrm{de}}(x) := \begin{cases} f(x) & 0 \leq x < N \\ x & N \leq x < 2^k \end{cases}. \tag{1}$$

However, this transform does bad in preserving lossiness, in particular in the case where N is close to 2^{k-1}. Indeed, if the lossiness factor of f is L then the lossiness factor of f_{de} is about $L_{\mathrm{de}} = 2 \cdot L/(L+1) < 2$. Note that such a small lossiness factor does not even imply one-wayness, i.e., the resulting LTF is, taken by itself, essentially useless. (Based on a result by Mol and Yilek [19] it can still be used to build IND-CCA secure encryption, but with considerably worse efficiency.) In [11, Sect. 4.4] also an alternative domain-extension technique was sketched that can be used to construct an LTF f_{de} with index-independent domain $\{0,1\}^{k+\log(L)}$ and lossiness factor $L_{\mathrm{de}} \approx L$. Here, every evaluation of f_{de} requires $\log(L)$ many applications of f. For interesting values of L this is again prohibitively inefficient.

ALL-BUT-ONE LOSSY TRAPDOOR FUNCTIONS. All-but-one lossy trapdoor functions (ABO-LTFs) are a generalization of LTFs. An ABO-LTF is associated with a set $\mathcal{B}r$ of branches. The corresponding generator algorithm is invoked on input a target branch $br^* \in \mathcal{B}r$ and outputs a trapdoor and a family of functions $(f_{br})_{br \in \mathcal{B}r}$ with the property that f_{br} is injective for all $br \neq br^*$ (and can be inverted using the trapdoor), but function f_{br^*} is lossy. Moreover, the lossy branch is hidden (computationally) by the description of the function family. ABO-LTFs with just two branches are equivalent to LTFs, and, similarly to LTFs, ABO-LTFs can have index-independent or index-dependent domains. Using the techniques of Peikert and Waters [21] an ABO-LTF with exponentially large branch set can be constructed from any LTF, but the latter is required to have a sufficiently large lossiness factor L. (This transformation also works for LTFs with index-dependent domains.) Many of the mentioned applications of LTFs require in fact ABO-LTFs.

KNOWN LTFs AND ABO-LTFs. Roughly speaking, cryptographic assumptions are typically rooted in one out of three different environments: over cyclic groups, over lattices, or over RSA moduli. Over cyclic groups as well as over lattices, constructions of LTFs and ABO-LTFs are known [21]. They have index-independent domain and can be instantiated to have an arbitrarily large lossiness factor L. In the RSA setting, the situation is different.[3] There are constructions known from

---

[3] When we say an LTF is "RSA-based" we mean it is defined in respect to some composite number $N = pq$ where p, q are primes. This shall not suggest its security relies on the RSA assumption (the hardness of computing e-th roots).

the quadratic residuosity assumption [11], Paillier's decisional composite residuosity assumption [11], and from the Phi-hiding assumption [9,17] (for a fourth one, see below). All constructions have index-dependent domains (the transform sketched above fixes this, but the results are essentially useless due to the small lossiness factor). Unfortunately, for the constructions based on the Phi-hiding assumption and the quadratic residuosity assumption the lossiness factor cannot be made arbitrarily large and, in particular, it is not sufficient to construct efficient ABO-TDFs. However, both an index-independent LTF and an ABO-LTF based on the decisional composite residuosity assumption are known [11].

As it is quite general, we describe in more detail the technique from [21] for building LTFs. Starting with an additively homomorphic encryption scheme, function indices correspond with element-wise encryptions of the identity matrix. The range of the construction consists of vectors of ciphertexts. If ElGamal encryption is used to instantiate the encryption scheme one obtains an LTF with security based on DDH. Constructions of LTFs and ABO-LTFs in the same spirit, but that achieve smaller index sizes and output lengths, are proposed in [6, 15]. Using a generalization of the Goldwasser–Micali homomorphic encryption scheme [12] allows this construction, in contrast to processing the LTF input bit-by-bit, to consider input values sequences of numbers of some fixed bit-length. The construction's security is based not only on the DDH assumption but also on the quadratic residuosity assumption for a restricted class of RSA moduli and an additional non-standard assumption, which can be removed by making further restrictions on the modulus.

While the described constructions from [6,15,21] achieve high lossiness factors, a common disadvantage is that their indices are ciphertext matrices and the function ranges are ciphertext vectors, and thus quite large. Further, [6,15] require strong hardness assumptions in a quite restricted RSA setting.

As shown in [27], collision-resistant hash functions, CPA- and CCA-secure public-key encryption, and deterministic encryption can be constructed from adversary-dependent lossy trapdoor functions and ABO-LTFs, a variant of LTFs and ABO-LTFs with relaxed security conditions. The authors give index-independent constructions of these primitives from the factoring assumption for semi-smooth RSA moduli. The proposed instantiations achieve high lossiness factors and have compact indices and ciphertexts of roughly the size of an RSA modulus.

1.1 Our Results

In this work we propose a new general domain-extension transformation that can be used to transform index-dependent LTPs into index-independent LTPs without sacrificing much lossiness. Concretely, our transformation decreases the lossiness factor by at most by a factor of 2. For the special cases of the LTP based on the Phi-hiding assumption and the LTP from [11] based on the quadratic residuosity assumption, a more refined analysis even shows that the lossiness factor effectively stays invariant. That is, ultimately we construct an LTP with index-independent domain $\{0,1\}^k$ and lossiness factor as large as $L = 2^{k/4}$ from the Phi-hiding assumption, and an LTP with index-independent domain $\{0,1\}^k$ and lossiness factor 2 from the quadratic residuosity assumption. In comparison, the index-independent variants obtained via the transform implicitly given in [11] would result in lossiness factors of 2 and 4/3 respectively. Furthermore, in the full version [1] we apply our transformation to the index-dependent LTF and ABO-LTF of [11] based on the decisional composite residuosity assumption. As a result we obtain index-independent variants with slightly larger domain and lossiness factor than the index-independent constructions given in [11]. Finally we construct the first ABO-LTP from (a variant of) the Phi-hiding assumption. We highlight that in particular our Phi-hiding based construction has particularly compact indices (of the size of an RSA modulus) and range elements.

DOMAIN EXTENSION FOR LTFs WITH INDEX-DEPENDENT DOMAINS. We explain our domain extension technique for the special case of a LTF $f \colon \mathbb{Z}_N \to \mathbb{Z}_N$ with index-dependent domain $\mathbb{Z}_N$ (with $2^{k-1} \leq N < 2^k$). We use a two-round construction in the spirit of Hayashi, Okamoto and Tanaka [13], who used a similar construction to extend the domain of the RSA one-way permutation. We define the function

$$f'_{\mathrm{de}} \colon \{0,1\}^k \to \{0,1\}^k, \quad f'_{\mathrm{de}}(x) := f_{\mathrm{de}}(\pi(f_{\mathrm{de}}(x))), \tag{2}$$

where f_{de} is defined in (1) and permutation $\pi \colon \{0,1\}^k \to \{0,1\}^k$ is given as $\pi(x) = x - (N-1) \bmod 2^k$. The intuition of this construction is that the LTF f is applied to every $x \in \{0,1\}^k$ at least once. Indeed, if f is one-way, then f'_{de} defined in (2) is one-way [13]. Our first main result states that if f is a LTF with index-dependent domain and lossiness factor L, then f'_{de} is a LTF with index-independent domain $\{0,1\}^k$ and lossiness factor $L'_{\mathrm{de}} = L/2$.

In the case of the RSA-based LTF f_{RSA} we can even prove that the lossiness factor of f'_{de} is completely preserved, i.e. $L'_{\mathrm{de}} = L$. Under the Phi-hiding assumption this gives us a LTP with index-independent domain and lossiness factor as large as $k^{1/4}$. We also show how to obtain index-independent LTPs from the quadratic residuosity and the decisional composite residuosity assumption (in the full version [1]), which have a larger lossiness factor than the constructions of [11].

AN ABO-LTP IN THE RSA SETTING. Our second main result is the construction of an ABO-LTP with index-dependent domain from the Phi-hiding assumption. Our generic domain extension technique also works for ABO-LTFs, so it can be transformed into an ABO-LTP with index-independent domain $\{0,1\}^k$.

Our construction essentially follows [16, Sect. 5.2] who construct an adaptive trapdoor function from the instance-independent RSA assumption, a decisional version of the RSA assumption. It makes use of a new primitive that we call *prime family generator* (PFG), an abstraction that may be of independent interest. An instance of a PFG indicates a fixed sequence of (distinct) primes $e_1, \ldots, e_{2^n}$ of some specified bit-length $l \geq n/2$. A specific programmability feature allows embedding any given prime at any given position, where the position remains hidden (computationally) from the instance. We give an information-theoretic construction of a PFG that is based on work by Cachin, Micali, and Stadler [9].

A PFG instance consists of l^2 bits and we leave it as an open problem to construct a (computationally secure) PFG with improved parameters, for example by using the PRF-based construction as implicitly in the work of Hohenberger and Waters [14].

Given a PFG we define our new RSA-setting based ABO-LTP for a branch $br \in \{0,1\}^n$ as

$$f_{br} \colon \mathbb{Z}_N \to \mathbb{Z}_N; \quad f_{br}(x) := x^{e_{br}},$$

where e_{br} is the br-th prime of the PFG prime sequence. To prove the ABO-LTF security property we first use the Phi-hiding assumption to change the distribution of the RSA modulus N to satisfy $e^* \mid \varphi_N$, for some random prime e^*. Next, we use the PFG's programmability feature to make sure that $e_{br^*} = e^*$, meaning the function $f_{br}(\cdot)$ is injective if $br \neq br^*$ and e^*-to-1 if $br = br^*$.[4]

APPLICATIONS. Our constructions of index-independent LTFs and LTPs over domain $\{0,1\}^k$ (and our techniques to build them) are mostly of theoretical interest with potential future applications. Whereas with our current knowledge we are not able to present a killer application, let us still discuss possible minor applications. Most importantly, correlated-product secure trapdoor functions [24] and IND-CCA secure public-key encryption [21] can be constructed from index-independent LTFs over domain $\{0,1\}^k$. Both require the lossiness factor L to be larger than $2^{k/2}$, whereas our construction based on the Phi-hiding assumption cannot go beyond $L = 2^{k/4}$. One can still apply the amplification result by Mol and Yilek [19] to build IND-CCA secure encryption. The efficiency loss will be smaller than with the previous constructions from the Phi-hiding assumption (having lossiness factor $L \approx 2$).

2 Preliminaries

2.1 Notation

If $a, b \in \mathbb{N}, a < b$, we use notations $[a \mathbin{..} b] = \{a, \ldots, b\}$, $[b] = [1 \mathbin{..} b]$, $[\![a \mathbin{..} b[\![= [a \mathbin{..} (b-1)]$, and $[\![b[\![= [0 \mathbin{..} (b-1)]$. We say $m \in \mathbb{N}$ is an l-bit number if $m \in [\![2^{l-1} \mathbin{..} 2^l]\!]$. For any set $M \subseteq \mathbb{N}$ we denote with $M_l := M \cap [\![2^{l-1} \mathbin{..} 2^l]\!]$ its subset of l-bit elements. We write $\{0,1\}^l$ for the set of strings of length l and denote the bit-wise exclusive-or operation of same-length strings with $\oplus$. For all $l \in \mathbb{N}$ we assume a canonic bijection $\#\colon [\![2^l[\![\to \{0,1\}^l$ and correspondingly denote with $\#x$ the interpretation of an element x of $[\![2^l[\![$ as a string in $\{0,1\}^l$. The support of a randomized algorithm A on input x, i.e., the set of values it outputs with non-zero probability, is denoted by $[A(x)]$. We annotate a disjoint union with $\uplus$.

---

[4] In fact this requires a slightly strengthened variant of the Phi-hiding assumption where for a larger set $\mathcal{E}$ it is known that precisely one element $e \in \mathcal{E}$ is a divisor of φ_N. We call this the *unique-divisor Phi-hiding assumption*, see Sect. 2.3.

2.2   (All-But-One) Lossy Trapdoor Permutations

We recall the concepts of lossy trapdoor functions and all-but-one lossy trapdoor functions as introduced by Peikert and Waters [21]. More precisely, we slightly deviate from their formalizations by restricting attention to permutations, supporting index-dependent domains [11], and considering permutations that are not perfectly correct.

Lossy Trapdoor Permutations. Let $\mathcal{X}$ be a domain, $\mathcal{Id}$ a universe of function indices, and for each index $id \in \mathcal{Id}$ let $\mathcal{X}(id) \subseteq \mathcal{X}$ be a specific (sub)domain. A *lossy trapdoor permutation* (LTP) for $\mathcal{X}, \mathcal{Id}$ then consists of a trapdoor space $\mathcal{Td}$ and three efficient algorithms $F = (\mathrm{FGen}, \mathrm{FEv}, \mathrm{FInv})$ for which the following hold: Algorithm

$$\{0,1\} \to \mathrm{FGen} \to_\$ \mathcal{Id} \times (\mathcal{Td} \cup \{\bot\})$$

is a randomized instance generator. Its input $b \in \{0,1\}$ specifies whether the generated instance is *injective* ($b = 1$) or *lossy* ($b = 0$). We require $[\mathrm{FGen}(1)] \subseteq \mathcal{Id} \times \mathcal{Td}$ and $[\mathrm{FGen}(0)] \subseteq \mathcal{Id} \times \{\bot\}$. In injective mode, if $(id, td) \in [\mathrm{FGen}(1)]$, we refer to td as the trapdoor corresponding to id. Algorithms

$$\mathcal{Id} \times \mathcal{X} \to \mathrm{FEv} \to \mathcal{X} \qquad \text{and} \qquad \mathcal{Td} \times \mathcal{X} \to \mathrm{FInv} \to \mathcal{X}$$

are the *evaluation* and *inversion* algorithms, respectively. We require it hold $\mathrm{FEv}(id, x) \in \mathcal{X}(id)$ for all $id \in \mathcal{Id}$ and $x \in \mathcal{X}(id)$. For correctness we further require that in injective mode the mapping $\mathcal{X}(id) \to \mathcal{X}(id)$ induced by FEv can be effectively inverted on (almost) all values if the trapdoor is known. Formally, we say that F is $(1 - \epsilon_1)$-correct if

$$\Pr[(id, td) \leftarrow_\$ \mathrm{FGen}(1), x \leftarrow_\$ \mathcal{X}(id), y \leftarrow \mathrm{FEv}(id, x) : \mathrm{FInv}(td, y) \neq x] \leq \epsilon_1.$$

This means that for $\epsilon_1 > 0$ the function implemented by $\mathrm{FEv}(id, \cdot)$ might technically not be a permutation. For security we require (a) that FEv lose information in lossy mode, and (b) that injective mode and lossy mode be indistinguishable. Concerning (a), we say the LTP is *L-lossy* if for all $(id, \bot) \in [\mathrm{FGen}(0)]$ we have $|\mathrm{FEv}(id, \mathcal{X}(id))| \leq |\mathcal{X}(id)|/L$.[5] Concerning (b), we say the LTP is (τ, ϵ_2)-*indistinguishable* if for all τ-time distinguishers $\mathcal{D}$ we have

$$\left| \begin{array}{l} \Pr[(id, td) \leftarrow_\$ \mathrm{FGen}(1) : \mathcal{D}(id) \Rightarrow 1] \\ \quad - \Pr[(id, \bot) \leftarrow_\$ \mathrm{FGen}(0) : \mathcal{D}(id) \Rightarrow 1] \end{array} \right| \leq \epsilon_2.$$

---

[5] According to our definition, L-lossiness indicates that the size of the lossy image is by a factor L smaller than the domain. The original definition by Peikert and Waters indicates the same quantity on a logarithmic scale, i.e., they report $\log_2(L)$ instead of L.

All-But-One Lossy Trapdoor Permutations. All-but-one LTPs are a generalization of LTPs where in addition to the universe of function indices there is a universe of branches; function FEv is lossy for one branch and injective for all others. In particular, a (regular) LTP is equivalent to an all-but-one LTP if the branch space consists of precisely two elements.

Let $\mathcal{Br}$ be a branch space, $\mathcal{X}$ a domain, $\mathcal{Id}$ a universe of function indices, and for each index $id \in \mathcal{Id}$ let $\mathcal{X}(id) \subseteq \mathcal{X}$ be a specific (sub)domain. An *all-but-one lossy trapdoor permutation* (ABO-LTP) for $\mathcal{Br}, \mathcal{X}, \mathcal{Id}$ then consists of a trapdoor space $\mathcal{Td}$ and three efficient algorithms A = (FGen, FEv, FInv) for which the following hold: Algorithm

$$\mathcal{Br} \to \text{FGen} \to_\text{s} \mathcal{Id} \times \mathcal{Td}$$

is an instance generator such that the invocation $(id, td) \leftarrow_\text{s} \text{FGen}(br)$, for a branch br, generates a function index id with trapdoor td. Similarly as for LTPs, algorithms

$$\mathcal{Br} \times \mathcal{Id} \times \mathcal{X} \to \text{FEv} \to \mathcal{X} \qquad \text{and} \qquad \mathcal{Br} \times \mathcal{Td} \times \mathcal{X} \to \text{FInv} \to \mathcal{X}$$

are the evaluation and inversion algorithms. We require that for all $br, br^* \in \mathcal{Br}$ and $(id, td) \in [\text{FGen}(br^*)]$ and $x \in \mathcal{X}(id)$, if $y = \text{FEv}(br, id, x)$ then $y \in \mathcal{X}(id)$. We further require that the mappings $\mathcal{X}(id) \to \mathcal{X}(id)$ induced by FEv on all branches with exception of br^* can be effectively inverted (on almost all values) if the trapdoor is known. Formally, we say that A is $(1 - \epsilon_1)$-correct if for all $br, br^* \in \mathcal{Br}$, $br \neq br^*$, we have

$$\Pr\left[(id, td) \leftarrow_\text{s} \text{FGen}(br^*), x \leftarrow_\text{s} \mathcal{X}(id) : \text{FInv}\left(br, td, \text{FEv}(br, id, x)\right) \neq x\right] \leq \epsilon_1.$$

For security we require that FEv lose information on its *lossy branch*, i.e., the branch br^* the instance was generated for. Further, it shall be unfeasible to identify the lossy branch. Concretely, we say the ABO-LTP is *L-lossy* if for all $br^* \in \mathcal{Br}$ and $(id, td) \in [\text{FGen}(br^*)]$ we have $|\text{FEv}(br^*, id, \mathcal{X}(id))| \leq |\mathcal{X}(id)|/L$, and we say it is (τ, ϵ_2)-*indistinguishable* if for all $br_0, br_1 \in \mathcal{Br}$ and all τ-time distinguishers $\mathcal{D}$ (that may depend on br_0, br_1) we have

$$\left| \begin{array}{l} \Pr[(id, td) \leftarrow_\text{s} \text{FGen}(br_0) : \mathcal{D}(id) \Rightarrow 1] \\ - \Pr[(id, td) \leftarrow_\text{s} \text{FGen}(br_1) : \mathcal{D}(id) \Rightarrow 1] \end{array} \right| \leq \epsilon_2.$$

Index-Dependent vs. Index-Independent LTPs/ABO-LTPs. In the above definition of LTPs, the domain $\mathcal{X}(id) \subseteq \mathcal{X}$ on which $\text{FEv}(id, \cdot)$ operates may depend on function index id. We say the LTP is index-independent if this restriction does not exist, i.e., if $\mathcal{X}(id) = \mathcal{X}$ for all id. For ABO-LTPs we say correspondingly. In later sections we show how to generically transform an index-dependent trapdoor permutation into an index-independent one.

2.3 Number Theoretic Assumptions

For $a, b \in \mathbb{N}, a \neq 0$, we write $a \mid b$ if a divides b, i.e., if there exists $d \in \mathbb{N}$ s.t. $b = da$. We further write $a \mid_1 b$ if a divides b exactly once, i.e., if $a \mid b \wedge a^2 \nmid b$. The greatest common divisor of a, b is denoted $\gcd(a, b)$. We denote the set of prime numbers with $\mathcal{P}$. Recall from Sect. 2.1 that $\mathbb{N}_l$ and $\mathcal{P}_l$ denote the sets of l-bit natural and prime numbers, respectively.

If k is an even number, a product $N = pq$ is a k-bit RSA $modulus$ if $N \in \mathbb{N}_k$, $p, q \in \mathcal{P}_{k/2}$, and $p \neq q$. The order of the multiplicative group $\mathbb{Z}_N^*$ is $\varphi_N := \varphi(N) = (p-1)(q-1)$. We denote the space of k-bit RSA moduli with $\mathcal{RSA}_k$. If we want to restrict attention to k-bit RSA moduli that fulfill a specific condition C, we write $\mathcal{RSA}_k[C]$. The set of k-bit Blum integers, i.e., RSA moduli where the prime factors satisfy $p \equiv q \equiv 3 \bmod 4$, is denoted by $\mathcal{BRSA}_k := \mathcal{RSA}_k[p \equiv q \equiv 3 \bmod 4]$.

Phi-Hiding Assumption. In standard RSA encryption, public exponent e is chosen constraint to $e \nmid \varphi_N$ so that the mapping $x \mapsto x^e$ is a bijection. Some applications in addition use exponents $e \mid_1 \varphi_N$ and require that it be hard, given (N, e), to decide whether $e \mid_1 \varphi_N$ or $e \nmid \varphi_N$. Roughly, the Phi-hiding assumption [9,17] for a set of primes $\mathcal{E}$ says that $N \in \mathcal{RSA}_k$ can be generated such that for uniformly picked $e \in \mathcal{E}$ the cases $N \in \mathcal{RSA}_k[e \nmid \varphi_N]$ and $N \in \mathcal{RSA}_k[e \mid_1 \varphi_N]$ are computationally indistinguishable. Formally, we say that the (τ, ϵ)-Phi-$hiding$ $assumption$ holds for $(k, \mathcal{E})$ if for all τ-time adversaries $\mathcal{D}$ we have

$$\left| \begin{array}{l} \Pr[e \leftarrow_{\mathrm{s}} \mathcal{E}; (N, \varphi_N) \leftarrow_{\mathrm{s}} \mathcal{RSA}_k[e \mid_1 \varphi_N] : \mathcal{D}(N, e) \Rightarrow 1] \\ \quad - \Pr[e \leftarrow_{\mathrm{s}} \mathcal{E}; (N, \varphi_N) \leftarrow_{\mathrm{s}} \mathcal{RSA}_k[e \nmid \varphi_N] : \mathcal{D}(N, e) \Rightarrow 1] \end{array} \right| \leq \epsilon.$$

In the probability expressions we write $(N, \varphi_N) \leftarrow_{\mathrm{s}} \mathcal{RSA}_k[C]$ for an algorithm that generates a k-bit RSA modulus satisfying condition C, and also outputs $\varphi_N = |\mathbb{Z}_N^*|$.

In this paper we also need a variant of this assumption: An added restriction is that precisely one $e \in \mathcal{E}$ shall be a divisor of φ_N, and, as before, if e divides φ_N then at most once.[6] This is expressed by condition

$$C(\mathcal{E}, \varphi_N, e) \quad :\Longleftrightarrow \quad e \mid \varphi_N \wedge \gcd(\mathcal{E}, \varphi_N/e) = 1,$$

where the gcd term encodes that φ_N/e is relative prime to all elements of $\mathcal{E}$; this in particular implies $e \mid_1 \varphi_N$. We say the unique-divisor (τ, ϵ)-Phi-$hiding$ $assumption$ holds for $(k, \mathcal{E})$ if for all τ-time adversaries $\mathcal{D}$ we have

$$\left| \begin{array}{l} \Pr[e_0 \leftarrow_{\mathrm{s}} \mathcal{E}; (N, \varphi_N) \leftarrow_{\mathrm{s}} \mathcal{RSA}_k[C(\mathcal{E}, \varphi_N, e_0)] : \mathcal{D}(N, e_0) \Rightarrow 1] \\ \quad - \Pr[e_0, e_1 \leftarrow_{\mathrm{s}} \mathcal{E}; (N, \varphi_N) \leftarrow_{\mathrm{s}} \mathcal{RSA}_k[C(\mathcal{E}, \varphi_N, e_0)] : \mathcal{D}(N, e_1) \Rightarrow 1] \end{array} \right| \leq \epsilon.$$

---

[6] While this assumption is stronger than the standard Phi-hiding assumption, we conjecture that it is rather mild (possibly in the same way as the strengthened Quadratic Residuosity assumption from [15] that is specialized towards defining the 2^k-th Power Residue symbol).

$\text{FGen}_{ii}(b)$	$\text{FEv}_{ii}(id, x)$	$\text{FInv}_{ii}(td, y)$
00 $(id, td) \leftarrow_\$ \text{FGen}(b)$	02 If $x \in \mathcal{X}(id)$:	08 If $y \in \mathcal{X}(id)$:
01 Return (id, td)	03 $x \leftarrow \text{FEv}(id, x)$	09 $y \leftarrow \text{FInv}(td, y)$
	04 $y \leftarrow \pi_{id}(x)$	10 $x \leftarrow \pi_{id}^{-1}(y)$
	05 If $y \in \mathcal{X}(id)$:	11 If $x \in \mathcal{X}(id)$:
	06 $y \leftarrow \text{FEv}(id, y)$	12 $x \leftarrow \text{FInv}(td, x)$
	07 Return y	13 Return x

Fig. 1. Transformation of index-dependent LTP into index-independent LTP. To make algorithm FInv_{ii} well-defined we assume implicitly that trapdoor td contains a copy of function index id. A visualization of the construction is in Fig. 2.

Quadratic Residuosity Assumption. Roughly, the quadratic residuosity assumption says that it is hard to distinguish quadratic residues modulo a Blum integer from quadratic non-residues that have positive Jacobi symbol.

Formally, for all $N \in \mathbb{N}$ denote with $\mathcal{QR}_N \subseteq \mathbb{Z}_N^*$ the set of quadratic residues modulo N and with $\mathcal{J}_N \subseteq \mathbb{Z}_N^*$ the set of numbers with positive Jacobi symbol. (In particular we have $\mathcal{QR}_N \subseteq \mathcal{J}_N$.) We say that the (τ, ϵ)-*quadratic residuosity assumption* holds for k if for all τ-time adversaries $\mathcal{D}$ we have

$$\left| \begin{array}{l} \Pr[(N, p, q) \leftarrow_\$ \mathcal{BRSA}_k, x \leftarrow_\$ \mathcal{QR}_N : \mathcal{D}(N, x) \Rightarrow 1] \\ - \Pr[(N, p, q) \leftarrow_\$ \mathcal{BRSA}_k, x \leftarrow_\$ \mathcal{J}_N \setminus \mathcal{QR}_N : \mathcal{D}(N, x) \Rightarrow 1] \end{array} \right| \leq \epsilon.$$

In the probability expressions we write $(N, p, q) \leftarrow_\$ \mathcal{BRSA}_k$ for an algorithm that generates a k-bit Blum integer and also outputs its prime factors. Note that sampling elements of $\mathcal{QR}_N$ and $\mathcal{J}_N \setminus \mathcal{QR}_N$ can be done efficiently if these factors are known.

3   From Index-Dependence to Index-Independence

Many natural constructions of lossy trapdoor permutations are index-dependent, i.e., for each index id the function $\text{FEv}(id, \cdot)$ operates on an individual set $\mathcal{X}(id) \subseteq \mathcal{X}$. However, for applications it might be necessary that there is only one domain: $\mathcal{X}(id) = \mathcal{X}$ for all id. In this section we convert index-dependent LTPs into index-independent LTPs. Some transforms of this type have been proposed before. For instance, [11] implicitly uses the somewhat trivial approach of leaving elements in $\mathcal{X} \setminus \mathcal{X}(id)$ untouched (i.e., elements in $\mathcal{X}(id)$ are processed with the LTP, the others are passed through without modification). As discussed in the introduction, the performance of this conversion is generally rather poor: In the worst case, if $|\mathcal{X}(id)| \ll |\mathcal{X}|$, lossiness is bounded by $L = 1$.

Below we study a two-round construction that was first proposed in [13], in a different context. There, the goal was to extend the domain of the RSA trapdoor permutation; aspects of lossiness were not studied. Further, our exposition is more generic. The idea behind the transformation is to ensure that FEv is applied to every point of $\mathcal{X}$ at least once. In both rounds the points of $\mathcal{X}(id)$ are permuted with FEv while the remaining points of $\mathcal{X}$ stay unchanged. To achieve

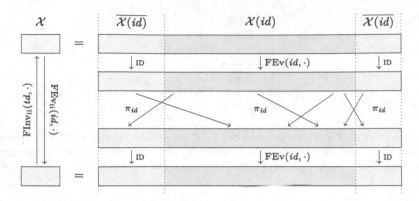

Fig. 2. Working principle of transformation of index-dependent LTP into index-independent LTP. The corresponding algorithms are in Fig. 1. Note that π_{id} is chosen such that every point in $\mathcal{X}$ is permuted by FEv at least once.

the property stated above, after the first round a permutation π_{id} is used to move into $\mathcal{X}(id)$ all those points that have not yet been touched by FEv.

Let F = (FGen, FEv, FInv) be a LTP with domain $\mathcal{X}$ and index space $\mathcal{Id}$. Assume F has index-dependent domains. For all $id \in \mathcal{Id}$ write $\overline{\mathcal{X}(id)} = \mathcal{X} \setminus \mathcal{X}(id)$ and let $\pi_{id} \colon \mathcal{X} \to \mathcal{X}$ be an efficiently computable and efficiently invertible permutation satisfying $\pi_{id}(\overline{\mathcal{X}(id)}) \subseteq \mathcal{X}(id)$ or, equivalently, $\pi_{id}^{-1}(\overline{\mathcal{X}(id)}) \subseteq \mathcal{X}(id)$. (Note that such a π_{id} can exist only if $|\mathcal{X}(id)| \geq |\mathcal{X}|/2$ for all id.) From F and $(\pi_{id})_{id \in \mathcal{Id}}$ we construct a LTP $F_{ii} = (FGen_{ii}, FEv_{ii}, FInv_{ii})$ with index-independent domain $\mathcal{X}$, i.e., $\mathcal{X}(id) = \mathcal{X}$ for all id. The algorithms are specified in Fig. 1 and illustrated in Fig. 2. The analysis is in Lemma 1 (which is proved in the full version [1]).

Lemma 1. *Let* F *be a* $(1 - \epsilon_1)$-*correct,* (τ, ϵ_2)-*indistinguishable* L-*lossy trapdoor permutation with index-dependent domain. Furthermore, let* $(\pi_{id})_{id \in \mathcal{Id}}$ *be a family of permutations on* $\mathcal{X}$ *as described. Then* F_{ii} *is an* $(1 - 2\epsilon_1)$-*correct,* (τ, ϵ_2)-*indistinguishable* L/2-*lossy trapdoor permutation with index-independent domain* $\mathcal{X}$. *In particular, if* F *is 1-correct, then so is* F_{ii}.

Analogously to the construction in Fig. 1 we can transform an index-dependent ABO-LTP A = (FGen, FEv, FInv) into an index-independent ABO-LTP A_{ii} = (FGen, FEv$_{ii}$, FInv$_{ii}$). Note that A_{ii} uses the same instance generator as A. Algorithms FEv$_{ii}$ and FInv$_{ii}$ work as their counterparts for LTPs defined in Fig. 1, the only difference being the use of the additional input br to evaluate FEv and FInv. We obtain the following.

Lemma 2. *Let* A *be a* $(1 - \epsilon_1)$-*correct,* (τ, ϵ_2)-*indistinguishable* L-*lossy ABO-LTP with index-dependent domain. Let* $(\pi_{id})_{id \in \mathcal{Id}}$ *be a family of permutations on* $\mathcal{X}$ *as described. Then* A_{ii} *is an* $(1 - 2\epsilon_1)$-*correct,* (τ, ϵ_2)-*indistinguishable* L/2-*lossy ABO-LTP with index-independent domain* $\mathcal{X}$. *In particular, if* A *is 1-correct, then so is* A_{ii}.

4   Lossy Trapdoor Permutations from Phi-Hiding

Fix an RSA modulus N and let $e \ll \varphi_N$ be prime. We say e is *injective* for N if $e \nmid \varphi_N$ and that it is *lossy* for N if $e \mid_1 \varphi_N$. In the injective case the mapping $E \colon \mathbb{Z}_N \to \mathbb{Z}_N$; $x \mapsto x^e$ is inverted by $D \colon y \mapsto y^d$, where d is such that $ed = 1 \bmod \varphi_N$. In the lossy case, the restriction $E|_{\mathbb{Z}_N^*}$ of E to domain $\mathbb{Z}_N^*$ is e-to-1, i.e., we have $|E(\mathbb{Z}_N^*)|/|\mathbb{Z}_N^*| = 1/e$. The Phi-hiding assumption from Sect. 2.3 then precisely says that it is hard to decide whether a candidate exponent e is injective or lossy for N.

We propose two LTPs in the RSA setting, both with security based on the Phi-hiding assumption. The first construction is quite natural but has index-dependent domains. The second construction is the index-independent analogue of the first, obtained via the transformation from Sect. 3. Here, our contribution is establishing a better bound on the lossiness than is possible with the generic result. (Our arguments are based on structures specific to the RSA setting.)

FGen(b)	FEv(id, x)	FEv*(id, x)
00 $e \leftarrow_{\$} \mathcal{E}$	09 $(N, e) \leftarrow id$	15 $(N, e) \leftarrow id$
01 If $b = 0$: (lossy mode)	10 $y \leftarrow x^e \bmod N$	16 If $x = 0$: Return 0
02 $(N, \varphi_N) \leftarrow_{\$} \mathcal{RSA}_k[e \mid_1 \varphi_N]$	11 Return y	17 If $x \notin \mathbb{Z}_N^*$:
03 $id \leftarrow (N, e)$; $td \leftarrow \bot$	FInv(td, y)	18 $p \leftarrow \gcd(x, N)$
04 If $b = 1$: (injective mode)	12 $(N, d) \leftarrow td$	19 $q \leftarrow N/p$
05 $(N, \varphi_N) \leftarrow_{\$} \mathcal{RSA}_k[e \nmid \varphi_N]$	13 $x \leftarrow y^d \bmod N$	20 $\varphi_N \leftarrow (p-1)(q-1)$
06 $d \leftarrow e^{-1} \bmod \varphi_N$	14 Return x	21 If $e \mid \varphi_N$: Return 0
07 $id \leftarrow (N, e)$; $td \leftarrow (N, d)$		22 $y \leftarrow x^e \bmod N$
08 Return (id, td)		23 Return y

Fig. 3. LTPs F and F* from Phi-hiding assumption (with index-dependent domains).

4.1   Index-Dependent Domain LTP from Phi-Hiding Assumption

Let k be an even number indicating a desired bit length of RSA moduli. Let $\mathcal{E}$ be a distribution of prime numbers such that the (τ, ϵ)-Phi-hiding assumption holds for $(k, \mathcal{E})$. Consider the constructions of LTPs F $=$ (FGen, FEv, FInv) and F* $=$ (FGen, FEv*, FInv) given by the algorithms in Fig. 3. Observe that condition $e \mid_1 \varphi_N$ in line 02 implies that no element of $\mathcal{E}$ can be longer than $k/2$ bits. Further, to protect from known attacks it is necessary that $\max \mathcal{E} \leq 2^{k/4}$.

The working principle of F is as follows: Function indices id correspond with RSA parameters (N, e). The domain corresponding to index id is $\mathcal{X}(id) = \mathbb{Z}_N$. In injective mode, (N, e) are chosen such that e is invertible modulo φ_N, i.e., such that a corresponding decryption exponent d exists. The FEv and FInv algorithms, in this case, are the standard RSA mappings $x \mapsto x^e$ and $y \mapsto y^d$ (lines 10 and 13). In lossy mode, e is a divisor of φ_N. In this case, mapping $x \mapsto x^e$ is e-to-1 for elements in $\mathbb{Z}_N^*$. The resulting overall lossiness (i.e., for full $\mathbb{Z}_N$) is analyzed in Lemma 3.

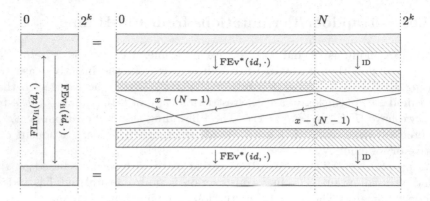

Fig. 4. Illustration of Phi-hiding based LTP F_{ii} with index-independent domain.

We next discuss F^*. This variant achieves better lossiness by building on the fact that given an element of $\mathbb{Z}_N \setminus \mathbb{Z}_N^*$ it is possible to effectively determine whether the function index (N, e) is injective or lossy. In the first case FEv^* uses the standard RSA map; in the second case elements in $\mathbb{Z}_N \setminus \mathbb{Z}_N^*$ are detected and explicitly mapped to 0. The identification of lossy indices and elements in $\mathbb{Z}_N \setminus \mathbb{Z}_N^*$ is handled in lines 17–21. Observe that the condition in line 17 can be checked efficiently.

We analyze constructions F and F^* in Lemma 3 (the proof of which is in the full version [1]). While the second LTP is more complicated to implement, the achieved lossiness bound is easier to work with.

Lemma 3. *If for $(k, \mathcal{E})$ the (τ, ϵ)-Phi-hiding assumption holds and $L \leq \min \mathcal{E}$ is a lower bound on the elements in the support of $\mathcal{E}$, LTP F is a 1-correct, (τ, ϵ)-indistinguishable $(1/L + 2^{-k/2+3})^{-1}$-lossy trapdoor function. Furthermore, LTP F^* is a 1-correct (τ, ϵ)-indistinguishable L-lossy trapdoor function. Both LTPs have index-dependent domain.*

4.2   Index-Independent Domain LTP from Phi-Hiding Assumption

The LTP F^* from Sect. 4.1 has index-dependent domains: for function index $id = (N, e)$, algorithm $FEv^*(id, \cdot)$ operates on domain $\mathcal{X}(id) = \mathbb{Z}_N$. By construction we have $N \in [\![2^{k-1} .. 2^k]\!]$ and thus $\mathcal{X}(id) \subseteq \mathcal{X}$ for $\mathcal{X} = [\![2^k]\!]$. To obtain an LTP F_{ii} with index-independent domain $[\![2^k]\!]$ we can apply to F^* the generic transform of Sect. 3. By Lemma 1, assuming appropriately chosen permutations (π_{id}), if F^* is L-lossy, then F_{ii} is $L/2$-lossy. The contribution of the current section is to show that for a specifically defined family (π_{id}) using direct (non-generic) arguments this result can be strengthened: If F^* is L-lossy, then also F_{ii} is L-lossy. In other words, there is no price to pay for switching from index-dependent domains to index-independent domains. (This holds for the lossiness; computation time might double.)

As a first step we identify a family (π_{id}) of permutations on $\mathcal{X}$ that suits the conditions of the transform from Sect. 3, namely $\pi_{id}(\mathcal{X}(id)) \subseteq \mathcal{X}(id)$ for all $id \in \mathcal{Id}$. Hence let $\mathcal{X} = [\![2^k]\!]$ and $(N, e) = id \in \mathcal{Id}$, where $N \in [\![2^{k-1} .. 2^k]\!]$. We define $\pi_{id} \colon \mathcal{X} \to \mathcal{X}; x \mapsto x - (N-1) \bmod 2^k$. Then π_{id} is a permutation on $\mathcal{X}$ and we have $N \leq x < 2^k \Rightarrow 1 \leq \pi_{id}(x) \leq 2^k - N < N$ (the last inequality follows from $2^{k-1} \leq N < 2^k$); this establishes $\pi_{id}(\mathcal{X}(id)) \subseteq \mathcal{X}(id)$. We illustrate the transform from Fig. 2 in conjunction with this family of bijections (π_{id}) in Fig. 4. In the following, we first state the generic result obtained by applying Lemma 1 to this setup. We then give the one established directly. The proof of Lemma 4 is in the full version [1].

Corollary 1. *Let $\mathcal{E}$ be a prime distribution and $L \leq \min \mathcal{E}$. Further, let $F^* = (\text{FGen}, \text{FEv}^*, \text{FInv})$ be the L-lossy LTP defined in Fig. 3, $(\pi_{id})_{id \in \mathcal{Id}}$ the permutation family defined above, and F_{ii} the conversion of F^* via Fig. 1. If for $(k, \mathcal{E})$ the (τ, ϵ)-Phi-hiding assumption holds, then F_{ii} is a 1-correct, (τ, ϵ)-indistinguishable L/2-lossy trapdoor function with index-independent domain $\mathcal{X} = [\![2^k]\!]$.*

Lemma 4. *Let $\mathcal{E}$ be a prime distribution and $L \leq \min \mathcal{E}$. Further, let $F^* = (\text{FGen}, \text{FEv}^*, \text{FInv})$ be the L-lossy LTF defined in Fig. 3, $(\pi_{id})_{id \in \mathcal{Id}}$ the permutation family defined above, and F_{ii} the conversion of F^* via Fig. 1. If for $(k, \mathcal{E})$ the (τ, ϵ)-Phi-hiding assumption holds, then F_{ii} is a 1-correct, (τ, ϵ)-indistinguishable $L/(1 + 2^{-k/2})$-lossy trapdoor function with index-independent domain $\mathcal{X} = [\![2^k]\!]$.*

5 Lossy Trapdoor Permutations from Quadratic Residuosity Assumption

In this section we recall the index-dependent lossy trapdoor function F of [10] based on the quadratic residuosity assumption and show how the transform of Sect. 3 can be used to obtain an index-independent variant F_{ii}. Since F has a lossiness factor of 2, using the generic bound is of no use in this case. However, by exploiting the algebraic structure of the construction we are able to establish that F_{ii} has essentially the same lossiness factor as F. This improves on the index-independent variant given in [10], which achieves a lossiness factor of 4/3.

5.1 Index-Dependent Domain LTP from Quadratic Residuosity

Let p, q be primes of bit length $k/2$ satisfying $p \equiv 3 \bmod 4$ and $q \equiv 3 \bmod 4$. Consider the functions $j_N \colon \mathbb{Z} \to \{0, 1\}$ and $h_N \colon \mathbb{Z} \to \{0, 1\}$ defined by

$$j_N(x) = \begin{cases} 0, & \text{if } x \in \mathcal{J}_N \cup (\mathbb{Z}_N \setminus \mathbb{Z}_N^*) \\ 1, & \text{if } x \in \mathbb{Z}_N^* \setminus \mathcal{J}_N \end{cases}$$

$$h_N(x) = \begin{cases} 0, & \text{if } x \leq N/2 \\ 1, & \text{if } x > N/2 \end{cases}.$$

FGen(b)

00 $(N, p, q) \leftarrow_\$ \mathcal{BRSA}_k$
01 $r \leftarrow_\$ \mathbb{Z}_N^* \setminus \mathcal{J}_N$
02 If $b = 0$:   (lossy mode)
03      $s \leftarrow_\$ \mathcal{QR}_N$
04      $id \leftarrow (N, r, s); \; td \leftarrow \bot$
05 If $b = 1$:   (injective mode)
06      $s \leftarrow_\$ \mathcal{J}_N \setminus \mathcal{QR}_N$
07      $id \leftarrow (N, r, s)$
08      $td \leftarrow (N, p, q, r, s)$
09 Return (id, td)

FEv(id, x)

10 $(N, r, s) \leftarrow id$
11 $d_j \leftarrow j_N(x)$
12 $d_h \leftarrow h_N(x)$
13 $y \leftarrow x^2 r^\iota s^\tau$
14 Return y

FInv(td, y)

15 If $y = 0$: return 0
16 $(N, p, q, r, s) \leftarrow td$
17 $d_j \leftarrow j_N(y)$
18 $y' \leftarrow yr^{-d_j}$
19 If $y' \in \mathbb{Z}_N \setminus \mathbb{Z}_N^*$:
20   If $y' \notin \mathcal{QR}_p \wedge y' \notin \mathcal{QR}_q$:
21          $d_h \leftarrow 1$
22   Else: $d_h \leftarrow 0$
23 Elseif $y' \in \mathcal{QR}_N$: $d_h \leftarrow 0$
24 Else: $d_h \leftarrow 1$
25 $y'' \leftarrow y' s^{-d_h}$
26 $x \leftarrow R_{d_j, d_h}(y'')$
27 Return x

Fig. 5. LTP F from Quadratic residuosity assumption (with index-dependent domains).

Note that both j_N and h_N can be efficiently computed given N. Let $d_j, d_h \in \{0, 1\}$. Then—as pointed out in [10]—for each $y \in \mathcal{QR}_N$ exactly one of the four solutions of the equation $x^2 = y \bmod N$ satisfies $j_N(x) = d_j$ and $h_N(x) = d_h$. We denote this square root of y by R_{d_j, d_h}. Furthermore for every $y \in \mathbb{Z}_N \setminus \mathbb{Z}_N^*$ with $y \in \mathcal{QR}_p \vee y \in \mathcal{QR}_q$ the equation $y = x^2 \bmod N$ has exactly two solutions—one being the negative of the other. Hence both solutions satisfy $j_N(x) = 0$ and for $d_h \in \{0, 1\}$ exactly one of the solutions satisfies $h_N(x) = d_h$. Analogous to the situation above we denote this solution by R_{0, d_h}. In [10] the authors construct a lossy trapdoor permutation with index-dependent domain $\mathbb{Z}_N$. The LTP's algorithms are depicted in Fig. 5. The idea of the construction is to map elements $x \in \mathbb{Z}_N$ to x^2, which is afterwards multiplied by some appropriately chosen group elements, which allow to reconstruct x^2 as well as both $j_N(x) =: d_j$ and $h_N(x) =: d_h$. Then the LTF can be inverted by computing R_{d_j, d_h}.

Lemma 5 ([10]). *Let* F $=$ (FGen, FEv, FInv) *the LTP of Fig. 5. If the* (τ, ϵ)-*Quadratic residuosity assumption holds for* k, *then* F *is an* (τ', ϵ)-*indistinguishable 2-lossy trapdoor function with index-dependent domain* $\mathcal{X}((N, r, s)) = \mathbb{Z}_N \subseteq [\![2^k]\!] = \mathcal{X}$, *where* $\tau' \approx \tau$.

5.2 Index-Independent Domain LTP from Quadratic Residuosity

In [10] the authors propose to modify the LTP F of Sect. 5.1 in the following way to obtain an LTP F_{ii}^* with index-independent domain $[\![2^k]\!]$. This is done by letting $\mathrm{F}_{ii}^*|_{\mathcal{X}(id)}(id, \cdot) := \mathrm{F}(id, \cdot)$ and $\mathrm{F}_{ii}^*|_{\overline{\mathcal{X}(id)}}(id, \cdot) := \mathrm{ID}$. The resulting LTP F_{ii}^* is a 4/3-lossy trapdoor function. In this section we show that using our transformation of Sect. 3 with an appropriate permutation yields an index-independent LTP based on the quadratic residuosity assumption having essentially the same lossiness factor as the underlying LTP F.

To be able to use our transformation we need a family of permutations on $\mathcal{X}$ that suits the conditions of Sect. 3. Since—as in the construction based on the Phi-hiding assumption—the index-dependent domain $\mathcal{X}(id)$ for some $id = (N, r, s)$ is $\mathbb{Z}_N$, we are able to use the same family of permutations. Hence for $id = (N, r, s) \in \mathcal{Id}$ define $\pi_{id} \colon \mathcal{X} \to \mathcal{X}; x \mapsto x - (N-1) \bmod 2^k$. Then π_{id} is a permutation on $\mathcal{X}$ and as in Sect. 4.2 we obtain $\pi_{id}(\mathcal{X}(id)) \subseteq \mathcal{X}(id)$.

Note that applying Lemma 1 would only yield a bound of $2/2 = 1$ on the lossiness factor of the transformed LTP, which is of no use. However, we are able to establish a desirable result directly using techniques similar to the ones used in the proof of Lemma 4. The proof of Lemma 6 is in the full version [1].

Lemma 6. *Let* $F = (FGen, FEv, FInv)$ *be the 1-correct, 2-lossy LTP defined in Fig. 5,* $(\pi_{id})_{id \in \mathcal{Id}}$ *the permutation family defined above, and* F_{ii} *the transformation of* F *via Fig. 1. If the* (τ, ϵ)-*Quadratic residuosity assumption holds for* k, F_{ii} *is a 1-correct* (τ', ϵ)-*indistinguishable* $2/(1 + 2^{-k/2})$-*lossy trapdoor function with index-independent domain* $\mathcal{X} = [\![2^k]\!]$, *where* $\tau' \approx \tau$.

6 Prime Family Generators

In Sect. 7 we construct all-but-one lossy trapdoor permutations from the unique divisor Phi-hiding assumption. As a building block we use prime family generators, a tool that deterministically derives prime numbers from a randomly picked seed. While this concept already appeared in [9], we need a variant of the tool with different functionality and security properties. Below, we first define syntax and functionality of prime family generators, and then give a construction based on polynomial evaluation.

Let $\mathcal{Q} \subseteq \mathcal{P}$ be a finite set of prime numbers and let $L \leq |\mathcal{Q}|$. For $(\mathcal{Q}, L)$, any instance of a *prime family generator* (PFG) indicates a sequence of distinct primes $q_1, \ldots, q_L \in \mathcal{Q}$. A specific programmability feature allows for embedding any given prime at any given position. Formally, an (ϵ_1, ϵ_2)-PFG for $(\mathcal{Q}, L)$ consists of a seed space $\mathcal{Sd}$ and three algorithms $PGen, PGet, PProg$ such that

$$PGen \to_{\$} \mathcal{Sd} \quad \text{and} \quad \mathcal{Sd} \times [L] \to PGet \to \mathcal{Q} \quad \text{and} \quad [L] \times \mathcal{Q} \to PProg \to_{\$} \mathcal{Sd}.$$

For functionality we demand (a) programmability: for all $i \in [L]$ we require

$$\Pr[q \leftarrow_{\$} \mathcal{Q}; sd \leftarrow_{\$} PProg(i, q) : PGet(sd, i) \neq q] \leq \epsilon_1.$$

(b) distinctness of outputs: for all $i \in [L]$ we require

$$\Pr[sd \leftarrow_{\$} PGen : \exists j \in [L], i \neq j : PGet(sd, i) = PGet(sd, j)] \leq \epsilon_2.$$

For security we require perfectly indistinguishable programmability: We demand that for all $i \in [L]$ and every distinguisher $\mathcal{D}$ (running in arbitrary time) we have

$$\left| \begin{array}{l} \Pr[sd \leftarrow_{\$} PGen : \mathcal{D}(sd) \Rightarrow 1] \\ \quad - \Pr[q \leftarrow_{\$} \mathcal{Q}; sd \leftarrow_{\$} PProg(i, q) : \mathcal{D}(sd) \Rightarrow 1] \end{array} \right| = 0.$$

6.1 Construction Based on Polynomial Evaluation

The PFG we construct here outputs (l-bit) primes from $\mathcal{Q} = \mathcal{P}_l$. While the construction is similar to one by [9], their PFG would also output primes shorter than l bits. Further, our analysis of probabilities is different, for being tailored towards our application: the construction of ABO-LTPs.

Concretely, for a set of chosen parameters $l, n, d, \lambda \in \mathbb{N}$ we construct a $(2^{-(\lambda+1)}, 2^{-\lambda})$-PFG for $\mathcal{Q} = \mathcal{P}_l$ and $L = 2^n$. The construction is based on a family $\{F_{sd}\}$ of d-wise independent hash functions and, roughly, works as follows (see Fig. 6). The PFG's seed space $\mathcal{S}d$ is equal to $\{F_{sd}\}$'s key space. For $sd \in \mathcal{S}d$ and $i \in [2^n]$, natural numbers are generated by evaluating F_{sd} at up to $d/2$ distinct points. PGet(sd, i)'s output is the first prime found. Since numbers of bit length l are tested for primality, the prime number theorem guarantees that PGen will succeed in finding a prime on average after roughly l attempts. Furthermore, if d is chosen large enough finding a prime in this way will succeed except with some negligible error probability. Concretely, we instantiate $\{F_{sd}\}$ with polynomial evaluation of degree d over the field GF(2^{l-1}). Programming a prime q into a particular point i is done by sampling a sequence of d-many values a_j in the image of F_{sd}. Then—if existent—the first prime in this sequence is replaced by q. By polynomial interpolation it is possible to find a seed sd such that F_{sd} evaluated at the j'th point equals a_j. The technical challenge is to prove that if q was a uniformly distributed prime then resulting seed sd has the correct distribution and, furthermore, with high probability satisfies $q = \text{PGet}(sd, i)$.

PGen
00 $sd \leftarrow_s \{0,1\}^{d(l-1)}$
01 Return sd

PGet(sd, i)
02 For $j \leftarrow 1$ to $d/2$:
03      $q \leftarrow F_{sd}(\#i \| \#j)$
04   If $q + 2^{l-1} \in \mathcal{P}_l$:
05   Return $q + 2^{l-1}$
06 Return $\perp$

PProg(i, q)
07 $(a_1, \ldots, a_d) \leftarrow_s [\![2^{l-1} .. 2^l]\!]^d$
08 Find smallest j with $a_j \in \mathcal{P}_l$
09      $a_j \leftarrow q$
10 $sd \leftarrow \text{FindC}(i, a_1 - 2^{l-1}, \ldots, a_d - 2^{l-1})$
11 Return sd

Fig. 6. PFG based on polynomial evaluation

We now specify the construction in detail. We start by imposing necessary restrictions on its parameters. Let $l, n, d, \lambda \in \mathbb{N}$ with d even and $l \geq 25$ such that

$$n \leq l - \lambda - \log_2(l) - 2 \tag{3}$$

$$2l(\lambda + 1)/\log_2(e) \leq d < 2^{l-1-n} \tag{4}$$

where e is Euler's number. The first inequality ensures the probability of two primes sampled uniformly from $\mathcal{P}_l$ colliding is small, the second inequality makes sure d on one hand is large enough that PGet finds a prime with high probability and on the other hand small enough, that numbers smaller than d can be encoded with few bits. Note that for $l = \mathcal{O}(\lambda)$ and $n = l/2$ Eq. (3) will typically be fulfilled and results in d being of order $\mathcal{O}(\lambda^2)$. The family of hash functions used in our construction is defined as follows. For $sd \in \mathrm{GF}(2^{l-1})^d$ let

$$F_{sd}: \{0,1\}^{l-1} \to [\![2^{l-1}]\!]; \ x \mapsto \sum_{k=0}^{d-1} sd_k x^k.$$

Here x is interpreted as element of $\mathrm{GF}(2^{l-1})$. Note that the function family $(F_{sd})_{sd \in \mathcal{S}d}$ is a d-wise independent hash function [25]. Finally, we define an algorithm FindC as follows. FindC receives as input a tuple $(i, a_1, \ldots, a_d)$, where $i \in [\![2^n]\!]$ and $a_1, \ldots, a_d \in [\![2^{l-1}]\!]$. It then uses Lagrange interpolation to find $sd_0, \ldots, sd_{d-1} \in \mathrm{GF}(2^{l-1})$ such that $F_{sd}(\#i\|\#j) = a_j$ for all $j \in [d]$, where $sd := (sd_0, \ldots, sd_{d-1})$ (see Sect. 2.1 for the $\#$ notation). Here we assume $\#j \in \{0,1\}^{l-1-n}$, which is possible since by Eq. 4 we have $j \le d < 2^{l-1-n}$. FindC's output is sd. Note that for every $i \in [\![2^n]\!]$ the function implemented by FindC$(i, \cdot)$ is a bijection between $[\![2^{l-1}]\!]^d$ and $\mathcal{S}d$. The description of the PFG P may be found in Fig. 6.

Note that in the definition we formally do not allow PGet to return elements that are not in $\mathcal{Q}$. However, P returns $\perp$ if after d tests no prime has been found. This issue could be solved by letting PGet return some fixed prime $q \in \mathcal{Q}$ in this case. We obtain the following result (the proof of which is in the full version [1]).

FGen(br^*)	FEv(br, id, x)	FInv(br, td, y)
00 $sd \leftarrow_\$ $ PGen	06 If $x = 0$: Return 0	16 $(N, sd, \varphi_N) \leftarrow td$
01 $e^* \leftarrow_\$ $ PGet(sd, br^*)	07 $(N, sd) \leftarrow id$	17 $e \leftarrow$ PGet(sd, br)
02 $(N, \varphi_N) \leftarrow_\$ \mathcal{RSA}_k[C(e^*, \varphi_N)]$	08 $e \leftarrow$ PGet(sd, br)	18 If $\gcd(e, \varphi_N) \ne 1$:
03 $id \leftarrow (N, sd)$	09 If $x \notin \mathbb{Z}_N^*$:	19 $\quad$ Return $\perp$
04 $td \leftarrow (N, sd, \varphi_N)$	10 $\quad p \leftarrow \gcd(x, N)$	20 $d \leftarrow e^{-1} \bmod \varphi_N$
05 Return (id, td)	11 $\quad q \leftarrow N/p$	21 $x \leftarrow y^d \bmod N$
	12 $\quad \varphi_N \leftarrow (p-1)(q-1)$	22 Return x
	13 $\quad$ If $e \mid \varphi_N$: Return 0	
	14 $y \leftarrow x^e \bmod N$	
	15 Return y	

Fig. 7. ABO from Phi-hiding assumption. $C(e^*, \varphi_N)$ denotes the condition defined in Sect. 2.3.

Theorem 1. *Let $l, n, d, \lambda \in \mathbb{N}$ as above. Then* P $=$ (PGen, PGet, PProg) *from Fig. 6 is a $(2^{-(\lambda+1)}, 2^{-\lambda})$-PFG for $(\mathcal{P}_l, 2^n)$ with seed space $\mathcal{S}d = \mathrm{GF}(2^{l-1})^d$.*

7 ABO-LTP with Index-Independent Domain from Unique-Divisor Phi-Hiding

We use a prime family generator (for instance the one from Sect. 6) to construct an ABO-LTP with index-independent domain, which can be shown secure under the unique-divisor Phi-hiding assumption. The construction resembles [16,

Sect. 5.2] who build an adaptive trapdoor function. As a starting point we first specify an ABO-LTP A having index-dependent domains. Using the transform from Sect. 3, A can be made index-independent. Due to the result of Lemma 4 the transformed ABO-LTP has essentially the same lossiness factor as A.

Index-Dependent ABO-LTP from Unique-Divisor Phi-Hiding. Let $n, l \in \mathbb{N}$. Consider the ABO-LTP defined in Fig. 7. We obtain the following result (the proof of which is in the full version [1]).

Lemma 7. *Let $n, l \in \mathbb{N}$ and let $P = (\mathrm{PGen}, \mathrm{PGet}, \mathrm{PProg})$ be a (ϵ_1, ϵ_2)-PFG for $(\mathcal{P}_l, 2^n)$. Consider $A = (\mathrm{FGen}, \mathrm{FEv}, \mathrm{FInv})$ from Fig. 7. If the unique-divisor (τ, ϵ)-Phi-hiding assumption holds for $(k, \mathcal{P}_l)$, A is a $(1 - \epsilon_2)$-correct, L-lossy, $(\tau', 2(\epsilon + \epsilon_1)/(1 - \epsilon_1))$-indistinguishable ABO-LTP with index-dependent domain $\mathcal{X} = [\![2^k]\!]$, where $L = 2^{l-1}$ and $\tau' \approx \tau$. Further, A has branching set $\mathcal{B}r = [2^n]$.*

Index-Independent ABO-LTP from Unique-Divisor Phi-Hiding. Using the technique from Sect. 3 it is possible to transform A into an index-independent ABO-LTP A_{ii}. Using the improved bound on the lossiness from Lemma 4 we obtain the following.

Corollary 2. *Let $n, l, k \in \mathbb{N}$ and $A = (\mathrm{FGen}, \mathrm{FEv}, \mathrm{FInv})$ be the ABO defined in Fig. 7. Further, for $(N, sd) = id \in \mathcal{Id}$ let π_{id} the permutation*

$$\pi_{id} \colon [\![2^k]\!] \to [\![2^k]\!]; x \mapsto (x - N + 1) \bmod N.$$

Let A_{ii} be the conversion of A via Fig. 1. If the unique-divisor (τ, ϵ)-Phi-hiding assumption holds for $(k, \mathcal{P}_l)$, then A_{ii} is a $(1 - 2\epsilon_2)$-correct, L-lossy, $(\tau', 2(\epsilon + \epsilon_1)/(1 - \epsilon_1)))$-indistinguishable index-independent ABO-LTP with domain $[\![2^k]\!]$ and branching set $[2^n]$, where $L = 2^{l-1}/(1 + 2^{-k/2})$ and $\tau' \approx \tau$.

Acknowledgments. Benedikt Auerbach was supported in part by the NRW Research Training Group SecHuman and by ERC Project ERCC (FP7/615074). Bertram Poettering conducted part of the research at Ruhr University Bochum, supported by ERC Project ERCC (FP7/615074). Eike Kiltz was supported in part by ERC Project ERCC (FP7/615074) and by DFG SPP 1736 Big Data.

References

1. Auerbach, B., Kiltz, E., Poettering, B., Schoenen, S.: Lossy trapdoor permutations with improved lossiness. Cryptology ePrint Archive, Report 2018/1183 (2018). https://eprint.iacr.org/2018/1183
2. Bellare, M., et al.: Hedged public-key encryption: how to protect against bad randomness. In: Matsui, M. (ed.) ASIACRYPT 2009. LNCS, vol. 5912, pp. 232–249. Springer, Heidelberg (2009). https://doi.org/10.1007/978-3-642-10366-7_14
3. Bellare, M., Fischlin, M., O'Neill, A., Ristenpart, T.: Deterministic encryption: definitional equivalences and constructions without random oracles. In: Wagner, D. (ed.) CRYPTO 2008. LNCS, vol. 5157, pp. 360–378. Springer, Heidelberg (2008). https://doi.org/10.1007/978-3-540-85174-5_20

4. Bellare, M., Hoang, V.T.: Resisting randomness subversion: fast deterministic and hedged public-key encryption in the standard model. In: Oswald, E., Fischlin, M. (eds.) EUROCRYPT 2015, Part II. LNCS, vol. 9057, pp. 627–656. Springer, Heidelberg (2015). https://doi.org/10.1007/978-3-662-46803-6_21

5. Bellare, M., Hofheinz, D., Yilek, S.: Possibility and impossibility results for encryption and commitment secure under selective opening. In: Joux, A. (ed.) EUROCRYPT 2009. LNCS, vol. 5479, pp. 1–35. Springer, Heidelberg (2009). https://doi.org/10.1007/978-3-642-01001-9_1

6. Benhamouda, F., Herranz, J., Joye, M., Libert, B.: Efficient cryptosystems from 2^k-th power residue symbols. J. Cryptology 30(2), 519–549 (2017)

7. Boldyreva, A., Fehr, S., O'Neill, A.: On notions of security for deterministic encryption, and efficient constructions without random oracles. In: Wagner, D. (ed.) CRYPTO 2008. LNCS, vol. 5157, pp. 335–359. Springer, Heidelberg (2008). https://doi.org/10.1007/978-3-540-85174-5_19

8. Brakerski, Z., Segev, G.: Better security for deterministic public-key encryption: the auxiliary-input setting. In: Rogaway, P. (ed.) CRYPTO 2011. LNCS, vol. 6841, pp. 543–560. Springer, Heidelberg (2011). https://doi.org/10.1007/978-3-642-22792-9_31

9. Cachin, C., Micali, S., Stadler, M.: Computationally private information retrieval with polylogarithmic communication. In: Stern, J. (ed.) EUROCRYPT 1999. LNCS, vol. 1592, pp. 402–414. Springer, Heidelberg (1999). https://doi.org/10.1007/3-540-48910-X_28

10. Freeman, D.M., Goldreich, O., Kiltz, E., Rosen, A., Segev, G.: More constructions of lossy and correlation-secure trapdoor functions. In: Nguyen, P.Q., Pointcheval, D. (eds.) PKC 2010. LNCS, vol. 6056, pp. 279–295. Springer, Heidelberg (2010). https://doi.org/10.1007/978-3-642-13013-7_17

11. Freeman, D.M., Goldreich, O., Kiltz, E., Rosen, A., Segev, G.: More constructions of lossy and correlation-secure trapdoor functions. J. Cryptology 26(1), 39–74 (2013)

12. Goldwasser, S., Micali, S.: Probabilistic encryption. J. Comput. Syst. Sci. 28(2), 270–299 (1984)

13. Hayashi, R., Okamoto, T., Tanaka, K.: An RSA family of trap-door permutations with a common domain and its applications. In: Bao, F., Deng, R., Zhou, J. (eds.) PKC 2004. LNCS, vol. 2947, pp. 291–304. Springer, Heidelberg (2004). https://doi.org/10.1007/978-3-540-24632-9_21

14. Hohenberger, S., Waters, B.: Short and stateless signatures from the RSA assumption. In: Halevi, S. (ed.) CRYPTO 2009. LNCS, vol. 5677, pp. 654–670. Springer, Heidelberg (2009). https://doi.org/10.1007/978-3-642-03356-8_38

15. Joye, M., Libert, B.: Efficient cryptosystems from 2^k-th power residue symbols. In: Johansson, T., Nguyen, P.Q. (eds.) EUROCRYPT 2013. LNCS, vol. 7881, pp. 76–92. Springer, Heidelberg (2013). https://doi.org/10.1007/978-3-642-38348-9_5

16. Kiltz, E., Mohassel, P., O'Neill, A.: Adaptive trapdoor functions and chosen-ciphertext security. In: Gilbert, H. (ed.) EUROCRYPT 2010. LNCS, vol. 6110, pp. 673–692. Springer, Heidelberg (2010). https://doi.org/10.1007/978-3-642-13190-5_34

17. Kiltz, E., O'Neill, A., Smith, A.: Instantiability of RSA-OAEP under chosen-plaintext attack. In: Rabin, T. (ed.) CRYPTO 2010. LNCS, vol. 6223, pp. 295–313. Springer, Heidelberg (2010). https://doi.org/10.1007/978-3-642-14623-7_16

18. Mironov, I., Pandey, O., Reingold, O., Segev, G.: Incremental deterministic public-key encryption. In: Pointcheval, D., Johansson, T. (eds.) EUROCRYPT 2012. LNCS, vol. 7237, pp. 628–644. Springer, Heidelberg (2012). https://doi.org/10.1007/978-3-642-29011-4_37

19. Mol, P., Yilek, S.: Chosen-ciphertext security from slightly lossy trapdoor functions. In: Nguyen, P.Q., Pointcheval, D. (eds.) PKC 2010. LNCS, vol. 6056, pp. 296–311. Springer, Heidelberg (2010). https://doi.org/10.1007/978-3-642-13013-7_18

20. Nishimaki, R., Fujisaki, E., Tanaka, K.: Efficient non-interactive universally composable string-commitment schemes. In: Pieprzyk, J., Zhang, F. (eds.) ProvSec 2009. LNCS, vol. 5848, pp. 3–18. Springer, Heidelberg (2009). https://doi.org/10.1007/978-3-642-04642-1_3

21. Peikert, C., Waters, B.: Lossy trapdoor functions and their applications. In: Ladner, R.E., Dwork, C. (eds.) 40th ACM STOC, pp. 187–196. ACM Press, May 2008

22. Peikert, C., Waters, B.: Lossy trapdoor functions and their applications. SIAM J. Comput. **40**(6), 1803–1844 (2011). https://doi.org/10.1137/080733954

23. Raghunathan, A., Segev, G., Vadhan, S.: Deterministic public-key encryption for adaptively chosen plaintext distributions. In: Johansson, T., Nguyen, P.Q. (eds.) EUROCRYPT 2013. LNCS, vol. 7881, pp. 93–110. Springer, Heidelberg (2013). https://doi.org/10.1007/978-3-642-38348-9_6

24. Rosen, A., Segev, G.: Chosen-ciphertext security via correlated products. In: Reingold, O. (ed.) TCC 2009. LNCS, vol. 5444, pp. 419–436. Springer, Heidelberg (2009). https://doi.org/10.1007/978-3-642-00457-5_25

25. Shoup, V.: A Computational Introduction to Number Theory and Algebra. Cambridge University Press, Cambridge (2005)

26. Xie, X., Xue, R., Zhang, R.: Efficient threshold encryption from lossy trapdoor functions. In: Yang, B.-Y. (ed.) PQCrypto 2011. LNCS, vol. 7071, pp. 163–178. Springer, Heidelberg (2011). https://doi.org/10.1007/978-3-642-25405-5_11

27. Yamakawa, T., Yamada, S., Hanaoka, G., Kunihiro, N.: Adversary-dependent lossy trapdoor function from hardness of factoring semi-smooth RSA subgroup moduli. In: Robshaw, M., Katz, J. (eds.) CRYPTO 2016, Part II. LNCS, vol. 9815, pp. 3–32. Springer, Heidelberg (2016). https://doi.org/10.1007/978-3-662-53008-5_1

Post-quantum EPID Signatures
from Symmetric Primitives

Dan Boneh, Saba Eskandarian[✉], and Ben Fisch

Stanford University, Stanford, USA
{dabo,saba,bfisch}@cs.stanford.edu

Abstract. EPID signatures are used extensively in real-world systems for hardware enclave attestation. As such, there is a strong interest in making these schemes post-quantum secure. In this paper we initiate the study of EPID signature schemes built only from symmetric primitives, such as hash functions and PRFs. We present two constructions in the random oracle model. The first is a scheme satisfying the EPID signature syntax and security definitions needed for private hardware attestation used in Intel's SGX. The second achieves significantly shorter signatures for many applications, including the use case of remote hardware attestation. While our EPID signatures for attestation are longer than standard post-quantum signatures, they are short enough for applications where the data being signed is large, such as analytics on large private data sets, or streaming media to a trusted display. We evaluate several instantiations of our schemes so that the costs and benefits of these constructions are clear. Along the way we also give improvements to the zero-knowledge Merkle inclusion proofs of Derler et al. (2017).

1 Introduction

Enhanced Privacy ID, or EPID, signatures allow members of a group to anonymously sign messages on behalf of the group, with the added property that a group manager can revoke the credentials of a misbehaving or compromised group member [15, 36].

In recent years, EPID signatures have become an important privacy mechanism in real-world systems, most prominently in trusted hardware attestation such as Intel's SGX. Attestation is a process by which a hardware enclave running on a client device proves the authenticity of its execution environment to a remote party. EPID lets the client device attest without revealing its identity to the remote party. However, EPID signatures used today are not post-quantum secure [15]. An adversary with a quantum computer could subvert the attestation process and break a hardware enclave's security in the worst possible way.

In light of the above, there is strong interest in developing post-quantum secure EPID signatures. One way to do so is to construct an EPID signature scheme using only symmetric primitives, which are believed to be post-quantum secure. This is analogous to constructing a standard signature scheme from hash

© Springer Nature Switzerland AG 2019
M. Matsui (Ed.): CT-RSA 2019, LNCS 11405, pp. 251–271, 2019.
https://doi.org/10.1007/978-3-030-12612-4_13

functions [9,16,20,43,44] to obtain a signature scheme whose post-quantum security is virtually assured.

Can we build efficient and secure EPID signatures from symmetric primitives? Bellare et al. [6] give a generic construction of a group signature [21], a related primitive, from a standard signature scheme, public-key encryption, and a non-interactive zero-knowledge (NIZK) proof. In this generic construction, the group manager adds a member to the group by signing that member's public key. The member can then sign messages anonymously by first using the private key to sign the message, and then computing a NIZK proof of knowledge of both this signature and the group manager's signature on the corresponding public key. This NIZK proof is the member's group signature. With some work, their framework can be adapted to support the EPID group signature definition of Brickell and Li [15] and to only use symmetric primitives. The NIZK can be built from the "MPC in the Head" technique of Ishai et al. [3,30,35] using random oracles, and the standard signature scheme can also be built from one-way functions and collision-resistant hashing [9,20,31,43]. Camenisch and Groth [17] give such a scheme from one-way functions and NIZKs. However, without careful optimization, this generic approach leads to very inefficient signatures due to the need for NIZK proofs on complex circuits (the proof size and prover time of these NIZKs is proportional to the number of multiplication gates in the arithmetic circuit representing the statement).

1.1   Our Contributions

We construct an EPID signature scheme from symmetric primitives, and take a significant step towards reducing the signature size.

Towards this goal, we build two signature schemes. Our first construction greatly reduces the size of the NIZK statement in the signature by using PRFs instead of signatures wherever possible. In particular, we are able to replace the inner group member's signature in the generic approach with a PRF evaluation. Our construction does not treat the given primitives as a black-box and performs best when instantiated with NIZK-friendly PRFs and CRHFs. In particular, we evaluate the scheme using the LowMC cipher [2], also including a comparison to AES to show the benefit of choosing the right instantiations for our primitives.

Next, we show how to significantly improve our EPID signature by adapting it to the specific real-world use case where signature verification requires an interaction with the group manager to ensure that the signer has not been revoked. We take advantage of this structure to dramatically reduce the signature size by moving many heavy verification steps outside of the NIZK, without compromising anonymity or affecting security. This significantly shrinks the signature size over the first construction.

Along the way, we develop a technique for proving membership in a Merkle tree, without revealing the leaf location, using a *third* preimage resistant hash function (Sect. 5.4). This also provides an improvement to the recent post-quantum accumulators of Derler et al. [24].

Performance and Use Cases. In Sect. 5 we discuss options for instantiating our schemes, and measure the sizes of the resulting signatures under different security assumptions. For the circuit sizes needed inside NIZKs in our construction, ZKB++ [20] provides the most efficient proofs. We report sizes for both the Random Oracle and Quantum Random Oracle models [11] (using the Fiat-Shamir [27] and Unruh [48] transforms, respectively), and find that our second signature scheme, designed for attestation, can support groups of over a million members with 3.45 MB signatures at 128-bit post-quantum security. While these signatures are not short, it is important to keep in mind that several megabytes of traffic for attestation is quite acceptable for many applications of trusted hardware, especially where the data transfer needs of the higher-level application dwarf the size of the attestation.

One example is the case of analytics over large private data sets, an area of heavy investment, both in terms of research and financial resources [29,51]. In this setting, nodes in a distributed network (or the server in a client-server setting) provide a single remote attestation and then exchange a great deal of data. As the quantity of data transferred exceeds millions of database records, the size of the initial attestation ceases to present a major bottleneck.

The case of digital rights management (DRM), for which hardware enclaves such as Intel SGX seem particularly well-suited [22], is another setting where the size of our signatures are acceptable. Consider the common situation where a content provider wishes to stream a movie (easily a few gigabytes in size) to a subscriber while preventing redistribution or unauthorized viewing of copyrighted content [50,52]. The few additional megabytes of an attestation do not matter next to a film or television series several hundred times its size.

1.2 Additional Related Work

Trusted Hardware and Attestation. Hardware enclaves, particularly Intel's SGX [22], have recently been used for a variety of security applications [28, 45]. One of the primary cryptographic components of SGX is its use of direct anonymous attestation, a primitive introduced by Brickell et al. [14]. The EPID attestation mechanism currently in use by SGX, is due to Brickell et al. [15,36].

Group Signatures. Anonymous attestation and EPID signatures bear a great deal of similarity to group signatures. Group signatures [21] allow members of a group to anonymously produce signatures on behalf of the group, with the added restriction that a group manager has the power to police the behavior of members, e.g. by revoking their group credentials or stripping their anonymity. The most frequently used definitions of group signatures are described by Bellare et al. [6,7]. Subsequent work on group signatures has led to various schemes, for example, those of Lysyanskaya and Camenisch [18,19], Boneh et al. [10,12], and a scheme of Groth [34]. These constructions are not post-quantum secure.

Post-quantum Signatures and Proofs. Lattice-based cryptography is a popular candidate for post-quantum security. Lattice group signatures were introduced by Gordon et al. [33] and extended in several subsequent works [39–42].

The resulting group signatures are shorter than the ones developed here, but rely on qualitatively stronger post-quantum assumptions.

Another set of post-quantum tools come from the "MPC in the Head" technique [35] for zero-knowledge proofs. This idea has been extended by ZKBoo [30], ZKB++ [20], and Ligero [3]. In particular, Chase et al. use ZKB++ to construt two post-quantum signature schemes Fish and Picnic [20]. The recent development of zk-STARKS [8] opens another avenue to post-quantum zero-knowledge proofs. In concurrent work, El Bansarkhani and Misoczki [4] describe a stateful group signature scheme based on hash functions. Their work features small signature sizes but large keys. Derler et al. [24] and Katz et al. [37] also concurrently study post-quantum group and ring signatures from symmetric primitives.

2   Preliminaries

Notation. Let $x \leftarrow F(y)$ denote the assignment of the output of $F(y)$ to x, and let $x \xleftarrow{\text{R}} S$ denote assignment to x of a uniformly random element sampled from set S. We use λ to refer to a security parameter and sometimes omit it if its presence is implicit. The notation $[k]$ represents the set of integers $1, 2, ..., k$, and $\emptyset$ denotes the empty set. We use $\mathcal{A}^H$ to denote that $\mathcal{A}$ has oracle access to some function H. A function $\mathsf{negl}(x)$ is *negligible* if for all $c > 0$, there is an x_0 such that for any $x > x_0$, $\mathsf{negl}(x) < \frac{1}{x^c}$. We omit x if the parameter is implicit. We use $f(x) \approx g(x)$ to mean that for two functions f, g, $|f(x) - g(x)| < \mathsf{negl}(x)$. PPT stands for probabilistic polynomial time. We use the notation $\mathsf{Func}_{\mathcal{A}, \mathcal{B}}\langle a, b \rangle$ to refer to a protocol Func between parties $\mathcal{A}$ and $\mathcal{B}$ with inputs a and b, respectively. Finally, we allow algorithms to output $\perp$ to indicate failure.

Proof Systems. We briefly review the definitions of proof systems that we will need in later sections. The main notion we will use is that of a non-interactive zero knowledge proof of knowledge in the random oracle model. We use the definitions of [26], which modify prior commom reference string-based definitions of non-interactive zero-knowledge for use in the Random Oracle Model.

Definition 1 (Non-interactive Proof System). *A non-interactive proof system Π for a relation R consists of prover algorithm that on input x, w outputs a proof π and a verifier algorithm that on input x, π outputs a bit b. We say that (P, V) is correct and sound if it satisfies the following properties:*

- $(x, w) \in R \rightarrow V(x, P(x, w)) = 1$
- $(x, w) \notin R \rightarrow \Pr[V(x, P^*(x, w)) = 1] < \mathsf{negl}$ *for any (potentially cheating) prover P^*.*

For convenience and clarity of notation, we use $P(\mathsf{public}(\cdot), \mathsf{private}(\cdot), R)$ to indicate that the public parts of the input to a prover P for relation R correspond to the statement x and that the private parts correspond to the witness w.

The zero-knowledge property [32] informally requires that a proof reveals nothing about (x, w) except that $(x, w) \in R$. Formally, we model this property by describing a *simulator* that can provide a legitimate proof given only x and not w [5].

Extractability, informally, is a strengthening of the soundness property that requires any acceptable proof to have an *extractor* algorithm that can efficiently recover w with high probability given the ability to interact with the prover. We refer to Bellare and Goldreich [5] for a full definition. Simulation-sound extractability [34,46,47] further strengthens the extractability requirement of proofs of knowledge to enable extracting a witness even after seeing many simulated proofs.

EPID Signatures. We construct our EPID signature to match the syntax and security requirements as defined by Brickel and Li [15]. In this section we state the EPID syntax and sketch security requirements. Full definitions and security games appear in the full version of this paper. First, anonymity must ensure that the group manager colluding with any number of group members cannot uncover the identity of the signer. In particular, we do not want the group manager to have a tracing key that lets it compromise a group member's identity from a signature. Nevertheles, we will later briefly explain how to extend our scheme to achieve traceability, if desired.

Second, we want a revocation property where a group manager can revoke a user's ability to sign by either:

- adding a revoked user's leaked signing key to a revocation list KEY-RL, or
- adding a revoked user's EPID signature to a revocation list SIG-RL.

A user is revoked if its key is included in the list KEY-RL, or if any of its signatures are included in the list SIG-RL.

With this setup, we define the syntax and security properties for an EPID signature scheme as follows.

Definition 2 (EPID Signature). *An EPID signature scheme $\mathcal{G}$ involving a group manager $\mathcal{M}$ and n group members, parties $\mathcal{P}_1$ to $\mathcal{P}_n$, consists of algorithms Init, Join, GPSign, GPVerify, RevokeKey and RevokeSig:*

- $(gsk, gpk) \leftarrow$ *Init(1^λ): This algorithm takes as input a security parameter 1^λ and outputs a key pair (gsk, gpk).*
- $\langle cert_i, (sk_i, cert_i) \rangle \leftarrow$ *Join$_{\mathcal{M},\mathcal{P}_i}\langle (gsk, gpk), gpk \rangle$: This is a protocol between the group manager and a group member $\mathcal{P}_i$ where each party has its keys as input, and both parties get party $\mathcal{P}_i$'s certificate as output. $\mathcal{P}_i$ also gets its secret key sk_i as an output.*
- $\perp/sig \leftarrow$ *GPSign$(gpk, sk_i, cert_i, m, SIG\text{-}RL)$: This algorithm takes as input the public key, a signature revocation list SIG-RL, and party $\mathcal{P}_i$'s secret key and certificate. The output is an EPID signature sig.*
- $1/0 \leftarrow$ *GPVerify$(gpk, m, KEY\text{-}RL, SIG\text{-}RL, sig)$: This algorithm verifies an EPID signature sig on a message m given the group public key and key/signature revocation lists KEY-RL, SIG-RL. It outputs 1 to accept the signature and 0 to reject it.*

- KEY-RL ← RevokeKey(gpk, KEY-RL, sk$_i$): *This algorithm adds a secret key* sk$_i$ *to a key revocation list, so signatures created with this key will no longer be accepted.*
- SIG-RL ← RevokeSig(gpk, KEY-RL, SIG-RL, m, sig): *This algorithm adds a signature* sig *to a signature revocation list, so signatures created with the same key as* sig *will no longer be accepted.*

The algorithms must satisfy Correctness, Anonymity, and Unforgeability.

For correctness, we require that if a group member has successfully completed the Join procedure and neither its key nor any of its signatures have been revoked, then that group member's signatures should successfully verify.

We define anonymity via the Anonymity game. Informally, the property of being Anonymous requires that signatures in $\mathcal{G}$ hide the identity of the signer against any coalition of group members (including the group manager) except the signer herself. The definition of anonymity also implies notions of unlinkability between a signer and her signatures. The game allows the adversary to create users, sign messages, and corrupt users of its choosing before attempting to distinguish which of two uncorrupted users produced a signature on a challenge message of the adversary's choice.

Finally, we define unforgeability. Our unforgeability game consists of an adversary who can add arbitrary parties to a group and corrupt arbitrarily many members of a group. Security holds if this adversary cannot forge the signature of an uncorrupted party on a message of its own choosing.

3   Post-quantum EPID Signatures

In this section we describe and prove the security of our first post-quantum EPID signature scheme. Our construction uses a standard signature scheme where each group member has its own key pair and a *certificate* from the group manager. Instead of signature keys, however, we construct our scheme so that each group member has a unique PRF secret key that will be used to issue EPID signatures. As we will see, this leads to significant savings over the general framework of Bellare et al. [6]. We still need a signature scheme for the group manager to produce certificates, but the NIZK proof is done over a circuit that verifies a single signature (the group manager's) along with a few evaluations of the PRF. An overview of the construction is as follows. Each member generates its own secret key sk for a PRF f. During the join procedure it obtains a challenge c from the group manager, sends $t = f(\mathsf{sk}, c)$ to the manager, and obtains back a signature σ on t. To sign a message, the member first reveals $t' = (f(\mathsf{sk}, r), r)$ for random r and then a signature of knowledge, where the proof witness is sk consistent with t' as well as σ, i.e. a signature on $f(\mathsf{sk}, c^*)$ for some c^*. Including t' in the clear is used for signature revocation. Note that signatures need to be verified relative to the same signature revocation lists under which they were signed.

Collision Resistant PRF. We state and prove security of our scheme using a function $f : \mathcal{K} \times \mathcal{X} \to \mathcal{Y}$ that is both a secure PRF and a collision resistant function. In fact, it suffices that f be collision-resistant *on the keyspace*, meaning that for a target input $x \in \mathcal{X}$ chosen by the adversary, it should be hard to find $k_0 \neq k_1 \in \mathcal{K}$ such that $f(k_0, x) = f(k_1, x)$. We explain how to construct an MPC-friendly function with this property in Sect. 5.

Construction 1 (EPID Signature). Our EPID signature scheme $\mathcal{G} = (\text{Init, Join,} \text{GPSign, GPVerify, RevokeKey, RevokeSig})$ with security parameter λ uses a signature scheme $\mathcal{S} = (\text{Keygen, Sign, Verify})$, a proof system $\Pi = (P, V)$, and a PRF f that also serves as a collision-resistant hash function.

- Init(1^λ): Group manager $\mathcal{M}$ runs Keygen(1^λ) to get (gpk, gsk) and outputs this tuple (gpk is published and gsk kept secret).
- Join$_{\mathcal{M}, \mathcal{P}_i}\langle(\text{gsk}, \text{gpk}), \text{gpk}\rangle$:
  - Group manager $\mathcal{M}$ sends challenge c_i to member $\mathcal{P}_i$.
  - $\mathcal{P}_i$ chooses $\text{sk}_i \xleftarrow{\text{R}} \{0,1\}^\lambda$ and sends $t_i^{\text{join}} = f(\text{sk}_i, c_i)$ back to $\mathcal{M}$.
  - $\mathcal{M}$ produces signature $\sigma_i = \text{Sign}(\text{gsk}, (t_i^{\text{join}}, c_i))$, and constructs $\text{cert}_i = (t_i^{\text{join}}, c_i, \sigma_i)$, sending a copy to $\mathcal{P}_i$. If the signature scheme is stateful, then algorithm Join must maintain a counter that is incremented for every user who joins the group.
  - The group member's private key is sk_i and both parties get copies of cert_i.
- GPSign(gpk, sk_i, cert_i, m, SIG-RL): Compute the following and output sig:
  - $r \xleftarrow{\text{R}} \{0,1\}^\lambda \backslash c_i$
  - $t \leftarrow (f(\text{sk}_i, r), r)$
  - $\pi \leftarrow P\big(\text{public}(\lambda, m, \text{gpk}, t, \text{SIG-RL}, \text{KEY-RL}), \text{private}(\text{sk}_i, \text{cert}_i), R_1\big)$
  - $\text{sig} \leftarrow (t, \pi)$.

  We define the relation R_1 in the proof of knowledge π for $(\text{sk}_i^*, \text{cert}_i^*)$ to be true when the following statements hold:
  - $t = (f(\text{sk}_i^*, r), r)$
  - $r \neq c_i^*$
  - $\text{Verify}(\text{gpk}, (t_i^{\text{join}*}, c_i^*), \sigma_i^*) = 1$
  - $t_i^{\text{join}*} = f(\text{sk}_i^*, c_i^*)$
  - for each $\text{sig}_j \in \text{SIG-RL}, t_{\text{sig}_j} \neq (f(\text{sk}_i^*, r_{\text{sig}_j}), r_{\text{sig}_j})$
- GPVerify(gpk, m, KEY-RL, SIG-RL, sig):
  - Verify proof π: check $V((\lambda, m, \text{gpk}, t, \text{SIG-RL}, \text{KEY-RL}), \pi) = 1$.
  - For each $\text{sk}_j \in \text{KEY-RL}$, check that $t \neq (f(\text{sk}_j, r), r)$.
  - Check that $\text{sig} \notin \text{SIG-RL}$.
  - Output 1 if all of the above checks return 1; otherwise, output 0.
- RevokeKey(gpk, KEY-RL, sk_i): Return $\text{KEY-RL} \cup \{\text{sk}_i\}$.
- RevokeSig(gpk, KEY-RL, SIG-RL, m, sig): return $\text{SIG-RL} \cup \{\text{sig}\}$ if GPVerify(gpk, m, KEY-RL, SIG-RL, sig) $= 1$. Otherwise, return SIG-RL.

Revocation. Although the difference between the two forms of revocation does not affect our scheme's security, the effect of revocation differs in practice depending on whether a group member is revoked by key or by signature. A revocation by key renders all signatures, past or future, invalid for that user, whereas a revocation by signature only applies to future signatures because past signatures need to be verified with respect to the SIG-RL in place at the time of signing. This does not matter for the purposes of the security game because the attempted forgery is always the last signature produced in the game. For the same reason, the decision to include the check that sig $\notin$ SIG-RL during GPVerify does not affect security for the purpose of the proof and can be omitted. We include it only to better capture behavior that may be expected of revocation in practice.

Traceable Signatures. Our approach can also be used to achieve *traceability*. Traceability requires that the group manager have the power to learn the identity of a signer. We presented our scheme without a tracing property in order to guarantee a stronger anonymity property against the group manager, but a similar approach could be used to achieve traceability. The group manager could give each group member a signed secret token sk_i'', and every signature would include the token $t' = (f(\mathsf{sk}_i'', r'), r')$, for a newly picked random r', along with a proof of knowledge of a signature on sk_i''. Now the group manager can trace a signature by trying to reconstruct t' with the value of sk_i'' for each signer, but anonymity will still hold against any other group member.

Camenisch and Groth [17] give a traceable group signature scheme from one-way functions and NIZKs. Although their scheme can be instantiated under the same assumptions as ours, they (loosely speaking) include a commitment to a credential for each group member in their public key and give a proof of knowledge that a signature corresponds to one of those credentials. By avoiding this cost, our scheme shrinks both the public key size and signature size by a factor $O(N)$. Our public key can also be published at group initialization time before any members have joined the group.

Security Theorems. We now state our various theorems regarding the security of our scheme and give a brief intuition to justify them. Proofs are deferred to the full version of this paper. Correctness follows almost immediately from the construction with the caveat that we must ensure that the revocation checks do not accidentally cause a signature from a legitimate key to be rejected.

Theorem 3. *Assuming the correctness of signature scheme S and proof system Π and the pseudorandomness of f, $\mathcal{G}$ is a correct EPID signature scheme.*

Anonymity follows from the zero-knowledge and pseudorandomness properties of the primitives used in our construction. Intuitively, the scheme achieves anonymity against the group manager by having each group member generate its own PRF secret key sk, and from all other parties because the signatures are zero-knowledge signatures of knowledge.

Theorem 4. *Assuming that Π is a zero-knowledge proof system and that f is a PRF, $\mathcal{G}$ is an anonymous EPID signature scheme.*

The high level intuition for unforgeability is as follows. If the adversary A has not obtained a signature from the group manager on $t = f(sk, c)$ then it cannot produce a PoK of valid signature on t by unforgeability of the group manager's signature scheme and soundness of the PoK. Second, if A does not know sk for some $t = f(sk, c)$ that has been signed, then even though it sees many $f(sk, r), r$ inside signatures it cannot produce $f(sk, c^*)$ on a fresh c^* by the security of the PRF. (Note that even if it were able to do this it has to actually learn sk to forge a signature as otherwise it breaks PoK extractability). Finally, collision-resistance of the PRF ensures that A who has a signature on $f(sk, c)$ for revoked sk cannot find $sk' \neq sk$ and r such that $f(sk', c) = t$ and $f(sk', r) \neq f(sk, r)$.

Theorem 5. *Assuming that Π is a zero knowledge proof of knowledge proof system with simulation-sound extractability, S is an unforgeable signature scheme, that f is a PRF, and that f is additionally a collision-resistant hash function, G is an unforgeable EPID signature scheme.*

4   Practical Post-quantum Signatures for Attestation

Attestation schemes (such as that used in Intel SGX [22,36]) involve interaction with an attestation service on every attestation, among other reasons to obtain an updated revocation list. In the case of SGX, this attestation service is also the group manager. In this section, we present a significantly smaller post-quantum EPID-like signature scheme appropriate for this setting where frequent interaction with the group manager is allowed.

The main bottleneck for signature size in our first construction was including verification of the group manager's signature on a group member's certificate inside the PoK (i.e. this contributed the most to arithmetic complexity). We remove this signature in our new scheme by making each group member's certificate a leaf in a Merkle tree. The group manager signs only the root, providing each group member an inclusion proof during Join. The signature on the root can be public as it leaks nothing about the identity of a member. Signers now only need to include the Merkle inclusion proof inside the proof of knowledge instead of a hash-based signature. The verification of an inclusion proof requires a much smaller circuit.

This modification has several implications for security. As a new Merkle tree root will need to be published each time a group member joins, this reduces the size of anonymity sets. In an extreme case the group manager could issue a sequence of Merkle roots where each tree only included a valid credential for one group member, uniquely identifying the member's signatures.

Fortunately, the continuing contact between group members and the group manager enforced by attestation in practice enable effective mitigations for these concerns. Group members can periodically "re-join" the group to update the Merkle root relative to which they provide membership proofs, thereby increasing the size of their anonymity sets. In practice, we can ensure that subsequent Merkle roots issued by the group manager only ever add new credentials to the group and never omit previous ones by using a *Merkle consistency proof* such as the one proposed by the Certificate Transparency standard [38] and proven secure by Dowling et al. [25]. We model the Merkle trees used in our proofs as accumulators with zero-knowledge membership proofs and discuss how we instantiate this primitive with an improved construction in Sect. 5.

4.1 Definitions

In this section we define accumulators and EPID-like signatures for attestation. We begin with a special case of the formalization of accumulators by [23].

Definition 6 (Accumulator). *A static accumulator is a tuple of efficient algorithms (AGen, AEval, AWitCreate, AVerify, AProveCon, ACheckCon) which are defined as follows:*

- *AGen(1^λ): This algorithm takes a security parameter λ and returns a public key $pk_\wedge$.*
- *AEval$(pk_\wedge, \mathcal{X})$: This deterministic algorithm takes a key $pk_\wedge$ and a set $\mathcal{X}$ to be accumulated and returns an accumulator $\Lambda_\mathcal{X}$.*
- *AWitCreate$(pk_\wedge, \Lambda_\mathcal{X}, \mathcal{X}, x_i)$: This algorithm takes a key $pk_\wedge$, an accumulator $\Lambda_\mathcal{X}$, the set $\mathcal{X}$, and a value x_i. It returns $\perp$ if $x_i \notin \mathcal{X}$ and a witness wit_{x_i} for x_i otherwise.*
- *AVerify$(pk_\wedge, \Lambda_\mathcal{X}, wit_{x_i}, x_i)$: This algorithm takes a public key $pk_\wedge$, an accumulator $\Lambda_\mathcal{X}$, a witness wit_{x_i}, and a value x_i. It returns 1 if wit_{x_i} is a witness for $x_i \in \mathcal{X}$ and 0 otherwise.*

We require accumulators to be correct, meaning that AVerify will accept an honestly generated witness for $x_i \in \mathcal{X}$. We also require a soundness property dubbed *collision-freeness*, formally defined below.

Definition 7 (Collision Freeness). *An accumulator is collision free if for all PPT adversaries $\mathcal{A}$, we have that*

$$Pr[\text{AVerify}(pk_\wedge, \Lambda^*, wit^*_{x_i}, x^*_i) = 1 \wedge x^*_i \notin \mathcal{X}^* |$$

$$pk_\wedge \leftarrow \text{AGen}(1^\lambda, \Lambda^*), \Lambda^* \leftarrow \text{Eval}_{r^*}(pk_\wedge, \mathcal{X}^*), (wit^*_{x_i}, x^*_i, \mathcal{X}^*) \leftarrow \mathcal{A}(pk_\wedge, \Lambda^*)] \leq negl(\lambda)$$

The setting of EPID signatures for attestation largely leaves the security definitions of Sect. 3 unaffected up to changes in syntax, so we present the updated syntax in the full version and omit statements of the security definitions. The only notable changes are that (1) in both security games the adversary can now choose to have a group member run the new GARejoin at any time it chooses, and (2) signatures are only indistinguishable for two signatures produced relative to the same accumulator.

4.2 EPID Signature Construction II

The full construction of the modified EPID signature scheme appears below. Structurally similar to the construction in Sect. 3, the main changes involve the introduction of a post-quantum accumulator and the resulting restructuring of what needs to be proven inside/outside the proof of knowledge π, as described informally at the beginning of this section.

Construction 2 (EPID Signature for Attestation). Our EPID signature scheme for attestation $\mathcal{GA} = (\mathsf{GAInit}, \mathsf{GAJoin}, \mathsf{GARejoin}, \mathsf{GASign}, \mathsf{GAVerify}, \mathsf{GARevokeKey}, \mathsf{GARevokeSig})$ with security parameter λ uses a signature scheme $\mathcal{S} = (\mathsf{Keygen}, \mathsf{Sign}, \mathsf{Verify})$, a proof system $\Pi = (P, V)$, a PRF f that also serves as a collision-resistant hash function, and an accumulator $\mathcal{Ac} = (\mathsf{AGen}, \mathsf{AEval}, \mathsf{AWitCreate}, \mathsf{AVerify})$.

- $\mathsf{GAInit}(1^\lambda)$: Group manager $\mathcal{M}$ runs $\mathsf{Keygen}(1^\lambda)$ to get $(\mathsf{pk_{gp}}, \mathsf{sk_{gp}})$ and runs $\mathsf{AGEN}(1^\lambda)$, to get $\mathsf{pk_\wedge}$. It outputs public key $\mathsf{gpk} = (\mathsf{pk_{gp}}, \mathsf{pk_\wedge})$ and secret key $\mathsf{gsk} = \mathsf{sk_{gp}}$.
- $\mathsf{GAJoin}_{\mathcal{M}, \mathcal{P}_i} \langle (\mathsf{gsk}, \mathsf{gpk}, \mathcal{X}), \mathsf{gpk} \rangle$:
  - Group manager $\mathcal{M}$ sends challenge c_i to member $\mathcal{P}_i$.
  - $\mathcal{P}_i$ picks $\mathsf{sk}_i \xleftarrow{\text{R}} \{0,1\}^\lambda$ and sends $t_i^{\mathsf{join}} = f(\mathsf{sk}_i, c_i)$ back to $\mathcal{M}$.
  - $\mathcal{M}$ defines $x_i = (t_i^{\mathsf{join}}, c_i)$, sets $\mathcal{X} = \mathcal{X} \cup x_i$, sets $\Lambda = \mathsf{AEval}(\mathsf{pk_\wedge}, \mathcal{X})$, and produces signature $\sigma_\wedge = \mathsf{Sign}(\mathsf{gsk}, \Lambda)$. Next, $\mathcal{M}$ creates $\mathsf{wit}_{x_i} = \mathsf{AWitCreate}(\mathsf{pk_\wedge}, \Lambda, \mathcal{X}, x_i)$ and constructs $\mathsf{cert}_i = (x_i, \mathsf{wit}_{x_i})$, sending a copy to $\mathcal{P}_i$ along with Λ and $\sigma_\wedge$.
  - The group member's private key is sk_i and both parties get copies of cert_i, Λ, and $\sigma_\wedge$.
- $\mathsf{GARejoin}_{\mathcal{M}, \mathcal{P}_i} \langle (\mathsf{gsk}, \mathsf{gpk}, \mathcal{X}, \Lambda, \sigma_\wedge), (\mathsf{gpk}, \mathsf{cert}_i) \rangle$:
  - $\mathcal{P}_i$ sends cert_i to $\mathcal{M}$.
  - First, $\mathcal{M}$ verifies the signature in cert_i, aborting in case of failure. Then it creates a new $\mathsf{wit}_{x_i} = \mathsf{AWitCreate}(\mathsf{pk_\wedge}, \Lambda, \mathcal{X}, x_i)$ and constructs the updated $\mathsf{cert}_i = (x_i, \mathsf{wit}_{x_i})$, sending a copy to $\mathcal{P}_i$ along with Λ and $\sigma_\wedge$.
  - $\mathcal{P}_i$ updates its values of cert_i, Λ, and $\sigma_\wedge$.
- $\mathsf{GASign}(\mathsf{gpk}, \mathsf{sk}_i, \mathsf{cert}_i, m, \mathsf{SIG\text{-}RL}, \Lambda, \sigma_\wedge)$: Compute the following and output sig:
  - $\mathsf{Verify}(\mathsf{pk_{gp}}, \sigma_\wedge, \Lambda)$ (abort if it outputs 0)
  - $r \xleftarrow{\text{R}} \{0,1\}^\lambda \backslash c_i$
  - $t = (f(\mathsf{sk}_i, r), r)$
  - $\pi = P(\mathsf{public}(\lambda, m, \mathsf{gpk}, t, \mathsf{SIG\text{-}RL}, \mathsf{KEY\text{-}RL}, \Lambda), \mathsf{private}(\mathsf{sk}_i, \mathsf{cert}_i), R_2)$
  - $\mathsf{sig} = (t, \pi, \Lambda, \sigma_\wedge)$.
  We define R_2 as a relation in the proof of knowledge of $(\mathsf{sk}_i^*, \mathsf{cert}_i^*)$ such that the following statements hold:
  - $t = (f(\mathsf{sk}_i^*, r), r)$
  - $r \neq c_i^*$
  - $\mathsf{AVerify}(\mathsf{pk_\wedge}, \Lambda, \mathsf{wit}_{x_i}^*, (t_i^{\mathsf{join}*}, c_i^*))$
  - $t_i^{\mathsf{join}*} = f(\mathsf{sk}_i^*, c_i^*)$
  - for each $\mathsf{sig}_j \in \mathsf{SIG\text{-}RL}, t_{\mathsf{sig}_j} \neq (f(\mathsf{sk}_i^*, r_{\mathsf{sig}_j}), r_{\mathsf{sig}_j})$
- $\mathsf{GAVerify}(\mathsf{gpk}, m, \mathsf{KEY\text{-}RL}, \mathsf{SIG\text{-}RL}, \mathsf{sig})$:
  - Verify signature $\sigma_\wedge$: check $\mathsf{Verify}(\mathsf{pk_{gp}}, \sigma_\wedge, \Lambda) = 1$
  - Verify proof π: check $V((\lambda, m, \mathsf{gpk}, t, \mathsf{SIG\text{-}RL}, \mathsf{KEY\text{-}RL}, \Lambda), \pi) = 1$.
  - For each $\mathsf{sk}_j \in \mathsf{KEY\text{-}RL}$, check that $t \neq (f(\mathsf{sk}_j, r), r)$.
  - Check that $\mathsf{sig} \notin \mathsf{SIG\text{-}RL}$.
  - If all of the above checks return 1, output 1. Else, output 0.
- $\mathsf{GARevokeKey}(\mathsf{gpk}, \mathsf{KEY\text{-}RL}, \mathsf{sk}_i)$: Return $\mathsf{KEY\text{-}RL} \cup \mathsf{sk}_i$.

- GARevokeSig(gpk, KEY-RL, SIG-RL, m, sig):   If   GAVerify(gpk, m, KEY-RL, SIG-RL, sig) = 1, return SIG-RL ∪ sig. Otherwise, return SIG-RL.

Security Theorems. Correctness and anonymity proofs for $\mathcal{GA}$ are almost completely unchanged from our standard EPID signature scheme, so we only state the corresponding theorems. The only proof that needs some tweaking is that of unforgeability, which we sketch in the full version of this paper.

Theorem 8. *Assuming the correctness of signature scheme $\mathcal{S}$, proof system Π, and accumulator $\mathcal{Ac}$, as well as the pseudorandomness of f, $\mathcal{GA}$ is a correct EPID signature scheme.*

Theorem 9. *Assuming that Π is a zero-knowledge proof system and that f is a PRF, $\mathcal{GA}$ is an anonymous EPID signature scheme.*

Theorem 10. *Assuming that Π is a proof system for zero-knowledge proofs of knowledge with simulation-sound extractability, $\mathcal{S}$ is an unforgeable signature scheme, that f is a PRF, that f is additionally a collision-resistant hash function, and that $\mathcal{Ac}$ is a collision-free (sound) accumulator, $\mathcal{GA}$ is an unforgeable EPID signature scheme.*

5   Instantiation of Protocols

We have now described and proven the security of our constructions, but the post-quantum security of each construction relies on the existence of post-quantum secure instantiations of the various primitives required. In particular we require a PRF that is also a collision-resistant hash function, a signature scheme, zero knowledge proofs of knowledge (ZKPoKs), and an accumulator. In this section we describe options for instantiating each primitive under different security assumptions about the underlying ciphers used and report the signature sizes of our instantiated schemes in both the Random Oracle (RO) and Quantum Random Oracle (QRO) models [11].

5.1   Zero Knowledge Proofs of Knowledge

In principle, standard symmetric primitives (AES, SHA) suffice for post-quantum security so long as we double our security parameters. However, our schemes uses these primitives in a non-black box manner by running them inside of a ZKPoK. In particular, the following ZKPoKs contribute significantly to signature sizes:

1. ZKPoK of a PRF key k such that $f(k, r) = t$, for a PRF that is collision-resistant on its key space.
2. ZKPoK of a signature σ on a message m such that Verify$(m, \sigma) = 1$ for a post-quantum signature scheme $\mathcal{S} = $ (Keygen, Sign, Verify).
3. ZKPoK of membership of element x_i in accumulator Λ for set $\mathcal{X}$.

We restrict our choice of ZKPoK proof system to those systems which rely only on symmetric primitives. This includes works following the "MPC in the Head" approach of Ishai et al. [35] – ZKBoo [30], ZKB++ [20], and Ligero [3] – as well as zk-STARKs [8]. Although Ligero and zk-STARKs offer proofs asymptotically sublinear in the size of the circuit to be proven, a preliminary analysis suggested that, for our relatively small proof circuits, ZKB++ provides the smallest signature sizes in practice without requiring heavy computing costs for the signer. Moreover, ZKB++ has proofs of security in both the Random Oracle and Quantum Random Oracle models, whereas Ligero and zk-STARKs only have proofs in the classical RO model. As such, we choose to instantiate our signatures and measure signature size using ZKB++ as our underlying ZKPoK.

In ZKB++ [20], the underlying statement to be proven is represented as an arithmetic circuit over $GF(2)$, and the proof size is proportional to the multiplicative complexity (i.e., number of AND gates) in the circuit. The most important practical consideration in signature schemes is signature size; therefore our main criterion in instantiating the PRF and outer signature scheme is to minimize their multiplicative complexity over $GF(2)$.

5.2 PRF and Collision-Resistant Hash Function

Recently the ciphers LowMC [2] and MiMC [1] have been proposed as alternatives to AES that have significantly lower multiplicative complexity as arithmetic circuits over finite fields.[1] Although relatively new and less extensively studied, these ciphers were shown to resist statistical cryptanalytic attacks, similar to other state-of-the-art designs. A number of works have already proposed using LowMC as the best candidate to-date for instantiating ciphers inside ZKB++-style proofs [20, 24]. The most recent public version of the LowMC cipher with parameters set for 128-bit post-quantum security (256-bit key, 256-bit block size) involves only 1374 AND gates, a significant improvement over the 7616 AND gates in AES-256 [2].

Derler et al. [24] also suggest using the LowMC round function in the sponge framework (as described in [1]) to construct a collision-resistant hash function with low multiplicative complexity. However, since only a collision-resistant compression function on a fixed message length is needed (rather than full-blown indifferentiability from a random oracle), we propose applying the much simpler Davies-Meyer transformation to the LowMC cipher. Collision resistance of Davies-Meyer is proved in the ideal cipher model [13], which is only marginally stronger than the security assumption underlying the sponge transformation. Given an ideal cipher $E(k, x)$ on equal sized key and message space, the Davies-Meyer compression function is $H(m_1 || m_2) = E(m_1, m_2) \oplus m_2$. For a collision-resistant PRF we would use $F(k, x) = E(k, x) \oplus x$; as long as E is a PRF then F is also a PRF. Note that the multiplicative complexity of F is the same as E.

---

[1] LowMC optimizes multiplicative complexity over $GF(2)$ while MiMC optimizes complexity over larger finite fields. In ZKB++ the underlying circuit is represented in $GF(2)$, which is why we prefer LowMC.

To obtain a PRF that is collision-resistant only on its keyspace we can rely on a slightly weaker assumption than the ideal cipher model. The ideal cipher model assumes that E with *any* key is indistinguishable from a random permutation, whereas we only need to assume there is an explicit fixed key k_{fix} on which $E(k_{\text{fix}}, \cdot)$ is indistinguishable from a random permutation. Then we can define $\Pi(y) = E(k_{\text{fix}}, y)$, and define $F'(k, x) = \Pi(E(k, x)) \oplus E(k, x)$. (The inner evaluation of $E(k, x)$ ensures the PRF property while $\Pi(y) \oplus y$ is collision resistant as a special case of Davies-Meyer).

5.3 Post-quantum Signature Scheme

Choices for post-quantum signatures that do not rely on stronger lattice assumptions include Merkle signatures [43], Goldreich's stateless signatures [31], SPHINCS signatures [9], or the Fish signatures of Chase et al. [20]. The recent literature on post-quantum signatures has focused on optimizing signature size. When using signatures outside of proofs (in our construction of EPID signatures for attestation) we propose using SPHINCS, which has the smallest signature size. However, since our main EPID signature construction involves verifying the group manager's post-quantum signature inside a ZKPoK, there we care about optimizing the arithmetic multiplicative complexity of signature verification rather than the signature size.

We examine two options for instantiating the group manager's signature scheme for signatures used inside a ZKPoK: one using stateful Merkle signatures, and other using Goldreich's stateless signatures.

Stateful Merkle Signatures. The signer runs a signature setup that generates a large number of one-time signature (OTS) keypairs. We would use Lamport signatures from one-way functions (instantiated with LowMC) for the OTS. The Lamport signature private key consists of 256 pairs of pseudorandom 256-bit strings the public key consists of the 256 pairs of outputs generated by applying the one-way function to each private key string. The signer finalizes the setup by computing a Merkle tree (using a 2-to-1 collision resistant compression function) over the OTS public keys at the leaves of the tree and publishing the root as the public verification key. Signing a message involves singing the message with one of the leaf OTS keys and proving membership of this OTS key in the Merkle tree. The signer needs to maintain state to ensure that no OTS key is used more than once. The stateful requirement is not prohibitive in the setting of managing a group of trusted hardware platforms. The preprocessing of a tree of up to 2^{30} members would take under a day on modern commodity hardware and would require the server to use only several GB of storage.

Stateless Goldreich Signatures. Instead of maintaining state in the Merkle signature scheme above, the signer could choose an OTS key at random. This requires squaring the size of the tree to make collisions unlikely. For a group of 2^{30} members storing a tree of size 2^{60} keys would be prohibitively expensive. However, Godlreich's scheme provides a way to generate this tree pseudorandomly from a small seed. In this scheme, the signer pseudorandomly generates an OTS keypair for each node of the tree, which can be done by evaluating a PRF on the index of the tree node. The OTS public key at the root of the tree is the overall public key. The OTS key pair on each node of the tree is used to sign the hash of the public keys on each of its two child nodes. To sign a message a random leaf is selected and the signature includes the OTS signatures along the path from this leaf to the root, where each signature signs either a child public key or the actual message at the leaf.

5.4   Reducing Circuit Size for Membership Proofs

As mentioned in Sect. 4, we will use Merkle trees to instantiate our accumulators. A recent work of Derler et al. [24] points out, however, that the circuit used to verify standard Merkle inclusion proofs differs based on the path from the Merkle root to the leaf x_i. The dependence arises based on whether the hash at depth j of the tree becomes the left or right input of the hash at depth $j - 1$. This dependence of the AVerify circuit on i must be removed in order to generically create a zero-knowledge inclusion proof with some zero-knowledge proof system. They suggest a modification to the standard inclusion proof that allows the same circuit to verify inclusion regardless of the index i whose inclusion is proven. The idea is as follows: suppose x_i resides in a subtree rooted at internal node a and that a has sibling and parent nodes b and c, respectively. At each level of the Merkle tree, instead of simply calculating $h(a, b)$ and only comparing the result to the root, they evaluate the expression $c = h(a, b) \lor c = h(b, a)$ and reject the inclusion proof if it is not satisfied. This allows the construction of a circuit AVerify' with a fixed ordering of inputs to each hash function, since as long as one ordering of inputs matches the node at the next level of the tree, correctness will hold. The cost of this transformation is an extra hash evaluation, an equality check, and a logical OR for each level of the tree.

We propose a solution that eliminates the need for equality checks at each level of the tree and replaces the OR with an XOR, allowing smaller and more efficient zero-knowledge membership proofs. Our idea is to replace the hash function h already used in computing the merkle root with a modified function $h'(x, y) = h(x, y) \oplus h(y, x)$. Using h' in place of h proves that the input x_i is a dth preimage of the merkle root for a tree of depth d without any dependence on the position i of x_i among the tree's leaves. Of course, h' is trivially neither collision-resistant nor second preimage resistant, as a swapping of the inputs x and y results in the same output. Below we prove that h' provides a *third* preimage resistance property and helps build the inclusion proofs we desire.

Definition 11 (Third Preimage Resistance). *We say a hash function H defined over $(\mathcal{M}, \mathcal{T})$ is third preimage resistant if given a random $m = a||b \in \mathcal{M}$ (with $|a| = |b|$) and a different $m' = b||a \in \mathcal{M}$ such that $H(m) = H(m')$, it is difficult to find an $m'' \in \mathcal{M}$ such that $H(m'') = H(m) = H(m')$.*

Lemma 12. *Assuming the hash function* $h : \mathcal{M} \times \mathcal{M} \rightarrow \mathcal{M}$ *is a random function, the hash function* $h'(x,y) = h(x,y) \oplus h(y,x)$ *for* $x, y \in \mathcal{M}$ *is third preimage resistant, provided* $x \neq y$.

Proof. $h'(x,y)$ admits a trivial collision $h'(y,x)$. We argue it is hard to find any other collision unless $x = y$ (since $h'(x,x) = 0$ for all x). To find a third preimage of $h'(x,y)$ an adversary must produce w, z such that either $h'(w,z) = h'(x,y)$ and either $w \neq x$ or $z \neq y$. Since h is a random function and $(x,y), (y,x), (w,z), (z,w)$ are all distinct tuples, $h(x,y)$, $h(y,x)$, $h(w,z)$, and $h(z,w)$ will all be independently random strings. The probability that $h(x,y) \oplus h(y,x) = h(w,z) \oplus h(z,w)$ is therefore negligible in the length $|x| + |y|$. Therefore no efficient adversary can find a third preimage for h'. $\square$

In order to replace h with h' in our merkle tree construction and retain security for the circuit AVerify', we only need to show that we will have no leaves $x \| y$ in the accumulator such that $x = y$. Fortunately, since the elements in the accumulator for our particular case are challenge/response pairs $(f(sk_i, c_i), c_i)$ that serve as group member credentials (where f is collision-resistant and a PRF), the probability that $x = y$ is negligible in our setting.

Practically, our new circuit AVerify' reduces the number of equality checks inside a ZKPoK from $2 \log_2(N)$ (where N is the group size) to 1. Additionally, $\log_2(N)$ OR gates are replaced with XORs which do not increase proof size.

5.5 Signature Sizes

As discussed above, we instantiate our signatures using LowMC, Merkle signatures (inside the ZKPoK), SPHINCS signatures (outside the ZKPoK), ZKB++, and Merkle tree accumulators with our modified membership proof circuit.

Figure 1 shows the sizes for our modified EPID signatures for various group sizes under (1) the assumption that LowMC is and ideal cipher and (2) the assumption that LowMC with a public fixed key is a random permutation. Figure 2 presents the same information, but uses the Unruh transform [48] instead of the Fiat-Shamir transform [27] to make the ZKB++ proof noninteractive. The Fiat-Shamir transform is proven secure in the Random Oracle model but only sometimes retains security in the Quantom Random Oracle model [11,49]. As visible from the figures, groups of size up to 2^{20} could use postquantum signatures of size 6.74 MB (3.45 MB in RO model) under our scheme, a sufficiently small size for attestation in applications with heavy data transfer requirements. For comparison, the same signatures instantiated with AES-256 would require 33.8 MB (16.9 MB in RO model), meaning the choice of LowMC enables a 5× improvement in signature size.

For comparison, our signature sizes are smaller than the recent ring signatures of Derler et al. [24], which require at least 10.4 MB (5.26 MB in RO Model) for signatures in a ring of 2^{20} members[2], despite providing a more elaborate

---

[2] This size represents an optimized version of the ring signatures instantiated assuming LowMC is an ideal cipher. The original Derler et al. paper claimed slightly larger signatures of size 11.88 MB (8 MB in RO Model) for this ring size.

Signature Sizes in RO Model

Group Size	Ideal Cipher	Random Permutation
2^7	1.37MB	2.28MB
2^{10}	1.85MB	3.21MB
2^{20}	3.45MB	6.31MB
2^{30}	5.05MB	9.41MB
2^{40}	6.65MB	12.5MB

Fig. 1. Signature sizes for construction II under various security assumptions on LowMC, using Fiat-Shamir [27] to make proofs of knowledge noninteractive.

Signature Sizes in QRO Model

Group Size	Ideal Cipher	Random Permutation
2^7	2.64MB	4.45MB
2^{10}	3.59MB	6.30MB
2^{20}	6.74MB	12.5MB
2^{30}	9.89MB	18.6MB
2^{40}	13.0MB	24.8MB

Fig. 2. Signature sizes for construction II under various security assumptions on LowMC, using the Unruh transform [48] to make proofs of knowledge noninteractive.

functionality. The improvement comes from our new accumulator membership proofs, as the accumulator constitutes the most costly component of both constructions. Note that subsequent to our paper, the Derler et al. paper has been updated with new results that shrink their signatures by a factor of 2. Their techniques can reduce signature sizes in our construction II as well.

Our general-purpose EPID signatures require 216.82 MB for signatures in a group of size 2^{30} assuming LowMC is an ideal cipher (110.81 MB in QRO Model), a much larger value than the variation designed for attestation. This motivates the question of how to generalize the specialized version of our construction to apply to a wider range of use-cases, which we leave as an open problem.

6   Conclusion

We presented a general-purpose post-quantum EPID signature scheme as well as a construction of a specialized variant designed for trusted hardware enclave attestation. We also gave an analysis of the concrete sizes of our signatures based on the best possible instantiations with current tools and showed that our signatures for attestation can achieve sizes acceptable for use in some applications.

EPID signatures play an important role in modern trusted hardware. Making them post-quantum secure is an important goal, and we hope this work will spur further research on this question that will further reduce the signature size.

Acknowledgments. We would like to thank David Wu for several helpful conversations. This work is supported by NSF, the DARPA/ARL SAFEWARE project, the Simons foundation, and a grant from ONR. The views expressed are those of the author and do not reflect the official policy or position of the Department of Defense, the National Science Foundation, or the U.S. Government.

References

1. Albrecht, M., Grassi, L., Rechberger, C., Roy, A., Tiessen, T.: MiMC: efficient encryption and cryptographic hashing with minimal multiplicative complexity. In: Cheon, J.H., Takagi, T. (eds.) ASIACRYPT 2016. LNCS, vol. 10031, pp. 191–219. Springer, Heidelberg (2016). https://doi.org/10.1007/978-3-662-53887-6_7
2. Albrecht, M.R., Rechberger, C., Schneider, T., Tiessen, T., Zohner, M.: Ciphers for MPC and FHE. In: Oswald, E., Fischlin, M. (eds.) EUROCRYPT 2015. LNCS, vol. 9056, pp. 430–454. Springer, Heidelberg (2015). https://doi.org/10.1007/978-3-662-46800-5_17
3. Ames, S., Hazay, C., Ishai, Y., Venkitasubramaniam, M.: Ligero: lightweight sublinear arguments without a trusted setup. In: CCS, pp. 2087–2104 (2017)
4. El Bansarkhani, R., Misoczki, R.: G-merkle: a hash-based group signature scheme from standard assumptions. IACR Cryptology ePrint Archive (2018)
5. Bellare, M., Goldreich, O.: On defining proofs of knowledge. In: Brickell, E.F. (ed.) CRYPTO 1992. LNCS, vol. 740, pp. 390–420. Springer, Heidelberg (1993). https://doi.org/10.1007/3-540-48071-4_28
6. Bellare, M., Micciancio, D., Warinschi, B.: Foundations of group signatures: formal definitions, simplified requirements, and a construction based on general assumptions. In: Biham, E. (ed.) EUROCRYPT 2003. LNCS, vol. 2656, pp. 614–629. Springer, Heidelberg (2003). https://doi.org/10.1007/3-540-39200-9_38
7. Bellare, M., Shi, H., Zhang, C.: Foundations of group signatures: the case of dynamic groups. In: Menezes, A. (ed.) CT-RSA 2005. LNCS, vol. 3376, pp. 136–153. Springer, Heidelberg (2005). https://doi.org/10.1007/978-3-540-30574-3_11
8. Ben-Sasson, E., Bentov, I., Horesh, Y., Riabzev, M.: Scalable, transparent, and post-quantum secure computational integrity. IACR Cryptology ePrint Archive (2018)
9. Bernstein, D.J., et al.: SPHINCS: practical stateless hash-based signatures. In: Oswald, E., Fischlin, M. (eds.) EUROCRYPT 2015. LNCS, vol. 9056, pp. 368–397. Springer, Heidelberg (2015). https://doi.org/10.1007/978-3-662-46800-5_15
10. Boneh, D., Boyen, X., Shacham, H.: Short group signatures. In: Franklin, M. (ed.) CRYPTO 2004. LNCS, vol. 3152, pp. 41–55. Springer, Heidelberg (2004). https://doi.org/10.1007/978-3-540-28628-8_3
11. Boneh, D., Dagdelen, Ö., Fischlin, M., Lehmann, A., Schaffner, C., Zhandry, M.: Random oracles in a quantum world. In: Lee, D.H., Wang, X. (eds.) ASIACRYPT 2011. LNCS, vol. 7073, pp. 41–69. Springer, Heidelberg (2011). https://doi.org/10.1007/978-3-642-25385-0_3
12. Boneh, D., Shacham, H.: Group signatures with verifier-local revocation. In: Proceedings of the 11th ACM Conference on Computer and Communications Security (CCS), pp. 168–177. ACM (2004)
13. Boneh, D., Shoup, V.: A Graduate Course in Applied Cryptography (2017)
14. Brickell, E.F., Camenisch, J., Chen, L.: Direct anonymous attestation. In: CCS, pp. 132–145 (2004)

15. Brickell, E., Li, J.: Enhanced privacy ID from bilinear pairing. IACR Cryptology ePrint Archive, 2009:95 (2009)
16. Buchmann, J., Dahmen, E., Hülsing, A.: XMSS - a practical forward secure signature scheme based on minimal security assumptions. In: Yang, B.-Y. (ed.) PQCrypto 2011. LNCS, vol. 7071, pp. 117–129. Springer, Heidelberg (2011). https://doi.org/10.1007/978-3-642-25405-5_8
17. Camenisch, J., Groth, J.: Group signatures: better efficiency and new theoretical aspects. In: Blundo, C., Cimato, S. (eds.) SCN 2004. LNCS, vol. 3352, pp. 120–133. Springer, Heidelberg (2005). https://doi.org/10.1007/978-3-540-30598-9_9
18. Camenisch, J., Lysyanskaya, A.: A signature scheme with efficient protocols. In: Cimato, S., Persiano, G., Galdi, C. (eds.) SCN 2002. LNCS, vol. 2576, pp. 268–289. Springer, Heidelberg (2003). https://doi.org/10.1007/3-540-36413-7_20
19. Camenisch, J., Lysyanskaya, A.: Signature schemes and anonymous credentials from bilinear maps. In: Franklin, M. (ed.) CRYPTO 2004. LNCS, vol. 3152, pp. 56–72. Springer, Heidelberg (2004). https://doi.org/10.1007/978-3-540-28628-8_4
20. Chase, M., et al.: Post-quantum zero-knowledge and signatures from symmetric-key primitives. In: CCS, pp. 1825–1842 (2017)
21. Chaum, D., van Heyst, E.: Group signatures. In: Davies, D.W. (ed.) EUROCRYPT 1991. LNCS, vol. 547, pp. 257–265. Springer, Heidelberg (1991). https://doi.org/10.1007/3-540-46416-6_22
22. Costan, V., Devadas, S.: Intel SGX explained. IACR Cryptology ePrint Archive 2016:86 (2016)
23. Derler, D., Hanser, C., Slamanig, D.: Revisiting cryptographic accumulators, additional properties and relations to other primitives. In: Nyberg, K. (ed.) CT-RSA 2015. LNCS, vol. 9048, pp. 127–144. Springer, Cham (2015). https://doi.org/10.1007/978-3-319-16715-2_7
24. Derler, D., Ramacher, S., Slamanig, D.: Post-quantum zero-knowledge proofs for accumulators with applications to ring signatures from symmetric-key primitives. IACR Cryptology ePrint Archive (2017)
25. Dowling, B., Günther, F., Herath, U., Stebila, D.: Secure logging schemes and certificate transparency. In: Askoxylakis, I., Ioannidis, S., Katsikas, S., Meadows, C. (eds.) ESORICS 2016. LNCS, vol. 9879, pp. 140–158. Springer, Cham (2016). https://doi.org/10.1007/978-3-319-45741-3_8
26. Faust, S., Kohlweiss, M., Marson, G.A., Venturi, D.: On the non-malleability of the fiat-shamir transform. In: Galbraith, S., Nandi, M. (eds.) INDOCRYPT 2012. LNCS, vol. 7668, pp. 60–79. Springer, Heidelberg (2012). https://doi.org/10.1007/978-3-642-34931-7_5
27. Fiat, A., Shamir, A.: How to prove yourself: practical solutions to identification and signature problems. In: Odlyzko, A.M. (ed.) CRYPTO 1986. LNCS, vol. 263, pp. 186–194. Springer, Heidelberg (1987). https://doi.org/10.1007/3-540-47721-7_12
28. Fisch, B., Vinayagamurthy, D., Boneh, D., Gorbunov, S.: IRON: functional encryption using intel SGX. In: CCS, pp. 765–782 (2017)
29. Fuller, B., et al.: Sok: cryptographically protected database search. In: IEEE Symposium on Security and Privacy (Oakland), pp. 172–191 (2017)
30. Giacomelli, I., Madsen, J., Orlandi, C.: ZKBoo: faster zero-knowledge for boolean circuits. In: USENIX Security, pp. 1069–1083 (2016)
31. Goldreich, O.: Foundations of Cryptography - Volume 2, Basic Applications. Cambridge University Press, Cambridge (2004)
32. Goldwasser, S., Micali, S., Rackoff, C.: The knowledge complexity of interactive proof systems. SIAM J. Comput. 18(1), 186–208 (1989)

33. Gordon, S.D., Katz, J., Vaikuntanathan, V.: A group signature scheme from lattice assumptions. In: Abe, M. (ed.) ASIACRYPT 2010. LNCS, vol. 6477, pp. 395–412. Springer, Heidelberg (2010). https://doi.org/10.1007/978-3-642-17373-8_23

34. Groth, J.: Simulation-sound NIZK proofs for a practical language and constant size group signatures. In: Lai, X., Chen, K. (eds.) ASIACRYPT 2006. LNCS, vol. 4284, pp. 444–459. Springer, Heidelberg (2006). https://doi.org/10.1007/11935230_29

35. Ishai, Y., Kushilevitz, E., Ostrovsky, R., Sahai, A.: Zero-knowledge proofs from secure multiparty computation. SIAM J. Comput. **39**(3), 1121–1152 (2009)

36. Johnson, S., Scarlata, V., Rozas, C., Brickell, E., Mckeen, F.: Intel® software guard extensions: EPID provisioning and attestation services (2016)

37. Katz, J., Kolesnikov, V., Wang, X.: Improved non-interactive zero knowledge with applications to post-quantum signatures. IACR Cryptology ePrint Archive 2018:475 (2018)

38. Laurie, B., Langley, A., Kasper, E.: Certificate transparency. RFC 6962 (2013)

39. Libert, B., Ling, S., Mouhartem, F., Nguyen, K., Wang, H.: Signature schemes with efficient protocols and dynamic group signatures from lattice assumptions. In: Cheon, J.H., Takagi, T. (eds.) ASIACRYPT 2016. LNCS, vol. 10032, pp. 373–403. Springer, Heidelberg (2016). https://doi.org/10.1007/978-3-662-53890-6_13

40. Libert, B., Ling, S., Nguyen, K., Wang, H.: Zero-knowledge arguments for lattice-based accumulators: logarithmic-size ring signatures and group signatures without trapdoors. In: Fischlin, M., Coron, J.-S. (eds.) EUROCRYPT 2016. LNCS, vol. 9666, pp. 1–31. Springer, Heidelberg (2016). https://doi.org/10.1007/978-3-662-49896-5_1

41. Ling, S., Nguyen, K., Wang, H.: Group signatures from lattices: simpler, tighter, shorter, ring-based. In: Katz, J. (ed.) PKC 2015. LNCS, vol. 9020, pp. 427–449. Springer, Heidelberg (2015). https://doi.org/10.1007/978-3-662-46447-2_19

42. Ling, S., Nguyen, K., Wang, H., Xu, Y.: Lattice-based group signatures: achieving full dynamicity with ease. In: Gollmann, D., Miyaji, A., Kikuchi, H. (eds.) ACNS 2017. LNCS, vol. 10355, pp. 293–312. Springer, Cham (2017). https://doi.org/10.1007/978-3-319-61204-1_15

43. Merkle, R.C.: A digital signature based on a conventional encryption function. In: Pomerance, C. (ed.) CRYPTO 1987. LNCS, vol. 293, pp. 369–378. Springer, Heidelberg (1988). https://doi.org/10.1007/3-540-48184-2_32

44. Naor, M., Yung, M.: Universal one-way hash functions and their cryptographic applications. In: STOC, pp. 33–43. ACM (1989)

45. Nayak, K., et al.: HOP: hardware makes obfuscation practical. In: NDSS (2017)

46. Sahai, A.: Non-malleable non-interactive zero knowledge and adaptive chosen-ciphertext security. In: FOCS, pp. 543–553 (1999)

47. De Santis, A., Di Crescenzo, G., Ostrovsky, R., Persiano, G., Sahai, A.: Robust non-interactive zero knowledge. In: Kilian, J. (ed.) CRYPTO 2001. LNCS, vol. 2139, pp. 566–598. Springer, Heidelberg (2001). https://doi.org/10.1007/3-540-44647-8_33

48. Unruh, D.: Non-interactive zero-knowledge proofs in the quantum random oracle model. In: Oswald, E., Fischlin, M. (eds.) EUROCRYPT 2015. LNCS, vol. 9057, pp. 755–784. Springer, Heidelberg (2015). https://doi.org/10.1007/978-3-662-46803-6_25

49. Unruh, D.: Post-quantum security of Fiat-Shamir. In: Takagi, T., Peyrin, T. (eds.) ASIACRYPT 2017. LNCS, vol. 10624, pp. 65–95. Springer, Cham (2017). https://doi.org/10.1007/978-3-319-70694-8_3

50. Yu, M., Gligor, V.D., Zhou, Z.: Trusted display on untrusted commodity platforms. In: CCS, pp. 989–1003 (2015)
51. Zheng, W., Dave, A., Beekman, J.G., Popa, R.A., Gonzalez, J.E., Stoica, I.: Opaque: an oblivious and encrypted distributed analytics platform. In: NSDI, pp. 283–298 (2017)
52. Zhou, Z., Gligor, V.D., Newsome, J., McCune, J.M.: Building verifiable trusted path on commodity x86 computers. In: IEEE Symposium on Security and Privacy (Oakland), pp. 616–630 (2012)

Assessment of the Key-Reuse Resilience
of NewHope

Aurélie Bauer[1], Henri Gilbert[1,2], Guénaël Renault[1,3(✉)], and Mélissa Rossi[4,5]

[1] ANSSI, Paris, France
{aurelie.bauer,henri.gilbert,guenael.renault}@ssi.gouv.fr
[2] UVSQ, Versailles, France
[3] Sorbonne Université, CNRS, Inria, Laboratoire d'Informatique de Paris 6, LIP6,
Équipe PolSys, Paris, France
[4] Thales, Gennevilliers, France
[5] Département d'informatique de l'Ecole normale supérieure, CNRS,
PSL Research University, Inria, Paris, France
melissa.rossi@ens.fr

Abstract. NewHope is a suite of two efficient Ring-Learning-With-Error based key encapsulation mechanisms (KEMs) that has been proposed to the NIST call for proposals for post-quantum standardization. In this paper, we study the security of NewHope when an active adversary takes part in a key establishment protocol and is given access to an oracle, called key mismatch oracle, which indicates whether her guess of the shared key value derived by the party targeted by the attack is correct or not. This attack model turns out to be relevant in private key reuse situations since an attacker may then be able to access such an oracle repeatedly – either directly or using faults or side channels, depending on the considered instance of NewHope. Following this model we show that, by using NewHope recommended parameters, several thousands of queries are sufficient to recover the full private key with high probability. This result has been experimentally confirmed using Magma CAS implementation. While the presented key mismatch oracle attacks do not break any of the designers' security claims for the NewHope KEMs, they provide better insight into the resilience of these KEMs against key reuse. In the case of the CPA-KEM instance of NewHope, they confirm that key reuse (e.g. key caching at server side) should be strictly avoided, even for an extremely short duration. In the case of the CCA-KEM instance of NewHope, they allow to point out critical steps inside the CCA transform that should be carefully protected against faults or side channels in case of·potential key reuse.

Keywords: PQ-crypto · Lattice based cryptography · Active attack ·
Side channels

This research has been partially funded by ANRT under the program CIFRE 2016/1583. We acknowledge the support of the French Programme d'Investissement d'Avenir under national project RISQ P141580. This work is also partially supported by the European Union PROMETHEUS project (Horizon 2020 Research and Innovation Program, grant 780701).

M. Matsui (Ed.): CT-RSA 2019, LNCS 11405, pp. 272–292, 2019.
https://doi.org/10.1007/978-3-030-12612-4_14

1   Introduction

The insecurity of the main asymmetric cryptosystems (RSA, (EC)DLP) in front of a potential quantum computer has led the crytographic community to investigate new quantum resistant primitives. In 2016, NIST has initiated a process to develop and standardize one or more public-key cryptographic algorithms which are supposed to be quantum safe. Cryptosystems based on lattices represent one of the most promising directions for such systems.

Key Encapsulation Mechanisms (or KEMs) are one of the most important asymmetric cryptographic primitives. The NIST call specifically asks for quantum resistant KEM proposals in order to replace number theory based Diffie-Hellman key establishment protocols, which can be broken in the quantum computation model. Potential candidates for post quantum key establishment include the ones based on the lattice based Ring Learning With Errors Problem (RING-LWE) introduced in [7,22]. Recently, GOOGLE conducted real life TLS experiments [6] with a RING-LWE based key exchange scheme: the NEWHOPE-USENIX system [6]. While these experiments show the efficiency of NEWHOPE-USENIX, the specification of the reconciliation step of the system is rather complex. The technicality of this step requires a large fraction of the algorithm description in the original paper [1]. This issue together with possible intellectual property right considerations led the designers to introduce a simplified new variant initially named NewHope-SIMPLE [25] where the *reconciliation-based* approach of NEWHOPE-USENIX is replaced by an *encryption-based* approach. Thanks to the combined use of *encoding* and *compression* techniques, the performance price to pay for this new version in terms of bandwith overhead is quite marginal. Now NewHope-Simple has been transformed into NewHope, a suite of two candidate KEM mechanisms of the NIST call for proposals [23] named NewHope-CPA-KEM and NewHope-CCA-KEM, in short CPA-KEM and CCA-KEM. Both mechanisms are encryption-based: they rely upon an auxiliary probabilistic public key encryption allowing to encrypt a 256-bit data named CPA-PKE, that is not submitted to the NIST call for proposals as a standalone mechanism.

NewHope-CPA-KEM, that is nearly identical to NewHope-SIMPLE, is only claimed to be a passively secure KEM. It can be viewed as the CPA-PKE encryption of a hashed secret random value ν followed by hashing ν on both sides. Unlike CPA-KEM, CCA-KEM is claimed to be secure with respect to adaptively chosen ciphertext attacks. It is derived from CPA-PKE in a less straightforward manner, by applying a variant of the Fujisaki-Okamoto transform [11]. An essential feature of this transform is that the encryption of ν is derandomized: this allows the decrypting party Alice to re-encrypt the decryption result, check that the result matches the received ciphertext, and use this test to prevent information leakages on the private key in active attacks where "dishonestly" derived ciphertext values are sent by an adversary.

While the specification of CPA-KEM and CCA-KEM does not formally prevent re-using the same CPA-PKE (public key, private key) pair in multiple key establishments, the design rationale section of the NewHope specification requires that such key pairs be never cached and that a fresh key pair be generated at each key establishment[1]. In the case of CPA-KEM, one of the main reasons for this requirement is that, unlike the classical Diffie-Hellman key establishment, the original RING-LWE based KEM with reconciliation is known to be vulnerable to a practical active attack in a key reuse situation as shown in [10]. Despite not being based on the reconciliation paradigm, CPA-KEM shares sufficiently many features with its predecessor for being conjectured also vulnerable to similar attacks. In the case of CCA-KEM, this requirement to reuse private keys could be justified by the fact that no real perfect forward privacy can be offered if private keys are not ephemeral[2].

Motivation

With its strong performance and its RING-LWE based security, NewHope is a high profile candidate of the NIST competition. There is a good chance for it to be implemented in the future for Internet protocols. So, studying its security under several attacker models is important.

In this paper, we investigate the resilience of the CPA-KEM and CCA-KEM versions of NewHope in a misuse situation where the same key pair is reused for multiple key establishment by the private key owner – who will be referred to as Alice in the sequel. Note that Alice is also the party who initiates the two-round key establishment in both schemes. We use the generic name of key mismatch oracle to refer to the private key recovery attack models we are considering, that are closely inspired from the adversary model considered in [10]. While slightly less powerful than a CCA attack against an encryption based KEM where a decryption oracle is available, attacks using a key mismatch oracle still belong to the active attack category. Their common feature is that the adversary is assumed to be able: (1) to actively interact with Alice by performing multiple KEM establishment where Alice uses the same key pair, (2) to produce each time a guess on the resulting secret key derived by Alice and (3) to access a binary oracle that indicates whether this guess is valid or not.

Our study is motivated by the belief that an in-depth understanding of the security offered by candidate KEM mechanisms submitted to the NIST call for

---

[1] The single potential exception to this requirement is the *publicseed* part of the public key, whose caching "for say a few hours" seems to be considered by the designers as a viable alternative in situations where the preferred solution of a systematic renewal would turn out to be prohibitively expensive.

[2] On the other hand this requirement is not fully in line with the former observation, in the NEWHOPE-USENIX paper, that "One could enable key caching with a transformation from the CPA-secure key establishment to a CCA-secure key establishment [...]". Given the performance advantage that may be provided by key caching at server side in certain applications, one can wonder whether it will be strictly followed in practice in all deployments of CCA-KEM if strong cryptanalytic arguments in favour of this conservative choice are not developed during the evaluation of the candidates to the NIST call.

proposals in key reuse situations is a useful part of their cryptanalytic evaluation, even for those candidates for which key reuse is considered as a misuse of the mechanism. Having an accurate estimate of the number of queries to the key mismatch oracle and of the complexity of the private key recovery really helps to assess the possible danger[3]. We focus here on a case study of the NewHope candidate KEMs. An advantage of this choice is that previous work on reconciliation-based RING-LWE schemes such as [10] can be partly leveraged. However, as will be seen in the sequel, the fact that the NewHope suite is encryption-based and is using encoding techniques induces substantial differences and non-trivially complicates the cryptanalysis. To the best of our knowledge, no investigation of attacks against a scheme without reconciliation in a key mismatch oracle model was published so far.

Previous Work

The danger of accessing a key mismatch oracle within some key agreement protocols in a key share reuse context has been already exposed several times. Early examples showing the vulnerability of some standardized Diffie-Hellman key agreement protocols in such a context were introduced in [20]. The potential danger of a somewhat related type of attack, namely so-called reaction attacks against PKE schemes [13], where an adversary can submit a chosen ciphertext to the legitimate private key owner and access a binary information about her reaction (whether the decryption succeeds or fails for instance), is probably even better known. Bleichenbacher's attack against RSA PKCS#1 of Crypto'98 [4] can been viewed as an early reaction attack. In 1999, Hall, Goldberg and Schneier presented reactions attacks against several PKE schemes [13]. In the particular case of lattice based cryptography, several notes on the vulnerability of NTRU to reaction attacks and its protection against such attacks were published [14,15]. In 2003, Howgrave-Graham et al. proposed a reaction attack on NTRUEncrypt that leverages decryption failures [17]. A recent example of reaction attack is Guo et al.'s key recovery attack on the code-based PKE QC-MDPC [12]. It is thus natural that NSA, in 2015, warns NIST Post-Quantum candidates against active attacks [19]. Few times later, the first concrete attacks on a RING-LWE based key establishment leveraging a key mismatch oracle was proposed by Fluhrer [10] (see also [8,9]).

These attacks rely on the fact that the reconciliation step can be exploited by an active adversary to retrieve some information on the secret static key. Despite the warnings issued in [19], certain NIST candidates are vulnerable to active attacks. Indeed, it is shown in [3] that the secret key of the NIST

---

[3] A similar need to investigate the resilience of candidate algorithms in misuse situations was encountered in the framework of the CAESAR competition aimed at selecting authenticated encryption primitives. In that competition, much analysis was conducted on the resistance of candidates to key recovery attacks in misuse cases such as nonce or decryption-misuse and this provided quite useful information for the algorithms selection process.

candidate HILA5 can be recovered in the key mismatch oracle setting following Fluhrer's approach. In summary, despite the raising awareness of the cryptography research community that key mismatch oracle attacks threaten many lattice based KEMs in case of key reuse, relatively few examples of such attacks have been published so far.

About the side channel protection of NewHope, no dedicated countermeasure has been proposed for NewHope so far, but in [21] a side channel protection for a similar scheme has been proposed. This paper describes a provably first-order secure masking scheme and its integration into a CCA conversion.

Our Contribution

In the following, we evaluate the security of NewHope when the attacker gets access to a key mismatch oracle. We concretely explain how the attacker can have access to such an oracle in different scenarios with the CPA-KEM and the CCA-KEM. We first introduce a straightforward way to recover such an oracle in the CPA-KEM. The adversary enters a key establishment with Alice, derives from her guess on the shared key produced by Alice a guess on the resulting session key she produces, and attempts to initiate a session with Alice under this guessed session key. The success or failure of this protected communication attempt provides the desired key mismatch oracle[4].

Then, at the end of the paper, we elaborate other scenarios on the CCA version which require side channels. Indeed, the CCA-KEM version induces major extra differences with formerly analyzed reconciliation-based schemes, that also deserve being analyzed. Because of the CCA transform, a key mismatch oracle cannot be accessed directly. But we show that for unsufficiently protected implementations, simple faults or side channels could bypass this transform and provide the desired key mismatch oracle. While unprotected versions of CCA-KEM are extremely efficient, its implementations must be very carefully protected against any key mismatch oracle leakage if key pairs are potentially reused. This might eventually come with a cost in terms of performance. This study may help the developers to protect the algorithms against a possible key mismatch oracle leakage.

The core of this work is the description of a new attack on NewHope using the key mismatch oracle. Even if the existence of previous work attacks (see [8,10]) casts suspicion on the resistance of NewHope CPA-KEM against active attacks in the same key-reuse setting, one has to take into account substantial differences between the reconciliation-based paradigm of the original NewHope and the encryption-based paradigm of CPA-KEM. Because of these differences, the detail of Fluhrer's attack [10] is not really inspiring for mounting an attack and any direct transposition attempt would be hopeless. Finding an efficient way

---

[4] It is worth noticing that the same direct access to a key mismatch oracle remains feasible if the KEM exchange is embedded in an authenticated key establishment protocol, under the sole condition that the adversary is the owner of a valid authentication (or signature) key.

of deriving information on the secret key from the key mismatch oracle with a low number of queries induces several issues. The main difficulty is to retrieve enough leakages after the application of the encoding and compression functions. We investigated how to leverage these functions in order to find a simple way to instantiate the oracle and identified precise elements in the polynomial ring that can be used by the adversary to recover the secret. Finally, we had to take into account the fact that NewHope coefficients are in $[-8, 8]$.

We experimented our attack with a Magma CAS proof of concept. Under NewHope parameters, we were able to recover exactly the secret **S** with on average 16, 700 queries for NewHope1024 which corroborates the expected performance of the model.

Paper Outline

In Sect. 2 we introduce some notation and describe the NewHope CPA scheme. In Sect. 3, we describe the notion of key mismatch oracle and how practical it can be for the CPA-KEM. In Sect. 4, we detail our attack using the key mismatch oracle. In Sect. 4.4, we present our experiments. In Sect. 5, we show how the key mismatch oracle can be retrieved with side channels with the CCA-KEM. Finally, in Sect. 6, we summarize our results and discuss future research.

2   Preliminaries

2.1   Notations

Let q be a prime number in $\mathbb{N}$ and let $\mathbb{Z}_q$ denote the ring elements $\mathbb{Z}/q\mathbb{Z}$. Depending on the context, the elements in $\mathbb{Z}_q$ can be equivalently represented as integers in $\{0, \ldots, q-1\}$ or in $\{-(\frac{q-1}{2}), \ldots, (\frac{q-1}{2})\}$. In the following, the notation $\mathcal{R}$ refers to the polynomial ring $\mathbb{Z}_q[x]/(x^N + 1)$ with N a power of 2. If **P** belongs to $\mathcal{R}$, it is a polynomial of degree $(N - 1)$ with coefficients $\mathbf{P}[i]$ belonging to the set $\mathbb{Z}_q$. Such elements can also be represented as vectors whose i-th coordinate is the coefficient related to x^i. In the sequel we use either the polynomial notation or the vectorial one. For readability, bold capital letters are used to refer to elements in $\mathcal{R}$ and bold lowercase letters will refer to compressed elements, i.e. elements in $\mathcal{R}$ with small coefficients.

Let us define $\mathcal{G}_a$ as the centered Gaussian distribution of standard deviation a and ψ_k the centered binomial distribution of parameter k. Its standard deviation is $\sqrt{k/2}$. One may sample from ψ_k for integer $k > 0$ by computing $\sum_{i=1}^{k} b_i - b_i'$, where the $b_i, b_i' \in \{0, 1\}$ are uniform independent bits.

Property 1. The elements generated according to a centered binomial distribution ψ_k of parameter k are in the interval $[-k, k]$. Thus, the coefficients of the small elements drawn from $\mathcal{R}$ in NewHope are in $[-8, 8]$.

In the figures and algorithms, the notation $\xleftarrow{\$} \mathcal{D}$ means picking an element in $\mathcal{R}$ having all its coefficients generated at random according to distribution $\mathcal{D}$. The notation $\xleftarrow{coin} \mathcal{D}$ means using a $coin \in \{0, ..., 255\}^{32}$ as a seed to pick a pseudorandom element in $\mathcal{R}$ having all its coefficients according to distribution $\mathcal{D}$. This is generally done using a hash function like SHAKE-128. In the paper we refer several times to $Sign(a)$ with $a \in \mathbb{Z}$ by using the convention that it is defined as *positive* when $a \geq 0$ and as *negative* when $a < 0$. If $x \in \mathbb{R}$, the integer $\lfloor x \rceil$ is defined as $\lfloor x + \frac{1}{2} \rfloor \in \mathbb{Z}$.

2.2   NewHope

NewHope [23,25] is a RING-LWE based key establishment scheme derived from NEWHOPE-USENIX [1], that is simplified because it does not use the reconciliation anymore. In this section, we describe NewHope, where we omit some details (e.g. the so-called NTT transform or the encoding of the messages) to simplify the presentation. This does not imply any loss of generality for our attack. To ease the understanding, we will describe the CPA-KEM version of NewHope in this section as the key mismatch oracle can be easily derived. We will present the CCA-KEM later in Sect. 5 when we present some ways to access a key mismatch oracle.

The polynomial ring $\mathcal{R}$ used in NewHope has the following parameters: $(N, q) = (1024, 12289)$ or $(N, q) = (512, 12289)$. The coefficients of the small elements drawn from $\mathcal{R}$ follow a centered binomial distribution ψ_k^N with $k = 8$. The standard deviation is $a = \sqrt{\frac{8}{2}} = 2$. We decided to focus on explaining the attack for $N = 1024$. Indeed, for $N = 512$ there is twice less redundancy and the attack is easier. Thus, we fix $N = 1024$. These elements will be seen as vectors of size N with integer components. We denote $s = 1536$ which is such that $q = 8s + 1$. The aim of the system is to share a key of size 256 bits following the exchange mechanism outlined below and represented in Fig. 1.

A public value $\mathbf{A} \in \mathcal{R}$ is derived from a published *seed*. Four specific functions are introduced: Encode, Decode, Compress and Decompress. They are described in Algorithms 1, 2, 3 and 4. Note that we partly deviate from the notation of the original specification of these algorithms, since we use the parameter s (the original description is in [25]). The following paragraphs describe these functions.

Compress and Decompress. The function Compress (Algorithm 3) takes as input a vector $\mathbf{C}$ in $\mathcal{R}$ and applies on each of its component a *modulus switching* to obtain an element c in $\mathbb{Z}_8[x]/(x^N + 1)$. Compressing a vector $\mathbf{C}$ essentially means keeping the 3 most significant bits of each coefficient. The function Decompress (Algorithm 4) shifts the bits of the input $c \in [0, 8[^N$ to place them among the most significant bits. These functions are not the inverse of each other.

Encode and Decode. The Encode function takes a n-bit input ν where $n = N/4$ and creates an element $\mathbf{K} \in \mathcal{R}$ which stores 4 times the element ν. The redundancy is used by the function Decode to recover ν with a noisy $\mathbf{K}$.

NewHope Key Encapsulation Mechanism. Let us now describe this scheme.

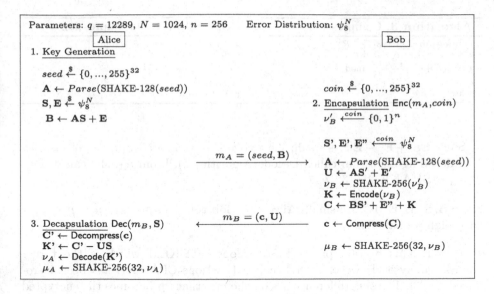

Fig. 1. Simplified NewHope

1. *Setup*: Alice generates 2 small secrets $\mathbf{S}$ and $\mathbf{E}$ in $\mathcal{R}$. She sends $\mathbf{B} = \mathbf{AS} + \mathbf{E}$ to Bob.

2. *Key Encapsulation*: From a random *coin* acting as a seed, Bob derives 3 small secrets $\mathbf{S}'$, $\mathbf{E}'$ and $\mathbf{E}''$ in $\mathcal{R}$ and a random element ν_B of size n which will be the encapsulated key. He computes $\mathbf{U} = \mathbf{AS}' + \mathbf{E}'$. He encodes ν_B into a redundant element $\mathbf{K}$ of $\mathcal{R}$ using the algorithm Encode (Algorithm 1). Bob uses Compress (Algorithm 3) to compress $\mathbf{C} = \mathbf{BS}' + \mathbf{E}'' + \mathbf{K}$ into an element with very small coefficients as described above. He sends $(\mathbf{c} = \mathsf{Compress}(\mathbf{C}), \mathbf{U})$ to Alice. He deduces the shared secret as $\mu_B = \mathrm{SHAKE}\text{-}256(32, \nu_B)$.

3. *Key Decapsulation*: Alice decompresses $\mathbf{c}$ with Decompress into $\mathbf{C}'$ (Algorithm 4). She computes $\mathbf{C}' - \mathbf{US}$ which is close to

$$\mathbf{C} - \mathbf{US} = \mathbf{ES}' + \mathbf{E}'' + \mathbf{K} - \mathbf{E}'\mathbf{S}. \tag{1}$$

Algorithm 1. Key Encoding	**Algorithm 2.** Key Decoding
1 **function** Encode($\nu \in \{0,1\}^n$)	1 **function** Decode($\mathbf{K} \in \mathcal{R}$)
2 $\mathbf{k} \leftarrow 0$	2 $\nu \leftarrow 0$
3 **for** $i := 0$ *to* $n-1$ **do**	3 **for** $i := 0$ *to* $n-1$ **do**
4 $\mathbf{K}_i \leftarrow \nu_i.4s$	4 $t \leftarrow \sum_{j=0}^{3} \left\| \mathbf{K}_{i+jn} - 4s \right\|$
5 $\mathbf{K}_{i+n} \leftarrow \nu_i.4s$	5 **if** $t < q$ **then** $\nu_i \leftarrow 1$ **else** $\nu_i \leftarrow 0$
6 $\mathbf{K}_{i+2n} \leftarrow \nu_i.4s$	6 **end**
7 $\mathbf{K}_{i+3n} \leftarrow \nu_i.4s$	7 Return ν
8 **end**	
9 Return $\mathbf{k}$	

Algorithm 3. Compression	Algorithm 4. Decompression
1 **function** Compress($C \in \mathcal{R}$) 2 **for** $i := 0$ *to* $N - 1$ **do** 3 $\quad \mid \quad c[i] \leftarrow \left\lceil \frac{8 \cdot C[i]}{q} \right\rfloor$ mod 8 4 **end** 5 **Return** c	1 **function** Decompress($c \in [0, 8[^N$) 2 **for** $i := 0$ *to* $N - 1$ **do** 3 $\quad \mid \quad$ C'$[i] \leftarrow \left\lceil \frac{q \cdot c[i]}{8} \right\rfloor$ 4 **end** 5 **Return** C'

Since $\mathbf{ES'} + \mathbf{E''} - \mathbf{E'S}$ is small, she recovers an estimated value ν_A of ν_B with a decoding algorithm called Decode(Algorithm 2). From ν_A, she can deduce $\mu_A = \text{SHAKE-256}(32, \nu_A)$.

Since $\mathbf{S}, \mathbf{S'}, \mathbf{E}, \mathbf{E'}, \mathbf{E''}$ are small, Alice and Bob get the same key $\mu = \mu_B = \mu_A$ with high probability.

Remark 1. This Section presented NewHope-CPA-KEM which is the target Sect. 4's analysis. However a PKE called NewHope-CPA-PKE has been introduced in [23]. The slim difference lies on the fact that ν_B becomes the encrypted message. The CCA security of the CCA version, called NewHope-CCA-KEM relies on the CPA security of NewHope-CPA-PKE (see Sect. 5).

3 The Key Mismatch Oracle

This section introduces the notion of key mismatch oracle and a way to access it in the CPA version. We will always consider a malicious active adversary, Eve, who acts as Bob. Her messages, key and intermediate values will be denoted as m_E, μ_E and ν_E instead of m_B, μ_B and ν_B.

Remark 2. One might wonder how a malicious Alice can recover Bob's secret in a case of key reuse by Bob. In NewHope, this can be done with 2 queries, see the full version of our paper [2].

The goal of the adversary is to recover Alice's static private keys $\mathbf{S}$ and $\mathbf{E}$ by using the following oracle several times. We will focus on recovering the secret $\mathbf{S}$. $\mathbf{E}$ can be derived from $\mathbf{S}$ with $\mathbf{E} = \mathbf{B} - \mathbf{AS}$.

Definition 1 (*key mismatch oracle*). *A key mismatch oracle is an oracle that outputs a bit of information on the possible mismatch at the end of the key encapsulation mechanism.*

In the NewHope context, the key mismatch oracle is the oracle that takes any message m_E and any key hypothesis μ_E as input and outputs the following

$$\mathcal{O}_1(m_E, \mu_E) = \begin{cases} 1 & \text{if } (\mu_A =) \text{ Decapsulation}(m_E, \mathbf{S}) = \mu_E \\ -1 & \text{otherwise} \end{cases} \tag{2}$$

Such an oracle should leak information on secret $\mathbf{S}$ because its output is clearly correlated to the value of $\mathbf{S}$. However, this oracle is less powerful than a CCA decryption oracle against CPA-PKE. Indeed, the only information given is a bit representing the possible key mismatch. The difficulty is to choose appropriate (m_E, μ_E) to retreive information of a small part of $\mathbf{S}$. In Sect. 4, we present how to recover the secret $\mathbf{S}$ from such an oracle.

The simplest way to access such an oracle is when the CPA-KEM is implemented with static secrets. In other words, Alice will keep her secrets $\mathbf{S}$ and $\mathbf{E}$ for several key establishment requests. We consider that Eve does not necessarily follow the scheme specification. She can "cheat" and generate a message m_E that is not derived from a coin or from random small secrets $\mathbf{S}', \mathbf{E}'$ and $\mathbf{E}''$. By definition, the CPA version of NewHope is passively secure, an attacker using a key mismatch oracle is outside of the security assumptions[5]. This has been well highlighted in paragraph 2.3, Section **No key caching** of the original paper of NEWHOPE-USENIX. However an implementation of NewHope which allows misuse cases (see [24]) cannot be completely excluded. Thus it is important to precisely evaluate such a threat and consider the following attack model.

Attack Model 1. *Alice will accept any syntactically correct message m_E and always try to use the corresponding shared key for communicating. When she derives the shared key, either she is able to decrypt messages exchanged after that with Eve (and thus Eve deduces that the shared key is the same) or she will notify Eve that something went wrong with the key agreement. Eve will then deduce that the key is different. In both cases, Eve gets the desired key mismatch oracle.*

In Sect. 5, we show how to get access to such an oracle with side channels in the CCA framework.

4   Attack on **NewHope** with **Key Mismatch Oracle**

We assume here that Eve, the attacker, has access to $\mathcal{O}_1$, a key mismatch oracle as defined in Sect. 3. Let us now explain how she proceeds to recover Alice's static secret key $\mathbf{S}$ following Attack Model 1.

---

[5] While key reuse is against the designers' requirements of the NIST submission NewHope, as expressed in the footnote in the design rationale on p. 16, this requirement does not seem to be formally reflected in the algorithm description of Sect. 1.2. This section indeed defines separate algorithms for key pairs generation, (en/de)capsulation, but does not state that a pair shall be used only once. Thus, though running NewHope with key reuse represents a misuse situation, analyzing the security of this scheme in this situation is definitely much more relevant question than considering variations in the formal specification of NewHope and investigating resulting weaknesses.

4.1   Rewriting the Key Mismatch Oracle

The use of the key mismatch oracle obviously leaks information on Alice's secret key S. But the task of recovering S entirely seems much more complicated. Indeed as defined in Sect. 3, the only information provided by the key mismatch oracle is a bit representing the success or mismatch of the key agreement. The difficulty for Eve is to choose appropriate (m_E, μ_E) pairs to get useful information on small parts of S.

In a first step, Eve simplifies her part of the protocol in such a way that the knowledge of the key mismatch oracle output bit $\mathcal{O}_1(m_E, \mu_E)$ can be easily exploited. To do so, she can fix for instance μ_E such that:

$$\nu_E = (1, 0, \ldots, 0) \text{ and thus } \mu_E = \text{SHAKE-256}(32, \nu_E). \tag{3}$$

The value of $\nu_E = (1, 0, \ldots, 0)$ has not been arbitrarily chosen; as we will see later, the 0 in positions 1 to $n - 1$ will help the success rate of the attack (see Proposition 3). From now on, the value of μ_E is *fixed* according to Eq. (3). Moreover, when replacing m_E by its definition: $m_E = (\mathbf{c}, \mathbf{U})$, the oracle $\mathcal{O}_1$ can be reformulated using the oracle $\mathcal{O}_2$ defined below.

Definition 2. *Let us introduce oracle $\mathcal{O}_2$ such that $\mathcal{O}_2(\mathbf{c}, \mathbf{U}) = \mathcal{O}_1((\mathbf{c}, \mathbf{U}), \mu_E)$.*

With this new definition, Eve can adapt the values of $\mathbf{c}$ and $\mathbf{U}$ to leverage Oracle $\mathcal{O}_2$ and retrieve information on S. In other words, since μ_E is fixed, the inputs $(\mathbf{c}, \mathbf{U})$ are the degrees of liberty for finding S.

From Alice's side, the link between ν_A and S passes through the functions Decode, Decompress (see the figures in full version of our paper [2].) and the element $\mathbf{K}'$: $\nu_A = \text{Decode}(\mathbf{k}') = \text{Decode}(\mathbf{C} - \mathbf{US}) = \text{Decode}(\text{Decompress}(\mathbf{c}) - \mathbf{US})$. Thus, from the definition of the Decode algorithm, the value of $\nu_A[i]$, the i-th component of ν_A, is deduced from the following sign computation:

$$Sign\left(\sum_{j=0}^{3} \left| (\text{Decompress}(\mathbf{c}) - \mathbf{U} \cdot \mathbf{S})[i + nj] - 4s \right| - q \right) \tag{4}$$

We recall here that 0 is positive by convention.

The problem for Eve is that she is unable to know the number of errors that will occur at the end of the decryption computations and the positions in which they appear. Indeed, the key mismatch oracle only gives one bit of information corresponding either to *mismatch* or *success*. If there is a mismatch, Eve knows that *at least* one bit of ν_A is different from ν_E but she can not determine which one (or which ones). Therefore, in order to mount an effective attack, Eve needs to restrict all these different possibilities by making the following hypothesis:

Hypothesis 1. *For i from 1 to $n - 1$, the component $\nu_A[i]$ is equal to 0.*

If Hypothesis 1 is verified, any failure in the communication comes from a single error in ν_A located in the very first component $\nu_A[0]$. Indeed, in that case, the success of the exchange only depends on the first computed value $\nu_A[0]$. In particular, if we assume this hypothesis, the oracle $\mathcal{O}_2$ depends only on the $\nu_A[0]$ and we obtain the following result.

Lemma 1. *Under Hypothesis 1, the initial oracle $\mathcal{O}_2$ can be rewritten as*

$$\mathcal{O}_2(c, U) = Sign\left(\sum_{j=0}^{j=3}\left|(Decompress(c) - US)[0 + nj] - 4s\right| - q\right)$$

For mounting her attack, Eve has to find pairs (c, U) that
1. target the smallest number of bits of S
2. verify Hypothesis 1

For item 1, since the Decode algorithm takes coefficients of S four by four, the size of the smallest target is a quadruplet of coefficients of S. Actually, for a given quadruplet of integers $\underline{\ell} = (\ell_0, \ell_1, \ell_2, \ell_3)$ and a target index k (i.e. an index corresponding to the components of S that Eve wants to retrieve), by taking

$$U = sx^{-k} \quad \text{and} \quad c = \sum_{j=0}^{3}\left((\ell_j + 4) \mod 8\right) \cdot x^{nj} \tag{5}$$

one can prove (see in Proposition 1) that Eve targets the quadruplet $(S[k + nj])_{j=0\cdots 3}$. Indeed, the element x^{-k} will "rotate" S in order to target $(S[k + nj])_{j=0\cdots 3}$ and c is induced by the quadruplet $\underline{\ell} = (\ell_0, \ell_1, \ell_2, \ell_3)$ that can vary.

About item 2, with this choice of (c, U), the Hypothesis 1 has good chances to be verified because the coefficients of c outside from the set $\{k + nj \mid j = 0 \cdots 3\}$ are 0. So, the same coefficients of $C - US$ have good chances to be small. Then, Alice is likely to derive 0 for these coefficients of ν_A. However, it is not always verified and this will impact the attack's success rate. We will discuss and compute this probability later in Proposition 3.

We can now introduce $\mathcal{O}_3$, a reformulation of $\mathcal{O}_2$ depending on target index k and the quadruplet $\underline{\ell}$ (see Eq. 5):

$$\mathcal{O}_3(k, \underline{\ell}) = \mathcal{O}_2\left(sx^{-k}, \sum_{j=0}^{3}\left((\ell_j + 4) \mod 8\right) \cdot x^{nj}\right)$$

This formulation of the key mismatch oracle is more convenient in order to explain how Eve will gather information on S from instantiations of $\underline{\ell}$. The following proposition shows a first result in this direction.

Proposition 1. *Final oracle. Let us assume that Hypothesis 1 is verified. Let k be a target index ($k \in [0, n - 1]$). For a given integer quadruplet $\underline{\ell}$ in $[-4, 3]^4$, the (c, U) explicited in Eq. 5 is such that*

$$\mathcal{O}_3(k, \underline{\ell}) = Sign\left(\sum_{j=0}^{j=3}\left|\ell_j - S[k + nj]\right| - 8\right)$$

Proof. The proof is given in the full version of our paper [2]. $\square$

In the next section, we explain how to effectively use the form $\mathcal{O}_3$ of the key mismatch oracle to extract the secret S.

4.2   Recovering Very Small Coefficients of S

Let us recall that the secret $\mathbf{S}$ is a polynomial in $\mathbb{Z}_q[x]/(x^N+1)$ with coefficients in $[-8,8]$, it can be seen as a vector of N components $\mathbf{S}[i]$. Eve will recover the coefficients of the secret $\mathbf{S}$ four by four. Let k be the index of the targeted quadruplet $[\mathbf{S}[k], \mathbf{S}[k+n], \mathbf{S}[k+2n], \mathbf{S}[k+3n]]$. The index k goes from 0 to $n-1$ and for each fixed k, Eve will call the oracle $\mathcal{O}_3(k, \ell)$ with several appropriate value of ℓ until she gets the secret values.

For simplicity, let us now **fix the index** k and denote $S_j = \mathbf{S}[k+nj]$.

The following proposition and corollary describe an algorithm that, when iterated (see Corollary 1), allows to recover S_j for j from 0 to 3.

Proposition 2. *Let us fix j in $[0,3]$. Under Hypothesis 1, if S_j is in $[-3,2]$ and $(S_i)_{i\neq j} \in [-4,4]$, there exists a probabilistic algorithm $\mathcal{A}$ which recovers the value S_j in 8 queries to oracle $\mathcal{O}_3$ with a success probability depending on the distribution of $(S_i)_{0\leq i\leq 3}$.*

Corollary 1. *Under Hypothesis 1, if S_j is in $[-3,2]$ and $(S_i)_{i\neq j} \in [-4,4]$, there exists a probabilistic algorithm $\mathcal{A}'$ which recovers the value S_j with an average number of queries to oracle $\mathcal{O}_3$ depending on the distribution of $(S_i)_{0\leq i\leq 3}$.*

In the sequel of this section, we give the proof of Proposition 2 by first presenting the construction of the algorithm and then by introducing a method to assess the success rate. We refer the reader to the full version of our paper [2] for the proof of Corollary 1.

Proof of Proposition 2

Description of $\mathcal{A}$. Let us prove the proposition by focusing on the secret S_0 and by explaining how it can be recovered in 8 queries to oracle $\mathcal{O}_3$. The process will then be exactly the same for the three other values S_1, S_2 and S_3.

The first step consists in taking the 3 values ℓ_1, ℓ_2, ℓ_3 at random inside the interval $[-4,3]$. Knowing that all S_j are fixed, the quantity $\sum_{j=0}^{3}|\ell_j - S_j| - 8$ can thus be expressed by $f_v(\ell_0) = |\ell_0 - S_0| + v - 8$ with $v = \sum_{i=1}^{3}|\ell_j - S_j|$ a fixed unknown constant (since all S_j are unknown). Let us now see how $f_v(\ell_0)$ behaves when ℓ_0 varies, see Fig. 2 for an illustration.

We now assume that one makes 8 queries to the oracle $\mathcal{O}_3$: one for each value of ℓ_0 varying inside $[-4,3]$. Such queries imply having access to $Sign\Big(f_v(\ell_0)\Big)$ $\forall \ell_0 \in [-4,3]$. The analysis can thus be split in 2 cases:

1. If $(v-8) \geq 0$ then all queries to oracle 1 obviously lead to "positive signs". It is quite clear when one looks at Fig. 2.
2. If $(v-8) < 0$, two subcases occur
   - In some cases, there exists two possible values $\tau_1 < \tau_2$ such that the function $|\ell_0 - S_0| + (v-8)$ goes from a positive value to a negative one at point τ_1 and then from a negative value to a positive one at point τ_2. We call this case the *favorable case*. Figure 3 provides a good illustration.

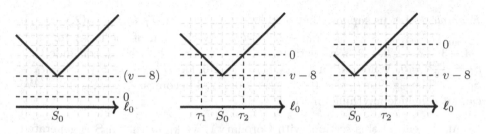

Fig. 2. If $v - 8 \geq 0$ **Fig. 3.** If $v - 8 > 0$ **Fig. 4.** If $v - 8 \gg 0$

$$\begin{array}{cccccccccccc} \ell_0 & -4 & \cdots & \tau_1 - 1 & \tau_1 & \tau_1 + 1 & \cdots & \tau_2 - 1 & \tau_2 & \tau_2 + 1 & \cdots & 3 \\ \mathcal{O} & + & \cdots & + & + & - & \cdots & - & + & + & \cdots & + \end{array}$$

- If $(v - 8) < 0$ and $v \ll 8$, only one change of sign will occur in the interval $[-4, 3]$. Figure 4 provides a good illustration.

Figure 3 illustrated what happens in the *favorable case*. Around S_0, the trace has a slope equal to $+$ or -1. Because of the symmetry, the value S_0 can simply be recovered by:

$$S_0 = \frac{\tau_2 + \tau_1}{2}. \tag{6}$$

If we are not in the *favorable case*, two such values τ_1 and τ_2 do not exist. This means that the constant v is not appropriate.

Termination of $\mathcal{A}$. For any $S_0 \in [-3, 2]$, $\mathcal{A}$ has a non zero success probability. Indeed, no matter the values of (S_1, S_2, S_3) in $[-4, 4]^3$, the 3-uple $(\ell_1, \ell_2, \ell_3) \in [-4, 3]^3$ defined by

$$\left(\ell_1 = S_1 - 2 \cdot Sign(S_1), \quad \ell_2 = S_2 - 2 \cdot Sign(S_2), \quad \ell_3 = S_3 - 3 \cdot Sign(S_3) \right)$$

is at least one of the choices inducing a favorable case. Actually, one can check that this choice implies that $v = 7$. Thus $v - 8 = -1$ which always gives a favorable case for finding $S_0 \in [-3, 2]$.

Table 1. Success probability of $\mathcal{A}$ for $(S_j)_{1 \leq j \leq 3}$ following ψ_4 distribution

S_0	-3	-2	-1	0	1	2
Probability (%)	14	27	39	39	27	14
Expected number of iterations ($1/probability$)	7.1	3.7	2.6	2.6	3.7	7.1

Success Probability. A precise probabilistic study on the $(S_j)_{1 \leq j \leq 3}$ to assess the success rate of algorithm $\mathcal{A}$ is detailed in the full version of our paper [2]. In Table 1, one can find the probability of success assuming that S_1, S_2, S_3 follow a binomial distribution ψ_4. The expected number of iterations is the average amount of tries before recovering the secret. $\quad\square$

Example 1. Let us suppose that $S_i = [0, -2, 1, -1]$. For $(\ell_1, \ell_2, \ell_3) = (2, -2, -1)$, $\sum_{j=0}^{3} |\ell_j - S_j| - 8 = |\ell_0 - S_0| - 2$. If we query the sign of the latter for $\ell_0 = -4, -3, -2, -1, 0, 1, 2, 3$, we get: +, +, +, -, -, -, +, +. We can conclude that $S_0 = \frac{1-1}{2} = 0$. Whereas, for $(\ell_1, \ell_2, \ell_3) = (-2, 0, 1)$, $\sum_{j=0}^{3} |\ell_j - S_j| - 8 = |\ell_0 - S_0| - 5$. The sign for $\ell_0 = -4, -3, -2, -1, 0, 1, 2, 3$ becomes: -, -, -,-, -, -, -, -. We cannot conclude anything on S_0.

At the end of this section, with Corollary 1, we know that if $\mathbf{S}$ is generated with coefficients following the ψ_4 distribution and if Hypothesis 1 is verified, there exist an algorithm that recovers each coefficient of $\mathbf{S}$ that is in $[-3, 2]$ (i.e. almost 96% of the coefficients). If a coefficient of $\mathbf{S}$ is not in $[-3, 2]$, no favorable case will appear and the coefficient will not be found. In the next section, we adapt this method for NewHope.

4.3   Recovering S for NewHope Parameters

In this section, we describe a way to recover $\mathbf{S}$ for NewHope parameters, *i.e.* when the binomial parameter is 8. According to Property 1, the coefficients of $\mathbf{S}[k]$ are in $[-8, 8]$. This is outside from the hypothesis made in Proposition 2. Indeed, the coefficients $\mathbf{S}[k]$ should lie in $[-3, 2]$. One can make the following change in order to fit with Proposition 2 hypothesis: $\mathbf{S}^1 = \frac{\mathbf{S}}{2}$. In order to target $\mathbf{S}^1$ instead of $\mathbf{S}$, one can change $\mathbf{U}$ from Eq. 5 to be the following $\mathbf{U} = \frac{s}{2}x^{-k}$.

Let us wrap up the attack into the following Proposition.

Proposition 3. *There exists a probabilistic algorithm $\mathcal{B}$ which recovers NewHope secret S with high probability using an average of $18,500$ queries for $N = 1024$.*

Proof. Let $k \in [0, n - 1]$. The distribution of probabilities for $\mathbf{S}[k]$ is in Table 2.

<u>Case 1</u>: $\mathbf{S}[k]$ **belongs to** $\{-8, -7, 5, 6, 7, 8\}$. The probability of this case is around 1%. In that case, at most one change of sign will always happen. Then, only the sign of $\mathbf{S}[k]$ can be recovered and a brute force should be done at the end of the attack to distinguish among the possible values. For $N = 1024$, on average 10 coefficients out of 1024 will not be found. When a positive value is not found, it has 8/10 chances to be a 5. At the end of the attack, a bruteforce step evaluating $\mathbf{B} - \mathbf{AS}$ and taking account of the probabilities can be done.

Table 2. Distribution ψ_8 (note that the probability is the same for negative values)

$\mathbf{S}[k]$	0	1	2	3	4	5	6	7	8
Probability $(\times 2^{16})$	12870	11440	8008	4368	1820	560	120	16	1

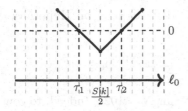

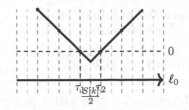

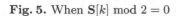

Fig. 5. When $\mathbf{S}[k] \bmod 2 = 0$ **Fig. 6.** When $\mathbf{S}[k] \bmod 3 = 1$

<u>**Case 2**</u>: $\mathbf{S}[k]$ **belongs to** $\{-6, ..., 4\}$. In that case, $\mathbf{S}^1[k]$ belongs in the interval $[-3, 2]$. The attack is the one from Proposition 2 with a different secret $\mathbf{S}^1[k] = \frac{\mathbf{S}[k]}{2}$. However, the results will not be as accurate as before. We will show that there is a subtelty that allows Eve to recover the exact value of $\mathbf{S}[k]$. There are 2 possible results depending on $\mathbf{S}[k] \bmod 2$:

- If $\mathbf{S}[k] \bmod 2 = 0$, then $\mathbf{S}^1[k] \in \{-3, -2, -1, 0, 1, 2\}$. Proposition 2 allows Eve to recover $\mathbf{S}^1$. In other words, Eve will recover a succession of signs where an odd number of $(-)$ occurs (see Fig. 5). She will then be able to recover $\frac{\mathbf{S}[k]}{2} = \frac{\tau_1 + \tau_2}{2}$ and then $\mathbf{S}[k]$.
- If $\mathbf{S}[k] \bmod 2 = 1$ then $\mathbf{S}^1[k] \in \{-2.5, -1.5, -0.5, 0.5, 1.5\}$. In a favorable case of Proposition 2, the situation will be different. As in Fig. 6, the number of $(-)$ is then even.

Wrap Up. Here is a procedure to recover $\mathbf{S}[k]$.

Case 1. If the number of $(-)$ is odd, then $\mathbf{S}[k]$ is even and $\mathbf{S}[k] = 2\frac{\tau_1 + \tau_2}{2} = \tau_1 + \tau_2$

Case 2. If the number of $(-)$ is even, then $\mathbf{S}[k] = 2\left\lfloor \frac{\tau_1 + \tau_2}{2} \right\rfloor + 1$

Case 3. If at most one change of sign occur, the procedure is restarted.

If the number of restarts is too large (say, $\geq M$), the procedure is stopped and the coefficient, placed in a bruteforce set, is found at the end of the attack.

Table 3. Average number of queries

Value	−6	−5	−4	−3	−2	−1	0	1	2	3	4	−8, −7, 5, 6, 7 or 8
Average queries	33	33	19	20	16	17	17	15	22	20	38	M

Number of Queries. The amount of queries is derived with the same technique as in the full version of our paper [2]. See Table 3 for the average number of queries. Let us set the threshold M to 50, to get the total average number of queries, we compute the expected number of queries for $\mathbf{S}[k]$ ($\approx$18) and multiply it by $N = 1024$.

Success Probability. The success probability depends only on Hypothesis 1 with $\mathbf{S}^1$, which becomes the following for $\mathbf{S}$.

Hypothesis 2. $\forall i, k \in [1, n - 1]$ $\sum_{j=0}^{j=3} \left| \frac{\mathbf{S}[k+i+nj \bmod N]}{2} + 4 \right| \geq 8$

Hypothesis 2 is true with a probability 94.6% for $N = 1024$. Indeed, to compute this probability, one can check whether each quadruplet verifies it. Only a few unlikely quadruplet (e.g. $[8, 8, 8, 8]$) do not verify the hypothesis. □

4.4 Experimental Results

We implemented a proof of concept with Magma CAS [5][6]. We coded NewHope according to its parameters and used the key mismatch oracle for the attack. We worked on a basic optimization of the number of queries. We ran 1000 experiments and recovered more than 95% of the secret keys in an average time of 30 minutes per key and 16,700 queries. We still think that the number of queries and the time can be better optimized.

5 Accessing the Key Mismatch Oracle with the CCA Version of NewHope

In order to be protected against active attacks, the CPA-KEM of NewHope has been transformed according to the Hofheinz, Hövelmanns and Kiltz CCA transformation [16] which is a variant of the Fujisaki-Okamoto transformation [11]. The CCA security is then based on the CPA security of the PKE. The CCA transformation of the algorithms defining this version of NewHope is detailed in Algorithms 5, 6 and 7. These algorithms use the underlying CPA-PKE of NewHope as defined in Sect. 1.2.1 of [23].

Algorithm 5. NewHope CCA-KEM Key Generation

```
1  function NewHope CCA-KEM.Gen()
2    (pk, sk) ← NewHope-CPA-PKE.Gen()
3    s ← {0, ..., 255}^32
4    return (pk, ŝk = (sk||pk||SHAKE-256(32, pk)||s)
```

Algorithm 6. NewHope-CCA-KEM Encapsulation

```
1  function NewHope-CCA-KEM-Encaps(pk)
2    coin ← {0, ...255}^32
3    μ ← SHAKE-256(32, coin) ∈ {0, ..., 255}^32
4    K||coin'||d ←
       SHAKE-256(96, μ||SHAKE-256(32, pk)) ∈
       {0, ..., 255}^{32+32+32}
5    c ← NewHope-CPA-PKE.Encrypt(pk, μ; coin')
6    ss ← SHAKE-256(32, K||SHAKE-256(32, c||d))
7    return (c̄ = c||d, ss)
```

One can note the main security measure in Algorithm 7 where the instruction in red corresponds to a double encryption to check if the message m_B has been honestly generated.

---

[6] The Magma code can be found at https://www.di.ens.fr/~mrossi/.

More precisely, in the key mismatch oracle, the message m_B can be adjusted by the attacker but with this CCA version of NewHope, Eve must follow the protocol and generate m_E according to a seed called $coin'$ that is derived from μ_E and another seed called $coin$ (a 32-byte random integer). Then, Alice will derive $coin'$ to check if μ_E was computed following the protocol. Then, a key mismatch will come from the following oracle

$$\mathcal{O}_4(coin, \mu_E) = \begin{cases} 1 & \text{if } \mathsf{Dec}(\mathsf{Enc}(m_A, coin), \mathbf{S}) = \mu_E \\ -1 & otherwise \end{cases} \tag{7}$$

This oracle is less convenient than $\mathcal{O}_1$ because with an honest behaviour, the error probability is claimed to be lower than 2^{-213} in the NIST specification (paragraph 4.2.7 of [23]). In the sequel, we point at critical steps inside the CCA transform that let Eve access oracle $\mathcal{O}_1$ using side channel or fault attacks.

On Using Side Channel or Fault Attack

When the attacker has access to a device implementing Alice's side of the exchange, the attack model should take into account situations where some algorithmic security measures may be bypassed by using hardware attacks.

Power Analysis. Here we consider that Eve is able to make a power analysis during the verification step of Alice decapsulation algorithm.

Algorithm 7. NewHope-CCA-KEM Decapsulation

```
1  function NewHope-CCA-KEM.Decaps (c̄, s̄k)
2  c||d ← c̄ ∈ {0, ..., 255}^NEWHOPE_CPAPKE_CIPHERTEXTBYTES+32
3  sk||pk||h||s ← s̄k ∈ {0, ..., 255}^32+32+32+32
4  μ' ← NewHope-CPA-PKE.Decrypt(c, sk)
5  K'||coin''|d' ← SHAKE-256(96, μ'||h) ∈ {0, ..., 255}^32+32+32
6  if c =NewHope-CPA-PKE.Encrypt(pk, μ'; coin'') and d = d'
7  then fail ← 0 else fail ← 1 end if
8  K_0 ← K'
9  K_1 ← s
10 return ss = (SHAKE-256(32, K_fail ||SHAKE-256(32, c||d)))
```

Attack Model 2. *We assume that Alice has done the CCA key generation. Eve sends messages m_E with a wrong coin. Alice will then reject any messages m_e because the verification is never passed. Eve, the attacker, is able to make a power analysis during the verification step of Alice's decapsulation algorithm.*

With a power analysis, Eve can easily get the desired key mismatch oracle with a low number of traces.

A first idea would be to target the computation of $d = d'$ with differential power analysis. The following code corresponds to NewHope-CCA-KEM verification step where $a = (c, d)$, $b = (\mathsf{NewHope\text{-}CPA\text{-}PKE.Encrypt}(pk, \mu'; coin''), d')$ and $len = 17/8 \cdot N + 32$.

```
* Name:            verify
* Description:  Compare two arrays for equality in constant time.
* Arguments:
* const unsigned char *a:  pointer to first byte array
* const unsigned char *b:  pointer to second byte array
* size_t len:              length of the byte arrays
* Returns 0 if the byte arrays are equal, 1 otherwise
**********************************************************/

int verify(const unsigned char *a, const unsigned char *b, size_t len)
{
    uint64_t r;
    size_t i;
    r = 0;

    for(i=0;i<len;i++)
        r |= a[i] ^ b[i];

    r = (-r) >> 63;
    return r;
}
```

This naive method actually works well in practice for an unprotected scheme because when $d = d'$, r is ored with 0 during $17/8 \cdot N$ iterations and when $d \neq d'$, r is ored with arbitrary values during $17/8 \cdot N$ iterations. With a single trace analysis, the equality $d = d'$ can be verified. One would argue reasonably that unprotected schemes are always vulnerable. The main aim of [21] is to propose a countermeasure to such an attack for a similar scheme which uses the CCA transform. It is an open problem, in this protected context, to extend this approach to a second order power analysis attack. A more realistic model relies on an invasive attack, this is what we present in the sequel.

Single Fault Attack. We consider inserting a fault during the computation of the verification step which cancels the CCA transform. The attack model becomes:

Attack Model 3. *We assume that Alice has done the **CCA** key generation. Eve, the attacker, is able to set the value r to 0 in the verification step of Alice's decapsulation algorithm.*

If Eve is able to set the value r to 0 anytime during the check $d = d'$, she can bypass the reencryption and the mismatch will appear only if $d \neq d'$. Then oracle $\mathcal{O}_1$ becomes accessible. Indeed, Eve can thus send any message m_E. Alice derives a wrong $coin'$ but the verification is skipped with the fault. If $d = d'$, Alice derives the shared key for initiating a communication. If $d \neq d'$, Alice will notice Eve that the key agreement failed. Eve will then deduce that the key is different. This vulnerability has been underlined in Sect. 3.6 of [21] for a similar scheme. But no countermeasure has been added to protect against this single fault attack, which can practically be induced by a laser. Countermeasures should have thus to be considered (see [18]), what may impact the efficiency of the verification.

6   Conclusion

The resilience of NIST post-quantum candidate algorithms in misuse situations is worth being investigated. It will help developers to propose implementations with countermeasures tightly designed to ensure the security in extreme contexts (e.g. smart card, IoT) without decreasing too much the efficiency. In this paper, we describe an active attack against NewHope-CPA-KEM with (public, private) key pair reuse. This clearly confirms that if the designers' caveat against any private key reuse (e.g. temporary caching) is not strictly followed, this results in a practical, low complexity, key recovery attack. Our study indeed indicates that setting an upper limit of a few hundreds on the number of authorized key reuses would not be conservative enough, and already expose private keys to significant information leakages. While unprotected versions of CCA-KEM are extremely efficient, implementations of this scheme must be very carefully protected against any key mismatch oracle leakage if key pairs are potentially reused. As explained in this paper, this is particularly true for countermeasures against fault attacks. This might eventually come with a cost in terms of performance. This consideration may become even more important if one considers second order side channel or combined attacks, which could be a sequel of this work.

References

1. Alkim, E., Ducas, L., Pöppelmann, T., Schwabe, P.: Post-quantum key exchange - a new hope. In: Holz, T., Savage, S. (eds.) 25th USENIX Security Symposium, USENIX Security 16, Austin, TX, USA, 10–12 August 2016, pp. 327–343. USENIX Association (2016)
2. Bauer, A., Gilbert, H., Renault, G., Rossi, M.: Assessment of the Key-Reuse Resilience of NewHope (2019, to appear)
3. Bernstein, D.J., Groot Bruinderink, L., Lange, T., Panny, L.: HILA5 pindakaas: on the CCA security of lattice-based encryption with error correction. In: Joux, A., Nitaj, A., Rachidi, T. (eds.) AFRICACRYPT 2018. LNCS, vol. 10831, pp. 203–216. Springer, Cham (2018). https://doi.org/10.1007/978-3-319-89339-6_12
4. Bleichenbacher, D.: Chosen ciphertext attacks against protocols based on the RSA encryption standard PKCS #1. In: Krawczyk, H. (ed.) CRYPTO 1998. LNCS, vol. 1462, pp. 1–12. Springer, Heidelberg (1998). https://doi.org/10.1007/BFb0055716
5. Bosma, W., Cannon, J., Playoust, C.: The Magma algebra system I. The user language. J. Symbolic Comput. 24(3–4), 235–265 (1997). Computational algebra and number theory (London, 1993)
6. Braithwaite, M.: Experimenting with Post-quantum Cryptography. Posting on the Google Security Blog (2016)
7. Ding, J.: A Simple Provably Secure Key Exchange Scheme Based on the Learning with Errors Problem. Cryptology ePrint Archive, Report 2012/688 (2012). https://eprint.iacr.org/2012/688
8. Ding, J., Alsayigh, S., Saraswathy, R.V., Fluhrer, S.R., Lin, X.: Leakage of signal function with reused keys in RLWE key exchange. In: IEEE International Conference on Communications, ICC 2017, pp. 1–6. IEEE (2017)
9. Ding, J., Fluhrer, S., Saraswathy, R.V.: Complete attack on RLWE key exchange with reused keys, without signal leakage. In: Susilo, W., Yang, G. (eds.) ACISP 2018. LNCS, vol. 10946, pp. 467–486. Springer, Cham (2018). https://doi.org/10.1007/978-3-319-93638-3_27
10. Fluhrer, S.: Cryptanalysis of Ring-LWE based Key Exchange with Key Share Reuse. Cryptology ePrint Archive, Report 2016/085 (2016). https://eprint.iacr.org/2016/085

11. Fujisaki, E., Okamoto, T.: Secure integration of asymmetric and symmetric encryption schemes. In: Wiener, M. (ed.) CRYPTO 1999. LNCS, vol. 1666, pp. 537–554. Springer, Heidelberg (1999). https://doi.org/10.1007/3-540-48405-1_34

12. Guo, Q., Johansson, T., Stankovski, P.: A key recovery attack on MDPC with CCA security using decoding errors. In: Cheon, J.H., Takagi, T. (eds.) ASIACRYPT 2016, Part I. LNCS, vol. 10031, pp. 789–815. Springer, Heidelberg (2016). https://doi.org/10.1007/978-3-662-53887-6_29

13. Hall, C., Goldberg, I., Schneier, B.: Reaction attacks against several public-key cryptosystem. In: Varadharajan, V., Mu, Y. (eds.) ICICS 1999. LNCS, vol. 1726, pp. 2–12. Springer, Heidelberg (1999). https://doi.org/10.1007/978-3-540-47942-0_2

14. Hoffstein, J., Silverman, J.H.: Protecting NTRU against chosen ciphertext and reaction attacks. Technical report 16, NTRU Cryptosystems Technical report (2000)

15. Hoffstein, J., Silverman, J.H.: Reaction attacks against the NTRU public key cryptosystem. Technical report 15, NTRU Cryptosystems Technical report (1999)

16. Hofheinz, D., Hövelmanns, K., Kiltz, E.: A modular analysis of the fujisaki-okamoto transformation. In: Kalai, Y., Reyzin, L. (eds.) TCC 2017. LNCS, vol. 10677, pp. 341–371. Springer, Cham (2017). https://doi.org/10.1007/978-3-319-70500-2_12

17. Howgrave-Graham, N., et al.: The impact of decryption failures on the security of NTRU encryption. In: Boneh, D. (ed.) CRYPTO 2003. LNCS, vol. 2729, pp. 226–246. Springer, Heidelberg (2003). https://doi.org/10.1007/978-3-540-45146-4_14

18. Joye, M., Tunstall, M. (eds.): Fault Analysis in Cryptography. Information Security and Cryptography. Springer, Heidelberg (2012). https://doi.org/10.1007/978-3-642-29656-7

19. Kirkwood, D., Lackey, B., McVey, J., Motley, M., Solinas, J., Tuller, D.: Failure is not an option: standardization issues for post-quantum key agreement. In: NIST Workshop on Cybersecurity in a Post Quantum World (2015)

20. Menezes, A., Ustaoglu, B.: On reusing ephemeral keys in Diffie-Hellman key agreement protocols. IJACT 2(2), 154–158 (2010)

21. Oder, T., Schneider, T., Pöppelmann, T., Güneysu, T.: Practical CCA2-secure and masked ring-LWE implementation. IACR Transactions on CHES (2016). https://eprint.iacr.org/2016/1109

22. Peikert, C.: Lattice cryptography for the internet. In: Mosca, M. (ed.) PQCrypto 2014. LNCS, vol. 8772, pp. 197–219. Springer, Cham (2014). https://doi.org/10.1007/978-3-319-11659-4_12

23. Pöppelmann, T., et al.: NewHope. Submission to Round 1 of NIST Post Quantum Cryptography Competition (2017)

24. Rogaway, P., Shrimpton, T.: A provable-security treatment of the key-wrap problem. In: Vaudenay, S. (ed.) EUROCRYPT 2006. LNCS, vol. 4004, pp. 373–390. Springer, Heidelberg (2006). https://doi.org/10.1007/11761679_23

25. Schwabe, P., Alkim, E., Ducas, L., Pöppelmann, T., Schwabe, P.: NewHope without Reconciliation. Cryptology ePrint Archive, Report 2016/1157 (2016). https://eprint.iacr.org/2016/1157

Universal Forgery and Multiple Forgeries of MergeMAC and Generalized Constructions

Tetsu Iwata[1], Virginie Lallemand[2], Gregor Leander[2], and Yu Sasaki[3(✉)]

[1] Nagoya University, Nagoya, Japan
tetsu.iwata@nagoya-u.jp
[2] Horst Görtz Institute for IT Security, Ruhr-Universität Bochum,
Bochum, Germany
{**virginie.lallemand,gregor.leander**}**@rub.de**
[3] NTT Secure Platform Laboratories, Tokyo, Japan
sasaki.yu@lab.ntt.co.jp

Abstract. This article presents universal forgery and multiple forgeries against MergeMAC that has been recently proposed to fit scenarios where bandwidth is limited and where strict time constraints apply. MergeMAC divides an input message into two parts, $m\|\tilde{m}$, and its tag is computed by $\mathcal{F}(\mathcal{P}_1(m) \oplus \mathcal{P}_2(\tilde{m}))$, where $\mathcal{P}_1$ and $\mathcal{P}_2$ are PRFs and $\mathcal{F}$ is a public function. The tag size is 64 bits. The designers claim 64-bit security and mention that it might be insecure to accept beyond-birthday-bound queries.

This paper presents the first third-party analysis of MergeMAC. Firstly, it is shown that limiting the number of queries up to the birthday bound is crucial, because a generic universal forgery against CBC-like MAC can be applied. Afterwards another attack is presented that works with very few queries, 3 queries and $2^{58.6}$ computations of $\mathcal{F}$, by applying a preimage attack against weak $\mathcal{F}$. This breaks the claimed security. The analysis is then generalized to a MergeMAC variant where $\mathcal{F}$ is replaced with a one-way function $\mathcal{H}$.

Finally, multiple forgeries are discussed in which the attacker's goal is to improve the ratio of the number of queries to the number of forged tags. It is shown that the number of achievable forgeries is quadratic in the number of queries in the sense of existential forgery, and this is tight when messages have a particular structure. For universal forgery, tags for $3q$ arbitrary chosen messages can be obtained by making $5q$ queries.

Keywords: MergeMAC · Universal forgery · Multiple forgeries ·
Public finalization · Preimage · Splice-and-cut

1 Introduction

Fully aware of the rapid expansion of pervasive computing and of what is usually referred to as the Internet of Things (IoT), symmetric cryptographers proposed solutions to ensure appropriate security for the new use cases. Lightweight

© Springer Nature Switzerland AG 2019
M. Matsui (Ed.): CT-RSA 2019, LNCS 11405, pp. 293–312, 2019.
https://doi.org/10.1007/978-3-030-12612-4_15

cryptography became a hot research topic as it was understood that finding the correct compromise between security and efficiency was challenging. Many cryptographers – whether from academic community, from government agencies or from private companies – proposed new primitives, starting with a myriad of lightweight block ciphers (like Present [9], Prince [10], SKINNY [5], CLE-FIA [18] and Simon [4] just to name a few). While in comparison the design of other primitives seems less popular, some lightweight stream ciphers and hash functions were also proposed[1]. The design of Message Authentication Codes was also addressed, with the publication of SipHash [3], Chaskey [15], of the MAC mode LightMAC [14] and very recently of MergeMAC [1].

MergeMAC was proposed by Ankele, Böhl and Friedberger at ACNS18. As for all the Message Authentication Codes, it intends to provide integrity and authenticity by producing a fixed-length tag from a message and a secret key. MergeMAC was designed to fit extremely constrained environments with strict time requirements and limited bandwidth, and in particular for the Controller Area Network (CAN) bus[2]. The necessity to bring authentication for this latter scenario comes from the fact that some of the components at play are also connected to the Internet, creating remote attack opportunities. The MAC construction proposed by Ankele et al. is based on 3 components: 2 variable input-length Pseudo-Random Functions (parameterized by independent keys), and a so-called MERGE function. Each PRF modifies one part of the input message, and the two outputs are recombined by the merge function.

Our Contributions. In this paper, we investigate the resistance of MergeMAC against forgery attacks in different scenarios.

First, we show that an attacker can take advantage of its special structure and forge messages by adapting the universal forgery attack proposed by Jia et al. [13], and this regardless of the choice of the PRF or of the MERGE function. This first technique has a data complexity slightly higher than the limit set by the designers, which shows its tightness.

Our second results is a universal forgery that breaks the security claim of MergeMAC by only requiring 3 queries to forge a tag. This attack exploits the details of the MERGE function (in particular its low diffusion and its feed-forward structure) to perform a preimage attack using the splice-and-cut Meet-in-the-Middle technique [2].

We also discuss the possibility of forgery attacks in the situation where the MERGE function is an ideal one-way function. We call this construction MergeMAC^{OW}. By using the fact that it is public and can be evaluated offline, we deduce possible tradeoffs that can be more practical than the generic attack, but still less efficient than the one using the specificities of the MERGE function.

Our last contribution is the analysis of MergeMAC to forge multiple tags: first in the case of existential forgeries, and next in the case of universal ones.

---

[1] We refer to [7] for a thorough review of lightweight constructions.

[2] The CAN bus is the standard system used in most modern cars to connect together the different components (engine control unit, airbags, audio system, doors, etc.).

Table 1. Overview of the universal forgeries presented in this paper. Constant factor in the complexities is omitted.

Merge func.	Queries	Complexity	Ref.
Any	2^{32}	Memory: 2^{32}, time: 2^{32}	Sect. 3.1
3-round Chaskey	3	Memory: 2^8, time: $2^{58.6}$	Sect. 3.2
One-way function	2^{24}	Memory: 2^{48}, time: 2^{48} (offline), 2^{24} (online)	Sect. 4

Table 2. Multiple forgeries presented in this paper.

Type of forgery	Forgeries	Queries	Ref.
Multiple existential	$(q-1)^2$	$2q-1$	Sect. 5.1
Multiple universal	$3\ell + r$	$5\ell + 2r$	Sect. 5.4

The problem is known as the MAC reforgeability [8], where one takes advantage of the computational efforts for the first forgery to reduce the complexity for the subsequent forgeries. In the case of existential forgery, we show that it is possible to forge $(q-1)^2$ tags by making $2q-1$ queries, i.e., we can obtain more forgeries than the number of queries. We also discuss the tightness on the number of queries. In the case of universal forgery, we show that we can forge q tags by making $2q-1$ queries, and we also show that this can be improved to forge $q = 3\ell + r$ tags $(0 \leq r < 3)$ by making $5\ell + 2r$ queries. We remark that no security claim has been made by the designers regarding multiple forgeries, and hence our analyses give the first insight about the security of MergeMAC in this attack scenario. Our results are summarized in Tables 1 and 2.

Paper Outline. Section 2 introduces specification of MergeMAC. Section 3 presents universal forgery against MergeMAC. Section 4 generalizes the analysis to MergeMAC^{OW}. Section 5 discusses multiple forgeries.

2 Specification of MergeMAC

MergeMAC is a new MAC construction that has been recently proposed by Ankele, Böhl and Friedberger [1] to fit scenarios where bandwidth is limited and where strict time constraints apply. More precisely, the designers aim for an efficient solution for authenticating messages on the CAN bus, a communication system widely used in modern cars to manage the different electronic components. In addition to the bandwidth constraint inherent to the CAN technology, the fact that the components in questions are as critical as brakes or airbags makes it plain that the MAC must have a low latency.

To meet these requirements, the solution proposed by Ankele et al. uses different techniques[3]: for instance, it saves bandwidth by not transmitting some

---

[3] We refer to the specification [1] for details.

low-entropy bits of the message, and it can be built from lightweight ciphers such as Prince [10] to limit the latency. One of the design ideas that impacted the most their construction was the wish to speed up MAC verifications by storing frequently needed intermediate parts in the cache instead of computing them again. This point leads them to a construction that combines the output of two PRFs (each operating on a part of the input message) into a merging function (see Fig. 1). The authors propose to precompute and cache the PRF outputs, and stress that this solution only requires simple computations, an advantage in comparison to other cache-able construction.

In what follows, we use the same notation as in the specification. As shown in Fig. 1, the input of MergeMAC is first split into two parts, m and $\tilde{m}$, each entering one of the PRFs $\mathcal{P}_1$, $\mathcal{P}_2$. These PRFs are of variable input length and depend on two k-bit keys K_1, K_2. The n-bit outputs of $\mathcal{P}_1$, $\mathcal{P}_2$ are denoted by ρ and $\tilde{\rho}$, respectively, and both enter the MERGE function which returns the n-bit tag.

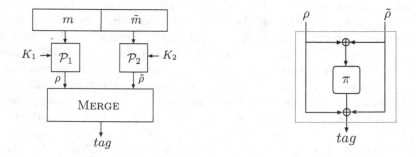

Fig. 1. MergeMAC construction (left) and MERGE function (right).

The authors state that any MAC scheme that is a secure PRF (as for example AES-CMAC or Chaskey) can be used to instantiate $\mathcal{P}_1$ and $\mathcal{P}_2$. To fit in with the constrained environment use-case, they propose to use Present [9] or Prince [10] in CMAC mode. The MERGE function follows a Davies-Meyer construction with $\rho \oplus \tilde{\rho}$ as input: $tag = \pi(\rho \oplus \tilde{\rho}) \oplus (\rho \oplus \tilde{\rho})$, where π is a permutation on n bits. The authors define π as a 3-round variant of CHASKEY [15] operating on 64-bit blocks (note that the reduced block size is required to achieve compatibility with the block size of Present/Prince). The other changes made to the round function can be read in Fig. 2.

The instantiation of MERGE can be viewed as an XOR-then-hash construction, i.e. the XOR of two inputs are processed by a public hash function (Fig. 3). We will use this view when it is convenient to understand our analysis.

Security Claim. The authors claim that their construction is a provably secure MAC, and in particular that it reaches n-bit security against forgery attacks. Their proof requires that $\mathcal{P}_1$ and $\mathcal{P}_2$ are secure PRFs and that the MERGE function satisfies Random Input Indistinguishability.

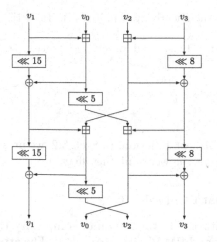

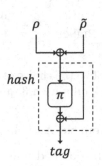

Fig. 2. One round of π in MERGE. Each wire represents 16 bits. The order of the variables $(1, 0, 2, 3)$ follow the one in the design document.

Fig. 3. Another view of MERGE.

To prove this last point, they provide a security analysis of the MERGE function with respect to various types of attacks. An argument that they use repeatedly in the discussion is that, since the input of the MERGE function is unknown and comes from a PRF, an attacker cannot force a specific property on it, which removes the threat of many attacks such as the ones based on differentials.

The authors also claim that finding a preimage of MERGE is "as hard as exhaustively guessing the internal state after the initial PRFs" so that MergeMAC is resistant to attacks based on Meet-in-the-Middle techniques. They justify the resistance to more advanced MitM attacks by the fact that "MergeMAC does not implement an inverse function for the merging function MERGE"[4].

The designers claim the security for each underlying primitive as in Table 3. The designers also notice the risk of using a small block size against birthday attacks demonstrated by the Sweet32 attack [6], and suggest that the amount of data blocks that are processed by the initial PRFs of MergeMAC must be limited appropriately. Although the designers do not specify the details of the appropriate level, Table 3 may be interpreted as security claims under the condition that key is renewed after the number of queries reaches the birthday bound.

3   Universal Forgery Against MergeMAC

In Sect. 3.1, we show that limiting the number of queries up to the birthday bound is almost tight because a generic universal forgery can be applied

---

[4] As we will show later in the paper, this argument turns wrong.

Table 3. Security claims according to the underlying primitives [1, Table 1].

Underlying BC	Block size	Key size	Existential forgery resistance
PRESENT	64	80	2^{-64}
PRESENT	64	128	2^{-64}
PRINCE	64	128	2^{-64}

irrelevant to the choice of PRFs and the MERGE function. In Sect. 3.2, we present an attack only with 3 queries by exploiting the weak mixing effect of π.

3.1   Generic Attacks with High Data Complexity

Jia et al. proposed universal forgery with the birthday-bound complexity that generally works against CBC-like MACs and PMAC-like MACs [13]. The attack can be directly applied to MergeMAC. Let $m\|\tilde{m}$ be a challenged message. The goal of the attacker is producing the tag t for this message without querying $m\|\tilde{m}$. The attack works as follows.

1. For distinct $x_i, 1 \leq i \leq 2^{n/2}$, query $x_i\|\tilde{m}$ to obtain a tag t_i.
2. For distinct $\tilde{y}_j, 1 \leq j \leq 2^{n/2}$, query $m\|\tilde{y}_j$ to obtain a tag t_j.
3. Find a collision of t_i and t_j. Let $\hat{i}, \hat{j}$ be the indices of the colliding pair.
4. Query $x_{\hat{i}}\|\tilde{y}_{\hat{j}}$ to obtain the corresponding tag t'.
5. Output t' as a valid tag for $m\|\tilde{m}$.

Analysis. We view MERGE as Fig. 3. We first evaluate the attack by replacing the hash function in MERGE with a permutation. Then, a collision of the tag implies a collision of the XOR of two PRF's outputs, namely

$$\mathcal{P}_1(x_{\hat{i}}) \oplus \mathcal{P}_2(\tilde{m}) = \mathcal{P}_1(m) \oplus \mathcal{P}_2(\tilde{y}_{\hat{j}}). \tag{1}$$

Therefore,

$$\mathcal{P}_1(x_{\hat{i}}) \oplus \mathcal{P}_2(\tilde{y}_{\hat{j}}) = \mathcal{P}_1(m) \oplus \mathcal{P}_2(\tilde{m}), \tag{2}$$

which shows that the tag for $m\|\tilde{m}$ is equal to the tag for $x_{\hat{i}}\|\tilde{y}_{\hat{j}}$.

The attack requires $2 \cdot 2^{n/2} + 1$ queries, which is roughly $O(2^{n/2})$ queries (and the computational cost of $O(2^{n/2})$ memory accesses to operate on the data).

Analysis for Non-injective Merge Function. We now evaluate the case with MERGE following the actual construction. Then, a collision of t_i and t_j does not imply Eq. (1). Suppose that $\mathcal{P}_1(x_{\hat{i}}) \oplus \mathcal{P}_2(\tilde{m}) = \alpha, \mathcal{P}_1(m) \oplus \mathcal{P}_2(\tilde{y}_{\hat{j}}) = \beta, \alpha \neq \beta$ and $\text{MERGE}(\alpha) = \text{MERGE}(\beta)$. Then Eq. (2) becomes

$$\mathcal{P}_1(x_{\hat{i}}) \oplus \mathcal{P}_2(\tilde{y}_{\hat{j}}) = \mathcal{P}_1(m) \oplus \mathcal{P}_2(\tilde{m}) \oplus \alpha \oplus \beta,$$

with unknown α and β. Hence, a tag for $m\|\tilde{m}$ cannot be computed.

This issue can be solved by iterating the attack (finding a collision between t_i and t_j) several times until the attacker probabilistically hits the case with $\alpha = \beta$ as follows. For an n-bit to n-bit function, the number of multicollisions can be upper bounded by n. Hence, by iterating the entire attack procedure n times, the attacker can predict the correct tag with probability $1/n$. The attack can be improved slightly. When the attacker makes $2^{n/2}$ queries of $x_i \| \tilde{m}$ and $m \| \tilde{y}_j$, the attacker can make $2^{n/2} \cdot \sqrt{n}$ queries. This generates $n \cdot 2^n$ pairs of i, j, thus n pairs of $\hat{i}, \hat{j}$, which is sufficient for the attack. In the end, the complexity of the application of the generic attack is upper bounded by $O(\sqrt{n} \cdot 2^{n/2})$.

The average complexity is smaller than the upper bound. The range size of an n-bit to n-bit function is e^{-1} times smaller than the domain size, where e is the base of the natural logarithm. Hence, an output value should have e distinct preimages on average. In the end, the average complexity of the generic attack is $O(\sqrt{e} \cdot 2^{n/2})$, which is $O(2^{n/2})$.

Complexity for MergeMAC. In MergeMAC, n is 64. Hence, the attack complexity is about $\sqrt{64} \cdot 2^{32} \approx 2^{35}$. Given that the authors imply to limit the number of queries up to an appropriate level in the context of the Sweet32 attack, the generic universal forgery may not break the claimed security but shows the tightness of their bounding data complexity.

Remarks on Existential Forgery Attacks. One of the reviewers mentioned that a simple existential forgery with a birthday-bound complexity can be performed. The attack first fixes the first part of the message m to an arbitrary value, and make queries of $O(2^{n/2})$ distinct $\tilde{m}$. The collision of the tags, with a high probability, indicates the collision of the two PRF outputs for $\tilde{m}$ and $\tilde{m}'$. Then, for an arbitrary choice of the first part of the message m^*, $m^* \| \tilde{m}$ and $m^* \| \tilde{m}'$ lead to the same tag.

3.2   Universal Forgery with Very Low Data Complexity

In this section we present a universal forgery with a very low data complexity but with a higher offline computational cost than that of the generic attack.

Attack Overview. The idea is to exploit the fact that the MERGE function mixes the data very lightly. Namely, we present a preimage attack against the 3-round Chaskey with the feed-forward operation used in MergeMAC.

Recall that the core idea of the generic attack is to obtain some information on the input to the MERGE function by finding collisions of the tag. To reduce the data complexity, we avoid searching for a collision (with many queries), instead invert the MERGE function by spending offline computational cost. Note that this strategy can only be applied when the finalization function is public, hence the following attack shows another feature particular to MergeMAC.

Let $m \| \tilde{m}$ be a target. If the attacker obtains the value of $\mathcal{P}_1(m) \| \mathcal{P}_2(\tilde{m})$, the tag can be forged by processing MERGE function offline. We notice that

$\mathcal{P}_1(m)\|\mathcal{P}_2(\tilde{m})$ can be recovered by 3 queries and 3 executions of the preimage attack. Let x and $\tilde{y}$ be the former half and the latter half of an arbitrary chosen message. Then, the attacker queries three messages $x\|\tilde{m}$, $m\|\tilde{y}$ and $x\|\tilde{y}$ to obtain the corresponding tags t_1, t_2, and t_3 that are expressed as follows.

$$t_1 \leftarrow \pi(\mathcal{P}_1(x) \oplus \mathcal{P}_2(\tilde{m})) \oplus \mathcal{P}_1(x) \oplus \mathcal{P}_2(\tilde{m})$$
$$t_2 \leftarrow \pi(\mathcal{P}_1(m) \oplus \mathcal{P}_2(\tilde{y})) \oplus \mathcal{P}_1(m) \oplus \mathcal{P}_2(\tilde{y})$$
$$t_3 \leftarrow \pi(\mathcal{P}_1(x) \oplus \mathcal{P}_2(\tilde{y})) \oplus \mathcal{P}_1(x) \oplus \mathcal{P}_2(\tilde{y})$$

Suppose that for a given o, the attacker can execute a preimage attack to find i such that $o \leftarrow \pi(i) \oplus i$. Then, by finding preimages of t_1, t_2, and t_3, the attacker obtains $\mathcal{P}_1(x) \oplus \mathcal{P}_2(\tilde{m})$, $\mathcal{P}_1(m) \oplus \mathcal{P}_2(\tilde{y})$ and $\mathcal{P}_1(x) \oplus \mathcal{P}_2(\tilde{y})$. The sum of those 3 values equals $\mathcal{P}_1(m) \oplus \mathcal{P}_2(\tilde{m})$, hence the attacker can compute the tag offline.

Preimage attacks on cryptographic functions have been discussed deeply. We follow the framework of meet-in-the-middle preimage attacks [2,17]. Due to the construction, the attack framework is closer to the preimage attack against the block-cipher based compression functions first demonstrated against AES in the Davies-Meyer mode [16].

Meet-in-the-Middle Preimage Attacks. Meet-in-the-Middle (MitM) attack [11] was originally proposed to recover a key of a block cipher. When a ciphertext c is computed with two encryption algorithms E_1 and E_2 with independent keys k_1 and k_2, i.e. $c = E_{2,k_2} \circ E_{1,k_1}(p)$, k_1 and k_2 can be recovered with a complexity $\min\{|k_1|, |k_2|\}$ instead of $|k_1| + |k_2|$.

Sasaki [16] presented a framework to apply the MitM attack to $t = P(x) \oplus x$ for recovering unknown x for a given t, where P consists of an iteration of a round function $\mathcal{R}$ with imperfect diffusion. Suppose that $\mathcal{R}$ consists of r rounds, namely t is computed from x as

$$V_0 \leftarrow x, \qquad V_i \leftarrow \mathcal{R}(V_{i-1}) \text{ for } i = 1, 2, \ldots, r, \qquad t \leftarrow V_r \oplus V_0.$$

The splice-and-cut technique [2] allows the attacker to regard the first and the last rounds as consecutive rounds. Indeed, t is computed by $V_r \oplus V_0$. For any fixed t, computing V_0 (resp. V_r) immediately fixes V_r (resp. V_0).

The overview of the attack framework is illustrated in Fig. 4. The attacker first determines a starting round p and matching round q, such that the computation from V_{p-1} to V_q (forward computation) and the computation from V_{p-1} to V_0, $V_r = t \oplus V_0$, and from V_r to V_q (backward computation) can be independently performed. The results of the two computations are matched on V_q.

More precisely, each bit of the state V_{p-1} is classified into three groups:

B^{for}: all possible values are examined during the forward computation.
B^{back}: all possible values are examined during the backward computation.
B^{fix}: the value is fixed during the independent computations.

Suppose that the value of B^{fix} is fixed. The attacker, for each possible value of B^{for}, proceeds the forward computation without using the value of B^{back}.

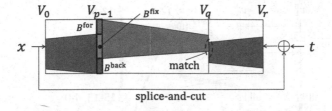

Fig. 4. Overview of meet-in-the-middle preimage attacks for $t = H(x) \oplus x$.

Algorithm 1. Meet-in-the-middle preimage attack for $t = P(x) \oplus x$

Require: $t, p, q, B^{\text{fix}}, B^{\text{for}}, B^{\text{back}}$
Ensure: x
 1: **for** all candidates of B^{fix} **do**
 2:    **for** all candidates of B^{for} **do**
 3:       Partially compute $V_i \leftarrow \mathcal{R}(V_{i-1})$ for $i = p, p+1, \cdots, q$, and store the result in a list L.
 4:    **end for**
 5:    **for** all candidates of B^{back} **do**
 6:       Partially compute $V_{i-1} \leftarrow \mathcal{R}^{-1}(V_i)$ for $i = p-1, p-2, \cdots, 1$.
 7:       Partially compute $V_r \leftarrow V_0 \oplus t$.
 8:       Partially compute $V_{i-1} \leftarrow \mathcal{R}^{-1}(V_i)$ for $i = r, r-1, \cdots, q+1$.
 9:       **if** the computed value exists in L **then**
10:          Set $v_{p-1} \leftarrow (B^{\text{fix}}, B^{\text{for}}, B^{\text{back}})$, and compute corresponding V_0 and V_r.
11:          **if** $V_0 \oplus V_r = T$ **then**
12:             **return** V_0.
13:          **end if**
14:       **end if**
15:    **end for**
16: **end for**

Because B^{back} is unknown, the forward computation cannot compute all bits of the state. However, when the diffusion of $\mathcal{R}$ is imperfect, the partial computation can be performed for a few rounds (until round q). Independently, the attacker computes the backward computation by examining all possible values of B^{back} without using the value of B^{for} (up to V_q). For a correct combination of $B^{\text{fix}}, B^{\text{for}}$, B^{back}, the partially computed values always match at V_q, and the correct value of V_{p-1} can be recovered efficiently. Finally, the MitM attack is iterated for the exhaustive guesses of B^{fix}. The algorithmic description is given by Algorithm 1.

Attacks on 3-Round Chaskey with Feed-Forward. As shown in Fig. 2, one round of π consists of two iterations of the half-round transformation. Hence, 3-round transformation of π is regarded as 6-round half-transformation of π. Let $(v_1^i, v_0^i, v_2^i, v_3^i)$ denote a 64-bit internal state which is an input to the ith half-transformation (or an output from the $(i-1)$th transformation), where

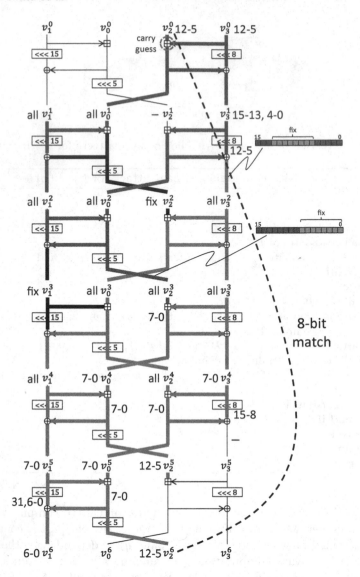

Fig. 5. Details of two independent computations for $\pi(x) \oplus x$. Numbers denote known bit positions in each independent computation.

$i = 0, 1, \ldots, 6$. We divide this transformation into two independent computations. Readers may refer to Fig. 5 for the illustration of the independent computations.

Choices of B^{for}, B^{back}, B^{fix}. In Fig. 4, the starting round is defined as an input state to some round. However, we can choose 64 bits of the state in different rounds as the starting position, as long as they fix the entire transformation. In our attack, we choose $(v_1^3, v_2^3, v_2^2, v_3^2)$ as a starting position. It is easy to see that all the possible internal state values can be simulated by exhaustively examining 2^{64} values of $(v_1^3, v_2^3, v_2^2, v_3^2)$. We then choose B^{for}, B^{back}, and B^{fix} as follows.

B^{for}: bit positions 0 to 4 and 13 to 15 of v_3^2 (total 8 bits)
B^{back}: bit positions 8 to 15 of v_2^3 (total 8 bits)
B^{fix}: v_1^3, v_2^2 and bit positions 5 to 12 of v_3^2 and bit positions 0 to 7 of v_2^3

The forward computation partially computes $(v_1^6, v_2^6, v_2^6, v_3^6) \oplus t$ and the backward computation partially computes $(v_1^0, v_2^0, v_2^0, v_3^0)$. We match the results of two independent computations in 8 bits.

Forward Computation. All bits of v_1^3, v_2^2 and v_2^3 are known, while bit positions 8 to 15 of v_3^2 are unknown. When we compute $v_0^4 \leftarrow v_2^3 \boxplus v_3^3$, we only can compute the 8 LSBs of v_0^4. Similarly, $v_3^4 \leftarrow v_0^4 \oplus (v_3^3 \lll 8)$ can be computed only in 8 LSBs. With the same analysis, as shown in Fig. 5, the forward computation can compute 8 bits of v_2^6 in bit positions 5 to 12, and thus the corresponding 8 bits after xoring the tag value. Note that all partial computations of the modular addition in the forward computation are done from the LSBs, thus we do not need to consider the unknown carry effect.

Backward Computation. All bits of v_1^3, v_2^2 and v_2^3 are known, while bit positions 0 to 4 and 13 to 15 of v_3^2 are unknown. All bits of v_0^1 can be computed while we can compute only 8 bits (bit positions 0 to 4 and 13 to 15) of $v_3^1 \leftarrow (v_2^2 \oplus v_0^2) \ggg 8$. This allows us to compute only 8 bits (bit positions 5 to 12) of $v_3^0 \leftarrow (v_0^1 \oplus v_3^1) \ggg 8$. Finally, we compute $v_2^0 \leftarrow v_0^1 \boxminus v_3^0$ in bit positions 5 to 12, where $\boxminus$ is a modular subtraction. We do not know the carry from bit position 4 to 5. Hence, we guess the carry and compute v_2^0 in both cases. Thus, we have 2^9 results of the backward computation.

Complexity Evaluation. For each fixed choice of B^{fix}, we obtain 2^8 and 2^9 results from two computations. They can match in 8 bits. Correct $B^{\text{for}}, B^{\text{back}}, B^{\text{fix}}$ always match, thus we obtain $(2^8 \cdot 2^9)/2^8 = 2^9$ candidates, which need to be tested further. The procedure is iterated for exhaustive guesses of B^{fix}. Hence, the complexity to find a preimage is $2^{48} \cdot 2^9 = 2^{57}$ computations of π. The attack requires 2^8 amount of memory to store the results of the forward computation.

Summary of Attacks. The attack requires 3 queries and 3 executions of the preimage attack. Hence, the data, time and memory complexities are 3, $2^{58.6} (\approx 3 \times 2^{57})$ and 2^8, respectively.

Analysis for Non-injective Merge Function. Let us finally discuss the analysis for non-injective MERGE function. As discussed before, each target has e preimages on average. The MitM preimage attack exhaustively examines all internal state values (in an efficient way), hence it collects all of e preimages with 1 execution. When we sum up preimages of t_1, t_2 and t_3, we have e^3 combinations on average. This can be regarded that the success probability of our attack is

$e^{-3} \approx 0.0498$. We can also store those e^3 values as candidates, and iterate the attack for another choice of x and $\tilde{y}$ to obtain another e^3 candidates. The correct internal state is included in both e^3 pools of candidates. In this case, the data and time complexities become 6 and $2^{59.6}$, respectively.

Discussion of the Attack. MergeMAC is a provably secure MAC under the assumption that $\mathcal{P}_1$ and $\mathcal{P}_2$ are secure PRFs and the MERGE function satisfies Random Input Indistinguishability (RII). The preimage attack on 3-round Chaskey with feed-forward presented in this section shows that, using the terminology of [1], there exists a (t, q, ϵ)-RII-adversary, where $t = 3 \times 2^{57}$, $q = 2$, and ϵ is close to 1. As a consequence, as far as we see, our attack contradicts the overall security claim on MergeMAC by the designers, but it does *not* contradict the provable security claim. More precisely, the provable security claim excludes the possibility of forgery attacks whose success probability is larger than about ϵ, i.e., the attack with a high success probability itself is not excluded once ϵ turns out to be large.

4   Analysis on MergeMAC^{OW}

In this section, the attack against MergeMAC is extended to MergeMAC^{OW}, in which the MERGE function of MergeMAC (3-round-Chaskey with feed-forward) is replaced with a one-way function $\mathcal{H}$.

The generic universal forgery discussed in Sect. 3.1 still works even if $\mathcal{H}$ is invertible. Our approach here is to exploit the feature that $\mathcal{H}$ is public, and thus can be evaluated offline. We preprocess $\mathcal{H}$ for various inputs and make a look-up table so that the attacker can look up the input x efficiently from the observed $\mathcal{H}(x)$. Namely, a precomputation phase is introduced to trade the data complexity in the online phase by the offline computational cost.

4.1   Definition of MergeMAC^{OW}

Let $\mathcal{P}_1, \mathcal{P}_2$ be two PRFs and $\mathcal{H}$ be a public one-way function. For a given message $m \| \tilde{m}$, MergeMAC^{OW} computes a tag t as follows.

$$\rho \leftarrow \mathcal{P}_1(m), \qquad \tilde{\rho} \leftarrow \mathcal{P}_2(\tilde{m}), \qquad t \leftarrow \mathcal{H}(\rho \oplus \tilde{\rho}).$$

4.2   Tradeoff Between Time and Data

As in Sect. 3, we first explain the attack by assuming that $\mathcal{H}$ is injective. The tradeoff is parameterized by the offline computational cost ℓ, where $\ell < n$. The intuition of this attack is as follows. We first evaluate $\mathcal{H}$ for 2^ℓ inputs offline to generate a *dictionary* to be looked up, i.e. the input is looked up from the output (instead of applying preimage attack in Sect. 3). Each query is included in the lookup table with probability $2^{-(n-\ell)}$ and as discussed in Sect. 3) we need to invert 3 tags, i.e. we need to satisfy an event with probability of $2^{-3(n-\ell)}$.

Hence, we make $2^{3(n-\ell)/2}$ distinct queries for each of the first half and the last half of the input. The detailed attack procedure is described below.

Offline Phase

1. For 2^ℓ distinct z, compute $\mathcal{H}(z)$ and store $(z, \mathcal{H}(z))$ in a list L_p.

Online Phase

2. For distinct x_i, where $i = 1, 2, \ldots, 2^{3(n-\ell)/2}$, query $x_i \| \tilde{m}$ to obtain the tag t_x. If t_x is included in L_p, store x_i and the corresponding $\mathcal{P}_1(x_i) \oplus \mathcal{P}_2(\tilde{m})$ in a list L_x.
3. For distinct $\tilde{y}_j$, where $j = 1, 2, \ldots, 2^{3(n-\ell)/2}$, query $m \| \tilde{y}_j$ to obtain the tag t_y. If t_y is included in L_p, store $\tilde{y}_j$ and the corresponding $\mathcal{P}_1(m) \oplus \mathcal{P}_2(\tilde{y}_j)$ in a list L_y.
4. For all combinations of x_i and $\tilde{y}_j$ in L_x and L_y, query $x_i \| \tilde{y}_j$ to obtain the corresponding tag t' until t' is included in L_p and thus the attacker obtains the value of $\mathcal{P}_1(x_i) \oplus \mathcal{P}_2(\tilde{y}_j)$.
5. Compute $\mathcal{P}_1(m) \oplus \mathcal{P}_2(\tilde{m})$ by

$$\big(\mathcal{P}_1(x_i) \oplus \mathcal{P}_2(\tilde{m})\big) \oplus \big(\mathcal{P}_1(m_1) \oplus \mathcal{P}_2(\tilde{y}_j)\big) \oplus \big(\mathcal{P}_1(x_i) \oplus \mathcal{P}_2(\tilde{y}_j)\big).$$

Compute $t = \mathcal{H}\big(\mathcal{P}_1(m) \oplus \mathcal{P}_2(\tilde{m})\big)$, and output t as a tag for $m \| \tilde{m}$.

Evaluation and Tradeoff

- In the offline phase (Step 1), time and memory complexities are 2^ℓ.
- In Step 2, $2^{3(n-\ell)/2}$ queries are made. Each tag is included in L_p with probability $2^{n-\ell}$, thus $2^{(n-\ell)/2}$ x_i are stored in L_x.
- In Step 3, $2^{3(n-\ell)/2}$ queries are made and $2^{(n-\ell)/2}$ $\tilde{y}_j$ are stored in L_y.
- In Step 4, $2^{(n-\ell)}$ queries are made and there exists one pair of $(x_i, \tilde{y}_j)$ such that t' is included in L_p.

Let T_{off}, D, and N be offline computational cost (2^ℓ), data complexity $(2^{3(n-\ell)/2})$, and a cardinality of the tag space (2^n), respectively. The tradeoff curve is represented as

$$T_{\text{off}}^{3/2} \cdot D = N^{3/2}. \tag{3}$$

Setting $T_{\text{off}} > 2^{2n/3}$ leads to $D < 2^{n/2}$, i.e. the number of online queries can be reduced compared to the generic attack in Sect. 3.1.

The attack requires to store 2^ℓ, $2^{n-\ell}$ and $2^{n-\ell}$ values for L_p, L_x and L_y, respectively. When $T_{\text{off}} > 2^{2n/3}$, $M = T_{\text{off}}$. The online computational complexity, T_{on}, is only for processing queried data, thus equals D. As long as $T_{\text{off}} > 2^{2n/3}$, T_{on} is negligible.

Example. MergeMAC supposes that $N = 2^{64}$. By spending $T_{\text{off}} = 2^{48}$ computational cost and memory amount, the number of online queries is reduced to $D = 2^{24}$ with online computational cost $T_{\text{on}} = 2^{24}$, which is more practical than the general attack with $D = 2^{32}$ queries.

Remarks. The dedicated low data complexity attack against MergeMAC in Sect. 3.2 succeeds with $T_{off} = 2^{58.6}$ and $D = 3$. This is more efficient than the generic attack against MergeMAC^{OW}. As long as it is available, using the preimage attack against $\mathcal{H}$ is more efficient.

5   Multiple Forgeries

In this section, we consider a problem of producing multiple forgeries by making as small number of queries as possible. This is known as the security notion called *MAC reforgeability* [8], where the adversary utilizes the computational complexity for the first forgery to reduce the complexity for the subsequent forgeries. This notion was also studied in the context of authenticated encryption [12].

5.1   Existential Forgery

We first consider the existential forgery, where we focus on producing as many forgeries as possible, but we do not care about the content of forged messages. From the results of Sect. 3.2, we see that given the tags of $(m_1, \tilde{m}_1)$, $(m_1, \tilde{m}_2)$, and $(m_2, \tilde{m}_1)$, we obtain the tag of $(m_2, \tilde{m}_2)$. In other words, we make 3 queries to output one forgery, and we need 3 preimage attacks. If we define the rate r as the number of queries needed to produce one forgery, i.e.,

$$r = \frac{\#\text{queries}}{\#\text{forgeries}},$$

then we have $r = 3$. We note that for an ideally secure MAC, if the rate to produce one forgery is r, then the rate remains the same for multiple forgeries.

Now we call it the basic attack, which can be represented by using the first matrix in Fig. 6: The matrix shows that we make queries $(m_i, \tilde{m}_j)$ for $(i, j) = (1, 1), (1, 2), (2, 1)$ that are shown with Q, and we obtain the forgery for $(i, j) = (2, 2)$ that is shown with X.

We show that, for $q \geq 2$, it is possible to output $(q - 1)^2$ forgeries by making $2q - 1$ queries. We first present a small example with $q = 3$. Consider the case where we make 5 queries represented by the second matrix in Fig. 6. Observe that we obtain the tag for $(i, j) = (2, 2)$ from the submatrix with $i \in \{1, 2\}$ and $j \in \{1, 2\}$, and once this is obtained, we obtain the tag for $(i, j) = (2, 3)$ from the submatrix with $i \in \{1, 2\}$ and $j \in \{2, 3\}$. At this point, we have the third matrix in Fig. 6: It is easy to see that we also obtain the tags for $(i, j) = (3, 2)$ and $(3, 3)$ from the submatrix with $i \in \{2, 3\}$ and $j \in \{1, 2\}$, and then from that with $i \in \{2, 3\}$ and $j \in \{2, 3\}$. In this case, we need to make 5 queries and 5 executions of the preimage attack to produce 4 forgeries. This gives the rate $r = 5/4 = 1.25$, which is lower than the case of the basic attack.

We now generalize this to arbitrarily $q \geq 2$. We start with the fourth matrix in Fig. 6: For each $i = 2, 3, \ldots, q$, we see that we can successively obtain the tag

$i \backslash j$	1	2
1	Q	Q
2	Q	X

$i \backslash j$	1	2	3
1	Q	Q	Q
2	Q		
3	Q		

$i \backslash j$	1	2	3
1	Q	Q	Q
2	Q	X	X
3	Q		

$i \backslash j$	1	2	$\cdots$	q
1	Q	Q	$\cdots$	Q
2	Q			
$\vdots$	$\vdots$			
q	Q			

Fig. 6. 1st (leftmost): Messages for basic attack. 2nd: 5 queries for the attack with $q = 3$. 3rd: middle status of the attack with $q = 3$ after forging 2 messages. 4th (rightmost): $(2q - 1)$ queries for the attack with arbitrary q.

for (i, j) with $j = 2, 3, \ldots, q$. We present the algorithmic description to show the details of this attack in Algorithm 2.

Algorithm 2. Producing $(q - 1)^2$ forgeries with $2q - 1$ queries

---

Require: q, the oracle $\mathcal{O}$ that computes the tag
1: fix $m_1, \ldots, m_q$ and $\tilde{m}_1, \ldots, \tilde{m}_q$, where m_i's are distinct and $\tilde{m}_j$'s are distinct.
2: for $i = 1, \ldots, q$, obtain the tag of $(m_i, \tilde{m}_1)$ by making queries to $\mathcal{O}$.
3: for $j = 2, \ldots, q$, obtain the tag of $(m_1, \tilde{m}_j)$ by making queries to $\mathcal{O}$.
4: **for** $i = 2, \ldots, q$ **do**
5:     **for** $j = 2, \ldots, q$ **do**
6:         compute the tag for $(m_i, \tilde{m}_j)$ from the tags of $(m_{i-1}, \tilde{m}_{j-1})$, $(m_{i-1}, \tilde{m}_j)$, and $(m_i, \tilde{m}_{j-1})$.
7:     **end for**
8: **end for**

Observe that we make $2q - 1$ queries and execute $2q - 1$ preimage attacks to obtain $(q - 1)^2$ forgeries, and this gives the rate $r = (2q - 1)/(q - 1)^2$.

It is interesting to note that for $q \geq 4$, the rate becomes smaller than 1, and thus we obtain more forgeries than the number of queries. However, we remark that when q is large, the time complexity exceeds 2^{64} as the time complexity of one preimage attack is 2^{57}.

5.2 Tightness of Existential Forgery

In this section, we consider a problem of the tightness on the rate in the existential forgery. More precisely, we consider the following problem setting:

- Suppose we are given q half messages $m_1, m_2, \ldots, m_q$ and q half messages $\tilde{m}_1, \tilde{m}_2, \ldots, \tilde{m}_q$.
- To obtain tags of all q^2 messages of the form $(m_i, \tilde{m}_j)$, where $i, j \in \{1, 2, \ldots, q\}$, how many queries are necessary?

We show that $2q - 1$ queries are necessary, showing the tightness of the attack presented in the previous section.

For $i, j \in \{1, \ldots, q\}$, let $t_{i,j}$ be the tag of $(m_i, \tilde{m}_j)$, and $s_{i,j}$ be the preimage of $t_{i,j}$, i.e., we let

$$\begin{cases} s_{i,j} \leftarrow \rho_i \oplus \tilde{\rho}_j, \\ t_{i,j} \leftarrow \pi(s_{i,j}) \oplus s_{i,j}, \end{cases}$$

where $\rho_i \leftarrow \mathcal{P}_1(m_i)$ and $\tilde{\rho}_j \leftarrow \mathcal{P}_2(\tilde{m}_j)$.

Now we observe that the relationship, $s_{i,j} \leftarrow \rho_i \oplus \tilde{\rho}_j$ for $i, j \in \{1, \ldots, q\}$, can be represented by using a binary $q^2 \times 2q$ matrix M as follows:

$$M \cdot \rho = s, \tag{4}$$

where ρ is a column vector of length $2q$ and s is a column vector of length q^2, and they are defined as

$$\begin{cases} \rho = [\rho_1, \ldots, \rho_q, \tilde{\rho}_1, \ldots, \tilde{\rho}_q]^T, \\ s = [s_{1,1}, \ldots, s_{1,q}, \ldots, s_{q,1}, \ldots, s_{q,q}]^T. \end{cases}$$

For instance when $q = 3$, Eq. (4) is

$$\begin{bmatrix} 1 & 0 & 0 & 1 & 0 & 0 \\ 1 & 0 & 0 & 0 & 1 & 0 \\ 1 & 0 & 0 & 0 & 0 & 1 \\ 0 & 1 & 0 & 1 & 0 & 0 \\ 0 & 1 & 0 & 0 & 1 & 0 \\ 0 & 1 & 0 & 0 & 0 & 1 \\ 0 & 0 & 1 & 1 & 0 & 0 \\ 0 & 0 & 1 & 0 & 1 & 0 \\ 0 & 0 & 1 & 0 & 0 & 1 \end{bmatrix} \cdot \begin{bmatrix} \rho_1 \\ \rho_2 \\ \rho_3 \\ \tilde{\rho}_1 \\ \tilde{\rho}_2 \\ \tilde{\rho}_3 \end{bmatrix} = \begin{bmatrix} s_{1,1} \\ s_{1,2} \\ s_{1,3} \\ s_{2,1} \\ s_{2,2} \\ s_{2,3} \\ s_{3,1} \\ s_{3,2} \\ s_{3,3} \end{bmatrix}.$$

Now the tightness problem is equivalent to prove the minimum number of $s_{i,j}$ that fully determines the linear system of Eq. (4) having q^2 equations and $2q$ variables. From its form, it is easy to see that the rank of the matrix M is $2q - 1$. As a consequence, we need at least $2q - 1$ values of $s_{i,j}$ to determine the system, and hence we need to make at least $2q - 1$ queries.

We remark that the tightness is obtained with respect to the problem setting mentioned as above, and there are cases that are not covered. We leave the tightness of a general case as an open question.

5.3   Universal Forgery

We next consider the universal forgery, where a list of messages to be forged is given as a challenge. Suppose that $(m_1, \tilde{m}_1), \ldots, (m_q, \tilde{m}_q)$ are the challenge messages. For simplicity, we assume that m_i's are all distinct, and $\tilde{m}_i$'s are all distinct.

We illustrate the case $q = 6$. Our goal is to output the tags shown with X in the left matrix given in Fig. 7. For this, we make queries represented by the middle matrix given in Fig. 7. At this point, we cannot obtain any of the

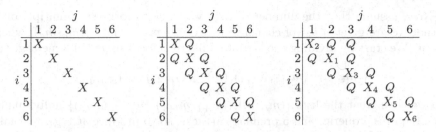

Fig. 7. Left: Messages to be forged given as a challenge. Middle: $2q-1$ queries we make for the attack. Right: One more query is sufficient to compute q tags for the challenge.

tags of the targets. However, observe that one more appropriate query allows us to obtain the entire q tags of the targets. For instance if we make a query $(m_1, \tilde{m}_3)$, then we obtain the right matrix in Fig. 7, and we see that it is possible to compute 6 tags with the order of $X_1, \ldots, X_6$.

This can be generalized to arbitrary q in an obvious way, and for completeness, we present the algorithmic description of the attack in Algorithm 3.

Algorithm 3. Producing q universal forgeries with $2q - 1$ queries

---

Require: $(m_1, \tilde{m}_1), \ldots, (m_q, \tilde{m}_q)$, the oracle $\mathcal{O}$ that computes the tag
 1: for $i = 1, \ldots, q-1$, obtain the tags of $(m_i, \tilde{m}_{i+1})$ and $(m_{i+1}, \tilde{m}_i)$ by making queries to $\mathcal{O}$.
 2: obtain the tag of $(m_1, \tilde{m}_3)$ by making a query to $\mathcal{O}$.
 3: compute the tag for $(m_2, \tilde{m}_2)$ from the tags of $(m_1, \tilde{m}_2)$, $(m_1, \tilde{m}_3)$, and $(m_2, \tilde{m}_3)$.
 4: compute the tag for $(m_1, \tilde{m}_1)$ from the tags of $(m_1, \tilde{m}_2)$, $(m_2, \tilde{m}_1)$, and $(m_2, \tilde{m}_2)$.
 5: for $i = 3, \ldots, q$ do
 6:     compute the tag for $(m_i, \tilde{m}_i)$ from the tags of $(m_{i-1}, \tilde{m}_{i-1})$, $(m_{i-1}, \tilde{m}_i)$, and $(m_i, \tilde{m}_{i-1})$.
 7: **end for**

With this attack, we make $2q - 1$ queries and it uses executions of $2q - 1$ preimage attack to obtain q forgeries, which gives the rate $r = (2q - 1)/q \approx 2$.

5.4 Universal Forgery with Better Rate

We show below that it is possible to arrange the queries differently in order to improve the previous rate and obtain one that is close to $5/3$. First, we remark that 3 tags can be forged by making 5 queries (and 5 preimage attacks), as can be seen from the following matrix:

$$
\begin{array}{c|ccc}
 & \multicolumn{3}{c}{j} \\
 & 1 & 2 & 3 \\
\hline
1 & X & Q & Q \\
i\;2 & Q & X & Q \\
3 & & Q & X \\
\end{array}
$$

Now, assume that the number of tags we want to forge is a multiple of 3, so that we are given a list of challenge messages $(m_1, \tilde{m}_1), \ldots, (m_q, \tilde{m}_q)$, where $q = 3\ell$. We start by dividing the list into ℓ lists, each consisting of 3 messages as

$$\{(m_i, \tilde{m}_i), (m_{i+1}, \tilde{m}_{i+1}), (m_{i+2}, \tilde{m}_{i+2})\}_{i=1,4,7,\ldots,q-2}$$

and we then treat the lists $\{(m_i, \tilde{m}_i), (m_{i+1}, \tilde{m}_{i+1}), (m_{i+2}, \tilde{m}_{i+2})\}$ individually. Each requires 5 queries and 5 preimage attacks, so to produce 3ℓ tags, we make 5ℓ queries and execute 5ℓ times the preimage attack, which gives a rate of $r = 5\ell/3\ell \approx 1.67$.

In case the number of challenges is not a multiple of 3 and is equal to $q = 3\ell + r$ with $0 < r < 3$, we proceed as before and forge each of the ℓ lists of 3 challenges with 5 queries and 5 preimage attacks. The remaining r tags can be forged by making 2 additional queries for each of them, as depicted on the following matrix:

		$\cdots$	$3\ell-2$	$3\ell-1$	3ℓ	$3\ell+1$	$3\ell+2$
	$\cdots$	$\cdots$					
	$3\ell-2$		X	Q	Q		
	$3\ell-1$		Q	X	Q		
i	3ℓ			Q	X	Q	
	$3\ell+1$				Q	X	Q
	$3\ell+2$					Q	X

We formalize this as follows. Assume we forged the first 3ℓ challenges with the previous technique. If $r = 1$, we query the tags corresponding to $(m_{3\ell+1}, \tilde{m}_{3\ell})$ together with $(m_{3\ell}, \tilde{m}_{3\ell+1})$. We combine them with the previously-forged $(m_{3\ell}, \tilde{m}_{3\ell})$ and we are able to forge $(m_{3\ell+1}, \tilde{m}_{3\ell+1})$. If $r = 2$ we also query the tags corresponding to $(m_{3\ell+2}, \tilde{m}_{3\ell+1})$ and to $(m_{3\ell+1}, \tilde{m}_{3\ell+2})$, and combine them with $(m_{3\ell+1}, \tilde{m}_{3\ell+1})$ to forge $(m_{3\ell+2}, \tilde{m}_{3\ell+2})$.

To sum up, $q = 3\ell + r$ tags (with $0 \leq r < 3$) can be forged by making $5\ell + 2r$ queries and the same number of preimage attacks, leading to a rate equal to $r = (5\ell + 2r)/(3\ell + r)$.

Note that we do not know the tightness of the rate, which is left as an open question.

6 Concluding Remarks

In this paper we presented several attacks and observations on MergeMAC. They are build around pre-image attacks on the merge functions that are possible as the merge function is public (generically) and not-one way (in the specific instance given).

We also studied the reforgeability of MergeMAC, with the result that the number of forgeries we can produce increases quadratically with the number of queries. For example, it is possible to produce roughly 2^{64} forgeries using

2^{33} forgeries and 2^{64} computation, so the cost per forgery becomes as small as legitimately computing one tag.

Finally, we like to mention interesting topics for future work. First, as stated above, we are not able to prove the tightness of the rate in the case of universal forgeries. We preformed a limited computer search for the optimal solution and were able to confirm that no solution with a better rate exist for up to 6 challenges. In our opinion, proving the optimality, or finding better strategies, is an interesting (but challenging) open question. As a second topic, generalizations of MergeMAC could be investigated, where instead of splitting the initial message into two parts, the message is split into t parts that are processed by t PRFs. The input to the merge function than becomes the xor of the t outputs of the PRFs. It would be interesting to see how our analysis could be adopted to this case.

Acknowledgments. The authors would like to thank organizers of Japan Days 2018 to provide us with an opportunity of the collaboration. We also would like to thank the anonymous reviewers of CT-RSA 2019 for helpful comments.

References

1. Ankele, R., Böhl, F., Friedberger, S.: MERGEMAC: a MAC for authentication with strict time constraints and limited bandwidth. In: Preneel, B., Vercauteren, F. (eds.) ACNS 2018. LNCS, vol. 10892, pp. 381–399. Springer, Cham (2018). https://doi.org/10.1007/978-3-319-93387-0_20
2. Aoki, K., Sasaki, Y.: Preimage attacks on one-block MD4, 63-step MD5 and more. In: Avanzi, R.M., Keliher, L., Sica, F. (eds.) SAC 2008. LNCS, vol. 5381, pp. 103–119. Springer, Heidelberg (2009). https://doi.org/10.1007/978-3-642-04159-4_7
3. Aumasson, J.-P., Bernstein, D.J.: SipHash: a fast short-input PRF. In: Galbraith, S., Nandi, M. (eds.) INDOCRYPT 2012. LNCS, vol. 7668, pp. 489–508. Springer, Heidelberg (2012). https://doi.org/10.1007/978-3-642-34931-7_28
4. Beaulieu, R., Shors, D., Smith, J., Treatman-Clark, S., Weeks, B., Wingers, L.: The SIMON and SPECK Families of Lightweight Block Ciphers. IACR Cryptology ePrint Archive 2013, 404 (2013)
5. Beierle, C., et al.: The SKINNY family of block ciphers and its low-latency variant MANTIS. In: Robshaw, M., Katz, J. (eds.) CRYPTO 2016, Part II. LNCS, vol. 9815, pp. 123–153. Springer, Heidelberg (2016). https://doi.org/10.1007/978-3-662-53008-5_5
6. Bhargavan, K., Leurent, G.: On the practical (in-)security of 64-bit block ciphers: collision attacks on HTTP over TLS and OpenVPN. In: Proceedings of the 2016 ACM SIGSAC Conference on Computer and Communications Security, Vienna, Austria, 24–28 October 2016, pp. 456–467 (2016)
7. Biryukov, A., Perrin, L.: State of the Art in Lightweight Symmetric Cryptography. IACR Cryptology ePrint Archive 2017, 511 (2017)
8. Black, J., Cochran, M.: MAC reforgeability. In: Dunkelman, O. (ed.) FSE 2009. LNCS, vol. 5665, pp. 345–362. Springer, Heidelberg (2009). https://doi.org/10.1007/978-3-642-03317-9_21
9. Bogdanov, A., et al.: PRESENT: an ultra-lightweight block cipher. In: Paillier, P., Verbauwhede, I. (eds.) CHES 2007. LNCS, vol. 4727, pp. 450–466. Springer, Heidelberg (2007). https://doi.org/10.1007/978-3-540-74735-2_31

10. Borghoff, J., et al.: PRINCE – a low-latency block cipher for pervasive computing applications. In: Wang, X., Sako, K. (eds.) ASIACRYPT 2012. LNCS, vol. 7658, pp. 208–225. Springer, Heidelberg (2012). https://doi.org/10.1007/978-3-642-34961-4_14

11. Diffie, W., Hellman, M.E.: Special feature exhaustive cryptanalysis of the NBS data encryption standard. IEEE Comput, **10**(6), 74–84 (1977)

12. Forler, C., List, E., Lucks, S., Wenzel, J.: Reforgeability of authenticated encryption schemes. In: Pieprzyk, J., Suriadi, S. (eds.) ACISP 2017, Part II. LNCS, vol. 10343, pp. 19–37. Springer, Cham (2017). https://doi.org/10.1007/978-3-319-59870-3_2

13. Jia, K., Wang, X., Yuan, Z., Xu, G.: Distinguishing and second-preimage attacks on CBC-like MACs. In: Garay, J.A., Miyaji, A., Otsuka, A. (eds.) CANS 2009. LNCS, vol. 5888, pp. 349–361. Springer, Heidelberg (2009). https://doi.org/10.1007/978-3-642-10433-6_23

14. Luykx, A., Preneel, B., Tischhauser, E., Yasuda, K.: A MAC mode for lightweight block ciphers. In: Peyrin, T. (ed.) FSE 2016. LNCS, vol. 9783, pp. 43–59. Springer, Heidelberg (2016). https://doi.org/10.1007/978-3-662-52993-5_3

15. Mouha, N., Mennink, B., Van Herrewege, A., Watanabe, D., Preneel, B., Verbauwhede, I.: Chaskey: an efficient MAC algorithm for 32-bit microcontrollers. In: Joux, A., Youssef, A. (eds.) SAC 2014. LNCS, vol. 8781, pp. 306–323. Springer, Cham (2014). https://doi.org/10.1007/978-3-319-13051-4_19

16. Sasaki, Y.: Meet-in-the-middle preimage attacks on AES hashing modes and an application to whirlpool. In: Joux, A. (ed.) FSE 2011. LNCS, vol. 6733, pp. 378–396. Springer, Heidelberg (2011). https://doi.org/10.1007/978-3-642-21702-9_22

17. Sasaki, Y., Aoki, K.: Finding preimages in full MD5 faster than exhaustive search. In: Joux, A. (ed.) EUROCRYPT 2009. LNCS, vol. 5479, pp. 134–152. Springer, Heidelberg (2009). https://doi.org/10.1007/978-3-642-01001-9_8

18. Shirai, T., Shibutani, K., Akishita, T., Moriai, S., Iwata, T.: The 128-bit blockcipher CLEFIA (extended abstract). In: Biryukov, A. (ed.) FSE 2007. LNCS, vol. 4593, pp. 181–195. Springer, Heidelberg (2007). https://doi.org/10.1007/978-3-540-74619-5_12

Linking Stam's Bounds with Generalized Truncation

Bart Mennink[✉]

Digital Security Group, Radboud University, Nijmegen, The Netherlands
b.mennink@cs.ru.nl

Abstract. One of the most prominent PRP-to-PRF designs is truncation, a method that found renewed interest with the GCM-SIV authenticated encryption scheme. A long line of research (from 1998 to 2018)
shows that truncating an n-bit random permutation to m bits achieves
tight $n - m/2$ security. However, it appeared that the result was a direct
consequence of a statistical result of Stam from 1978. In this work, we
aim to gain better understanding in the possibilities and impossibilities
of truncation. We take a closer look at the ancient result, observe that it
is much more general, and link it with a generalized truncation function
that uses an arbitrary post-processing function after the evaluation of the
permutation. The main conclusion is that generalized truncation with
any balanced post-processing achieves the same security bound as plain
truncation. For unbalanced post-processing, security degrades gradually
with the amount of unbalancedness. The results in particular exhibit a
use of the Kullback-Leibler divergence for cryptographic indistinguishability proofs, without resorting to the recently popularized chi-squared
method.

Keywords: Truncation · Generalization · PRF · Stam's bounds

1 Introduction

The dominant building block for symmetric cryptographic modes is a pseudorandom permutation (PRP), such as AES [22]. However, for many such modes, most
notably stream-based (authenticated) ciphers [24,28,39] and message authentication codes [5,11,16,49], security is determined by the level at which the
underlying primitive behaves like a *random function* rather than a *random permutation*. Stated differently, these modes benefit from being instantiated with
a pseudorandom function (PRF) instead of a PRP. Yet, with an extreme abun-
dance in PRP candidates [1–4,13,14,22] (to name a few), and only very few
dedicated PRFs [10,41], people have resorted to generic methods of transforming a PRP into a PRF.

The well-known PRP-PRF switch [7,9,17,30,31] shows that an n-bit PRP
behaves as a PRF up to approximately $2^{n/2}$ evaluations. This "birthday bound"
could be inadequate for lightweight block ciphers, and various "beyond birthday bound" modes, schemes that achieve security beyond $2^{n/2}$ evaluations,

M. Matsui (Ed.): CT-RSA 2019, LNCS 11405, pp. 313–329, 2019.
https://doi.org/10.1007/978-3-030-12612-4_16

have appeared. These include the xor of permutations [6,8,18,23,38,42,44–46], EDM [19,23,40], EDMD [40], and truncation [6,12,25–27,30,47]. We refer to Mennink and Neves [40,41] for an extensive discussion of the four variants. In this work, we focus on truncation.

1.1 History of Truncation

Let $n, m \in \mathbb{N}$ be such that $m \leq n$, and let p be an n-bit PRP. Truncation is defined as simply returning the m leftmost bits of p:

$$\mathsf{Trunc}^p(x) = \mathsf{left}_m(p(x)). \tag{1}$$

Hall et al. [30], introduced the truncation construction, and demonstrated security up to around $2^{n-m/2}$ evaluations, but not for the entire parameter spectrum. Bellare and Impagliazzo [6] gave an improved analysis that demonstrates security for a broader selection of n and m. Gilboa and Gueron [25] resolved the remaining gaps by proving security up to $2^{n-m/2}$ evaluations for any choice of n and m. It turned out, however, that the problem was already solved in 1978 by Stam [47], and that Stam's bound is stronger than the bounds of [6,25,30] altogether. Bhattacharya and Nandi [12] transformed Stam's analysis to the chi-squared method [23], deriving an identical bound. We elaborate on this upper bound in Sect. 4.1. Gilboa et al. [27] presented a detailed comparison of the bounds of Hall et al. [30], Bellare and Impagliazzo [6], Gilboa and Gueron [25], and Stam [47].

With respect to insecurity, Hall et al. [30] also argued tightness of their bound by sketching a distinguisher. Gilboa and Gueron [26] presented a formal derivation of a lower bound, for various choices of n, m, and the number of evaluations. They showed that the best distinguisher's success probability is close to 1 for around $2^{n-m/2}$ evaluations. See Sect. 4.1 for the lower bound.

The truncated permutation construction found application as key derivation function in GCM-SIV [28,29,37], although its use is disputed [15,32].

1.2 Stam's Bounds

Stam's 1978 bound [47] is more general than suggested in Sect. 1.1. Intuitively (a formal treatment of Stam's bounds is given in Sect. 3), it covers the idea of 2^n possible outcomes being grouped into 2^m colors (the number of occurrences per color not necessarily equal) and measures the distance between sampling with or without replacement, where the observer learns the color of every sample. In a later publication in 1986, Stam [48] generalized this result to the case where the number of colors and the grouping of the outcomes into the colors differs per sample.

The analysis of Stam is based on the Kullback-Leibler divergence $KL(X;Y)$ [36] (see Sect. 2.1 for the details), and Pinsker's inequality [21,34,35] stating that

$$\Delta(X, Y) \leq \left(\frac{1}{2} KL(X; Y)\right)^{1/2}, \tag{2}$$

where $\Delta(X, Y)$ denotes the statistical distance between X and Y. The exact same statistical tools were used in the chi-squared method of Dai et al. [23]. However, Dai et al. make an additional step, namely that the Kullback-Leibler divergence $KL(X; Y)$ is at most the chi-squared divergence $\chi^2(X; Y)$ (see, again, Sect. 2.1 for the details). In this work, we rely on Stam's results and perform analysis at the level of the Kullback-Leibler divergence.

1.3 Generalized Truncation

The goal of this work is to fully understand the implication of Stam's bounds to truncation. To do so, we describe a generalized truncation function GTrunc in Sect. 4. The function generalizes simple truncation by the evaluation of a post-processing function post : $\{0, 1\}^n \times \{0, 1\}^n \to \{0, 1\}^m$ after permutation:

$$\mathsf{GTrunc}^p(x) = \mathsf{post}(x, p(x)). \tag{3}$$

The function is depicted in Fig. 1. It covers plain truncation of (1) by taking the post-processing function that ignores its first input and evaluates left_m on its second input.

However, GTrunc is much more general than Trunc. Most importantly, it feed-forwards its input x to the post-processing function post. This, on the one hand, gives an adversary more power, but on the other hand, frustrates statistical analysis as the output function is not purely a post-processing function on the output of the permutation p. We consider the security of GTrunc for various types of post-processing functions. In Sect. 4.2 we consider a simplified variant where post is balanced and no feed-forward is involved, and show security-wise equivalence of the resulting construction with Trunc. In Sect. 4.3 we consider the general GTrunc construction with balanced post-processing and link it with the bounds of Stam [47,48]. The result shows that, in fact, GTrunc achieves the same level of security as Trunc, regardless of the choice of post-processing function post (as long as it is balanced). Finally, we extend the result to arbitrary (possibly unbalanced) post, and derive a security bound that is slightly worse, depending on the unbalancedness of post. The derivation is based on Stam's bounds, with in addition an analysis of the statistical distance between unbalanced and balanced random samplings with replacement using the Kullback-Leibler divergence.

We comment on the affect of including a pre-processing function pre in Sect. 5.

2 Security Model

Consider two natural numbers $n, m \in \mathbb{N}$. We denote by $\{0, 1\}^n$ the set of n-bit strings. The set $\mathsf{func}(n, m)$ denotes the set of all n-to-m-bit functions, and $\mathsf{perm}(n)$ the set of all n-bit permutations. If $m \leq n$, the function $\mathsf{left}_m : \{0, 1\}^n \to \{0, 1\}^m$ returns the left m bits of its input. We denote by $(m)_n$ the falling factorial $m(m - 1) \cdots (m - n + 1) = m!/(m - n)!$. For a finite set $\mathcal{X}$, $x \xleftarrow{\$} \mathcal{X}$ denotes the uniform random drawing of x from $\mathcal{X}$.

2.1   Statistical Tools

For two distributions X, Y over a finite space Ω, the statistical distance between X and Y is defined as

$$\Delta(X, Y) = \frac{1}{2} \sum_{\omega \in \Omega} \left| \mathbf{Pr}\left(X = \omega\right) - \mathbf{Pr}\left(Y = \omega\right) \right| \tag{4}$$

$$= \max_{\Omega^* \subseteq \Omega} \left\{ \sum_{\omega \in \Omega^*} \mathbf{Pr}\left(X = \omega\right) - \mathbf{Pr}\left(Y = \omega\right) \right\}. \tag{5}$$

The Kullback-Leibler divergence [36] between X and Y is defined as

$$KL(X; Y) = \sum_{\omega \in \Omega} \mathbf{Pr}\left(X = \omega\right) \log \left(\frac{\mathbf{Pr}\left(X = \omega\right)}{\mathbf{Pr}\left(Y = \omega\right)} \right), \tag{6}$$

with the condition that $\mathbf{Pr}\left(Y = \omega\right) > 0$ for all $\omega \in \Omega$ and the convention that $0 \log(0) = 0$. Pinsker's inequality [21, 34, 35] gives

$$\Delta(X, Y) \leq \left(\frac{1}{2} KL(X; Y) \right)^{1/2}. \tag{7}$$

Remark 1. Dai et al. [23] recently introduced the chi-squared method to cryptography. The chi-squared method also relies on Pinsker's inequality (7), but *in addition* uses that

$$KL(X; Y) \leq \chi^2(X; Y), \tag{8}$$

where

$$\chi^2(X; Y) = \sum_{\omega \in \Omega} \frac{\left(\mathbf{Pr}\left(X = \omega\right) - \mathbf{Pr}\left(Y = \omega\right) \right)^2}{\mathbf{Pr}\left(Y = \omega\right)} \tag{9}$$

is the chi-squared divergence [20, 43]. What then remains in order to bound $\Delta(X, Y)$ is an analysis of the chi-squared divergence between X and Y. In our work, we do not go that far, but instead, stop at the Kullback-Leibler divergence. (This is no critique on the chi-squared method; in many applications, bounding $\chi^2(X; Y)$ may be easier to do than bounding $KL(X; Y)$).

2.2   Pseudorandom Functions

A distinguisher $\mathcal{D}$ is an algorithm that is given access to an oracle $\mathcal{O}$; it can make a certain amount of queries to this oracle, and afterwards it outputs $b \in \{0, 1\}$. We focus on computationally unbounded distinguishers, whose complexities are measured by the number of oracle queries only. As usual, a scheme is secure if it withstands the strongest possible distinguisher, and we can without loss of generality restrict our focus to deterministic distinguishers. The reason for this is that for any probabilistic distinguisher there exists a deterministic distinguisher with the same success probability.

Let $n, m \in \mathbb{N}$ such that $m \leq n$. Let $p \in \mathsf{perm}(n)$, and consider a function $F^p \in \mathsf{func}(n, m)$. We define the pseudorandom function (PRF) security of F^p as a random function against a distinguisher $\mathcal{D}$ by

$$\mathbf{Adv}_F^{\mathrm{prf}}(\mathcal{D}) = \left| \mathbf{Pr}\left(\mathcal{D}^{F^p} = 1 \right) - \mathbf{Pr}\left(\mathcal{D}^f = 1 \right) \right|, \tag{10}$$

where the first probability is taken over the random drawing of $p \xleftarrow{\$} \mathsf{perm}(n)$ and the second probability over $f \xleftarrow{\$} \mathsf{func}(n, m)$. (Recall that $\mathcal{D}$ is a deterministic distinguisher).

The definition of PRF security relates to the statistical distance of (4–5) in the following manner. Let $q \in \mathbb{N}$, and consider a deterministic distinguisher $\mathcal{D}$ making q queries. Let X denote the probability distribution of interactions with F^p and Y the probability distribution of interactions with f. Let Ω_1 denote the set of query-response tuples for which distinguisher $\mathcal{D}$ outputs 1. Then,

$$\mathbf{Adv}_F^{\mathrm{prf}}(\mathcal{D}) = \left| \sum_{\omega \in \Omega_1} \mathbf{Pr}\left(X = \omega \right) - \mathbf{Pr}\left(Y = \omega \right) \right| \leq \Delta(X, Y). \tag{11}$$

Equality is achieved for distinguisher $\mathcal{D}$ that returns 1 for any query-response tuple in Ω^*, where Ω^* is the set for which (5) achieves its maximum [12].

Remark 2. The above security model considers F^p to be "keyed" with a random permutation $p \xleftarrow{\$} \mathsf{perm}(n)$. A standard hybrid argument allows us to transform all results in this work to a complexity-theoretic setting where p is, instead, a block cipher E with secret key K, and the distinguisher's capabilities are also bounded by a time parameter t.

3   Stam's Bounds

Consider a finite set of N elements, of M types/colors. Denote the partition of the N elements into the M colors by $A_1 \cup \cdots \cup A_M$. For color j, write $a_j = |A_j| > 0$, such that

$$a_1 + \cdots + a_M = N. \tag{12}$$

Let $q \in \mathbb{N}$. Denote by X the probability distribution of the obtained colors when sampling q elements *without* replacement, and by Y the probability distribution of the obtained colors when sampling *with* replacement. Both X and Y have range $\{1, \ldots, M\}^q$. Stam [47] measures the distance between X and Y, and proves the following bound[1].

---

[1] Note that our definition of distance has a factor $\frac{1}{2}$ compared to that of Stam.

Theorem 1 (Stam's bound [47, Theorems 2.2 and 2.3]**).** *Let* $q, N, M \in \mathbb{N}$ *such that* $M \leq N$, *and consider the configuration of* M *colors of color sizes* $(a_1, \ldots, a_M)$ *as in (12). Consider the two distributions* X *and* Y *over range* $\{1, \ldots, M\}^q$. *We have,*

$$\Delta(X, Y) \leq \frac{1}{2} \left(\frac{(M-1)q(q-1)}{(N-1)(N-q+1)} \right)^{1/2}. \tag{13}$$

Proof. We include Stam's proof (in our terminology) for completeness.

Write $X = (X_1, \ldots, X_q)$ and $Y = (Y_1, \ldots, Y_q)$. Denote, for brevity, $\boldsymbol{X}_i = (X_1, \ldots, X_i)$ and $\boldsymbol{Y}_i = (Y_1, \ldots, Y_i)$ for $i = 1, \ldots, q$. The Kullback-Leibler divergence (6) can be rewritten as

$$KL(X; Y) \leq KL(X_1; Y_1) + \sum_{i=1}^{q-1} KL(X_{i+1}; Y_{i+1} \mid \boldsymbol{X}_i, \boldsymbol{Y}_i), \tag{14}$$

where

$$KL(X_{i+1}; Y_{i+1} \mid \boldsymbol{X}_i, \boldsymbol{Y}_i) = \sum_{\boldsymbol{j}_i \in \{1, \ldots, M\}^i} \mathbf{Pr}\left(\boldsymbol{X}_i = \boldsymbol{j}_i\right) \cdot$$

$$\sum_{j=1}^{M} \mathbf{Pr}\left(X_{i+1} = j \mid \boldsymbol{X}_i = \boldsymbol{j}_i\right) \log \left(\frac{\mathbf{Pr}\left(X_{i+1} = j \mid \boldsymbol{X}_i = \boldsymbol{j}_i\right)}{\mathbf{Pr}\left(Y_{i+1} = j \mid \boldsymbol{Y}_i = \boldsymbol{j}_i\right)} \right). \tag{15}$$

We have

$$\mathbf{Pr}\left(X_{i+1} = j \mid \boldsymbol{X}_i = \boldsymbol{j}_i\right) = \frac{a_j - h}{N - i}, \tag{16}$$

$$\mathbf{Pr}\left(Y_{i+1} = j \mid \boldsymbol{Y}_i = \boldsymbol{j}_i\right) = \frac{a_j}{N}, \tag{17}$$

where h denotes the number of occurrences of j in sample $\boldsymbol{j}_i$. Thus,

$$KL(X_{i+1}; Y_{i+1} \mid \boldsymbol{X}_i, \boldsymbol{Y}_i) \tag{18}$$

$$= \sum_{j=1}^{M} \sum_{\boldsymbol{j}_i \in \{1, \ldots, M\}^i} \mathbf{Pr}\left(\boldsymbol{X}_i = \boldsymbol{j}_i\right) \cdot \frac{a_j - h}{N - i} \cdot \log \left(\frac{\frac{a_j - h}{N - i}}{\frac{a_j}{N}} \right) \tag{19}$$

$$= \sum_{j=1}^{M} \sum_{h=0}^{\min\{i, a_j-1\}} \mathbf{Pr}\left(HG_{a_j}^N(i) = h\right) \cdot \frac{a_j - h}{N - i} \cdot \log \left(\frac{\frac{a_j - h}{N - i}}{\frac{a_j}{N}} \right), \tag{20}$$

where $HG_{a_j}^N(i)$ is a random variable of i hypergeometrically distributed draws from N elements with a_j success elements. We have

$$\mathbf{Pr}\left(HG_{a_j}^N(i) = h\right) \cdot \frac{a_j - h}{N - i} = \binom{i}{h} \frac{(a_j)_h (N - a_j)_{i-h}}{(N)_i} \cdot \frac{a_j - h}{N - i} \tag{21}$$

$$= \binom{i}{h} \frac{(a_j - 1)_h (N - a_j)_{i-h}}{(N-1)_i} \cdot \frac{a_j}{N} \tag{22}$$

$$= \mathbf{Pr}\left(HG_{a_j-1}^{N-1}(i) = h\right) \cdot \frac{a_j}{N}. \tag{23}$$

Note furthermore that

$$\sum_{h=0}^{\min\{i,a_j-1\}} h \cdot \mathbf{Pr}\left(HG_{a_j-1}^{N-1}(i) = h\right) = \mathbf{Ex}\left(HG_{a_j-1}^{N-1}(i)\right) = \frac{i(a_j-1)}{N-1}. \qquad (24)$$

We subsequently derive the following for (20), where in the first bounding we use Jensen's inequality (log is concave) and in the second bounding we use that $\log(\alpha) \leq \alpha - 1$ (for any $\alpha > 0$):

$$KL(X_{i+1}; Y_{i+1} \mid \boldsymbol{X}_i, \boldsymbol{Y}_i) \qquad (25)$$

$$= \sum_{j=1}^{M} \frac{a_j}{N} \cdot \sum_{h=0}^{\min\{i,a_j-1\}} \mathbf{Pr}\left(HG_{a_j-1}^{N-1}(i) = h\right) \cdot \log\left(\frac{\frac{a_j-h}{N-i}}{\frac{a_j}{N}}\right) \qquad (26)$$

$$\leq \sum_{j=1}^{M} \frac{a_j}{N} \cdot \log\left(\sum_{h=0}^{\min\{i,a_j-1\}} \mathbf{Pr}\left(HG_{a_j-1}^{N-1}(i) = h\right) \cdot \frac{\frac{a_j-h}{N-i}}{\frac{a_j}{N}}\right) \qquad (27)$$

$$= \sum_{j=1}^{M} \frac{a_j}{N} \cdot \log\left(\frac{N}{a_j(N-i)}\left(a_j - \mathbf{Ex}\left(HG_{a_j-1}^{N-1}(i)\right)\right)\right) \qquad (28)$$

$$= \sum_{j=1}^{M} \frac{a_j}{N} \cdot \log\left(\frac{N}{a_j(N-i)}\left(a_j - \frac{i(a_j-1)}{N-1}\right)\right) \qquad (29)$$

$$= \sum_{j=1}^{M} \frac{a_j}{N} \cdot \log\left(1 + \frac{(N-a_j)i}{a_j(N-1)(N-i)}\right) \qquad (30)$$

$$\leq \sum_{j=1}^{M} \left(1 - \frac{a_j}{N}\right) \cdot \frac{i}{(N-1)(N-i)} \qquad (31)$$

$$= \frac{(M-1)i}{(N-1)(N-i)}. \qquad (32)$$

The theorem is concluded by combining (7), (14), and (32).   □

It is interesting to note that the bound depends on q, N, and M, *but not on the a_i's*. This is caused by the observation that the outcomes are hypergeometrically distributed and that the a_j's drop out due to concavity of the function log.

This fact allowed Stam to generalize his result to partitions varying with $i = 1, \ldots, q$ at little effort [48]. More formally, consider a finite set of N elements, this time with q partitions into M_i types/colors $A_{i,1} \cup \cdots \cup A_{i,M_i}$ for $i = 1, \ldots, q$. For color j in sample i, write $a_{i,j} = |A_{i,j}| > 0$, such that for all $i = 1, \ldots, q$,

$$a_{i,1} + \cdots + a_{i,M_i} = N. \qquad (33)$$

Let $q \in \mathbb{N}$. Denote by X the probability distribution of the obtained colors when sampling q elements *without* replacement, and by Y the probability distribution of the obtained colors when sampling *with* replacement. Both X and Y have range

$$\{1,\ldots,M_1\} \times \cdots \times \{1,\ldots,M_q\}. \tag{34}$$

Stam [48] proves the following bound for the distance between X and Y.

Theorem 2 (Stam's bound [48, Theorem 1]). *Let $q, N, M_1, \ldots, M_q \in \mathbb{N}$ such that $M_1, \ldots, M_q \leq N$, and consider the configuration of M_i colors of color sizes $\{(a_{i,1}, \ldots, a_{i,M_i})\}$ for $i = 1, \ldots, q$ as in (33). Consider the two distributions X and Y over range $\{1, \ldots, M_1\} \times \cdots \times \{1, \ldots, M_q\}$. We have,*

$$\Delta(X,Y) \leq \frac{1}{2} \left(\sum_{i=1}^{q-1} \frac{2(M_{i+1} - 1)i}{(N-1)(N-q+1)} \right)^{1/2}. \tag{35}$$

Proof. The proof is a straightforward extension of that of Theorem 1: the only differences are that the indices in the summations and summands of (15) are updated to the new range $\{1, \ldots, M_1\} \times \cdots \times \{1, \ldots, M_q\}$ and color sizes $a_{i+1,j}$. In particular, *for fixed $i \in \{1, \ldots, q\}$*, (31–32) is superseded by

$$KL(X_{i+1}; Y_{i+1} \mid \boldsymbol{X}_i, \boldsymbol{Y}_i) \leq \sum_{j=1}^{M_{i+1}} \left(1 - \frac{a_{i+1,j}}{N} \right) \frac{i}{(N-1)(N-i)} \tag{36}$$

$$= \frac{(M_{i+1} - 1)i}{(N-1)(N-i)}. \tag{37}$$

The result then immediately follows. □

If $M_1 = \cdots = M_q = M$ (but not necessarily with identical color sizes $\{(a_{i,1}, \ldots, a_{i,M})\}$ for every sampling), the bound of Theorem 2 obviously simplifies to that of Theorem 1.

4   Generalized Truncation

We consider a generalization of Trunc of (1) to arbitrary post-processing function. As before, let $n, m \in \mathbb{N}$ such that $m \leq n$, and $p \in \mathsf{perm}(n)$. Let post $: \{0,1\}^n \times \{0,1\}^n \to \{0,1\}^m$ be an arbitrary post-processing function. Generalized truncation is defined as

$$\mathsf{GTrunc}^p(x) = \mathsf{post}(x, p(x)). \tag{38}$$

Generalized truncation is depicted in Fig. 1. For fixed $x \in \{0,1\}^n$ and $y \in \{0,1\}^m$, we define

$$\mathsf{post}[x]^{-1}(y) = \{z \in \{0,1\}^n \mid \mathsf{post}(x,z) = y\}. \tag{39}$$

The differences between GTrunc and Trunc are subtle but quite significant, depending on the choice of post.

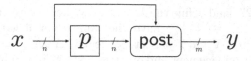

Fig. 1. GTrunc of (38) based on n-bit permutation $p \in \mathsf{perm}(n)$. post is any function.

- The generalized description covers Trunc of (1) by setting $\mathsf{post}(x, z) = \mathsf{left}_m(z)$. In Sect. 4.1, we revisit the state of the art on Trunc and re-derive the best security bound;
- In Sect. 4.2, we consider GTrunc with *balanced and x-independent post-processing*, i.e., where the feed-forward of x is discarded, and demonstrate that its security is equivalent to the security of Trunc;
- In Sect. 4.3, we consider GTrunc with *balanced post-processing* (not necessarily discarding the feed-forward). In this case a direct reduction to Trunc seems impossible but we resort to Stam's generalized bound of Theorem 2;
- In Sect. 4.4, we consider GTrunc with *arbitrary post-processing*. Also in this case, we resort to Theorem 2, but additional analysis is needed to make the result carry over.

We elaborate on using a pre-processing function in Sect. 5.

4.1   Plain Truncation

We consider the case of plain truncation: Trunc of (1), or equivalently GTrunc of (38) with $\mathsf{post}(x, z) = \mathsf{left}_m(z)$.

Truncation first appeared in Hall et al. [30]. It is known to be secure up to approximately $2^{n-m/2}$ queries [6,12,25,30,47]. We describe the bound as a direct implication of Stam's bound of Theorem 1. For educational interest, Bhattacharya and Nandi [12] gave a self-contained proof of this result in the chi-squared method: they derived the exact same bound, which should not come as surprise in light of Remark 1 in Sect. 2.1.

Theorem 3 (Security of Trunc). *Let $q, n, m \in \mathbb{N}$ such that $m \leq n$. Consider GTrunc of (38) with $\mathsf{post}(x, z) = \mathsf{left}_m(z)$. For any distinguisher $\mathcal{D}$ making at most q queries,*

$$\mathbf{Adv}_{\mathsf{Trunc}}^{\mathrm{prf}}(\mathcal{D}) \leq \frac{1}{2} \left(\frac{(2^m - 1)q(q-1)}{(2^n - 1)(2^n - q + 1)} \right)^{1/2}. \tag{40}$$

Proof. Fix a deterministic distinguisher $\mathcal{D}$ that makes q queries. Let X^{Trunc^p} denote the probability distribution of interactions with Trunc^p for $p \xleftarrow{\$} \mathsf{perm}(n)$, and Y^f the probability distribution of interaction with $f \xleftarrow{\$} \mathsf{func}(n, m)$. By (11),

$$\mathbf{Adv}_{\mathsf{Trunc}}^{\mathrm{prf}}(\mathcal{D}) \leq \Delta(X^{\mathsf{Trunc}^p}, Y^f). \tag{41}$$

Put $N = 2^n$, $M = 2^m$, and define the M colors by the first m bits of the sampling, i.e., two elements $z, z' \in \{0,1\}^n$ have the same color if $\mathsf{left}_m(z) = \mathsf{left}_m(z')$. Consider the samplings X and Y of Sect. 3. Clearly, $\Delta(X, X^{\mathsf{Trunc}^P}) = 0$: in X^{Trunc^P} one samples without replacement and only reveals the first m bits of the drawing, which is equivalent to revealing the color. As all color sets are of equal size $a_1 = \cdots = a_{2^m} = 2^{n-m}$, we also have $\Delta(Y^f, Y) = 0$. Thus, by the triangle inequality,

$$\mathbf{Adv}_{\mathsf{Trunc}}^{\mathrm{prf}}(\mathcal{D}) \leq \Delta(X^{\mathsf{Trunc}^P}, Y^f) = \Delta(X, Y). \tag{42}$$

The result now immediately follows from Theorem 1. $\square$

A simple simplification simplifies the bound of Theorem 3 to $\left(\binom{q}{2}/2^{2n-m}\right)^{1/2}$. The bound is known to be tight: Hall et al. [30] already presented a distinguisher $\mathcal{D}$ meeting this bound up to a constant, but their distinguisher did not come with an exact analysis. Gilboa and Gueron presented a more detailed attack [26], and we repeat a simplification of their bound.

Theorem 4 (Insecurity of Trunc [26, Proposition 2, simplified]). *Let $n, m \in \mathbb{N}$ such that $m \leq n$. Consider GTrunc of (38) with $\mathsf{post}(x,z) = \mathsf{left}_m(z)$. There exists a distinguisher $\mathcal{D}$ making $q = 2^{n-m/2-3}$ queries, such that*

$$\mathbf{Adv}_{\mathsf{Trunc}}^{\mathrm{prf}}(\mathcal{D}) \geq \frac{1}{400}\left(1 - e^{-1/306}\right). \tag{43}$$

4.2 Balanced and x-Independent Post-processing

We consider security of GTrunc in a limited setting where post is independent of its first input x ($\mathsf{post}(\cdot, z)$ is constant for all z) and where it is balanced (the set $\mathsf{post}[x]^{-1}(y)$ is of the same size for all x, y). Already in the original introduction, Hall et al. [30] remarked that the analysis of Trunc carries over to balanced post-processing functions, and it also follows immediately from Theorem 1 (with different color sets, but still all of equal size 2^{n-m} as the function is balanced). As a bonus, we present an analysis of this case that reduces the security of GTrunc with balanced and x-independent post to Trunc.

Theorem 5 (Security of GTrunc with balanced and x-independent post). *Let $q, n, m \in \mathbb{N}$ such that $m \leq n$. Consider GTrunc of (38) with balanced and x-independent post. For any distinguisher $\mathcal{D}$,*

$$\mathbf{Adv}_{\mathsf{GTrunc}}^{\mathrm{prf}}(\mathcal{D}) = \mathbf{Adv}_{\mathsf{Trunc}}^{\mathrm{prf}}(\mathcal{D}). \tag{44}$$

Proof. Without loss of generality, consider $\mathsf{post} : \{0,1\}^n \to \{0,1\}^m$ and write GTrunc^P as

$$\mathsf{GTrunc}^P(x) = \mathsf{post} \circ p(x). \tag{45}$$

As post is balanced, there exists a balanced function $post' : \{0,1\}^n \to \{0,1\}^n$ such that

$$post = left_m \circ post'. \tag{46}$$

Let $p \xleftarrow{\$} perm(n)$, and consider any distinguisher $\mathcal{D}$ whose goal it is to distinguish $GTrunc^p$ from $f \xleftarrow{\$} func(n,m)$. Defining $p' = post' \circ p$, we obtain that

$$GTrunc^p = post \circ p = left_m \circ post' \circ p = left_m \circ p' = Trunc^{p'}, \tag{47}$$

and thus that

$$\mathbf{Adv}^{prf}_{GTrunc}(\mathcal{D}) = \mathbf{Adv}^{prf}_{Trunc}(\mathcal{D}), \tag{48}$$

as $p' \xleftarrow{\$} perm(n)$ iff $p \xleftarrow{\$} perm(n)$ (because $post'$ is n-to-n and balanced). □

4.3 Balanced Post-processing

We consider security of GTrunc in a more general setting: post is any *balanced* function. We consider this to be the most interesting configuration, as for unbalanced post-processing, security decreases (see Sect. 4.4).

Theorem 6 (Security of GTrunc with balanced post). *Let $q, n, m \in \mathbb{N}$ such that $m \leq n$. Consider GTrunc of (38) with balanced post. For any distinguisher $\mathcal{D}$ making at most q queries,*

$$\mathbf{Adv}^{prf}_{Trunc}(\mathcal{D}) \leq \frac{1}{2} \left(\frac{(2^m - 1)q(q-1)}{(2^n - 1)(2^n - q + 1)} \right)^{1/2}. \tag{49}$$

Proof. Fix a deterministic distinguisher $\mathcal{D}$ that makes q queries. Let X^{GTrunc^p} denote the probability distribution of interactions with $GTrunc^p$ for $p \xleftarrow{\$} perm(n)$, and Y^f the probability distribution of interaction with $f \xleftarrow{\$} func(n,m)$. By (11),

$$\mathbf{Adv}^{prf}_{GTrunc}(\mathcal{D}) \leq \Delta(X^{GTrunc^p}, Y^f). \tag{50}$$

Put $N = 2^n$, $M = 2^m$. For ease of reasoning, assume (for now) that the distinguisher makes queries $x_1, \ldots, x_q$. For each query x_i ($i = 1, \ldots, q$), define the M colors by the sets $A_{i,j} := post^{-1}[x_i](j)$ for $j \in \{0,1\}^m$. The q queries thus define q partitions of the N elements into M colors $A_{i,1} \cup \cdots \cup A_{i,M}$ for $i = 1, \ldots, q$. Consider the samplings X and Y of Sect. 3. Clearly, $\Delta(X, X^{GTrunc^p}) = 0$ as in the proof of Theorem 3. As post is balanced, all color sets are of equal size $a_{i,1} = \cdots = a_{i,M} = 2^{n-m}$ for $i = 1, \ldots, q$. We therefore also have $\Delta(Y^f, Y) = 0$. Thus, by the triangle inequality,

$$\mathbf{Adv}^{prf}_{GTrunc}(\mathcal{D}) \leq \Delta(X, Y). \tag{51}$$

We obtain our bound on the remaining distance from Theorem 2. As this bound holds for any possible distinguisher, and any possible selection of inputs $x_1, \ldots, x_q$, we can maximize over all possible deterministic distinguishers. (Formally, the analysis of Theorem 2 consists of a *per-query* analysis of $KL(X_{i+1}; Y_{i+1} \mid \boldsymbol{X}_i, \boldsymbol{Y}_i)$, where the derived bound in (37) is independent of the $a_{i+1,j}$'s and thus of the input x_{i+1}.) This completes the proof. $\qquad\square$

It is not straightforward to analyze tightness for the general GTrunc construction, i.e., to derive a lower bound. As demonstrated by Gilboa and Gueron [26], the analysis for plain truncation is already highly involved: including a feed-forward of the input only frustrates the analysis, and influences the per-query probability of a response to occur (unlike the case of plain Trunc of Sect. 4.1 and GTrunc without feed-forward of Sect. 4.2). However, it is possible to argue tightness for a reasonable simplification of GTrunc. In detail, if post : $\{0,1\}^n \times \{0,1\}^n \to \{0,1\}^m$ is linear in x, i.e.,

$$\mathsf{post}(x,y) = \mathbf{A} \cdot x \oplus \mathsf{post}'(y) \tag{52}$$

for some matrix $\mathbf{A} \in \{0,1\}^{m \times n}$ and arbitrary post' : $\{0,1\}^n \to \{0,1\}^m$, an adversary can "undo the feed-forward" by deciding to attack

$$(\mathsf{GTrunc}')^p(x) = \mathsf{GTrunc}^p(x) \oplus \mathbf{A} \cdot x \tag{53}$$
$$= \mathsf{post}'(p(x)). \tag{54}$$

In this way, it returns to the simpler case of Theorem 5. More involved post-processing functions, where x is used to transform y (e.g., by rotation or multiplication) do not fall victim to this technique.

4.4 Arbitrary Post-processing

We finally consider GTrunc with arbitrary post-processing, where we only assume that any value $y \in \{0,1\}^m$ occurs with positive probability. Let $\gamma \in \mathbb{N} \cup \{0\}$ be such that $|\mathsf{post}^{-1}[x](y) - 2^{n-m}| \le \gamma$ for any $x \in \{0,1\}^n$ and $y \in \{0,1\}^m$. This value γ measures the unbalancedness of post: for γ close to 0, post is close to a balanced function.

Theorem 7 (Security of GTrunc with arbitrary post). *Let $q, n, m \in \mathbb{N}$ such that $m \le n$. Consider GTrunc of (38) with arbitrary post. For any distinguisher $\mathcal{D}$ making at most q queries,*

$$\mathbf{Adv}^{\mathrm{prf}}_{\mathsf{Trunc}}(\mathcal{D}) \le \frac{1}{2} \left(\frac{(2^m - 1)q(q-1)}{(2^n - 1)(2^n - q + 1)} \right)^{1/2} + \left(\frac{1}{2} q \left(\frac{\gamma}{2^{n-m}} \right)^2 \right)^{1/2}. \tag{55}$$

Proof. The proof is identical to that of Theorem 6, with one important exception: post does not need to be balanced, and hence $\Delta(Y^f, Y) \ge 0$. We will use Pinsker's inequality (7) on the chi-squared divergence (9) to bound this term. For any $i = 1, \ldots, q, \boldsymbol{j}_{i-1} \in \{1, \ldots, 2^m\}^{i-1}$, and $j \in \{1, \ldots, 2^m\}$,

$$\mathbf{Pr}\left((Y^f)_i = j \mid (\boldsymbol{Y}^f)_{i-1} = \boldsymbol{j}_{i-1} \right) = \mathbf{Pr}\left((Y^f)_i = j \right) = \frac{1}{2^m}, \tag{56}$$

$$\mathbf{Pr}\left(Y_i = j \mid \boldsymbol{Y}_{i-1} = \boldsymbol{j}_{i-1} \right) \qquad = \mathbf{Pr}\left(Y_i = j \right) \quad = \frac{a_{i,j}}{2^n}. \tag{57}$$

In particular, for both Y^f and Y the drawing of the i-th element is independent of the first $i - 1$ samples. From the chi-squared divergence (9), for which we translate its inductive formula [23] to our setting, we obtain

$$\chi^2(Y; Y^f) \le \sum_{i=1}^{q} \sum_{j=1}^{2^m} \frac{\left(\mathbf{Pr}\left(Y_i = j \right) - \mathbf{Pr}\left((Y^f)_i = j \right) \right)^2}{\mathbf{Pr}\left((Y^f)_i = j \right)} \tag{58}$$

$$= \sum_{i=1}^{q} \sum_{j=1}^{2^m} \frac{1}{2^{2n-m}} \left(a_{i,j} - 2^{n-m} \right)^2. \tag{59}$$

Using that $|a_{i,j} - 2^{n-m}| \le \gamma$, we can proceed:

$$\chi^2(Y; Y^f) \le \sum_{i=1}^{q} \sum_{j=1}^{2^m} \frac{\gamma^2}{2^{2n-m}} \tag{60}$$

$$= q \left(\frac{\gamma}{2^{n-m}} \right)^2. \tag{61}$$

The proof is completed using Pinsker's inequality (7).   □

The first part of the bound of Theorem 7 is identical to that of Theorem 6, and the comments on tightness carry over. The second part of the bound comes from the bounding of $\Delta(Y^f, Y)$, and in this bounding we use the estimation $|a_{i,j} - 2^{n-m}| \le \gamma$, which is non-tight for most of the choices for (i, j). We see no way of attacking the scheme with query complexity around $(2^{n-m}/\gamma)^2$, but it is reasonable to assume that the security degrades with the bias in the balancedness of post.

It is interesting to note that, had we used the Kullback-Leibler divergence (6) instead of the chi-squared divergence (9), we would have derived

$$KL(Y; Y^f) \le q \left(1 + \frac{\gamma}{2^{n-m}} \right) \log \left(1 + \frac{\gamma}{2^{n-m}} \right), \tag{62}$$

which is in turn at most

$$q \left(1 + \frac{\gamma}{2^{n-m}} \right) \left(\frac{\gamma}{2^{n-m}} \right) \tag{63}$$

as $\log(\alpha) \le \alpha - 1$ (for any $\alpha > 0$). In other words, the non-tightness of $|a_{i,j} - 2^{n-m}| \le \gamma$ would have amplified into a slightly worse overall bound. We remark that this does not contradict (8).

5   Note on Including Pre-processing Function

One might consider generalizing GTrunc of (38) even further to include an arbitrary pre-processing function $\mathsf{pre} : \{0, 1\}^n \to \{0, 1\}^n$ as well:

$$(\mathsf{GTrunc}')^p(x) = \mathsf{post}(x, p(\mathsf{pre}(x))). \tag{64}$$

However, we see no justification for doing so. If pre is balanced, it is necessarily invertible and one can "absorb" it into p as done in the analysis of Sect. 4.2. If it is unbalanced, this means that there exist distinct x, x' such that $\mathsf{pre}(x) = \mathsf{pre}(x')$, and consequently, the evaluations $(\mathsf{GTrunc}')^p(x)$ and $(\mathsf{GTrunc}')^p(x')$ use the same source of randomness:

$$p(\mathsf{pre}(x)) = p(\mathsf{pre}(x')). \tag{65}$$

This does not immediately lead to an attack, most importantly as post only outputs $m \leq n$ bits. If, in particular, $m \ll n$, a distinguisher may not note that the same randomness is employed. Nevertheless, unbalanced pre's seem to set the stage for a weaker generalized truncation.

Acknowledgments. Bart Mennink is supported by a postdoctoral fellowship from the Netherlands Organisation for Scientific Research (NWO) under Veni grant 016.Veni.173.017. The author would like to thank the reviewers for their detailed comments and suggestions.

References

1. Adams, C.: The CAST-128 encryption algorithm. Request for Comments (RFC) 2144, May 1997. http://tools.ietf.org/html/rfc2144
2. Aoki, K., et al.: Specification of Camellia – a 128-bit Block Cipher, Version 2.0 (2001). https://info.isl.ntt.co.jp/crypt/eng/camellia/dl/01espec.pdf
3. Banik, S., Pandey, S.K., Peyrin, T., Sasaki, Y., Sim, S.M., Todo, Y.: GIFT: a small present - towards reaching the limit of lightweight encryption. In: Fischer, W., Homma, N. (eds.) CHES 2017. LNCS, vol. 10529, pp. 321–345. Springer, Cham (2017). https://doi.org/10.1007/978-3-319-66787-4_16
4. Beierle, C., et al.: The SKINNY family of block ciphers and its low-latency variant MANTIS. In: Robshaw, M., Katz, J. (eds.) CRYPTO 2016. LNCS, vol. 9815, pp. 123–153. Springer, Heidelberg (2016). https://doi.org/10.1007/978-3-662-53008-5_5
5. Bellare, M., Guérin, R., Rogaway, P.: XOR MACs: new methods for message authentication using finite pseudorandom functions. In: Coppersmith, D. (ed.) CRYPTO 1995. LNCS, vol. 963, pp. 15–28. Springer, Heidelberg (1995). https://doi.org/10.1007/3-540-44750-4_2
6. Bellare, M., Impagliazzo, R.: A tool for obtaining tighter security analyses of pseudorandom function based constructions, with applications to PRP to PRF conversion. Cryptology ePrint Archive, Report 1999/024 (1999). http://eprint.iacr.org/1999/024
7. Bellare, M., Kilian, J., Rogaway, P.: The security of cipher block chaining. In: Desmedt, Y.G. (ed.) CRYPTO 1994. LNCS, vol. 839, pp. 341–358. Springer, Heidelberg (1994). https://doi.org/10.1007/3-540-48658-5_32
8. Bellare, M., Krovetz, T., Rogaway, P.: Luby-Rackoff backwards: increasing security by making block ciphers non-invertible. In: Nyberg, K. (ed.) EUROCRYPT 1998. LNCS, vol. 1403, pp. 266–280. Springer, Heidelberg (1998). https://doi.org/10.1007/BFb0054132

9. Bellare, M., Rogaway, P.: The security of triple encryption and a framework for code-based game-playing proofs. In: Vaudenay, S. (ed.) EUROCRYPT 2006. LNCS, vol. 4004, pp. 409–426. Springer, Heidelberg (2006). https://doi.org/10.1007/11761679_25

10. Bernstein, D.J.: SURF: simple unpredictable random function (1997). https://cr.yp.to/papers.html#surf

11. Bernstein, D.J.: How to stretch random functions: the security of protected counter sums. J. Cryptol. **12**(3), 185–192 (1999). https://doi.org/10.1007/s001459900051

12. Bhattacharya, S., Nandi, M.: A note on the chi-square method: a tool for proving cryptographic security. Cryptogr. Commun. **10**(5), 935–957 (2018). https://doi.org/10.1007/s12095-017-0276-z

13. Biham, E., Anderson, R., Knudsen, L.: Serpent: a new block cipher proposal. In: Vaudenay, S. (ed.) FSE 1998. LNCS, vol. 1372, pp. 222–238. Springer, Heidelberg (1998). https://doi.org/10.1007/3-540-69710-1_15

14. Bogdanov, A., et al.: PRESENT: an ultra-lightweight block cipher. In: Paillier, P., Verbauwhede, I. (eds.) CHES 2007. LNCS, vol. 4727, pp. 450–466. Springer, Heidelberg (2007). https://doi.org/10.1007/978-3-540-74735-2_31

15. Bose, P., Hoang, V.T., Tessaro, S.: Revisiting AES-GCM-SIV: multi-user security, faster key derivation, and better bounds. In: Nielsen, J.B., Rijmen, V. (eds.) EUROCRYPT 2018. LNCS, vol. 10820, pp. 468–499. Springer, Cham (2018). https://doi.org/10.1007/978-3-319-78381-9_18

16. Brassard, G.: On computationally secure authentication tags requiring short secret shared keys. In: Chaum, D., Rivest, R.L., Sherman, A.T. (eds.) Advances in Cryptology, pp. 79–86. Springer, Boston, MA (1983). https://doi.org/10.1007/978-1-4757-0602-4_7

17. Chang, D., Nandi, M.: A short proof of the PRP/PRF switching lemma. Cryptology ePrint Archive, Report 2008/078 (2008). http://eprint.iacr.org/2008/078

18. Cogliati, B., Lampe, R., Patarin, J.: The indistinguishability of the XOR of k permutations. In: Cid, C., Rechberger, C. (eds.) FSE 2014. LNCS, vol. 8540, pp. 285–302. Springer, Heidelberg (2015). https://doi.org/10.1007/978-3-662-46706-0_15

19. Cogliati, B., Seurin, Y.: EWCDM: an efficient, beyond-birthday secure, nonce-misuse resistant MAC. In: Robshaw, M., Katz, J. (eds.) CRYPTO 2016. LNCS, vol. 9814, pp. 121–149. Springer, Heidelberg (2016). https://doi.org/10.1007/978-3-662-53018-4_5

20. Csiszár, I.: Eine informationstheoretische Ungleichung und ihre Anwendung auf den Beweis der Ergodizitat von Markoffschen Ketten. Magyar. Tud. Akad. Mat. Kutató Int. Közl **8**, 85–108 (1963)

21. Csiszár, I.: Information-type measure of difference of probability distributions and indirect observations. Stud. Sci. Math. Hung. **2**, 299–318 (1967)

22. Daemen, J., Rijmen, V.: The Design of Rijndael: AES - The Advanced Encryption Standard. Information Security and Cryptography. Springer, Heidelberg (2002). https://doi.org/10.1007/978-3-662-04722-4

23. Dai, W., Hoang, V.T., Tessaro, S.: Information-theoretic indistinguishability via the chi-squared method. In: Katz, J., Shacham, H., (eds.) [33], pp. 497–523. https://doi.org/10.1007/978-3-319-63697-9_17

24. Dworkin, M.: NIST SP 800–38A: Recommendation for block cipher modes of operation: methods and techniques (2001)

25. Gilboa, S., Gueron, S.: Distinguishing a truncated random permutation from a random function. Cryptology ePrint Archive, Report 2015/773 (2015). http://eprint.iacr.org/2015/773

26. Gilboa, S., Gueron, S.: The advantage of truncated permutations. CoRR abs/1610.02518 (2016). http://arxiv.org/abs/1610.02518
27. Gilboa, S., Gueron, S., Morris, B.: How many queries are needed to distinguish a truncated random permutation from a random function? J. Cryptol. **31**(1), 162–171 (2018). https://doi.org/10.1007/s00145-017-9253-0
28. Gueron, S., Langley, A., Lindell, Y.: AES-GCM-SIV: specification and analysis. Cryptology ePrint Archive, Report 2017/168 (2017). http://eprint.iacr.org/2017/168
29. Gueron, S., Lindell, Y.: GCM-SIV: full nonce misuse-resistant authenticated encryption at under one cycle per byte. In: Ray, I., Li, N., Kruegel, C. (eds.) Proceedings of the 22nd ACM SIGSAC Conference on Computer and Communications Security, Denver, CO, USA, 12–16 October 2015, pp. 109–119. ACM, New York (2015). https://doi.org/10.1145/2810103.2813613
30. Hall, C., Wagner, D., Kelsey, J., Schneier, B.: Building PRFs from PRPs. In: Krawczyk, H. (ed.) CRYPTO 1998. LNCS, vol. 1462, pp. 370–389. Springer, Heidelberg (1998). https://doi.org/10.1007/BFb0055742
31. Impagliazzo, R., Rudich, S.: Limits on the provable consequences of one-way permutations. In: Goldwasser, S. (ed.) CRYPTO 1988. LNCS, vol. 403, pp. 8–26. Springer, New York (1990). https://doi.org/10.1007/0-387-34799-2_2
32. Iwata, T., Seurin, Y.: Reconsidering the security bound of AES-GCM-SIV. IACR Trans. Symmetric Cryptol. **2017**(4), 240–267 (2017). https://doi.org/10.13154/tosc.v2017.i4.240-267
33. Katz, J., Shacham, H. (eds.): Advances in Cryptology - CRYPTO 2017-37th Annual International Cryptology Conference, Santa Barbara, CA, USA, 20–24 August 2017, Proceedings, Part III. LNCS, vol. 10403. Springer, Heidelberg (2017). https://doi.org/10.1007/978-3-319-63697-9
34. Kemperman, J.H.: On the optimum rate of transmitting information. Ann. Math. Stat. **40**(6), 2156–2177 (1969). https://doi.org/10.1214/aoms/1177697293
35. Kullback, S.: A lower bound for discrimination information in terms of variation (corresp.). IEEE Trans. Inf. Theory **13**(1), 126–127 (1967). https://doi.org/10.1109/TIT.1967.1053968
36. Kullback, S., Leibler, R.A.: On information and sufficiency. Ann. Math. Stat. **22**(1), 79–86 (1951). https://doi.org/10.1214/aoms/1177729694
37. Lindell, Y., Langley, A., Gueron, S.: AES-GCM-SIV: Nonce Misuse-Resistant Authenticated Encryption. Internet-Draft draft-irtf-cfrg-gcmsiv-05, Internet Engineering Task Force, May 2017, Work in Progress. https://datatracker.ietf.org/doc/html/draft-irtf-cfrg-gcmsiv-05
38. Lucks, S.: The sum of PRPs is a secure PRF. In: Preneel, B. (ed.) EUROCRYPT 2000. LNCS, vol. 1807, pp. 470–484. Springer, Heidelberg (2000). https://doi.org/10.1007/3-540-45539-6_34
39. McGrew, D.A., Viega, J.: The security and performance of the Galois/Counter Mode (GCM) of operation. In: Canteaut, A., Viswanathan, K. (eds.) INDOCRYPT 2004. LNCS, vol. 3348, pp. 343–355. Springer, Heidelberg (2004). https://doi.org/10.1007/978-3-540-30556-9_27
40. Mennink, B., Neves, S.: Encrypted Davies-Meyer and its dual: towards optimal security using mirror theory. In: Katz, J., Shacham, H. (eds.) CRYPTO 2017. LNCS, vol. 10403, pp. 556–583. https://doi.org/10.1007/978-3-319-63697-9_19
41. Mennink, B., Neves, S.: Optimal PRFs from blockcipher designs. IACR Trans. Symmetric Cryptol. **2017**(3), 228–252 (2017). https://doi.org/10.13154/tosc.v2017.i3.228-252

42. Mennink, B., Preneel, B.: On the XOR of multiple random permutations. In: Malkin, T., Kolesnikov, V., Lewko, A.B., Polychronakis, M. (eds.) ACNS 2015. LNCS, vol. 9092, pp. 619–634. Springer, Cham (2015). https://doi.org/10.1007/978-3-319-28166-7_30

43. Morimoto, T.: Markov processes and the H-theorem. J. Phys. Soc. Jpn. **18**(3), 328–331 (1963). https://doi.org/10.1143/JPSJ.18.328

44. Patarin, J.: A proof of security in $O(2^n)$ for the Xor of two random permutations. In: Safavi-Naini, R. (ed.) ICITS 2008. LNCS, vol. 5155, pp. 232–248. Springer, Heidelberg (2008). https://doi.org/10.1007/978-3-540-85093-9_22

45. Patarin, J.: Introduction to mirror theory: analysis of systems of linear equalities and linear non equalities for cryptography. Cryptology ePrint Archive, Report 2010/287 (2010). http://eprint.iacr.org/2010/287

46. Patarin, J.: Security in $O(2^n)$ for the Xor of two random permutations - proof with the standard h technique-. Cryptology ePrint Archive, Report 2013/368 (2013). http://eprint.iacr.org/2013/368

47. Stam, A.J.: Distance between sampling with and without replacement. Stat. Neerl. **32**(2), 81–91 (1978). https://doi.org/10.1111/j.1467-9574.1978.tb01387.x

48. Stam, A.J.: A note on sampling with and without replacement. Stat. Neerl. **40**(1), 35–38 (1986). https://doi.org/10.1111/j.1467-9574.1986.tb01162.x

49. Wegman, M.N., Carter, L.: New hash functions and their use in authentication and set equality. J. Comput. Syst. Sci. **22**(3), 265–279 (1981). https://doi.org/10.1016/0022-0000(81)90033-7

Poly-Logarithmic Side Channel Rank Estimation via Exponential Sampling

Liron David[(✉)] and Avishai Wool[(✉)]

School of Electrical Engineering, Tel Aviv University,
Ramat Aviv, 69978 Tel Aviv, Israel
lirondavid@gmail.com, yash@eng.tau.ac.il

Abstract. Rank estimation is an important tool for a side-channel evaluations laboratories. It allows estimating the remaining security after an attack has been performed, quantified as the time complexity and the memory consumption required to brute force the key given the leakages as probability distributions over d subkeys (usually key bytes). These estimations are particularly useful where the key is not reachable with exhaustive search.

We propose ESrank, the first rank estimation algorithm that enjoys provable poly-logarithmic time- and space-complexity, which also achieves excellent practical performance. Our main idea is to use exponential sampling to drastically reduce the algorithm's complexity. Importantly, ESrank is simple to build from scratch, and requires no algorithmic tools beyond a sorting function. After rigorously bounding the accuracy, time and space complexities, we evaluated the performance of ESrank on a real SCA data corpus, and compared it to the currently-best histogram-based algorithm. We show that ESrank gives excellent rank estimation (with roughly a 1-bit margin between lower and upper bounds), with a performance that is on-par with the Histogram algorithm: a run-time of under 1 s on a standard laptop using 6.5 MB RAM.

1 Introduction

1.1 Background

Side-channel attacks (SCA) represent a serious threat to the security of cryptographic hardware products. As such, they reveal the secret key of a cryptosystem based on leakage information gained from physical implementation of the cryptosystem on different devices. Information provided by sources such as timing [14], power consumption [13], electromagnetic emulation [23], electromagnetic radiation [2,11] and other sources, can be exploited by SCA to break cryptosystems.

A security evaluation of a cryptographic device should determine whether an implementation is secure against such an attack. To do so, the evaluator needs to determine how much time, what kind of computing power and how

© Springer Nature Switzerland AG 2019
M. Matsui (Ed.): CT-RSA 2019, LNCS 11405, pp. 330–349, 2019.
https://doi.org/10.1007/978-3-030-12612-4_17

much storage a malicious attacker would need to recover the key given the side-channel leakages. The leakage of cryptographic implementations is highly device-specific, therefore the usual strategy for an evaluation laboratory is to launch a set of popular attacks, and to determine whether the adversary can break the implementation (i.e., recover the key) using "reasonable" efforts.

Most of the attacks that have been published in the literature are based on a "divide-and-conquer" strategy. In the first "divide" part, the cryptanalyst recovers multi-dimensional information about different parts of the key, usually called subkeys (e.g., each of the $d = 16$ AES key bytes can be a subkey). In the "conquer" part the cryptanalyst combines the information all together in an efficient way via key enumeration [7,21,25]. In the attacks we consider in this paper, the information that the SCA provides for each subkey is a probability distribution over the N candidate values for that subkey, and the SCA probability of a full key is the product of the SCA probabilities of its d subkeys.

A security evaluator knows the secret key and aims to estimate the number of decryption attempts the attacker needs to do before he reaches to the correct key, assuming the attacker uses the SCA's probability distribution. Clearly enumerating the keys in the optimal SCA-predicted order is the best strategy the evaluator can follow. However, this is limited by the computational power of the evaluator. This is a worrying situation because it is hard to decide whether an implementation is "practically secure". For example, one could enumerate the 2^{50} first keys for an AES implementation (in the optimal order) without finding the correct key, and then conclude that the implementation is practically secure because the attacker needs to enumerate beyond 2^{50} number of keys. But, this does not provide any hint whether the concrete security level is 2^{51} or 2^{120}. This makes a significant difference in practice, especially in view of the possibility of improved measurement setups, signal processing, information extraction, etc., that should be taken into account for any physical security evaluation, e.g., via larger security margins.

In this paper, we introduce a new method to estimate the rank of a given secret key in the optimal SCA-predicted order. Our algorithm enjoys simplicity, accuracy and provable poly-logarithmic time and memory efficiency and excellent practical performance.

The Rank Estimation Problem: Given d independent subkey spaces each of size N with their corresponding probability distributions $P_1, \ldots, P_d$ such that P_i is sorted in decreasing order of probabilities, and given a key k^* indexed by $(k_1, \ldots, k_d)$, let $p^* = P_1(k_1) \cdot P_2(k_2) \cdot \ldots \cdot P_d(k_d)$ be the probability of k^* to be the correct key. The evaluator would like to estimate the number of full keys with probability higher than p^*, when the probability of a full key is defined as the product of its subkey's probabilities.

In other words, the evaluator would like to estimate k^*'s rank: the position of the key k^* in the sorted list of N^d possible keys when the list is sorted in decreasing probability order, from the most likely key to the least. If the dimensions, or k^*'s rank are small, one can easily compute the rank of the correct key by a straightforward key enumeration. However, for a key with a high rank r, any optimal-order key enumeration requires $\Omega(r)$ time—which may be prohibitive, and the currently-best optimal-order key enumeration algorithm [25] requires $\Omega(N^{d/2})$ space, which again may be prohibitive. Hence developing fast and low-memory algorithms to estimate the rank without enumeration is of great interest.

1.2   Related Work

The best key enumeration algorithm so far, in terms of optimal-order, was presented by Veyrat-Charvillon, Gérard, Renauld and Standaert in [25]. However, its worst case space complexity is $\Omega(N^{d/2})$ when d is the number of subkey dimensions and N is the number of candidates per subkey - and its space complexity is $\Omega(r)$ when enumerating up to a key at rank $r \leq N^{d/2}$. Thus its space complexity becomes a bottleneck on real computers with bounded RAM in realistic SCA attacks.

Since then several near-optimal key enumeration were proposed [4,5,7,12,15–17,19,20,22,24,28]. However, none of these key enumeration algorithms enumerate the whole key space within a realistic amount of time and with a realistic amount of computational power: enumerating an exponential key space will always come at an exponential cost. Hence the need for efficient and accurate rank estimation for keys that have a high rank.

The first rank estimation algorithm was proposed by Veyrat-Charvillon et al. [26]. They suggested to organize the keys by sorting their subkeys according to the a-posteriori probabilities provided, and to represent them as a high-dimensional dataspace. The full key space can then be partitioned in two volumes: one defined by the key candidates with probability higher than the correct key, one defined by the key candidates with probability lower than the correct key. Using this geometrical representation, the rank estimation problem can be stated as the one of finding bounds on these "higher" and "lower" volumes. It essentially works by carving volumes representing key candidates on each side of their boundary, progressively refining the lower and upper bounds on the key rank. Refining the bounds becomes exponentially difficult at some point.

A number of works have investigated solutions to improve upon [26]. In particular, Glowacz et al. [12] presented a rank estimation algorithm that is based on a convolution of histograms and allows obtaining tight bounds for the key rank of (even large) keys. This Histogram algorithm is currently the best rank estimation algorithm we are aware of. The space complexity of this algorithm is $O(dB)$ where d is the number of dimensions and B is a design parameter controlling the number of the histogram bins. A comparable result was developed independently by Bernstein et al. [4].

Martin et al. [20] used a score-based rank enumeration, rather than a probability based rank estimation. They mapped the rank estimation to a knapsack problem, which can be simplified and expressed as path counting. Subsequently, in [18] Martin et al. show that their algorithm [20] is mathematically equivalent to the Histogram algorithm [12] for a suitable choice of their respective discretization parameter, thus they can both be equally accurate. Since the two algorithms are equivalent we compared our algorithm's performance only to that of the Histogram algorithm [12].

Ye et al. investigated an alternative solution based on a weak Maximum Likelihood (wML) approach [28], rather than a Maximum Likelihood (ML) one for the previous examples. They additionally combined this wML approach with the possibility to approximate the security of an implementation based on "easier to sample" metrics, e.g., starting from the subkey Success Rates (SR) rather than their likelihoods. Later Duc et al. [9] described a simple alternative to the algorithm of Ye et al. and provided an "even easier to sample" bound on the subkey SR, by exploiting their formal connection with a Mutual Information metric. Recently, Wang et al. [27] presented a rank estimation for at dependent score lists.

Choudary et al. [6] presented a method for estimating Massey's guessing entropy (GM) which is the statistical expectation of the position of the correct key in the sorted distribution. Their method allows to estimate the GM within a few bits. However, the *actual* guessing entropy (GE), i.e., the *rank* of the correct key, is sometimes quite different from the expectation. In contrast, our algorithm focuses on the real GE.

1.3   Contribution

In this paper we propose a simple and effective new rank estimation method called ESrank, that is fundamentally different from previous approaches. We have rigorously analyzed its accuracy, time and space complexities. Our main idea is to use exponential sampling to drastically reduce the algorithm's complexity. We prove ESrank has a poly-logarithmic time- and space-complexity: for a design parameter $1 < \gamma \leq 2$ ESrank has $O(\frac{d^2}{4}(\log_\gamma N)^2 \log(\log_\gamma N))$ time and $O(d \log_\gamma N + \frac{d^2}{16}(\log_\gamma N)^2)$ space, and it can be driven to any desired level of accuracy (trading off time and space against accuracy). Importantly, ESrank is simple to build from scratch, and requires no algorithmic tools beyond a sorting function.

Beyond asymptotic analysis, we evaluated the performance of ESrank through extensive simulations based on a real SCA data corpus, and compared it to the currently-best histogram-based algorithm. We showed that ESrank gives excellent rank estimation (with roughly a 1-bit margin between lower and upper bounds), with a performance that is on-par with the Histogram algorithm: a run-time of under 1s, for all ranks up to 2^{128}, on a standard laptop using at most 6.5 MB RAM. Hence ESrank is a useful addition to the SCA evaluator's toolbox.

2   The ESrank Algorithm for the Case $d = 2$

We start with describing the idea of our algorithm in case $d = 2$, then we shall extend this idea for the general case $d \geq 2$.

Algorithm 1. Exact rank.

Input: Two non-decreasing probability distributions P_1, P_2 of size N each, the correct key $k^* = (k_1, k_2)$ and its probability $p^* = P_1[k_1] \cdot P_2[k_2]$.

Output: $Rank(k^*)$.

```
1  i = 1; j = N; rank = 0;
2  while i ≤ N and j ≥ 1 do
3      p = P₁[i] · P₂[j];
4      if p ≥ p* then
5          rank = rank + j;
6          i = i + 1;
7      else
8          j = j − 1;
9  return rank;
```

2.1   An Exact Rank Estimation for $d = 2$

Definition 1 ($Rank(k^*)$). *Let d non-increasing subkey probability distributions P_i for $1 \le i \le d$ and the correct key $k^* = (k_1, \ldots, k_d)$ be given. Let $p^* = P_1[k_1] \cdot \ldots \cdot P_d[k_d]$ be the probability of the correct key. Then, define $Rank(k^*)$ to be the number of keys $(x_1, \ldots, x_d)$ s.t. $P_1[x_1] \cdot \ldots \cdot P_d[x_d] \ge p^*$.*

Definition 2. *Let 2 non-increasing subkey probability distributions P_1 and P_2, each of size N, the correct key $k^* = (k_1, k_2)$ and an index $1 \le i \le N$ be given. Let $p^* = P_1[k_1] \cdot P_2[k_2]$ be the probability of the correct key. Then define H_i to be the number of points (i, j) such that $P_1[i] \cdot P_2[j] \ge p^*$, i.e.,*

$$H_i(k^*) = |\{(i, j) | P_1[i] \cdot P_2[j] \ge p^*\}|.$$

The idea of the algorithm is to find $H_i(k^*)$ for each i. The rank of the correct key k^* is the sum of $H_i(k^*)$ over $1 \le i \le N$, i.e.,

$$Rank(k^*) = \sum_{i=1}^{N} H_i(k^*).$$

The pseudo code is described in Algorithm 1. The correctness of Algorithm 1 stems from the observation that $H_i \ge H_{i+1}$ for all $1 \le i \le N - 1$. Therefore, to find H_{i+1}, j starts from H_i and it is decreased until H_{i+1} is found.

Proposition 1. *The running time of Algorithm 1 is $\Theta(N)$.*

Proof: In the technical report [8].

Algorithm 1 is reminiscent of the Threshold key enumeration algorithm of [17].

2.2   Exponential Sampling with $d = 2$

To make this algorithm faster, we use exponential sampling. Intuitively, we sample a set of indices SI and run Algorithm 1 on the $SI \times SI$ grid. On the sampled indices Algorithm 1 is no longer exact, but we can modify it to produce lower and upper bounds on $Rank(k^*)$. As we shall see, if we use exponential sampling, we can bound the inaccuracy introduced by the sampling.

Given a non-increasing subkey probability distribution P of size N, the exponential sampling process returns a sampled probability distribution (SI, SP) of size N_s where $N_s = O(\log N)$. SI contains the sampled indices and SP contains their corresponding probabilities such that $SP[i] = P[SI[i]]$ for all $i \leq N_s$.

The goal of the exponential sampling is to maintain an invariant on the ratio between sampled indices. Let $1 < \gamma \leq 2$ be given and let b be the smallest i such that $i/(i-1) \leq \gamma$. The first b sampled indices are the first b indices of P. The rest of the sampled indices are sampled from P at powers of γ. Formally,

Definition 3. *Given a non-increasing subkey probability distribution P of size N, the exponential sampling process returns a sampled probability distribution (SI, SP) of size N_s such that for all $i \leq N_s - 1$:*

$$\begin{cases} SI[i] = i & \text{if } i \leq b \\ SI[i]/SI[i-1] \leq \gamma \text{ and } SI[i+1]/SI[i-1] > \gamma & \text{otherwise.} \end{cases} \tag{1}$$

E.g., if $\gamma = 2$ then $b = 2$, and for $SI = \{1, 2, 4, 8, \ldots, N\}$ invariant (1) holds. The pseudo code of this sampling is described in Algorithm 2. Note that the indices 1 and N are always included in SI.

Lemma 1. *If SI is the output of Algorithm 2 then for any index $i \geq b + 1$ in SI it holds that*

$$SI[i] = \lfloor \gamma \cdot SI[i-1] \rfloor.$$

and

$$SI[i] - SI[i-1] = \lfloor (\gamma - 1) \cdot SI[i-1] \rfloor.$$

Proof: In the technical report [8].

Proposition 2. *Let $N_s = |SI|$ be the size the sample returned by Algorithm 2. Then $b + \log_\gamma(N/b) \leq N_s < b + \log_\gamma(N/(b-1))$.*

Proof: Since $b \cdot \gamma^{N_s} \geq N$ and $b \cdot \gamma^{N_s-1} < N$.

To calculate the upper and lower bounds of the correct key $k^* = (k_1, k_2)$ given two sampled probability distributions, we generalize $H_i(k^*)$ for the sampled case:

Definition 4. *Let two sampled probability distributions $(SI, SP_1), (SI, SP_2)$, each of size N_s, the correct key $k^* = (k_1, k_2)$, its probability p^* and an index $1 \leq i \leq N_s$ be given. Then define H_i^S to be the number of points (i, j) s.t. $1 \leq j \leq N$ and $SP_1[i] \cdot P_2[j] \geq p^*$, i.e.,*

$$H_i^S(k^*) = |\{(i, j) | 1 \leq j \leq N \text{ and } SP_1[i] \cdot P_2[j] \geq p^*\}|.$$

Algorithm 2. Exponential Sampling Process.

Input: A probability distribution P of size N, b, γ.
Output: A sampled probability distribution (SI, SP).
1 **for** $i = 1$ *to* b **do**
2 $\quad |\quad SI[i] = i;\ SP[i] = P[i];$
3 $j = b;\ i = j + 1;\ c = j + 1;$
4 **while** $i < N$ **do**
5 $\quad |\quad$ **if** $i/j \leq \gamma$ *and* $(i + 1)/j > \gamma$ **then**
6 $\quad |\quad\quad |\quad SI[c] = i;\ SP[c] = P[i];$
7 $\quad |\quad\quad |\quad c = c + 1;\ j = i;$
8 $\quad |\quad i = i + 1;$
9 $SI[c] - N;\ SP[c] = P[N];$
10 **return** (SI, SP);

The difference between every two successive indices in the sampled probability distributions might be bigger than 1, i.e., $SI[i + 1] - SI[i] > 1$ therefore, besides counting H_i^S for each $i \leq N_s$ we also need to add the number of points (i', j) such that $SI[i] < i' < SI[i+1]$ for each $i \leq N_s - 1$. Recall that Algorithm 2 always includes $i = N$ in SI.

Definition 5. *Let two sampled probability distributions* $(SI, SP_1), (SI, SP_2)$, *each of size* N_s, *the correct key* $k^* = (k_1, k_2)$, *its probability* p^* *and an index* $1 \leq i \leq N_s$ *be given. Then define* $H_{a,b}^S$ *be the number of* (i, j) *s.t.* $1 \leq j \leq N$ *and* $SI[a] < i < SI[b]$ *and* $SP_1[i] \cdot P_2[j] \geq p^*$, *i.e.,*

$$H_{a,b}^S(k^*) = |\{(i,j) | 1 \leq j \leq N \text{ and } P_1[i] \cdot P_2[j] \geq p^* \text{ and } SI[a] < i < SI[b]\}|.$$

The idea of Algorithm 3 is to find $H_i^S(k^*)$ for each $i \in \{1, \ldots, N_s\}$ and $H_{i,i+1}^S(k^*)$ for each $i \in \{1, \ldots, N_s - 1\}$. The rank of the correct key k^* is the following sum:

$$Rank(k^*) = \sum_{i=1}^{N_s} H_i^S(k^*) + \sum_{i=1}^{N_s-1} H_{i,i+1}^S(k^*).$$

Since we are given sampled distributions, we cannot calculate the exact values of $H_i^S(k^*)$ and $H_{i,i+1}^S(k^*)$. Instead we calculate upper and lower bounds for each $H_i^S(k^*)$ and $H_{i,i+1}^S(k^*)$ as illustrated in Fig. 1.

Definition 6. *Let* $up(H_i^S(k^*))$ *be an upper bound of* $H_i^S(k^*)$ *and let* $up(H_{i,i+1}^S(k^*))$ *be an upper bound of* $H_{i,i+1}^S(k^*)$, *i.e.,*

$$H_i^S(k^*) \leq up(H_i^S(k^*)) \text{ and } H_{i,i+1}^S(k^*) \leq up(H_{i,i+1}^S(k^*)).$$

Definition 7. *Let* $low(H_i^S(k^*))$ *be a lower bound of* $H_i^S(k^*)$ *and let* $low(H_{i,i+1}^S(k^*))$ *be a lower bound of* $H_{i,i+1}^S(k^*)$, *i.e.,*

$$H_i^S(k^*) \geq low(H_i^S(k^*)) \text{ and } H_{i,i+1}^S(k^*) \geq low(H_i^S(k^*)).$$

Algorithm 3. Calculating Upper and Lower bounds.

Input: Sampled probability distributions SP_1, SP_2 each of size N_s, b, the correct key $k^* = (k_1, k_2)$ and it probability p^*.

Output: Upper and lower bounds on $Rank(k^*)$.

```
1  iLast = Ns; jLast = Ns;
2  if k1 == 1 then jLast = k2;
3  if k2 == 1 then iLast = k1;
4  i = 1; j = jLast; ub = 0; lb = 0;
5  while i ≤ iLast and j ≥ 1 do
6  │   pCurr = SP1[i] · SP2[j];
7  │   if pCurr ≥ p* then
8  │   │   u = l = SI2[j]; uPrev = u;
9  │   │   ub = ub + u; lb = lb + l;
10 │   │   if i ≥ b + 1 then
11 │   │   │   ub = ub + uPrev · (SI[i] − SI[i − 1] − 1);
12 │   │   │   lb = lb + l · (SI[i] − SI[i − 1] − 1);
13 │   │   i = i + 1;
14 │   else if j > 1 then
15 │   │   pNext = SP1[i] · SP2[j − 1];
16 │   │   if pNext < p* < pCurr then
17 │   │   │   u = SI[j] − 1; l = SI[j − 1]; uPrev = u;
18 │   │   │   ub = ub + u; lb = lb + l;
19 │   │   │   if i ≥ b + 1 then
20 │   │   │   │   ub = ub + uPrev · (SI[i] − SI[i − 1] − 1);
21 │   │   │   │   lb = lb + l · (SI[i] − SI[i − 1] − 1);
22 │   │   │   i = i + 1;
23 │   │   else
24 │   │   │   j = j − 1;
25 │   else
26 │   │   j = j − 1;
27 if j < 1 and i ≤ iLast then
28 │   ub = ub + uPrev · (SI[i] − SI[i − 1] − 1);
29 return (lb, ub);
```

Therefore, it holds

$$\sum_{i=1}^{N_s} low(H_i(k^*)) + \sum_{i=1}^{N_s-1} low(H_{i,i+1}(k^*)) \leq Rank(k^*)$$

$$\leq \sum_{i=1}^{N_s} up(H_i(k^*)) + \sum_{i=1}^{N_s-1} up(H_{i,i+1}(k^*)). \tag{2}$$

Our algorithm is intuitively similar to exponential searching [3]; note that in our case the parameter γ is fractional.

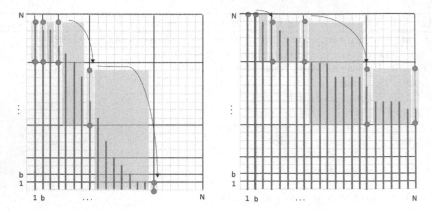

Fig. 1. The red bars represent the un-sampled H_i's, and the black grid represents the sampled indices in SI. For each sampled index $1 \le i \le N_s$ the blue circles are upper and lower bounds on $H_i^S(k^*)$. The yellow-shaded rectangles represent $H_{i,i+1}^S(k^*)$ for each $b \le i \le N_s - 1$, for two different keys. Note that the yellow-shaded rectangles stop exactly one index before the sampled indices, in both dimensions. (Color figure online)

2.3   Bounding the Sampled Distributions

Given two probability distributions P_1 and P_2, each of size N, we first sample the indices using Algorithm 2. We get sampled probability distributions (SI, SP_1) and (SI, SP_2) each of size N_s when SI is the set of sampled indices and SP_1, SP_2 are the corresponding sampled probabilities. Given these sampled probability distributions, the next step is to calculate an upper bound and a lower bound for $Rank(k^*)$. This is done in Algorithm 3.

To do this, it keeps two variables: ub for the upper bound and lb for the lower bound. At the beginning, both ub and lb are initialized to 0.

Definition 8. *Given a key k^*, and given $1 \le i \le N_s$, let u_i be the value of u at iteration i in Algorithm 3 and let l_i be the value of l at iteration i in Algorithm 3.*

Algorithm 3 starts with $i = 1$ and $j = N_s$. It decreases j until one of the two options happens:
(a) (line 16) We reach the highest j such that

$$SP_1[i] \cdot SP_2[j] < p^* < SP_1[i] \cdot SP_2[j-1].$$

In this case $(i, j) \in H_i^S(k^*)$ but $(i, j-1) \notin H_i^S(k^*)$, therefore

$$SI[j-1] \le H_i^S(k^*) \le SI[j] - 1.$$

Therefore the values of l_i and u_i become

$$l_i = SI[j-1] \text{ and } u_i = SI[j] - 1, \tag{3}$$

and the running totals ub and lb are updated (line 9).
(b) (line 7) We reach the highest j such that

$$SP_1[i] \cdot SP_2[j] \geq p^*.$$

In this case we have the exact value of $H_i^S(k^*)$ which is

$$H_i^S(k^*) = SI[j].$$

Therefore the values of l_i and u_i become

$$l_i = u_i = SI[j], \tag{4}$$

and the running totals ub and lb are updated (line 18).

In the next step, after finding bounds on H_i^S, the algorithm moves to $i+1$ and finds bounds on H_{i+1}^S. Since $H_i^S \geq H_{i+1}^S$ we start from j of the previous iteration i.e., j s.t. $SI[j-1] \leq H_i^S \leq SI[j]$ and decrease it to get the corresponding bounds on H_{i+1}^S.

Once $i \geq b+1$ (lines 10, 19) the difference $SI[i] - SI[i-1] \geq 1$ therefore $H_{i-1,i}^S(k^*) \geq 1$ and it should be added. To upper bound this number we multiply the upper bound of H_{i-1}^S, which is $uPrev_i = u_{i-1}$, by the width of $H_{i-1,i}^S(k^*)$, which is $(SI[i] - SI[i-1] - 1)$ (lines 11, 20). To lower bound $H_{i-1,i}^S(k^*)$ we multiply the lower bound of H_i^S, which is l_i by the width of $H_{i-1,i}^S(k^*)$, (lines 12, 21); see Fig. 1.

Theorem 1. *Let two sampled probability distributions SP_1 and SP_2, which are sampled from the probability distributions P_1 and P_2 respectively using Algorithm 2 with $\gamma > 1$ be given and let b be the smallest i such that $i/(i-1) \leq \gamma$. For a key k^*, let ub and lb be the outputs of Algorithm 3. Then $ub/lb \leq \gamma^2$.*

Proof: From Eq. (2) it holds that

$$ub = \sum_{i=1}^{N_s} up(H_i(k^*)) + \sum_{i=1}^{N_s-1} up(H_{i,i+1}(k^*)).$$

Since

$$up(H_i^S(k^*)) = u_i \text{ and } up(H_{i,i+1}(k^*)) = u_i \cdot (SI[i+1] - SI[i] - 1)$$

we get

$$ub = \sum_{i=1}^{N_s} u_i + \sum_{i=1}^{N_s-1} u_i \cdot (SI[i+1] - SI[i] - 1).$$

Since $SI[i+1] - SI[i] = 1$ for all $1 \le i \le b-1$, the first $b-1$ elements of the second sum are 0.

$$ub = \sum_{i=1}^{N_s} u_i + \sum_{i=b}^{N_s-1} u_i \cdot (SI[i+1] - SI[i]) - 1)$$

$$\sum_{i=1}^{b-1} u_i + \sum_{i=b}^{N_s-1} \left(u_i + u_i \cdot (SI[i+1] - SI[i] - 1) \right) + u_{N_s}$$

$$\sum_{i=1}^{b-1} u_i + \sum_{i=b}^{N_s-1} u_i \cdot (SI[i+1] - SI[i])) + u_{N_s}$$

Separating the b'th term from the second sum we get

$$ub \le \left(\sum_{i=1}^{b-1} u_i \right) + u_b \cdot (SI[b+1] - SI[b]) + u_{N_s} + \sum_{i=b+1}^{N_s-1} u_i \cdot (SI[i+1] - SI[i]). \quad (5)$$

Similarly from Eq. (2) it holds that

$$lb = \sum_{i=1}^{N_s} low(H_i(k^*)) + \sum_{i=1}^{N_s-1} low(H_{i,i+1}(k^*)).$$

Since

$$low(H_i^S(k^*)) = l_i \text{ and } low(H_{i,i+1}(k^*)) = l_{i+1} \cdot (SI[i+1] - SI[i] - 1)$$

(Note the shift in indices where the multiplication is by the lower bound of $i+1$) we get

$$lb = \sum_{i=1}^{N_s} l_i + \sum_{i=1}^{N_s-1} l_{i+1} \cdot (SI[i+1] - SI[i] - 1).$$

Again the first $b-1$ elements of the second sum are 0, therefore

$$lb = \sum_{i=1}^{N_s} l_i + \sum_{i=b}^{N_s-1} l_{i+1} \cdot (SI[i+1] - SI[i] - 1).$$

By shifting index i by 1 in the second sum, we get

$$lb = \sum_{i=1}^{N_s} l_i + \sum_{i=b+1}^{N_s} l_i \cdot (SI[i] - SI[i-1] - 1)$$

$$= \sum_{i=1}^{b} l_i + \sum_{i=b+1}^{N_s} \left(l_i + l_i \cdot (SI[i] - SI[i-1] - 1) \right)$$

$$= \sum_{i=1}^{b} l_i + \sum_{i=b+1}^{N_s} l_i \cdot (SI[i] - SI[i-1])$$

$$\ge \sum_{i=1}^{b} l_i + \sum_{i=b+1}^{N_s-1} l_i \cdot (SI_1[i] - SI_1[i-1]).$$

(6)

In order to show $ub/lb \leq \gamma^2$, we prove the following two Lemmas:

Lemma 2.

$$\left(\sum_{i=b+1}^{N_s-1} u_i \cdot (SI[i+1] - SI[i]) \right) \Big/ \left(\sum_{i=b+1}^{N_s-1} l_i \cdot (SI[i] - SI[i-1]) \right) \leq \gamma^2$$

Lemma 3.

$$\left(\left(\sum_{i=1}^{b-1} u_i \right) + u_b \cdot (SI[b+1] - SI[b]) + u_{N_s} \right) \Big/ \left(\sum_{i=1}^{b} l_i \right) \leq \gamma^2.$$

3   The General Case $d > 2$

Given $d > 2$ sampled probability distributions $(SI_1, SP_1), \ldots, (SI_d, SP_d)$, and the correct key $k^* = (k_1, \ldots, k_d)$, we now follow the intuition of the $d = 2$ case to solve the general case. To do so, we organize the d distributions into pairs, merge the pairs into $d/2$ joint distributions, sub-sample the joint distributions, and continue in the same way until we get to a single pair of distributions sampled from the $N^{d/2}$-dimensioned half-keys. We achieve this via a sequence of algorithms described below.

3.1   Merging Two Sampled Distributions into a Joint Distribution

Given two sampled non-increasing probability distributions (SI_1, SP_1), (SI_2, SP_2), each of size N_s, we wish to merge them into one non-increasing distribution, and compute lower and upper bounds on the ranks of the points. Algorithm 4 implements this task.

First, the algorithm goes over the grid of N_s^2 points (i, j) such that $1 \leq i \leq N_s$ and $1 \leq j \leq N_s$. For each point (i, j) it calculates the point's probability $SP_1[i] \cdot SP_2[j]$. Then, it sorts these points in decreasing order of their probabilities.

Given two consecutive points (i_1, j_1) and (i_2, j_2) in the sorted order such that $Prob(i_1, j_1) \geq Prob(i_2, j_2)$, all the points whose probability is greater than $Prob(i_1, j_1)$ are also greater than $Prob(i_2, j_2)$, therefore, all the points in the rank of (i_1, j_1) are contained in the rank of (i_2, j_2). Relying on this observation, if we know the order of the N_s^2 points according to their probabilities, we can bound the accumulative rank of these points while going over them from the most likely point to the least. In this way, the upper-bound of the rank of the current point (i_c, j_c) is the upper bound of the previous point (i_p, j_p) plus the following expressions:

$$\begin{aligned} &+ (SI[j_p+1] - SI[j_p]) \cdot (SI[i_p+1] - SI[i_p] - 1) \\ &+ SI[j_p+1] - SI[j_p] - 1 \\ &+ 1 \\ &= (SI[j_p+1] - SI[j_p]) \cdot (SI[i_p+1] - SI[i_p]). \end{aligned} \tag{7}$$

Algorithm 4. Calculating the joint probability distribution.

Input: Sampled probability distributions SP_1, SP_2 each of size N_s.

Output: Joint probability distribution.

```
1  r = 1;
2  for i = 1 to N_s do
3  |    for j = 1 to N_s do
4  |    |    Y(r, 1) = SP_1[i] · SP_2[j];  Y(r, 2) = (i, j);
5  |    |    r = r + 1;
6  Y = Sort(Y) in decreasing order of Y(r, 1) ;
7  ub(1, 1) = 1;  ub(1, 2) = SP_1[1] · SP_2[1];
8  lb(1, 1) = 1;  lb(1, 2) = SP_1[1] · SP_2[1];
9  for r = 2 to N_s^2 do
10 |    (i_c, j_c) = Y(r, 2);  (i_p, j_p) = Y(r − 1, 2);
11 |    ub(r, 1) = ub(r − 1, 1) + (SI(j_p + 1) − SI(j_p)) · (SI(i_p + 1) − SI(i_p));
12 |    lb(r, 1) = lb(r − 1, 1) + (SI(j_c) − SI(j_c − 1)) · (SI(i_c) − SI_1(i_c − 1));
13 |    ub(r, 2) = lb(r, 2) = Y(r, 2);
14 return (ub, lb);
```

The first term in (7), $(SI[j_p + 1] − SI[j_p]) · (SI[i_p + 1] − SI[i_p] − 1)$, represents the number of points that might come after the previous point and before the current point, which are not on the SI grid. I.e., these are the points (i, j) s.t.

$$SI[i_p] < i < SI[i_p + 1] \text{ and } SI[j_p] \le j < SI[j_p + 1].$$

$SI[j_p + 1]$ is not included since we haven't reached that point yet.

The second term in (7), $SI[j_p + 1] − SI[j_p] − 1$, represents the number of points that might come after the previous point and before the current point which *are* on the SI grid. I.e., these are the points (i, j) s.t.

$$i = SI[i_p] \text{ and } SI[j_p] < j < SI[j_p + 1].$$

$SI[j_p]$ is not included since the point $(SI[i_p], SI[j_p])$ is the previous point and it was already included and $SI[j_p + 1]$ is not included since we haven't reached that point yet.

The last addition in (7) is 1, accounting for the current point itself.

The resulting expression can be seen in Algorithm 4 (line 11). A similar derivation can be done for the lower bound (omitted).

3.2   Sampling the Joint Probability Distribution

The output of Algorithm 4 is a distribution over N_s^2 elements. We now show that we can sub-sample this distribution, via exponential sampling, using the *same* parameters b and γ used to create the one-dimension samples. Theorem 2 below shows that a sub-sampling with the same b and γ always exists.

We would like to sample this joint probability distribution using Algorithm 2, using b and γ, except now instead of the 1-dimensional ranks we sample using the rank-upper/lower-bounds, See Algorithm 5.

Algorithm 5. Sub-Sampling the joint distribution.

Input: A joint probability distribution $(inSI, inSP)$ of size N_s^2, b, γ.
Output: A sampled probability distribution (SI, SP).
1 **for** $i = 1$ *to* b **do**
2     $SI[i] = inSI[i]$; $SP[i] = inSP[i]$;
3 $j = b$; $i = j + 1$; $c = j + 1$;
4 **while** $i < N_s^2$ **do**
5   **if** $inSI[i]/inSI[j] \leq \gamma$ *and* $inSI[i+1]/inSI[j] > \gamma$ **then**
6        $SI[c] = inSI[i]$; $SP[c] = inSP[i]$;
7        $c = c + 1$; $j = i$;
8     $i = i + 1$;
9 $SI[c] = inSI[N_s^2]$; $SP[c] = inSP[N_s^2]$;
10 **return** (SI, SP);

For this, we shall prove in Lemma 5 that the first b indices of the joint probability distribution are $1, \ldots, b$ and we shall prove in Theorem 2 that the ratio between any two successive ranks is at most γ.

Lemma 4. *For any index $i \geq b + 1$ in SI it holds that*

$$SI[i] - SI[i - 1] \leq (\gamma - 1) \cdot SI[i - 1].$$

Lemma 5. *Given two sampled probability distributions (SI_1, SP_1) and (SI_2, SP_2) that are sampled by Algorithm 2 merged by Algorithm 4. The first b upper ranks in the upper joint probability distribution are the integers $1, \ldots, b$ and the first b lower ranks in the lower joint probability distribution are the integers $1, \ldots, b$.*

Proof: According to the sampling process in Algorithm 2 it holds: $\forall i \leq b$ $SI_1[i] = i$ and $SI_2[i] = i$. Therefore, the joint probability contains the indices of $(i, j) \in \{1, \ldots, b\} \times \{1, \ldots, b\}$. Since the first b points with the highest probabilities are somewhere in the square: $\{1, \ldots, b\} \times \{1, \ldots, b\}$. The rank of the first b composed only from points in this square, therefore for $i \leq b$, the upper bound and lower bound of the i'th element in the joint distribution are equal to each other and equal to i.

Theorem 2. *Given the joint probability distribution of the sampled probability distributions $(SI_1, SP_1), (SI_2, SP_2)$, The ratio between any two consecutive upper (lower) ranks is at most γ, where $1 < \gamma \leq 2$.*

Proof: In the technical report [8].

Theorem 2 shows that in the joint $N_s \times N_s$ distribution, the upper (lower) bounds of every two consecutive points (in sorted order) obey the invariant $ub(i_c, j_c) \leq \gamma \cdot ub(i_p, j_p)$.

Corollary 1: *The sample produced by Algorithm 5 on an input distribution of size N_s^2 consists of $O(N_s)$ ranks.*

Algorithm 6. ESrank: Calculating the upper and lower bounds for $d > 2$.

Input: The probability distributions $P_1, ..., P_d$, the correct key $k^* = (k_1, ..., k_d)$, b and γ.

Output: Upper and lower bounds of $rank(k^*)$.

```
1  for i = 1 to d do
2  │   (SI_i, SP_i) = Alg2(P_i, b, γ) ;              // Sample the input distributions
3  dim = d;
4  while dim ≠ 2 do
5  │   for i = 1 to dim/2 do
6  │   │   (ub_i, lb_i) = Alg4((SI_{2i-1}, SP_{2i-1}), (SI_{2i}, SP_{2i})) ;        // Merge
7  │   │   (SI_i, SP_i) = Alg5(ub_i) ;                                         // Sub-Sample
8  │   dim = dim/2;
9  (ub', lb') = Alg3((SI_1, SP_1), (SI_2, SP_2)) ;          // Calculate upper bound
10 dim = d;
11 while dim ≠ 2 do
12 │   for i = 1 to dim/2 do
13 │   │   (ub_i, lb_i) = Alg4((SI_{2i-1}, SP_{2i-1}), (SI_{2i}, SP_{2i})) ;        // Merge
14 │   │   (SI_i, SP_i) = Alg5(lb_i) ;                                         // Sub-Sample
15 │   dim = dim/2;
16 (ub'', lb'') = Alg3((SI_1, SP_1), (SI_2, SP_2)) ;        // Calculate lower bound
17 return (ub', lb'');
```

3.3 The ESrank Algorithm: Putting it all Together

Given $d > 2$ sampled probability distributions $(SI_1, SP_1), ..., (SI_d, SP_d)$, and the correct key $k^* = (k_1, ..., k_d)$, we first merge the d sampled probability distributions into $d/2$ sampled joint distributions, so that we get $d/2$ sampled upper- and lower-bounded distributions. Now, We take the $d/2$ upper-bounded distributions and merge them into $d/4$ sampled upper-bounded distributions, and similarly for the lower bounded distribution. We continue in the same way until we get two pairs of joint distributions: one pair of upper sampled joint distributions and one pair of lower sampled joint distributions. Now, we apply Algorithm 3 on the upper pair sampled joint distribution to get the upper bound of $Rank(k^*)$ and again, we apply Algorithm 3 on the lower pair sampled joint distribution to get the lower bound of $Rank(k^*)$. Algorithm 6 shows the complete pseudo-code for ESrank.

3.4 Theoretical Performance

Time Complexity. At each level of Algorithm 6 it uses Algorithm 4 to merge the sampled distributions received from the previous level. Algorithm 4 goes over

N_s^2 pairs, calculates their probabilities using $\Theta(N_s^2)$ time, and sorts them using $\Theta(N_s^2 \cdot \log N_s)$ time. Let $T(d, \gamma)$ be the total the running time. Then

$$T(d, \gamma) \leq \sum_{i=1}^{\log d - 2} \frac{d}{2^i} (2^{i-1} \log_\gamma N)^2 \log (2^{i-1} \log_\gamma N)^2$$

$$\leq \frac{d^2}{4} (\log_\gamma N)^2 \log(\log_\gamma N).$$

I.e., we see that ESrank has a poly-logarithmic time complexity (in N).

Accuracy. Assume the correct key is $k^* = (k_1, \ldots, k_d)$. For a key (k_i, k_{i+1}) and $(SI_i, SP_i), (SI_{i+1}, SP_{i+1})$ let $k_{i,i+1}$ be the real rank of (k_i, k_{i+1}). At the lowest level Theorem 1 and Algorithm 3 give that $up(k_i, k_{i+1}) \leq \gamma^2 k_{i,i+1}$. In the next level, each rank in the sampled joint distribution is multiplied by at most γ^2, therefore each term in the sum that composes $up(\gamma^2 k_{i,i+1}, \gamma^2 k_{i+2,i+3})$ is multiplied by at most γ^4. Hence $up(\gamma^2 k_{i,i+1}, \gamma^2 k_{i+2,i+3}) \leq \gamma^4 up(k_{i,i+1}, k_{i+2,i+3}) \leq \gamma^4 \gamma^2 k_{i,i+1,i+2,i+3} = \gamma^6 k_{i,i+1,i+2,i+3}$. We continue in the same way, and get

$$up(Rank(k^*))/Rank(k^*) \leq \gamma^{\sum_{i=1}^{\log d} 2^i} = \gamma^{2d-2}.$$

Since $rank(k^*)$ might be any value in $[low(Rank(k^*)), up(Rank(k^*))]$, we get

$$accuracy(d, \gamma) = up(Rank(k^*))/low(Rank(k^*)) \leq \gamma^{2d-2}.$$

E.g., for AES-128 with a preprocessing step of merging the 16 8-bit distributions into $d = 8$ 16-bit distributions we get $2d - 2 = 14$.

Space Complexity. In the first step we need to store d distributions of size $\log_\gamma N$ from Algorithm 2. In order to merge each pair of distributions into one, we need addition memory of $(\log_\gamma N)^2$. After merging 2 distributions each of size $(\log_\gamma N)$, we get one sampled distribution of size $(\log_\gamma N^2)$ which is $2(\log_\gamma N)$. Since we do not need the original pair any more, we can overwrite this space of size $2(\log_\gamma N)$ and store the new distribution into it. In the same way, in order to merge two distributions of size $\log_\gamma N^2$ we need additional space of $(\log_\gamma N^2)^2$, and the merged distribution will overwrite the original pair. In the last step, we need to merge 4 distributions, each of size $N^{d/4}$, therefore the maximum additional space we need is $(\log_\gamma N^{d/4})^2$. In total we get $d \log_\gamma N + (\log_\gamma N^{d/4})^2$ which is

$$space(d, \gamma) = d \log_\gamma N + \frac{d^2}{16} (\log_\gamma N)^2.$$

4   Empirical Evaluation

We evaluated the performance of the ESrank algorithm through an extensive simulation study. We compared our algorithm to the currently best rank estimation algorithm: the Histogram algorithm of [12]. We implemented both in

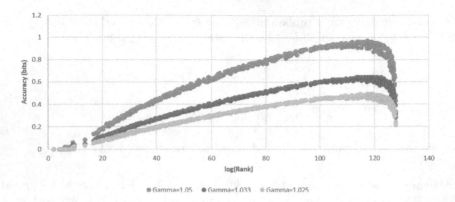

Fig. 2. The accuracy ($\log_2$ of the ratio between the upper- and lower-bounds) for the ESrank algorithm as a function of $\log_2(Rank(k^*))$ for different parameter settings: $\gamma = 1.05$ (green), $\gamma = 1.033$ (blue), $\gamma = 1.025$ (yellow). (Color figure online)

Matlab. We ran both algorithms on a 2.80 GHz i7 PC with 8 GB RAM running Microsoft windows 7, 64bit.

For the performance evaluation we used the data of [10]. Within this data corpus there are 611 probability distribution sets gathered from a specific SCA. The SCA of [10] was against AES [1] with 128-bits keys running on an embedded processor with an unstable clock. Each set represents a particular setting of the SCA: number of traces used, whether the clock was jittered, and the values of tunable attack parameters. The attack grouped the key bits into 16 8-bit subkeys, and hence its output probability distributions are over these byte values. Each set in the corpus consists of the correct secret key and 16 distributions, one per subkey. The distributions are sorted in non-increasing order of probability, each of length 2^8. We used the same technique suggested in [12]: merge the $d = 16$ probability lists of size $N = 2^8$ into $d = 8$ lists of size $N = 2^{16}$. We measured the upper bound, lower bound, time and space for each trace using ESrank and the Histogram rank estimation.

Bound Tightness. Figure 2 shows that the analytical performance of Sect. 3.4 indeed agrees with the empirical results. For different values of γ we get accuracy which corresponds to at most γ^{14}: e.g., when $\gamma = 1.05$ Fig. 2 shows a margin of at most 0.9 bits. We can see that as γ becomes closer to 1, the accuracy becomes closer to 0. As we expected, the maximum gap between the upper bound and the lower bound happens for ranks around $100 - 120$ since the difference between any two successive indices in the sampled set becomes greater when the indices becomes greater.

Time and Space Analysis. Table 1 shows the time, the space and the percentage of the traces for which the accuracy is better than 1 bit, for ESrank with $\gamma = 1.025, 1.033, 1.05, 1.065$ and for Histogram [12] with $B = 50,000, 35,000,$

Table 1. Performance summary of the ESrank and Histogram algorithms. The Accuracy column indicates the percentage of traces for which the difference between the upper- and lower-bounds of the estimated ranks was below 1 bit.

	Time (Seconds)	Space (MB)	Accuracy < 1 bit (%)
$\gamma = 1.025$	0.59	6.48	100
$\gamma = 1.033$	0.3	3.68	100
$\gamma = 1.05$	0.16	1.60	99.83
$\gamma = 1.065$	0.05	0.96	56.95
$B = 50K$	0.62	3.20	100
$B = 35K$	0.29	2.24	100
$B = 20K$	0.12	1.28	100
$B = 5K$	0.01	0.32	99.83

20,000, 5,000. As we can see, the two algorithms, using the described parameters - all take less than 0.6 s and use under 6.5 MB of memory. In a practical sense ESrank is on-par with the Histogram algorithm: both exhibit a run-time of under 1 s using less than 6.5 MB, to get a 1-bit margin of uncertainty in the rank for all ranks up to 2^{128}.

5   Conclusion

In this paper we proposed a simple and effective new rank estimation method. We have rigorously analyzed its accuracy, and its time and space complexities. Our main idea is to use exponential sampling to drastically reduce the algorithm's complexity. We proved ESrank has a poly-logarithmic time- and space-complexity, and it can be driven to any desired level of accuracy (trading off time and space against accuracy). Importantly, ESrank is simple to build from scratch, and requires no algorithmic tools beyond a sorting function.

We evaluated the performance of ESrank through extensive simulations based on a real SCA data corpus, and compared it to the currently-best histogram-based algorithm. We showed that ESrank gives excellent rank estimation (with roughly a 1-bit margin between lower and upper bounds), with a performance that is practically on-par with the Histogram algorithm: a run-time of under 1 s, for all ranks up to 2^{128}, on a standard laptop. Hence ESrank is a useful addition to the SCA evaluator's toolbox.

Acknowledgement. Liron David was partially supported by The Yitzhak and Chaya Weinstein Research Institute for Signal Processing.

References

1. FIPS PUB 197, advanced encryption standard (AES), 2001. U.S. Department of Commerce/National Institute of Standards and Technology (NIST)
2. Agrawal, D., Archambeault, B., Rao, J.R., Rohatgi, P.: The EM side—channel(s). In: Kaliski, B.S., Koç, K., Paar, C. (eds.) CHES 2002. LNCS, vol. 2523, pp. 29–45. Springer, Heidelberg (2003). https://doi.org/10.1007/3-540-36400-5_4
3. Jon Louis Bentley and Andrew Chi-Chih Yao: An almost optimal algorithm for unbounded searching. Inf. Process. Lett. 5(3), 82–87 (1976)
4. Daniel J Bernstein, Tanja Lange, and Christine van Vredendaal. Tighter, faster, simpler side-channel security evaluations beyond computing power. IACR Cryptology ePrint Archive, 2015:221, 2015
5. Bogdanov, A., Kizhvatov, I., Manzoor, K., Tischhauser, E., Witteman, M.: Fast and memory-efficient key recovery in side-channel attacks. In: Dunkelman, O., Keliher, L. (eds.) SAC 2015. LNCS, vol. 9566, pp. 310–327. Springer, Cham (2016). https://doi.org/10.1007/978-3-319-31301-6_19
6. Choudary, M.O., Popescu, P.G.: Back to Massey: impressively fast, scalable and tight security evaluation tools. In: Fischer, W., Homma, N. (eds.) CHES 2017. LNCS, vol. 10529, pp. 367–386. Springer, Cham (2017). https://doi.org/10.1007/978-3-319-66787-4_18
7. David, L., Wool, A.: A bounded-space near-optimal key enumeration algorithm for multi-subkey side-channel attacks. In: Handschuh, H. (ed.) CT-RSA 2017. LNCS, vol. 10159, pp. 311–327. Springer, Cham (2017). https://doi.org/10.1007/978-3-319-52153-4_18
8. Liron David and Avishai Wool. Poly-logarithmic side channel rank estimation via exponential sampling. Cryptology ePrint Archive, Report 2018/867 (2018). https://eprint.iacr.org/2018/867
9. Duc, A., Faust, S., Standaert, F.-X.: Making masking security proofs concrete. In: Oswald, E., Fischlin, M. (eds.) EUROCRYPT 2015. LNCS, vol. 9056, pp. 401–429. Springer, Heidelberg (2015). https://doi.org/10.1007/978-3-662-46800-5_16
10. Fledel, D., Wool, A.: Sliding-window correlation attacks against encryption devices with an unstable clock. In: Proceedings of 25th Conference on Selected Areas in Cryptography (SAC), Calgary, August 2018
11. Gandolfi, K., Mourtel, C., Olivier, F.: Electromagnetic analysis: concrete results. In: Koç, Ç.K., Naccache, D., Paar, C. (eds.) CHES 2001. LNCS, vol. 2162, pp. 251–261. Springer, Heidelberg (2001). https://doi.org/10.1007/3-540-44709-1_21
12. Glowacz, C., Grosso, V., Poussier, R., Schüth, J., Standaert, F.-X.: Simpler and more efficient rank estimation for side-channel security assessment. In: Leander, G. (ed.) FSE 2015. LNCS, vol. 9054, pp. 117–129. Springer, Heidelberg (2015). https://doi.org/10.1007/978-3-662-48116-5_6
13. Kocher, P., Jaffe, J., Jun, B.: Differential power analysis. In: Wiener, M. (ed.) CRYPTO 1999. LNCS, vol. 1666, pp. 388–397. Springer, Heidelberg (1999). https://doi.org/10.1007/3-540-48405-1_25
14. Kocher, P.C.: Timing attacks on implementations of Diffie-Hellman, RSA, DSS, and other systems. In: Koblitz, N. (ed.) CRYPTO 1996. LNCS, vol. 1109, pp. 104–113. Springer, Heidelberg (1996). https://doi.org/10.1007/3-540-68697-5_9
15. Li, Y., Meng, X., Wang, S., Wang, J.: Weighted key enumeration for EM-based side-channel attacks. In: 2018 IEEE International Symposium on Electromagnetic Compatibility and 2018 IEEE Asia-Pacific Symposium on Electromagnetic Compatibility (EMC/APEMC), pp. 749–752. IEEE (2018)

16. Li, Y., Wang, S., Wang, Z., Wang, J.: A strict key enumeration algorithm for dependent score lists of side-channel attacks. In: Eisenbarth, T., Teglia, Y. (eds.) CARDIS 2017. LNCS, vol. 10728, pp. 51–69. Springer, Cham (2018). https://doi.org/10.1007/978-3-319-75208-2_4

17. Longo, J., Martin, D.P., Mather, L., Oswald, E., Sach, B., Stam, M.: How low can you go? Using side-channel data to enhance brute-force key recovery. IACR Cryptology ePrint Archive, 2016:609 (2016)

18. Martin, D.P., Mather, L., Oswald, E.: Two sides of the same coin: counting and enumerating keys post side-channel attacks revisited. In: Smart, N.P. (ed.) CT-RSA 2018. LNCS, vol. 10808, pp. 394–412. Springer, Cham (2018). https://doi.org/10.1007/978-3-319-76953-0_21

19. Martin, D.P., Mather, L., Oswald, E., Stam, M.: Characterisation and estimation of the key rank distribution in the context of side channel evaluations. In: Cheon, J.H., Takagi, T. (eds.) ASIACRYPT 2016. LNCS, vol. 10031, pp. 548–572. Springer, Heidelberg (2016). https://doi.org/10.1007/978-3-662-53887-6_20

20. Martin, D.P., O'Connell, J.F., Oswald, E., Stam, M.: Counting keys in parallel after a side channel attack. In: Iwata, T., Cheon, J.H. (eds.) ASIACRYPT 2015. LNCS, vol. 9453, pp. 313–337. Springer, Heidelberg (2015). https://doi.org/10.1007/978-3-662-48800-3_13

21. Pan, J., van Woudenberg, J.G.J., den Hartog, J.I., Witteman, M.F.: Improving DPA by peak distribution analysis. In: Biryukov, A., Gong, G., Stinson, D.R. (eds.) SAC 2010. LNCS, vol. 6544, pp. 241–261. Springer, Heidelberg (2011). https://doi.org/10.1007/978-3-642-19574-7_17

22. Poussier, R., Standaert, F.-X., Grosso, V.: Simple key enumeration (and rank estimation) using histograms: an integrated approach. In: Gierlichs, B., Poschmann, A.Y. (eds.) CHES 2016. LNCS, vol. 9813, pp. 61–81. Springer, Heidelberg (2016). https://doi.org/10.1007/978-3-662-53140-2_4

23. Quisquater, J.-J., Samyde, D.: ElectroMagnetic Analysis (EMA): measures and counter-measures for smart cards. In: Attali, I., Jensen, T. (eds.) E-smart 2001. LNCS, vol. 2140, pp. 200–210. Springer, Heidelberg (2001). https://doi.org/10.1007/3-540-45418-7_17

24. Martin, D.P., Montanaro, A., Oswald, E., Shepherd, D.: Quantum key search with side channel advice. In: Adams, C., Camenisch, J. (eds.) SAC 2017. LNCS, vol. 10719, pp. 407–422. Springer, Cham (2018). https://doi.org/10.1007/978-3-319-72565-9_21

25. Veyrat-Charvillon, N., Gérard, B., Renauld, M., Standaert, F.-X.: An optimal key enumeration algorithm and its application to side-channel attacks. In: Knudsen, L.R., Wu, H. (eds.) SAC 2012. LNCS, vol. 7707, pp. 390–406. Springer, Heidelberg (2013). https://doi.org/10.1007/978-3-642-35999-6_25

26. Veyrat-Charvillon, N., Gérard, B., Standaert, F.-X.: Security evaluations beyond computing power. In: Johansson, T., Nguyen, P.Q. (eds.) EUROCRYPT 2013. LNCS, vol. 7881, pp. 126–141. Springer, Heidelberg (2013). https://doi.org/10.1007/978-3-642-38348-9_8

27. Wang, S., Li, Y., Wang, J.: A new key rank estimation method to investigate dependent key lists of side channel attacks. In: 2017 Asian Hardware Oriented Security and Trust Symposium (AsianHOST), pp. 19–24. IEEE (2017)

28. Ye, X., Eisenbarth, T., Martin, W.: Bounded, yet sufficient? How to determine whether limited side channel information enables key recovery. In: Joye, M., Moradi, A. (eds.) CARDIS 2014. LNCS, vol. 8968, pp. 215–232. Springer, Cham (2015). https://doi.org/10.1007/978-3-319-16763-3_13

Efficient Fully-Leakage Resilient
One-More Signature Schemes

Antonio Faonio[✉]

IMDEA Software Institute, Madrid, Spain
antonio.faonio@imdea.org

Abstract. In a recent paper Faonio, Nielsen and Venturi (ICALP 2015) gave new constructions of leakage-resilient signature schemes. The signature schemes proposed remain unforgeable against an adversary leaking arbitrary information on the entire state of the signer, including the random coins of the signing algorithm. The main feature of their signature schemes is that they offer a graceful degradation of security in situations where standard existential unforgeability is impossible. The notion, put forward by Nielsen, Venturi, and Zottarel (PKC 2014), defines a *slack parameter* γ which, roughly speaking, describes how gracefully the security degrades. Unfortunately, the standard-model signature scheme of Faonio, Nielsen and Venturi has a slack parameter that depends on the number of signatures queried by the adversary.

In this paper we show two new constructions in the standard model where the above limitation is avoided. Specifically, the first scheme achieves slack parameter $O(1/\lambda)$ where λ is the security parameter and it is based on standard number theoretic assumptions, the second scheme achieves optimal slack parameter (i.e. $\gamma = 1$) and it is based on knowledge of the exponent assumptions. Our constructions are efficient and have leakage rate $1 - o(1)$, most notably our second construction has signature size of only 8 group elements which makes it the leakage-resilient signature scheme with the shortest signature size known to the best of our knowledge.

Keywords: Signature scheme · Leakage resilience · Efficient scheme · Knowledge assumptions

1 Introduction

In the last years a lot of effort has been put into constructing cryptographic primitives that remain secure even in case the adversary obtains partial information of the secrets used within the system. This effort is motivated by the existence of the so-called side-channel attacks (see, e.g. [19, 26, 27]) which can break provably secure cryptosystems exploiting physical characteristics of the crypto-devices where such schemes are implemented.

A common way to model leakage attacks is to give to the adversary a leakage oracle. Such oracle stores the current secret state of the cryptosystem under attack (let it be α), takes as input leakage functions f_i and returns $f_i(\alpha)$.

© Springer Nature Switzerland AG 2019
M. Matsui (Ed.): CT-RSA 2019, LNCS 11405, pp. 350–371, 2019.
https://doi.org/10.1007/978-3-030-12612-4_18

The leakage functions need to belong to a restricted set of functions, as otherwise there is no hope for security. In this paper we consider the *bounded leakage model* where we assume that the total bit-length of the leakage obtained via the leakage functions is smaller than some a priori determined leakage bound ℓ. Leakage-resilient schemes in this model include public-key, identity-based encryption, signature schemes and identification schemes [2–4,7,8,10,13,28,29].

Graceful Degradation. For any existentially unforgeable signature scheme in the bounded leakage model, necessarily, the length of a signature is larger than the leakage bound, as otherwise an adversary could simply leak a forgery. The main consequence is that, if the goal is to tolerate large amount of leakage then, the signature size needs to be very large but the latter makes the schemes unpractical. Recently Nielsen, Venturi and Zottarel [30] addressed this issue introducing a new notion of security for signature schemes which requires that an adversary should not be able to produce more forgeries than what he could have leaked via leakage queries.

In particular, if s is the length in bits of a signature of size and ℓ is the leakage bound, to break unforgeability, an adversary must produce n forgeries where $n \approx \ell/(\gamma \cdot s)+1$, where $\gamma \in (0,1]$ is a value that we call the "slack parameter". Roughly speaking, the slack parameter measures how close to optimal security the scheme is. When $\gamma = 1$ we say that the scheme has *optimal* graceful degradation of security, as the number of forged signatures requested is exactly one more than what an adversary could possibly leak. When γ is a constant smaller then 1 we say that the scheme has *almost-optimal* graceful degradation, as in this case, the number of forged signature requested is a constant factor more than what an adversary could leak[1]. Notably, this new security notion enables to design signature schemes where the size of the secret key (and the leakage bound) does not depend on the signature size, leading to short signatures.

Subsequently, Faonio, Nielsen and Venturi [14] (journal version in [15]), extended the model to the fully-leakage resilient setting, where the adversary can leak arbitrary information of the entire secret state, including all the random coins of the signing algorithm.

Interestingly, while in the (not-fully) leakage-resilient regime the authors of [30] showed a signature scheme with almost-optimal graceful degradation, in the fully-leakage-resilient regime the best signature scheme known (in the standard model) has slack parameter $\gamma = O(1/q)$ where q is the number of signature oracle queries performed by the adversary. While the latter result still allows for some meaningful applications, in practice, the leakage security of the scheme is hard to estimate as it degrades as function of the number of signatures which in principle could be really big.

---

[1] In [30], the authors show that the notion, even for small value of the slack parameter, allows for interesting applications such as leakage-resilient identification schemes.

Our Contributions. In this paper we solve the above problem by constructing two new fully leakage-resilient signature schemes in the bounded leakage model where the slack parameter does not depend on the number of signatures issued.

The first signature scheme has slack parameter $O(1/\lambda)$. The construction makes use of an All-but-Many Encryption scheme (Fujisaki [17]) and a Non-Interactive Witness-Indistinguishable system and is instantiated under standard number theoretic assumptions.

The second signature scheme has optimal graceful degradation. The construction is based on a specific extractable and perfectly hiding commitment scheme (Abe and Fehr [1]) and on a quasi-adaptive NIZK for linear space (Jutla and Roy [24]). For technical reason, we need a NIZK system with a weak form of knowledge soundness. As minor contribution of independent interest, we show how to modify the elegant construction of Kiltz and Wee [25] to get an efficient quasi-adaptive NIZK system for linear-space relationship with (weak) knowledge soundness. Both the components of the second schemes are instantiated under the knowledge of the exponent assumption (see, e.g. [1,5,9,21]).

A Technical Overview. We recall the scheme of [30], for future reference we call it NVZ14. The secret key of NVZ14 is a polynomial δ in $\mathbb{Z}_p[X]$ of degree d and a signature for a message $m \in \mathbb{Z}_p$ is composed by a commitment C^* to the evaluation of the polynomial δ on the point m together with a sim-extractable NIZK that the commitment, indeed, commits to such evaluation. The polynomial δ is published in the verification key using an homomorphic commitment scheme (for example, the classical Pedersen's commitment scheme [32]). The verification of a signature works in two stages: first from the verification key it derives (using the homomorphic property of the commitment scheme) a commitment C_m to the evaluation of the polynomial δ on point m, second it verifies the NIZK for the statement (C^*, C_m) which proves that the commitments C_m and C^* open to the same value, therefore proving that the commitment C^* commits to an evaluation of δ on the point m. The leakage bound of the scheme is roughly $\ell \approx d \log p$ and the slack parameter is a constant. The key idea for the unforgeability is that from $n \approx d + 1$ signatures we can extract $d + 1$ evaluations of the polynomial δ, however, because of the bound on the leakage performed, at most d evaluation points could be possibly be uniquely defined. The latter implies that one of the commitment produced by the adversary can be opened in two different way therefore breaking the binding property of the commitment scheme.

The construction proposed by [14] follows the same blue print. Their main idea is to convert leakage functions over the full state (namely, the secret key and the randomness) to leakage functions of the secret key only. In this way, they reduce the task of proving fully leakage resilient to the easier task of proving (standard) leakage resilience.

We give a glimpse of their technique with a toy example. As in the scheme NVZ14, in the construction of [14], a signature $\sigma = (C^*, \pi)$ is composed by a commitment C^* and a proof of consistency for the commitment π. So the randomness of a signature is equal to (r, t) where r is the randomness for the commitment and t is the randomness for the NIZK. Their first idea is to use an equivocable commitment scheme. Recall that a commitment scheme is equivocable if, roughly speaking, we can sample a fake commitment C such that, given a trapdoor, for any message m we can produce randomness r' such that $C = \mathsf{Com}(\mathsf{vk}, m, r')$, namely, the fake commitment C opens to the message m. For the sake of this toy example, let us consider a leakage function $f(\delta, r)$ that does not depend on the randomness t of the NIZK. In [14], the authors show that we can construct a new leakage function $\hat{f}(\delta)$ that first computes r' equivocating the commitment C^* to $\delta(m)$ and then it computes $f(\delta, r')$. The function $\hat{f}$ converts the leakage on the randomness as leakage of the secret key only.

The main technical problem that [14] had to solve is that standard equivocable commitments scheme were not sufficient. In fact two contrasting requirements are necessary: on one hand, both the commitment scheme and the NIZK need to be equivocable (so that we can reduce fully-leakage resilience to standard leakage resilience as shown in the toy example above), on the other hand, to extract the n evaluations of the polynomial δ we need that either the commitment scheme or the NIZK system is perfectly binding. To solve this problem the authors of [14] showed a construction of a commitment scheme where any commitment created is perfectly binding with probability $1/q$ and equivocable with probability $1-1/q$. In this way, almost all the signatures queried by the adversary will be perfectly hiding while over the $n \approx O(q \cdot \ell)$ forged signatures (so that $\gamma = O(1/q)$) strictly more than $(\ell/\log p) + 1$ signatures are perfectly binding (with overwhelming probability). The unforgeability of the scheme follows because a winning adversary gets in input exactly ℓ bits of information about δ and outputs strictly more than ℓ bits of information about δ: this adversary cannot exist as otherwise a basic information-theoretic principle would be violated.

New Ideas. We describe our two new signature schemes. For the first construction we substitute the commitment scheme of [14] with an All-But-Many Encryption (ABM-Enc) scheme. Roughly speaking, an ABM-Enc is an encryption scheme where all the ciphertexts created by the adversary can be successfully decrypted (knowing the secret key) while, with the knowledge of a special trapdoor, we can create an unbounded number of fake ciphertexts that are equivocable. The proof of security is quite straight-forward (actually even easier than in [14]): with the knowledge of the trapdoor all the signatures are equivocated and with the knowledge of the secret key of the ABM-Enc all the forged signature are extracted. Fujisaki [17], building over a paper of Hofheinz [23], showed two constructions of ABM-Enc. The first construction achieves constant overhead (the ratio between ciphertext size and message size) and it is based on the decision Composite Residuosity (DCR) assumption while the latter is based on DDH and achieves $\lambda/\log\lambda$ overhead (where λ is the security parameter). At first sight, by plugging the constant-overhead ABM-Enc of Fujisaki in our signature scheme we would get a fully-leakage resilient signature with almost-optimal slack parameter, the problem is that efficient NIZK [22] and the Fujisaki's construction over DCR groups do not quite match. In particular, a Groth-Sahai proof for the needed statement would commit the witness bit-by-bit so that the total size of the signature is $O(\lambda^2)$ groups elements. Since each forged signature carries only $\log p$ bits of information this, unfortunately, implies that the slack parameter is $1/\text{poly}(\lambda)$. Luckily, the ABM-Enc based on DDH of Fujisaki fits better with the NIZK of Groth-Sahai, as to prove the necessary statement we need only a constant number, in the size of the ciphertext, of pairing-product equations.

The second construction is inspired by the following observation: if we used a zk-SNARK [20,21,31] instead of Groth-Sahai then the construction sketched above would have signature size $O(\lambda)$ and therefore almost-optimal slack parameter. However, at second thought, employing a zk-SNARK is an over killing, as what we need is the ability of simultaneously equivocate and extract the commitments, and in particular, we do not need succinctness. Therefore, instead of naively use zk-SNARKs, we "open the box" of zk-SNARKs. In particular, we consider the commitment scheme of Abe and Fehr [1] based on the knowledge of the exponent assumption (KEA3) of Bellare and Palacio [5] (see also Damgård [9]). Nicely, for this kind of commitments, we can reduce the relation that two commitments open to the same message to the fact that a certain vector in $\mathbb{G}^2$ lies in a specific subspace. The latter allows us to get faster and shorter signatures, thanks to recent advances in efficiency of quasi-adaptive NIZK systems for linear relations (see for example, [24,25]).

More in details, the proof technique for the second construction diverges significantly to the proof technique of [14]. The main reason is that the commitment scheme of Abe and Fehr is simultaneously extractable and perfect hiding but it is not efficiently equivocable[2]. Our strategy is to first apply all the computational steps and then use the fact that the commitment scheme is perfectly hiding. Therefore we can "equivocate" a commitment by brute force it and open it to the desired value.

Comparison. We compare our signature schemes with the signature schemes of [30] and [14,15] (see Table 1). Four different signature schemes are presented in [15], we select the three most interesting[3] and we denote them with FNV15_1, FNV15_2 and FNV15_3. The third column in the Table 1 (namely, "No Erasure") refers to a weaker model of fully leakage resilient signature considered in [14]. Specifically, the scheme FNV15_1 is proved secure under the assumption that the cryptographic device can perfectly erase the random coins used in the previous invocations. We call $\mathcal{SS}_1$ the signature scheme based on ABM-Enc scheme and $\mathcal{SS}_2$ the scheme based on knowledge of the exponent assumption. From an efficiency point of view we notice that $\mathcal{SS}_1$ is less efficient than FNV15_2 but achieves asymptotically better graceful degradation. On the other hand, $\mathcal{SS}_1$ is both less efficient and with worse graceful degradation respect to FNV15_1 and FNV15_3, however, FNV15_1 needs perfect erasure of the randomness and FNV15_3 is only

---

[2] Intuitively, any trapdoor for equivocation would break the knowledge of the exponent assumption.

[3] As the forth scheme is a variation of FNV15_1 and it achieves worse efficiency parameters.

Table 1. Comparison of known efficient leakage-resilient one-more signature schemes in the bounded leakage model. The * symbol means the scheme is in the random oracle model; G.D. stands for graceful degradation. The signature size is computed in number of group elements. The value ϵ is parameter set at initialization phase and it can be any inverse polynomial of the security parameter. DLIN stands for the decision linear assumption, BDH stands for the bilinear Diffie-Hellman assumption, SXDH stands for the external decisional diffie-hellman assumption.

Scheme	Fully	No Erasure	KGen	G. D.	Assumption	Efficiency	
						leak	signature size
NVZ14	✗	-	-	$O(1)$	DLIN	$\frac{1}{2} - o(1)$	$O(1)$
$FNV15_1$	✓	✗	✓	$O(1)$	DLIN	$1 - \epsilon$	$O(\epsilon^{-1})$
$FNV15_2$	✓	✓	✓	$O(1/q)$	DLIN	$1 - \epsilon$	$O(\epsilon^{-1} \cdot \log \lambda)$
$FNV15_3$	✓	✓	✓	$O(1)$	BDH*	$1 - \epsilon$	$O(\epsilon^{-1} \cdot \log \lambda)$
SS_1	✓	✓	✓	$O(1/\lambda)$	SXDH	$1 - \epsilon$	$O(\epsilon^{-1} \cdot \lambda)$
SS_2	✓	✓	✗	1	KerLin$_2$+q-KE*	$1 - \epsilon$	8λ

proved secure in the random oracle model. The signature scheme SS_2 is proved secure in a fully-leakage model where the key generation phase is leak free. We consider this a reasonable assumption, in fact, in almost all practical scenarios we could safely assume that the cryptographic devices are initialized in a safe environment before being used *in the wild*. The technical reason behind this limitation is that the commitment scheme based on the knowledge of the exponent assumption does not admit oblivious sampling of the parameters. The scheme SS_2 achieves optimal graceful degradation, the signature size is independent of the ϵ and, notably, more compact (both asymptotically and practically) even than the signature scheme $FNV15_3$ in the random oracle model.

2 Notations and Preliminaries

Throughout the paper we let λ denote the security parameter. We say that a function f is negligible in the security parameter λ, and we write $f \in \texttt{negl}(\lambda)$, if it vanishes asymptotically faster than the inverse of any polynomial. We use the classic notion of probabilistic polynomial time (PPT) algorithms. We write $x \leftarrow \$ \, \mathcal{D}$ (resp. $x \leftarrow \$ \, \mathsf{A}(y)$) to denote that x is chosen at random from the distribution $\mathcal{D}$ (resp. an PPT algorithm A run on input y), and we write $x \leftarrow \mathsf{A}(y; r)$ to denote that we assign to x the output of A run with randomness r. For two ensembles $\mathcal{X} = \{X_\lambda\}_{\lambda \in \mathbb{N}}$ and $\mathcal{Y} = \{Y_\lambda\}_{\lambda \in \mathbb{N}}$, we write $\mathcal{X} \equiv \mathcal{Y}$ to denote that $\mathcal{X}$ and $\mathcal{Y}$ are identically distributed, and $\mathcal{X} \approx_s \mathcal{Y}$ (resp., $\mathcal{X} \approx_c \mathcal{Y}$) to denote that $\mathcal{X}$ and $\mathcal{Y}$ are statistically (resp., computationally) indistinguishable. Vectors and matrices are typeset in boldface. Given an element $m \in \mathbb{Z}$ and a vector $\boldsymbol{v}$ of length d, we denote $\boldsymbol{v}(m) := \boldsymbol{v}^T \cdot (1, m^1, \ldots, m^{d-1})^T$, meaning the evaluation of the polynomial with coefficients $\boldsymbol{v}$ at point m. We consider also the natural extension of the notion to matrix, $\boldsymbol{V}(m) := \boldsymbol{V} \cdot (1, m^1, \ldots, m^{d-1})^T$. All the algorithms take as input (group) parameters prm, for readability, whenever it is clear from the context we consider them implicit. A (bilinear) group generator Setup_{BG} is an algorithm that upon input the security parameter 1^λ outputs the description $(\mathbb{G}_1, \mathbb{G}_2, \mathbb{G}_T, p, G_1, G_2, G_T, e)$ of three groups equipped with a (non-degenerate) bilinear map $e : \mathbb{G}_1 \times \mathbb{G}_2 \to \mathbb{G}_T$. We use additive notation for the group operation, and we denote group elements using the bracket notation introduced by Escala *et al.* in [11]. Namely, for a $y \in \mathbb{Z}_p$ we let $[y]_X$ be the element $y \cdot G_X \in \mathbb{G}_X$ for $X \in \{1, 2, T\}$. Given $[x]_1$ and $[y]_2$ we write $[x \cdot y]_T$ as shorthand for $e([x]_1, [y]_2)$. We denote with the tuple of PPT algorithms $(\mathsf{Gen}_{CRH}, \mathsf{H})$ a collision-resistant hash function (CRH).

Knowledge of the Exponent Assumption. Consider the experiment in Fig. 1 between an adversary A, a randomness sampler $\mathcal{S}$, an extractor Ext and a bilinear group generator Setup_{BG}.

Experiment $\mathbf{Exp}^{q-\mathsf{KE}^*}_{\mathsf{A},\mathcal{S},\mathsf{Ext},\mathsf{Setup}_{BG}}(1^\lambda)$:

1. Let $\mathtt{prm} = (\mathbb{G}_1, \mathbb{G}_2, \mathbb{G}_T, p, G_1, G_2, G_T, e) \leftarrow \mathsf{Setup}_{BG}(1^\lambda)$;
2. Sample $\boldsymbol{g} \leftarrow_\$ \mathbb{Z}_p^q$, $\alpha \leftarrow_\$ \mathbb{Z}_p$ and $r \leftarrow_\$ \{0,1\}^\lambda$, set $\mathbf{M} \leftarrow (\boldsymbol{g} \cdot (1, \alpha))^T \in \mathbb{Z}_p^{2,q}$;
3. Let $\omega \leftarrow \mathcal{S}([\mathbf{M}]_1, [\alpha]_2; r)$;
4. Let $[\boldsymbol{y}]_1 \leftarrow \mathsf{A}([\mathbf{M}]_1, [\alpha]_2, \omega)$ and $\boldsymbol{z} \leftarrow \mathsf{Ext}([\mathbf{M}]_1, [\alpha]_2, \omega)$;
5. Output 1 iff $\boldsymbol{y} \in Span((1, \alpha)^T)$ and $[\boldsymbol{y}]_1 \neq [\mathbf{M}]_1 \cdot \boldsymbol{z}$.

Fig. 1. The experiment of the q-KE* assumption.

Definition 1. *Given a bilinear group generator Setup_{BG} and a value $q \in \mathbb{N}$, we say that the q-KE* assumption holds for Setup_{BG} if for any deterministic PT A and any PPT sampler $\mathcal{S}$ there exists a PT Ext such that:*

$$\mathbf{Adv}^{q-KE^*}_{\mathsf{A},\mathsf{Ext},\mathsf{Setup}_{BG}}(\lambda) := \Pr\left[\mathbf{Exp}^{q-\mathsf{KE}^*}_{\mathsf{A},\mathsf{Ext},\mathsf{Setup}_{BG}}(1^\lambda) = 1\right] \in \mathsf{negl}(\lambda).$$

In contrast with the standard definition of the knowledge of the exponent assumption, in our definition we additionally have a sampler $\mathcal{S}$. The technical reason is that we deal with adversaries with oracle access (for example, to the signature oracle or the leakage oracle). In fact, in this setting, as shown by Fiore and Nitulescu [16], we need to take particular care on how the adversary can interact with its oracles. In particular, as we will show in the proof of security in Sect. 5, with the help of the sampler, we can reduce the queries of the adversary to be non adaptive. Notice, in bilinear groups the test $[\boldsymbol{y}]_1 \in Span([1, \alpha]_1^T)$ can be efficiently performed using the bilinear map $e([\boldsymbol{y}_0]_1, [\alpha]_2) = e([\boldsymbol{y}_1]_1, [1]_2)$. Also, we can naturally scale down the assumption to non bilinear groups, in this case, the adversary does not get $[\alpha]_2$. Given a (non-bilinear) group generator Setup_G the assumption for $q = 1$ is not stronger than the KEA [9] for non-uniform PT adversaries, while for $q = 3$ is not stronger than the KEA3 assumption [5] for non-uniform PT adversaries. For a bilinear group Setup_{BG}, and any polynomial q, the q-KE* assumption is not stronger than the q-PKE assumption of [21], indeed it is easy to show that if q-PKE holds than also q-KE* holds, however, the reverse implication is not known. The extractability assumptions for non-uniform adversaries consider an extractor that works for any auxiliary inputs. As shown in [6] this sometimes can be dangerous. Notice that in our assumption the only "auxiliary input" is generated by the random sampler $\mathcal{S}$ which does not take the secret material $g, \alpha \in \mathbb{Z}_p$ on clear[4].

Homomorphic Trapdoor Commitment Schemes. A trapdoor commitment scheme $\mathcal{COM} = (\mathsf{Setup}, \mathsf{Com}, \mathsf{ECom}, \mathsf{EOpen})$ is a tuple of algorithms where: (1) Algorithm Setup takes as input the security parameter and outputs a verification key ϑ and a trapdoor ψ; (2) Algorithm Com takes as input a message $m \in \mathcal{M}$, randomness $r \in \mathcal{R}$, the verification key ϑ and outputs a value $Com \in \mathcal{C}$. To open a commitment Com we output (m, r); an opening is valid if and only if $Com = \mathsf{Com}(\vartheta, m; r)$. (3) Algorithm ECom takes as input ψ and outputs a pair (Com, aux); (4) Algorithm EOpen takes as input (ψ, m, aux) and outputs $r \in \mathcal{R}$. We recall the standard security notions of *trapdoor hiding* and *computationally binding*. Roughly speaking, the former says that given a trapdoor is possible to create *fake commitments* using ECom which later on can be equivocated to open to any message in a indistinguishable way. The latter instead says that no PPT adversary can open the same commitment to two different messages without the knowledge of the trapdoor ψ. For simplicity in the exposition we set $\mathcal{M}$ and $\mathcal{R}$ to be $\mathbb{Z}_p$ for a prime p. We say that $\mathcal{COM}$ is *linearly homomorphic* if given commitments Com and Com' (that commit to m and m') and $a \in \mathbb{Z}_p$, one can compute the commitment $Com^* := a \cdot Com + Com'$ that opens to $a \cdot m + m'$. We write the mappings as $Com^* = \mathsf{Com}(\vartheta, a \cdot m + m'; a \cdot r + r')$.

Moreover, we require the following additional property. Let $(\vartheta, \psi) \leftarrow \mathsf{Setup}(1^\lambda)$, $(Com_1, aux_1) \leftarrow \mathsf{ECom}(\vartheta, \psi)$ and $(Com_2, aux_2) \leftarrow \mathsf{ECom}(\vartheta, \psi)$. We can use the auxiliary information $a \cdot aux_1 + aux_2$ to equivocate the commitment $a \cdot Com_1 + Com_2$. Finally, we consider commitment schemes with an additional algorithm $\widetilde{\mathsf{Setup}}$ which samples the verification key *obliviously*.

Quasi-Adaptive NIZK and NIWI Argument Systems. Let $\mathcal{R} \subseteq \{0,1\}^* \times \{0,1\}^*$ be an NP-relation, the language associated with $\mathcal{R}$ is $\mathcal{L}_\mathcal{R} := \{x : \exists w \text{ s.t. } (x, w) \in \mathcal{R}\}$. We assume that $(x, w) \in \mathcal{R}$ is efficiently verifiable. An non-interactive argument system $\mathcal{NIZK} := (\mathsf{Init}, \mathsf{P}, \mathsf{V})$ for $\mathcal{R}$ is a tuple of PPT algorithms where: (1) The initialization algorithm Init takes as input the security parameter 1^λ, and creates a common reference string (CRS) $\mathsf{crs} \in \{0,1\}^*$; (2) The prover algorithm P takes as input the CRS crs, a pair (x, w) such that $(x, w) \in \mathcal{R}$, and produces a proof $\pi \leftarrow_\$ \mathsf{P}(\mathsf{crs}, x, w)$; (3) The verifier algorithm V takes as input the CRS crs, a pair (x, π), and outputs a decision bit

---

[4] Also notice that we quantify the extractor after the sampler, so to avoid pathological situation where the adversary A simply forwards the output of the sampler $\mathcal{S}$.

$V(crs, x, \pi)$. Additionally, we say that an argument system is quasi-adaptive if the CRS generator algorithm Init takes as additional input the NP-relation $\mathcal{R}$ (or more formally a description of it). We consider distribution $\mathcal{D}_R$ over NP-relation. As for all the algorithms in this paper, the distribution can depends on the parameters prm. We require the standard notion of completeness, meaning that for any CRS crs output by $Init(1^\lambda)$ (or for any $\mathcal{R}$ and any crs output by $Init(1^\lambda, \mathcal{R})$ in the quasi-adaptive case), and for any pair $(x, w) \in \mathcal{R}$, we have that $V(crs, x, P(crs, x, w)) = 1$ with all but a negligible probability. We consider argument systems that admit oblivious sampling of the CRS and we denote it with $\tilde{Init}$. We require the following security properties.

- **Perfect zero-knowledge:** Proofs do not reveal anything beyond the validity of the statement, meaning that they can be perfectly simulated given only the statement itself and a trapdoor information.
- **Perfect witness-indistinguishability:** Given two different witnesses valid for the same instance, a proof generated with the first witness is equivalently distributed to a proof generated with the second witness.
- **Adaptive weak knowledge soundness:** For any PPT adversary that on input the CRS produces a valid NIZK proof for a statement x there exists a PPT extractor that outputs a witness w such that $(x, w) \in \mathcal{R}$.
- **Adaptive soundness:** No PPT adversary can forge a verifying proof for an adaptively chosen invalid statement.

2.1   All-but-Many Encryption

An all-but-many encryption scheme (ABM-Enc) is a tuple $\mathcal{ABM} =$ (Gen, Sample, Enc, Dec, EquivEnc, FakeEnc) such that: (1) Gen upon input the security parameter 1^λ outputs $(pk, (sk^s, sk^e))$. The public key pk defines an *tag space* that we denote with $\mathcal{U}$ and a message space $\mathcal{M}$. (2) Sample upon input (pk, sk^e) and $t \in \{0, 1\}^\lambda$ outputs $u \in \mathcal{U}_{pk}$. (3) Enc upon input $pk, (t, u)$ and a message $\mu \in \mathcal{M}$ outputs a ciphertext C. (4) Dec upon input $sk^e, (t, u)$ and a ciphertext C outputs a message μ. (5) FakeEnc upon input $pk, (t, u), sk^s$ outputs a ciphertext C and auxiliary information aux. (6) EquivEnc upon input (t, u) and aux and a message μ outputs random coins r; Let $\mathcal{L}_{pk}^s = \{(t, u) : t \in \{0, 1\}^\lambda, u \leftarrow Sample(pk, sk^e, t)\}$ and let $\mathcal{L}_{pk}^e = \{0, 1\}^\lambda \times \mathcal{U}_{pk} \setminus \mathcal{L}_{pk}^s$. (For simplicity we will omit the subscript pk when it is clear from the context.) We require that an ABM-Enc satisfies the following properties:

- **Pseudorandomness:** The algorithm $Sample(pk, sk^s, \cdot)$ is a pseudo-random[5] function with domain $\{0, 1\}^\lambda$ and co-domain $\mathcal{U}_{pk}$.
- **Unforgeability:** It is hard to forge a fresh tuple $(t^*, u^*) \in \mathcal{L}^s$ even given oracle access to $Sample(pk, sk^s, \cdot)$.

---

[5] The adversary gets to see the public key pk for uniformly sampled keys $pk, sk^s, sk^e \leftarrow_\$ Gen(1^\lambda)$.

- **Dual Mode:** The scheme can work in two different modes: (1) *decryption mode*, for all the tags $(t, u) \in \mathcal{L}^e$ the scheme defines a correct encryption scheme; (2) *trapdoor mode*, for all tags $(t, u) \in \mathcal{L}^s$ it is possible to sample fake ciphertexts using the algorithm FakeEnc that later on can be equivocated to any message using the algorithm EquivEnc. The fake ciphertext and randomness are indistinguishable from a real ciphertext and its randomness.

For space reason, we give the formal definition in the full version [12].

Theorem 1 (Fujisaki, [18]). *If DDH assumption holds in* Setup$_G$ *then there exists an ABM-Enc scheme. Moreover, the scheme admits an algorithm* $\tilde{\mathsf{Gen}}$ *that obliviously samples the public parameter.*

3   Fully-Leakage One-More Unforgeability

A signature scheme is a triple of algorithms $\mathcal{SS} = (\mathsf{Gen}, \mathsf{Sign}, \mathsf{Verify})$ where: (1) The key generation algorithm takes as input the security parameter λ and outputs a verification key/signing key pair $(\mathsf{vk}, \mathsf{sk}) \leftarrow \mathsf{Gen}(1^\lambda)$; (2) The signing algorithm takes as input a message $m \in \mathcal{M}$ and the signing key sk and outputs a signature $\sigma \leftarrow \mathsf{Sign}(\mathsf{sk}, m)$; (3) The verification algorithm takes as input the verification key vk and a pair (m, σ) and outputs a bit $\mathsf{Verify}(\mathsf{vk}, (m, \sigma)) \in \{0, 1\}$.

Given a signature scheme $\mathcal{SS}$, consider the experiments in Fig. 2 running with a PPT adversary A and parametrized by the security parameter $\lambda \in \mathbb{N}$, the leakage parameter $\ell \in \mathbb{N}$, and the slack parameter $\gamma := \gamma(\lambda)$.

$\mathbf{Exp}_{\mathcal{SS},\mathsf{A}}^{\text{one-more}}(\lambda, \ell, \gamma)$ and $\boxed{\mathbf{Exp}_{\mathcal{SS},\mathsf{A}}^{\text{one-more}^*}(\lambda, \ell, \gamma)}$:

1. $(\mathsf{vk}, \mathsf{sk}) \leftarrow_\$ \mathsf{Gen}(1^\lambda; r_0)$, return vk to A; let $\alpha = r_0$, $\boxed{\text{let } \alpha = \mathsf{sk}}$.
2. Run A(vk) with oracle access to $\mathsf{Sign}(\mathsf{sk}, \cdot)$ and the leakage oracle.
   - Upon query $m \in \mathcal{M}$ to the signature oracle, let $\sigma := \mathsf{Sign}(\mathsf{sk}, m; r)$, $r \leftarrow_\$ \{0, 1\}^\lambda$ and update the state $\alpha := \alpha \cup \{r\}$.
   - Upon query f to the leakage oracle, return $f(\alpha)$ where α is the current state.
3. Let $\mathcal{Q}$ be the set of signing queries issued by A, and let $\Lambda \in \{0, 1\}^*$ be the concatenation of all the leakage. A outputs n pairs $(m_1^*, \sigma_1^*), \ldots, (m_n^*, \sigma_n^*)$.
4. The experiment outputs 1 if and only if the following conditions are satisfied:
   (a) $\mathsf{Verify}(\mathsf{vk}, (m_i^*, \sigma_i^*)) = 1$ and $m_i^* \notin \mathcal{Q}$, for all $i \in [n]$.
   (b) The messages $m_1^*, \ldots, m_n^*$ are pairwise distinct.
   (c) $n \geq \lceil \ell/(\gamma \cdot s) \rceil + 1$, where $s := |\sigma|$ and $|\Lambda| \leq \ell$.

Fig. 2. The fully-leakage one-more unforgeability experiment and the fully-leakage one-more unforgeability experiment with leak-free key gen. The second experiment is equal to the first but it additionally executes the operations described the box.

Definition 2 (Fully-leakage one-more unforgeability). *We say that* $SS =$ (Gen, Sign, Verify) *is* (ℓ, γ)*-fully-leakage one-more unforgeable if for every PPT adversary* A *we have that:*

$$\text{Adv}_{SS,A}^{\text{one-more}}(\lambda, \ell, \gamma) := \Pr\left[\textbf{Exp}_{SS,A}^{\text{one-more}}(\lambda, \ell, \gamma) = 1\right] \in \text{negl}(\lambda).$$

Moreover, We say that SS *is* (ℓ, γ)*-fully-leakage one-more unforgeable with leak-free keygen if for every PPT adversary* A *we have that:*

$$\text{Adv}_{SS,A}^{\text{one-more}^*}(\lambda, \ell, \gamma) := \Pr\left[\textbf{Exp}_{SS,A}^{\text{one-more}^*}(\lambda, \ell, \gamma) = 1\right] \in \text{negl}(\lambda).$$

The number of signatures the adversary musts forge depends on the length of the leakage. In particular (ℓ, γ)-fully-leakage one-more unforgeability implies standard unforgeability for any adversary asking no leakage. The slack parameter γ specifies how close the signature scheme SS is to the optimal security SS. In particular, in the case $\gamma = 1$ one-more unforgeability requires that the adversary A cannot forge even a single signature more than what it could have (partially) leaked via leakage queries. As γ decreases, so does the strength of the signature scheme (the extreme case being $\gamma = |\mathcal{M}|^{-1}$, where we have no security).

4   Signature Scheme Based on ABM-Encryption

Our scheme SS = (Gen, Sign, Verify) has message space equal to $\mathbb{Z}_p$ and is described in Fig. 3. The scheme is based on a homomorphic commitment scheme $\mathcal{COM}$, an ABM-Enc scheme $\mathcal{ABM}$, a NIWI argument system $\mathcal{NIWI}$ and a CRH function (Gen$_{CRH}$, H). The scheme follows the basic template described in Sect. 1, however instead of using just one single polynomial $\delta \in \mathbb{Z}_p[X]$ of degree d, we use $\mu \in \mathbb{N}$ different polynomials arranged in the matrix $\boldsymbol{\Delta}$. The correctness follows from the completeness of the NIWI argument system, and from the linearly homomorphic property.

Theorem 2. *Let* $\mu \in \mathbb{N}$. *Assume that: (i) the commitment scheme* $\mathcal{COM}$ *is trapdoor hiding and linearly homomorphic with message space* $\mathbb{Z}_p^\mu$; *(ii) the* $\mathcal{ABM}$ *is a secure ABME-Enc scheme with message space* $\mathbb{Z}_p^\mu$ *and ciphertexts of length* s_1 *bits; (iii)* $\mathcal{NIWI}$ *is a perfect NIWI argument system for the relation* $\mathcal{R}$ *described in Fig. 3 with proofs of length* s_2 *bits. Then, let* $s = s_1 + s_2$ *and let* $\gamma = \mu \log p / s$, *for any* $0 \leq \ell \leq ((d+1)\mu \log p) - \lambda$, *the signature scheme* SS_1 *is* (ℓ, γ)*-fully-leakage one-more unforgeable.*

For space reason, the proof will appear in the full version of the paper [12]. Here we provide a sketch. The proof is similar to the proof of [14], the following proof sketch highlights the main differences. We denote with $(r_0, \boldsymbol{\Delta}, \mathbf{r}, (s_j, t_j)_{j\in[q]})$ the full secret state. Notice that, because of the oblivious sampling of the parameters, the randomness r_0 such that $\text{vk}, \text{sk} = \text{KGen}(1^\lambda; r_0)$ can be computed efficiently as function of both vk and sk, we therefore omit r_0 from the state α. The first hybrid $\mathbf{H}_0$ is the fully-leakage one-more unforgeability

---

Key Generation. Let $d, \mu \in \mathbb{N}$ be parameters. Let $\mathcal{NIWI} = (\mathsf{Init}, \mathsf{P}, \mathsf{V})$ be a NIWI argument system for the following polynomial-time relation:

$$\mathcal{R} := \left\{ (\vartheta, \mathsf{pk}, \tau, Com, C); (m^*, r^*, s) \, \middle| \, \begin{array}{l} Com = \mathsf{Com}(\vartheta, m^*; r^*) \\ C = \mathsf{Enc}(\mathsf{pk}, \tau, m^*; s) \end{array} \right\} .$$

Run $hk \leftarrow_{\$} \mathsf{Gen}_{CRH}(1^\lambda)$ $\mathsf{crs} \leftarrow \tilde{\mathsf{Init}}(1^\lambda)$, $\vartheta \leftarrow \tilde{\mathsf{Setup}}(1^\lambda)$ and $\mathsf{pk} \leftarrow_{\$} \tilde{\mathsf{Gen}}(1^\lambda)$.
Sample $\boldsymbol{\Delta} \leftarrow_{\$} \mathbb{Z}_p^{\mu, d+1}$ and $\mathbf{r} = (r_0, \ldots, r_d) \leftarrow_{\$} \mathcal{R}^{d+1}$, and compute $Com_i \leftarrow \mathsf{Com}(\vartheta, \boldsymbol{\delta}_i; r_i)$ for $i \in [0, d]$, where $\boldsymbol{\delta}_i \in \mathbb{Z}_p^\mu$ is the j-th column of $\boldsymbol{\Delta}$. Let $\boldsymbol{Com} = (Com_0, \ldots, Com_d)$
Output
$$\mathsf{sk} = (\boldsymbol{\Delta}, \mathbf{r}) \qquad \mathsf{vk} = (\mathsf{crs}, \vartheta, \mathsf{pk}, \boldsymbol{Com}).$$

Signature. To sign a message $m \in \mathbb{Z}_p$ compute $m^* \leftarrow \boldsymbol{\Delta}(m)$ and $r^* \leftarrow \mathbf{r}(m)$. Pick $u \leftarrow \mathcal{U}_{\mathsf{pk}}$ and set $\tau = (\mathsf{H}(hk, m), u)$ and compute $C \leftarrow \mathsf{Enc}(\mathsf{pk}, \tau, m^*; s)$ where $s \leftarrow_{\$} \mathcal{R}$. Generate a NIWI argument π for $(\vartheta, \mathsf{pk}, \tau, \boldsymbol{Com}(m), C)$, using the witness (m^*, r^*, s). Output $\sigma = (C, \tau, \pi)$.

Verification. Given a pair (m, σ) and vk, parse σ as $(C, \tau = (t, u), \pi)$ and parse vk as $(\mathsf{crs}, \vartheta, \mathsf{pk}, \boldsymbol{Com})$. Output 1 if and only if $\mathsf{H}(hk, m) = t$ and $\mathsf{V}(\mathsf{crs}, \pi, (\vartheta, \mathsf{pk}, \tau, \boldsymbol{Com}(m), C))$.

Fig. 3. The signature scheme $\mathcal{SS}_1$.

game but we additionally condition on the validity of the forged proofs. By the adaptive soundness of the NIWI the real experiment and $\mathbf{H}_0$ are indistinguishable. In the next hybrid $\mathbf{H}_1$ we switch the way the parameters are sampled, so that we gets the secret keys $\mathsf{sk}^s, \mathsf{sk}^e$ of the ABM-Enc and the equivocation trapdoor ψ of the commitment scheme. The hybrids $\mathbf{H}_0$ and $\mathbf{H}_1$ are indistinguishable because of the dual mode property of the ABM-Enc and the equivocability of the commitment scheme.

In the hybrid $\mathbf{H}_2$ we equivocate the commitments $\boldsymbol{Com}$ in the public key. Notice that the full secret state α can be written as $((\boldsymbol{\Delta}, \mathbf{r}(\boldsymbol{\Delta})), (s_j, z_j)_{i \in [q]})$ where $\mathbf{r}(\boldsymbol{\Delta})$ is a function of the secret key computed by EOpen.

In the hybrid $\mathbf{H}_3$ for each signature oracle query we sample the tag $\tau = (t, u)$ such that $u = \mathsf{Sample}(\mathsf{pk}, \mathsf{sk}^s, t)$. The indistinguishability comes from the pseudorandomness property of the ABM-Enc scheme.

Thanks to the last change, in the hybrid $\mathbf{H}_4$, for each signature oracle query we can sample the encryption C using the trapdoor mode FakeEnc. Notice that the full secret state α can be written as $((\boldsymbol{\Delta}, \mathbf{r}(\boldsymbol{\Delta})), (s_j(\boldsymbol{\Delta}), z_j)_{i \in [q]})$ where for any j, the value $s_j(\boldsymbol{\Delta})$ is a function of the secret key $\boldsymbol{\Delta}$ computed using the algorithm EquivEnc. The dual mode property of the ABM-Enc scheme assures that the two hybrids are indistinguishable.

In the hybrid $\mathbf{H}_5$ we compute the NIWI proof using the witness $(0, r', s')$ where r' is an opening of the equivocated commitment $\boldsymbol{Com}(m)$ to 0 and s' is an opening of the fake encryption to 0. This step follows exactly as in the proof of security in [14].

In this last hybrid the full secret state α can be written as $((\boldsymbol{\Delta}, \boldsymbol{r}(\boldsymbol{\Delta})), (s_j(\boldsymbol{\Delta}), z_j(\boldsymbol{\Delta}))_{i \in [q]})$, namely, all the state can be written as a deterministic function of the secret polynomials $\boldsymbol{\Delta}$. In particular, any function $f(\alpha)$ could be rephrased as a function $f'(\boldsymbol{\Delta})$.

The last part of the proof proceeds similarly as in [14] so here we give just an intuition. Informally, an adversary A that wins the fully-leakage one-more unforgeability game with probability ϵ will wins with probability negligibly close to ϵ in the hybrid $\mathbf{H_5}$. Recall that a winning adversary returns $n := \lceil \ell/\mu \log p \rceil + 1$ valid signatures. By the unforgeability of the ABM Encryption and the change introduced in $\mathbf{H_0}$, from the forged signatures $(m_i^*, \sigma^* = (C_i^*, \tau_i^*, \pi_i^*))_{i \in [n]}$, by decrypting the ciphertext C_i^*, we can extract the values $\boldsymbol{\Delta}(m_i^*)$. Notice that each $\boldsymbol{\Delta}(m_i^*)$ gives us $\mu \log p$ bits of information about $\boldsymbol{\Delta}$. Putting all together, with probability negligibly close to ε from the adversary we can extract $n \cdot (\mu \log p) > \ell$ bits of information about $\boldsymbol{\Delta}$. On the other hand, in $\mathbf{H_5}$, the adversary gets at most ℓ bits of information about $\boldsymbol{\Delta}$, the latter implies that ε must be negligible.

Concrete Instantiation. We instantiate the ABM-Scheme with the construction $\mathcal{ABM}_{DDH}$ of [18] based on DDH assumption, the NIWI argument system with Groth-Sahai [22] and the trapdoor commitment with the Pedersen's commitment scheme. A ciphertext C of $\mathcal{ABM}_{DDH}$ is composed by $5\lambda/\log(\lambda)$ groups elements and the encryption procedure can be described by $5\lambda \log(\lambda)$ pairing-product equations. The message space can be parsed as $\mathbb{Z}_n^{\lambda/\log \lambda}$ where $n = \texttt{poly}(\lambda)$ and its "encoded in the exponent". We additionally need $O(\lambda/\log \lambda)$ equations to describe that the plaintext and the opening of the commitment match. Summing up, the value s in the theorem is equal to $O(\lambda/\log \lambda)$. Finally, we notice that since we use the same groups for NIWI and $\mathcal{ABM}_{DDH}$ we need to use the external Diffie-Hellman (SXDH) assumption.

Let $\mathcal{COM} := (\mathsf{Setup}, \mathsf{Com})$ be the following commitment scheme:

Setup. The algorithm Setup parses prm as $(\mathbb{G}_1, \mathbb{G}_2, \mathbb{G}_T, p, G_1, G_2, G_T)$, picks at a random $[\boldsymbol{g}]_1 \leftarrow_\$ \mathbb{G}_1^\mu$, $\alpha \leftarrow_\$ \mathbb{Z}_p$ and $[h]_1 \leftarrow_\$ \mathbb{G}_1$, sets $[\mathcal{M}]_1 \leftarrow (1, \alpha)^T \cdot [\boldsymbol{g}^T, h]_1$, sets $[\boldsymbol{h}]_1 = [h, \alpha \cdot h]_1^T$ be the last column of $[\mathcal{M}]_1$, and sets $[\alpha]_2$. It outputs the verification key $\vartheta = ([\mathcal{M}]_1, [\alpha]_2) \in (\mathbb{G}_1^{2, \mu+1} \times \mathbb{G}_2)$.

Commit. The algorithm Com on input $[\mathcal{M}]_1, [\alpha]_2$ and a message $\boldsymbol{m} \in \mathbb{Z}_p^\mu$, samples $r \leftarrow_\$ \mathbb{Z}_p$ and sets $Com = [\mathcal{M}] \cdot (\boldsymbol{m}^T, r)^T \in \mathbb{G}_1^2$. The opening of the commitment is the r.

Fig. 4. The commitment scheme $\mathcal{COM}$

5 A Signature Scheme Based on KEA

Before describing the signature scheme we give more details on the building blocks. Consider the commitment scheme $\mathcal{COM} := (\mathsf{Setup}, \mathsf{Com})$ (with implicit parameters an integer μ and a group generator Setup_{BG}) described in Fig. 4. Notice that for any two messages m_0, m_1 and randomness r_0 there exists an unique assignment for r_1 such that $[\mathcal{M}]_1 \cdot (m_0^T, r_0)^T = [\mathcal{M}]_1 \cdot (m_0^T, r_1)^T$ holds, therefore $\mathcal{COM}$ is perfectly hiding.

The second building block is a quasi-adaptive non-interactive perfect zero-knowledge argument of knowledge $\mathcal{NIZK}_{ext}$. The argument system is adaptive weak knowledge sound[6]. Roughly speaking, the NIZK is a two-fold version of the scheme of Kiltz and Wee. For space reason we defer the details of the NIZK in the full version of this paper, here we state the following theorem:

Theorem 3. *The scheme $\mathcal{NIZK}_{ext}$ is a quasi-adaptive perfect zero-knowledge argument system and if both the $\mathcal{D}_k$-KerMDH assumption and the 1-KE* assumption hold for Setup_{BG} then it is adaptive weak knowledge sound.*

Let $\mathcal{SS}_2 = (\mathsf{KGen}, \mathsf{Sign}, \mathsf{Verify})$ with message space $\mathbb{Z}_p$ be defined as follow:

Key Generation. Let $d, \mu \in \mathbb{N}$ be parameters. Let $\mathsf{prm} \leftarrow_\$ \mathsf{Setup}_{BG}(1^\lambda)$ be parameter describing an asymmetric bilinear group , let $\vartheta = ([\mathcal{M}]_1, [\alpha]_2) \leftarrow_\$ \mathsf{Setup}(\mathsf{prm})$ and let $[h]_1$ be the last column of $[\mathcal{M}]_1$. Consider the NP relation $\mathcal{R}$ defined as follow:

$$\mathcal{R} = \{([y]_1, r) : [y]_1 = r \cdot [h]_1\}$$

Run $\mathsf{crs}, tp \leftarrow \mathsf{Init}(1^\lambda, \mathcal{R})$, sample $\boldsymbol{\Delta} \leftarrow_\$ \mathbb{Z}_p^{\mu, d+1}$ and $\mathbf{r} = (r_0, \ldots, r_d) \leftarrow_\$ \mathbb{Z}_p^{d+1}$, and compute commitments $Com_i \leftarrow \mathsf{Com}(\vartheta, \boldsymbol{\delta}_i; r_i)$ for $i \in [0, d]$, where $\boldsymbol{\delta}_i \in \mathbb{Z}_p^\mu$ is the j-th column of $\boldsymbol{\Delta}$. Let $\boldsymbol{Com} = (Com_i)_{i=0}^d$ and output

$$\mathsf{sk} = (\boldsymbol{\Delta}, \mathbf{r}) \qquad \mathsf{vk} = (\mathsf{crs}, \vartheta, \boldsymbol{Com}).$$

Signature. To sign a message $m \in \mathbb{Z}_p$ compute $m^* = \boldsymbol{\Delta}(m)$ and let $C \leftarrow \mathsf{Com}(\vartheta, m^*, s)$ where $s \leftarrow_\$ \mathbb{Z}_p$, and compute $\pi \leftarrow \mathsf{P}(\mathsf{crs}, (\mathbf{r}(m) - s) \cdot [h], \mathbf{r}(m) - s)$. Output $\sigma = (C, \pi)$.

Verification. Given a pair (m, σ) and the verification key vk, parse σ as (C, π) and parse vk as $(\mathsf{crs}, \vartheta, \boldsymbol{Com})$. Output 1 if and only if $\mathsf{V}(\mathsf{crs}, \boldsymbol{Com}(m) - C, \pi)$ and $e(C_0, [1]_2) = e(C_1, [\alpha]_2)$.

Fig. 5. The signature scheme $\mathcal{SS}_2$.

The Signature Scheme. The signature scheme $\mathcal{SS}_2$ is described in Fig. 5. We show that the scheme is correct. For any tuple m, σ where σ is a valid signature for m with the verification key $\mathsf{vk} = (\mathsf{crs}, \vartheta, \boldsymbol{Com})$, let parse σ as (C, π), we have:

---

[6] We reverse the order of the quantifiers in the usual definition of knowledge soundness. Namely, for each adversary A there exists an extractor Ext.

$$Com(m) - C = \sum_i Com_i \cdot m^i - C = \sum_i [\mathcal{M}]_1 \cdot (\delta_i^T, r_i)^T \cdot m^i - [\mathcal{M}]_1 \cdot (\Delta(m)^T, s)^T$$
$$= [\mathcal{M}]_1 \cdot \sum_i (\delta_i^T, r_i)^T \cdot m^i - [\mathcal{M}]_1 \cdot (\Delta(m)^T, s)^T$$
$$= [\mathcal{M}]_1 \cdot ((\Delta(m)^T, \mathbf{r}(m))^T - (\Delta(m)^T, s)^T) = [\mathbf{h}]_1 \cdot (\mathbf{r}(m) - s).$$

The last equation follows because $[\mathbf{h}]_1$ is the last column on $[\mathcal{M}]_1$. The correctness of the signature scheme follows by the equation above and the correctness of the quasi-adaptive NIZK scheme.

Theorem 4. *Let $\mu, d \in \mathbb{N}$ and $\mu > 8$. If the $(\mu + 1)$-KE^* assumption and the* KerLin_2 *assumption hold over* Setup_{BG} *then, for any* $0 \leq \ell \leq ((d+1) \log \lambda) - \lambda$, *the signature scheme* $\mathcal{SS}_2$ *described Fig. 5 is* $(\ell, 1)$-*fully-leakage one-more unforgeable with leak-free key generation.*

We give an intuition of the proof. In particular, we explain how to use the knowledge of the exponent assumption of Definition 1. The main idea is to define a sampler that, roughly speaking, executes the fully-leakage one-more unforgeability experiment. More in details, the sampler $\mathcal{S}$ samples all the randomness needed, including the secret key, the randomness for the signatures and the random tape of the adversary, with the only exception of the parameters of the KEA* assumption. The sampler proceeds with executing the experiment up to the moment before the adversary outputs its forgeries. Eventually the sampler outputs the full view of the adversary including the queried signatures, the leakage and the random tape of the adversary, let View be such value.

At this point we can deterministically execute the adversary feeding it with the view produced by the sampler. This adversary produces n commitment values (one for each forgery) for which, thanks to the knowledge of the exponent assumption he must know the opening.

Notice we do not incur in any problem of recursive composition of extractors. In fact the adversary outputs all its commitments at once. More in details, given the adversary code, for any $i \in [n]$, we can define the adversary A_i which outputs only the i-th commitment of A. Using the knowledge of the exponent assumption, for any index i, there musts exist an extractor Ext_i for the adversary A_i. Crucially, the computational complexity of the extractor Ext_i depends only on A_i and not on Ext_j for an index $j \neq i$.

The proof continues showing that the extracted values are indeed evaluations of the polynomial Δ sampled by the sampler. To argue this we use the adaptive weak knowledge soundness of the NIZK. We give more details about this step in the formal proof.

Now, consider the predictor that on input the random variable View first runs the extractors $\mathsf{Ext}_1, \ldots, \mathsf{Ext}_n$ obtaining n evaluation points of the polynomial Δ and then guesses a random polynomial that interpolates the evaluation points. The probability that this predictor guesses the polynomial Δ is roughly $\varepsilon p^{-(d-n)\mu}$ where ε is the winning probability of the adversary A. On the other hand, we prove that, thanks to perfect hiding and perfect zero-knowledge, no predictor can guess the polynomial Δ with probability more than $2^\ell p^{-(d+1)\mu}$. We complete the proof by noticing that the two bounds are in contradiction when ε is noticeable in the security parameter.

Proof (of Theorem 4). Let A be an adversary such that $\mathsf{Adv}^{\text{one-more}^*}_{\mathsf{A},\mathcal{SS}_2}(\lambda, \ell, 1) = \varepsilon$ for parameter ℓ as described in the statement of the theorem. Let $\mathbf{H}_0(\lambda)$ be the experiment $\mathbf{Exp}^{\text{one-more}^*}_{\mathcal{SS},\mathsf{A}}(\lambda)$. Denote with $((m_1^*, (C_1^*, \pi_1^*)), \ldots, (m_n^*, (C_n^*, \pi_n^*)))$ the list of forgeries of A. During the experiment the adversary has oracle access to $\alpha = (\boldsymbol{\Delta}, \mathbf{r}, (s_j, z_j)_{j \in [q]})$ where s_j is the randomness used by Com and z_j is the randomness used by P (the prover of the NIZK proof system). The proof proceeds with an hybrid argument. In particular, the proof has seven main hybrid experiments named $\mathbf{H}_0, \ldots, \mathbf{H}_7$ and other sub-hybrids that we name with $\mathbf{H}_{i,j}$ for $i \in \{2, 3\}$ and $j \in [n]$. Let Forge_i (resp. $\mathsf{Forge}_{i,j}$) be the event that $\mathbf{H}_i$ (resp. $\mathbf{H}_{i,j}$) returns 1, so that $\mathsf{P}[\mathsf{Forge}_0] = \varepsilon$.

Hybrid 1. The hybrid $\mathbf{H}_1$ runs the same as the hybrid $\mathbf{H}_0$ but with a slightly different syntax. More in details, consider the following sampler $\mathcal{S}$:

Sampler $\mathcal{S}([\mathcal{M}]_1, [\alpha]_2)$:

1. Sample $r_\mathsf{A} \leftarrow \{0,1\}^\lambda$ and $\boldsymbol{\Delta} \leftarrow_\$ \mathbb{Z}_p^{\mu, d+1}, \mathbf{r} \leftarrow \mathbb{Z}_p^{d+1}$, set $\mathsf{sk} = (\boldsymbol{\Delta}, \mathbf{r})$ and compute the verification key vk as described in KGen using $[\mathcal{M}]_1$; Sample the randomness $(s_j, z_j)_{j \in [q]}$ and set $\alpha = (\mathsf{sk}, \mathbf{r}, (s_j, z_j)_{j \in [q]})$.
2. Run $\mathsf{A}(\mathsf{vk}; r_\mathsf{A})$ and answer all the signature oracle queries using $\mathsf{Sign}(\mathsf{sk}, \cdot)$ and the leakage oracle queries with the state α. Let $\mathsf{View} = (\sigma_1, \ldots, \sigma_q, \mathsf{Leak})$ be the full transcript of the interactions between A and the oracles;
3. Output $(\mathsf{vk}, \mathsf{View}, r_\mathsf{A})$.

The hybrid $\mathbf{H}_1$ executes three steps: (1) it creates the parameters $(\mathsf{prm}_{BG}, [\mathcal{M}]_1, [\alpha]_2)$, (2) it executes the sampler $(\mathsf{vk}, \mathsf{View}, r_\mathsf{A}) \leftarrow_\$ \mathcal{S}([\mathcal{M}]_1, [\alpha]_2)$, (3) it runs $\mathsf{A}(\mathsf{vk}; r_\mathsf{A})$ and answers all the oracle queries using the information in View. The change between the two hybrids is only syntactical, therefore $\varepsilon_0 = \varepsilon_1$.

Hybrid 2.i. The hybrid $\mathbf{H}_{2.i}$ takes as parameters i different extractors $\mathsf{Ext}_1, \ldots, \mathsf{Ext}_i$ and runs the same as the hybrid $\mathbf{H}_1$ but, also, it runs the extractors and outputs 1 if and only if the extracted values match the commitments $C_1^*, \ldots, C_i^*$. More in details, the hybrid $\mathbf{H}_{2.i}$ first creates the parameters $(\mathsf{prm}_{BG}, [\mathcal{M}]_1, [\alpha]_2)$, then it executes the sampler $(\mathsf{vk}, \mathsf{View}, r_\mathsf{A}) \leftarrow \mathcal{S}([\mathcal{M}]_1, [\alpha]_2)$, then it runs $\mathsf{A}(\mathsf{vk}; r_\mathsf{A})$ and answers all the oracle queries using the information in View. Eventually, A outputs its forgeries $(m_1^*, \sigma_1^*), \ldots, (m_n^*, \sigma_n^*)$ where $\sigma_i^* = (C_i^*, \pi_i^*)$, and for $j = 1, \ldots, i$ the hybrid $\mathbf{H}_{1.i}$ computes $\boldsymbol{x}_i \leftarrow \mathsf{Ext}_i(((\mathcal{M}]_1, [\alpha]_2), (\mathsf{vk}, \mathsf{View}, r_\mathsf{A}))$ and outputs 1 if and only if:

(a) all the forged signatures verify correctly for vk and all the messages are different and,
(b) for any $j = 1, \ldots, i$ we have $C_j^* = [\mathcal{M}]_1 \cdot \boldsymbol{x}_j$.

Claim. There exist PPT extractors $\mathsf{Ext}_1, \ldots, \mathsf{Ext}_n$ such that for any $i > 1$, $|\varepsilon_{1.i-1} - \varepsilon_{1.i}| \in \mathtt{negl}(\lambda)$. Moreover, $\varepsilon_1 = \varepsilon_{2.0}$.

Proof. First we prove second sentence of the claim. The change between $\mathbf{H}_1$ and $\mathbf{H}_{2.0}$ is only syntactical. In fact, the winning condition is the same in both hybrids, as $\mathbf{H}_{2.0}$ does not check the condition (b). Now we prove the first sentence. We define an adversary A'_i for the $(\mu + 1)$-KE^* assumption:

Adversary $\mathsf{A}'_i([\mathcal{M}]_1; r')$:

1. Parse r' as $(\mathsf{vk}, \mathsf{View}, r_\mathsf{A})$;
2. Run $\mathsf{A}(\mathsf{vk}; r_\mathsf{A})$ and answers all the oracle queries using the information in View;
3. Eventually, A outputs its forgeries $(m_1^*, \sigma_1^*), \ldots, (m_n^*, \sigma_n^*)$;
4. If all the forged signatures verify correctly for vk and all the messages are different parse σ_i^* as (C_i^*, π_i^*) and output $[\boldsymbol{y}]_1 := C_i^*$.

For any PPT Ext_i the two hybrids diverge when $[\mathcal{M}]_1 \cdot \boldsymbol{x}_i \neq [\boldsymbol{y}]_1$, where $\boldsymbol{x}_i$ is the output of the extractor, but the signature σ_i^* verifies correctly. Notice that the verification algorithm checks that $e([y_0]_1, [\alpha]_2) = e([y_1]_1, [1]_2)$, where $\boldsymbol{y} = (y_0, y_1)$ and so $[\boldsymbol{y}]_1 \in Span([1, \alpha]_1)$. Therefore:

$$|\varepsilon_{1.i-1} - \varepsilon_{1.i}| \leq \Pr\left[[\mathcal{M}]_1 \cdot \boldsymbol{x}_i \neq Y \ \wedge \ Y \in Span([1, \alpha]_1)\right]$$

We can apply the security of the $\mu + 1$-KE^* assumption. In particular, there musts exist an extractor Ext_i such that the difference above is negligible.

Hybrid 3.*i*. The hybrid $\mathbf{H}_{3.i}$ takes as parameters n different PPT extractors $\mathsf{Ext}_1, \ldots, \mathsf{Ext}_n$ plus i different PPT extractors $\mathsf{Ext}'_1, \ldots, \mathsf{Ext}'_i$ and runs the same as the hybrid $\mathbf{H}_{2.n}$ but also <u>for any $j = 1, \ldots, i$ it computes $w_i \leftarrow$ $\mathsf{Ext}'_i(\mathsf{crs}, tp, r')$ where $r' = (\boldsymbol{\Delta}, \mathbf{r}, [\boldsymbol{g}, h], \alpha)$</u> and the winning conditions are changed as follow:

(a) All the forged signatures verify correctly for vk and all the messages are different,
(b) for any $j = 1, \ldots, n$ we have $C_j^* = [\mathcal{M}]_1 \cdot \boldsymbol{x}_j$ and,
(c) <u>for any $j = 1, \ldots, i$ check $\boldsymbol{Com}(m_i^*) - C_i^* = w_i \cdot [h, \alpha h]$.</u>

Claim. For any PPT $\mathsf{Ext}_1, \ldots, \mathsf{Ext}_n$ there exist PPT extractors $\mathsf{Ext}'_1, \ldots, \mathsf{Ext}'_n$ such that for any $i > 1$, $|\varepsilon_{1.i-1} = \varepsilon_{2.i}| \in \mathtt{negl}(\lambda)$. Moreover, $\varepsilon_{3.0} = \varepsilon_{2.n}$.

The claim follows by the weak knowledge soundness of $\mathcal{NIZK}_{ext}$. For space reasons the proof of the Claim is deferred to the full version [12].

Hybrid 4. The hybrid $\mathbf{H}_4$ is the same as $\mathbf{H}_{3.n}$ but the winning conditions are changed as follow:

(a) All the forged signatures verify correctly for vk and all the messages are different,

(b) for any $j = 1, \ldots, n$ we have $C_j^* = [\mathcal{M}]_1 \cdot \boldsymbol{x}_j$,

(c) for any $j = 1, \ldots, n$ check $\boldsymbol{Com}(m_i^*) - C_i^* = w_i \cdot [h, \alpha h]_1$ and,

(d) for any $j = 1, \ldots, n$, let $\boldsymbol{x}_j'$ be the projection of $\boldsymbol{x}_j$ to the first μ coordinates, check $\boldsymbol{x}_j' = \boldsymbol{\Delta}(m_j^*)$.

Claim. $|\varepsilon_{3.n} = \varepsilon_4| \in \mathtt{negl}(spar)$.

The claim follows by a simple reduction to the DLOG problem. For space reasons the proof of the Claim is deferred to the full version [12].

Hybrid 5. The hybrid $\mathbf{H}_5$ is the same as $\mathbf{H}_4$ but we revert the changes introduced in the hybrids $\mathbf{H}_{2,i}$ for all $i \in [n]$. The winning conditions are changed and in particular they are less stringent as do not consider the condition (c). As the condition is not checked then the hybrid does not need to execute the extractors Ext_i' for $i \in [n]$. Notice that the set of conditions are relaxed, so the probability of the event cannot decrease, namely $\varepsilon_5 \geq \varepsilon_4$.

The Predictor P. The predictor runs the same as the hybrid $\mathbf{H}_5$ but the sampler $\mathcal{S}$ is run *externally*. In particular, the parameters for $\mathcal{S}$ are sampled, then first the sampler is executed and then the predictor P is executed with input the output produced by $\mathcal{S}$. Eventually, the predictors (which runs internally A) receives n forgeries $(m_1^*, \sigma_1^*), \ldots, (m_n^*, \sigma_n^*)$. The predictor checks the winning conditions (a), (b), (d) of the hybrid $\mathbf{H}_5$ and if they hold, for $j \in [\mu]$ it samples a polynomial δ_j^* in $\mathbb{Z}_p[X]$ of degree d such that $\delta_j(m_i^*) = x_{i,j}'$ for $i \in [n]$, and it outputs $\boldsymbol{\Delta}^* = (\delta_1^*, \ldots, \delta_\mu^*)$.

Recall that the advantage of A in the one-more unforgeability game is ε.

Lemma 1. $\Pr\left[\mathsf{P}(\mathcal{S}([\mathcal{M}]_1, [\alpha]_2)) = \boldsymbol{\Delta}\right] \geq \exp(((n - d) \cdot \mu) \log p) \cdot (\varepsilon - \mathtt{negl}(\lambda))$.

Proof. By the triangular inequality and the claims above we have that $\varepsilon_5 \geq \varepsilon - \mathtt{negl}(\lambda)$. When the event $\mathtt{Forge}_5$ happens then $\boldsymbol{\Delta}(m_i^*) = \boldsymbol{x}_i'$ for $i \in [n]$ so the event that $\boldsymbol{\Delta}^* = \boldsymbol{\Delta}$ is equivalent to the event that the predictor P correctly guesses the remaining $d - n$ zeros of the polynomials δ_i for $i \in [\mu]$ which is equal to $1/p^{\mu(d-n)} = \exp(((n - d) \cdot \mu) \log p)$.

Lemma 2. *For any* $\mathsf{prm} \leftarrow_\$ \mathsf{Setup}_{BG}(1^\lambda)$, *any* $([\mathcal{M}]_1, [\alpha]_2) \in \mathbb{G}_1^{2,\mu+1} \times \mathbb{G}_2$ *and any predictor* P' *we have* $\Pr\left[\mathsf{P}'(\mathcal{S}([\mathcal{M}]_1, [\alpha]_2)) = \boldsymbol{\Delta}\right] \leq \exp(-(d + 1)\mu \log p + \ell)$.

Proof. We define two samplers $\mathcal{S}_1$ and $\mathcal{S}_2$, we prove that their output distributions $(\mathsf{vk}, (\sigma_1, \ldots, \sigma_q, \mathsf{Leak}), r_A)$ are equivalent to the distribution of $\mathcal{S}$, and moreover, the components $\mathsf{vk}, \sigma_1, \ldots, \sigma_q, r_A$ are independent of $\boldsymbol{\Delta}$ as sampled by $\mathcal{S}$. Both the sampler $\mathcal{S}_1$ and $\mathcal{S}_2$ are not efficiently computable, however, this is not a problem as we are proving that their distributions are identically distributed to the distribution of $\mathcal{S}$.

The sampler $\mathcal{S}_1$ executes the same of $\mathcal{S}$ but the elements $\boldsymbol{Com}$, the signature queries, and the leakage oracle queries are computed in the following way:

- The elements $\boldsymbol{Com}$ are sampled as uniformly element from $Span([g, \alpha g])$.
- At the j-th signature oracle query with message m the element C_j is sampled as uniformly element from $Span([g, \alpha g])$.
- Define the function $\mathbf{r}(\boldsymbol{\Delta})$ that outputs the vector $(r_0, \ldots, r_d)$ computing r_i such that $Com_i = [\mathcal{M}]_1 \cdot (\boldsymbol{\delta}_i^T, r_i)^T$. Similarly, define the functions $s_j(\boldsymbol{\Delta})$ that output the vector s_j such that $C_j = [\mathcal{M}]_1 \cdot (\boldsymbol{\delta}_i^T, s_j)^T$. For each leakage oracle query f the answer of f is computed as $f(\boldsymbol{\Delta}, \mathbf{r}(\boldsymbol{\Delta}), (s_i(\boldsymbol{\Delta}), z_i)_{i \leq q})$.

Claim. For any parameter $\mathtt{prm} \leftarrow_\$ \mathsf{Setup}_{BG}(1^\lambda)$ and any $([\mathcal{M}]_1, [\alpha]_2) \in \mathbb{G}_1^{2, \mu+1} \times \mathbb{G}_2$ the outputs of the samplers $\mathcal{S}$ and $\mathcal{S}_1$ are identically distributed.

Proof. We notice that for any m the commitment to m is uniformly distributed over $Span([1, \alpha])$. Therefore, for any Com_i (resp. C_i), it always exists such r_i (resp. s_i), and moreover, once $\boldsymbol{\Delta}$ and $\boldsymbol{Com}$ (resp. C_i) are fixed its value is uniquely defined.

The sampler $\mathcal{S}_2$ executes the same of $\mathcal{S}_1$ but, for all the signatures, the NIZK proofs π_i are computed using the simulator S of NIZK and, moreover, the randomness z_i is uniformly sampled over the set[7]

$$\{z_i : \pi_i = \mathsf{P}(\mathsf{crs}, (\mathbf{r}(\boldsymbol{\Delta})(m_i) - \mathbf{s}(\boldsymbol{\Delta})) \cdot [\mathbf{h}], (\mathbf{r}(\boldsymbol{\Delta})(m_i) - \mathbf{s}(\boldsymbol{\Delta})))\}$$

where $\mathbf{r}(\boldsymbol{\Delta})$ is the vector of the randomness as computed by $\mathcal{S}_1$.

Claim. For any parameter $\mathtt{prm} \leftarrow_\$ \mathsf{Setup}_{BG}(1^\lambda)$ and any $([\mathcal{M}]_1, [\alpha]_2) \in \mathbb{G}_1^{2, \mu+1} \times \mathbb{G}_2$ the outputs of the samplers $\mathcal{S}_1$ and $\mathcal{S}_2$ are identically distributed, $\mathcal{S}_1([\mathcal{M}]_1, [\alpha]_2) \equiv \mathcal{S}_2([\mathcal{M}]_1, [\alpha]_2)$.

Proof. By the perfect zero-knowledge property of the quasi-adaptive NIZK, the proofs π_i are distributed equivalently to the real proofs. Notice that perfect zero-knowledge implies that the set of the simulated proofs and the set of real proofs (for any instance and witness) is exactly the same. Moreover, for all i, we sample s_i' uniformly at random from the set of possible randomness that match with the proof π_i, therefore s_i' is equivalently distributed to s_i, the randomness used to compute the proofs in $\mathcal{S}_1$. We write $z_i(\boldsymbol{\Delta})$ to stress that z_i is computed as function of $\boldsymbol{\Delta}$, for each leakage oracle query f the answer of f is computed as $f(\boldsymbol{\Delta}, \mathbf{r}(\boldsymbol{\Delta}), (s_i(\boldsymbol{\Delta}), z_i(\boldsymbol{\Delta}))_{i \leq q})$.

Claim. For any P' we have $\Pr[\mathsf{P}'(\mathcal{S}_2([\mathcal{M}]_1, [\alpha]_2)) = \boldsymbol{\Delta}] \leq \exp(-(d+1)\mu \log p + \ell)$.

Proof. Let q be the number of signature queries made by A and let Leak the concatenation of all the leakage performed by A. For any predictor P'

$$\Pr\left[\mathsf{P}'(\mathcal{S}_2([\mathcal{M}]_1, [\alpha]_2)) = \boldsymbol{\Delta}\right] = \Pr\left[\mathsf{P}'(\mathsf{Leak}) = \boldsymbol{\Delta}\right] \tag{1}$$

$$= \sum_L \Pr\left[\mathsf{P}'(L) = \boldsymbol{\Delta} \mid \mathsf{Leak} = L\right] \Pr\left[\mathsf{Leak} = L\right]$$

$$\leq 2^\ell \max_D \Pr\left[\boldsymbol{\Delta} = D\right]. \tag{2}$$

---

[7] Namely, the set of assignment for the randomness z_i for which the execution of P with randomness z_i and the appropriate tuple instance and witness does compute exactly the proof π_i.

where Eq. 1 holds because vk, r_A and the signatures $\sigma_1, \ldots, \sigma_q$ are sampled independently from Δ, while Eq. 2 holds applying the chain rule of the average conditional min-entropy. Finally we notice that Δ is sampled uniformly at random so the statement of the claim follows.

By putting together the first two claims we have that the probability of guessing Δ by a predictor given in input the output produced by $\mathcal{S}_2$ is the same as it gets in input the output produced by $\mathcal{S}_1$, by the last claim, therefore, the lemma follows.

Returning to the proof of the theorem, we can put together the inequalities of Lemmas 1 and 2, and by taking the logarithms we have:

$$-d\mu \log p + \ell \geq -(d - n)\mu \log p + \log(\varepsilon - \mathsf{negl}(\lambda))$$

By adding $d\mu \log p$ to both sides we derive that $\ell \geq n\mu \log p + \log(\varepsilon - \mathsf{negl}(\lambda))$, and by the fact that $n > \frac{\ell}{s \cdot \gamma} + 1$ and $\gamma = 1$ we derive that $-\log(\varepsilon - \mathsf{negl}(\lambda)) > s \geq \lambda$. For the equation above to hold, necessarily, ε is negligible in λ.

Acknowledgements. Research leading to these results has been supported by the Spanish Ministry of Economy under the projects Dedetis (ref. TIN2015-70713-R) and Datamantium (ref. RTC-2016-4930-7), and by the Madrid Regional Government under project N-Greens (ref. S2013/ICE-2731).

I would like to thank Dario Fiore for a conversation we had on his paper [16]. Also, I would like to thank Dennis Hofheinz which suggested to me the paper of Fujisaki on ABM Encryption.

References

1. Abe, M., Fehr, S.: Perfect NIZK with adaptive soundness. In: Vadhan, S.P. (ed.) TCC 2007. LNCS, vol. 4392, pp. 118–136. Springer, Heidelberg (2007). https://doi.org/10.1007/978-3-540-70936-7_7

2. Alwen, J., Dodis, Y., Naor, M., Segev, G., Walfish, S., Wichs, D.: Public-key encryption in the bounded-retrieval model. In: Gilbert, H. (ed.) EUROCRYPT 2010. LNCS, vol. 6110, pp. 113–134. Springer, Heidelberg (2010). https://doi.org/10.1007/978-3-642-13190-5_6

3. Alwen, J., Dodis, Y., Wichs, D.: Leakage-resilient public-key cryptography in the bounded-retrieval model. In: Halevi, S. (ed.) CRYPTO 2009. LNCS, vol. 5677, pp. 36–54. Springer, Heidelberg (2009). https://doi.org/10.1007/978-3-642-03356-8_3

4. Ateniese, G., Faonio, A., Kamara, S.: Leakage-resilient identification schemes from zero-knowledge proofs of storage. In: Groth, J. (ed.) IMACC 2015. LNCS, vol. 9496, pp. 311–328. Springer, Cham (2015). https://doi.org/10.1007/978-3-319-27239-9_19

5. Bellare, M., Palacio, A.: The knowledge-of-exponent assumptions and 3-round zero-knowledge protocols. In: Franklin, M. (ed.) CRYPTO 2004. LNCS, vol. 3152, pp. 273–289. Springer, Heidelberg (2004). https://doi.org/10.1007/978-3-540-28628-8_17

6. Bitansky, N., Canetti, R., Paneth, O., Rosen, A.: On the existence of extractable one-way functions. In: 46th ACM STOC, pp. 505–514 (2014)

7. Boyle, E., Segev, G., Wichs, D.: Fully leakage-resilient signatures. In: Paterson, K.G. (ed.) EUROCRYPT 2011. LNCS, vol. 6632, pp. 89–108. Springer, Heidelberg (2011). https://doi.org/10.1007/978-3-642-20465-4_7

8. Brakerski, Z., Kalai, Y.T., Katz, J., Vaikuntanathan, V.: Overcoming the hole in the bucket: public-key cryptography resilient to continual memory leakage. In: 51st FOCS, pp. 501–510 (2010)

9. Damgård, I.: Towards practical public key systems secure against chosen ciphertext attacks. In: Feigenbaum, J. (ed.) CRYPTO 1991. LNCS, vol. 576, pp. 445–456. Springer, Heidelberg (1992). https://doi.org/10.1007/3-540-46766-1_36

10. Dodis, Y., Haralambiev, K., López-Alt, A., Wichs, D.: Cryptography against continuous memory attacks. In: 51st FOCS, pp. 511–520 (2010)

11. Escala, A., Herold, G., Kiltz, E., Ràfols, C., Villar, J.: An algebraic framework for Diffie-Hellman assumptions. In: Canetti, R., Garay, J.A. (eds.) CRYPTO 2013. LNCS, vol. 8043, pp. 129–147. Springer, Heidelberg (2013). https://doi.org/10.1007/978-3-642-40084-1_8

12. Faonio, A.: Efficient fully-leakage resilient one-more signature schemes. Cryptology ePrint Archive, Report 2018/1140 (2018). https://eprint.iacr.org/2018/1140

13. Faonio, A., Nielsen, J.B.: Fully leakage-resilient codes. In: Fehr, S. (ed.) PKC 2017. LNCS, vol. 10174, pp. 333–358. Springer, Heidelberg (2017). https://doi.org/10.1007/978-3-662-54365-8_14

14. Faonio, A., Nielsen, J.B., Venturi, D.: Mind your coins: fully leakage-resilient signatures with graceful degradation. In: Halldórsson, M.M., Iwama, K., Kobayashi, N., Speckmann, B. (eds.) ICALP 2015. LNCS, vol. 9134, pp. 456–468. Springer, Heidelberg (2015). https://doi.org/10.1007/978-3-662-47672-7_37

15. Faonio, A., Nielsen, J.B., Venturi, D.: Fully leakage-resilient signatures revisited: graceful degradation, noisy leakage, and construction in the bounded-retrieval model. Theoret. Comput. Sci. **660**, 23–56 (2017)

16. Fiore, D., Nitulescu, A.: On the (in)security of SNARKs in the presence of oracles. In: Hirt, M., Smith, A. (eds.) TCC 2016. LNCS, vol. 9985, pp. 108–138. Springer, Heidelberg (2016). https://doi.org/10.1007/978-3-662-53641-4_5

17. Fujisaki, E.: All-but-many encryption. In: Sarkar, P., Iwata, T. (eds.) ASIACRYPT 2014. LNCS, vol. 8874, pp. 426–447. Springer, Heidelberg (2014). https://doi.org/10.1007/978-3-662-45608-8_23

18. Fujisaki, E.: All-but-many encryption. J. Cryptol. **31**(1), 226–275 (2018)

19. Gandolfi, K., Mourtel, C., Olivier, F.: Electromagnetic analysis: concrete results. In: Koç, Ç.K., Naccache, D., Paar, C. (eds.) CHES 2001. LNCS, vol. 2162, pp. 251–261. Springer, Heidelberg (2001). https://doi.org/10.1007/3-540-44709-1_21

20. Gennaro, R., Gentry, C., Parno, B., Raykova, M.: Quadratic span programs and succinct NIZKs without PCPs. In: Johansson, T., Nguyen, P.Q. (eds.) EUROCRYPT 2013. LNCS, vol. 7881, pp. 626–645. Springer, Heidelberg (2013). https://doi.org/10.1007/978-3-642-38348-9_37

21. Groth, J.: Short pairing-based non-interactive zero-knowledge arguments. In: Abe, M. (ed.) ASIACRYPT 2010. LNCS, vol. 6477, pp. 321–340. Springer, Heidelberg (2010). https://doi.org/10.1007/978-3-642-17373-8_19

22. Groth, J., Sahai, A.: Efficient non-interactive proof systems for bilinear groups. In: Smart, N. (ed.) EUROCRYPT 2008. LNCS, vol. 4965, pp. 415–432. Springer, Heidelberg (2008). https://doi.org/10.1007/978-3-540-78967-3_24

23. Hofheinz, D.: All-but-many lossy trapdoor functions. In: Pointcheval, D., Johansson, T. (eds.) EUROCRYPT 2012. LNCS, vol. 7237, pp. 209–227. Springer, Heidelberg (2012). https://doi.org/10.1007/978-3-642-29011-4_14

24. Jutla, C.S., Roy, A.: Shorter quasi-adaptive NIZK proofs for linear subspaces. In: Sako, K., Sarkar, P. (eds.) ASIACRYPT 2013. LNCS, vol. 8269, pp. 1–20. Springer, Heidelberg (2013). https://doi.org/10.1007/978-3-642-42033-7_1
25. Kiltz, E., Wee, H.: Quasi-adaptive NIZK for linear subspaces revisited. In: Oswald, E., Fischlin, M. (eds.) EUROCRYPT 2015. LNCS, vol. 9057, pp. 101–128. Springer, Heidelberg (2015). https://doi.org/10.1007/978-3-662-46803-6_4
26. Kocher, P.C.: Timing attacks on implementations of Diffie-Hellman, RSA, DSS, and other systems. In: Koblitz, N. (ed.) CRYPTO 1996. LNCS, vol. 1109, pp. 104–113. Springer, Heidelberg (1996). https://doi.org/10.1007/3-540-68697-5_9
27. Kocher, P., Jaffe, J., Jun, B.: Differential power analysis. In: Wiener, M. (ed.) CRYPTO 1999. LNCS, vol. 1666, pp. 388–397. Springer, Heidelberg (1999). https://doi.org/10.1007/3-540-48405-1_25
28. Malkin, T., Teranishi, I., Vahlis, Y., Yung, M.: Signatures resilient to continual leakage on memory and computation. In: Ishai, Y. (ed.) TCC 2011. LNCS, vol. 6597, pp. 89–106. Springer, Heidelberg (2011). https://doi.org/10.1007/978-3-642-19571-6_7
29. Naor, M., Segev, G.: Public-key cryptosystems resilient to key leakage. In: Halevi, S. (ed.) CRYPTO 2009. LNCS, vol. 5677, pp. 18–35. Springer, Heidelberg (2009). https://doi.org/10.1007/978-3-642-03356-8_2
30. Nielsen, J.B., Venturi, D., Zottarel, A.: Leakage-resilient signatures with graceful degradation. In: Krawczyk, H. (ed.) PKC 2014. LNCS, vol. 8383, pp. 362–379. Springer, Heidelberg (2014). https://doi.org/10.1007/978-3-642-54631-0_21
31. Parno, B., Howell, J., Gentry, C., Raykova, M.: Pinocchio: nearly practical verifiable computation. In: 2013 IEEE Symposium on Security and Privacy, pp. 238–252 (2013)
32. Pedersen, T.P.: Non-interactive and information-theoretic secure verifiable secret sharing. In: Feigenbaum, J. (ed.) CRYPTO 1991. LNCS, vol. 576, pp. 129–140. Springer, Heidelberg (1992). https://doi.org/10.1007/3-540-46766-1_9

MILP-Based Differential Attack on Round-Reduced GIFT

Baoyu Zhu[1][iD], Xiaoyang Dong[2(✉)][iD], and Hongbo Yu[1,3(✉)][iD]

[1] Department of Computer Science and Technology, Tsinghua University,
Beijing, People's Republic of China
yuhongbo@mail.tsinghua.edu.cn
[2] Institute for Advanced Study, Tsinghua University,
Beijing, People's Republic of China
xiaoyangdong@tsinghua.edu.cn
[3] Science and Technology on Communication Security Laboratory,
Chengdu, People's Republic of China

Abstract. At Asiacrypt 2014, Sun et al. proposed a MILP model [20] to search for differential characteristics of bit-oriented block ciphers. In this paper, we improve this model to search for differential characteristics of GIFT [2], a new lightweight block cipher proposed at CHES 2017. GIFT has two versions, namely GIFT-64 and GIFT-128. For GIFT-64, we find the best 12-round differential characteristic and a number of iterative 4-round differential characteristics with our MILP-based model. We give a key-recovery attack on 19-round GIFT-64. For GIFT-128, we find a 18-round differential characteristic and give the first attack on 23-round GIFT-128.

Keywords: GIFT · Differential cryptanalysis ·
Lightweight block cipher · MILP

1 Introduction

In recent years, research on lightweight block ciphers has received a lot of attentions. Lightweight block ciphers are widely used in Internet of things and wireless communication because their structures are simple and they can be run in low-power environment. Many lightweight block ciphers such as PRESENT [5], CLEFIA [17], LED [10], PRINCE [6], SIMON and SPECK [3] have been published in last decades. GIFT [2] is a new lightweight block cipher proposed by Banik et al. at CHES 2017, which is designed to celebrate 10 years of PRESENT. GIFT has an SPN structure which is similar to PRESENT. It has two versions,

Supported by the National Key Research and Development Program of China (No. 2017YFA0303903 No. 2018YFB0803400) and National Cryptography Development Fund (No. MMJJ20170121, MMJJ20180101) and Foundation of Science and Technology on Information Assurance Laboratory (No. 61421120103162112008).

M. Matsui (Ed.): CT-RSA 2019, LNCS 11405, pp. 372–390, 2019.
https://doi.org/10.1007/978-3-030-12612-4_19

namely GIFT-64 and GIFT-128, whose block sizes are 64 and 128, and the round numbers are 28 and 40 respectively.

Many classical cryptanalysis methods could be converted to mathematical optimization problems which aims to achieve the minimal or maximal value of an objective function under certain constraints. Mixed-integer Linear Programming (MILP) is the most widely studied technique to solve these optimization problems. One of the most successful applications of MILP is to search for differential and linear trails. Mouha et al. first applied MILP method to count active S-boxes of word-based block ciphers [12]. Then, at Asiacrypt 2014, Sun et al. extended this technique to search for differential and linear trails [20], whose main idea is to derive some linear inequalities through the H-Representation of the convex hull of all differential patterns and linear bias of S-box. Xiang et al. [21] introduced a MILP model to search for integral distinguisher, Sasaki et al. [16] and Cui et al. [7] gave the MILP-based impossible differential search model independently. There are many MILP-based tools proposed already, such as MILP-based differential/linear search model for ARX ciphers [8], MILP-based conditional cube attacks [11] on Keccak [4], etc.

Our Contributions

The designers of GIFT provided many analysis result about GIFT in [2]. They use MILP to compute the lower bounds for the number of active S-boxes in differential cryptanalysis firstly. Then they presented round-reduced differential probabilities. For GIFT-64, they provided a 9-round differential characteristic with probability of $2^{-44.415}$ and they expected that the differential probability of 13-round GIFT-64 will be lower than 2^{-63}. For GIFT-128, they provided a 9-round differential probability of 2^{-47} and they expected that the differential probability of 26-round GIFT-128 will be lower than 2^{-127}. The designers did not present actual attack on GIFT in [2].

In this paper, we generalize an efficient two-stage MILP-based model inspired by Sun et al.'s two-stage model [18]. Our model includes two interactive submodels, denoted as outer-MILP and inner-MILP part. The outer-MILP part obtains the minimal active S-boxes, namely, the truncated differential. Then the inner-MILP part produces the differential characteristic with maximal probability, the differential characteristic should match the truncated differential. With our two-stage model, we find some 12-round differential characteristics of GIFT-64, some of the differential characteristics are iterative. Moreover, using a 12-round differential characteristic with probability of 2^{-60}, we give an attack on 19-round reduced GIFT-64 (out of 28 full rounds) with time complexity 2^{112}, memory complexity 2^{80} and data complexity 2^{63}.

In addition, we also improved our search model to find differential characteristics of GIFT-128. Firstly, the algorithm solves a sub-MILP-model to obtain an acceptable differential characteristic with small number of rounds. The output difference of a sub-MILP-model should be served as input difference of the following sub-MILP-model. The sub-MILP-model is iterated until the probability of the whole differential characteristic is higher than the given bound. Using our algorithm, we find some new differential characteristics, including a new 18-

round differential characteristic with probability 2^{-109}. We give the first attack on 23-round GIFT-128 (out of 40 full rounds) with the 18-round differential characteristic. All of the source code is uploaded to GitHub (https://github.com/zhuby12/MILP-basedModel).

The summary of differential analysis of GIFT is shown in Table 1.

Table 1. Summary of cryptography analysis on GIFT

	Type	Rounds	Time	Memory	Data	Source
GIFT-64	Integral	14	2^{96}	2^{63}	2^{63}	[2]
GIFT-64	MitM	15	2^{120}	2^{8}	2^{64}	[2]
GIFT-64	MitM	15	2^{112}	2^{16}	2^{64}	[14]
GIFT-64	Differential	19	2^{112}	2^{80}	2^{63}	Ours
GIFT-128	Differential	23	2^{120}	2^{86}	2^{120}	Ours

2   Preliminaries

2.1   Description of GIFT

GIFT has an SPN structure which is similar to PRESENT. It has two versions, namely GIFT-64 and GIFT-128, whose block sizes are 64 and 128 and round numbers are 28 and 40 respectively. Both versions have a key length of 128 bits.

Each round of GIFT consists of three steps: SubCells, PermBits and AddRoundKey. The round function of GIFT-64 is shown in Fig. 1. Similarly, GIFT-128 adopts thirty-two 4-bit S-boxes for each round.

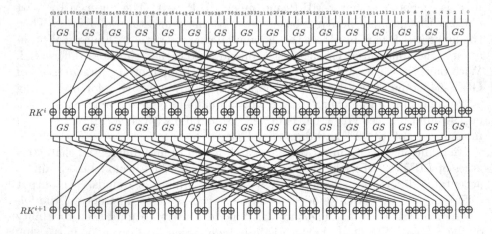

Fig. 1. Two rounds of GIFT-64

SubCells. Both versions of GIFT use the same invertible 4-bit S-box, which is the only nonlinear component of the algorithm. The action of this S-box in hexadecimal notation is given in Table 2.

Table 2. Sbox of GIFT

x	0	1	2	3	4	5	6	7	8	9	a	b	c	d	e	f
GS(x)	1	a	4	c	6	F	3	9	2	d	b	7	5	0	8	e

PermBits. The bit permutation used in GIFT-64 and GIFT-128 are given in Table 3.

AddRoundKey. The round key RK is extracted from the key state. A round key is *first* extracted from the key state before the key state update.

For GIFT-64, two 16-bit words of the key state are extracted as the round key $RK = U\|V$. U and V are XORed to b_{4i+1} and b_{4i} of the cipher state respectively. b_i represents the *i-th* bit of the cipher state. u_i and v_i represent the *i-th* bit of U and V.

$$U \leftarrow k_1, V \leftarrow k_0$$

$$b_{4i+1} \leftarrow b_{4i+1} \oplus u_i, b_{4i} \leftarrow b_{4i} \oplus v_i, \forall i \in \{0, \cdots, 15\}$$

For GIFT-128, four 16-bit words of the key state are extracted as the round key $RK = U\|V$. U and V are XORed to b_{4i+2} and b_{4i+1} of the cipher state respectively.

$$U \leftarrow k_5\|k_4, V \leftarrow k_1\|k_0$$

$$b_{4i+2} \leftarrow b_{4i+2} \oplus u_i, b_{4i+1} \leftarrow b_{4i+1} \oplus v_i, \forall i \in \{0, \cdots, 31\}$$

The key state for two versions are updated as follows,

$$k_7\|k_6\| \cdots \|k_1\|k_0 \leftarrow k_1 \ggg 2\|k_0 \ggg 12\| \cdots \|k_3\|k_2$$

Round Constants. For both versions of GIFT, a single bit "1" and a 6-bit constant $C = \{c_5, c_4, c_3, c_2, c_1, c_0\}$ are XORed into the cipher state at bit position n-1,23,19,15,11,7,3 respectively in each round. For GIFT-64, n-1 is 63 and for GIFT-128, n-1 is 127. $\{c_5, c_4, c_3, c_2, c_1, c_0\}$ are initialized to "0", and they are updated as follow:

$$(c_5, c_4, c_3, c_2, c_1, c_0) \leftarrow (c_4, c_3, c_2, c_1, c_0, c_5 \oplus c_4 \oplus 1)$$

Table 3. Specifications of GIFT bit permutation

GIFT-64	i	0	1	2	3	4	5	6	7	8	9	10	11	12	13	14	15
	$P_{64}(i)$	0	17	34	51	48	1	18	35	32	49	2	19	16	33	50	3
	i	16	17	18	19	20	21	22	23	24	25	26	27	28	29	30	31
	$P_{64}(i)$	4	21	38	55	52	5	22	39	36	53	6	23	20	37	54	7
	i	32	33	34	35	36	37	38	39	40	41	42	43	44	45	46	47
	$P_{64}(i)$	8	25	42	59	56	9	26	43	40	57	10	27	24	41	58	11
	i	48	49	50	51	52	53	54	55	56	57	58	59	60	61	62	63
	$P_{64}(i)$	12	29	46	63	60	13	30	47	44	61	14	31	28	45	62	15
GIFT-128	i	0	1	2	3	4	5	6	7	8	9	10	11	12	13	14	15
	$P_{128}(i)$	0	33	66	99	96	1	34	67	64	97	2	35	32	65	98	3
	i	16	17	18	19	20	21	22	23	24	25	26	27	28	29	30	31
	$P_{128}(i)$	4	37	70	103	100	5	38	71	68	101	6	39	36	69	102	7
	i	32	33	34	35	36	37	38	39	40	41	42	43	44	45	46	47
	$P_{128}(i)$	8	41	74	107	104	9	42	75	72	105	10	43	40	73	106	11
	i	48	49	50	51	52	53	54	55	56	57	58	59	60	61	62	63
	$P_{128}(i)$	12	45	78	111	108	13	46	79	76	109	14	47	44	77	110	15
	i	64	65	66	67	68	69	70	71	72	73	74	75	76	77	78	79
	$P_{128}(i)$	16	49	82	115	112	17	50	83	80	113	18	51	48	81	114	19
	i	80	81	82	83	84	85	86	87	88	89	90	91	92	93	94	95
	$P_{128}(i)$	20	53	86	119	116	21	54	87	84	117	22	55	52	85	118	23
	i	96	97	98	99	100	101	102	103	104	105	106	107	108	109	110	111
	$P_{128}(i)$	24	57	90	123	120	25	58	91	88	121	26	59	56	89	122	27
	i	112	113	114	115	116	117	118	119	120	121	122	123	124	125	126	127
	$P_{128}(i)$	28	61	94	127	124	29	62	95	92	125	30	63	60	93	126	31

2.2 Notations

K_i^j	The j-th bit of the i-th round key
ΔP	The differential in the plaintext
ΔX_S^i	The differential in the output of the i-th round's Sbox
ΔX_P^i	The differential in the output of the i-th round's Permutation
ΔX_K^i	The differential in the output of the i-th round's AddKey
$\Delta X_{S,P,K}^i$	ΔX_S^i or ΔX_P^i or ΔX_K^i
$\Delta X_{S,P,K}^i\{m\}$	The m-th bit of $\Delta X_{S,P,K}^i$
$\Delta X_{S,P,K}^i\{m_l\text{-}m_t\}$	The $(m_t\text{-}m_l+1)$ bits totally from the m_l-th bit to the m_t-th bit of $\Delta X_{S,P,K}^i$

3 Related Works

3.1 Mouha et al.'s Framework for Word-Oriented Block Ciphers

Mouha et al. [12] introduced MILP model to count the number of differentially active S-boxes for word-oriented block ciphers.

Definition 1. *Consider a differential characteristic state Δ consisting of n bytes $\Delta = (\Delta_0, \Delta_1, \ldots, \Delta_{n-1})$. Then, the difference vector $x = (x_0, x_1, \ldots, x_{n-1})$ corresponding to Δ is defined as*

$$x_i = \begin{cases} 0 & \text{if } \Delta_i = 0, \\ 1 & \text{otherwise.} \end{cases} \tag{1}$$

Based on Definition 1, Mouha et al. translated the XOR operation and the linear transformation to linear inequalities as follows:

- **Equations describing the XOR operation:** Suppose the input difference vector for the XOR operation be $(x_{in1}^{\oplus}, x_{in2}^{\oplus})$ and the corresponding output difference vector be $x_{out}^{\oplus}$. The following constraints will make sure that when $x_{in1}^{\oplus}$, $x_{in2}^{\oplus}$ and $x_{out}^{\oplus}$ are not all zero, then there are at least two of them are nonzero:

$$\begin{cases} x_{in1}^{\oplus} + x_{in2}^{\oplus} + x_{out}^{\oplus} \geq 2d_{\oplus} \\ d_{\oplus} \geq x_{in1}^{\oplus}, d_{\oplus} \geq x_{in2}^{\oplus}, d_{\oplus} \geq x_{out}^{\oplus} \end{cases} \tag{2}$$

  where $d_{\oplus}$ is a dummy variable taking values in $\{0, 1\}$.
- **Equations describing the linear transformation:** Assume linear transformation L transforms the input difference vector $(x_1^L, x_2^L, \ldots, x_{m-1}^L)$ to the output difference vector $(y_1^L, y_2^L, \ldots, y_{m-1}^L)$. Given the differential branch number $\mathcal{B}_D$. The following constraints can describe the relation between the input and output difference vectors, they should be subject to:

$$\begin{cases} \sum_i^{m-1} x_i^L + \sum_i^{m-1} y_i^L \geq \mathcal{B}_D d^L \\ d^L \geq x_i^L, d^L \geq y_i^L, i \in \{0, \ldots, m-1\} \end{cases} \tag{3}$$

  where d^L is a dummy variable taking values in $\{0, 1\}$.

3.2 Sun et al.'s Framework for Bit-Oriented Block Ciphers

At Asiacrypt 2014, Sun et al. [20] extended Mouha et al.'s framework [12] to bit-oriented ciphers. For bit-oriented ciphers, Mouha et al.'s descriptions of XOR operation and linear transformation are also suitable.

Definition 2. *Consider a differential characteristic state Δ consisting of n bits $\Delta = (\Delta_0, \Delta_1, \ldots, \Delta_{n-1})$. Then, the difference vector $x = (x_0, x_1, \ldots, x_{n-1})$ corresponding to Δ is defined as*

$$x_i = \begin{cases} 0 & if\ \Delta_i = 0, \\ 1 & if\ \Delta_i = 1. \end{cases} \tag{4}$$

Based on Definition 2, Sun et al. translated the S-box operation to linear inequalities as follow:

- **Equations describing the S-box operation:** Suppose $(x_0, \ldots, x_{w-1})$ and $(y_0, \ldots, y_{v-1})$ are the input and output bit-level differences of an $w \times v$ S-box. A is a dummy variable taking values in $\{0,1\}$ to describe whether the S-box is active or not. $A = 1$ holds if and only if $x_0, x_1, \ldots, x_{w-1}$ are not all zero. The following constraints should be obeyed:

$$\begin{cases} A - x_i \geq 0, i \in \{0, \ldots, w-1\} \\ \sum_i^{w-1} x_i - A \geq 0 \end{cases} \tag{5}$$

3.3 Valid Cutting-Off Inequalities from the Convex Hull of S-Box

The convex hull of a set Q of discrete points in $\mathbb{R}^n$ is the smallest convex that contains Q. A convex hull in $\mathbb{R}^n$ can be described as the common solutions of a set of finitely many linear equalities and inequalities.

Suppose $p = (x, y) = (x_0, \ldots, x_{w-1}, y_0, \ldots, y_{v-1})$ is a differential pattern of a $w \times v$ S-box, in which x is the input differential vector and y is the output differential vector. If we treat a differential pattern of a $w \times v$ S-box as a discrete point in $\mathbb{R}^{w+v}$, then we can get a set of finitely discrete points which includes all possible differential patterns of the S-box. We can describe this definite set with the following inequalities:

$$\begin{cases} \alpha_{0,0}x_0 + \ldots + \alpha_{0,w-1}x_{w-1} + \beta_{0,0}y_0 + \ldots + \beta_{0,v-1}y_{v-1} + \gamma_0 \geq 0 \\ \ldots \\ \alpha_{n,0}x_0 + \ldots + \alpha_{n,w-1}x_{w-1} + \beta_{n,0}y_0 + \ldots + \beta_{n,v-1}y_{v-1} + \gamma_n \geq 0 \end{cases} \quad (6)$$

This is called the H-Representation of a $w \times v$ S-box, in which α and β are constant. With the help of SageMath [1], hundreds of linear inequalities can be derived by the differential distribution table of a S-box. But the inequalities is redundant in general, for example, the number of inequalities of GIFT S-box given by SageMath is 237. Because the efficiency of the MILP optimizer is reduced radically when the amount of linear inequalities increase, adding all of the inequalities to the MILP model will make the model insolvable in practical time.

In order to minimize the number of the set of inequalities, Sasaki et al. raised a MILP-based reduction algorithm in [15] to find the optimal combination with minimal number of linear inequalities from hundreds of inequalities in the H-representation of the convex hull. The algorithm considers each impossible pattern in the DDT of S-box. An impossible pattern should be excluded from the solution space by at least one inequality. Under these constraints, we can minimize the number of inequalities by using MILP optimizer.

4   MILP-Based Model to Search Differential Characteristic for GIFT-64

4.1 MILP-Based Two-Stage Algorithm to Search for Differential Characteristic

Two-stage search strategy to find differential characteristics of block ciphers is used in [9,13,18]. In the first step, truncated differential characteristics with minimal active S-box will be found. Then, concrete differential characteristics matching the truncated differential characteristic can be found in a subroutine algorithm. In previous works, one first chose a prespecified threshold of the number of active S-box. However, it is possible that the characteristic with the highest probability do not have the minimal number of active S-box. In this section, we propose Algorithm 1 to search for the best or better differential characteristic.

Algorithm 1. MILP-based differential characteristic searching algorithm

---

Require: r-round block cipher; valid cutting-off inequalities from the convex hull of the S-box; Mr is the minimal number of active S-boxes in all of the r-round differential characteristics.

Ensure: The highest probability; differential characteristics with high probability.

1: Define $MPr = 2^{-64}$ as the initial differential probability of GIFT-64.

2: In the Outer-MILP part, construct a model $\mathcal{M}_1$ describing the differential behavior of the cipher. The target value of $\mathcal{M}_1$ is a truncated differential characteristic, which active S-boxes number is minimum in current solution space. Define $Mr_{bound} = Mr$ as the lower bound of the number of active S-box in $\mathcal{M}_1$.

3: Solve the model $\mathcal{M}_1$ using an MILP optimizer.

4: **if** A feasible solution TD is found in $\mathcal{M}_1$, save it to a file. **then**

5:    $\Diamond$ *begin of Inner-MILP part*

6:    Construct a MILP model $\mathcal{M}_2$ describing the differential behavior of the cipher and add the truncated differential characteristic TD as a constraint to $\mathcal{M}_2$. The objective function of $\mathcal{M}_2$ is the differential characteristic with maximal probability.

7:    Solve the model using an MILP optimizer. If a feasible solution x is found, save x and its probability Pr to the file. If $Pr > MPr$, set MPr equal to Pr.

8:    $\Diamond$ *end of Inner-MILP part*

9: **end if**

10: Remove the truncated differential TD from the feasible region of $\mathcal{M}_1$.

11: Solve $\mathcal{M}_1$ again. If a new solution TD is found and its active S-boxes number is equal to Mr, save it and go to step 5. Else go to step 12.

12: If the number of active S-boxes of is more than Mr and less than $Mr + 3$, set Mr_{bound} equal to $Mr_{bound} + 1$, go to step 5. If a new solution TD is not found or the number of active S-boxes of TD is greater than or equal to $Mr + 3$, **return** MPr and the collection of solution x.

Algorithm 1 does not need the predefined threshold and could get the characteristic with highest probability definitely. Algorithm 1 includes two interactive sub-models, denoted as outer-MILP part and inner-MILP part. The two stages are interactive. In the outer-MILP part, the objective function is the minimal active S-boxes. When a solution is found in the outer-MILP part, the truncated differential that contains the information of the positions of active S-boxes will input the inner-MILP part as constraints. In the inner-MILP part, it produces the differential characteristic with maximal probability that matches the truncated differential. Then the algorithm goes to the outer-MILP part with the truncated differential removed from its feasible region.

In addition, the maximal probability of the derived differential characteristic is also used to reduce the feasible region of the outer-MILP part dynamically. In details, if a differential characteristic with larger probability could be found in the next loops, the number of active S-boxes produced in outer-MILP part must be lower than a certain bound. The bound is dynamically computed by the current maximal probability. When the outer-MILP part is infeasible, the algorithm returned.

We apply Algorithm 1 to search for differential characteristics for GIFT-64, and get some interesting results.

4.2 Search for Differentials of GIFT-64

Algorithm 1 needs two convex hulls about the S-box in the outer-MILP part and the inner-MILP part respectively. First, we compute the H-representation of convex hull of differential patterns of S-box in Appendix A. Using SageMath, 237 inequalities are produced in the H-Representation of the convex hull of GIFT S-box, then after selecting inequalities by the method introduced in [15], we get 21 inequalities. Second, we study the convex hull of differential patterns with probabilities of the S-box. Sun et al. introduced the differential distribution probability of S-box to MILP-model in [19]. Since, for GIFT S-box, there are 4 possible probabilities, i.e. $1, 2^{-1.415}, 2^{-2}, 2^{-3}$, we need three extra bits (p_0, p_1, p_2) to encode the differential patterns with probability. The new differential pattern is $(x_0, x_1, x_2, x_3, y_0, y_1, y_2, y_3; p_0, p_1, p_2) \in \mathbb{F}_2^{8+3}$ which satisfies Eq. 7.

$$\begin{cases} (p_0, p_1, p_2) = (0,0,0), \text{if } \Pr_s[(x_0, x_1, x_2, x_3) \rightarrow (y_0, y_1, y_2, y_3)] = 1 = 2^{-0} \\ (p_0, p_1, p_2) = (0,0,1), \text{if } \Pr_s[(x_0, x_1, x_2, x_3) \rightarrow (y_0, y_1, y_2, y_3)] = 6/16 = 2^{-1.415} \\ (p_0, p_1, p_2) = (0,1,0), \text{if } \Pr_s[(x_0, x_1, x_2, x_3) \rightarrow (y_0, y_1, y_2, y_3)] = 4/16 = 2^{-2} \\ (p_0, p_1, p_2) = (1,0,0), \text{if } \Pr_s[(x_0, x_1, x_2, x_3) \rightarrow (y_0, y_1, y_2, y_3)] = 2/16 = 2^{-3} \end{cases}$$
$$(7)$$

Then the objective function is changed to minimize $\sum(3 \times p_0 + 2 \times p_1 + 1.415 \times p_2)$.

We implement the Algorithm 1 to search for differential characteristics for GIFT-64. In the Outer-MILP part of the Algorithm 1, the objective function is to minimize active S-boxes. We get the tight bound of number of active S-boxes

Table 4. 12-round differential characteristic with probability 2^{-59}

Round	Differential-1	Probability
Input	0c00 0000 0060 0000	1
1st round	0000 0000 0000 4020	2^{-4}
2nd round	0005 0000 0005 0000	2^{-8}
3rd round	0000 0000 2020 0000	2^{-14}
4th round	0050 0000 0050 0000	2^{-18}
5th round	0000 0000 0000 2020	2^{-24}
6th round	0005 0000 0005 0000	2^{-28}
7th round	0000 0000 2020 0000	2^{-34}
8th round	0050 0000 0050 0000	2^{-38}
9th round	0000 0000 0000 2020	2^{-44}
10th round	0000 0000 0005 000a	2^{-49}
11th round	0080 0000 0000 0001	2^{-54}
12th round	1008 0000 0002 2000	2^{-59}

Table 5. 4-round differential characteristic with probability 2^{-20}

Round	Differential-1	Probability
Input	0000 0000 0000 1010	1
1st round	0000 000a 0000 000a	2^{-6}
2nd round	0000 0000 0000 0101	2^{-10}
3rd round	000a 0000 000a 0000	2^{-16}
4th round	0000 0000 0000 1010	2^{-20}

for 11-round and 12-round reduced GIFT-64, which are 22 and 24 respectively. Using the Algorithm 1, we find many 12-round differential characteristics. The highest probability of 12-round differential characteristic is 2^{-59}, the 12-round differential characteristic with highest probability is shown in Table 4. Meanwhile we get dozens of differential characteristics with probability 2^{-60}.

We observe that some of 12-round characteristics are iterative. As a result, we get eight 4-round differential characteristics with probability 2^{-20} totally. These 4-round characteristics are iterative, namely, their input states are identical to their output states. One of them is shown in Table 5, and these characteristics can be extended to more rounds. So we get one of 12-round differential characteristics cycled by three 4-round differential characteristics with probability 2^{-60} in Table 6. A 13-round characteristic with probability 2^{-64} can also be generated by adding another round at the beginning of 12-round differential characteristic. Note that the designers of GIFT claimed that the differential probability of 13-round GIFT-64 will be lower than 2^{-63}. Our result does not violate the claim, however the gap is very small.

4.3 Attack on 19-Round GIFT-64

Using the 12-round differential characteristic with probability 2^{-60} in Table 6, we could launch a key-recovery attack against 19-round GIFT-64. We choose this differential characteristic because its active bits in the head and tail is less than others. As shown in Table 7, we add three rounds at its beginning and four rounds at the end of the differential characteristic. Therefore, we can attack 19-round GIFT-64. According to the key schedule, the round key used in 1-st, 2-nd, 16-th, 17-th, 18-th and 19-th round corresponds to (k_1, k_0), (k_3, k_2), $(k_7 \ggg 6, k_6 \ggg 4)$, $(k_1 \ggg 8, k_0)$, $(k_3 \ggg 8, k_2)$ and $(k_5 \ggg 8, k_4)$ in initial key state $(k_7, k_6, k_5, k_4, k_3, k_2, k_1, k_0)$, respectively.

Data Collection

Since GIFT-64 does not have whitening key layer at the beginning, after the P permutation of the first round, we could build 2^n structures. Each structure traverses the sixteen bits undetermined in ΔX_P^1, i.e. the bit labeled by "?" in ΔX_P^1 of Table 7, thus it can generate $2^{16 \times 2 - 1} = 2^{31}$ pairs obeying the differential. Therefore, 2^n structures can generate $2^n \times 2^{31} = 2^{n+31}$ pairs.

Table 6. 12-round differential characteristic with probability 2^{-60}

Round	Differential	Probability
Input	0000 0000 0000 1010	1
1st round	0000 000a 0000 000a	2^{-6}
2nd round	0000 0000 0000 0101	2^{-10}
3rd round	000a 0000 000a 0000	2^{-16}
4th round	0000 0000 0000 1010	2^{-20}
5th round	0000 000a 0000 000a	2^{-26}
6th round	0000 0000 0000 0101	2^{-30}
7th round	000a 0000 000a 0000	2^{-36}
8th round	0000 0000 0000 1010	2^{-40}
9th round	0000 000a 0000 000a	2^{-46}
10th round	0000 0000 0000 0101	2^{-50}
11th round	000a 0000 000a 0000	2^{-56}
12th round	0000 0000 0000 1010	2^{-60}

Table 7. 19-round differential attack on GIFT-64

ΔP	???? ???? ???? ???? ???? ???? ???? ???? ???? ???? ???? ???? ???? ???? ???? ????
ΔX_S^1	?000 0?00 00?0 000? ?000 0?00 00?0 000? ?000 0?00 00?0 000? ?000 0?00 00?0 000?
ΔX_P^1	0000 0000 0000 0000 0000 0000 0000 0000 0000 0000 0000 0000 ???? ???? ???? ????
ΔX_K^1	0000 0000 0000 0000 0000 0000 0000 0000 0000 0000 0000 0000 ???? ???? ???? ????
ΔX_S^2	0000 0000 0000 0000 0000 0000 0000 0000 0000 0000 0000 0000 0?0? 10?0 0?0? 10?0
ΔX_P^2	0000 0000 0000 1??? 0000 0000 0000 0000 0000 0000 0000 1??? 0000 0000 0000 0000
ΔX_K^2	0000 0000 0000 1??? 0000 0000 0000 0000 0000 0000 0000 1??? 0000 0000 0000 0000
ΔX_S^3	0000 0000 0000 0001 0000 0000 0000 0000 0000 0000 0000 0001 0000 0000 0000 0000
ΔX_P^3	0000 0000 0000 0000 0000 0000 0000 0000 0000 0000 0000 0000 0001 0000 0001 0000
ΔX_K^3	0000 0000 0000 0000 0000 0000 0000 0000 0000 0000 0000 0000 0001 0000 0001 0000
4th round input	0000 0000 0000 0000 0000 0000 0000 0000 0000 0000 0000 0000 0001 0000 0001 0000
⋮	⋮
15th round output	0000 0000 0000 0000 0000 0000 0000 0000 0000 0000 0000 0000 0001 0000 0001 0000
ΔX_S^{16}	0000 0000 0000 0000 0000 0000 0000 0000 0000 0000 0000 0000 ???? 0000 ???? 0000
ΔX_P^{16}	0000 0000 0000 0?0? 0000 0000 0000 ?0?0 0000 0000 0000 0?0? 0000 0000 0000 ?0?0
ΔX_K^{16}	0000 0000 0000 0?0? 0000 0000 0000 ?0?0 0000 0000 0000 0?0? 0000 0000 0000 ?0?0
ΔX_S^{17}	0000 0000 0000 ???? 0000 0000 0000 ???? 0000 0000 0000 ???? 0000 0000 0000 ????
ΔX_P^{17}	?000 ?000 ?000 ?000 0?00 0?00 0?00 0?00 00?0 00?0 00?0 00?0 000? 000? 000? 000?
ΔX_K^{17}	?000 ?000 ?000 ?000 0?00 0?00 0?00 0?00 00?0 00?0 00?0 00?0 000? 000? 000? 000?
ΔX_S^{18}	???? ???? ???? ???? ???? ???? ???? ???? ???? ???? ???? ???? ???? ???? ???? ????
ΔX_P^{18}	???? ???? ???? ???? ???? ???? ???? ???? ???? ???? ???? ???? ???? ???? ???? ????
ΔX_K^{18}	???? ???? ???? ???? ???? ???? ???? ???? ???? ???? ???? ???? ???? ???? ???? ????
ΔX_S^{19}	???? ???? ???? ???? ???? ???? ???? ???? ???? ???? ???? ???? ???? ???? ???? ????
ΔX_P^{19}	???? ???? ???? ???? ???? ???? ???? ???? ???? ???? ???? ???? ???? ???? ???? ????
ΔX_K^{19}	???? ???? ???? ???? ???? ???? ???? ???? ???? ???? ???? ???? ???? ???? ???? ????

For such a pair, it has an average probability of 2^{-16} to meet the differential in 4-*th* round in Table 7. Then, the pair encrypted with the right key will obey the differential after 15th round with probability of 2^{-60}. While the pair with a wrong key will obey it with a random probability of 2^{-64}. Therefore, with the right key guess, $2^{n+31} \times 2^{-16} \times 2^{-60} = 2^{n-45}$ pairs will obey the differential after 15th round. Here we choose $n = 47$. So the data complexity is $2^{47} \times 2^{16} = 2^{63}$.

Key Recovery

When processing the key recovery, the guessing key bits include: k_1^3, k_1^2, k_1^1, k_1^0, k_0^3, k_0^2, k_0^1, k_0^0 in 1st round, k_7^{12}, k_2^{12}, k_3^4, k_2^4 in 2nd round; k_7^6, k_6^8, k_7^{14}, k_6^0 in 16th round, k_1^{15}, k_1^{14}, k_1^{13}, k_1^{12}, k_0^3, k_0^2, k_0^1, k_0^0 in 17th round, as well as all 64 key bits in 18th, 19th round. Totally, we construct 2^{80} counters for the possible values of the 80 key bits above. The whole attack procedure is a guess and filter approach. Guess two key bits k_1^0, k_0^0, then we can partially encrypt the plaintexts.

Table 8. Round keys of GIFT-64

Round	Key bit
1st round	$k_1^{15}, k_1^{14}, k_1^{13}, k_1^{12}, k_1^{11}, k_1^{10}, k_1^9, k_1^8, k_1^7, k_1^6, k_1^5, k_1^4, k_1^3, k_1^2, k_1^1, k_1^0$
	$k_0^{15}, k_0^{14}, k_0^{13}, k_0^{12}, k_0^{11}, k_0^{10}, k_0^9, k_0^8, k_0^7, k_0^6, k_0^5, k_0^4, k_0^3, k_0^2, k_0^1, k_0^0$
2nd round	$k_3^{15}, k_3^{14}, k_3^{13}, k_3^{12}, k_3^{11}, k_3^{10}, k_3^9, k_3^8, k_3^7, k_3^6, k_3^5, k_3^4, k_3^3, k_3^2, k_3^1, k_3^0$
	$k_2^{15}, k_2^{14}, k_2^{13}, k_2^{12}, k_2^{11}, k_2^{10}, k_2^9, k_2^8, k_2^7, k_2^6, k_2^5, k_2^4, k_2^3, k_2^2, k_2^1, k_2^0$
16th round	$k_7^5, k_7^4, k_7^3, k_7^2, k_7^1, k_7^0, k_7^{15}, k_7^{14}, k_7^{13}, k_7^{12}, k_7^{11}, k_7^{10}, k_7^9, k_7^8, k_7^7, k_7^6$
	$k_6^3, k_6^2, k_6^1, k_6^0, k_6^{15}, k_6^{14}, k_6^{13}, k_6^{12}, k_6^{11}, k_6^{10}, k_6^9, k_6^8, k_6^7, k_6^6, k_6^5, k_6^4$
17th round	$k_1^7, k_1^6, k_1^5, k_1^4, k_1^3, k_1^2, k_1^1, k_1^0, k_1^{15}, k_1^{14}, k_1^{13}, k_1^{12}, k_1^{11}, k_1^{10}, k_1^9, k_1^8$
	$k_0^{15}, k_0^{14}, k_0^{13}, k_0^{12}, k_0^{11}, k_0^{10}, k_0^9, k_0^8, k_0^7, k_0^6, k_0^5, k_0^4, k_0^3, k_0^2, k_0^1, k_0^0$
18th round	$k_3^7, k_3^6, k_3^5, k_3^4, k_3^3, k_3^2, k_3^1, k_3^0, k_3^{15}, k_3^{14}, k_3^{13}, k_3^{12}, k_3^{11}, k_3^{10}, k_3^9, k_3^8$
	$k_2^{15}, k_2^{14}, k_2^{13}, k_2^{12}, k_2^{11}, k_2^{10}, k_2^9, k_2^8, k_2^7, k_2^6, k_2^5, k_2^4, k_2^3, k_2^2, k_2^1, k_2^0$
19th round	$k_5^7, k_5^6, k_5^5, k_5^4, k_5^3, k_5^2, k_5^1, k_5^0, k_5^{15}, k_5^{14}, k_5^{13}, k_5^{12}, k_5^{11}, k_5^{10}, k_5^9, k_5^8$
	$k_4^{15}, k_4^{14}, k_4^{13}, k_4^{12}, k_4^{11}, k_4^{10}, k_4^9, k_4^8, k_4^7, k_4^6, k_4^5, k_4^4, k_4^3, k_4^2, k_4^1, k_4^0$

As the middle values of right pairs should obey $\Delta X_S^2\{0\} = 0$, $\Delta X_S^2\{2\} = 0$, $\Delta X_S^2\{3\} = 1$, the (*plaintext, ciphertext*) pairs can be filtered with a probability of 2^{-3}. Similarly, guessing $k_1^i, k_0^i, i = 1, 2, 3$ and partially encrypt, corresponding conditions in $\Delta X_S^2\{5, 7\}$, $\Delta X_S^2\{8, 10, 11\}$, $\Delta X_S^2\{13, 15\}$ can filter the pairs with 2^{-2}, 2^{-3} and 2^{-2}. Totally 1st round provide a filtering probability of 2^{-10}.

Similarly, the encryption at 2-*nd*, 16-*th*, 17-*th*, 18-*th* round can filter the pairs with probability 2^{-6}, 2^{-8}, 2^{-8}, 2^{-48} while all 32 key bits in 19th round need to be guessed. Thus, 2^{-2} pairs will be left for a random key, while 4 pairs should be left for a right key.

The time complexity is $2^2 \times 2^{31+47} \times 2^{32} = 2^{112}$, the data complexity is 2^{63} and the memory complexity is 2^{80}.

5   Improved MILP-Based Method to Find Differential for GIFT-128

GIFT-128 adopts 128 bits state and has thirty-two 4-bit S-boxes in each round. The variables and constrains are twice as many as GIFT-64. The designers of GIFT [2] gives 9-round differential characteristics of GIFT-128. We test Algorithm 1 on 9-round GIFT-128 and obtain the designers' conclusion. But it costs days to solve. In this section, we devise a segmented MILP-based method to search for longer differential characteristics for GIFT-128.

Suppose we aim to find a r-round differential characteristic for a block cipher. We first divide it as r_i-round ($i = 1, 2, ..., t$) sub-ciphers and $\sum_1^t r_i = r$. We choose probability thresholds for r_1-round, r_2-round,...,r_t-round ciphers as $P_{r_1}, P_{r_2}, ..., P_{r_t}$, so that the probability p_{r_i} for r_i-round sub-cipher should be larger than P_{r_i}. Choose a threshold value P_{target} for r-round. If $p_{r_1}p_{r_2} \ldots p_{r_t}$ is larger than P_{target}, an acceptable solution is found.

As shown in Fig. 2, for r_i-round sub-cipher, the input state are fixed as the output state of the differential characteristic $\mathcal{D}_{i-1}$ of r_{i-1}-round sub-cipher, and construct the MILP model $\mathcal{M}_{r_i}$. If $\mathcal{M}_{r_i}$ is feasible, we continue to construct $\mathcal{M}_{r_{i+1}}$ for r_{i+1}-round sub-cipher; else, we remove $\mathcal{D}_{i-1}$ from $\mathcal{M}_{r_{i-1}}$, and solve it again. The search terminates until we find the differential characteristics of r_1-round,r_2-round,...,r_t-round sub-ciphers that could be connected to produce a r-round differential characteristic.

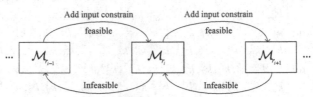

Fig. 2. The framework of our search algorithm

We apply this model to search for differential characteristics for GIFT-128. It is indeed a heuristic and empirical process. For GIFT-128, it is time consuming to solve a more than 6-round MILP model. In order to keep the efficiency, we choose $r_i < 6$. P_{r_i} is chosen more flexible. According to the designers' analysis in [2], for 3/4/5-round GIFT-128, the numbers of minimum active S-boxes are 3, 5, and 7, respectively. The length of the sub-cipher can neither be too short nor be too long. If the number of rounds is smaller than 2, this sub-MILP-model is unnecessary to solve. On the other hand, if the number of rounds is bigger than 6 or 7, it costs too much time to solve the sub-model that we cannot bear. We do not want the probability of r_i-round differential characteristic of GIFT-128 to be much smaller than the highest one. So P_{r_i} are chosen according to the minimum active S-boxes of r_i-round GIFT-128. In this section, we choose $P_{r_i=3} = 2^{-30}$, $P_{r_i=4} = 2^{-40}$ and $P_{r_i=5} = 2^{-50}$ to act as the exact lower bound of differential probability of each sub-model.

We use this model and the strategies above choosing parameters to search for differential characteristics for GIFT-128. We list some results in Table 9. The 12-round and 14-round differential characteristics are shown in Appendix C.

Table 9. Probabilities of some differential characteristics of GIFT-128

Round	Parameters for r_i	Probability	Source
9	–	2^{-47}	[2]
12	$r_1 = r_2 = r_3 = r_4 = 3$	$2^{-62.415}$	Ours
14	$r_1 = r_2 = 4$ and $r_3 = 6$	2^{-85}	Ours
18	$r_1 = r_2 = r_3 = 4$ and $r_4 = 6$	2^{-109}	Ours

The 18-round characteristic, shown in Table 10 is constructed by the connection of the following three 4-round differential characteristics and a 6-round differential characteristic:

$(0000\ 0000\ 7060\ 0000\ 0000\ 0000\ 0000\ 0000) \xrightarrow{4-round,\ 2^{-12}} (0020\ 0000\ 0010\ 0000\ 0000\ 0000\ 0000\ 0000)$

$(0020\ 0000\ 0010\ 0000\ 0000\ 0000\ 0000\ 0000) \xrightarrow{4-round,\ 2^{-29}} (0000\ 0000\ 0000\ 0011\ 0000\ 0000\ 0000\ 0000)$

$(0000\ 0000\ 0000\ 0011\ 0000\ 0000\ 0000\ 0000) \xrightarrow{4-round,\ 2^{-32}} (0000\ 0000\ 0a00\ 0a00\ 0000\ 0000\ 0000\ 0000)$

$(0000\ 0000\ 0a00\ 0a00\ 0000\ 0000\ 0000\ 0000) \xrightarrow{6-round,\ 2^{-36}} (0000\ 0100\ 0020\ 0800\ 0014\ 0404\ 0002\ 0202)$

Table 10. 18-round differential characteristic of GIFT-128

Round	Input Difference	Probability
Input	0000 0000 7060 0000 0000 0000 0000 0000	1
1st	0000 0000 0000 0000 0000 0000 00a0 0000	2^{-5}
2nd	0000 0010 0000 0000 0000 0000 0000 0000	2^{-7}
3rd	0000 0000 0800 0000 0000 0000 0000 0000	2^{-10}
4th	0020 0000 0010 0000 0000 0000 0000 0000	2^{-12}
5th	0000 0000 0000 0000 4040 0000 2020 0000	2^{-17}
6th	0000 5050 0000 0000 0000 5050 0000 0000	2^{-25}
7th	0000 0000 0000 0000 0000 0000 0a00 0a00	2^{-37}
8th	0000 0000 0000 0011 0000 0000 0000 0000	2^{-41}
9th	0008 0000 0008 0000 0000 0000 0000 0000	2^{-47}
10th	0000 0000 0000 0000 2020 0000 1010 0000	2^{-51}
11th	0000 5050 0000 0000 0000 5050 0000 0000	2^{-61}
12th	0000 0000 0a00 0a00 0000 0000 0000 0000	2^{-73}
13th	0000 0000 0011 0000 0000 0000 0000 0000	2^{-77}
14th	0090 0000 00c0 0000 0000 0000 0000 0000	2^{-83}
15th	1000 0000 0080 0000 0000 0000 0000 0000	2^{-89}
16th	0010 0000 0000 0000 0000 0000 8020 0000	2^{-94}
17th	0000 0000 8000 0020 0000 0050 0000 0020	2^{-101}
18th	0000 0100 0020 0800 0014 0404 0002 0202	2^{-109}

With the 18-round differential characteristic, we can add three rounds at its beginning and two rounds at the end to attack 23-round reduced GIFT-128. The attack procedure is similar to Subsect. 4.3. The time complexity is 2^{120} which is bounded by the data complexity and the memory complexity is 2^{86} bits to store the key counters.

6   Conclusion

In this paper, first, we design a more efficient MILP-based differential search model. Using this model, we give a 12-round differential characteristic with probability 2^{-60} and get the first 19-round key-recovery attack on GIFT-64. Second, we improve our MILP-based model for block ciphers with large state size. With this model, we give 18-round differential characteristic with probability 2^{-109} and obtain the first 23-round key-recovery attack on GIFT-128.

MILP can efficiently find high-probabilistic differential characteristics when attacking algorithms whose permutation layer will not cause diffusion. In the future work, we can try to apply heuristic method to constrain global variables, so as to find a higher probability differential characteristics.

A   Difference Distribution Table (DDT) of GIFT S-Box

See Table 11.

Table 11. DDT of GIFT S-box

	0	1	2	3	4	5	6	7	8	9	a	b	c	d	e	f
0	16	0	0	0	0	0	0	0	0	0	0	0	0	0	0	0
1	0	0	0	0	0	2	2	0	2	2	2	2	2	0	0	2
2	0	0	0	0	0	4	4	0	0	2	2	0	0	2	2	0
3	0	0	0	0	0	2	2	0	2	0	0	2	2	2	2	2
4	0	0	0	2	0	4	0	6	0	2	0	0	0	2	0	0
5	0	0	2	0	0	2	0	0	2	0	0	0	2	2	2	4
6	0	0	4	6	0	0	0	2	0	0	2	0	0	0	2	0
7	0	0	2	0	0	2	0	0	2	2	2	4	2	0	0	0
8	0	0	0	4	0	0	0	4	0	0	0	4	0	0	0	4
9	0	2	0	2	0	0	2	2	2	0	2	0	2	2	0	0
a	0	4	0	0	0	0	4	0	0	2	2	0	0	2	2	0
b	0	2	0	2	0	0	2	2	2	2	0	0	2	0	2	0
c	0	0	4	0	4	0	0	0	2	0	2	0	2	0	2	0
d	0	2	2	0	4	0	0	0	0	0	2	2	0	2	0	2
e	0	4	0	0	4	0	0	0	2	2	0	0	2	2	0	0
f	0	2	2	0	4	0	0	0	0	2	0	2	0	0	2	2

B   Some 4-Round Iterative Differential Characteristics of GIFT-64

See Table 12.

Table 12. 4-round iterative differential characteristics

Round	Input difference	Probability
Input	0005 0000 0005 0000	1
1st	0000 0000 2020 0000	2^{-6}
2nd	0050 0000 0050 0000	2^{-10}
3rd	0000 0000 0000 2020	2^{-16}
4th	0005 0000 0005 0000	2^{-20}
Input	0000 000a 0000 000a	1
1st	0000 0000 0000 0101	2^{-4}
2nd	000a 0000 000a 0000	2^{-10}
3rd	0000 0000 0000 1010	2^{-14}
4th	0000 000a 0000 000a	2^{-20}
Input	0000 00a0 0000 00a0	1
1st	0101 0000 0000 0000	2^{-4}
2nd	a000 0000 a000 0000	2^{-10}
3rd	0000 0000 1010 0000	2^{-14}
4th	0000 00a0 0000 00a0	2^{-20}
Input	0000 0000 0101 0000	1
1st	00a0 0000 00a0 0000	2^{-6}
2nd	1010 0000 0000 0000	2^{-10}
3rd	0000 a000 0000 a000	2^{-16}
4th	0000 0000 0101 0000	2^{-20}
Input	0000 0202 0000 0000	1
1st	0000 0500 0000 0500	2^{-4}
2nd	0202 0000 0000 0000	2^{-10}
3rd	0000 5000 0000 5000	2^{-14}
4th	0000 0202 0000 0000	2^{-20}
Input	0000 1010 0000 0000	1
1st	0000 0a00 0000 0a00	2^{-6}
2nd	0000 0101 0000 0000	2^{-10}
3rd	0a00 0000 0a00 0000	2^{-16}
4th	0000 1010 0000 0000	2^{-20}
Input	0000 0050 0000 0050	1
1st	0000 0000 0000 0202	2^{-6}
2nd	0000 0005 0000 0005	2^{-10}
3rd	0000 0000 0202 0000	2^{-16}
4th	0000 0050 0000 0050	2^{-20}
Input	0500 0000 0500 0000	1
1st	2020 0000 0000 0000	2^{-6}
2nd	5000 0000 5000 0000	2^{-10}
3rd	0000 2020 0000 0000	2^{-16}
4th	0500 0000 0500 0000	2^{-20}

C 12-Round and 14-Round Differential Characteristics of GIFT-128

See Tables 13 and 14.

Table 13. 12-round differential characteristic

Round	Input Difference	Probability
Input	0000 0000 7060 0000 0000 0000 0000 0000	1
1st	0000 0000 0000 0000 0000 0000 00a0 0000	2^{-5}
2nd	0000 0010 0000 0000 0000 0000 0000 0000	2^{-7}
3rd	0000 0000 0800 0000 0000 0000 0000 0000	2^{-10}
4th	0020 0000 0010 0000 0000 0000 0000 0000	2^{-12}
5th	0000 0000 0000 0000 4040 0000 2020 0000	2^{-17}
6th	0000 5050 0000 0000 0000 5050 0000 0000	2^{-25}
7th	0000 0000 0a00 0a00 0000 0000 0000 0000	2^{-37}
8th	0000 0000 0011 0000 0000 0000 0000 0000	2^{-41}
9th	0090 0000 0000 0000 0060 0000 0000 0000	2^{-47}
10th	1000 0000 0000 0000 0000 0000 0000 2000	2^{-52}
11th	0000 0004 0000 0002 0000 0000 8000 0000	2^{-57}
12th	0000 0000 0404 0020 0200 0010 0101 0000	$2^{-62.415}$

Table 14. 14-round differential characteristic

Round	Input Difference	Probability
Input	0000 0000 0000 0000 0000 0706 0000 0000	1
1st	0000 0000 0000 0000 0000 0a00 0000 0000	2^{-5}
2nd	0000 0000 0000 0100 0000 0000 0000 0000	2^{-7}
3rd	0000 0000 0000 0000 0008 0000 0000 0000	2^{-10}
4th	0000 0000 0000 0000 0000 2000 0000 1000	2^{-12}
5th	0000 0404 0000 0202 0000 0000 0000 0000	2^{-17}
6th	0000 0000 0505 0000 0000 0000 0505 0000	2^{-25}
7th	00a0 00a0 0000 0000 0000 0000 0000 0000	2^{-37}
8th	1100 0000 0000 0000 0000 0000 0000 0000	2^{-41}
9th	6000 0000 0000 0000 0000 0000 c000 0000	2^{-47}
10th	0000 0000 2000 0020 0000 0000 0000 0000	2^{-51}
11th	0041 0000 0000 0000 0014 0000 0000 0000	2^{-55}
12th	9000 0000 0000 c000 0000 0000 3000 1000	2^{-66}
13th	0000 0000 0002 0000 0000 0000 8000 0088	2^{-77}
14th	0000 0001 0040 0020 0000 0012 0010 0003	2^{-85}

References

1. http://www.sagemath.org/
2. Banik, S., Pandey, S.K., Peyrin, T., Sasaki, Y., Sim, S.M., Todo, Y.: GIFT: a small present - towards reaching the limit of lightweight encryption. In: Fischer, W., Homma, N. (eds.) CHES 2017. LNCS, vol. 10529. Springer, Cham (2017). https://doi.org/10.1007/978-3-319-66787-4_16
3. Beaulieu, R., Shors, D., Smith, J., Treatman-Clark, S., Weeks, B., Wingers, L.: The SIMON and SPECK families of lightweight block ciphers. Cryptology ePrint Archive, Report 2013/404 (2013). https://eprint.iacr.org/2013/404
4. Berton, G., Daemen, J., Peeters, M., Assche, G.V.: The Keccak sponge function family. http://keccak.noekeon.org/
5. Bogdanov, A., et al.: PRESENT: an ultra-lightweight block cipher. In: Paillier, P., Verbauwhede, I. (eds.) CHES 2007. LNCS, vol. 4727, pp. 450–466. Springer, Heidelberg (2007). https://doi.org/10.1007/978-3-540-74735-2_31
6. Borghoff, J., et al.: PRINCE – a low-latency block cipher for pervasive computing applications - extended abstract. In: Wang, X., Sako, K. (eds.) ASIACRYPT 2012. LNCS, vol. 7658, pp. 208–225. Springer, Heidelberg (2012). https://doi.org/10.1007/978-3-642-34961-4_14
7. Cui, T., Jia, K., Fu, K., Chen, S., Wang, M.: New automatic search tool for impossible differentials and zero-correlation linear approximations. IACR Cryptology ePrint Archive 2016, p. 689 (2016). http://eprint.iacr.org/2016/689
8. Fu, K., Wang, M., Guo, Y., Sun, S., Hu, L.: MILP-based automatic search algorithms for differential and linear trails for speck. In: Peyrin, T. (ed.) FSE 2016. LNCS, vol. 9783, pp. 268–288. Springer, Heidelberg (2016). https://doi.org/10.1007/978-3-662-52993-5_14
9. Gerault, D., Minier, M., Solnon, C.: Constraint programming models for chosen key differential cryptanalysis. In: Rueher, M. (ed.) CP 2016. LNCS, vol. 9892, pp. 584–601. Springer, Cham (2016). https://doi.org/10.1007/978-3-319-44953-1_37
10. Guo, J., Peyrin, T., Poschmann, A., Robshaw, M.: The LED block cipher. In: Preneel, B., Takagi, T. (eds.) CHES 2011. LNCS, vol. 6917, pp. 326–341. Springer, Heidelberg (2011). https://doi.org/10.1007/978-3-642-23951-9_22
11. Li, Z., Bi, W., Dong, X., Wang, X.: Improved conditional cube attacks on keccak keyed modes with MILP method. In: Takagi, T., Peyrin, T. (eds.) ASIACRYPT 2017. LNCS, vol. 10624, pp. 99–127. Springer, Cham (2017). https://doi.org/10.1007/978-3-319-70694-8_4
12. Mouha, N., Wang, Q., Gu, D., Preneel, B.: Differential and linear cryptanalysis using mixed-integer linear programming. In: Wu, C.-K., Yung, M., Lin, D. (eds.) Inscrypt 2011. LNCS, vol. 7537, pp. 57–76. Springer, Heidelberg (2012). https://doi.org/10.1007/978-3-642-34704-7_5
13. Fouque, P.-A., Jean, J., Peyrin, T.: Structural evaluation of AES and chosen-key distinguisher of 9-round. In: Canetti, R., Garay, J.A. (eds.) CRYPTO 2013. LNCS, vol. 8042, pp. 183–203. Springer, Heidelberg (2013). https://doi.org/10.1007/978-3-642-40041-4_11
14. Sasaki, Y.: Integer linear programming for three-subset meet-in-the-middle attacks: application to GIFT. In: Inomata, A., Yasuda, K. (eds.) IWSEC 2018. LNCS, vol. 11049, pp. 227–243. Springer, Cham (2018). https://doi.org/10.1007/978-3-319-97916-8_15

15. Sasaki, Y., Todo, Y.: New algorithm for modeling S-box in MILP based differential and division trail search. In: Farshim, P., Simion, E. (eds.) SecITC 2017. LNCS, vol. 10543, pp. 150–165. Springer, Cham (2017). https://doi.org/10.1007/978-3-319-69284-5_11

16. Sasaki, Y., Todo, Y.: New impossible differential search tool from design and cryptanalysis aspects. In: Coron, J.-S., Nielsen, J.B. (eds.) EUROCRYPT 2017. LNCS, vol. 10212, pp. 185–215. Springer, Cham (2017). https://doi.org/10.1007/978-3-319-56617-7_7

17. Shirai, T., Shibutani, K., Akishita, T., Moriai, S., Iwata, T.: The 128-bit blockcipher CLEFIA (extended abstract). In: Biryukov, A. (ed.) FSE 2007. LNCS, vol. 4593, pp. 181–195. Springer, Heidelberg (2007). https://doi.org/10.1007/978-3-540-74619-5_12

18. Sun, S., et al.: Analysis of AES, SKINNY, and others with constraint programming. IACR Trans. Symmetric Cryptol. **2017**(1), 281–306 (2017). https://tosc.iacr.org/index.php/ToSC/article/view/595

19. Sun, S., et al.: Towards finding the best characteristics of some bit-oriented block ciphers and automatic enumeration of (related-key) differential and linear characteristics with predefined properties. Cryptology ePrint Archive, Report 2014/747 (2014). http://eprint.iacr.org/2014/747

20. Sun, S., Hu, L., Wang, P., Qiao, K., Ma, X., Song, L.: Automatic security evaluation and (related-key) differential characteristic search: application to SIMON, PRESENT, LBlock, DES(L) and other bit-oriented block ciphers. In: Sarkar, P., Iwata, T. (eds.) ASIACRYPT 2014. LNCS, vol. 8873, pp. 158–178. Springer, Heidelberg (2014). https://doi.org/10.1007/978-3-662-45611-8_9

21. Xiang, Z., Zhang, W., Bao, Z., Lin, D.: Applying MILP method to searching integral distinguishers based on division property for 6 lightweight block ciphers. In: Cheon, J.H., Takagi, T. (eds.) ASIACRYPT 2016. LNCS, vol. 10031, pp. 648–678. Springer, Heidelberg (2016). https://doi.org/10.1007/978-3-662-53887-6_24

Quantum Chosen-Ciphertext Attacks Against Feistel Ciphers

Gembu Ito[1], Akinori Hosoyamada[1,2], Ryutaroh Matsumoto[1,3], Yu Sasaki[2], and Tetsu Iwata[1(✉)]

[1] Nagoya University, Nagoya, Japan
g_itou@echo.nuee.nagoya-u.ac.jp,
{ryutaroh.matsumoto,tetsu.iwata}@nagoya-u.jp
[2] NTT Secure Platform Laboratories, Tokyo, Japan
{hosoyamada.akinori,sasaki.yu}@lab.ntt.co.jp
[3] Aalborg University, Aalborg, Denmark

Abstract. Seminal results by Luby and Rackoff show that the 3-round Feistel cipher is secure against chosen-plaintext attacks (CPAs), and the 4-round version is secure against chosen-ciphertext attacks (CCAs). However, the security significantly changes when we consider attacks in the quantum setting, where the adversary can make superposition queries. By using Simon's algorithm that detects a secret cycle-period in polynomial-time, Kuwakado and Morii showed that the 3-round version is insecure against quantum CPA by presenting a polynomial-time distinguisher. Since then, Simon's algorithm has been heavily used against various symmetric-key constructions. However, its applications are still not fully explored.

In this paper, based on Simon's algorithm, we first formalize a sufficient condition of a quantum distinguisher against block ciphers so that it works even if there are multiple collisions other than the real period. This distinguisher is similar to the one proposed by Santoli and Schaffner, and it does not recover the period. Instead, we focus on the dimension of the space obtained from Simon's quantum circuit. This eliminates the need to evaluate the probability of collisions, which was needed in the work by Kaplan et al. at CRYPTO 2016. Based on this, we continue the investigation of the security of Feistel ciphers in the quantum setting. We show a quantum CCA distinguisher against the 4-round Feistel cipher. This extends the result of Kuwakado and Morii by one round, and follows the intuition of the result by Luby and Rackoff where the CCA setting can extend the number of rounds by one. We also consider more practical cases where the round functions are composed of a public function and XORing the subkeys. We show the results of both distinguishing and key recovery attacks against these constructions.

Keywords: Feistel cipher · Quantum chosen-ciphertext attacks · Simon's algorithm

© Springer Nature Switzerland AG 2019
M. Matsui (Ed.): CT-RSA 2019, LNCS 11405, pp. 391–411, 2019.
https://doi.org/10.1007/978-3-030-12612-4_20

1 Introduction

A block cipher is an important cryptographic primitive that is widely adopted in various secure communication protocols and security products. A block cipher is a pseudo-random permutation (PRP), i.e. it takes a key as input and provides distinct permutations that cannot be distinguished from a random permutation for distinct key inputs.

Designing an efficient block cipher is a long-term challenge in symmetric-key cryptography. One of the most popular approaches is to use the Feistel network, in which an n-bit state is divided into $n/2$-bit halves denoted by a_i and b_i, and the state is updated by iteratively applying the following two operations;

$$b_{i+1} \leftarrow a_i \oplus F_{K_i}(b_i), \qquad a_{i+1} \leftarrow b_i,$$

where F_{K_i} is a keyed function taking a subkey K_i as input. The construction is known as the Luby-Rackoff construction. In this paper, we call it *Feistel-F* to make the name consistent with other constructions. The diagram of the construction is drawn in the left of Fig. 1. Luby and Rackoff [19] proved that when F_{K_i} is a pseudo-random function (PRF), 3-round and 4-round Feistel ciphers are PRPs up to $O(2^{n/4})$ queries against chosen-plaintext attacks (CPAs) and chosen-ciphertext attacks (CCAs), respectively. Luby and Rackoff also showed the tightness of the number of rounds by demonstrating efficient attacks against 2 and 3 rounds in the corresponding attack models.

While the provable security bounds derived by Luby and Rackoff are attractive, using a PRF for F_{K_i} requires significant implementation costs, and this is often practically infeasible. To design a block cipher for practical usage, the subkey space is often limited to $\{0,1\}^{n/2}$, and $F_{K_i}(b_i)$ is defined as

$$b_{i+1} \leftarrow a_i \oplus F(K_i \oplus b_i), \qquad a_{i+1} \leftarrow b_i,$$

where F is a public function. In this paper, we call this construction *Feistel-KF*. See the middle figure of Fig. 1. Feistel-KF includes a lot of practical designs, e.g. DES [20] and Camellia [1], where the function $x \mapsto F(K_i \oplus x)$ is not a PRF, and generic attacks on this construction have been widely studied, e.g. impossible differential attacks [15], meet-in-the-middle attacks [10,12], dissection attacks [5] and division property [24].

It is also possible to inject a subkey $K_i \in \{0,1\}^{n/2}$ outside the F function as

$$b_{i+1} \leftarrow a_i \oplus F(b_i) \oplus K_i, \qquad a_{i+1} \leftarrow b_i.$$

We call this construction *Feistel-FK*, which is illustrated on the right of Fig. 1. This construction provides implementation advantages and can be seen in several lightweight designs e.g. Piccolo [22], Simon [2] and Simeck [25].

The discussion so far is about the classical computation setting, while the security of symmetric-key schemes against quantum computers has become active recently. Owing to less mathematical structure in symmetric-key schemes than public-key schemes, there was a belief that simply doubling the key size in

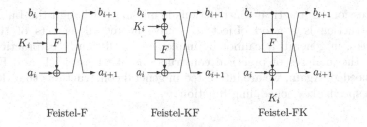

Fig. 1. Our target constructions.

order to resist the exhaustive key search by Grover's algorithm [9] is sufficient to protect symmetric-key schemes from quantum computers. However, Kuwakado and Morii [16] demonstrated that, by exploiting Simon's algorithm [23], the Feistel ciphers can be distinguished from a random permutation only in polynomial-time of the output size under the assumption that the adversary can make quantum superposition queries. Since then, many polynomial-time attacks using Simon's algorithm have been proposed e.g. key recovery against Even-Mansour construction [17], forgery on various CBC-like MACs [14], and cryptanalysis of AEZ [3]. Moreover, Leander and May [18] showed a clever method to combine Grover's and Simon's algorithms to recover the key against the FX construction. See also [21].

The attack model that adversaries can make quantum queries is worth investigating. This model is a natural extension of the classical attack models, and theoretically interesting. Any symmetric scheme broken in this model should not be implemented on a quantum computer. Moreover, the threat of this attack model becomes significant if an adversary has access to its white-box implementation. Because arbitrary classical circuit can be converted into quantum one, the adversary can construct a quantum circuit from the classical source code given by the white-box implementation.

There are several attacks on Feistel ciphers in the quantum setting. Besides the first work in [16], a meet-in-the-middle attack in the quantum setting was discussed in [11] and appending key-recovery rounds by applying the algorithm by Leander and May [18] was discussed in [7,8,11]. However, the following important issues have not been discussed by the previous work.

– Security analysis of Feistel ciphers against chosen-ciphertext adversaries is missing. In the classical setting, the tight bound of the number of rounds is known for the Feistel-F construction, and clarifying the number of rounds that can be attacked in the quantum setting leads us a deeper understanding of the Feistel-F construction. Furthermore, the quantum setting assumes strong power of adversaries, hence considering CCAs is more reasonable. We note that there are results in a CCA setting on Feistel ciphers with a specific key scheduling function called 2 key- or 4 key-alternation Feistel ciphers and their variants [4,6], however, we are considering more general constructions.

– Discussion on practical constructions is missing. Although the Luby-Rackoff construction is a good object to study theoretical aspects of the Feistel ciphers, in general, it cannot be implemented efficiently in practice. Therefore, the analyses of practical constructions like Feistel-KF and Feistel-FK are needed. Again, we are interested in general constructions that do not rely on a specific key scheduling function.

Our Contributions. In this paper, we further investigate the security of the Feistel ciphers against quantum adversaries. In particular, we show CCA distinguishers that can distinguish more rounds than the previous CPA distinguishers. In addition, we extend the distinguishers to key recovery attacks for the practical constructions, i.e. Feistel-KF and Feistel-FK.

We start with several fundamental observations about Simon's algorithm that detects a secret cycle-period in polynomial-time. The usage of Simon's algorithm in the previous work can be classified into two types; the first type uses Simon's algorithm for key recovery attacks, namely, the recovered secret cycle-period corresponds to the key of the construction such as [17] and [14], whereas the second type uses Simon's algorithm for distinguishers, e.g. to distinguish the construction from an ideal one [16,21] or to distinguish the right key guess from wrong key guesses [7,8,11,18].

We observe that, for the second type, recovering the secret cycle-period is not necessary as long as a non-ideal behavior is detected. If we follow [14] to recover the secret cycle-period by using Simon's algorithm, one has to derive the upper bound on the probability of a collision other than the period. However, there are cases where obtaining the upper bound is non-obvious, and it may be difficult to prove it in attacks on complicated constructions. This motivates us to relax the requirement of recovering the period in Simon's algorithm. Technically, we focus on the property that the dimension of the space spanned by the vectors in Simon's algorithm, instead of the exact period s. Namely, the dimension of the space is at most $\ell - 1$ if the target function has a period s, where $\{0,1\}^\ell$ is the domain of the function evaluated by Simon's algorithm. This modification eliminates the need to derive the upper bound on the probability of a collision other than the period s. Note that Santoli and Schaffner pointed out a similar observation [21], and we are dealing with a general class of block ciphers, and we also formalize a sufficient condition so that the distinguisher works.

We then apply the above observations to attack several Feistel ciphers. For the Feistel-F construction, we show that a cycle-period can be formed for 4 rounds in the CCA setting. This leads to a 4-round polynomial-time CCA distinguisher, which is 1-round longer than the CPA distinguisher by Kuwakado and Morii [16]. The attack is then extended to the practical constructions; Feistel-KF and Feistel-FK. For Feistel-KF, although the distinguisher is the same as the one for Feistel-F, we can now discuss the key recovery attack owing to the practical size of the secret key. We obtain 7-round key recovery attacks that recover $7n/2$-bit key with $O(2^{3n/4})$ complexity. For Feistel-FK, the CCA distinguisher is extended to 6 rounds and we obtain 9-round key recovery attacks that recover

Table 1. Comparison of the number of attacked rounds in various settings. "Dist." and "KR" denote distinguisher and key recovery attack, respectively. Superscript ^{P} denotes that the attack complexity is only a polynomial of the function's output size, while the others require exponential complexity.

Construction	Classic-CPA		Classic-CCA		Quantum-CPA		Quantum-CCA	
	Dist.	KR	Dist.	KR	Dist.	KR	Dist.	KR
Feistel-F	2 [19]	-	3 [19]	-	3^P [16]	-	4^P Ours	-
Feistel-KF	5 [10]	6 [10]	5 [10]	6 [10]	5 [11] 3^P [16]	6 [11]	4^P Ours	7 Ours
Feistel-FK	-	-	-	-	5^P Ours	8 Ours	6^P Ours	9 Ours

$9n/2$-bit key with $O(2^{3n/4})$ complexity. In addition, the CPA distinguisher is extended to 5 rounds and we obtain 8-round key recovery attacks that recover $8n/2$-bit key with $O(2^{3n/4})$ complexity. A comparison of the number of attacked rounds is given in Table 1. Note that Table 1 focuses on attacks with complexity at most $O(2^n)$, and it does not include attacks with higher complexities. Also, we consider only general constructions, so it does not include attacks against constructions with a particular key scheduling function such as [4,6].

Paper Outline. This paper is organized as follows. Section 2 describes preliminaries. Section 3 introduces previous works. Section 4 explains the formalization of a distinguishing technique that relaxes Simon's algorithm. Section 5 presents our CCA distinguisher against the 4-round Feistel-F constructions. The attack is then applied to chosen-ciphertext key-recovery attacks on Feistel-KF constructions in Sect. 6. Section 7 explains distinguishing and key-recovery attacks against Feistel-FK constructions in both CCA and CPA settings. We conclude the paper in Sect. 8.

2 Preliminaries

2.1 Notation

For a positive integer n, let $\{0,1\}^n$ be the set of all n-bit strings. Let $\text{Perm}(n)$ be the set of all permutations on $\{0,1\}^n$, and let $\text{Func}(n)$ be the set of all functions from $\{0,1\}^n$ to $\{0,1\}^n$. For bit strings a and b, $a \parallel b$ denotes their concatenation. We also regard a and b as binary vectors, and let $|a|$ be the dimension of the vector a. When $|a| = |b|$, we denote their inner product as $a \cdot b$. In this paper, e denotes Napier's number. For a finite set $\mathcal{X}$, we write $X \xleftarrow{\$} \mathcal{X}$ for the process of sampling an element uniformly from $\mathcal{X}$ and assigning the result to X.

2.2 Simon's Algorithm

In this section, we describe Simon's algorithm [23] that is used in our quantum algorithms. Throughout this paper, we assume that readers have basic knowledge about quantum computation. Simon's algorithm can solve the following problem.

Problem 1. Given a function $f : \{0,1\}^n \to \{0,1\}^n$, assume that there exists a period $s \in \{0,1\}^n \backslash \{0^n\}$ such that for any distinct $x, x' \in \{0,1\}^n$, it holds that $f(x) = f(x') \Leftrightarrow x' = x \oplus s$. The goal is to find the period s.

We assume that Simon's algorithm has access to the quantum oracle U_f, which is defined as $U_f \, |x\rangle \, |z\rangle = |x\rangle \, |z \oplus f(x)\rangle$. We use the Hadamard transform $H^{\otimes n}$ that is applied on n-qubit state $|x\rangle$ and gives $H^{\otimes n} \, |x\rangle = \frac{1}{\sqrt{2^n}} \sum_{y \in \{0,1\}^n} (-1)^{x \cdot y} \, |y\rangle$. Simon proposed a circuit $\mathcal{S}_f$ that computes vectors that are orthogonal to s by using the quantum oracle U_f. $\mathcal{S}_f$ is described as $(H^{\otimes n} \otimes I_n) \cdot U_f \cdot (H^{\otimes n} \otimes I_n)$ and works as follows:

1. We first apply the Hadamard transform $H^{\otimes n}$ on the first n qubits of $2n$-qubit state $|0^n\rangle \, |0^n\rangle$ to obtain the state $\frac{1}{\sqrt{2^n}} \sum_x |x\rangle \, |0^n\rangle$.

2. Then, we apply the unitary operator U_f to obtain the state $\frac{1}{\sqrt{2^n}} \sum_x |x\rangle \, |f(x)\rangle$.

3. Finally, we apply the Hadamard transform $H^{\otimes n}$ on the first n qubits to obtain the state

$$\frac{1}{2^n} \sum_{x,y} (-1)^{x \cdot y} \, |y\rangle \, |f(x)\rangle. \tag{1}$$

As we assume that f satisfies $f(x) = f(x') \Leftrightarrow x' = x \oplus s$, we have $|y\rangle \, |f(x)\rangle = |y\rangle \, |f(x \oplus s)\rangle$ for each y and x. Therefore, Eq. (1) is described as

$$\frac{1}{2^n} \sum_{x \in V, y} \left((-1)^{x \cdot y} + (-1)^{(x \oplus s) \cdot y} \right) |y\rangle \, |f(x)\rangle,$$

where V is a linear subspace of $\{0,1\}^n$ of dimension $n-1$ that partitions $\{0,1\}^n$ into cosets V and $V + s$. The vector y such that $y \cdot s \equiv 1 \pmod 2$ will satisfy $(-1)^{x \cdot y} + (-1)^{(x \oplus s) \cdot y} = 0$. Thus, we will obtain a random vector y such that $y \cdot s \equiv 0 \pmod 2$ by measuring the first n qubits. By repeating this routine that obtains a random vector y for $O(n)$ times, with a high probability, we obtain $n - 1$ linearly independent such vectors, and then the period s can be recovered by solving the system of linear equations.

We note that, in Simon's algorithm, we assume that the function f has a period s. In latter sections, we will use the circuit $\mathcal{S}_f$ to a function f that may not have any period, or may have multiple periods.

2.3   Kaplan et al.'s Observation

To apply Simon's algorithm, the function f has to satisfy $f(x) = f(x') \Leftrightarrow x' = x \oplus s$. We call this property Simon's promise. If f does not satisfy this property and has other collisions in addition to s, then there is no guarantee that Simon's algorithm works. However, Kaplan et al. showed that Simon's algorithm can find s even if f has partial periods, where the partial period is defined as $t \neq s$ such that $f(x) = f(x \oplus t)$ holds for some x [14].

More precisely, suppose that a function $f : \{0,1\}^\ell \to \{0,1\}^m$ satisfies only the condition that $f(x) = f(x') \Leftarrow x' = x \oplus s$ for any distinct $x, x' \in \{0,1\}^\ell$. Since now the counter condition $f(x) = f(x') \Rightarrow x' = x \oplus s$ does not always hold, there may exist partial periods of f. Intuitively, if there exist many partial periods $t_1, t_2, \ldots$ which are very close to complete periods (i.e., $\Pr_x [f(x) = f(x \oplus t_j)]$ is close to 1 for each j), then it becomes hard to recover s. To describe this intuition formally, Kaplan et al. introduced the parameter $\epsilon(f, s)$ defined as

$$\epsilon(f, s) = \max_{t \in \{0,1\}^\ell \setminus \{0^\ell, s\}} \Pr_x [f(x) = f(x \oplus t)]. \tag{2}$$

This shows the maximum probability of partial periods of f. Notice that if f is a constant function, then $\epsilon(f, s) = 1$ and s cannot be recovered. On the other hand, if f satisfies Simon's promise, then $\epsilon(f, s) = 0$. The following theorem about the success probability of Kaplan et al.'s observation was proved.

Theorem 1 ([14]). *If $\epsilon(f, s) \leq p_0$ for some positive number $p_0 < 1$, the probability that Simon's algorithm returns s after $c\ell$ queries is at least $1 - (2(\frac{1+p_0}{2})^c)^\ell$.*

This theorem shows that we still obtain s with $O(\ell)$ quantum queries and the complexity does not increase significantly.

3 Previous Works

3.1 Quantum Distinguisher Against the 3-Round Feistel Cipher

Here we review the distinguishing algorithm of the 3-round Feistel cipher by Kuwakado and Morii [16]. Kuwakado and Morii considered the case where F_{K_i} in Fig. 1 is a random permutation, and we write P_i for F_{K_i}.

Let FP$_3$ denote the encryption algorithm of the 3-round Feistel cipher, where random permutations $P_1, P_2, P_3 \overset{\$}{\leftarrow} \mathrm{Perm}(n/2)$ are used as internal functions. FP$_3$ takes a plaintext $(a, b) \in (\{0,1\}^{n/2})^2$ as input and outputs a ciphertext $(c, d) \in (\{0,1\}^{n/2})^2$, where

$$c = b \oplus P_2(a \oplus P_1(b)),$$
$$d = a \oplus P_1(b) \oplus P_3(b \oplus P_2(a \oplus P_1(b))).$$

Figure 2 illustrates FP$_3$.

Kuwakado and Morii considered the following problem.

Problem 2. Let $\mathcal{O} : \{0,1\}^n \to \{0,1\}^n$ be either FP$_3$ or a random permutation $\Pi \overset{\$}{\leftarrow} \mathrm{Perm}(n)$. Given access to the quantum oracle $U_{\mathcal{O}} : |x\rangle |y\rangle \mapsto |x\rangle |y \oplus \mathcal{O}(x)\rangle$, where $x, y \in \{0,1\}^n$, the goal is to distinguish the two cases.

Let $\alpha_0, \alpha_1 \in \{0,1\}^{n/2}$ be arbitrary distinct constants. For $\beta \in \{0,1\}$ and $x \in \{0,1\}^n$, Kuwakado and Morii used (x, α_β) as the plaintext (a, b). When $\mathcal{O}$ is FP$_3$, the lower half c of the ciphertext is described as

$$c = \alpha_\beta \oplus P_2(x \oplus P_1(\alpha_\beta)).$$

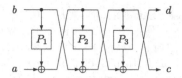

Fig. 2. The 3-round Feistel cipher with $P_i \xleftarrow{\$} \mathrm{Perm}(n/2)$ being used as the internal function.

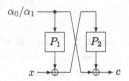

Fig. 3. $\mathrm{FP}_3(x, \alpha_\beta)$ and the lower half c of the ciphertext.

Fig. 4. $P_2(x \oplus P_1(\alpha_\beta))$.

Figure 3 illustrates c. Then, we see that $c \oplus \alpha_\beta = P_2(x \oplus P_1(\alpha_\beta))$ holds, which is illustrated in Fig. 4. If we change the value of β, i.e., if we let β to $\beta \oplus 1$, we see that the input value of P_2 remains the same value by changing x to $x \oplus P_1(\alpha_0) \oplus P_1(\alpha_1)$. Thus, we can construct a function $f^{\mathcal{O}}(\beta \parallel x)$ that has the period $1 \parallel P_1(\alpha_0) \oplus P_1(\alpha_1)$ by defining $f^{\mathcal{O}}$ as

$$f^{\mathcal{O}} : \{0,1\} \times \{0,1\}^{n/2} \to \{0,1\}^{n/2}$$
$$(\beta \parallel x) \mapsto c \oplus \alpha_\beta, \quad \text{where } (c, d) = \mathcal{O}(x, \alpha_\beta). \tag{3}$$

Note that $f^{\mathcal{O}}$ can also be evaluated in quantum superpositions. We can realize the unitary operator $U_{f^{\mathcal{O}}} : |x\rangle |y\rangle \mapsto |x\rangle |y \oplus f^{\mathcal{O}}(x)\rangle$ which makes $O(1)$ quantum queries to $U_{\mathcal{O}}$. If $\mathcal{O}$ is FP_3, then the function $f^{\mathcal{O}}$ is described as

$$f^{\mathcal{O}}(\beta \parallel x) = \alpha_\beta \oplus P_2(x \oplus P_1(\alpha_\beta)) \oplus \alpha_\beta$$
$$= P_2(x \oplus P_1(\alpha_\beta)),$$

and the following lemma holds.

Lemma 1. *If $\mathcal{O}$ is FP_3, the function $f^{\mathcal{O}}$ satisfies $f^{\mathcal{O}}(\beta \parallel x) = f^{\mathcal{O}}(\beta' \parallel x') \Leftrightarrow \beta' \parallel x' = (\beta \parallel x) \oplus (1 \parallel P_1(\alpha_0) \oplus P_1(\alpha_1))$ for any $x, x' \in \{0,1\}^{n/2}$ such that $x \neq x'$. That is, $f^{\mathcal{O}}$ has the period $s = 1 \parallel (P_1(\alpha_0) \oplus P_1(\alpha_1))$.*

For completeness, a proof is presented in [13].

Lemma 1 guarantees that the function $f^{\mathcal{O}}$ defined in Eq. (3) satisfies Simon's promise if $\mathcal{O}$ is FP_3, and we can recover the period s by applying Simon's algorithm to $f^{\mathcal{O}}$. Define a unitary operator $\mathcal{S}_{f^{\mathcal{O}}}$ by $\mathcal{S}_{f^{\mathcal{O}}} = (H^{\otimes n/2+1} \otimes I_{n/2}) \cdot U_{f^{\mathcal{O}}} \cdot (H^{\otimes n/2+1} \otimes I_{n/2})$. The quantum distinguisher by Kuwakado and Morii works as follows.

1. Measure the first $n/2 + 1$ qubits of $\mathcal{S}_{f^{\mathcal{O}}} |0^{n+1}\rangle$ to obtain the vector $y \in \{0,1\}^{n/2+1}$.

2. Repeat Step 1 until we obtain $n/2$ linearly independent vectors. If obtained, compute s by solving the system of linear equations.
3. Choose $\beta \in \{0,1\}$ and $z \in \{0,1\}^{n/2}$ randomly, and compute $f^{\mathcal{O}}(\beta \parallel z)$ and $f^{\mathcal{O}}((\beta \parallel z) \oplus s)$. If $f^{\mathcal{O}}(\beta \parallel z) = f^{\mathcal{O}}((\beta \parallel z) \oplus s)$, then output "$\mathcal{O}$ is FP$_3$," otherwise output "$\mathcal{O}$ is Π."

If $\mathcal{O}$ is FP$_3$, we obtain the period s in Step 2 with a high probability and it passes the test in Step 3. On the other hand, according to [16], if $\mathcal{O}$ is Π, with a high probability, Simon's algorithm returns a random string s', and the probability that $f^{\mathcal{O}}(\beta \parallel z) = f^{\mathcal{O}}((\beta \parallel z) \oplus s')$ is about $2^{-n/2}$. Therefore, the distinguisher above returns a correct answer by making $O(n)$ quantum queries.

Remark 1. We need to truncate outputs of $\mathcal{O}$ for constructing the function $f^{\mathcal{O}}$, since we use only the lower $n/2$ bits of the output of $\mathcal{O}$. However, the oracle may return outputs of which the lower and upper parts are entangled, and it is not trivial to truncate such outputs without destroying the entanglement, as pointed out by Kaplan et al. [14]. To solve this problem, Hosoyamada and Sasaki showed how to simulate truncation of outputs of the oracles without destroying quantum entanglements [11], and the same technique can be used in our case.

3.2 Key Recovery Attacks Against the Feistel-KF Construction

Next, we introduce the idea of the key recovery attacks against the Feistel-KF construction by Hosoyamada and Sasaki [11], and Dong and Wang [8]. They combined the quantum distinguisher against the 3-round Feistel cipher (see Sect. 3.1) with the Grover search. The attack is a quantum chosen-plaintext attack, and recovers the keys of the r-round Feistel cipher in time $\tilde{O}(2^{(r-3)n/4})$.

Attack Idea. Given the quantum encryption oracle of the r-round Feistel-KF construction, run the following procedures (on a quantum circuit).

1. Implement a quantum circuit which
   - takes the intermediate state value after the first $(r - 3)$ rounds and the subkeys for the first $(r - 3)$ rounds as input,
   - computes the plaintext by decrypting the first $(r - 3)$ rounds,
   - makes a quantum query of the computed plaintext to the oracle,
   - and returns the oracle output.
   The input and output of this circuit correspond to those of the last 3 rounds. We denote this circuit by $\mathcal{E}$, which is depicted in Fig. 5.
2. Guess the subkeys of the first $(r - 3)$ rounds.
3. For each guess, check its correctness with the following procedure.
   (a) Apply the 3-round distinguisher to $\mathcal{E}$.
   (b) If the distinguisher returns that "this is a random permutation", then judge that the guess is wrong. Otherwise judge that the guess is correct.

Attack Complexity. The total length of the subkeys of the first $(r - 3)$ rounds is $((r - 3)n/2)$ bits. Thus the exhaustive search of the first $(r - 3)$ rounds can be

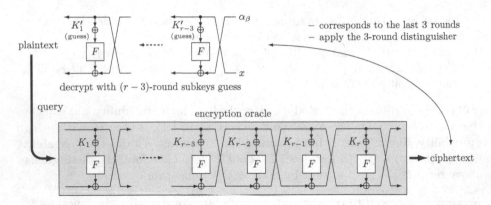

Fig. 5. Construction of $\mathcal{E}$ in the key recovery attack against the r-round Feistel-KF construction. The ciphertext corresponds to the output of the 3-round Feistel-KF construction which takes (K_{r-2}, K_{r-1}, K_r) as subkeys and (x, α_β) as input.

done in time $O(\sqrt{2^{(r-3)n/2}})$ by using the Grover search. Moreover, the 3-round distinguisher in the third step runs in time $O(n)$ for each subkeys guess. The running time of the attack is $O(\sqrt{2^{(r-3)n/2}}) \times O(\text{poly}(n)) = \tilde{O}(2^{(r-3)n/4})$.

Although how to formally combine the Grover search and the 3-round distinguisher is non-trivial, the technique developed by Leander and May [18] guarantees that those can be combined. See the previous papers [8,11] for details.

4   Relaxing Simon's Algorithm

This section presents quantum distinguishers that are based on the relaxed version of Simon's algorithm [23]. In a nutshell, we discuss that it is enough to obtain several vectors that are orthogonal to the period, and thus we eliminate the need to recover the actual period. This is similar to the one by Santoli and Schaffner [21], while we are dealing with a general class of block ciphers, and we also formalize a sufficient condition so that the distinguisher works.

In more detail, instead of using the period for the basis of the distinguisher, we focus on the dimension of the space spanned by the vectors $y_1, y_2, \ldots$ that are obtained by using $\mathcal{S}_f$ (recall that $\mathcal{S}_f$ is defined in Sect. 2.2). If f has the non-zero period s, then the dimension is at most $|s| - 1$, since the vectors $y_1, y_2, \ldots$ are all orthogonal to the period s. On the other hand, as we prove in Theorem 2 below, if the function f does not have any period, the dimension of the space spanned by the vectors $y_1, y_2, \ldots$ can reach $|s|$ with a high probability. In other words, we can distinguish f by checking the dimension of the space spanned by the vectors $y_1, y_2, \ldots$ without computing the actual period s. Thus, there will not be a problem if there are several partial periods or periods other than s because our distinguisher does not need the period s.

Note that this technique works only if we do not need the value of s. This technique cannot be applied to the key recovery attacks on Even-Mansour construction and forgery attacks on authentication and authenticated encryption schemes since the goal of these attacks needs s [14].

Below we formally explain how our distinguisher works. Let $\mathcal{O} : \{0,1\}^n \rightarrow \{0,1\}^n$ be either an encryption scheme E_K or a random permutation $\Pi \xleftarrow{\$} \mathrm{Perm}(n)$, and suppose that the quantum oracles of $\mathcal{O}$ and $\mathcal{O}^{-1}$ are given. Our goal is to distinguish whether $\mathcal{O} = E_K$ or $\mathcal{O} = \Pi$. In what follows, when we use the symbol π for a permutation, we consider that π is a fixed (or constant) permutation.

Settings. Our distinguisher can be applied when there is a function family $\{f^\pi : \{0,1\}^\ell \rightarrow \{0,1\}^m\}_{\pi \in \mathrm{Perm}(n)}$ that satisfies the following conditions:

1. There is a (classical) algorithm $\mathcal{A}$ that makes black-box access to π, π^{-1}, and computes f^π. That is, for each permutation π, $\mathcal{A}^{\pi,\pi^{-1}}$ computes $f^\pi(x)$ if x is given as input. We assume that $\mathcal{A}$ makes $O(1)$ queries and runs in time $O(\mathrm{poly}(\ell, m))$.
2. For the encryption scheme E and any key K, f^{E_K} has a period, i.e., there exists $s \in \{0,1\}^\ell$ such that $f^{E_K}(x \oplus s) = f^{E_K}(x)$ holds for all x (note that s depends on K).

Moreover, informally we expect that f^Π has no period with a high probability when Π is a random permutation. Note that the first condition implies that we can make a quantum circuit that realizes the unitary operator $U_{f^\mathcal{O}} : |x\rangle |z\rangle \mapsto |x\rangle |z \oplus f^\mathcal{O}(x)\rangle$ by making $O(1)$ quantum queries to $\mathcal{O}$ and $\mathcal{O}^{-1}$, since any classical deterministic algorithm can be converted to a corresponding quantum algorithm.

Description of the Distinguisher. Let $\mathcal{S}_{f^\mathcal{O}}$ be the unitary operator that is defined as in Sect. 2. Recall that $\mathcal{S}_{f^\mathcal{O}} = (H^{\otimes \ell} \otimes I_m) \cdot U_{f^\mathcal{O}} \cdot (H^{\otimes \ell} \otimes I_m)$. Our distinguisher is described in Algorithm 1.

Analysis of the Distinguisher. Our distinguisher always returns the correct answer if $\mathcal{O} = E_K$, since by assumption, f^{E_K} has a period for any K, and thus the dimension of the space spanned by $\mathcal{Y}$ becomes strictly less than ℓ. Our distinguisher fails only if $\mathcal{O} = \Pi$ and the dimension of the space spanned by $\mathcal{Y}$ becomes less than ℓ. Below we analyze the failure probability, assuming that η (the number of iterations in Step 2) is sufficiently large.

Algorithm 1. Distinguisher without recovering the period

---
1. Prepare an empty set $\mathcal{Y}$.
2. For $1 \leq i \leq \eta$, do:
3.   Measure the first ℓ qubits of $\mathcal{S}_{f^\mathcal{O}} |0^{\ell+m}\rangle$ and add the obtained vector y to $\mathcal{Y}$.
4. End For
5. Calculate the dimension d of the vector space spanned by $\mathcal{Y}$.
6. If $d = \ell$, then output "$\mathcal{O}$ is Π." If $d < \ell$, output "$\mathcal{O}$ is E_K."

The failure probability increases if the distribution of y in Step 3 is highly biased. Moreover, we obtain a vector y which is orthogonal to a partial period t of f^Π with a high probability in Step 3 if $\Pr_x\left[f^\Pi(x) = f^\Pi(x \oplus t)\right]$ is large (i.e., t is close to a complete period) by definition of $\mathcal{S}_{f^\mathcal{O}}$. To capture how much the distribution of y is biased under the condition that random permutation Π matches a fixed permutation π, we introduce a parameter ϵ_f^π defined as

$$\epsilon_f^\pi = \max_{t \in \{0,1\}^\ell \setminus \{0^\ell\}} \Pr_x \left[f^\pi(x) = f^\pi(x \oplus t)\right]. \tag{4}$$

We expect that, if π is chosen uniformly at random, this parameter ϵ_f^π is small on average.

Now take a small constant $0 \leq \delta < 1$ arbitrarily and say that a permutation π is irregular if $\epsilon_f^\pi > 1 - \delta$, i.e., ϵ_f^π is relatively large. In addition, define the set of irregular permutations irr_f^δ as

$$\mathrm{irr}_f^\delta = \{\pi \in \mathrm{Perm}(n) \mid \epsilon_f^\pi > 1 - \delta\}. \tag{5}$$

Our intuition is that the failure probability becomes small if $\Pr_\Pi[\Pi \in \mathrm{irr}_f^\delta]$ is sufficiently small, and actually the following theorem holds.

Theorem 2. *Let ℓ and m be positive integers that are $O(n)$. Assume that we have a quantum circuit with $O(\mathrm{poly}(\ell, m))$ qubits which computes $f^\mathcal{O}$ by making $O(1)$ queries to $\mathcal{O}$, and runs in time $T = T(\ell, m)$. Then, our distinguisher makes $O(\eta)$ quantum queries, runs in time $O(\eta T + \ell^3)$, and distinguishes E_K from Π with probability at least*

$$1 - 2^\ell/e^{\delta\eta/2} - \Pr_\Pi[\Pi \in \mathrm{irr}_f^\delta]. \tag{6}$$

A proof is presented in [13]. This theorem guarantees that we can distinguish E_K from Π if $2^\ell/e^{\delta\eta/2}$ and $\Pr_\Pi[\Pi \in \mathrm{irr}_f^\delta]$ are small. In later sections, we apply the above theorem with $\eta = 2\ell/\delta$, in which case we have $2^\ell/e^{\delta\eta/2} = (2/e)^\ell$.

If we use the technique by Kaplan et al. (Theorem 1) to analyze a success probability of a distinguisher, we have to upper bound the parameter $\epsilon(f^{E_K}, s)$ that depends on the real construction E_K, which may become hard if E_K has a complex structure. On the other hand, our technique (Theorem 2) requires only upper bounds of the terms that are not related to the real construction. Thus our technique makes analysis of a distinguisher easier than the technique by Kaplan et al. We remark that the probability evaluation in the ideal case that is similar to the last term of Eq. (6) is needed in the previous works [7,14,16] as well.

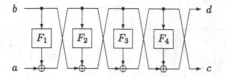

Fig. 6. The 4-round Feistel-F construction. $F_i \in \mathrm{Func}(n/2)$.

5   Quantum Distinguishing Attacks Against Feistel-F

In this section, we present our distinguisher against the 4-round Feistel-F construction with quantum chosen-ciphertext attacks. Based on this, we present in Sect. 6 quantum distinguishing attacks and key recovery attacks against the Feistel-KF construction.

We write F_{K_i} as F_i. Note that F_i is still a keyed function and the absence of K_i does not imply that it is a keyless function. Let FF_4 denote the encryption algorithm of the 4-round Feistel-F construction, and FF_4^{-1} denote its decryption algorithm. Figure 6 illustrates FF_4. Let $F_1, \ldots, F_4 \in \mathrm{Func}(n/2)$ be the round functions of Feistel-F. FF_4 takes a plaintext $(a, b) \in (\{0,1\}^{n/2})^2$ as input and outputs a ciphertext $(c, d) \in (\{0,1\}^{n/2})^2$, where $\mathrm{FF}_4 : (a, b) \mapsto (c, d)$ is

$$c = a \oplus F_1(b) \oplus F_3(b \oplus F_2(a \oplus F_1(b))),$$
$$d = b \oplus F_2(a \oplus F_1(b)) \oplus F_4\Big(a \oplus F_1(b) \oplus F_3(b \oplus F_2(a \oplus F_1(b)))\Big).$$

The decryption $\mathrm{FF}_4^{-1} : (c, d) \mapsto (a, b)$ is defined as

$$a = c \oplus F_3(d \oplus F_4(c)) \oplus F_1\Big(d \oplus F_4(c) \oplus F_2(c \oplus F_3(d \oplus F_4(c)))\Big),$$
$$b = d \oplus F_4(c) \oplus F_2(c \oplus F_3(d \oplus F_4(c))).$$

Let $\Pi \xleftarrow{\$} \mathrm{Perm}(n)$ be a random permutation and Π^{-1} be the inverse permutation of Π. Π takes a plaintext $(a, b) \in (\{0,1\}^{n/2})^2$ as input and outputs a ciphertext $(c, d) \in (\{0,1\}^{n/2})^2$, and Π^{-1} takes a ciphertext (c, d) as input and outputs a plaintext (a, b).

Given the quantum oracles of $\mathcal{O}$ and $\mathcal{O}^{-1}$, where $\mathcal{O}$ is either the 4-round Feistel-F FF_4 or a random permutation $\Pi \xleftarrow{\$} \mathrm{Perm}(n)$, our goal is to distinguish the two cases. We now construct the function $f^{\mathcal{O}}$ to use Algorithm 1. We first fix two arbitrary distinct constants $\alpha_0, \alpha_1 \in \{0,1\}^{n/2}$, and we define the function $f^{\mathcal{O}}$ as

$$f^{\mathcal{O}} : \{0,1\} \times \{0,1\}^{n/2} \to \{0,1\}^{n/2}$$
$$(\beta \,\|\, x) \mapsto b \oplus \alpha_\beta, \quad \text{where } (c, d) = \mathcal{O}(x, \alpha_\beta),$$
$$(a, b) = \mathcal{O}^{-1}(c, d \oplus \alpha_0 \oplus \alpha_1).$$

That is, $f^{\mathcal{O}}$ is obtained by first encrypting (x, α_β) to obtain the ciphertext (c, d), then decrypting $(c, d \oplus \alpha_0 \oplus \alpha_1)$ to obtain the plaintext (a, b), and we define $f^{\mathcal{O}}$ as $b \oplus \alpha_\beta$.

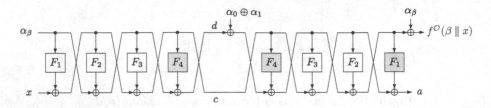

Fig. 7. The function $f^{\mathcal{O}}$ with FF_4 and FF_4^{-1}, where $\mathcal{O}$ is FF_4.

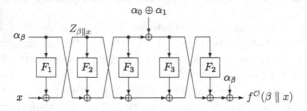

Fig. 8. A circuit that is equivalent to $f^{\mathcal{O}}$.

If $\mathcal{O}$ is FF_4, then by connecting FF_4 and FF_4^{-1}, our function $f^{\mathcal{O}}$ can be illustrated as in Fig. 7. We observe that F_4 has no effect on the computation of $f^{\mathcal{O}}$, and F_1 in FF_4^{-1} does not contribute to $f^{\mathcal{O}}$. They are shown in gray in Fig. 7. We see that Fig. 7 is equivalent to Fig. 8, and the function $f^{\mathcal{O}}$ is described as

$$f^{\mathcal{O}}(\beta \parallel x) = \alpha_0 \oplus \alpha_1 \oplus F_2(x \oplus F_1(\alpha_\beta))$$
$$\oplus F_2\Big(x \oplus F_1(\alpha_\beta) \oplus F_3(\alpha_\beta \oplus F_2(x \oplus F_1(\alpha_\beta)))$$
$$\oplus F_3(\alpha_\beta \oplus \alpha_0 \oplus \alpha_1 \oplus F_2(x \oplus F_1(\alpha_\beta)))\Big). \tag{7}$$

Our main observation is the following lemma.

Lemma 2. *If $\mathcal{O} = FF_4$, $f^{\mathcal{O}}$ satisfies $f^{\mathcal{O}}(\beta \parallel x) = f^{\mathcal{O}}(\beta \oplus 1 \parallel x \oplus F_1(\alpha_0) \oplus F_1(\alpha_1))$. That is, $f^{\mathcal{O}}$ has the period $s = 1 \parallel F_1(\alpha_0) \oplus F_1(\alpha_1)$.*

Proof. Let $Z_{\beta \parallel x} = x \oplus F_1(\alpha_\beta)$ (See Fig. 8). We prove the lemma based on two claims. The first claim is that $Z_{\beta \parallel x}$ already has the period $s = 1 \parallel F_1(\alpha_0) \oplus F_1(\alpha_1)$, and the second claim is that the subsequent computation of $f^{\mathcal{O}}$ does not depend on β nor x.

First, $Z_{\beta \parallel x}$ has the period s, since

$$Z_{(\beta \parallel x) \oplus s} = x \oplus F_1(\alpha_0) \oplus F_1(\alpha_1) \oplus F_1(\alpha_{\beta \oplus 1})$$
$$= x \oplus F_1(\alpha_\beta)$$
$$= Z_{\beta \parallel x}.$$

We next show that the subsequent computation of $f^\mathcal{O}$ does not depend on β nor x. If we describe $f^\mathcal{O}$ in Eq. (7) by using $Z_{\beta\|x}$, then we obtain

$$f^\mathcal{O}(\beta \| x) = \alpha_0 \oplus \alpha_1 \oplus F_2(Z_{\beta\|x})$$
$$\oplus F_2\Big(Z_{\beta\|x} \oplus F_3(\alpha_\beta \oplus F_2(Z_{\beta\|x})) \oplus F_3(\alpha_\beta \oplus \alpha_0 \oplus \alpha_1 \oplus F_2(Z_{\beta\|x}))\Big).$$

Now this is equivalent to

$$f^\mathcal{O}(\beta \| x) = \alpha_0 \oplus \alpha_1 \oplus F_2(Z_{\beta\|x})$$
$$\oplus F_2\Big(Z_{\beta\|x} \oplus F_3(\alpha_0 \oplus F_2(Z_{\beta\|x})) \oplus F_3(\alpha_1 \oplus F_2(Z_{\beta\|x}))\Big) \qquad (8)$$

since $\{\alpha_\beta, \alpha_\beta \oplus \alpha_0 \oplus \alpha_1\} = \{\alpha_0, \alpha_1\}$. We see that $f^\mathcal{O}$ depends on $Z_{\beta\|x}$ that has the period $s = 1 \| F_1(\alpha_0) \oplus F_1(\alpha_1)$, and hence the lemma follows. $\qquad\square$

Therefore, we can construct a distinguisher against the 4-round Feistel-F construction by using the function $f^\mathcal{O}$. From Theorem 2, the success probability of the distinguisher with measuring $(2n + 4)$ times is $1 - (2/e)^{n/2+1} - \Pr_\Pi[\Pi \in \mathrm{irr}_f^{1/2}]$, where we use $\delta = 1/2$ and $\eta = 2n + 4$.

It is clear that $\Pr_\Pi[\Pi \in \mathrm{irr}_f^{1/2}]$ is a small value, since it is highly unlikely that $f^\mathcal{O}$ obtained from a random permutation has periods. In [13], we present experimental results for small values of n to show that $\Pr_\Pi[\Pi \in \mathrm{irr}_f^{1/2}]$ is indeed a small value.

6   Quantum Attacks Against Feistel-KF

The distinguisher in the previous section can obviously be applied to the 4-round Feistel-KF construction, and we can distinguish it from random permutations in polynomial time. Similarly to the previous key recovery attacks against the Feistel-KF [8,11] construction (see Sect. 3.2), our 4-round distinguisher can be combined with the Grover search to develop key recovery attacks. Our new key recovery attack recovers the keys of the r-round Feistel-KF construction in time $\tilde{O}(2^{(r-4)n/4})$ in the quantum CCA setting.

Attack Idea. Our attack idea is almost the same as that of the previous attacks [8, 11], except that our attack uses not only the encryption oracle but also the decryption oracle. Given the quantum encryption and decryption oracles of the r-round Feistel-KF construction, run the following procedures (on a quantum circuit).

1. Implement a quantum circuit $\mathcal{E}$ that takes the intermediate state value after the first $(r - 4)$ rounds and the subkeys for the first $(r - 4)$ rounds as input, and computes the last 4 rounds, in the same way as the first step of the attack idea in Sect. 3.2.
2. Implement a quantum circuit $\mathcal{D}$ that computes the inverse of $\mathcal{E}$. That is, implement a quantum circuit which

- takes the ciphertext and the subkeys for the first $(r-4)$ rounds as input,
- makes a quantum decryption query of the ciphertext to the oracle to obtain the plaintext,
- computes the intermediate state value after the first $(r-4)$ rounds from the plaintext and the subkeys for the first $(r-4)$ rounds,
- and returns the intermediate state.

3. Guess the subkeys of the first $(r-4)$ rounds.
4. For each guess, check its correctness with the following procedure.
   (a) Apply the 4-round distinguisher to $\mathcal{E}$ and $\mathcal{D}$.
   (b) If the distinguisher returns that "this is a random permutation", then judge that the guess is wrong. Otherwise judge that the guess is correct.

Attack Complexity. The length of the first $(r-4)$-round subkeys is $((r-4)n/2)$ bits in total. Thus the exhaustive search on the first $(r-4)$ rounds can be done in time $O(\sqrt{2^{(r-4)n/2}})$ by using the Grover search. Moreover, the 4-round distinguisher in the fourth step runs in time $O(n)$ for each candidate subkeys. Therefore the running time of the attack becomes $O(\sqrt{2^{(r-4)n/2}}) \times O(\text{poly}(n)) = \tilde{O}(2^{(r-4)n/4})$.

Our new attack reduces the time complexity $\tilde{O}(2^{(r-3)n/4})$ of the previous attacks to $\tilde{O}(2^{(r-4)n/4})$, by using our new CCA 4-round distinguisher instead of the previous CPA 3-round distinguisher by Kuwakado and Morii. Our attack is a chosen-ciphertext attack unlike that the previous attacks are chosen-plaintext attacks, since our 4-round distinguisher is a CCA distinguisher.

7 Quantum Attacks Against Feistel-FK

In Sect. 7.1, we show a quantum distinguishing attack against Feistel-FK. Based on this, we present in Sect. 7.2 a key recovery attack. The main difference from the previous sections is that the number of the distinguishable rounds increases. In Sect. 7.3, we present a quantum chosen-plaintext attack.

7.1 Distinguishers Against Feistel-FK

We present our distinguisher against the 6-round Feistel-FK construction with quantum chosen-ciphertext attacks. This attack is based on the distinguisher against the 4-round Feistel-F construction described in Sect. 5. We increase the number of rounds by adding the first and last rounds, and this is possible because we can compute the output of the first F function and the last F function in encryption (or decryption) without knowing the subkeys.

Let $(a, b) \in (\{1, 0\}^{n/2})^2$ denote a plaintext and $(c, d) \in (\{1, 0\}^{n/2})^2$ denote a ciphertext. Let $\text{FFK}_6 : (a, b) \mapsto (c, d)$ denote the encryption algorithm of the 6-round Feistel-FK construction, and $\text{FFK}_6^{-1} : (c, d) \mapsto (a, b)$ denote its decryption algorithm. Figure 9 illustrates the 6-round Feistel-FK construction.

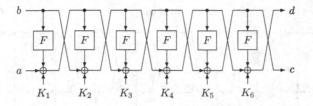

Fig. 9. The 6-round Feistel-FK construction.

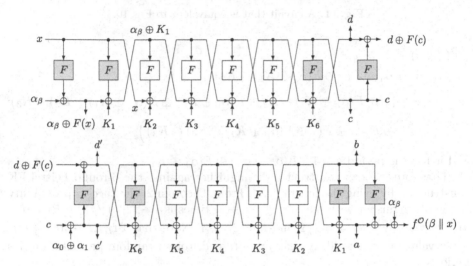

Fig. 10. The function $f^{\mathcal{O}}$ with FFK_6 and FFK_6^{-1}, where $\mathcal{O}$ is FFK_6. $c' = c \oplus \alpha_0 \oplus \alpha_1$ and $d' = d \oplus F(c) \oplus F(c \oplus \alpha_0 \oplus \alpha_1)$.

Given the quantum oracles of $\mathcal{O}$ and $\mathcal{O}^{-1}$, we define the function $f^{\mathcal{O}}$ as

$$f^{\mathcal{O}} : \{0,1\} \times \{0,1\}^{n/2} \to \{0,1\}^{n/2}$$
$$(\beta \| x) \quad \mapsto a \oplus F(b) \oplus \alpha_\beta$$
$$\text{where } (c,d) = \mathcal{O}(\alpha_\beta \oplus F(x), x),$$
$$(a,b) = \mathcal{O}^{-1}(c \oplus \alpha_0 \oplus \alpha_1, d \oplus F(c) \oplus F(c \oplus \alpha_0 \oplus \alpha_1)).$$

If $\mathcal{O}$ is FFK_6, then our function $f^{\mathcal{O}}$ can be illustrated as in Fig. 10. We observe that the F functions shown in gray in Fig. 10 and the subkeys K_6 have no effect on the computation of $f^{\mathcal{O}}$. By connecting FFK_6 and FFK_6^{-1}, we obtain Fig. 11 that is equivalent to Fig. 10. If we replace α_β with $\alpha_\beta \oplus K_1$ and $F_i(x)$ with $F(x) \oplus K_{i+1}$ in Fig. 7, we see that Fig. 7 is equivalent to Fig. 11. Therefore, from Eqs. (7) and (8), the function $f^{\mathcal{O}}$ is described as

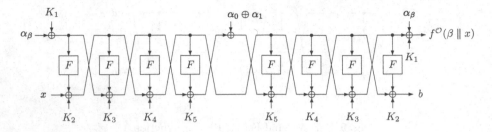

Fig. 11. A circuit that is equivalent to Fig. 10.

$$f^{\mathcal{O}}(\beta \parallel x)$$
$$= \alpha_0 \oplus \alpha_1 \oplus F(x \oplus F(\alpha_\beta \oplus K_1) \oplus K_2)$$
$$\oplus F\Big(x \oplus F(\alpha_\beta \oplus K_1) \oplus K_2 \oplus F\big(\alpha_0 \oplus F(x \oplus F(\alpha_\beta \oplus K_1) \oplus K_2) \oplus K_3\big)$$
$$\oplus F\big(\alpha_1 \oplus F(x \oplus F(\alpha_\beta \oplus K_1) \oplus K_2) \oplus K_3\big)\Big)$$

and it has the period $s = 1 \parallel F(\alpha_0 \oplus K_1) \oplus F(\alpha_1 \oplus K_1)$.

Therefore, we can construct a distinguisher against the 6-round Feistel-FK construction by using the function $f^{\mathcal{O}}$. From Theorem 2, the success probability of the distinguisher with measuring $(2n + 4)$ times is $1 - (2/e)^{n/2+1} - \Pr_\Pi[\Pi \in \mathrm{irr}_f^{1/2}]$, where we set $\delta = 1/2$ and $\eta = 2n + 4$. Note that $\Pr_\Pi[\Pi \in \mathrm{irr}_f^{1/2}]$ is a small value, as it is unlikely that $f^{\mathcal{O}}$ obtained from a random permutation has periods.

7.2   Key Recovery Attacks Against Feistel-FK

Similarly to the key recovery attacks against the Feistel-KF construction in Sect. 6, the distinguisher introduced above can be combined with the Grover search to develop key recovery attacks. We can recover keys of the r-round Feistel-FK construction in time $\tilde{O}(2^{(r-6)n/4})$ in the quantum CCA setting.

Our attack idea follows the attack against the Feistel-KF construction in Sect. 6. Recall that the attack in Sect. 6 guesses the first $(r-4)$-round subkeys since a 4-round distinguisher is available. On the other hand, as for the Feistel-FK construction, we can use the 6-round distinguisher in Sect. 7.1 instead of the 4-round distinguisher. Hence it is sufficient to guess only the first $(r-6)$-round subkeys (instead of the first $(r-4)$-round subkeys) when we attack the Feistel-FK construction. The time complexity of our attack becomes $\tilde{O}(2^{(r-6)n/4})$, since the Grover search on the first $(r-6)$-round subkeys ($\frac{(r-6)n}{2}$ bits in total) requires $O(\sqrt{2^{(r-6)n/2}}) = O(2^{(r-6)n/4})$ evaluations.

7.3   Quantum CPA Attacks Against Feistel-FK

We can also construct a distinguisher and recover the key of the Feistel-FK construction in the quantum CPA setting. As in Sect. 7.1, we can construct a 5-round distinguisher by following the 3-round distinguisher in Sect. 3.1 and by computing the output of the first F function and the last F function in encryption. Specifically, we use $(\alpha_\beta \oplus F(x), x)$ as the input of the oracle $\mathcal{O}$ and use $d \oplus F(c) \oplus \alpha_\beta$ as the output of the function $f^{\mathcal{O}}(\beta \parallel x)$, where $(c, d) = \mathcal{O}(\alpha_\beta \oplus F(x), x)$. This function has the period $s = 1 \parallel F(\alpha_0 \oplus K_1) \oplus F(\alpha_1 \oplus K_1)$.

Combined with the 5-round distinguisher, we can recover the subkeys of the r-round Feistel-FK construction as in Sect. 6. The time complexity of our key recovery attack is $\tilde{O}(2^{(r-5)n/4})$, since the Grover search on the first $(r-5)$-round subkeys ($\frac{(r-5)n}{2}$ bits in total) requires $O(\sqrt{2^{(r-5)n/2}}) = O(2^{(r-5)n/4})$ evaluations.

8 Concluding Remarks

In this paper, we first formalized a distinguishing algorithm against block ciphers that does not recover the period. We then considered quantum chosen-ciphertext attacks against Feistel ciphers. We gave a new quantum CCA distinguisher against Feistel ciphers that can distinguish more rounds than the previous CPA distinguishers. Our quantum CCA distinguishers can distinguish the 4-round Feistel-F and Feistel-KF constructions, and the 6-round Feistel-FK construction, from random permutations in polynomial-time of the output size. Moreover, we extended the distinguishers to key recovery attacks for the Feistel-KF and Feistel-FK constructions. Our quantum CCA key recovery attacks against the r-round Feistel-KF and Feistel-FK constructions recover keys in time $\tilde{O}(2^{(r-4)n/4})$ and $\tilde{O}(2^{(r-6)n/4})$, and quantum CPA key recovery attacks against the r-round Feistel-FK constructions recover keys in time $\tilde{O}(2^{(r-5)n/4})$, respectively.

There are interesting open questions. First, we still do not know the tight bound on the number of rounds that we can distinguish the Feistel-F construction. From the result of Kuwakado and Morii, we know that the 3-round construction can be distinguished with quantum CPA, and this paper shows that the 4-round construction can be distinguished with quantum CCA. However, there is a possibility that these rounds can be extended, and deriving the tight number of rounds remains as a challenging question. Improving the complexity or extending the number of rounds of the attacks against Feistel-KF and Feistel-FK constructions is also an interesting question.

Acknowledgments. The authors would like to thank participants of Dagstuhl seminar 18021, Symmetric Cryptography, for insightful feedback. We also would like to thank the anonymous reviewers of CT-RSA 2019 for helpful comments.

References

1. Aoki, K., et al.: *Camellia*: a 128-bit block cipher suitable for multiple platforms—design and analysis. In: Stinson, D.R., Tavares, S. (eds.) SAC 2000. LNCS, vol. 2012, pp. 39–56. Springer, Heidelberg (2001). https://doi.org/10.1007/3-540-44983-3_4
2. Beaulieu, R., Shors, D., Smith, J., Treatman-Clark, S., Weeks, B., Wingers, L.: The SIMON and SPECK lightweight block ciphers. In: Proceedings of the 52nd Annual Design Automation Conference, pp. 175:1–175:6. ACM (2015)

3. Bonnetain, X.: Quantum key-recovery on full AEZ. In: Adams, C., Camenisch, J. (eds.) SAC 2017. LNCS, vol. 10719, pp. 394–406. Springer, Cham (2018). https://doi.org/10.1007/978-3-319-72565-9_20

4. Bonnetain, X., Naya-Plasencia, M., Schrottenloher, A.: On quantum slide attacks. IACR Cryptology ePrint Archive 2018, 1067 (2018)

5. Dinur, I., Dunkelman, O., Keller, N., Shamir, A.: New attacks on Feistel structures with improved memory complexities. In: Gennaro, R., Robshaw, M. (eds.) CRYPTO 2015. LNCS, vol. 9215, pp. 433–454. Springer, Heidelberg (2015). https://doi.org/10.1007/978-3-662-47989-6_21

6. Dong, X., Dong, B., Wang, X.: Quantum attacks on some Feistel block ciphers. IACR Cryptology ePrint Archive 2018, 504 (2018)

7. Dong, X., Li, Z., Wang, X.: Quantum cryptanalysis on some generalized Feistel schemes. IACR Cryptology ePrint Archive 2017, 1249 (2017)

8. Dong, X., Wang, X.: Quantum key-recovery attack on Feistel structures. IACR Cryptology ePrint Archive 2017, 1199 (2017)

9. Grover, L.K.: A fast quantum mechanical algorithm for database search. In: Miller, G.L. (ed.) STOC 1996, pp. 212–219. ACM (1996)

10. Guo, J., Jean, J., Nikolić, I., Sasaki, Y.: Meet-in-the-middle attacks on generic Feistel constructions. In: Sarkar, P., Iwata, T. (eds.) ASIACRYPT 2014. LNCS, vol. 8873, pp. 458–477. Springer, Heidelberg (2014). https://doi.org/10.1007/978-3-662-45611-8_24

11. Hosoyamada, A., Sasaki, Y.: Quantum Demiric-Selçuk meet-in-the-middle attacks: applications to 6-round generic Feistel constructions. In: Catalano, D., De Prisco, R. (eds.) SCN 2018. LNCS, vol. 11035, pp. 386–403. Springer, Cham (2018). https://doi.org/10.1007/978-3-319-98113-0_21

12. Isobe, T., Shibutani, K.: Generic key recovery attack on Feistel scheme. In: Sako, K., Sarkar, P. (eds.) ASIACRYPT 2013. LNCS, vol. 8269, pp. 464–485. Springer, Heidelberg (2013). https://doi.org/10.1007/978-3-642-42033-7_24

13. Ito, G., Hosoyamada, A., Matsumoto, R., Sasaki, Y., Iwata, T.: Quantum chosen-ciphertext attacks against Feistel ciphers. IACR Cryptology ePrint Archive 2018, 1193 (2018). Full version of this paper

14. Kaplan, M., Leurent, G., Leverrier, A., Naya-Plasencia, M.: Breaking symmetric cryptosystems using quantum period finding. In: Robshaw, M., Katz, J. (eds.) CRYPTO 2016. LNCS, vol. 9815, pp. 207–237. Springer, Heidelberg (2016). https://doi.org/10.1007/978-3-662-53008-5_8

15. Knudsen, L.R.: The security of Feistel ciphers with six rounds or less. J. Cryptol. 15(3), 207–222 (2002)

16. Kuwakado, H., Morii, M.: Quantum distinguisher between the 3-round Feistel cipher and the random permutation. In: ISIT 2010, pp. 2682–2685. IEEE (2010)

17. Kuwakado, H., Morii, M.: Security on the quantum-type Even-Mansour cipher. In: ISITA 2012, pp. 312–316. IEEE (2012)

18. Leander, G., May, A.: Grover meets Simon – quantumly attacking the FX-construction. In: Takagi, T., Peyrin, T. (eds.) ASIACRYPT 2017. LNCS, vol. 10625, pp. 161–178. Springer, Cham (2017). https://doi.org/10.1007/978-3-319-70697-9_6

19. Luby, M., Rackoff, C.: How to construct pseudorandom permutations from pseudorandom functions. SIAM J. Comput. 17(2), 373–386 (1988)

20. National Bureau of Standards: Data encryption standard. FIPS 46, January 1977

21. Santoli, T., Schaffner, C.: Using Simon's algorithm to attack symmetric-key cryptographic primitives. Quantum Inf. Comput. 17(1&2), 65–78 (2017)

22. Shibutani, K., Isobe, T., Hiwatari, H., Mitsuda, A., Akishita, T., Shirai, T.: *Piccolo*: an ultra-lightweight blockcipher. In: Preneel, B., Takagi, T. (eds.) CHES 2011. LNCS, vol. 6917, pp. 342–357. Springer, Heidelberg (2011). https://doi.org/10. 1007/978-3-642-23951-9_23
23. Simon, D.R.: On the power of quantum computation. SIAM J. Comput. **26**(5), 1474–1483 (1997)
24. Todo, Y.: Structural evaluation by generalized integral property. In: Oswald, E., Fischlin, M. (eds.) EUROCRYPT 2015. LNCS, vol. 9056, pp. 287–314. Springer, Heidelberg (2015). https://doi.org/10.1007/978-3-662-46800-5_12
25. Yang, G., Zhu, B., Suder, V., Aagaard, M.D., Gong, G.: The Simeck family of lightweight block ciphers. In: Güneysu, T., Handschuh, H. (eds.) CHES 2015. LNCS, vol. 9293, pp. 307–329. Springer, Heidelberg (2015). https://doi.org/10. 1007/978-3-662-48324-4_16

Automatic Search for a Variant of Division Property Using Three Subsets

Kai Hu and Meiqin Wang[✉]

Key Laboratory of Cryptologic Technology and Information Security,
Ministry of Education, Shandong University, Jinan 250100, China
hukai@mail.sdu.edu.cn, mqwang@sdu.edu.cn

Abstract. The division property proposed at Eurocrypt'15 is a novel technique to find integral distinguishers, which has been applied to most kinds of symmetric ciphers such as block ciphers, stream ciphers, and authenticated encryption, *etc.* The original division property is word-oriented, and later the bit-based one was proposed at FSE'16 to get better integral property, which is composed of conventional bit-based division property (two-subset division property) and bit-based division property using three subsets (three-subset division property). Three-subset division property has more potential to achieve better integral distinguishers compared with the two-subset division property. The bit-based division property could not be to apply to ciphers with large block sizes due to its unpractical complexity. At Asiacrypt'16, the two-subset division property was modeled using Mixed Integral Linear Programming (MILP) technique, and the limits of block sizes were eliminated. However, there is still no efficient method searching for three-subset division property. The propagation rule of the XOR operation for $\mathbb{L}$ (The definition of $\mathbb{L}$ and $\mathbb{K}$ is introduced in Sect. 2.), which is a set used in the three-subset division property but not in two-subset one, requires to remove some specific vectors, and new vectors generated from $\mathbb{L}$ should be appended to $\mathbb{K}$ when Key-XOR operation is applied, both of which are difficult for common automatic tools such as MILP, SMT or CP. In this paper, we overcome one of the two challenges, concretely, we address the problem to add new vectors into $\mathbb{K}$ from $\mathbb{L}$ in an automatic search model. Moreover, we present a new model automatically searching for a variant three-subset division property (VTDP) with STP solver. The variant is weaker than the original three-subset division property (OTDP) but it is still powerful in some ciphers. Most importantly, this model has no constraints on the block size of target ciphers, which can also be applied to ARX and S-box based ciphers. As illustrations, some improved integral distinguishers have been achieved for SIMON32, SIMON32/48/64(102), SPECK32 and KATAN/KTANTAN32/48/64 according to the number of rounds or number of even/odd-parity bits.

Keywords: Division property · Three-subset · STP · Automatic research

© Springer Nature Switzerland AG 2019
M. Matsui (Ed.): CT-RSA 2019, LNCS 11405, pp. 412–432, 2019.
https://doi.org/10.1007/978-3-030-12612-4_21

1   Introduction

Division property, a generalization of the integral property [6], was proposed by Todo at Eurocrypt'15 [12], which has been applied to most kinds of symmetric ciphers, such as block ciphers, stream ciphers and authenticated encryption [13, 14], *etc.* The most impressive application is that it was used to break, for the first time, the full MISTY1 at CRYPTO'15 [13]. Furthermore, the division property made significant progress in the cube attack because the limits of practical data complexity have been eliminated [14].

Since the division property was put forward, this cryptanalytic technique has been further investigated. The original division property [12] is word-oriented, and it can only describe the algebraic degree of S-box instead of the particular Boolean function. In order to further consider the Boolean function of S-box, Boura *et al.* gave more precise description for S-box in division property at CRYPTO'16 [3].

At FSE'16, Todo and Morii [15] introduced the bit-based division property which depicts the components of target primitive at bit level so that more information of the cipher structures can be utilized. Compared with the original word-level division property, the bit-based one is more likely to find better integral characteristics. Bit-based division property family proposed in [15] includes two-subset and three-subset division property. The two- and three-subset division property classify all vectors $u \in \mathbb{F}_2^n$ into two and three subsets, respectively, according to the parity of a Boolean polynomial related to u. In detail, the parity is even or unknown for two-subset division property while even, odd or unknown for three-subset division property. Because the odd-parity set is extracted from the unknown set in three-subset division property, it means that more information of Boolean function is traced. Therefore, three-subset division property has more potential to achieve better integral distinguishers. For example, the 14-round integral characteristic of SIMON32 has been found by two-subset division property while 15-round integral characteristic was found by three-subset division property [15].

Although the bit-based division property under Todo and Morri's framework is quite effective to find integral distinguishers, unfortunately, they can only work on ciphers with small block sizes because of the huge memory and time requirements. As pointed in [15], for a cipher with block size n, the time and memory complexities are upper bounded by 2^n. Xiang *et al.* have solved the problem of searching for two-subset division property by utilizing the MILP tools at Asiacrypt'16 [17]. They transformed the search problem into an MILP problem which can be used to find division property for ciphers with large block size. Automatic tools such as MILP solvers can describe the set with some constraints and conduct some inner optimization automatically, which do not need to go through all the vectors. Xiang *et al.*'s method has been extended and applied to improve the integral attacks on many ciphers [5,9,10,16]. Especially, the MILP model to search division property was used to extend the cube attack, which has improved the attacks on Trivium, Grain128a, and Acorn [14].

Since the automatic search model for three-subset division property is still not constructed, it can be merely used on ciphers with small size until now. For two-subset division property, we only trace the set $\mathbb{K}$ but both the set $\mathbb{K}$ and $\mathbb{L}$ should be considered for three-subset division property. There are two challenges to face when we construct the automatic search model by MILP, SMT or CP. In one hand, the propagation rules for $\mathbb{L}$ are very different because some vectors which appear an even number of times should be removed from $\mathbb{L}$ and the propagation rule of XOR should remove the vectors occurring an even number of times, too. On the other hand, some new vectors generated from vectors in $\mathbb{L}$ will be added into $\mathbb{K}$.

In common MILP, SMT or CP models, the constraints are used only to narrow the range of the sets which the variables belong to. There are no direct methods which can solve the two following problems as far as we know,

1. decide the duplicated vectors which appear even times and remove them dynamically.
2. extend the range of a set which the specific variable belongs to.

In this paper, we introduce one new technique by an STP solver to overcome the second problem directly. We do not remove the duplicated vectors in $\mathbb{L}$ and then we get a variant of three-subset division property. Although VTDP is not more efficient than OTDP, we prove that the results of VTDP are valid and useful. Most importantly, we can automatically search for VTDP without the limits of block sizes. It can also be applied to S-box based and ARX ciphers.

1.1   Our Contributions

1.1.1   Automatic Search Algorithm for VTDP

In this paper, we introduce VTDP and construct a general model of automatic search for it. The details of our technical contributions are three-fold, which are listed as follows.

VTDP and Variant Three-Subset Division Trail. We describe the method to obtain VTDP from OTDP and prove the validity of this variant. Compared with OTDP, VTDP does not remove any duplicated vector in $\mathbb{L}$ and modify the propagation rule of XOR for $\mathbb{L}$. As a result, we can prove that the integral distinguishers found by VTDP are valid according to OTDP. To construct the automatic search model for VTDP, we introduce the definition of variant three-subset division trail. The definition of division trail to illustrate the propagation of two-subset division property is introduced in [17]. Similarly, we define the variant three-subset division trail in order to construct the automatic search model for VTDP. With this definition, the problem of searching for VDTP can be transformed to a problem of searching for a valid variant three-subset division trail.

Table 1. Results of VTDP for some ciphers

Cipher	Data	Round	Number of even/odd-parity bits	Time	Reference
SIMON32	2^{31}	14	32		[17]
		15	**3**	**27 s**	[15], Sect. 4.1
SIMON32(102)	2^{31}	20	1		[17]
		20	**3**	**25 s**	Sect. 4.1
SIMON48(102)	2^{47}	28	1		[17]
		28	**3**	**9.3 s**	Sect. 4.1
SIMON64(102)	2^{63}	36	1		[17]
		36	**3**	**1.1 h**	Sect. 4.1
KATAN/KTANTAN32	2^{31}	99	1		[9]
		101	**1**	**5.6 h**	Sect. 4.4
KATAN/KTANTAN48	2^{47}	63.5	1		[9]
		64	**1**	**16 h**	Sect. 4.4
KATAN/KTANTAN64	2^{63}	72.3	1		[9]
		72.3	**2**	**18 h**	Sect. 4.4
SPECK32	2^{31}	6	1		[11]
		6	**2**	**3.5 m**	Sect. 4.2

Models of Key-Independent Components for $\mathbb{L}$. To search for VTDP, we should build the models for propagation for $\mathbb{K}$ and $\mathbb{L}$. For $\mathbb{K}$, the models are the same as those in the two-subset division property [11,17], which can be referred directly. However, we should construct the models of all kinds of operations for $\mathbb{L}$. We first give a variant propagation rule of XOR for $\mathbb{L}$ and construct the automatic search models for common component such as Copy, AND and XOR. Then, to make our models more general, we consider Modular Addition and S-box also.

Model for Key-XOR. The difficult problem in constructing the models for VTDP is how to update the set $\mathbb{K}$ with the set $\mathbb{L}$ when a Key-XOR operation is applied to the state. By introducing the logical OR operation in STP, which is a simple but efficient solver for the theory of quantifier-free bit vectors, we succeed to solve this difficult problem. Thus, we can give a model for Key-XOR based on STP.

1.1.2 Applications

We apply our model to search for integral distinguishers of SIMON [1], SIMECK [18], SIMON(102) [7], SPECK [1], KATAN/KTANTAN [4]. The results are shown in Table 1. Note our model are also suitable to the ciphers with larger size and the S-box based ciphers but no better results can be obtained.

1.2   Organization of the Paper

We briefly recall some background knowledge about the bit-based division property in Sect. 2. In Sect. 3, we introduce VTDP and construct the whole automatic search model for it. We show some applications of our model in Sect. 4. At last, we conclude the paper in Sect. 5.

2   Preliminaries

2.1   Bit-Based Division Property

At Eurocrypt'15, the division property, a generalization of the integral property, was proposed [12], where better integral distinguishers for word-oriented cryptographic primitives have been detected. Later, Todo and Morii introduced the bit-based division property [15] where the propagation of integral characteristic can be described in a more dedicated manner for the concrete structures of the target primitives. As a result, more rounds of integral characteristics have been found with this new technique. For example, the integral distinguishers of SIMON32 have been improved from 10-round to 15-round.

Bit-based division property traces the propagation of vectors $u \in \mathbb{F}_2^n$ according to the parity of $\pi_u(x)$ for all x, where $\pi_u(x)$ is a polynomial $\pi_u(x) = \Pi_i x_i^{u_i}$ and x_i, u_i are the i-th bit of vector u and v. For the traditional bit-based division property, only two cases are considered where u can be classified into two sets according to that the parity of $\pi_u(x)$ is even or unknown. In this paper, we name it as *two-subset bit-based division property*.

Definition 1 (Two-Subset Bit-Based Division Property [15]). *Let $\mathbb{X}$ be a multiset whose elements take a value of $\mathbb{F}_2^n$. Let $\mathbb{K}$ be a set whose elements take an n-dimensional bit vector. When the multiset $\mathbb{X}$ has the division property $\mathcal{D}_{\mathbb{K}}^{1^n}$, it fulfils the following conditions:*

$$\bigoplus_{x \in \mathbb{X}} \pi_u(x) = \begin{cases} unknown, & \text{if there exist } k \in \mathbb{K} \text{ s.t. } u \succeq k, \\ 0, & \text{otherwise,} \end{cases}$$

where $u \succeq k$ if $u_i \geqslant k_i$ for all i.

The two-subset bit-based division property uses the set $\mathbb{K}$ to represent the subset of u such that the parity of $\pi_u(x)$ is unknown. According to [15], the two-subset bit-based division property is insufficient to find more accurate integral characteristic because it cannot exploit the fact that the parity of $\pi_u(x)$ is definitely odd. Motivated by this fact, the three-subset bit-based division property is introduced in [15].

The three-subset bit-based division property classifies u into three sets on the basis of what the parity of $\bigoplus_{x \in \mathbb{X}} \pi_u(x)$ is unknown, definitely even or odd. Therefore, the set $\mathbb{K}$ is used to represent the set of u with unknown $\bigoplus_{x \in \mathbb{X}} \pi_u(x)$, and the set $\mathbb{L}$ is used to denote the set of u with $\bigoplus_{x \in \mathbb{X}} \pi_u(x)$ equal to one.

Definition 2 (Three-Subset Bit-Based Division Property [15]). *Let* $\mathbb{X}$ *be a multiset whose elements take a value of* $\mathbb{F}_2^n$. *Let* $\mathbb{K}$ *and* $\mathbb{L}$ *be two sets whose elements take n-dimensional bit vectors. When the multiset* $\mathbb{X}$ *has the division property* $\mathcal{D}_{\mathbb{K},\mathbb{L}}^{1^n}$, *it fulfills the following conditions:*

$$\bigoplus_{x \in \mathbb{X}} \pi_u(x) = \begin{cases} unknown, & \text{if there exist } k \in \mathbb{K} \text{ s.t. } u \succeq k \\ 1, & \text{else if there is } l \in \mathbb{L} \text{ s.t. } u = l \\ 0, & \text{otherwise} \end{cases}.$$

According to [15], if there are $k \in \mathbb{K}$ and $k' \in \mathbb{K}$ satisfying $k \succeq k'$, then k is redundant. Moreover, if there are $l \in \mathbb{L}$ and $k \in \mathbb{K}$, the vector l is also redundant if $l \succeq k$. The redundant vectors in $\mathbb{K}$ and $\mathbb{L}$ will not affect the parity of $\pi_u(x)$ for any u.

Since we only focus on the bit-based division property in this paper, all notations of division property is for the bit level by default if we do not declare it.

Propagation Rules

Those for $\mathbb{K}$ are the same as those of two-subset one.

Rule 1 (Copy [15]). *Let* F *be a copy function, where the input* $(x_1, x_2, \ldots, x_m)$ *takes values of* $(\mathbb{F}_2)^n$, *and the output is calculated as* $(x_1, x_1, x_2, x_3, \ldots, x_m)$. *Let* $\mathbb{X}$ *and* $\mathbb{Y}$ *be the input and output multiset, respectively. Assume that* $\mathbb{X}$ *has* $\mathcal{D}_{\mathbb{K},\mathbb{L}}^{1^m}$, $\mathbb{Y}$ *has* $\mathcal{D}_{\mathbb{K}',\mathbb{L}'}^{1^{m+1}}$, *where* $\mathbb{K}'$ *and* $\mathbb{L}'$ *are computed as*

$$\mathbb{K}' \leftarrow \begin{cases} (0, 0, k_2, \ldots, k_m), & \text{if } k_1 = 0 \\ (1, 0, k_2, \ldots, k_m), (0, 1, k_2, \ldots, k_m), & \text{if } k_1 = 1 \end{cases},$$

$$\mathbb{L}' \leftarrow \begin{cases} (0, 0, l_2, \ldots, l_m), & \text{if } l_1 = 0 \\ (1, 0, l_2, \ldots, l_m), (0, 1, l_2, \ldots, l_m), (1, 1, l_2, \ldots, l_m), & \text{if } l_1 = 1 \end{cases}.$$

from $k \in \mathbb{K}$ *and* $l \in \mathbb{L}$, *respectively.*

Rule 2 (AND [15]). *Let* F *be a function compressed by an* AND, *where the input* $(x_1, x_2, \ldots, x_m)$ *takes values of* $(\mathbb{F}_2)^m$, *and the output is calculated as* $(x_1 \wedge x_2, x_3, \ldots, x_m)$. *Let* $\mathbb{X}$ *and* $\mathbb{Y}$ *be the input and output multiset, respectively. Assume that* $\mathbb{X}$ *has* $\mathcal{D}_{\mathbb{K},\mathbb{L}}^{1^m}$, $\mathbb{Y}$ *has* $\mathcal{D}_{\mathbb{K}',\mathbb{L}'}^{1^{m-1}}$, *where* $\mathbb{K}'$ *is computed from* $k \in \mathbb{K}$ *as*

$$\mathbb{K}' \leftarrow \left(\left\lceil \frac{k_1 + k_2}{2} \right\rceil, k_3, k_4, \ldots, k_m \right).$$

Moreover, $\mathbb{L}'$ *is computed from* $l \in \mathbb{L}$ *s.t.* $(l_1, l_2) = (0, 0)$ *or* $(1, 1)$ *as*

$$\mathbb{L}' \leftarrow \left(\left\lceil \frac{l_1 + l_2}{2} \right\rceil, l_3, l_4, \ldots, l_m \right).$$

Rule 3 (XOR [15]). *Let F be a function compressed by an XOR, where the input $(x_1, x_2, \ldots, x_m)$ takes values of $(\mathbb{F}_2)^m$, and the output is calculated as $(x_1 \oplus x_2, x_3, \ldots, x_m)$. Let $\mathbb{X}$ and $\mathbb{Y}$ be the input and output multiset, respectively. Assume that $\mathbb{X}$ has $\mathcal{D}_{\mathbb{K},\mathbb{L}}^{1^m}$, $\mathbb{Y}$ has $\mathcal{D}_{\mathbb{K}',\mathbb{L}'}^{1^{m-1}}$, where $\mathbb{K}'$ is computed from $\mathbf{k} \in \mathbb{K}$ s.t. $(k_1, k_2) = (0,0), (1,0),$ or $(0,1)$ as*

$$\mathbb{K}' \leftarrow (k_1 + k_2, k_3, k_4, \ldots, k_m).$$

Moreover, $\mathbb{L}'$ is computed from $\mathbf{l} \in \mathbb{L}$ s.t. $(l_1, l_2) = (0,0), (1,0),$ or $(0,1)$ as

$$\mathbb{L}' \xleftarrow{x} (l_1 + l_2, l_3, l_4, \ldots, l_m),$$

where $\mathbb{L} \xleftarrow{x} \mathbf{l}$ means

$$\mathbb{L} = \begin{cases} \mathbb{L} \cup \{\mathbf{l}\} & \text{if the original } \mathbb{L} \text{ does not include } \mathbf{l}, \\ \mathbb{L} \backslash \{\mathbf{l}\} & \text{if the original } \mathbb{L} \text{ includes } \mathbf{l}. \end{cases}$$

Boura *et al.* presented the propagation rules of S-box for $\mathbb{K}$ at bit-level in [3] for the first time. We summarize the technique in Rule 4.

Rule 4 (Bit-Based S-box for $\mathbb{K}$ [3]). *Let $F : \mathbb{F}_2^m \to \mathbb{F}_2^n$ be a function of substitution composed of $(f_1, f_2, \ldots, f_n)$, where the input $\mathbf{x} = (x_1, x_2, \ldots, x_m)$ takes values of $(\mathbb{F}_2)^m$, and the output $\mathbf{y} = (y_1, y_2, \ldots, y_n)$ is calculated as*

$$y_1 = f_1(x_1, x_2, \ldots, x_m),$$
$$y_2 = f_2(x_1, x_2, \ldots, x_m),$$
$$\vdots$$
$$y_n = f_n(x_1, x_2, \ldots, x_m).$$

For each vector $\mathbf{u} \in \mathbb{K}$ representing the input division property, check each vector $\mathbf{v} \in \mathbb{F}_2^n$ whether the polynomial $\pi_v(\mathbf{y})$ contains any monomial $\pi_{k'}(\mathbf{x})$ that $\mathbf{k}' \succeq \mathbf{k}$. If so, then $(\mathbf{u}, \mathbf{v})$ is a valid division trail for the S-box function.

Modular Addition is the nonlinear component of ARX ciphers. The **Modular Addition** operation can be decomposed into a series of basic operations such as **Copy**, **AND** and **XOR**. Let $\mathbf{x} = (x_0, x_1, \ldots, x_{n-1})$, $\mathbf{y} = (y_0, y_1, \ldots, y_{n-1})$ and $\mathbf{z} = (z_0, z_1, \ldots, z_{n-1})$. If $\mathbf{z} = \mathbf{x} \boxplus \mathbf{y}$, the Boolean function of z_i can be iteratively expressed as follows,

$$z_{n-1} = x_{n-1} \oplus y_{n-1} \oplus c_{n-1}, c_{n-1} = 0,$$
$$z_i = x_i \oplus y_i \oplus c_i, c_i = x_{i+1} \cdot y_{i+1} \oplus (x_{i+1} \oplus y_{i+1}) \cdot c_{i+1},$$
$$i = n - 2, n - 3, \ldots, 0.$$

With some auxiliary variables, Sun *et al.* modeled **Modular Addition** at Aisacrypt'17 in [11] as follows.

Rule 5 (ModularAddition for $\mathbb{K}$ [11]). *Let* $(a_0, a_1, \ldots, a_{n-1}, b_0, b_1, \ldots, b_{n-1},$ $d_0, d_1, \ldots, d_{n-1})$ *be a division trail of n-bit* Modular Addition *operation, to describe the division property propagation, the* Copy, AND *and* XOR *models should be applied in a specific order.*

Rule 6 (Key − XOR). *Assuming F is a component of* Key-XOR, $(\mathbb{K}, \mathbb{L})$ *and* $(\mathbb{K}', \mathbb{L}')$ *are the input and output division property, respectively. According to [15], the propagation is as follows,*

$$\mathbb{L}' \leftarrow l, \text{ for } l \in \mathbb{L},$$
$$\mathbb{K}' \leftarrow k, \text{ for } k \in \mathbb{K},$$
$$\mathbb{K}' \leftarrow (l_1, l_2, \ldots l_i \vee 1, \ldots, l_m), \text{ for } l \in \mathbb{L} \text{ satisfying } l_i = 0, 1 \leqslant i \leqslant m.$$

2.2 Automatic Search for Bit-Based Division Property

As pointed in [15], the time and memory complexities for bit-based division property are upper-bounded by 2^n, where n denotes the block length. Therefore, the bit-based division property was just applied to SIMON32 and SIMECK32 in [15].

Recently, the techniques of automatic search for distinguishers have developed a lot. Automatic search can trace the transitions of sets in an efficient way. The propagation of vectors can be modeled by a serial of constrained optimization or decision statements. The technique has been used to find better differential and linear characteristics. Especially, it is very efficient to search for the division property.

Xiang *et al.* transformed the problem of finding two-subset division property into an MILP problem for the first time [17]. With the help of MILP solver Gurobi, they can find division property for ciphers with large block sizes, e.g., SIMON128 or PRESENT. To search for two-subset bit-based division property, they introduced the definition of two-subset division trail.

Definition 3 (Two-Subset Division Trail [17]). *Let us consider the propagation of the division property* $\{k\} \stackrel{def}{=} \mathbb{K}_0 \to \mathbb{K}_1 \to \ldots \to \mathbb{K}_r$. *Moreover, for any vector* $k^*_{i+1} \in \mathbb{K}_{i+1}$, *there must exit a vector* $k^*_i \in \mathbb{K}_i$ *such that* k^*_i *can propagate to* k^*_{i+1} *by the propagation rules of the division property. Furthermore, for* $(k_0, k_1, \ldots, k_r) \in \mathbb{K}_0 \times \mathbb{K}_1 \times \ldots \times \mathbb{K}_r$ *if* k_i *can propagate to* k_{i+1} *for all* $i \in \{0, 1, \ldots, r-1\}$, *we call* $(k_0 \to k_1 \to \ldots \to k_r)$ *an r-round division trail.*

2.2.1 Models of Propagation with SMT/SAT

Since we will use STP solver to implement our model, we introduce the SMT/SAT models for $\mathbb{K}$ describing the basic components Copy, AND, XOR and complex components Modular Addition according to Rule 5.

Model 1 (Bit-Based Copy for $\mathbb{K}$ [11]). *Denote* $(a) \xrightarrow{Copy} (b_0, b_1)$ *a division trail of* Copy *operation, the following logical equations are sufficient to depict the propagation of bit-based division trail,*

$$\begin{cases} \bar{b}_0 \vee \bar{b}_1 = 1 \\ a \vee b_0 \vee \bar{b}_1 = 1 \\ a \vee \bar{b}_0 \vee b_1 = 1 \\ \bar{a} \vee b_0 \vee b_1 = 1 \end{cases}.$$

Model 2 (Bit-Based XOR for $\mathbb{K}$ [11]). *Denote* $(a_0, a_1) \xrightarrow{XOR} (b)$ *a division trail of XOR function, the following logical equations are sufficient to evaluate the bit-based division trail through XOR operation,*

$$\begin{cases} \bar{a}_0 \vee \bar{a}_1 = 1 \\ a_0 \vee a_1 \vee \bar{b} = 1 \\ a_0 \vee \bar{a}_1 \vee b = 1 \\ \bar{a}_0 \vee a_1 \vee b = 1 \end{cases}.$$

Model 3 (Bit-Based AND for $\mathbb{K}$ [11]). *Denote* $(a_0, a_1) \xrightarrow{AND} (b)$ *a division trail of AND function, the following logical equations are sufficient to evaluate the bit-based division trail through AND operation,*

$$\begin{cases} \bar{a}_1 \vee b = 1 \\ a_0 \vee a_1 \vee \bar{b} = 1 \\ \bar{a}_0 \vee b = 1 \end{cases}.$$

Model 4 (Bit-Based ModularAddition for $\mathbb{K}$ [11]). *According to Rule 5, we can use the models of basic operations Copy, AND and XOR and some auxiliary variables to implement the Modular Addition.*

2.2.2 Initial and Stopping Rules of Two-Subset Division Property

An MILP or SMT/SAT model to search for two-subset bit-based division property needs to set proper initial and stopping rules, i.e., assign values to the initial and output variables in the division trail.

Assume that $(a_0^0, a_1^0, \ldots, a_{n-1}^0) \rightarrow \ldots \rightarrow (a_0^r, a_1^r, \ldots, a_{n-1}^r)$ is an r-round division trail for an n-bit length cipher. Let $\mathcal{D}_k^{1^n}$ denote the initial division property with $\mathbf{k} = (k_0, k_1, \ldots, k_{n-1})$, and then we append the following constraints to the search model,

$$a_i^0 = k_i, \ i = 0, 1, 2, \cdots, n - 1.$$

To check whether the i_0-th ($0 \leqslant i_0 \leqslant n - 1$) output bit is balanced or not, we just add constraints on a_i^r ($i = 0, 1, \ldots, n - 1$) that

$$a_i^r = \begin{cases} 1, & if \ i = i_0, \\ 0, & else. \end{cases}$$

If there is a division trail, the i_0-th output bit is decided as unknown; otherwise, the i_0-th output bit is balanced.

3   Search for Variant Three-Subset Division Property

3.1   Variant of Three-Subset Division Property

Firstly, we introduce a compromising propagation rule of XOR for $\mathbb{L}$ for VTDP as follows,

Rule 7 (Variant XOR). *Let F be a function compressed by an XOR, where the input $(x_1, x_2, \ldots, x_m)$ takes values of $(\mathbb{F}_2)^m$, and the output is calculated as $(x_1 \oplus x_2, x_3, \ldots, x_m)$. Let $\mathbb{X}$ and $\mathbb{Y}$ be the input and output multiset, respectively. Assuming that $\mathbb{X}$ has $\mathcal{D}_{\mathbb{K},\mathbb{L}}^{1^m}$, $\mathbb{Y}$ has $\mathcal{D}_{\mathbb{K}',\mathbb{L}'}^{1^{m-1}}$, where $\mathbb{K}'$ is computed from $\mathbf{k} \in \mathbb{K}$ s.t. $(k_1, k_2) = (0,0), (1,0),$ or $(0,1)$ as*

$$\mathbb{K}' \leftarrow (k_1 + k_2, k_3, k_4, \ldots, k_m).$$

Moreover, $\mathbb{L}'$ is computed from $\boldsymbol{l} \in \mathbb{L}$ s.t. $(l_1, l_2) = (0,0), (1,0),$ or $(0,1)$ as

$$\mathbb{L}' \leftarrow (l_1 + l_2, l_3, l_4, \ldots, l_m),$$

In VTDP, we do not remove the duplicated vectors which appear even number of times in $\mathbb{L}$, and there are no other differences between VTDP and OTDP.

In VTDP, some duplicated vectors which appear even times will further generate some unexpected vectors in $\mathbb{L}$ and $\mathbb{K}$ by Key-XOR. As a result, there are many unexpected division trails in $\mathbb{K}$ and $\mathbb{L}$. Note that these extra trails will not change the original division trails inherited from OTDP if we do not remove the redundant vectors. Let $\mathbb{K}_V$ and $\mathbb{L}_V$ be the set containing all the division trails from all the duplicated vectors which appears even times and $\mathbb{K}_O$ and $\mathbb{L}_O$ be the set containing all the division trails which are from the OTDP. The following proposition describes the relationships between VTDP and OTDP.

Proposition 1. *Regarding one fixed bit of ciphertext, the VTDP will determine the parity of this bit by checking the vectors in $\mathbb{K}$ and $\mathbb{L}$ after r-round encryption. Compared with the results from OTDP, those from VTDP satisfy the following three properties.*

1. *If VTDP indicates that the parity of the bit is not unknown (even or odd), the parity of this bit is not unknown, too, according to OTDP.*
2. *If VTDP indicates that the parity of the bit is even, the parity of this bit is really even.*
3. *If VTDP indicates that the parity of the bit is odd, the parity of this bit will be constant.*

The proof is provided in the full version of this paper. According to Proposition 1, we can illustrate the relationship between VTDP and OTDP by Fig. 1. In Fig. 1, the colors represent the results based on OTDP while the line patterns stand for those based on VTDP. If one bit is determined as an odd-parity bit, we can know the bit is definitely not unknown. Therefore, we can still obtain some useful information from these results. In practice, we can encrypt all possible plaintexts by traversing all active plaintext bits under a random key, and Xor all the corresponding considered ciphertext bits to determine the parity of the considered ciphertext bits. This parity result holds for any key, which can be applied to attack the target cipher with any key. In other words, with our searching result, the test for only one key can achieve the available integral distinguisher for any key. Thus, our searching result is significant for attack. It is reasonable to encrypt the plaintexts because we need all the details of the cipher structure except the key-schedule to construct the model to search for VTDP. Note that the requirement also lies in the algorithm to search for OTDP [15].

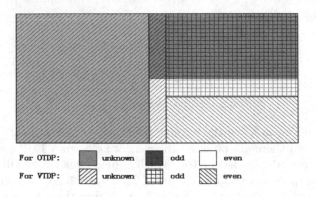

Fig. 1. Relationship between VTDP and OTDP.

3.2   Variant Three-Subset Division Trail

To model the automatic search for VTDP, we introduce the variant three-subset division trail.

Definition 4 (Variant Three-Subset Division Trial). *Let us consider the propagation of the division property* $\{(k, l)\} \overset{def}{=} \mathbb{K}_0 \times \mathbb{L}_0 \to \mathbb{K}_1 \times \mathbb{L}_1 \to \cdots \to \mathbb{K}_r \times \mathbb{L}_r$. *Moreover, for any vector tuple* (k_{i+1}^*, l_{i+1}^*), $k_{i+1}^* \in \mathbb{K}_{i+1}$ *and* $l_{i+1}^* \in \mathbb{L}_{i+1}$, *there must exit a vector tuple* (k_i^*, l_i^*), $k_i^* \in \mathbb{K}_i$ *and* $l_i^* \in \mathbb{L}_i$, *such that* (k_i^*, l_i^*) *can propagate to* (k_{i+1}^*, l_{i+1}^*) *by the propagation rules of the division property for* $i = 0, 1, \ldots, r - 1$. *Furthermore, for* $((k_0, l_0), (k_1, l_1), \ldots, (k_r, l_r)) \in \mathbb{K}_0 \times \mathbb{L}_0 \times \mathbb{K}_1 \times \mathbb{L}_1 \times \cdots \times \mathbb{K}_r \times \mathbb{L}_r$, *if* (k_i, l_i) *can propagate to* (k_{i+1}, l_{k+1}) *for all* $i \in \{0, 1, \ldots, r - 1\}$, *we call* $(k_0, l_0) \to (k_1, l_1) \to \cdots \to (k_r, l_r)$ *an r-round variant three-subset division trail.*

Similar to methods in [17], we decide the parity of one output bit by checking whether certain division trails exist. Therefore, we need to transform the propagation rules of each component into constraints and solve the problem by an MILP or SMT/SAT tool. We divide all components into key-independent and key-dependent components according to whether there are secret keys involved.

For key-independent components, we construct the models of Copy, AND, XOR and Modular Addition operations for $\mathbb{L}$ according to Rule 1, 2, 5 and 7. Since there is no rule of S-box for $\mathbb{L}$, we give the rule and then model the S-box in Sect. 3.3 for the first time.

For key-dependent components, we concentrate only on the Key-XOR operation. We introduce a new technique that we can use the logical OR operation of STP solver to model the dependencies between $\mathbb{K}$ and $\mathbb{L}$ when a Key-XOR component is applied.

Note 1. Since redundant vectors do not affect the result of $\bigoplus_{x \in \mathbb{X}} \pi_u(x)$, our model will not remove them.

3.3 Models of VTDP for Key-Independent Components

Assuming that f is a key-independent component of a cipher, $(\mathbb{K}, \mathbb{L})$ and $(\mathbb{K}', \mathbb{L}')$ are the input and output division property of f, respectively. In our automatic search model, we allocate variables to represent the vectors in $\mathbb{K}$, $\mathbb{L}$, $\mathbb{K}'$ and $\mathbb{L}'$ at the bit level at first and then the constraints are added on these variables according to the propagation rule of f. Note that the propagations of $\mathbb{K} \xrightarrow{f} \mathbb{K}'$ and $\mathbb{L} \xrightarrow{f} \mathbb{L}'$ are conducted separately according to their own rules.

In this paper, we use STP solver to implement our model. STP is a simple but efficient solver for the theory of quantifier-free bit vectors. It is first introduced to find optimal differential characteristic by Mouha and Preneel [8]. At Asiacrypt'17, Sun et al. took it to search for division property [11]. We can describe the propagation rules in CNF formulas using the method proposed in [11]. The automatic search models for $\mathbb{K}$ has been listed in Sect. 2.1. We construct models for the basic operations Copy, AND, XOR and Modular Addition for $\mathbb{L}$ in a similar way.

For Copy operation, let a, b_0 and b_1 be three binary variables and $(a) \xrightarrow{\text{Copy}} (b_0, b_1)$ be the division trail. There are four possible division trails according to Rule 1, which are $(0) \rightarrow (0,0)$, $(1) \rightarrow (0,1)$, $(1) \rightarrow (1,0)$ and $(1) \rightarrow (1,1)$. To make (a, b_0, b_1) follow these four division trails only we put constraints on a, b_0 and b_1 as follows.

Model 5 (Bit-Based Copy for $\mathbb{L}$). *Denote (a, b_0, b_1) a division trail of Copy function, the following logical equations are sufficient to evaluate the bit-based division trail through Copy operation,*

$$\begin{cases} a \vee b_0 \vee \bar{b}_1 = 1 \\ \bar{a} \vee b_0 \vee b_1 = 1 \, . \\ a \vee \bar{b}_0 = 1 \end{cases}$$

For AND operation, let a_0, a_1 and b be three binary variables and $(a_0, a_1) \xrightarrow{\text{AND}} (b)$ be the division trail. There are two possible division trails according to Rule 2, which are $(0,0) \rightarrow (0)$ and $(1,1) \rightarrow (1)$, To make (a_0, a_1, b) follow these two division trails only we add constrains on a_0, a_1 and b as follows.

Model 6 (Bit-Based AND for $\mathbb{L}$). *Denote* (a_0, a_1, b) *a division trail of AND function, the following logical equations are sufficient to evaluate the bit-based division trail trough AND operation,*

$$\begin{cases} a_0 = b \\ a_1 = b \end{cases}.$$

For XOR operation, we follow the Rule 7 rather than Rule 3, let a_0, a_1 and b be three binary variables and $(a_0, a_1) \xrightarrow{\text{XOR}} (b)$ be the division trail. There are three possible division trails according to Rule 7, which are $(0,0) \to (0)$, $(0,1) \to (1)$ and $(1,0) \to (1)$. To make (a_0, a_1, b) follow these three division trails only we append constraints on a_0, a_1 and b as follows.

Model 7 (Bit-Based Variant XOR for $\mathbb{L}$). *Denote* (a_0, a_1, b) *a division trail of XOR function, the following logical equations are sufficient to evaluate the bit-based division trail trough XOR operation,*

$$\begin{cases} a_0 \vee a_1 \vee \bar{b} = 1 \\ \bar{a}_1 \vee b = 1 \\ \bar{a}_0 \vee a_1 \vee b = 1 \\ \bar{a}_0 \vee \bar{a}_1 \vee \bar{b} = 1 \end{cases}.$$

Model 8 (Bit-Based ModularAddition for $\mathbb{L}$). *The model of Modular Addition for $\mathbb{L}$ is totally same with that for $\mathbb{K}$ except that we use basic models of Copy, AND and variant XOR for $\mathbb{L}$ rather than $\mathbb{K}$.*

Modeling S-box for $\mathbb{L}$

The rule to calculate all the division trails of an S-box for $\mathbb{K}$ was presented in [3,17]. Here we introduce the rules to find all the division trails for $\mathbb{L}$.

Let $F : (\mathbb{F}_2)^m \to (\mathbb{F}_2)^n$ be a function of substitution composed of $(f_1, f_2, \ldots, f_n)$, where the input $\boldsymbol{x} = (x_1, x_2, \ldots, x_m)$ takes values of $(\mathbb{F}_2)^m$, and the output $\boldsymbol{y} = (y_1, y_2, \ldots, y_n)$ is calculated as

$$y_1 = f_1(x_1, x_2, \ldots, x_m),$$
$$y_2 = f_2(x_1, x_2, \ldots, x_m),$$
$$\vdots$$
$$y_n = f_n(x_1, x_2, \ldots, x_m).$$

Similar to Rule 4, for each input vector $\boldsymbol{u} \in \mathbb{L}$, we consider each output vector $\boldsymbol{v} \in \mathbb{F}_2^n$ seperately to derive all the valid division trails. According to Definition 2, for each vector $\boldsymbol{v} \in \mathbb{F}_2^n$, $(\boldsymbol{u}, \boldsymbol{v})$ is a valid division trail if the polynomial $\pi_{\boldsymbol{v}}(\boldsymbol{y})$ contains the monomial $\pi_{\boldsymbol{u}}(\boldsymbol{x})$ but does not contain the monomial $\pi_{\boldsymbol{u}'}(\boldsymbol{x})$ for any $\boldsymbol{u}'$ satisfying $\boldsymbol{u}' \succ \boldsymbol{u}$.

Algorithm 1. Calculating Division Trails of S-box for $\mathbb{L}$

Input: a vector u representing the input division property
Output: A set $\mathbb{L}$ of vectors representing the output division property

1 $\bar{\mathbb{S}} = \{\bar{u}|\bar{u} \succ u\}$;
2 $F(X) = \{\pi_{\bar{u}}(x)|\bar{u} \in \bar{\mathbb{S}}\}$;
3 $Allocate \mathbb{L} = \varnothing$;
4 **for** *each* $v \in \mathbb{F}_2^n$ **do**
5 $\quad$ **if** $\pi_v(y)$ *does not contain any monomial in* $F(X)$ *and* $\pi_v(y)$ *contains*
   $\quad\quad \pi_u(x)$ **then**
6 $\quad\quad$ $\lfloor$ $\mathbb{L} \leftarrow v$;

7 **return** $\mathbb{L}$;

We give Algorithm 1 to calculate all the valid division trails of S-box for $\mathbb{L}$.

To implement the model for S-box, firstly we use Algorithm 1 to compute all the division trails. Then we need to describe these trails in STP solver. We define an array variable to store all the trails and then use this array to add constraints on the variables representing the input and output division property[1].

3.4   Model of VTDP for Key-XOR

For Key-XOR operation f_k, the input and output division properties are $\{\mathbb{K}, \mathbb{L}\}$ and $\{\mathbb{K}', \mathbb{L}'\}$, respectively. In our model, we use four n-bit variables $\mathcal{K}, \mathcal{L}, \mathcal{K}'$ and $\mathcal{L}'$ to denote them, where n is the block size. Because the dependencies between $\mathbb{K}$ and $\mathbb{L}$ work on the block rather than a single bit, we use n-bit variables rather than binary variables.

According to Rule 6, f_k does not affect the propagation from $\mathbb{L}$ to $\mathbb{L}'$. Therefore, the constraint on $\mathcal{L}$ and $\mathcal{L}'$ is $\mathcal{L}' = \mathcal{L}$.

In many ciphers, round key is only XORed with a part of block. Without loss of generality, we assume that the round key is XORed with the left s $(1 \leqslant s \leqslant n)$ bits. This operation can be divided into two steps.

1. Allocate n-bit variables $\mathcal{V}_j$ $(j \in \{0, 1, 2, \ldots, s-1\})$. Check each bit of $\mathcal{L}$, i.e., $\mathcal{L}[0], \mathcal{L}[1], \ldots, \mathcal{L}[s-1]$, and assign $\mathcal{V}_j$ as follows,

$$\mathcal{V}_j = \begin{cases} \mathcal{L} \vee e_j, & \text{if } \mathcal{L}[j] = 0, \\ 1, & otherwise, \end{cases}$$

where e_j is an n-bit unit vector whose bit j is one and $\mathbf{1}$ is the vector with all components one. If $\mathcal{L}[j] \neq 0$, we set $\mathcal{V}_j$ as $\mathbf{1}$ because we use the STP statement IF-THEN-ELSE to implement it, which follows a strict grammar. Note that $\mathbf{1}$ has no effect on the search results.

2. Let $\{\mathcal{K}'\} = \{\mathcal{K}\} \cup \{\mathcal{V}_0\} \cup \{\mathcal{V}_1\} \cup \cdots \cup \{\mathcal{V}_{s-1}\}$.

---

[1] We can implement the model of S-box using the exclusion method as those of Copy, AND and XOR, also.

In STP solver, we can implement the first step with an IF-THEN-ELSE branch statement as follows,

ASSERT $\mathcal{L}^j$ = IF $\mathcal{L}[j] = 0$ THEN $\mathcal{L} \vee e_j$ ELSE 1 ENDIF;

For the second step, we use the following statement with the logical OR operation in STP to implement,

ASSERT $\mathcal{K}' = \mathcal{K}$ OR $\mathcal{K}' = \mathcal{V}_0$ OR $\mathcal{K}' = \mathcal{V}_1$ OR ... OR $\mathcal{K}' = \mathcal{V}_{s-1}$;

Algorithm 2 concludes the model of the Key-XOR operation.

Algorithm 2. Generating Constraints of Propagation Rule of Key-XOR

Input: n-bit variables $\mathcal{K}, \mathcal{K}', \mathcal{L}, \mathcal{L}'$.
Output: A set $\mathbb{C}$ with constraints on $\mathcal{K}, \mathcal{K}', \mathcal{L}, \mathcal{L}'$.
1 Allocate $\mathbb{C}$ as $\varnothing$;
2 $\mathbb{C} \leftarrow \mathcal{L}' = \mathcal{L}$;
3 Allocate n-bit variables $\mathcal{V}_j$ $(j = 0, 1, \ldots, s-1)$;
4 **for** $j = 0; j < s; j = j + 1$ **do**
5 $\quad$ **if** $\mathcal{L}[j] == 0$ **then**
6 $\qquad \lfloor \mathbb{C} \leftarrow \mathcal{V}_j = \mathcal{L} \vee e_j$;
7 $\quad$ **else**
8 $\qquad \lfloor \mathbb{C} \leftarrow \mathcal{V}_j = 1$;

9 $\mathbb{C} \leftarrow \mathcal{K}' = \mathcal{K}$ OR $\mathcal{K}' = \mathcal{V}_0$ OR $\mathcal{K}' = \mathcal{V}_1$ OR $\cdots$ OR $\mathcal{K}' = \mathcal{V}_{s-1}$;
10 **return** $\mathbb{C}$;

Note 2. We just know that the STP solver supports the logical OR operation, so our model relies on it. However, any tool that can implement the two steps is suitable to our algorithm also.

3.5   Initial and Stopping Rules for VTDP

Initial Rule

In [15], to search for three-subset division property, Todo and Morii set the initial division property as $(k = 1, l)$, where the active bits of l are set as one or zero for constant bits. It is the same for VTDP. For example, if we find integral characteristic for SIMON32 using 2^{31} chosen-plaintexts with first bit constant, the initial division property is then set as $(k = 1, l = \text{7fffffff})$. Let $((\mathcal{K}_0^0, \mathcal{K}_1^0, \ldots, \mathcal{K}_{n-1}^0), (\mathcal{L}_0^0, \mathcal{L}_1^0, \ldots, \mathcal{L}_{n-1}^0))$ denote the initial division property, where n is the block size. The constraints on $\mathcal{K}_i^0$ and $\mathcal{L}_i^0$ are

$$\mathcal{K}_i^0 = 1, \text{for } i = 0, 1, 2, \ldots, n-1.$$

$$\mathcal{L}_i^0 = \begin{cases} 1, & \text{if the } i\text{-th bit is active,} \\ 0, & \text{otherwise.} \end{cases}$$

Stopping Rule

Our automatic search model only focuses on the parity of one output bit. Without loss of generality, we consider the i_0-th output bit. According to Definition 2, the first step is to examine whether there is a unit vector $e_{i_0} \in \mathbb{K}$ for the r-th round, so we only need to set the constraints on $(\mathcal{K}_0^r, \mathcal{K}_1^r, \ldots, \mathcal{K}_{n-1}^r)$ as follows,

$$\mathcal{K}_i^r = \begin{cases} 1, & \text{if } i = i_0, \\ 0, & \text{otherwise.} \end{cases}$$

If the constraint problem has solutions, the i_0-th bit is unknown, and our algorithm stops. Otherwise, we need to remove the constraints on $\mathcal{K}_i^r$ ($0 \leqslant i \leqslant n-1$) and add the following constraints on $(\mathcal{L}_0^r, \mathcal{L}_1^r, \ldots, \mathcal{L}_{n-1}^r)$,

$$\mathcal{L}_i^r = \begin{cases} 1, & \text{if } i = i_0, \\ 0, & \text{otherwise.} \end{cases}$$

If there is still no solution, the i_0-th bit is balanced, otherwise the parity of the i_0-th bit is even or odd.

3.6 Connection Between Key-Independent and Key-XOR Components

Note that we use bit-level variables to model the key-independent components in Sect. 3.3, but the implementations for key-XOR are based on n-bit variables. Therefore, in order to connect bit variables and n-bit variables, the concatenation operation "@" in STP is used to link them. Let the bit variables $(\mathcal{L}_0, \mathcal{L}_1, \ldots, \mathcal{L}_{n-1})$ denote the output division property for $\mathbb{L}$ of a key-independent component, whose following operation is Key-XOR with input division property $\mathcal{L}' \in \mathbb{F}_2^n$. The link constraint on them is

$$\text{ASSERT } \mathcal{L}' = \mathcal{L}_0 @ \mathcal{L}_1 @ \ldots @ \mathcal{L}_{n-1};$$

Conversely, if $\mathcal{L}'$ is the output of Key-XOR while $(\mathcal{L}_0, \mathcal{L}_1, \ldots, \mathcal{L}_{n-1})$ are the input of next key-independent component, we use the statement above, too.

4 Applications

In this section, we apply our model to SIMON, SIMECK, SIMON(102), SPECK, PRESENT and KATAN/KTANTAN. All our experiments are implemented on a server with 48 Intel(R) Xeon(R) CPU E5-2670 v3 @ 2.30 GHz and 96 GB memory. And some of the programs run in a parallel way as long as the memory is enough. In our illustrations, the character '?' represents unknown, '*' represents even or odd and '0' stands for even. All the programs for these algorithms are public in website https://github.com/VTDP/submission_for_ctrsa/.

4.1 VTDP of SIMON-Like Ciphers

SIMON [1] is a family of lightweight block ciphers published by the U.S. National Security Agency (NSA) in 2013. SIMON adopts Feistel structure and it has a very compact round function which only involves bit-wise And, XOR and Circular Shift. According to the block size, SIMON family is composed of SIMON32, SIMON48, SIMON64, SIMON96, SIMON128.

For SIMON32, we identify a 15-round integral characteristic which is as follows,

$$(\texttt{7fff,ffff}) \xrightarrow{14r} (\texttt{????,????,????,????,?*??,????,*???,???*}).$$

Then we can encrypt the corresponding 2^{31} chosen-plaintexts and determine the three bits represented by '*' are all even, which is the same result as that in [15]. However, our automatic algorithm takes about 27 s which is much more efficient than that in [15]. Unfortunately, the results for SIMON48/64/96/128 with VTDP have no improvements compared with the previous distinguishers.

SIMECK is a family of lightweight block cipher proposed at CHES'15 [18]. The round function of SIMECK is very like SIMON except the rotation constants. We apply our automatic search algorithm to 15-, 18- and 21-round SIMECK32/48/64, respectively. All the integral characteristics from our algorithm are the same as those found by Xiang *et al.*

In [7], another variant of SIMON family named SIMON(102) is proposed with rotation constants (1, 0, 2).

For 20-round SIMON32(102), we find the following improved integral distinguisher

$$(\texttt{7fff,ffff}) \xrightarrow{19r} (\texttt{????,????,????,????,0*??,????,????,???*}),$$

which has two additional odd or even parity bits compared with the previous best results,

$$(\texttt{7fff,ffff}) \xrightarrow{19r} (\texttt{????,????,????,????,0???,????,????,????}).$$

Similarly, for 28-round SIMON48(102) and 35-round SIMON64(102), a new distinguisher with two extra odd or even parity bits have been found, respectively.

$$(\texttt{7fff,ffff,ffff}) \xrightarrow{27r}$$
$$(\texttt{????,????,????,????,????,????,0*??,????,????,????,???*}).$$

$$(\texttt{7fff,ffff,ffff,ffff}) \xrightarrow{35r}$$
$$(\texttt{????,????,????,????,????,????,????,????,\ 0*??,????,????,????,????,????,????,???*}).$$

4.2 VTDP of ARX Cipher SPECK

SPECK [1] is a family of lightweight block ciphers published by NSA, too. Different from SIMON, SPECK takes the Modular Addition as its nonlinear operation. According to the block size, SPECK family has 5 members, SPECK32,

SPECK48, SPECK64, SPECK96 and SPECK128. shift by i bits and $\boxplus$ represents the Modular Addition operation.

For SPECK32, there only exists one two-subset bit-based integral distinguisher for 6 rounds with 2^{31} chosen-plaintexts as follows,

$$(\texttt{ffff},\texttt{ffdf}) \xrightarrow{6r} (\texttt{????},\texttt{????},\texttt{????},\texttt{???0},\texttt{????},\texttt{????},\texttt{????},\texttt{????}).$$

However, based on VTDP, we can find one more distinguisher besides the above one,

$$(\texttt{ffff},\texttt{ffbf}) \xrightarrow{6r} (\texttt{????},\texttt{????},\texttt{????},\texttt{???*},\texttt{????},\texttt{????},\texttt{????},\texttt{????}).$$

4.3 VTDP of S-Box Based Cipher PRESENT

PRESENT [2] is an SP-network block cipher, of which the linear layers are bit permutations.

In [17], Xiang et al. found a 9-round integral distinguisher with 2^{60} chosen-plaintexts under the two-subset division property framework. Our algorithm achieves the same result. Furthermore, If we use more data complexity such as 2^{63} chosen-plaintexts with the leftmost 63 bits active, we find a new distinguisher with 28 balanced bits which is listed as follows,

$$(\texttt{ffff},\texttt{ffff},\texttt{ffff},\texttt{fffe}) \xrightarrow{9r}$$
$$(\texttt{???0},\texttt{???0},\texttt{???0},\texttt{0000},\texttt{???0},\texttt{???0},\texttt{???0},\texttt{0000},\texttt{???0},\texttt{???0},\texttt{???0},\texttt{0000},\texttt{???0},\texttt{???0},\texttt{???0},\texttt{0000}).$$

Note that this distinguisher can be found by Xiang et al.'s model.

4.4 VTDP of KATAN/KTANTAN Family

KATAN and KTANTAN [4] are two families of hardware oriented block ciphers and have three variants of 32-bit, 48-bit, 64-bit block. KATAN/KTANTAN takes a very simple structure composed of two LFSR's.

KATAN/KTANTAN32, 48, 64 conduct the round function once, twice and three times in one round with the same round key, respectively. The only difference between KATAN and KTANTAN is the key schedule.

Compared with the previous results [9], we obtained the longer integral distinguishers for KATAN/KTANTAN32 and 48 with our automatic algorithm for VTDP. Moreover, our identified integral characteristic for $72\frac{1}{3}$-round KATAN/KTANTAN64 has two more balanced bits.

For KATAN/KTANTAN32, Sun et al. found the following 99-round integral characteristic with the two-subset division property [9],

$$(\texttt{fffb},\texttt{ffff}) \xrightarrow{99r} (\texttt{????},\texttt{????},\texttt{????},\texttt{????},\texttt{????},\texttt{????},\texttt{????},\texttt{???0}).$$

However, our new distinguishers based on VTDP are listed as follows,

$$(\texttt{fffb}, \texttt{ffff}) \xrightarrow{100r} (????,????,????,????,????,????,????,??*0),$$

$$(\texttt{fffb}, \texttt{ffff}) \xrightarrow{101r} (????,????,????,????,????,????,????,???*).$$

For 64- and $72\frac{1}{2}$-round KATAN/KTANTAN48 and KATAN/KTANTAN64, respectively, the search program requires too much time to get VTDP. Therefore, we introduce a compromising strategy to simplify some propagation of vectors. For two-subset division property, we only trace $\mathbb{K}$, but for three-subset division property, $\mathbb{K}$ and $\mathbb{L}$ are considered. In general, the program of two-subset division property will take less time than that of the three-subset one. In our program, we can trace $\mathbb{K}$ and $\mathbb{L}$ for the first N rounds only; and append $\boldsymbol{u}$ to $\mathbb{K}$ for all $\boldsymbol{u} \in \mathbb{L}$ at the N-th round; then trace the modified $\mathbb{K}$ merely. Since after N rounds, the program becomes a two-subset division property, the stopping rules should follow that of the two-subset division property.

With the compromising strategy, we still find better integral distinguishers for KATAN/KTANTAN48 and 64 than those in [9].

For 64-round KATAN/KTANTAN48, the distinguisher we found is presented as follows ($N = 100$),

$$(\texttt{ffff}, \texttt{efff}, \texttt{ffff}) \xrightarrow{64r}$$
$$(????,????,????,????,????,????,????,????,????,????,???0),$$

which covers half more round than that in [9]. For KATAN/KTANTAN64, we find the same length of integral distinguisher with the previous best one [9] but ours has one more balanced bit as follows ($N = 50$),

$$(\texttt{ffff}, \texttt{ffbf}, \texttt{ffff}, \texttt{ffff}) \xrightarrow{72.3r}$$
$$(????,????,????,????,????,????,????,????,????,????,????,????,????,????,??00).$$

5   Conclusions

In this paper, we proposed an automatic search model for a variant of three-subset division property and it can be applied to ciphers with large block sizes. Furthermore, we give the rules of S-box and Modular Addition for $\mathbb{L}$, which extend the usage of three-subset division property. With this model, the better integral distinguishers have been found compared with the previous results.

Acknowledgement. The authors would like to thank Yosuke Todo for his important comments and suggestions to this paper. This work is supported by National Cryptography Development Fund (MMJJ20170102), National Natural Science Foundation of China (Grant No. 61572293) and Major Scientific and Technological Innovation Projects of Shandong Province, China (2017CXGC0704).

References

1. Beaulieu, R., Shors, D., Smith, J., Treatman-Clark, S., Weeks, B., Wingers, L.: The SIMON and SPECK lightweight block ciphers. In: PADAC 2015, pp. 175:1–175:6 (2015)
2. Bogdanov, A., et al.: PRESENT: an ultra-lightweight block cipher. In: Paillier, P., Verbauwhede, I. (eds.) CHES 2007. LNCS, vol. 4727, pp. 450–466. Springer, Heidelberg (2007). https://doi.org/10.1007/978-3-540-74735-2_31
3. Boura, C., Canteaut, A.: Another view of the division property. In: Robshaw, M., Katz, J. (eds.) CRYPTO 2016. LNCS, vol. 9814, pp. 654–682. Springer, Heidelberg (2016). https://doi.org/10.1007/978-3-662-53018-4_24
4. De Cannière, C., Dunkelman, O., Knežević, M.: KATAN and KTANTAN—a family of small and efficient hardware-oriented block ciphers. In: Clavier, C., Gaj, K. (eds.) CHES 2009. LNCS, vol. 5747, pp. 272–288. Springer, Heidelberg (2009). https://doi.org/10.1007/978-3-642-04138-9_20
5. Funabiki, Y., Todo, Y., Isobe, T., Morii, M.: Improved integral attack on HIGHT. In: Pieprzyk, J., Suriadi, S. (eds.) ACISP 2017. LNCS, vol. 10342, pp. 363–383. Springer, Cham (2017). https://doi.org/10.1007/978-3-319-60055-0_19
6. Knudsen, L., Wagner, D.: Integral cryptanalysis. In: Daemen, J., Rijmen, V. (eds.) FSE 2002. LNCS, vol. 2365, pp. 112–127. Springer, Heidelberg (2002). https://doi.org/10.1007/3-540-45661-9_9
7. Kölbl, S., Leander, G., Tiessen, T.: Observations on the SIMON block cipher family. In: Gennaro, R., Robshaw, M. (eds.) CRYPTO 2015. LNCS, vol. 9215, pp. 161–185. Springer, Heidelberg (2015). https://doi.org/10.1007/978-3-662-47989-6_8
8. Mouha, N., Preneel, B.: Towards finding optimal differential characteristics for ARX: application to salsa20. Cryptology ePrint Archive, Report 2013/328 (2013)
9. Sun, L., Wang, W., Liu, R., Wang, M.: MILP-aided bit-based division property for ARX-based block cipher. IACR Cryptology ePrint Archive 2016:1101 (2016)
10. Sun, L., Wang, W., Wang, M.: MILP-aided bit-based division property for primitives with non-bit-permutation linear layers. IACR Cryptology ePrint Archive 2016:811 (2016)
11. Sun, L., Wang, W., Wang, M.: Automatic search of bit-based division property for ARX ciphers and word-based division property. In: Takagi, T., Peyrin, T. (eds.) ASIACRYPT 2017. LNCS, vol. 10624, pp. 128–157. Springer, Cham (2017). https://doi.org/10.1007/978-3-319-70694-8_5
12. Todo, Y.: Structural evaluation by generalized integral property. In: Oswald, E., Fischlin, M. (eds.) EUROCRYPT 2015. LNCS, vol. 9056, pp. 287–314. Springer, Heidelberg (2015). https://doi.org/10.1007/978-3-662-46800-5_12
13. Todo, Y.: Integral cryptanalysis on full MISTY1. In: Gennaro, R., Robshaw, M. (eds.) CRYPTO 2015. LNCS, vol. 9215, pp. 413–432. Springer, Heidelberg (2015). https://doi.org/10.1007/978-3-662-47989-6_20
14. Todo, Y., Isobe, T., Hao, Y., Meier, W.: Cube attacks on non-blackbox polynomials based on division property. In: Katz, J., Shacham, H. (eds.) CRYPTO 2017. LNCS, vol. 10403, pp. 250–279. Springer, Cham (2017). https://doi.org/10.1007/978-3-319-63697-9_9
15. Todo, Y., Morii, M.: Bit-based division property and application to SIMON family. In: Peyrin, T. (ed.) FSE 2016. LNCS, vol. 9783, pp. 357–377. Springer, Heidelberg (2016). https://doi.org/10.1007/978-3-662-52993-5_18

16. Wang, Q., Grassi, L., Rechberger, C.: Zero-sum partitions of PHOTON permutations. IACR Cryptology ePrint Archive 2017:1211 (2017)
17. Xiang, Z., Zhang, W., Bao, Z., Lin, D.: Applying MILP method to searching integral distinguishers based on division property for 6 lightweight block ciphers. In: Cheon, J.H., Takagi, T. (eds.) ASIACRYPT 2016. LNCS, vol. 10031, pp. 648–678. Springer, Heidelberg (2016). https://doi.org/10.1007/978-3-662-53887-6_24
18. Yang, G., Zhu, B., Suder, V., Aagaard, M.D., Gong, G.: The Simeck family of lightweight block ciphers. In: Güneysu, T., Handschuh, H. (eds.) CHES 2015. LNCS, vol. 9293, pp. 307–329. Springer, Heidelberg (2015). https://doi.org/10.1007/978-3-662-48324-4_16

Constructing TI-Friendly Substitution Boxes Using Shift-Invariant Permutations

Si Gao[✉], Arnab Roy, and Elisabeth Oswald

University of Bristol, Bristol, UK
si.gao@bristol.ac.uk

Abstract. The threat posed by side channels requires ciphers that can be efficiently protected in both software and hardware against such attacks. In this paper, we proposed a novel Sbox construction based on iterations of shift-invariant quadratic permutations and linear diffusions. Owing to the selected quadratic permutations, all of our Sboxes enable uniform 3-share threshold implementations, which provide first order SCA protections without any fresh randomness. More importantly, because of the "shift-invariant" property, there are ample implementation trade-offs available, in software as well as hardware. We provide implementation results (software and hardware) for a four-bit and an eight-bit Sbox, which confirm that our constructions are competitive and can be easily adapted to various platforms as claimed. We have successfully verified their resistance to first order attacks based on real acquisitions. Because there are very few studies focusing on software-based threshold implementations, our software implementations might be of independent interest in this regard.

Keywords: Shift-invariant · Threshold implementation · Sbox

1 Introduction

In the past decade, side channel analysis (SCA) has become a serious threat to various cryptographic devices. In this adversarial model, an attacker may observe information leakage from a device operating some key-related information. For cryptographic engineers, efficiently implementing a good cipher is then no longer enough. They must also mitigate against the threat of such leakage and integrate a proper countermeasure, which often is a non-trivial task.

Since they were proposed, Threshold Implementations (TI) [1,2] have become a recognised countermeasure for power analysis when hardware implementations are considered. Unlike Boolean masking schemes, TI requires more shares, but the "non-completeness" property of TI ensures that in each computation logic gate, at least one of the (input) shares is missing. As a consequence, even in the presence of hardware glitches, this missing share guarantees that the observed leakage will not give out information about any secret intermediate value [2] and

© Springer Nature Switzerland AG 2019
M. Matsui (Ed.): CT-RSA 2019, LNCS 11405, pp. 433–452, 2019.
https://doi.org/10.1007/978-3-030-12612-4_22

thus robustly protects against so-called first-order attacks. In this paper, we only consider threshold implementations that provide first order protections.

One obstacle in threshold implementations is that there is no trivial efficient constructions for arbitrary cryptographic components. Take 3-share TI schemes for instance: in theory, any arbitrary quadratic function can be re-written in a TI-shared form with 3 shares. In practice, however, considering the requirement of "uniformity", a uniform 3-share TI scheme may not exist [2]. For smaller components (eg. Sboxes), this issue has been extensively studied up to affine equivalence [3–6]. For larger components, there is no generic construction available. On the other hand, solutions for uniform TIs may exist with higher implementation costs, such as increasing the number of shares or adding fresh randomness. Recently, De Meyer, Moradi and Wegener proposed a bit-serialized implementation of the Sbox of AES [7]: although their implementation with AES can be easily deployed in many applications, it comes with the price of adding fresh randomness. Daemen proposed a technique called "Changing of the Guards", which significantly eases the dilemma between uniformity and fresh randomness [8]. As the "Changing of the Guards" technique borrows randomness from the shares of other concurrent components, engineers no longer need to ensure uniformity for their TI schemes, as long as there are a few extra random bits available in the beginning of the encryption. Considering that the overhead of TI is already high, it is imperative to keep any extra cost as low as possible. Therefore, in this paper, we would like to avoid any fresh randomness and minimize the number of shares.

Instead of searching for efficient TI representations for existing Sboxes, we can also construct new Sboxes that are intrinsically suitable for TI protections. The TI forms of all 4×4 Sboxes were described in [3]. Boss et al. constructed several 8-bit Sboxes with round-based balanced Feistel, MISTY, SPNs structures, where the core building blocks are 4-bit Sboxes with easier TI protections [9]. The main focus of their paper was in finding Sboxes with efficient hardware TI implementations. However, the authors claimed their approach also "enables an efficient and low-cost implementation in software" (their "software implementation" refers to masked bitslice implementations, rather than TI-based software implementations). De Meyer and Varici further extended this approach to several new constructions (such as Generalized Feistel, Lai-Massey, Asymmetric SPN etc.) and provided implementation costs in terms of ASIC logic area [10].

It is not surprising that very few papers actually consider using TI-based software implementations. To the best of our knowledge, the only available TI constructions on software are TI-based PRESENT on an 8-bit micro-controller [11] and TI-based ARX ciphers [12]. The reason behind this is straightforward: the main concern that TI solves — glitches — do not exist in software[1]. The overhead of using TI-based countermeasures is usually much higher than using (bit-sliced) masking. Thus in theory, there is little point in applying TI to software

---

[1] Technically, glitches still exist within one instruction. However, the threat that glitches may bring—mixing between different data shares—does not usually show up.

implementations. In practice however, it has been observed that d-order bitsliced maskings sometimes fail to provide d-order SCA protections. This is because the internal architecture of micro-processors is not publicly accessible. Now even if a cryptographic engineer carefully writes his/her code in assembly, some implicit operations/registers may still mix different shares and produce exploitable leakage such as demonstrated in [13,14].

Our Contribution. In this paper, we aim to find several Sboxes that come with easier first order TI protections, in both software and hardware platforms. In contrast to Boss et al.'s work [9] we use shift-invariant quadratic permutations instead of smaller Sboxes [15]. Similar to the χ^2 function [16], any coefficient Boolean function of these permutations is simply a "rotated" version of another. In other words, the bit-width of the elementary computation logic —which we called "granularity" in this paper — can be 1. Combined with the idea of serial threshold implementations [17,18], the granularity of first order TI implementation can then be 1. Finer granularity brings more flexibility for cryptographic engineers, giving them more fine-grained trade-off options between executing time, logic area as well as power consumption. Specifically, the benefits of such protected Sboxes include:

- No fresh randomness.
- Easier software implementations. Since the shared version of our TI function preserves the "shift-invariant" property to some extent, bit-slicing such protected Sbox becomes easier.
- Flexible hardware implementations. As the granularity of such TI Sboxes is 1, in hardware, it is possible to implement only 1 computation unit, then get all other shared bits by shifting. Such strategy can lead to a very compact footprint, in the price of taking more cycles to execute.
- Full implementations/security evaluations. Despite the fact that all the implementations in this paper follow exactly the same rules as standard TI-s, we have verified these implementations with real-world acquisitions.

Outline. In Sect. 2 we explain a few essential concepts, including the cryptographic properties for Sboxes, the principle of threshold implementations and our Sbox searching strategies. Section 3 first introduces the concept of shift-invariance, then presents a search for quadratic TI-uniform shift-invariant permutations. Based on the results of this search, we further construct Sboxes with an SPN network. Sections 4 and 5 discuss the possible implementation tradeoffs on software/hardware platforms, respectively. Section 6 presents TVLA-based security evaluation results on both an ARM M0 core and a Kintex 7 FPGA.

2 Preliminaries

2.1 Cryptanalytic Properties for Sboxes

In a block cipher the Sbox provides the desired non-linear properties. A newly constructed Sbox must be evaluated for cryptographic properties e.g. differential uniformity, linearity, to thwart the differential and linear attacks. Let : $\mathbb{F}_{2^n} \rightarrow \mathbb{F}_{2^n}$ be a function.

Definition 1 *(**Differential uniformity** [19]). For any pair $(a, b) \in \mathbb{F}_{2^n}$, define the set*

$$D^F(a \rightarrow b) = \{x \in \mathbb{F}_{2^n} | F(x \oplus a) \oplus F(x) = b\}.$$

The differential uniformity of F is defined as $\delta(F) := \max_{a \neq 0, b} |D^F(a \rightarrow b)|$ where the $|D^F(a \rightarrow b)|$ denotes the cardinality of the set $D^F(a \rightarrow b)$ and is determined by the entry at the position (a, b) in the difference distribution table of F.

The Walsh transformation of the function F is defined as $W : \mathbb{F}_{2^n} \times \mathbb{F}_{2^n} \rightarrow \mathbb{Z}$ and is given as

$$W^F(a, b) = \sum_{x \in \mathbb{F}_{2^n}} (-1)^{a \cdot x + b \cdot F(x)}.$$

The linearity of an Sbox gives a measure of its best linear approximation. The linearity of F is defined as follows,

Definition 2. *The linearity of F is defined as $L(F) = \max_{a, b \neq 0} W^F(a, b)$.*

Besides, an Sbox should not have any algebraic properties e.g. low degree of the polynomial, which may be exploited by an adversary to mount an attack. It is known that the maximum algebraic degree of an m-bit permutation Sbox will be $m - 1$.

2.2 Threshold Implementation

In side channel research, threshold implementation (TI) usually refers to a countermeasure that based on secret sharing. For an $m \times n$ vectorial Boolean function f where each input x is shared as an s-length vector $\mathbf{x} = (x^{(1)}, .., x^{(s)})$, TI implements a few shared functions $f^{(j)}$ that satisfy:

- Correctness. The sum of all shared functions is equal to the original unshared function f (i.e. $\sum_{j=1}^{s} f^{(j)} = f$).
- Non-completeness. Every shared function $f^{(j)}$ is independent of at least one share of x. Specifically, for a d-order TI scheme, the combination of d $f^{(j)}$ functions is still independent of at least one share.
- Uniformity. For any unshared input value $x = x^{(1)} \oplus x^{(2)} \oplus ... \oplus x^{(s)}$, the corresponding output shares $\mathbf{y} = (y^{(1)}, .., y^{(s)})$ are uniformly distributed on all $\mathbf{y}$-s that satisfy $f(x) = y^{(1)} \oplus y^{(2)} \oplus ... \oplus y^{(s)}$.

To ensure uniformity for permutations ($m = n$), we can simply check if the shared version of f is an $m \times s$-bit permutation [3] (or prove it is invertible [8]).

2.3 Constructing TI Sboxes

To ensure non-completeness, threshold implementations need more shares for Boolean functions with higher degrees. As the implementation cost increases with the number of shares, the cheapest protected non-linear functions are quadratic ($deg = 2$) Boolean functions. For Sbox constructions, it is favourable to use permutations rather than arbitrary quadratic vectorial Boolean functions. Previous studies have successfully found uniform TI schemes for many quadratic permutations, including 3×3 and 4×4 Sboxes [3], 5-bit permutations [20] as well as a few observations on 6-bit quadratic permutations [21].

All the results above serve as a perfect building block for larger Sboxes: although directly applying TI is difficult, we can always use smaller Sboxes/quadratic permutations with known TIs to build large Sboxes. Boss et al. started searching for 8-bit Sboxes with Feistel (Fig. 1(a)), SPN (Fig. 1(b)), and MISTY structures, using 4-bit TI Sboxes as building blocks [9]. De Meyer and Varici extended this search to other constructions, such as Double Misty, Asymmetric SPN and Generalized Feistel structures [10].

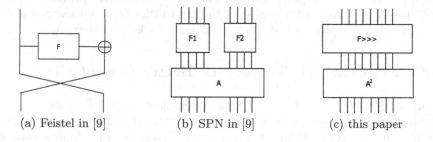

| (a) Feistel in [9] | (b) SPN in [9] | (c) this paper |

Fig. 1. Structure overview

Since the building blocks are smaller Sboxes/permutations, such constructions give much more compact 8-bit Sboxes in hardware [9,10]. Generally speaking, for an n-bit Sbox, its 3-share TI form would be a $3n$-bit permutation. Although each share can be computed with only 2 input shares ($2n$-bit), in hardware, increasing inputs usually boosts the area cost. Using smaller TI-Sboxes as building blocks significantly reduces the overall implementation cost, but it is unclear whether such constructions can provide flexibility when considering other platforms. Neither of these papers discusses the possibilities of serial TI— an extra trade-off proposed back in 2013 [17]. Boss et al.'s work did mention software implementations, yet their argument is that fewer AND gates lead to more efficient bit-sliced masking in software, rather than any TI protection [9]. None of these papers present security evaluations of their final implementations.

2.4 The Notion of Granularity

Irrespective of considering hardware or software implementations, constructions that feature multiple identical computation tasks usually give the cryptographic engineer more flexibility for the speed/cost trade-off. Taking hardware implementations for instance, all 4 bits in a PRESENT Sbox must be implemented with combinational logic, because all 4 bits are based on different Boolean functions [22]. Meanwhile, for the Keccak 5-bit χ^2 function, it is possible to implement only the circuit to do a 1 bit computation, as other 4 output bits can be computed through rotating the inputs [16] using the same circuit.

In this paper, we denote the output size of the smallest "gadget" to compute an Sbox as the "granularity". Clearly, the granularity for an unprotected PRESENT Sbox is 4, whereas for an unprotected 5-bit χ^2 function is 1. A finer granularity gives crypto engineers more opportunities for trade-offs: for instance, they can opt for a serial (slower) implementation, or a parallel (faster) implementation in hardware. Granularity also plays a critical role in software implementations. As most processors have intrinsic bit-widths (8,32 or 64), when performing bitwise operations, most of the bit-width will be wasted unless all the bits require the same operation. In order to take full advantage of the bit-width, a bit-slice implementation usually "slices" the same bits from multiple Sboxes to one register. As the CPU processes multiple Sboxes simultaneously, the overall throughput increases. Implementations with finer granularity provide intrinsic parallelism, which may take the most of the bit-width of our processors without manually "slicing" from a lot of concurrent data blocks (eg. Sboxes).

3   Constructing TI-Sboxes with Better Granularity

In this section, we present our TI-Sboxes search strategy. To achieve better implementation flexibility, we choose a different type of building blocks: instead of using 4 bit Sboxes with known TIs, our search utilizes the "Shift-invariant" [15] permutations. Such constructions usually lead to finer granularity (for each elemental operation) and give better implementation trade-offs for not only the Sbox itself, but also its TI-protection.

3.1   Shift-Invariant: Concept and Previous Works

Technically, an $n \times n$ vectorial Boolean function F is shift-invariant if for any rotated shift τ and any state x, $F(\tau(x)) = \tau(F(x))$ [15]. As stated in Daemen's thesis [15], "shift-invariant transformations can be implemented as an interconnected array of identical 1-bit output 'processors'" (granularity 1). Daemen further studied both linear and non-linear shift-invariant transformations, exploring their invertibility, local propagation and correlation properties [15]. As shift-invariance is closely linked to the concept of cellular automaton, Mariot, Picek , Leporati and Jakobovic searched up to 7×7 Sboxes from a cellular automaton perspective [23]. The most well known output of this direction is the χ^2 function in Keccak. However, it worth mentioning that without any other trick, χ^2 itself does not have a uniform 3-share TI.

3.2   Quadratic Shift-Invariant Permutation with Uniform TI

For an unprotected Sbox, shift-invariance ensures its granularity is equal to 1. However, considering the requirements of first order TI, its granularity also grows with the number of shares. Further reducing the granularity requires not only shift-invariance, but also its TI property: for any Boolean function f, if its direct shared form (i.e. Sect. 4.2 in [3]) is uniform, its granularity can be reduced to 1, using a serial TI implementation [17,18]. Thus, for granularity, our best option would be using quadratic shift-invariant permutations with a uniform direct sharing threshold implementation.

Therefore, our main building blocks for Sbox constructions are quadratic shift-invariant permutations with uniform 3-share TI-s. Although Daemen's thesis gave many useful results, it did not cover all possible nonlinear shift-invariant transformations. Fortunately, the search space for common Sbox sizes ($n = 4$ or $n = 8$) is small enough. For $n \times n$ shift-invariant transformations, the number of all possible quadratic transformations are equal to the number of n-bit quadratic Boolean functions $2^{\sum_{i=0}^{2} \binom{n}{i}}$. The search space for 4 bit building blocks is 2^{11}, whereas for the 8 bit case is 2^{37}. Among these transformations, we are interested in those satisfy:

- The transformation itself is an n-bit permutation.
- Its direct 3-share TI is uniform.

Both properties are easy to check: for TI uniformity we simply check whether the shared form is still a $3n \times 3n$ permutation. For early abortion in this permutation check we first examine whether the coefficient Boolean function f is balanced. If it is not balanced, the transformation it derived cannot be a permutation. Additionally, we further limit our search to functions that satisfy:

- For bit y_0, its Boolean function always contains bit x_0. If not, we can always find a shift transformation τ that ensures $F' = F \circ \tau$ (F is the shift-invariant transformation f derived)[2]. For a shift-invariant F', τ and F are commutative. This means for lower rounds (1 or 2) of SPN network, τ can be integrated into the initial/final linear transformation, which does not affect the cryptographic properties.
- f does not have a constant term. For a shift-invariant transformation, the constant term can be either all-0 or all-1. As an all-1 constant has little impact on the cryptographic property of F, we simply discard these choices.

For 4-bit quadratic functions, we found that 960 out of 2048 functions contain x_0 and 0 as their constant terms. 400 of them are balanced, whereas only 28 f lead to a 4×4 permutation F. Fortunately, all of the direct 3-shares schemes are actually 12×12 permutations (i.e. satisfy uniformity) (Table 1).

On the other hand, for 8 bit permutations, the search space of f is 2^{37}. Almost half of the f-s have $x_0 = c = 0$, while only a quarter of f-s are balanced. 520 128 ($\approx 2^{19}$) can generate an 8-bit shift-invariant permutation F: interestingly, all of these permutations have uniform direct 3-share TI (Table 2).

---

[2] Note that here we only need x_0 to appear, rather than appearing as a linear term [15].

Table 1. Shift-invariant quadratic TI permutations: $n = 4$

n	All f	Has x_0 & $c = 0$	Balanced	Permutation	TI permutation
4	2048	960	400	28	28

Table 2. Shift-invariant quadratic TI permutations: $n = 8$

n	All f	Has x_0 & $c = 0$	Balanced	Permutation	TI permutation
8	2^{37}	68451041152	29986581632	520128	520128

3.3   Constructing Sboxes

In this section, we further construct cryptographically good 4/8-bit Sboxes with these quadratic permutations. The Sbox search follows exactly the same strategy as previous works [9,10], although the granularity further complicates the situation here.

Design Architectures. As shift-invariance ensures each bit can be computed in the same way, generally speaking, we would like to avoid more branches. Take two-branch balanced Feistel structure for instance: although the round function may still have granularity 1, the other branch also contributes to the granularity for the whole Sbox. To this end, we perform our Sbox search with full range Substitution-Permutation Network (SPN) (Fig. 1(c)).

Permutation Layer. As the substitution layer is chosen from those quadratic TI permutations, the only decision left to make is the permutation layer. Clearly, the most efficient construction would be using shift-invariant linear permutation or nothing at all. Although shift-invariance is a good property for software/hardware implementations, considering the threat of rotational cryptanalysis [24], we prefer not to preserve it in the final Sbox. Thus, our linear transformation here needs to stop the propagation of shift-invariance. In general, the cheapest option would be using non-shift bit-permutations. However, a bit-permutation usually have a larger granularity (as each bit has to be implemented respectively), which leads to a penalty on its software performance. Instead, in this paper, we consider a linear transformation that is similar to AES's "xtime". More specifically, we search for invertible matrices that satisfy:

$$\mathbf{A} = \begin{bmatrix} a_{1,1} & 1 & 0 & \dots & 0 \\ a_{2,1} & 0 & 1 & \dots & 0 \\ \dots & \dots & \dots & \dots & \dots \\ a_{n-1,1} & 0 & 0 & \dots & 1 \\ 1 & 0 & 0 & \dots & 0 \end{bmatrix}$$

Let $\mathbf{a_1} = \{a_{1,1}, a_{1,2}, ..., a_{n-1,1}, 1\}$, if $\mathbf{A}$ is indeed invertible, in software, it can be implemented with a shift and a conditional XOR.

$$\mathbf{A}x = \begin{cases} (x << 1) \oplus \mathbf{a_1}, & \text{if } hsb(x) = 1 \\ (x << 1), & \text{otherwise} \end{cases}$$

As the conditional branch is prone to cache attack, most implementations tend to use a multiplication instruction to achieve a constant control flow

$$\mathbf{A}x = (x << 1) \oplus (\mathbf{a_1} \times hsb(x))$$

As the n-bit state x is operated as a word, the granularity is determined by this 1-bit multiplication: since this equation only holds 1 bit values, the overall granularity gets coarser. Nonetheless, from an implementation perspective, it is still much better than arbitrary binary matrix multiplication. To achieve a better diffusion property, in our Sbox search, we use two layers of $\mathbf{A}$ ($\mathbf{A}^2$) as our permutation layer.

Selection Criteria. In order to achieve a balance between the implementation cost and the cryptographic properties, we have defined a selection criteria for the candidate Sboxes. Specifically, for 4-bit Sboxes,

- the differential uniformity is ≤ 4 and,
- the linearity is ≤ 8

For 8-bit Sboxes,

- the differential uniformity is ≤ 8 and,
- the linearity is ≤ 72

Besides, the algebraic degree and the degree of the interpolation polynomial should be large enough to resistent algebraic attack and interpolation attack, respectively.

3.4   Results

4-Bit Case. For 4-bit Sboxes, such selection criteria only accepts optimal Sboxes (differential uniformity = 4, linearity = 8) [25]. By enumerating all possible choices of A and quadratic permutations, we can find 16 such 4-bit Sboxes within 2 rounds. One such Sbox is presented as follow. The algebraic degree of this Sbox is 3, whereas the degree of the interpolation polynomial is 15 (Table 3).

$$\mathbf{A} = \begin{bmatrix} 1 & 1 & 0 & 0 \\ 1 & 0 & 1 & 0 \\ 1 & 0 & 0 & 1 \\ 1 & 0 & 0 & 0 \end{bmatrix}$$

Table 3. Shift-invariant quadratic TI permutation for S4

0	1	2	3	4	5	6	7	8	9	A	B	C	D	E	F
0	1	2	9	4	A	3	7	8	C	5	B	6	D	E	F

Table 4. Final Sbox for S4

0	1	2	3	4	5	6	7	8	9	A	B	C	D	E	F
0	4	8	A	F	C	6	9	1	E	B	D	7	5	3	2

8-Bit Case. For $n = 8$, the overall search space is around 2^{26}, which is quite feasible for most PCs. 6 Sboxes appear within 3 rounds: all of them have differential uniformity 8 whereas their linearity vary from 64 to 72. Due to the space limit, we present the best one (differential uniformity = 8, linearity = 64) in the extended version of this paper. The algebraic degree of the presented Sbox is 6 and the degree of interpolation polynomial is 252 (Table 4).

4   Software Implementation

The major benefit of an Sbox with small granularity, is that it can be efficiently implemented in both software and hardware platforms. Although software based TIs tend to have higher overhead, in terms of security, they might have their own advantages [17]. In this section, we implement our selected Sboxes with first order TI protections in software and discuss a few possible trade-off options.

4.1   Target Platform

For software implementations, the most common platforms are smart cards or high-end processors (ARM/AMD/Intel). Although different processors may have different instruction sets, for bit-slice computations, most required bit-wise instructions can be found easily in all instruction sets. The major difference lies in the bit-width of the target processor, which determines how many bits can be computed in parallel. In this paper, our implementation chooses the most common bit-width—32. Implementations for 8-bit and 64-bit follow exactly the same rule. Because our target chip is an NXP ARM M0 core, we wrote our Sbox implementations using the Thumb instruction set [26]. In order to demonstrate the difference between Thumb and ARM instruction sets [27], we also show how those Sboxes can be computed on a more advanced core like the ARM M3.

4.2   Implementation Trade-Offs

No Optimization. It is worth mentioning that finer granularity only provides a possibility for further implementation trade-off: when such trade-off is not necessary, engineers can always do a TI implementation with $3n$ variables. Such an implementation achieves its best performance when there are 32 concurrent data blocks (Sboxes) available. As the available bit-width is already fully occupied, the shift-invariant property will not provide any benefit in this case.

Size-Based Optimization. As each bit can be computed in the same way, with shift-invariant transformations, we can pack all n bits into one register. Take an 8 bit Sbox for instance, if there are 4 concurrent Sbox computations for $x^{[1]}$, $x^{[2]}$, $x^{[3]}$ and $x^{[4]}$, a 32-bit register can be filled with

$$\left(x_1^{[1]}, x_1^{[2]}, x_1^{[3]}, x_1^{[4]}, ..., x_8^{[1]}, x_8^{[2]}, x_8^{[3]}, x_8^{[4]} \right)$$

where x_i is the i-th bit of x. Correspondingly, each computation will be adjusted to ensure it takes the right input bit. Note that the rotated shift is still available in this form: instead of rotating 1 bit, now we are rotating 4 bits. Readers can verify that the transformation can still be computed correctly in this form, while the number of required concurrent data blocks shrinks from 32 to 4. Similar to the unprotected Sbox, the TI protection can be computed in exactly the same way. If all three shares are computed separately, such an optimization does not contradict with any TI requirement.

Extreme Optimization. In theory, since the granularity of the TI protection is still 1, packing all 3 shares into one register is possible. Whether it contradicts with TI's security requirement (i.e. non-completeness) is debatable: ideally, if bit-wise instructions' leakage can be regarded as a sum of the leakages of all candidate bits (i.e. no "bit-interactions"), such implementation should be as secure as a hardware-based TI[3]. However, current results seem to suggest this may not always be the case: Sasdrich et al.'s work shows that for lookup tables (i.e. LDR instruction) on smart cards, bit-interaction clearly exists [17]. Our experiments with ARM M0 processors also prove the shift instructions (LSL, LSR, ROR) have the same issue. Moreover, as different bits and shares both get placed in one register, shifting becomes trickier. Only one of the shifts, whether shift bits or shares, can be operated with rotated shift instructions. The other one must be done manually with a few shifts and data masks. Considering the security loss and potential performance gain, we believe this is not a reasonable option.

4.3   Implementation on ARM M0/M3

Throughout this section, our evaluation is based on the size-based optimization. For the quadratic permutation S, we simply computed the TI-protected permutation according to its Algebraic Normal Form (ANF). Further customized optimizations may be possible but are out of the scope of this paper. To limit

---

[3] Unlike its hardware counterpart, "coupling" effect [28] and "voltage fluctuation" are not the only concerns for the software TI. An AND instruction may not have the same leakage as 32 1-bit-AND gates, unless all the other combinational logic cells in the ALU are actually "silent".

the usage of registers or memories, we compute all shifted results online, even if some of them appear repeatedly in the computation. Although this sounds far from ideal, as most commodity processors have a limited number of general purpose registers, such a compromise is inevitable in practice. For the linear transformation P, as the multiplication operation can only handle 1 bit at a time, all n-bit data shares must be executed one by one.

Despite the fact that our Sbox is computed online (rather than using pre-computed lookup tables), architecturally, its computation procedure is not that different from Sasdrich et al.'s implementation of PRESENT's Sbox [11]. Depending on the context, leakage might still show up when the CPU switches from one TI-shared function to another. Nonetheless, as the number of shared functions in TI is quite limited (compared with the number of AND-s in masking), implementing TI correctly requires much less effort than implementing bit-slice Boolean masking.

Table 5 illustrates the software implementation costs of our selected Sboxes, along with a few other well-known protected Sboxes, such as AES and PRESENT. It is not hard to see there is a significant performance difference between Thumb [26] and ARM [27] instruction sets. The major difference lies in rotation: as Thumb's ROR only shifts with a register rather than a constant, rotating r1 by n and storing the result in r2 has to be implemented as

$$\text{MOV r3}, \#n$$
$$\text{MOV r2, r1}$$
$$\text{ROR r2, r3}$$

However, with the "Flexible Operand 2" [27] in ARM instruction set, such procedure can be implemented with only one line. In terms of executing cycles, implementations with ARM instructions have a significant bonus.

$$\text{MOV r2, r1, ROR} \#n$$

As the results in Table 5 are most likely parallel implementations for multiple Sboxes, we have listed the number of parallel Sboxes with the operation cycles. For our $S4$, Table 5 suggests it takes 870 cycles to compute 8 Sboxes simultaneously.[4] For 4 bit Sboxes, our shift-invariant Sbox has similar performance as the PRESENT Sbox based on quadratic decomposition (654 v.s. 686). With bitslice masking, PRESENT Sbox can be much more efficient [29]. On the other hand, for the 8 bit case, both the KHL and bit-sliced masking are quite efficient, running twice faster than our shift-invariant Sbox. However, we would like to stress that the comparison of Table 5 is not as trivial as comparing the numbers of cycles. First of all, our implementation does not take any fresh randomness. As we can see in Table 5, all other Sboxes use quite a lot of random

---

[4] Note that this does not mean each Sbox can be computed only 109 cycles: if there is only one Sbox to compute, it will still take 870 cycles, as most of the bit-width will be wasted.

Table 5. Software performance of various Sboxes

	Size	Diff.	Lin.	Deg.	1st order protected		
					Randomness	Cycles	
						Thumb	ARM
PRESENT (BS) [29]	4	4	8	3	64	n/a	796/16
PRESENT ($F \circ G$) [29]	4	4	8	3	128	n/a	686/8
$S4$ (our result)	4	4	8	3	0	870/8	654/8
AES (BS) [29]	8	4	32	7	512	n/a	4698/16
AES (KHL) [29]	8	4	32	7	192	n/a	2309/8
$S8$ (our result)	8	8	64	6	0	3627/4	2169/4

bits, even if they do not use any mask refreshing. Considering the cost of producing (pseudo)random numbers, it is clearly desirable to avoid fresh randomness. On the other hand, although all Sboxes in Table 5 claim first order security, a TI scheme has 3 shares whereas a bit-slice masking only has 2. Since the authors did not give any real traces based SCA evaluation [29], it is hard to argue whether these bit-sliced masking schemes provide the same security level as our threshold implementations. If we simply believe in the order-reduction theorem [30], a fair comparison would be using the second order bit-slice masking (3 shares), which degrades their performance to the same level of ours [29]. Last but not least, enormous effort has been invested in optimizing the implementations of both AES's Sbox and PRESENT's Sbox. In fact, the advantage of bit-slice masking is mainly inherited from the circuit optimization of the unprotected Sbox. On the contrary, we simply implemented the ANF of our shift-invariant Sboxes: further optimizations may be possible but they are out of the scope of this paper.

Another interesting observation would be our granularity gains. Technically, granularity determines how many concurrent Sbox computations we need to achieve the best possible throughput. For PRESENT and AES in Table 5, granularity does not cause an issue: both ciphers use SPN networks with many same Sboxes as their confusion layers. However, if the cipher uses smaller round functions with less concurrent Sboxes or a confusion layer with different Sboxes, it would be difficult to find enough data to "slice" within one plaintext block. Thanks to the fine granularity of our new Sboxes, in short encryption request, our construction has a better chance to reach its maximal throughput.

5   Hardware Implementation

5.1   Implementation Trade-Off

Unlike software platforms, TI on hardware has been extensively studied for years. The only difference our Sboxes bring is a "double-rotating" feature: not only the 3 shares can be generated by rotating the inputs with the same circuit (i.e. serial

TI [17]), all n-bit output can also be generated by rotating inputs. Note that these two rotations are different operations: one is rotating bits, the other is rotating shares. On software platforms, since there is only one rotation instruction, implementing both efficiently is not trivial. On hardware, double-rotation can be simply implemented with multiplexers. Thanks to the fine granularity, now we can implement only 1 bit Boolean function and compute the other $3n-1$ bits through rotations (Fig. 2).

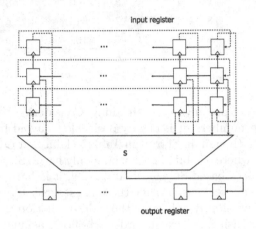

Fig. 2. Hardware schematic of shift invariant transformation S

As all other implementations are relatively trivial, in this section, our evaluation only uses this 1-bit serial implementation. Note that this implementation is by no means our "reference" design. The point of having a granularity 1 Sbox is that the engineers have the flexibility to choose the right trade-off. Although this 1-bit implementation leads to a very compact logic footprint, it trades area advantages with executing cycles. It takes $3 * n$ cycles to finish a 3-share n-bit Sbox computation. Besides, the multiple data paths cause the control logic to increase, which may compensate some of the footprint gain. Depending on the specific applications, engineers can also use a "single rotation" version, where only the shares or the bits are generated by rotations.

5.2 Pre-charge Issue

A well known issue for serial threshold implementation, is some first-order leakage might appear during the "shift-shares" procedure [31]. The reason behind is that the leakage for a combinational logic during an input transition depends on not only the current state, but also the previous state. The solution would be simply eliminating any transition of input shares in the combinational logic: i.e. add a pre-charge stage which charges the combinational logic with all zero between these two states. Obviously, this pre-charge stage penalizes the overall performance by one extra cycle. Interestingly, as our double-rotating design takes more cycles to proceed, the percentage of pre-charge time becomes smaller. Note that a pre-charge stage is only required when we are switching between different shares, not between different bits.

5.3 Implementation on ASIC

In order to evaluate their performance on hardware, we have implemented our Sboxes with first order TI protections in Verilog. For synthesis, we used Synopsys Design Compiler with the TSMC 180 nm standard cell library. Their area requirements as well as clock cycles are presented in Table 6. Note that only the combinational part is documented in Table 6: as most previous works excluded the multiplexers and registers as "required extra logic", we cannot further compare the whole design[5]. For clarity, Table 6 only shows one 8 bit Sbox and one 4 bit Sbox: other alternatives can be found in the full version of this paper.

Table 6. Hardware evaluation of various Sboxes

	Size	Diff.	Lin.	Deg.	Rounds	Protected		
						Area (GE)	Delay (ns)	Cycles
PRESENT [17]	4	4	8	3	n/a	151	—	6
GIFT [18]	4	6	8	3	n/a	172.5	—[a]	6
$S4$	4	4	8	3	2	54	0.72	28
AES [32]	8	4	32	7	n/a	2224	—	3
SB_1 [9]	8	16	64	6	8	51	1.09	8
SB_4 [9]	8	8	56	7	5	202	2.10	5
$S8$	8	8	64	6	3	181	1.89	78

[a] Not given.

Since most results in Table 6 are uniform first order threshold implementations, we did not present their fresh randomness requirements. Only the AES Sbox uses 32 random bits; all others do not take fresh randomness. Thanks to its fine granularity, our protected Sboxes can be implemented with 1-bit combinational logic, which leads to very compact implementations (Table 6). However, this is nothing more than a trade-off: the number of cycles clearly shows the price to pay. Besides, for a larger n, shift-invariant constructions lose most of their charms. Table 6 shows the area gain for 8 bit Sbox is neglectable (if any, considering a serial implementation uses more MUX-es), compared with Boss et al.'s construction. The reason for this roots in the philosophy of shift invariance: shift invariance saves area by reducing the outputs of a logic circuit, but not the inputs. Our 1-bit implementation is still a $2n$-variate Boolean function. Boss

---

[5] Depending on the specific implementation, such "extra logic" can actually predominates the overall area cost. To this end, we would like the stress that our serial implementation is only worthwhile if it has a significant advantage in area cost.

et al.'s construction uses smaller Sboxes, which reduces the input scale of the protected circuit. Technically, for an arbitrary vectorial Boolean function, the implementation cost grows linearly with its output, but exponentially with its input. Having said that, the main advantage of our construction is providing flexible implementation trade-offs, on both software and hardware platforms. Although Boss et al.'s paper also mentioned software-efficiency, their prediction is actually based on the number of AND-s. We believe that software performance evaluation should use actual assembly code: due to the limited resources available (eg. instructions, registers, buses, etc.), high-level estimations could be misleading.

6 Security Evaluation

6.1 Software: ARM M0

In order to evaluate our protected Sbox in practice, we have implemented such Sboxes on both software and hardware platforms. For software implementation, our target chip is an NXP LPC1114 (ARM Cortex M0) processor. The measurement point connects to a $100\,\Omega$ resistor on the VCC end. Power traces were captured with a PicoScope 2206B running at a sampling rate of $125\,\mathrm{MSa/s}$. The clock speed of the target core was set to $8\,\mathrm{MHz}$. For leakage detection, we use the non-specific fix-vs-random T-test [33]. In order to increase the detection power, we force all parallel Sboxes to use the same input shares (i.e. all the concurrent Sbox computations are exactly the same). Figure 3 shows the evaluation results for our 4 bit Sbox with 1 million traces:

Considering the Sbox computation includes 25000 time points, we increase the T-test threshold to 5 [34]. With 1 million traces, a first order T-test cannot find any significant leakage. As we have only implemented a first order TI protection, second order attacks are still feasible. In theory, the most efficient 2nd order attack should be multi-variate attacks which combine 2 independent samples on the trace. In practice, significant leakage can be detected by simply performing the same T-test on the second moment (Fig. 3). Therefore, we did not enumerate all possible second order sample combinations on the trace. The 8-bit case is quite similar: due to the limited space, we present the results for S_8 in the extended version.

6.2 Hardware: SAKURA-X FPGA

For hardware implementations, we have tested our Sboxes on the SAKURA-X board with Xilinx Kintex-7 FPGA. In order to increase the signal-to-noise ratio, an Agilent 25 db amplifier is connected to the measured signal. Moreover, considering our all-serial implementation has very limited power consumption, we extended a $3n$-bit protected Sbox to a 384-bit design: for the 4 bit case, this means there are 32 parallel Sboxes implemented on the board. For 8 bit Sboxes, there are 16 parallel Sboxes. Similar to software implementations, all

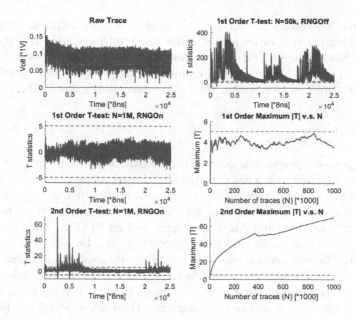

Fig. 3. Software evaluation of S4

the implemented Sboxes were given the same input shares. Our FPGA design run at 3 MHz, while our Lecroy Waverunner 700 Zi scope was capturing traces at 500 MSa/s. Obvious outliers were removed before T-test. Figure 4 shows the

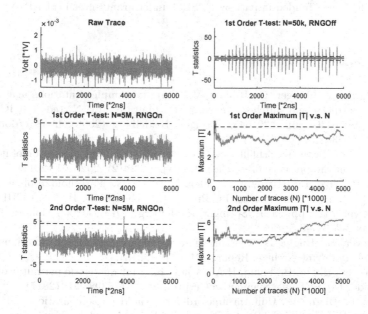

Fig. 4. Hardware evaluation of S4

leakage detection results for our 4 bit Sbox after 5 million traces. Clearly, our protected design is first order secure. Since our implementation is a serial one, technically, the second order detection should use multi-variate T-test. However, it is not hard to see that the second moment already shows some clear leakage. Like the software case, we present the 8-bit results in the Appendix.

7   Conclusion

In this paper, we propose a novel Sbox construction using quadratic shift-invariant transformations. Thanks to the shift-invariant property, our Sbox constructions have a fine "granularity" which contributes to more flexible implementation trade-offs. Both software and hardware implementations have been discussed and evaluated (on ARM processors and an FPGA). The strong point of our Sboxes is that their first order protection can be efficiently tuned for the needs in different applications without using any fresh randomness. Experiments suggest our TI protection has effectively eliminated the 1-st order leakage. Meanwhile, to the best of our knowledge, this is the first computation based TI Sbox implementation in software (rather than the table-based TI implementation in [17]). Considering masked software implementations do not always back their security claims (eg. [11]), utilizing threshold implementations on software is of independent interest.

Acknowledgements. We would like to thank all anonymous reviewers for improving the quality of this paper as well as providing insights from some other perspectives. This work has been funded in part by EPSRC under grant agreement EP/N011635/1 (LADA).

References

1. Nikova, S., Rechberger, C., Rijmen, V.: Threshold implementations against side-channel attacks and glitches. In: Ning, P., Qing, S., Li, N. (eds.) ICICS 2006. LNCS, vol. 4307, pp. 529–545. Springer, Heidelberg (2006). https://doi.org/10.1007/11935308_38
2. Nikova, S., Rijmen, V., Schläffer, M.: Secure hardware implementation of nonlinear functions in the presence of glitches. J. Cryptol. **24**(2), 292–321 (2011)
3. Bilgin, B., Nikova, S., Nikov, V., Rijmen, V., Stütz, G.: Threshold implementations of all 3×3 and 4×4 S-boxes. In: Prouff, E., Schaumont, P. (eds.) CHES 2012. LNCS, vol. 7428, pp. 76–91. Springer, Heidelberg (2012). https://doi.org/10.1007/978-3-642-33027-8_5
4. De Meyer, L., Bilgin, B.: Classification of balanced quadratic functions. IACR Cryptology ePrint Archive, Report 2018/113 (2018)
5. Bozilov, D., Bilgin, B., Sahin, H.A.: A note on 5-bit quadratic permutations' classification. IACR Trans. Symmetric Cryptol. **2017**(1), 398–404 (2017)
6. Beyne, T., Bilgin, B.: Uniform first-order threshold implementations. In: Avanzi, R., Heys, H. (eds.) SAC 2016. LNCS, vol. 10532, pp. 79–98. Springer, Cham (2017). https://doi.org/10.1007/978-3-319-69453-5_5

7. De Meyer, L., Moradi, A., Wegener, F.: Spin me right round rotational symmetry for FPGA-specific AES. IACR Trans. Cryptogr. Hardw. Embed. Syst. **2018**(3), 596–626 (2018)
8. Daemen, J.: Changing of the guards: a simple and efficient method for achieving uniformity in threshold sharing. In: Fischer, W., Homma, N. (eds.) CHES 2017. LNCS, vol. 10529, pp. 137–153. Springer, Cham (2017). https://doi.org/10.1007/978-3-319-66787-4_7
9. Boss, E., Grosso, V., Güneysu, T., Leander, G., Moradi, A., Schneider, T.: Strong 8-bit Sboxes with efficient masking in hardware extended version. J. Cryptogr. Eng. **7**(2), 149–165 (2017)
10. Meyer, L.D., Varici, K.: More constructions for strong 8-bit S-boxes with efficient masking in hardware. In: Proceedings of the 38th Symposium on Information Theory in the Benelux, Delft, NE, p. 11. Werkgemeenschap voor Informatie- en Communicatietheorie (2017)
11. Sasdrich, P., Bock, R., Moradi, A.: Threshold implementation in software. In: Fan, J., Gierlichs, B. (eds.) COSADE 2018. LNCS, vol. 10815, pp. 227–244. Springer, Cham (2018). https://doi.org/10.1007/978-3-319-89641-0_13
12. Jungk, B., Petri, R., Stottinger, M.: Efficient side-channel protections of ARX ciphers. IACR Trans. Cryptogr. Hardw. Embed. Syst. **2018**(3), 627–653 (2018)
13. Balasch, J., Gierlichs, B., Reparaz, O., Verbauwhede, I.: DPA, bitslicing and masking at 1 GHz. In: Güneysu, T., Handschuh, H. (eds.) CHES 2015. LNCS, vol. 9293, pp. 599–619. Springer, Heidelberg (2015). https://doi.org/10.1007/978-3-662-48324-4_30
14. de Groot, W., Papagiannopoulos, K., de La Piedra, A., Schneider, E., Batina, L.: Bitsliced masking and ARM: friends or foes? In: Bogdanov, A. (ed.) LightSec 2016. LNCS, vol. 10098, pp. 91–109. Springer, Cham (2017). https://doi.org/10.1007/978-3-319-55714-4_7
15. Daemen, J.: Cipher and hash function design, strategies based on linear and differential cryptanalysis. Ph.D. thesis, K. U. Leuven (1995). http://jda.noekeon.org/
16. Bertoni, G., Daemen, J., Peeters, M., Van Assche, G.: Keccak. In: Johansson, T., Nguyen, P.Q. (eds.) EUROCRYPT 2013. LNCS, vol. 7881, pp. 313–314. Springer, Heidelberg (2013). https://doi.org/10.1007/978-3-642-38348-9_19
17. Kutzner, S., Nguyen, P.H., Poschmann, A., Wang, H.: On 3-share threshold implementations for 4-bit S-boxes. In: Prouff, E. (ed.) COSADE 2013. LNCS, vol. 7864, pp. 99–113. Springer, Heidelberg (2013). https://doi.org/10.1007/978-3-642-40026-1_7
18. Gupta, N., Jati, A., Chattopadhyay, A., Sanadhya, S.K., Chang, D.: Threshold implementations of GIFT: a trade-off analysis. IACR Cryptology ePrint Archive, Report 2017/1040 (2017)
19. Nyberg, K.: Differentially uniform mappings for cryptography. In: Helleseth, T. (ed.) EUROCRYPT 1993. LNCS, vol. 765, pp. 55–64. Springer, Heidelberg (1994). https://doi.org/10.1007/3-540-48285-7_6
20. Božilov, D., Bilgin, B., Sahin, H.: A note on 5-bit quadratic permutations' classification. IACR Trans. Symmetric Cryptol. **2017**(1), 398–404 (2017)
21. Meyer, L.D., Bilgin, B.: Classification of balanced quadratic functions. Cryptology ePrint Archive, Report 2018/113 (2018). https://eprint.iacr.org/2018/113
22. Bogdanov, A., et al.: PRESENT: an ultra-lightweight block cipher. In: Paillier, P., Verbauwhede, I. (eds.) CHES 2007. LNCS, vol. 4727, pp. 450–466. Springer, Heidelberg (2007). https://doi.org/10.1007/978-3-540-74735-2_31
23. Mariot, L., Picek, S., Leporati, A., Jakobovic, D.: Cellular automata based S-boxes. Cryptogr. Commun. **11**, 41–62 (2018)

24. Khovratovich, D., Nikolić, I.: Rotational cryptanalysis of ARX. In: Hong, S., Iwata, T. (eds.) FSE 2010. LNCS, vol. 6147, pp. 333–346. Springer, Heidelberg (2010). https://doi.org/10.1007/978-3-642-13858-4_19

25. Leander, G., Poschmann, A.: On the classification of 4 bit S-boxes. In: Carlet, C., Sunar, B. (eds.) WAIFI 2007. LNCS, vol. 4547, pp. 159–176. Springer, Heidelberg (2007). https://doi.org/10.1007/978-3-540-73074-3_13

26. ARM: Arm and thumb-2 instruction set. http://infocenter.arm.com/help/topic/com.arm.doc.qrc0006e/QRC0006_UAL16.pdf

27. ARM: Thumb 16-bit instruction set. http://infocenter.arm.com/help/topic/com.arm.doc.qrc0001m/QRC0001_UAL.pdf

28. De Cnudde, T., Bilgin, B., Gierlichs, B., Nikov, V., Nikova, S., Rijmen, V.: Does coupling affect the security of masked implementations? In: Guilley, S. (ed.) COSADE 2017. LNCS, vol. 10348, pp. 1–18. Springer, Cham (2017). https://doi.org/10.1007/978-3-319-64647-3_1

29. Goudarzi, D., Rivain, M.: How fast can higher-order masking be in software? In: Coron, J.-S., Nielsen, J.B. (eds.) EUROCRYPT 2017. LNCS, vol. 10210, pp. 567–597. Springer, Cham (2017). https://doi.org/10.1007/978-3-319-56620-7_20

30. Balasch, J., Gierlichs, B., Grosso, V., Reparaz, O., Standaert, F.-X.: On the cost of lazy engineering for masked software implementations. In: Joye, M., Moradi, A. (eds.) CARDIS 2014. LNCS, vol. 8968, pp. 64–81. Springer, Cham (2015). https://doi.org/10.1007/978-3-319-16763-3_5

31. Wegener, F., Moradi, A.: A first-order SCA resistant AES without fresh randomness. In: Fan, J., Gierlichs, B. (eds.) COSADE 2018. LNCS, vol. 10815, pp. 245–262. Springer, Cham (2018). https://doi.org/10.1007/978-3-319-89641-0_14

32. Bilgin, B., Gierlichs, B., Nikova, S., Nikov, V., Rijmen, V.: Trade-offs for threshold implementations illustrated on AES. IEEE Trans. CAD Integr. Circuits Syst. **34**(7), 1188–1200 (2015)

33. Goodwill, G., Jun, B., Jaffe, J., Rohatgi, P.: A testing methodology for side channel resistance validation. Technical report, CRI (2011)

34. Ding, A.A., Zhang, L., Durvaux, F., Standaert, F.-X., Fei, Y.: Towards sound and optimal leakage detection procedure. In: Eisenbarth, T., Teglia, Y. (eds.) CARDIS 2017. LNCS, vol. 10728, pp. 105–122. Springer, Cham (2018). https://doi.org/10.1007/978-3-319-75208-2_7

Fast Secure Comparison for Medium-Sized Integers and Its Application in Binarized Neural Networks

Mark Abspoel[1,2]([✉]), Niek J. Bouman[3]([✉]), Berry Schoenmakers[3],
and Niels de Vreede[3]

[1] Centrum Wiskunde & Informatica (CWI), Amsterdam, The Netherlands
abspoel@cwi.nl
[2] Philips Research Eindhoven, Eindhoven, The Netherlands
[3] Technische Universiteit Eindhoven, Eindhoven, The Netherlands
n.j.bouman@tue.nl

Abstract. In 1994, Feige, Kilian, and Naor proposed a simple protocol for secure 3-way comparison of integers a and b from the range $[0, 2]$. Their observation is that for $p = 7$, the Legendre symbol $(x \mid p)$ coincides with the sign of x for $x = a - b \in [-2, 2]$, thus reducing secure comparison to secure evaluation of the Legendre symbol. More recently, in 2011, Yu generalized this idea to handle secure comparisons for integers from substantially larger ranges $[0, d]$, essentially by searching for primes for which the Legendre symbol coincides with the sign function on $[-d, d]$. In this paper, we present new comparison protocols based on the Legendre symbol that additionally employ some form of error correction. We relax the prime search by requiring that the Legendre symbol encodes the sign function in a noisy fashion only. Practically, we use the majority vote over a window of $2k + 1$ adjacent Legendre symbols, for small positive integers k. Our technique significantly increases the comparison range: e.g., for a modulus of 60 bits, d increases by a factor of 2.8 (for $k = 1$) and 3.8 (for $k = 2$) respectively. We give a practical method to find primes with suitable noisy encodings.

We demonstrate the practical relevance of our comparison protocol by applying it in a secure neural network classifier for the MNIST dataset. Concretely, we discuss a secure multiparty computation based on the binarized multi-layer perceptron of Hubara et al., using our comparison for the second and third layers.

1 Introduction

Secure integer comparison has been a primitive of particular interest since the inception of multiparty computation (MPC). In 1982, even before general multiparty computation had been realized, Yao introduced the *Millionaires' Problem* [21], where two millionaires want to determine who of them has greater wealth without revealing any information beyond the outcome of this comparison to

© Springer Nature Switzerland AG 2019
M. Matsui (Ed.): CT-RSA 2019, LNCS 11405, pp. 453–472, 2019.
https://doi.org/10.1007/978-3-030-12612-4_23

each other or to any third party. Secure comparison has been investigated extensively since. A whole range of solutions is available with every solution aiming for a particular trade-off. Nonetheless, with respect to arithmetic-secret-sharing-based MPC, secure comparison remains among the most expensive basic operations in terms of round complexity. Hence, for applications that require many comparisons, achieving high throughput (important for privacy-preserving data processing applications) or low latency (crucial for certain applications, like blind auctions for real-time advertisement sales) can be challenging.

1.1 Related Work

Whereas most secure comparison protocols work over finite fields of arbitrary order, Yu [22] presents a comparison protocol that only works for specifically chosen prime moduli. Although this clearly poses a restriction in terms of applicability, the main benefit is that the specifically chosen prime modulus p enables Yu to perform a comparison *in a single round of communication* in the online phase (the offline preprocessing phase requires three communication rounds), albeit in a range that is small compared to p (see Sect. 3.4 for explicit bounds). Namely, he chooses p such that the pattern of quadratic residues and non-residues modulo p coincides with the sign function on a given interval symmetric around zero, which is an idea that goes back to a protocol due to Feige, Kilian, and Naor [3], who use it to compute the sign of an element $x \in [-2, 2]$ in $\mathbb{F}_7$. Yu's comparison protocol for comparing arbitrary elements $a, b \in \mathbb{F}_p$ essentially works by breaking up the full-range comparison into several medium-range comparisons of the above type by performing a digit decomposition.

1.2 This Paper

In this paper, we pursue the line of work initiated by Yu [22]. Our main contribution is that we achieve an improvement in the comparison range while keeping the bit-length of the prime modulus fixed. Concretely, we propose a protocol that, for a fixed prime-length, achieves close to a *two-fold increase of the comparison range* (over Yu's results), while still enjoying a single-round online phase, at the cost of a constant amount of additional communication and some additional local computations. Also, we present a two-online-rounds protocol that achieves more than a *three-fold increase in the comparison range* when compared to Yu's approach. In other words, to compare two integers that lie in a given range (symmetric around zero), our methods require a smaller prime than the prime required for the protocol from [22]. Keeping the finite-field modulus as small as possible or within the machine's word size could be important, for example, in a setting where MPC protocols run on constrained hardware platforms. On such platforms, the complexity of prime-field arithmetic (which is directly related to the prime size) can have a significant impact on the runtime performance. Our protocols can be found in Sect. 5.

The main idea is to somewhat relax the constraints on the prime modulus p: instead of requiring that the Legendre symbols of *all* elements in the interval

$[-d, d]$, for a given positive integer d, coincide with the sign function, we only require this coincidence for *most* elements (in a specific sense). Let us, for some fixed prime p, say that there is an *error* at position $x \in [-d, d]$ if $(x \mid p) \neq \text{sgn}(x)$. Our improvement is based on exploiting a "local redundancy" property enjoyed by the sign function that lets us correct such errors as long as they are sufficiently "sparse", by means of inspecting also the Legendre symbols of some neighboring positions and then performing a majority vote.

This new approach raises the question of how to find primes that give rise to increased ranges. In Sect. 4, we present some results that considerably simplify this search, including tables of suitable primes for various bit lengths.

1.3   Application: Efficient Neural Network Evaluation in MPC

To demonstrate the practical value of our work, we apply our new comparison protocol to the problem of securely evaluating a neural network, in which the sign function is used as non-linearity. We use a binarized multi-layer perceptron (BMLP) for recognizing handwritten digits, as described in [7], which is trained (in the clear) on the well-known MNIST handwritten-digits data set. We consider an MPC scenario in which the input images are secret-shared between the parties, which then securely evaluate the BMLP to obtain the estimated digit in secret-shared form.

2   Preliminaries

Arithmetic Black Box. We suppose that we are given a secure arithmetic black-box (ABB) functionality that can securely evaluate multiplication and linear forms over the finite field $\mathbb{F}_p$. We write $[x]$ for the residue class $x \in \mathbb{F}_p$ encrypted under the ABB (e.g., x is secret-shared among a set of parties, or perhaps encrypted under some homomorphic encryption scheme). Abusing notation, for small $x \in \mathbb{F}_p$ we will also refer to x as an integer in $\mathbb{Z}$, given as the canonical lift of the residue class to the integers $[-\lfloor \frac{p}{2} \rfloor, \lfloor \frac{p}{2} \rfloor]$.

Sign vs. Binary Sign. The sign function and the binary sign function are respectively defined as

$$
\text{sgn}(z) = \begin{cases} 1 & \text{if } z > 0, \\ 0 & \text{if } z = 0, \\ -1 & \text{if } z < 0. \end{cases} \qquad \text{bsgn}(z) = \begin{cases} 1 & \text{if } z \geq 0, \\ -1 & \text{if } z < 0. \end{cases}
$$

Comparing two integers a and b is achieved by evaluating the sign (or bsgn) of their difference $a - b$. The sgn function gives rise to a three-way comparison, while the bsgn function corresponds to two-way comparison. In this paper, we will start our analysis in terms of the sgn function, but for reasons that will become clear later our protocols evaluate the bsgn function (i.e., achieve two-way comparison). We will sometimes be a bit sloppy and use the word "sign" also for the bsgn function; the precise meaning should nonetheless still be clear from its context.

The Legendre Symbol. Recall that for any odd prime p and any integer a, the Legendre symbol is defined as the integer

$$(a \mid p) = \begin{cases} 0 & \text{if } a \equiv 0 \pmod{p}, \\ 1 & \text{if } a \text{ is a quadratic residue modulo } p, \\ -1 & \text{otherwise.} \end{cases}$$

The Legendre symbol is a completely multiplicative function, which means that $(a \mid p)(b \mid p) = (ab \mid p)$ for all $a, b \in \mathbb{Z}$. The identity $(a \mid p) \equiv a^{\frac{p-1}{2}} \pmod{p}$ is known as *Euler's criterion*. The *law of quadratic reciprocity* asserts that for odd primes p and q,

$$(p \mid q)(q \mid p) = (-1)^{\frac{p-1}{2} \frac{q-1}{2}}.$$

Securely Evaluating Legendre Symbols. In principle, we can securely evaluate the Legendre symbol via Euler's criterion, which would require $O(\log p)$ secure multiplications. The complete multiplicativity of the Legendre symbol enables the following constant-rounds protocol for securely evaluating the Legendre symbol in the preprocessing model with an single-round online phase. In the preprocessing phase, we generate a secret-shared pair $([r], [(r \mid p)])$ of a random non-zero class r together with its Legendre symbol. In the online (input-dependent) phase, we securely multiply $[a] \cdot [r]$, open the result and then compute

$$[(a \mid p)] = (ar \mid p)[(r \mid p)].$$

Note that the security of the protocol requires that $a \not\equiv 0 \pmod{p}$, which should be taken into account when using this protocol.

Blum Primes. A prime p for which $p \equiv 3 \pmod{4}$ is called a *Blum prime*. By Euler's criterion, -1 is a quadratic non-residue modulo p if and only if p is a Blum prime. Hence, for any Blum prime p, the map $x \mapsto (x \mid p)$ is an odd function for $x \in [-\lfloor p/2 \rfloor, \lfloor p/2 \rfloor]$ (which follows immediately from the multiplicativity property of the Legendre symbol), i.e., it enjoys the same symmetry around the origin as the sign function.

3   Evaluating the Sign Function Using Legendre Symbols

3.1   Redundancy Property of the Sign Function

In this section we show that the sign function enjoys a "local redundancy" property, which lets us correct sign-flip errors by means of majority-decoding as long as those errors occur sparsely (in a sense defined below).

Definition 1. *Let $k \geq 0$ be an integer, and let $\mathcal{T} = [t_1, t_2]$ be an interval of integers with $t_2 - t_1 \geq 2k$. We say that a function $e : \mathcal{T} \to \{0, 1\}$ is an error function on $\mathcal{T}$ admissible for k if $e(x) = 0$ for all $x \in [-(k+1), k+1] \cap \mathcal{T}$ and if $\sum_{i=-k}^{k} e(y + i) \leq k$ holds for all $y \in [t_1 + k, t_2 - k]$.*

Lemma 1. *Let k and T be as in Definition 1, and let e be an error function on T admissible for k. Then,*

$$\mathrm{sgn}\left(\sum_{i=-k}^{k} (-1)^{e(x+i)} \mathrm{sgn}(x+i) \right) = \mathrm{sgn}(x)$$

holds for all $x \in [t_1 + k, t_2 - k]$.

The proof will clarify why we require in Definition 1 that an admissible error function $e(x)$ has an "error-free" region around $x = 0$; informally speaking, the reason is that the sign function undergoes its sign change at $x = 0$, which means that there is "less room" for errors under majority-decoding in this region.

Proof. We will prove the statement for $T = [-a, a]$ where $a \geq k$ is any integer. This implies the claim for any subinterval of T of cardinality at least $2k+1$. Note that because of symmetry (in the sign function as well as in the definition of an admissible error function), it suffices to prove the statement for $x \geq 0$. We distinguish three cases for x. If $x = 0$, we have $\sum_{i=-k}^{k} (-1)^{e(i)} \mathrm{sgn}(i) = \sum_{i=-k}^{k} \mathrm{sgn}(i) = \mathrm{sgn}(x) = 0$, where the first equality follows because e is admissible for k and the second equality follows from the fact that summing an odd function over an interval symmetric around zero gives the value zero.

Second, if $x > k$, we have

$$\sum_{i=-k}^{k} (-1)^{e(x+i)} \mathrm{sgn}(x+i) = \sum_{i=-k}^{k} (-1)^{e(x+i)} > 0,$$

where the equality follows because $\mathrm{sgn}(x+i) = 1$ for all $i \in [-k, k]$ and the inequality follows because e is admissible for k.

For the third (and final) case, suppose that $x \in [1, k]$. We have

$$\sum_{i=-k}^{k} (-1)^{e(x+i)} \mathrm{sgn}(x+i) = \sum_{i=-k}^{k-x+1} \mathrm{sgn}(x+i) + \sum_{i'=k-x+2}^{k} (-1)^{e(x+i')} \mathrm{sgn}(x+i')$$

$$= \sum_{j=x-k}^{k+1} \mathrm{sgn}(j) + \sum_{j'=k+2}^{k+x} (-1)^{e(j')} \mathrm{sgn}(j')$$

$$= 1 + x + \sum_{j'=k+2}^{k+x} (-1)^{e(j')}$$

$$\geq (1 + x) + (1 - x) = 2$$

$\square$

3.2   The Legendre Symbol as a "Noisy" Sign

Suppose that p is a Blum prime. We can view the Legendre symbol $(x \mid p)$ for $x \in \mathbb{F}_p$ as a "noisy" version of the sign of x:

$$(x \mid p) = (-1)^{e(x)} \mathrm{sgn}(x), \tag{1}$$

where $e(x)$ is the error function that is determined by p. If we now plug (1) into Lemma 1, we can conclude that we may compute the sign of x as the sign of the sum of the Legendre symbols of positions in a length-$(2k+1)$ interval centered at x, for all $x \in [t_1 + k, t_2 - k]$, if e is an error function on the interval $[t_1, t_2]$ admissible for k.

Because p is a Blum prime, the pattern of Legendre symbols has odd symmetry, which implies that we can w.l.o.g. define $\mathcal{T}$ such that it is symmetric around zero. A natural question, for a given Blum prime p, non-negative integer k, and $\mathcal{T} = [-d, d]$ for a positive integer $d \geq k$, is how large d can maximally be such that e is an error function on $\mathcal{T}$ that is admissible for k. This gives rise to the following equivalent definition, in which we leave the error function implicit.

Definition 2. *Let k be a non-negative integer, and let $p > 2k + 1$ be a Blum prime. We define the k-range of p, denoted $d_k(p)$, to be the largest integer d such that for all integers x with $1 \leq x \leq d$ it holds that*

$$\sum_{i=-k}^{k} (x + i \mid p) > 0, \tag{2}$$

and we set $d_k(p) = 0$ if no such d exists.

Note that $d_0(p)$ tells us the maximum size of Yu's "Consecutive Quadratic Residues and Non-Residues Sign Module" for a given prime p, i.e., in Yu's terminology and notation: a Blum prime p *qualifies* for $\pm\ell$-CQRN for all $\ell \leq d_0(p)$.

Lower Bound on $d_k(p)$. If $p > 2k + 1$ and $d_0(p) > k$, then $d_k(p) \geq d_0(p)$.

Example. Let us illustrate Definition 2 by means of an example. Let us take $p = 23$; note that this is a Blum prime. Below, we have evaluated the first 16 Legendre symbols.

x	0	1	2	3	4		5	6		7	8	9	10	11	12	13	14	15	...
$(x \mid p)$	0	1	1	1	1		-1	1		-1	1	1	-1	-1	1	1	-1	-1	

We can now read off that $d_0(23) = 4$. Furthermore, it is easy to verify that $d_1(23) = 5$, $d_2(23) = 8$, and $d_3(23) = 7$.

3.3 Avoiding Zero by Restricting to Odd Positions

As mentioned in the preliminaries, if we use the single-online-round protocol for securely evaluating the Legendre symbol, we may not evaluate the Legendre symbol on the zero element. A simple trick to avoid zero (also used in [22]) is to restrict to evaluation of odd inputs by using the map $x \mapsto 2x + 1$. Note that this implies that we cannot compute $\text{sgn}(x)$ using the single-online-round protocol; instead we will evaluate $\text{bsgn}(x)$. Removing the conditions on the Legendre symbols at even positions gives rise to the following definition.

Definition 3. *Let k be a non-negative integer, and let $p > 2k + 1$ be a Blum prime. We define $d_k^*(p)$ as the largest integer d such that for all integers x with $1 \le x \le d$ it holds that*

$$\sum_{i=-k}^{k} (2(x + i) + 1 \mid p) > 0, \tag{3}$$

and we set $d_k^*(p) = 0$ if no such d exists.

Note that for any Blum prime p for which $d_0(p) > 1$ (which implies that $d_0(p)$ is even), it is easy to see that it holds that $d_0^*(p) = \frac{1}{2}d_0(p) - 1$. For $k > 0$, such simple relations do not seem to exist. This means, for example, that a prime p that gives rise to a high value for $d_1(p)$, does not necessarily give a high value for $d_1^*(p)$, and vice versa.

3.4 Bounds on $d_0(p)$

The value $d_0(p)$ can be interpreted as the position just before the appearance of the first quadratic non-residue. Let $n_1(p)$ denote the smallest quadratic non-residue. Finding bounds on $n_1(p)$ is a well-known problem in number theory, with important contributions from Polyà, Vinogradov and Burgess, among others. The best explicit upper bound that is currently known (for p a Blum prime) is due to Treviño [19]:

$$d_0(p) + 1 = n_1(p) \le 1.1 \sqrt[4]{p} \log p.$$

Graham and Ringrose [5] proved an unconditional asymptotic lower bound (improving on a previous result by, independently,[1] Fridlender [4] and Salié [14]), namely, that there exist infinitely many primes for which

$$d_0(p) + 1 = n_1(p) \ge c \cdot \log(p) \cdot \log \log \log p.$$

for some absolute constant c.[2]

Lamzouri *et al.* [10] prove that conditional on the Generalized Riemann Hypothesis, for all primes $p \ge 5$ it holds that

$$d_0(p) + 1 = n_1(p) < (\log p)^2.$$

3.5 Bounds on $d_1(p)$

Hudson [8] proves an upper bound on the least *pair* of quadratic non-residues. Formally, let $n_2(p)$ be the smallest value such that $n_2(p)$ and $n_2(p) + 1$ are quadratic non-residues. For $k = 1$, it must hold that $d_1(p) < n_2(p)$, because an

---

[1] Ankeny [2] attributes this result to Chowla, but does not provide a reference.

[2] In the literature, this is also written as $n_1(p) = \Omega(\log(p) \cdot \log \log \log p)$, where Ω is Hardy–Littlewood's Big Omega: $f(n) = \Omega(g(n)) \iff \limsup_{n \to \infty} |f(n)/g(n)| > 0$.

"error pattern" consisting of two consecutive quadratic non-residues (such that $n_2(p) \in [1, (p-3)/2]$) cannot be corrected using a majority vote in a window of length $2k + 1 = 3$. Hudson's bound is as follows. For every $p \geq 5$ we have that

$$d_1(p) < n_2(p) \leq (n_1(p) - 1)q_2,$$

where q_2 is the second smallest prime that is a quadratic non-residue modulo p. Hildebrand [6] also proves an upper bound on $n_2(p)$:

$$d_1(p) < n_2(p) \leq p^{1/(4\sqrt{e})+\epsilon} \quad p \geq p_0(\epsilon),$$

for every $\epsilon > 0$ and $p_0(\epsilon)$ a sufficiently large constant depending on ϵ.

Sun [17] gives a construction for generating all elements n in $\mathbb{F}_p$ such that n and $n + 1$ are quadratic non-residues.

Lemma 2 ([17]). *Let p be an odd prime and let g be a primitive root of p. Then,*

$$\mathcal{U} := \left\{ n \in \mathbb{F}_p \mid (n \mid p) = (n+1 \mid p) = -1 \right\}$$

$$= \left\{ u_k \in \mathbb{F}_p \mid u_k \equiv \frac{(g^{2k-1} - 1)^2}{4g^{2k-1}} \pmod{p}, \quad k = 1, \ldots, \left\lfloor \frac{p-1}{4} \right\rfloor \right\}$$

We can interpret this lemma as giving a collection of upper bounds on $d_1(p)$, that is, $d_1(p) < n_2(p) \leq u_k$ holds for every $k = 1, \ldots, \lfloor (p-1)/4 \rfloor$.

An error pattern that consists of two quadratic non-residues that are separated by one arbitrary position can also not be corrected using a majority vote in a window of length $2k + 1 = 3$. Inspired by Sun, we prove the following lemma.

Lemma 3. *Let p be a Blum prime, let $b = ((2 \mid p) + 1)/2 \in \{0, 1\}$ and let g be a primitive root of p. Then,*

$$\mathcal{V} := \left\{ n \in \mathbb{F}_p \mid (n \mid p) = (n+2 \mid p) = -1 \right\}$$

$$= \left\{ v_k \in \mathbb{F}_p \mid v_k \equiv \frac{(g^{2k-b} - 1)^2}{2g^{2k-b}} \mod p, \quad k = 1, \ldots, (p-3)/4 \right\}.$$

Also this lemma can be viewed as giving a collection of upper bounds on $d_1(p)$. If $(n \mid p) = (n+2 \mid p) = -1$, then a decoding error (under majority decoding with $k = 1$) will occur at position $n + 1$, hence we have that $d_1(p) \leq v_k$ holds (instead of strict inequality) for every $k = 1, \ldots, (p-3)/4$.

Proof. Let $\chi(x) = (x \mid p)$ for all $x \in \mathbb{F}_p$. Jacobsthal [9] proves that for p a Blum prime,

$$\left| \{ n \in \mathbb{F}_p \mid \chi(n) = \chi(n+2) = -1 \wedge \chi(n+1) = 1 \} \right| = \frac{p-1+2(2 \mid p)}{8},$$

$$\text{and} \quad \left| \{ n \in \mathbb{F}_p \mid \chi(n) = \chi(n+1) = \chi(n+2) = -1 \} \right| = \frac{p-5-2(2 \mid p)}{8}.$$

Hence, by summing the cardinalities of the above sets, we get that

$$\left|\{n \in \mathbb{F}_p \mid \chi(n) = \chi(n+2) = -1\}\right| = \frac{p-3}{4}.$$

For $j = 1, 2, \ldots, (p-3)/2$, let $r_j \equiv (g^j - 1)^2/(2g^j) \mod p$. Then, $r_j + 2 \equiv (g^j + 1)^2/(2g^j) \mod p$. It now follows that $\chi(r_j) = \chi(r_j + 2) = (-1)^j\chi(2)$ for all $j = 1, 2, \ldots, (p-3)/2$. Hence, $\chi(r_{2k-(\chi(2)+1)/2}) = \chi(r_{2k-(\chi(2)+1)/2} + 2) = -1$ for all $k = 1, 2, \ldots, (p-3)/4$.

It remains to prove that $r_s \not\equiv r_t \mod p$ for all $s, t \in [1, (p-3)/2]$ with $t \neq s$; for this part we can re-use Sun's proof technique used in the proof of Lemma 2. Namely, for all $s, t \in [1, (p-3)/2]$ with $t \neq s$, we have that $g^{s+t} \not\equiv 1 \mod p$ (since g is a primitive root), which implies that $g^s - g^t \not\equiv (g^s - g^t)/g^{s+t} \mod p$. Hence, $g^s + g^{-s} \not\equiv g^t + g^{-t} \mod p$ from which we obtain that $r_s \not\equiv r_t \mod p$. We can now conclude that

$$\{n \in \mathbb{F}_p \mid \chi(n) = \chi(n+2) = -1\} = \{r_{2k-b} \in \mathbb{F}_p \mid k \in [1, (p-3)/4]\},$$

and the claim follows. □

4   Finding a Prime for a Given k-Range

In order to find a prime that, for given integers k and D_k, gives rise to $d_k(p) \geq D_k$, we could in principle take a naive approach by letting a computer exhaustively enumerate the primes in increasing order and compute the Legendre symbols at $a = 1, \ldots, D_k$, and stop when they are all 1. Although this approach works for small values of k and D_k (say for $D_1 < 200$), for larger D_k this will become intractable.

We can speed up the calculation of d_k by using the multiplicativity of the Legendre symbol, the law of quadratic reciprocity and the Chinese Remainder Theorem (CRT). Moreover, we may speed up the computation by enumerating over values p that already satisfy some conditions on the Legendre symbols, using a *wheel data structure* [13,16]. We will first review the problem for the case $k = 0$ and then extend the method to the case $k = 1$. Our approach also works for arbitrary k, and we supply the relevant extensions, but we note that its practicality rapidly diminishes as k increases.

4.1   Finding Primes with High $d_0(p)$

Recall that finding a prime p' such that $d_0(p') \geq D$, for some D, means that p' must be a Blum prime such that the elements $1, \ldots, D$ are quadratic residues modulo p'. By the complete multiplicativity of the Legendre symbol, it suffices to find a Blum prime p such that all primes $q \leq D$ are quadratic residues modulo p.

Proposition 1. *Let q be an odd prime, and p a Blum prime. Then, it holds that*

$$(q \mid p) = (-p \mid q).$$

Proof. It holds that $(q \mid p) = (p \mid q)^{-1} (-1)^{\frac{p-1}{2} \frac{q-1}{2}} = (p \mid q)(-1)^{\frac{q-1}{2}} = (p \mid q)(-1 \mid q) = (-p \mid q)$, where the first equality holds by the law of quadratic reciprocity, the second holds because p is a Blum prime, the third follows from Euler's criterion and the fourth follows from the multiplicativity property of the Legendre symbol.   □

Let $\mathcal{R}_q = \{r \bmod q : (-r \mid q) = 1\}$. Then, q is a quadratic residue modulo p if and only if

$$(p \bmod q) \in \mathcal{R}_q. \tag{4}$$

This represents an (exclusive) disjunction of linear congruences:

$$p \equiv r_1 (\bmod q) \vee \ldots \vee p \equiv r_\ell (\bmod q),$$

where $\mathcal{R}_q = \{r_1 \bmod q, \ldots, r_\ell \bmod q\}$.

Let $q_1, \ldots, q_m$ denote all odd primes that are in $[1, D]$. The condition that all integers $[1, D]$ are quadratic residues modulo x thus gives rise to the following system of *simultaneous disjunctions* of linear congruences:

$$x \equiv 7 (\bmod 8) \text{ (guarantees that } (-1 \mid x) = -1 \text{ and } (2 \mid x) = 1),$$
$$(x \bmod q_1) \in \mathcal{R}_{q_1},$$
$$(x \bmod q_2) \in \mathcal{R}_{q_2}, \tag{5}$$
$$\vdots$$
$$(x \bmod q_m) \in \mathcal{R}_{q_m}.$$

Suppose for each $i = 1, \ldots, m$ we choose a residue class $a_i \in \mathcal{R}_{q_i}$, and we regard the resulting vector $(a_1, \ldots, a_m)$. We may choose the a_i independently since the q_i are distinct primes. An element $(a_1, \ldots, a_m) \in \mathcal{R}_{q_1} \times \cdots \times \mathcal{R}_{q_m} =: \mathcal{R}$ is in one-to-one correspondence with an arithmetic progression of solutions to the above system of congruences, that is, $x, x + Q, x + 2Q, \ldots$ where $Q = 8 \prod_{i \in [m]} q_i$. Linnik's theorem [11] (combined with Xylouris' bound [20]) asserts that there will be a prime in this arithmetic progression whose size is bounded as $O(Q^5)$.

Finding the Smallest Such Prime. Finding *some* prime that satisfies the above system is relatively easy, since we may fix a vector $(a_1, \ldots, a_m) \in \mathcal{R}$. We can then enumerate all positive integers x such that $x \bmod q_i = a_i$ via the constructive proof of the CRT, and output the first solution that is prime. However, finding the *smallest* prime that satisfies the above system is a (much) harder task, as it involves searching over the full set $\mathcal{R}$, whose cardinality is exponential in m.

In practice, we may simply enumerate all integers x in ascending order, and check whether x satisfies the system of Eq. (5) rather than computing the Legendre symbols at $1, \ldots, D_0$ explicitly. We can speed up the computation by precomputing the sets $\mathcal{R}_{q_i}$ and storing them in memory. We can check many congruences at once by combining sets of congruences using the CRT. For example, for moduli q, q' we have that $(x \bmod q) \in \mathcal{R}_q$ and $(x \bmod q') \in \mathcal{R}_{q'}$ if and only if $(x \bmod qq') \in \mathcal{R}_{qq'}$,

$$\mathcal{R}_{qq'} := (\mathcal{R}_q + \{0, q', \ldots, (\ell/q' - 1)q'\}) \cap (\mathcal{R}_{q'} + \{0, q, \ldots, (\ell/q - 1)q\}), \tag{6}$$

where $\ell = \text{lcm}(q, q')$ and '+' denotes Minkowski addition. Note that we have abused notation here slightly, and represented the sets $\mathcal{R}_m$ for each modulus m as the set of integers in $[0, m-1]$ that are the canonical lifts of the residue classes mod m. By recursion, the above extends to combining more than two sets of congruences.

4.2   Finding Primes with High $d_1(p)$

For $k > 0$, for $d_k(p) \geq D$ to hold for some positive integer D, it is no longer necessary that p satisfies each disjunction of congruences in Eq. (5); instead, some subsets suffice. For example, for $d_1(p) \geq 6$ we need $(2 \mid p) = 1$ and at least one of $(5 \mid p) = 1$ or $(6 \mid p) = (2 \mid p)(3 \mid p) = (3 \mid p) = 1$, otherwise Eq. (2) fails to hold for $a = 5$.

In order for Eq. (2) to hold, we have one set of congruences for every length-$(2k + 1)$ subinterval of $[-k, d]$; even for $k = 1$ this quickly grows prohibitively large for non-trivial lower bounds D on $d_k(p)$. While for $k > 0$ the density of primes p satisfying $d_k(p) \geq D$ is greater than for $k = 0$, the search becomes a lot more expensive.

For $k = 1$, we simplify our search for p with $d_1(p) \geq D_1$ with an extra condition: we also require $d_0(p) \geq D_0$ where $D_1 \leq (D_0)^2$. This ensures that each integer in $(D_0, D_1]$ has at most one prime factor greater or equal to D_1. Under this restriction, we get a condition equivalent to $d_1(p) \geq D_1$ which requires fewer computations to check.

Definition 4. *Let D_0, D_1 be non-negative integers with $D_0 < D_1 \leq (D_0)^2$. Let q, q' be distinct primes. We say that $\{q, q'\}$ is a* related pair *on $(D_0, D_1]$ if $D_0 < q, q' \leq D_1$ and there exist positive integers $x, y < D_0$ such that $|xq - yq'| \leq 2$ and $\max\{xq, yq'\} \leq D_1$.*

Proposition 2. *Let D_0, D_1 be non-negative integers with $D_0 < D_1 \leq (D_0)^2$, and let p be a Blum prime with $d_0(p) \geq D_0$. Then $d_1(p) \geq D_1 - 1$ if and only if the following condition holds: for every related pair of primes $\{q, q'\}$ on $(D_0, D_1]$ it holds that $(q \mid p) = 1 \vee (q' \mid p) = 1$.*

Proof. Let a be any positive integer such that $a \leq D_1$. First, we show that $(a \mid p) = -1$ if and only if a has a prime factor $q > D_0$ and $(q \mid p) = -1$. Suppose a has a prime factor $q > D_0$ with $(q \mid p) = -1$. Since $\frac{a}{q} < \frac{a}{D_0} \leq \frac{D_1}{D_0} \leq D_0$, we have $(a/q \mid p) = 1$, hence $(a \mid p) = -1$. If a does not have a prime factor $q > D_0$ with $(q \mid p) = -1$, then taking any prime factor $q' \mid a$, it must hold that $q' > D_0$, in which case $(q' \mid p) = 1$ by assumption, or $q' \leq D_0$, in which case $(q' \mid p) = 1$ by $d_0(p) \geq D_0$.

We now finish the proof by showing $d_1(p) < D_1 - 1$ if and only if there is some related pair q, q' such that $(q \mid p) = (q' \mid p) = -1$. We have $d_1(p) < D_1 - 1$ if and only if there exists an integer x such that $1 < x \leq D_1 - 1$ and $(x - 1 \mid p) + (x \mid p) + (x + 1 \mid p) < 0$. This latter inequality holds if and only if at least two of $\{x - 1, x, x + 1\}$ have Legendre symbol -1. By the above, this holds if and only if two of these numbers have respective prime factors $q, q' > D_0$ and $(q \mid p) = (q' \mid p) = -1$. For these q, q', we have that they constitute a related pair, since they each have a multiple in $\{x-1, x, x+1\}$ and $x+1 \leq D_1$. Conversely, for any related pair there exists such an interval $\{x-1, x, x+1\}$ with $1 < x \leq D_1 - 1$.

$\square$

Proposition 2 gives sufficient conditions for $d_1(p) > D_1 - 1$ in terms of related pairs of primes that have to satisfy certain disjunctions of congruences. If we want to include those disjunctions in a system as shown in Eq. (5), we need to represent them in the same form. For every pair of related primes $\{q, q'\}$, the condition that $(q \mid p) = 1 \lor (q' \mid p) = 1$ in Proposition 2 corresponds to taking the *union* of the associated residue sets $\mathcal{R}_q$ and $\mathcal{R}'_q$ of the related primes q and q'. That is, let $\ell = \mathrm{lcm}(q, q')$, then

$$\mathcal{R}_{q,q'} := (\mathcal{R}_q + \{0, q, \ldots, (\ell/q - 1)q\}) \cup (\mathcal{R}'_q + \{0, q', \ldots, (\ell/q' - 1)q'\}),$$

where '+' denotes Minkowski addition, and again we abuse notation and canonically lift residue classes modulo m to the integers $[0, m-1]$. We can now express the related-primes disjunction of congruences as

$$(x \bmod \ell) \in \mathcal{R}_{q,q'}.$$

Since this disjunction of congruences has exactly the same form as the other disjunctions in Eq. (5) we can also take intersections (using Eq. (6)) between a related-primes congruence $\mathcal{R}_{q,q'}$ and another disjunction of congruences.

We can naturally extend the approach for searching primes with high $d_1(p)$ to an approach for finding primes with high $d_k(p)$ for $k > 1$. This involves imposing constraints on sets of $k + 1$ distinct primes that are related in a suitably defined way. Note, however, that the use of this for high k is limited, given that we still constrain $D_k \leq (D_0)^2$, and we do not elaborate on this.

4.3   Finding Primes with High $d_k^*(p)$

To find primes p with large $d_k^*(p)$ we use the following results.

Definition 5. *Let D_0, D_k be non-negative integers with $D_0 < D_k \leq (D_0)^2$. Let $Q = \{q_0, \ldots, q_k\}$ be a set of $k+1$ distinct primes. We say that Q is a $*$-related set on $(D_0, D_k]$ if $Q \subseteq (D_0, D_k]$ and there exist positive odd integers $x_0, \ldots, x_k < D_0$ such that:*

1. *for any i with $0 \leq i \leq k$ we have $x_i q_i \leq D_k$*
2. *for any i, j with $0 \leq i < j \leq k$ it holds that $|x_i q_i - x_j q_j| \in \{2, 4, 6, \ldots, 4k\}$*

Proposition 3. *Let D_0, D_k be non-negative integers with $D_0 < D_k \leq (D_0)^2$, and let p be a Blum prime with $d_0^*(p) \geq \frac{1}{2} D_0$. Then $d_k^*(p) \geq \frac{1}{2} D_k - k$ if and only if the following condition holds: for every set Q of $k+1$ distinct primes $*$-related on $(D_0, D_k]$, it holds that there exists some $q \in Q$ with $(q \mid p) = 1$.*

4.4   Implementation and Results

We have implemented a search algorithm for primes p with minimal $d_k(p)$ and $d_k^*(p)$ for $k = 0, 1, 2$ using the precomputation of linear congruences as detailed above. We have enumerated all minimal p up to 64 bits with ascending $d_1(p)$ and with $d_0(p) \geq 64$, and likewise for ascending $d_1^*(p)$ with $d_0^*(p) \geq 32$. Our implementation is written in Rust and uses the wheel method from [16]. It is publicly available on GitHub [1].

Table 1 shows results of our search for primes that give rise to as high as possible values of $d_1^*(p)$ and $d_2^*(p)$. Because of space constraints, we refer the reader to the full version of our paper (IACR ePrint, Report 2018/1236) for tables for $d_1(p)$ and $d_2(p)$. See Fig. 1 for a plot of the overall results.

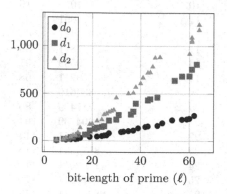 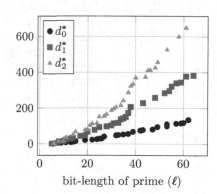

bit-length of prime (ℓ)   bit-length of prime (ℓ)

Fig. 1. Graphical comparison of the comparison range achieved by Yu's method (d_0 and d_0^*) vs. our method. The data for d_0 is taken from [12, Table 6.23] (and for all points shown here it holds that $d_0^* = d_0/2$).

5   Secure Protocols for bsgn

In this section we present three protocols for evaluating the bsgn function, for $k = 1$ and $k = 2$. Note that these immediately imply comparison protocols; from the triangle inequality it follows that correctness for comparison is guaranteed if both inputs lie in $[-\lfloor d/2 \rfloor, \lfloor d/2 \rfloor]$, where $[-d, d]$ is the input range of the bsgn protocol. Throughout this section, we suppose that p is a Blum prime.

We first describe a protocol for securely evaluating the Legendre symbol, which we call Legendre. We describe the protocol in terms of black-box invocations of protocols for sampling a random element from $\mathbb{F}_p^*$ (denoted as RandomElem($\mathbb{F}_p^*$)) and for sampling a random bit $\{0, 1\} \subset \mathbb{F}_p$ called RandomBit.

5.1   Secure Medium-Range bsgn Protocol for $k = 1$

In our protocol for $k = 1$, shown as Protocol 2, we compute the binary sign of the sum of the Legendre symbols by means of the multivariate polynomial

$$f(x, y, z) = \frac{x + y + z - xyz}{2},$$

Table 1. Sequence of primes in increasing order (and their bit-lengths ℓ) for which $d_k^*(p)$ is strictly increasing, for $k \in \{1, 2\}$. Primes below the dashed lines have been found via our sieving method, which means that there could exist smaller primes (missed by the sieving method) that give rise to the same or higher values of $d_1^*(p)$ resp. $d_2^*(p)$. For the primes above the dashed lines, it holds that the prime is the smallest possible for a given $d_k^*(p)$. The primes below "$\star\star\star$" are 64 bit primes with the best known k-range.

ℓ	p	$d_1^*(p)$	ℓ	p	$d_2^*(p)$
5	23	1	6	47	3
6	47	4	7	83	6
7	83	5	8	131	8
8	131	7	8	179	15
8	239	8	10	1019	16
8	251	14	11	1091	26
10	1019	16	11	1427	31
11	1091	24	11	1811	36
13	4259	30	14	9539	51
14	10331	33	15	19211	68
14	12011	34	19	334619	78
17	74051	42	20	717419	80
17	96851	44	21	1204139	104
19	420731	47	22	2808251	114
20	831899	52	24	8774531	116
20	878099	53	24	11532611	117
20	954971	68	25	18225611	152
23	5317259	78	27	98962211	155
25	19127891	79	28	247330859	166
25	31585979	94	30	738165419	174
28	140258219	98	30	1030152059	188
30	697955579	104	31	1456289579	197
31	1452130811	112	32	2451099251	206
31	1919592419	115	34	11159531291	207
33	4323344819	116	34	13730529419	216
33	4499001491	117	35	17221585499	219
33	6024587819	118	35	19186524419	232
34	9259782419	138	35	26203369331	242
35	19846138451	143	37	92830394411	248
36	34613840351	151	37	128808841619	287
37	73773096179	153	38	232481520059	324
- - - - - - - - - - - - - - - - - - -			39	408727560491	335
37	119607747731	174	40	807183995411	370
38	163030664579	182	- - - - - - - - - - - - - - - - - - -		
38	170361409391	207	44	15869813229371	373
43	4754588149211	229	45	19379613618119	411
48	171772053182831	242	46	46760546950211	412

(*continued*)

Table 1. (*continued*)

48	178774759690511	243	48	240160967391791	425
48	205152197251811	258	49	294269750529611	456
52	2950193919326891	259	53	8755197891979139	526
52	3705750905778011	284	57	85283169141238571	528
54	10624213337944379	296	58	148892345027857499	599
55	26259748609914431	321	61	1915368196138563011	648
57	141840650661890879	340		$\star\,\star\,\star$	
59	321961111376298371	345	64	10807930853257193939	623
61	1158960903343074191	348			
61	1561357330831673339	378			
64	9409569905028393239	383			

Protocol 1. Legendre($[x]$)

Offline Phase
1: $[a] \leftarrow$ RandomElem($\mathbb{F}_p^*$)
2: $[b] \leftarrow$ RandomBit()
3: $[s] \leftarrow 2[b] - 1$
4: $[r] \leftarrow [s] \cdot [a^2]$

Online Phase
5: $c \leftarrow [x] \cdot [r]$
6: $[z] \leftarrow (c \mid p) \cdot [s]$
7: **return** $[z]$

---

which can be evaluated securely in two rounds using ordinary secure multiplication. It is easy to verify that f correctly computes the sign of the sum of $x, y, z \in \{-1, +1\}$.

Protocol 2. bsgn1Simple($[a]$), $|a| \leq d_1^*(p)$

1: $[x] \leftarrow$ Legendre($2[a] - 1$), $[y] \leftarrow$ Legendre($2[a] + 1$), $[z] \leftarrow$ Legendre($2[a] + 3$)
2: $[s] \leftarrow ([x] + [y] + [z] - [x][y][z])/2$
3: **return** $[s]$

Decreasing the Round Complexity in the Online Phase. Protocol bsgn1Simple requires three rounds in the online phase. We can bring this down to a single round by premultiplying the random Legendre symbols produced in the offline phase of the Legendre protocol. This is shown in Protocol 3. The random bit protocol has been concretely instantiated in the offline phase of Protocol 3 to show that the product of the three random Legendre symbols can be computed in parallel to the preparation of their corresponding random elements. The offline phase requires two rounds in addition to the round complexity of securely sampling random elements of $\mathbb{F}_p^*$.

Protocol 3. bsgn1SingleRound([a]), $|a| \leq d_1^*(p)$

Offline Phase

1: **for** $i \in \{1, 2, 3\}$ **do** $[t_i] \leftarrow$ RandomElem$(\mathbb{F}_p^*)$; $[u_i] \leftarrow$ RandomElem$(\mathbb{F}_p^*)$

2: **for** $i \in \{1, 2, 3\}$ **do** $[v_i] \leftarrow [t_i] \cdot [t_i]$; $w_i \leftarrow [u_i] \cdot [u_i]$

   $[m] \leftarrow [u_1] \cdot [u_2]$

3: **for** $i \in \{1, 2, 3\}$ **do** $[r_i] \leftarrow [v_i] \cdot [u_i] \cdot w_i^{-1/2}$; $[s_i] \leftarrow [u_i] \cdot w_i^{-1/2}$

   $[n] \leftarrow [m] \cdot [u_3] \cdot \prod_{i=1}^{3} w_i^{-1/2}$

4: **return** $([r_1], [s_1], [r_2], [s_2], [r_3], [s_3], [n])$

Online Phase

5: **for** $i \in \{1, 2, 3\}$ **do** $c_i \leftarrow (2[a] - 3 + 2i) \cdot [r_i]$

6: **return** $2^{-1} \left(\sum_{i=1}^{3} [s_i] \cdot (c_i \mid p) - [n] \cdot \prod_{i=1}^{3} (c_i \mid p) \right)$

5.2   Secure Medium-Range bsgn Protocol for $k = 2$

In our protocol for $k = 2$, shown as Protocol 4, we compute the binary sign of the sum of the five Legendre symbols by means of another invocation of Legendre. In the latter (outer) invocation of Legendre, we need not apply the $x \mapsto 2x + 1$ map because we sum an odd number of values in $\{-1, +1\}$ which cannot become zero. Note that this requires that $d_0(p) \geq 5$ for correctness of the protocol.

Protocol 4. bsgn2([a]), $|a| \leq d_2^*(p)$, $d_0(p) \geq 5$

1: $[x_1] \leftarrow$ Legendre$(2[a] - 3)$, $[x_2] \leftarrow$ Legendre$(2[a] - 1)$, $[x_3] \leftarrow$ Legendre$(2[a] + 1)$

   $[x_4] \leftarrow$ Legendre$(2[a] + 3)$, $[x_5] \leftarrow$ Legendre$(2[a] + 5)$

2: $[s] \leftarrow$ Legendre$([x_1] + [x_2] + [x_3] + [x_4] + [x_5])$

3: **return** $[s]$

6   Application: Fast Neural Network Evaluation in MPC

In this section we demonstrate the usefulness of our secure binary-sign evaluation technique for securely evaluating a neural network.

6.1   Binarized Multi-layer Perceptron for MNIST

For our experiments, we take the binarized multi-layer perceptron of Courbariaux et al. for recognizing handwritten digits from the well-known MNIST benchmark data set [7], which we refer as BMLP below. The BMLP network uses the sign function as its non-linear activation function, and is designed to be evaluated using integer arithmetic only, which allows for a natural MPC implementation.

The MNIST data set contains images of 28-by-28 pixels, where the intensity of each pixel is represented by a byte, i.e., an integer in $\mathcal{B} := [0, 255]$ (0 represents black, 255 represents white, and the values in between represent shades of gray). For the BMLP network, an input image is represented as a byte *vector* $x \in \mathcal{B}^{784}$. Note that by reshaping a two-dimensional image into a (one-dimensional) vector the spatial structure is lost, but this is not a problem for multi-layer perceptrons (as opposed to convolutional neural networks, for instance).

Let n denote the number of neurons per layer. The BMLP network consists of four layers, and uses $n = 4096$. We view each layer L_i, $i \in [1, 4]$, as a map between an input and output vector:

$$L_1 : \qquad \mathcal{B}^{784} \to \{-1, +1\}^n,$$
$$L_i : \{-1, +1\}^n \to \{-1, +1\}^n, \qquad i \in \{2, 3\}$$
$$L_4 : \{-1, +1\}^n \to \mathbb{Z}^{10}.$$

Let $k_1 = k_2 = k_3 = m_2 = m_3 = m_4 = n$ and $k_4 = 10$ and $m_1 = 784$. In [7], the output of L_i is computed as

$$L_i(x) := \begin{cases} \text{BinarySign}(\text{BatchNorm}_{\Theta_i}^{k_i}(W_i x + b_i)), & i \in \{1, 2, 3\} \\ \text{BatchNorm}_{\Theta_i}^{k_i}(W_i x + b_i) & i = 4. \end{cases}$$

Here $W_i \in \{-1, +1\}^{k_i \times m_i}$ is a matrix of weights, and $b_i \in \mathbb{Z}^{k_i}$ is a vector of bias values. The function BatchNorm, which applies *batch normalization* element-wise, is defined as

$$\text{BatchNorm}_{\Theta_i}^{\ell} : \qquad \mathbb{Z}^{\ell} \qquad \to \mathbb{Z}^{\ell}$$
$$(x_1, \ldots, x_\ell) \mapsto (f_{\Theta_i, 1}(x_1), \ldots, f_{\Theta_i, \ell}(x_\ell))$$

where $\Theta_i := (\mu_i, \tilde{\sigma}_i, \gamma_i, \beta_i)$ are the batch norm parameters for the ith layer: $\mu_i = (\mu_{i,1}, \ldots, \mu_{i,\ell})$, $\tilde{\sigma}_i = (\tilde{\sigma}_{i,j})_{j \in [1,\ell]}$, $\gamma = (\gamma_{i,j})_{j \in [1,\ell]}$, and $\beta = (\beta_{i,j})_{j \in [1,\ell]}$, and

$$f_{\Theta_i, j}(x) := \gamma_{i,j}\left(\frac{x - \mu_{i,j}}{\tilde{\sigma}_{i,j}}\right) + \beta_{i,j}.$$

The function BinarySign applies the bsgn function element-wise,

$$\text{BinarySign} : \qquad \mathbb{Z}^n \qquad \to \{-1, +1\}^n$$
$$(x_1, \ldots, x_n) \mapsto (\text{bsgn}(x_1), \ldots, \text{bsgn}(x_n)).$$

To obtain the final output of the BMLP, which is an integer $y \in [0, 9]$, we apply an (oblivious) argmax operation to the output of L_4:

$$y := \arg\max L_4(L_3(L_2(L_1(x)))).$$

Training the Network. We have trained the BMLP on a GPU using Courbariaux' original implementation (described in [7]) which is publicly available on GitHub.

6.2   Eliminating Redundant Parts of Batch Normalization

In layers 1–3, the BinarySign function is applied directly to the output of the BatchNorm function. Because the bsgn function is invariant to multiplying its input by a positive scalar, the BatchNorm function might perform some operations that are immediately undone by the bsgn function. Indeed, it actually turns out that the BatchNorm function (when followed by the BinarySign function) reduces to an additional bias term; the authors of [7] seem to have overlooked this. Formally,

$$f_i(x) = \gamma_i \left(\frac{x - \mu_i}{\tilde{\sigma}_i} \right) + \beta_i = \frac{\gamma_i}{\tilde{\sigma}_i} \left(x - \mu_i + \frac{\beta_i \tilde{\sigma}_i}{\gamma_i} \right),$$

$$\mathrm{bsgn}(f_i(x)) = \mathrm{bsgn}\left(x - \mu_i + \frac{\beta_i \tilde{\sigma}_i}{\gamma_i} \right), \qquad \gamma_i, \tilde{\sigma}_i > 0.$$

Hence, we update the bias vector in all layers except the last as follows,

$$\boldsymbol{b}'_i := \boldsymbol{b}_i - \boldsymbol{\mu}_i + \frac{\beta_i \tilde{\sigma}_i}{\gamma_i}$$

where all operations (addition, subtraction, multiplication, and division) in the above expression are performed element-wise. With this modification, evaluation of the BMLP network simplifies to

$$L_i(\boldsymbol{x}) = \begin{cases} \mathrm{BinarySign}(W_i \boldsymbol{x} + \boldsymbol{b}'_i), & i \in \{1,2,3\} \\ \mathrm{BatchNorm}^{k_i}_{\Theta_i}(W_i \boldsymbol{x} + \boldsymbol{b}_i) & i = 4. \end{cases}$$

6.3   Instantiating the BinarySign Function per Layer

Our aim is to instantiate the BinarySign function using our medium-range bsgn protocols. Nonetheless, for layer L_1, the magnitudes of the elements in the vector $W_1 \boldsymbol{x} + \boldsymbol{b}'_1$ for some image $\boldsymbol{x} \in \mathcal{B}^{784}$ will typically be way too large compared to the input range on which our bsgn protocols guarantee a correct answer. Hence, for L_1 we instantiate BinarySign as the element-wise application of an "off-the-shelf" large-range bsgn protocol, such as Toft's comparison protocol [18].

For layers L_2 and L_3 we instantiate BinarySign with (element-wise applications of) Protocol bsgn1Simple using a 64-bit prime modulus p for which $d_1^*(p) = 383$, and, in a separate experiment, with bsgn2 using a 64-bit modulus p' for which $d_2^*(p') = 594$.[3] Also for these layers, there seems to be a mismatch between the input ranges of bsgn1Simple and bsgn2 on which they guarantee correctness, i.e., $[-383, 383]$ and $[-594, 594]$ respectively, and the magnitudes of the elements in the vector $W_i \boldsymbol{y} + \boldsymbol{b}'_i$ for $i \in \{2,3\}$, where $\boldsymbol{y} \in \{-1, +1\}^n$. The first term in this sum (the vector $W_i \boldsymbol{y}$), can have elements with magnitude equal to n in the worst case, where $n = 4096$. Nonetheless, the distribution of values in the vector $W_i \boldsymbol{y} + \boldsymbol{b}'_i$ for all $i \in \{2,3\}$ is strongly concentrated around zero, hence

---

[3] The prime moduli are $p = 9409569905028393239$ and $p' = 15569949805843283171$.

Table 2. Classification performance of the BMLP on 10,000 MNIST test images

	Full-range sign	bsgn1Simple	bsgn2
Number of misclassifications	248	227	247
Error rate	0.0248	0.0227	0.0247

we will just ignore the fact that our bsgn-protocols will be invoked a number of times on values outside the range for which they guarantee correctness. As we show quantitatively in Table 2, this does not deteriorate the classification performance compared to a network where the full-range sign protocol is also used in layers L_2 and L_3. (Surprisingly, using bsgn1Simple even slightly improves the performance on the MNIST test set.)

6.4 Experimental Results (Neural Network Evaluation)

We have implemented the neural network in MPyC, a Python framework for secure multiparty computation [15]. For $k = 1$ we used a mixture of Protocols 2 and 3, and for $k = 2$ we used Protocol 4, in all cases expanding the calls to Protocol 1 to parallelize the secure computations of the Legendre symbol as much as possible. As a baseline we use the MPyC built-in secure comparison protocol, which is based on Toft's protocol [18]. For a meaningful performance evaluation, we set the bit length to 10 bits for the built-in comparisons used in layers 2 and 3. We have also vectorized the code for all these comparison protocols, handling $n = 4096$ comparisons at the same time for layers 1–3, which increases the speed considerably.

We have run our experiments on a 3PC-LAN setup (CPUs: Intel four-core 4th generation Core i7 3.6 GHz). A complete evaluation between three parties on a secret-shared input image, using secret-shared weights and bias vectors, runs in 60 s for $k = 1$, in 62 s for $k = 2$, and in 67 s for full-range comparisons. For evaluation of a batch of 10 input images the times are 223, 235, and 302 s, respectively. The times for processing all comparisons in layers 2 and 3 are 20, 34, and 99 s, respectively. Hence, in this experiment the Legendre-based comparisons with $k = 1$ are about 5 times faster than full-range comparisons. Similar speedups may be expected with other MPC frameworks for applications with comparisons restricted to medium-sized integers.

To determine the error rate for our particular BMLP, we have also implemented it in Python (including the Python counterparts of the Protocols bsgn1Simple and bsgn2, producing exactly the same errors outside their input ranges). The results measured for the 10,000 MNIST test images are shown in Table 2.

Acknowledgments. We thank Frank Blom for running all our 3-party experiments on his 3PC-LAN setup. This work has received funding from the European Union's Horizon 2020 research and innovation program under grant agreements No 731583 (SODA) and No 780477 (PRIViLEDGE).

References

1. Abspoel, M.: Search for primes with high d_1, d_2 (2018). https://github.com/abspoel/dk-search
2. Ankeny, N.C.: The least quadratic non residue. Ann. Math. **55**(1), 65–72 (1952)
3. Feige, U., Kilian, J., Naor, M.: A minimal model for secure computation (extended abstract). In: Proceedings of STOC 1994, pp. 554–563 (1994)
4. Fridlender, V.R.: On the least nth power non-residue. Dokl. Akad. Nauk. SSSR **66**, 351–352 (1949)
5. Graham, S.W., Ringrose, C.J.: Lower bounds for least quadratic non-residues. In: Berndt, B.C., et al. (eds.) Analytic Number Theory: Proceedings of a Conference in Honor of Paul T. Bateman, vol. 85, pp. 269–309. Springer, Boston (1990). https://doi.org/10.1007/978-1-4612-3464-7_18
6. Hildebrand, A.: On the least pair of consecutive quadratic nonresidues. Mich. Math. J. **34**(1), 57–62 (1987)
7. Hubara, I., Courbariaux, M., Soudry, D., El-Yaniv, R., Bengio, Y.: Quantized neural networks: training neural networks with low precision weights and activations. J. Mach. Learn. Res. **18**(187), 1–30 (2018)
8. Hudson, R.H.: The least pair of consecutive character non-residues. J. Reine Angew. Math. (281), 219–220 (1976)
9. Jacobsthal, E.: Anwendungen einer Formel aus der Theorie der quadratischen Reste. Ph.D. thesis, Friedrich-Wilhelms-Universität, Berlin, Germany (1906)
10. Lamzouri, Y., Li, X., Soundararajan, K.: Conditional bounds for the least quadratic non-residue and related problems. Math. Comput. **84**(295), 2391–2412 (2015)
11. Linnik, U.V.: On the least prime in an arithmetic progression. I. The basic theorem. Rec. Math. [Mat. Sbornik] N.S. **15**(57), 139–178 (1944)
12. Lukes, R.F.: A very fast electronic number sieve. Ph.D. thesis, University of Manitoba, Winnipeg, Canada (1995)
13. Pritchard, P.: A sublinear additive sieve for finding prime numbers. Commun. ACM **24**(1), 18–23 (1981)
14. Salié, H.: Über den kleinsten positiven quadratischen Nichtrest nach einer Primzahl. Math. Nachr. **3**(1), 7–8 (1949)
15. Schoenmakers, B.: MPyC - secure multiparty computation in Python, v0.4.7. GitHub (2018). https://github.com/lschoe/mpyc
16. Sorenson, J.P.: The pseudosquares prime sieve. In: Hess, F., Pauli, S., Pohst, M. (eds.) ANTS 2006. LNCS, vol. 4076, pp. 193–207. Springer, Heidelberg (2006). https://doi.org/10.1007/11792086_15
17. Sun, Z.H.: Consecutive numbers with the same Legendre symbol. Proc. Am. Math. Soc. **130**(9), 2503–2507 (2002)
18. Toft, T.: Primitives and applications for multi-party computation. Ph.D. thesis, Aarhus Universitet, Denmark (2007)
19. Treviño, E.: The least kth power non-residue. J. Number Theory **149**, 201–224 (2015)
20. Xylouris, T.: Über die Nullstellen der Dirichletschen L-Funktionen und die kleinste Primzahl in einer arithmetischen Progression. Ph.D. thesis, Rheinischen Friedrich-Wilhelms-Universität Bonn, Germany (2011)
21. Yao, A.C.: Protocols for secure computations. In: 23rd Annual Symposium on FOCS 1982, pp. 160–164 (1982)
22. Yu, C.H.: Sign modules in secure arithmetic circuits. Cryptology ePrint Archive, Report 2011/539 (2011). http://eprint.iacr.org/2011/539

EPIC: Efficient Private Image Classification (or: Learning from the Masters)

Eleftheria Makri[1,2], Dragos Rotaru[1,3], Nigel P. Smart[1,3(✉)],
and Frederik Vercauteren[1]

[1] imec-COSIC, KU Leuven, Leuven, Belgium
{eleftheria.makri,dragos.rotaru,nigel.smart,
frederik.vercauteren}@esat.kuleuven.be
[2] ABRR, Saxion University of Applied Sciences, Enschede, The Netherlands
[3] University of Bristol, Bristol, UK

Abstract. Outsourcing an image classification task raises privacy concerns, both from the image provider's perspective, who wishes to keep their images confidential, and from the classification algorithm provider's perspective, who wishes to protect the intellectual property of their classifier. We propose EPIC, an efficient private image classification system based on support vector machine (SVM) learning, secure against malicious adversaries. EPIC builds upon transfer learning techniques known from the Machine Learning (ML) literature and minimizes the load on the privacy-preserving part. Our solution is based on Multiparty Computation (MPC), it is 34 times faster than Gazelle (USENIX'18) –the state-of-the-art in private image classification– and it improves the communication cost by 50 times, with a 7% higher accuracy on CIFAR-10 dataset. For the same accuracy as Gazelle achieves on CIFAR-10, EPIC is 700 times faster and the communication cost is reduced by 500 times.

1 Introduction

Visual object recognition is an important machine learning application, deployed in numerous real-life settings. Machine Learning as a Service (MLaaS) is becoming increasingly popular in the era of cloud computing, data mining, and knowledge extraction. Object recognition is such a machine learning task that can be provided as a cloud service. However, in most application scenarios, straightforward outsourcing of the object recognition task is not possible due to privacy concerns. Generally, the *image holder* who wishes to perform the image classification process, requires their input images to remain confidential. On the other hand, the *classification algorithm provider* wishes to commercially exploit their algorithm; hence, requires the algorithm parameters to remain confidential.

We consider an approach, which facilitates the outsourcing of the image classification task to an external classification algorithm provider, without requiring

© Springer Nature Switzerland AG 2019
M. Matsui (Ed.): CT-RSA 2019, LNCS 11405, pp. 473–492, 2019.
https://doi.org/10.1007/978-3-030-12612-4_24

the establishment of trust, contractually or otherwise, between the involved parties. We focus on the evaluation task (i.e., labeling a new unclassified image), and not the learning task. Our proposal is based on secure Multiparty Computation (MPC), and allows for private image classification without revealing anything about the private images of the image holder, nor about the parameters of the classification algorithm. Unlike previous work [4,5,20], we can fully outsource the task at hand, in such a way that the classification algorithm provider does not need to be the same entity as the *cloud computing provider*. Although any of the involved parties (i.e., the classification algorithm provider, and the image holder) can play the role of one of the MPC servers, this is not a requirement for guaranteeing the security of our proposal. MPC allows distribution of trust to two or more parties. As long as the image holder (resp. the classification algorithm provider) trusts at least one of the MPC servers, their input images (resp. their classification algorithm parameters) remain secret.

MPC allows a set of mutually distrusting parties to jointly compute a function on their inputs, without revealing anything about these inputs (other than what can be inferred from the function output itself). Currently, MPC allows one to compute relatively simple functions on private data; arbitrarily complex functions can be supported, but with an often prohibitive computational cost. EPIC, our privacy-preserving image classification solution, combines the techniques of transfer learning feature extraction, support vector machine (SVM) classification, and MPC. In this work we use recently developed techniques for generic image classification (within the ImageNet competition) such as transfer learning to extract powerful generic features. Transfer learning using raw Convolutional Neural Network (CNN) features has been studied extensively by Azizpour et al. [3], and Yosinski et al. [55]. Then, the computation done in the MPC setting is minimized to only evaluate a simple function with secret shared inputs.

We focus on classification via SVM, as opposed to using more sophisticated techniques, such as Neural Networks (NNs), in the privacy-preserving domain to minimize the computational cost. While the field of private image classification is shifting towards NN-based approaches [25,33,43], we show that it is not necessary to use private NNs, as we can achieve classification with better accuracy by using generic NNs to improve the feature extraction techniques used. Although CNNs are the state-of-the-art for image classification [23], we confirm that SVMs can achieve high accuracy, as long as they are provided with good quality features. Transforming a NN to a privacy-preserving one results in inefficient solutions (e.g., 570 s for one image classification by CryptoNets [20]).

A schematic representation of the application scenario treated by EPIC is given in Fig. 1. Using additive secret sharing techniques both the *classification algorithm provider*, and the *image holder* share their inputs to the $n \geq 2$ *MPC servers*. Note that no information about the actual secret inputs can be gained by the individual shares alone. Thus, each MPC server learns nothing about the inputs of the two parties. The cluster of the MPC servers comprise the *cloud computing provider*, which together execute the MPC protocol to produce the final classification result. The MPC servers communicate via authenticated channels to accomplish what the protocol prescribes. The protocol completes its execution by having all MPC servers sending their share of the final classification result to the designated party, who can then reconstruct the result by combining the received shares. This party can be the *image holder*, or an external *analyst*, assigned to examine the classification results, without getting access to the underlying private images. The involved parties (image holder, classification algorithm provider, and –potentially– analyst), may play the role of the MPC servers themselves, avoiding completely the outsourcing to the cloud provider(s).

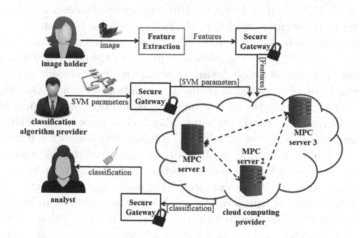

Fig. 1. A schematic representation of the private image classification scenario.

A key aspect of our work is how the data is processed before the MPC engine is used to perform the classification. The SVM classification is performed on so-called feature vectors, and not directly on the images. The way one determines these feature vectors not only affects accuracy, but it also has an impact on security. As shown in Fig. 1 the image holder performs the feature extraction on the input image before it is passed to the secure gateway. Thus this feature extraction must not be specific to the algorithm classification provider; otherwise the extracted features could reveal information about exactly what is being classified. We apply a generic feature extraction method, which is independent of the underlying classification task.

In particular, we employ TensorFlow [1], to extract features based on the activation of a deep CNN (specifically the Inception-v3 [47] CNN) trained on a set of object recognition tasks, *different* from the target task. This method is known as CNN-off-the-shelf in the ML literature, and it has been successfully applied in various image recognition tasks [15,42]. Since the CNN is generic, it can be released in the clear, and hence become part of the image holder's preprocessing. This not only gives us a security benefit, but it also significantly improves the accuracy of our method. There are many public CNNs available online for generic feature extraction in Caffe's Model Zoo, which can be used with our EPIC solution to add a privacy dimension to a typical ML problem [24]. In our paper we selected Inception-v3 as the public CNN to extract features, because it suits many generic image recognition tasks, and allows us to benchmark EPIC against previous solutions on traditional datasets such as CIFAR-10.

We also present a second variant of EPIC, which aims at allowing a tradeoff between the accuracy of the classifier's predictions, and its performance. It does so by deploying a kernel approximation method, on top of Inception-v3 features for dimensionality reduction.

We implemented our solution using SPDZ [7], which was introduced by Damgård et al. [12,13]; it is based on additive secret sharing, and it is proven secure in the active security model, in the full versions of the papers [12,13]. We assume the reader to be familiar with MPC, but we discuss preliminaries on the techniques used by EPIC for completeness in the full version of our paper [34]. EPIC outperforms the state-of-the-art in secure neural network inference [25], both in terms of efficiency, and in terms of prediction accuracy. Our implementation shows that privacy-preserving image classification has become practical. As shown in Table 1, we are the only provably secure work in the active security model, which is a property we inherit by the chosen implementation frameworks. A system like EPIC could find application in numerous real-life cases, such as in purchase scenarios where visual inspection is performed, or when targeted surveillance is required without compromising non-targets' privacy.

Our contributions are thus four fold: (i) We enable full outsourcing of privacy-preserving image classification to a third independent party using a simple technique yet much faster and accurate than others, which require complicated machinery. (ii) Our solution does not leak *any* information about the private images, nor the classifier, while being the first to provide active security. (iii) We show how to deploy a data-independent feature extraction method to alleviate the privacy-preserving computations, while increasing accuracy and efficiency. (iv) We demonstrate the practicality of our approach, both in terms of efficiency, and in terms of accuracy, by conducting experiments on realistic datasets.

2   Related Work

Privacy-preserving machine learning can focus either on providing a secure training phase, a secure classification phase, or both secure training and classification phases. The first research works in the field aimed at designing a privacy-preserving training phase. Recently, due to the advent of cloud computing, and Machine Learning as a Service, more and more works focus on the design of a privacy-preserving classification phase. Fewer works have attempted to address both the training, and the classification phases in a privacy-preserving manner.

To facilitate an easy comparison of the related work, we summarize the main features of each proposal in Table 1.

- The first column of Table 1 is the reference to the corresponding paper.
- The second column indicates whether the work considers secure training (T), secure training and classification (T + C), or only secure classification (C).
- The third column indicates the security model, under which the proposed protocols are secure, where P stands for passive security, and A stands for active security. N/A (not applicable) refers to differential privacy techniques, which are designed to protect against inference about the inputs from the outputs, and thus are orthogonal to the issue of securing the computation which we deal with.
- The fourth column denotes the method used to preserve privacy. DP stands for differential privacy; SP stands for selective privacy, and refers to the unique characteristic of the work of Shokri and Shmatikov [46] allowing the users to decide how much private information about their learned models they wish to reveal. SHE stands for Somewhat Homomorphic Encryption, 2-PC for 2-Party Computation, and MPC stands for Multiparty Computation (which could include 2-PC).
- The fifth column lists the training method(s) used. N-L SVM stands for non-linear SVM, NN for Neural Networks, LM for Linear Means, FLD for Fisher's Linear Discriminant, HD for hyperplane decision, LIR for linear regression, LOR for logistic regression, and DT for decision trees.
- The sixth column lists the information that is revealed by the protocol execution. C stands for information about the classifier, and TD for information about the training data. We note with boldface letters the information that is intentionally revealed by the protocol execution, and we mark with an asterisk the information that is protected by means of differential privacy techniques. Information that can potentially, and unintentionally be leaked is noted with normal, non-boldface letters.
- The last column indicates whether the work provides an implementation.

Training an SVM in a privacy-friendly way, has been previously considered based on techniques of differential privacy [30,31]. Despite the little overhead that these techniques incur, which makes them competitive from an efficiency perspective, they do not consider the security of the actual *computation* during the training or classification. Shokri and Shmatikov [46] achieve such privacy-preserving collaborative deep learning with multiple participants, while refraining from using cryptographic techniques. Their work focuses on learning the NN, but they also consider protecting the privacy of each individual's NN, allowing the participants to decide how much information to share about their models.

A lot of research has been devoted to provable privacy-preserving techniques for training a classifier. Privacy-preserving data mining has been an active research area since the seminal work of Lindell and Pinkas [32]. More recently, Vaidya et al. [51] showed how to train a SVM classifier, in a privacy-preserving manner, based on vertically, horizontally, and arbitrarily partitioned training data. In follow-up work, Teo et al. [48] improved upon the efficiency of the solution of Vaidya et al. [51], and showed that their approach scales well to address the challenges of data mining on big data. Chase et al. [9] combine MPC techniques with differential privacy techniques to achieve private neural network learning. Their work provides provable security guarantees for the learning

Table 1. Comparison of the related work.

	Func.	Sec. model	Privacy mthd	Train mthd	Info leak	Impl.
[30]	T	N/A	DP	N-L SVM	C; TD*	✓
[31]	T	N/A	DP	N-L SVM	C; TD*	✓
[46]	T	P	SP	NN	C	✓
[51]	T	P	MPC	N-L SVM	C	✓
[48]	T	P	MPC; DP	N-L SVM	C	✓
[9]	T	P	MPC; DP	NN	C*	✓
[21]	T + C	P	SHE	LM; FLD	No	✓
[2]	T + C	P	SHE	Bayes; random forests	No	✓
[29]	T + C	P	2-PC	N-L SVM	No	✗
[10]	T + C	P	2-PC	NN	TD	✗
[35]	T + C	P	2-PC	NN; LIR; LOR	No	✓
[20]	C	P	SHE	NN	No	✓
[4]	C	P	SHE	N-L SVM	C	✓
[8]	C	P	SHE	NN	No	✗
[6]	C	P	SHE; 2-PC	HD; Bayes; DT	No	✓
[41]	C	P	2-PC	N-L SVM	No	✓
[5]	C	P	2-PC	NN	C	✗
[36]	C	P	2-PC	NN	No	✓
[45]	C	P	2-PC	NN	No	✓
[33]	C	P	2-PC	NN	Filter size	✓
[43]	C	P	2-PC	NN; SVM	No	✓
[25]	C	P	2-PC	NN	No	✓
EPIC	C	A	MPC	SVM	No	✓

phase (in the passive security model), and adds noise to the resulting network to protect its privacy during classification.

A parallel research line aiming to address the same challenge, namely privacy-preserving data mining, is based on homomorphic encryption (instead of MPC). The notion of homomorphic encryption dates back to the work of Rivest et al. [44], but only recently fully homomorphic encryption was devised [19]. This type of homomorphic encryption allows the computation of any polynomial function on the encrypted data, and unlike MPC, it does not require communication, as the task can be outsourced to one single party. Since the seminal work of Gentry [19], somewhat homomorphic encryption schemes have been proposed, allowing computations of polynomial functions of a limited degree. Graepel et al. [21] consider both machine learning training, and classification based on encrypted data, with their solutions being secure in the passive model. Due to the selected homomorphic encryption scheme, Graepel et al. [21] cannot treat comparisons efficiently, which excludes SVM-based solutions. Addressing both learning, and classification based on extremely random forests, and naïve Bayes networks, Aslett et al. [2], also work on homomorphically encrypted data.

One of the first private SVM classifiers was proposed by Laur et al. [29], which addresses both the training and the classification in a privacy-preserving manner.

Their work combines the techniques of homomorphic encryption, secret sharing, and circuit evaluation, into a passively secure 2-PC solution. Concurrently, and independently Dahl [10] is working on using the same MPC framework as in our work, to realize both the training, and the classification of CNN based privacy-preserving algorithms. While Dahl [10] is deploying CNNs instead of SVM, he needs to apply them in a non-black-box fashion. The protocol of Dahl [10] allows some leakage of information during the training phase, which is not the case with our approach. SecureML [35] also considers both training and classification in the 2-PC setting, and the passive security model. These approaches [10, 29, 35] can only treat the two-party setting, and cannot be trivially extended to allow the classifier provider to be a different entity than the cloud provider.

Other works focus particularly on the private image classification problem, instead of the training of the model. Gilad-Bachrach et al. [20] propose a solution applicable to the image classification problem, based on homomorphically encrypted data. The resulting *CryptoNets* [20] provide an accuracy of 99% for the MNIST dataset, and can make on average 51739 predictions per hour. However, this is only the case when the predictions are to be made simultaneously; for a single prediction the task takes 570 s to complete.

Recent work by Barnett et al. [4] demonstrated the potential of polynomial-kernel SVM to be used for classification in a privacy-preserving manner. Specifically, Barnett et al. apply SVM techniques for the classification –as in our work– but on encrypted data. Although they mention the potential of an MPC approach to be more efficient in this setting, they do not consider it, because direct translation of the protocols to MPC would require interaction between the client and the classification algorithm provider during the computations. We overcome this limitation by extending the application scenario in a way that allows the classification task to be fully outsourced to a cluster of independent third parties. We implement their approach using SPDZ in a more secure way by keeping the PCA components private (they choose to make them public). This implementation is more expensive than EPIC, due to the non-linearity of the polynomial SVM, and it is also less accurate. Albeit inefficient and inaccurate, it provides an initial benchmark, and it shows the gap between an FHE and an MPC approach (see details in Sect. 4). Chabanne et al. [8] attempted to approximate commonly used functions used in NN-based classification in a SHE-friendly manner. Despite the high prediction accuracy that their work achieves, Chabanne et al. do not provide any performance evaluation results.

In the 2-PC setting, Bost et al. [6], and Rahulamathavan et al. [41] focus on the problem of private classification, where both the classifier parameters, and the client's input to be classified need to remain private. The latter approach does not consider linear SVM, while both approaches only offer passive security. Barni et al. [5] propose private NN-based data classification, also in the 2-PC setting and passive security model. They suggest three protocols, which offer different privacy guarantees for the classifier owner, while always protecting fully the client's input. Follow up work by Orlandi et al. [36] extends the work of Barni et al. in terms of privacy. DeepSecure [45] is another work in the

2-PC setting, and the passive security model, using Garbled-Circuit techniques. A direct performance comparison of DeepSecure versus CryptoNets [20] confirmed a significant efficiency improvement achieved by DeepSecure.

The recently proposed MiniONN [33] is one of the latest NN-based data classification approaches in the 2-PC setting. MiniONN demonstrates a significant performance increase compared to CryptoNets, without loss of accuracy, as well as better accuracy compared to SecureML [35], combined with increased performance. However, it still operates in the 2-PC setting, which is more restricted than the MPC setting we consider, and it only offers passive security. Under a comparable configuration as MiniONN, and still in the passive security model, Chameleon [43] achieves a 4.2 times performance improvement. Chameleon operates in the 2-PC setting, under the assumption that a Semi-Honest Third Party (STP) is engaged in the offline phase to generate correlated randomness. Despite the strong STP assumption, Chameleon does not need the third party for the online phase, while it gets a significant performance increase from this STP.

Gazelle [25], the latest work on secure NN classification, outperforms, in terms of efficiency, the best previous solutions in the literature [20, 33, 43], by carefully selecting which parts of the CNN to carry out using a packed additively homomorphic encryption, and which parts using garbled circuits. EPIC performs better than Gazelle, while also being secure in the active security model. This is because EPIC only treats linear computations in the privacy-preserving domain.

To the best of our knowledge, we are the first to provide a privacy-preserving image classification tool combining SVM classification with transfer learning feature extraction, offering active security. EPIC is more efficient than previous work and achieves prediction accuracy higher than that of the related work on the same datasets, although it does not deploy sophisticated NN-based classification on the private inputs. Interestingly, EPIC is not limited to the 2-PC setting, allowing a broad range of application scenarios to be treated by our solution.

3   EPIC

The proposed private image classification solution, EPIC, is based on transfer learning techniques [49] for feature extraction. The EPIC algorithm for image classification runs in two phases. In the first phase the image is passed through a generic feature extraction method. Being generic, i.e., not task specific, this method can be published in-the-clear and hence can be applied by the image holder before passing the output securely to the MPC engine. In the second phase the actual classification, via an SVM, is applied. This SVM is specific to the task at hand, and hence needs to be securely passed to the MPC engine. We thus have two problems to solve: Feature Extraction and SVM classification.

Feature Extraction. High quality features are key to the accuracy of a trained classifier. We ensure high quality feature extraction by deploying the techniques of transfer learning. Specifically, we perform feature extraction based on Inception-v3 [47], which is a *public* CNN classifier trained on a set of non-privacy-sensitive object recognition tasks. Commonly, the training for such a

CNN classifier is performed on large datasets, which enhances the prediction accuracy of the classifier. In our context, the trained classifier extracts features based on the activation of a deep convolutional network. Our work shows that powerful feature extraction is essential to the quality of the final classification accuracy. In fact, we demonstrate that the high-complexity (CNN) tasks can be learned on non-private datasets, and still use their power for feature extraction of unrelated tasks. Eventually, this allows us to deploy only linear functions for the actual classification, which enables accurate, and efficient privacy-preserving solutions.

SVM Classification. Despite the increasing popularity and high effectiveness of CNN classification techniques, the direct deployment of CNN techniques requires large training datasets [14] that are potentially difficult to obtain when the underlying data is privacy sensitive. In addition, black-box transformation of CNN-based methods to their privacy-preserving equivalents will result in classifiers that are computationally prohibitive to use. Thus using a light-weight classification method such as SVMs can be beneficial in privacy sensitive environments, and their evaluation can be done (as we show) in a secure manner. With the CNN features, an SVM can learn quickly from very few positive examples, which shows that they are useful to perform one-shot learning [15]. Thus, we opted for the design of a private SVM classifier, while using the techniques of CNN-based *transfer learning* in the context of feature extraction, which does not raise privacy concerns.

To classify a new unlabeled input with our classifier trained with a linear SVM, we need to securely evaluate the following equation:

$$\mathsf{class}(\mathbf{h}) = \arg\max_i (\mathbf{x_i} \cdot \mathbf{h} + b_i), \tag{1}$$

where:

- $\mathbf{h}$ is the vector representing the client's image, and has been provided to the MPC servers in shared form;
- b_i is the model intercept (aka bias), calculated by the classification algorithm provider during the learning phase and secret shared to the MPC servers;
- $\mathbf{x_i}$ are the n support vectors.

The support vectors $\mathbf{x_i}$, and the model intercepts b_i are assumed to need protection, as they represent the intellectual property of the learned model.

Feature Reduction. To achieve efficient training of kernel machines (such as SVM) aimed at non-linear problems, several approximation methods (e.g., the method of Rahimi and Recht [39]) have been proposed. Such approaches have the goal to alleviate the (cleartext) computational, and storage cost of the training, incurred by the high dimensionality of the data, especially when the training datasets are large. The approximation generally is implemented by mapping the input data to a low-dimensional feature space, such that the inner products of the mapped data are approximately equal to the features of a more complex (e.g., Gaussian) kernel. This is known as the kernel trick. These features are then combined with linear techniques (e.g., linear SVM), yielding an efficient training, but also an efficient classification, which we are able to implement in a privacy-preserving way.

One of the first successful approaches for kernel approximations, achieving high accuracy, was proposed by Rahimi and Recht [39], and is based on random features, which are independent of the training data. To the contrary, Nyström based kernel approximations [16,53], are data dependent. Although Nyström approximations outperform randomly extracted features [54] in terms of accuracy, being data dependent makes them unfit for our purposes, as they require applying non-linear functions on the private inputs. From a computational, and storage efficiency perspective, data independent approximations are favored.

We discovered that a variant of the method proposed by Rahimi and Recht [40] is presented in the scikit-learn package [37]. This implements an RBF (Radial Basis Function) sampler, which allows to transform the features without using the training data. This dimensionality reduction (like the feature extraction) is deployed both for the training, and for the data classification. Since the feature selection is random (i.e., data independent), it can be performed on the cleartext data, both by the classification algorithm provider, and by the client, without raising privacy concerns.

Our second variant of EPIC (see below) supports dimensionality reduction for free, by placing all the computational load on the cleartext. This variant makes use of an algorithm implementing the RBF sampler listed in Fig. 2. In our application scenario, the algorithm provider broadcasts the RBF sampler parameters, namely the γ parameter and the feature size. The γ parameter does not reveal any information about the dataset. Note that γ is a floating point number, which is varied to match a cross-validation score on the training data. The shape variable is the feature size of a point (set to 2048), which is the output of Inception-v3.

Scikit-learn variant of Random Kitchen Sinks [37].

Init: Set γ, shape, state$_{random}$, nc.
Fit:
    1. Select weights$_{random} = \sqrt{2 * \gamma} \cdot$ state$_{random}.\mathcal{N}(0,1)$ of size nc $\times$ shape, with mean 0 and standard deviation 1.
    2. Assign offset$_{random} =$ state$_{random}.\mathcal{U}(0, 2 \cdot \pi)$ of size nc.
Transform(x):
    1. projection $= x \cdot$ weights$_{random} +$ offset$_{random}$.
    2. projection $= \cos$ (projection).
    3. projection $=$ projection $\cdot (\sqrt{2}/\sqrt{nc})$

Fig. 2. RBF sampler.

EPIC – Simple Variant: The classification algorithm provider has already trained their SVM classifier. The parameters for the SVM classification are shared to the MPC servers by the classification algorithm provider and are never revealed to the image holder (nor the analyst). The image holder applies the Inception-v3 feature extraction to their image, and takes the second to last layer, which has a feature size of 2048, as their output. The resulting features are then shared (via the secure gateway) to the MPC servers by the image holder, and thus are kept secret from the classification algorithm provider. We indicate secret shared data in square brackets (Fig. 1). The MPC engine then evaluates the SVM securely on the features and outputs the result to the analyst (or image holder).

Note that although EPIC does not allow any information leakage about the private SVM parameters, recent work by Tramèr et al. [50] showed that only black-box access to the classifiers can still serve to recover an (near-)equivalent model. We consider this problem to be out of this work's scope, as it can easily be tackled by restricting the number of queries an external party is allowed to perform on the MPC Engine. This type of attacks has not been averted by any of the secure computation solutions in the related work.

EPIC – Complex Variant: The second variant of the EPIC protocol is summarized in Fig. 3. This EPIC variant trades a small percentage of the classification accuracy to increase efficiency. It achieves this tradeoff by deploying the *kernel approximation* dimensionality reduction explained above, and in particular the kernel approximation sub-step is also considered to be part of the feature extraction phase. Here the algorithm provider needs to publish the feature size of a point (in our case 2048) and the parameter γ from above. At first sight it might seem that γ reveals information about the training data, but we noticed that for our datasets one can fix $\gamma = 2^{-13}$ to a small value and modify the regularization parameter C of the SVM. This parameter C will always remain private to the algorithm provider, hence there is no information leakage. We stress again that for both cases, the CNN feature extraction is input independent, so privacy is maintained for the image holder and algorithm provider.

Specifically, the protocol starts with the Setup phase, where the algorithm provider (AP) performs the kernel approximation (from Fig. 2) on its own dataset, and broadcasts the type of CNN used, and the Init parameters necessary for the feature reduction at the image holder (IH) side. Then, the algorithm provider secret shares the SVM parameters to the MPC Engine (Eng). Secret shared values are denoted in double square brackets. In the evaluation phase, the image holder performs the feature extraction locally (given the previously obtained parameters), and secret shares the new point to be classified by Eng. Then, the MPC protocol computes Eq. 1.

4   Experiments

Experimental Setup. Our experiments are conducted on two MPC servers, which yields the most efficient solution, but we also show how the proposed sys-

---

EPIC Protocol with kernel approximation as feature reduction

Setup:
1. Algorithm Provider (AP) broadcasts the type of CNN used for feature extraction.
2. AP computes γ from Fig.2 on its own training data. Then AP broadcasts the Init variables from Fig. 2 and secret shares the support vectors x_i, b_i to the MPC engine (Eng). These are stored on Eng as $[\![x_i]\!], [\![b_i]\!]$.

Evaluate:
1. Image Holder (IH) uses public CNN to extract features h' from its image. Then IH maps $h' \mapsto h$ locally using the RBF sampler initialized with the γ broadcasted by AP to obtain a smaller number of features. The new point h is further secret shared to the Eng and stored as $[\![h]\!]$.
2. Eng uses $[\![x_i]\!], [\![b_i]\!], [\![h]\!]$ to compute Eq. 1 with a shared result: $[\![\text{class}(\mathbf{h})]\!]$.

Fig. 3. Protocol for SVM classification with RBF sampler.

tem scales with more than two MPC servers. We assume a protocol-independent, input-independent preprocessing phase that takes place prior to the protocol execution between the MPC servers. The inputting parties do not need to be aware, nor contribute to this phase. The preprocessing creates the randomness needed to boost the efficiency of the online phase, and allows the inputting parties (image holder and classification algorithm provider) to securely share their inputs.

The online phase begins with the image holder, and the algorithm provider sharing their inputs (reduced CNN features, and SVM parameters, resp.) to the MPC servers. This is performed by executing an interactive protocol between each inputting party and the two MPC servers, as Damgård et al. [11] proposed. Then, the actual private image classification task is executed only between the two MPC servers, as in the **Evaluate** phase of Fig. 3. In the end, each MPC server sends their resulting share to the image holder, or the analyst, who can combine the shares and reconstruct the cleartext result, which is the desired class label.

From Fixed Point Arithmetic to Integers. For the secure integer comparison sub-protocols that EPIC deploys, we selected the statistical security parameter to be $\kappa = 40$ bits. We stress that everywhere the computational security parameter is set to $\lambda = 128$. We observed experimentally after running the scikit-learn's RBF (see Fig. 2) on top of Inception-v3 that each feature is bounded by $\text{abs}(x_i) \leq 15$ where $\text{len}(x) \leq 2048$.

To avoid the costly fixed point arithmetic, we scale each feature x_i by a factor f, and then perform arithmetic on integers. Particularly, we compute $x_i \cdot f$ and then floor it to the nearest integer. We varied f, and evaluated the SVM's accuracy. We experimentally concluded that setting $f = 2^8$ gives sufficient accuracy, as if working on floating point numbers, while lowering the scale factor f decreased the accuracy by more than 1%. If $f = 2^8$ then to compute a class score from Eq. 1 becomes: $s = \sum_{j=1}^{2048}(2^8 \cdot x_{ij} \cdot 2^8 \cdot h_j) + 2^{16} \cdot b_i$ since we need to scale both the support vectors x_i as well the features h. Using the fact that each component is bounded by 15 then clearly $s \leq 2^{35}$.

To improve the underlying MPC performance we wanted to aim for using a 64-bit prime modulus for the underlying linear secret sharing scheme. Unfortunately, if our inputs are of 35 bit size then there is no room left to perform the secure comparisons in $\arg\max$ with 40 bits statistical security, as $35 + 40 > 64$. Since some of the x_{ij}'s are negative and roughly uniform around zero then we can conclude that s is bounded by 20 bits which was confirmed for all our datasets. Hence, we could run everything modulo a 64-bit prime with 40-bit statistical security, while ensuring there is no information leak from the comparisons. We can achieve an even tighter bounding by normalizing the features using the L2-Norm, after the RBF-Sampler invocation. In our setting this is not necessary, since the expected bound on s is already low (20 bits). We also experimented (see later) with higher statistical security of 100 bits by using 128-bit prime fields.

For the feature reduction we considered whether to use RBF or PCA, and concluded that RBF is more suitable for our purposes. Despite the accuracy loss that RBF incurs compared to PCA, it is justified to use RBF for reasons of computational and communication efficiency. For a more detailed comparison between RBF and PCA feature reduction in our setting, we refer the reader to the full version of our paper [34].

Datasets. We selected three image datasets: CIFAR-10, MIT-67, and Caltech-101, to show how EPIC scales in terms of performance, when increasing the number of classes, and to illustrate its classification accuracy.

- **CIFAR-10** [28]: This is a dataset of 60000 32×32 color images, out of which 50000 are training images and 10000 are test images. CIFAR-10 features 10 classes of objects, with 6000 images per class. The accuracy metric is the quotient between correctly classified samples and total number of samples.
- **MIT-67** [38]: MIT-67 has 15620 indoor images from 67 scene categories. We used 80 images per class for training, and the rest of the pictures for testing. The accuracy metric used here is the mAP (mean Accuracy Precision), which consists of calculating the average over the accuracies of each class.
- **Caltech-101** [17]: This dataset contains pictures of objects of 102 categories. Each class has at least 31 images and we chose to use 30 images from each class for the training. The accuracy metric is mAP, just as in MIT-67.

Training. We trained the SVM on the cleartext versions of the aforementioned datasets. Feature extraction was done after resizing each image to 256×256. We trained Linear SVMs based on the one-versus-all strategy (OvA) [52], because it is more efficient to evaluate n classifiers in MPC instead of $n(n-1)/2$. Note that we chose to avoid the data augmentation trick, and adopted the training method presented in DeCAF [15] using the original datasets, and raw features from Inception-v3 [15]. To find parameters that yield high classification accuracy, we have done a grid search for the γ required in the RBF, and the parameter C, which denotes the size-margin hyperplane for the SVM decision function.

We stress that EPIC achieves a sufficient classification accuracy. Given that EPIC workings have been purposely kept simple to allow for efficient secure computations, we consider the classification accuracy of EPIC comparable to that achieved by the state-of-the-art (non-privacy-preserving) works in the ML community. The best classification accuracy in-the-clear on the CIFAR-10 dataset is 97.14% [18], while EPIC achieves 88.8%. On the MIT-67 dataset, EPIC achieves 72.2% accuracy, while the state-of-the-art in-the-clear solution [27] reports an accuracy of 83.1%. More interestingly, on Caltech-101, the state-of-the-art accuracy in-the-clear is still 93.42% [22], while EPIC achieves 91.4%.

Classification Accuracy and Performance Evaluation. We executed our experiments, simulating the two MPC servers on two identical desktop computers equipped with Intel i7-4790 processor, at 3.60 GHz over a 1 Gbps LAN with an average round-trip ping of 0.3 ms.

Our algorithm hand matches the one listed in Fig. 3, where the **Evaluate** step from Fig. 3 was implemented using the SPDZ software [7]. The preprocessing phase for this step was estimated using the LowGear protocol by Keller et al. [26], which is the fastest known protocol to produce triples for multiple parties with active security. We do not report on the timings for the feature extraction and reduction, since they can be done in the clear, locally by the external parties, which provide inputs to the MPC engine, and they are not privacy-sensitive.

EPIC – Simple Variant: We evaluated the computational performance, data sent over the network, and classification accuracy of EPIC on the default 2048 length feature from the output of Inception-v3. We report these experiment results in Table 2. Increasing the number of classes n (from 10, to 67, to 102) has a worsening effect on the performance, as the amount of data sent over the network scales linearly with n. The runtime of the online phase is affected less as n increases. Going from 10 classes (CIFAR-10) with 0.005 s runtime, to 102 classes (Caltech) with 0.03 s, is an increase factor of six, whereas for all other metrics it is roughly ten (i.e., linear in the number of classes).

In Table 3 we show that EPIC improves over Gazelle [25] in terms of every relevant metric on CIFAR-10: accuracy with 7%, total communication by 50x, and total runtime by 34x. This is because we start with secret shared (powerful) features obtained from public CNNs, whereas Gazelle [25] starts with an encrypted image. We expect Gazelle's timings to considerably improve, if they adopt our approach, starting from encrypted features produced by a public CNN.

EPIC – Complex Variant: To increase the performance of EPIC even further, we tried to minimize the feature size used, while still matching the classification accuracy achieved by Gazelle [25] or MiniONN [33] for CIFAR-10. In the end, we settled with nc = 128, and then performed a grid search on γ for the MIT and Caltech datasets. Our results are reported in Table 4. Since the number of features decreases considerably from 2048 to 128 the timings decrease as well. For example, if we look at the online runtime compared to Gazelle [25], our solution improves by a factor of 700x and the total communication cost decreases by almost 500x. We do recognize that our setting is different from the one considered by Gazelle [25], but we see more the similarities, since the end goal is the same, namely to classify secret shared (or encrypted) images.

Our results indicate that general image recognition, and user's privacy can go well together. In fact we showed that securing the private classification comes nearly for free. A stronger case for why CNN features with a Linear SVM should be considered, as a baseline benchmark is done by Razavian et al. [42].

Other Optimizations: Note that one of the major improvements came from running the dot products on multiple threads, and doing the argmax operation in a tree-wise manner to decrease the number of communication rounds required.

Table 2. 1 Gbps LAN timings for EPIC – simple variant on different datasets with a linear SVM.

Dataset	Runtime (s)			Communication (MB)			Accuracy %
	Offline	Online	Total	Offline	Online	Total	
CIFAR	0.36	0.005	0.37	24	0.33	24.33	88.8
MIT	2.43	0.02	2.45	161.94	2.24	164.18	72.2
Caltech	3.71	0.03	3.74	246.59	3.41	250	91.4

Table 3. 1 Gbps LAN timings for CIFAR-10 dataset on different frameworks. The EPIC – simple variant is compared to the state-of-the-art private classification solutions, and outperforms them in all metrics.

Framework	Runtime (s)			Communication (MB)			Accuracy %
	Offline	Online	Total	Offline	Online	Total	
MiniONN [33]	472	72	544	3046	6226	9272	81.61
Gazelle [25]	9.34	3.56	12.9	940	296	1236	81.61
EPIC	0.36	0.005	0.37	24	0.33	24.33	88.8

Table 4. 1 Gbps LAN timings for EPIC – complex variant on different datasets with a RBF-SVM and a 128 feature size.

Dataset	Runtime (s)			Communication (MB)			Accuracy %
	Offline	Online	Total	Offline	Online	Total	
CIFAR	0.037	0.0003	0.037	2.472	0.027	2.5	81.74
MIT	0.259	0.002	0.261	17.22	0.180	17.4	64.4
Caltech	0.395	0.004	0.399	26.27	0.273	26.543	85.56

Multiparty Setting. We benchmarked EPIC on different number of computers with the RBF-128 variant on the CIFAR-10 dataset and measured throughput (operations per second) for the online and offline phases in Fig. 4. For the two party case our protocol can carry around 2650 evaluations per second. The throughput decreases with a growing number of parties and reaches 870 ops per second for the five parties case. Notice that the main bottleneck when executing these protocols is still the preprocessing phase, generating the necessary triples.

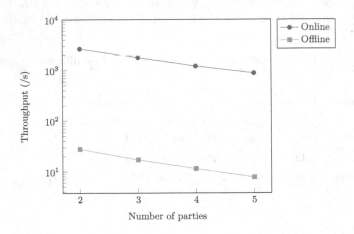

Fig. 4. Throughput of CIFAR-10 evaluations of secret features with RBF-128 EPIC for multiple parties.

Similar Work. It is worth mentioning that we also implemented the method of Barnett et al. [4] in SPDZ, after fixing some security bugs such as cleartext PCA coefficients. They report 124 s for one binary classification thus to extrapolate this to 10 classes takes roughly 1240 s. To translate the work for Barnett et al. in SPDZ we used a feature extraction algorithm based on Histogram of Oriented Gradients (HOG) and then reduced their dimension using PCA. The reduced points were then plugged into a polynomial SVM to classify the inputs. This methodology yielded a 6.7 s execution time of the online phase, and an expensive preprocessing phase of 12 h for CIFAR-10. The classification accuracy was also poor (58%). This showed that the input dependent phase in MPC is faster than in FHE, by at least two orders of magnitude, confirming that our EPIC solution outperforms traditional attempts at classifying images using SVMs.

The closest work to ours that tried to solve the issue of linear SVM classification is a semi-honest 2-PC protocol due to Bost et al. [6]. In this work party A owns the model and party B holds the features to be classified. To compare our method with theirs in an accurate manner we took their open sourced code and tailored it to our feature length (2048), input size (27 bits) and computational security $\lambda = 128$ and ran it on our computers; whilst maintaining their statistical security of 100 bits. In Table 5 the method of Bost et al. [6] is benchmarked with the recent libraries (NTL-11.3.0, HElib, etc.). We then compare with EPIC using the same parameters as the ones used in the experiments of Bost et al., namely statistical security $\kappa = 100$ and computational security $\lambda = 128$, where the shares live in $\mathbb{F}_p$ and $p \approx 2^{128}$. For more details on the selection of the security parameters, we refer the reader to the full version of our paper [34]. EPIC has a faster online phase than Bost et al., by at least a factor of 20, at the cost of a slower preprocessing phase. This shows that the main bottleneck in the entire protocol is the triple generation, which deploys expensive cryptographic tools.

Table 5. 1 Gbps LAN timings for EPIC – simple variant and Bost et al. with different number of classes.

Method	Classes	Runtime (s)			Communication (MB)		
		Offline	Online	Total	Offline	Online	Total
[6]	10	0	0.48	0.48	0	5.36	5.36
EPIC	10	1.04	0.014	1.054	46.35	0.66	47.01
[6]	102	0	1.67	1.67	0	54.85	54.85
EPIC	102	10.72	0.083	10.8	475.96	6.68	482.64

5   Conclusion and Future Work

We have introduced EPIC, a private image classification system, trained with SVM, while having the input features extracted based on the techniques of transfer learning. We showed how to achieve privacy-preserving image classification in such a way that the task can be fully outsourced to a third, independent party. For our solution we deployed generic MPC tools and showed how to avoid the restricted two-party setting. Unlike all previous work, our approach provides active security, does not leak any information about the private images, nor about the classifier parameters, and it is orders of magnitude more efficient than the privacy-preserving classification solutions proposed in the literature.

Due to their highly accurate predictions, especially for multiclass classification tasks, CNNs have superseded SVM as the state-of-the-art for image classification. However, our work shows that in the privacy-preserving domain, SVM classification can still produce accurate results, as long as it is provided with high quality features. Thus, we chose to focus on improving the feature extraction phase, using a transfer learning, CNN-based approach, while avoiding the execution of such complex functions in the MPC domain. An interesting advantage of our solution is that it can be applied to the homomorphic encryption domain, since performing the linear operations has depth 1, and the costlier operation is computing the argmax, which requires to branch on secret comparisons.

Our experiments confirmed that there is a tradeoff between the complexity, and therefore also accuracy of the classification algorithms used, versus the efficiency of the privacy-preserving variants of the proposed solutions. In the active security model that we consider in this work, deploying CNNs in the same manner as they are used on cleartext data, is computationally prohibitive with current privacy-preserving methods.

Acknowledgements. This work has been supported in part by ERC Advanced Grant ERC-2015-AdG-IMPaCT, by the Defense Advanced Research Projects Agency (DARPA) and Space and Naval Warfare Systems Center, Pacific (SSC Pacific) under contract No. N66001-15-C-4070. This work has been supported in part by the Research Council KU Leuven grants C14/18/067 and STG/17/019.

References

1. Abadi, M., et al.: TensorFlow: a system for large-scale machine learning. In: OSDI, pp. 265–283 (2016)
2. Aslett, L.J., Esperança, P.M., Holmes, C.C.: Encrypted statistical machine learning: new privacy preserving methods. arXiv:1508.06845 (2015)
3. Azizpour, H., Razavian, A.S., Sullivan, J., Maki, A., Carlsson, S.: Factors of transferability for a generic convnet representation. IEEE Trans. Pattern Anal. Mach. Intell. **38**(9), 1790–1802 (2016)
4. Barnett, A., et al.: Image classification using non-linear support vector machines on encrypted data. IACR Cryptology ePrint Archive: 2017/857 (2017)
5. Barni, M., Orlandi, C., Piva, A.: A privacy-preserving protocol for neural-network-based computation. In: Multimedia and Security Workshop, pp. 146–151. ACM (2006)
6. Bost, R., Popa, R.A., Tu, S., Goldwasser, S.: Machine learning classification over encrypted data. In: Network and Distributed System Security Symposium (2015)
7. Bristol Crypto: SPDZ-2: Multiparty computation with SPDZ, MASCOT, and Overdrive offline phases (2018). https://github.com/bristolcrypto/SPDZ-2
8. Chabanne, H., de Wargny, A., Milgram, J., Morel, C., Prouff, E.: Privacy-preserving classification on deep neural network. IACR Cryptology ePrint Archive: 2017/35 (2017)
9. Chase, M., Gilad-Bachrach, R., Laine, K., Lauter, K., Rindal, P.: Private collaborative neural network learning. IACR Cryptology ePrint Archive: 2017/762 (2017)
10. Dahl, M.: Private image analysis with MPC: training CNNs on sensitive data using SPDZ (2018). https://mortendahl.github.io/2017/09/19/private-image-analysis-with-mpc/
11. Damgård, I., Damgård, K., Nielsen, K., Nordholt, P.S., Toft, T.: Confidential benchmarking based on multiparty computation. IACR Cryptology ePrint Archive: 2015/1006 (2015)
12. Damgård, I., Keller, M., Larraia, E., Pastro, V., Scholl, P., Smart, N.P.: Practical covertly secure MPC for dishonest majority – or: breaking the SPDZ limits. In: Crampton, J., Jajodia, S., Mayes, K. (eds.) ESORICS 2013. LNCS, vol. 8134, pp. 1–18. Springer, Heidelberg (2013). https://doi.org/10.1007/978-3-642-40203-6_1
13. Damgård, I., Pastro, V., Smart, N., Zakarias, S.: Multiparty computation from somewhat homomorphic encryption. In: Safavi-Naini, R., Canetti, R. (eds.) CRYPTO 2012. LNCS, vol. 7417, pp. 643–662. Springer, Heidelberg (2012). https://doi.org/10.1007/978-3-642-32009-5_38

14. Deng, J., Dong, W., Socher, R., Li, L.J., Li, K., Fei-Fei, L.: Imagenet: a large-scale hierarchical image database. In: CVPR, pp. 248–255. IEEE (2009)
15. Donahue, J., et al.: DeCAF: a deep convolutional activation feature for generic visual recognition. In: ICML, pp. 647–655 (2014)
16. Drineas, P., Mahoney, M.W.: On the Nyström method for approximating a gram matrix for improved kernel-based learning. J. Mach. Learn. Res. **6**(Dec), 2153–2175 (2005)
17. Fei-Fei, L., Fergus, R., Perona, P.: Learning generative visual models from few training examples: an incremental bayesian approach tested on 101 object categories. In: CVPR, pp. 178–178. IEEE (2004)
18. Gastaldi, X.: Shake-Shake regularization. arXiv:1705.07485 (2017)
19. Gentry, C.: Fully homomorphic encryption using ideal lattices. In: STOC, pp. 169–178 (2009)
20. Gilad-Bachrach, R., Dowlin, N., Laine, K., Lauter, K., Naehrig, M., Wernsing, J.: CryptoNets: applying neural networks to encrypted data with high throughput and accuracy. In: ICML, pp. 201–210 (2016)
21. Graepel, T., Lauter, K., Naehrig, M.: ML confidential: machine learning on encrypted data. In: Kwon, T., Lee, M.-K., Kwon, D. (eds.) ICISC 2012. LNCS, vol. 7839, pp. 1–21. Springer, Heidelberg (2013). https://doi.org/10.1007/978-3-642-37682-5_1
22. He, K., Zhang, X., Ren, S., Sun, J.: Spatial pyramid pooling in deep convolutional networks for visual recognition. In: Fleet, D., Pajdla, T., Schiele, B., Tuytelaars, T. (eds.) ECCV 2014. LNCS, vol. 8691, pp. 346–361. Springer, Cham (2014). https://doi.org/10.1007/978-3-319-10578-9_23
23. Huang, G., Liu, Z., van der Maaten, L., Weinberger, K.Q.: Densely connected convolutional networks. In: CVPR, pp. 4700–4708. IEEE (2017)
24. Jia, Y., et al.: Caffe: convolutional architecture for fast feature embedding. In: ACMMM, pp. 675–678. ACM (2014)
25. Juvekar, C., Vaikuntanathan, V., Chandrakasan, A.: GAZELLE: a low latency framework for secure neural network inference. In: USENIX, pp. 1651–1668 (2018)
26. Keller, M., Pastro, V., Rotaru, D.: Overdrive: making SPDZ great again. In: Nielsen, J.B., Rijmen, V. (eds.) EUROCRYPT 2018. LNCS, vol. 10822, pp. 158–189. Springer, Cham (2018). https://doi.org/10.1007/978-3-319-78372-7_6
27. Khan, F.S., van de Weijer, J., Anwer, R.M., Bagdanov, A.D., Felsberg, M., Laaksonen, J.: Scale coding bag of deep features for human attribute and action recognition. Mach. Vis. Appl. **29**(1), 55–71 (2018)
28. Krizhevsky, A., Hinton, G.: Learning multiple layers of features from tiny images. Technical report, University of Toronto (2009)
29. Laur, S., Lipmaa, H., Mielikäinen, T.: Cryptographically private support vector machines. In: SIGKDD, pp. 618–624. ACM (2006)
30. Lin, K.P., Chen, M.S.: Privacy-preserving outsourcing support vector machines with random transformation. In: SIGKDD, pp. 363–372. ACM (2010)
31. Lin, K.P., Chen, M.S.: On the design and analysis of the privacy-preserving SVM classifier. Knowl. Data Eng. **23**(11), 1704–1717 (2011)
32. Lindell, Y., Pinkas, B.: Privacy preserving data mining. In: Bellare, M. (ed.) CRYPTO 2000. LNCS, vol. 1880, pp. 36–54. Springer, Heidelberg (2000). https://doi.org/10.1007/3-540-44598-6_3
33. Liu, J., Juuti, M., Lu, Y., Asokan, N.: Oblivious neural network predictions via MiniONN transformations. In: SIGSAC, pp. 619–631. ACM (2017)

34. Makri, E., Rotaru, D., Smart, N.P., Vercauteren, F.: EPIC: efficient private image classification (or: learning from the masters). IACR Cryptology ePrint Archive: 2017/1190 (2017)
35. Mohassel, P., Zhang, Y.: SecureML: a system for scalable privacy-preserving machine learning. In: S&P, pp. 19–38. IEEE (2017)
36. Orlandi, C., Piva, A., Barni, M.: Oblivious neural network computing via homomorphic encryption. EURASIP J. Inf. Secur. **2007**(1), 1–11 (2007)
37. Pedregosa, F., et al.: Scikit-learn: machine learning in python. J. Mach. Learn. Res. **12**, 2825–2830 (2011)
38. Quattoni, A., Torralba, A.: Recognizing indoor scenes. In: CVPR, pp. 413–420. IEEE (2009)
39. Rahimi, A., Recht, B.: Random features for large-scale kernel machines. In: NIPS, pp. 1177–1184 (2008)
40. Rahimi, A., Recht, B.: Weighted sums of random kitchen sinks: replacing minimization with randomization in learning. In: NIPS, pp. 1313–1320 (2009)
41. Rahulamathavan, Y., Phan, R.C.W., Veluru, S., Cumanan, K., Rajarajan, M.: Privacy-preserving multi-class support vector machine for outsourcing the data classification in cloud. IEEE Trans. Dependable Secure Comput. **11**(5), 467–479 (2014)
42. Razavian, A.S., Azizpour, H., Sullivan, J., Carlsson, S.: CNN features off-the-shelf: an astounding baseline for recognition. In: CVPRW, pp. 512–519. IEEE (2014)
43. Riazi, M.S., Weinert, C., Tkachenko, O., Songhori, E.M., Schneider, T., Koushanfar, F.: Chameleon: a hybrid secure computation framework for machine learning applications. In: ASIACCS, pp. 707–721. ACM (2018)
44. Rivest, R.L., Adleman, L., Dertouzos, M.L.: On data banks and privacy homomorphisms. Found. Secure Comput. **4**(11), 169–180 (1978)
45. Rouhani, B.D., Riazi, M.S., Koushanfar, F.: DeepSecure: scalable provably-secure deep learning. In: ACM/ESDA/DAC, pp. 1–6. IEEE (2018)
46. Shokri, R., Shmatikov, V.: Privacy-preserving deep learning. In: SIGSAC, pp. 1310–1321. ACM (2015)
47. Szegedy, C., Vanhoucke, V., Ioffe, S., Shlens, J., Wojna, Z.: Rethinking the inception architecture for computer vision. In: CVPR, pp. 2818–2826. IEEE (2016)
48. Teo, S.G., Han, S., Lee, V.C.: Privacy preserving support vector machine using non-linear kernels on Hadoop Mahout. In: CSE, pp. 941–948. IEEE (2013)
49. Thrun, S.: Is learning the n-th thing any easier than learning the first? In: NIPS, pp. 640–646 (1996)
50. Tramèr, F., Zhang, F., Juels, A., Reiter, M.K., Ristenpart, T.: Stealing machine learning models via prediction APIs. In: USENIX, pp. 601–618 (2016)
51. Vaidya, J., Yu, H., Jiang, X.: Privacy-preserving SVM classification. Knowl. Inf. Syst. **14**(2), 161–178 (2008)
52. Vapnik, V.N.: Statistical Learning Theory, vol. 3. Wiley, New York (1998)
53. Williams, C.K., Seeger, M.: Using the Nyström method to speed up kernel machines. In: NIPS, pp. 682–688 (2001)
54. Yang, T., Li, Y.F., Mahdavi, M., Jin, R., Zhou, Z.H.: Nyström method vs random Fourier features: a theoretical and empirical comparison. In: NIPS, pp. 476–484 (2012)
55. Yosinski, J., Clune, J., Bengio, Y., Lipson, H.: How transferable are features in deep neural networks? In: NIPS, pp. 3320–3328 (2014)

Context Hiding Multi-key Linearly Homomorphic Authenticators

Lucas Schabhüser$^{(\boxtimes)}$, Denis Butin, and Johannes Buchmann

Technische Universität Darmstadt, Darmstadt, Germany
{lschabhueser,dbutin,buchmann}@cdc.informatik.tu-darmstadt.de

Abstract. Demanding computations are increasingly outsourced to cloud platforms. For such outsourced computations, the efficient verifiability of results is a crucial requirement. When sensitive data is involved, the verification of a computation should preserve the privacy of the input values: it should be context hiding. Context hiding verifiability is enabled by existing homomorphic authenticator schemes. However, until now, no context hiding homomorphic authenticator scheme supports multiple independent clients, e.g. multiple keys. Multi-key support is necessary for datasets involving input authenticated by different clients, e.g. multiple hospitals in e-health scenarios. In this paper, we propose the first perfectly context hiding, publicly verifiable multi-key homomorphic authenticator scheme supporting linear functions. Our scheme is provably unforgeable in the standard model, and succinct. Verification time depends only linearly on the number of clients, in an amortized sense.

Keywords: Delegated computation · Homomorphic authenticators · Context hiding

1 Introduction

Today, it is common practice to outsource time-consuming computations to the cloud. In such a situation, it is desirable to be able to verify the outsourced computation. The verification must be *efficient*, by which we mean that the verification procedure is significantly faster than the verified computation itself. Otherwise, the verifier could as well carry out the computation by himself, negating the advantage of outsourcing. In addition, there are scenarios in which the verification is required to provide *input privacy*, i.e. the verification does not reveal anything about the input to the computation. For instance, a cloud service may collect health data of individuals and compute statistics on them. These statistical evaluations are then given to third parties, such as insurance companies. While these third parties must be able to learn the statistical outcome, for privacy reasons, they must not learn the individual health data. Furthermore, many interesting statistics involve *multiple identities*; for instance, computing on health data across datasets provided by multiple hospitals. Keeping identities separate instead of merging all data supports fine-grained authenticity.

© Springer Nature Switzerland AG 2019
M. Matsui (Ed.): CT-RSA 2019, LNCS 11405, pp. 493–513, 2019.
https://doi.org/10.1007/978-3-030-12612-4_25

Furthermore, using different keys instead of copies of a shared key avoids a single point of failure. With multiple keys, the loss of a single key does not result in a total security loss, in contrast with the shared key approach.

Homomorphic Authenticators. In practice, the efficient verifiability of outsourced computation can be realised using *homomorphic authenticators*. The general idea of homomorphic authenticators is the following. Before delegating inputs to a function, the input values are authenticated. The homomorphic property allows the server to compute an authenticator to the output of a given function from the authenticators to the inputs to said function. In the public key setting, homomorphic authenticators are called *homomorphic signatures*. In the private key setting, they are called *homomorphic MACs*. Input privacy for homomorphic authenticators has been formalized in the form of the *context hiding* property.

State of the Art. Using such authenticators, there are solutions for efficient context hiding verifiability for the case of a *single* client, and for the equivalent case of multiple clients sharing a single secret key [4,8,20]. However, no context hiding solution for multiple clients with different keys exists. Fiore et al. [12] already presented multi-key homomorphic authenticators. However, their constructions are not context hiding. Hence the challenge to design efficient and context hiding verification procedures for outsourced computing that support multiple clients.

1.1 Contribution Overview

In this paper, we present the first publicly verifiable homomorphic authenticator scheme providing efficient and context hiding verification in the setting of multiple clients (allowing for multiple keys). We construct a multi-key linearly homomorphic signature scheme, and thus focus on the public key setting. We first define the context hiding property in the multi-key case. We then describe our main contribution, a new publicly verifiable multi-key linearly homomorphic authenticator scheme. Our scheme allows to generate an authenticator on the function value of a linear function from authenticators on the input values of various identities without knowledge of the authentication key. Furthermore, our scheme is perfectly context hiding, i.e. the authenticator to the output value does not leak any information about the input values. Using our multi-key homomorphic authenticator scheme, the verification procedure for outsourced computations of linear functions can be implemented as follows. The various clients each upload data, signed under their personal private key, to the cloud. The cloud server computes the result of the given function over these data. It also generates an authenticator to this result from the signatures on the inputs. The verifier uses this authenticator to check for correctness of the computation, by using the verification keys associated to the clients providing input to the computation. Regarding performance, verification time depends only on the number of identities involved (in an amortized sense).

Context Hiding Security for Multiple Clients. On a high level, we first define the context hiding property in the multi-key setting. Intuitively, this property provides some measure of input privacy, i.e. an authenticator to the output of a computation does not leak information about the input to the computation. In the multi-key setting, the question who exactly is meant to be prevented from learning about the input values becomes relevant. In particular, we differentiate between an external adversary—one that has not corrupted any of the identities involved in a computation—and an internal adversary, who has this additional knowledge. Thus we capture the two slightly different notions of keeping the input values private with respect to some outside party (*externally context hiding*), versus keeping the input values confidential with respect to an identity that also provided inputs to the computation (*internally context hiding*).

Our Construction. Then, we provide a concrete instantiation of a publicly verifiable multi-key linearly homomorphic authenticator scheme, i.e. a homomorphic signature scheme with these properties. Our authenticator size is $\mathcal{O}(k)$, where k is the number of identities involved in the computation, thus achieving succinctness. A homomorphically derived authenticator consists of both components associated to an identity id and global elements. In order to prevent the elements associated to id from leaking information about the inputs provided by id, the authenticators are randomized, and the global elements are used to deal with the randomization in order to preserve the homomorphic property. Our verification procedure naturally splits into two parts, only one of which involves the actual outcome of the computation. The other part only depends on the public verification key vk and the function to be evaluated, and can thus be pre-computed. This allows for amortized efficient verification, i.e. after an expensive function-dependent one-time precomputation, all subsequent verifications occur in constant time.

Proving Unforgeability. A significant part of this paper is the security reduction used to prove our scheme's unforgeability. In Sect. 4, we present a series of games, followed by several lemmata considering the difference between the games. Most games only differ if a forgery of a specific type is produced by the adversary, i.e. a special case of a forgery, where one or several of the components are correct. We bound the probability of these events and can show that such forgeries imply solving the Discrete Logarithm, the Decisional Diffie–Hellman and the Flexible Diffie–Hellman Inversion problem (introduced by Catalano, Fiore and Nizzardo at CRYPTO 2015 [8]), respectively. Our security reduction is performed in the standard model. Our scheme does not use Fiore et al.'s lattice-based construction [12] and thus features a different structure. Consequently, our proof strategy is also novel. As is common in homomorphic authenticator schemes, we use identifiers or labels. They uniquely identify the position of an input in a dataset. There are elements in the public verification key associated to these labels. When simulating (some of) these security games, the simulator does not have access to the secret signing key and thus cannot run the algorithm

Auth. By embedding a trapdoor into the elements associated to labels in the verification key the simulator can perfectly simulate authenticators when presented with a Flexible Diffie–Hellman Inversion instance (and thus not knowing the secret key).

Outline. We recall relevant definitions for homomorphic authenticator schemes in Sect. 2 and define the context hiding property in the multi-key setting. In Sect. 3, we present our publicly verifiable multi-key homomorphic authenticator scheme for linear functions. We then address its properties, notably correctness and context hiding. In Sect. 4, we provide a security reduction for our scheme. Next, in Sect. 5, we compare our contribution to existing work on homomorphic authenticators and verifiable computation. Finally, in Sect. 6, we summarize our results and give an outlook to future work and open problems.

2   Formalising Multi-key Homomorphic Authenticators

In this section, we provide the necessary background for homomorphic authenticators and their properties. We recall the definitions for correctness and unforgeability, ass well as efficiency properties in the form of succinctness and efficient verification. Then we present our generalization of the context hiding property to the multi-key setting. Finally we state the computational assumptions on which the security of our scheme is based.

To accurately describe both correct and legitimate operations for homomorphic authenticators, we use *multi-labeled programs* similarly to Backes, Fiore, and Reischuk [5]. The basic idea is to append a function by several identifiers, in our case *input identifiers* and *dataset identifiers*. Input identifiers label in which order the input values are to be used and dataset identifiers determine which authenticators can be homomorphically combined. The idea is that only authenticators created under the same dataset identifier can be combined. We now give formal definitions.

A *labeled program* $\mathcal{P}$ consists of a tuple $(f, \tau_1, \ldots, \tau_n)$, where $f : \mathcal{M}^n \to \mathcal{M}$ is a function with n inputs and $\tau_i \in \mathcal{T}$ is a label for the ith input of f from some set $\mathcal{T}$. Given a set of labeled programs $\mathcal{P}_1, \ldots, \mathcal{P}_N$ and a function $g : \mathcal{M}^N \to \mathcal{M}$, they can be composed by evaluating g over the labeled programs, i.e. $\mathcal{P}^* = g(\mathcal{P}_1, \ldots, \mathcal{P}_N)$. The identity program with label τ is given by $\mathcal{I}_\tau = (f_{id}, \tau)$, where $f_{id} : \mathcal{M} \to \mathcal{M}$ is the identity function. The program $\mathcal{P} = (f, \tau_1, \ldots, \tau_n)$ can be expressed as the composition of n identity programs $\mathcal{P} = f(\mathcal{I}_{\tau_1}, \ldots, \mathcal{I}_{\tau_n})$.

A *multi-labeled program* $\mathcal{P}_\Delta$ is a pair $(\mathcal{P}, \Delta)$ of the labeled program $\mathcal{P}$ and a dataset identifier Δ. Given a set of k multi-labeled programs with the same dataset identifier Δ, i.e. $(\mathcal{P}_1, \Delta), \ldots, (\mathcal{P}_N, \Delta)$, and a function $g : \mathcal{M}^N \to \mathcal{M}$, a composed multi-labeled program $\mathcal{P}_\Delta^*$ can be computed, consisting of the pair $(\mathcal{P}^*, \Delta)$, where $\mathcal{P}^* = g(\mathcal{P}_1, \ldots, \mathcal{P}_N)$. Analogously to the identity program for labeled programs, we refer to a multi-labeled identity program by $\mathcal{I}_{(\tau, \Delta)} = ((f_{id}, \tau), \Delta)$.

In particular, we use labeled programs to identify the different clients. Our multi-key homomorphic authenticators allow the verification of linear functions evaluated over data signed by different keys. Following the convention of [12], we assume every client has an identity id in some identity space ID, and that public keys can be linked to an identity id. This can, for instance, be achieved by a public-key infrastructure (PKI). In order to identify which inputs (labeled by τ) were authenticated by id, our messages are assigned with a label $l \leftarrow (\mathsf{id}, \tau)$, where id is a client's identity and τ is an input identifier. Following convention, messages are grouped within datasets Δ and homomorphic evaluation is only supported over the same dataset. $[n]$ denotes the interval of integers from 1 to n.

Definition 1 (Multi-key Homomorphic Authenticator ([12]). *A multi-key homomorphic authenticator scheme* MKHAuth *is a tuple of the following probabilistic polynomial time (PPT) algorithms:*

Setup(1^λ): *On input a security parameter λ, the algorithm returns a set of public parameter* pp, *consisting of (at least) the description of a tag space $\mathcal{T}$, an identity space* ID, *a message space $\mathcal{M}$, and a set of admissible functions $\mathcal{F}$. Given $\mathcal{T}$ and* ID *the label space of the scheme is defined as $\mathcal{L} = \mathsf{ID} \times \mathcal{T}$. The public parameters* pp *will implicitly be inputs to all following algorithms even if not explicitly specified.*

KeyGen(pp): *On input the public parameters* pp, *the algorithm returns a key triple* (sk, ek, vk), *where* sk *is the secret key authentication key,* ek *is a public evaluation key, and* vk *is a verification key that can be either private or public.*

Auth(sk, Δ, l, m): *On input a secret key* sk, *a dataset identifier Δ, a label $l = (\mathsf{id}, \tau)$, and a message m, the algorithm returns an authenticator σ.*

Eval($f, \{(\sigma_i, \mathsf{EKS}_i)\}_{i \in [n]}$): *On input a function $f : \mathcal{M}^n \to \mathcal{M}$ and a set $\{(\sigma_i, \mathsf{EKS}_i)\}_{i \in [n]}$ of authenticators and evaluation keys, the algorithm returns an authenticator σ.*

Ver($\mathcal{P}_\Delta, \{\mathsf{vk}_{\mathsf{id}}\}_{\mathsf{id} \in \mathcal{P}}, m, \sigma$): *On input a multi-labeled program $\mathcal{P}_\Delta$, a set of verification key $\{\mathsf{vk}_{\mathsf{id}}\}_{\mathsf{id} \in \mathcal{P}}$, corresponding to the identities* id *involved in the program $\mathcal{P}$, a message $m \in \mathcal{M}$, and an authenticator σ , the algorithm returns either 1 (accept), or 0 (reject).*

If the class $\mathcal{F}$ of admitted functions is the set of linear functions, we call MKHAuth a *multi-key linearly homomorphic authenticator*. If vk is private, we call MKHAuth a *multi-key homomorphic MAC*, while for a public vk we call it a *multi-key homomorphic signature*.

We now define properties relevant for the analysis of multi-key homomorphic authenticator schemes: authentication correctness, evaluation correctness, succinctness, unforgeability, efficient verification and context hiding.

Correctness naturally comes in two forms. We require both authenticators created directly with a secret signing key as well as those derived by the homomorphic property to verify correctly.

Definition 2 (Authentication Correctness). *A multi-key homomorphic authenticator scheme* (Setup, KeyGen, Auth, Eval, Ver) *satisfies* authentication correctness *if, for any security parameter* λ, *any public parameters* pp $\leftarrow$ Setup(1^λ), *any key triple* (sk, ek, vk) $\leftarrow$ KeyGen(pp), *any label* $l = (\text{id}, \tau) \in \mathcal{L}$, *any dataset identifier* $\Delta \in \{0,1\}^*$, *any message* $m \in \mathcal{M}$, *and any authenticator* $\sigma \leftarrow$ Auth(sk, Δ, l, m) *we have* Ver($\mathcal{I}_{(l,\Delta)}$, vk, m, σ) = 1, *where* $\mathcal{I}_{l,\Delta}$ *is the multi-labeled identity program.*

Definition 3 (Evaluation Correctness). *A multi-key homomorphic authenticator scheme* (Setup, KeyGen, Auth, Eval, Ver) *satisfies* authentication correctness *if, for any security parameter* λ, *any public parameters* pp $\leftarrow$ Setup(1^λ), *any set of key triples* $\{(\text{sk}_{\text{id}}, \text{ek}_{\text{id}}, \text{vk}_{\text{id}})\}_{\text{id}\in\tilde{\text{ID}}}$, *with* $(\text{sk}_{\text{id}}, \text{ek}_{\text{id}}, \text{vk}_{\text{id}}) \xleftarrow{\$} $ KeyGen(pp) *for all* id $\in \tilde{\text{ID}}$, *for some subset* $\tilde{\text{ID}} \subset$ ID, *for any dataset identifier* $\Delta \in \{0,1\}^*$, *and any set of program/message/authenticator triples* $\{(\mathcal{P}_i, m_i, \sigma_i)\}_{i\in[N]}$, *such that* Ver($\mathcal{P}_{i,\Delta}$, $\{\text{vk}_{\text{id}}\}_{\text{id}\in\mathcal{P}_i}, m_i, \sigma_i$) = 1 *the following holds: Let* $m^* = g(m_1, \ldots, m_N), \mathcal{P}^* = g(\mathcal{P}_1, \ldots, \mathcal{P}_N)$, *and* $\sigma^* = $ Eval($g, \{(\sigma_i, \text{EKS}_i)\}_{i\in[N]}$) *where* $\text{EKS}_i = \{\text{ek}_{\text{id}}\}_{\text{id}\in\mathcal{P}_i}$. *Then* Ver($\mathcal{P}^*_\Delta$, $\{\text{vk}_{\text{id}}\}_{\text{id}\in\mathcal{P}^*}, m^*, \sigma^*$) = 1 *holds.*

We now consider two properties impacting the practicality of homomorphic authenticator schemes. Succinctness on a high level guarantees that bandwidth requirements for deploying such a scheme are low. Efficient verification allows for low computational effort on behalf of the verifier.

Definition 4 (Succinctness [12]). *A multi-key homomorphic authenticator scheme* (Setup, KeyGen, Auth, Eval, Ver) *is said to be succinct if the size of every authenticator depends only logarithmically on the size of a dataset. However, we allow authenticators to depend on the number of keys involved in the computation. More formally, let* pp $\leftarrow$ Setup(1^λ), $\mathcal{P} = (f, l_1, \ldots, l_n)$, *with* $l_i = (\text{id}_i, \tau_i)$, $\{(\text{sk}_{\text{id}}, \text{ek}_{\text{id}}, \text{vk}_{\text{id}}) \leftarrow$ KeyGen(pp)$\}_{\text{id}\in\mathcal{P}}$, *and* $\sigma_i \leftarrow$ Auth($\text{sk}_{\text{id}_i}, \Delta, l_i, m_i$) *for all* $i \in [n]$. *A multi-key homomorphic authenticator is said to be succinct if there exists a fixed polynomial* p *such that* $|\sigma| = p(\lambda, k, \log n)$, *where* $\sigma = $ Eval($f, \{\sigma_i, \text{ek}_{\text{id}_i}\}_{i\in[n]}$) *and* $k = |\{\text{id} \in \mathcal{P}\}|$.

We explicitly allow the size of the authenticators to depend on the number of identities $k = |\{\text{id} \in \mathcal{P}\}|$ involved in the computation.

Like Libert and Yung [19], we call a key *concise* if its size is independent of the input size n.

Definition 5 (Efficient Verification [8]). *A multi-key homomorphic authenticator scheme for multi-labeled programs allows for* efficient verification *if there exist two additional algorithms* (VerPrep, EffVer) *such that:*

VerPrep($\mathcal{P}, \{\text{vk}_{\text{id}}\}_{\text{id}\in\mathcal{P}}$): *Given a labeled program* $\mathcal{P} = (f, l_1, \ldots, l_n)$, *and a set of verification keys* $\{\text{vk}_{\text{id}}\}_{\text{id}\in\mathcal{P}}$ *this algorithm generates a concise verification key* $\text{vk}_\mathcal{P}$. *This does* not *depend on a dataset identifier* Δ.

EffVer($\text{vk}_\mathcal{P}, \Delta, m, \sigma$): *Given a concise verification key* $\text{vk}_\mathcal{P}$, *a dataset* Δ, *a message* m, *and an authenticator* σ, *it outputs* 1 *or* 0.

The above algorithms are required to satisfy the following two properties:

Correctness: *Let* $\{(\mathsf{sk}_{\mathsf{id}}, \mathsf{ek}_{\mathsf{id}}, \mathsf{vk}_{\mathsf{id}})\}_{\mathsf{id} \in \mathsf{ID}}$ *be a set of honestly generated keys and* $(\mathcal{P}_\Delta, m, \sigma)$ *be a tuple such that,* $\mathsf{Ver}(\mathcal{P}_\Delta, \{\mathsf{vk}_{\mathsf{id}}\}_{\mathsf{id} \in \mathcal{P}}, m, \sigma) = 1$. *Then, for every* $\mathsf{vk}_\mathcal{P} \xleftarrow{\$} \mathsf{VerPrep}(\mathcal{P}, \{\mathsf{vk}_{\mathsf{id}}\}_{\mathsf{id} \in \mathcal{P}})$, $\Pr[\mathsf{EffVer}(\mathsf{vk}_\mathcal{P}, \Delta, m, \sigma) = 0] = \mathsf{negl}(\lambda)$, *where* $\mathsf{negl}(\lambda)$ *denotes any function negligible in the security parameter* λ.

Amortized Efficiency: *Let* $\mathcal{P}$ *be a program, let* $m_1, \ldots, m_n$ *be valid input values and let* $t(n)$ *be the time required to compute* $\mathcal{P}(m_1, \ldots, m_n)$ *with output* m. *Then, for any* $\mathsf{vk}_\mathcal{P} \xleftarrow{\$} \mathsf{VerPrep}(\mathcal{P}, \{\mathsf{vk}_{\mathsf{id}}\}_{\mathsf{id} \in \mathcal{P}})$, *and any* $\Delta \in \{0,1\}^*$ *the time required to compute* $\mathsf{EffVer}(\mathsf{vk}_\mathcal{P}, \Delta, m, \sigma)$ *is* $t' = o(t(n))$, *where* $\sigma_i \leftarrow \mathsf{Auth}(\mathsf{sk}_{\mathsf{id}_i}, \Delta, l_i, m_i)$ *for* $i \in [n]$, *and* $\sigma \leftarrow \mathsf{Eval}(f, \{(\sigma_i, \mathsf{EKS}_i)\}_{i \in [n]})$.

Here, *efficiency* is used in an amortized sense. There is a function-dependent pre-processing phase, so that verification cost amortizes over multiple datasets.

For the notion of unforgeability of a multi-key homomorphic authenticator scheme (Setup, KeyGen, Auth, Eval, Ver), we define the following experiment between an adversary $\mathcal{A}$ and a challenger $\mathcal{C}$. During the experiment, the adversary $\mathcal{A}$ can adaptively query the challenger $\mathcal{C}$ for authenticators on messages of his choice under labels of his choice. He can also make verification queries and corrupt clients. Intuitively, the homomorphic property allows anyone (with access to the evaluation keys) to derive new authenticators. This can be checked by the use of the corresponding program in the verification algorithm. An adversary should however not be able to derive authenticators beyond that. Preventing forgeries on programs involving inputs of corrupted clients is impossible in many cases (e.g. for any linear function), as knowledge of the secret key allows the creation of arbitrarily many authenticators under any multi-label (l, Δ). However, this security definition captures that knowledge of one client's secret key does not allow any forgeries on a computation not involving this corrupted client.

Definition 6 ($\mathsf{HomUF} - \mathsf{CMA}_{\mathcal{A}, \mathsf{MKHAuth}}(\lambda)$).

Setup: $\mathcal{C}$ runs $\mathsf{Setup}(1^\lambda)$ *to obtain the public parameters* pp *that are sent to* $\mathcal{A}$.
Authentication Queries: $\mathcal{A}$ can adaptively submit queries of the form (Δ, l, m) *where* Δ *is a dataset identifier,* $l = (\mathsf{id}, \tau) \in \mathcal{L}$ *is a label, and* $m \in \mathcal{M}$ *is a message of its choice. $\mathcal{C}$ answers as follows:*

If (Δ, l, m) *is the first query for the dataset* Δ, *$\mathcal{C}$ initializes an empty list* $L_\Delta = \varnothing$ *and proceeds as follows.*
If (Δ, l, m) *is the first query with identity* id, *$\mathcal{C}$ generates keys* $(\mathsf{sk}_{\mathsf{id}}, \mathsf{ek}_{\mathsf{id}}, \mathsf{vk}_{\mathsf{id}})$ $\xleftarrow{\$} \mathsf{KeyGen}(\mathsf{pp})$ *(that are implicitly assigned to identity* id*), gives* $(\mathsf{ek}_{\mathsf{id}}, \mathsf{vk}_{\mathsf{id}})$ *to $\mathcal{A}$ and proceeds as follows.*
If (Δ, l, m) *is such that* $(l, m) \notin L_\Delta$, *$\mathcal{C}$ computes* $\sigma_l \leftarrow \mathsf{Auth}(\mathsf{sk}_{\mathsf{id}}, \Delta, l, m)$ *($\mathcal{C}$ has already generated keys for the identity* id*), returns* σ_l *to $\mathcal{A}$ and updates the list* $L_\Delta \leftarrow L_\Delta \cup (l, m)$.
If (Δ, l, m) *is such that* $(l, \cdot) \in L_\Delta$ *(which means that the adversary had already made a query* (Δ, l, m') *for the identity* id*), then $\mathcal{C}$ ignores the query.*

Verification Queries: $\mathcal{A}$ *is also given access to a verification oracle. Namely the adversary can submit a query* $(\mathcal{P}_\Delta, m, \sigma)$ *and* $\mathcal{C}$ *replies with the output of* $\mathsf{Ver}(\mathcal{P}_\Delta, \{\mathsf{vk}_{\mathsf{id}}\}_{\mathsf{id} \in \mathcal{P}}, m, \sigma)$.

Corruption Queries: *The adversary* $\mathcal{A}$ *has access to a corruption oracle. At the beginning of the experiment, the challenger* $\mathcal{C}$ *initializes an empty list* $L_{\mathsf{corr}} = \varnothing$ *of corrupted identities. During the game* $\mathcal{A}$ *can adaptively query identities* $\mathsf{id} \in \mathsf{ID}$. *If* $\mathsf{id} \notin L_{\mathsf{corr}}$ *then* $\mathcal{C}$ *replies with the triple* $(\mathsf{sk}_{\mathsf{id}}, \mathsf{ek}_{\mathsf{id}}, \mathsf{vk}_{\mathsf{id}})$ *(that is generated using* KeyGen *if not done before) and updates the list* $L_{\mathsf{corr}} \leftarrow L_{\mathsf{corr}} \cup \mathsf{id}$. *If* $\mathsf{id} \in L_{\mathsf{corr}}$, *then* $\mathcal{C}$ *replies with the triple* $(\mathsf{sk}_{\mathsf{id}}, \mathsf{ek}_{\mathsf{id}}, \mathsf{vk}_{\mathsf{id}})$ *assigned to* id *before.*

Forgery: *In the end,* $\mathcal{A}$ *outputs a tuple* $(\mathcal{P}^*_{\Delta^*}, m^*, \sigma^*)$. *The experiment outputs* 1 *if the tuple returned by* $\mathcal{A}$ *is a forgery as defined below (see Definition 7), and* 0 *otherwise.*

This describes the case of publicly verifiable multi-key homomorphic authenticators. For multi-key homomorphic MACs, only the verification keys $\mathsf{vk}_{\mathsf{id}}$ received from the corruption oracle are given to the adversary $\mathcal{A}$ during the security experiment.

Definition 7 (Forgery [12]). *Consider a run of* $\mathsf{HomUF} - \mathsf{CMA}_{\mathcal{A}, \mathsf{MKHAuth}}(\lambda)$ *where* $(\mathcal{P}^*_{\Delta^*}, m^*, \sigma^*)$ *is the tuple returned by the adversary in the end of the experiment, with* $\mathcal{P}^* = (f^*, l^*_1, \ldots, l^*_n)$. *This is a forgery if* $\mathsf{Ver}(\mathcal{P}^*_{\Delta^*}, \{\mathsf{vk}_{\mathsf{id}}\}_{\mathsf{id} \in \mathcal{P}^*}, m^*, \sigma^*) = 1$, $\mathsf{id} \notin L_{\mathsf{corr}}$ *(i.e. no identity involved in* $\mathcal{P}^*$ *is corrupted), and at least one of the following properties is satisfied:*

Type 1: *The list* L_{Δ^*} *was not initialized during the security experiment, i.e. no message was ever committed under the dataset identifier* Δ^*.

Type 2: $\mathcal{P}^*_{\Delta^*}$ *is well defined with respect to list* L_{Δ^*} *and* m^* *is not the correct output of the computation, i.e.* $m^* \neq f^*(m_1, \ldots, m_n)$

Type 3: $\mathcal{P}^*_{\Delta^*}$ *is not well defined with respect to* L_{Δ^*} *(see Definition 8).*

Definition 8 (Well Defined Program). *A labeled program* $\mathcal{P} = (f, l_1, \ldots, l_n)$ *is* well defined *with respect to a list* $L \subset \mathcal{L} \times \mathcal{M}$ *if one of the two following cases holds: First, there are messages* $m_1, \ldots, m_n$ *such that* $(l_i, m_i) \in L$ $\forall i \in [n]$. *Second, there is an* $i \in \{1, \ldots, n\}$ *such that* $(l_i, \cdot) \notin L$ *and* $f(\{m_j\}_{(l_j, m_j) \in L} \cup \{m'_k\}_{(l_k, \cdot) \notin L})$ *is constant over all possible choices of* $m'_k \in \mathcal{M}$.

If f is a linear function, the labeled program $\mathcal{P} = (f, l_1, \ldots, l_n)$, with $f(m_1, \ldots, m_n) = \sum_{i=1}^n f_i m_i$ fulfills the second condition if and only if $f_k = 0$ for all $(l_k, \cdot) \notin L$.

Definition 9 (Unforgeability). *A multi-key homomorphic authenticator scheme* $\mathsf{MKHAuth}$ *is* unforgeable *if for any PPT adversary* $\mathcal{A}$ *we have*

$$\Pr[\mathsf{HomUF} - \mathsf{CMA}_{\mathcal{A}, \mathsf{MKHAuth}}(\lambda) = 1] = \mathsf{negl}(\lambda).$$

Additionally, we will use the following statement:

Lemma 1. *Let* MKHAuth $=$ (Setup, KeyGen, Auth, Eval, Ver) *be a multi-key linearly homomorphic authenticator scheme over a message space* $\mathcal{M} \subset R^t$ *for some ring* R *and integer* t. *If* MKHAuth *is secure against Type 2 forgeries, then* MKHAuth *is also secure against Type 3 forgeries.*

Proof. This is an immediate corollary of a result by Freeman [13, Proposition 2.3].

We also consider a relaxation of the unforgeability definition in which the adversaries ask for corruptions in a non-adaptive way. More precisely, we say that an adversary $\mathcal{A}$ makes non-adaptive corruption queries if for every identity id asked to the corruption oracle, id was not queried earlier in the game to the authentication oracle or the verification oracle. For this class of adversaries, corruption queries are of no help as the adversary can generate keys on its own. We will use the following lemma:

Lemma 2 ([12, Proposition 1]). MKHAuth *is unforgeable against adversaries that do not make corruption queries if and only if* MKHAuth *is unforgeable against adversaries that make non-adaptive corruption queries.*

We are now ready to provide our notion of input privacy, in the form of the context hiding property and adapting this to the multi-key setting.

Our definition for the context hiding property is inspired by Gorbunov et al.'s definition [15] for the single-key case. However, in our case, the simulator is explicitly given the circuit for which the authenticator is supposed to verify. With respect to this difference, our definition is more general. We stress that the circuit is not hidden in either of these notions. Furthermore, we differentiate between an external adversary and an internal adversary, that corrupts some of the various identities involved in a computation, i.e. knows their secret keys and inputs to a computation. Such an adversary will learn more than the outcome of the computation, since it knows some of the secret keys. It is however desirable for any non-corrupted party to achieve context hiding privacy even against other parties involved in the computation, as far as that is possible. We now formally define context hiding for both kinds of adversaries.

Definition 10 (Context Hiding). *A multi-key homomorphic authenticator scheme for multi-labeled programs is* externally context hiding *if there exist two additional PPT procedures* $\tilde{\sigma} \leftarrow$ Hide($\{vk_{id}\}_{id \in \mathcal{P}}, m, \sigma$) *and* HideVer($\{vk_{id}\}_{id \in ID},$ $\mathcal{P}_\Delta, m, \tilde{\sigma}$) *such that:*

Correctness: *For any* pp $\leftarrow$ Setup(1^λ), $(sk_{id}, ek_{id}, vk_{id}) \leftarrow$ KeyGen(pp) *and any tuple* $(\mathcal{P}_\Delta, m, \sigma)$, *such that* Ver($\mathcal{P}_\Delta, \{vk_{id}\}_{id \in \mathcal{P}}, m, \sigma$) $= 1$, *and* $\tilde{\sigma} \leftarrow$ Hide($\{vk_{id}\}_{id \in ID}, m, \sigma$), *it holds that* HideVer($\{vk_{id}\}_{id \in ID}, \mathcal{P}_\Delta, m, \tilde{\sigma}$) $= 1$.

Unforgeability: *The homomorphic authenticator scheme is unforgeable (Definition 9) when replacing the algorithm* Ver *with* HideVer *in the security experiment.*

Context Hiding Security: *There is a simulator* Sim *such that, for any fixed (worst-case) choice of* $\{(\mathsf{sk_{id}}, \mathsf{ek_{id}}, \mathsf{vk_{id}}) \leftarrow \mathsf{KeyGen}(\mathsf{pp})\}_{\mathsf{id} \in \mathcal{P}}$, *any multi-labeled program* $\mathcal{P}_\Delta = (f, l_1, \ldots, l_n, \Delta)$, *messages* $m_1, \ldots, m_n$, *and distinguisher* $\mathcal{D}$ *there exists a function* $\epsilon(\lambda) = \mathsf{negl}(\lambda)$ *such that* $|\Pr[\mathcal{D}(\mathsf{Hide}(\{\mathsf{vk_{id}}\}_{\mathsf{id} \in \mathcal{P}}, m, \sigma)) = 1] - \Pr[\mathcal{D}(\mathsf{Sim}(\{\mathsf{sk_{id}}\}_{\mathsf{id} \in \mathcal{P}}, \mathcal{P}_\Delta, m)) = 1]| = \epsilon(\lambda)$, *where* $\sigma_i \leftarrow \mathsf{Auth}(\mathsf{sk_{id_i}}, \Delta, l_i, m_i)$, $m \leftarrow f(m_1, \ldots, m_n)$, $\sigma \leftarrow \mathsf{Eval}(f, \{(\sigma_i, \mathsf{EKS}_i)\}_{i \in [n]})$, *and the probabilities are taken over the randomness of* Auth, Hide *and* Sim.

If $\epsilon(\lambda) = \mathsf{negl}(\lambda)$, *we call the multi-key homomorphic authenticator scheme statistically externally context hiding. If* $\epsilon(\lambda) = 0$, *we call it* perfectly externally context hiding.

If for the context hiding security we even have $|\Pr[\mathcal{D}(\mathcal{I}, \mathsf{Hide}(\mathsf{vk}, m, \sigma)) = 1] - \Pr[\mathcal{D}(\mathsf{Sim}(\{\mathsf{sk_{id}}\}_{\mathsf{id} \in \mathcal{P}}, \mathcal{I}, \mathcal{P}_\Delta, m)) = 1]| = \epsilon(\lambda)$, *where* $\mathcal{I} = (\{\mathsf{sk_{id}}\}_{\mathsf{id} \in \tilde{\mathsf{ID}}}, \{(m_{(\tau, \mathsf{id})}, \sigma_{(\tau, \mathsf{id})})\}_{\mathsf{id} \in \tilde{\mathsf{ID}}})$, $\tilde{\mathsf{ID}} \subset \mathsf{ID}$ *is a set of corrupted identities and the rest is like before, we call the multi-key homomorphic authenticator scheme (statistically or perfectly, depending on* $\epsilon(\lambda)$ *as above)* internally context hiding.

2.1 Computational Assumptions

We recall the computational assumptions on which our schemes are based.

Definition 11 (Asymmetric bilinear groups). *An* asymmetric bilinear group *is a tuple* $\mathsf{bgp} = (p, \mathbb{G}_1, \mathbb{G}_2, \mathbb{G}_T, g_1, g_2, e)$, *such that:*

- $\mathbb{G}_1, \mathbb{G}_2$, *and* $\mathbb{G}_T$ *are cyclic groups of prime order* p,
- $g_1 \in \mathbb{G}_1$ *and* $g_2 \in \mathbb{G}_2$ *are generators for their respective groups,*
- *The Discrete Logarithm (DL) assumption holds in* $\mathbb{G}_1, \mathbb{G}_2$, *and* $\mathbb{G}_T$,
- $e : \mathbb{G}_1 \times \mathbb{G}_2 \rightarrow \mathbb{G}_T$ *is bilinear, i.e.* $e(g_1{}^a, g_2{}^b) = e(g_1, g_2)^{ab} \; \forall \, a, b \in \mathbb{Z}$,
- e *is non-degenerate, i.e.* $e(g_1, g_2) \neq 1$, *and*
- e *is efficiently computable.*

We will write $g_t = e(g_1, g_2)$.

Definition 12. *Let* $\mathcal{G}$ *be a generator of asymmetric bilinear groups and let* $\mathsf{bgp} = (p, \mathbb{G}_1, \mathbb{G}_2, \mathbb{G}_T, g_1, g_2, e) \xleftarrow{\$} \mathcal{G}(1^\lambda)$. *We say the Decisional Diffie–Hellman assumption (DDH) holds in* $\mathbb{G}_1$ *if, for every PPT adversary* $\mathcal{A}$,

$$|\Pr[\mathcal{A}(\mathsf{bgp}, g_1^x, g_1^y, g_1^{xy}) \mid x, y \xleftarrow{\$} \mathbb{Z}_p] - \Pr[\mathcal{A}(\mathsf{bgp}, g_1^x, g_1^y, g_1^z) \mid x, y, z \xleftarrow{\$} \mathbb{Z}_p]| = \mathsf{negl}(\lambda)$$

We also use the Flexible Diffie–Hellman Inversion hardness assumption, introduced by Catalano, Fiore and Nizzardo [8]. In the extended version of their CRYPTO2015 paper, they formally investigate the hardness of this assumption and analyse it in the generic group model.

Definition 13 ([8]). *Let* $\mathcal{G}$ *be a generator of asymmetric bilinear groups and let* $\mathsf{bgp} = (p, \mathbb{G}_1, \mathbb{G}_2, \mathbb{G}_T, g_1, g_2, e) \xleftarrow{\$} \mathcal{G}(1^\lambda)$. *We say the Flexible Diffie–Hellman Inversion (FDHI) assumption holds in* bgp *if, for every PPT adversary* $\mathcal{A}$,

$$\Pr[W \in \mathbb{G}_1 \backslash \{1_{\mathbb{G}_1}\} \wedge W' = W^{\frac{1}{z}} \mid (W, W') \leftarrow \mathcal{A}(g_1, g_2, g_2^z, g_2^v, g_1^{\frac{z}{v}}, g_1^r, g_1^{\frac{r}{v}}) \mid$$
$$z, r, v \xleftarrow{\$} \mathbb{Z}_p] = \mathsf{negl}(\lambda).$$

3 A Publicly Verifiable Multi-key Linearly Homomorphic Authenticator Scheme

In this section, we present our multi-key homomorphic signature scheme, i.e. a publicly verifiable homomorphic authenticator. It supports linear functions. We analyse it with respect to its correctness, its succinctness and efficient verifiability. Finally, we prove that our scheme is indeed perfectly context hiding. Unforgeability is dealt with in the next section.

3.1 Our Construction

Notation. If we have n possibly distinct messages $m_1, \ldots, m_n$, we denote by m_i the ith message. Since our messages are vectors, i.e. $m \in \mathbb{Z}_p^T$, we write $m[j]$ to indicate the jth entry of message vector m for $j \in [T]$. Therefore $m_i[j]$ denotes the jth entry of the ith message. Given a linear function f, its ith coefficient is denoted by f_i, i.e. $f(m_1, \ldots, m_n) = \sum_{i=1}^n f_i m_i$. If we have n possibly distinct authenticator components, e.g. $\Lambda_1, \ldots, \Lambda_n$, we denote by Λ_i the ith component. A single authenticator comprises different components, corresponding to different identities. For authenticator Λ, we denote by Λ_{id} the component for identity id. We denote by $\Lambda_{\text{id},i}$ the component of the ith authenticator corresponding to identity id. We use a regular signature scheme $\mathsf{Sig} = (\mathsf{KeyGen}_{sig}, \mathsf{Sign}_{sig}, \mathsf{Ver}_{sig})$ as a building block. $(\mathsf{sk}_{sig}, \mathsf{pk}_{sig})$ denotes a secret/public key pair for Sig. $\|$ denotes concatenation.

$\mathsf{Setup}(1^\lambda)$: On input a security parameter λ, this algorithm chooses the parameters $k, n, T \in \mathbb{Z}$, a bilinear group $\mathsf{bgp} = (p, \mathbb{G}_1, \mathbb{G}_2, \mathbb{G}_T, g_1, g_2, e) \overset{\$}{\leftarrow} \mathcal{G}(1^\lambda)$, the message space $\mathcal{M} = \mathbb{Z}_p^T$, the tag space $\mathcal{T} = [n]$, and the identity space $\mathsf{ID} = [k]$. Additionally it fixes a pseudorandom function $F : \mathcal{K} \times \{0,1\}^* \to \mathbb{Z}_p$, as well as a signature scheme Sig. It chooses $H_1, \ldots H_T \in \mathbb{G}_1$ uniformly at random. It outputs the public parameters $\mathsf{pp} = (k, n, T, \mathsf{bgp}, H_1, \ldots, H_T, F, \mathsf{Sig}, \lambda)$.

$\mathsf{KeyGen}(\mathsf{pp})$: On input the public parameters pp, the algorithm chooses $K \in \mathcal{K}$ uniformly at random. It runs $(\mathsf{sk}_{sig}, \mathsf{pk}_{sig}) \leftarrow \mathsf{KeyGen}_{sig}(1^\lambda)$. It chooses $x_1, \ldots, x_n, y \in \mathbb{Z}_p$ uniformly at random. It sets $h_i = g_1^{x_i}$ for all $i \in [n]$, as well as $Y = g_2^y$. It sets $\mathsf{sk} = (K, \mathsf{sk}_{sig}, x_1, \ldots x_n, y)$, $\mathsf{ek} = \varnothing$, $\mathsf{vk} = (\mathsf{pk}_{sig}, h_1, \ldots, h_n, Y)$ and outputs $(\mathsf{sk}, \mathsf{ek}, \mathsf{vk})$. Each identity performs KeyGen individually, and hence obtains its own key tuple $(\mathsf{sk}_{\text{id}}, \mathsf{ek}_{\text{id}}, \mathsf{vk}_{\text{id}})$.

$\mathsf{Auth}(\mathsf{sk}, \Delta, l, m)$: On input a secret key sk, a dataset identifier Δ, a label $l = (\text{id}, \tau)$, and a message m, the algorithm computes $z = F_K(\Delta)$, sets $Z = g_2^z$ and binds this parameter to the dataset by signing it, i.e. it computes $\sigma_\Delta \leftarrow \mathsf{Sign}_{sig}(\mathsf{sk}_{sig}, Z\|\Delta)$. Then it chooses $r, s \in \mathbb{Z}_p$ uniformly at random and sets $R = g_1^{r-s}, S = g_2^{-s}$. It parses $l = (\text{id}, \tau)$ and computes $A = \left(g_1^{x_l + r} \cdot \prod_{j=1}^T H_j^{m[j]} \right)^{\frac{1}{z}}$ and $C = \left(g_1^s \cdot \prod_{j=1}^T H_j^{m[j]} \right)^{\frac{1}{y}}$. It sets $\Lambda = \{(\text{id}, \sigma_\Delta, Z, A, C)\}$ and outputs $\sigma = (\Lambda, R, S)$.

$\mathsf{Eval}(f, \{(\sigma_i, \mathsf{EKS}_i)\}_{i \in [n]})$: On input an function $f : \mathcal{M}^n \rightarrow \mathcal{M}$ and a set $\{(\sigma_i, \mathsf{EKS}_i)\}_{i \in [n]}$ of authenticators and evaluation keys (in our construction, no evaluation keys are needed, so this set contains only authenticators), the algorithm parses $f = (f_1, \dots f_n)$ as a coefficient vector. It parses each σ_i as (Λ_i, R_i, S_i) and sets $R = \prod_{i=1}^n R_i^{f_i}$, $S = \prod_{i=1}^n S_i^{f_i}$. Set $L_{\mathsf{ID}} = \bigcup_{i=1}^n \{\mathsf{id}_i\}$. For each $\mathsf{id} \in L_{\mathsf{ID}}$ it chooses a pair $(\sigma_{\Delta,\mathsf{id}}, Z_{\mathsf{id}})$ uniformly at random such that a tuple $(\mathsf{id}, \sigma_{\Delta,\mathsf{id}}, Z_{\mathsf{id}}, A, C)$ is contained in one of the Λ_i. More formally, it chooses $(\sigma_{\Delta,\mathsf{id}}, Z_{\mathsf{id}}) \overset{\$}{\leftarrow} \{(\sigma, Z) \mid \exists A, C \mid (\mathsf{id}, \sigma_\Delta, Z, A, C) \in \bigcup_{i=1}^n \Lambda_i\}$. Then it computes $A_{\mathsf{id}} = \prod_{\substack{i=1 \\ \mathsf{id}_i = \mathsf{id}}}^n A_i^{f_i}$, $C_{\mathsf{id}} = \prod_{\substack{i=1 \\ \mathsf{id}_i = \mathsf{id}}}^n C_{\mathsf{id}_i}^{f_i}$, and sets $\Lambda_{\mathsf{id}} = \{(\mathsf{id}, \sigma_{\Delta,\mathsf{id}}, Z_{\mathsf{id}}, A_{\mathsf{id}},$ $C_{\mathsf{id}})\}$. Set $\Lambda = \bigcup_{\mathsf{id} \in L_{\mathsf{ID}}} \Lambda_{\mathsf{id}}$. It returns $\sigma = (\Lambda, R, S)$.

$\mathsf{Ver}(\mathcal{P}_\Delta, \{\mathsf{vk}_{\mathsf{id}}\}_{\mathsf{id} \in \mathcal{P}}, m, \sigma)$: On input a multi-labeled program $\mathcal{P}_\Delta$, a set of verification key $\{\mathsf{vk}_{\mathsf{id}}\}_{\mathsf{id} \in \mathcal{P}}$, corresponding to the identities id involved in the program $\mathcal{P}$, a message $m \in \mathcal{M}$, and an authenticator σ , the algorithm parses $\sigma = (\Lambda, R, S)$. For each id such that $(\mathsf{id}, \sigma_{\Delta,\mathsf{id}}, Z_{\mathsf{id}}, A_{\mathsf{id}}, C_{\mathsf{id}}) \in \Lambda$ it takes $\mathsf{pk}_{sig,\mathsf{id}}$ from $\mathsf{vk}_{\mathsf{id}}$ and checks whether $\mathsf{Ver}_{sig}(\mathsf{pk}_{sig,\mathsf{id}}, Z_{\mathsf{id}}||\Delta, \sigma_{\Delta,\mathsf{id}}) = 1$ holds, i.e. whether there is a valid signature on $(Z_{\mathsf{id}}||\Delta)$. If any check fails it returns 0. Otherwise it checks whether the following equations hold: $\prod_{\mathsf{id} \in \mathcal{P}} e(A_{\mathsf{id}}, Z_{\mathsf{id}}) = \prod_{i=1}^n h_{l_i}^{f_i} \cdot \prod_{\mathsf{id} \in \mathcal{P}} e(C_{\mathsf{id}}, Y_{\mathsf{id}}) \cdot e(R, g_2)$, as well as $e(g_1, S) \cdot \prod_{\mathsf{id} \in \mathcal{P}} e(C_{\mathsf{id}}, Y_{\mathsf{id}}) = e\left(\prod_{j=1}^T H_j^{m[j]}, g_2\right)$. If they do, it outputs 1, otherwise it outputs 0.

Our authenticators σ consist of several components, so we have $\sigma = (\Lambda, R, S)$, where Λ is a list of elements, each associated to some identity id, i.e. $\Lambda = \{(\mathsf{id}, \sigma_{\Delta,\mathsf{id}}, Z_{\mathsf{id}}, A_{\mathsf{id}}, C_{\mathsf{id}})\}_{\mathsf{id} \in \mathcal{P}}$. The R and S components are global. Note, that the $A_{\mathsf{id}}, C_{\mathsf{id}}$ are randomized in order for the scheme to be internally context hiding and the global components are used to preserve the homomorphic property.

3.2   Correctness and Efficiency

We now analyse our scheme with respect to its correctness and efficiency. An obvious requirement for a homomorphic authenticator scheme is to be correct. Due to the homomorphic property, there are two different types of correctness to consider (see Definitions 2 and 3). The former ensures, that our scheme MKHAuth can be used as a conventional signature scheme, by verifying it with respect to the identity program. The latter property ensures a correct homomorphic evaluation will also be verified as correct.

Theorem 1. *The scheme* MKHAuth *presented in Subsect. 3.1 satisfies authentication correctness (see Definition 2), if* Sig *is a correct signature scheme.*

Proof. Take any public parameters $\mathsf{pp} \leftarrow \mathsf{Setup}(1^\lambda)$, any key triple $(\mathsf{sk}, \mathsf{ek}, \mathsf{vk}) \leftarrow \mathsf{KeyGen}(\mathsf{pp})$, any label $l = (\mathsf{id}, \tau) \in \mathcal{L}$, any dataset identifier $\Delta \in \{0,1\}^*$, and any authenticator $\sigma \leftarrow \mathsf{Auth}(\mathsf{sk}, \Delta, l, m)$. Then we have $\sigma = (\Lambda, R, S)$ and $\Lambda = (\mathsf{id}, \sigma_\Delta, Z, A, C)$. By construction we have $\sigma_\Delta \leftarrow \mathsf{Sign}_{sig}(\mathsf{sk}_{sig}, Z||\Delta)$ and if Sig is a correct signature scheme then $\mathsf{Ver}_{sig}(\mathsf{pk}_{sig,\mathsf{id}}, Z_{\mathsf{id}}||\Delta, \sigma_{\Delta,\mathsf{id}}) = 1$

holds. We have by construction $e(A, Z) = e\left(\left(g_1^{x_l+r} \cdot \prod_{j=1}^{T} H_j^{m[j]}\right)^{\frac{1}{z}}, g_2^z\right) =$

$e\left(g_1^{x_l+r-s} \cdot g_1^s \cdot \prod_{j=1}^{T} H_j^{m[j]}, g_2\right) = g_t^{x_l+r-s} \cdot e\left(g_1^{\frac{s}{y}} \cdot \prod_{j=1}^{T} H_j^{\frac{1}{y}m[j]}, g_2^y\right) = h_l \cdot$

$e(C, Y) \cdot e(R, g_2)$, and $e(g_1, S) \cdot e(C, Y) = g_t^{-s} \cdot g_t^s \cdot e\left(\prod_{j=1}^{T} H_j^{\frac{1}{z}m[j]}, g_2^y\right) =$

$e\left(\prod_{j=1}^{T} H_j^{m[j]}, g_2\right)$, and thus $\mathsf{Ver}(\mathcal{I}_{l,\Delta}, \mathsf{vk}, m, \sigma) = 1$ holds.

Theorem 2. *The scheme* MKHAuth *presented in Subsect. 3.1 satisfies evaluation correctness (see Definition 3), if* Sig *is a correct signature scheme.*

Proof. We have $\mathcal{P}_\Delta^* = g(\mathcal{P}_{\Delta,1}^*, \ldots \mathcal{P}_{\Delta,N}^*)$. Since Sig is a correct signature scheme, $\mathsf{Ver}_{sig}(\mathsf{pk}_{sig,\mathsf{id}}, Z_{\mathsf{id}} \| \Delta, \sigma_{\Delta,\mathsf{id}}) = 1$ holds for all $\mathsf{id} \in \mathcal{P}^*$. If $\mathsf{Ver}(\mathcal{P}_{i,\Delta}, \{\mathsf{vk}_{\mathsf{id}}\}_{\mathsf{id} \in \mathcal{P}_i}, m_i, \sigma_i) = 1$ holds, then in particular

$$\prod_{\mathsf{id} \in \mathcal{P}_{i,\Delta}} e(A_{\mathsf{id},i}, Z_{\mathsf{id}}) = \prod_{k=1}^{n} h_{l_{i,k}}^{f_{i,k}} \cdot e\left(\prod_{\mathsf{id} \in \mathcal{P}_{i,\Delta}} C_{\mathsf{id},i}, Y_{\mathsf{id}}\right) \cdot e(R_i, g_2)$$

holds as well as $e(g_1, S_i) \cdot \prod_{\mathsf{id} \in \mathcal{P}_{i,\Delta}} e(C_{\mathsf{id},i}, Y_{\mathsf{id}}) = e\left(\prod_{j=1}^{T} H_j^{m_i[j]}, g_2\right)$ for all $i \in [N]$. Write g as a coefficient vector $(c_1, \ldots c_N)$. Without loss of generality let $\{\mathsf{id} \in \mathcal{P}_{i,\Delta}\} = \{\mathsf{id} \in \mathcal{P}_{j,\Delta}\}$ for all $i, j \in [n]$. Let f_k for $k \in [n]$ denote the coefficients describing $\mathcal{P} = g(\mathcal{P}_1, \ldots, \mathcal{P}_N)$. Then we have $f_k = \sum_{i=1}^{N} c_i f_{i,k}$. We have

$$\prod_{i=1}^{N} \left(\prod_{\mathsf{id} \in \mathcal{P}_{i,\Delta}} e(A_{\mathsf{id},i}, Z_{\mathsf{id},i})\right)^{c_i} = \prod_{i=1}^{N} \left(\prod_{k=1}^{n} h_{l_{i,k}}^{f_{i,k}} \cdot \prod_{\mathsf{id} \in \mathcal{P}_{i,\Delta}} e(C_{\mathsf{id},i}, Y_{\mathsf{id}}) \cdot e(R_i, g_2)\right)^{c_i}$$

and

$$\prod_{\mathsf{id} \in \mathcal{P}_\Delta^*} e(A_{\mathsf{id}}^*, Z_{\mathsf{id}}^*) = \prod_{i=1}^{N} \left(\prod_{\mathsf{id} \in \mathcal{P}_{i,\Delta}} e(A_{\mathsf{id},i}, Z_{\mathsf{id},i})\right)^{c_i}$$

$$= \prod_{k=1}^{n} h_{l_k}^{f_k} \cdot \prod_{\mathsf{id} \in \mathcal{P}_\Delta^*} e(C_{\mathsf{id}}^*, Y_{\mathsf{id}}^*) \cdot e(R^*, g_2)$$

We also have
$e(g_1, S^*) \cdot \prod_{\mathsf{id} \in \mathcal{P}^*} e(C_{\mathsf{id}}^*, Y_{\mathsf{id}}) = e\left(g_1, \prod_{i=1}^{N} S_i^{g_i}\right) \cdot \prod_{\mathsf{id} \in \mathcal{P}^*} e\left(\prod_{i=1}^{N} C_{i,\mathsf{id}}^{g_i}, Y_{\mathsf{id}}\right)$

$$= \prod_{i=1}^{N} e\left(\prod_{j=1}^{T} H_j^{m_i[j]}, g_2\right)^{g_i} = e\left(\prod_{j=1}^{T} H_j^{\sum_{i=1}^{N} g_i m_i[j]}, g_2\right) = e\left(\prod_{j=1}^{T} H_j^{m^*[j]}, g_2\right)$$

Thus all checks of Ver pass.

We now consider our scheme's efficiency properties, first w.r.t. bandwidth, in the form of succinctness, and then w.r.t. verification time.

A trivial solution to constructing a homomorphic signature scheme is to (conventionally) sign every input, and during Eval to just concatenate all the signatures along with the corresponding values. Verification then consists of checking every input value and then redoing the computation. This naive solution is obviously undesirable in terms of bandwidth, efficiency and does not provide any privacy guarantees.

Succinctness guarantees that a homomorphically derived signature is still small, thus keeping bandwidth requirements low. Efficient verification ensures that the time required to check an authenticator is low. This is achieved by splitting Ver into two sub-algorithms, one of which can be precomputed, and the other one EffVer can be faster than natively computing the function itself.

Theorem 3. *The scheme* MKHAuth *in Subsect. 3.1 is succinct (Definition 4).*

Proof. An authenticator consists of (at most) $k + 1$ elements of $\mathbb{G}_1$, k elements of $\mathbb{G}_2$, k identities id $\in$ ID, and k (conventional) signatures. None of this depends on the input size n. Therefore MKHAuth is succinct.

Theorem 4. MKHAuth *allows for efficient verification (Definition 5).*

Proof. We describe the algorithms (VerPrep, EffVer):

VerPrep($\mathcal{P}, \{vk_{id}\}_{id \in \mathcal{P}}$): On input a labeled program $\mathcal{P} = (f, l_1, \ldots, l_n)$, with f given by its coefficient vector $(f_1, \ldots f_n)$, the algorithm takes $(Y_{id}, pk_{sig,id})$ from vk_{id}. For label $l_i = (id_i, \tau_i)$ it takes h_{l_i} from vk_{id_i}. It computes $h_{\mathcal{P}} \leftarrow \prod_{i=1}^{n} h_{l_i}^{f_i}$ and outputs $vk_{\mathcal{P}} \leftarrow (h_{\mathcal{P}}, \{(Y_{id}, pk_{sig,id})\}_{id \in \mathcal{P}})$. This is independent of the input size n.

EffVer($vk_{\mathcal{P}}, \Delta, m, \sigma$): On input a concise verification key $vk_{\mathcal{P}}$, a dataset Δ, a message m, and an authenticator σ, the algorithm parses $\sigma = (\Lambda, R, S)$. For each id $\in \mathcal{P}$ it checks whether $Ver_{sig}(pk_{sig,id}, Z_{id}||\Delta, \sigma_{\Delta,id}) = 1$ holds. If not, it outputs 0. Otherwise, it checks whether the following equation holds: $\prod_{id \in \mathcal{P}} e(A_{id}, Z_{id}) = h_{\mathcal{P}} \cdot \prod_{id \in \mathcal{P}} e(C_{id}, Y_{id}) \cdot e(R, g_2)$ as well as $e(g_1, S) \cdot \prod_{id \in \mathcal{P}} e(C_{id}, g_2^{y_{id}}) = e\left(\prod_{j=1}^{T} H_j^{m[j]}, g_2\right)$. If they do, it outputs 1, otherwise it outputs 0.

This obviously satisfies correctness. We can see that the runtime of EffVer is $\mathcal{O}(k)$, and is independent of the input size n. Thus, for $n \gg k$, MKHAuth allows for efficient verification.

3.3   Context Hiding

We now showcase our scheme's privacy property. On a high level, we want an authenticator to the output of a computation not to leak information about the inputs to the computation, which we have formalized in Definition 10. Intuitively, the outcome of a function (e.g. the average) reveals significantly less information than the individual inputs to the computation. In our scenario, multiple clients upload data to a cloud server that performs the computation, and allows for public verification of the result due to the use of homomorphic authenticators. The context hiding property ensures that the verifier cannot use the authenticators provided to him to derive additional information about the inputs, beyond his knowledge of the output.

Theorem 5. *The scheme* MKHAuth *in Subsect. 3.1 is perfectly internally context hiding (Definition 10) and thus also externally context hiding.*

Proof. First, in our case, the algorithm Hide is just the identity function. More precisely, we have $\mathsf{Hide}(\{\mathsf{vk}_{\mathsf{id}}\}_{\mathsf{id}\in\mathsf{ID}}, m, \sigma) = \sigma$, for all possible verification keys $\mathsf{vk}_{\mathsf{id}}$, messages m and authenticators σ. Thus we have $\mathsf{HideVer} = \mathsf{Ver}$, so correctness and unforgeability hold by Theorems 1, 2 and 6.

We show how to construct a simulator Sim that outputs authenticators perfectly indistinguishable from the ones obtained by running Eval. Consider that for all linear functions f, we have $f(m_1, \ldots, m_n) = \sum_{i=1}^{n} f_i m_i = \sum_{i\in\mathcal{I}} f_i m_i + \sum_{j\in\mathcal{J}} f_j m_j$, for each $\mathcal{I}, \mathcal{J} \subset [n]$, with $\mathcal{I} \cup \mathcal{J} = [n]$ and $\mathcal{I} \cap \mathcal{J} = \varnothing$.

$\mathcal{S}$ can simulate the corrupted parties perfectly. By the identity shown before, we can in our case therefore reduce internal context hiding security to external context hiding security. We now show external context hiding security. Parse the simulator's input as $\mathsf{sk}_{\mathsf{id}} = (K_{\mathsf{id}}, K'_{\mathsf{id}}, \mathsf{sk}_{sig,\mathsf{id}}, x_{1,\mathsf{id}}, \ldots x_{n,\mathsf{id}}, y)$, $m = (m[1], \ldots, m[T])$, and $\mathcal{P}_\Delta = (f, l_1, \ldots, l_n, \Delta)$. With this information, the simulator computes:

$$
\begin{aligned}
&Z'_{\mathsf{id}} = g_2^{z_{\mathsf{id}}} \text{ where } z_{\mathsf{id}} \leftarrow F_{K_{\mathsf{id}}}(\Delta) && \sigma'_{\Delta,\mathsf{id}} \xleftarrow{\$} \mathsf{Sign}_{sig}(\mathsf{sk}_{sig,\mathsf{id}}, Z_{\mathsf{id}}||\Delta) \\
&r'_{\mathsf{id}} \xleftarrow{\$} \mathbb{Z}_p && r' = \sum_{l=(\tau,\mathsf{id})\in\mathcal{P}} f_l r'_{\mathsf{id}} \\
&s'_{\mathsf{id}} \xleftarrow{\$} \mathbb{Z}_p && s' = \sum_{\mathsf{id}\in\mathcal{P}} y_{\mathsf{id}} s_{\mathsf{id}} \\
&A'_{\mathsf{id}} = \left(g_1^{\sum_{(\mathsf{id},\tau)\in\mathcal{P}} x_l f_l + r'} \cdot \prod_{j=1}^{T} H_j^{y m[j]}\right)^{\frac{1}{z_{\mathsf{id}}}} && \mathsf{id}^* \xleftarrow{\$} \mathsf{ID} \\
&C'_{\mathsf{id}} = g_1^{-s'_{\mathsf{id}}} \text{ for all } \mathsf{id} \neq \mathsf{id}^* && C'_{\mathsf{id}^*} = g_1^{-s'_{\mathsf{id}^*}} \cdot \prod_{j=1}^{T} \frac{1}{y} H_j^{m[j]} \\
&R' = g_1^{r' + \sum_{\mathsf{id}\in\mathcal{P}} y_{\mathsf{id}} s'_{\mathsf{id}}} && S' = g_2^{-s'} \\
&\Lambda' = \bigcup_{\mathsf{id}\in\mathcal{P}} \{(A'_{\mathsf{id}}, Z'_{\mathsf{id}}, \sigma'_{\Delta,\mathsf{id}})\} &&
\end{aligned}
$$

The simulator outputs the authenticator $\sigma' = (\Lambda', R', S')$. We now show that this simulator allows for perfectly context hiding security. We fix arbitrary key pairs $(\mathsf{sk}_{\mathsf{id}}, \mathsf{pk}_{\mathsf{id}})$, a multi-labeled program $\mathcal{P}_\Delta$, and messages $m_1, \ldots, m_n \in \mathbb{Z}_p^T$. Let $\sigma \leftarrow (f, \{(\sigma_i, \mathsf{EKS}_i)\}_{i\in[n]})$ and parse it as $\sigma = (\Lambda, R, S)$. We look at each component of the authenticator. We have $Z_{\mathsf{id}} = F_{K_{\mathsf{id}}}(\Delta)$ by definition and therefore also $Z_{\mathsf{id}} = Z'_{\mathsf{id}}$. Y_{id} and Y'_{id} are both taken from the public keys and therefore identical. In particular we also have $z_{\mathsf{id}} = z'_{\mathsf{id}}$. We have $\sigma_{\Delta_{\mathsf{id}}} = \mathsf{Sign}_{sig}(\mathsf{sk}', Z_{\mathsf{id}}||\Delta)$ by definition and $\sigma'_{\Delta_{\mathsf{id}}} = \mathsf{Sign}_{sig}(\mathsf{sk}', Z'_{\mathsf{id}}||\Delta)$. Since $Z_{\mathsf{id}} = Z'_{\mathsf{id}}$, for all $\mathsf{id} \in \mathcal{P}$, $\sigma_{\Delta_{\mathsf{id}}}$ and $\sigma'_{\Delta_{\mathsf{id}}}$ are perfectly indistinguishable to any distinguisher $\mathcal{D}$. Thus these components are perfectly indistinguishable to any distinguisher $\mathcal{D}$.

A'_{id} is a uniformly random (u.r.) element of $\mathbb{G}_1$, as r'_{id} is also u.r. A_{id} is a u.r. element of $\mathbb{G}_1$, as $r_{\mathsf{id}} = \sum_{\mathsf{id} \in l} f_l r_l$ is u.r. as a linear combination of u.r. elements. C'_{id} is a u.r. element of $\mathbb{G}_1$, as s'_{id} is also u.r. C_{id} is a u.r. element of $\mathbb{G}_1$, as $s_{\mathsf{id}} = \sum_{\mathsf{id} \in l} f_l y s_l$ is u.r. as a linear combination of u.r. elements. R' is a u.r. element of $\mathbb{G}_1$, as all r'_{id} are also u.r. R is a u.r. element of $\mathbb{G}_1$, as $r = \sum_{\mathsf{id} \in \mathcal{P}} r_{\mathsf{id}}$ is u.r. as a linear combination of u.r. elements. The $A'_{\mathsf{id}}, C'_{\mathsf{id}}$ as well as R' uniquely define S' and $A_{\mathsf{id}}, C_{\mathsf{id}}$ as well as R uniquely define S. Thus, all simulated elements have the identical distribution as the ones from the real evaluation. They correspond to a different choice of randomness during Auth. This holds even if all secret keys $\mathsf{sk}_{\mathsf{id}}$ are known to $\mathcal{D}$. Hence σ and σ' are perfectly indistinguishable for any (computationally unbounded) distinguisher $\mathcal{D}$.

4   Unforgeability

In delegated computations, the question of the correctness of the result arises. Homomorphic authenticators aim at making these computations verifiable, thus allowing for the detection of incorrect results. It should therefore be infeasible for any adversary to produce a authenticator that passes the Ver algorithm, that has not been produced by honestly performing the Eval algorithm. This has been formalized in Definition 6. In this section, we present the security reduction for the unforgeability of our scheme. To this end, we first describe a sequence of games, allowing us to argue about different variants of forgeries. In the extended version of this work [21], we prove a series of lemmata where we bound the difference between those games.

Since our authenticators have multiple components, we consider specific types of forgeries in the various games, i.e. ones where one or multiple components are indeed correct, and in our final security reduction we consider the generic case. When simulating the final two games, the issue of providing signatures, without knowing the correct secret key arises. Here we use the elements $h_{\mathsf{id},i}$ taken from the public keys associated to the label $l = (\mathsf{id}, i)$ and embed an information theoretically hidden trapdoor into them, which we use to answer signing queries.

Theorem 6. *The scheme* MKHAuth *is unforgeable (see Definition 9), if* Sig *is an unforgeable (EU-CMA [14]) signature scheme, F is a pseudorandom function and $\mathcal{G}$ is a bilinear group generator, such that the DL assumption, the DDH assumption (see Definition 12) and the FDHI assumption (see Definition 13) hold.*

Proof. We can deal with corruptions via our generic result of Lemma 2. It is thus sufficient to prove the security against adversaries that make no corruptions. Recall that any corrupted party provides their key tuples $(\mathsf{sk}_{\mathsf{id}}, \mathsf{ek}_{\mathsf{id}}, \mathsf{vk}_{\mathsf{id}})$ to the adversary, giving the adversary additional knowledge in order for him to adaptively query messages. To prove Theorem 6, we define a series of games with the adversary $\mathcal{A}$ and we show that the adversary $\mathcal{A}$ wins, i.e. any game outputs 1, only with negligible probability. Following the notation of [8], we write $G_i(\mathcal{A})$ to denote that a run of game i with adversary $\mathcal{A}$ returns 1. We use flag values bad_i, initially set to false. If, at the end of each game, any of these previously defined flags is set to true, the game simply outputs 0. Let Bad_i denote the event that bad_i is set to true during game i. Using Lemma 1, any adversary who outputs a Type 3 forgery (see Definition 7) can be converted into one that outputs a Type 2 forgery. Hence we only have to deal with Type 1 and Type 2 forgeries.

Game 1 is the security experiment $\mathsf{HomUF-CMA}_{\mathcal{A},\mathsf{MKHAuth}}(\lambda)$ between an adversary $\mathcal{A}$ and a challenger $\mathcal{C}$, where $\mathcal{A}$ makes no corruption queries and only outputs Type 1 or Type 2 forgeries.

Game 2 is defined as Game 1, except for the following change: Whenever $\mathcal{A}$ returns a forgery $(\mathcal{P}^*_{\Delta^*}, m^*, \sigma^*)$ and the list L_{Δ^*} has not been initialized by the challenger during the queries, then Game 2 sets $\mathsf{bad}_2 = \mathsf{true}$. It is worth noticing that after this change the game never outputs 1 if $\mathcal{A}$ returns a Type 1 forgery. In the extended version we show that Bad_2 cannot occur if Sig is unforgeable.

Game 3 is defined as Game 2, except that the keyed pseudorandom function F_K is replaced by a random function $\mathcal{R} : \{0,1\}^* \to \mathbb{Z}_p$. In the extended version, we show that these two games are indistinguishable if F is pseudorandom.

Game 4 is defined as Game 3, except for the following changes. It computes $\hat{m} = f^*(m_1, \ldots, m_n)$, as well as $\hat{\sigma} = \mathsf{Eval}(f^*, \{(\sigma_i, \mathsf{EKS}_i)\}_{i \in [n]})$, i.e. it runs an honest computation over the queried messages and generated authenticators in dataset Δ^*. The challenger runs an additional check. If $\prod_{j=1}^{T} H_j^{m^*[j]} = \prod_{j=1}^{T} H_j^{\hat{m}[j]}$ and $\hat{m} \neq m^*$ it sets $\mathsf{bad}_4 = \mathsf{true}$. We clearly have $|\Pr[G_3(\mathcal{A})] - \Pr[G_4(\mathcal{A})]| \leq \Pr[\mathsf{Bad}_4]$. In the extended version, we show that any adversary $\mathcal{A}$ for which Bad_4 occurs implies a solver for the DL problem.

Game 5 is defined as Game 4, except for the following change. The challenger runs an additional check. If $C^* = \hat{C}$ and $m^* \neq \hat{m}$ it sets $\mathsf{bad}_5 = \mathsf{true}$, where C^* is a component of the forged authenticator σ^* and $\hat{C}$ is a component of the honest execution of Eval over the queried data set, as defined in Game 4. We have $|\Pr[G_4(\mathcal{A})] - \Pr[G_5(\mathcal{A})]| \leq \Pr[\mathsf{Bad}_5]$. In the extended version, we show that any adversary $\mathcal{A}$ for which Bad_5 occurs implies a solver for the DDH problem.

Game 6 is defined as Game 5, except for the following change. At the beginning $\mathcal{C}$ chooses $\mu \in [Q]$ uniformly at random, with $Q = \mathsf{poly}(\lambda)$ is the number of queries made by $\mathcal{A}$ during the game. Let $\Delta_1, \ldots, \Delta_Q$ be all the datasets queried by $\mathcal{A}$. Then, if in the forgery $\Delta^* \neq \Delta_\mu$, set $\mathsf{bad}_6 = \mathsf{true}$. In the extended version, we show that $\Pr[G_5(\mathcal{A})] = Q \cdot \Pr[G_6(\mathcal{A})]$.

Game 7 is defined as Game 6, except for the following change. The challenger runs an additional check. If $\mathsf{Ver}(\mathcal{P}^*_{\Delta^*}, \{\mathsf{vk}_{\mathsf{id}}\}_{\mathsf{id} \in \mathcal{P}^*}, m^*, \sigma^*) = 1$ as well as $\hat{m} \neq m^*$ and $\prod_{\mathsf{id} \in \mathcal{P}^*} e\left(\hat{A}_{\mathsf{id}}, Z^*_{\mathsf{id}}\right) = \prod_{\mathsf{id} \in \mathcal{P}^*} e(A^*_{\mathsf{id}}, Z^*_{\mathsf{id}})$, where $\hat{A}_{\mathsf{id}}, A^*_{\mathsf{id}}$ are the components taken from $\hat{\sigma}$ and σ^* respectively, then $\mathcal{C}$ sets $\mathsf{bad}_7 = \mathsf{true}$. We have $|\Pr[G_6(\mathcal{A})] - \Pr[G_7(\mathcal{A})]| \leq \Pr[\mathsf{Bad}_7]$. In the extended version, we show that any adversary $\mathcal{A}$ for which Bad_7 occurs implies a solver for the FDHI problem.

Finally, in the extended version we show that any adversary $\mathcal{A}$ that wins Game 7 implies a solver for the FDHI problem. This proves Theorem 6 and we have
$$\Pr[\mathcal{G}(\mathcal{A})] \leq \mathsf{Adv}_{\mathsf{Sig},\mathcal{F}}^{\mathsf{UF-CMA}}(\lambda) + \mathsf{Adv}_{F,D}^{PRF}(\lambda) + (1 - \tfrac{1}{p}) \cdot \mathsf{Adv}_{\mathcal{S}}^{DL}(\lambda) + \mathsf{Adv}_{\mathcal{S}}^{DDH}(\lambda) + 2Q\mathsf{Adv}_{\mathcal{S}}^{FDHI}(\lambda).$$

5   Related Work

We review related work on homomorphic authenticators and verifiable computation, considering multi-key support separately for both scheme categories.

Homomorphic Authenticators. Homomorphic authenticators have received substantial attention in previous work, focusing either on the public key setting, in the form of homomorphic signatures or on the private key setting, in the form of homomorphic MACs. The notion of homomorphic signatures was originally proposed by Johnson et al. [17]. The first published schemes were homomorphic only for linear functions (e.g. [2–4,6–8,20]), and found important applications in network coding and proofs of retrievability. Schemes supporting functions of higher degree also exist (e.g. [5,9]). The work by Catalano et al. [9] contains the first mechanism to verify signatures faster than the running time of the verified function. Gorbunov et al. [15] have proposed the first homomorphic signature scheme that can evaluate arbitrary boolean circuits of bounded polynomial depth over signed data. However, none of the above schemes support multiple keys.

Multi-key Homomorphic Authenticators. Works considering multi-key homomorphic authenticators are more directly comparable to our scheme. Agrawal et al. [1] considered a notion of multi source signatures for network coding, and proposed a solution for linear functions. Network coding signatures are one application of homomorphic signatures, where signed data is combined to produce new signed data. Their solution allows for the usage of different keys in combining signatures, but differ slightly in their syntax and homomorphic property, as formalized in our definition of evaluation correctness. Unlike this work, our scheme achieves efficient verification and is perfectly context hiding. Fiore et al. [12] have even constructed multi-key homomorphic authenticators for boolean circuits of bounded depth. While our scheme only supports linear functions, it allows the authentication of field elements, while in the case of [12] each single bit is signed individually. Thus our authenticators are significantly smaller. Both their and our solution achieve fast amortized verification, independently of function complexity. Their solution, however, is not context hiding. Lai et al. [18] proposed a generic constructions of multi-key homomorphic authenticators from zk-SNARGs. So far, zk-SNARGs are only known to exist under non-falsifiable assumptions. Their constructions only allows for an a priori set bound of applications of Eval on authenticators that have been produced by Eval. Our construction has no such bound.

Verifiable Computation. Verifiable computation also aims at detecting incorrect results in delegated computations. In this setting, a client wants to delegate the computation of a function f on input x to an untrusted server. If the server outputs y, the client's goal is to verify that indeed $y = f(x)$ at a faster runtime than an evaluation of f. For a detailed overview of this line of research, we refer to Demirel et al. [11]. Using homomorphic authenticators, clients can authenticate various (small) pieces of data independently and without storing previously outsourced data, thus allowing for incremental updates of data. In contrast, for other verifiable computation schemes, it is necessary to encode the entire input data before delegation and often such encoding can be used in a single computation only. Another advantage of homomorphic authenticators is their natural composition property. The outputs of some computations on authenticated data are already authenticated, and can be input to further computations.

Multi-client Verifiable Computation. Verifiable computation has also been considered in the multi-key setting [10, 16]. Here the verifier is always one of the clients providing inputs to the functions, whereas our construction is publicly verifiable. Existing multi-client verifiable computation schemes also require a message from the verifier to the server, where it has to provide an encoding of the function f, which is not necessary for our homomorphic authenticators. Furthermore, the communication between the server and the verifier is at least linear in the total number of inputs of f, whereas in the case of succinct multi-key homomorphic authenticators the communication between server and verifier is proportional only to the number of clients. Finally, in multi-client verifiable computation, an encoding of one input can only be used in a single computation. Any input to be used in multiple computations has to be uploaded for each computation. In contrast, multi-key homomorphic authenticators allow the one-time authentication of every input and allow it to be used in an unbounded number of computations.

6   Conclusions

In this paper, we investigated the problem of constructing a context hiding publicly verifiable multi-key homomorphic authenticator scheme. We first presented two different definitions of the context hiding property in this setting, thereby distinguishing between adversaries with inside knowledge of the computation and purely external adversaries. We present the first scheme that fulfils both of these requirements. The context hiding property, both against internal and external adversaries holds in an information theoretic sense, allowing not even computationally unbounded adversary to gain additional knowledge about inputs.

Our authenticators are succinct, i.e. their size is independent of the number of inputs to a computation, thus keeping bandwidth low. Our verification procedure can be split into two parts, only one of which actually requires the signature to be verified. The other part can thus be precomputed, allowing for faster verification time. Regarding performance, verification time depends only on the number of identities involved (after a one time preprocessing), thus leading to efficient verification. We furthermore showed how to reduce the security of our scheme to the discrete logarithm, the decisional Diffie–Hellman and the Flexible Diffie–Hellman Inversion problems in the standard model.

In the future, we intend to investigate the viability of context hiding multi-key homomorphic authenticators for functions of higher degree. Another interesting question is whether authenticators can be constructed, whose size does not even depend on the number of identities involved.

Acknowledgments. This work has received funding from the European Union's Horizon 2020 research and innovation program under Grant Agreement No. 644962.

References

1. Agrawal, S., Boneh, D., Boyen, X., Freeman, D.M.: Preventing pollution attacks in multi-source network coding. In: Nguyen, P.Q., Pointcheval, D. (eds.) PKC 2010. LNCS, vol. 6056, pp. 161–176. Springer, Heidelberg (2010). https://doi.org/10.1007/978-3-642-13013-7_10
2. Attrapadung, N., Libert, B.: Homomorphic network coding signatures in the standard model. In: Catalano, D., Fazio, N., Gennaro, R., Nicolosi, A. (eds.) PKC 2011. LNCS, vol. 6571, pp. 17–34. Springer, Heidelberg (2011). https://doi.org/10.1007/978-3-642-19379-8_2
3. Attrapadung, N., Libert, B., Peters, T.: Computing on authenticated data: new privacy definitions and constructions. In: Wang, X., Sako, K. (eds.) ASIACRYPT 2012. LNCS, vol. 7658, pp. 367–385. Springer, Heidelberg (2012). https://doi.org/10.1007/978-3-642-34961-4_23
4. Attrapadung, N., Libert, B., Peters, T.: Efficient completely context-hiding quotable and linearly homomorphic signatures. In: Kurosawa, K., Hanaoka, G. (eds.) PKC 2013. LNCS, vol. 7778, pp. 386–404. Springer, Heidelberg (2013). https://doi.org/10.1007/978-3-642-36362-7_24
5. Backes, M., Fiore, D., Reischuk, R.M.: Verifiable delegation of computation on outsourced data. In: ACM CCS 2013, pp. 863–874. ACM (2013)
6. Boneh, D., Freeman, D.M.: Linearly homomorphic signatures over binary fields and new tools for lattice-based signatures. In: Catalano, D., Fazio, N., Gennaro, R., Nicolosi, A. (eds.) PKC 2011. LNCS, vol. 6571, pp. 1–16. Springer, Heidelberg (2011). https://doi.org/10.1007/978-3-642-19379-8_1
7. Boneh, D., Freeman, D., Katz, J., Waters, B.: Signing a linear subspace: signature schemes for network coding. In: Jarecki, S., Tsudik, G. (eds.) PKC 2009. LNCS, vol. 5443, pp. 68–87. Springer, Heidelberg (2009). https://doi.org/10.1007/978-3-642-00468-1_5
8. Catalano, D., Fiore, D., Nizzardo, L.: Programmable hash functions go private: constructions and applications to (homomorphic) signatures with shorter public keys. In: Gennaro, R., Robshaw, M. (eds.) CRYPTO 2015. LNCS, vol. 9216, pp. 254–274. Springer, Heidelberg (2015). https://doi.org/10.1007/978-3-662-48000-7_13

9. Catalano, D., Fiore, D., Warinschi, B.: Homomorphic signatures with efficient verification for polynomial functions. In: Garay, J.A., Gennaro, R. (eds.) CRYPTO 2014. LNCS, vol. 8616, pp. 371–389. Springer, Heidelberg (2014). https://doi.org/10.1007/978-3-662-44371-2_21

10. Choi, S.G., Katz, J., Kumaresan, R., Cid, C.: Multi-client non-interactive verifiable computation. In: Sahai, A. (ed.) TCC 2013. LNCS, vol. 7785, pp. 499–518. Springer, Heidelberg (2013). https://doi.org/10.1007/978-3-642-36594-2_28

11. Demirel, D., Schabhüser, L., Buchmann, J.: Privately and Publicly Verifiable Computing Techniques. SCS. Springer, Cham (2017). https://doi.org/10.1007/978-3-319-53798-6

12. Fiore, D., Mitrokotsa, A., Nizzardo, L., Pagnin, E.: Multi-key homomorphic authenticators. In: Cheon, J.H., Takagi, T. (eds.) ASIACRYPT 2016. LNCS, vol. 10032, pp. 499–530. Springer, Heidelberg (2016). https://doi.org/10.1007/978-3-662-53890-6_17

13. Freeman, D.M.: Improved security for linearly homomorphic signatures: a generic framework. In: Fischlin, M., Buchmann, J., Manulis, M. (eds.) PKC 2012. LNCS, vol. 7293, pp. 697–714. Springer, Heidelberg (2012). https://doi.org/10.1007/978-3-642-30057-8_41

14. Goldwasser, S., Micali, S., Yao, A.C.: Strong Signature Schemes. In: STOC 1983, pp. 431–439. ACM (1983)

15. Gorbunov, S., Vaikuntanathan, V., Wichs, D.: Leveled fully homomorphic signatures from standard lattices. In: STOC 2015, pp. 469–477. ACM (2015)

16. Gordon, S.D., Katz, J., Liu, F.-H., Shi, E., Zhou, H.-S.: Multi-client verifiable computation with stronger security guarantees. In: Dodis, Y., Nielsen, J.B. (eds.) TCC 2015. LNCS, vol. 9015, pp. 144–168. Springer, Heidelberg (2015). https://doi.org/10.1007/978-3-662-46497-7_6

17. Johnson, R., Molnar, D., Song, D., Wagner, D.: Homomorphic signature schemes. In: Preneel, B. (ed.) CT-RSA 2002. LNCS, vol. 2271, pp. 244–262. Springer, Heidelberg (2002). https://doi.org/10.1007/3-540-45760-7_17

18. Lai, R.W.F., Tai, R.K.H., Wong, H.W.H., Chow, S.S.M.: Multi-key homomorphic signatures unforgeable under insider corruption. In: Peyrin, T., Galbraith, S. (eds.) ASIACRYPT 2018. LNCS, vol. 11273, pp. 465–492. Springer, Cham (2018). https://doi.org/10.1007/978-3-030-03329-3_16

19. Libert, B., Yung, M.: Concise mercurial vector commitments and independent zero-knowledge sets with short proofs. In: Micciancio, D. (ed.) TCC 2010. LNCS, vol. 5978, pp. 499–517. Springer, Heidelberg (2010). https://doi.org/10.1007/978-3-642-11799-2_30

20. Schabhüser, L., Buchmann, J., Struck, P.: A linearly homomorphic signature scheme from weaker assumptions. In: O'Neill, M. (ed.) IMACC 2017. LNCS, vol. 10655, pp. 261–279. Springer, Cham (2017). https://doi.org/10.1007/978-3-319-71045-7_14

21. Schabhüser, L., Butin, D., Buchmann, J.: Context hiding multi-key linearly homomorphic authenticators. Cryptology ePrint Archive, Report 2018/629 (2018). https://eprint.iacr.org/2018/629

Revisiting the Secret Hiding Assumption Used in Verifiable (Outsourced) Computation

Liang Zhao[✉]

College of Cybersecurity, Sichuan University, Chengdu, China
zhaoliangjapan@scu.edu.cn

Abstract. Privacy-preserving Verifiable (outsourced) Computation (PVC) is a hopeful primitive that enables a resource-constrained client to outsource expensive and sensitive workloads to powerful but possibly untrusted servers and to verify the correctness of the returned results. Specifically, the privacy property is of significance for this type of primitive. Then, how to provide the privacy property has become a central interest of many researchers. At ACM-ASIACCS 2010, Atallah and Frikken introduced a new hardness assumption called the Secret Hiding assumption (SH), which includes the Weak SH assumption (WSH) and Strong SH assumption (SSH). Moreover, for the outsourcing of the multiplication of large-scale matrices, the authors constructed two concrete PVC protocols whose privacy is based on the decisional-WSH assumption and decisional-SSH assumption, respectively.

Until our work, to the best of our knowledge, there is no paper that precisely explored the hardnesses of the WSH assumption and SSH assumption. Thus, in this paper, we first propose an analysis method, using the rank distribution of the matrix as the basic strategy, to evaluate the hardnesses of two problems corresponding to the decisional-WSH assumption and decisional-SSH assumption. Unfortunately, our analysis can efficiently break the decisional-WSH assumption and decisional-SSH assumption for a wide range of parameters with overwhelming probability. Then we employ the idea of the above analysis for breaking the SH assumption to similarly break the privacy of Atallah and Frikken's PVC protocols. The results show that the adversary's advantages are non-negligible. Finally, we present some detailed experimental results to support our theoretical argument.

Keywords: Privacy-preserving verifiable (outsourced) computation ·
Indistinguishability · Rank · Linear relation

1 Introduction

1.1 Background

Privacy-preserving Verifiable (outsourced) Computation (PVC), characterized by four properties [8], i.e., correctness, security, privacy and efficiency, has

© Springer Nature Switzerland AG 2019
M. Matsui (Ed.): CT-RSA 2019, LNCS 11405, pp. 514–534, 2019.
https://doi.org/10.1007/978-3-030-12612-4_26

attracted many researchers from the cryptography and information security community. Various protocols [2–6,8,9,15,16] have been proposed to solve the problems related to the outsourcing of computations on general and specific functions. In particular, for those protocols, privacy is a significant property guaranteeing that the information hidden in the data structure related to the input and output of the outsourced computation cannot be revealed to any unauthorised entity who has access to the data. The analysis of privacy is based on the notion of indistinguishability (see [7] about this notion). This implies that the input and output data are semantically hidden to the unauthorised entity.

To construct the PVC protocols for outsourcing expensive linear algebraic computations, at ACM-ASIACCS 2010, Atallah and Frikken [2] introduced a new hardness assumption called the Secret Hiding assumption (SH) (see Sect. 2.1). Specifically, the authors presented two concrete versions, i.e., the Weak SH assumption (WSH) and the Strong SH assumption (SSH), respectively. The WSH assumption, informally, states that it is hard to distinguish (with knowing the prime p) between the uniform distribution over $\mathbb{Z}_p^{n \times m}$ and the distribution $\chi(p)^{n \times m}$ that outputs the matrix with $\lambda + 1$ rows $[\Sigma_{j=1}^{\lambda} a_{1,j} \cdot k_r^j \ldots \Sigma_{j=1}^{\lambda} a_{m,j} \cdot k_r^j]$ and λ rows uniformly distributed over $\mathbb{Z}_p^m$, where $n = 2 \cdot \lambda + 1$, where $\lambda \in \mathbb{N}_+$, $m \in \mathbb{N}_+$ (e.g., $m = 2 \cdot \lambda + 1$), $\forall r \in \{1, \ldots, \lambda + 1\} k_r$ is chosen from $\mathbb{Z}_p^*$ uniformly at random, and $\forall i \in \{1, \ldots, m\}, j \in \{1, \ldots, \lambda\} a_{i,j}$ is chosen from $\mathbb{Z}_p$ uniformly at random. The SSH assumption is similar to the WSH assumption, and it states that the uniform distribution over $\mathbb{Z}_p^{n \times m}$ is computationally indistinguishable from the distribution $\chi(p)^{n \times m}$ that outputs the matrix with $\lambda + e + 1$ rows $[\Sigma_{j=1}^{\lambda} a_{1,j} \cdot k_r^j \ldots \Sigma_{j=1}^{\lambda} a_{m,j} \cdot k_r^j]$ and $\lambda + e + 1$ rows uniformly distributed over $\mathbb{Z}_p^m$, where $n = 2 \cdot \lambda + 2 \cdot e + 2$, where $e \in \mathbb{N}_+$ (e.g., $e = \lambda$). To validate the plausible hardnesses of the above assumptions, Atallah and Frikken provided a proof to show that the SH assumption (i.e., the WSH assumption) implies the existence of one-way functions. This means that proving the SH assumption is at least as hard as proving P $\neq$ NP [2].

Based on the SH assumption, Atallah and Frikken [2] proposed two concrete PVC protocols for efficiently outsourcing the multiplication of large-scale matrices (see Sect. 2.3). Specifically, these two provably private protocols can be seen as the ingenious extensions of Shamir's secret sharing [14], and they are always regarded as the typical work in the PVC community. Atallah and Frikken first introduced a protocol based on the WSH assumption under the two non-colluding servers model (denoted by AF-PVC$_{two}$). In this warm-up protocol, a client needs to generate λ and $2 \cdot \lambda + 1$ pairs of matrices for each server, respectively. The servers perform $O(\lambda)$ matrix multiplications. Then, the authors developed a protocol based on the SSH assumption under the single server model (denoted by AF-PVC$_{single}$). In this main protocol, a client must create $4 \cdot \lambda + 2$ pairs of matrices for the single server, and this server also perform $O(\lambda)$ matrix multiplications. Furthermore, the authors provided a method to make the protocol under the single server model hold the security (i.e., the property related to the integrity verification). Of course, there exist some other researchers who are also interested in the SH assumption. For example, Laud and Pankova [12] tried to construct a PVC protocol for outsourcing solutions of linear programming problems based on the SSH assumption.

1.2   Our Contributions

Atallah and Frikken have given some theoretical consequences related to the SH assumption, but whether the SH problem corresponding to the assumption is a hard problem is still a worthwhile research area, particularly when the assumption is proposed for applications in the concrete real-world scenarios. In this paper, we present some rigorous analyses, targeting the SH problem and the Atallah-Frikken PVC Protocols for matrix multiplication, as follows:

- We present the decisional and search variants of the SH problem in Sect. 2, which are more standard problems when compared with the originals.
- We propose an analysis, discussed in Sect. 3, to break the decisional variant of the SH assumption (including the WSH assumption and SSH assumption) in a wide range of parameters. Our precise analysis focusing on evaluating the rank of a matrix shows that the decisional-SH problem (including the decisional-WSH problem and decisional-SSH problem) is not a hard problem, and the given SH distribution $\chi(p)^{n \times m}$ can be distinguished from the uniform distribution over $\mathbb{Z}_p^{n \times m}$ with overwhelming probability.
- We invoke the idea of the analysis for solving the decisional-SH problem to undermine the privacy of AF-PVC$_{two}$ and AF-PVC$_{single}$ in Sect. 3. Our analyses running in polynomial-time take advantage of the distinctions between the rank distributions of two types of given ciphertext matrices (see Theorems 7 and 8 for the two types of ciphertext matrices). The success probabilities of the analyses are close to 1, which shows that neither of those protocols is private against passive eavesdropping (i.e., a ciphertext-only attack (COA) (see Definition 3)) and also a chosen-plaintext attack (CPA) (see Definition 4).
- We implement the simulation experiments on our theoretical analyses for solving the decisional-SH problem and breaking the privacy of AF-PVC$_{two}$ and AF-PVC$_{single}$. The experimental results, presented in Sect. 4, confirm our analyses, which demonstrates that the decisional-SH problem is not a hard problem for a wide range of parameters, and AF-PVC$_{two}$ and AF-PVC$_{single}$ are not semantically private PVC protocols.

1.3   Organization of the Rest of the Paper

The remainder of the paper is organized as follows. Section 2 introduces the decisional and search versions of the SH assumption (including the WSH assumption and SSH assumption), the Atallah and Frikken's theoretical exploration on the SH assumption, the PVC protocols AF-PVC$_{two}$ and AF-PVC$_{single}$ and the formal definition of privacy. Section 3 describes the adversary's strategy and the detailed theoretical analyses for solving the decisional-SH problem and breaking the privacy of AF-PVC$_{two}$ and AF-PVC$_{single}$. Section 4 gives some detailed experimental verifications about our theoretical analyses in Sect. 3. The paper is concluded in Sect. 5 with a direction for future research.

Notation: Throughout the paper, we generally do math modulo p for some prime p. We denote by bold lower-case letters vectors over $\mathbb{Z}_p^n$ for $n \geq 2$, and by bold upper-case letters matrices over $\mathbb{Z}_p^{n \times m}$ for $n, m \geq 2$, where $\mathbb{Z}_p$ is a finite field of size p. We refer a set of elements from a row or a column of a matrix to as a vector. We denote by $x_{i,j}$ the individual element in the ith row and j^{th} column of a matrix $\mathbf{X}$. For any integer n, we denote the set $\{1, \ldots, n\}$ by $[n]$. We denote a security parameter by $\lambda \in \mathbb{N}_+$. We denote the transpose of x by x^T, the rank of a matrix $\mathbf{X}$ by $\mathsf{rank}(\mathbf{X})$, and the minimum of two values by $\min(\cdot, \cdot)$. We denote the class of polynomial functions in λ by $\mathsf{poly}(\lambda)$, and some unspecified negligible function in λ by $\mathsf{negl}(\lambda)$. We use $x \xleftarrow{\$} \Psi$ to denote the operation of uniformly sampling an element x from a finite set Ψ. For some probability distribution χ, $x \leftarrow \chi$ refers to sampling x according to χ.

2   Preliminaries

In this section, we recall the SH assumption, AF-PVC$_{two}$ and AF-PVC$_{single}$ proposed by Atallah and Frikken at ACM-ASIACCS 2010 [2]. We also present the formal definition of privacy for the PVC protocol.

2.1   The SH Assumption

We first describe the probability distribution $\chi(p)^{n \times m}$ that results from the following steps, where $n \in \{2 \cdot \lambda + 1, 2 \cdot \lambda + 2 \cdot e + 2\}$ and $m = \mathsf{poly}(\lambda) \geq 2$, where $e \in \mathbb{N}_+$.

1. Choose a uniformly random matrix $\mathbf{A} \xleftarrow{\$} \mathbb{Z}_p^{m \times \lambda}$, where each element $a_{i,j} \xleftarrow{\$} \mathbb{Z}_p$ for $i \in [m]$ and $j \in [\lambda]$. Choose $\ell = \lambda + 1$ (resp. $\ell = \lambda + e + 1$) distinct values $k_1, \ldots, k_\ell \xleftarrow{\$} \mathbb{Z}_p^*$.
2. For $r \in [\lambda + 1]$ (resp. $r \in [\lambda + e + 1]$), compute $\mathbf{d}_r = (\mathbf{A} \cdot \mathbf{k}_r)^T$, where $\mathbf{k}_r = [k_r k_r^2 \ldots k_r^\lambda]^T$. Obtain $\ell = \lambda + 1$ (resp. $\ell = \lambda + e + 1$) row vectors $\mathbf{d}_1, \ldots, \mathbf{d}_\ell$, where $\mathbf{d}_r = [\Sigma_{j=1}^\lambda a_{1,j} \cdot k_r^j \ldots \Sigma_{j=1}^\lambda a_{m,j} \cdot k_r^j]$ for $r \in [\lambda + 1]$ (resp. $r \in [\lambda + e + 1]$).
3. For $r \in [\lambda]$ (resp. $r \in [\lambda + e + 1]$), choose $\mathbf{u}_r \xleftarrow{\$} \mathbb{Z}_p^m$. Obtain $\tau = \lambda$ (resp. $\tau = \lambda + e + 1$) row vectors $\mathbf{u}_1, \ldots, \mathbf{u}_\tau$.
4. Combine the $\ell = \lambda + 1$ (resp. $\ell = \lambda + e + 1$) row vectors $\mathbf{d}_1, \ldots, \mathbf{d}_\ell$ with the $\tau = \lambda$ (resp. $\tau = \lambda + e + 1$) row vectors $\mathbf{u}_1, \ldots, \mathbf{u}_\tau$ to generate an $n \times m$ matrix $\mathbf{R}$. Choose a random permutation of the set $[n]$ to permute the rows of $\mathbf{R}$. The permuted matrix is the final matrix.

Then, we present the WSH problem and SSH problem as follows:

Definition 1 (WSH Problem). *Let $n = 2 \cdot \lambda + 1$ and $m = \mathsf{poly}(\lambda) \geq 2$. The WSH distribution $\chi(p)^{n \times m}$ for a given prime p is the set of the permuted matrices, where each matrix includes $\lambda + 1$ row vectors $\boldsymbol{d}_1, \ldots, \boldsymbol{d}_{\lambda+1}$ and λ row vectors $\boldsymbol{u}_1, \ldots, \boldsymbol{u}_\lambda$.*

- *The decisional-WSH problem is: For some fixed prime p and given arbitrarily many samples (i.e., a polynomial number of samples) from $\mathbb{Z}_p^{n \times m}$, to computationally distinguish whether these samples are distributed uniformly or whether they are distributed as $\chi(p)^{n \times m}$.*
- *The search-WSH problem is: For some fixed prime p and given n samples from the distribution $\chi(p)^m$ (i.e., a sample from $\chi(p)^{n \times m}$), to find $k_1, \ldots, k_{\lambda+1}$ (or $\boldsymbol{A}$).*

Definition 2 (SSH Problem). *Let $n = 2 \cdot \lambda + 2 \cdot e + 2$ and $m = \mathsf{poly}(\lambda) \geq 2$, where $e \in \mathbb{N}_+$. The SSH distribution $\chi(p)^{n \times m}$ for a given prime p is the set of the permuted matrices, where each matrix includes $\lambda + e + 1$ row vectors $\boldsymbol{d}_1, \ldots, \boldsymbol{d}_{\lambda+e+1}$ and $\lambda + e + 1$ row vectors $\boldsymbol{u}_1, \ldots, \boldsymbol{u}_{\lambda+e+1}$.*

- *The decisional-SSH problem is: The description of this problem is the same as that of the decisional version in Definition 1.*
- *The search-SSH problem is: The description of this problem is the same as that of the search version in Definition 1. The aim is to find $k_1, \ldots, k_{\lambda+e+1}$ (or $\boldsymbol{A}$).*

According to Atallah and Frikken's opinion, the WSH assumption denotes that no polynomial-time adversary solve the decisional and search WSH problem, and the SSH assumption means that no polynomial-time adversary can solve the decisional and search SSH problem. Specifically, the decisional-WSH assumption and the decisional-SSH assumption state that the distribution $\chi(p)^{n \times m}$ is computationally indistinguishable from the uniform distribution over $\mathbb{Z}_p^{n \times m}$ for $n \in \{2 \cdot \lambda + 1, 2 \cdot \lambda + 2 \cdot e + 2\}$. Then, this implies that, for any polynomial-time adversary $\mathcal{A}$, we have

$$\mathsf{Adv}_{\mathcal{A},\mathrm{SH}}(p, n, m) \overset{\text{def}}{=} \left| \mathsf{Suc}_{\mathcal{A},\mathrm{SH}}(p, n, m) - \tfrac{1}{2} \right| \leq \mathsf{negl}(\lambda), \tag{1}$$

where SH is either the WSH distribution or the SSH distribution, $\mathsf{Suc}_{\mathcal{A},\mathrm{SH}}(p, n, m)$ denotes the probability of $\mathcal{A}$'s successful guess employing some adversary's strategy for the distribution of the sample $\mathbf{X}$ from $\mathbb{Z}_p^{n \times m}$, and $\mathsf{Adv}_{\mathcal{A},\mathrm{SH}}(p, n, m)$ denotes the advantage of $\mathcal{A}$'s guess for the distribution. Note that, $\mathcal{A}$'s guess for the sample $\mathbf{X} \in \mathbb{Z}_p^{n \times m}$ can be based on the following experiment:

1. $b \overset{\$}{\leftarrow} \{0,1\}$.
2. If $b = 1$ then $\mathbf{X} \leftarrow \chi(p)^{n \times m}$ else $\mathbf{X} \overset{\$}{\leftarrow} \mathbb{Z}_p^{n \times m}$.
3. If $\mathcal{A}(\mathbf{X}) = b$ then $\mathcal{A}$ wins else $\mathcal{A}$ loses.

2.2 Atallah-Frikken Theorems Related to the SH Assumption

For the above WSH assumption and SSH assumption, Atallah and Frikken introduced some associated consequences below.

Lemma 1 ([2], Lemma 1). *Given a set of ℓ special row vectors $d_1, \ldots, d_\ell$, where $\ell < \lambda + 1$, this set of row vectors is distributed identically to a set of ℓ uniformly random row vectors from $\mathbb{Z}_p^m$.*

Theorem 1 ([2], Corollary 2). *Consider a $(\lambda + 1) \times m$ matrix that includes $\lambda + 1$ randomly permuted rows consisting of ℓ special row vectors $d_1, \ldots, d_\ell$ and $\lambda + 1 - \ell$ uniformly random row vectors from $\mathbb{Z}_p^m$, where $\ell < \lambda + 1$. This type of matrix is distributed identically to the uniformly sampled matrix from $\mathbb{Z}_p^{(\lambda+1) \times m}$.*

Theorem 2 ([2], Theorem 6). *Consider an $n \times m$ matrix sampled from $\chi(p)^{n \times m}$, where $n = 2 \cdot \lambda + 2 \cdot e + 2$. Choose a set of $\lambda + 1$ row vectors from this matrix uniformly at random. The probability that all the $\lambda + 1$ row vectors come from the $\lambda + e + 1$ special row vectors $d_1, \ldots, d_{\lambda+e+1}$ is negligible in λ.*

In [2], Atallah and Frikken did not prove the WSH assumption and SSH assumption from first principles, but the authors confirmed the hardness of the WSH problem and proposed the following theorem.

Theorem 3 ([2], Theorem 9). *Assume that the decisional-WSH assumption holds, the function that outputs an $n \times m$ matrix by invoking the generation steps of the distribution $\chi(p)^{n \times m}$ is a one-way function, where $n = 2 \cdot \lambda + 1$.*

Actually, from Theorem 3, the difficulty for distinguishing between the uniform distribution over $\mathbb{Z}_p^{n \times m}$ and the distribution $\chi(p)^{n \times m}$ shows the lower bound of the difficulty for finding $k_1, \ldots, k_{\lambda+1}$ (or $\mathbf{A}$). This means that the hardness of the decisional-WSH problem implies the hardness of the search-WSH problem. We refer to [2] for more details.

2.3 Atallah-Frikken PVC Protocols for Matrix Multiplication

Since decisional version is more handy for applications, Atallah and Frikken proposed two PVC protocols $\mathsf{AF\text{-}PVC}_{two}$ and $\mathsf{AF\text{-}PVC}_{single}$ based on the plausible hardnesses of the decisional-WSH problem and decisional-SSH problem, respectively. Specifically, these protocols consist of a tuple of Probabilistic Polynomial-Time (PPT) algorithms $\mathsf{PVC} = (\mathsf{KeyGen}, \mathsf{ProbGen}, \mathsf{Compute}, \mathsf{ResuGen})$, where KeyGen is a private-key generation algorithm, $\mathsf{ProbGen}$ a problem generation algorithm that produces some ciphertext inputs for an outsourced function, $\mathsf{Compute}$ a function computation algorithm that is run by the server to produce some ciphertext outputs of the outsourced function, and $\mathsf{ResuGen}$ a result generation algorithm that produces the real output. The details of these two protocols are as follows:

The Two-Server Case: Given a security parameter λ, the matrix size $v = \mathsf{poly}(\lambda)$, the size of the message space $p = \mathsf{poly}(\lambda)$ and the degree of a polynomial

$h = \lambda$. For two $v \times v$ matrices $\mathbf{M}_1, \mathbf{M}_2 \in \mathbb{Z}_p^{v \times v}$, a quadruple of PPT algorithms AF-PVC$_{two}$ is defined by

1. AFT.KeyGen(1^λ): Choose a uniformly random matrix $\mathbf{A} \xleftarrow{\$} \mathbb{Z}_p^{2 \cdot v^2 \times h}$, $2 \cdot \lambda + 1$ distinct values $k_1, \ldots, k_{2 \cdot \lambda + 1} \xleftarrow{\$} \mathbb{Z}_p^*$ and a random permutation θ of the set $[2 \cdot \lambda + 1]$. Output a fresh key $\mathsf{sk} = (\mathbf{A}, \{k_1, \ldots, k_{2 \cdot \lambda + 1}\}, \theta)$.

2. AFT.ProbGen($\mathsf{sk}, \mathbf{M}_1, \mathbf{M}_2$): Run $\mathbf{A} \cdot \mathbf{k}$ to obtain a vector $\mathbf{d}$ that involves $2 \cdot v^2 h$-degree polynomials, where $\mathbf{k} = [k \; k^2 \ldots k^h]^T$, where k is an indeterminate. Use these h-degree polynomials to mask each element of $\mathbf{M}_1$ and $\mathbf{M}_2$, and generate two ciphertexts $\mathbf{C}_1$ and $\mathbf{C}_2$. Specifically, $\forall i, j \in [v]$, $i' \in [2 \cdot v^2]$ $c_{i,j} = \Sigma_{s=1}^h a_{i',s} \cdot k^s + m_{i,j}$. For $r \in [2 \cdot \lambda + 1]$, let $k = k_r$ and compute $\mathbf{C}_1(k_r)$ and $\mathbf{C}_2(k_r)$. This implies that $c_{i,j}(k_r) = \Sigma_{s=1}^h a_{i',s} \cdot k_r^s + m_{i,j}$. Choose $2 \cdot \lambda$ uniformly random matrices $\mathbf{B}_1, \ldots, \mathbf{B}_{2 \cdot \lambda} \xleftarrow{\$} \mathbb{Z}_p^{v \times v}$ and create λ pairs $(\mathbf{B}_1, \mathbf{B}_2), \ldots, (\mathbf{B}_{2 \cdot \lambda - 1}, \mathbf{B}_{2 \cdot \lambda})$. A client sends a set of matrix pairs $U^{(1)} = \{(\mathbf{C}_1(k_1), \mathbf{C}_2(k_1)), \ldots, (\mathbf{C}_1(k_\lambda), \mathbf{C}_2(k_\lambda))\}$ to the first server. Moreover, the client permutes the $2 \cdot \lambda + 1$ matrix pairs of the set $U^{(2)} = \{(\mathbf{C}_1(k_{\lambda+1}), \mathbf{C}_2(k_{\lambda+1})), \ldots, (\mathbf{C}_1(k_{2 \cdot \lambda + 1}), \mathbf{C}_2(k_{2 \cdot \lambda + 1})), (\mathbf{B}_1, \mathbf{B}_2), \ldots, (\mathbf{B}_{2 \cdot \lambda - 1}, \mathbf{B}_{2 \cdot \lambda})\}$ using θ, and sends the permuted set $U^{(2)}$ to the second server.

3. AFT.Compute($U^{(1)}, U^{(2)}$): The products of all matrix pairs in $U^{(1)}$ and $U^{(2)}$ are computed by those two servers and put in two sets $Q^{(1)}$ and $Q^{(2)}$, respectively. These two sets $Q^{(1)}$ and $Q^{(2)}$ are sent back to the client.

4. AFT.ResuGen($\mathsf{sk}, Q^{(1)}, Q^{(2)}$): Based on θ, choose some matrices from $Q^{(1)}$ and $Q^{(2)}$, which correspond to $\mathbf{M}_1$ and $\mathbf{M}_2$. Interpolate these matrices to find the real result of $\mathbf{M}_1 \cdot \mathbf{M}_2$.

The Single-Server Case: Given a security parameter λ, the matrix size $v = \mathsf{poly}(\lambda)$, the size of the message space $p = \mathsf{poly}(\lambda)$ and the degree of a polynomial $h = \lambda$. For two $v \times v$ matrices $\mathbf{M}_1, \mathbf{M}_2 \in \mathbb{Z}_p^{v \times v}$, a quadruple of PPT algorithms AF-PVC$_{single}$ is defined as

1. AFS.KeyGen(1^λ): Choose a uniformly random matrix $\mathbf{A} \xleftarrow{\$} \mathbb{Z}_p^{2 \cdot v^2 \times h}$, $2 \cdot \lambda + 1$ distinct values $k_1, \ldots, k_{2 \cdot \lambda + 1} \xleftarrow{\$} \mathbb{Z}_p^*$ and a random permutation θ of the set $[4 \cdot \lambda + 2]$. Output a fresh key $\mathsf{sk} = (\mathbf{A}, \{k_1, \ldots, k_{2 \cdot \lambda + 1}\}, \theta)$.

2. AFS.ProbGen($\mathsf{sk}, \mathbf{M}_1, \mathbf{M}_2$): Run $\mathbf{A} \cdot \mathbf{k}$ to obtain a vector $\mathbf{d}$ that includes $2 \cdot v^2 h$-degree polynomials, where $\mathbf{k} = [k \; k^2 \; \ldots \; k^h]^T$, where k is an indeterminate. Use these h-degree polynomials to mask each element of $\mathbf{M}_1$ and $\mathbf{M}_2$, and generate two ciphertexts $\mathbf{C}_1$ and $\mathbf{C}_2$. Specifically, $\forall i, j \in [v]$, $i' \in [2 \cdot v^2] c_{i,j} = \Sigma_{s=1}^h a_{i',s} \cdot k^s + m_{i,j}$. For $r \in [2 \cdot \lambda + 1]$, let $k = k_r$ and compute $\mathbf{C}_1(k_r)$ and $\mathbf{C}_2(k_r)$, where $\forall i, j \in [v], i' \in [2 \cdot v^2] c_{i,j}(k_r) = \Sigma_{s=1}^h a_{i',s} \cdot k_r^s + m_{i,j}$. Choose $4 \cdot \lambda + 2$ uniformly random matrices $\mathbf{B}_1, \ldots, \mathbf{B}_{4 \cdot \lambda + 2} \xleftarrow{\$} \mathbb{Z}_p^{v \times v}$ and create $2 \cdot \lambda + 1$ pairs $(\mathbf{B}_1, \mathbf{B}_2), \ldots, (\mathbf{B}_{4 \cdot \lambda + 1}, \mathbf{B}_{4 \cdot \lambda + 2})$. A client permutes the $4 \cdot \lambda + 2$ matrix pairs of the set $U = \{(\mathbf{C}_1(k_1), \mathbf{C}_2(k_1)), \ldots, (\mathbf{C}_1(k_{2 \cdot \lambda + 1}), \mathbf{C}_2(k_{2 \cdot \lambda + 1})), (\mathbf{B}_1, \mathbf{B}_2), \ldots, (\mathbf{B}_{4 \cdot \lambda + 1}, \mathbf{B}_{4 \cdot \lambda + 2})\}$ using θ, and sends the permuted set U to a server.

3. AFS.Compute(U): The products of all matrix pairs in U are computed by the server and put in a set Q. The set Q is sent back to the client.
4. AFS.ResuGen(sk, Q): Based on θ, choose some matrices from Q, which correspond to $\mathbf{M}_1$ and $\mathbf{M}_2$. Interpolate these matrices to find the real result of $\mathbf{M}_1 \cdot \mathbf{M}_2$.

For AF-PVC$_{single}$, Atallah and Frikken introduced a method to verify the result returned from a server who is lazy or malicious. This verification algorithm is a probabilistic verification process that means successfully detecting a cheating server with non-negligible probability. Since our work focuses on the privacy property of the PVC protocol, we refer to [2] for more details about the verification process.

2.4 Privacy Definition

According to [2], a property of AF-PVC$_{two}$ and AF-PVC$_{single}$, from an informal ciphertext indistinguishability statement, is that it is infeasible for any passive PPT adversary $\mathcal{A}$ to computationally distinguish the ciphertexts over two distinct inputs. Specifically, a ciphertext is a set of matrix pairs (i.e., $U^{(1)}, U^{(2)}, U$). This computational problem is linked to the notion of privacy against passive adversary. Based on different attack models, two formal definitions are given below.

Definition 3 (Privacy Against Passive Eavesdropping). *For a PVC protocol PVC = (KeyGen, ProbGen, Compute, ResuGen), the following experiment associated with a PPT eavesdropping adversary $\mathcal{A}$ is considered:*
    Experiment $Exp_{\mathcal{A}}^{ind\text{-}priv^{coa}}[PVC, \lambda]$:

$((\mathbf{M}_{1(0)}, \mathbf{M}_{2(0)}), (\mathbf{M}_{1(1)}, \mathbf{M}_{2(1)})) \leftarrow \mathcal{A}(1^\lambda)$;
$sk \leftarrow KeyGen(1^\lambda)$;
$b \xleftarrow{\$} \{0, 1\}$;
$U_b \leftarrow ProbGen(sk, \mathbf{M}_{1(b)}, \mathbf{M}_{2(b)})$;
$b' \leftarrow \mathcal{A}((\mathbf{M}_{1(0)}, \mathbf{M}_{2(0)}), (\mathbf{M}_{1(1)}, \mathbf{M}_{2(1)}), U_b)$;
If $b' = b$, output 1; else, output 0,

where U_b is called a challenge ciphertext. The computation of U_b is done by the performer of the experiment. Then, we define the advantage of $\mathcal{A}$ in the experiment above as follows:

$$Adv_{\mathcal{A}}^{ind\text{-}priv^{coa}}(PVC, \lambda) = \left| \Pr[Exp_{\mathcal{A}}^{ind\text{-}priv^{coa}}[PVC, \lambda] = 1] - \tfrac{1}{2} \right|.$$

PVC is IND-COA private if, for any $\mathcal{A}$, there exists a negligible function negl such that

$$Adv_{\mathcal{A}}^{ind\text{-}priv^{coa}}(PVC, \lambda) \leq negl(\lambda).$$

Definition 4 (Privacy Against A Chosen-Plaintext Attack). *For a PVC protocol PVC = (KeyGen, ProbGen, Compute, ResuGen), the following experiment associated with a PPT adversary $\mathcal{A}$ is considered:*
    Experiment $Exp_{\mathcal{A}}^{ind\text{-}priv}[PVC, \lambda]$:

$$((M_{1(0)}, M_{2(0)}), (M_{1(1)}, M_{2(1)})) \leftarrow \mathcal{A}^{PrivProbGen(KeyGen(1^\lambda), \cdot, \cdot)}(1^\lambda);$$
$$sk \leftarrow KeyGen(1^\lambda);$$
$$b \xleftarrow{\$} \{0, 1\};$$
$$U_b \leftarrow ProbGen(sk, M_{1(b)}, M_{2(b)});$$
$$b' \leftarrow \mathcal{A}^{PrivProbGen(KeyGen(1^\lambda), \cdot, \cdot)}((M_{1(0)}, M_{2(0)}), (M_{1(1)}, M_{2(1)}), U_b);$$
$$\text{If } b' = b, \text{ output } 1; \text{ else, output } 0,$$

where the oracle $PrivProbGen(KeyGen(1^\lambda), M_1, M_2)$ asks $ProbGen(KeyGen(1^\lambda), M_1, M_2)$ to obtain a set of matrix pairs U and send it back. The output from $PrivProbGen(KeyGen(1^\lambda), M_1, M_2)$ is probabilistic. Then, we can define the advantage of $\mathcal{A}$ in the experiment above as follows:

$$Adv_{\mathcal{A}}^{ind-priv}(PVC, \lambda) = \left| \Pr[Exp_{\mathcal{A}}^{ind-priv}[PVC, \lambda] = 1] - \tfrac{1}{2} \right|.$$

PVC is IND-CPA private if, for any $\mathcal{A}$, there exists a negligible function negl such that

$$Adv_{\mathcal{A}}^{ind-priv}(PVC, \lambda) \leq negl(\lambda).$$

Remark 1. From Katti et al.'s work [11], privacy against passive eavesdropping is equivalent to IND-COA privacy. If a PVC protocol satisfies IND-CPA privacy based on Definition 4, it must also satisfy IND-COA privacy based on Definition 3. However, if a PVC protocol does not satisfy IND-COA privacy, it also does not satisfy IND-CPA privacy.

In [2], Atallah and Frikken gave the detailed proofs for privacy of AF-PVC$_{two}$ and AF-PVC$_{single}$ and the following theorems.

Theorem 4 ([2], Theorem 5). *Assume that the two servers do not collude and the decisional-WSH assumption holds. Then, AF-PVC$_{two}$ is IND-CPA private.*

Theorem 5 ([2], Sect. 4.5.3). *Assume that the decisional-SSH assumption holds. Then, AF-PVC$_{single}$ is IND-CPA private.*

3   Breaking the Decisional-SH Assumption

In this section, we first present a rigorous analysis for breaking the decisional-WSH assumption and decisional-SSH assumption. Then, we show how the analysis for solving the decisional-SH problem extends naturally to AF-PVC$_{two}$ and AF-PVC$_{single}$, thus demonstrating that both of them are not IND-COA private.

3.1   Adversary's Strategy

For the decisional-WSH problem (resp. decisional-SSH problem) in Definition 1 (resp. Definition 2), if a polynomial-time adversary $\mathcal{A}$ wants to solve this problem with non-negligible advantage, she must employ some unexpected strategy. In general, the adversary's direct strategy is that she tries to find a set that involves ℓ special row vectors $\mathbf{d}_1, \ldots, \mathbf{d}_\ell$ efficiently and evaluate the distinction between the set of ℓ special row vectors and a set of ℓ uniformly random vectors over $\mathbb{Z}_p^m$. As stated in Theorem 1, any set of $\lambda + 1$ row vectors that include at least one uniformly random vector over $\mathbb{Z}_p^m$ is distributed identically to the set of $\lambda + 1$ uniformly random vectors over $\mathbb{Z}_p^m$. This implies that $\mathcal{A}$ needs to find at least $\ell = \lambda + 1$ special row vectors $\mathbf{d}_1, \ldots, \mathbf{d}_{\lambda+1}$. However, Atallah and Frikken argued that $\mathcal{A}$ is unlikely to find $\mathbf{d}_1, \ldots, \mathbf{d}_{\lambda+1}$ with significant probability (e.g., Theorem 2)[1].

Then, we take a step back and consider such a question: if we sample a matrix from a distribution which is either the WSH distribution (resp. the SSH distribution) or uniformly random, what type of factor about this matrix do we need to analyze and evaluate? We believe that one of the important factors is the rank of a matrix. This means that the adversary's strategy can be based on the analysis for the rank of a matrix. From this point of view, we propose an adversary's strategy that proceeds in two steps.

Strategy Overview: Let $\mathbf{X}$ be an $n \times m$ matrix that is sampled from a distribution which is either the WSH distribution (resp. the SSH distribution) $\chi(p)^{n \times m}$ or the uniform distribution over $\mathbb{Z}_p^{n \times m}$.

1. Compute the rank of $\mathbf{X}$, denoted by $\mathsf{rank}(\mathbf{X})$.
2. Check whether $\mathsf{rank}(\mathbf{X})$ is below some value $\varepsilon \leq \min(n, m)$ or not below this value. If $\mathsf{rank}(\mathbf{X})$ is below ε, $\mathbf{X}$ is sampled from $\chi(p)^{n \times m}$; otherwise, $\mathbf{X}$ is sampled from the uniform distribution over $\mathbb{Z}_p^{n \times m}$.

Why the Rank-Based Analysis Works? The idea of the proposed strategy is remarkably simple. It focuses on a distinguishing problem about the distributions of ranks of matrices from those two distributions. Specifically, the value ε can be seen as a threshold rank that is the critical factor of the proposed strategy. To motivate why computing the rank of a matrix is useful for solving the decisional-WSH problem and decisional-SSH problem, we list the following two facts:

- **Fact 1:** Consider an $n \times m$ matrix $\mathbf{X}$ over $\mathbb{Z}_p^{n \times m}$. W.l.o.g. assume that $n \leq m$. If there are $\ell < n$ linearly dependent row vectors in $\mathbf{X}$, all the n row vectors of $\mathbf{X}$ are linearly dependent. This implies that the rank of $\mathbf{X}$ must be below n (i.e., $\mathsf{rank}(\mathbf{X}) < n$).
- **Fact 2:** Consider an $n \times m$ matrix $\mathbf{X}$ sampled from the uniform distribution over $\mathbb{Z}_p^{n \times m}$. W.l.o.g. assume that $n \leq m$. With high probability, the n row vectors of $\mathbf{X}$ are linearly independent, and the rank of $\mathbf{X}$ is n (i.e., $\mathsf{rank}(\mathbf{X}) = n$).

Specifically, based on Linial and Weitz's work [13] (see Eq. (2)), we verify the **Fact 2** concretely. To implement this verification, we choose parameters $p > 4 \cdot \lambda + 2$, $n = 2 \cdot \lambda + 1$ and $m \geq n$, and compute the results on the probabilities of the full-row-rank matrices for different parameters. The verification

---

[1] In Sect. 5, we show that $\mathbf{d}_1, \ldots, \mathbf{d}_{\lambda+1}$ can be found (with overwhelming probability) by employing our adversary's strategy. Here, we want to show that these vectors are unlikely to be found without using our adversary's strategy.

results show that the probability of a uniformly random matrix having rank n is nearly 1, i.e., $\Pr[\text{rank}(\mathbf{X}) = n] \approx 1$, which can show the rank distribution of the uniformly random matrices over $\mathbb{Z}_p^{n \times m}$. For more details about the verification results, we refer the reader to the full version of our paper.

$$\Pr[\text{rank}(\mathbf{X}) = z] = \frac{1}{p^{(n-z)\cdot(m-z)}} \cdot \prod_{i=0}^{z-1} \frac{(1 - p^{i-n}) \cdot (1 - p^{i-m})}{1 - p^{i-z}} \qquad (2)$$

According to **Fact 1** and **Fact 2**, if the matrices sampled from some distribution over $\mathbb{Z}_p^{n \times m}$ always have some linearly dependent row vectors, the ranks of these matrices are always below the matrix sizes, and the rank distribution is distinguished from the rank distribution of the uniformly random matrices over $\mathbb{Z}_p^{n \times m}$ with non-negligible advantage.

Then, based on the above analysis, if $\mathcal{A}$ employs the proposed strategy to solve the decisional-WSH problem and decisional-SSH problem, the crux is that whether there are $\lambda + 1$ linearly dependent special row vectors $\mathbf{d}_1, \ldots, \mathbf{d}_{\lambda+1}$ and what is the probability that $\mathbf{d}_1, \ldots, \mathbf{d}_{\lambda+1}$ are linearly dependent. Assume that $\mathbf{d}_1, \ldots, \mathbf{d}_{\lambda+1}$ must be linearly dependent, then the rank of a matrix sampled from $\chi(p)^{n \times m}$ can leak information about the matrix structure. In what follows, we focus on exploring the linear relation of the $\lambda + 1$ special row vectors $\mathbf{d}_1, \ldots, \mathbf{d}_{\lambda+1}$ and give the answer.

3.2   Analysis for the Decisional-SH Assumption

To show the linear relation of the $\lambda + 1$ special row vectors $\mathbf{d}_1, \ldots, \mathbf{d}_{\lambda+1}$, we consider a set of the transposes of the $\lambda + 1$ vectors $[(\mathbf{d}_1)^T \ldots (\mathbf{d}_{\lambda+1})^T]$ as the product of two matrices $\mathbf{A} \cdot \mathbf{K}$, where $\mathbf{A}$ is an $m \times \lambda$ uniformly random matrix where the ith column is $\mathbf{a}_i$ for $i \in [\lambda]$, and $\mathbf{K}$ is a $\lambda \times (\lambda+1)$ matrix where the rth column is $\mathbf{k}_r = [k_r\ k_r^2\ \ldots\ k_r^\lambda]^T$ for $r \in [\lambda + 1]$. Specifically, according to **Fact 2**, our following analysis focuses on the case with high probability that the vectors $\mathbf{a}_1, \ldots, \mathbf{a}_\lambda$ are linearly independent[2].

Lemma 2. *Consider an* $m \times (\lambda + 1)$ *matrix* $(\mathbf{A} \cdot \mathbf{K})$*. Assume that* $m = poly(\lambda) > \lambda$*, and the column vectors* $\mathbf{a}_1, \ldots, \mathbf{a}_\lambda$ *are linearly independent. Then,* $\text{rank}(\mathbf{A} \cdot \mathbf{K}) < min(m, \lambda + 1)$*, which implies that the special row vectors* $\mathbf{d}_1, \ldots, \mathbf{d}_{\lambda+1}$ *are linearly dependent.*

Proof. The result in this lemma is immediate, actually. For the formal proof, we refer the reader to the full version of our paper.

According to Eq. (2), the probability that the column vectors $\mathbf{a}_1, \ldots, \mathbf{a}_\lambda$ are linearly independent (i.e., $\text{rank}(\mathbf{A}) = \lambda$) is $\Pi_{i=0}^{\lambda-1}(1-p^{i-m})$. Then, the probability that the row vectors $\mathbf{d}_1, \ldots, \mathbf{d}_{\lambda+1}$ are linearly dependent is also $\Pi_{i=0}^{\lambda-1}(1-p^{i-m})$. Specifically, if p is a large prime (e.g., $p > 4 \cdot \lambda + 2$), the row vectors $\mathbf{d}_1, \ldots, \mathbf{d}_{\lambda+1}$ are likely to be linearly dependent.

Then, based on the proposed adversary's strategy and Lemma 2, we show our main analysis results for solving the decisional-WSH problem and decisional-SSH problem.

---

[2] In the full version of our paper, we will present an analysis that also considers the case that the vectors $\mathbf{a}_1, \ldots, \mathbf{a}_\lambda$ are linearly dependent.

Lemma 3. *Consider a sample X from either the WSH distribution (resp. the SSH distribution) $\chi(p)^{n \times m}$ or the uniform distribution over $\mathbb{Z}_p^{n \times m}$, where $n \in \{2 \cdot \lambda + 1, 2 \cdot \lambda + 2 \cdot e + 2\}$. Assume that $m > 2 \cdot \lambda$ (resp. $m > 2 \cdot \lambda + e + 1$), and p is a large prime, e.g., $p > 4 \cdot \lambda + 2$. Let $\varphi = \Pi_{i=0}^{\lambda-1}(1 - p^{i-m})$. Let $\eta = Pr[rank(X) = z]$, where the probability is for the case that X is uniformly random, and $z = min(n, m)$. If $rank(X) < min(n, m)$, the probability that X is sampled from $\chi(p)^{n \times m}$ satisfies $Pr[X \leftarrow \chi(p)^{n \times m} | rank(X) < min(n, m)] \geq \frac{1}{1+\frac{1-\eta}{\varphi}}$, and if $rank(X) = min(n, m)$, the probability that X is uniformly random satisfies $Pr[X \xleftarrow{\$} \mathbb{Z}_p^{n \times m} | rank(X) = min(n, m)] \geq \frac{1}{1+\frac{1-\varphi}{\eta}}$.*

Proof. For the detailed proof, we refer the reader to the full version of our paper.

In Lemma 3, since p is a large prime, we can obtain $Pr[X \leftarrow \chi(p)^{n \times m} | rank(X) < min(n, m)] \approx 1$ and $Pr[X \xleftarrow{\$} \mathbb{Z}_p^{n \times m} | rank(X) = min(n, m)] \approx 1$.

Theorem 6. *Let $\varphi = \Pi_{i=0}^{\lambda-1}(1 - p^{i-m})$. Let $\eta = Pr[rank(X) = z]$ denote the probability that the rank of any $n \times m$ uniformly random matrix X is z, where $z = min(n, m)$, where $n \in \{2 \cdot \lambda + 1, 2 \cdot \lambda + 2 \cdot e + 2\}$. Assume that $m > 2 \cdot \lambda$ (resp. $m > 2 \cdot \lambda + e + 1$), and p is a large prime, e.g., $p > 4 \cdot \lambda + 2$. Then there exists an adversary $\mathcal{A}$ running in polynomial-time t for solving the decisional-WSH problem (resp. decisional-SSH problem) with*

$$Adv_{\mathcal{A},SH}(p, n, m) \geq \tfrac{1}{2} \cdot (\varphi + \eta) - \tfrac{1}{2},$$

where t is used to compute the rank of a matrix. Specifically, since p is a large prime, $\mathcal{A}$ has advantage $Adv_{\mathcal{A},SH}(p, n, m) \approx \tfrac{1}{2}$ in solving the decisional-WSH problem (resp. decisional-SSH problem).

Proof. Let $Unif(\mathbb{Z}_p^{n \times m})$ denote the uniform distribution over $\mathbb{Z}_p^{n \times m}$. The adversary $\mathcal{A}$ has access to an oracle that is either $\chi(p)^{n \times m}$ or $Unif(\mathbb{Z}_p^{n \times m})$. She calls the oracle arbitrarily many times (i.e., a polynomial number of times) to obtain samples of the form X_i and uses the rank-based adversary's strategy to evaluate each sample. If $rank(X_i) < min(n, m)$, $\mathcal{A}$ outputs $\chi(p)^{n \times m}$. If $rank(X_i) = min(n, m)$, $\mathcal{A}$ returns $Unif(\mathbb{Z}_p^{n \times m})$.

We first look at the probability distribution of the rank of X_i when the oracle that $\mathcal{A}$ has access to is $Unif(\mathbb{Z}_p^{n \times m})$. In this case it's easy to see that $Pr[rank(X_i) = min(n, m)] = \eta$ and $Pr[rank(X_i) < min(n, m)] = 1 - \eta$.

If the oracle is $\chi(p)^{n \times m}$, as discussed earlier, we have $Pr[rank(X_i) = min(n, m)] \leq 1 - \varphi$ and $Pr[rank(X_i) < min(n, m)] \geq \varphi$.

Thus, based on Lemma 3, we obtain the success probability (see Sect. 2.1)

$Suc_{\mathcal{A},SH}(p, n, m)$
$= Pr[\mathcal{A}(X) = b | rank(X) < min(n, m)] \cdot Pr[rank(X) < min(n, m)]+$
$\quad Pr[\mathcal{A}(X) = b | rank(X) = min(n, m)] \cdot Pr[rank(X) = min(n, m)]$
$= Pr[X \leftarrow \chi(p)^{n \times m} | rank(X) < min(n, m)] \cdot Pr[rank(X) < min(n, m)]+$
$\quad Pr[X \xleftarrow{\$} \mathbb{Z}_p^{n \times m} | rank(X) = min(n, m)] \cdot Pr[rank(X) = min(n, m)]$
$\geq \frac{\varphi}{\varphi+1-\eta} \cdot \frac{1-\eta+\varphi}{2} + \frac{1}{2} \cdot \eta = \frac{1}{2} \cdot \varphi + \frac{1}{2} \cdot \eta$

This means that $\mathsf{Adv}_{\mathcal{A},\mathrm{SH}}(p,n,m) \geq \frac{1}{2} \cdot \varphi + \frac{1}{2} \cdot \eta - \frac{1}{2}$. Specifically, when p is a large prime, the value of φ is close to 1. Moreover, as discussed in Sect. 3.1, η is also close to 1 if p is not a small prime. Then, $\mathsf{Adv}_{\mathcal{A},\mathrm{SH}}(p,n,m)$ is close to $\frac{1}{2}$, which confirms our theorem.

Theorem 6 demonstrates that we can break the decisional-WSH assumption and decisional-SSH assumption efficiently for a wide range of parameters. The final result contradicts Atallah and Frikken's result in Eq. (1). However, this does not imply that we can solve the search-WSH problem and search-SSH problem efficiently, which shows the inaccuracy of Theorem 3.

3.3   Analysis for AF-PVC$_{two}$ and AF-PVC$_{single}$

Now we want to present the formal analysis for privacy of AF-PVC$_{two}$ and AF-PVC$_{single}$. Specifically, it is straightforward to use the idea of the analysis for the decisional-WSH assumption and decisional-SSH assumption to undermine the privacy of AF-PVC$_{two}$ and AF-PVC$_{single}$. This means that an adversary $\mathcal{A}$ employs the rank-based strategy to evaluate a given ciphertext matrix. Note that, our analysis is based on the IND-COA experiment (see Definition 3), where an eavesdropping adversary $\mathcal{A}$ running in polynomial-time has non-negligible advantage to show that both protocols are not IND-COA private (and thus not IND-CPA private).

Lemma 4. *Given a uniformly random matrix $\boldsymbol{A} \in \mathbb{Z}_p^{2 \cdot v^2 \times \lambda}$ where the ith column is $\boldsymbol{a}_i$ for $i \in [\lambda]$, a $\lambda \times n$ matrix $\boldsymbol{K}$ where the rth column is $\boldsymbol{k}_r = [k_r\ k_r^2\ \ldots\ k_r^\lambda]^T$ for $r \in [n]$, and a $2 \cdot v^2 \times n$ matrix $\boldsymbol{S}$ where the elements of the ith column $\boldsymbol{s}_i$ are the same as the corresponding elements of the jth column $\boldsymbol{s}_j$ for $i, j \in [n]$, where $\boldsymbol{s}_i \xleftarrow{\$} \mathbb{Z}_p^{2 \cdot v^2}{}^3$. Let p be a large prime (e.g., $p > 4 \cdot \lambda + 2$), $v = \mathsf{poly}(\lambda) > \sqrt{\frac{\lambda}{2}}$ and $n \in \{\lambda + 1, 2 \cdot \lambda + 1\}$. Assume that the column vectors $\boldsymbol{a}_1, \ldots, \boldsymbol{a}_\lambda, \boldsymbol{s}_i$ are linearly independent. Then, for the $2 \cdot v^2 \times n$ matrix $(\boldsymbol{A} \cdot \boldsymbol{K} + \boldsymbol{S})$, we have $\mathsf{rank}(\boldsymbol{A} \cdot \boldsymbol{K} + \boldsymbol{S}) = \lambda + 1$.*

Proof. For the formal proof, we refer the reader to the full version of our paper.

Corollary 1. *Consider two $2 \cdot v^2 \times n$ matrices $(\boldsymbol{A} \cdot \boldsymbol{K} + \boldsymbol{S})$ and $(\boldsymbol{A} \cdot \boldsymbol{K} + \boldsymbol{Z})$, where the definitions of $\boldsymbol{A}, \boldsymbol{K}$ and $\boldsymbol{S}$ are in Lemma 4, and $\boldsymbol{Z}$ is a $2 \cdot v^2 \times n$ zero matrix. Let $v = \mathsf{poly}(\lambda) > \sqrt{\frac{\lambda}{2}}$ and $n \in \{\lambda + 1, 2 \cdot \lambda + 1\}$. Then the probability $Pr[\mathsf{rank}(\boldsymbol{A} \cdot \boldsymbol{K} + \boldsymbol{S}) = \lambda + 1] = \Pi_{i=0}^{\lambda}(1 - p^{i - 2 \cdot v^2})$, and the probability $Pr[\mathsf{rank}(\boldsymbol{A} \cdot \boldsymbol{K} + \boldsymbol{Z}) < \lambda + 1] = \Pi_{i=0}^{\lambda - 1}(1 - p^{i - 2 \cdot v^2})$ for the case that the vectors $\boldsymbol{a}_1, \ldots, \boldsymbol{a}_\lambda, \boldsymbol{s}_i$ are linearly independent.*

Proof. We again refer the reader to the full version of our paper for the detailed proof.

---

[3] For column vectors $\mathbf{s}_1, \mathbf{s}_2, \ldots, \mathbf{s}_n$, since $\mathbf{s}_1 = \mathbf{s}_2 = \cdots = \mathbf{s}_n$, $\mathbf{S} = [\mathbf{s}_1\ \mathbf{s}_1\ \ldots\ \mathbf{s}_1]$, where $\mathbf{s}_1 \xleftarrow{\$} \mathbb{Z}_p^{2 \cdot v^2}$.

Based on Lemma 4 and Corollary 1, we present the following theorems of breaking the privacy of AF-PVC$_{two}$ and AF-PVC$_{single}$.

Theorem 7. *The protocol AF-PVC$_{two}$ does not satisfy IND-COA privacy based on Definition 3 under the condition that the size of the message space p is a large prime (e.g., $p > 4 \cdot \lambda + 2$) and the matrix size $v > \sqrt{\lambda}$. Specifically, the advantage of an PPT adversary $\mathcal{A}$ for breaking the privacy of this protocol is close to $\frac{1}{2}$.*

Proof. According to Definition 3, for the experiment $\mathsf{Exp}_{\mathcal{A}}^{\text{ind-priv}^{\text{coa}}}[\text{AF-PVC}_{two}, \lambda]$, an PPT adversary $\mathcal{A}$ chooses two pairs of $v \times v$ matrices $(\mathbf{M}_{1(0)}, \mathbf{M}_{2(0)})$, $(\mathbf{M}_{1(1)}, \mathbf{M}_{2(1)})$. Specifically, $(\mathbf{M}_{1(0)}, \mathbf{M}_{2(0)}) \xleftarrow{\$} \mathbb{Z}_p^{v \times v} \times \mathbb{Z}_p^{v \times v}$, and $(\mathbf{M}_{1(1)}, \mathbf{M}_{2(1)})$ are two zero matrices. The challenge ciphertext is the matrix set U_b that comes from the second server (i.e., $U_b^{(2)}$). $\mathcal{A}$ flattens out each pair of matrices of U_b into a list of $2 \cdot v^2$ values to generate a $(2 \cdot \lambda + 1) \times 2 \cdot v^2$ matrix $\mathbf{E}_b$. $\mathbf{E}_b$ involves either all rows of the matrix $(\mathbf{A} \cdot \mathbf{K} + \mathbf{S})^T$ or all rows of the matrix $(\mathbf{A} \cdot \mathbf{K} + \mathbf{Z})^T$, where the descriptions of the transposes of these two matrices are in Corollary 1. For winning the experiment in Definition 3, $\mathcal{A}$ employs a PPT distinguisher $\mathcal{D}$ based on the proposed adversary's strategy as follows:

Distinguisher $\mathcal{D}$:

- For the case $\mathsf{rank}(\mathbf{E}_b) = 2 \cdot \lambda + 1$, $\mathcal{A}$ outputs $b' = 0$.
- For the case $\mathsf{rank}(\mathbf{E}_b) < 2 \cdot \lambda + 1$, $\mathcal{A}$ outputs $b' = 1$.

The positive integer $2 \cdot \lambda + 1$ is regarded as the threshold rank. If $\mathsf{Adv}_{\mathcal{A}}^{\text{ind-priv}^{\text{coa}}}$ (AF-PVC$_{two}$, λ) is non-negligible, then AF-PVC$_{two}$ is not IND-COA private. In what follows, we show this result by considering a large prime p (e.g., $p > 4 \cdot \lambda + 2$) and a matrix size $v > \sqrt{\lambda}$.

$$\begin{aligned}
&\Pr[\mathsf{Exp}_{\mathcal{A}}^{\text{ind-priv}^{\text{coa}}}[\text{AF-PVC}_{two}, \lambda] = 1] \\
&= \Pr[\mathbf{E}_b = \mathbf{E}_0 | \mathsf{rank}(\mathbf{E}_b) = 2 \cdot \lambda + 1] \cdot \Pr[\mathsf{rank}(\mathbf{E}_b) = 2 \cdot \lambda + 1] \\
&\quad + \Pr[\mathbf{E}_b = \mathbf{E}_1 | \mathsf{rank}(\mathbf{E}_b) < 2 \cdot \lambda + 1] \cdot \Pr[\mathsf{rank}(\mathbf{E}_b) < 2 \cdot \lambda + 1]
\end{aligned}$$

Specifically, from Corollary 1, we obtain

$$\begin{cases}
\Pr[\mathsf{rank}(\mathbf{E}_b) = 2 \cdot \lambda + 1 | \mathbf{E}_b = \mathbf{E}_0] = \prod_{i=0}^{\lambda} (1 - p^{i-2 \cdot v^2}) \cdot \prod_{i=0}^{2 \cdot \lambda} (1 - p^{i-2 \cdot v^2}) \\
\Pr[\mathsf{rank}(\mathbf{E}_b) < 2 \cdot \lambda + 1 | \mathbf{E}_b = \mathbf{E}_1] \geq \prod_{i=0}^{\lambda-1} (1 - p^{i-2 \cdot v^2})
\end{cases}$$

Thus, we have

$$\begin{aligned}
&\Pr[\mathsf{Exp}_{\mathcal{A}}^{\text{ind-priv}^{\text{coa}}}[\text{AF-PVC}_{two}, \lambda] = 1] \\
&\geq \frac{1}{2} \cdot \prod_{i=0}^{\lambda} (1 - p^{i-2 \cdot v^2}) \cdot \prod_{i=0}^{2 \cdot \lambda} (1 - p^{i-2 \cdot v^2}) + \frac{1}{2} \cdot \prod_{i=0}^{\lambda-1} (1 - p^{i-2 \cdot v^2}) \\
&= \frac{1}{2} \cdot \prod_{i=0}^{\lambda-1} (1 - p^{i-2 \cdot v^2}) \cdot ((1 - p^{\lambda-2 \cdot v^2}) \cdot \prod_{i=0}^{2 \cdot \lambda} (1 - p^{i-2 \cdot v^2}) + 1)
\end{aligned}$$

Since p is a large prime, as discussed earlier, we can obtain $\Pr[\mathsf{Exp}_{\mathcal{A}}^{\text{ind-priv}^{\text{coa}}}[\mathsf{AF\text{-}PVC}_{two}, \lambda] = 1] \approx 1$. This means that $\mathsf{Adv}_{\mathcal{A}}^{\text{ind-priv}^{\text{coa}}}$ $(\mathsf{AF\text{-}PVC}_{two}, \lambda) \approx \frac{1}{2} \nleq \mathsf{negl}(\lambda)$.

Theorem 8. *The protocol $\mathsf{AF\text{-}PVC}_{single}$ does not satisfy IND-COA privacy based on Definition 3 under the condition that the size of the message space p is a large prime (e.g., $p > 4 \cdot \lambda + 2$) and the matrix size $v > \sqrt{\frac{3 \cdot \lambda + 1}{2}}$. Specifically, the advantage of an PPT adversary $\mathcal{A}$ for breaking the privacy of this protocol is close to $\frac{1}{2}$.*

Proof. The proof follows a similar procedure to that for Theorem 7. For the experiment $\mathsf{Exp}_{\mathcal{A}}^{\text{ind-priv}^{\text{coa}}}[\mathsf{AF\text{-}PVC}_{single}, \lambda]$ in Definition 3, an PPT adversary $\mathcal{A}$ also chooses two pairs of $v \times v$ matrices $(\mathbf{M}_{1(0)}, \mathbf{M}_{2(0)})$ and $(\mathbf{M}_{1(1)}, \mathbf{M}_{2(1)})$, where $(\mathbf{M}_{1(0)}, \mathbf{M}_{2(0)}) \xleftarrow{\$} \mathbb{Z}_p^{v \times v} \times \mathbb{Z}_p^{v \times v}$, and $(\mathbf{M}_{1(1)}, \mathbf{M}_{2(1)})$ are two zero matrices. The challenge ciphertext is the matrix set U_b. $\mathcal{A}$ flattens out each pair of matrices of U_b into a list of $2 \cdot v^2$ values to generate a $(4 \cdot \lambda + 2) \times 2 \cdot v^2$ matrix $\mathbf{E}_b$. $\mathbf{E}_b$ includes either all rows of the matrix $(\mathbf{A} \cdot \mathbf{K} + \mathbf{S})^T$ or all rows of the matrix $(\mathbf{A} \cdot \mathbf{K} + \mathbf{Z})^T$. To win the experiment in Definition 3, $\mathcal{A}$ employs a PPT distinguisher $\widehat{\mathcal{D}}$ based on the proposed adversary's strategy as follows:

Distinguisher $\widehat{\mathcal{D}}$:

– For the case $\mathsf{rank}(\mathbf{E}_b) = 3 \cdot \lambda + 2$, $\mathcal{A}$ outputs $b' = 0$.
– For the case $\mathsf{rank}(\mathbf{E}_b) < 3 \cdot \lambda + 2$, $\mathcal{A}$ outputs $b' = 1$.

The positive integer $3 \cdot \lambda + 2$ is regarded as the threshold rank. If $\mathsf{Adv}_{\mathcal{A}}^{\text{ind-priv}^{\text{coa}}}$ $(\mathsf{AF\text{-}PVC}_{single}, \lambda)$ is non-negligible, then $\mathsf{AF\text{-}PVC}_{single}$ is not IND-COA private. In what follows, we show this result by considering a large prime p (e.g., $p > 4 \cdot \lambda + 2$) and a matrix size $v > \sqrt{\frac{3 \cdot \lambda + 1}{2}}$.

$$\Pr[\mathsf{Exp}_{\mathcal{A}}^{\text{ind-priv}^{\text{coa}}}[\mathsf{AF\text{-}PVC}_{single}, \lambda] = 1]$$
$$= \Pr[\mathbf{E}_b = \mathbf{E}_0 | \mathsf{rank}(\mathbf{E}_b) = 3 \cdot \lambda + 2] \cdot \Pr[\mathsf{rank}(\mathbf{E}_b) = 3 \cdot \lambda + 2]$$
$$+ \Pr[\mathbf{E}_b = \mathbf{E}_1 | \mathsf{rank}(\mathbf{E}_b) < 3 \cdot \lambda + 2] \cdot \Pr[\mathsf{rank}(\mathbf{E}_b) < 3 \cdot \lambda + 2]$$

Specifically, from Corollary 1, we have

$$\begin{cases} \Pr[\mathsf{rank}(\mathbf{E}_b) = 3 \cdot \lambda + 2 | \mathbf{E}_b = \mathbf{E}_0] = \prod_{i=0}^{\lambda}(1 - p^{i-2 \cdot v^2}) \cdot \prod_{i=0}^{3 \cdot \lambda + 1}(1 - p^{i-2 \cdot v^2}) \\ \Pr[\mathsf{rank}(\mathbf{E}_b) < 3 \cdot \lambda + 2 | \mathbf{E}_b = \mathbf{E}_1] \geq \prod_{i=0}^{\lambda - 1}(1 - p^{i-2 \cdot v^2}) \end{cases}.$$

Then, we can obtain

$$\Pr[\mathsf{Exp}_{\mathcal{A}}^{\text{ind-priv}^{\text{coa}}}[\mathsf{AF\text{-}PVC}_{single}, \lambda] = 1]$$
$$\geq \frac{1}{2} \cdot \prod_{i=0}^{\lambda}(1 - p^{i-2 \cdot v^2}) \cdot \prod_{i=0}^{3 \cdot \lambda + 1}(1 - p^{i-2 \cdot v^2}) + \frac{1}{2} \cdot \prod_{i=0}^{\lambda - 1}(1 - p^{i-2 \cdot v^2})$$
$$= \frac{1}{2} \cdot \prod_{i=0}^{\lambda - 1}(1 - p^{i-2 \cdot v^2}) \cdot ((1 - p^{\lambda - 2 \cdot v^2}) \cdot \prod_{i=0}^{3 \cdot \lambda + 1}(1 - p^{i-2 \cdot v^2}) + 1)$$

Since p is a large prime, as discussed earlier, the above success probability $\Pr[\mathsf{Exp}_{\mathcal{A}}^{\text{ind-priv}^{\text{coa}}}[\mathsf{AF\text{-}PVC}_{single}, \lambda] = 1] \approx 1$. This implies that the adversary's advantage $\mathsf{Adv}_{\mathcal{A}}^{\text{ind-priv}^{\text{coa}}}(\mathsf{AF\text{-}PVC}_{single}, \lambda) \approx \frac{1}{2} \not\leq \mathsf{negl}(\lambda)$.

3.4   Discussion

In order to make the readers fully understood our rank-based analyses, we present some concrete discussions below.

Parameters: The parameter choice is significant for our analyses of solving the decisional-SH problem and breaking the privacy of $\mathsf{AF\text{-}PVC}_{two}$ and $\mathsf{AF\text{-}PVC}_{single}$.

First, for the size of the message space p, it should be set as a large prime that is at least larger than λ, e.g., $p > 4 \cdot \lambda + 2$. On the one hand, as shown in Sect. 3.1, if p is large enough, with high probability, the vectors from an uniformly random matrix are linearly independent. This is necessary for our analyses. On the other hand, if a client wants to outsource the multiplication of some matrix pair $(\mathbf{M}_1, \mathbf{M}_2) \in \mathbb{Z}_p^{v \times v} \times \mathbb{Z}_p^{v \times v}$ to a powerful server, then the message space of each element in these two matrices should be large, which makes the client hard to run the expensive computation. Otherwise, there is no need to do the outsourcing, and the client can carry out the computation locally. This means that the decisional-SH problem and the feasible protocols $\mathsf{AF\text{-}PVC}_{two}$ and $\mathsf{AF\text{-}PVC}_{single}$ with a suitable large parameter p are the targets of our analyses.

Second, for the matrix size v (resp. the matrix size m involved in the decisional-SH problem), it should satisfy $v > \sqrt{\lambda}$ (see Theorem 7) or $v > \sqrt{\frac{3 \cdot \lambda + 1}{2}}$ (see Theorem 8) (resp. $m > 2 \cdot \lambda$ or $m > 2 \cdot \lambda + e + 1$ for $e \in \mathbb{N}_+$ (see Theorem 6)[4]). On the one hand, for an $n \times 2 \cdot v^2$ (resp. $n \times m$) matrix, where $n \in \{2 \cdot \lambda + 1, 4 \cdot \lambda + 2$ (resp. $2 \cdot \lambda + 2 \cdot e + 2)\}$, since the rank of the matrix is dependent on $\min(n, 2 \cdot v^2$ (resp. $m))$, if v (resp. m) does not satisfy the above condition, the rank-based adversary's strategy no longer has any effect. This means that our analyses cannot solve the decisional-SH problem and break the privacy of $\mathsf{AF\text{-}PVC}_{two}$ and $\mathsf{AF\text{-}PVC}_{single}$. On the other hand, if a client wants to outsource the multiplication of some matrix pair to a powerful server, a key requirement is that these two matrices should be large-scale, which makes the outsourcing practical. If the matrix size does not satisfy the above condition, e.g., $v \leq \sqrt{\lambda}$, the amount of work performed by the client for the outsourcing may be not substantially cheaper than performing the computation on its own. This implies that the outsourcing may be impractical. Therefore, this demonstrates that our analyses focus on the meaningful decisional-SH problem and protocols $\mathsf{AF\text{-}PVC}_{two}$ and $\mathsf{AF\text{-}PVC}_{single}$.

Adversary's Cost: The cost of our analyses is generated by computing the rank of a matrix. We can employ any existing algorithm for obtaining the rank of a matrix. In general, for a matrix from $\mathbb{Z}_p^{n \times m}$ with rank $z \leq \min(n, m)$, using Gaussian elimination, we may compute the rank of the matrix in $O(z \cdot n \cdot m)$

---

[4] $2 \cdot v^2$ is equivalent to m.

field operations and storage of $n \cdot m$ field elements [17]. Of course, the rank of a matrix can be computed probabilistically by invoking the blackbox approaches, e.g., the Wiedemann method [10,18]. More concretely, if our analyses employ the blackbox method, for a matrix from $\mathbb{Z}_p^{(2 \cdot \lambda + 1) \times (2 \cdot \lambda + 1)}$ with rank $2 \cdot \lambda$, we need to take $\tilde{O}(2 \cdot \lambda \cdot (2 \cdot \lambda + 1)^2)$ time and use $\tilde{O}(2 \cdot \lambda + 1)$ storage to obtain the rank of this matrix, where we employ the "$soft - Oh$" (i.e., $\tilde{O}$) notation to suppress log factors.

4   Experimental Verifications

In order to give the reader a glance at the practical results of our analyses for solving the decisional-SH problem and breaking the privacy of AF-PVC$_{two}$ and AF-PVC$_{single}$. We implemented our analyses in Sect. 3 and reported the adversary's advantages and costs.

4.1   Setup

Hardware and Software: We conducted the real example experiments on a Lenovo ThinkStation (Intel(R) Xeon(R) E5-2620, 24 hyperthreaded cores at 2.00 GHz, 8 GB RAM at 2.00 GHz), on Windows (Windows 7, x64_64). Our implementations are single-threaded. We used the NTL library [1] version 10.5.0 for the field operations over $\mathbb{Z}_p$ and the matrix operations.

Parameters Choice: In our implementations we covered $\lambda = 80, 128, 192$ and 256 privacy. These selections lead to the parameters in Table 1, where $e = \lambda, n \in \{2 \cdot \lambda + 1, 2 \cdot \lambda + 2 \cdot e + 2\}$, $m \in \{2 \cdot \lambda + 1, 3 \cdot \lambda + 1\}$ for $n = 2 \cdot \lambda + 1$ and $m \in \{3 \cdot \lambda + 1, 4 \cdot \lambda + 2\}$ for $n = 2 \cdot \lambda + 2 \cdot e + 2, p > 4 \cdot \lambda + 2$, $v = \lceil \sqrt{\lambda} + 1 \rceil$ for $n = 2 \cdot \lambda + 1$ and $v = \lceil \sqrt{\frac{3 \cdot \lambda + 1}{2}} + 1 \rceil$ for $n = 2 \cdot \lambda + 2 \cdot e + 2^5$, and $h = \lambda$.

Table 1. The used parameters for our analyses

λ	e	n	m	v	p	h
80	N/A	161	161, 241	10	353, 401	80
	80	322	241, 322	12		
128	N/A	257	257, 385	13	631, 701	128
	128	514	385, 514	15		
192	N/A	385	385, 577	15	809, 907	192
	192	770	577, 770	18		
256	N/A	513	513, 769	17	1069, 1187	256
	256	1026	769, 1026	21		

---

[5] $n = 4 \cdot \lambda + 2$.

4.2   Results and Timings

The experimental results are presented in Tables 2, 3, 4 and 5. Specifically, the adversary's advantages and timings for solving the decisional-WSH problem and decisional-SSH problem are shown in Tables 2 and 3, and the adversary's advantages and timings for breaking the privacy of AF-PVC$_{two}$ and AF-PVC$_{single}$ are reported in Tables 4 and 5. To obtain these results, we compute the advantages that the adversaries answer correctly in the whole experiment process (i.e., 200 experiments). Note that, for each experiment of solving the decisional-WSH problem (resp. the decisional-SSH problem), a fresh sample from either the distribution $\chi(p)^{n \times m}$ or the uniform distribution over $\mathbb{Z}_p^{n \times m}$ is used for the guess. For each experiment of breaking the privacy of AF-PVC$_{two}$ (resp. AF-PVC$_{single}$), a fresh key sk used by AF-PVC$_{two}$ (resp. AF-PVC$_{single}$) is generated to complete the matrix masking. Moreover, for each timing in the tables, the value is the average value over 200 experiments.

Table 2. Results on the decisional-WSH problem

(n, m, p)	$\mathsf{Adv}_{\mathcal{A}, \mathrm{WSH}}(p, n, m)$	Timing (second)
$(161, 161, 353)$	0.495	0.725
$(161, 241, 353)$	0.495	0.998
$(161, 161, 401)$	0.500	0.723
$(161, 241, 401)$	0.500	0.997
$(257, 257, 631)$	0.500	2.843
$(257, 385, 631)$	0.500	4.646
$(257, 257, 701)$	0.495	2.832
$(257, 385, 701)$	0.500	4.633
$(385, 385, 809)$	0.500	9.304
$(385, 577, 809)$	0.500	15.253
$(385, 385, 907)$	0.500	9.284
$(385, 577, 907)$	0.500	15.137
$(513, 513, 1069)$	0.500	21.558
$(513, 769, 1069)$	0.500	35.944
$(513, 513, 1187)$	0.500	21.629
$(513, 769, 1187)$	0.500	35.997

As reported in Tables 2, 4 and 5, all the experimental results about the adversary's advantage are in accord with the analyses of Theorems 6, 7 and 8, and demonstrate that there exists a PPT adversary algorithm that (almost) always succeeds in guessing the distribution of a given sample or the bit b in the eavesdropping indistinguishability experiment (see Definition 3). For the results in

Table 3. Results on the decisional-SSH problem

(n, m, p)	$\mathsf{Adv}_{\mathcal{A},\mathrm{SSH}}(p, n, m)$	Timing (second)
(322, 241, 353)	0.005	2.543
(322, 322, 353)	0.500	3.843
(322, 241, 401)	0.010	4.447
(322, 322, 401)	0.495	3.746
(514, 385, 631)	0.030	9.610
(514, 514, 631)	0.500	15.348
(514, 385, 701)	0.050	9.476
(514, 514, 701)	0.495	14.253
(770, 577, 809)	0.025	30.900
(770, 770, 809)	0.495	46.268
(770, 577, 907)	0.040	30.098
(770, 770, 907)	0.500	46.374
(1026, 769, 1069)	0.040	71.009
(1026, 1026, 1069)	0.500	109.091
(1026, 769, 1187)	0.020	71.436
(1026, 1026, 1187)	0.500	108.871

Table 4. Results on AF-PVC$_{two}$

(n, v, p)	$\mathsf{Adv}_{\mathcal{A}}^{\mathrm{ind\text{-}priv}^{\mathrm{coa}}}(\text{AF-PVC}_{two}, \lambda)$	Timing (second)
(161, 10, 353)	0.500	0.854
(161, 10, 401)	0.495	0.849
(257, 13, 631)	0.500	3.549
(257, 13, 701)	0.500	3.648
(385, 15, 809)	0.500	11.064
(385, 15, 907)	0.500	10.336
(513, 17, 1069)	0.500	23.037
(513, 17, 1187)	0.500	22.666

Table 3, when $n = m$, the adversary's advantages validate the analysis in Theorem 6, which is based on the fact that $m > 3 \cdot \lambda + 1$. However, when $n > m$, the adversary's advantages are close to 0. This is because the rank of a given matrix from one of those two distributions is dependent on m if $m \leq 3 \cdot \lambda + 1$. Then, in this case, the proposed rank-based strategy is invalid for distinguishing the SSH distribution from the uniform distribution over $\mathbb{Z}_p^{n \times m}$, and the adversary must guess randomly.

Moreover, the timings of all the example experiments in Tables 2, 3, 4 and 5 show that our rank-based analyses for solving the decisional-SH problem and

Table 5. Results on AF-PVC$_{single}$

(n, v, p)	$\mathsf{Adv}_{\mathcal{A}}^{\text{ind-priv}^{\text{coa}}}(\text{AF-PVC}_{single}, \lambda)$	Timing (second)
$(322, 12, 353)$	0.500	2.976
$(322, 12, 401)$	0.500	3.026
$(514, 15, 631)$	0.500	11.499
$(514, 15, 701)$	0.500	11.509
$(770, 18, 809)$	0.500	36.407
$(770, 18, 907)$	0.500	34.566
$(1026, 21, 1069)$	0.500	82.436
$(1026, 21, 1187)$	0.500	83.199

breaking the privacy of AF-PVC$_{two}$ and AF-PVC$_{single}$ are really efficient. Specifically, for some small matrix sizes (e.g., $(n, m) = (161, 161)$ in Table 2), our analyses take less than a second.

5   Conclusions

In this paper, we propose an efficient analysis method for solving the decisional-WSH problem and decisional-SSH problem introduced by Atallah and Frikken [2]. Specifically, the strategy of our analysis takes advantage of the rank distribution of the matrix to distinguish between the samples from the WSH distribution (resp. the SSH distribution) $\chi(p)^{n \times m}$ and the samples from the uniform distribution over $\mathbb{Z}_p^{n \times m}$. The adversary's advantage of our analysis on a wide range of parameters is close to 0.5. Moreover, we employ a similar approach to break the privacy of AF-PVC$_{two}$ and AF-PVC$_{single}$. The analysis results show that both protocols are not IND-COA private.

Solving the Search Variant of the SH Problem? Our rank-based analysis can break the decisional-WSH assumption and decisional-SSH assumption, but this does not implies that we can also break the search versions efficiently. Actually, for breaking the search-WSH assumption and search-SSH assumption, our rank-based analysis may be regarded as a preprocessing step. To check whether a row of a matrix sampled from $\chi(p)^{n \times m}$ is a row vector from $\mathbf{d}_1, \ldots, \mathbf{d}_\ell$ or from $\mathbf{u}_1, \ldots, \mathbf{u}_\tau$, the adversary first replaces the row that needs to be tested by a row vector chosen from $\mathbb{Z}_p^m$ uniformly at random, and then computes the rank of the matrix where the tested row has been replaced. According to our analysis in Sect. 3.2, if the obtained rank increases (compared with the rank of the matrix sampled from $\chi(p)^{n \times m}$), this implies that the tested row is from the row vectors $\mathbf{d}_1, \ldots, \mathbf{d}_\ell$. The above procedure can be run at most $n - 1$ times (with overwhelming probability) to reveals all the vectors $\mathbf{d}_1, \ldots, \mathbf{d}_\ell$. However, this result is not equivalent to finding $k_1, \ldots, k_\ell$ (or $\mathbf{A}$). Therefore, how to break the search variant of the SH assumption efficiently is an interesting open problem.

Acknowledgements. The author would like to thank the anonymous reviewers of CT-RSA 2019 for providing their helpful comments. This work was supported in part by the National Natural Science Foundation of China under Grant 61302161, in part by the Doctoral Fund, Ministry of Education, China, under Grant 20130181120076.

References

1. NTL 10.5.0 (2017). http://www.shoup.net/ntl/
2. Atallah, M.J., Frikken, K.B.: Securely outsourcing linear algebra computations. In: ASIACCS (2010)
3. Benjamin, D., Atallah, M.J.: Private and cheating-free outsourcing of algebraic computations. In: PST (2008)
4. Choi, S.G., Katz, J., Kumaresan, R., Cid, C.: Multi-client non-interactive verifiable computation. In: Sahai, A. (ed.) TCC 2013. LNCS, vol. 7785, pp. 499–518. Springer, Heidelberg (2013). https://doi.org/10.1007/978-3-642-36594-2_28
5. Chung, K.-M., Kalai, Y., Vadhan, S.: Improved delegation of computation using fully homomorphic encryption. In: Rabin, T. (ed.) CRYPTO 2010. LNCS, vol. 6223, pp. 483–501. Springer, Heidelberg (2010). https://doi.org/10.1007/978-3-642-14623-7_26
6. Fiore, D., Gennaro, R., Pastro, V.: Efficiently verifiable computation on encrypted data. In: CCS (2014)
7. Goldreich, O.: Foundations of Cryptography: Volume I Basic Tools. Cambridge University Press, Cambridge (2001)
8. Gennaro, R., Gentry, C., Parno, B.: Non-interactive verifiable computing: outsourcing computation to untrusted workers. In: Rabin, T. (ed.) CRYPTO 2010. LNCS, vol. 6223, pp. 465–482. Springer, Heidelberg (2010). https://doi.org/10.1007/978-3-642-14623-7_25
9. Gordon, S.D., Katz, J., Liu, F.-H., Shi, E., Zhou, H.-S.: Multi-client verifiable computation with stronger security guarantees. In: Dodis, Y., Nielsen, J.B. (eds.) TCC 2015. LNCS, vol. 9015, pp. 144–168. Springer, Heidelberg (2015). https://doi.org/10.1007/978-3-662-46497-7_6
10. Kaltofen, E., David Saunders, B.: On Wiedemann's method of solving sparse linear systems. In: Mattson, H.F., Mora, T., Rao, T.R.N. (eds.) AAECC 1991. LNCS, vol. 539, pp. 29–38. Springer, Heidelberg (1991). https://doi.org/10.1007/3-540-54522-0_93
11. Katti, R.S., Srinivasan, S.K., Vosoughi, A.: On the security of randomized arithmetic codes against ciphertext-only attacks. IEEE Trans. Inf. Forensics Secur. **6**(1), 19–27 (2011)
12. Laud, P., Pankova, A.: On the (im)possibility of privately outsourcing linear programming. In: CCSW (2013)
13. Linial, N., Weitz, D.: Random vectors of bounded weight and their linear dependencies (2000). http://www.drorweitz.com/ac/pubs/rand_mat.pdf
14. Shamir, A.: How to share a secret. Commun. ACM **22**(11), 612–613 (1979)
15. Salinas, S., Luo, C., Chen, X., Li, P.: Efficient secure outsourcing of large-scale linear systems of equations. In: INFOCOM (2015)
16. Salinas, S., Luo, C., Liao, W., Li, P.: Efficient secure outsourcing of large-scale quadratic programs. In: ASIACCS (2016)
17. Saunders, B.D., Youse, B.S.: Large matrix, small rank. In: ISSAC (2009)
18. Wiedemann, D.H.: Solving sparse linear equations over finite fields. IEEE Trans. Inf. Theory **32**(1), 54–62 (1986)

Delegatable Anonymous Credentials from Mercurial Signatures

Elizabeth C. Crites[✉] and Anna Lysyanskaya[✉]

Brown University, Providence, RI 02912, USA
{elizabeth_crites,anna_lysyanskaya}@brown.edu

Abstract. In a delegatable anonymous credential system, participants may use their credentials anonymously as well as anonymously delegate them to other participants. Such systems are more usable than traditional anonymous credential systems because a popular credential issuer can delegate some of its responsibilities without compromising users' privacy. They also provide stronger privacy guarantees than traditional anonymous credential systems because the identities of credential issuers are hidden. The identity of a credential issuer may convey information about a user's identity even when all other information about the user is concealed.

The only previously known constructions of delegatable anonymous credentials were prohibitively inefficient. They were based on non-interactive zero-knowledge (NIZK) proofs. In this paper, we provide a simple construction of delegatable anonymous credentials and prove its security in the generic group model. Our construction is direct, not based on NIZK proofs, and is therefore considerably more efficient. In fact, in our construction, only five group elements are needed per link to represent an anonymous credential chain.

Our main building block is a new type of signature scheme, a *mercurial signature*, which allows a signature σ on a message M under public key pk to be transformed into a signature σ' on an equivalent but unlinkable message M' under an equivalent but unlinkable public key pk'.

Keywords: Anonymous credentials · Signature schemes · Generic group model

1 Introduction

Anonymous Credentials. Anonymous credentials allow a user to prove possession of a set of credentials, issued by some trusted issuer or issuers, that allow access to a resource. What makes them *anonymous* is the fact that the user's proof is zero-knowledge and credentials can be obtained anonymously: an issuer need not know the user's identity in order to issue a credential.

Supported by NSF grant 1422361.

As a result of decades of research, there are anonymous credential systems that are provably secure and efficient enough for practical use [Cha86,LRSW99, CL01,Lys02,CL04,CKL+14,CDHK15]. These results have attracted wide attention beyond the cryptographic community: they have been implemented by industry leaders such as IBM, incorporated into industrial standards (such as the TCG standard), and underpinned government policy.

And yet traditional anonymous credentials *do not in fact protect users' privacy*. The traditional anonymous credential model assumes that the verifying party, such as an access provider, knows the public key of the credential issuer. This can reveal a lot of information about a user. In the US, for example, the identity of the issuer of a user's driver's license (the local DMV) might reveal the user's zip code. If, in addition, the user's date of birth and gender are leaked (as could happen in the context of a medical form), this is enough to uniquely identify the user the majority of the time [Swe97]. To remedy this, a user could prove possession of a credential from one issuer in a long list instead of from a particular issuer (local DMV), but this solution is undesirable for two reasons: (1) it incurs a significant slowdown, proportional to the number of potential issuers, and (2) it requires the user herself to know who the issuer is.

Delegatable Anonymous Credentials. A more promising approach is to use delegatable anonymous credentials [CL06,BCC+09]. First, a non-anonymous delegatable credential scheme can be constructed as follows. A certification chain is rooted at some authority and ends at the public key of the user in question, who then needs to demonstrate that she knows the corresponding secret key to prove that she is authorized. The simplest case, when the trusted authority issues certificates *directly* to each user (so each certification chain is of length 1), is inconvenient because it requires the authority to do too much work. A system in which the authority delegates responsibility to other entities is more convenient: an entity with a certification chain of length ℓ can issue certification chains of length $\ell + 1$. A conventional signature scheme immediately allows delegatable credentials: Alice, who has a public signing key pk_A and a certification chain of length ℓ, can sign Bob's public key pk_B, giving Bob a chain of length $\ell + 1$.

Delegatable anonymous credentials allow users to enjoy much more privacy. Even the users themselves do not know the actual identities of the links on their certification chains. They only know what they need to know. For example, consider a discount program for senior citizens. An online shopper proves that she is eligible for the discount by presenting a level-3 credential from the government administering the program as follows. Government official Alice receives a credential directly from the government. She gives a credential to a local grocer, Bob, who does not need to know who she is or to whom she has issued credentials. Bob's job is to issue credentials to his customers who are senior citizens and he gives such a credential to Carol. Carol need not know who Bob is, who gave him the credential, or who else received credentials from him. Now Carol can use her credential to shop online with a discount. Her credential does not reveal the identity of anyone on her credential chain. Thus, even if Bob issues a discount credential to no other customer, Carol's anonymity is still preserved.

Delegatable anonymous credentials (DACs) were first proposed by Chase and Lysyanskaya [CL06], who gave a proof of concept construction based on non-interactive zero-knowledge (NIZK) proof systems for NP. Their construction incurred a blow-up that was exponential in L, the length of the certification chain. Even for constant L it was not meant for use in practice. Belenkiy et al. [BCC+09] showed that, given a commitment scheme and a signature scheme that "play nicely" with randomizable NIZK (which they defined and realized), DACs with only linear dependency on L could be achieved. They also showed that their approach could be instantiated using Groth-Sahai commitments and an NIZK proof system [GS08]. Although this was a significant efficiency improvement over previous work, the resulting scheme's use of heavy machinery, such as the Groth-Sahai proof system, rendered it unsuitable for use in practice. (A back-of-the-envelope calculation shows that several hundred group elements would be required to represent a certification chain of length two.) Chase et al. [CKLM13] gave a conceptually novel construction of DACs that relied on controlled-malleable signatures and achieved stronger security; however, their instantiation of controlled-malleable signatures still required Groth-Sahai proofs, so the resulting construction was essentially as inefficient as that of Belenkiy et al. A recent paper by Camenisch et al. [CDD17] suggests a solution in which one can indeed prove possession of a credential chain in a privacy-preserving manner, but one cannot obtain credentials anonymously.

Our Contribution. We provide a simple and efficient construction of delegatable anonymous credentials. Our construction does not rely on heavy machinery such as NIZK proofs; it relies on bilinear groups, where only five group elements per level of delegation are needed to represent a credential chain. (If Alice obtains a credential from the certification authority and delegates it to Bob, who in turn delegates it to Carol, Carol's credential chain can be represented using fifteen group elements.) Our construction is provably secure in the generic group model. We also give what we believe to be a simpler definition of DACs.

Our Approach. The main building block of our construction is a new type of signature scheme, which we call a *mercurial* signature scheme[1]. Given a mercurial signature σ on a message M under public key pk, one can, without knowing the secret key sk, transform it into a new signature σ' on an equivalent message M' under an equivalent public key pk', for some equivalence relations on messages and public keys. Moreover, for an appropriate choice of message space and public key space, this can be done in such a way that the new M' cannot be linked to the original M, and the new public key pk' cannot be linked to pk.

The approach to constructing DACs from mercurial signatures is as follows. Suppose that the certification authority (CA) with public key pk_0 has issued a credential to Alice, whose pseudonym is some public key pk_A. Alice's certification

---

[1] No relationship to mercurial commitments [CHK+05].

chain (of length 1) will have the form $(\mathsf{pk}_A, \sigma_A)$, where σ_A is the CA's signature on pk_A. Alice interacts with Bob, who knows her under a different public key, pk_A'. The public keys pk_A and pk_A' are equivalent—they both belong to Alice and have the same underlying secret key—but Bob cannot link them. Mercurial signatures allow her to translate σ_A into σ_A', which is the CA's signature on her pk_A'. Alice delegates her credential to Bob, after which Bob's certification chain has the form $((\mathsf{pk}_A', \mathsf{pk}_B), (\sigma_A', \sigma_B))$, where pk_B is the pseudonym under which Bob is known to Alice, and σ_B is the signature on pk_B under the public key pk_A'. Now suppose that Bob wants to delegate to Carol, who is known to him under the pseudonym pk_C. He first uses the properties of the mercurial signature scheme in order to make his credential chain unrecognizable. He transforms pk_A' into an equivalent pk_A'' and pk_B into an equivalent pk_B', taking care to also transform the signatures appropriately. Finally, he signs pk_C under pk_B'.

Our mercurial signatures were inspired by the paper of Fuchsbauer, Hanser and Slamanig [FHS14] on structure-preserving signatures on equivalence classes (SPS-EQ). SPS-EQ does not include the feature of transforming a public key into an equivalent one; this is new with our mercurial signatures. It does introduce the property that a signature on a message M can be transformed into one on an equivalent message M', where M' cannot be linked to M. It also presents a construction of SPS-EQ that is secure in the generic group model. Our construction of mercurial signatures is adapted from theirs, but our notion of security requires that the adapted construction is still unforgeable even when the forger is given the added freedom to modify the public key. In addition, it requires that we prove pk_A and pk_A' are unlinkable even when given signatures under these keys. A recent, independent work by Backes et al. [BHKS18] considers signatures with flexible public keys but not flexible messages.

Open Problems. Our paper leaves open the question of how to construct efficient DACs with desirable features that have been explored in the context of anonymous credentials, such as credential attributes (e.g. expiration dates), revocation, identity escrow and conditional anonymity.

2   Definition of Mercurial Signatures

For a relation $\mathcal{R}$ over strings, let $[x]_{\mathcal{R}} = \{y \mid \mathcal{R}(x, y)\}$. If $\mathcal{R}$ is an equivalence relation, then $[x]_{\mathcal{R}}$ denotes the equivalence class of which x is a representative. We say (somewhat loosely) that a relation $\mathcal{R}$ is *parameterized* if it is well-defined as long as some other parameters are well-defined. For example, if $\mathbb{G}$ is a cyclic group with generators g and h, then the decisional Diffie-Hellman (DDH) relation $\mathcal{R} = \{(x, y) \mid \exists \alpha \text{ such that } x = g^{\alpha} \wedge y = h^{\alpha}\}$ is parameterized by $\mathbb{G}$, g, and h and is well-defined as long as $\mathbb{G}$, g, and h are well-defined.

Definition 1 (Mercurial signature). *A mercurial signature scheme for parameterized equivalence relations $\mathcal{R}_M$, $\mathcal{R}_{\mathsf{pk}}$, $\mathcal{R}_{\mathsf{sk}}$ is a tuple of the following polynomial-time algorithms, which are deterministic algorithms unless otherwise stated:*

PPGen(1^k) → PP: On input the security parameter 1^k, this probabilistic algorithm outputs the public parameters PP. This includes parameters for the
parameterized equivalence relations $\mathcal{R}_M$, $\mathcal{R}_{pk}$, $\mathcal{R}_{sk}$ so they are well-defined.
It also includes parameters for the algorithms sample$_\rho$ and sample$_\mu$, which
sample key and message converters, respectively.

KeyGen(PP, ℓ) → (pk, sk): On input the public parameters PP and a length
parameter ℓ, this probabilistic algorithm outputs a key pair (pk, sk). The
message space $\mathcal{M}$ is well-defined from PP and ℓ. This algorithm also
defines a correspondence between public and secret keys: we write (pk, sk) ∈
KeyGen(PP, ℓ) if there exists a set of random choices that KeyGen could make
that would result in (pk, sk) as the output.

Sign(sk, M) → σ: On input the signing key sk and a message $M \in \mathcal{M}$, this
probabilistic algorithm outputs a signature σ.

Verify(pk, M, σ) → 0/1: On input the public key pk, a message $M \in \mathcal{M}$, and a
purported signature σ, output 0 or 1.

ConvertSK(sk, ρ) → s̃k: On input sk and a key converter $\rho \in$ sample$_\rho$, output a
new secret key s̃k ∈ $[sk]_{\mathcal{R}_{sk}}$.

ConvertPK(pk, ρ) → p̃k: On input pk and a key converter $\rho \in$ sample$_\rho$, output
a new public key p̃k ∈ $[pk]_{\mathcal{R}_{pk}}$. (Correctness of this operation, defined below,
will guarantee that if pk corresponds to sk, then p̃k corresponds to s̃k =
ConvertSK(sk, ρ).)

ConvertSig(pk, M, σ, ρ) → σ̃: On input pk, a message $M \in \mathcal{M}$, a signature σ,
and key converter $\rho \in$ sample$_\rho$, this probabilistic algorithm returns a new
signature σ̃. (Correctness of this will require that whenever Verify(pk, M, σ) =
1, it will also be the case that Verify(p̃k, M, σ̃) = 1.)

ChangeRep(pk, M, σ, μ) → (M', σ'): On input pk, a message $M \in \mathcal{M}$, a signature σ, and a message converter $\mu \in$ sample$_\mu$, this probabilistic algorithm
computes a new message $M' \in [M]_{\mathcal{R}_M}$ and a new signature σ' and outputs (M', σ'). (Correctness of this will require that Verify(pk, M, σ) = 1 ⇒
Verify(pk, M', σ') = 1.)

Similar to a standard cryptographic signature [GMR88], a mercurial signature
must be correct and unforgeable.

Definition 2 (Correctness). *A mercurial signature scheme* (PPGen, KeyGen,
Sign, Verify, ConvertSK, ConvertPK, ConvertSig, ChangeRep) *for parameterized
equivalence relations* $\mathcal{R}_M$, $\mathcal{R}_{pk}$, $\mathcal{R}_{sk}$ *is correct if it satisfies the following conditions for all k, for all $PP \in$ PPGen(1^k), for all $\ell > 1$, for all* (pk, sk) ∈
KeyGen(PP, ℓ):

Verification. For all $M \in \mathcal{M}$, for all $\sigma \in$ Sign(sk, M), Verify(pk, M, σ) = 1.

Key conversion. For all $\rho \in$ sample$_\rho$, (ConvertPK(pk, ρ), ConvertSK(sk, ρ))
∈ KeyGen(PP, ℓ). Moreover, ConvertSK(sk, ρ) ∈ $[sk]_{\mathcal{R}_{sk}}$ and ConvertPK(pk, ρ)
∈ $[pk]_{\mathcal{R}_{pk}}$.

Signature conversion. For all $M \in \mathcal{M}$, for all σ such that Verify(pk, M, σ)
= 1, for all $\rho \in$ sample$_\rho$, for all σ̃ ∈ ConvertSig(pk, M, σ, ρ), Verify(ConvertPK
(pk, ρ), M, σ̃) = 1.

Change of message representative. For all $M \in \mathcal{M}$, for all σ such that Verify(pk, M, σ) = 1, for all $\mu \in$ sample$_\mu$, Verify(pk, M', σ') = 1, where $(M', \sigma') =$ ChangeRep(pk, M, σ, μ). Moreover, $M' \in [M]_{\mathcal{R}_M}$.

Let us discuss the intuition for the correctness property. Correct verification is simply the standard correctness property for signature schemes. Correct key conversion means that if the same key converter ρ is applied to a valid key pair (pk, sk), the result is a new valid key pair ($\tilde{\text{pk}}, \tilde{\text{sk}}$) from the same pair of equivalence classes. Correct signature conversion means that if the same key converter ρ is applied to a public key pk to obtain $\tilde{\text{pk}}$ and to a valid signature σ on a message M to obtain $\tilde{\sigma}$, then the new signature $\tilde{\sigma}$ is a valid signature on the same message M under the new public key $\tilde{\text{pk}}$. Finally, correct change of message representative ensures that if a message converter μ is applied to a valid message-signature pair (M, σ), the result is a new valid message-signature pair (M', σ'), where the new message M' is in the same equivalence class as M.

Definition 3 (Unforgeability). *A mercurial signature scheme* (PPGen, KeyGen, Sign, Verify, ConvertSK, ConvertPK, ConvertSig, ChangeRep) *for parameterized equivalence relations* $\mathcal{R}_M$, $\mathcal{R}_{\text{pk}}$, $\mathcal{R}_{\text{sk}}$ *is unforgeable if for all polynomial-length parameters* $\ell(k)$ *and all probabilistic, polynomial-time (PPT) algorithms* $\mathcal{A}$ *having access to a signing oracle, there exists a negligible function* ν *such that:*

$$\Pr[PP \leftarrow \text{PPGen}(1^k); (\text{pk}, \text{sk}) \leftarrow \text{KeyGen}(PP, \ell(k)); (Q, \text{pk}^*, M^*, \sigma^*) \leftarrow$$
$$\mathcal{A}^{\text{Sign}(\text{sk}, \cdot)}(\text{pk}) : \forall M \in Q, [M^*]_{\mathcal{R}_M} \neq [M]_{\mathcal{R}_M} \wedge [\text{pk}^*]_{\mathcal{R}_{\text{pk}}} = [\text{pk}]_{\mathcal{R}_{\text{pk}}}$$
$$\wedge \text{Verify}(\text{pk}^*, M^*, \sigma^*) = 1] \leq \nu(k)$$

where Q *is the set of queries that* $\mathcal{A}$ *has issued to the signing oracle.*

The unforgeability property here is similar to existential unforgeability (EUF-CMA) for signature schemes, except the adversary's winning condition is somewhat altered. As in the EUF-CMA game, the adversary is given the public key pk and is allowed to issue signature queries to the oracle that knows the corresponding secret key sk. Eventually, the adversary outputs a public key pk*, a message M^*, and a purported signature σ^*. Unlike the EUF-CMA game, the adversary has the freedom to output a forgery under a different public key pk*, as long as pk* is in the same equivalence class as pk. This seemingly makes the adversary's task easier. At the same time, the adversary's forgery is not valid if the message M^* is in the same equivalence class as a previously queried message, making the adversary's task harder. We can more formally relate our definitions to the standard definitions of existential unforgeability and correctness for signature schemes as follows. Suppose the relations $\mathcal{R}_M$, $\mathcal{R}_{\text{pk}}$, $\mathcal{R}_{\text{sk}}$ are equality relations (i.e. $(a, b) \in \mathcal{R} \Leftrightarrow a = b$). Let ConvertSK, ConvertPK, ConvertSig, ChangeRep be algorithms that do nothing but simply output their input sk, pk, $\sigma, (M, \sigma)$, respectively. Then, it is easy to see that (PPGen, KeyGen, Sign, Verify) is a correct and existentially unforgeable signature scheme if and only if the mercurial signature scheme (PPGen, KeyGen, Sign, Verify, ConvertSK, ConvertPK, ConvertSig, ChangeRep) for $\mathcal{R}_M$, $\mathcal{R}_{\text{pk}}$, $\mathcal{R}_{\text{sk}}$ is correct and unforgeable.

If one disregards insignificant differences in input-output specification and the emphasis on structure-preserving properties (not important for the security definition), our mercurial signatures are a generalization of Fuchsbauer, Hanser and Slamanig's [FHS14] structure-preserving signatures on equivalence classes (SPS-EQ) and in fact were inspired by signatures on equivalence classes in that paper. In an SPS-EQ signature for an equivalence relation $\mathcal{R}_M$, the ChangeRep algorithm is present, but there are no ConvertSK, ConvertPK, ConvertSig algorithms. The correctness requirement boils down to our correct verification and correct change of message representative requirements. Unforgeability of SPS-EQ is similar to unforgeability of mercurial signatures, except that $\mathcal{A}$ does not have the freedom to pick a different public key pk^*; the forgery must verify under the original public key pk. We can more formally relate our definitions to the definitions of existential unforgeability and correctness for signatures on equivalence classes as follows. Suppose the relations $\mathcal{R}_{\mathsf{pk}}$ and $\mathcal{R}_{\mathsf{sk}}$ are equality relations. Let ConvertSK, ConvertPK, ConvertSig be algorithms that do nothing but simply output their input $\mathsf{sk}, \mathsf{pk}, \sigma$, respectively. Then, (PPGen, KeyGen, Sign, Verify, ChangeRep) is a correct and unforgeable signature scheme for the equivalence relation $\mathcal{R}_M$ if and only if the mercurial signature scheme (PPGen, KeyGen, Sign, Verify, ConvertSK, ConvertPK, ConvertSig, ChangeRep) for $\mathcal{R}_M, \mathcal{R}_{\mathsf{pk}}, \mathcal{R}_{\mathsf{sk}}$ is correct and unforgeable.

Class- and Origin-Hiding of Mercurial Signatures. It is important for our application that the relations $\mathcal{R}_M$ and $\mathcal{R}_{\mathsf{pk}}$ be *class-hiding*. Class-hiding for messages [FHS14] means that given two messages, M_1 and M_2, it should be hard to tell whether or not $M_1 \in [M_2]_{\mathcal{R}_M}$. Class-hiding for public keys means that, given two public keys, pk_1 and pk_2, and oracle access to the signing algorithm for both of them, it is hard to tell whether or not $\mathsf{pk}_1 \in [\mathsf{pk}_2]_{\mathcal{R}_{\mathsf{pk}}}$.

An additional property we will need for our application is that, even if pk^* is adversarial, a message-signature pair obtained by running ChangeRep(pk^*, M_0, σ_0, μ_0) is distributed the same way as a pair obtained by running ChangeRep($\mathsf{pk}^*, M_1, \sigma_1, \mu_1$), as long as M_0 and M_1 are in the same equivalence class. Thus, seeing the resulting message-signature pair hides its origin, whether it came from M_0 or M_1. Similarly, even for an adversarial pk^*, a signature on a message M output by ConvertSig hides whether ConvertSig was given pk^* as input or another pk in the same equivalence class.

Definition 4 (Class- and origin-hiding). *A mercurial signature scheme* (PPGen, KeyGen, Sign, Verify, ConvertSK, ConvertPK, ConvertSig, ChangeRep) *for parameterized equivalence relations* $\mathcal{R}_M, \mathcal{R}_{\mathsf{pk}}, \mathcal{R}_{\mathsf{sk}}$ *is class-hiding if it satisfies the following two properties:*

Message class-hiding: For all polynomial-length parameters $\ell(k)$ and all probabilistic polynomial-time (PPT) adversaries $\mathcal{A}$, there exists a negligible function ν such that:

$$\Pr[PP \leftarrow \mathsf{PPGen}(1^k); M_1 \leftarrow \mathcal{M}; M_2^0 \leftarrow \mathcal{M}; M_2^1 \leftarrow [M_1]_{\mathcal{R}_M};$$
$$b \leftarrow \{0,1\}; b' \leftarrow \mathcal{A}(PP, M_1, M_2^b) \; : \; b' = b] \leq \frac{1}{2} + \nu(k)$$

Public key class-hiding: For all polynomial-length parameters $\ell(k)$ and all PPT adversaries $\mathcal{A}$, there exists a negligible function ν such that:

$$\Pr[PP \leftarrow \mathsf{PPGen}(1^k); (\mathsf{pk}_1, \mathsf{sk}_1) \leftarrow \mathsf{KeyGen}(PP, \ell(k)); (\mathsf{pk}_2^0, \mathsf{sk}_2^0) \leftarrow \mathsf{KeyGen}(PP,$$
$$\ell(k)); \rho \leftarrow \mathsf{sample}_\rho(PP); \mathsf{pk}_2^1 = \mathsf{ConvertPK}(\mathsf{pk}_1, \rho); \mathsf{sk}_2^1 = \mathsf{ConvertSK}(\mathsf{sk}_1, \rho);$$
$$b \leftarrow \{0,1\}; b' \leftarrow \mathcal{A}^{\mathsf{Sign}(\mathsf{sk}_1, \cdot), \mathsf{Sign}(\mathsf{sk}_2^b, \cdot)}(\mathsf{pk}_1, \mathsf{pk}_2^b) \; : \; b' = b] \leq \frac{1}{2} + \nu(k)$$

A mercurial signature is also *origin-hiding* if the following two properties hold:

Origin-hiding of ChangeRep: For all k, for all $PP \in \mathsf{PPGen}(1^k)$, for all pk^* (in particular, adversarially generated ones), for all M, σ, if $\mathsf{Verify}(\mathsf{pk}^*, M, \sigma) = 1$, if $\mu \leftarrow \mathsf{sample}_\mu$, then $\mathsf{ChangeRep}(\mathsf{pk}^*, M, \sigma, \mu)$ outputs a uniformly random $M' \in [M]_{\mathcal{R}_M}$ and a uniformly random $\sigma' \in \{\hat{\sigma} \mid \mathsf{Verify}(\mathsf{pk}^*, M', \hat{\sigma}) = 1\}$.

Origin-hiding of ConvertSig: For all k, for all $PP \in \mathsf{PPGen}(1^k)$, for all pk^* (in particular, adversarially generated ones), for all M, σ, if $\mathsf{Verify}(\mathsf{pk}^*, M, \sigma) = 1$, if $\rho \leftarrow \mathsf{sample}_\rho$, then $\mathsf{ConvertSig}(\mathsf{pk}^*, M, \sigma, \rho)$ outputs a uniformly random $\tilde{\sigma} \in \{\hat{\sigma} \mid \mathsf{Verify}(\mathsf{ConvertPK}(\mathsf{pk}^*, \rho), M, \hat{\sigma}) = 1\}$, and $\mathsf{ConvertPK}(\mathsf{pk}^*, \rho)$ outputs a uniformly random element of $[\mathsf{pk}^*]_{\mathcal{R}_{\mathsf{pk}}}$.

3   Construction of Mercurial Signatures

Let $e : \mathbb{G}_1 \times \mathbb{G}_2 \to \mathbb{G}_T$ be a Type III bilinear pairing for multiplicative groups $\mathbb{G}_1, \mathbb{G}_2,$ and $\mathbb{G}_T$ of prime order p. Let $P, \hat{P},$ and $e(P, \hat{P})$ be generators, respectively. (See full version [CL18] for a review.) The message space for our mercurial signature scheme will consist of vectors of group elements from $\mathbb{G}_1^*$, where $\mathbb{G}_1^* = \mathbb{G}_1 \backslash \{1_{\mathbb{G}_1}\}$. The space of secret keys will consist of vectors of elements from $\mathbb{Z}_p^*$. The space of public keys, similar to the message space, will consist of vectors of group elements from $\mathbb{G}_2^*$. Once the prime p, $\mathbb{G}_1^*$, $\mathbb{G}_2^*$, and ℓ are well-defined, the equivalence relations of interest to us are as follows:

$$\mathcal{R}_M = \{(M, M') \in (\mathbb{G}_1^*)^\ell \times (\mathbb{G}_1^*)^\ell \mid \exists r \in \mathbb{Z}_p^* \text{ such that } M' = M^r\}$$
$$\mathcal{R}_{\mathsf{sk}} = \{(\mathsf{sk}, \tilde{\mathsf{sk}}) \in (\mathbb{Z}_p^*)^\ell \times (\mathbb{Z}_p^*)^\ell \mid \exists r \in \mathbb{Z}_p^* \text{ such that } \tilde{\mathsf{sk}} = r \cdot \mathsf{sk}\}$$
$$\mathcal{R}_{\mathsf{pk}} = \{(\mathsf{pk}, \tilde{\mathsf{pk}}) \in (\mathbb{G}_2^*)^\ell \times (\mathbb{G}_2^*)^\ell \mid \exists r \in \mathbb{Z}_p^* \text{ such that } \tilde{\mathsf{pk}} = \mathsf{pk}^r\}$$

where $M^r = (M_1^r, \ldots, M_\ell^r)$ for a message $M = (M_1, \ldots, M_\ell) \in (\mathbb{G}_1^*)^\ell$. Note that messages, secret keys, and public keys are restricted to vectors consisting of only non-identity group elements. Without this restriction and the restriction that $r \neq 0$, the resulting relation would not be an equivalence one.

We introduce our mercurial signature construction with message space $(\mathbb{G}_1^*)^\ell$, but a mercurial signature scheme with message space $(\mathbb{G}_2^*)^\ell$ can be obtained by simply switching $\mathbb{G}_1^*$ and $\mathbb{G}_2^*$ throughout.

$\mathsf{PPGen}(1^k) \to PP$: Compute $\mathsf{BG} \leftarrow \mathsf{BGGen}(1^k)$. Output $PP = \mathsf{BG} = (\mathbb{G}_1, \mathbb{G}_2, \mathbb{G}_T, P, \hat{P}, e)$. Now that BG is well-defined, the relations $\mathcal{R}_M, \mathcal{R}_{\mathsf{pk}}, \mathcal{R}_{\mathsf{sk}}$ are also well-defined. sample_ρ and sample_μ are the same algorithm, namely the one that samples a random element of $\mathbb{Z}_p^*$.

$\mathsf{KeyGen}(PP, \ell) \to (\mathsf{pk}, \mathsf{sk})$: For $1 \leq i \leq \ell$, pick $x_i \leftarrow \mathbb{Z}_p^*$ and set secret key $\mathsf{sk} = (x_1, \ldots, x_\ell)$. Compute public key $\mathsf{pk} = (\hat{X}_1, \ldots, \hat{X}_\ell)$, where $\hat{X}_i = \hat{P}^{x_i}$ for $1 \leq i \leq \ell$. Output $(\mathsf{pk}, \mathsf{sk})$.

$\mathsf{Sign}(\mathsf{sk}, M) \to \sigma$: On input $\mathsf{sk} = (x_1, \ldots, x_\ell)$ and $M = (M_1, \ldots, M_\ell) \in (\mathbb{G}_1^*)^\ell$, pick a random $y \leftarrow \mathbb{Z}_p^*$ and output $\sigma = (Z, Y, \hat{Y})$, where $Z = \left(\prod_{i=1}^\ell M_i^{x_i} \right)^y$, $Y = P^{\frac{1}{y}}$, and $\hat{Y} = \hat{P}^{\frac{1}{y}}$.

$\mathsf{Verify}(\mathsf{pk}, M, \sigma) \to 0/1$: On input $\mathsf{pk} = (\hat{X}_1, \ldots, \hat{X}_\ell)$, $M = (M_1, \ldots, M_\ell)$, and $\sigma = (Z, Y, \hat{Y})$, check whether $\prod_{i=1}^\ell e(M_i, \hat{X}_i) = e(Z, \hat{Y}) \wedge e(Y, \hat{P}) = e(P, \hat{Y})$. If it holds, output 1; otherwise, output 0.

$\mathsf{ConvertSK}(\mathsf{sk}, \rho) \to \tilde{\mathsf{sk}}$: On input $\mathsf{sk} = (x_1, \ldots, x_\ell)$ and a key converter $\rho \in \mathbb{Z}_p^*$, output the new secret key $\tilde{\mathsf{sk}} = \rho \cdot \mathsf{sk}$.

$\mathsf{ConvertPK}(\mathsf{pk}, \rho) \to \tilde{\mathsf{pk}}$: On input $\mathsf{pk} = (\hat{X}_1, \ldots, \hat{X}_\ell)$ and a key converter $\rho \in \mathbb{Z}_p^*$, output the new public key $\tilde{\mathsf{pk}} = \mathsf{pk}^\rho$.

$\mathsf{ConvertSig}(\mathsf{pk}, M, \sigma, \rho) \to \tilde{\sigma}$: On input pk, message M, signature $\sigma = (Z, Y, \hat{Y})$, and key converter $\rho \in \mathbb{Z}_p^*$, sample $\psi \leftarrow \mathbb{Z}_p^*$. Output $\tilde{\sigma} = (Z^{\psi \rho}, Y^{\frac{1}{\psi}}, \hat{Y}^{\frac{1}{\psi}})$.

$\mathsf{ChangeRep}(\mathsf{pk}, M, \sigma, \mu) \to (M', \sigma')$: On input pk, M, $\sigma = (Z, Y, \hat{Y})$, $\mu \in \mathbb{Z}_p^*$, sample $\psi \leftarrow \mathbb{Z}_p^*$. Compute $M' = M^\mu$, $\sigma' = (Z^{\psi \mu}, Y^{\frac{1}{\psi}}, \hat{Y}^{\frac{1}{\psi}})$. Output (M', σ').

Proofs of the following theorems can be found in the full version [CL18].

Theorem 1 (Correctness). *The construction described above is correct.*

Theorem 2 (Unforgeability). *The construction described above is unforgeable in the generic group model for Type III bilinear groups.*

To prove unforgeability, we construct a reduction to the unforgeability of the SPS-EQ signature scheme. Suppose a PPT algorithm $\mathcal{A}$ produces a successful forgery $(M^*, \sigma^*, \mathsf{pk}^*)$ for a mercurial signature scheme with non-negligible probability. Then, by definition, there exists some α in $\mathbb{Z}_p^*$ such that $\mathsf{pk}^* = \mathsf{pk}^\alpha$, where pk is the challenge public key for unforgeability of SPS-EQ. We show that a PPT reduction $\mathcal{B}$ is able to obtain this α and produce a successful forgery $((M^*)^\alpha, \sigma^*, \mathsf{pk})$ for the SPS-EQ scheme, contradicting its proven security in the generic group model. The full proof can be found in the full version [CL18].

Theorem 3 (Class-hiding). *The construction described above is class-hiding in the generic group model for Type III bilinear groups.*

Message class-hiding follows from message class-hiding of the SPS-EQ scheme. Specifically, $(\mathbb{G}_i^*)^\ell$ is a class-hiding message space if and only if the decisional Diffie-Hellman assumption (DDH) holds in $\mathbb{G}_i$ [FHS14].

For public key class-hiding, consider public keys written additively, so that $\mathsf{pk} = (x_i \hat{X})_{i \in [\ell]}$. We must show that an adversary's view in a game in which the challenger computes independent public keys $\mathsf{pk}_1 = (x_i^{(1)}\hat{X})_{i\in[\ell]}$ and $\mathsf{pk}_2 = (x_i^{(2)}\hat{X})_{i\in[\ell]}$ (Game 0) is the same as his view in a game in which $\mathsf{pk}_2 = \alpha\mathsf{pk}_1 = (\alpha x_i^{(1)}\hat{X})_{i\in[\ell]}$ for some $\alpha \in \mathbb{Z}_p^*$ (Game 3). We achieve this by constructing two intermediate games (Game 1 and Game 2). In Game 1, pk_1 and pk_2 are independent, but $\mathcal{C}$'s responses to $\mathcal{A}$'s group oracle and signing queries are computed as formal multivariate Laurent polynomials in the variables $x_1^{(1)}, \ldots, x_\ell^{(1)}, x_1^{(2)}, \ldots, x_\ell^{(2)}, y_1, \ldots y_q$, where y_i is the secret value the challenger uses for the ith Sign query. In Game 2, $\mathsf{pk}_2 = \alpha\mathsf{pk}_1$ for some $\alpha \in \mathbb{Z}_p^*$, and $\mathcal{C}$'s responses to the oracle queries are again computed as formal multivariate Laurent polynomials, but now in the variables $x_1^{(1)}, \ldots, x_\ell^{(1)}, y_1, \ldots y_q$, and α. Demonstrating that $\mathcal{A}$'s view is the same in Game 0 as it is in Game 1 is a direct application of the Schwartz-Zippel lemma, which guarantees that the probability that a formal polynomial in Game 1, in which the variables $x_1^{(1)}, \ldots, x_\ell^{(1)}, x_1^{(2)}, \ldots, x_\ell^{(2)}, y_1, \ldots y_q$ are given to $\mathcal{A}$ as handles, collides with a formal polynomial in Game 0, in which the handles correspond to the variables that were fixed at the beginning of the game, is negligible. The same argument applies to Game 2 vs. Game 3.

It is nontrivial to prove that $\mathcal{A}$'s view is the same in Game 1 as it is in Game 2. First, we must show that for computations carried out by the challenger in each of the three groups, $\mathbb{G}_1^*, \mathbb{G}_2^*$, and $\mathbb{G}_T$, $\mathcal{A}$'s view is the same in both games. In $\mathbb{G}_2^*$, for example, we prove that two group oracle queries to $\mathbb{G}_2^*$ in Game 1 result in distinct formal polynomials if and only if the same two queries in Game 2 result in distinct polynomials. Then, the same must be shown, by induction, for signature queries too. If this sounds vague, it is because of the difficulty in conveying the details, which involve many variables and groups, in a high-level proof sketch. Please see the full version [CL18] for the full proof.

Theorem 4 (Origin-hiding). *The construction described above is origin-hiding in the generic group model for Type III bilinear groups.*

4   Definition of Delegatable Anonymous Credentials

Delegatable anonymous credentials have been studied before and previous definitions exist. The first paper to study the subject, due to Chase and Lysyanskaya [CL06], does not contain a definition of security. The next paper, by Belenkiy et al. [BCC+09], contains a simulation-extraction style definition. Anonymity means there is a simulator that, when interacting with the adversary on behalf of honest parties, creates for each interaction a transcript whose distribution is independent on the identity of the honest party interacting with the adversary. The extractability part means there is an extractor that "de-anonymizes" the parties under the adversary's control and guarantees that the adversary cannot prove possession of a credential that "de-anonymizes" to a credential chain not corresponding to a sequence of credential issue instances that have actually occurred. A subsequent paper, by Chase et al. [CKLM13], suggested modifying the Belenkiy et al. definition but preserved the simulation-extraction style.

Our definitional approach is more traditional: we have a single security game, in which the adversary interacts with the system and attempts to break it either by forging a credential or de-anonymizing a user, or both. Thus, we do not rely on the definitional machinery of simulation and extraction that Belenkiy et al. "inherited" from non-interactive zero-knowledge proof of knowledge (NIZK PoK) systems. This makes our definition weaker than the Belenkiy et al. definition (as we will discuss below), but at the same time, doing away with simulation and extraction requirements means that it can be satisfied with cryptographic building blocks, such as mercurial signatures and (interactive) zero-knowledge proofs, that do not necessarily imply NIZK PoK.

Definition 5 (Delegatable anonymous credentials). *A delegatable anonymous credential scheme consists of algorithms* (Setup, KeyGen, NymGen) *and protocols for issuing/receiving a credential and proving/verifying possession of a credential as follows:*

Setup(1^k) → (*params*): A PPT algorithm that generates the public parameters *params* for the system.

KeyGen(*params*) → (pk, sk): A PPT algorithm that generates an "identity" of a system participant, which consists of a public and secret key pair (pk, sk). sk is referred to as the user's *secret identity key*, while pk is its *public identity key*. WLOG, sk is assumed to include both *params* and pk so that they need not be given to other algorithms as separate inputs. A root authority runs the same key generation algorithm as every other participant.

NymGen(sk, $L(\check{pk}_0)$) → (nym, aux): A PPT algorithm that, on input a user's secret identity key sk and level $L(\check{pk}_0)$ under the root authority whose public key is $\check{pk}_0$, outputs a pseudonym nym for this user and the auxiliary information aux needed to use nym.

Issuing a credential:

[Issue($L_I(\check{pk}_0)$, $\check{pk}_0$, sk_I, nym_I, aux_I, $cred_I$, nym_R) ↔ Receive($L_I(\check{pk}_0)$, $\check{pk}_0$, sk_R, nym_R, aux_R, nym_I)] → ($cred_R$): This is an interactive protocol between an issuer of a credential, who runs the Issue side of the protocol, and a receiver, who runs the Receive side. The issuer takes as input his own credential at level $L_I(\check{pk}_0)$ under root authority $\check{pk}_0$ together with all information associated with it. Specifically, this includes $L_I(\check{pk}_0)$, the length of the issuer's credential chain; $\check{pk}_0$, the public key of the root authority; sk_I, the issuer's secret key; nym_I, the pseudonym by which the issuer is known to the receiver and its associated auxiliary information, aux_I; and $cred_I$, the issuer's credential chain. The issuer also takes as input nym_R, the pseudonym by which the receiver is known to him. The receiver takes as input the same $L_I(\check{pk}_0)$ and $\check{pk}_0$, the same nym_I and nym_R, her own secret key sk_R, and the auxiliary information aux_R associated with her pseudonym nym_R. The receiver's output is her credential $cred_R$.

Remarks. Note that there is a single protocol any issuer, including a root authority, runs with any recipient. A root authority does not use a pseudonym, so our convention in that case is $L_I(\check{pk}_0) = 0$, $nym_I = \check{pk}_0$, and $aux_I = cred_I = \perp$. Also, note that credentials, like levels, are dependent on $\check{pk}_0$ (i.e. $cred_I = cred_I(\check{pk}_0)$), but this dependency has been omitted for clarity.

Proof of possession of a credential:
[CredProve($L_P(\check{pk}_0), \check{pk}_0, sk_P, nym_P, aux_P, cred_P$) $\leftrightarrow$ CredVerify(*params*, L_P $(\check{pk}_0), \check{pk}_0, nym_P$)] $\rightarrow$ output (0 or 1): This is an interactive protocol between a prover, who is trying to prove possession of a credential and runs the CredProve side of the protocol, and a verifier, who runs the CredVerify side. The prover takes as input his own credential at level $L_P(\check{pk}_0)$ under root authority $\check{pk}_0$ together with all information associated with it. Specifically, this includes $L_P(\check{pk}_0)$, the length of the prover's credential chain; $\check{pk}_0$, the public key of the root authority; sk_P, the prover's secret key; nym_P, the pseudonym by which the prover is known to the verifier and its associated auxiliary information, aux_P; and $cred_P$, the prover's credential chain. The verifier takes as input *params* and the same $L_P(\check{pk}_0)$, $\check{pk}_0$, and nym_P. The verifier's output is 1 if it accepts the proof of possession of a credential and 0 otherwise.

A delegatable anonymous credential (DAC) system must be correct and secure. We provide a description of the security game along with a definition of unforgeability and anonymity for DAC under a single certification authority.

Definition 6 (Correctness of DAC). *A delegatable anonymous credential scheme is correct if, whenever* Setup*,* KeyGen *and* NymGen *are run correctly and the* Issue-Receive *protocol is executed correctly on correctly generated inputs, the receiver outputs a certification chain that, when used as input to the prover in an honest execution of the* CredProve-CredVerify *protocol, is accepted by the verifier with probability 1.*

Security game. The security game is parameterized by (hard-to-compute) functions f, f_{cred}, and f_{demo}. An adversary $\mathcal{A}$ interacts with a challenger $\mathcal{C}$, who is responsible for setting up the keys and pseudonyms of all the honest participants in the system and for acting on their behalf when they issue, receive, prove possession of, or verify possession of credential chains. Throughout the game, $\mathcal{C}$ maintains the following state information:

1. A directed graph $G(\check{pk}_0) = (V(\check{pk}_0), E(\check{pk}_0))$ that will consist of a single tree and some singleton nodes. The root of the tree is the node called *root*, and it has public key $\check{pk}_0$.
2. Corresponding to every node $v \in V(\check{pk}_0)$, the following information:
   (a) v's level $L(\check{pk}_0, v)$ (i.e. v's distance to *root* $\check{pk}_0$).
   (b) $status(v)$, which specifies whether v corresponds to an honest or adversarial user.
   (c) If $status(v) = honest$, then
       – $pk(v)$, the public key associated with v;

- $\mathsf{sk}(v)$, the secret key corresponding to $\mathsf{pk}(v)$;
- all pseudonyms $\mathsf{nym}_1(v), \ldots, \mathsf{nym}_n(v)$ associated with v (if they exist) and their corresponding auxiliary information $\mathsf{aux}_1(v), \ldots, \mathsf{aux}_n(v)$;
- the user's credential $\mathsf{cred}_v := \mathsf{cred}_v(\check{\mathsf{pk}}_0)$ (if it exists);
- a value $\hat{\mathsf{pk}}_v$, determined using the function f. (As we will see, $\hat{\mathsf{pk}}_v = f(\mathsf{pk}(v)) = f(\mathsf{nym}_i(v))$ for $\mathsf{nym}_i(v) \in \{\mathsf{nym}_1(v), \ldots, \mathsf{nym}_n(v)\}$.)

(d) If $status(v) = adversarial$, a value $\hat{\mathsf{pk}}_v$, determined using the function f, that will be used as this node's identity. As we will see, $\hat{\mathsf{pk}}_v = f(\mathsf{nym}(v))$ if $\mathsf{nym}(v)$ is a pseudonym used by the adversary on behalf of node v. Note that for two different adversarial nodes v, v', it is possible that $\hat{\mathsf{pk}}_v = \hat{\mathsf{pk}}_{v'}$. This is not possible for honest nodes.

3. A `forgery` flag, which is set to true if the adversary forges a credential.
4. An anonymity bit $b \in \{0, 1\}$, a pair of anonymity challenge nodes (u_0, u_1), and the status of the anonymity attack. Define S to be the set of pairs of pseudonyms $(\mathsf{nym}(u_b), \mathsf{nym}(u_{\bar{b}}))$ that the adversary has seen for the anonymity challenge node u_b and the other node in the pair, $u_{\bar{b}}$, where $\bar{b} = 1 - b$. The challenger keeps track of S along with the auxiliary information for the pairs of pseudonyms it contains.

The security game is initialized as follows. The $params$ are generated and given to the adversary $\mathcal{A}$. $\mathcal{A}(params)$ specifies whether the status of the root node is going to be $honest$ or $adversarial$. If it is $honest$, the challenger $\mathcal{C}$ generates the root key pair, $(\check{\mathsf{pk}}_0, \check{\mathsf{sk}}_0) \leftarrow \mathsf{KeyGen}(params)$; else, $\mathcal{A}$ supplies $\check{\mathsf{pk}}_0$ to $\mathcal{C}$. Next, $\mathcal{C}$ sets the `forgery` flag to false and picks a random value for the anonymity bit b: $b \leftarrow \{0, 1\}$. At this point, the anonymity attack has not begun yet, so its status is $undefined$. $\mathcal{C}$ stores $G(\check{\mathsf{pk}}_0) = (V(\check{\mathsf{pk}}_0), E(\check{\mathsf{pk}}_0)) = (\{root\}, \emptyset)$ (i.e. the graph consisting of the root node and no edges) and sets $status(root)$ to be as specified by $\mathcal{A}$: $\mathsf{pk}(root) = \check{\mathsf{pk}}_0$, and when $status(root) = honest$, $\mathsf{sk}(root) = \check{\mathsf{sk}}_0$. Next, $\mathcal{A}$ can add nodes/users to $G(\check{\mathsf{pk}}_0)$, both honest and adversarial, and have these users obtain, delegate, and prove possession of credentials by interacting with $\mathcal{C}$ using the following oracles (see full version [CL18] for details):

AddHonestParty(u): $\mathcal{A}$ invokes this oracle to create a new, honest node u. $\mathcal{C}$ runs $(\mathsf{pk}(u), \mathsf{sk}(u)) \leftarrow \mathsf{KeyGen}(params)$, sets $L(\check{\mathsf{pk}}_0, u) = \infty$, returns $\mathsf{pk}(u)$ to $\mathcal{A}$.

SeeNym(u): $\mathcal{A}$ invokes this oracle to see a fresh pseudonym for honest node u. $\mathcal{C}$ runs $(\mathsf{nym}(u), \mathsf{aux}(u)) \leftarrow \mathsf{NymGen}(\mathsf{sk}(u), L(\check{\mathsf{pk}}_0, u))$, returns $\mathsf{nym}(u)$ to $\mathcal{A}$.

CertifyHonestParty$(\check{\mathsf{pk}}_0, u, v)$: $\mathcal{A}$ invokes this oracle to have the honest party associated with u issue a credential to the honest party associated with v. $\mathcal{A}$ selects pseudonyms $\mathsf{nym}(u), \mathsf{nym}(v)$ that he has seen for u, v (unless $u = root$), and $\mathcal{C}$ runs the protocols: $[\mathsf{Issue}(L(\check{\mathsf{pk}}_0, u), \check{\mathsf{pk}}_0, \mathsf{sk}(u), \mathsf{nym}(u), \mathsf{aux}(u), \mathsf{cred}_u, \mathsf{nym}(v)) \leftrightarrow \mathsf{Receive}(L(\check{\mathsf{pk}}_0, u), \check{\mathsf{pk}}_0, \mathsf{sk}(v), \mathsf{nym}(v), \mathsf{aux}(v), \mathsf{nym}(u))] \rightarrow \mathsf{cred}_v$. If $u = root$, then $\check{\mathsf{pk}}_0$ is given as input instead of $\mathsf{nym}(u)$. $\mathcal{C}$ adds the edge (u, v) to the graph and sets $L(\check{\mathsf{pk}}_0, v) = L(\check{\mathsf{pk}}_0, u) + 1$.

VerifyCredFrom$(\check{\mathsf{pk}}_0, u)$: The honest party associated with u proves to $\mathcal{A}$ that it has a credential at level $L(\check{\mathsf{pk}}_0, u)$. $\mathcal{A}$ selects a pseudonym $\mathsf{nym}(u)$

that he has seen for u, and C runs the CredProve protocol with $\mathcal{A}$: CredProve$(L(\check{\mathsf{pk}}_0, u), \check{\mathsf{pk}}_0, \mathsf{sk}(u), \mathsf{nym}(u), \mathsf{aux}(u), \mathsf{cred}_u) \leftrightarrow \mathcal{A}$.

GetCredFrom$(\check{\mathsf{pk}}_0, u, \mathsf{nym}_R)$: The honest party associated with u issues a credential to $\mathcal{A}$, whom it knows by nym_R. C creates a new adversarial node v and sets its identity to be $\hat{\mathsf{pk}}_v = f(\mathsf{nym}_R)$. $\mathcal{A}$ selects a pseudonym $\mathsf{nym}(u)$ that he has seen for u (unless $u = root$), and C runs the Issue protocol with $\mathcal{A}$: Issue$(L(\check{\mathsf{pk}}_0, u), \check{\mathsf{pk}}_0, \mathsf{sk}(u), \mathsf{nym}(u), \mathsf{aux}(u), \mathsf{cred}_u, \mathsf{nym}_R) \leftrightarrow \mathcal{A}$. If $u = root$, then $\check{\mathsf{pk}}_0$ is given as input instead of $\mathsf{nym}(u)$. C adds the edge (u, v) to the graph and sets $L(\check{\mathsf{pk}}_0, v) = L(\check{\mathsf{pk}}_0, u) + 1$.

GiveCredTo$(\check{\mathsf{pk}}_0, L_I(\check{\mathsf{pk}}_0), \mathsf{nym}_I, v)$: $\mathcal{A}$ issues a credential to the honest party associated with v under a pseudonym nym_I (or $\check{\mathsf{pk}}_0$ if he is the root). $\mathcal{A}$ selects a pseudonym $\mathsf{nym}(v)$ that he has seen for v, and C runs the Receive protocol with $\mathcal{A}$: $[\mathcal{A} \leftrightarrow \mathsf{Receive}(L_I(\check{\mathsf{pk}}_0), \check{\mathsf{pk}}_0, \mathsf{sk}(v), \mathsf{nym}(v), \mathsf{aux}(v), \mathsf{nym}_I)] \to \mathsf{cred}_v$. If $\mathcal{A}$ is the *root*, then $\check{\mathsf{pk}}_0$ is given as input instead of nym_I. If $\mathsf{cred}_v \neq \bot$, C sets $L(\check{\mathsf{pk}}_0, v) = L_I(\check{\mathsf{pk}}_0) + 1$ and computes the function f_{cred} on v's credential, $f_{cred}(\mathsf{cred}_v) = (\hat{\mathsf{pk}}_0, \hat{\mathsf{pk}}_1, \ldots, \hat{\mathsf{pk}}_{L_I})$, revealing the identities in v's credential chain. If $\hat{\mathsf{pk}}_0 \neq \check{\mathsf{pk}}_0$, $\hat{\mathsf{pk}}_{L_I} \neq f(\mathsf{nym}_I)$, or $\hat{\mathsf{pk}}_{L_I} = f(\mathsf{nym}(u))$ for an honest user u, then C sets the forgery flag to true. Additionally, if according to C's data structure, there is some $\hat{\mathsf{pk}}_i$ in this chain such that $\hat{\mathsf{pk}}_i = f(\mathsf{nym}(u))$ for an honest user u, but $\hat{\mathsf{pk}}_{i+1} \neq f(\mathsf{nym}(v'))$ for any v' that received a credential from u, then C sets the forgery flag to true. If $\mathsf{cred}_v \neq \bot$ and the forgery flag remains false, C fills in the gaps in the graph as follows. Starting from the nearest honest ancestor of v, C creates a new node for each (necessarily adversarial) identity in the chain between that honest node and v and sets its identity to be the appropriate $\hat{\mathsf{pk}}_j$. C then adds edges between the nodes on the chain from the nearest honest ancestor of v to v.

DemoCred$(\check{\mathsf{pk}}_0, L_P(\check{\mathsf{pk}}_0), \mathsf{nym}_P)$: $\mathcal{A}$ proves possession of a credential at level L_P $(\check{\mathsf{pk}}_0)$. C runs the Verify protocol with $\mathcal{A}$: $[\mathcal{A} \leftrightarrow \mathsf{CredVerify}(params, L_P(\check{\mathsf{pk}}_0), \check{\mathsf{pk}}_0, \mathsf{nym}_P)] \to$ output $(0$ or $1)$. If output $= 1$, C computes the function f_{demo} on the transcript of the output, $f_{demo}(transcript) = (\hat{\mathsf{pk}}_0, \hat{\mathsf{pk}}_1, \ldots, \hat{\mathsf{pk}}_{L_P})$, and determines if a forgery has occurred as in GiveCredTo. If output $= 1$ and the forgery flag remains false, C creates a new adversarial node v for the identity $\hat{\mathsf{pk}}_{L_P}$ and sets $L(\check{\mathsf{pk}}_0, v) = L_P(\check{\mathsf{pk}}_0)$. C fills in the gaps in the graph as in GiveCredTo.

SetAnonChallenge(u_0, u_1): $\mathcal{A}$ will try to distinguish between the honest parties associated with u_0 and u_1.

SeeNymAnon: $\mathcal{A}$ invokes this oracle to see fresh pseudonyms for u_b and $u_{\bar{b}}$. C runs $(\mathsf{nym}(u_b), \mathsf{aux}(u_b)) \leftarrow \mathsf{NymGen}(\mathsf{sk}(u_b), L(\check{\mathsf{pk}}_0, u_b))$, repeats this for $u_{\bar{b}}$, and returns $(\mathsf{nym}(u_b), \mathsf{nym}(u_{\bar{b}}))$ to $\mathcal{A}$.

CertifyHonestAnon$(\check{\mathsf{pk}}_0, u)$: $\mathcal{A}$ invokes this oracle to have the honest party associated with u issue credentials to u_b and $u_{\bar{b}}$. $\mathcal{A}$ selects pseudonyms $(\mathsf{nym}(u_b), \mathsf{nym}(u_{\bar{b}}))$ and $\mathsf{nym}(u)$ that he has seen for $u_b, u_{\bar{b}}$, and u, and C runs the protocols: $[\mathsf{Issue}(L(\check{\mathsf{pk}}_0, u), \check{\mathsf{pk}}_0, \mathsf{sk}(u), \mathsf{nym}(u), \mathsf{aux}(u), \mathsf{cred}_u, \mathsf{nym}(u_b)) \leftrightarrow \mathsf{Receive}(L(\check{\mathsf{pk}}_0, u), \check{\mathsf{pk}}_0, \mathsf{sk}(u_b), \mathsf{nym}(u_b), \mathsf{aux}(u_b), \mathsf{nym}(u))] \to \mathsf{cred}_{u_b}$. If $u = root$, then $\check{pk}_0$ is given as input instead of $\text{nym}(u)$. $\mathcal{C}$ adds the edge (u, u_b) to the graph and sets $L(\check{pk}_0, u_b) = L(\check{pk}_0, u) + 1$. $\mathcal{C}$ repeats these steps for $u_{\bar{b}}$, using the same $\text{nym}(u)$ (if $u \neq root$).

CertifyAnonHonest$(\check{pk}_0, b^*, v)$: $\mathcal{A}$ invokes this oracle to have one of the anonymity challenge nodes, u_{b^*}, where $b^* = b$ or $\bar{b}$, issue a credential to the honest party associated with v. $\mathcal{C}$ checks that the two paths from u_{b^*} and $u_{\bar{b}^*}$ to the root $\check{pk}_0$ consist entirely of honest nodes, with the exception that $\check{pk}_0$ may be adversarial. If this check fails, $\mathcal{C}$ updates the status of the anonymity attack to *forfeited*. $\mathcal{A}$ selects pseudonyms $(\text{nym}(u_{b^*}), \text{nym}(u_{\bar{b}^*}))$ and $\text{nym}(v)$ that he has seen for $u_{b^*}, u_{\bar{b}^*}$, and v, and $\mathcal{C}$ runs the protocols: $[\text{Issue}(L(\check{pk}_0, u_{b^*}), \check{pk}_0, \text{sk}(u_{b^*}), \text{nym}(u_{b^*}), \text{aux}(u_{b^*}), \text{cred}_{u_{b^*}}, \text{nym}(v)) \leftrightarrow \text{Receive}(L(\check{pk}_0, u_{b^*}), \check{pk}_0, \text{sk}(v), \text{nym}(v), \text{aux}(v), \text{nym}(u_{b^*}))] \rightarrow \text{cred}_v$. $\mathcal{C}$ adds the edge (u_{b^*}, v) to the graph and sets $L(\check{pk}_0, v) = L(\check{pk}_0, u_{b^*}) + 1$.

VerifyCredFromAnon$(\check{pk}_0)$: The honest parties associated with u_b and $u_{\bar{b}}$ prove to $\mathcal{A}$ that they have credentials at level $L(\check{pk}_0, u_b) = L(\check{pk}_0, u_{\bar{b}})$. $\mathcal{C}$ checks the two paths from u_b and $u_{\bar{b}}$ to the root $\check{pk}_0$ as in CertifyAnonHonest. Next, $\mathcal{A}$ selects pseudonyms $(\text{nym}(u_b), \text{nym}(u_{\bar{b}}))$ that he has seen for u_b and $u_{\bar{b}}$, and $\mathcal{C}$ runs the CredProve protocol with $\mathcal{A}$: CredProve$(L(\check{pk}_0, u_b), \check{pk}_0, \text{sk}(u_b), \text{nym}(u_b), \text{aux}(u_b), \text{cred}_{u_b}) \leftrightarrow \mathcal{A}$. $\mathcal{C}$ repeats this step for $u_{\bar{b}}$.

GetCredFromAnon$(\check{pk}_0, b^*, \text{nym}_R)$: The honest party associated with u_{b^*}, where $b^* = b$ or $\bar{b}$, issues a credential to $\mathcal{A}$, whom it knows by nym_R. $\mathcal{C}$ checks the two paths from u_{b^*} and $u_{\bar{b}^*}$ to the root $\check{pk}_0$ as in CertifyAnonHonest. Next, $\mathcal{C}$ creates a new adversarial node v and sets its identity to be $\hat{pk}_v = f(\text{nym}_R)$. Note that $\mathcal{A}$ can have $u_{b^*}, u_{\bar{b}^*}$ issue credentials to two different adversarial nodes v, v', respectively, with the same underlying adversarial identity $\hat{pk}_v = \hat{pk}_{v'}$. $\mathcal{A}$ selects pseudonyms $(\text{nym}(u_{b^*}), \text{nym}(u_{\bar{b}^*}))$ that he has seen for u_{b^*} and $u_{\bar{b}^*}$, and $\mathcal{C}$ runs the Issue protocol with $\mathcal{A}$: Issue$(L(\check{pk}_0, u_{b^*}), \check{pk}_0, \text{sk}(u_{b^*}), \text{nym}(u_{b^*}), \text{aux}(u_{b^*}), \text{cred}_{u_{b^*}}, \text{nym}_R) \leftrightarrow \mathcal{A}$. $\mathcal{C}$ adds the edge (u_{b^*}, v) to the graph and sets $L(\check{pk}_0, v) = L(\check{pk}_0, u_{b^*}) + 1$.

GiveCredToAnon$(\check{pk}_0, L_I(\check{pk}_0), \text{nym}_I)$: $\mathcal{A}$ issues credentials to u_b and $u_{\bar{b}}$ under a pseudonym nym_I (or $\check{pk}_0$ if he is the root). $\mathcal{A}$ selects pseudonyms $(\text{nym}(u_b), \text{nym}(u_{\bar{b}}))$ that he has seen for u_b and $u_{\bar{b}}$, and $\mathcal{C}$ runs the Receive protocol with $\mathcal{A}$: $[\mathcal{A} \leftrightarrow \text{Receive}(L_I(\check{pk}_0), \check{pk}_0, \text{sk}(u_b), \text{nym}(u_b), \text{aux}(u_b), \text{nym}_I)] \rightarrow \text{cred}_{u_b}$. If $\mathcal{A}$ is the root, then $\check{pk}_0$ is given as input instead of nym_I. $\mathcal{C}$ repeats this step for $u_{\bar{b}}$. If both $\text{cred}_{u_b} \neq \bot$ and $\text{cred}_{u_{\bar{b}}} \neq \bot$, $\mathcal{C}$ sets $L(\check{pk}_0, u_b) = L_I(\check{pk}_0) + 1$, computes the function f_{cred} on u_b's credential, $f_{cred}(\text{cred}_{u_b}) = (\hat{pk}_0, \hat{pk}_1, \ldots, \hat{pk}_{L_I})$, and determines if a forgery has occurred as in GiveCredTo. $\mathcal{C}$ repeats this step for $u_{\bar{b}}$. If both $\text{cred}_{u_b} \neq \bot$ and $\text{cred}_{u_{\bar{b}}} \neq \bot$ and the **forgery** flag remains false, $\mathcal{C}$ fills in the gaps in the graph as follows. If there is already an adversarial node v corresponding to the pseudonym nym_I with an edge connecting it to an honest parent, then $\mathcal{C}$ only adds an edge between v and u_b. Else, $\mathcal{C}$ creates a chain of edges and (adversarial) nodes from the nearest honest ancestor of u_b to u_b as in GiveCredTo. $\mathcal{C}$ repeats this step for $u_{\bar{b}}$.

GuessAnon(b'): If $b' = b$, the status of the anonymity attack is set to *success*.

Definition 7 (Unforgeability and Anonymity). *A delegatable anonymous credential scheme is unforgeable and anonymous if there exist functions f, f_{cred}, and f_{demo} such that for all PPT $\mathcal{A}$, there exists a negligible function ν such that:*

1. *the probability that the **forgery** flag will be true in the single-authority game is at most $\nu(k)$, where k is the security parameter.*
2. *the probability that the status of the anonymity attack in the single-authority game will be* success *is at most $1/2 + \nu(k)$.*

Strengthening Anonymity. Note that this flavor of anonymity is weaker than the previous one by Belenkiy et al., and not only because it is not based on simulatability. In our anonymity game, two nodes, u_0 and u_1, may have credentials at the same level but still may not be appropriate candidates for the anonymity challenge; the two paths from u_0 and u_1 to the root must consist entirely of honest nodes, with the exception that the root may be adversarial. The reason is that our definition allows the adversary to recognize himself on a credential chain, so if he were on u_0's credential chain but not u_1's, he would be able to distinguish the two. It would be relatively straightforward to "fix" our definition to not allow this: we would just need to remove the requirement that u_0 and u_1 have entirely honest paths to the root. Unfortunately, our construction only satisfies the weaker anonymity notion in which this requirement must be met.

Other Types of Composition. Note that in our definition, the adversary invokes the oracles *sequentially*. Our definition gives no security guarantees when the oracles are invoked concurrently and the adversary orchestrates the order in which protocol messages are exchanged. There are standard techniques for turning certain sequentially secure protocols into concurrently secure ones; there are also well-known subtleties [Dam00, Lin03b, Lin03a]. As far as stronger types of composition, such as universal composition [Can01], are concerned, our definition, even if modified somewhat, does not seem to provide this level of security.

5   Construction of DAC from Mercurial Signatures

Suppose we have a mercurial signature scheme such that the space of public keys is a subset of the message space and $\mathcal{R}_M = \mathcal{R}_{pk}$. Furthermore, suppose it has the property that $\mathsf{sample}_\mu = \mathsf{sample}_\rho$ and on input $\mathsf{ChangeRep}(pk, M, \sigma, \mu)$, where $M = pk'$, it outputs (M', σ') such that $M' = \mathsf{ConvertPK}(pk', \mu)$.

To generate a key pair, each participant runs the KeyGen algorithm of the mercurial signature scheme to get (pk, sk). To generate a new pseudonym and its auxiliary information, pick ρ and let $\mathsf{nym} = \mathsf{ConvertPK}(pk, \rho)$, $\mathsf{aux} = \rho$.

A credential chain of length L will consist of a series of pseudonyms $(\mathsf{nym}_1, \ldots, \mathsf{nym}_L)$ and a series of signatures $(\sigma_1, \ldots, \sigma_L)$ such that (1) σ_1 is a signature on the message nym_1 under the certification authority's public key $\check{\text{pk}}_0$; (2) for $2 \leq i \leq L$, σ_i is the signature on the message nym_i under the public key nym_{i-1}. This is possible because the message space contains the space of public keys and the relations $\mathcal{R}_M$ and $\mathcal{R}_{\text{pk}}$ are the same.

A credential chain can be randomized so as to be unrecognizable by using the ConvertSig and ChangeRep algorithms as follows. The input to this step is $(\text{nym}_1, \ldots, \text{nym}_L)$ and $(\sigma_1, \ldots, \sigma_L)$. In order to randomize it, pick random $(\rho_1, \ldots, \rho_L) \leftarrow \text{sample}_\rho^L$. Define $\text{nym}_0' = \check{\text{pk}}_0$, $\tilde{\sigma}_1 = \sigma_1$. Now, perform two steps: (1) for $2 \leq i \leq L$, set $\tilde{\sigma}_i = \text{ConvertSig}(\text{nym}_{i-1}, \text{nym}_i, \sigma_i, \rho_{i-1})$, and (2) for $1 \leq i \leq L$, set $(\text{nym}_i', \sigma_i') = \text{ChangeRep}(\text{nym}_{i-1}', \text{nym}_i, \tilde{\sigma}_i, \rho_i)$. This way, nym_i' is the new, unrecognizable pseudonym corresponding to the same underlying identity as nym_i, and σ_i' is a signature attesting to that fact, which verifies under the already updated pseudonym nym_{i-1}' (treated as a public key for the purposes of message verification). Finally, output $(\text{nym}_1', \ldots, \text{nym}_L')$ and $(\sigma_1', \ldots, \sigma_L')$.

In order to issue a credential, the issuer first has the receiver prove, via an interactive zero-knowledge proof of knowledge (ZKPoK), that the receiver knows the secret key associated with his pseudonym, nym_R. Then, the issuer randomizes his certification chain as described above and uses the last pseudonym on the randomized chain, nym_L', as his issuer's pseudonym nym_I. (Alternatively, he can give a zero-knowledge proof that the two are equivalent.) He then computes $\sigma_{L+1} = \text{Sign}(\text{sk}_I, \text{nym}_R)$, where sk_I is the secret key that corresponds to nym_I. He sends the randomized chain as well as σ_{L+1} to the receiver, who stores the resulting credential chain $(\text{nym}_1', \ldots, \text{nym}_L', \text{nym}_R)$ and $(\sigma_1', \ldots, \sigma_L', \sigma_{L+1})$. In order to prove possession of a credential, a prover first randomizes the credential chain, reveals it to the verifier, and proves knowledge of the secret key that corresponds to the last pseudonym, nym_L', on the certification chain.

Unfortunately, we do not know of a construction of a mercurial signature in which the public key space is a subset of the message space. Our mercurial signature construction does not enjoy that property because messages are vectors in $\mathbb{G}_1^*$, while public keys are vectors in $\mathbb{G}_2^*$. However, we know how to construct a pair of mercurial signature schemes in which the public key space of one is the message space of the other, and vice versa. That is accomplished by just switching $\mathbb{G}_1^*$ and $\mathbb{G}_2^*$ in one of the schemes; the secret key space is the same in both. We can use this pair of mercurial signature schemes to construct delegatable anonymous credentials similar to the intuitive way described above, except that we must invoke different algorithms for even positions on the certification chain than we do for odd positions.

Let MS_1 = $(\text{PPGen}_1, \text{KeyGen}_1, \text{Sign}_1, \text{Verify}_1, \text{ConvertSK}_1, \text{ConvertPK}_1, \text{ConvertSig}_1, \text{ChangeRep}_1)$ and MS_2 = $(\text{PPGen}_2, \text{KeyGen}_2, \text{Sign}_2, \text{Verify}_2, \text{ConvertSK}_2, \text{ConvertPK}_2, \text{ConvertSig}_2, \text{ChangeRep}_2)$ be two mercurial signature schemes that share the same parameter generation algorithm $\text{PPGen}_1 = \text{PPGen}_2$. Let $\mathcal{R}_1, \mathcal{R}_2, \mathcal{R}_{\text{sk}}$ be parameterized relations such that MS_1 has message relation $\mathcal{R}_1$, public key relation $\mathcal{R}_2$, and secret key relation $\mathcal{R}_{\text{sk}}$, while MS_2 has message relation $\mathcal{R}_2$, public key relation $\mathcal{R}_1$, and the same secret key relation $\mathcal{R}_{\text{sk}}$. Suppose $\text{sample}_\mu = \text{sample}_\rho$ for both schemes and that the message space for the first scheme consists of public keys for the second one, and vice versa. Finally, suppose that both schemes satisfy class- and origin-hiding.

Our construction consists of the following algorithms and protocols. Initially, a user runs KeyGen to obtain two key pairs, an odd pair and an even pair. Once a user receives a credential, her level is fixed, so she only uses the relevant key pair - the odd pair to be used at an odd level and the even pair at an even level.

Setup$(1^k) \to (params)$: Compute $PP \leftarrow \mathsf{PPGen}_1(1^k) = \mathsf{PPGen}_2(1^k)$ and output $params = PP$.

KeyGen$(params) \to (\mathsf{pk}, \mathsf{sk})$: There are two cases. For the root authority, compute $(\mathsf{p\breve{k}}_0, \mathsf{s\breve{k}}_0) \leftarrow \mathsf{KeyGen}_1(PP, \ell)$ and output it. For others, compute $(\mathsf{pk}_{even}, \mathsf{sk}_{even}) \leftarrow \mathsf{KeyGen}_1(PP, \ell)$ and $(\mathsf{pk}_{odd}, \mathsf{sk}_{odd}) \leftarrow \mathsf{KeyGen}_2(PP, \ell)$ and output both pairs of keys $(\mathsf{pk}_{even}, \mathsf{sk}_{even}), (\mathsf{pk}_{odd}, \mathsf{sk}_{odd})$.

NymGen$(\mathsf{sk}, L(\mathsf{p\breve{k}}_0)) \to (\mathsf{nym}, \mathsf{aux})$: If $L(\mathsf{p\breve{k}}_0) = 0$, output $(\mathsf{p\breve{k}}_0, \perp)$. Otherwise, pick random key converters ρ_{even}, ρ_{odd} and compute $\mathsf{s\breve{k}}_{even} \leftarrow \mathsf{ConvertSK}_1(\mathsf{sk}_{even}, \rho_{even})$ and $\mathsf{nym}_{even} \leftarrow \mathsf{ConvertPK}_1(\mathsf{pk}_{even}, \rho_{even})$. Similarly, compute $\mathsf{s\breve{k}}_{odd} \leftarrow \mathsf{ConvertSK}_2(\mathsf{sk}_{odd}, \rho_{odd})$ and $\mathsf{nym}_{odd} \leftarrow \mathsf{ConvertPK}_2(\mathsf{pk}_{odd}, \rho_{odd})$. Output both pairs $(\mathsf{nym}_{even}, \rho_{even}), (\mathsf{nym}_{odd}, \rho_{odd})$.

In the following protocols, each algorithm is either from MS_1 or MS_2, but the even/odd subscripts have been omitted for clarity. For example, $\sigma_1 \leftarrow \mathsf{Sign}(\mathsf{s\breve{k}}_0, \mathsf{nym}_1)$ is computed as $\sigma_1 \leftarrow \mathsf{Sign}_1(\mathsf{s\breve{k}}_0, \mathsf{nym}_{1,odd})$ since the user nym_1 is fixed at odd level 1.

Issuing a credential:

Issue$(L_I(\mathsf{p\breve{k}}_0)), \mathsf{p\breve{k}}_0, \mathsf{sk}_I, \mathsf{nym}_I, \mathsf{aux}_I, \mathsf{cred}_I, \mathsf{nym}_R)$ $\leftrightarrow$ Receive$(L_I(\mathsf{p\breve{k}}_0)), \mathsf{p\breve{k}}_0, \mathsf{sk}_R,$
    $\mathsf{nym}_R, \mathsf{aux}_R, \mathsf{nym}_I)] \quad \to \quad \mathsf{cred}_R: \quad \{(\mathsf{nym}'_1, \dots, \mathsf{nym}'_{L_I}, \mathsf{nym}_R), (\sigma'_1, \dots, \sigma'_{L_I},$
    $\sigma_{L_I+1})\}$

The issuer first has the receiver prove, via an interactive ZKPoK, that the receiver knows the secret key, sk_R, associated with his pseudonym, nym_R.

Issue: If the ZKPoK accepts, proceed as follows; else, abort.

Randomize credential chain.

1. If $L_I(\mathsf{p\breve{k}}_0) = 0$, $\mathsf{cred}_I = \perp$. Define $\mathsf{nym}'_0 = \mathsf{p\breve{k}}_0$, $\tilde{\sigma}_1 = \sigma_1$.
   Compute $\sigma_1 \leftarrow \mathsf{Sign}(\mathsf{s\breve{k}}_0, \mathsf{nym}_1)$.
   Output $\mathsf{cred}_R = (\mathsf{nym}_1, \sigma_1)$ and send it to the receiver.

2. If $L_I(\mathsf{p\breve{k}}_0) \neq 0$, $\mathsf{cred}_I = \{(\mathsf{nym}_1, \dots, \mathsf{nym}_{L_I}), (\sigma_1, \dots, \sigma_{L_I})\}$.
   Pick random $(\rho_1, \dots, \rho_{L_I}) \leftarrow \mathsf{sample}_\rho^{L_I}$.
   If $L_I(\mathsf{p\breve{k}}_0) = 1$, $\mathsf{nym}'_0 = \mathsf{p\breve{k}}_0$, $\tilde{\sigma}_1 = \sigma_1$ as above.
   Compute $(\mathsf{nym}'_1, \sigma'_1) \leftarrow \mathsf{ChangeRep}(\mathsf{nym}'_0, \mathsf{nym}_1, \tilde{\sigma}_1, \rho_1)$.
   If $L_I(\mathsf{p\breve{k}}_0) > 1$, for $2 \leq i \leq L_I$,
   Compute $\tilde{\sigma}_i \leftarrow \mathsf{ConvertSig}(\mathsf{nym}_{i-1}, \mathsf{nym}_i, \sigma_i, \rho_{i-1})$.
   Then, compute $(\mathsf{nym}'_i, \sigma'_i) \leftarrow \mathsf{ChangeRep}(\mathsf{nym}'_{i-1}, \mathsf{nym}_i, \tilde{\sigma}_i, \rho_i)$.
   Finally, output $(\mathsf{nym}'_1, \dots, \mathsf{nym}'_{L_I})$ and $(\sigma'_1, \dots, \sigma'_{L_I})$.
   Compute $\sigma_{L_I+1} \leftarrow \mathsf{Sign}(\mathsf{sk}_{L_I}, \mathsf{nym}_R)$.
   Send the randomized chain as well as σ_{L_I+1} to the receiver.
   Note: The issuer uses nym'_{L_I} as his issuer's pseudonym, nym_I.

Receive: If $\mathsf{Verify}(\mathsf{nym}'_{i-1}, \mathsf{nym}'_i, \sigma'_i) = 1 \; \forall \; 1 < i < L_I$ and $\mathsf{Verify}(\mathsf{nym}'_{L_I}, \mathsf{nym}_R, \sigma_{L_{I+1}}) = 1$, store the resulting credential chain cred_R : $\{(\mathsf{nym}'_1, \ldots, \mathsf{nym}'_{L_I}, \mathsf{nym}_R), (\sigma'_1, \ldots, \sigma'_{L_I}, \sigma_{L_{I+1}})\}$; else, output $\perp$.

Proof of possession of a credential:

$[\mathsf{CredProve}(L_P(\check{\mathsf{pk}}_0), \check{\mathsf{pk}}_0, \mathsf{sk}_P, \mathsf{nym}_P, \mathsf{aux}_P, \mathsf{cred}_P) \quad \leftrightarrow \quad \mathsf{CredVerify}(\mathit{params},$
$L_P(\check{\mathsf{pk}}_0), \check{\mathsf{pk}}_0, \mathsf{nym}_P)] \to$ output (0 or 1)

CredProve: Randomize the credential chain $\mathsf{cred}_P = \{(\mathsf{nym}_1, \ldots, \mathsf{nym}_{L_P}), (\sigma_1, \ldots, \sigma_{L_P})\}$ as above and send the chain to the verifier. The prover then proves knowledge of the secret key that corresponds to the last pseudonym, nym'_{L_P}, on the randomized chain, which he uses as nym_P.

CredVerify: If the ZKPoK accepts, $\mathsf{cred}_P \neq \perp$, and $\mathsf{Verify}(\mathsf{nym}'_{i-1}, \mathsf{nym}'_i, \sigma'_i) = 1$ $\forall \; 1 < i < L_P$, output 1; else, output 0.

Theorem 5 *The construction presented in Sect. 5 is correct, unforgeable, and anonymous in the single-authority security game.*

Unforgeability follows from unforgeability of mercurial signatures, while anonymity follows from class- and origin-hiding. The proof is in the full version [CL18].

Efficiency Analysis. Consider this scheme instantiated with our mercurial signature construction (Sect. 3). We need to establish an appropriate value for the length parameter ℓ. For our purposes, $\ell = 2$ is good enough, so public keys and messages consist of two group elements each. (If $\ell = 1$, all messages and all public keys are equivalent.) A certification chain of length L will then have two group elements per pseudonym on the chain and three group elements per signature (according to our construction). Therefore, it takes $5L$ group elements to represent a credential chain of length L.

Trust Assumptions. Note that the only system-wide setup that needs to take place is the generation of the system parameters. When instantiated with mercurial signatures, this boils down to just the bilinear pairing setup. Even if the setup is carried out by a less-than-trustworthy party, it is unclear that this party can introduce trapdoors that would allow it to forge credentials or break anonymity. This is in contrast with previous constructions, in which the setup had to be carried out by a completely trustworthy process because trapdoors would allow simulation and extraction, thus breaking both unforgeability and anonymity.

References

[BCC+09] Belenkiy, M., Camenisch, J., Chase, M., Kohlweiss, M., Lysyanskaya, A., Shacham, H.: Randomizable proofs and delegatable anonymous credentials. In: Halevi, S. (ed.) CRYPTO 2009. LNCS, vol. 5677, pp. 108–125. Springer, Heidelberg (2009). https://doi.org/10.1007/978-3-642-03356-8_7

[BHKS18] Backes, M., Hanzlik, L., Kluczniak, K., Schneider, J.: Signatures with flexible public key: a unified approach to privacy-preserving signatures (full version). Cryptology ePrint Archive, Report 2018/191 (2018). https://eprint.iacr.org/2018/191

[Can01] Canetti, R.: Universally composable security: a new paradigm for cryptographic protocols. In: 42nd FOCS, pp. 136–145. IEEE Computer Society Press (2001)

[CDD17] Camenisch, J., Drijvers, M., Dubovitskaya, M.: Practical UC-secure delegatable credentials with attributes and their application to blockchain. In: ACM CCS 2017, pp. 683–699. ACM Press (2017)

[CDHK15] Camenisch, J., Dubovitskaya, M., Haralambiev, K., Kohlweiss, M.: Composable and modular anonymous credentials: definitions and practical constructions. In: Iwata, T., Cheon, J.H. (eds.) ASIACRYPT 2015. LNCS, vol. 9453, pp. 262–288. Springer, Heidelberg (2015). https://doi.org/10.1007/978-3-662-48800-3_11

[Cha86] Chaum, D.: Showing credentials without identification. In: Pichler, F. (ed.) EUROCRYPT 1985. LNCS, vol. 219, pp. 241–244. Springer, Heidelberg (1986). https://doi.org/10.1007/3-540-39805-8_28

[CHK+05] Canetti, R., Halevi, S., Katz, J., Lindell, Y., MacKenzie, P.: Universally composable password-based key exchange. In: Cramer, R. (ed.) EUROCRYPT 2005. LNCS, vol. 3494, pp. 404–421. Springer, Heidelberg (2005). https://doi.org/10.1007/11426639_24

[CKL+14] Camenisch, J., Krenn, S., Lehmann, A., Mikkelsen, G.L., Neven, G., Pedersen, M.Ø.: Formal treatment of privacy-enhancing credential systems. Cryptology ePrint Archive, Report 2014/708 (2014). http://eprint.iacr.org/2014/708

[CKLM13] Chase, M., Kohlweiss, M., Lysyanskaya, A., Meiklejohn, S.: Malleable signatures: complex unary transformations and delegatable anonymous credentials. Cryptology ePrint Archive, Report 2013/179 (2013). http://eprint.iacr.org/2013/179

[CL01] Camenisch, J., Lysyanskaya, A.: An efficient system for non-transferable anonymous credentials with optional anonymity revocation. In: Pfitzmann, B. (ed.) EUROCRYPT 2001. LNCS, vol. 2045, pp. 93–118. Springer, Heidelberg (2001). https://doi.org/10.1007/3-540-44987-6_7

[CL04] Camenisch, J., Lysyanskaya, A.: Signature Schemes and Anonymous Credentials from Bilinear Maps. In: Franklin, M. (ed.) CRYPTO 2004. LNCS, vol. 3152, pp. 56–72. Springer, Heidelberg (2004). https://doi.org/10.1007/978-3-540-28628-8_4

[CL06] Chase, M., Lysyanskaya, A.: On signatures of knowledge. In: Dwork, C. (ed.) CRYPTO 2006. LNCS, vol. 4117, pp. 78–96. Springer, Heidelberg (2006). https://doi.org/10.1007/11818175_5

[CL18] Crites, E.C., Lysyanskaya, A.: Delegatable anonymous credentials from mercurial signatures. http://eprint.iacr.org/2001/064 (2018)

[Dam00] Damgård, I.: Efficient concurrent zero-knowledge in the auxiliary string model. In: Preneel, B. (ed.) EUROCRYPT 2000. LNCS, vol. 1807, pp. 418–430. Springer, Heidelberg (2000). https://doi.org/10.1007/3-540-45539-6_30

[FHS14] Fuchsbauer, G., Hanser, C., Slamanig, D.: Structure-preserving signatures on equivalence classes and constant-size anonymous credentials. Cryptology ePrint Archive, Report 2014/944 (2014). http://eprint.iacr.org/2014/944

[GMR88] Goldwasser, S., Micali, S., Rivest, R.L.: A digital signature scheme secure against adaptive chosen-message attacks. SIAM J. Comput. **17**(2), 281–308 (1988)

[GS08] Groth, J., Sahai, A.: Efficient non-interactive proof systems for bilinear groups. In: Smart, N. (ed.) EUROCRYPT 2008. LNCS, vol. 4965, pp. 415–432. Springer, Heidelberg (2008). https://doi.org/10.1007/978-3-540-78967-3_24

[Lin03a] Lindell, Y.: Bounded-concurrent secure two-party computation without setup assumptions. In: 35th ACM STOC, pp. 683–692. ACM Press (2003)

[Lin03b] Lindell, Y.: Brief announcement: impossibility results for concurrent secure two-party computation. In: 22nd ACM PODC, p. 200. ACM, July 2003

[LRSW99] Lysyanskaya, A., Rivest, R.L., Sahai, A., Wolf, S.: Pseudonym systems. In: Heys, H., Adams, C. (eds.) SAC 1999. LNCS, vol. 1758, pp. 184–199. Springer, Heidelberg (2000). https://doi.org/10.1007/3-540-46513-8_14

[Lys02] Lysyanskaya, A.: Signature schemes and applications to cryptographic protocol design. Ph.D. thesis, Massachusetts Institute of Technology, Cambridge, Massachusetts, September 2002

[Swe97] Sweeney, L.: Weaving technology and policy together to maintain confidentiality. Int. J. Law Med. Ethics **25**(2–3), 98–110 (1997)

Accountable Tracing Signatures from Lattices

San Ling, Khoa Nguyen, Huaxiong Wang, and Yanhong Xu[✉]

Division of Mathematical Sciences, School of Physical and Mathematical Sciences,
Nanyang Technological University, Singapore, Singapore
{lingsan,khoantt,hxwang,xu0014ng}@ntu.edu.sg

Abstract. Group signatures allow users of a group to sign messages anonymously in the name of the group, while incorporating a tracing mechanism to revoke anonymity and identify the signer of any message. Since its introduction by Chaum and van Heyst (EUROCRYPT 1991), numerous proposals have been put forward, yielding various improvements on security, efficiency and functionality. However, a drawback of traditional group signatures is that the opening authority is given too much power, i.e., he can indiscriminately revoke anonymity and there is no mechanism to keep him accountable. To overcome this problem, Kohlweiss and Miers (PoPET 2015) introduced the notion of accountable tracing signatures (ATS) - an enhanced group signature variant in which the opening authority is kept accountable for his actions. Kohlweiss and Miers demonstrated a generic construction of ATS and put forward a concrete instantiation based on number-theoretic assumptions. To the best of our knowledge, no other ATS scheme has been known, and the problem of instantiating ATS under post-quantum assumptions, e.g., lattices, remains open to date.

In this work, we provide the first lattice-based accountable tracing signature scheme. The scheme satisfies the security requirements suggested by Kohlweiss and Miers, assuming the hardness of the Ring Short Integer Solution (RSIS) and the Ring Learning With Errors (RLWE) problems. At the heart of our construction are a lattice-based key-oblivious encryption scheme and a zero-knowledge argument system allowing to prove that a given ciphertext is a valid RLWE encryption under some hidden yet certified key. These technical building blocks may be of independent interest, e.g., they can be useful for the design of other lattice-based privacy-preserving protocols.

1 Introduction

Group signature is a fundamental cryptographic primitive introduced by Chaum and van Heyst [12]. It allows members of a group to anonymously sign messages on behalf of the group, but to prevent abuse of anonymity, there is an opening authority (OA) who can identify the signer of any message. While such a tracing mechanism is necessary to ensure user accountability, it grants too much power to the opening authority. Indeed, in traditional models of group signatures, e.g., [2,

© Springer Nature Switzerland AG 2019
M. Matsui (Ed.): CT-RSA 2019, LNCS 11405, pp. 556–576, 2019.
https://doi.org/10.1007/978-3-030-12612-4_28

3, 7, 8, 22, 23, 52], the OA can break users' anonymity whenever he wants, and we do not have any method to verify whether this trust is well placed or not.

One existing attempt to restrict the OA's power is the proposal of group signatures with message-dependent opening (MDO) [51], in which the OA can only identify the signers of messages admitted by an additional authority named admitter. However, this solution is still unsatisfactory. Once the OA has obtained admission to open a specific message, he can identify all the users, including some innocent ones, who have ever issued signatures on this specific message. Furthermore, by colluding with the admitter, the OA again is able to open all signatures.

To tackle the discussed above problem, Kohlweiss and Miers [24] put forward the notion of accountable tracing signatures (ATS), which is an enhanced variant of group signatures that has an additional mechanism to make the OA accountable. In an ATS scheme, the role of the OA is incorporated into that of the group manager (GM), and there are two kinds of group users: traceable ones and non-traceable ones. Traceable users are treated as in traditional group signatures, i.e., their anonymity can be broken by the OA/GM. Meanwhile, it is infeasible for anyone, including the OA/GM, to trace signatures generated by non-traceable users. When a user joins the group, the OA/GM first has to determine whether this user is traceable and then he issues a corresponding (traceable/nontraceable) certificate to the user. In a later phase, the OA/GM reveals which user he deems traceable using an "accounting" algorithm, yielding an intriguing method to enforce his accountability.

As an example, let us consider the surveillance controls of a building, which is implemented using an ATS scheme. On the one hand, the customers in this building would like to have their privacy protected as much as possible. On the other hand, the police who are conducting security check in this building would like to know as much as they can. To balance the interests of these two parties, the police can in advance narrow down some suspects and asks the OA/GM to make these suspected users traceable and the remaining non-suspected users non-traceable. To check whether the suspects entered the building, the police can ask the OA/GM to open all signatures that were used for authentication at the entrance. Since only the suspects are traceable, the group manager can only identify them if they indeed entered this building. However, if a standard group signature scheme (e.g., [1–3,6]) were used, then the privacy of innocent users would be seriously violated. In this situation, one might think that a traceable signature scheme, as suggested by Kiayias, Tsiounis and Yung [22], would work. By requesting a user-specific trapdoor from the OA/GM, the police can trace all the signatures created by the suspects. However, this only achieves privacy of innocent users against the *police*, but not against the *group authorities*. In fact, in a traceable signature scheme, the OA/GM has the full power to identify the signers of all signatures and hence can violate the privacy of all users without being detected. In contrast, if an ATS scheme is used, then the OA/GM must later reveal which user he chose to be traceable, thus enabling his accountability.

In [24], besides demonstrating the feasibility of ATS under generic assumptions, Kohlweiss and Miers also presented an instantiation based on number-theoretic assumptions, which remains the only known concrete ATS construction to date. This scheme, however, is vulnerable against quantum computers due to Shor's algorithm [53]. For the sake of not putting all eggs in one basket, it is therefore tempting to build schemes based on post-quantum foundations. In this paper, we investigate the design of accountable tracing signatures based on lattice assumptions, which are currently among the most viable foundations for post-quantum cryptography. Let us now take a look at the closely related and recently active topic of lattice-based group signatures.

LATTICE-BASED GROUP SIGNATURES. The first lattice-based group signature scheme was introduced by Gordon, Katz and Vaikuntanathan in 2010 [19]. Subsequently, numerous schemes offering improvements in terms of security and efficiency have been proposed [9,11,25,27,29,33,46,49]. Nevertheless, regarding the supports of advanced functionalities, lattice-based group signatures are still way behind their number-theoretic-based counterparts. Indeed, there have been known only a few lattice-based schemes [27,30,31,34,35] that depart from the BMW model [2] - which deals solely with static groups and which may be too inflexible to be considered for a wide range of real-life applications. In particular, although there was an attempt [30] to restrict the power of the OA in the MDO sense, the problem of making the OA accountable in the context of lattice-based group signatures is still open. This somewhat unsatisfactory state-of-affairs motivates our search for a lattice-based instantiation of ATS. As we will discuss below, the technical road towards our goal is not straightforward: there are challenges and missing building blocks along the way.

OUR RESULTS AND TECHNIQUES. In this paper, we introduce the first lattice-based accountable tracing signature scheme. The scheme satisfies the security requirements suggested by Kohlweiss and Miers [24], assuming the hardness of the Ring Short Integer Solution (RSIS) problem and the Ring Learning With Errors (RLWE) problem. As all other known lattice-based group signatures, the security of our scheme is analyzed in the random oracle model. For a security parameter λ, our ATS scheme features group public key size and user secret key size $\widetilde{\mathcal{O}}(\lambda)$. However, the accountability of the OA/GM comes at a price: the signature size is of order $\widetilde{\mathcal{O}}(\lambda^2)$ compared with $\widetilde{\mathcal{O}}(\lambda)$ in a recent scheme by Ling et al. [35].

Let us now give an overview of our techniques. First, we recall that in an ordinary group signature scheme [2,3], to enable traceability, the user is supposed to encrypt his identifying information and prove the well-formedness of the resulting ciphertext. In an ATS scheme, however, not all users are traceable. We thus would need a mechanism to distinguish between traceable users and non-traceable ones. A possible method is to let traceable users encrypt their identities under a public key (pk) such that only the OA/GM knows the underlying secret key (sk), while for non-traceable users, no one knows the secret key. However, there seems to be no incentive for users to deliberately make themselves traceable. We hence should think of a way to choose traceable users obliviously.

An interesting approach is to randomize pk to a new public key epk so that it is infeasible to decide how these keys are related without the knowledge of the secret key and the used randomness. More specifically, when a user joins the group, the OA/GM first randomizes pk to epk and sends the latter to the user together with a certificate. The difference between traceable users and non-traceable ones lies in whether OA/GM knows the underlying secret key. Thanks to the obliviousness property of the randomization, the users are unaware of whether they are traceable. Then, when signing messages, the user encrypts his identity using his own randomized key epk (note that this "public key" should be kept secret) and proves the well-formedness of the ciphertext. Several questions regarding this approach then arise. What special kind of encryption scheme should we use? How to randomize the public key in order to get the desirable obliviousness? More importantly, how could the user prove the honest execution of encryption if the underlying encryption key is secret?

To address the first two questions, Kohlweiss and Miers [24] proposed the notion of key-oblivious encryption (KOE) - a public-key encryption scheme in which one can randomize public keys in an oblivious manner. Kohlweiss and Miers showed that a KOE scheme can be built from a key-private homomorphic public-key encryption scheme. They then gave an explicit construction based on the ElGamal cryptosystem [17], where epk is obtained by multiplying pk by a ciphertext of 1. When adapting this idea into the lattice setting, however, one has to be careful. In fact, we observe that an implicit condition for the underlying key-private public-key encryption scheme is that its public key and ciphertext should have *the same algebraic form*[1], which is often not the case for the schemes in the lattice setting, e.g., [18,50]. Furthermore, lattice-based encryption schemes from the Learning with Errors (LWE) problem or its ring version RLWE often involve noise terms that grow quickly when one performs homomorphic operations over ciphertexts. Fortunately, we could identify a suitable candidate: the RLWE-based encryption scheme proposed by Lyubashevsky, Peiker and Regev (LPR) [42], for which both the public key and the ciphertext consist of a pair of ring elements. Setting the parameters carefully to control the noise growth in LPR, we are able to adapt the blueprint of [24] into the lattice setting and obtain a lattice-based KOE scheme.

To tackle the third question, we need a zero-knowledge (ZK) protocol for proving well-formedness of the ciphertext under a hidden encryption key, which is quite challenging to build in the RLWE setting. Existing ZK protocols from lattices belong to two main families. One line of research [4,5,36,37,40,43] designed very elegant approximate ZK proofs for (R)LWE and (R)SIS relations by employing rejection sampling techniques. While these proofs are quite efficient and compact, they only handle linear relations. In other words, they can only prove knowledge of a short vector $\mathbf{x}$ satisfying $\mathbf{y} = \mathbf{A} \cdot \mathbf{x} \bmod q$, for *public* $\mathbf{A}$ and public $\mathbf{y}$. This seems insufficient for our purpose. Another line of research [13,28,29,32,33,35] developed decomposition/ extension/permutation

---

[1] This condition is needed so that epk can be computed as pk $\cdot$ enc(1) (multiplicative homomorphic) or pk $+$ enc(0) (additive homomorphic).

techniques that operate in Stern's framework [55]. Although Stern-like protocols are less practical than those in the first family, they are much more versatile and can even deal with quadratic relations [28]. More precisely, as demonstrated by Libert et al. [28] one can employ Stern-like techniques to prove knowledge of *secret-and-certified* **A** together with short secret vector **x** satisfying $\mathbf{y} = \mathbf{A} \cdot \mathbf{x} \bmod q$. Thus, Libert et al.'s work appears to be the "right" stepping stone for our case. However, in [28], quadratic relations were considered only in the setting of general lattices, while here we have to deal with the ring setting, for which the multiplication operation is harder to express, capture and prove in zero-knowledge. Nevertheless we manage to adapt their techniques into the ring lattices and obtain the desired technical building block.

As discussed so far, we have identified the necessary ingredients - the LPR encryption scheme and Stern-like ZK protocols - for upgrading a lattice-based ordinary group signature to a lattice-based accountable tracing signature. Next, we need to find a lattice-based ordinary group signature scheme that is compatible with the those ingredients. To this end, we work with Ling et al.'s scheme [35], that also employs the LPR system for its tracing layer and Stern-like techniques for proving knowledge of a valid user certificate (which is a Ducas-Micciancio signature [14,15] based on the hardness of the Ring Short Integer Solution (RSIS) problem). We note that the scheme from [35] achieves constant-size signatures, which means that the signature size is independent of the number of users. As a by-product, our signatures are also constant-size (although our constant is larger, due to the treatment of quadratic relations).

A remaining aspect is how to enable the accountability of the OA/GM. To this end, we let the latter reveal the choice (either traceable or non-traceable) for a given user together with the randomness used to obtain the randomized public key. The user then checks whether his epk was computed as claimed. However, the OA/GM may claim a traceable user to be non-traceable by giving away malicious randomness and accusing that the user had changed epk by himself. To ensure non-repudiation, OA/GM is required to sign epk and the users' identifying information when registering the user into the group. This mechanism in fact also prevents dishonest users from choosing non-traceable epk by themselves.

The obtained ATS scheme is then proven secure in the random oracle model under the RSIS and RLWE assumptions, according to the security requirements put forward by Kohlweiss and Miers [24]. On the efficiency front, as all known lattice-based group signatures with advanced functionalities, our scheme is still far from being practical. We, however, hope that our result will inspire more efficient constructions in the near future.

2   Background

NOTATIONS. For a positive integer n, define the set $\{1, 2, \ldots, n\}$ as $[n]$, the set $\{0, 1, \ldots, n\}$ as $[0, n]$, and the set containing all the integers from $-n$ to n as $[-n, n]$. Denote the set of all positive integers as $\mathbb{Z}^+$. If S is a finite set, then $x \xleftarrow{\$} S$ means that x is chosen uniformly at random from S. Let $\mathbf{a} \in \mathbb{R}^{m_1}$ and

$\mathbf{b} \in \mathbb{R}^{m_2}$ be two vectors for positive integers m_1, m_2. Denote $(\mathbf{a}\|\mathbf{b}) \in \mathbb{R}^{m_1+m_2}$, instead of $(\mathbf{a}^\top, \mathbf{b}^\top)^\top$, as the concatenation of these two vectors.

2.1 Rings, RSIS and RLWE

Let $q \geq 3$ be a positive integer and let $\mathbb{Z}_q = [-\frac{q-1}{2}, \frac{q-1}{2}]$. In this work, let us consider rings $R = \mathbb{Z}[X]/(X^n + 1)$ and $R_q = (R/qR)$, where n is a power of 2.

Let τ be the coefficient embedding $\tau : R_q \to \mathbb{Z}_q^n$ that maps a ring element $v = v_0 + v_1 \cdot X + \ldots + v_{n-1} \cdot X^{n-1} \in R_q$ to a vector $\tau(v) = (v_0, v_1, \ldots, v_{n-1})^\top$ over $\mathbb{Z}_q^n$. When working with vectors and matrices over R_q, we generalize the notations τ in the following way. For a vector $\mathbf{v} = (v_1, \ldots, v_m)^\top \in R_q^m$, define $\tau(\mathbf{v}) = (\tau(v_1)\| \cdots \|\tau(v_m)) \in \mathbb{Z}_q^{mn}$.

For $a = a_0 + a_1 \cdot X + \ldots + a_{n-1} \cdot X^{N-1} \in R$, we define $\|a\|_\infty = \max_i(|a_i|)$. Similarly, for vector $\mathbf{b} = (b_1, \ldots, b_m)^\top \in R^m$, we define $\|\mathbf{b}\|_\infty = \max_j(\|b_j\|_\infty)$.

We now recall the average-case problems RSIS and RLWE associated with the rings R, R_q, as well as their hardness results.

Definition 1 ([38, 39, 48]). *Given a uniform matrix $\mathbf{A} = [a_1|a_2|\cdots|a_m]$ over $R_q^{1\times m}$, the $\mathsf{RSIS}^\infty_{n,m,q,\beta}$ problem asks to find a ring vector $\mathbf{b} = (b_1, b_2, \ldots, b_m)^\top$ over R^m such that $\mathbf{A} \cdot \mathbf{b} = a_1 \cdot b_1 + a_2 \cdot b_2 + \cdots + a_m \cdot b_m = 0$ over R_q and $0 < \|\mathbf{b}\|_\infty \leq \beta$.*

For polynomial bounded m, β and $q \geq \beta \cdot \widetilde{\mathcal{O}}(\sqrt{n})$, it was proven that the $\mathsf{RSIS}^\infty_{n,m,q,\beta}$ problem is no easier than the SIVP_γ problem in any ideal in the ring R, where $\gamma = \beta \cdot \widetilde{\mathcal{O}}(\sqrt{nm})$ (see [26, 38, 48]).

Definition 2 ([41, 42, 54]). *For positive integers $n, m, q \geq 2$ and a probability distribution χ over the ring R, define a distribution $A_{s,\chi}$ over $R_q \times R_q$ for $s \overset{\$}{\leftarrow} R_q$ in the following way: it first samples a uniformly random element $a \in R_q$, an error element $e \hookleftarrow \chi$, and then outputs $(a, a \cdot s + e)$. The target of the $\mathsf{RLWE}_{n,m,q,\chi}$ problem is to distinguish m samples chosen from a uniform distribution over $R_q \times R_q$ and m samples chosen from the distribution $A_{s,\chi}$ for $s \overset{\$}{\leftarrow} R_q$.*

Let $q \geq 2$ and $B = \widetilde{\mathcal{O}}(\sqrt{n})$ be positive integers. χ is a distribution over R which efficiently outputs samples $e \in R$ with $\|e\|_\infty \leq B$ with overwhelming probability in n. Then there is a quantum reduction from the $\mathsf{RLWE}_{n,m,q,\chi}$ problem to the SIVP_γ problem and the SVP_γ problem in any ideal in the ring R, where $\gamma = \widetilde{\mathcal{O}}(\sqrt{n} \cdot q/B)$ (see [10, 26, 41, 47]). It is shown that the hardness of the RLWE problem is preserved when the secret s is sampled from the error distribution χ (see [10, 41]).

2.2 Decompositions

In this work, we employ the decomposition technique from [32]. For any positive integer B, let $\delta_B := \lfloor \log_2 B \rfloor + 1 = \lceil \log_2(B+1) \rceil$ and the sequence $B_1, \ldots, B_{\delta_B}$, where $B_j = \lfloor \frac{B+2^{j-1}}{2^j} \rfloor$, for any $j \in [\delta_B]$. Then there is a decomposition procedure that on input $v \in [0, B]$, it outputs $\mathsf{idec}_B(a) = (a^{(1)}, a^{(2)}, \ldots, a^{(\delta_B)})^\top \in \{0, 1\}^{\delta_B}$ satisfying $(B_1, B_2, \ldots, B_{\delta_B}) \cdot \mathsf{idec}_B(a) = a$.

In [35], the above decomposition procedure is also utilized to deal with polynomials in the ring R_q. Specifically, for $B \in [1, \frac{q-1}{2}]$, define the injective function rdec_B that maps $a \in R_q$ with $\|a\|_\infty \leq B$ to $\mathbf{a} \in R^{\delta_B}$ with $\|\mathbf{a}\|_\infty \leq 1$, which works as follows.

1. Let $\tau(a) = (a_0, \ldots, a_{n-1})^\top$. For each i, let $\sigma(a_i) = 0$ if $a_i = 0$; $\sigma(a_i) = -1$ if $a_i < 0$; and $\sigma(a_i) = 1$ if $a_i > 0$.
2. $\forall i$, compute $\mathbf{w}_i = \sigma(a_i) \cdot \mathsf{idec}_B(|a_i|) = (w_{i,1}, \ldots, w_{i,\delta_B})^\top \in \{-1, 0, 1\}^{\delta_B}$.
3. Form the vector $\mathbf{w} = (\mathbf{w}_0 \| \ldots \| \mathbf{w}_{n-1}) \in \{-1, 0, 1\}^{n\delta_B}$, and let $\mathbf{a} \in R^{\delta_B}$ be the vector such that $\tau(\mathbf{a}) = \mathbf{w}$.
4. Output $\mathsf{rdec}_B(a) = \mathbf{a}$.

When working with vectors of ring elements, e.g., $\mathbf{v} = (v_1, \ldots, v_m)\top$ such that $\|\mathbf{v}\|_\infty \leq B$, then we let $\mathsf{rdec}_B(\mathbf{v}) = (\mathsf{rdec}_B(v_1) \| \cdots \| \mathsf{rdec}_B(v_m)) \in R^{m\delta_B}$. Now, $\forall m, B \in \mathbb{Z}^+$, we define matrices $\mathbf{H}_B \in \mathbb{Z}^{n \times n\delta_B}$ as

$$\mathbf{H}_B = \begin{bmatrix} B_1 \ldots B_{\delta_B} & & \\ & \ddots & \\ & & B_1 \ldots B_{\delta_B} \end{bmatrix}.$$

Then we have

$$\tau(a) = \mathbf{H}_B \cdot \tau(\mathsf{rdec}_B(a)) \bmod q.$$

For simplicity reason, when $B = \frac{q-1}{2}$, we will use the notation rdec instead of $\mathsf{rdec}_{\frac{q-1}{2}}$, and $\mathbf{H}$ instead of $\mathbf{H}_{\frac{q-1}{2}}$.

2.3   A Variant of the Ducas-Micciancio Signature Scheme

We recall the stateful and adaptively secure version of Ducas-Micciancio signature scheme [14,15], which is used to enroll new users in our construction.

Following [14,15], throughout this work, for any real constants $c > 1$ and $\alpha_0 \geq \frac{1}{c-1}$, define a series of sets $\mathcal{T}_j = \{0, 1\}^{c_j}$ of lengths $c_j = \lfloor \alpha_0 c^j \rfloor$ for $j \in [d]$, where $d \geq \log_c(\omega(\log n))$. For each tag $t = (t_0, t_1, \ldots, t_{c_j})^\top \in \mathcal{T}_j$ for $j \in [d]$, associate it with a ring element $t(X) = \sum_{k=0}^{c_j} t_k \cdot X^k \in R_q$. Let $c_0 = 0$ and then define $t_{[i]}(X) = \sum_{k=c_{i-1}}^{c_i-1} t_k \cdot X^k$ and $t_{[i]} = (t_{c_{i-1}}, \ldots, t_{c_i-1})^\top$ for $i \in [j]$. Then one can check $t = (t_{[1]} \| t_{[2]} \| \cdots \| t_{[j]})$ and $t(X) = \sum_{i=1}^j t_{[i]}(X)$.

This variant works with the following parameters.

- Let n, m, q, k be some positive integers such that $n \geq 4$ is a power of 2, $m \geq 2\lceil \log q \rceil + 2$, and $q = 3^k$. Define the rings $R = \mathbb{Z}[X]/(X^n + 1)$ and $R_q = R/qR$.
- Let the message dimension be $m_s = \mathrm{poly}(n)$. Also, let $\ell = \lfloor \log \frac{q-1}{2} \rfloor + 1$, and $\overline{m} = m + k$ and $\overline{m}_s = m_s \cdot \ell$.

- Let integer $\beta = \widetilde{\mathcal{O}}(n)$ and integer d and sequence $c_0, \ldots, c_d$ be as above.
- Let $S \in \mathbb{Z}$ be a state that is 0 initially.

The public verification key consists of the following:

$$\mathbf{A}, \mathbf{F}_0 \in R_q^{1 \times \overline{m}}; \quad \mathbf{A}_{[0]}, \ldots, \mathbf{A}_{[d]} \in R_q^{1 \times k}; \quad \mathbf{F} \in R_q^{1 \times \ell}; \quad \mathbf{F}_1 \in R_q^{1 \times \overline{m}_s}; \quad u \in R_q$$

while the secret signing key is a Micciancio-Peikert [44] trapdoor matrix $\mathbf{R} \in R_q^{m \times k}$.

When signing a message $\mathsf{m} \in R_q^{m_s}$, the signer first computes $\overline{\mathsf{m}} = \mathsf{rdec}(\mathsf{m}) \in R^{\overline{m}_s}$, whose coefficients are in the set $\{-1, 0, 1\}$. He then performs the following steps.

- Set the tag $t = (t_0, t_1 \ldots, t_{c_d-1})^\top \in \mathcal{T}_d$, where $S = \sum_{j=0}^{c_d-1} 2^j \cdot t_j$, and compute $\mathbf{A}_t = [\mathbf{A} | \mathbf{A}_{[0]} + \sum_{i=1}^d t_{[i]} \mathbf{A}_{[i]}] \in R_q^{1 \times (\overline{m}+k)}$. Update S to $S + 1$.
- Choose $\mathbf{r} \in R^{\overline{m}}$ with $\|\mathbf{r}\|_\infty \leq \beta$.
- Let $y = \mathbf{F}_0 \cdot \mathbf{r} + \mathbf{F}_1 \cdot \overline{\mathsf{m}} \in R_q$ and $u_p = \mathbf{F} \cdot \mathsf{rdec}(y) + u \in R_q$.
- Employing the trapdoor matrix $\mathbf{R}$, produce a ring vector $\mathbf{v} \in R^{\overline{m}+k}$ with $\mathbf{A}_t \cdot \mathbf{v} = u_p$ over the ring R_q and $\|\mathbf{v}\|_\infty \leq \beta$.
- Return the tuple $(t, \mathbf{r}, \mathbf{v})$ as a signature for the message m.

To check the validity of the tuple $(t, \mathbf{r}, \mathbf{v})$ with respect to message $\mathsf{m} \in R_q^{m_s}$, the verifier first computes the matrix $\mathbf{A}_t$ as above and verifies the following conditions:

$$\begin{cases} \mathbf{A}_t \cdot \mathbf{v} = \mathbf{F} \cdot \mathsf{rdec}(\mathbf{F}_0 \cdot \mathbf{r} + \mathbf{F}_1 \cdot \mathsf{rdec}(\mathsf{m})) + u, \\ \|\mathbf{r}\|_\infty \leq \beta, \quad \|\mathbf{v}\|_\infty \leq \beta. \end{cases}$$

He outputs 1 if all these three conditions hold and 0 otherwise.

Lemma 1 ([14,15]). *Given at most polynomially bounded number of signature queries, the above variant is existentially unforgeable against adaptive chosen message attacks assuming the hardness of the* $\mathsf{RSIS}_{n,\overline{m},q,\widetilde{\mathcal{O}}(n^2)}$ *problem.*

2.4   Stern-Like Zero-Knowledge Argument of Knowledge

The statistical zero-knowledge arguments of knowledge (ZKAoK) presented in this work are Stern-like [55] protocols. In particular, they are Σ-protocols in the generalized sense defined in [4,20] (where 3 valid transcripts are needed for extraction, instead of just 2). Stern's protocol was originally proposed in the context of code-based cryptography, and was later adapted into the lattice setting by Kawachi et al. [21]. Subsequently, it was empowered by Ling et al. [32] to handle the matrix-vector relations where the secret vectors are of small infinity norm, and further developed to design various lattice-based schemes. Libert et al. [27] put forward an abstraction of Stern's protocol to capture a wider range lattice-based relations.

2.5   Key-Oblivious Encryption

We next recall the definitions of key-oblivious encryption (KOE), as introduced in [24]. A KOE scheme consists of the following polynomial-time algorithms.

Setup(λ): On input the security parameter λ, it outputs public parameter pp. pp is implicit for all algorithms below if not explicitly mentioned.

KeyGen(pp): On input pp, it generates a key pair (pk, sk).

KeyRand(pk): On input the public key pk, it outputs a new public key pk' for the same secret key.

Enc(pk, m): On inputs pk and a message m, it outputs a ciphertext ct on this message.

Dec(sk, ct): On inputs sk and ct, it outputs the decrypted message m'.

CORRECTNESS. The above scheme must satisfy the following correctness requirement: For all λ, all pp $\leftarrow$ Setup(λ), all (pk, sk) $\leftarrow$ KeyGen(pp), all pk' $\leftarrow$ KeyRand(pk), all m,

$$Dec(sk, Enc(pk', m)) = m.$$

SECURITY. The security requirements of a KOE scheme consist of *key randomizability* (KR), *plaintext indistinguishability under key randomization* (INDr), and *key privacy under key randomization* (KPr). Details of these requirements are referred to [24] or the full version of this paper.

2.6   Accountable Tracing Signatures

An ATS scheme [24] involves a group manager (GM) who also serves as the opening authority (OA), a set of users, who are potential group members. As a standard group signature scheme (e.g. [2,3]), GM is able to identify the signer of a given signature. However, if GM is able to do so, there is an additional *accounting* mechanism that later reveals which user he chose to trace (traceable user). Specifically, if a user suspects that he was traceable by group manager who had claimed non-traceability of this user, then the user can resort to this mechanism to check whether group manager is honest/accountable or not. An ATS scheme consists of the following polynomial-time algorithms.

Setup(λ): On input the security parameter λ, it outputs public parameter pp. pp is implicit for all algorithms below if not explicitly mentioned.

GKeyGen(pp): This algorithm is run by GM. On input pp, GM generates group public key gpk and group secret keys: issue key ik and opening key ok.

UKeyGen(pp): Given input pp, it outputs a user key pair (upk, usk).

Enroll(gpk, ik, upk, tr): This algorithm is run by GM. Upon receiving a user public key upk from a user, GM determines the value of the bit tr $\in \{0, 1\}$, indicating whether the user is traceable (tr $= 1$) or not. He then produces a certificate cert for this user according to his choice of tr. GM then registers this user to the group and stores the registration information and the witness w^{escrw} to the bit tr, and sends cert to the user.

Sign(gpk, cert, usk, M): Given the inputs gpk, cert, usk and message M, this algorithm outputs a signature Σ on this message M.

Verify(gpk, M, Σ): Given the inputs gpk and the message-signature pair (M, Σ), this algorithm outputs 1/0 indicating whether the signature is valid or not.

Open(gpk, ok, M, Σ): Given the inputs gpk, ok and the pair (M, Σ), this algorithm returns a user public key upk' and a proof Π_{open} demonstrating that user upk' indeed generated the signature Σ. In case of upk' $= \bot$, $\Pi_{open} = \bot$.

Judge(gpk, M, Σ, upk', Π_{open}): Given all the inputs, this algorithm outputs 1/0 indicating whether it accepts the opening result or not.

Account(gpk, cert, w^{escrw}, tr): Given all the inputs, this algorithm returns 1 confirming the choice of tr and 0 otherwise.

CORRECTNESS. The above ATS scheme requires that: for any honestly generated signature, the Verify algorithm always outputs 1. Furthermore, if the user is traceable, then Account algorithm outputs 1 when tr $= 1$, and the Open algorithm can identify the signer and generate a proof Π_{open} that will be accepted by the Judge algorithm. On the other hand, if the user is non-traceable, then the Account algorithm outputs 1 when tr $= 0$, and the Open algorithm outputs $\bot$.

Remark 1. There is a minor difference between the syntax we describe here and that presented by Kohlweiss and Miers [24]. Specifically, we omit the time epoch when the user joins the group, since we do not consider forward and backward tracing scenarios as in [24].

SECURITY. The security requirements of an ATS scheme consist of *anonymity under tracing* (AuT), *traceability* (Trace), and *non-frameability* (NF), *anonymity with accountability* (AwA) and *trace-obliviousness* (TO). Details of these requirements are referred to [24] or the full version of this paper.

3 Key-Oblivious Encryption from Lattices

In [24], Kohlweiss and Miers constructed a KOE scheme based on ElGamal cryptosystem [17]. To adapt their blueprint into the lattice setting, we would need a key-private homomorphic encryption scheme whose public keys and ciphertexts should have the same algebraic form (e.g., each of them is a pair of ring elements). We observe that, the LPR RLWE-based encryption scheme, under appropriate setting of parameters, does satisfy these conditions. We thus obtain an instantiation of KOE which will then serve as a building block for our ATS construction in Sect. 4.

3.1 Description

Our KOE scheme works as follows.

Setup(λ): Given the security parameter λ, let $n = \mathcal{O}(\lambda)$ be a power of 2 and $q = \tilde{\mathcal{O}}(n^4)$. Also let $\ell = \lfloor \log \frac{q-1}{2} \rfloor + 1$. Define the rings $R = \mathbb{Z}[X]/(X^n + 1)$ and $R_q = R/qR$. Let the integer bound B be of order $\tilde{\mathcal{O}}(\sqrt{n})$ and χ be a B-bounded distribution over the ring R. This algorithm then outputs public parameter $\mathsf{pp} = \{n, q, \ell, R, R_q, B, \chi\}$.

KeyGen(pp): Given the input pp, this algorithm samples $s \hookleftarrow \chi$, $\mathbf{e} \hookleftarrow \chi^\ell$ and $\mathbf{a} \xleftarrow{\$} R_q^\ell$. Set $\mathsf{pk} = (\mathbf{a}, \mathbf{b}) = (\mathbf{a}, \mathbf{a} \cdot s + \mathbf{e}) \in R_q^\ell \times R_q^\ell$ and $\mathsf{sk} = s$. It then returns $(\mathsf{pk}, \mathsf{sk})$.

KeyRand(pk): Given the public key $\mathsf{pk} = (\mathbf{a}, \mathbf{b})$, it samples $g \hookleftarrow \chi$, $\mathbf{e}_1 \hookleftarrow \chi^\ell$ and $\mathbf{e}_2 \hookleftarrow \chi^\ell$. Compute

$$(\mathbf{a}', \mathbf{b}') = (\mathbf{a} \cdot g + \mathbf{e}_1, \ \mathbf{b} \cdot g + \mathbf{e}_2) \in R_q^\ell \times R_q^\ell.$$

This algorithm then outputs randomized public key as $\mathsf{pk}' = (\mathbf{a}', \mathbf{b}')$.

Enc(pk', p): Given the public key $\mathsf{pk}' = (\mathbf{a}', \mathbf{b}')$ and a message $p \in R_q$, it samples $g' \in \chi$, $\mathbf{e}_1' \in \chi^\ell$ and $\mathbf{e}_2' \in \chi^\ell$. Compute

$$(\mathbf{c}_1, \mathbf{c}_2) = (\mathbf{a}' \cdot g' + \mathbf{e}_1', \ \mathbf{b}' \cdot g' + \mathbf{e}_2' + \lfloor q/4 \rfloor \cdot \mathsf{rdec}(p)) \in R_q^\ell \times R_q^\ell.$$

This algorithm returns ciphertext as $\mathsf{ct} = (\mathbf{c}_1, \mathbf{c}_2)$.

Dec(sk, ct): Given $\mathsf{sk} = s$ and $\mathsf{ct} = (\mathbf{c}_1, \mathbf{c}_2)$, the algorithm proceeds as follows.

1. It computes
$$\mathbf{p}'' = \frac{\mathbf{c}_2 - \mathbf{c}_1 \cdot s}{\lfloor q/4 \rfloor}.$$

2. For each coefficient of $\mathbf{p}''$,
   - if it is closer to 0 than to -1 and 1, then round it to 0;
   - if it is closer to -1 than to 0 and 1, then round it to -1;
   - if it is closer to 1 than to 0 and -1, then round it to 1.
3. Denote the rounded $\mathbf{p}''$ as $\mathbf{p}' \in R_q^\ell$ with coefficients in $\{-1, 0, 1\}$.
4. Let $p' \in R_q$ such that $\tau(p') = \mathbf{H} \cdot \tau(\mathbf{p}')$. Here, $\mathbf{H} \in \mathbb{Z}_q^{n \times n\ell}$ is the decomposition matrix for elements of R_q (see Sect. 2.2).

3.2 Analysis

CORRECTNESS. Note that

$$\begin{aligned}
\mathbf{c}_2 - \mathbf{c}_1 \cdot s &= \mathbf{b}' \cdot g' + \mathbf{e}_2' + \lfloor q/4 \rfloor \cdot \mathsf{rdec}(p) - (\mathbf{a}' \cdot g' + \mathbf{e}_1') \cdot s \\
&= \mathbf{e} \cdot g \cdot g' + \mathbf{e}_2 \cdot g' - \mathbf{e}_1 \cdot s \cdot g' + \mathbf{e}_2' - \mathbf{e}_1' \cdot s + \lfloor q/4 \rfloor \cdot \mathsf{rdec}(p)
\end{aligned}$$

where $s, g, g', \mathbf{e}, \mathbf{e}_1, \mathbf{e}_2, \mathbf{e}'_1, \mathbf{e}'_2$ are B-bounded. Hence we have:

$$\|\mathbf{e} \cdot g \cdot g' + \mathbf{e}_2 \cdot g' - \mathbf{e}_1 \cdot s \cdot g' + \mathbf{e}'_2 - \mathbf{e}'_1 \cdot s\|_\infty \leq 3n^2 \cdot B^3 = \widetilde{\mathcal{O}}(n^{3.5}) \leq \lceil \frac{q}{10} \rceil = \widetilde{\mathcal{O}}(n^4).$$

With overwhelming probability, the rounding procedure described in the Dec algorithm recovers $\mathsf{rdec}(p)$ and hence outputs p. Therefore, our KOE scheme is correct.

SECURITY. The security of our KOE scheme is stated in the following theorem.

Theorem 1. *Under the* RLWE *assumption, the described key-oblivious encryption scheme satisfies: (i) key randomizability; (ii) plaintext indistinguishability under key randomization; and (iii) key privacy under key randomization.*

The proof of Theorem 1 is deferred to the full version of this paper.

4 Accountable Tracing Signatures from Lattices

In this section, we construct our ATS scheme based on: (i) The Ducas-Micciancio signature scheme (as recalled in Sect. 2.3); (ii) The KOE scheme described in Sect. 3; and (iii) Stern-like ZK argument systems. Due to space restriction, the details of our Stern-like ZK protocol are deferred to the full version.

4.1 Description of Our ATS Scheme

We assume there is a trusted setup such that it generates parameters of the scheme. Specifically, it generates a public matrix $\mathbf{B}$ for generating users' key pairs, and two secret-public key pairs of our KOE scheme such that the secret keys are discarded and not known by any party. The group public key then consists of three parts: (i) the parameters from the trusted setup, (ii) a verification key of the Ducas-Micciancio signature, (iii) two public keys of our KOE scheme such that the group manager knows both secret keys. The issue key is the Ducas-Micciancio signing key, while the opening key is any one of the corresponding secret keys of the two public keys. Note that both the issue key and the opening key are generated by the group manager.

When a user joins the group, it first generates a secret-public key pair $(\mathbf{x}, p)$ such that $\mathbf{B} \cdot \mathbf{x} = p$. It then interacts with the group manager, who will determine whether user p is traceable or not. If the user is traceable, group manager sets a bit $\mathsf{tr} = 1$, randomizes the two public key generated by himself, and then generates a Ducas-Micciancio signature σ_{cert} on user public key p and the two randomized public keys $(\mathsf{epk}_1, \mathsf{epk}_2)$. If the user is non-traceable, group manager sets a bit $\mathsf{tr} = 0$, randomizes the two public key generated from the trusted setup, and then generates a signature on p and $\mathsf{epk}_1, \mathsf{epk}_2$. If it completes successfully, the group manager sends certificate $\mathsf{cert} = (p, \mathsf{epk}_1, \mathsf{epk}_2, \sigma_{\mathsf{cert}})$ to user p, registers this user to the group, and keeps himself the witness w^{escrw} that was ever used for randomization.

Once registered as a group member, the user can sign messages on behalf of the group. To this end, the user first encrypts his public key p twice using his two randomized public keys, and obtains ciphertexts c_1, c_2. The user then generates a ZKAoK such that (i) he has a valid secret key x corresponding to p; (ii) he possesses a Ducas-Micciancio signature on p and epk_1, epk_2; and (iii) c_1, c_2 are correct ciphertexts of p under the randomized keys epk_1, epk_2, respectively. Since the ZKAoK protocol the user employs has soundness error $2/3$ in each execution, it is repeated $\kappa = \omega(\log \lambda)$ times to make the error negligibly small. Then, it is made non-interactive via the Fiat-Shamir heuristic [16]. The signature then consists of the non-interactive zero-knowledge argument of knowledge (NIZKAoK) Π_{gs} and the two ciphertexts. Note that the ZK argument together with double encryption enables CCA-security of the underlying encryption scheme, which is known as the Naor-Yung transformation [45].

To verify the validity of a signature, it suffices to verify the validity of the argument Π_{gs}. Should the need arises, the group manager can decrypt using his opening key. If a user is traceable, the opening key group manager possesses can be used to correctly identify the signer. However, if a user is non-traceable, then his anonymity is preserved against the manager.

To prevent corrupted opening, group manager is required to generate a NIZKAoK of correct opening Π_{open}. Only when Π_{open} is a valid argument, we then accept the opening result. Furthermore, there is an additional accounting mechanism for group manager to reveal which users he had chosen to be traceable. This is done by checking the consistency of tr and the randomized public keys in user's certificate with the help of the witness w^{escrw}.

We describe the details of our scheme below.

Setup(λ): Given the security parameter λ, it generates the following public parameter.

- Let $n = \mathcal{O}(\lambda)$ be a power of 2, and modulus $q = \widetilde{\mathcal{O}}(n^4)$, where $q = 3^k$ for $k \in \mathbb{Z}^+$. Let $R = \mathbb{Z}[X]/(X^n + 1)$ and $R_q = R/qR$.
  Also, let $m \geq 2\lceil \log q \rceil + 2$, $\ell = \lfloor \log \frac{q-1}{2} \rfloor + 1$, $m_s = 4\ell + 1$, and $\overline{m} = m + k$ and $\overline{m}_s = m_s \cdot \ell$.
- Let integer d and sequence $c_0, \ldots, c_d$ be described in Sect. 2.3.
- Let $\beta = \widetilde{\mathcal{O}}(n)$ and $B = \widetilde{\mathcal{O}}(\sqrt{n})$ be two integer bounds, and χ be a B-bounded distribution over the ring R.
- Choose a collision-resistant hash function $\mathcal{H}_{FS} : \{0,1\}^* \to \{1,2,3\}^\kappa$, where $\kappa = \omega(\log \lambda)$, which will act as a random oracle in the Fiat-Shamir heuristic [16].
- Choose a statistically hiding and computationally binding commitment scheme from [21], denoted as COM, which will be employed in our ZK argument systems.
- Let $B \xleftarrow{\$} R_q^{1 \times m}$, $a_1^{(0)} \xleftarrow{\$} R_q^\ell$, $a_2^{(0)} \xleftarrow{\$} R_q^\ell$, $s_{-1}, s_{-2} \hookleftarrow \chi$, $e_{-1}, e_{-2} \hookleftarrow \chi^\ell$.
  Compute

$$\mathbf{b}_1^{(0)} = \mathbf{a}_1^{(0)} \cdot s_{-1} + \mathbf{e}_{-1} \in R_q^\ell; \quad \mathbf{b}_2^{(0)} = \mathbf{a}_2^{(0)} \cdot s_{-2} + \mathbf{e}_{-2} \in R_q^\ell.$$

This algorithm outputs the public parameter pp:

$$\{n, q, k, R, R_q, \ell, m, m_s, \overline{m}, \overline{m}_s, d, c_0, \cdots, c_d,$$

$$\beta, B, \chi, \mathcal{H}_{\mathsf{FS}}, \kappa, \mathsf{COM}, \mathbf{B}, \{\mathbf{a}_i^{(0)}, \mathbf{b}_i^{(0)}\}_{i \in \{1,2\}}\}.$$

pp is implicit for all algorithms below if not explicitly mentioned.

GKeyGen(pp): On input pp, GM proceeds as follows.

– Generate verification key

$$\mathbf{A}, \mathbf{F}_0 \in R_q^{1 \times \overline{m}}; \ \mathbf{A}_{[0]}, \ldots, \mathbf{A}_{[d]} \in R_q^{1 \times k}; \ \mathbf{F} \in R_q^{1 \times \ell}; \ \mathbf{F}_1 \in R_q^{1 \times \overline{m}_s}; \ u \in R_q$$

and signing key $\mathbf{R} \in R_q^{m \times k}$ for the Ducas-Micciancio signature from Sect. 2.3.
– Initialize the Naor-Yung double-encryption mechanism [45] with the key-oblivious encryption scheme described in Sect. 3.1. Specifically, sample $s_1, s_2 \hookleftarrow \chi$, $\mathbf{e}_1, \mathbf{e}_2 \hookleftarrow \chi^\ell$, $\mathbf{a}_1^{(1)} \xleftarrow{\$} R_q^\ell$, $\mathbf{a}_2^{(1)} \xleftarrow{\$} R_q^\ell$ and compute

$$\mathbf{b}_1^{(1)} = \mathbf{a}_1^{(1)} \cdot s_1 + \mathbf{e}_1 \in R_q^\ell; \quad \mathbf{b}_2^{(1)} = \mathbf{a}_2^{(1)} \cdot s_2 + \mathbf{e}_2 \in R_q^\ell.$$

Set the group public key gpk, the issue key ik and the opening key ok as follows:

$$\mathsf{gpk} = \{\mathsf{pp}, \mathbf{A}, \{\mathbf{A}_{[j]}\}_{j=0}^d, \mathbf{F}, \mathbf{F}_0, \mathbf{F}_1, u, \mathbf{a}_1^{(1)}, \mathbf{b}_1^{(1)}, \mathbf{a}_2^{(1)}, \mathbf{b}_2^{(1)}\},$$

$$\mathsf{ik} = \mathbf{R}, \qquad \mathsf{ok} = (s_1, \mathbf{e}_1).$$

GM then makes gpk public, sets the registration table $\mathbf{reg} = \emptyset$ and his internal state $S = 0$.

UKeyGen(pp): Given the public parameter, the user first chooses $\mathbf{x} \in R^m$ such that the coefficients are uniformly chosen from the set $\{-1, 0, 1\}$. He then calculates $p = \mathbf{B} \cdot \mathbf{x} \in R_q$. Set $\mathsf{upk} = p$ and $\mathsf{usk} = \mathbf{x}$.

Enroll(gpk, ik, upk, tr): Upon receiving a user public key upk from a user, GM determines the value of the bit $\mathsf{tr} \in \{0, 1\}$, indicating whether the user is traceable. He then does the following:

– Randomize two pairs of public keys $(\mathbf{a}_1^{(\mathsf{tr})}, \mathbf{b}_1^{(\mathsf{tr})})$ and $(\mathbf{a}_2^{(\mathsf{tr})}, \mathbf{b}_2^{(\mathsf{tr})})$ as described in Sect. 3.1. Specifically, sample $g_1, g_2 \hookleftarrow \chi$, $\mathbf{e}_{1,1}, \mathbf{e}_{1,2} \hookleftarrow \chi^\ell$, $\mathbf{e}_{2,1}, \mathbf{e}_{2,2} \hookleftarrow \chi^\ell$. For each $i \in \{1, 2\}$, compute

$$\mathsf{epk}_i = (\mathbf{a}_i', \mathbf{b}_i') = (\mathbf{a}_i^{(\mathsf{tr})} \cdot g_i + \mathbf{e}_{i,1}, \ \mathbf{b}_i^{(\mathsf{tr})} \cdot g_i + \mathbf{e}_{i,2}) \in R_q^\ell \times R_q^\ell. \tag{1}$$

– Set the tag $t = (t_0, t_1 \ldots, t_{c_d - 1})^\top \in \mathcal{T}_d$, where $S = \sum_{j=0}^{c_d - 1} 2^j \cdot t_j$, and compute $\mathbf{A}_t = [\mathbf{A}|\mathbf{A}_{[0]} + \sum_{i=1}^d t_{[i]} \mathbf{A}_{[i]}] \in R_q^{1 \times (\overline{m} + k)}$.
– Let $\mathfrak{m} = (p \| \mathbf{a}_1' \| \mathbf{b}_1' \| \mathbf{a}_2' \| \mathbf{b}_2') \in R_q^{m_s}$.

– Generate a signature $\sigma_{\text{cert}} = (t, \mathbf{r}, \mathbf{v})$ on message $\text{rdec}(\mathfrak{m}) \in R^{\overline{m}_s}$ - whose coefficients are in $\{-1, 0, 1\}$ - using his issue key $\text{ik} = \mathbf{R}$. As in Sect. 2.3, we have $\mathbf{r} \in R^{\overline{m}}$, $\mathbf{v} \in R^{\overline{m}+k}$ and

$$\begin{cases} \mathbf{A}_t \cdot \mathbf{v} = \mathbf{F} \cdot \text{rdec}(\mathbf{F}_0 \cdot \mathbf{r} + \mathbf{F}_1 \cdot \text{rdec}(\mathfrak{m})) + u, \\ \|\mathbf{r}\|_\infty \leq \beta, \quad \|\mathbf{v}\|_\infty \leq \beta. \end{cases} \tag{2}$$

Set certificate cert and w^{escrw} as follows:

$$\text{cert} = (p, \mathbf{a}'_1, \mathbf{b}'_1, \mathbf{a}'_2, \mathbf{b}'_2, t, \mathbf{r}, \mathbf{v}), \quad w^{\text{escrw}} = (g_1, \mathbf{e}_{1,1}, \mathbf{e}_{1,2}, g_2, \mathbf{e}_{2,1}, \mathbf{e}_{2,2}).$$

GM sends cert to the user p, stores $\mathbf{reg}[S] = (p, \text{tr}, w^{\text{escrw}})$, and updates the state to $S + 1$.

$\text{Sign}(\text{gpk}, \text{cert}, \text{usk}, M)$: To sign a message $M \in \{0, 1\}^*$ using the certificate $\text{cert} = (p, \mathbf{a}'_1, \mathbf{b}'_1, \mathbf{a}'_2, \mathbf{b}'_2, t, \mathbf{r}, \mathbf{v})$ and $\text{usk} = \mathbf{x}$, the user proceeds as follows.

– Encrypt the ring vector $\text{rdec}(p) \in R_q^\ell$ whose coefficients are in $\{-1, 0, 1\}$ twice. Namely, sample $g'_1, g'_2 \hookleftarrow \chi$, $\mathbf{e}'_{1,1}, \mathbf{e}'_{1,2} \hookleftarrow \chi^\ell$, and $\mathbf{e}'_{2,1}, \mathbf{e}'_{2,2} \hookleftarrow \chi^\ell$. For each $i \in \{1, 2\}$, compute $\mathbf{c}_i = (\mathbf{c}_{i,1}, \mathbf{c}_{i,2}) \in R_q^\ell \times R_q^\ell$ as follows:

$$\mathbf{c}_{i,1} = \mathbf{a}'_i \cdot g'_i + \mathbf{e}'_{i,1}; \quad \mathbf{c}_{i,2} = \mathbf{b}'_i \cdot g'_i + \mathbf{e}'_{i,2} + \lfloor q/4 \rfloor \cdot \text{rdec}(p).$$

– Generate a NIZKAoK Π_{gs} to demonstrate the possession of a valid tuple ζ of the following form

$$\zeta = (p, \mathbf{a}'_1, \mathbf{b}'_1, \mathbf{a}'_2, \mathbf{b}'_2, t, \mathbf{r}, \mathbf{v}, \mathbf{x}, g'_1, \mathbf{e}'_{1,1}, \mathbf{e}'_{1,2}, g'_2, \mathbf{e}'_{2,1}, \mathbf{e}'_{2,2}) \tag{3}$$

such that
(i) The conditions in (2) are satisfied.
(ii) $\mathbf{c}_1$ and $\mathbf{c}_2$ are correct encryptions of $\text{rdec}(p)$ with B-bounded randomness $g'_1, \mathbf{e}'_{1,1}, \mathbf{e}'_{1,2}$ and $g'_2, \mathbf{e}'_{2,1}, \mathbf{e}'_{2,2}$, respectively.
(iii) $\|\mathbf{x}\|_\infty \leq 1$ and $\mathbf{B} \cdot \mathbf{x} = p$.

This is achieved by running our Stern-like ZK protocol. The protocol is repeated $\kappa = \omega(\log \lambda)$ times and made non-interactive via Fiat-Shamir heuristic [16] as a triple $\Pi_{\text{gs}} = (\{\text{CMT}_i\}_{i=1}^\kappa, \text{CH}, \{\text{RSP}_i\}_{i=1}^\kappa)$ where the challenge CH is generated as $\text{CH} = \mathcal{H}_{\text{FS}}(M, \{\text{CMT}_i\}_{i=1}^\kappa, \xi)$ with ξ of the following form

$$\xi = (\mathbf{A}, \mathbf{A}_{[0]}, \ldots, \mathbf{A}_{[d]}, \mathbf{F}, \mathbf{F}_0, \mathbf{F}_1, u, \mathbf{B}, \mathbf{c}_1, \mathbf{c}_2) \tag{4}$$

– Output the group signature $\Sigma = (\Pi_{\text{gs}}, \mathbf{c}_1, \mathbf{c}_2)$.

$\text{Verify}(\text{gpk}, M, \Sigma)$: Given the inputs, the verifier performs in the following manner.

– Parse Σ as $\Sigma = (\{\text{CMT}_i\}_{i=1}^\kappa, (Ch_1, \ldots, Ch_\kappa), \{\text{RSP}\}_{i=1}^\kappa, \mathbf{c}_1, \mathbf{c}_2)$.
If $(Ch_1, \ldots, Ch_\kappa) \neq \mathcal{H}_{\text{FS}}(M, \{\text{CMT}_i\}_{i=1}^\kappa, \xi)$, output 0, where ξ is as in (4).

- For each $i \in [\kappa]$, run the verification phase of our Stern-like ZK protocol to verify the validity of RSP_i corresponding to CMT_i and Ch_i. If any of the verification process fails, output 0.
- Output 1.

Open(gpk, ok, M, Σ): Let $ok = (s_1, e_1)$ and $\Sigma = (\Pi_{gs}, c_1, c_2)$. The group manager proceeds as follows.

- Use s_1 to decrypt $c_1 = (c_{1,1}, c_{1,2})$ as in the decryption algorithm from Sect. 3.1. The result is $p' \in R_q$.
- He then searches the registration information. If **reg** does not include an element p', then return $\perp$.
- Otherwise, he produces a NIZKAoK Π_{open} to show the knowledge of a tuple $(s_1, e_1, \mathbf{y}) \in R_q \times R_q^\ell \times R_q^\ell$ such that the following conditions hold.

$$\begin{cases} \|s_1\|_\infty \leq B; \ \|e_1\|_\infty \leq B; \ \|\mathbf{y}\|_\infty \leq \lceil q/10 \rceil; \\ \mathbf{a}_1^{(1)} \cdot s_1 + e_1 = \mathbf{b}_1^{(1)}; \\ c_{1,2} - c_{1,1} \cdot s_1 = \mathbf{y} + \lfloor q/4 \rfloor \cdot \mathsf{rdec}(p'). \end{cases} \quad (5)$$

Since the conditions in (5) only encounter linear secret objects with bounded norm, we can easily handled them using the Stern-like techniques. Therefore, we are able to have a statistical ZKAoK for the above statement. Furthermore, the protocol is repeated $\kappa = \omega(\log \lambda)$ times and made non-interactive via the Fiat-Shamir heuristic, resulting in a triple $\Pi_{\mathsf{Open}} = (\{\mathrm{CMT}_i\}_{i=1}^\kappa, \mathrm{CH}, \{\mathrm{RSP}\}_{i=1}^\kappa)$, where $\mathrm{CH} \in \{1, 2, 3\}^\kappa$ is computed as

$$\mathrm{CH} = \mathcal{H}_{\mathsf{FS}}\big(\{\mathrm{CMT}_i\}_{i=1}^\kappa, \mathbf{a}_1^{(1)}, \mathbf{b}_1^{(1)}, M, \Sigma, p'\big). \quad (6)$$

- Output $(p', \Pi_{\mathsf{Open}})$.

Judge($gpk, M, \Sigma, p', \Pi_{open}$): Given all the inputs, this algorithm does the following.

- If Verify algorithm outputs 0 or $p' = \perp$, return 0.
- This algorithm then verifies the argument Π_{Open} with respect to common input $(\mathbf{a}_1^{(1)}, \mathbf{b}_1^{(1)}, M, \Sigma, p')$, in the same way as in the algorithm Verify. If verification of the argument Π_{open} fails, output 0.
- Else output 1.

Account($gpk, \mathsf{cert}, w^{\mathsf{escrw}}, \mathsf{tr}$): Let the certificate be $\mathsf{cert} = (p, \mathbf{a}_1', \mathbf{b}_1', \mathbf{a}_2', \mathbf{b}_2', t, \mathbf{r}, \mathbf{v})$ and witness be $w^{\mathsf{escrw}} = (g_1, e_{1,1}, e_{1,2}, g_2, e_{2,1}, e_{2,2})$ and the bit tr, this algorithm proceeds as follows.

- It checks whether $(t, \mathbf{r}, \mathbf{v})$ is a valid Ducas-Micciancio signature on the message $(p, \mathbf{a}_1', \mathbf{b}_1', \mathbf{a}_2', \mathbf{b}_2')$. Specifically, it verifies whether cert satisfies the conditions in (2). If not, output 0.

– Otherwise, it then checks if $(\mathbf{a}_1', \mathbf{b}_1')$ and $(\mathbf{a}_2', \mathbf{b}_2')$ are randomization of $(\mathbf{a}_1^{(\mathrm{tr})}, \mathbf{b}_1^{(\mathrm{tr})})$ and $(\mathbf{a}_2^{(\mathrm{tr})}, \mathbf{b}_2^{(\mathrm{tr})})$ with respect to randomness $(g_1, \mathbf{e}_{1,1}, \mathbf{e}_{1,2})$ and $(g_2, \mathbf{e}_{2,1}, \mathbf{e}_{2,2})$, respectively. Specifically, it verifies whether the conditions in (1) hold. If not, output 0.
– Else output 1.

4.2   Analysis of Our ATS Scheme

EFFICIENCY. We first analyze the efficiency of our scheme from Sect. 4.1 in terms of the security parameter λ.

– The bit-size of the public key gpk is of order $\mathcal{O}(\lambda \cdot \log^3 \lambda) = \widetilde{\mathcal{O}}(\lambda)$.
– The bit-size of the membership certificate cert is of order $\mathcal{O}(\lambda \cdot \log^2 \lambda) = \widetilde{\mathcal{O}}(\lambda)$.
– The bit-size of a signature Σ is determined by that of the Stern-like NIZKAoK Π_{gs}, which is of order $\mathcal{O}(\lambda^2 \cdot \log^3 \lambda) \cdot \omega(\log \lambda) = \widetilde{\mathcal{O}}(\lambda^2)$.
– The bit-size of the Stern-like NIZKAoK Π_{open} is of order $\mathcal{O}(\lambda \cdot \log^3 \lambda) \cdot \omega(\log \lambda) = \widetilde{\mathcal{O}}(\lambda)$.

CORRECTNESS. For an honestly generated signature Σ for message M, we first show that the Verify algorithm always outputs 1. Due to the honest behavior of the user, when signing a message in the name of the group, this user possesses a valid tuple ζ of the form (3). Therefore, Π_{gs} will be accepted by the Verify algorithm with probability 1 due to the perfect completeness of our argument system.

If an honest user is traceable, then $\mathsf{Account}(\mathsf{gpk}, \mathsf{cert}, w^{\mathrm{escrw}}, 1)$ will output 1, implied by the correctness of Ducas-Micciancio signature scheme and honest behaviour of group manager. In terms of the correctness of the Open algorithm, we observe that $\mathbf{c}_{1,2} - \mathbf{c}_{1,1} \cdot s_1 =$

$$(\mathbf{b}_1^{(\mathrm{tr})} - \mathbf{a}_1^{(\mathrm{tr})} \cdot s_1) \cdot g_1 \cdot g_1' + \mathbf{e}_{1,2} \cdot g_1' - \mathbf{e}_{1,1} \cdot s_1 \cdot g_1' + \mathbf{e}_{1,2}' - \mathbf{e}_{1,1}' \cdot s_1 + \lfloor q/4 \rfloor \cdot \mathsf{rdec}(p),$$

denoted as $\widetilde{\mathbf{e}} + \lfloor q/4 \rfloor \cdot \mathsf{rdec}(p)$. In this case, $\mathsf{tr} = 1$, $\mathbf{b}_1^{(\mathrm{tr})} - \mathbf{a}_1^{(\mathrm{tr})} \cdot s_1 = \mathbf{e}_1$, and $\|\widetilde{\mathbf{e}}\|_\infty \leq \lceil \frac{q}{10} \rceil$. The decryption can recover $\mathsf{rdec}(p)$ and hence the real signer due to the correctness of our key-oblivious encryption from Sect. 3.1. Thus, correctness of the Open algorithm follows. What is more, Π_{open} will be accepted by the Judge algorithm with probability 1 due to the perfect completeness of our argument system.

If an honest user is non-traceable, then again $\mathsf{Account}(\mathsf{gpk}, \mathsf{cert}, w^{\mathrm{escrw}}, 1)$ will output 1. For the Open algorithm, since $\mathbf{b}_1^{(0)} - \mathbf{a}_1^{(0)} \cdot s_1 = \mathbf{a}_1^{(0)} \cdot (s_{-1} - s_1) + \mathbf{e}_{-1}$, then we obtain

$$\mathbf{c}_{1,2} - \mathbf{c}_{1,1} \cdot s_1 = \mathbf{a}_1^{(0)} \cdot (s_{-1} - s_1) \cdot g_1 \cdot g_1' + \widetilde{\mathbf{e}} + \lfloor q/4 \rfloor \cdot \mathsf{rdec}(p),$$

where $\|\widetilde{\mathbf{e}}\|_\infty \leq \lceil \frac{q}{10} \rceil$. Observe that $\mathbf{a}_1^{(0)} \xleftarrow{\$} R_q^\ell$, and $s_{-1} \neq s_1$ with overwhelming probability. Over the randomness of g_1, g_1', the decryption algorithm described in Sect. 3.1 will output a random element $p' \in R_q$. Then, with overwhelming probability, p' is not in the registration table and the Open algorithm outputs $\perp$. It then follows that our scheme is correct.

SECURITY. In Theorem 2, we prove that our scheme satisfies the security requirements of accountable tracing signatures, as specified by Kohlweiss and Miers.

Theorem 2. *Under the* RLWE *and* RSIS *assumptions, the accountable tracing signature scheme described in Sect. 4.1 satisfies the following requirements in the random oracle model: (i) anonymity under tracing; (ii) traceability; (iii) non-frameability; (iv) anonymity with accountability; and (v) trace-obliviousness.*

The proof of Theorem 2 is deferred to the full version of this paper.

Acknowledgements. The research is supported by Singapore Ministry of Education under Research Grant MOE2016-T2-2-014(S). Khoa Nguyen is also supported by the Gopalakrishnan – NTU Presidential Postdoctoral Fellowship 2018.

References

1. Ateniese, G., Camenisch, J., Joye, M., Tsudik, G.: A practical and provably secure coalition-resistant group signature scheme. In: Bellare, M. (ed.) CRYPTO 2000. LNCS, vol. 1880, pp. 255–270. Springer, Heidelberg (2000). https://doi.org/10.1007/3-540-44598-6_16
2. Bellare, M., Micciancio, D., Warinschi, B.: Foundations of group signatures: formal definitions, simplified requirements, and a construction based on general assumptions. In: Biham, E. (ed.) EUROCRYPT 2003. LNCS, vol. 2656, pp. 614–629. Springer, Heidelberg (2003). https://doi.org/10.1007/3-540-39200-9_38
3. Bellare, M., Shi, H., Zhang, C.: Foundations of group signatures: the case of dynamic groups. In: Menezes, A. (ed.) CT-RSA 2005. LNCS, vol. 3376, pp. 136–153. Springer, Heidelberg (2005). https://doi.org/10.1007/978-3-540-30574-3_11
4. Benhamouda, F., Camenisch, J., Krenn, S., Lyubashevsky, V., Neven, G.: Better zero-knowledge proofs for lattice encryption and their application to group signatures. In: Sarkar, P., Iwata, T. (eds.) ASIACRYPT 2014. LNCS, vol. 8873, pp. 551–572. Springer, Heidelberg (2014). https://doi.org/10.1007/978-3-662-45611-8_29
5. Benhamouda, F., Krenn, S., Lyubashevsky, V., Pietrzak, K.: Efficient zero-knowledge proofs for commitments from learning with errors over rings. In: Pernul, G., Ryan, P.Y.A., Weippl, E. (eds.) ESORICS 2015. LNCS, vol. 9326, pp. 305–325. Springer, Cham (2015). https://doi.org/10.1007/978-3-319-24174-6_16
6. Boneh, D., Boyen, X., Shacham, H.: Short group signatures. In: Franklin, M. (ed.) CRYPTO 2004. LNCS, vol. 3152, pp. 41–55. Springer, Heidelberg (2004). https://doi.org/10.1007/978-3-540-28628-8_3
7. Boneh, D., Shacham, H.: Group signatures with verifier-local revocation. In: CCS 2004, pp. 168–177. ACM (2004)
8. Bootle, J., Cerulli, A., Chaidos, P., Ghadafi, E., Groth, J.: Foundations of fully dynamic group signatures. In: Manulis, M., Sadeghi, A.-R., Schneider, S. (eds.) ACNS 2016. LNCS, vol. 9696, pp. 117–136. Springer, Cham (2016). https://doi.org/10.1007/978-3-319-39555-5_7

9. Boschini, C., Camenisch, J., Neven, G.: Floppy-sized group signatures from lattices. In: Preneel, B., Vercauteren, F. (eds.) ACNS 2018. LNCS, vol. 10892, pp. 163–182. Springer, Cham (2018). https://doi.org/10.1007/978-3-319-93387-0_9

10. Brakerski, Z., Gentry, C., Vaikuntanathan, V.: (Leveled) fully homomorphic encryption without bootstrapping. In: ITCS 2012, pp. 309–325. ACM (2012)

11. Camenisch, J., Neven, G., Rückert, M.: Fully anonymous attribute tokens from lattices. In: Visconti, I., De Prisco, R. (eds.) SCN 2012. LNCS, vol. 7485, pp. 57–75. Springer, Heidelberg (2012). https://doi.org/10.1007/978-3-642-32928-9_4

12. Chaum, D., van Heyst, E.: Group signatures. In: Davies, D.W. (ed.) EUROCRYPT 1991. LNCS, vol. 547, pp. 257–265. Springer, Heidelberg (1991). https://doi.org/10.1007/3-540-46416-6_22

13. Cheng, S., Nguyen, K., Wang, H.: Policy-based signature scheme from lattices. Des. Codes Cryptogr. **81**(1), 43–74 (2016)

14. Ducas, L., Micciancio, D.: Improved short lattice signatures in the standard model. In: Garay, J.A., Gennaro, R. (eds.) CRYPTO 2014. LNCS, vol. 8616, pp. 335–352. Springer, Heidelberg (2014). https://doi.org/10.1007/978-3-662-44371-2_19

15. Ducas, L., Micciancio, D.: Improved short lattice signatures in the standard model. IACR Cryptology ePrint Archive 2014, 495 (2014)

16. Fiat, A., Shamir, A.: How to prove yourself: practical solutions to identification and signature problems. In: Odlyzko, A.M. (ed.) CRYPTO 1986. LNCS, vol. 263, pp. 186–194. Springer, Heidelberg (1987). https://doi.org/10.1007/3-540-47721-7_12

17. ElGamal, T.: A public key cryptosystem and a signature scheme based on discrete logarithms. In: Blakley, G.R., Chaum, D. (eds.) CRYPTO 1984. LNCS, vol. 196, pp. 10–18. Springer, Heidelberg (1985). https://doi.org/10.1007/3-540-39568-7_2

18. Gentry, C., Peikert, C., Vaikuntanathan, V.: Trapdoors for hard lattices and new cryptographic constructions. In: STOC 2008, pp. 197–206. ACM (2008)

19. Gordon, S.D., Katz, J., Vaikuntanathan, V.: A group signature scheme from lattice assumptions. In: Abe, M. (ed.) ASIACRYPT 2010. LNCS, vol. 6477, pp. 395–412. Springer, Heidelberg (2010). https://doi.org/10.1007/978-3-642-17373-8_23

20. Jain, A., Krenn, S., Pietrzak, K., Tentes, A.: Commitments and efficient zero-knowledge proofs from learning parity with noise. In: Wang, X., Sako, K. (eds.) ASIACRYPT 2012. LNCS, vol. 7658, pp. 663–680. Springer, Heidelberg (2012). https://doi.org/10.1007/978-3-642-34961-4_40

21. Kawachi, A., Tanaka, K., Xagawa, K.: Concurrently secure identification schemes based on the worst-case hardness of lattice problems. In: Pieprzyk, J. (ed.) ASIACRYPT 2008. LNCS, vol. 5350, pp. 372–389. Springer, Heidelberg (2008). https://doi.org/10.1007/978-3-540-89255-7_23

22. Kiayias, A., Tsiounis, Y., Yung, M.: Traceable signatures. In: Cachin, C., Camenisch, J.L. (eds.) EUROCRYPT 2004. LNCS, vol. 3027, pp. 571–589. Springer, Heidelberg (2004). https://doi.org/10.1007/978-3-540-24676-3_34

23. Kiayias, A., Yung, M.: Secure scalable group signature with dynamic joins and separable authorities. Int. J. Secur. Netw. **1**(1), 24–45 (2006)

24. Kohlweiss, M., Miers, I.: Accountable metadata-hiding escrow: a group signature case study. PoPETs **2015**(2), 206–221 (2015)

25. Laguillaumie, F., Langlois, A., Libert, B., Stehlé, D.: Lattice-based group signatures with logarithmic signature size. In: Sako, K., Sarkar, P. (eds.) ASIACRYPT 2013. LNCS, vol. 8270, pp. 41–61. Springer, Heidelberg (2013). https://doi.org/10.1007/978-3-642-42045-0_3

26. Langlois, A., Stehlé, D.: Worst-case to average-case reductions for module lattices. Des. Codes Cryptogr. **75**(3), 565–599 (2015)

27. Libert, B., Ling, S., Mouhartem, F., Nguyen, K., Wang, H.: Signature schemes with efficient protocols and dynamic group signatures from lattice assumptions. In: Cheon, J.H., Takagi, T. (eds.) ASIACRYPT 2016. LNCS, vol. 10032, pp. 373–403. Springer, Heidelberg (2016). https://doi.org/10.1007/978-3-662-53890-6_13

28. Libert, B., Ling, S., Mouhartem, F., Nguyen, K., Wang, H.: Zero-knowledge arguments for matrix-vector relations and lattice-based group encryption. In: Cheon, J.H., Takagi, T. (eds.) ASIACRYPT 2016. LNCS, vol. 10032, pp. 101–131. Springer, Heidelberg (2016). https://doi.org/10.1007/978-3-662-53890-6_4

29. Libert, B., Ling, S., Nguyen, K., Wang, H.: Zero-knowledge arguments for lattice-based accumulators: logarithmic-size ring signatures and group signatures without trapdoors. In: Fischlin, M., Coron, J.-S. (eds.) EUROCRYPT 2016. LNCS, vol. 9666, pp. 1–31. Springer, Heidelberg (2016). https://doi.org/10.1007/978-3-662-49896-5_1

30. Libert, B., Mouhartem, F., Nguyen, K.: A lattice-based group signature scheme with message-dependent opening. In: Manulis, M., Sadeghi, A.-R., Schneider, S. (eds.) ACNS 2016. LNCS, vol. 9696, pp. 137–155. Springer, Cham (2016). https://doi.org/10.1007/978-3-319-39555-5_8

31. Ling, S., Nguyen, K., Roux-Langlois, A., Wang, H.: A lattice-based group signature scheme with verifier-local revocation. Theor. Comput. Sci. **730**, 1–20 (2018)

32. Ling, S., Nguyen, K., Stehlé, D., Wang, H.: Improved zero-knowledge proofs of knowledge for the ISIS problem, and applications. In: Kurosawa, K., Hanaoka, G. (eds.) PKC 2013. LNCS, vol. 7778, pp. 107–124. Springer, Heidelberg (2013). https://doi.org/10.1007/978-3-642-36362-7_8

33. Ling, S., Nguyen, K., Wang, H.: Group signatures from lattices: simpler, tighter, shorter, ring-based. In: Katz, J. (ed.) PKC 2015. LNCS, vol. 9020, pp. 427–449. Springer, Heidelberg (2015). https://doi.org/10.1007/978-3-662-46447-2_19

34. Ling, S., Nguyen, K., Wang, H., Xu, Y.: Lattice-based group signatures: achieving full dynamicity with ease. In: Gollmann, D., Miyaji, A., Kikuchi, H. (eds.) ACNS 2017. LNCS, vol. 10355, pp. 293–312. Springer, Cham (2017). https://doi.org/10.1007/978-3-319-61204-1_15

35. Ling, S., Nguyen, K., Wang, H., Xu, Y.: Constant-size group signatures from lattices. In: Abdalla, M., Dahab, R. (eds.) PKC 2018. LNCS, vol. 10770, pp. 58–88. Springer, Cham (2018). https://doi.org/10.1007/978-3-319-76581-5_3

36. Lyubashevsky, V.: Fiat-Shamir with aborts: applications to lattice and factoring-based signatures. In: Matsui, M. (ed.) ASIACRYPT 2009. LNCS, vol. 5912, pp. 598–616. Springer, Heidelberg (2009). https://doi.org/10.1007/978-3-642-10366-7_35

37. Lyubashevsky, V.: Lattice signatures without trapdoors. In: Pointcheval, D., Johansson, T. (eds.) EUROCRYPT 2012. LNCS, vol. 7237, pp. 738–755. Springer, Heidelberg (2012). https://doi.org/10.1007/978-3-642-29011-4_43

38. Lyubashevsky, V., Micciancio, D.: Generalized compact knapsacks are collision resistant. In: Bugliesi, M., Preneel, B., Sassone, V., Wegener, I. (eds.) ICALP 2006. LNCS, vol. 4052, pp. 144–155. Springer, Heidelberg (2006). https://doi.org/10.1007/11787006_13

39. Lyubashevsky, V., Micciancio, D., Peikert, C., Rosen, A.: SWIFFT: a modest proposal for FFT hashing. In: Nyberg, K. (ed.) FSE 2008. LNCS, vol. 5086, pp. 54–72. Springer, Heidelberg (2008). https://doi.org/10.1007/978-3-540-71039-4_4

40. Lyubashevsky, V., Neven, G.: One-shot verifiable encryption from lattices. In: Coron, J.-S., Nielsen, J.B. (eds.) EUROCRYPT 2017. LNCS, vol. 10210, pp. 293–323. Springer, Cham (2017). https://doi.org/10.1007/978-3-319-56620-7_11

41. Lyubashevsky, V., Peikert, C., Regev, O.: On ideal lattices and learning with errors over rings. In: Gilbert, H. (ed.) EUROCRYPT 2010. LNCS, vol. 6110, pp. 1–23. Springer, Heidelberg (2010). https://doi.org/10.1007/978-3-642-13190-5_1

42. Lyubashevsky, V., Peikert, C., Regev, O.: On ideal lattices and learning with errors over rings. J. ACM **60**(6), 43:1–43:35 (2013)

43. Lyubashevsky, V., Seiler, G.: Short, invertible elements in partially splitting cyclotomic rings and applications to lattice-based zero-knowledge proofs. In: Nielsen, J.B., Rijmen, V. (eds.) EUROCRYPT 2018. LNCS, vol. 10820, pp. 204–224. Springer, Cham (2018). https://doi.org/10.1007/978-3-319-78381-9_8

44. Micciancio, D., Peikert, C.: Trapdoors for lattices: simpler, tighter, faster, smaller. In: Pointcheval, D., Johansson, T. (eds.) EUROCRYPT 2012. LNCS, vol. 7237, pp. 700–718. Springer, Heidelberg (2012). https://doi.org/10.1007/978-3-642-29011-4_41

45. Naor, M., Yung, M.: Public-key cryptosystems provably secure against chosen ciphertext attacks. In: STOC 1990, pp. 427–437. ACM (1990)

46. Nguyen, P.Q., Zhang, J., Zhang, Z.: Simpler efficient group signatures from lattices. In: Katz, J. (ed.) PKC 2015. LNCS, vol. 9020, pp. 401–426. Springer, Heidelberg (2015). https://doi.org/10.1007/978-3-662-46447-2_18

47. Peikert, C., Regev, O., Stephens-Davidowitz, N.: Pseudorandomness of ring-LWE for any ring and modulus. In: STOC 2017, pp. 461–473. ACM (2017)

48. Peikert, C., Rosen, A.: Efficient collision-resistant hashing from worst-case assumptions on cyclic lattices. In: Halevi, S., Rabin, T. (eds.) TCC 2006. LNCS, vol. 3876, pp. 145–166. Springer, Heidelberg (2006). https://doi.org/10.1007/11681878_8

49. del Pino, R., Lyubashevsky, V., Seiler, G.: Lattice-based group signatures and zero-knowledge proofs of automorphism stability. IACR Cryptology ePrint Archive, 2018:779 (2018). Accepted to ACM CCS 2018

50. Regev, O.: On lattices, learning with errors, random linear codes, and cryptography. In: STOC 2005, pp. 84–93. ACM (2005)

51. Sakai, Y., Emura, K., Hanaoka, G., Kawai, Y., Matsuda, T., Omote, K.: Group signatures with message-dependent opening. In: Abdalla, M., Lange, T. (eds.) Pairing 2012. LNCS, vol. 7708, pp. 270–294. Springer, Heidelberg (2013). https://doi.org/10.1007/978-3-642-36334-4_18

52. Sakai, Y., Schuldt, J.C.N., Emura, K., Hanaoka, G., Ohta, K.: On the security of dynamic group signatures: preventing signature hijacking. In: Fischlin, M., Buchmann, J., Manulis, M. (eds.) PKC 2012. LNCS, vol. 7293, pp. 715–732. Springer, Heidelberg (2012). https://doi.org/10.1007/978-3-642-30057-8_42

53. Shor, P.W.: Algorithms for quantum computation: discrete logarithms and factoring. In: FOCS 1994, pp. 124–134. IEEE Computer Society (1994)

54. Stehlé, D., Steinfeld, R., Tanaka, K., Xagawa, K.: Efficient public key encryption based on ideal lattices. In: Matsui, M. (ed.) ASIACRYPT 2009. LNCS, vol. 5912, pp. 617–635. Springer, Heidelberg (2009). https://doi.org/10.1007/978-3-642-10366-7_36

55. Stern, J.: A new paradigm for public key identification. IEEE Trans. Inf. Theory **42**(6), 1757–1768 (1996)

Author Index

Printed in the United States
By Bookmasters